A HISTORY OF
american_literature_

DISCARD

To
Sheona

DISCARD

A HISTORY OF american literature

RICHARD **GRAY**

Blackwell Publishing

© 2004 by Richard Gray

BLACKWELL PUBLISHING

350 Main Street, Malden, MA 02148-5020, USA
9600 Garsington Road, Oxford OX4 2DQ, UK
550 Swanston Street, Carlton, Victoria 3053, Australia

The right of Richard Gray to be identified as the Author of this Work has been asserted in accordance with the UK Copyright, Designs, and Patents Act 1988.

All rights reserved. No part of this publication may be reproduced, stored in a retrieval system, or transmitted, in any form or by any means, electronic, mechanical, photocopying, recording or otherwise, except as permitted by the UK Copyright, Designs, and Patents Act 1988, without the prior permission of the publisher.

First published 2004 by Blackwell Publishing Ltd

4   2005

Library of Congress Cataloging-in-Publication Data

Gray, Richard J.
    A history of American literature / Richard Gray.
        p. cm.
    Includes bibliographical references and index.
        ISBN 0-631-22134-4 (alk. paper) – ISBN 0-631-22135-2 (pbk.: alk. paper)
        1. American literature–History and criticism. 2. United States–Literatures–History and criticism. I. Title.

    PS88.G73 2003
    810.9–dc21

                                                                  2003004958

ISBN-13: 978-0-631-22134-0 (alk. paper) – ISBN-13: 978-0-631-22135-7 (pbk.: alk. paper)

A catalogue record for this title is available from the British Library.

Set in 10.5/13 pt Minion
by Graphicraft Ltd, Hong Kong
Printed and bound in the United Kingdom
by TJ International, Padstow, Cornwall

The publisher's policy is to use permanent paper from mills that operate a sustainable forestry policy, and which has been manufactured from pulp processed using acid-free and elementary chlorine-free practices. Furthermore, the publisher ensures that the text paper and cover board used have met acceptable environmental accreditation standards.

For further information on
Blackwell Publishing, visit our website:
www.blackwellpublishing.com

contents

preface and acknowledgements

In this history of American literature, I have tried to be responsive to the immense changes that have taken place over the past thirty to forty years in the study of literature in general and American literature in particular: changes that, among other things, have put the whole issue of just what is American and exactly what constitutes literature into contention. Interdisciplinary studies, gender, ethnic and popular culture studies, critical and cultural theory have all complicated and problematized our notion of what literature is. And the debates initiated by these newly developed fields of study have, very often, gathered around and found their focus in American books. I have also tried to tell a story: about the continued inventing of communities, and the sustained imagining of nations, that constitute the literary history of the part of the American continent which came to be known as the United States. My story has had to be a selective one. Most readers will soon discover some authors to whom I have given less than their due, in terms of attention and discussion, and others to whom I have not even managed to give a mention. Apart from apologizing for this, pleading the excuse all literary historians have eventually to give – the excuse, that is, which Herman Melville famously summarized as the limited draughts of time, strength, cash and patience on which all mortals draw – I should perhaps add one thing. While necessarily being selective, I have nevertheless tried to be as true as I can be to the whole range of American diversity and difference: the multiple and often conflicting communities that have been involved in writing their region or nation. What I have been after here, in short, is to tell a tale of an ongoing series of texts resistant to any simply totalizing vision: to write, not so much the literary history as the literary histories of America.

Another way of putting this might be to say that my aim here – shaped by the emphasis recent American literary scholarship has placed on the authority of difference – has been to 'uninvent' the reading of American literature that sees America in monolithic and millennial terms, and that restricts attention to literature in the sense of the published and widely distributed poem, fiction and play. The more widely available and canonical material of course constitutes a substantial and significant element in what I look at, but it is not the only one. I have tried to be responsive to the fundamentally plural character of American history and culture by acknowledging and talking about other powerful traditions, some of them oral, political or popular, others marginalized and denied publication until recently. My hope is that what the reader will find here, as a result, is the story of a literature that is, and always has been, multiple, conflicted. But what he or she will also find here, if I have had any success at all in realizing my aims, is the story of a vast number of individuals and communities animated by a connected series of aims and by the sense of a past held, however cruelly or painfully, in common. This history, while aimed at unravelling any simple, singular notion of its subject, has also been driven by a related set of arguments – and, more particularly, by an interest in that process by which communities and nations continually remake themselves.

My debts here are vast, to generations of scholars in the field and, in particular, to all those who have enlarged the materials and the meanings of American literature over the past three or four decades. To that extent, this book situates itself as one fragment, one small voice in a much larger and continuing debate. But for the preliminary critical model for the whole story I am trying to tell, I have specific debts to acknowledge, since it is based on the premise that, as Fredric Jameson has argued, historical epochs are not monolithic integrated social formations. On the contrary, they are complex overlays of different methods of production that serve as the bases of different social groups and classes and, consequently, of their world views. It is because of this that, in any given epoch, a variety of antagonisms can be discerned, conflicts between different interest groups. One culture may well be dominant, but there will also be – to borrow Raymond Williams's useful terms – a residual culture, formed in the past but still active in the cultural process, and an emergent culture, prescribing new meanings and practices. Writers, according to this model, like any other members of society, are not the victims or agents of some totalizing structure, since – to quote Williams – 'no dominant culture ever in reality includes or exhausts all human practices, human energy and human intention'. So they are able, and perhaps even obliged, to insert themselves in the space between warring interests and practices and then dramatize the contradictions the conflict engenders. Throughout their work, by means of a mixture of voices, a free play of various languages (and sometimes even genres), they can represent the reality of their culture as multiple, complex and internally antagonistic. They can achieve a realization of both synchrony and diachrony: a demonstration both of the continuities between past and present and of the processes by which those continuities are challenged, dissolved and reconstituted. They consequently have more chance than most members of their society do of realizing what Hayden White has called 'the human capacity to endow lived contradictions with intimations of their possible transcendence'. They have the opportunity, in other words, of getting 'into' history, participating in its processes, and, in a perspectival sense at least, of getting 'out' of it too – enabling us, the readers, to begin to understand just how those processes work.

All this may sound intolerably abstract; it probably does. It is, however, a way for me to tease out, and to underscore, what I see as three fundamental points: points that are never really foregrounded or argued out in this history but are nevertheless there, feeding into and informing everything I try to say and providing me with something like a structure, a narrative pattern. First, social stability is an illusion, the preserve of pastoral dream and utopian vision – and, for that matter, of that idea of the writing into life of a New Eden that has tended to monopolize readings of American literature. At some moments, the pace of change may accelerate but change is the one constant, guaranteeing the plural character of any culture. Second, American culture and writing are surely only properly understood in these terms, as multiple and layered, composed of many different groups all trying to make sense of their lives and changes – and, in the process, construct their own imaginative community. And third, if anyone at all is likely to help us understand the exact forms that change has taken in America, the plurality of its cultures and the conflicting forces at work there, it is writers precisely because of the chance their writing gives them to live both 'in' and 'out' of history. Writers can help more than most to disclose to us the continuing acts of imagination that constitute the making of a nation.

There are other more personal debts, among them to the many students and colleagues who have helped me to what little I have learned about American literature over the past thirty years. I would like to thank all those I have met and communicated with in the British Association for American Studies, particularly during my stints as Associate Editor and then Editor of the *Journal of American Studies*, and my fellow scholars in the European Association for American Studies and the Southern Studies Forum. Friends at the British Academy, particularly Andrew Hook, Jon Stallworthy and Wynn Thomas, are to be thanked, for the advice and support they have given. So are colleagues at other universities in the United Kingdom, notably Susan Castillo, Kate Fullbrook, Mick Gidley, Judie Newman and Helen Taylor, at other universities in other parts of Europe, especially Jan Nordby Gretlund, Lothar Honnighausen and Waldemar Zacharasiewicz, in Asia, particularly Bob Lee, and in the United States, where I owe a special debt of gratitude to Saki Bercovitch, George Dekker and Marjorie Perloff. At the University of Essex, I have especially to thank my friend and colleague of over thirty years Herbie Butterfield, John Gillies and Peter Hulme, and my doctoral students, with particular thanks to one former doctoral student, Owen Robinson, who has now become a colleague. I would like to thank Brigitte Lee, too, for being such a meticulous, thoughtful and creative copy-editor. Acknowledgements should also be made to the University of Essex, the British Academy, and the Arts and Humanities Research Board for making some limited support available, and to the several universities and conferences that enabled me to try out my ideas – often persuading me to change them. More personally, I want to thank Andrew McNeillie at Blackwell, the best, most supportive and inspiring of editors and a good friend. On a more personal note still, my greatest debt is, as always, to my family. My older daughter, Catharine, now herself an academic in the United States, I want to thank here for her quick wit, grace and subtle understanding, and for providing me with a delightful American son-in-law, Ricky, and two wonderful American grandsons, Sam and Zack. My older son, Ben, I thank in turn for keeping me on my intellectual toes, or trying to, for his good humour, thoughtfulness and commitment and, not least, for always being there when I need him. My younger daughter, Jessica, I want to thank for her lovely spirit, her lively intelligence and kindness, the constant delight of her conversation and company, and for never taking me or my work too – or even at all – seriously. My younger son, Jack, I owe a debt of gratitude for his gentleness, his vitality and for his ability to teach me about the poverty of words sometimes: being without language, he has reminded me of other, deeper ways of communicating. He and my other children and my grandchildren, thanks to their energy, their apparently endless funds of resilience, have also helped give me faith in the future, despite everything. The final and deepest debt of all is, as ever, to my wife, Sheona. By encouraging and advising me, especially when the work hit a problem or the possibility of ever completing it seemed to recede, she became, in a real sense, one of the hidden authors of this book. More than that, she has given me memories and hope, not just while researching and writing this but always. That is why, as one small token of my gratitude for all she has given me, this history of a subject that has consumed my interests and attention for all my professional career, is dedicated to her.

Preface and Acknowledgements

1

the first americans
american literature before and during the colonial and revolutionary periods

Imagining Eden

'America is a poem in our eyes: its ample geography dazzles the imagination, and it will not wait long for metres.' The words are those of Ralph Waldo Emerson, and they sum up that desire to turn the New World into words which has seized the imagination of so many Americans. But 'America' was only one of the several names for a dream dreamed in the first instance by Europeans. 'He invented America: a very great man,' one character observes of Christopher Columbus in a Henry James novel; and so, in a sense, he did. Columbus, however, was following a prototype devised long before him and surviving long after him, the idea of a new land outside and beyond history: 'a Virgin Countrey,' to quote one early, English settler, 'so preserved by Nature out of a desire to show mankinde fallen into the Old Age of Creation, what a brow of fertility and beauty she was adorned with when the world was vigorous and youthfull.' For a while, this imaginary America obliterated the history of those who had lived American lives long before the Europeans came. And, as Emerson's invocation of 'America . . . a poem' discloses, it also erased much sense of American literature as anything other than the writing into existence of a New Eden.

Not that the first European settlers were unaware of the strangeness of America: in October 1492, for example, Christopher Columbus (1451–1506) confided to his journals that there were 'a thousand kinds of herbs and flowers' in this New World, 'of all of which I remain in ignorance as to their properties'. His ignorance extended, famously, into areas he was hardly aware of: convinced that he had arrived at the continent of India, he christened the people he encountered Indians. 'Their language I do not understand,' admitted Columbus. And their customs he found either odd or abhorrent. The 'natives' went about 'with firebrands in their hands', Columbus along with other early European explorers observed, 'these they call by the name of *tabacos*'. 'They draw the smoke by sucking, this causes a drowsiness and sort of intoxication', but, he concluded, 'I do not see what relish or benefit they could find in them.' More seriously, they were 'without any religion that could be discovered'. An 'inoffensive, unwarlike people', 'without the knowledge of iniquity', they were nevertheless strangers to the blessings of religion. This, however, was a problem ripe for the solving, since the 'gentle race' in the New World could surely be introduced to the truths of the Old. 'They very quickly learn such prayers as we repeat to them,' Columbus reported, 'and also to make the sign of the cross.' So, he advised his royal masters, 'Your Highnesses should adopt the resolution of converting them to Christianity'. Such a project, he explained without any trace of irony, 'would suffice to gain to our holy faith multitudes of people, and to Spain great riches and immense dominion'.

Conversion was one strategy Columbus and other early Europeans had for dealing with America and the Americans they encountered. Comparison was another: the New World could be understood, perhaps, by discovering likeness with the Old. 'Everything looked as green as in April in Andalusia,' reported Columbus of what he thought was India but was, in fact, Cuba. 'The days here are hot, and the nights mild like May in Andalusia,' he added, and 'the isle is full of pleasant mountains after the manner of Sicily.' Naming was another ploy: Columbus was not the first nor the last to believe that the strange could be familiarized by being given a familiar label. The strange people he met seemed less strange once he had convinced himself they were 'Indians'; the strange places he visited became more understandable once they were given the names of saints. To map the New World meant either to deny its newness, by coming up with a name or a comparison associated with the Old, or to see that newness as precisely what had to be changed. 'I have no doubt, most serene Princes,' Columbus reported,

> that were proper devout and religious persons to come among the natives and learn their language, it would be an easy matter to convert them all to Christianity, and I hope in our Lord that your Highnesses will . . . bring into the church so many multitudes, inasmuch as you have exterminated those who refused to confess the Father, Son, and Holy Ghost.

Fundamental to this project of mapping the New World was the myth of Eden, according to which the European settlers were faced not so much with another culture as with nature, and not really with encountering a possible future but, on the contrary, returning to an imagined past. 'These people go naked,' Columbus observed, 'except that the women wear a very slight covering at the loins'; and, while he was willing to confess that 'their manners are very decent', he could see this only as a sign of their aboriginal innocence. Stripped of culture, as well as clothes and Christianity, they were primitives, a recollection of natural man. In this, Columbus was not unusual; the only difference, if any, between him and many other early European explorers and settlers was that he eventually took the dream of Eden to its logical conclusion and a literal extreme. All his life, Columbus continued to believe he had discovered the Indies and only had to venture over the next hill or stream to find the legendary cities of gold and silver described by Marco Polo. When one discovery after another failed to confirm this belief, Columbus consoled himself with the conviction that what he had found was, literally, the Garden of Eden. 'Each time I sailed from Spain to the Indies,' Columbus recalled towards the end of his life, 'I reached a point when the heavens, the stars, the temperature of the air and the waters of the sea abruptly changed.' 'It was as if the seas sloped upward at this point,' he remembered; and the odd behaviour of his navigation equipment led him to conclude, finally, that the globe was not round. One hemisphere, he claimed, 'resembles the half of a round pear with a raised stalk, like a woman's nipple on a round ball'. 'I do not hold that the earthly Paradise has the form of a rugged mountain,' Columbus insisted, 'as it is shown in pictures, but that it lies at the summit of what I have described as the stalk of a pear.' 'I do not find any Greek or Latin writings which definitely state the worldly situation of the earthly Paradise,' Columbus wrote, 'and I believe that the earthly Paradise lies here' just beyond the strange new world he had found. He did not, he admitted, believe 'that anyone can ascend to the top' and so enter the Garden of Eden. But he was firmly convinced that the streams and rivers he had discovered 'flow out of the earthly Paradise' and that, accordingly, he had been closer than anyone to the place where 'Our Lord placed the Tree of Life'.

The evidence Columbus adduced for associating the New World with Eden was an odd but, for its time, characteristic mix of scientific and pseudo-scientific argument, Biblical exegesis and imaginative rhetoric. Not of least importance here was his rapt account of the vegetation and the native inhabitants of his earthly Paradise. 'The land and trees were very green and as lovely as the orchards of Valencia in April,' he remembered, 'and the inhabitants were lightly built and fairer than most of the other people we had seen in the Indies'; 'their hair was long and straight and they were quicker, more intelligent, and less cowardly.' This is natural man as innocent rather than savage, reminding Europeans of their aboriginal, unfallen state rather than inviting conversion. The Indian as savage and the Indian as innocent were and are, of course, two sides of the same coin. Both map Native Americans, and the land they and their forebears had lived in for more than thirty thousand years, as somehow absent from history: existing in a timeless void, a place of nature and a site of myth. But, in mapping the New World and its inhabitants in this way, in trying to accommodate strange sights and experiences to familiar signs and legends, Columbus and other early European explorers were at least beginning a story of American literature: a story, that is, of encounters between cultures that leaves both sides altered. If there is one truth in the history of American writing, it is the truth of process and plurality. The American writer has to write in and of a world of permeable borders and change. Although he was hardly aware of it, Columbus was forging a narrative that was neither precisely Old World (because of the sights he had seen), nor exactly New World either (because of the signs he had used), but a mix or synthesis of both. Telling of meetings between strangers, oddly syncretic in its language and vision, it was in its own way an American tale he was telling.

Native American Oral Traditions

If Columbus thought some of his Indians were close to Paradise, then some of those Indians thought they came from heaven. Or so Columbus said. Some of the native inhabitants themselves tell a different story. Among some Native Americans of the Southeast, for example, there was the legend that white people came across the water to visit them. Treated hospitably, the whites then disappeared, leaving behind them only 'a keg of something which we know was whiskey'. The people began smelling it, tasting it, then 'some went so far as to drink a little', whereupon 'they began to reel and stagger and butt each other with their heads'. It was then that the white people came back for their real purpose: trade. Other Native Americans related the Europeans to their own myths of origin. Among the inhabitants of the Southeast, the Yuchis were not unusual in calling themselves 'offspring of the sun'. If they were from the sun, then, the Yuchis felt, the whites clearly originated from the sea. 'It was out upon the ocean,' Yuchi legend goes. 'Some sea-foam formed against a big log floating there. Then a person emerged from the sea-foam and crawled out upon the log.' This was a white man. 'Another person crawled up, on the other side of the log.' This was a white woman. After meetings on sea and land, many more white people came 'with a great many ships'. They told the Yuchis 'that their land was very strong and fertile' and asked them 'to give a portion that they might live on it'. The Yuchis agreed, the tale concludes, 'the white people came to shore, and they have lived there ever since'.

At the moment when the inhabitants of the Old World and the New first met and began to describe the meeting, there were more than ten million Native Americans speaking more than 350 languages. There are still two million of their descendants living in the United States and in North America there may be as many as 200 languages still spoken. Columbus left a written record and had others leave written accounts for him. The Yuchis told tales to each other that were passed from one generation to the next, as they were transplanted from their home on the southern Appalachians to new territory west of the Mississippi in the notorious removals of the 1830s. For Europeans, encounter with Native Americans may have coincided with the age of the book, but for Native Americans literature remained a matter of speech and performance. Although it may resonate with certain common themes and a shared idiom, each song or tale has its own verbal particularity each time it is sung or spoken. And although it may be modulated by a framework of expectations and prescribed ritual, each performance is unrepeatable, unique. What we read now, when we read a Native American story, is the result of an act of textualization, something that necessarily rips the story out of the living tissue of the world in which it was formed and changed. It is no longer part of a communal dialogue, a continuous process of mythmaking, but a text set in the apparent authority and fixity of print. What we read now is also the result of an act of translation: any version we have of a Native American tale is precisely that, a version shaped by the use of a written alphabet if not also by prevailing notions of what is appropriately literary. Quite apart from problems of textualization and transcription, there are those of historical and geographical difference. The stories vary, of course, according to a people's way of life, the place where they live, the food they eat and the way they get it. The world of the Pueblo Indians of the Southwest, for instance, is bounded by four sacred mountains, where holy men still journey on pilgrimages to gather herbs and pray for rain. Their lives governed by the rhythms of planting and harvesting, the coming of corn and the changing seasons, they tell tales very different from those of the nomadic buffalo hunters of the Plains – or the people of the Northwest who make their living from the sea and fill their stories with ocean monsters, heroic boatbuilders and harpooneers.

When we read Native American texts, however, with all due acknowledgement that what we are reading *is* a text and a translation, certain themes and preoccupations tend to recur. There are stories of world creation and the evolution of the sun, moon and stars; there are tales of human and cultural emergence, involving the discovery of rituals or resources such as corn, buffalo, horses, salt, tobacco or peyote vital to the tribe. There are the legends of culture heroes, sometimes related to history such as Hiawatha, sometimes purely mythic like the recurring figures of twin brothers; and, not unrelated to this, there are stories of tricksters, such as Coyote, Rabbit and Spider Man. There are, invariably, tales of love and war, animals and spirits, mythic versions of a particular tribal history and mythic explanations of the geography, the place where the tribe now lives. Along with myths of origin, the evolution of the world out of water and primal mud, there are also myths of endings, although very often the ending is simply the prelude to another beginning. In one tale told among the Brule Sioux, for example, the 'Creating Power' is thinking of other endings and beginnings even while he is creating our present world and telling the people 'what tribes they belonged to'. 'This is the third world I have made,' he declares. 'The first world I made was bad; the creatures on it were bad. So I burned it up.' 'The second world I made was bad too. So I burned it up.' 'If you make this world bad and ugly,' he warns the men and women he has fashioned out of mud, 'then I will destroy this world too. It's up to you.' Then:

> The Creating Power gave the people the pipe. 'Live by it,' he said. He named this land the Turtle Continent because it was there that the turtle came up with the mud out of which the third world was made. 'Someday there might be a fourth world,' the Creating Power thought. Then he rested.

Beginnings and endings in these tales are sometimes linked to the coming of the whites: in this case, the ending of peace and primal unity and the beginning of loss and division. 'In the old, old days, before Columbus "discovered" us, as they say,' one White River Sioux story goes, 'we were even closer to the animals than we are now. Many people could understand the animal languages; they could talk to a bird, gossip with a butterfly. Animals could change themselves into people and people into animals.' These are common refrains in Native American tales: the vitality and unity of creation ('The earth was once a human being,' one Okanogan story goes. 'Earth is alive yet'), the vital thread of language that once connected humans and animals and the equally vital thread of being that still links them, the belief that this is a universe of metamorphosis, motion and mutuality. What gives stories like that of the White River Sioux an extra edge is this conviction that the white man ruined things, at least for the time being. To the claim of Columbus that the New World was the earthly Paradise, the implicit response is, yes it was but you spoiled it. So, in one story told by the Papago, or Bear People, of the Southwest, the Creator or 'Great Mystery Power' is imagined punishing his people by sending 'the locust flying far across the eastern waters' to summon 'a people in an unknown land' whose 'face and bodies were full of hair, who rode astride strange beasts, who were encased in iron, wielding iron weapons' and 'who had magic hollow sticks spitting fire, thunder, and destruction'. In another, Kiowa tale, the buffalo who 'were the life of the Kiowa' finally leave because of 'war between the buffalo and the white man'. Threatened with extinction at the hands of white soldiers, hunters and developers, the buffalo retreat into a 'green and fresh' world inside a local mountain 'never to be seen again'. 'The buffalo saw that their day was over', the tale relates; and, since 'everything the Kiowas had came from the buffalo', the unspoken message is that so too is the day of the Kiowa people.

Among the most apocalyptic of these tales of the encounter between European settler and native inhabitant is one told by the Brule Sioux. 'Many years ago,' the tale begins, 'Iktomo the Spider Man, trickster and bringer of bad news, went from village to village and tribe to tribe' to announce 'there is a new generation coming, a new nation, a new kind of man who is going to run over everything.' Spider Man, like many trickster figures, is a combination of liar and prophet, cheat and hero, with a metamorphic capacity for changing between spider and human and the ability to speak any language. And, as he moves from tribe to tribe, he spins out his warning about 'the White Long-legs' who is imminent, telling of his lies, his cunning, his greed; 'he is coming', Spider Man warns, 'to steal all the four directions of the world'. 'Watch the buffalo,' Spider Man advises, 'when this new man comes, the buffalo will go into a hole in the mountain. Guard the buffalo, because the White Long-legs will take them all.' 'He will bring four things,' the tribes are told, '*wicocuye* – sickness; *wawoya* – hate; *wawiwagele* – prejudice; *waunshilap-sni* – pitilessness.' After Spider Man leaves, however, the people soon forget his prophecies, until one morning two Sioux women, out gathering chokecherries, see 'a black smog' covering the place where they are. Out of this blackness, they see 'a strange creature' emerging; 'his skin was pale, his hair was yellow, and his eyes were blue'. 'He was hairy all over,' the women notice. 'When he spoke, it did not sound like human speech,' and 'he was sitting on a large, strange animal as big as a large moose, but it was not a moose.' In one hand, 'this weird man' carried a cross and in the other 'a fearful firestick which spat lightning and made a noise like thunder'. He offered the women a drink from a water bag, and 'when they tried it, the strange water burned their throats and made their heads swim'. 'The man was covered with an evil sickness,' the tale concludes, 'and this sickness jumped on the women's skin like many unnumbered pustules and left them dying.' 'You shall know him as *washi-manu*, steal-all,' Spider Man had prophesied of the 'new kind of man' he saw coming, 'or better by the name of fat-taker, *wasichu*, because he will take the fat of the land. He will eat up everything.' Now, the women realize, 'the *wasichu* had arrived, finally he was among them, and everything would be changed'.

Stories of apocalypse like this one may rehearse themes and figures common to Native American tales of many ages – creation from the water, the holy mountain, the trickster-prophet – but they do clearly pivot on one significant moment of historical encounter. They are about the time when Columbus 'invented America'. Many other stories are less bound to a specific time and place – although, of course, they are meant to explain the times and places in which the storytellers live – and among these, notably, are the stories of origin and emergence. These are often complex, symbolic narratives that characteristically project the tribal under-standing of the origins of the earth and its people, confirm the fundamental rela-tionships between the different elements of creation from the sun to the humblest plant, define the roles and rituals of the tribe, account for the distinctive climate and terrain of the homeland, and describe the origins of various social processes and activities. In short, they reveal the grounds of being for the storyteller and his audience: they explain the who, what, why, where and how of their existence. 'In the beginning the earth was covered with water,' begins a tale of origins told among the Jicarilla Apache. This is a common theme. 'And all living things were below in the underworld.' This Jicarilla Apache tale, in fact, brings together the two most recurrent elements in accounts of origin: the emergence story, in which the people are led up from below the earth to find their place on the surface, very often near the place of emergence, and the story that begins with the primal element of water. Here, 'all the people' come up from the underworld once the surface of the earth has become dry. 'But the Jicarillas continued to circle around the hole where they had come up from the underworld,' the tale reveals. 'Three times they went around it' before 'the Ruler' of the universe took them to 'the middle of the earth,' 'a place very near Taos,' where 'the Jicarillas made their home.'

What the Jicarilla story does not have is the earth-diver theme. In many stories that begin with the primal element of water, a creature dives beneath the ocean to bring up enough mud to create the world and its inhabitants. The creature may be a deity, like 'the Great Chief Above' in a Yakima tale. It may be an animal, such as the turtle in one story told among the Caddo. Or it may be a figure familiar from many other narratives, such as the trickster-hero Coyote who, in one account of origins told by the Crow, 'took up a handful of mud, and out of it made people' – dropping his clowning to become a creator. In a Yuma story, it is twins. Twins are common culture heroes in Native American legend. Sometimes, the twins are female – as they are in, say, the story of origins popular among the Acoma people of the Southwest, reflecting the matrilineal nature of their society. More often, as in Yuma myth, they are male; and, in the case of the Yuma myth as in many others, in order to account for the contraries and mysteries of existence, one is good and one is evil – and both are coextensive with their father. 'This is how it all began,' the Yuma story announces. 'There was only water – there was no land, only nothingness.' 'Deep down' in the waters was 'Kokomaht – the Creator'. 'He was bodiless, nameless, breathless, motionless, and he was two beings – twins.' In this densely symbolic tale, the beginning of creation is marked by the emergence of Kokomaht, the Creator as 'the first twin, the good twin'; Kokomaht, the Creator then names himself 'Kokomaht-All-Father'. Having assumed bodily form, he proceeds to create the body of the earth and its inhabitants: 'the four directions' of the north, south, east and west, six series of four tribes, the creatures of the earth and sky, and the moon and stars. All that 'Bakutahl, the Evil Blind One', who emerges shortly after his brother, creates are the symptoms of his own incompetence, 'creatures without hands or feet, toes or fingers'; 'these were the fish and other water animals'.

There are touches of sly humour to some later versions of this legend. White people, we are told, Kokomaht 'left for last' as the least of his creations. When the white man began to cry 'because his hair was faded' and 'his skin was pale and washed out', Kokomaht tried to shut him up with the gift of a horse; 'so the greedy one was satisfied – for a while'. More fundamental, and more characteristic of most tales of emergence, the Yuma legend describes the beginnings of birth and death. 'Without help from a woman', Kokomaht, the All-Father sires a son 'Kumashtam'hu' and tells men and women 'to join together and rear children'. 'I taught the people to live,' Kokomaht, the All-Father declares. 'Now I must teach them how to die, for without death there will be too many people on the earth.' The lesson is one of example. Kokomaht, the All-Father dies, and his son buries him, in the process teaching the people the proper rituals that follow a man's death: which are, of course, the Yuma rituals of burning his house and belongings so they may 'follow him to the spirit land'. Explaining birth and death, this tale of origins is typical also in explaining the special place and destiny of its tellers. Having taught the Yuma people the appropriate rites, Kumashtam'hu offers them the gift of corn and other 'useful seeds from the four corners of the world'. He scatters the other tribes 'over all the world', but keeps the Yuma near him beside the Colorado River 'because they were the special people he loved'. 'I cannot stay with you forever,' he warns his people. 'I am now only one, but I will become four': four eagles that, after Kumashtam'hu no longer dwells among the Yuma 'in the shape of a man', still keep watch over them and enter their dreams to give them 'power from Kokomaht'. 'Everything that is good comes from Kokomaht,' the legend ends, 'and everything evil comes from Bakutahl.' For Bakutahl, 'the Evil Blind One', survives beneath and 'does bad things'. To him, for instance, are attributable all storms and earthquakes; when such things erupt, 'then the people are afraid and say, "The Blind One is stirring down below"'.

What is remarkable about the Yuma legend of Kokomaht and Bakutahl is that, like so many Native American myths of origin, it combines what might appear contraries: the mystical and the material, the universal and the local, the spiritual and the sexual, the heroic and the comic. It is a tale about the origins of human-ity and about how the Yuma people happen to live where they do; it is about the earth and about Yuma rites and diet. Much the same could be said for such stories as the Zuni account of how the two children of the sun led the people up from beneath the earth, eventually settling them at 'the place called since the first begin-ning, Halona-Itiwana' – the sacred name of Zuni Pueblo, 'the Middle Ant Hill of the World'. So, too, could it be said for the Navajo myth of their own origins and habitation. Guided by 'Changing Woman', embodying the cyclical rhythms of nature, advised by 'Spider Woman', a grandmotherly figure whose wisdom is at the service of humanity, and helped by heroic twins, the Navajo people in this myth make an arduous and perilous journey to a place of destiny that is also their appointed homeplace, marked by the sacred mountains – Hesperus Peak, the Sangre de Cristo, Mount Taylor, the San Francisco Peak – that still measure the boundaries of their land. Along the way, they encounter mythical places that are also actual locations, the legend helping to account for the way they are. A peak named 'the Head', for instance, forty miles northeast of Mount Taylor, is said to be the head of a giant, cut off by one of the heroic twins when the giant barred the jour-ney of the people, a lava flow not far away his coagulated blood. And, at their destination, they establish the sacred rites of the Navajo: songs acknowledging the power of Changing Woman and the sun, the first Scalp Dance celebrating victory over the enemy while also cleansing the warrior of the effects of contact with the enemy dead.

Not all tales of origin resemble those of the Yuma people – and, to a lesser extent, those of the Zuni and the Navajo – in attempting to explain the creation of the world, perhaps the evolution of sun, moon and stars, and human and cultural emergence all in one narrative. There is, for example, the tale told by the Hopi people about a poor little boy who becomes a warrior and kills many. His power comes from his discovery that he is the son of the sun, but the tale is less about this than it is about the specifics of Hopi culture. The enemies the boy kills are all hunter-gatherers, reflecting the fear felt by the Pueblo farmers towards marauding nomadic tribes; and, having killed his enemies, the boy returns to the Hopi village where he proceeds to 'teach the people the right way to live'. On the other hand, there is a legend popular among the Tsimshian, featuring Raven the Giant, a favourite hero among Northwest coast tribes, which is precisely about how daylight came into the world. A shifting, metamorphic creature, the hero of this legend assumes the form of a raven, cedar leaf, child and then raven again, while stealing light from 'the chief of heaven'. More specifically still, there are tales that con-centrate on explaining the existence of a staple or ritual. A Blackfoot story tells how a young man called Bull-by-Himself was taught by the beavers how to grow and smoke tobacco: 'Bull-by-Himself and his wife brought the sacred tobacco to the tribes,' the story ends, 'who have been smoking it in a sacred manner ever since.' A Brule Sioux story tells of a vision quest that became the foundation of all others. An old woman, journeying to 'the top of a lonely hill', finds the 'holy herb' of peyote after strenuous prayers and visions; and she returns to the tribe to introduce them to 'the sacred herb, the drum, the gourd, the fire, the water, the cedar' – everything needed, from sweat lodge to solitary vigil, to achieve a visionary state. Sometimes, the tone of these stories is humorous. A Pima tale, for instance, suggests that white and black people are a mistake of creation, burned too little or too long in the oven of 'the Man Maker', whereas the Pueblo Indian is 'exactly right', perfectly baked and beautiful. Similarly, a Blackfoot story about the discovery of sex has its male and female discoverers smiling with sly delight after the event – 'their whole bodies were smiling, it seemed'. Sometimes, on the contrary, the tone is serious, even rapt. So a Cheyenne legend simply explains how 'Maheu the Creator' first taught the sun dance 'that represents the making of this universe', 'the great medicine dance' to a medicine man and his wife. And a more complex tale, told among the Brule Sioux, tells how 'White Buffalo Woman' brought the sacred pipe that 'stands for all that grows on the earth' to the tribe and then transformed herself from woman into buffalo. 'As soon as she vanished,' the story goes, 'buffalo in great herds appeared' furnishing the people with 'everything they needed – meat for their food, skins for their clothes and tipis, bones for their many tools.' Having given the pipe that holds creation together, White Buffalo Woman then effectively gives herself to hold the tribe together, offering her flesh that others might live. This story of origins is typical in its celebration of the special nature of the story-tellers: in this case, their possession of the pipe and the ties that bind them to what are called here 'our relations, the buffalo'.

The heroes and tricksters who are described creating humanity out of mud, leading the people to their homeplace, appointing the rituals and furnishing corn or buffalo, are permitted many other adventures and activities. Very often, the birth of the hero is shrouded in mystery. In the legends of the Northern Cheyenne, the hero Sweet Medicine is born to a woman 'no man has touched' but who became pregnant after voices and visions appeared to her on four consecutive nights. Even more often, the hero faces trials that vary widely from tribe to tribe: most tribes, though, tell of a ferocious monster that must be evaded – an ogre in a cliff, a sea monster, a gluttonous creature often in the shape of a bull or bear that swallows people – and ordeal by fire or water. Like other legendary beings associated with a different order in time – a time before the floods, perhaps, or before the arrival of Columbus – the hero is able to speak to animals and they are able to speak to him; often, he assumes their shape or they carry and conceal him. Sometimes, the hero is actually an animal, or more likely a human who is at the same time an animal, like Spider Woman, Man-Eagle, Bear-Man, Wakinyan Tanka the Great Thunderbird, or Old Man Coyote. And creatures they have to fight usually assume shapes and personalities as remarkable as theirs. Many tribes, for instance, tell of a great water monster, Unktehi or Uncegila to the Sioux, whose fossil bones are now scattered across the Badlands of Nebraska and the Dakotas. More bizarre is No Body, the Great Rolling Head, a creature who tumbles over mountain and prairie, destroying everything in its way and devouring people with its monstrous teeth. Other legendary monsters include Delgeth, a ferocious man-eating antelope, the Lord Killer of the Whales, Yeitso the terrible giant of the East, and a giant so gigantic that Coyote walks into its belly believing it to be a mountain cave. And in several tales the monster assumes the shape of a white man. In one Chinook legend, for example, the hero is confronted with a 'thing' that 'looked like a bear' but with 'the face of a human being'. It emerges from 'something out in the water', just like any sea monster: only, in this case, this 'strange something' is 'covered with copper', has 'two spruce trees upright on it' with 'ropes tied to the spruce trees'. And it loses its power when the 'strange thing' carrying it is set on fire.

What these tales of heroes rehearse, among other things, are clearly the fears and aspirations of the tribe. Set in some mythical time, but also a product of collective memory, they describe actions that require not only retelling but ritual re-enactment: the tellers would be likely to imitate the heroic manoeuvres of the hero, his saving gestures, as the tale is told. And, eliding very often with tales of origin, they may explain life and the location of the tribe: why the tribe is as and where it is, the legendary past that has made the actual present. In one story told among the Passamaquoddy, for instance, a hero and medicine man called Glooscap destroys a monster, slits open his belly, and the wound he makes becomes 'a mighty stream' 'flowing by the village and on to the great sea of the East'. 'That should be enough water for the people,' Glooscap observes: a comment that acquires its point once we know that the Passamaquoddy were fishermen living on the East coast – their name, in fact, comes from *peskede makadi* meaning 'plenty of herring'. Glooscap is ensuring the survival of the tribe. In another story, told by the Iroquois, a hero based on an actual historical figure, Hiawatha, is at the centre. He here becomes Ta-ren-ya-wa-gon, the Creator and 'upholder of heavens' who 'chose to be a man and took the name of Hiawatha' in order to unite the Iroquois tribes. After bringing the tribes together and instructing them in the right practices and ceremonies, he steps into his 'white mystery canoe' and slowly rises into the sky. 'Hiawatha was gone,' so the legend concludes, 'but his teachings survive in the hearts of the people.'

Fear and awe are mingled in the Cheyenne story of one of their great heroes, Sweet Medicine, the offspring of a virgin birth. Abandoned by his mother on the prairie, raised by an old woman, he already has 'grown-up wisdom and hunting skill' when he is only ten years old. Intimations that he is the chosen one are scattered through the account of his early years. As a child of ten, he kills a miraculous calf and so ends a famine in his village: 'however much they ate of the calf,' the tale reveals, 'there was always more.' And, although for a time he is banished from the village, a prophet without honour in his own country, he reaps advantage from exile. 'Wandering alone on the prairie', Sweet Medicine is led by a mysterious voice inside 'the sacred mountain called Bear Butte'. There he has a meeting with spirits, who instruct him in 'the many useful things by which people could live', give him 'the sacred four arrows' ('two arrows are for war and two for hunting'), and teach him 'how to make a special tipi in which the sacred arrows were to be kept'. With these gifts, Sweet Medicine then makes 'the long journey home', where he finds his people suffering from another famine. 'People of the Cheyenne,' he declaims four times as he approaches the village, 'with great power I am approaching.

Be joyful. The sacred arrows I am bringing.' Instructing his people in 'the sacred laws', teaching them 'what the spirits inside the holy mountain taught him', he establishes 'the true Cheyenne nation' and appeases 'the One Above'. 'At daybreak', after instruction, ceremony and the smoking of 'the sacred tobacco', the story reveals, 'the people emerged from the sacred arrow lodge' and 'found the prairie around them covered with buffalo'. The famine is over. For the duration of four lives, Sweet Medicine lives among his people making the Cheyenne 'a proud tribe respected throughout the Plains'. But 'only the rocks and mountains last forever'. When he knows his end is near, Sweet Medicine instructs his people to carry him to 'a place near the Sacred Bear Butte' and there build him a lodge to die in. He withdraws into the hut to die, but, before doing so, he offers his people one final word of prophecy – or, rather, warning. 'I have seen in my mind,' he announces,

> that some time after I am dead – and may the time be long – light-skinned, bearded men will arrive with sticks spitting fire. They will conquer the land and drive you before them. They will kill the animals who give their flesh that you might live . . . They will take your land until there is nothing left for you.

The future, as Sweet Medicine describes it, seems inexorably fated. All he can offer the people, by way of advice, is the courage to face it and to fight for survival. 'You must be strong,' his parting words are, or 'the Cheyenne will cease to be.'

Courage is one strategy of survival, cunning is another. They are by no means mutually exclusive, of course, which is why so often in Native American legend the hero is also a trickster. The trickster is, however, less a lawgiver usually than a breaker of laws, a rebel against authority and a violator of taboos. And one remarkable feature of Native American tales is just how quickly the great culture bringer can turn into an imp, metamorphosing from creator to clown and then back again. The great trickster figure in these tales is Coyote. There are many others. Blue Jay, Rabbit, Raven, Mink and Ground Squirrel all play their part as troublemakers. So do such human or semi-human characters as Iktome the Sioux Spider Man, Whisky Jack of the Cree and Saultaux, Old Man of the Crow and Blackfoot tribes, Manabozho of the central woodlands and Great Lakes regions and Veeho of the Cheyenne. But it is Coyote who can be found everywhere in tales of the trickster. Certainly, his character may vary from tribe to tribe. In the Plains and plateau regions, stories about Coyote give equal measure to his cleverness and to his clowning, his lechery and cheating, whereas in the North Pacific Coast area there is more attention given to his sharp wit than to his buffoonery. But, even when a tribe has a trickster of its own, Coyote often appears as his companion in mischief. And certain traits are common to Coyote wherever he is found: not least, his spontaneity, his skill at disguise and his gift for metamorphosis.

In one White River Sioux story, for instance, Coyote gives his blanket to a rock and then takes it back again. Trickster tales carry the Native American habit of giving animate life to the supposedly inanimate – trees talk and walk, a lump of pitch fights for his life in these tales – and this one is no exception. The rock demands the blanket back and, when refused, rolls down and flattens Coyote. It is routine for Coyote to be given his comeuppance, in this case for his churlish gift-giving, but it is also routine for him to survive. The flattened-out Coyote is mistaken for a rug by a rancher, who takes it home and puts it in front of the fireplace. But 'whenever Coyote is killed, he can make himself come to life again', the story tells us. Within a night, he has puffed himself up 'into his usual shape'. 'I just saw your rug running away,' the rancher's wife tells her husband. The surreal quality of this story is matched by a Cheyenne tale in which Coyote dances with a star: falling to earth after the dance, he is 'flattened out like a tanned, stretched deerskin' when he hits the ground and is dead for 'quite a few winters' before he is able to 'puff himself up again into his old shape'. Surreal and obscene at the same time is a story told by the Alsea tribe from western Oregon in which Coyote steals the vulvas of two frog women, to provide him with sexual satisfaction when he needs it; 'for this reason frogs, they say, have no female organs'. Explanations of the whys and wherefores of things, as this observation shows, are not unusual in Coyote and other trickster tales. In one Pima story, for instance, we learn that Coyote is 'dust-coloured all over' because one day, in his arrogance, he did not look where he was going and 'ran into a stump so hard that it threw him down in the dirt'. While in another legend, popular among the Karok, a tribe of salmon fishers, we are told how Coyote got his cunning. It was compensation, apparently, for being made among the weakest of the animals by Kareya, 'the god who in the very beginning created the world'.

Fundamental to the character of the trickster is resistance to authority, a celebration of the subversive impulse. Authority, after the arrival of Columbus, gradually came to be associated with the whites – or, to be more exact, a claim to authority – and so it is no surprise to find that, in many versions of these stories, the victim of trickery is white. In one variation on the tales of sharp trading popular in Anglo-American folklore as well as Native American, Coyote meets a white man who believes that 'nobody ever got the better of him' in a trade. 'I've cheated all the Indians around here,' he boasts. But Coyote fools and robs him, by persuading the white trader to lend him his horse and his clothes while he goes to get his 'cheating medicine' so that they can engage in a cheating contest. This Brule Sioux story of a trickster outwitting a white man, and making an idiot of him into the bargain, finds a more complex variation in a White Mountain Apache tale. Coyote fools some white traders into giving him a horse, clothes, saddle and pistol, fools some white soldiers into buying a tree on which he has strung up some money ('I'm going to tell you about this tree,' he informs the soldiers. 'Money grows on it and I want to sell it'), then fools 'the big man in charge' of the town by selling him a burro whose excrement, so he claims, is money – 'and it comes out of him every day'. In stories like this, the boundaries between trickster and hero are more than usually permeable, since Coyote is clearly getting back at and getting even with the figure who, historically, got the better of the encounter between Old World and New. The celebration of the spontaneous in life, cunning and carnival, is here also a reversal of the familiar rhythms of power: for once, the white man gets the raw end of the deal.

Not all the animals that appear in Native American tales are tricksters, of course. Animals are a constant, talkative presence in these stories and their contacts with the human world are incessant and intimate. The animal and human realms merge in Native American belief, humans metamorphose into animals and vice versa, and there are frequent marriages across the shifting, elusive boundaries that divide the two. In one tale told among the Pomo tribe in northern California, a girl marries a rattlesnake and bears him 'four rattlesnake boys'. She visits her parents for a while, but then happily returns to 'Rattlesnake's house' and, we learn, 'has lived there ever since'. In other stories circulated in the Southwest and the Plains, people marry buffaloes, in others from the Northwest the spouse is a whale. In Passamaquoddy legend, it is the great horned owl who carries off his human bride, using his skill on the flute to seduce her. The girl, so the legend goes, 'eventually became used to being married to the great horned owl. Women have to get used to their husbands, no matter who they are'. That laconic, stoical conclusion does not perhaps register the mystery, the magic to be found in many of these tales of marriage between man, or more frequently woman, and beast. More characteristic, in this respect, is the tale of a union between a girl and a bear told by the Haida people. To express his love for his wife, the bear composes a song in her honour, in which he declares, 'I will give her berries from the hill and roots from the ground. I will do all I can to please her'. 'This is the Song of the Bears,' the story explains, 'whoever can sing it has their lasting friendship'; 'that song to this day is known among the children of the Haidas', many of whom claim their descent from the union between the author of the song and its subject. It is a testimony to the vital relation between the human and animal, just as in its way the tale itself is.

Animals are familiar creatures in Native American lore; they are sacred; they are also an important source of food. There is no necessary contradiction here, since the animating belief is that what binds animals and humans together is a living web of mutual aid and respect. A Brule Sioux story illustrates this. It tells of four brothers who go hunting buffalo. They find and kill one and then, all at once, they hear 'the voice of the buffalo making human talk'. 'Take the meat to nourish yourselves,' the voice commands, 'but put the skin, head, hooves, and tail together, every part in its place.' The three older brothers ignore the command, feasting on the buffalo hump and then falling asleep. But the youngest brother obeys. Having put the skin, head, hooves and tail together, he then sees 'all the parts of the buffalo' reunite to form 'a fine strong buffalo who bellowed loudly' before disappearing into the hills. The survival of the buffalo, as a source of food and an object of reverence, is assured for the tribe. The three older brothers, having failed to participate in this rite ensuring survival, are punished by being turned into rattlesnakes. Even as rattlesnakes, however, they have their part to play in the tale of mutuality. The youngest brother returns to them 'four-times-four-days' after their metamorphosis, and they furnish him with the 'snake medicine' that will enable him to become a true warrior. Led by the youngest brother, all the people of the tribe come to them as well, with offerings of 'tobacco and good red meat'. From then on, so the tale goes, 'they protected the people with powerful snake medicine every time we go to war'. 'Rattlesnakes are our cousins': that is one lesson learned from this story. They are an intimate and magical wellspring of power for the Sioux. And the buffalo are just as closely, mystically related: that is the other lesson. The buffalo, as this story puts it, 'gave his flesh so the people might live'. Which is why, having killed the buffalo, the youngest brother then prays to it: it is part of nature, part of him and part of the simultaneously mundane and miraculous connection between the two.

Stories of love between humans and animals often modulate into stories of love between humans, one or both of whom may then turn out to be or become animals – or of animals who may then become human. There is, for instance, the tale told by the Coos tribe in Oregon about one of their women who married a merman and gradually turned into a sea creature. 'Every summer and winter,' the tale reveals, the two lovers 'would put ashore two whales as a gift to their kinsmen above the sea.' Or there is the Maidu legend of a woman who pursues a butterfly, falls asleep exhausted by the pursuit, and awakens to find the butterfly has turned into a man. 'You have followed me this far,' the 'butterfly man' tells her, 'perhaps you would like to follow me always.' 'If so,' he warns, 'you must pass through a lot of my people.' The woman then chases the man now transformed back into a butterfly again, but, when they approach a valley filled with his 'people', the butterflies, she becomes distracted, running after one or other of them, so that she loses the original object of her pursuit. So she dies, still chasing after butterflies; 'and now when people speak of olden times,' the legend tells us, 'they say this woman lost her lover, and tried to get others but lost them, and went crazy and died.' These are tales of longing, pursuit of an elusive object of desire, but there are also more straightforward accounts of desire satisfied: love and lust coexist easily in Native American legend. One story popular among the Ponca tribe of South Dakota, for example, plays on the ancient myth of vagina dentata but opts for a happy consummation. The lover, desperate with desire, 'knocked out the teeth in the girl's vagina', the story discloses, '– except for one blunt tooth that was very thrilling when making love'.

Native American legend is not unusual in frequently linking love and death. There are, for instance, several tales that offer variations on the story associated with Orpheus in western myth. In the variation known among the Zuni people of the Southwest, a young man follows his wife as she passes to the Land of the Dead but, when she sinks to 'the spirit land at the bottom of the lake', he is unable to continue. The young man 'buried his face in his hands', as the legend has it, 'and wept'. Presently, an owl appears and takes him to a cave 'full of owl-men and owl-women', where he is given sleep medicine which, he is told, will transport him to 'some other place' while he slumbers. 'When you awake, you will walk toward the Morning Star,' the owl advises him. 'Following the trail to the middle anthill, you will find your spirit-wife there.' As always in versions of this legend, along with the advice there is a warning. 'Let not your desire to touch and embrace her get the better of you,' the young man is told, 'for if you touch her before bringing her safely home to the village of your birth, she will be lost to you forever.' And, as always, the warning is eventually forgotten, the taboo is momentarily violated. The owls rescue the spirit wife from the Land of the Dead beneath the lake, bringing her to the appointed place to meet her husband when he wakes up. 'When the husband awoke,' the legend reveals, 'he saw first the Morning Star, then the middle anthill, and his wife at his side, still in deep slumber.' When she too wakes up, they begin the long journey home; and 'on the fourth day they arrived at Thunder Mountain and came to the river that flows by Salt Town'. Here, they lie down to rest. And, at that moment, the young man can no longer control himself. 'Gazing at her loveliness,' as his spirit-wife sleeps, 'desire so strong that he could not resist it' overcomes him 'and he stretched out and touched her'. At once, she awakens, weeping, and disappears. 'If the young lover had controlled his desire,' the story concludes, 'then death would have been overcome.' For everyone, 'there would have been no journeying to the land below the lake, and no mourning for others lost'. But then, 'if there were no death, men would crowd each other'. There would be 'more people on this earth than the earth could hold'. There would be 'hunger and war', if there were no death, 'with people fighting over a tiny patch of earth, over an ear of corn, over a scrap of meat'. So, 'maybe what happened was for the best'.

The Zuni tale of a young man and woman not unlike Orpheus and Eurydice is remarkable in a number of ways that take us back to the heart of Native American legend. There is the acceptance, even celebration, of the cycle of life, the necessity of death and the inevitability of renewal. Story is inseparable from ritual in Native American life, since both are forms of re-enactment – that is, rehearsal of the past in the present to ensure continuance in the future – so it is hardly surprising to find the same celebratory acknowledgement of that cycle in Native American ceremony: in, for instance, the songs as well as the stories of the Zuni. Every year, in a complex and ancient ritual called Shalako, the Zuni work to ensure and praise the renewal of life. The formal title of the ritual means 'the Coming of the Gods'. And it derives that name from the belief that the kachinas, who are at once patron spirits of the earth's forces and the Zuni ancestral dead, promised at the beginning of time to return every December to the Zuni homeplace in New Mexico with seeds and moisture to renew life for the coming year. The gods return incarnated in the persons of masked, costumed men, who have spent most of the preceding year in rigorous preparation for their duties. And the poem chanted in unison by the Shalako priests, over the eighth night of Shalako, praises 'Our father, Kawulia Pautiwa', the creator of life: who, 'perpetuating what had been since the first beginning, / Again assumed form / Carrying his waters, / Carrying his seeds' to the people. The performance of the entire poem, with accompanying rituals and repetition, takes about six hours. It confirms that, more than 'maybe', 'death happened for the best' because it is a pivotal part of the cycle of life. And it insists on interdependence as well as continuance. That is, it knits sun, earth, water, humanity, plants and all animate beings together in one complex web of mutually sustaining existence – as in this passage where the growth of the corn ('they') is attributed to divine, human and natural agencies, all working together to ensure that, as the song puts it elsewhere, 'the earth is clothed anew':

> Your earth is enriched with living waters.
> Then in all your water-filled fields,
> These, with which you will renew yourselves,
> Your mothers,
> And the different kinds of corn,
> Within your earth mother
> You will lay down.
> With our earth mother's living waters,
> They will once more become living beings.
> Into the daylight of our sun father
> They will come out standing.
> They will stand holding out their hands to all directions.
> Calling for water.
> And from somewhere,
> Our fathers with their fresh water
> Will come to them.

That sense of the mutuality of all forms of life, announced in the arrival of the corn, is a second remarkable feature of the Zuni tale of the young man and his spirit-wife. It is, after all, their friends the 'owl-men' and 'owl-women' who bring the lovers back together for a while, with magic, advice and warning. A similar sense animates nearly all Native American song and story. It is at work, for instance, in these lines from an Inuit song, set in the bleak environment of Alaska, about what is called 'the Great Weather', a mysterious being that informs sea, wind and sky and moves human beings in directions they do not always understand:

> The great sea stirs me.
>   . . .
> The sky's height stirs me.
> The strong wind blows through my mind.
> It carries me away
> And moves my inward parts with joy.

And then there is the way the Zuni story of the lovers and their owl friends is anchored in a familiar geography. The young man succumbs to the desire to touch the woman he loves, forgetting the owl's warning, at Thunder Mountain close to 'the river that flows by Salt Town'. The owl advised him, earlier on in the story, that he would find his spirit-wife at 'the middle anthill'; and, to catch the resonance of that, we have only to remember that the Zuni myth of origin has their people end their journey from the place of emergence in the Middle, a site of achievement and balance from which no further movement is necessary – and that the sacred

---

name of Zuni Pueblo means the Middle Anthill of the World. Native American myths are about living as and where you are, staying or wandering, and the rhythms that pulse through all creation binding the place where you live to the story of the world and the story of time. They are about continuities between all animate beings, between the living and the dead and future generations, between the mysterious and the mundane – and between the universal and the immediate, furnishing legend with a local habitation and a name. Continuities like these, all of them, are measured in the concluding words of the poem chanted on the eighth night of the Zuni ceremony of the Coming of the Gods: when the man in whom the spirits of the earth and the dead are incarnated, after intense preparation, calls for the life-giving aid ('the breath') of the ancestors ('the fathers') to renew the community ('add your breath') in the here and now. 'Let no one despise the breath of the fathers,' he declares. 'But into your bodies, / Draw their breath.' 'That yonder to where the road of our sun father comes out,' he continues,

> Your roads may reach;
> That clasping hands,
> Holding one another fast,
> You may finish your roads.
> To this end I add your breath now.
> Verily, so long as we enjoy the light of day
> May we greet one another with love,
> Verily, so long as we enjoy the light of day
> May we wish one another well.
> Verily may we pray for one another.
> To this end, my fathers,
> My mothers,
> My children:
> May you be blessed with light;
> May your roads be fulfilled;
> May you grow old;
> May you be blessed in the chase;
> To where the life-giving road of your sun father comes out
> May your roads reach;
> May your roads all be fulfilled.

Spanish and French Encounters with America

The Zuni were the first Pueblo encountered by the Spanish. A party led by Alvar Nuñez Cabeza de Vaca in 1528 had heard tales of an area far to the north where the natives told of the 'Seven Cities of Cibula' overflowing with wealth. So when, some years later, another explorer, the Franciscan Fray Marcos de Niza (1495?– 1542), saw the Zuni village from afar, its light adobe walls glistening in the evening sun, he was convinced that he had discovered the Seven Cities, their streets paved with gold; and he reported back to that effect to the Spanish viceroy in Mexico City. 'I continued my journey till I came in sight of Cibula,' he wrote in 1539 in *A Relation of the Reverend Fray Marcos de Niza, Touching His Discovery of the Kingdom of Ceuola or Cibula*. 'It appeared to be a very beautiful city.' And although he decided not to enter it at this time, 'considering my danger' as he put it, 'and that if I died I would not be able to give an account of that country', he was sure that it was 'bigger than the city of Mexico', that there was 'much gold in it' and that 'the natives of it deal in vessels and jewels for the ears and little plates with which they relieve themselves of sweat'. Furthermore, he reported, his Native American scouts had told him that 'it was the least of the seven cities'; one other 'much bigger and better than all the seven' had 'so many houses and people' that there was 'no end to it'. Such fabulous wealth clearly had to be in the right hands, and its present caretakers taught the twin blessings of Christianity and civilization. 'It occurred to me to call this country the new kingdom of St Francis,' Fray Marcos de Niza recalled; and there, outside the city, 'with the aid of the Indians', he 'made a heap of stones' with 'on top of it' 'a small, slender cross'. The cross was a sign, he explained, that 'all the seven cities' had been taken 'in the name of Don Antonio de Mendoza, viceroy and governor of New Spain for the Emperor, our Lord'. With one simple stroke, announcing both spiritual dominion and material appropriation, the Old World declared that it would take control of the New.

The accounts of fabulous wealth waiting to be possessed, and a native population ripe for conquest and conversion, encouraged a full-scale expedition in 1540 headed by a protégé of the viceroy of New Spain, one Francisco Vasquez de Coronado. Coronado found no gold, of course, even though some members of the expedition journeyed as far as what would later be Kansas, where they encountered the Wichita tribe. One Native American scout, a Plains Indian nicknamed 'the Turk', lured them on with promises that they would soon find the city of their dreams. But eventually, in 1542, the Spanish explorers returned south, having garroted 'the Turk' as a punishment for misleading them, their only consolation being that they had subdued and stolen from the Pueblo Indians. They had not found streets paved with gold. However, as the account of the Coronado expedition written by Pedro de Casteñeda (1520?–1570?) over twenty years later (translated and published in 1904 as *The Journey of Coronado 1540–1542*) reveals, they had found something else: the vastness of America, the immense emptiness of the plains, over which every now and then great herds of buffalo would appear. 'Many fellows were lost at this time,' Pedro de Casteñeda writes, 'who went out hunting and did not get back to the army for two or three days, wandering about the country as if they were crazy, in one direction or another, not knowing where they started from.' If space is the central fact of American experience, as writers from Walt Whitman to Charles Olson have claimed, then this was the European discovery of it. Along with that, as in so many American stories and poems, went the discovery of the sense of being lost in America – sometimes exhilarating and at others, as here, genuinely terrifying. The Spanish could not get over the size and strangeness of everything. 'All over the plains' Pedro de Casteñeda reported, there were vast numbers of bulls: 'the number of those that were without any cows was something incredible.' There were also 'large numbers of animals like squirrels and a great number of their holes': the first recorded account of the prairie dog towns common in the Southwest. Pedro de Casteñeda's narrative of the Coronado expedition captures the abundance together with the vastness of the New World: herds of buffalo, packs of prairie dogs, great seas of 'unripe grapes and currants and wild marjoram', numerous streams all flowing 'into the mighty river of the Holy Spirit which the men with Don Hernando de Soto discovered' – in other words, the Mississippi. What is remarkable about accounts of exploration and conquest like those of Coronado or Columbus is that along with the American dream of success (the Garden of Eden, the Seven Cities) goes the discovery of bafflement. The speech of Europe has no name for either the space or the plenitude of America at this stage. To describe it requires a new language, neither entirely of the Old World or the New: which is another way of describing the evolution of American literature.

'I found myself lost in the woods, going now on this side now on that, without being able to recognize my position.' In this case, the European lost in America is French, Samuel de Champlain (1570?–1635), describing his explorations in *The Voyages to the Great River St Lawrence, 1608–1612* (included in *The Voyages of Samuel de Champlain, 1604–1618* [1907]). There is, however, the same sense of negotiating a terrain that is terrifyingly unfamiliar, uncharted and unnamed. 'I had forgotten to bring with me a small compass which would have put me on the right road, or nearly so,' Champlain wrote. 'I began to pray to God to give me the will and courage to sustain patiently my misfortune.' Eventually, he finds his way back to his Native American companions; and his delight at finding them is matched only by their relief in seeing him again. 'They begged me not to stray off from them any more,' he explains. This is not, clearly, simple solicitude for his welfare on their part. Nor is this episode as a whole just another rehearsal of a common story: the European lost in a world only too familiar to its native inhabitants. Samuel de Champlain's companions admit to him their fear of being accused of killing him, should he have never appeared again; their freedom, honour and even their lives would have been put in jeopardy, had he remained lost. Implicitly, they are acknowledging a dependence on him in the new order of things: their lives have been changed by the arrival of the European, so much so that they need him to be there and are fearful when he is not. The European is, in short, assuming centrality and power: something that Champlain registers in the customary way by naming his surroundings as he looks around him, just like Adam in the Garden of Eden – notably, a great expanse of water that he chooses to call Lake Champlain.

As the narrative progresses, Samuel de Champlain offers further revelations of how the encounter between Old World and New transformed both. He comes across a 'strange fish', his account tells us, that for now neither he nor any other European has a name for. 'This makes war upon all others in the lakes and rivers' and is 'called by the savages of the country, *Chaousaroo*'; it will eventually be christened, although not by Champlain, 'garpike'. 'There are also many beavers,' Champlain observes: a casual remark that acquires point when we remember that he was involved in the fur trade. Samuel de Champlain may not have imagined encountering cities of gold but he had his own, more easily realizable dream of success, his own way of making America a site of profit and power. In the course of his *Voyages*, Champlain also reveals how he promoted the French alliance with the Hurons against the Iroquois and introduced his allies to firearms. During one Iroquois attack, he tells the reader, he loaded his musket with four balls and, as a result, killed two of the enemy and fatally wounded a third with one shot. 'The Iroquois were greatly astonished that two men had been so quickly killed,' he reports triumphantly, 'although they were equipped with armour woven from cotton thread, and with wood which was proof against arrows'; and, as more shots rang out from Champlain and his companions, they hastily fled. The Iroquois had begun the attack by walking 'at a slow pace', 'with a dignity and assurance which greatly amused me', Champlain recalls. For the Native American, warfare was a ceremony, brutal but full of magic. For the European, however, it was or had become a much more practical, more straightforwardly ruthless affair. A moment like this marks the appearance of a new element in Native American life: a change that has an immediate, devastating effect on the bodies of Native Americans and other, subtler and more long-term implications for their beliefs and customary behaviour.

Samuel de Champlain professed himself amused by the strangeness of the 'savages' he encountered. Other early explorers and colonizers claimed simply to be shocked by their savagery and idolatry. So, the French Huguenot René Goulaine de Laudonnière (fl. 1562–82), in his *A Notable Historie Containing Four Voyages Made by Certaine French Captaines unto Florida* (1587), describes a bloodthirsty ritual witnessed by some of his men – at the time of establishing a colony in 1564 – with a mixture of incredulity and horror. Invited to a feast, Laudonnière tells us, the white men saw one of the Native Americans, who sat 'alone in one of the corners of the hall', being stabbed by some of the others. When 'he that had been struken fell down backwards', then the son of the chief appeared 'apparelled in a long white skin, fel down at the feet of him that was fallen backward, weeping bitterly half a quarter of an hour'. Two others 'clad in like apparel' joined him and also began to 'sigh pitifully', after which 'a company of young girls' appeared and, 'with the saddest gestures they could devyse', carried the corpse away to an adjoining house. Asked by the visitors 'for what occasion the Indian was so persecuted in their presence', the chief explained 'that this was nothing else but a kind of ceremony' by which he and his tribe 'would call to mind the death and persecution of . . . their ancestors executed by their enemy'. The explanation does not, however, satisfy either those who witnessed the event or Laudonnière who reports it. It remains for all of them just another example of the pointless cruelty of the local inhabitants (Laudonnière, in fact, follows this example with several others) and their consequent need to be conquered, converted and civilized.

While there might be general agreement that, if they were not to be slaughtered, then the Native Americans needed to be converted as well as subdued, there was disagreement about what conversion involved. To the king of Spain, the colony established by René Goulaine de Laudonnière represented a violation of the true faith of Catholicism. What is more, it threatened his power and dominion in the New World, and so he ordered its elimination. Pedro Menéndez de Avilés (1519–74), who became captain-general under Philip II, carried out the order with ruthless efficiency, in the process founding St Augustine, the oldest permanent city of European origin in the United States. While carrying out the royal command, however, Menéndez de Avilés was also pursuing his own dream, which was to settle as large an area of the conquered territory as possible. Menéndez de Avilés overstretched himself; and, in a series of increasingly desperate letters, he wrote back to those with the resources, including Philip II himself, begging for help. The letters show how very closely the narratives, and the rhetoric, of conversion and conquest were intertwined, and how, in fact, the projects of spiritual dominion and material gain were seen as mutually dependent. The elimination of the French would 'leave us more free to implant the Gospel in these parts', Menéndez de Avilés explained in a letter to Philip II written in 1565. It would enable him 'to enlighten the natives, and bring them to allegiance to Your Majesty'. 'Forasmuch as this land is very large,' he went on, 'there will be much to do these fifty years'; with the proper support and supplies, though, 'I hope in Our Lord that He will give me success in everything, that I and my descendants may give these Kingdoms to Your Majesty free and unobstructed, and that the people thereof may become Christians.' 'Being master of Florida,' Menéndez de Avilés reminded his king, 'you will secure the Indies and the navigation thereto.' 'I assure Your Majesty that henceforth you can sustain Florida at very little cost,' he added, and 'it will yield Your Majesty much money, and will be worth more to Spain than New Spain or even Peru.' All he asked or rather prayed for at this juncture was 'to be provided with great diligence', since he and his fellow settlers were enduring 'very great hunger' and, without immediate help, many would 'pass away from this world from starvation'.

Writing to 'a Jesuit friend' in 1565 in a very similar vein, Menéndez de Avilés told terrible tales of Native American idolatry. 'The ceremonies of these people consist in great measure in adoring the sun and moon,' he tells his correspondent, 'and the dead deer and other animals they hold as idols.' Many of the natives had, however, 'begged' him 'to let them become Christians'; 'and I have replied', he said, 'that I am expecting your worships'. 'It has done the greatest harm,' he warned, 'that none of your worships, nor any other learned religious' had 'come to instruct these people' since they were 'great traitors and liars' and desperately needed 'the preaching of the Holy Gospel'. And to press his point home, Menéndez de Avilés even resorted to prayer. 'May Our Lord inspire the Good Society of Jesus to send to these parts as many as six of its members,' he implored, '– may they be such – for they will certainly reap the greatest reward.' Menéndez de Avilés was clearly hoping that an investment of priests by the Society of Jesus would be the first investment in a series that would allow his settlement to prosper. To encourage this, he was not averse to suggesting that the return on such an investment would not just be a spiritual one: the Jesuits, he intimated, would reap souls if they came

The First Americans

over as missionaries but also a more tangible harvest. It was the same readiness to associate spiritual and material conquest that had led Fray Marcos de Niza to use the sign of the cross to announce that Spain had taken possession of the legendary Seven Cities of gold. Mastery of souls and mastery of the land shared a story and a vocabulary; they were part of one great imperial project.

That project was also the subject of and inspiration for the first American epic poem of European origin, *Historia de la Nueva Mexico*, published in 1610. The poem was written by Gaspar Pérez de Villagrá (1555–1620), who was the official chronicler of the expedition led by Juan de Oñate that established Spanish settlements in north central New Mexico. 'I sing of arms and the heroic man', the poem begins, echoing the opening lines of the *Aeneid*, the epic poem by Virgil celebrating the founding of Rome. That captures the form, style and the fundamental aim of the *Historia*. The conventions of the traditional epic poem, and high rhetoric, are deployed here to celebrate the founding of a new empire, the mission of which is to civilize the wilderness and convert its native inhabitants. Addressing the 'great King' of Spain in these opening lines, Villagrá asks him to lend 'attentive ear' while the poet tells him about

> the load of toil
> Of calumny, affliction under which
> Did plant the evangel holy and the Faith of Christ
> That Christian Achilles whom you wished
> To be employed in such heroic work.

The 'Christian Achilles' is, of course, Oñate; and Villagrá presents his expedition as an early religious version of Manifest Destiny. Conversion is seen, in other words, as part of the destined westward expansion of the Catholic church, moving from Jerusalem to Asia Minor to Rome and, now, to 'nations barbarous, remote / From the bosom' of the true faith. What may seem surprising about this poem is that it allows the 'barbarous' people whom Oñate has to civilize, the Acomas, an epic dignity. During the battles with the Spanish, the Acomas are presented as courageous. Prior to one battle, Zutapacan the Acoma leader – who, for the most part, is the chief villain of the poem – is even allowed a romantic episode, as he takes leave of his bride with elaborate expressions of regret and admiration for her beauty: her eyes, he declares, offer 'peace and light' to him, her lips conceal 'lovely, oriental pearls'. But this, after all, is the dignity of the noble savage, whose strength and weakness derive precisely from his simplicity and simple ignorance of the true faith. To a large extent, the native inhabitants of the West are treated in this poem just as, traditionally, the peoples of the East have been by European writers: as strange, exotic and, above all, 'other'. This is surely why the eventual levelling of the Acoma village, the killing of eight hundred Acomas and the enslavement of many more are all seen as not only inevitable but right. It is part of an imaginative venture that, like the historical enterprise it celebrates, refuses to see the Native Americans and their culture on anything like their own terms.

Where there was closer contact between the early Spanish settlers and native peoples the story could, however, get more complicated. That closer contact often meant captivity. An account of the expedition of Hernando De Soto of 1539–43, for instance, by an anonymous 'Gentleman of Elvas' (fl. 1537–57), *The Discovery and Conquest of Terra Florida* (1557; translated by Richard Hakluyt, 1611), tells how members of the party came upon a group of 'ten or eleven Indians'. Among them, we learn, 'was a Christian, which was naked and scorched with the sunne, and had his arms razed after the Indians, and differed nothing at all from them'. When the Spanish party approached, the account goes on, the naked Christian 'began to crie out, Sirs, I am a Christian, slay me not, nor these Indians for they have saved my life'. The Christian turns out to be Spanish; and he explains how he was captured, prepared for death but saved by the mediation of an Indian woman, a daughter of the chief. His story anticipates one that was to become common, made most famous in the tale of Pocahontas saving John Smith. Quite probably, it reveals European misunderstanding of a Native American ritual: the visitor is being 'saved' in a ceremony of welcome and bonding. Certainly, it allows for acknowledgement of the humanity, the saving graces of at least some of the 'savages'. What is more remarkable here, though, is the recognition of how the Christian may be changed by the Indian rather than change him. The Christian, so we are told, has come to differ 'nothing at all' from his captors; his is a story, not of conquest, but of acculturation.

That story is told at more length by Alvar Nuñez Cabeza de Vaca (1490?–1556?), who accompanied an expedition to the Gulf Coast in 1528 led by Pánfilo de Narváez. After floating on rafts from Florida to Texas, nearly all in the expedition were lost. Cabeza de Vaca and three companions, drifting somewhere off the coast of Texas or Louisiana, were captured and enslaved by Indians. However, they adapted to Indian customs over the several years of their captivity, so much so that they were trusted to move freely between tribes. Eventually, journeying through the Southwest into northern Mexico, they came across Spanish settlements and were returned to Spain. There Cabeza de Vaca wrote his memoirs, published in 1542 and later translated as *Relation of Alvar Nuñez Cabeza de Vaca* (1871), which were intended both to justify him and to promote royal support for further expeditions to the New World. He could hardly claim conquest. So what he did was to write a captivity narrative, one of the first, in which the experiences of being lost in America and then living among its natives were all seen as part of one providential plan. As Cabeza de Vaca describes it, his perilous journey through the wilderness was attended by miracles. On one occasion, 'thanks to God', he found 'a burning tree' in the chill and darkness of the woods, 'and in the warmth of it passed the cold night'. On another, he survived by making 'four fires, in the form of a cross'. And, on still another, he prayed and 'through the mercy of God, the wind did not blow from the north' any more; 'otherwise', he says, 'I would have died'. 'Walking naked as I was born,' Cabeza de Vaca recalls, stripped of all the signs of his civilization except his faith, he is captured but then proceeds to convert his captors. Like one of the early saints, he becomes both missionary and saviour, using the beliefs of the Old World and the herbs of the New to heal the sick and creating a new religion out of Christian prayer and Native American custom. Captivity tale, in effect, modulates into conversion narrative; and, in a way that was to become familiar in American writing, material failure is reimagined as spiritual success. The hero is one of God's elect, according to this pattern; and not only his survival, but every moment in his life is reinterpreted as the work of providence.

In the closing chapters of his memoirs, Cabeza de Vaca turns from his captivity, and his life as a missionary, to his return to civilization. It is an uneasy, ambiguous return. Cabeza de Vaca and his fellow captives have some Indians with them; and, when some Spanish soldiers first catch sight of the group, they evidently do not know what to make of what they see. 'They were astonished at the sight of me, so strangely habited as I was,' Cabeza de Vaca recalls, 'and in company with Indians.' The unease grows as, it turns out, the Spanish show signs of wanting to make slaves of the Indians. Not only that, despite the threat to their freedom, the Indians make it clear that they want Cabeza de Vaca and the other captives to return with them; 'if they returned without doing so', Cabeza de Vaca explains, 'they were afraid they should die'. 'Our countrymen became jealous at this,' Cabeza de Vaca goes on, giving the Indians to understand 'that we were of them, and for a long time had been lost; that they were lords of the land who must be obeyed . . . while we were persons of mean condition.' The reply to this is simple and forceful. 'The Indians,' Cabeza de Vaca reports,

> said the Christians lied: that we had come whence the sun rises, and they whence it goes down; we healed the sick, they killed the sound; that we had come naked and barefooted, while they had arrived in clothing and on horses with lances; that we were not covetous of anything . . . ; that the others had only the purpose to rob whosoever they found.

'Even to the last,' Cabeza de Vaca concludes later, 'I could not convince the Indians that we were of the Christians.' What we have here is the tacit admission by the author of this extraordinary account that, according to the perception of most people around them, 'we' – that is, he and his fellow captives – are now no longer 'Christian' nor 'Indian' but in between, a curious and debatable hybrid. Anticipating many later heroes and heroines in American literature, they occupy a border area between one culture, one version of experience and another. They are mixed New World beings now; and their tale, finally, is about neither conquest nor captivity but about the making of Americans.

Anglo-American Encounters

Into that making, from its earliest stages, went not only the Spanish and the Portuguese, the French and the Native Americans, but also the English and their immediate neighbours in Scotland, Wales and Ireland. From the beginning, the story of America is a story neither of a monolith nor a melting pot but a mosaic: a multicultural environment in which individuals negotiate an identity for themselves between the different traditions they encounter. And the tale of American literature has been one of pluralism: collision, conflict and even congruence between different languages and literatures, each of them struggling to articulate the experience of being in the world. The congruence is certainly there. English settlers, and those promoting English settlement of America, undoubtedly shared with Columbus and others a dream of Eden. Or, if they were simply trying to sell the idea of colonization to businessmen or aristocratic investors, they at least claimed to believe in that dream. America, one writer quoted earlier on insisted, was a 'Virgin Countrey' sealed in its aboriginal state so as to remind humanity, and more particularly visitors from the Old World, what the earth was like when it was 'vigorous and youthfull', before it had fallen into decrepitude and dismay, 'the Old Age of Creation'. It unfolded visions of lost innocence and innocence regained, past perfection and future promise. That writer, the author of this not untypical piece of nostalgic utopianism, was one Edward Williams (fl. 1650). He was writing in 1650, in one of the pamphlets ('Virginia, more especially the South Part thereof Richly and Truly Valued') supporting the colonizing enterprises of the London Company in what was then known as Virginia. And it is in the literature dealing with the English colonization of this area that the sheer abundance of the New World, its fertility and the opportunity it offered for the recovery of a mythical good life, is most energetically and unambiguously expressed.

In the early years of English exploration of Virginia, as it was then understood, this sense that the New World might offer a new start was expressed in a relatively tentative way. So, the elder Richard Hakluyt (?–1591), in a pamphlet for the Virginia enterprise, merely proposed for the reader's consideration the idea that 'the poor and idle persons which are either burdensome or hurtfull to this Realm at home may become profyttable members by ymploying theme . . . in these Countreyes'; while one Sir George Peckham (?–1608) simply mentioned in passing that the 'great number of men which doe now live ydely at home' might 'imploy [them]selves . . . in matters of husbandry' across the seas. The younger Richard Hakluyt (1552–1616) was a little more forthright. In his *Discourse Concerning Western Planting* addressed to Elizabeth I (and eventually included, along with the pamphlet of the elder Hakluyt, in *The Original Writings and Correspondence of the Two Richard Hakluyts* [1935]), he gave careful attention to the possibility of using the New World as a means of release and revival. He began by citing the example of other countries. This in itself was not a new device. Other writers had suggested a parallel between the condition of England and that, say, of ancient Rome before it became an imperial power. Here, for example, are some typical lines from a poem, 'M. J. H., His Opinion of the Intended Voyage', which, like the comments of Sir George Peckham, served as a preface to an account of English adventuring called *The Voyages and Colonising Enterprises of Sir Humprey Gilbert* (1610):

The Romans when the number of their people grewe so great,
As neither warres could waste, nor Rome suffice them for a seate,
They led them forth by swarming troops, to foreign lands amaine,
And founded divers Colonies, unto the Roman raigne.
Th' athenians us'de the like devise . . .

But to this use of example Hakluyt added another element, the sense of rivalry with the two great contemporary powers of exploration and exploitation. 'Portingale and Spain,' he declared, '. . . by their discoveries, have founde such occasion of employmente, that this many yere we have not herde scarcely of any pirate of these two nations.' Not only that, Hakluyt played on the fear, rife in Elizabethan England, that overpopulation, the enclosure of the common land and the eviction of those working it might lead to widespread poverty, starvation and even civil strife. 'They can hardly lyve one by another,' he said of the English people, 'nay they are ready to eat up one another.' The only solution was emigration to Virginia, where emigrants could find work 'in plantinge of sugar cane, in maynetenaunce and increasing of silk worms, . . . in gatherings of cotton . . . in tilling of the soil there for grains, in dressing of vines'. A safety-valve for dissent in England, the restoration of individual fortunes and the creation of a new commonwealth would all, as a consequence, be assured.

Following on the younger Hakluyt, later writers became still more positive about the promise of the New World. 'God himself is the founder and favourer of this Plantation,' asserted one William Crashaw (1572–1626) in 1617, in his 'Epistle Dedicatorie' to a pamphlet about Virginia, 'Good Newes from Virginia' (1617) by Alexander Whitaker (fl. 1617). In order to drive the point home, Crashaw and others compared Virginia to the Promised Land and its potential immigrants to the Israelites. It became commonplace to 'prove' the providential nature of the place by such things as the miraculous escape of two early English explorers, called Gates and Somers, from shipwreck and their subsequent discovery of Bermuda. It became equally commonplace to describe in detail the fertility and beauty of the countryside, as in this passage from 'Virginia . . . Richly and Truly Valued' by Williams, suggesting how the supposed virginity of the new country was accompanied by a pleasing ripeness:

Nor is the present wilderness of it without a particular beauty, being all over a natural Grove of Oaks, Pines, Cedars, Cypress, Mulberry, Chestnut, Laurel, Sassafras, Cherry, Plumtree, and Vines, all of so delectable an aspect, that the melancholiest eye in the World cannot look upon it without contentment or admiration. No shrubs or underwoods choke up your passage, and in its season your foot can hardly direct itself where it will not be dyed in the blood of large and delicious Strawberries.

In effect, the pamphleteers claimed that, as one Ralph Hamor (fl. 1615) put it in 'A True Discourse of the Present Estate of Virginia' (1615), this was 'a land more like the garden of Eden, which the Lord planted, than any part also of the earth'. A cross between Arcadia and that place 'in which it pleased God himself to set the first man and most excellent creature Adam in his innocency' – as a preacher William Symonds (1556–1616?) claimed, in 'Virginia: A Sermon Preached at White-Chapel' (1609) – it inspired some to visionary rhetoric. Others were driven to sing their praises of the newly discovered land in verse, as in these rather creaking lines from 'News from Virginia' by Robert Rich (1587–1688), published in 1610:

> There is no fear of hunger here,
>   for Corne much store here grows,
> Much fish the gallant Rivers yield,
>   in truth, without suppose.
>
> Great stores of Fowle, of Venison,
>   of Grapes, and Mulberries,
> Of Chestnuts, Walnuts, and such like
>   of fruits and Strawberries.
>
> There is indeed no want at all . . .

In this ideal atmosphere, observers, pamphleteers and preachers like William Symonds argued, Englishmen could once more flourish in the occupation of Adam, 'that most wholesome, profitable, and pleasant work of planting'. All they had to do – and here it is Robert Rich speaking – was 'but freely cast corn into the ground, and with patience wait for a blessing'. The blessing would be as much spiritual as material. For, working with a land that would 'yield much more fruit to independent labours' than the tired, cramped soil of their native land, English settlers would recover their independence, the means and so the will to rely on nobody but themselves. Returned to conditions where 'he maie have ground for nothing more than he can manure', each settler would recover his ancient, Anglo-Saxon virtues – his pride, his thrift, his generosity and hospitality. That was intimated or insisted on time and again, in pamphlets like the ones from which the two comments just quoted are taken, 'A True Discourse of the Present Estate of Virginia' (1615) by Ralph Hamor and 'Good Newes from Virginia' by Alexander Whitaker. What the New World was seen or believed to promise was the newest and yet the oldest of societies, the recovery of an ancient sense of community and sociability:

> If any fall sick and cannot compass to follow his crop which if not followed, will soon be lost, the adjoining neighbour will . . . join together and work on it by spells . . . and that gratis. Let any travel, it is without charge, and at every house is entertainment as in a hostelry, and with it a hearty welcome are stranger entertained.

This vision of a return, not just to Eden but to antique English virtues, was announced by John Hammond (fl. 1655–6) in 'Leah and Rachel; or, The Two

The First Americans

Fruitfull Sisters, Virginia and Maryland', in 1656. In another pamphlet, 'Virginia Impartially Examined' by William Bullock (1594–1650), published a year earlier, the vision was accompanied by an elaborate social programme. Following the utopian impulses common among so many writers of the time (Sir Thomas More's *Utopia* [1516] was an early example), Bullock devoted most of his attention to an elaborate plan for a social, economic and political system that had the good farmer at its centre and the restoration and perpetuation of self-reliance and self-subsistence as its ultimate aim. The details of the plan, which Bullock seriously proposed for the English colonies in Virginia, hardly matter. What does matter is that this was symptomatic of a general tendency to see the New World, particularly in the South, as a new Eden that might and should develop into a new commonwealth: a new England in which would be recovered the lost virtues of the old. That tendency was to have a profound impact, not only on individual writers and thinkers like Thomas Jefferson, but on the whole project of imagining America.

The name most often associated with the early English settlement of Virginia is not that of William Bullock, however, or of John Hammond – or, for that matter, of any of the other pamphleteers – but that of Captain John Smith (1580–1631). In 1606, when the Virginia Company sent out its first colonists, Smith, who already had a life of adventure behind him, sailed with them as one of seven councillors. The organizers of the Virginia Company, and many of the settlers, had the Spanish model of colonization in mind: profit for the company's investors was to be acquired through conquest and the discovery of gold. But, even before he became president of the settlement in 1608, Smith had a very different aim. For him, survival not profit was the priority. To this end, he spent time exploring the region and negotiating with the Native Americans for food. He sent men out to live with the natives to learn their language, customs and system of agriculture. And he framed a policy summed up in his formula that 'he who does not work shall not eat'. Smith's policy proved unpopular among many of his fellow colonizers, who were expecting the easy pickings promised by a city of gold or the easy living promised in a new Eden. Smith was replaced by the Virginia Company in 1609. He went back to England, never to return to Virginia. Soon shifting his vision to the region he would name New England, he travelled there in 1614 to gather information about its climate and terrain. And, when his further efforts to colonize New England were stymied, he devoted his time to writing about a project in which he was no longer allowed to participate, in the North as well as the South. *A True Relation of Virginia* had already appeared in 1608. This was now followed by *A Description of New England* (1616), *The Generall Historie of Virginia, New England, and the Summer Isles* (1624) and *The True Travels, Adventures, and Observations of Captaine John Smith* (1630).

Smith was quick to explain in these books how he differed from other travel writers like the Hakluyts. 'I am no Compiler by hearsay, but have been a real Actor,' he proudly asserted at the beginning of *The Generall Historie*. He had had first-hand experience. So, he felt, he could speak with authority about the New

World and 'the Salvages' he had found there. As all his books reveal, however, that experience seems only to have compounded his sense of European superiority. The Virginia Company recommended a tactful, even gentle policy toward Native Americans, no doubt because they were aware of just how easily local enmity could threaten their investment. Despite that, though, and despite the fact that Smith and his companions in Virginia were dependent on the local tribe, the Powhatans, for food, Smith never ceased to think of Native Americans as inferior and was never reluctant to intimidate them with a show of force. Even while he was negotiating with the Powhatans for provisions, Smith refused their request for him and his men to lay aside their arms during negotiations. 'Many doe informe me,' Smith records the Powhatan chief as saying, 'your coming hither is not for trade, but to invade my people, and possesse my Country.' 'To free us of this feare,' the chief implores, 'leave aboord your weapons, for here they are needless, we being all friends.' Smith proudly remembers how he refused the request, which is dismissed as a 'subtill discourse' or probable trick. The 'Salvages' were frightened by the guns, and what they might portend, and he wanted to exploit that fear.

Even the most famous story in *The Generall Historie*, of how the daughter of the Powhatan chief, Pocahontas, saved John Smith from execution, is not quite the celebration of Native American courage and grace under pressure that, in the retelling over generations, it has tended to become. As Smith originally tells the story, it has quite other implications that reflect his own sense of his mission, to tame the wilderness and make it fit for civilization. 'Two great stones were brought . . . then as many as could layd hands on him . . . and thereon laid his head,' Smith recalls, here as elsewhere telling the tale of his captivity in the third person. The 'Salvages', having dragged Smith to a place of execution, are then 'ready with their clubs, to beate out his brains'; and Smith is only rescued when '*Pocahontas* the Kings dearest daughter, when no intreaty could prevail, got his head in her armes, and laid her owne upon his to save him from death'. The moment does not occur in Smith's earlier account of his captivity in *A True Relation*, which has led some to doubt that it really happened. Whether it happened or not, though, it becomes here part of a narrative pattern that subsumes it, making it one episode in a tale telling how the '*Barbarians*' were mastered. The chief, Pocahontas's father, is momentarily appeased; and Smith is returned to confinement. Then, a few days later, the reader is told, the chief comes to where Smith is being held. He is dressed up 'more like a devill than a man, with some two hundred more as blacke as himself' accompanying him. He orders Smith to go to Jamestown to acquire 'two great gunnes' for the Powhatan. Not having much choice, Smith goes with '12 guides' to keep an eye on him. He expects 'every houre to be put to one death or another' by his guards, 'but almightie God (by his divine providence) had mollified the hearts of those sterne Barbarians', Smith records with gratitude. He survives, returns with two cannon and then, by the simple expedient of firing them off, persuades the Powhatans not to take them. On hearing the noise of cannon fire, 'the poor Salvages ran away halfe dead with fear', Smith explains with a mixture of amusement and contempt. After this terrifying experience, all the Powhatans want by way of gift or trade is not guns but mere 'toys'. Not for the first time, by his own account, Smith uses the fear and ignorance of the Powhatans to get what he wants, to assert the superiority of his own claims. And, seen in the context of that account as a whole, Pocahontas's saving gesture seems less the act of a noble savage that it later came to be – and more part of an evolutionary tale in which the savage yields to the advance of the civilized. Pocahontas's evident readiness to sacrifice her life for John Smith, in other words, becomes here a romantic variation on the theme that runs through all this particular captivity tale. The Native American, according to this theme, acknowledges both the superiority and the inevitability of the European and is overpowered or, as in this specific case, offers her acknowledgement in the form of personal sacrifice.

The civilization that John Smith anticipated coming to the New World, and pushing aside the Native American, was one that he came more and more to associate with New England rather than Virginia. This was hardly surprising, because the Massachusetts Bay Colony was much more driven by the ideas of settlement, private property and the establishment of a body politic than many of the early Virginia investors and adventurers were. It came much closer to Smith's own preferences and his emphasis on useful toil. 'Who can desire more content, that hath small meanes . . . then to tread, and plant that ground hee hath purchased by the hazard of his life?' Smith asked in *A Description of New England*. 'If he have but the taste of virtue . . . what to such a mind can bee more pleasant, then planting and building a foundation for his Posteritie, gotte from the rude earth . . . ?' For Smith, appealing for settlers to plant a colony in New England, prosperity would flow naturally to anyone of middling condition who was willing to venture as he had done. It would come 'by Gods blessing and . . . industrie', as a sign of special election and a reward for hard work. Anyone in England with only 'small wealth to live on' could 'by their labour . . . live exceeding well' in America, Smith declared. And they could add to the usefulness of their toil by 'converting those poor Salvages' who lived there 'to the knowledge of God', by instruction, admonition and the power of example, showing their faith by their works. Like others eager to promote settlement, Smith was not reluctant to use national pride, and a sense of rivalry with other imperial powers, to promote his cause. Nor was the dream of Eden and its recovery ever very far from his thoughts. '*Adam* and *Eve* did first beginne this innocent worke, To plant the earth to remaine to posteritie,' he pointed out. '*Noe* [Noah], and his family, beganne againe the second plantation; and their seed as it still increased, hath still planted new Countries, and one countrie another.' Without such devotion to the planting of seeds and faith, Smith insisted, 'wee our selves, had at this present beene as Salvage, and as miserable as the most barbarous Salvage yet uncivilized'; the European, in short, would have been as benighted and as desperate as the Native American. Now it was up to Smith's own contemporaries to show similar devotion: so that the spread of civilization and Christianity could continue and a plantation much like Eden wrested out of the wilderness of the New World.

Writing of the Colonial and Revolutionary Periods

There were, of course, those who dissented from this vision of a providential plan, stretching back to Eden and forward to its recovery in America. They included those Native Americans for whom the arrival of the white man was an announcement of the apocalypse. As one of them, an Iroquois chief called Handsome Lake, put it at the end of the eighteenth century, 'white men came swarming into the country bringing with them cards, money, fiddles, whiskey, and blood corruption'. They included those countless, uncounted African Americans brought over to America against their will, starting with the importation aboard a Dutch vessel of 'Twenty Negars' into Jamestown, Virginia, in 1619. They even included some European settlers, those for whom life in America was not the tale of useful toil rewarded that John Smith so enthusiastically told. This was especially the case with settlers of very limited means, like those who went over as indentured servants, promising their labour in America as payment for their passage there. In a series of letters to his parents the indentured servant Richard Frethorne (fl. 1623), for instance, complained of sickness, starvation and living 'in fear of the enemy every hour' in Virginia. 'For God's sake send beef and cheese and butter,' he wrote to them in 1623. Shortly after, the entreaties became more urgent. 'I pray you . . . not to forget me, but by any means redeem me,' he wrote, '. . . release me from this bondage and save my life.' Frethorne did not suggest that he was alone in his suffering. On the contrary, 'people cry out day and night – Oh! That they were in England without their limbs', he averred, '– and would not care to lose a limb to be in England again, yea, though they beg from door to door'. His sense of the extremity of his suffering, though, did lead him to compare himself in particular, not to Adam, but to 'holy Job'. 'I . . . curse the time of my birth,' he confessed, 'I thought no head had been able to hold so much water as doth daily flow from mine eyes'. And the sheer bitterness of his sense of exile in the wilderness offers a useful corrective to the dominant European version of early settlement in the New World.

Puritan narratives

Dominant that version was, though, and in its English forms, along with the writings of John Smith, it was given most powerful expression in the work of William Bradford (1590–1657) and John Winthrop (1588–1649). Bradford was one of the Puritan Separatists who set sail from Leyden in 1620 and disembarked at Plymouth. He became governor in 1621 and remained in that position until his death in 1657. In 1630, he wrote the first book of his history, *Of Plymouth Plantation*; working on it sporadically, he brought his account of the colony up to 1646, but he never managed to finish it. Nevertheless, it remains a monumental achievement. At the very beginning of *Of Plymouth Plantation*, Bradford announces that he will write in the Puritan 'plain style, with singular regard to the simple truth in all things', as far as his 'slender judgement' will permit. This assures a tone of humility, and a narrative that cleaves to concrete images and facts. But it still allows Bradford to unravel the providential plan that he, like other Puritans, saw at work in history. The book is not just a plain, unvarnished chronicle of events in the colony year by year. It is an attempt to decipher the meaning of those events, God's design for his 'saints', that exclusive, elect group of believers destined for eternal salvation. The 'special work of God's providence', as Bradford calls it, is a subject of constant analysis and meditation in *Of Plymouth Plantation*. Bradford's account of the arrival of the Pilgrim Fathers in the New World is notable, for instance, for the emphasis he puts on the perils of the 'wilderness'. 'For the season was winter,' he points out, 'and they that know the winters of that country know them to be sharp and violent.' 'Besides,' he adds, all the Pilgrims could see was 'but a hideous and desolate wilderness, full of wild beasts and wild men'; 'the whole country . . . represented a wild and savage hue' and, 'if they looked behind them', all these 'poor people' could see there 'was the mighty ocean which they had passed and was now a main bar and gulf to separate them from all the civil parts of the world.' 'What could now sustain them but the Spirit of God and His Grace?' Bradford asks rhetorically. The survival of the Puritans during and after the long voyage to the New World is seen as part of the divine plan. For Bradford, America was no blessed garden originally, but the civilizing mission of himself and his colony was precisely to make it one: to turn it into evidence of their election and God's infinite power and benevolence.

This inclination or need to see history in providential terms sets up interesting tensions and has powerful consequences, in Bradford's book and similar Puritan narratives. *Of Plymouth Plantation* includes, as it must, many tales of human error and wickedness, and Bradford often has immense difficulty in explaining just how they form part of God's design. He can, of course, and does fall back on the primal fact of Original Sin. He can see natural disasters issuing from 'the mighty hand of the Lord' as a sign of His displeasure and a test for His people; it is notable that the godly weather storms and sickness far better than the godless do in this book, not least because, as Bradford tells it, the godly have a sense of community and faith in the ultimate benevolence of things to sustain them. Nevertheless, Bradford is hard put to it to explain to himself and the reader why 'sundry notorious sins' break out so often in the colony. Is it that 'the Devil may carry a greater spite against the churches of Christ and the Gospel here . . . ?' Bradford wonders. Perhaps it is the case with evil 'as it is with waters when their streams are stopped or dammed up'; 'wickedness being stopped by strict laws', it flows 'with more violence' if and when it 'breaks out'. Perhaps, he suggests, it is simply that 'here . . . is not more evils in this kind' but just clearer perception of them; 'they are here more discovered and seen and made public by due search, inquisition and due punishment'. Bradford admits himself perplexed. And the fact that he does so adds dramatic tension to the narrative. Like so many great American stories, *Of Plymouth Plantation* is a search for meaning. It has a narrator looking for what might lie behind the mask of the material event: groping, in the narrative present, for the possible significance of what happened in the past.

Which suggests another pivotal aspect of Bradford's book and so much Puritan narrative. According to the Puritan idea of providence at work in history, every material event does have meaning; and it is up to the recorder of that event to find out what it is. At times, that may be difficult. At others, it is easy. Bradford has no problem, for example, in explaining the slaughter of four hundred of the Pecquot tribe, and the burning of their village, by the English. 'It was a fearful sight to see them thus frying in the fire and the streams of blood quenching the same,' Bradford admits, '. . . but the victory seemed a sweet sacrifice.' The battle is seen as one in a long line waged by God's chosen people, part of the providential plan; and Bradford regards it as entirely appropriate that, once it is over, the victors should give 'the praise thereof to God, who had wrought so wonderfully for them, thus to . . . give them so speedy a victory over so proud and insulting an enemy'. Whether difficult or not, however, this habit of interpreting events with the help of a providential vocabulary was to have a profound impact on American writing – just as, for that matter, the moralizing tendency and the preference for fact rather than fiction, 'God's truth' over 'men's lies', also were. That habit encouraged a tendency towards allegory and symbol: something that was to lead Ralph Waldo Emerson, for example, to regard every material fact as the symbol of some spiritual truth – and writers like Nathaniel Hawthorne and Herman Melville to worry constantly about what significance, if any, might lurk beneath the surfaces of human behaviour.

Of Plymouth Plantation might emphasize the sometimes mysterious workings of providence. That, however, does not lead it to an optimistic, millennial vision of the future. On the contrary, as the narrative proceeds, it grows ever more elegiac. Bradford notes the passing of what he calls 'the Common Course and Condition'. As the material progress of the colony languishes, he records, 'the Governor' – that is, Bradford himself – 'gave way that they should set corn every man for his own particular'; every family is allowed 'a parcel of land, according to the proportion of their number'. The communal nature of the project is correspondingly diluted. 'The experience that was had in this common course and condition, tried sundry years and that amongst godly and sober men,' Bradford sadly observes, 'may well evince the vanity of that conceit of Plato's . . . that the taking away of property and bringing in community into a commonwealth would make them happy and flourishing'. The communitarian spirit of the first generation of immigrants, those like Bradford himself whom he calls 'Pilgrims', slowly vanishes. The next generation moves off in search of better land and further prosperity; 'and thus', Bradford laments, 'was this poor church left, like an ancient mother grown old and forsaken of her children'. The passing of the first generation and the passage of the second generation to other places and greater wealth inspires Bradford to that sense of elegy, the intimations of a vision recovered for a moment and then lost, that was to become characteristic of narratives dramatizing the pursuit of dreams in America. It also pushes *Of Plymouth Plantation* towards a revelation of the central paradox in the literature of immigration – to be revealed again and again in American books – that material success leads somehow and ineluctably to spiritual failure.

Ten years after Bradford and his fellow Pilgrims landed at Plymouth, John Winthrop left for New England with nearly four hundred other Congregationalist Puritans. The Massachusetts Bay Company had been granted the right by charter to settle there and, prior to sailing, Winthrop had been elected governor of the colony, a post he was to hold for twelve of the nineteen remaining years of his life. As early as 1622, Winthrop had called England 'this sinfull land'; and, playing variations on the by now common themes of poverty and unemployment, declared that 'this Land grows weary of her Inhabitants'. Now, in 1630, aboard the *Arbella* bound for the New World, Winthrop took the opportunity to preach a lay sermon, *A Modell of Christian Charity*, about the good society he and his fellow voyagers were about to build. As Winthrop saw it, they had an enormous responsibility. 'Thus stands the cause betweene God and us,' Winthrop insisted, 'wee are entered into Covenant with him for this worke': that is, they had entered into a contract with God of the same kind He had once had with the Israelites, according to which He would protect them if they followed His word. Not only the eyes of God but 'the eyes of all people are upon us', Winthrop declared. They were a special few, chosen for an errand into the wilderness. That made their responsibility all the greater; the divine punishment was inevitably worse for the chosen people than for the unbelievers. What was 'a truthe in profession onely' among those left behind in the churches of England had to be 'familiar and constant practice' amongst them. 'Wee must love, brotherly, without dissimulation,' Winthrop told his congregation; 'wee must love one another with a pure heart fervently; wee must bear one anothers burthens.'

Written as a series of questions, answers and objections that reflect Winthrop's legal training, *A Modell of Christian Charity* is, in effect, a plea for a community in which 'the care of the public must oversway all private respects'. It is fired with a sense of mission and visionary example. 'Wee shall finde that the God of Israell is among us, when tenn of us shall be able to resist a thousand of our enemies,' Winthrop explained; 'when hee shall make us a prayse and glory, that men shall say of succeeding plantacions: the lord make it like that of New England; for wee must Consider that wee shall be as a Citty upon a Hill.' To achieve this divinely sanctioned utopia, he pointed out to all those aboard the *Arbella*, 'wee must delight in each other, make others Condicions our owne . . . allwayes having before our eyes our Commission and Community in the worke, our Community as members of the same body'. This utopia would represent a translation of the ideal into the real, a fulfilment of the prophecies of the past, 'a story and a by-word through the world' in the present, and a beacon, a living guide for the future. It would not exclude social difference and distinction. Quite the contrary, Winthrop began his sermon by explaining how 'God Almightie in his . . . providence hath soe disposed of the Condicion of mankinde, as in all times some must be rich some poore; some high and eminent in power and dignitie; others meane and in subjecion'. But it would be united as the various organs of the human body were. 'All true Christians are of one body in Christ,' Winthrop argued; 'the ligaments of this body which knitt together are love'; and the community he and his fellows were about to found would be a living analogue of this – a body politic in which, as he put it, 'the sensiblenes and Sympathy of each others Condicions will necessarily infuse into each parte a native desire and endeavour, to strengthen, defend, preserve, and comfort the other'.

Along with the sense of providence and special mission, Winthrop shared with Bradford the aim of decoding the divine purpose, searching for the spiritual meanings behind material facts. He was also capable of a similar humility. His spiritual autobiography, for instance, *John Winthrop's Christian Experience* – which was written in 1637 and recounts his childhood and early manhood – makes no secret of his belief that he was inclined to 'all kind of wickednesse' in his youth, then was allowed to come 'to some peace and comfort in God' through no merit of his own. But there was a greater argumentativeness in Winthrop, more of an inclination towards analysis and debate. This comes out in his journal, which he began aboard the *Arbella*, and in some of his public utterances. In both a journal entry for 1645, for instance, and a speech delivered in the same year, Winthrop developed his contention that true community did not exclude social difference and required authority. This he did by distinguishing between what he called natural and civil liberty. Natural liberty he defined in his journal as something 'common to man with beasts and other creatures'. This liberty, he wrote, was 'incompatible and inconsistent with authority and cannot endure the least restraint'. Civil liberty, however, was 'maintained and exercised in a way of subjection to authority'; it was the liberty to do what was 'good, just, and honest'. It was 'the same kind of liberty wherewith Christ hath made us free', Winthrop argued. 'Such is the liberty of the church under the authority of Christ', and also of the 'true wife' under the authority of her husband, accounting 'her subjection her honor and freedom'. Like the true church or true wife, the colonist should choose this liberty, even rejoice in it, and so find a perfect freedom in true service.

Challenges to the Puritan oligarchy

John Winthrop found good reason for his belief in authority, and further demands on his capacity for argument, when faced with the challenge of Anne Hutchinson (1591–1643). A woman whom Winthrop himself described in his journal as being 'of ready wit and bold spirit', Hutchinson insisted that good works were no sign of God's blessing. Since the elect were guaranteed salvation, she argued, the mediating role of the church between God and man became obsolete. This represented a serious challenge to the power of the Puritan oligarchy, which of course had Winthrop at its head. It could hardly be countenanced by them and so, eventually, Hutchinson was banished. Along with banishment went argument: Winthrop clearly believed that he had to meet the challenge posed by Hutchinson in other ways, and his responses in his work were several. In his spiritual autobiography, for instance, he pointedly dwells on how, as he puts it, 'it pleased the Lord in my family exercise to manifest unto mee the difference between the Covenant of Grace and the Covenant of workes'. This was because, as he saw it, Hutchinson's heresy was based on a misinterpretation of the Covenant of Grace. He also dwells on his own personal experience of the importance of doing good. In a different vein, but for a similar purpose, in one entry in his journal for 1638, Winthrop reports a story that, while travelling to Providence, Rhode Island, after banishment, Hutchinson 'was delivered of a monstrous birth' consisting of 'twenty-seven several lumps of man's seed, without any alteration or mixture of anything from the woman'. This, Winthrop notes, was interpreted at the time as a sign of possible 'error'; and he does not resist that interpretation since, after all, Hutchinson has been guilty of a monstrous resistance. She has not accepted that 'subjection to authority' that is the mark of the true Christian and the good woman. Rumour and argument, personal experience and forensic expertise are all deployed in Winthrop's writings to meet the challenges he saw to his ideal community of the 'Citty upon a Hill'. The threat to the dominant theme of civilizing and Christianizing mission is, in effect, there, not only in Bradford's elegies for a communitarian ideal abandoned, but also in Winthrop's urgent attempts to meet and counter that threat by any rhetorical means necessary.

William Bradford also had to face challenges, threats to the purity and integrity of his colony; and Anne Hutchinson was not the only, or even perhaps the most serious, challenge to the project announced on board the *Arbella*. The settlement Bradford headed for so long saw a threat in the shape of Thomas Morton (1579?– 1642?); and the colony governed by Winthrop had to face what Winthrop himself described as the 'divers new and dangerous opinions' of Roger Williams (1603?– 1683). Both Morton and Williams wrote about the beliefs that brought them into conflict with the Puritan establishment; and, in doing so, they measured the sheer diversity of opinion and vision among English colonists, even in New England. Thomas Morton set himself up in 1626 as head of a trading post at Passonagessit which he renamed 'Ma-re Mount'. There, he soon offended his Puritan neighbours at Plymouth by erecting a maypole, revelling with the Indians and, at least according to Bradford (who indicated his disapproval by calling the place where Morton lived 'Merry-mount'), selling the 'barbarous savages' guns. To stop what Bradford called Morton's 'riotous prodigality and excess', the Puritans led by Miles Standish arrested him and sent him back to England in 1628. He was to return twice, the first time to be rearrested and returned to England again and the second to be imprisoned for slander. Before returning the second time, though, he wrote his only literary work, *New English Canaan*, a satirical attack on Puritanism and the Separatists in particular, which was published in 1637.

In *New English Canaan*, Morton provides a secular, alternative version of how he came to set up 'Ma-re Mount,' how he was arrested and then banished. It offers a sharp contrast to the account of those same events given in *Of Plymouth Plantation*. As Bradford describes it, Morton became 'Lord of Misrule' at 'Merry-mount', and 'maintained (as it were) a School of Atheism'. Inviting 'the Indian women for their consorts' and then dancing around the maypole, Morton and his companions cavorted 'like so many fairies, or furies, rather', 'as if they had anew revised and celebrated the feasts of the Roman goddess Flora, or the beastly practices of the mad Bacchanalians'. Worse still, Bradford reports, 'this wicked man' Morton sold 'evil instruments' of war to the Indians: 'O, the horribleness of this villainy!' Morton makes no mention of this charge. What he does do, however, is describe how he and his fellows set up a maypole 'after the old English custom' and then, 'with the help of Salvages, that came thether of purpose to see the manner of our Revels', indulge in some 'harmeles mirth'. A sense of shared values is clearly suggested between the Anglicanism of Morton and his colleagues and the natural religion of the Native Americans. There is a core of common humanity here, a respect for ordinary pleasures, for custom, traditional authority and, not least, for the laws of hospitality that, according to Morton, the Puritans lack. 'These people,' Morton says of the local tribe, 'leades the more happy and freer life, being voyde of care, which torments the mindes of so many Christians.' Acting 'according to humane reason, guided onely by the light of nature', they have an instinctive sense of the divine, they are satisfied with a modest sufficiency, 'they are not delighted in baubles, but in usefull things', and they live as a true community – indeed, 'Platoes Commonwealth is so much practiced by these people'. The Puritans, on the other hand, fear natural pleasure, they are treacherous and inhospitable – Morton describes them, for instance, killing their Indian guests, having invited them to a feast. Respecting neither their divinely appointed leader, the king, nor the authority of church tradition, they live only for what they claim is the 'spirit' but Morton believes is material gain, the accumulation of power and property.

New English Canaan, as its title implies, is a promotional tract as well as a satire. It sets out to show that New England is indeed a Canaan or Promised Land, a naturally abundant world inhabited by friendly and even noble savages. Deserving British colonization, all that hampers its proper development, Morton argues, is the religious fanaticism of the Separatists and other Puritans. Morton divides his book in three. A celebration of what he calls 'the happy life of the Salvages', and their natural wisdom, occupies the first section, while the second is devoted to the natural wealth of the region. The satire is concentrated in the third section of what is not so much a history as a series of loosely related anecdotes. Here, Morton describes the general inhumanity of the Puritans and then uses the mock-heroic mode to dramatize his own personal conflicts with the Separatists. Morton himself is ironically referred to as 'the Great Monster' and Miles Standish, his principal opponent and captor, 'Captain Shrimp'. And, true to the conventions of mock-heroic, the mock-hero Shrimp emerges as the real villain, while the mock-villain becomes the actual hero, a defender of traditional Native American and English customs as well as a victim of Puritan zeal and bigotry. There is considerable humour here. For instance, Standish and his eight brothers in arms, surrounding Morton's house prior to capturing him, are compared to 'the nine worthies coming before the Denne of this supposed Monster (this seven headed hydra, as they termed him)'. And their assault on the house is likened to that of 'Don Quixote against the Windmill'. But that humour can scarcely conceal Morton's bitterness. Confined on an island, just before his removal to England, Morton reveals, he was brought 'bottles of strong liquor' and other comforts by 'Salvages'; by such gifts, they showed just how much they were willing to 'unite themselves in a league of brotherhood with him'. 'So full of humanity are these infidels before those Christians,' he remarks acidly. At such moments, Morton appears to sense just how far removed his vision of English settlement is from the dominant one. Between him and the Native Americans, as he sees it, runs a current of empathy; while between him and most of his fellow colonists there is only enmity – and, on the Puritan side at least, fear and envy.

That William Bradford feared and hated Morton is pretty evident. It is also clear that he had some grudging respect for Roger Williams, describing him as 'godly and zealous' but 'very unsettled in judgement' and holding 'strange opinions'. The strange opinions Williams held led to him being sentenced to deportation back to England in 1635. To avoid this, he fled into the wilderness to a Native American settlement. Purchasing land from the Nassagansetts, he founded Providence, Rhode Island, as a haven of dissent to which Anne Hutchinson came with many other runaways, religious exiles and dissenters. Williams believed, and argued for his belief, that the Puritans should become Separatists. This clearly threatened the charter under which the Massachusetts Bay colonists had come over in 1630, including Williams himself, since it denied the royal prerogative. He also insisted that the Massachusetts Bay Company charter itself was invalid because a Christian king had no right over heathen lands. That he had no right, according to Williams, sprang from Williams's seminal belief, and the one that got him into most trouble: the separation of church and state and, more generally, of spiritual from material matters. Christianity had to be free from secular interests, Williams declared, and from the 'foul embrace' of civil authority. The elect had to be free from civil constraints in their search for divine truth; and the civil magistrates had no power to adjudicate over matters of belief and conscience. All this Williams argued in his most famous work, *The Bloody Tenent of Persecution*, published in 1644. Here, in a dialogue between Truth and Peace, he pleaded for liberty of conscience as a natural right. He also contended that, since government is given power by the people, most of whom are unregenerate, it could not intervene in religious matters because the unregenerate had no authority to do so. But religious freedom did not mean civil anarchy. On the contrary, as he wrote in his letter 'To the Town of Providence' in 1655, liberty of conscience and civil obedience should go hand in hand. Williams used the analogy of the ocean voyage. 'There goes many a Ship to Sea, with many a Hundred Souls in One Ship,' he observed. They could include all kinds of faiths, '*Papists* and *Protestants*, *Jews* and *Turks*', each going to 'their own particular Prayers or Worship'. 'Notwithstanding this liberty,' Williams pointed out, 'the Commander of this Ship ought to command the Ship's Course; Yea, and also to command that Justice, Peace, and Sobriety, be kept and practised.' This was 'a true Picture of a Common-Wealth, or an human Combination, or Society'.

Like Thomas Morton, Williams was also drawn to the Native Americans: those whom writers like Bradford and Winthrop tended to dismiss as 'savage barbarians'. His first work, *A Key into the Language of America*, published in 1643, actually focuses attention on them. 'I present you with a *key*,' Williams tells his readers in the Preface, 'I have not heard of the like, yet framed, since it pleased God to bring that mighty *Continent of America* to light.' 'Others of my Countrey-men have often, and excellently, . . . written of the *Countrey*,' he concedes. But 'this *key*, respects the *Native Language* of it, and happily may unlocke some Rarities concerning the *Natives* themselves, not yet discovered'. Each chapter of Williams's *Key* begins with an 'Implicit Dialogue', a list of words associated with a particular topic, the Nassagansett words on the left and their English equivalents on the right. This is followed by an 'Observation' on the topic; and the topics in these chapters range from food, clothing, marriage, trade and war to beliefs about nature, dreams and religion. A 'generall Observation' is then drawn, with cultural inferences and moral lessons being offered through meditation and analogy. Finally, there is a conclusion in the form of a poem that contrasts Indian and 'English-man'. These poems, in particular, show Williams torn between his admiration for the natural virtues of Native Americans, and their harmony with nature, and his belief that the 'Natives' are, after all, pagans and so consigned to damnation. Implicit here, in fact, and elsewhere in the *Key* is an irony at work in a great deal of writing about the 'noble savage'. His natural nobility is conceded, even celebrated: but the need for him to be civilized and converted has to be acknowledged too. Civilized, however, he would invariably lose those native virtues that make him an object of admiration in the first place. And he could not then be used as Williams frequently uses him here, as a handy tool for attacking the degenerate habits of society.

Williams was clearly drawn to the simplicity and what he saw as the humility of Native American life. When he writes of the Nassagansett religion in his *Key*, for instance, he points out that the Nassagansetts have instinctively understood the 'two great points' of belief: '1. That God is. 2. That hee is a rewarder of all them that diligently seek him.' He is even intrigued by what he sees as their apprehension of a spiritual presence in everything. 'They conceive that there are many Gods or divine Powers within the body of a man,' he observes of the Nassagansetts. 'There is a generall Custome among them, at the apprehension of any Excellency in Men, Women, Birds, Beasts, Fish &c,' he adds, 'to cry out Manittoo, that is, it is a God.' The intrigue, or even sympathy, however, quickly shades into suspicion, since such a custom cannot but remind him, he admits, of the 'Papists'. And inevitably, inexorably towards the end of his chapter on religion and its vocabularies, Williams feels obliged to point out that the Nassagansetts may well be one of 'the wandring Generations of *Adams* lost posteritie': one of the ten lost tribes of Israel, that is, whose ignorance is a sign of their spiritual exile. The chapter concludes, appropriately enough, with a vision of judgement. 'Two sorts of men shall naked stand,' Williams solemnly announces, 'Before the burning ire / Of him that shortly shalle appeare / In dreadful flaming fire'. The Indian belongs with the millions who 'know not God' and his fate is a warning. For, 'If woe to *Indians*, Where shall *Turk*, / Where shall appeare the *Jew*?' For that matter, 'Where shall stand the Christian false? / O blessed then the True'. The Native American may have native virtues but they place him, in the hierarchy of final judgement, only slightly above those degenerates of civilization who embrace a false religion or are false to the true one.

He remains below all those who follow the true path. Williams's *Key* is an immense and imaginative project, founded on a recognition many later writers were to follow that the right tool for unlocking the secrets of America is a language actually forged there. But it remains divided between the natural and the civilized, the native and the colonist, the 'false' and the 'true'. Which is not at all to its disadvantage: quite the opposite, that is the source of its interest – the measure of its dramatic tension and the mark of its authenticity.

Some Colonial poetry

While Puritans were willing to concede the usefulness of history of the kind Bradford wrote or of sermons and rhetorical stratagems of the sort Winthrop favoured, they were often less enthusiastic about poetry. 'Be not so set upon poetry, as to be always poring on the passionate and measure pages,' the New England cleric Cotton Mather warned; 'beware of a boundless and sickly appetite for the reading of . . . poems . . . and let not the Circean cup intoxicate you.' Nor were such suspicions about the seductions of verse confined to Puritan New England. 'At this day / All poetry there's many to gainsay', wrote Elizabeth Sowle Bradford (1663?– 1731), a Quaker who settled in New York. 'If any book in verse, they chance to spy, /' she observed, 'Away profane, they presently do cry'. Yet Bradford herself wrote verse, citing the Biblical examples of David and Solomon. Poetry, she averred, 'hath been the delight of kings', 'I'm apt to think that angels do embrace it'. The Book of Revelation, she pointed out, foretold that the saints in heaven would sing 'a new song before the throne' (Rev. 14:5). Or, as she put it, 'And though God give't here but in part to some, / Saints shall have't perfect in the world to come'. That was a characteristic defence of those who disagreed with people like Cotton Mather. Poetry was to be found in the Bible; it was a resource of saints and angels; it could be a vehicle for understanding and communicating religious truth. Not all colonists saw poetry in these terms, of course. Some adopted classical models, or imitated popular English poets like Ben Jonson and John Donne, John Milton and John Dryden. John Saffin (1626–1710), an inhabitant of Massachusetts, for instance, wrote poems in praise of women that mixed classical references with elegant wit. 'Fair Venus, and Minerva both combine: / Resplendently, to make their graces thine,' he wrote in an 'Acrostic on Mrs Winifred Griffin' (unpublished until 1928); 'Each in her proper station; Wit and Beauty / Take thee for mistress out of bounden duty.' In turn, George Alsop (1636–73?) from Maryland wrote a poem in praise of trade, 'Trafique is Earth's Great Atlas' (1666); 'Trafique is Earth's great *Atlas*,' it begins, 'that supports / The pay of Armies, and the height of Courts.' Benjamin Tompson (1642–1714) of Massachusetts composed an epic poem about war with the Algonquin Indians, *New Englands Crisis* (1676), revised as *New Englands Tears* (1676). Richard Steere (1643?–1721) from Connecticut wrote, among other things, allegories of nature like 'On a Sea-Storm Nigh the Coast' (1700) and *The Daniel Catcher* (1713), an anti-Catholic response to the English poem *Absalom and Achitophel* (1681–2) by John Dryden. And Sarah Whipple Goodhue (1641–81) of Massachusetts left some touching 'Lines to Her Family' (1681) to be read after her death, as a testament to the 'natural affection' she said she felt for them all. Verse was prized among some colonists, at least, as a way of commemorating public events and personal experiences. It could take the form of lyric, elegy, ballad or epic, acrostic, satire. It was commonly a means of making sense of things, connecting the particular with the general. But only in New England was the general defined mainly in religious and Biblical terms. Elsewhere, and particularly in the South, it was likely to reflect the classical education of the author and his or her interest in matters of love, politics and public exchange.

Of the verse that survives from this period, however, most of the finest and most popular among contemporaries inclines to the theological. The most popular is represented by *The Day of Doom*, a resounding epic about Judgement Day written by Michael Wigglesworth (1631–1705), *The Bay Psalm Book* (1640) and *The New England Primer* (1683?). *The Day of Doom* was the biggest-selling poem in colonial America. In 224 stanzas in ballad metre, Wigglesworth presents the principal Puritan beliefs, mostly through a debate between sinners and Christ. This stanza, one of the many describing the torments of the damned, is typical:

> *Luke 13:28*   They wring their hands, their caitiff hands
> and gnash their teeth for terrour;
> They cry, they roar for anguish sore,
> and gnaw their tongues for horrour
> But get away without delay,
> Christ pities not your cry:
> Depart to Hell, there may you yell
> *Prov. 1:26*   and roar eternally.

The simple diction, the driving rhythms and the constant marginal references to Biblical sources are all part of Wigglesworth's didactic purpose. This is poetry intended to drive home its message, to convert some and to restore the religious enthusiasm of others. Many Puritan readers committed portions of the poem to memory; still more read it aloud to their families. The sheer simplicity and fervour of its message made it an ideal instrument for communicating and confirming faith. So it is, perhaps, hardly surprising that Cotton Mather could put aside his distrust of poetry when it came to a work like *The Day of Doom*. At Wigglesworth's death, in fact, Mather confessed his admiration for the poet: who, Mather said, had written for 'the Edification of such Readers, as are for Truth's dressed up in *Plaine Meeter*'.

Even more popular than *The Day of Doom*, however, were *The Bay Psalm Book* and *The New England Primer*. Only the Bible was more widely owned in colonial New England. *The Bay Psalm Book* was the first publishing project of the Massachusetts Bay Colony, and offered the psalms of David translated into idiomatic English and adapted to the basic hymn stanza form of four lines with eight beats in each line and regular rhymes. Here, for example, are the opening lines of Psalm 23:

> The Lord to me a shepherd is,
>> Want therefore shall not I.
> He in the folds of tender grass
>> Doth cause me down to lie.

The work was a collaborative one, produced by twelve New England divines. One of them, John Cotton, explained in the Preface that what they had in mind was 'Conscience rather than Elegance, fidelity rather than poetry'. 'We have . . . done our endeavour to make a plain and familiar translation,' Cotton wrote. 'If therefore the verses are not always so smoothe and elegant as some may desire . . . , let them consider that God's Altar need not our polishings.' What was needed, Cotton insisted, was 'a plain translation'. And, if the constraints imposed by the hymn stanza form led sometimes to a tortured syntax, then neither the translators nor the audience appear to have minded. The psalms were intended to be sung both in church and at home, and they were. *The Bay Psalm Book* was meant to popularize and promote faith, and it did. Printed in England and Scotland as well as the colonies, it went through more than fifty editions over the century following its first appearance. It perfectly illustrated the Puritan belief in an indelible, divinely ordained connection between the mundane and the miraculous, the language and habits of everyday and the apprehension of eternity. And it enabled vast numbers of people, as Cotton put it, to 'sing the Lord's songs . . . in our English tongue'.

The New England Primer had a similar purpose and success. Here, the aim was to give every child 'and apprentice' the chance to read the catechism and digest improving moral precepts. With the help of an illustrated alphabet, poems, moral statements and a formal catechism, the young reader was to learn how to read and how to live according to the tenets of Puritan faith. So, for instance, the alphabet was introduced through a series of rhymes designed to offer moral and religious instruction:

A	In *Adams* Fall
	We sinned all
B	Thy life to mend
	This *Book* attend
	. . .
Y	*Youth* forward slips
	Death soonest nips

Clearly, the *Primer* sprang from a belief in the value of widespread literacy as a means of achieving public order and personal salvation. 'Now the Child being entred in his Letters and Spelling,' it announces at the end of the alphabet, 'let him learn these and such like Sentences by Heart, whereby he will be both instructed in his Duty, and encouraged in his Learning.' Equally clearly, as time passed and the *Primer* went through numerous revisions, the revised versions reflected altering priorities. The 1758 revision, for instance, declares a preference for 'more grand noble Words' rather than 'diminutive Terms'; a 1770 version describes literacy as more a means of advancement than a route to salvation; and an 1800 edition opts for milder versified illustrations of the alphabet ('A was an apple pie'). But this tendency to change in response to changing times was a reason for the durability and immense popularity of the *Primer*: between 1683 and 1830, in fact, it sold over five million copies. And, at its inception at least, it was further testament to the Puritan belief that man's word, even in verse, could be used as a vehicle for God's truth.

That belief was not contested by the two finest poets of the colonial period, Anne Bradstreet (1612?–1672) and Edward Taylor (1642?–1729). It was, however, set in tension with other impulses and needs that helped make their poetry exceptionally vivid and dramatic. With Bradstreet, many of the impulses, and the tensions they generated, sprang from the simple fact that she was a woman. Bradstreet came with her husband to Massachusetts in 1630, in the group led by John Winthrop. Many years later, she wrote to her children that, at first her 'heart rose' when she 'came into this country' and 'found a new world and new manners'. 'But,' she added, 'after I was convinced it was the way of God, I submitted to it and joined the church in Boston.' What she had to submit to was the orthodoxies of faith and behaviour prescribed by the Puritan fathers ('Many times hath Satan troubled me concerning the verity of the Scriptures,' she confessed, 'many times by atheism how could I know there was a God . . . ?'). Along with this submission to patriarchal authority, both civil and religious, went acknowledgement of – or, at least, lip service to – the notion that, as a woman, her primary duties were to her family, as housekeeper, wife and mother. Bradstreet raised eight children. She also found time to write poetry that was eventually published in London in 1650 as *The Tenth Muse Lately Sprung Up in America*. Publication was arranged by Bradstreet's brother-in-law, who added a preface in which he felt obliged to point out that the poetry had not been written to the neglect of family duties. Readers of *The Tenth Muse* might well wonder, he admitted, 'whether it be a woman's work, and ask, is it possible?' He was happy to reassure them that the poems were, indeed, the work of a woman 'honored and esteemed' for 'her gracious demeanour . . . her pious conversation, her courteous disposition, her exact diligence in her place, and discreet managing of family occasions'. The poetry was 'the fruit but of some few hours, curtailed from her sleep and other refreshments'. Poet she might be, but there was no reason to suspect that Bradstreet had forgotten, for a moment, her role and responsibilities as a female.

Writing in a climate of expectations such as this, Bradstreet made deft poetic use of what many readers of the time would have seen as her oxymoronic title of woman poet. One of her strategies was deference. In 'The Prologue' to *The Tenth Muse*, for instance, Bradstreet admitted that 'To sing of wars, captains, and of kings, / Of cities founded, commonwealths begun,' was the province of men. Her 'mean pen', she assured the reader, would deal with other matters; her 'lowly lines' would concern themselves with humbler subjects. The deference, however, was partly assumed. It was, or became, a rhetorical device; a confession of humility could and did frequently lead on to the claim that her voice had its own song to sing in the great chorus. 'I heard the merry grasshopper . . . sing, /' she wrote in 'Contemplations', 'The black-clad cricket bear a second part'. 'Shall creatures abject thus their voices raise /', she asked, 'And in their kind resound their Maker's praise, / Whilst I, as mute, can warble forth higher lays?' Playing upon what her readers, and to a certain extent what she herself, expected of a female, she also aligned her creativity as a woman with her creativity as a writer. So, in 'The Author to her Book' (apparently written in 1666 when a second edition of her work was being considered), her poems became the 'ill-form'd offspring' of her 'feeble brain', of whom she was proud despite their evident weaknesses. 'If for thy father asked,' she tells her poems, 'say thou had'st none: / And for thy mother, she alas is poor, / Which caus'd her thus to send thee out of door.' Identifying herself as a singular and single mother here, Bradstreet plays gently but ironically with Puritan sensibilities, including her own. This is a gesture of at once humility and pride, since it remains unclear whether Bradstreet's 'ill-form'd offspring' have no father in law or in fact. They might be illegitimate or miraculous. Perhaps they are both.

An edition of the poems of Bradstreet was published in Boston six years after her death, with a lot of new material, *Several Poems Compiled with Great Variety of Wit and Learning*. It contains most of her finest work. It is here, in particular, that the several tensions in her writing emerge: between conventional subject matter and personal experience, submission to and rebellion against her lot as a woman in a patriarchal society, preparation for the afterlife and the pleasures of this world, and between simple humility and pride. The focus switches from the public to the private, as she writes about childbirth ('Before the Birth of One of Her Children'), married love ('To My Dear and Loving Husband'), her family growing up ('In reference to Her Children, 23 June, 1659'), about personal loss and disaster ('Upon the Burning of Our House, July 10th, 1666') and, in particular, about bereavement ('In memory of My Dear Grandchild Elizabeth Bradstreet, Who Deceased August, 1665, Being a Year and Half Old'; 'On My Dear Grandchild Simon Bradstreet; Who Died on 16 November, 1669, being but A Month, and One Day Old'). What is especially effective and memorable about, say, the poems of married love is their unabashed intimacy. 'If ever two were one, then surely we. / If ever man were loved by wife then thee,' she writes in 'To My Dear and Loving Husband'. And, in 'A Letter to Her Husband, Absent Upon Public Employment', she consoles herself while her beloved is gone by looking at their children: 'true living pictures of their father's face', as she calls them, 'fruits which through thy heat I bore'. There is ample time to dwell here on what Bradstreet calls her 'magazine of earthly store', and to reflect that, even when she is 'ta'en away unto eternity', testimony to the pleasures of the things and thoughts of time will survive – in the 'dear remains' of her 'little babes' and her verse. And the one dear remains will find delight and instruction in the other. 'This book by any yet unread, / I leave for you when I am dead, /' she writes in a poem addressed 'To My Dear Children', 'That being gone, here you may find / What was your living mother's mind'.

The tensions between time and eternity, earthly and heavenly love, are particularly acute in the poems about loss and bereavement. Her poem on the burning of the family home, for example, may end by seeking the conventional consolation. 'Thou hast an house on high erect, / Framed by that mighty Architect', Bradstreet reminds herself, which, 'With glory richly furnished, / Stands permanent though this be fled'. But this seems of only a little comfort, given that most of the poem is devoted to the terrible experience of seeing 'pleasant things in ashes lie'. Not only that, the sense of loss is rendered acutely sharp and painful by focusing on the destruction not so much of household goods as of the delights and comforts of home – and of a possible future as well as a pleasurable past. 'Under thy roof no guest shall sit, / Nor at thy table eat a bit /', she reflects as she gazes at the ruins. 'No pleasant tale shall e'er be told, /' she muses, 'Nor things recounted done of old. / No candle e'er shall shine in thee, / Nor bridegroom's voice e'er heard shall be'. Similarly, in her poems on the deaths of her grandchildren in infancy, the acknowledgement that God's will should and will be done hardly begins to resolve or explain things for Bradstreet – as these lines on the death of her granddaughter suggest:

> Farewell dear babe, my heart's too much content,
> Farewell sweet babe, the pleasure of mine eye,
> Farewell fair flower that for a space was lent,
> Then ta'en away into eternity.
> Blest babe, why should I bewail thy fate,
> Or sigh thy days so soon were terminate,
> Sith thou art settled in an everlasting state.

The grieving repetitions of the first three lines here yield only slightly to the consolatory note of the last three: a note that is, in any event, muted by the continuing emphasis on love ('Blest babe') and lamentation ('sigh thy days') and by being sounded as a rhetorical question. 'Time brings down what is both strong and tall, /' Bradstreet declares at the end of the poem, 'But plants new set to be eradicate, / And buds new blown to have so short a date, / Is by His hand alone that guides nature and fate.' The acquiescence in the workings of 'His hand' is set, finally, against scarcely suppressed astonishment at workings that, in this instance at least, seem so premature, even unnatural. Experiencing the pleasures and pains of this world, Bradstreet's heart rises up, as it does here. It may then try to submit to the will of man or God, in the shape of convention or faith. But it never quite can or will do so. This is the source of the drama and the intimacy of her best poems; and that is why they achieve exactly what Bradstreet herself had hoped for them – the sense that we are listening to a still living voice.

A similar sense of intimacy and engagement is one of the secrets of the work of Edward Taylor, which was virtually unpublished during his lifetime – a collected edition, *The Poetical Works of Edward Taylor*, did not appear, in fact, until 1939. Like Bradstreet, Taylor was born in England; he then left to join the Massachusetts Bay Colony in 1668. After studying at Harvard, he settled into the profession of minister for the rest of his life. Marrying twice, he fathered fourteen children, many of whom died in infancy. He began writing poetry even before he joined his small, frontier congregation in Westfield, but his earliest work tended towards the public and conventional. It was not until 1674 that, experimenting with different forms and styles, he started over the next eight or nine years to write in a more personal and memorable vein: love poems to his wife-to-be ('Were but my Muse an Huswife Good'), spiritual meditations on natural events or, as Taylor called them, 'occurrants' ('The Ebb & Flow'; 'Upon the Sweeping Flood'), and emblematic, allegorical accounts of the smaller creatures of nature and domestic objects ('Upon a Spider Catching a Fly'; 'Huswifery'). These poems already manifest some of Taylor's characteristic poetic habits. 'Upon a Spider Catching a Fly', for instance, written around 1680–2, begins with the kind of minute particularization of nature that was to become typical of later New England poets like Emily Dickinson and Robert Frost:

> Thou Sorrow, venom elfe
> Is this thy ploy,
> To spin a web out of thyselfe
> To catch a Fly?
> For Why?

Gradually, the intimate tone of address is switched to God, who is asked to 'break the Cord' with which 'Hells Spider', the Devil, would 'tangle Adams race'. What is memorable about the poem is how closely Taylor attends to both the material facts of the spider and the spiritual truth it is chosen to emblematize: symbolic meaning is not developed at the expense of concrete event. And what is just as memorable is the way Taylor uses an elaborate conceit and intricate stanzaic form as both a discipline to his meditations and a means of channelling, then relaxing, emotion. So, in the final stanza, the poet anticipates eventually singing to the glory of God, 'when pearcht on high' – 'And thankfully, /' he concludes, 'For joy'. That short last line, consisting of just two words, at once acts as a counterpoint to the conclusion of the first stanza ('For Why?') and allows Taylor to end his poem on a moment of pure, spiritual elation.

The experience of bereavement moved Taylor immensely, just as it did Bradstreet. 'Upon Wedlock, & Death of Children', for example, probably written in 1682, explores loss just as Bradstreet's poem about her granddaughter does, by comparing children to the things of nature, in this case flowers. The difference is that Taylor, characteristically, extends the comparison into an elaborate conceit. He plays, among other things, on the connections between the perfume of flowers ascending to the skies, prayers rising on offerings of incense and the souls of children climbing up to heaven. Also, and equally characteristically, he manages to resolve his loss of spiritual resolution, trust in the will of God, in a way that Bradstreet cannot quite, or will not. Without undervaluing his grief ('Grief o're doth flow', he admits), he seems to find genuine consolation in the belief that his children are now with the Lord – not only that, but also in the belief that, as he puts it, 'I piecemeal pass to Glory bright in them'. 'I joy,' he ends by declaring to

God, 'may I sweet Flowers for Glory breed, / Whether thou getst them green, or lets them Seed.' That simple but striking image, of his children passing 'green' to God, is at once elegiac and triumphant, an expression of loss certainly but also of faith.

The experience of faith was, in fact, central to Taylor's life and his work. About 1647, he began writing metrical paraphrases of the Psalms. Recalling the *Bay Psalm Book*, it is nevertheless in these poems that Taylor's distinctively meditative voice starts to be given freer rein. More important, he also began to bring together his vision of the history of salvation to produce his first major work, *Gods Determinations touching his Elect*. A collection of thirty-five poems, this traces the 'Glorious Handywork' of creation, dramatizes a debate between Justice and Mercy over the fate of humankind, then describes the combat between Christ and Satan for human souls. *Gods Determinations* is, in effect, both a visionary narrative and a didactic debate, recording the progress of the soul from the beginnings of life, through the Fall and Redemption, to the triumph of the Resurrection. It is also a work that demonstrates Taylor's ability to domesticate Christian mystery, using humble, everyday imagery to explore the transcendent, the ineffable. This is nowhere more evident than in 'The Preface' to the sequence, where Taylor considers the mysteries of time and infinity, aboriginal nothing and original creation. 'Infinity,' he announces,

> when all things it beheld
> In Nothing, and of Nothing all did build,
> Upon what Base was fixed the Lath, wherein
> He turn'd this Globe, and riggalld it so trim?
> Who blew the Bellows of his Furnace Vast?
> Or held the Mould wherein the world was Cast?

'Who in this Bowling Alley bowld the Sun?' he asks a few lines later. That question is typical of a poet who habitually uses wit to address serious matters and the mundane to anchor the mysterious.

Some years after beginning *Gods Determinations*, in 1682, Taylor turned to what is his finest longer work, *Preparatory Meditations before My Approach to the Lords Supper*. Usually composed after he had prepared a sermon or preaching notes, the two hundred and seventeen poems comprising this sequence are personal meditations 'Chiefly upon the Doctrine preached upon the Day of administration'. In them, Taylor tries to learn lessons gathered from the Sacrament day's Biblical text, which also acts as the poem's title. They are at once a form of spiritual discipline, with the poet subjecting himself to rigorous self-examination; petitions to God to prepare him for the immediate task of preaching and administering the Lord's Supper; and a private diary or confession of faith. And, as in so many of his poems, Taylor uses an intricate verse form, elaborate word play and imagery to organize his meditations and release his emotions. In the eighth meditation, for example, on *Job. 6.51. I am the Living Bread*, Taylor weaves together a series of different

Biblical texts and themes: Christ's flesh and blood as elements of the Lord's Supper, the manna that God provided daily for the Israelites, Christ's miracle of feeding the five thousand with loaves and fishes. Christ is 'the Bread of Life', Taylor intimates, the only way of meeting a 'Celestiall Famine sore'. 'The Creatures field no food for Souls e're gave'; the soul requires 'soul bread' not 'the Worlds White Loaf', the 'Bread of Heaven' ground from 'The Purest Wheate in Heaven' and then 'Disht on thy Table up by Angells Hands'. 'Yee Angells, help,' Taylor implores, 'This fill would to the brim / Heav'ns whelm'd-down Chrystall meete Bowle, yea and higher.' In an image at once homely and apocalyptic, the new heavens promised by God are envisioned as an inverted crystal bowl, eternally radiant. And that triumphant vision leads naturally back to the dominant image of the poem, another object on the table 'Disht . . . up by Angells Hands'. 'This Bread of Life,' Taylor announces, 'dropt in thy mouth, doth Cry / Eate, Eate, Soul, and thou shall never dy.' Characteristically, the meditation is resolved in understanding and joy.

Taylor belongs in a great tradition of meditative writing, certainly, one that includes the English poets George Herbert and John Donne, and an equally great tradition of New England writing: one in which the imaginative anticipation of dying becomes a means of understanding how to live. So it is perhaps not surprising that, after suffering a severe illness in 1720, he wrote three versions of 'A Valediction to all the World preparatory for Death 3d of the 11th 1720' and two versions of 'A Fig for thee Oh! Death'. What perhaps is surprising, and moving, is how these poems acknowledge the loveliness of the world while bidding it farewell. Saying goodbye to the 'Realm of Senses', for instance, in 'A Valediction', Taylor bids his last adieu 'Unto the Eare's enchanting Melodies Skill, / Unto the Eyes enticing Beauteous Sights / And to the Touch silk downy soft delights'. The strength of his feeling for the things of the earth, and even more for family and vocation, becomes here a measure of the strength of his faith. It is only faith, evidently, and the firm conviction that (as he puts it in one of the *Preparatory Meditations*) his heart 'loaded with love' will 'ascend / Up to . . . its bridegroom, bright, & Friend' that makes him content to give up all that he has not only come to know but also to cherish. In Taylor's poems, we find not so much conflict as continuity: not tension but a resolution founded on tough reasoning and vigorous emotion, patient attention to the ordinary and passionate meditation on the mysterious – above all, on a firmly grounded, fervently sustained faith. It is surely right to say that Taylor, as he reveals himself in his work, believes in the truths of the spirit not despite but because of his attachment to the facts of the matter. He loves the world, in short, but he loves God more.

Enemies within and without

The Puritan faith that Edward Taylor expressed and represented so vividly found itself challenged, very often, by enemies within and without. As for the enemies outside the Puritan community, they included above all the people the settlers had displaced, the Native Americans. The challenge posed by what one Puritan called 'this barbarous Enemy' was most eloquently expressed by those who had come under the enemy's power, however briefly. In February 1676, a woman named Mary White Rowlandson (1637?–1711) was captured by a group of Nassagansett Indians, along with her children. Many of her neighbours and relatives were also captured or killed, one of her children died soon after being captured, and the other two became separated from her. Rowlandson herself was finally released and returned to her husband in the following May; and the release of her two surviving children was effected several weeks later. Six years after this, she published an account of her experience, the full title of which gives some flavour of its approach and a clue to its purpose: *The Sovereignty and Goodness of* GOD, *Together With the Faithfulness of His Promises Displayed: Being a Narrative of the Captivity and Restauration of Mrs Mary Rowlandson*. The book was immensely popular, and remained so on into the nineteenth century; and it helped to inaugurate a peculiarly American literary form, the captivity narrative. There had, of course, been captivity narratives since the earliest period of European exploration, notably the accounts of their own experiences as prisoners written by Cabeza de Vaca and John Smith. But Rowlandson's account established both the appeal of such narratives and the form they would usually take: combining, as it does, a vivid portrait of her sufferings and losses with an emphatic interpretation of their meaning. The moral framework of the *Narrative* is, in fact, clearly and instructively dualistic: on the one side are the 'Pagans' and on the other the Christians. The Native Americans are, variously, 'ravenous Beasts', 'Wolves', 'black creatures' resembling the Devil in their cruelty, savagery and capacity for lying. Christians like Rowlandson who suffer at their hands are upheld only by 'the wonderfull mercy of God' and the 'remarkable passages of providence' that enable them to survive and sustain their faith.

'One principall ground of my setting forth these Lines,' Rowlandson explains during the course of the *Narrative*, is 'To declare the Works of the Lord, and his wonderfull Power in carrying us along, preserving us in the Wilderness, while under the Enemies hand.' Another aim of the account, and one that is equally foregrounded, is to identify the Native Americans as fit inhabitants of 'the Wilderness': these are no noble savages, dwelling in another Eden, but 'Barbarous Creatures' whose 'savageness and bruitishness' help turn the land where they dwell into 'a lively resemblance of hell'. There are pragmatic considerations at work here. The translation of the Native American into 'bloody heathen' helped to justify their removal from land the whites coveted; while the testimony to the power of Rowlandson's faith, and the precious support God gave to those who believed in Him, was a useful weapon at a time when church membership was declining. The *Narrative* is more than a demonstration of a divine thesis, however. It is that, certainly: Rowlandson never misses an opportunity to attribute a fortunate event, such as meeting with her son or the acquisition of a Bible, to the merciful intervention of God; and she rarely finds any redeeming features in her captors. But it is also a remarkable account of one woman's endurance in the face of exile, opposition and traumatic loss. Not only that, it is thoughtful and reflective enough to present Native Americans as possible instruments of providence, designed by God as 'a scourge to his People', and Rowlandson herself as someone indelibly changed by her encounter with them. So, while the 'Pagans' of the 'Wilderness' are represented in almost entirely negative terms, the idea of a scourge makes the depiction of the Puritans less than totally positive. 'Our perverse and evil carriages in the sight of the Lord,' Rowlandson observes, 'have so offended him, that instead of turning his hand against them [the Nassagansetts], the Lord feeds them up to be a scourge to the whole Land.' It also, eventually, complicates Rowlandson's presentation of herself. Returned to her husband and community, her children restored to her, Rowlandson confesses that she remains uncomfortable, even alienated. 'When all are fast about me, and no eye open, but his who ever waketh,' she reveals, 'my thoughts are upon things past.' Sleepless, she recalls 'how the other day I was in the midst of thousands of enemies, and nothing but death before me: It is then hard work to perswade my self, that ever I should be satisfied with bread again'. 'Now I see the Lord had his time to scourge and chasten me,' Rowlandson explains; 'the Lord hath shewed me the vanity of . . . outward things . . . they are but a shadow, a blast, a bubble, and things of no continuance.' She has learned from her late encounter with the enemy; and what she has learned has made her not quite a member, any more, of the community from which she was abducted. Captivity has led her into a kind of exile.

The enemy without in the captivity narrative is mainly the Native American, as in the account of Mary Rowlandson and in those, say, of John Gyles and Elizabeth Meader Hanson. It is, however, not always and entirely so. In 1704, for instance, John Williams (1664–1729) was captured after a raid on his village by French Canadians and Abnakis and Caughnawaga Mohawks during the French and Indian wars. Along with his wife and five of his children, he was then marched to Canada. He was, however, a captive of the Indians for only eight weeks. Most of the time, until his release in 1706, he was held by the French. And, according to his account of his experiences, *The Redeemed Captive Returning to Zion* published in 1707, French Jesuits tried earnestly and continually to convert him to 'Romish superstition'. Williams's book is consequently a description of a desperate struggle against two enemies to truth, the 'heathenish cruelty' of one and the 'popish rage' of the other. As he explains it, he had not only to endure extreme hardship and loss, including the killing of two of his children during the initial raid and the death of his 'dear wife' shortly after capture; he had also to fight, sometimes in the face of death threats, against the attempts to make him bow to 'idolatrous superstitions'. At the time when Williams was suffering capture and then putting down on paper an account of his sufferings, the Puritan community was feeling more threatened than it ever had previously: among other things, by an influx of new immigrants, most of whom had no interest in Puritanism. In 1650, the European population of America was 52,000, by 1700 it was 250,000, it had more than doubled by 1730, and by 1775 it was to become two and a half million. So it is perhaps not surprising that Williams's captivity narrative is also a jeremiad. Faced with the irrefutable fact of decline, like many other writers of the time Williams responded by discovering and announcing 'the anger of God' towards his 'professing people' at work in history. Rowlandson sees her captivity, and the presence and power of the 'Pagans', as corrective scourges, personal and communal. But Williams goes further. The story of his captivity is set, for him, in a larger narrative in which events are a sign of divine disfavour and an indication that things must change. For Williams, in *The Redeemed Captive*, 'the judgement of God [does] not slumber': his sufferings are part of a larger providential pattern designed to promote a return to earlier piety – and, in the meantime, to encourage patience among those of true faith who are suffering 'the will of God in very trying public calamities.'

As for the enemies within, nothing illustrated the Puritan fear of them more than the notorious witch trials that took place in Salem, Massachusetts, in 1692, during the course of which nineteen people were hanged, one was pressed to death, fifty-five were frightened or tortured into confessions of guilt, one hundred and fifty were imprisoned, and more than two hundred were named as deserving arrest. What brought those trials about, the sense of a special mission now threatened and the search for a conspiracy, an enemy to blame and purge from the common-wealth, is revealed in a work first published in 1693, *The Wonders of the Invisible World* by Cotton Mather (1663–1728). Mather, the grandson of two important religious leaders of the first generation of Puritan immigrants (including John Cotton, after whom he was named), wrote his book at the instigation of the Salem judges. 'The New Englanders are a people of God settled in those, which were once the devil's territories,' Mather announces; 'and it may easily be supposed that the devil was exceedingly disturbed, when he perceived such a people accomplishing the promise of old made unto our blessed Jesus, that He should have the utmost parts of the earth for His possession.' For Mather, the people, mostly women, tried and convicted at Salem represent a 'terrible plague of evil angels'. They form part of 'an horrible plot against the country' which 'if it were not seasonably discov-ered, would probably blow up, and pull down all the churches'. 'The devil is now making one attempt more upon us,' Mather warns, to recover his territories; 'if we get well through, we shall soon enjoy halcyon days with all the vultures of hell trodden under our feet.' A feeling of immediate crisis and longer-term decline is explained as the result of a conspiracy, the work of enemy insiders who need to be discovered and despatched if the community is to recover, then realize its earlier utopian promise. It is the dark side of the American dream, the search for someone or something to blame when that dream appears to be failing. Mather was sounding a sinister chord here that was to be echoed by many later Americans, and opening up a vein of reasoning and belief that subsequent American writers were to subject to intense, imaginative analysis.

But Cotton Mather was more than just the author of one of the first American versions of the conspiracy theory. He produced over four hundred publications during his lifetime. Among them were influential scientific works, like *The Christian Philosopher* (1720), and works promoting 'reforming societies' such as *Bonifacius; or, Essays to Do Good* (1710), a book that had an important impact on Benjamin Franklin. He also encouraged missionary work among African American slaves, in *The Negro Christianized* (1706), and among Native Americans, in *India Christiana*

(1721). But here, too, in his encouragement of Christian missions to those outside the true faith, a darker side of Puritanism, or at least of the Cotton Mather strain, is evident. Mather's belief in the supreme importance of conversion led him, after all, to claim that a slave taught the true faith was far better off than a free black; and it sprang, in the first place, from a low opinion of both African and Native Americans, bordering on contempt. For example, in his life of John Eliot, 'the apostle of the Indians' whom Nathaniel Hawthorne was later to praise, Mather made no secret of his belief that 'the natives of the country now possessed by New Englanders' had been 'forlorn and wretched' ever since 'their first herding here'. They were 'miserable savages', 'stupid and senseless', Mather declared. They had 'no *arts*', 'except just so far as to maintain their brutish conversation', 'little, if any, tradition . . . worthy of . . . notice'; reading and writing were 'altogether unknown to them' and their religion consisted of no more than 'diabolical rites', 'extravagant ridiculous devotions' to 'many gods'. Furthermore, they did not even know how to use the abundant resources of the New World. 'They live in a country full of the best ship timber under heaven,' Mather insisted, 'but never saw a ship till some came from Europe.' '*We* now have all the conveniences of human life,' he claimed proudly; 'as for *them*, their *housing* is nothing but a few mats tyed about poles,' 'their *clothing* is but skin of a beast,' and 'their *diet* has not a greater dainty' than 'parched meal, with a spoonful of water.' Such were 'the miserable people' Eliot set out to save and, in view of their condition, he had 'a double work incumbent on him'. He had, Mather concluded, 'to make men' of the Native Americans 'ere he could hope to see them saints'; they had to be '*civilized* ere they could be *Christianized*'.

Mather's account of Eliot's work among the Indians shows just how much for him, as for other early European settlers, the projects of civilization and conversion, creating wealth and doing good, went hand in hand. It comes from his longest and arguably most interesting work, *Magnalia Christi Americana; or, the Ecclesiastical History of New England* published in 1702. This book is an immensely detailed history of New England and a series of eminent lives, and it reflects Mather's belief that the past should be used to instruct the present and guide the future. Each hero chosen for description and eulogy, like Eliot, is made to fit a common saintly pattern, from the portrait of his conversion to his deathbed scene. Yet each is given his own distinctive characteristics, often expressive of Mather's own reforming interests and always illustrating his fundamental conviction that, as he puts it, 'The *First Age* was the *Golden Age*'. 'To return unto *That*' first age 'will make a man a *Protestant*,' Mather explains, 'and I may add, a *Puritan*.' And, for his contemporary readers to learn how to make that return, all they had to do was learn the history of those 'powerful *Brethren*, driven to seek a place for the Exercise of the *Protestant Religion* . . . in the Desarts of *America*'. This is exemplary history, then. It is also an American epic, one of the very first, in which the author sets about capturing in words what he sees as the promise of the nation. 'I WRITE the *Wonders* of the CHRISTIAN RELIGION,' Mather announces in 'A General Introduction' to *Magnalia Christi Americana*:

flying from the Depravations of *Europe*, to the *American Strand*. And, assisted by the Holy Author of that *Religion*, I do, With all Conscience of *Truth*, required there . . . by Him, who is The *Truth* itself, Report the *Wonderful Displays* of His Infinite Power, Wisdom, Goodness, and Faithfulness, wherewith His Divine Providence hath *Irradiated* an *Indian Wilderness*.

The echo of the *Aeneid* is an intimation of what Mather is after. He is hoping to link the story of his people to earlier epic migrations. As later references to the 'American Desart' testify, he is also suggesting a direct analogy with the journey of God's chosen people to the Promised Land. His subject is a matter of both history and belief: like so many later writers of American epic, in other words, he is intent on describing both an actual and a possible America.

Not everyone involved in the Salem witchcraft trials remained convinced that they were justified by the need to expose a dangerous enemy within. Among those who came to see them as a serious error of judgement, and of morality, was one of the judges at the trials, Samuel Sewall (1652–1730). An intensely thoughtful man, Sewall wrote a journal from 1673 to 1728, which was eventually published as *The Diary of Samuel Sewall* in 1973. It offers an insight into the intimate thoughts, the trials and private tribulations of someone living at a time when Puritanism no longer exerted the power it once did over either the civil or religious life of New England. Sewall notes how in 1697 he felt compelled to make a public retraction of his actions as one of the Salem judges, 'asking pardon of man' for his part in the proceedings against supposed witches, and, he adds, 'especially desiring prayers that God, who has an Unlimited Authority, would pardon that Sin' he had committed. He also records how eventually, following the dictates of his conscience, he felt 'call'd' to write something against 'the Trade fetching Negroes from Guinea'. 'I had a strong inclination to Write something about it,' he relates in an entry for 19 June 1700, 'but it wore off'. Only five days after this, however, a work authored by Sewall attacking the entire practice of slavery, *The Selling of Joseph: A Memorial*, was published in Boston. In it, he attacked slavery as a violation of Biblical precept and practice, against natural justice since 'all men, as they are the Sons of *Adam*, are Coheirs; and have equal Right unto Liberty', and destructive of the morals of both slaves and masters – not least because 'it is well known what Temptations Masters are under to connive at the fornications of their Slaves'. Sewall was a man eager to seek divine counsel on all matters before acting. This was the case whether the matter was a great public one, like the issues of witchcraft and the slave trade, or a more private one, such as the question of his marrying for a third time. His journals reveal the more private side of Puritanism: a daily search for the right path to follow in order to make the individual journey part of the divine plan. They also reveal a habit of meditation, a scrupulously detailed mapping of personal experiences, even the most intimate, that was to remain ingrained in American writing long after the Puritan hegemony had vanished.

The power of Puritanism was, in fact, waning in New England well before the end of the eighteenth century. The number of 'unchurched' colonists had been large to begin with, and they grew in number and power over the years. At the best of times for Puritanism, a high degree of political control had been made possible by restricting the suffrage to male church members. But that practice was soon modified, and then abolished in 1691 when it was replaced by a property qualification. Outside New England, the absence of one controlling cultural group was still more evident, since by 1775 half the population was of non-English origin. Scotch Irish, Scottish, German, French Huguenot and Dutch immigrants flooded the eastern seaboard; the Spanish settled a vast area over which they held dominion stretching from California to the Gulf Coast; and, by the end of the eighteenth century, more than 275,000 African slaves had been brought to America, mainly to the South. A rising standard of living encouraged Benjamin Franklin to claim, in 1751, that in the next century 'the greatest Number of Englishmen will be on this side of the water'. It certainly helped to promote the growing secular tendencies of the age. Religion was still strong; and it was, in fact, made stronger by a sweeping revivalist movement known as the Great Awakening, in the third and fourth decades of the eighteenth century. 'Under Great Terrors of Conscience,' as the preacher Jonathan Edwards put it, many thousands of people 'had their natures overborn under strong convictions.' They were born again, in an experience of radical conversion; and they banded together in evangelical communities, convinced of the power of 'Christ shedding blood for sinners' and the incalculable, more than rational nature of faith. The Great Awakening, however, was itself a reaction of what was rightly felt to be the dominant trend: the growing tendency among colonists to accept and practise the ideas of the Enlightenment, albeit usually in popularized form. Those ideas emphasized the determining influence of reason and common sense and the imperatives of self-help, personal and social progress. According to the philosophy of the Enlightenment, the universe was a rational, mechanical phenomenon which, as the English philosopher John Locke put it, ran rather like a self-winding watch. Once set in motion by its creator, God or an abstract First Cause, it no longer required His help or intervention. And man, using his reason and good sense, could ascertain the laws of this mechanism. He could then use those laws for his own profit, the betterment of society and his own improvement since, as Franklin put it, 'the one acceptable service to God is doing good to man'. It was an ethic with an obvious attraction for new generations of immigrants eager to stake their place and improve their lot in a new land with such abundant resources. Even for those, the vast majority, who had never heard of the Enlightenment, the secular gospel of reason, common sense, use, profit and progress became part of the American way.

The travel journals of two writers of this period, Sarah Kemble Knight (1666–1727) and William Byrd of Westover (1674–1744), suggest the increasingly secular tendencies of this era. Both Knight and Byrd wrote accounts of their journeys through parts of America that tend to concentrate on the social, the curious people and manners they encountered along the way. There is relatively little concern, of the kind shown in earlier European accounts of travels in the New World, with the abundance of nature, seen as either Eden or Wilderness. Nor is there any sense at all of being steered by providence: God may be mentioned in these journals, but rarely as a protective guide. Knight composed her journal as a description of a trip she took from Boston to New York and then back again in 1704–5. It did not reach printed form until the next century, when it appeared as *The Journals of Madam Knight* (1825): but it was 'published' in the way many manuscripts were at the time, by being circulated among friends. Her writings reveal a lively, humorous, gossipy woman alert to the comedy and occasional beauty of life in early America – and aware, too, of the slightly comic figure she herself sometimes cuts, 'sitting Stedy', as she puts it, 'on my Nagg'. She describes in detail how she is kept awake at night in a local inn by the drunken arguments of 'some of the Town tope-ers in [the] next Room'. She records, with a mixture of disbelief and amused disgust, meeting a family that is 'the picture of poverty' living in a 'little Hutt' that was 'one of the wretchedest I ever saw'. 'I Blest myself that I was not one of this miserable crew,' Knight remembers; and 'the Impressions' that their 'wretchedness' made on her inspired her to a series of verse couplets, which she then quotes. 'Their Lodgings thyn and hard, their Indian fare, / The mean Apparel which the wretches wear, /' she proclaims in her impromptu poem, 'And their ten thousand ills wch can't be told, / Makes nature er'e 'tis middle ag'd look old.' Sometimes, Knight is struck by the beauty of the landscape she passes through. She recalls, for instance, how moved she was by the sight of the woods lit up by the moon – or, as she has it, by 'Cynthia', 'the kind Conductress of the night'. Even here, however, the terms in which she expresses her excitement are a sign of her true allegiances. 'The Tall and thick trees at a distance,' she explains, 'when the moon glar'd through the branches, fill'd my Imagination with the pleasant delusion of a Sumpteous citty, fill'd with famous Buildings and churches, with their spiring steeples, Balconies, Galleries and I know not what.' Nature is most beautiful, evidently, when it evokes thoughts of culture; 'the dolesome woods', as she calls them elsewhere in her journal, are at their best when they excite memories of, or better still lead to, town.

The situation is more complicated with William Byrd of Westover. Born the heir of a large estate in Virginia, Byrd was educated in England and only made Virginia his permanent home in 1726. Byrd claimed, in one of his letters (published eventually in 1977 in *The Correspondence of the Three William Byrds*), that in America he lived 'like . . . the patriarchs'. And, to the extent that this was possible in a new country, he certainly did. For he was one of the leading members of what eventually became known as the 'first families of Virginia', those people who formed the ruling class by the end of the eighteenth century – in the colony of Virginia and, arguably, elsewhere in the South. The 'first families' claimed to be of noble English origin. Some of them no doubt were. But it is likely that the majority of them were, as one contemporary writer Robert Beverley II (1673–1722) put it in *The History and Present State of Virginia* (1722), 'of low Circumstances . . . such as were willing to seek their Fortunes in a Foreign Country'. Whatever their origins, they had to work hard since as one of them, William Fitzhugh (1651–1701), pointed out in a letter written in 1691, 'without a constant care and diligent Eye, a well-made plantation will run to Ruin'. ''Tis no small satisfaction to me,' wrote another great landowner, Robert 'King' Carter (1663–1732), in 1720, 'to have a pennyworth for my penny'; and to this end he, and other Virginia gentlemen like him, were scrupulous in the supervision of their landholdings. Nevertheless, they were keen to use their painstakingly acquired wealth to assume the manners and prerogatives of an aristocracy, among which was the appearance of a kind of aristocratic indolence – what one writer of the time, Hugh Jones (1670–1760), described in *The Present State of Virginia* (1724) as the gentleman's 'easy way of living'. William Fitzhugh, for example, a first-generation immigrant and the son of a woollen draper, eagerly set about acquiring a coat of arms and the other paraphernalia of an aristocrat once he had land and wealth. His sister was then invited to join him in the New World, but not before he had arranged for her to be 'handsomely and genteelly and well clothed, with a maid to wait on her'. 'The method I have taken for your coming in,' he informed her with clear unease, in one of several letters written to make these arrangements in 1686, 'I would advise you by all means to follow.' Such arrangements would, Fitzhugh told his sister, 'give us both credit and reputation, without which it's uncomfortable living'. The message was plain. Fitzhugh had transformed himself from an ordinary person into an aristocrat; now he expected his relatives, if he was to acknowledge them, to undergo a similar transformation.

Byrd, of course, did not have to struggle to acquire wealth, he inherited it. Once he had done so, however, he worked hard to sustain that wealth and even acquire more. He personally supervised his properties, once he settled in Virginia, arranging for the planting of crops, orchards and gardens; he also attended to his duties within his own community and in the county and the colony. And he was just as intent as his wealthy neighbours were on assuming the appearance of idle nobility. When writing back to friends in England, for instance, he tended to turn his life in Virginia into a version of the pastoral – as these two passages from two separate letters, one written in 1726 and one undated, amply testify:

> we sit securely under our vines and fig trees without any danger to our property . . . Thus, my Lord, we are very happy in our Canaans if we could but forget the onions and fleshpots of Egypt.

> We that are banish't from the polite pleasures [of London] . . . take up with rural entertainments. A Library, a garden, a grove, and a purling stream are the innocent scenes that divert our leisure . . .

As these small hymns to Southern pastoral intimate, the desire to paint plantation life as a kind of idyll sprang from two related things, for Byrd and others like him:

a feeling of exile from the centres of cultural activity and a desire to distance the spectres of provincialism and money-grubbing. Exiled from the 'polite pleasures' of the mother country, in a place that he elsewhere described as the 'great wilderness' of America, Byrd was prompted to describe his plantation home as a place of natural abundance, ripe simplicity and indolence. Describing it in this way, he also separated himself from the work ethic that prevailed further north. A clear dividing line was being drawn between him, and the life he and his social equals in Virginia led, and, on the one hand, England, on the other, New England. In the process, Byrd was dreaming and articulating what was surely to become the dominant image of the South.

That Byrd and the first families attempted to live according to this image there is no doubt. Both Byrd himself and Robert 'King' Carter, for example, assumed the role and function of feudal patriarch on their plantations. Considering themselves the guardians of the physical and moral welfare of their slaves – whom they often chose to refer to as their 'people' – they considered it an important part of their social duty to act as benevolent overlords: punishing the lazy 'children' – as they also sometimes referred to their slave labour – rewarding the industrious, and having all 'imaginable care', as one Virginia planter, Landon Carter (1710–78), put it in his diary for 1752, of such 'poor creatures' as were sick. That Byrd and others also felt exiled sometimes, in the Southern colonies, there can be no doubt either. 'The Habits, Life, Customs, Computations, etc of the Virginians,' declared Hugh Jones, 'are much the same as about London, which they esteem their home.' Byrd himself never ceased to think of England as, in many ways, the right place for him – a centre of culture, entertainment, as opposed to what he called, in a letter written in 1726, 'this silent country'. His writings are full of references to the scenes and life of London, as if language and, more specifically, imagery could make up for what he lacked in life. For example, after finding some horses that had strayed near the misty, mainly marshy region known as the Dismal Swamp, Byrd wrote: 'They were found standing indeed, but as motionless as the equestrian statues in Charing Cross.' The contrast between the scene described and the mode of description could hardly be more striking: on the one hand, a world of immense and disturbing strangeness, on the other, a cultural referent that is comfortingly familiar and known. In its own way, the remark appears to sum up the process of accommodation to which so many of the great planters like Byrd committed themselves: their effort, that is, to create a sense of connection, as well as division, between the Old World and the New.

That description of the horses in the Dismal Swamp comes from *The History of the Dividing Line betwixt Virginia and North Carolina*, Byrd's account of his participation in the 1728 survey of the southern border of Virginia. In this travel journal, written in 1729 and first published in 1841, Byrd considers a number of divisions quite apart from the one announced in the title. He talks, for instance, about the difference or division between the 'Frugal and Industrious' settlers of the northern colonies and the less energetic settlers to the south. 'For this reason,' he explains, 'New England improved much faster than Virginia.' He talks about the division between Indians and whites, particularly the early European explorers. The Indians, Byrd reflects, 'are healthy & Strong, with Constitutions untainted by Lewdness'. 'I cannot think', he adds, 'the Indians were much greater Heathens than the first Adventurers, who, had they been good Christians' would have found that the 'only method of converting Natives to Christianity' was to marry them – since 'a sprightly Lover is the most prevailing Missionary'. He talks about the divisions between men and women. 'The distemper of laziness seizes the men', in the backwoods, he suggests, 'much oftener than the women'. And he talks about the differences, the division between his homeplace and North Carolina. For him, North Carolina is 'Lubberland'. 'Surely there is no place in the world where the inhabitants live with less labour than North Carolina,' Byrd writes. The men 'make their wives rise out of their beds early in the morning, at the same time they lie and snore till the sun has risen one-third of his course'. Then, 'after stretching and yawning for half an hour, they light their pipes'. 'When the weather is mild', Byrd wryly observes, they may venture outside, to 'stand leaning with both their arms upon the cornfield fence'. But, 'if it happens to be never so little cold they quickly return shivering into the chimney corner'. 'Plenty and a warm sun', Byrd avers, confirm all North Carolinians, and especially the men, 'in their disposition to laziness for their whole lives'; 'they loiter away their lives, like Solomon's sluggard, with their arms across, and at the winding up of the year scarcely have bread to eat'.

Byrd's comic description of the inhabitants of North Carolina anticipates the Southwestern humorists of the nineteenth century, and all those other American storytellers who have made fun of life off the beaten track. It is also sparked off by one of a series of divisions in *The History of the Dividing Line* that are determined by the difference between sloth and industry: perhaps reflecting Byrd's suspicion that his own life, the contrast between its surfaces and its reality, measures a similar gap. Quite apart from such dividing lines, Byrd's account of his journey is as frank and lively as Knight's is. What emerges from its pages is the sense of an educated, energetic and broadminded man. So, he discovers with appreciation 'the three great articles of natural religion' at work among the Indians: belief in a god, 'the moral division betwixt good and evil', 'the expectation of rewards and punishments in another world'. And he and his companions discover with even more appreciation the erotic effect of eating bear meat. Thanks to this diet, 'all the married men of our company were joyful fathers within forty weeks after they got home', Byrd reveals, 'and most of the single men had children sworn to them within the same time'. Byrd's tone is even franker and livelier in *The Secret History of the Dividing Line*, an account of the same expedition as the one *The History of the Dividing Line* covers, first published in 1929. In *The Secret History*, as its title implies, what Byrd dwells on is the private exploits of the surveyors: their drinking, gambling, joking, squabbling and their encounters with more than one 'dark angel' or 'tallow-faced wench'. Throughout his adventures, 'Steddy', as Byrd calls himself in both histories, keeps his course and maintains his balance: negotiating his journey through divisions with the appearance of consummate ease.

Of course, the ease was very often just that, a matter of appearance, here in the histories of the dividing line and elsewhere. Or, if not that simply, it was a matter of conscious, calculated choice. As an alternative to the ruminative Puritan or the industrious Northerner, Byrd and others like him modelled themselves on the idea of the indolent, elegant aristocrat: just as, as an alternative to the noise and bustle of London, they modelled their accounts of their homeplace in imitation of the pastoral ideal. The divisions and accommodations they were forced into, or on occasion chose, were the product of the conflict between their origins and aspirations, the given facts and the assumed aims of their lives. They were also a consequence of the differences they perceived between the world they were making in their part of the American colonies and the ones being made in other parts. And they were also, and not least, a probable response to their own sense that the blood of others was on their hands. Anticipating the later Southern argument in defence of slavery, they turned their slaves, rhetorically, into 'children' who positively needed the feudal institution of an extended family, with a benevolent patriarch at its head, for guidance, support and protection. Perhaps the last word on all this, though, should be left with Byrd himself. In his diaries, kept in shorthand and only deciphered and published in the twentieth century (*The Secret Diary* [1941]; *Another Secret Diary* [1942]; *The London Diary* [1958]), he recounted the events of his everyday life, even the most trivial, and this, taken almost at random, is the entry for one fairly typical day. It happens to be 12 February 1709:

> I rose at 6 o'clock and read a chapter in Hebrew and two hundred verses in Homer's 'Odyssey'. I said my prayers . . . I read law. Toney came to tell me . . . that the hogs were ready . . . In the evening I walked around the plantation. I said my prayers. I had good health, good thoughts, and good humor, and good understanding this day, thanks be to God Almighty. Daniel came to let me know the sloop was almost loaded.

Byrd was, of course, exceptional as far as the range of his interests and his accomplishments as a writer were concerned, but not so exceptional that he cannot stand as an example here. As a planter, his life was not so very different from that of his neighbours: a life combining business activity with at least some attempt to cultivate manners, knowledge and the arts. Like others, in fact, he tried to apply an inherited model of belief and behaviour to new historical circumstances. That model was, in some ways, inappropriate, and destructively so: but, in others, it did help at least to ameliorate the harshness of a strange New World. Byrd expressed an impulse held in common with many of his fellow colonists – an impulse intended, as this diary entry shows, to make life more manageable, more tolerable and liveable. And, for good and ill, that impulse had an enormous impact on how writers write and many others talk about one vital part of the American nation.

The trend towards the secular in the work of Knight and Byrd is also noticeable in the poetry of the period. In the earlier part of the eighteenth century, the work of Nathaniel Evans (1742–67) was typical. Evans was an ordained minister. However, the subjects of his poetry, posthumously published as *Poems on Several Occasions* (1772), were rarely religious. He wrote of the changing seasons ('Hymn to May'), illustrious public figures ('To Benjamin Franklin, Occasioned by Hearing Him Play on the *Harmonica*') and friends closer to home ('Ode to the Memory of Mr Thomas Godfrey'). Certainly, he could lament what he saw as the greed and immorality of the times. As he put it in an 'Ode to My Ingenious Friend', 'we are in a climate cast / . . . / Where all the doctrine now that's told, / Is that a shining heap of gold / Alone can man embellish'. But, as these lines indicate, the criticism was framed in terms of an apparently secular morality, and the forms drawn from classical models – the ode, the elegy, the pastoral. More interesting, perhaps, than writers like Evans were those women poets of the time who often brought a self-consciously female perspective to familiar themes, and sometimes wrote about specifically female subjects, such as childbearing or their difficult role in society. 'How wretched is a woman's fate, /' complained one anonymous poet of the time in 'Verses Written by a Young Lady, on Women Born to be Controll'd' (1743), 'Subject to man in every state. / How can she then be free from woes?' The solution, as another anonymous poet, in 'The Lady's Complaint' (1736), put it, was for 'equal laws' that would 'neither sex oppress': a change that would 'More freedom give to womankind, / Or give to mankind less'. Not many poems of the time were quite as categorical as this. On the contrary, there was a tendency to find satisfaction in the admittedly restricted role reserved for women. 'Love, will then recompense my loss of freedom,' the anonymously written 'The Maid's Soliloquy' (1751) concludes. And this was a consolatory note sounded in other poems, both anonymous ones such as 'Impromptu, on Reading an Essay on Education. By a Lady' (1773; 'There is no blessing like conjugal love', the poem insists) and those attributed to a named or pseudonymous author, like 'A Poetical Epistle. Addressed by a Lady of New Jersey to Her Niece, upon Her Marriage' (1786) by Annis Boudinot Stockton (1736–1801). 'With reverence treat in every place, / The chosen patron of your future days, /' Stockton advises her niece. 'For when you show him but the least neglect, / Yourself you rifle of your due respect.'

Stockton also wrote poetry addressed to her friend Elizabeth Graeme Fergusson (1737–1801), one of the best-known poets of the eighteenth century, under Fergusson's pen name of 'Laura' ('To Laura' [1757]). Both Stockton and Fergusson composed poems on married love ('Epistle to Lucius' [1766]; 'An Ode Written on the Birthday of Mr Henry Fergusson'[1774]); Stockton also wrote about public figures ('The Vision, an Ode to Washington' [1789]) and Fergusson about conventional and philosophical topics, such as the transience of love ('On a Beautiful Damask Rose, Emblematical of Love and Wedlock' [1789]) and the primacy of self-love ('On the Mind's Being Engrossed by One Subject' [1789]). Both women were known, as well, for the literary salons over which they presided prior to the American Revolution, Stockton in Princeton and Fergusson near Philadelphia. They belonged, in short, to a coterie of women writers who knew each other, corresponded with each other, and frequently exchanged their work. One of

Fergusson's surviving commonplace books was apparently prepared for Stockton. And, just as Stockton addressed a poem to Fergusson, so another woman poet of the time, Sarah Wentworth Morton (1759–1846), wrote an 'Ode Inscribed to Mrs M Warren' (1790), that is, Mercy Otis Warren (1728–1814), poet, dramatist and historian. Warren, in turn, wrote a verse letter to another female writer and critic of the time, Elizabeth Robinson Montagu (1720–1800), titled 'To Mrs Montague. Author of "Observations on the Genius and Writings of Shakespeare"' (1790), thanking Montagu for praising one of Warren's plays. What is remarkable about many of these poems written by women is their sense of a shared suffering and dignity, sometimes associated with the core experience of childbirth. 'Thrice in my womb I've found the pleasing strife, / In the first struggles of my infant's life: /' observes Jane Colman Turell (1708–35) in a poem published in 1741 that remained untitled. 'But O how soon by Heaven I'm call'd to mourn, / While from my womb a lifeless babe is born?' 'What man is there, that thus shall dare / Woman to treat with scorn, /' asks Bridget Richardson Fletcher (1726–70) in 'Hymn XXXVI. The Greatest Dignity of a Woman, Christ Being Born of One' (1773), 'Since God's own son, from heav'n did come, / Of such an one was born'. That sense of shared suffering and dignity can also extend beyond the specifically female sphere. In later life, Morton, for example, acquired a considerable readership for a powerfully expressed anti-slavery poem, 'The African Chief' (1823). While someone from quite outside this privileged circle of educated white women, Lucy Terry (1730–1821), an African slave who eventually settled as a free black in Vermont, composed a poem called 'Bars Fight' (published in 1855, after being handed down by word of mouth for nearly a century) that records the pain experienced and the courage witnessed during a battle between whites and Indians.

Cotton Mather had attacked poetry as the food of 'a boundless and sickly appetite', for its fictive origins and sensual appeal. Benjamin Franklin, the presiding genius of the American Enlightenment, was inclined to dismiss it because it was not immediately useful, functional; it did not help in the clearing of woods or the building of farms, schoolhouses and character. 'To America, one schoolmaster is worth a dozen poets,' Franklin argued, 'and the invention of a machine or the improvement of an implement is of more importance than a masterpiece of Raphael.' 'Nothing is good or beautiful but in the measure that it is useful', he explained, and a 'more refined state of society' would have to emerge before 'poetry, painting, music (and the stage as their embodiment)' could become 'necessary and proper gratifications'. However, to this charge that poetry makes nothing happen, others replied to the contrary: that it did clear the ground and break new wood – in short, that it helped in the making of Americans. The full force of that reply had to wait until the Revolution, when writers and critics began to insist that the new American nation needed an American literature, and more specifically an American poetry, in order to announce and understand itself. But, even before that, there were poets in the colonies who were trying to turn the old European forms to new American uses. Even Cotton Mather, after all, tried to identify and celebrate the 'Wonders' of the New World and so wrote a proto-epic, *Magnalia Christi Americana*.

The First Americans

Another writer, Joel Barlow, was to make his own attempt, towards the end of the eighteenth century, at a more specifically poetic epic in *The Vision of Columbus*, a much enlarged and revised version of which was to appear early in the next century as *The Columbiad*. And two notable writers, well before that, tried their hands at producing American versions of the two other most common forms of early eighteenth-century poetry besides the epic, both of them also derived from neo-classical models, the satire and the pastoral. The two writers were Ebenezer Cook (1667–1733) and Richard Lewis (1700?–1734).

Cook divided his time between London and Maryland. He was a prolific writer, as well as a planter and tobacco merchant, but his claim to fame rests on a satirical poem he published in 1708, *The Sot-weed Factor; or, a Voyage to Maryland &c.* Written in the form of Hudibrastic verse – so named after the English poet Samuel Butler's satire of the Puritans, *Hudibras* (1662–77) – *The Sot-weed Factor* presents us with a narrator who visits America only to be robbed, cheated, stripped of his guide, horse and clothes, and, in general, appalled by what he sees as the anarchy and squalor of his new surroundings. The rollicking tetrameter lines, odd rhymes and syntax help to paint a carnival portrait of life on the frontier and in the backwoods, in small towns and in '*Annapolis* . . . / A City Situate on a Plain'. And, having left '*Albion's* Rocks' in the opening lines, the narrator eagerly returns there at the conclusion some seven hundred lines later. 'Embarqu'd and waiting for a Wind, / I left this dreadful Curse behind, /' he declares, damning America as he departs. 'May Canniballs transported o'er the Sea / Prey on these Slaves, as they have done on me, /' is how he begins his condemnation. 'May never Merchant's trading sails explore / This Cruel, this Inhospitable Shoar.' Rising to new heights of invective, he then prays for America to be 'left abandon'd by the World to starve' and for Americans to 'sustain the Fate they will deserve' by turning 'Savage, or as *Indians* Wild'. Finally, he calls on God to complete the damnation of America. 'May Wrath Divine then lay those regions wast /', he prays, 'Where no Mans faithful, nor a Woman Chast.' The bombastic character of the curses, like the representation of the narrator throughout *The Sot-weed Factor*, alerts the reader to what is happening here. The satire apparently directed at American vulgarity is, in fact, being levelled at English snobbery, preciousness and self-satisfaction. Cook has taken an English form and turned it to American advantage. In the process, he has developed a peculiarly American style of comedy: in which the contrast between the genteel and the vernacular is negotiated, to the advantage of the latter, through a use of language that is fundamentally ironic.

Richard Lewis was just as prolific a writer as Cook; and, in the time he could spare from being a politician in Maryland, he wrote, among other things, forms of the pastoral that implied or even asserted the superiority of American nature. 'A Journey from Patapsko to Annapolis, April 4, 1730' (1732), for instance, begins by acknowledging its illustrious ancestry, with a quotation from the first pastoral poem, the *Georgics* of Virgil. Lewis then includes, later on in his poetical journey, allusions to the *Seasons* (1726–30) by the Scottish poet James Thomson and John Dryden's translation of the *Georgics* (1697). But, while deferring in this way to the

European model he is using and the European masters who have preceded him, Lewis is nevertheless eager to insist on the specific advantages and special beauties of the countryside around him. So he dwells on the idyllic life lived here by 'the *Monarch-Swain*', with 'His *Subject-Flocks*' and 'well-tilled Lands'. In a way, this is a commonplace of European pastoral too. Lewis, however, devotes more attention than his European predecessors tended to do to the ideas of patient toil rewarded, the value of self-subsistence and the pleasures of abundance. The farmer and his '*Sons* robust' their 'daily Labours share', Lewis tells us. Thanks to 'Viands unbought', gathered from his own land, the farmer can see 'smiling *Plenty* wait upon his Board'; thanks to 'their Toils', the family can enjoy 'sweet Success'; and all around them are the further blessings of 'Delicious Fruits', 'Blooms thick-springing', 'Evolving Odours', 'vocal Vallies' filled with birdsong – 'So fruitful is the Soil – so mild the Skies'. As Lewis turns his attention from the happy farmer and his family to the burgeoning countryside around him, he espies a humming-bird, the beauty of whose 'ever-flutt'ring wings' becomes a paradigm for and measure of the superiority of American nature. 'Oh had that *Bard* in whose heart-leaping Lines, / The *Phoenix* in a Blaze of Glory shines, / Beheld those Wonders which are shewn in Thee, /' Lewis tells the humming-bird, 'That *Bird* had lost his Immortality! / Thou in His Verse hadst stretch'd thy fluttering Wing / Above all other Birds, – their beauteous King.' The phoenix, the bird of classical myth, pales beside the American bird, just as the site of pastoral in the Old World pales beside what Lewis now calls the 'blooming Wilderness' of the New. Not content to stop there, the poet then asks us to behold the wonders of 'the out-stretch'd *Land*' beyond wood and plantation: a vista 'O'er which the Sight exerts a wide Command; / The fertile Vallies, and the naked Hills'. We turn our eyes, in effect, to what so many American poets were to take as the primary fact of their land: space, its apparent endlessness. After this, admittedly, the poetical journey concludes in conventional fashion, with references to the journey of life and prayers to the 'great CREATOR'. But Lewis has already staked a claim for difference. He has already, earlier on in the poem, broken new ground in the depiction of the American landscape and the development of the American pastoral form.

Although the eighteenth century in America witnessed a growing trend towards the secular, it would be wrong to deny the continuing importance and power of religious influences and writing. In the Southwest, for example, the century witnessed a significant growth of interest in and worship of the Virgin of Guadalupe. According to legend, the Virgin appeared to a poor Indian in 1531 on a sacred site associated with an Indian goddess of fertility. She asked for a cathedral to be built to her over the site of an Aztec place of worship, which it then was. The first account of this miraculous encounter was eventually written down a century later, in 1649, in Nahuatl, the language of the Aztecs. The Virgin was and remains a syncretic religious figure. The 'somewhat dark' face and Indian features attributed to her in the original account, and in the numerous paintings and statues of her created ever since, make her a Native American Virgin; the word 'Guadalupe' is itself most probably a hybrid, derived from the Nahuatl word for 'snake' and the

Spanish word for 'crush' and referring to a gesture often given to the Virgin Mary in statues, of crushing the snake. During the eighteenth century, however, the miscegenation of Spanish and Indian that marked the original legend became less important than the use of the Virgin of Guadalupe as an emblem of New World hybridity, the *mestizo*. She became a potent religious, cultural and political icon for Mexican Americans. She remains so, her figure turning up everywhere, in churches, homes and religious and political activities, in Chicano literature. And she is a measure of just how far removed many Americans of the time were from the creed or even the influence of the Enlightenment.

The same is true for some American writers situated further east. In 1755, for instance, *Some Account of the Fore part of the Life of Elizabeth Ashbridge . . . Written by her own Hand many years ago* was published. Little is known of its author, other than what is contained in her book, but from that it is clear that the central fact of her life was her conversion. After emigrating to America as an indentured servant, Elizabeth Ashbridge (1713–55) discovered that her master, whom she had taken for 'a very religious man', was, in fact, cruel and hypocritical. Buying her own freedom, she married a man who, she says, 'fell in love with me for my dancing'. But, when she embraced the Quaker religion, the dancing stopped; and her husband, in his anger and disappointment, began to beat her. The beatings only ended, Ashbridge explains, when her husband died. Then she was able to marry again, this time to someone who shared her faith. That faith, and her conversion to it, are described with simple power; just as they are in the *Journal* that another Quaker, John Woolman (1720–72), kept intermittently between 1756 and his death – and which was published by the Society of Friends in 1774. 'I have often felt a motion of love to leave some hints in writing of my experience of the goodness of God,' Woolman confesses at the start of the *Journal*, 'and now, in the thirty-sixth year of my age, I begin the work.' What follows is the story of a life lived in the light of faith that is, nevertheless, remarkable for its simplicity and humility of tone. Woolman describes how he eventually gave up trade and his mercantile interests to devote himself to his family and farm, and to work as a missionary. He travelled thousands of miles, Woolman reveals, driven by 'a lively operative desire for the good of others'. The desire not only prompted him towards missionary work but also impelled him to champion the rights of Native Americans and to attack slavery, which he described as a 'dark gloominess hanging over the land'. 'To say we love God as unseen and at the same time exercise cruelty towards the least creature moving by His life,' Woolman insists in his *Journal*, is 'a contradiction in itself.' Just like Ashbridge, Woolman shows how many Americans even in an increasingly secular age relied on what Woolman himself termed 'the judgements of God' and 'the infallible standard: Truth' to steer their lives and direct their choices, rather than the touchstones of reason and use.

The case is more complicated, however, with the greatest American embodiment of faith in the eighteenth century, Jonathan Edwards (1703–58). Edwards was born in East Windsor, Connecticut. His father and grandfather were both clergymen and, even before he went to college, he had decided to follow their example: not least because, as he discloses in his *Personal Narrative*, written some time after 1739, he had felt 'a sense of the glorious majesty and grace of God'. 'I walked abroad alone, in a solitary place in my father's pasture, for contemplation', he recalls, and 'looking upon the sky and clouds' there came into his mind 'so sweet a sense' that he knew 'not how to express': a vision of 'a high, and great, and holy gentleness'. After that, Edwards explains, 'the appearance of everything was altered' since 'there seemed to be . . . a calm, sweet cast, or appearance of divine glory, in almost everything'. He felt compelled to meditate, 'to sit and view the moon . . . the clouds and the sky', 'to behold the sweet glory of God in these things', as he puts it, 'in the meantime, singing forth, with a low voice my contemplations of the Creator and Redeemer'. He also felt compelled to review and discipline the conduct of his life. Some time in 1722–3, he composed seventy *Resolutions* designed to improve himself in the light of his faith. 'Being sensible that I am unable to do anything without God's help,' he wrote at the start of them, 'I do humbly entreat him by his grace, to keep these Resolutions, so far as they are agreeable to his will, for Christ's sake.' What follows very much reflects the old New England habit of seeing death as the defining, determining event of life. 'Resolved,' Edwards announces in *Resolution 7*, 'Never to do anything, which I shall be afraid to do, if it were the last hour of my life.' 'Resolved,' goes *Resolution 9*, 'To think much, on all occasions, of my own dying, and of the common circumstances which attend death.' This is a self-help manual of a special kind, shaped by a belief in human impotence and a profound sense of mortality. The experience of conversion confirmed what Edwards had, in any event, learned from his deeply orthodox religious upbringing: that God was the ground and centre, not only of faith but of all conduct and existence.

Further confirmation came when Edwards moved to Northampton, Massachusetts, to become pastor there. In 1734, he preached a number of sermons stressing the passivity of the convert before the all-powerful offer of grace from God; and the sermons provoked a strong reaction amongst many of his congregation, who appeared to experience exactly the kind of radical conversion Edwards was preaching about and had himself undergone. Encouraged to prepare an account of this awakening of faith in his community, Edwards wrote a pamphlet that then became a book, *A Faithful Narrative of the Surprising Work of God*, published in 1737. 'Some under Great Terrors of Conscience have had Impressions on their Imaginations,' Edwards reported; 'they have had . . . Ideas of Christ shedding blood for sinners, his blood Running from his veins.' 'There have been several Persons that have had their natures overborn under strong Convictions,' Edwards added, 'have trembled, and hadn't been able to stand, they have had such a sense of divine wrath.' But, then, having been convinced of their guilt and damnation, and resigning themselves to God's justice, these same people discovered as Edwards had the power of God's grace. 'Persons are often revived out of their dead and dark frames,' Edwards revealed; 'their souls are carried away into holy exercises with abundant pleasure.' Anticipating the Great Awakening that was to sweep through many parts of the American colonies in the next few years, the Northampton congregation, many of

The First Americans

them, found themselves born again, into a new life grounded in 'the beauty and excellency of Christ', just as their pastor had been before them.

Both his own personal experience, then, and the 'surprising' conversions among his congregation were enough to convince Edwards of the supreme importance of divine grace and human faith. But that did not make him averse to science and systematic thinking. On the contrary, he made his own contribution to the philosophical debates of the time. In *A Treatise Concerning Religious Affections* (1746), for instance, Edwards attempted to construct a clear theory of the place of emotion in religion, so as the better to understand the emotional experience of converts. Similarly, in *A Careful and Strict Enquiry into the Modern Prevailing Notions of that Freedom of Will, Which is Supposed to be essential to . . . Praise and Blame* (1754), he made a conscientious effort to rescue philosophers from what he saw as their confusion, while resolving the potential contradiction between the doctrines of divine omnipotence and human responsibility. Just how much Edwards wanted to harness reason in the service of faith and, if necessary, to defend mystery with logic is nowhere better illustrated than in his arguments – developed in such works as *The Great Christian Doctrine of Original Sin Defended* (1758) and *Two Dissertations* (1765) – concerning the total depravity of human nature and the infinite grace of God. True virtue, Edwards argued, borrowing his definitions from Enlightenment philosophers like Hutcheson and Shaftesbury, consists in disinterested benevolence towards humankind in general. It involves pure selflessness. But, Edwards then insisted, humanity can never be selfless. All human actions, no matter how creditable their effects, are dictated by self-interest. Everything a human being does springs from considerations of self because, Edwards went on, now borrowing his definitions from an earlier Enlightenment figure, Descartes, he or she can never get outside the self. A man, or woman, can never escape from their own senses and sense impressions. So, they are incapable of true virtue. Each is imprisoned in his or her own nature. Each is corrupt, fallen and evil, and the only thing that can save them is something beyond human power to control: that is, the irresistible grace of God. 'All moral good,' Edwards concluded, 'stems from God.' God is the beginning and end, the ground and meaning of all moral existence.

And not only moral existence: Edwards was careful to argue that God was the ground of all created life, including our understanding of ourselves and our world: 'There is no identity or oneness in the world, but what depends on the *arbitrary* constitution of the Creator,' he explained. This was because existence and our knowledge of it depend on continuity, a connection between 'successive effects'; and such continuity 'depends on nothing but the *divine* will' which, in turn, 'depends on nothing but the *divine* wisdom'. Without God, as Edwards saw and argued it, the world and life not only became a moral desert; they also ceased to exist. Like a precious object precariously balanced, once the source of support was taken away, they lost identity as well as value. Or, as Edwards boldly put it, 'the whole *course* of *nature*, with all that belongs to it, all its laws and methods, and constancy and regularity, continuance and proceeding, is an *arbitrary constitution*'. Edwards's relation to the prevailing rationalism of his times certainly drew him towards

---

complex philosophical argument, the use of authorities like Descartes and Locke and the notion of the human being as a creature dependent on the impressions of the senses. But it never tempted him to deviate from the straight and narrow path of faith, or to surrender a vision of human experience that was rapt and apocalyptic, swinging between the extremes of human impotence and divine power, human unworthiness and divine grace and, above all, damnation and redemption.

A sermon like Edwards's most well-known piece of work, *Sinners in the Hands of an Angry God*, delivered in 1741 and published the same year, describes the alternative of damnation. In it, Edwards uses all the rhetorical devices at his disposal, above all vivid imagery and incremental repetition, to describe in gruesome detail the 'fearful danger' the 'sinner' is in. 'You hang by a slender thread,' he warns his flock, 'with the flames of divine wrath flashing about it,' that are 'ready every moment to . . . burn it asunder,' consigning all those who hang there to 'a great furnace of wrath, a wide and bottomless pit, full of the fire and wrath.' The other alternative, of conversions and salvation, is figured, for example, in Edwards's description in 1723 of the woman who became his wife, Sarah Pierrepoint. Like so many of Edwards's writings – or, for that matter, work by others inspired by the Puritan belief that material facts are spiritual signs – it is at once intimate and symbolic. This is, at once, his own dear beloved and an emblem of any redeemed soul in communion with God:

> They say that there is a young lady who is beloved of that Great Being who made and rules the world . . . She will sometimes go about from place to place, singing sweetly; and seems to be always full of joy and pleasure; and no one knows for what. She loves to be alone, walking in the fields and groves, and seems to have some one invisible always conversing with her.

'The Son of God created the world for this very end', Edwards wrote elsewhere, in 'Covenant of Redemption: "Excellency of Christ"', 'to communicate Himself in an image of His own excellency', 'By this we may discover the beauty of many of those metaphors and similes, which to an unphilosophical person do seem uncouth,' he infers; since everywhere in nature we may consequently behold emblems, 'the emanations of the sweet benevolence of Jesus Christ'. That belief in the spiritual and symbolic nature of the perceived world animates Edwards's writing, as here in his portrait of the woman he married. So does his fervent belief that all existence, natural and moral, depends on God, and his equally fervent conviction that all human faculties, including reason, must be placed in the service of faith in Him. It is all this that makes the writing, and Edwards himself, so typical of his time in some ways and, in others, so extraordinarily exceptional.

Towards the Revolution

It is possible to see Jonathan Edwards as a distillation of one side of the Puritan inheritance: that is, the spiritual, even mystical strain in Puritan thought that emphasized the inner life, the pursuit of personal redemption, and the ineffable character of God's grace. In which case, it is equally possible to see Edwards's great contemporary, Benjamin Franklin (1706–90), as a distillation and development of another side: that tendency in Puritanism that stressed the outer life, hard work and good conduct, and the freedom of the individual will. Edwards, to an extent, takes up the idealistic, sometimes pessimistic strain in Puritanism that claimed people were helpless, focused on death as the determining event in life, and set its sights on what lay beyond this world. The world, from this viewpoint, was a forest of symbols, signs given by God to teach people the ways of providence. In Franklin, by contrast, we see traces of a quite different strain, which said that people should strive mightily, focused on personal behaviour as the decisive factor in human experience, and made its immediate target a community of *visible* saints. The world, taken from this approach, was a matter of fact, a place where everyone proved their worth by adherence to the work ethic and the practice of such eminently social virtues as sobriety, self-control and charity. Of course, Edwards did not deny the importance of conduct, and Franklin was prepared to acknowledge the idea of ultimate reward or punishment in an afterlife. There is no doubt, however, where their fundamental priorities lay. 'This world is not our abiding place,' Edwards once declared. 'Man's days on the earth are as a shadow,' he went on. 'If we spend our lives in the pursuit of temporal happiness; as riches, or sensual pleasures; credit and esteem from men . . . All these things will be of little significancy to us. Death blows up all our hopes.' Franklin, at most, gave lip service to such notions, and sometimes not even that. If we look at him, after looking at Edwards, what we see, in fact, is the collapse in the eighteenth century of that perilous equilibrium that, earlier, the Puritans had managed somehow to maintain, and its replacement by a series of warring opposites.

Another way of putting it is to say that Franklin embodied the new spirit of America, emerging in part out of Puritanism and in part out of the Enlightenment, that was coming to dominate the culture. And he knew it. That is clear from his account of his own life in his most famous work, the *Autobiography*, which he laboured on at four different times (1771, 1784, 1788, 1788–9), revised extensively but left unfinished at the time of his death; an American edition was published in 1818, but the first complete edition of what he had written only appeared nearly a hundred years after his death, in 1867. Uncompleted though it is, the *Autobiography* nevertheless has a narrative unity. It is divided into three sections: first, Franklin's youth and early manhood in Boston and Philadelphia, second, Franklin's youthful attempts to achieve what he terms 'moral perfection', and third, Franklin's use of the principles discovered in the first section and enumerated in the second to enable him to rise to prosperity and success as a scientist, politician and philanthropist. Throughout all three sections, Franklin is keen to present his life as exemplary and typical: proof positive that anyone can make it, especially in America, 'the Land of Labour' where 'a general happy Mediocrity prevails' – as long as they apply themselves to useful toil. Like the good scientist, Franklin the narrator looks at the events of Franklin the autobiographical character's life and tries to draw inferences from them. Or he tries to see how his own moral hypotheses worked, when he put them to the test of action. This means that he is more than just remembering in his *Autobiography*. He is also demonstrating those truths, about human nature, human society, and God, which, as he sees it, should be acknowledged by all reasonable men. Exactly how he does this is anticipated in the opening pages of the book, where, addressing his 'Dear Son', Franklin explains his reasons for putting pen to paper. He did it, Franklin admits, 'partly to gratify my own vanity', being persuaded that a moderate indulgence of any personal desire is not necessarily a bad thing. He also did it, he points out, so as to discover his faults, the errors committed in his life, for himself. Not only that, he wrote his *Autobiography* in the hope that, by detailing just how he 'emerged from poverty and obscurity' to 'a state of affluence and some degree of reputation in the world', he could offer an instructive example to his family and future generations. The motives Franklin ascribes to himself are a mixture of the selfish and the social. What is more, they are seen as reinforcing rather than conflicting with each other. As he tells it, Franklin's personal reasons for writing his book complement, or even strengthen, those reasons that reflect his concern for the greater good, the betterment of others. He is pursuing his own interests *and* those of the community. The explanation that begins the *Autobiography*, in effect, illustrates one of the great commonplaces of Enlightenment thought: that, in a properly ordered world, self-help and helping others can coincide. It also announces the fundamental project of the book: which is to show how Franklin opened up the way to wealth and a better life for both himself and his society – how he helped the community by following the path of enlightened self-interest.

Just how much Franklin presents his story as a prototypical American one is measured in the first section of the *Autobiography*. His 'first entry' into the city of Philadelphia in 1723, for instance, is described in detail. And what he emphasizes is his sorry appearance and poverty. 'I was in my working dress,' he tells the reader, 'my best clothes being to come round by sea.' 'I was dirty from my journey,' he adds, 'and I knew no soul nor where to look for lodging.' 'Fatigued with travelling', 'very hungry', and with a 'stock of cash' consisting only of 'a Dutch dollar, and about a shilling in copper', all he could purchase for himself to eat was 'three great puffy rolls'. Munching disconsolately on these, he then walked through the streets of Philadelphia 'passing by the door of Mr Read, my future wife's father', Franklin explains, 'when she, standing at the door, saw me, and thought I made, as I certainly did, a most awkward, ridiculous appearance'. Whatever the truth of this story, Franklin is also clearly constructing a myth here, one that was to become familiar in American narratives. This is the self-made man as hero, on his first appearance, poor and unknown and unprotected, entering a world that he then proceeds to conquer.

That Franklin was able to rise to affluence and reputation from these humble beginnings was due, he tells the reader, not only to self-help and self-reliance but to self-reinvention. In the second section of his *Autobiography*, he explains how he 'conceived the bold and arduous project of arriving at moral perfection'. Wanting 'to live without committing any fault at any time', he drew up a list of the 'moral virtues', such as 'temperance', 'silence', 'order', 'resolution' and 'frugality'. He then gave 'a week's attention to each of the virtues successively'. 'My great goal', Franklin says, 'was to avoid even the least offence' against the moral virtue for that week, 'leaving the other virtues to their ordinary chance'. A complicated chart was drawn up for the week; and, if ever he committed a least offence against that week's moral virtue, he would mark it on the chart, his obvious aim being to keep it 'clean of spots'. Since he had enumerated thirteen virtues, he could 'go through a course complete' in moral re-education in thirteen weeks, and 'four courses in a year'. Franklin compared his scheme to horticulture: he was, he said, like someone 'who, having a garden to weed, does not eradicate all the bad herbs at once, which would exceed his reach and his strength, but works on one of the beds at a time'. Springing from a fundamental belief that the individual could change, improve and even recreate himself, with the help of reason, common sense and hard work, Franklin's programme for himself was one of the first great formulations of the American dream. Rather than being born into a life, Franklin is informing his readers, a person can make that life for himself. He can be whoever he wants to be. All he needs is understanding, energy and commitment to turn his own best desires about himself into a tangible reality.

And that, as he tells it and indeed lived it, is exactly what Franklin did. By 1748, when he was still only forty-two, he had made enough money to retire from active business. By this time, he had also become quite famous thanks to his newspaper, the *Pennsylvania Gazette*, and a little book he published annually from 1733. Almanacs were popular in early America, their principal purpose being to supply farms and traders with information about the weather and fluctuations in the currency. Franklin kept this tradition going, but he changed it by adding and gradually expanding a section consisting of proverbs and little essays, a kind of advice column that reflected his philosophy of economic and moral individualism. Eventually, many of the proverbs were brought together in one book, in 1758, that was to become known as *The Way to Wealth*; this was a nationwide best-seller and was reprinted several hundred times. Always, the emphasis here is on the virtues of diligence, thrift and independence. 'Diligence is the mother of good luck,' declares one proverb. 'Plough deep, while sluggards sleep,' says another, 'and you shall have corn to sell and keep.' 'Beware of little expenses; a small leak will sink a great ship.' 'The borrower is a slave to the lender.' 'Get all you can, and what you get, hold.' As a whole, the proverbs reflect the single-mindedness that had helped Franklin himself along the way to wealth. But they also show Franklin's wit. As early as 1722, Franklin had perfected a literary style that combined clarity of expression with sharpness and subtlety, and frequently humour of perception, in a series of essays called the 'Silence Dogood' papers, after the name of the narrator. In these, Franklin used a fictitious speaker, the busybody widow Silence Dogood, to satirize follies and vices ranging from poor poetry to prostitution. And, throughout his life, Franklin was not only an inventor of proverbial wisdom but a masterly essayist, using his skills to promote philanthropic and political projects (*A Proposal for*

Promoting Useful Knowledge [1743]; *Proposals Relating to the Education of Youth in Pennsylvania* [1749]), to attack violence against Native Americans or the superstition that led people to accuse women of witchcraft (*A Narrative of the Late Massacres* [1764]; 'A Witch Trial at Mount Holly' [1730]), and to satirize the slave trade and British imperialism ('On the Slave Trade' [1790]; 'An Edict by the King of Prussia' [1773]). Here, he developed his persona, 'the friend of all good men', and his characteristic argumentative strategy, also enshrined in his *Autobiography*, of weaving seamlessly together the imperatives of self-help and altruism, personal need and the claims of society.

Here, and elsewhere, Franklin also elaborated his belief in America. His homeplace, Franklin explained in 'Information to Those Who Would Remove to America' (1784), was a place where 'people do not inquire concerning a Stranger, *What is he?* But, *What can he do?*' Anyone with 'any useful Art' was welcome. And all 'Hearty young Labouring Men' could 'easily establish themselves' there. Not only that, they could soon rise to a reasonable fortune. They could increase and multiply, since 'the salubrity of the Air, the healthiness of the Climate, the plenty of good Provision, and the Encouragement to early Marriages by the certainty of Subsistence in cultivating the Earth' – all these made the growth of population 'very rapid in America'. Finally, they could live good lives. 'The almost general Mediocrity of Fortune that prevails in America', Franklin explained, obliged all people 'to follow some Business for subsistence'. So, 'those Vices, that arise usually from Idleness, are in a great measure prevented'; 'Industry and constant Employment' were the 'great preservatives of the Morals and Virtue' of the New World. For Franklin, America really was the land of opportunity. It was also a land of tolerance, common sense and reason, where people could and should be left free to toil usefully for themselves and their community, as he had done. Typically, he turned such beliefs into a matter of political practice as well as principle, working on behalf of his colonial home, then his country, for most of his life. In 1757 and 1775, for example, he made two lengthy trips to England, to serve as colonial agent. After the second trip, he returned to Philadelphia just in time to serve in the Continental Congress and to be chosen as a member of that committee which eventually drafted the Declaration of Independence. He spent two years in Paris, negotiating an alliance between France and America. Then, in 1783, he was one of the three American signatories to the treaty that ended the Revolutionary War. Finally, after some years in France as American ambassador, he became a member of that convention which drafted the Constitution of the United States. Characteristically, on the last day of the convention, he confessed that he did not 'entirely approve of this Constitution at present'. But, he then added, 'the older I get, the more apt I am to doubt my own judgement'. 'Thus, I consent, Sir, to this Constitution,' he concluded, 'because I expect no better, and because I am not sure that it is not the best. The opinion I have had of its *errors* I sacrifice to the public good.' Franklin was, in short, at the heart of the American Revolution from its origins to its conclusion. And he shows, more clearly than any other figure of the time does, just how much that Revolution owed to the principles of the Enlightenment. By

his presence and comments he also suggests just how much the founding documents of the American nation were rooted in a project that he himself embraced
and emblematized, based on the principles of natural rights and reason, self-help
and self-reinvention.

'What then is the American this new man?' asked J. Hector St Jean de Crèvecoeur
(1735–1813) in his *Letters from an American Farmer*, published in 1782. Answering
his own question, Crèvecoeur then suggested that 'the American is a new man,
who acts upon new principles; he must therefore entertain new ideas, and form
new opinions'. That was a common theme in the literature surrounding the American Revolution. As the American colonies became a new nation, the United States
of America, writers and many others applied themselves to the task of announcing
just what this new nation represented, and what the character and best hopes of
the American might be. Crèvecoeur was especially fascinated because of his mixed
background: born in France, he spent time in England and Canada before settling
as a planter in New York State. He was also, during the Revolution, placed in a
difficult position. As a Tory or Loyalist (that is, someone who continued to claim
allegiance to Britain), he found himself suspected by the Revolutionaries; as someone with liberal sympathies, however, he also fell under suspicion among the other
Tories. So in 1780 he returned to France; and it was in London that *Letters* was first
published. Following a form very popular in the eighteenth century, Crèvecoeur's
book (which was reprinted many times) consists of twelve letters written by a
fictional narrator, James, a Quaker and a farmer, describing his life on the farm
and his travels to places such as Charlestown, South Carolina. *Letters* is an epistolary
narrative; it is a travel and philosophical journal; and it also inaugurates that
peculiarly American habit of mixing fiction and thinly disguised autobiography.
James shares many of the experiences and opinions of Crèvecoeur but, unlike his
creator, he is a simple, relatively uneducated man and, of course, a Quaker – which
Crèvecoeur most certainly was not.

At the heart of *Letters* are three animating beliefs that Crèvecoeur shared with
many of his contemporaries, and that were to shape subsequent American thought
and writing. There is, first, the belief that American nature is superior to European
culture: at once older than even 'the half-ruined amphitheatres' of the Old World
and, because it is subject to perpetual, seasonal renewal, much newer and fresher
than, say, 'the musty ruins of Rome'. Second, there is the belief that America is the
place where the oppressed of Europe can find freedom and independence as 'tillers
of the earth'. America is 'not composed, as in Europe, of great lords who possess
everything, and a herd of people who have nothing', the narrator of *Letters* explains.
'We are all animated with the spirit of an industry which is unfettered and unrestrained, because each person works for himself.' Thanks to this, America offers the
pleasing spectacle of a return to 'the very beginnings and outlines of human society'.
Americans have 'regained the ancient dignity of our species', we learn; their 'laws
are simple and just'; and 'a pleasing uniformity of decent competence appears
throughout' the land. 'We are,' the narrator triumphantly declares, 'the most perfect
society now existing in the world.' The 'new man' at the centre of this perfect

society reflects the third belief animating this book. The American, as *Letters* describes him, is the product of 'the new mode of life he has embraced, the new government he obeys, and the new rank he holds'. 'Americans are the western pilgrims', the narrator proudly declaims; 'here individuals of all nations are melted into a new race of men'. And what lies at the end of this journey to a Promised Land, what rises out of the melting pot, is a self-reliant individual, whose 'labour is founded on the basis of nature, self-interest'. Working with his family in fields 'whence exuberant crops are to arise to feed and clothe them all', the American owes no allegiance to 'a despotic prince, a rich abbot, or a mighty lord'. Even 'religion demands little of him' other than 'a small voluntary salary to the minister, and gratitude to God'. He works for himself and his loved ones; he can think for himself; and the contribution he makes to his community and society is freely given, without fear or favour.

There are, certainly, moments of doubt and even despair in *Letters*. Travelling to South Carolina, James is reminded of the obscenity and injustice of slavery: not least, when he comes across the grotesque spectacle of a slave suspended in a cage in the woods, starving to death, his eyes pecked out by hungry birds. The slave, a 'living spectre', is being punished for killing an overseer; and this, together with other experiences in the South, leads James to reflect on a terrible exception to the American norm of just laws and useful toil rewarded. 'Day after day they drudge on without any prospect of ever reaping for themselves', James observes of the slaves: that cannot help but throw his own pleasing visions into doubt. James is similarly disturbed when he visits the frontier. Here, he notes, men are 'often in a perfect state of war; that of man against man' and 'appear to be no better than carnivorous animals of superior rank'. On this occasion, though, he can find consolation in the thought that the frontier represents only the 'feeble beginnings and laborious rudiments' of society. As in his own homeplace, this ugly but perhaps necessary first stage in social development will soon give way, James assures his readers and himself, to the 'general decency of manners' to be found in a settled farming community. *Letters* does then end on a disconsolate note, dwelling on the threat posed to the 'tranquillity' of 'this new land' by the Revolution. But, despite that – despite, even, the suspicion that the presence of slavery makes a mockery of any talk of a 'perfect society' – the general thrust of the book is towards celebration of both the promise and the perfection of America. Crèvecoeur's work is driven by certain convictions, about nature and natural rights, a new man and society, that he certainly shared with other American writers of the time – and, indeed, with some of his Romantic counterparts in Europe. But nowhere are such convictions given clearer or more charged expression. *Letters* begins with the claim that to 'record the progressive steps' of an 'industrious farmer' is a nobler project for a writer than any to be found in European literature. That claim is supported, and the project pursued with enthusiasm in the ensuing pages, where the hero is, quite simply, 'the American'.

A writer who shared Crèvecoeur's belief in the possibilities of American society was Thomas Paine (1737–1809). Unlike Crèvecoeur, however, Paine was unambiguously enthusiastic about the Revolution. Born in England, Paine arrived in America in 1774. He remained for only thirteen years, but his impact on America's developing vision of itself was enormous. In 1776, Paine published *Common Sense*, which argued for American independence and the formation of a republican government. 'In the following pages I offer nothing more than simple facts, plain arguments, and common sense,' Paine declared in the opening pages. That reflected the contemporary belief in the power of reason, which Paine shared, and the contemporary shift in political commentaries from arguments rooted in religion to more secular ones. It did not, however, quite do justice to, or prepare the reader for, the power of Paine's rhetoric. 'The blood of the slain, the weeping voice of the nation cries, 'TIS TIME TO PART,' Paine declaims at one point in *Common Sense*. 'O! receive the fugitive', he announces elsewhere to those in America who 'dare oppose not only the tyranny but the tyrant', 'and prepare in time an asylum for mankind'. That gift for firing arguments into life, often with the help of an imaginative use of maxims, is even more in evidence in the *Crisis* papers. With Washington defeated and in retreat at the end of 1776, Paine tried to rouse the nation to further resistance in the first of sixteen papers. 'These are the times that try men's souls,' he began. On this memorable opening he then piled a series of equally memorable maxims, clearly designed for the nation to take to and carry in its heart:

> The summer soldier and the sunshine patriot will, in this crisis, shrink from the service of their country; but he that stands it *now*, deserves the love and thanks of man and woman. Tyranny, like hell, is not easily conquered; yet we have this consolation with us, that the harder the conflict, the more glorious the triumph. What we obtain too cheap, we esteem too lightly: it is dearness only that gives every thing its value.

The last of the *Crisis* papers appeared in 1783, at the end of the Revolution. Only four years later, Paine returned to England. There, he wrote *The Rights of Man* (1791–2), intended as a reply to *Reflections on the Revolution in France* (1790) by Edmund Burke. It was immensely popular but, because Paine argued against a hereditary monarchy in *The Rights of Man*, he was charged with sedition and was forced to flee to France. There, his protest against the execution of Louis XVI led to imprisonment. He was only released when the American ambassador to Paris, James Madison, intervened. Paine returned to America. But the publication of his last major work, *The Age of Reason* (1794–5), led to further notoriety and unpopularity in his adoptive homeplace. In *The Age of Reason*, Paine attacks the irrationality of religion and, in particular, Christianity. In the name of reason, he denies the truth of such primary tenets of the Christian faith as the Virgin Birth, the Holy Trinity, miracles and revelation, and the divinity and resurrection of Jesus. 'The study of theology as it stands in Christian churches, is the study of nothing,' Paine declares with his customary rhetorical power; 'it is founded on nothing; it rests on no principles; it proceeds by no authorities; it has no data;

it can demonstrate nothing; and admits of no conclusion . . . it is therefore the study of nothing.' Paine did not deny the existence of 'one God' and, like Franklin, he insisted that, as he put it, 'religious duties consist in doing justice, loving mercy, and endeavouring to make our fellow-creatures happy'. But that did not enable him to escape the anger of many Americans: he was vilified in papers and on pulpits as a threat to both Christian and democratic faiths. 'My own mind is my own church,' Paine insisted in *The Age of Reason*. 'The Creation speaketh an universal language, independently of human speech,' he added; 'it preaches to all nations and to all worlds; and this *word of God* reveals to man all that is necessary for man to know of God.' Such impeccably deistic sentiments were entirely consistent with all that Paine had ever written; they were marked by his customary belief in the determining importance of reason and his customary use of maxim, epigram and antithesis to get his point across. There was little here that Franklin or many of the other founding fathers of the republic would have found fault with: but times had changed and, in any event, such an unrestrained and unambiguous assault on Christian mystery would have been likely to provoke a backlash in early America at any time. Not surprisingly, Paine lived his last few years in obscurity.

Obscurity was never to be the fate of Thomas Jefferson (1724–1826). A person of eclectic interests – and, in that, the inheritor of a tradition previously best illustrated by William Byrd of Westover – Jefferson's very myriad-mindedness has led to quite contradictory interpretations of both his aims and his achievement. He has been seen, for instance, as a man of the frontier and a cultivated planter, an idealist and a utilitarian, as the advocate of the rights of all and as a spokesman for the farmer in particular. What is incontestable, however, is the central part he played in the formation of America as a nation. His *A Summary View of the Rights of British America*, for example, published in 1774, was immensely influential. In it, Jefferson argued that Americans had effectively freed themselves from British authority by exercising 'a right which nature has given to all men, of departing from the country in which chance, not choice, has placed them'. 'God, who gave us life gave us liberty at the same time,' Jefferson insisted. 'Kings are servants, not the proprietors of the people.' Such stirring words earned him a place, in 1776, on the committee assigned the task of drafting the Declaration of Independence. And, if any one person can be called the author of that Declaration, it is undoubtedly Jefferson. This founding document of the American nation enshrines the beliefs that Jefferson shared with so many other major figures of the Enlightenment: that 'all men are created equal', that they are endowed with certain 'inalienable rights' and notably the right to 'life, liberty, and the pursuit of happiness'; and that 'to secure those rights, governments are instituted among men'. Like many great American documents, the Declaration of Independence describes an idea of the nation, an ideal or possibility against which its actual social practices can and must be measured – and, it might well be, found wanting.

Jefferson relied on the principle of natural rights and the argumentative tool of reason to construct a blueprint of the American nation. When it came to filling in the details, however, he relied as Crèvecoeur and many others did on his belief in the independent farmer. 'I know no condition happier than that of a Virginia farmer,' Jefferson wrote to a friend in 1787. 'His estate supplies a good table, clothes himself and his family with their ordinary apparel, furnishes a small surplus to buy salt, coffee, and a little finery for his wife and daughter, . . . and furnishes him pleasing and healthy occupation.' 'Cultivators of the earth are the most valuable citizens,' he declared in another letter, written in 1804. 'They are the most vigorous, the most independent, the most virtuous, and they are tied to their country, and wedded to its interests, by the most lasting bonds.' Fortunately, in his opinion, America would remain an agricultural country for the foreseeable future; small farmers would therefore remain 'the true representatives of the Great American interests' and the progress and prosperity of the new republic was consequently assured. 'The small landowners are the most precious part of a state,' Jefferson confided in a letter to his friend and fellow Virginian James Madison in 1772. In a more public vein, he made this famous statement:

> Those who labour in the earth are the chosen people of God, if ever he had a chosen people, whose breasts he has made his peculiar deposit for substantial and genuine virtue . . . Corruption of morals . . . is the mark set on those, who not looking . . . to their own soil and industry, as does the husbandman, for their subsistence, depend for it on the casualties and caprice of customers . . . generally speaking, the proportion which the aggregate of other classes of citizens bears in any state to that of its husbandmen, is the proportion of its unsound to its healthy parts.

It is the definitive statement of a determining American myth.

That statement comes from the one full-length book Jefferson published, in 1787, *Notes on the State of Virginia*. Written in response to a questionnaire sent to him about his home state while he was serving as governor, *Notes* is at once a scientific treatise and a crucial document of cultural formation. Jefferson examines and documents the natural and cultural landscape of the New World and, at the same time, considers the promise and possibilities of the new nation. One of his several aims in the book is to rebut the argument embraced by many leading European naturalists of the time that the animals and people of the New World were inherently smaller, less vigorous and more degenerate than their Old World counterparts. This gives him the opportunity to write in praise of the Native American. Jefferson was willing to accept the idea that Native Americans were still a 'barbarous people', lacking such advantages of civilization as 'letters' and deference towards women. But he insisted on their primitive strength, 'their bravery and address in war' and 'their eminence in oratory'. As he saw it, they were strong, courageous, 'faithful to the utmost extremity' and as far advanced in all respects as their relatively early stage in cultural evolution would allow. Rebutting European claims of this nature also allowed Jefferson to enumerate white American achievements in such fields as 'philosophy and war', government, oratory, painting and 'the plastic art', and to express the firm conviction that, in other areas too,

America would soon have 'her full quota of genius'. Of Great Britain, he declared that it had taken a long time for that nation to produce 'a Shakespeare and Milton'; 'the run of her glory is fast descending to the horizon' and it would no doubt soon be America's turn.

Like Crèvecoeur, Jefferson also felt compelled to confront the challenge to his idyllic vision of America posed by the indelible fact of slavery. He condemned the peculiar institution in his *Notes* and argued for emancipation. But emancipation, for him, was linked to repatriation: once freed, the slaves should be sent to some other colony, Jefferson insisted, where they could become 'a free and independent people'. Removal was necessary, Jefferson felt, because the 'deep rooted prejudices' of the whites and a lingering sense of injustice felt by the blacks would make coexistence impossible. Not only that, Jefferson was willing to entertain the idea that physical and moral differences between the two races further underlined the need for freed blacks to go elsewhere. 'In general, their existence appears to participate more of sensation than reflection,' Jefferson observed of African Americans. Among other things, this made them deficient as artists and writers. 'Never yet could I find that a black had uttered a thought above the level of plain narration,' he maintained. 'Religion has indeed produced a Phyllis Whateley [Phillis Wheatley]' but 'the compositions published under her name are below the dignity of criticism.' All the arguments that black people were inferior to white 'in the endowments both of body and mind' were advanced, Jefferson assured the reader 'as a suspicion only'. He was willing to consider evidence to the contrary, and to ascribe supposed differences, such as an alleged 'disposition to theft', to their situation rather than 'depravity of the moral sense'. But the general burden of the argument in *Notes* is clearly towards black inferiority. And the belief that, once freed, blacks should be 'removed beyond the reach of mixture' is stated consistently and categorically. So, for that matter, is the belief that, if black people are not freed soon, the American republic will reap a terrible harvest. 'Indeed, I tremble for my country when I reflect that God is just,' Jefferson famously declared in *Notes*. There might, he thought, be 'a revolution in the wheel of fortune, an exchange of situation'. But then, he added hopefully, there might be a more fortunate turn of events. 'The spirit of the master is abating, that of the slave is rising from the dust,' Jefferson told his readers, and 'the way I hope preparing . . . for total emancipation . . . disposed . . . to be with the consent of the masters, rather than by their extirpation.' It was a sign of Jefferson's intellectual honesty that he wrestled with the problem of slavery in the first place. It was also a sign that he was, after all, a man of his times imbued with many of its prejudices that he could not disentangle the ideal of black freedom from the ideas of separation and removal. His doubts about the radical threat to the new republic posed by its clear violation of its own clearly stated belief in natural rights were, in the last analysis, subdued by his conviction that reason, as he construed it, would prevail. That is the measure of his capacity for optimism, and of his belief that, as he put it in *Notes*, 'reason and free inquiry are the only effective agents against error'. It is also, perhaps, a measure of a capacity for self-delusion that was by no means uniquely his.

The First Americans

In 1813, Jefferson began a correspondence with John Adams (1735–1826), repairing the breach in their friendship that had occurred when Jefferson defeated Adams in the presidential elections of 1800; they were published separately and in full in 1959. The first vice-president and the second president, Adams was a lively intellectual of a sceptical turn of mind and the founder of a family dynasty that would produce another president, John Quincy Adams, and the historian, novelist and autobiographer Henry Adams. Discussing literature, history and philosophy, Jefferson pitted his idealism against Adams's acid wit and pessimistic turn of mind. To Jefferson's insistence that 'a natural aristocracy' of 'virtue and talents' would replace 'an artificial aristocracy founded on wealth and birth' Adams replied that the distinction would not 'help the matter'. 'Both artificial aristocracy, and Monarchy,' Adams argued, 'have grown out of the natural Aristocracy of "Virtue and Talents".' 'The five pillars of Aristocracy, are Beauty, Wealth, Birth, Genius, and Virtues'; and, Adams suggested, 'any one of the three first, can at any time over bear any one of the two last'. Adams's scepticism and, in particular, his sense that in time the purest republic becomes tainted by the hereditary principle or, at least, the evolution of a ruling class led him to think less well of the American future than Jefferson did. Part of this stemmed from a patrician distrust of the people: in one letter, written in November 1813, for example, he claimed to be ready to weep at 'the Stupidity with which the more numerous multitude' not only became 'the Dupes' of those 'who are allowed an aristocratical influence' but also even loved 'to be Taken in by their Tricks'. Whatever its sources, it prompted Adams to meet Jefferson's optimism with irony. 'Many hundred years must roll away before We shall be corrupted,' he declared sarcastically. 'Our pure, virtuous, public spirited federative Republick will last for ever, govern the Globe and introduce the perfection of Man.'

Alternative voices of Revolution

The letters between Adams and Jefferson reveal two contrary visions of the new American republic and its fate. So, in a different way, do the letters that passed between John Adams and his wife Abigail. Inevitably, perhaps, the tone is more intimate, even teasing. But Abigail Adams (1744–1818) raises, consistently, the serious issue of freedom and equality for women. 'I long to hear that you have declared an independency,' she wrote to her husband in 1776, 'and by the way in the new Code of Laws which I suppose it will be necessary for you to make I desire you would Remember the Ladies.' Abigail Adams urged John Adams and his colleagues, as they prepared the new laws of the nation, to be 'more generous and favourable' to women than their 'ancestors' had been. 'Do not put such unlimited power into the hands of the Husbands,' she wrote. 'Remember all Men would be tyrants if they could.' 'That your Sex are Naturally Tyrannical is a Truth so thoroughly established as to admit of no dispute,' she suggested, 'but such of you as wish to be happy willingly give up the harsh title of Master for the more endearing one of Friend.' If 'persistent care and attention' were not taken to observe the rights of women, Abigail Adams warned, 'we are determined to foment a Rebellion, and will not hold ourselves bound by any Laws in which we have no voice, or Representation'. The tone was playful, but it made adroit and serious use of one of the primary beliefs of the leaders of the Revolution: that, as Jefferson put it in his *Notes*, 'laws to be just, must give a reciprocation of rights . . . without this, they are mere arbitrary rules of conduct, founded on force'. Unfortunately, all Abigail Adams received in response was the playful claim from John that he, and all husbands, 'have only the Name of Masters'. All men, he insisted, were 'completely subject' 'to the Despotism of the Petticoat'.

Adams wrote to his wife, adding gentle insult to injury, that he could not choose but laugh at her 'extraordinary Code of Laws'. 'We have been told that our Struggle has loosened the bands of Government everywhere,' he explained: 'that Children and Apprentices were disobedient – that schools and Colledges were grown turbulent – that Indians slighted their Guardians and Negroes grew insolent to their Masters.' Now, he added, what she wrote to him made him aware that 'another Tribe more numerous and powerfull than all the rest were grown discontented' amidst the revolutionary turmoil of 1776. The remark was clearly intended to put Abigail Adams down, however playfully, to dismiss her claims for the natural rights of women by associating women with other, supposedly undeserving groups. But, inadvertently, it raised a serious and central point. 'All men are created equal', the Declaration of Independence announced. That explicitly excluded women. Implicitly, it also excluded 'Indians' and 'Negroes', since what it meant, of course, was all *white* men. An idealist like Jefferson might wrestle conscientiously with such exclusions (while, perhaps, painfully aware that he himself was a slaveholder); a man like John Adams might insist on them, however teasingly. But they could not go unnoticed, and especially by those, like Abigail Adams, who were excluded. The literature of the revolutionary period includes not only the visionary rhetoric and rational arguments of those men by and for whom the laws of the new republic were primarily framed but also the writings of those who felt excluded, ignored or left out. As John Adams, for all his irony, was forced to acknowledge, the political and social turmoil of the times was bound to make disadvantaged, marginalized groups more acutely aware of their plight. After all, he had his wife to remind him.

Among the leading voices of the American Revolution, there are some who, at least, were willing to recognize the rights of women. Notably, Thomas Paine spoke of the need for female equality. 'If we take a survey of ages and countries,' he wrote in 'An Occasional Letter on the Female Sex' (1775), 'we shall find the women, almost – without exception – at all times and in all places, adored and oppressed.' Man, Paine argued, never overlooked 'an opportunity of exerting his power'. While 'paying homage' to the beauty of females, he 'always availed himself of their weakness'; 'he has been at once their tyrant and their slave'. That neatly rebutted the claims of men like Adams that they were subject to 'the Despotism of the Petticoat'. So, at greater length, did the writings of Judith Sargent Murray (1751–1820). Murray wrote, among other things, two plays and a number of poems; she also wrote two essay series for the *Massachusetts Magazine* from 1792 to 1794. One essay series, *The Repository*, was largely religious in theme. The other, *The Gleaner*, considered a number of issues, including federalism, literary nationalism and the equality of the sexes. A three-volume edition of *The Gleaner* was published in 1798; and in it is to be found her most influential piece, 'On the Equality of the Sexes' (1790), which establishes her claim to be regarded as one of the first American feminists. Here, Murray argued that the capacities of memory and imagination are equal in women and men and that, if women are deficient as far as the two other faculties of the mind, reason and judgement, are concerned, it is because of a difference in education. If only women were granted equal educational opportunities, Sargent insisted, then they would be the equal of men in every respect. Or, as she put it, 'if we are allowed an equality of acquirement, let serious studies equally employ our minds, and we will bid our souls arise to equal strength'.

Murray's arguments were built on a firm belief in the equality of male and female souls. 'The same breath of God, enlivens, and invigorates us,' she told her male readers, 'we are not fallen lower than yourselves.' Domestic employments were consequently not enough for women. 'I would calmly ask, is it reasonable,' she wrote, 'that a candidate for immortality, . . . an intelligent being, . . . should be so degraded, as to be allowed no other ideas, than those which are suggested by the meachanism of a pudding, or the sewing the seams of a garment.' A young woman should be addressed 'as a rational being', she declared in a 1784 essay ('Desultory Thoughts upon the Utility of encouraging a degree of Self-Complacency especially in Female Bosoms'); she should be taught 'a reverence for self', and she should be encouraged to aspire, since 'ambition is a noble principle'. Murray was inspired as many of her contemporaries were by the events and rhetoric of the times. Her other works include, for instance, a patriotic poem celebrating the 'genius' of George Washington and anticipating the moment when the arts and sciences would flourish in 'blest Columbia' ('Occasional Epilogue to the *Contrast*; a Comedy, Written by Royal Tyler, Esq' [1794]). Unlike most of her contemporaries, however, that inspiration led Murray to consider the anomalous position of her own sex and to argue that the anomaly could and should be rectified. Appealing to the principle of equality enshrined in the laws of the new republic, to rational justice and Christian faith, she helped raise an issue that was to be foregrounded in the next century – not least, at the Seneca Falls Women's Rights Convention. There, at the Convention in 1848, a 'Declaration of Sentiments' was framed that gave succinct expression to Murray's beliefs by making a simple change to the original Declaration. 'We hold these truths to be self-evident,' it announced, 'that all men and women are created equal.'

'The great men of the United States have their liberty – they begin with new things, and now they endeavour to lift us up the Indians from the ground, that we may stand up and walk ourselves.' The words are those of Hendrick Aupaumut (?–1830), a Mahican Indian educated by Moravians. They come from *A Short Narration of my Last Journey to the Western Country*, which was written about 1794 but not published until 1827. Aupaumut, as this remark suggests, was intensely loyal to the

United States; and he clearly believed, or at least hoped, that his people would be afforded the same rights and opportunities as 'the great men' of the new nation. Because of his loyalty, he served as an intermediary between the government and Native Americans in the 1790s. This involved travelling among the tribes; and it was evidently after a journey among the Delawares, Shawnees and others that he wrote his book. Often awkward in style, the *Narration* reflects the desperate effort of at least one Native American, working in a second language, to record the history and customs of his peoples – and to convince them, and perhaps himself, that the leaders of the American republic would extend its rights and privileges to those who had lived in America long before Columbus landed. 'I have been endeavouring to do my best in the business of peace,' Aupaumut explains in the *Narration*, 'and according to my best knowledge with regard to the desires of the United States.' That best consisted, fundamentally, of assuring the Native Americans he met of the good intentions of the whites. 'I told them, the United States will not speak wrong,' Aupaumut recalls, 'whatever they promise to Indians they will perform.' Part of the assurance, we learn, rested on laying the blame for previous injustices on 'the Law of the great King of England'. 'Now they have new Laws,' Aupaumut insists, 'and by these Laws Indians cannot be deceived as usual.' The *Narration* is, in effect, a powerful declaration of faith in the universality of the principle of natural rights, and an equally powerful statement of the belief that this principle would now be put into practice. In the light of what happened to Native Americans after this it has, of course, acquired a peculiar pathos and irony that Aupaumut never for once intended.

A Native American who was less convinced that the American Revolution was a good cause was Samson Occom (1723–92). Quite the contrary, during the Revolutionary War Occom urged the tribes to remain neutral because that war was, he insisted, the work of the Devil. Born a Mohegan, Occom was converted by missionaries when he was sixteen. He then became an itinerant minister, devoting most of his energies to preaching and working on behalf of the Indian people. Only two books by him were published during his lifetime, but they were immensely successful. The first was a sermon written at the request of a fellow Mohegan who had been sentenced to death for murder, *A Sermon Preached by Samson Occom, Minister of the Gospel, and Missionary to the Indians; at the Execution of Moses Paul an Indian* (1772). Reflecting Occom's own evangelical convictions, and focusing, in the tradition of all execution sermons, on the omnipresence of death and the necessity for immediate, radical conversion, it was immensely popular. Its popularity encouraged the publication of the second book, *Collection of Hymns and Spiritual Songs* (1774), which became the first Indian best-seller. All Occom's work is marked by a fervent belief in the power of grace, and by his insistence that, as he put it in the execution sermon, 'we are all dying creatures' who had to seek that grace at once. It is marked, as well, by a fervent rhetorical style and an equally fervent belief that all his people, the Mohegans and other tribes, were in particular need of Christian redemption. Passing through it, however, is another current, less openly acknowledged but undeniably there: the suspicion that many of the miseries of his life were there 'because', as he expressed it, 'I am a poor Indian', that this was true of all other 'poor Indians' too, and that the way to deal with this was to build a separate community. Quite apart from consistently arguing that his people should not become involved in the quarrels of whites, such as the Revolution and the 1812 war between the United States and England, he became an enthusiastic disciple of a project to remove the Christian Indians of New England to a settlement in New York. The project was never realized, but Occom's enthusiasm for it shows how differently he felt from Aupaumut about the promise of the new republic. For him as for many Native Americans – and despite a passionate commitment to a religion learned from white people – the only solution was to come apart and be separate.

The rage felt by many African Americans, enslaved or freed, at the obvious and immense gap between the rhetoric of the Revolution and the reality of their condition was memorably expressed by Lemuel Haynes (1753–1833). As an evangelical minister, Haynes, along with Jupiter Hammon and Phillis Wheatley, helped to produce the first significant body of African American writing, founded on revivalist rhetoric and revolutionary discourse. His address, 'Liberty Further Extended: Or Free Thoughts on the Illegality of Slave-Keeping' (written early in his career but not published until 1983), begins by quoting the Declaration of Independence to the effect that 'all men are created Equal' with 'Ceartain unalienable rights'. Haynes then goes on to argue that 'Liberty, & freedom, is an innate principle, which is unmoveably placed in the human Species'. It is a 'Jewel', Haynes declares, 'which was handed Down to man from the cabinet of heaven, and is Coeval with his Existance'. And, since it 'proceeds from the Supreme Legislature of the univers, so it is he which hath a sole right to take away'. So, anyone who 'would take away a mans Liberty assumes a prerogative that Belongs to another, and acts out of his own domain', he assumes the power and prerogatives of God. In short, *the practise of Slave-keeping, which so much abounds in this Land is illicit*. Skilfully using the founding documents of the nation, and quotations from the Bible such as the pronouncement that God made *of one blood all nations of men, for to dwell upon the face of the earth*, Haynes weaves a trenchant argument against slavery. '[L]iberty is Equally as pre[c]ious to a *Black man*, as it is to a *white* one,' he insists; 'even an african, has Equally as good a right to his Liberty in common with Englishmen.' The message is rammed home, time and again, that the white people of the new republic are in breach of divine law and their own professed allegiance to 'natural rights'. ''Twas an Exelent note that I Lately read in a modern piece and it was this,' Haynes remembers, 'O when shall America be consistantly Engaged in the Cause of Liberty!' And he concludes with a prayer addressed to white Americans: 'If you have any Love to yourselves, or any Love to this Land, if you have any Love to your fellow-man, Break these intollerable yoaks.'

A similar commitment to the idea of brotherhood characterizes the work of Prince Hall (1735?–1807). Hall was a member of the Masonic order. He considered it the duty of Masons, as he put it in 'A Charge Delivered to the African Lodge, June 24, 1797, at Menotomy' (1797), to show 'love to all mankind', and 'to sympathise with our fellow men under their troubles'. The author of numerous petitions on behalf of Masons and free blacks in general, for support of plans for blacks to emigrate to Africa and for public education for children of tax-paying black people, he was also a strong opponent of slavery. His petition, 'To the Honorable Council & House of Representatives for the State of Massachusetts-Bay in General Court assembled January 13th 1777' (1788), asks for the emancipation of 'a great number of Negroes who are detained in a state of Slavery in the Bowels of a free & Christian Country'. And, in it, like Haynes, Hall uses the rhetoric of the Revolution against its authors. Slaves, he points out, 'have, in common with all other Men, a natural & unalienable right to that freedom, which the great Parent of the Universe hath bestowed equally on all Mankind'. Freedom is 'the natural right off all Men – & their Children (who were born in this Land of Liberty) may not be held as Slaves after they arrive at the age of twenty one years'. In short, the peculiar institution that still survives and flourishes 'Among a People professing the mild Religion of Jesus – A People not insensible of the sweets of rational freedom' is 'in Violation of the Laws of Nature & of Nation & in defiance of all tender feelings of humanity'. Hall was tireless in his support of any scheme intended to advance the cause of black freedom and equality. He was also acutely aware of how different were the futures of the different races in 'this Land of Liberty': 'thus my brethren', he declared once, 'we see what a chequered world we live in'. And he was never reluctant to use republican, as well as Biblical, rhetoric, to point that difference out.

Haynes was born into freedom. Hall was born into slavery and then freed. Olaudah Equiano (1745–97) was born into freedom in Africa; he was enslaved, transported first to Barbados and then to Virginia, bought by a British captain to serve aboard his ship, and then finally in 1776 became a free man again. All this became the subject of a two-volume autobiography, *The Interesting Narrative of the Life of Olaudah Equiano, or Gustavus Valla, the African, Written by Himself.* Published in 1787 and subscribed to by many of the leading abolitionists, it established the form of the slave narrative and so, indirectly or otherwise, it has influenced American writing – and African American writing in particular – to the present day. 'I offer here the history of neither a saint, a hero, nor a tyrant,' Equiano announces. 'I might say my sufferings were great,' he admits, 'but when I compare my lot with that of most of my countrymen, I regard myself as a *particular favorite of heaven*, and acknowledge the mercies of Providence in every occurrence of my life.' As that remark suggests, Equiano follows the tradition of spiritual autobiography derived from St Augustine and John Bunyan and used by American Puritans and Quakers, but he adds to it the new dimension of social protest. He also begins by painting an idyllic portrait of life in Africa. The manner of living in the place where he spent his childhood, Equiano explains, was 'simple' and 'plain'; he and his family and community lived 'in a country where nature is prodigal of her favor' and where wants were 'few and easily supplied'. Agriculture was the employment of everyone; all were 'habituated to labor' from their earliest years; everyone consequently con-tributed to 'the common stock' and, as a whole, the community was 'unacquainted with idleness'. What was more, his people were beautiful ('Deformity', Equiano claims, was 'unknown among us') and even pious, after a fashion, since they believed that there was 'one Creator of all things'. Just in case the reader does not grasp the point, Equiano then makes it clear. There is a 'strong analogy', he suggests, between 'the manners and customs of my countrymen', the companions of his childhood, 'and those of the Jews before they reached the land of promise, and particularly the patriarchs while they were yet in that pastoral state which is described in Genesis'. This is Eden, a prelapsarian world of innocence, simplicity and bliss where people enjoy a natural freedom and equality and nobody wants for the fruits of the earth.

Then, as Equiano tells it, came the fall. At the age of eleven, he was seized from his family and sold into slavery. Taken to the African coast, he was terrified by the sight of white people. 'I was now persuaded that I had gotten into a world of bad spirits,' he remembers, 'and that they were going to kill me.' And the strange complexions of those into whose hands he had come, 'their long hair, and the language they spoke', all united to confirm him in this belief. He feared he would be eaten, Equiano tells the reader, ironically throwing back upon its authors a common European myth about other peoples; and, when he is not eaten but 'put down under the decks' on ship and then transported across the ocean, his distress is hardly alleviated. Beaten savagely, chained for most of the time, gradually learning all the hardships of capture and the 'accursed trade' of slavery, Equiano becomes convinced that his new masters are 'savages'. Preparing the ground for later slave narratives, Equiano memorably traces the major events of his enslavement and the miseries he shared with his slaves: the breaking up of families, the imposition of new names, the strangeness and squalor, the fear of the black and the brutality of the whites. He also interlaces the narrative with a series of powerful declamatory statements. 'O, ye nominal Christians!' he declares while describing a slave market, 'might not an African ask you – learned you this from your God, who says to you, Do unto all men as you would men should do unto you?' There are, certainly, moments of relief. Aboard one ship, Equiano befriends a white man, 'a young lad'. Their close friendship, which is cut short by the white man's death, serves as an illustration of the superficiality of racial barriers, indicates the possibility of white kindness and a better way for free blacks and, besides, anticipates a powerful theme in later American writing – of interracial and often homoerotic intimacy. Gradually, too, Equiano manages to rise up from slavery. He learns to read. He manages to purchase his freedom. Finally, he experiences a religious vision and, as he puts it, is 'born again' to become one of 'God's children'. But the horror of Equiano's capture and enslavement, the long voyage to America and the even longer voyage to escape from the 'absolute power' exerted by the white master over his black property: that remains indelibly marked on the reader's memory. *The Interesting Narrative of . . . Olaudah Equiano* is the first in a great tradition of American narratives that juxtapose the dream of freedom with the reality of oppression, the Edenic myth (of Africa here, of America usually elsewhere) with a history of fall and redemption – all while telling us the story of an apparently ordinary, but actually remarkable, man.

In verse, an important tradition was inaugurated by two African American poets of the time, Jupiter Hammon (1711–1806?) and Phillis Wheatley (1753–84). Lucy Terry had, of course, become known earlier for her poem, 'Bars Fight', but Hammon was the first African American poet to have his work published, since Terry's was handed down for a while in the oral tradition. Born a slave, Hammon published a broadside, *Evening Thought: Salvation by Christ, With Penitential Cries*, a series of twenty-two quatrains, in 1760, and then a prose work, *Address to the Negroe: In the State of New York*, in 1787. The poetry is notable for its piety, the prose for its argument that black people must reconcile themselves to the institution of slavery. Some of Hammon's thinking here is registered in his poem to Phillis Wheatley, 'An Address to Miss Phillis Wheatly, Ethiopian Poetess, in Boston, who came from Africa at eight years of age, and soon became acquainted with the gospel of Jesus Christ' (1778). 'O Come you pious youth: adore / The wisdom of thy God, /' the poem begins, 'In bringing thee from distant shore, / To learn his holy word.' It then goes on to argue that it was 'God's tender mercy' that brought Wheatley in a slave ship across the Atlantic to be 'a pattern' to the 'youth of Boston town'. 'Thou hast left the heathen shore, / Thro' mercy of the Lord, /' Hammon declaims, addressing Wheatley directly, 'Among the heathen live no more, / Come magnify thy God.' It is worth emphasizing that all Hammon's publications are prefaced by an acknowledgement to the three generations of the white family he served. Anything of his that saw print was, in effect, screened by his white masters, and, in writing, was probably shaped by his awareness that it would never get published without their approval. That anticipated a common pattern in African American writing. Slave narratives, for instance, were commonly prefaced by a note or essay from a white notable, mediating the narrative for what was, after all, an almost entirely white audience – and giving it a white seal of approval. And it has to be borne in mind when reading what Hammon has to say about slavery: which, in essence, takes up a defence of the peculiar institution that was to be used again by Southern apologists in the nineteenth century – that slavery could and should be seen as a civilizing influence and a providential instrument of conversion.

African American writers of the time, and later, were, in effect, in a different position from their white counterparts. The growth in readership and printing presses, the proliferation of magazines, almanacs, manuals and many other outlets for writing all meant that the literary culture was changing. A system of literary patronage was being replaced by the literary marketplace. Poets like Hammon and Wheatley, however, were still dependent on their white 'friends' and patrons. For Equiano, fortunately, the friends, subscribers and readers were abolitionists. For Hammon, the friends were, quite clearly, otherwise. Phillis Wheatley enjoyed the cooperation and patronage of Susanne Wheatley, the woman who bought her in a Boston slave market when she was seven years old, and the Countess of Huntingdon. It was with their help that her *Poems* appeared in 1773 in London, the first volume of poetry known to have been published by an African American. The poetry reflects the neo-classical norms of the time. It also sometimes paints a less than flattering picture of Africa, the land from which Wheatley was snatched when she was still a child. ''Twas not long since I left my native shore / The land of errors, and *Egyptian* gloom: /' she writes in 'To the University of Cambridge, in New England (1773)', adding, 'Father of mercy, 'twas thy gracious hand / Brought me in safety from those dark abodes'. Sometimes, however, Wheatley leans towards a more Edenic and idyllic image of her birthplace, of the kind favoured by Equiano. 'How my bosom burns! /' she declares in one of her poems ('Philis's [*sic*] Reply to the Answer in our Last by the Gentleman in the Navy' [1774]), 'and pleasing Gambia on my soul returns, / With native grace in spring's luxurious reign, / Smiles the gay mead, and Eden blooms again.' A lengthy description of 'Africa's blissful plain' then follows, one that transforms it into a version of the pastoral. 'The various bower, the tuneful flowing stream', the 'soil spontaneous' that 'yields exhaustless stores', the 'soft retreats', the 'verdant shores' and 'bending harvest' ripening 'into gold': all this, and more, works against Wheatley's claims made elsewhere (in 'On Being Brought from Africa to America' [1773] and 'To His Excellency General Washington' [1776]) that she is grateful to have been taken away from 'my *Pagan* land' to 'Columbia's state'.

Wheatley is, in fact, a far subtler and more complicated poet than is often acknowledged. The pleas for freedom are sometimes clear enough in her prose as well as her poetry. 'In every human breast God has implanted a principle, which we call love of freedom,' she wrote in her 'Letter to Samson Occom' (1774). 'It is impatient of oppression . . . and by the leave of our modern Egyptians I will assert, that the same principle lives in us.' That is echoed in poems like 'Liberty and Peace' (1785) and 'To the Right Honourable William, Earl of Dartmouth, His Majesty's Principal Secretary of State for North America, &c' (1770). In both of these, she links the longing for freedom felt and expressed by the American colonists to her own experience of oppression. 'I, young in life, by seeming cruel fate / Was snatch'd from *Afric's* fancy'd happy seat,' she reveals in the latter poem. 'Such, such my case. And can I then but pray / Others may never feel tyrannic sway?' Even when the plea is not as clear as that, however, and the description of her present plight not quite so critical, there is still a measured sense of her own dignity, and a quiet intimation of the rights and potential of her race. Despite her references to her own 'fault'ring music' and 'grov'ling mind' in 'To Maecenas' (1770), for instance, she is still ambitious enough to invoke the example of the classical poet Terence (who, Wheatley notes, 'was an *African* by birth' – like her), and bold enough to ask Maecenas, the friend and patron of the great Roman poet Horace, to be her patron too. 'Then grant, *Maecenas*, thy paternal rays, /' she concludes, 'Hear me propitious, and defend my lays.' On a broader scale, one of her best-known poems, 'On being Brought from Africa to America', may well begin by suggesting that it was 'mercy' that brought her 'benighted soul' from Africa to experience 'redemption' in the New World. But it then goes on to use that experience of redemption as a measure of possibility for all African Americans. 'Some view our sable race with scornful eye', she admits, but then adds, pointing an admonitory finger at her, inevitably white, audience: 'Remember *Christians*, *Negros*, black as *Cain*, / May be refin'd and join th'angelic train.' That conclusion is a perfect example of how Wheatley could develop consciousness of self into an exploration of the black community, its experiences and its potential. It is also an illustration of how she could strike a pose, for herself and others of '*Afric's* sable race', that both deferred to white patrons and audience and subtly made a claim for dignity, even equality – that, in short, combined Christian humility with a kind of racial pride.

The difficult position of African American poets in the emerging literary marketplace is, perhaps, suggested by Wheatley's failure to find many readers for her published poetry – or, after 1773, to publish any further collections of her work. As late as 1778, she could complain about 'books that remain unsold'; her *Poems* were never reprinted during her lifetime; and all her many proposals for publication in Boston were rejected. One projected volume that never saw publication was advertised by the printers with the remark that they could scarcely credit 'ye performances to be by a Negro'. The work was evidently too good, or too literate, to suggest such a source to them. That measures the extent of the problem poets like Hammon and Wheatley faced. Poetry, even perhaps literacy, was seen as the prerogative of white poets, like Philip Freneau (1752–1832), Timothy Dwight (1752–1817), and Joel Barlow (1754–1826). Of these three poets who set out to explore and celebrate the new republic in verse, Freneau was probably the most accomplished. Born in New York City, of a French Huguenot father and a Scottish mother, he began his poetic career as a celebrant of 'Fancy, regent of the mind', and the power Fancy gave him to roam far to 'Britain's fertile land', 'her proud command' or empire around the globe, then back to 'California's golden shore' ('The Power of Fancy' [1770]). Events, however, soon conspired to turn his interests in a more political and less Anglophile direction. With college friends, Hugh Brackenridge and James Madison, he wrote some *Satires Against the Tories* (1775); and with Brackenridge he also wrote a long poem in celebration of *The Rising Glory of America*. *The Rising Glory of America*, written in 1771, published a year later, then drastically revised in 1786, marked Freneau's full conversion to the American cause: a cause that he was later to serve both as a satirical poet and as a strongly partisan editor and journalist. Yet for all its rhetorical energy this poem about the emerging splendour of the New World is as much a tribute to the continuing importance of the Old World, at least in matters cultural and intellectual, as anything else. The theme may be new. The form, however, is basically imitative. So is the style, a pale echo of the English poet John Milton and Miltonic orotundities. 'A Canaan here, / Another Canaan shall excel the old, /' the poem announces, 'And from a fairer Pisgah's top be seen.' 'Such days the world, / And such America at last shall have /', it concludes, looking boldly to the future of the nation, 'When ages, yet to come, shall run their round, / And future years of bliss alone remain.' In short, *The Rising Glory of America* tends to confirm the power of the mother country even while Freneau and Brackenridge struggle to deny it.

Freneau was, as it happened, acutely aware of this power. A poem like 'A Political Litany' (1775) is a bitter diatribe against the political domination of Britain, 'a kingdom that bullies, and hectors, and swears'. More interestingly, a poem such as 'Literary Importation' (1788) admits to a feeling of cultural domination. 'Can we never be thought to have learning or grace /', Freneau asks here, 'Unless it be brought from that damnable place.' The 'damnable place' was, of course, Britain; and Freneau must have suspected that his own literary importations of style and manner answered him in the negative. He was writing, as he perhaps sensed, in the wrong place and time. There was the continuing cultural influence of the Old World. And there was also, as Freneau intimates in another poem, 'To An Author' (1788), the problem of writing poetry at a moment of conflict and in a society dedicated to common sense and use. 'On these bleak climes by Fortune thrown, / Where rigid Reason reigns alone,' Freneau asks the 'Author' (who is, almost certainly, himself), 'Tell me, what has the muse to do?' 'An age employed in edging steel /', he adds bitterly, 'Can no poetic raptures feel.' Yet, despite that, Freneau continued to indulge in 'poetic raptures'. There are poems on philosophical issues ('On the Universality and Other Attributes of God in Nature' [1815]), on politics ('On the Causes of Political Degeneracy' [1798]), on nature ('On Observing a Large Red-Streak Apple' [1827]), and on moral and social issues such as his attack on slavery ('To Sir Toby' [1792]). There are also pieces in which Freneau makes a genuine attempt to arrive at universal significance in and through a firm sense of the local. 'The Indian Burying Ground' (1788) is an instance, one of the first attempts made by any poet to understand the new country in terms of a people who had themselves become an integral part of it – those who are called here 'the ancients of the lands'. So is 'The Wild Honey Suckle' (1788), in which Freneau focuses his attention on a detail of the American scene, the 'fair flower' of the title, and discovers in that detail one possible truth about the American psyche: its fundamental loneliness and privacy, the apartness of what Walt Whitman was to call 'the essential me'. As Freneau meditates on this one, small, frail plant, that chooses to 'shun the vulgar eye' in its 'silent, dull retreat', he also adopts a quieter style and more attentive tone. In contrast to the florid gestures of his early couplets, there is an inclination towards a more precise and simpler language here, concrete and appropriate to the delineation of minute particulars. In some of his poetry, at least, Freneau was working towards a form of literary emancipation, an approach and aesthetic less obviously learned from 'that damnable place'.

This modest degree of success was not achieved by Dwight and Barlow, at least not in what they considered their major work. A grandson of Jonathan Edwards, Dwight wrote much and variously, including some attacks on slavery in both prose and verse. His most ambitious work, however, was a poem written in imitation of the pastoral and elegiac modes of British writers of the Augustan period like Alexander Pope and Oliver Goldsmith. Titled *Greenfield Hill: A Poem in Seven Parts*, it was published in 1794, and it offers an idyllic portrait of life in the American countryside. In and around a 'sweet-smiling village', the narrator introduces us to a world where 'every farmer reigns a little king', where there are no extremes of wealth or poverty and 'one extended class embraces all'. The poem becomes a hymn to an ideal of self-reliance and modest sufficiency that Franklin and Jefferson also celebrated. Dwight describes it as 'Competence'. The hymn allows the narrator to attack various social iniquities in passing – and, in particular, what he calls the 'luxury', the brutishness and inequity, of slavery. Time is also found to look back at the earlier inhabitants of this land, the Native Americans, at their sufferings and eventual eviction. But, despite Dwight's references to 'Indian woes' – his admission that 'savages are men' and probably did not deserve the brutal treatment they received – his basic message is that their removal was a necessary step in the march of progress. Sympathy for the defeated and banished Native Americans is qualified by the clearly stated belief that they had to give way to the better and brighter forces of civilization represented by the pilgrims, and then later by other Anglo-Americans. For that matter, celebration of this particular American dream is vitiated by the fact that it is conducted in such conflicted and derivative terms. The poet endorses peace, tranquillity but also necessary, sometimes violent, progress. It speaks approvingly of 'Competence', modest sufficiency, but also, and with equal approval, of a kind of survival of the fittest. Also, in a familiar pattern, it uses old forms to write about the new: this hymn to American virtues and uniqueness is sung in a voice that is still definitively European.

That is just as true of the attempts Joel Barlow made at an American epic, *The Vision of Columbus* (1787) and *The Columbiad* (1807). Like Dwight, Barlow was a member of a pro-Federalist group known as the 'Connecticut Wits'. He travelled and wrote extensively. His work includes a number of patriotic poems ('The Prospect of Peace' [1778]) and poems attacking the monarchism and imperialism of Europe ('Advice to a Raven in Russia: December, 1812' [unpublished until 1938]). His most anthologized piece is 'The Hasty Pudding: A Poem in Three Cantos' (1793), a work about home thoughts from abroad that praises Yankee virtues by celebrating a peculiarly Yankee meal. *The Columbiad*, his much revised and extended version of *The Vision of Columbus*, was, however, his stab at a great work. 'My object is altogether of a moral and political nature,' he announced in the preface to his 1807 epic; 'I wish to encourage and strengthen, in the rising generation, a sense of the importance of republican institutions, as being the great foundation of public and private happiness.' 'This is the moment in America to give such a direction to poetry, painting and the other fine arts,' he added, 'that true and useful ideas of glory may be implanted in the minds of men here, to take [the] place of the false and destructive ones that have degraded the species in other countries.' Barlow was not the first to want to write an American epic. And by his time the idea of announcing the new nation in the form traditionally dedicated to such a project was becoming a commonplace. Even the congenitally cautious and sceptical John Adams could dream of such a thing. 'I should hope to live to see our young America in Possession of an Heroick Poem, equal to those the most esteemed in any Country,' he wrote. But this was the first major attempt made to realize this ambition, shared by so many, to see something that memorialized the American nation in verse just as, say, Rome and its founding had been memorialized in the *Aeneid*, to turn the hope expressed by Adams into a reality.

The Columbiad begins in traditional epic fashion: 'I sing the Mariner who first unfurl'd / An eastern banner o'er the western world / And taught mankind where future empires lay.' Contrary to the impression given by these opening lines, however, Barlow does not go on to sing of the actions of Columbus but rather of the inexorable progress of free institutions in the Americas as he anticipates them. To Columbus, in prison, comes Hesper, the guardian genius of the Western continent, who leads him to a mount of vision. The poem then proceeds in a series of visions of the American future, extending forward through colonial and revolutionary times to the establishment of peace and the arts in a new America. The final vision is of a time when the American federal system will extend 'over the whole earth'. The American, we are told, finding 'FREEDOM' to be 'his new Prometheus' will lead the way to utopia. There, in that blessed future, 'one confederate, codependent sway' will 'spread with the sun and bound the walks of day'; throughout the globe, 'one centred system, one all ruling soul' will 'live through the parts and regulate the whole'. Here, in the announcement of this ultimate vision, and elsewhere, the tone and style tend towards the declamatory, the derivative and didactic. What is more, the poem as a whole lacks the essential ingredient of epic: a hero, or heroic mind, engaged in heroic action. Columbus cannot be a hero. He is from the beginning completely passive. He observes, he is troubled, he hopes for the future and he is reassured by Hesper. He cannot do anything and is, in fact, closer to being an ideal type of the reader of an American epic than to being a hero. *The Columbiad* clearly poses the problem of how to write a democratic epic, a heroic poem of the common man or woman, but it comes nowhere near solving it. That would have to wait for Walt Whitman and *Leaves of Grass*.

While Joel Barlow was busy trying to write an American epic, Royall Tyler (1756–1826) was devoting his energies to establishing an American tradition in drama. Tyler wrote seven plays, but his reputation rests on *The Contrast*, written in 1787, produced in 1790 and published two years later. The first comedy by someone born in America to receive a professional production, it was hailed by one reviewer as 'proof that these new climes are particularly favorable to the cultivation of arts and sciences'. *The Contrast* was written after Tyler had attended a performance of *The School for Scandal* (1777) by Richard Brinsley Sheridan and is clearly influenced by the English social comedies of the eighteenth century. It is, however, impeccably American in theme, since the contrast of the title is between Bill Dimple, an embodiment of European affectation, and Colonel Manly, a representative of American straightforwardness and republican honesty. The intensely Anglophile Dimple, described by one character as a 'flippant, palid, polite beau', flirts with two women, Letitia and Charlotte, despite the fact that a match has been arranged with a third, Maria van Rough, by her father. Manly, a patriot and veteran of the Revolutionary War, is in love with Maria. And when Dimple, having gambled away his fortune, decides to marry the wealthy Letitia instead, Maria's father, discovering Dimple's baseness, gives his blessing to Manly's suit. Dimple is then finally thwarted in his ambition to cure his insolvency when Letitia learns of his flirtation with Charlotte. And he leaves the scene, ousted but unabashed, underlining the contrast between himself and Manly as he does so. 'Ladies and gentlemen,' he announces, 'I take my leave; and you will please to observe in the case of my deportment the contrast between a gentleman who has . . . received the polish of Europe and an unpolished, untravelled American.'

Manly himself emphasizes this contrast, through his simplicity and natural gentility of manner and through his comments on the times. In one long speech, for example, he attacks the 'luxury' to which, as he sees it, far too many Americans, like Dimple, are prone. 'Luxury! which enervates both soul and body, by opening a thousand new sources of enjoyment, opens, also a thousand sources of contention and want,' he declares. 'Luxury! which renders a people weak at home, and accessible to bribery, corruption, and force from abroad.' The aim of the play is clearly to address the different possibilities available to the new republic and to promote civic virtue and federal high-mindedness. 'Oh! That America! Oh that my country, would, in this her day, learn the things which belong to peace!' Manly prays. And he shows what those 'things' are in the impeccable character of his beliefs and behaviour. A subplot draws a similar lesson, by presenting another contrast in national manners, between Dimple's servant, the arrogant and duplicitous Jessamy, and Manly's servant, Jonathan, who is a plain, goodhearted and incorruptible Yankee. It is typical of Jonathan that he refuses, in fact, to be called a servant. 'I am Colonel Manly's waiter,' he insists. And, when Jessamy snootily suggests that this is 'a true Yankee distinction, egad, without a difference', he quickly responds. 'I am a true blue son of liberty,' Jonathan explains; 'father said I should come as Colonel Manly's waiter, to see the world . . . but no man shall master me. My father has as good a farm as the colonel.' In the 'Prologue' to *The Contrast*, given to the actor playing Jonathan to recite, the didactic and exemplary purposes of the play are emphasized. 'Our Author', the audience is forewarned, has confined himself to 'native themes' so as to expose 'the fashions and the follies of the times' and celebrate the 'genuine sincerity' and 'homespun habits' Americans have inherited from their 'free-born ancestors'. Tyler cannily used social comedy to explore issues that were particularly pressing for his fellow countrymen, with the emergence of a new political and social dispensation. In the process, he produced a work that answers Crèvecoeur's question, 'What is an American?', in a clear and thoroughly earnest way, and with an occasional wit that Crèvecoeur himself could hardly have imagined.

The urge to point a moral evident in *The Contrast* is even more openly at work in those books that can lay claim to being the first American novels, *The Power of Sympathy* (1789) by William Hill Brown (1765–93), *Charlotte Temple* (1794) by Susanna Haswell Rowson (1762–1824) and *The Coquette; or, The History of Eliza Wharton* (1797) by Hannah Webster Foster (1758–1840). *The Power of Sympathy*, the first American novel, was published anonymously to begin with. It was originally attributed to the Boston writer Sarah Wentworth Morton because it deals with a contemporary scandal of incest and suicide in the Morton family. It was not until 1894 that Brown, also from Boston, was recognized as the author. An epistolary romance, its didactic purpose is announced in the preface: *The Power of Sympathy* was written, the reader is told, 'To Expose the dangerous Consequences of Seduction' and to set forth 'the Advantages of Female Education'. The main plot deals with a threatened incestuous marriage between two characters called Harrington and Harriet Fawcett. They are both children of the elder Harrington, the first by his legitimate marriage and the second by his mistress, Maria. When the relationship is discovered, Harriet dies of shock and sadness and Harrington commits suicide. Hardly distinguished in itself, the book nevertheless establishes a currency common to all three of these early American novels: a clear basis in fact, actuality (so anticipating and meeting any possible objections to fiction, imaginative self-indulgence or daydreaming), an even clearer moral purpose (so anticipating and meeting any possible objections from Puritans or utilitarians), and a narrative that flirts with sensation and indulges in sentiment (so encouraging the reader to read on). Even more specifically, *The Power of Sympathy* shares the same currency as the books by Rowson and Foster in the sense that it places a young woman and her fate at the centre of the narrative, and addresses other young women as the intended recipients of its message. This reflected an economic reality: in the new, vastly expanded literary marketplace of America, as in Europe, women constituted the main readership for fiction. It also, perhaps, had an ideological dimension: the novel was where women, and especially young women, could go to find a dramatic reflection of their problems, economic, social and moral – some sense, and appreciation, of the way they lived, or had to live, now.

This further dimension is more noticeable, inevitably perhaps, in novels actually written by women. Susanna Haswell Rowson's *Charlotte Temple* was published in London in 1791 and then in the United States three years later, where it became the first American best-seller. By 1933, it had gone through 161 editions; and it has been estimated that it has been read by a quarter to a half million people. In the preface to her novel, Rowson explains that the circumstances in which she founded the novel were related to her by 'an old lady who had personally known Charlotte'. 'I have thrown over the whole a slight veil of fiction,' she adds, 'and substituted names and places according to my own fancy.' And what she has written, she insists, has a fundamentally moral purpose. 'For the perusal of the young and thoughtless of the fair sex, this Tale of Truth is designed,' Rowson declares. *Charlotte Temple* is 'not merely the effusion of Fancy, but . . . a reality' because it is grounded in fact *and* because it is intended as a manual of conduct, a guide to young women as they negotiate their way through life. 'If the following tale should save one hapless fair one from the errors that ruined poor Charlotte', Rowson tells the reader, then she will pronounce herself happy. The tale that follows this is essentially a simple one. Charlotte, a girl of fifteen in a school for young ladies, is seduced by an army officer called Montraville. Montraville is aided by an unscrupulous teacher whom Charlotte trusts, Mlle La Rue. After considerable hesitation, Charlotte elopes with Montraville from England to New York. There, she is deserted by both Montraville and Mlle La Rue, gives birth to a daughter, Lucy, and dies in poverty. What adds force, and a measure of complexity, to the tale are two things: Rowson's consistent habit of addressing the reader and her subtle pointers to the fact that, while Charlotte thinks she is in control of her fate, she fundamentally is not – she is at the mercy of male power and the machinations of others.

'Oh my dear girls – for to such only I am writing,' Rowson declares early on in *Charlotte Temple*. That is characteristic: the narrator turns constantly from her young woman character to the young women who are reading her story. As she does so, she underlines Charlotte's innocence, her ignorance. 'A young woman is never more in danger than when attempted by a young soldier,' she points out; 'the mind of youth eagerly catches at promised pleasure,' she says elsewhere, 'pure and innocent by nature, it thinks not of the dangers lurking beneath . . . till too late.' Charlotte believes in the best intentions of both her teacher and her lover. She is ready to confide in the one, unaware that she is intriguing against her pupil; and she believes she can rely on the goodwill and affection of the other when, as it turns out, he is ready to use force to impose his will on her. Quite apart from establishing the American blueprint for a long line of stories about a young woman affronting her destiny, this is a subtle acknowledgement of the conflicted position in which young women, rich or poor, found themselves in the new republic. A more fluid social position for wealthy women, and relatively greater economic opportunities for the poorer ones, might persuade them all that they had more control over their destinies. Real control, however, still lay elsewhere. Coming to America does not empower or liberate Charlotte; on the contrary, as Rowson shows, it simply subjects her to the discovery of 'the dangers lurking beneath' the surfaces of life. This is melodrama with a purpose. And that purpose, conceived within the sentimental constraints of the time and expressed in its conventional ethical language, is to give the people for whom it was written, the 'dear girls' whom the narrator constantly addresses, a way of measuring and meeting their condition as women.

Something similar could be said about a brief novel by Judith Sargent Murray, *The Story of Margaretta* (1798), included in *The Gleaner* essays: in which, in a manner clearly meant to illustrate the author's beliefs, the heroine Margaretta manages to escape the usually dire consequences of seduction, thanks to her superiority of soul and education, and is rewarded with a loving husband. More persuasively and interestingly, it could also be said of *The Coquette*, an epistolary novel and a best-seller for which Hannah Webster Foster was not given credit until 1866. Until then, the author was known simply as 'A Lady of Massachusetts'. In a series of seventy-four letters, mainly from the heroine Eliza Wharton to her friend Lucy Freeman, another tale of seduction and abandonment is told. Eliza is the coquette of the title, but she is also a spirited young woman. 'I am young, gay, volatile,' she proudly announces, 'I don't know how it is, I am certainly very much the taste of the other sex.' Thoroughly aware of her own needs and charms, she is unwilling to bury herself in a conventional marriage. She is saved from a match with an elderly clergyman, Mr Haly, when he dies before her parents can get them both to the altar. Another clergyman, the Reverend Boyer, courts her; however, she finds him dull. She would, she protests, gladly enter the kind of marriage enjoyed by her friends the Richmans, who share 'the purest and most ardent affection, the greatest consonance of taste and disposition, and the most congenial virtue and wishes'. But such intimacy between equals seems rare to her. 'Marriage is the tomb of friendship,' she confides to Lucy; 'it appears to me a very selfish state. Why do people, in general, as soon as they are married, centre all their cares, and pleasure in their own families?' For now, she declares, 'let me . . . enjoy that freedom which I so highly prize'. Longing for adventure, though, she meets the self-confessed 'rake' Peter Sanford and is entranced. Boyer, discovering the intimacy between Eliza and Sanford, gives Eliza up. Sanford deserts Eliza for an heiress. Still attracted, Eliza has an affair with Sanford; becoming pregnant, she leaves home and friends, and dies in childbirth; and Sanford, now finally admitting that Eliza was 'the darling of my soul', leaves his wife and flees the country. The customary claim that the entire story was 'founded on fact' is made by the author – and naturally so, since it was based on the experiences of a distant cousin. So is the customary invocation of moral purpose: Lucy Freeman, in particular, is never reluctant to offer what Eliza sardonically refers to as 'moral lectures', 'monitorial lessons and advice' to her friend and correspondent. What stays in the reader's mind, however, is the adventurous spirit of the heroine, despite its tragic, or rather melodramatic, consequences. 'From the melancholy story of Eliza Wharton,' the novel concludes, 'let the American fair learn to reject with disdain every insinuation derogatory to their true dignity and honor . . . To associate is to approve; to approve is to be betrayed!' That may be one thematic level of *The Coquette*. But another, slyly subverting it, is Eliza's quest for freedom; her clearsighted recognition of what marriage entails for most women, given the laws and customs of the day, and her ardent longing for what she calls 'opportunity, unbiassed by opinion, to gratify my disposition'. On this level, *The Coquette* charts the difference between what women want and what they are likely to get. In the process, it poses a question to be explored more openly and fundamentally in many later American narratives: is it possible for an individual to remain free in society or to survive outside it?

Social questions about the new American republic were at the centre of another significant prose narrative of this period, *Modern Chivalry* by Hugh Henry Brackenridge (1746–1816). Published in instalments between 1792 and 1815, *Modern Chivalry* was later described by Henry Adams as 'a more thoroughly American book than any written before 1833'. Its American character does not spring from its narrative structure, however, which is picaresque and clearly borrowed from the Spanish author Cervantes, but from its location and themes. The book is set in rural Pennsylvania and offers the first extended portrait of backwoods life in American fiction. Its two central characters are Captain John Farrago and his Irish servant Teague O'Regan, American versions of Don Quixote and Sancho Panza. And, as they travel around, their adventures provide an occasion for satirizing the manners of post-Revolutionary America. Farrago is a rather stuffy, aristocratic landowner: but narrative sympathy tends to be with him, or at least with his politics, since he is presented as an intelligent democrat, part Jeffersonian and part independent, inclining to the ideas of Thomas Paine. O'Regan, on the other hand, is portrayed as a knave and a fool, whose extraordinary self-assurance stems from his ignorance. At every stage of their journey, the two men meet some foolish group that admires O'Regan and offers him opportunities – as preacher, Indian treaty maker, potential husband for a genteel young lady – for which he is totally unequipped. The captain then has to invent excuses to stop such honours being bestowed on his servant; and each adventure is followed by a chapter of reflection on the uses and abuses of democracy. The satirical edge of *Modern Chivalry* anticipates the later Southwestern humorists. The disquisitions on democracy, in turn, reflect debates occurring at the time over the possible direction of the American republic. A notable contribution to these debates was the series of essays now called the *Federalist* papers (1787–8) written by Alexander Hamilton (1757–1804), John Jay (1745–1829) and James Madison (1751–1836). The authors of these essays argued that, since people were 'ambitious, vindictive, and rapacious', a strong central government was required to control 'factions and convulsions'. Furthermore, Madison (who was, in fact, a friend of Brackenridge) insisted that, in order to control faction without forfeiting liberty, it was necessary to elect men 'whose wisdom', as Madison put it, 'may best discern the true interests of their country, and whose patriotism and love of justice, will be least likely to sacrifice it to temporary or partial considerations'. *Modern Chivalry* tends towards similar conclusions. The portrait of Teague O'Regan, after all, betrays the same distrust as the *Federalist* papers do of what Hamilton and his colleagues called 'theoretic politicians' who believed that faction could be cured by 'reducing mankind to a perfect equality in their political rights'. In the novel, and in the papers, there is the same suspicion of populism, of ordinary people denied the guidance and control of their natural leaders, and a similar need to emphasize what Madison chose to term 'the great points of difference between a Democracy and a Republic'.

Brackenridge was not a professional author, he earned his living as a lawyer, neither were William Hill Brown, Rowson and Foster; the person who has earned the title of first in this category in America is Charles Brockden Brown (1771–1810), although it is now fairly clear that Brown was one among several men and women who laboured between 1776 and 1810 to earn their income from their writings. Under the influence of the English writer William Godwin, Brown wrote and published *Alcuin: A Dialogue* (1798), a treatise on the rights of women. Then, further stimulated by Godwin's novel *Caleb Williams* (1794) and his own critical ideas about fiction, he wrote his four best novels in just two years: *Wieland; or, The Transformation* (1798), *Arthur Mervyn; or, Memoirs of the Year 1793* (1799–1800), *Ormond; or, The Secret Witness* (1799) and *Edgar Huntly; or, Memoirs of a Sleep-Walker* (1799). All four reveal a confluence of influences: to the moral and social purpose of Godwin was added the sentimentalism and interest in personal psychology of the English novelist Samuel Richardson and, above all perhaps, the horrors and aberrations of the Gothic school of fiction. To this was added Brown's own sense of critical mission. He believed in writing novels that would be both intellectual and popular: that would stimulate debate among the thoughtful, while their exciting plots and often bizarre or romantic characters would attract a larger audience. Brown was also strongly committed to using distinctively American materials: in the preface to *Edgar Huntly*, for example, he talks about rejecting 'superstitious and exploded manners, Gothic castles and chimeras' in favour of 'incidents of Indian hostility and perils of the Western Wilderness'. The result of these ambitions and influences is a series of books that translate the Gothic into an American idiom, and that combine sensational elements such as murder, insanity, sexual aggression and preternatural events with brooding explorations of social, political and philosophical questions. These books also make art out of the indeterminate: the reader is left at the end with the queer feeling that there is little, perhaps nothing, a person can trust – least of all, the evidence of their senses.

Brown's first novel, *Wieland*, is a case in point. The older Wieland, a German mystic, emigrates to Pennsylvania, erects a mysterious temple on his estate, and dies there one night of spontaneous combustion. His wife dies soon afterwards, and their children Clara and the younger Wieland become friends with Catharine Pleyel and her brother Henry. Wieland marries Catharine, and Clara falls in love with Henry, who has a fiancée in Germany. A mysterious stranger called Carwin then enters the circle of friends; and, shortly after, a series of warnings is heard from unearthly voices. Circumstances, or perhaps the voices, persuade Henry that Clara and Carwin are involved with each other; he returns to his fiancée and marries her. Wieland, inheriting the fanaticism of his father, is evidently driven mad by the voices and murders his wife and children. Carwin then confesses to Clara that he produced the voices by the 'art' of *biloquium*, a form of ventriloquism that enables him to mimic the voices of others and project them over some distance. He was 'without malignant intentions', he claims, and was simply carried away by his curiosity and his 'passion for mystery'. Wieland, escaping from an asylum, is about to murder Clara when Carwin, using his 'art' for the last time, successfully orders him to stop. The unhappy madman then commits suicide, Carwin departs for a remote area of Pennsylvania, and Clara marries Henry Pleyel after the death of his first wife. These are the bare bones of the story, but what gives those bones flesh is the sense that the characters, and for that matter the reader, can never be quite sure what is the truth and what is not. Brown, for instance, was one of the first American writers to discover the uses of the unreliable narrator. Carwin professes the innocence of his intentions, but he also talks about being driven by a 'mischievous daemon'. More to the point, the entire novel is cast in the form of a letter from Clara, the last surviving member of the Wieland family, to an unnamed friend. And Clara does not hesitate to warn the reader that she is not necessarily to be trusted as a reporter of events. 'My narrative may be invaded by inaccuracy and confusion,' she confesses. 'What but ambiguities, abruptness, and dark transitions, can be expected from the historian who is, at the same time, the sufferer of these disasters?'

The indeterminacy goes further. 'Ideas exist in our minds that can be accounted for by no established laws,' Clara observes. And it is never quite clear, not only whether or not she and Carwin are telling the truth, but how complicit Henry Pleyel and the younger Wieland are with the voices they hear. In his portraits of Henry and Wieland, Brown is exploring the two prevailing systems of thought in early America: respectively, the rationalism of the Enlightenment and the mysticism of Christianity. He is also casting both into doubt. When Henry 'overhears' something that suggests Carwin and Clara are having an affair, he is convinced, he later admits, 'by . . . the testimony of my ears'. He has become accustomed to trusting the evidence of his senses, even though in this case – and many others, Brown intimates – that evidence is wrong. Similarly, when Wieland hears what he takes to be the voice of God, commanding him to kill his family as proof of his faith, he eagerly accepts the command. 'God is the object of my supreme passion,' he insists; 'I have thirsted for knowledge of his will. I have burnt with ardour to approve my faith and my obedience.' Just as it remains unclear whether or not the voice commanding Wieland has been projected by Carwin with malignant or innocent intention, so it is equally unclear whether or not, given his fanaticism and the history of fanaticism in his family, Wieland would have killed in any event. All that is clear is how unstable the instruments of reason and faith are, and how little we can believe what our senses or our more spiritual premonitions tell us. Like other authors of the time, Brown liked to emphasize that his fictions were based on fact. He pointed out, in his prefatory 'Advertisement' for his first novel, that there had recently been 'an authentic case, remarkably similar to Wieland'. Similarly, in both *Ormond* and *Arthur Mervyn*, he made use of an outbreak of yellow fever that had actually occurred in Philadelphia in 1793; and in *Edgar Huntly* he relied not only on familiar settings but on the contemporary interest in such diverse topics as Indians and somnambulism. What Brown built on this base, however, was unique: stories that were calculated to melt down the barrier between fact and fiction by suggesting that every narrative, experience or judgement is always and inevitably founded on quite uncertain premises and assumptions.

Brown was read eagerly by a number of other, distinguished writers of the time, among them Sir Walter Scott, John Keats and Percy Bysshe Shelley. But he never achieved the wider popularity he desired. He wrote two other novels, *Clara Howard* (1801) and *Jane Talbot* (1801), in an apparent attempt to exploit the growing market for sentimental fiction. These were similarly unsuccessful. So, more and more, he turned to journalism to earn a living. In 1799, he founded the *Monthly Magazine and American Review*, which collapsed within a year. He then edited the *Literary Magazine and American Register* from 1803 until 1807, which was more successful. *Memoirs of Carwin*, a sequel to *Wieland*, began to appear in this periodical, but the story remained unfinished at the time of his death. In the last years of his life, his interest turned more to politics and history, a shift marked by his starting the semi-annual *American Register, or General Repository of History, Politics, and Science*. Deprived of the popularity and income that he craved during his lifetime, Brown has continued to receive less than his due share of attention. This is remarkable, not least because he anticipates so much of what was to happen in American fiction in the nineteenth century. His fascination with aberrant psychology, deviations in human thought and behaviour, foreshadows the work of Edgar Allan Poe; so, for that matter, does his use of slippery narrators. His use of symbolism, and his transformation of Gothic into a strange, surreal mix of the extraordinary and the everyday, prepares the way for the fiction of Nathaniel Hawthorne and Herman Melville. Even his relocation of incidents of peril and adventure to what was then the Western wilderness clears a path for the romances of James Fenimore Cooper. Written at the turn of the century, the four major novels of Brown look back to the founding beliefs of the early republic and the founding patterns of the early novel. They also look forward to a more uncertain age, when writers were forced to negotiate a whole series of crises, including the profound moral, social and political crisis that was to eventuate in civil war. The subtitle of the first novel Brown ever wrote, but never published, was 'The Man Unknown to Himself'. That captures the indeterminism at the heart of his work. It also intimates a need that was to animate so much later American writing: as it engaged, and still does, in a quest for identity, personal and national – a way of making the unknown known.

2

inventing americas
the making of american literature, 1800–1865

Making a Nation

At the beginning of the nineteenth century, the American nation consisted of sixteen states and stretched across one-third of the American continent. By 1853, however, it had achieved the continental dimensions it would keep for over a century, until Alaska and Hawaii were admitted as states. In 1760, the population of the thirteen colonies was slightly more than a million and a half. By 1820, the population of the United States was more than nine and a half million, and by 1860 it had risen to nearly thirty-one and a half million. This was partly the result of the acquisition of new territory: the vast Louisiana territory was purchased from France in 1803, the Florida and Oregon territories (or claims to them) were ceded by Spain and Great Britain, and huge areas in the Southwest were taken from Mexico over a period of thirty years. And it was partly the result of an enormous influx of immigrants. For the first four decades after the Revolution, the number of immigrants was comparatively small and those who came were mostly from the British Isles. Beginning in 1820, though, the stream of immigration rapidly increased, with greatly improved means of ocean transport helping to further the movement of vast multitudes from old worlds to new; and immigrants came from many areas of Europe and the world. The United States was becoming a large and self-confidently, even brazenly, expansionist nation. It was becoming, too, even more than before, a multicultural one. That met with resistance: the immigration of Irish Catholics in the East, for instance, and Chinese in the West provoked violence and stimulated the growth of political organizations hostile to foreigners. America was changing rapidly, it was sensed, and many did not like it.

The real change, however, the one that was most radical and potentially troubling, had little to do with growth in the size and diversity of the population. The change that really mattered, and perhaps unnerved, was an economic one. The economic base of the country was shifting from agriculture to industry, and its population was moving from the country to the town. The changes in transportation taking place in the United States during this period are particularly striking here, since they illustrate the economic shift and facilitated it. In 1800, if Americans travelled in their country at all, they travelled by wagon or water, and, if by water, their vessels were propelled by current, sail or oar. Seven years later, the first steamboat appeared on an American waterway. Far more important, twenty-three years after that, in 1830, the first locomotive was manufactured in the United States; it reached the staggering speed of twelve miles an hour and lost a race with a horse. Ten years after this, in turn, in 1840, there were roughly as many miles of railroad track as there were miles of canals: 3,328, all built in the previous twenty-five years. And by 1860, there were no fewer than 30,000 miles of track. What Walt Whitman called 'type of the modern', the age of the railroad, had definitely arrived. Rail transformed trade and travel. It encouraged farmers to produce cash crops, on ever larger agricultural units, for market. It allowed labourers to go where the demand for their labour was. It stimulated the growth of a whole new range of industries, among them lumbering, mining and the production of machine tools. And it also indirectly promoted immigration, since immigrants were among those who notionally benefited from a more mobile labour market and vastly increased, significantly more fluid systems of production and consumption. In short, the railroads were at once an agent and paradigm, an enabler and an emblem, of a newer, more powerful and expansionist America.

If there was any change for African Americans, however, it was for the worse. All hope some of the founding fathers might have had, that slavery would die out or slaves gradually be freed, was extinguished by the invention of the cotton gin, and the vast expansion in the demand for cotton in Great Britain. Slavery was a profitable enterprise, so was the breeding of slaves; and, if anything, the living standards of slaves during this period deteriorated, their working and general conditions grew harsher. Laws against teaching slaves to read and write began to be rigorously enforced; opportunities for slaves to acquire a trade or hire out their time, and so perhaps buy their freedom eventually, began to disappear. A whole series of political compromises, meant to resolve the differences between slaveholding and free states, seemed likely to cement the status quo and postpone the different possibilities Jefferson had sketched out for emancipation indefinitely. So did the insistence of the Southern states that they had the right to define the social forms existing within their borders, without any federal interference. Three events, occurring in 1831, were pivotal. A slave insurrection led by Nat Turner succeeded briefly in Virginia; the Virginia legislature actually discussed a proposal for freeing all slaves within state borders only to reject it; and William Lloyd Garrison founded the anti-slavery journal, *The Liberator*. The growth of the abolitionist movement and the fear of slave insurrection, the sense of enemies without and within, encouraged the South to close ranks to defend its peculiar institution. The 1831 debate in Virginia turned out to be the last time the abolition of slavery was given such a public airing below the Mason-Dixon line. From then on, there would be increasingly urgent demands for abolition from the North, from writers both black and white, and an increasingly virulent defence of slavery and states rights from spokespeople from the South. And a path was opened up to civil war.

For Native Americans, this was also a period of change for the worse. The policy of the United States was a simple one: removal. Under the terms of the 1830 Removal Act, tribes gave up their lands east of the Mississippi for land to the west. 'Their cultivated fields; their constructed habitations . . . are undoubtedly by the law of nature theirs,' conceded John Quincy Adams, president from 1825 to 1829, 'but what is the right of the huntsman to the forest of a thousand miles which he has accidentally ranged in quest of prey?' As it happened, this was a distinction without a difference as far as practical policy was concerned. The Cherokees of Georgia and North Carolina turned themselves into a successful farming people and, in 1827, even adopted a constitution for themselves modelled on that of the United States. It was no use. They, too, were forced to move west, following what became known as the 'Trail of Tears' to the remote, infertile Oklahoma territory. At least four thousand of them died, either in the concentration camps where they were assembled for deportation or during the removal itself. By 1844, most tribes had been removed west. But even there they were not safe. The rapid westward movement of population, which in 1828 led to the election of the first president from a region west of the Appalachians, Andrew Jackson, meant that whites soon wanted some or most of the land to which the Native American peoples had been removed. Jackson had claimed that his policy of removal would put the tribes 'beyond the reach of injury and oppression' and under the 'paternal care of the General Government'. In fact, the policy of the government now turned towards concentrating them in ever smaller reservations. Another president, William Henry Harrison, who served briefly in 1841, summed up the thinking that subjected Native Americans during this period to dispossession and decimation. 'Is one of the fairest portions of the globe to remain in a state of nature, the haunt of a few wretched savages,' he asked, 'when it seems destined by the Creator to give support to a large population and to be the seat of civilisation?' The question was in every sense a rhetorical one since it was clear, from their policies, what the answer of successive governments was.

There were many who were ready to speak out on behalf of Native Americans, however. And many of these, like those who spoke out in favour of the abolition of slavery or the rights of women, were fired by their belief in a specifically social gospel. In 1790, it has been estimated, only one in twenty Americans was a church member. As a result of a series of religious revivals called the Second Great Awakening, though, by the 1830s about three in four Americans belonged to a church. Most of those churches were evangelical and Protestant; and, although no one church dominated, the Baptist and Methodist groups were predominant. Many of the newly converted subscribed to a faith that emphasized a purely spiritual redemption. If their beliefs had any social implications at all, that was only because they tended to identify the arrival of God's kingdom with the political destiny of the United States. The progress of democracy at home and elsewhere was taken as a measure of progress towards the millennium. But some, at least, believed that the coming of the kingdom of God depended on perfecting human society: by eradicating poverty, alcoholism, discrimination against women, oppressive policies against Native Americans, and, above all, slavery. This was an age of belief, or at the very least the search for belief. Both those who opposed and those who supported slavery claimed to be acting in obedience to God. And when the American Anti-Slavery Convention met in 1834, its Declaration certainly invoked the Declaration of Independence, with its thoroughly rationalist allegiance to natural rights. But the authors of that Declaration then went on to distinguish between the founding fathers and their own gathering. 'These principles led them to wage war against their oppressors,' the 'Declaration of the American Anti-Slavery Convention' pointed out, 'and to spill human blood like water in order to be free.' '*Ours* forbid the doing of evil that good may come,' it then went on to insist; 'and lead us to reject, and to entreat the oppressed to reject the use of all carnal weapons for deliverance from bondage, relying solely upon those which are spiritual and mighty through God to the pulling down of strongholds.'

There was a split in the anti-slavery movement on the use of violence, however. There were those, like John Brown, who believed that violent action was necessary to end ignorance and evil: even when that action was regarded as treason or insurrection, an offence against the state. There were also those, like Henry David Thoreau, who were willing to support such action. Thoreau was even willing to compare John Brown to Jesus. 'The same indignation that is said to have cleared the temple once will clear it again,' Thoreau declared. 'The question is not about the weapon, but the spirit in which you use it.' There was a split in the women's movement too, although of a very different kind. On the one hand, there were those like Catharine Beecher who believed in separate 'spheres' for men and women. Along with her sister, Harriet Beecher Stowe, she argued that a woman had the responsibility, and the privilege, to sustain and instil domestic female values as an alternative to the competitive, and frequently ruthless, principles of the marketplace that more and more governed the life of man. On the other, there were women like Margaret Fuller and Elizabeth Cady Stanton who argued that separation meant demotion for women, since the spheres were essentially unequal. In response to Beecher's argument, that running a household requires expertise equal to that of a lawyer or a doctor, they insisted that women could and should be lawyers or doctors if they wanted to be – that, indeed, they might take up any activity or profession as long as they had the talent and the commitment. Fuller and Stanton were arguing against the economic and cultural trends of the time, however, since women were still confined to very limited spheres of activity. Poorer white women were forced into menial jobs if they lived in town; they constituted much of the workforce for the new industries, the mills and sweatshops. Middle-class white women usually enjoyed better educational opportunities while they were young. More went to school, a substantial number went on to college, most could enjoy the increasing number of books and magazines available. But, once educated, if they did not want to enter the sphere of domesticity, there were few professions available to them. One of the few available options, in fact, was to become a writer.

The option was there, in part, because of the huge growth in publishing outlets. The United States had one of the most literate populations in the world at this time. Eager for entertainment and information, Americans flocked to the lectures and debates held at debating societies and lyceums. The lecture circuit attracted literary personalities from abroad, like Charles Dickens, and local cultural luminaries such as Ralph Waldo Emerson. It also drew those, like the abolitionists and feminists, who wished to speak on behalf of a cause. Americans also turned to newspapers, magazines and books in increasing numbers. Newspapers proliferated – there were 1,200 by 1830 – so did magazines; and many writers of this period learned their trade or earned their living as editors. William Cullen Bryant and Walt Whitman both ran newspapers. Edgar Allan Poe, Margaret Fuller, Frederick Douglass and Nathaniel Hawthorne were among many to edit magazines. Some of the newspapers gave a voice to the underprivileged or dispossessed. The *Cherokee Phoenix*, set up in 1828, was the first paper published by an Indian tribe and the first to appear in a native language as well as English. One year earlier, *Freedom's Journal* started to appear, the first of seventeen newspapers owned and edited by African Americans to be published before the Civil War. Other, more mainstream publications gave women, in particular, a chance to earn a living and shape taste. Sara Josepha Hale (1788–1879), for example, became editor of one of the most influential magazines of the period, *Godey's Lady's Book*. The absence of an international copyright law until 1891 certainly mitigated against American writers supporting themselves by their writing, since it meant that the market could be flooded with cheap pirated editions of famous British authors. Still, many tried and some succeeded in living, partly or entirely, by the products of their pen. One of the memorable features of the period, in fact, is the number of women who turned to writing, for income and self-expression. In the process, they established a tradition of work that is on the whole more realistic and domestic than the mythic, romantic fiction of, say, Poe, Hawthorne and Herman Melville: a tradition that focuses on community and family, and uses sentiment to explore fundamental social and moral issues. Another, equally remarkable feature of the time is just how many of the best-sellers were written by women: *The Wide, Wide World* (1850) by Susan Warner (1819–85) (which was the first American novel to sell more than a million copies), *The Lamplighter* (1854) by Maria Cummins (1827–66), *The Hidden Hand* (1859) by E. D. E. N. Southworth (1819–99), and, of course, *Uncle Tom's Cabin* by Harriet Beecher Stowe. Some women writers may have felt it necessary to deprecate their literary works. Some concealed their identities behind pen names. Others, like Mary E. Bryan in 'How Should Women Write' (1860), complained that men tried to restrict women to 'the surface of life', telling them that 'with metaphysics, they have nothing to do' – advising women writers that they should not 'grapple with those great social and moral problems with which every strong soul is now wrestling', then condemning their efforts, should they follow such advice, as 'tame and commonplace'. Still, women made a vital and significant contribution to the popularity of imaginative writing during this time, and, even more, to its quality.

The Making of American Myths

Myths of an emerging nation

One of the first writers to take advantage of the greater opportunities for publication that were opening up, in the process becoming one of the first American writers to achieve international fame, was Washington Irving (1783–1859). Irving was born into a prosperous merchant family in New York City, the youngest of eleven children. He studied law and contributed to two newspapers edited by one of his brothers, the *Morning Chronicle* and *The Corrector*. For the *Chronicle* he wrote 'The Letters of Jonathan Oldstyle, Gent.', a series of youthful satires on New York society. Published in 1802–3, they won him instant recognition. To restore his failing health, he then made the first of many trips to Europe; later, in fact, he was to live for protracted periods in England, to travel in France and Germany extensively, and to have spells of government service in Spain. But in 1806 he returned to New York City. There, a year later, he began to publish *Salmagundi; or, The Whim-Whams and Opinions of Launcelot Langstaff Esq., and Others* (1807–8), a series of satirical miscellanies concerned with New York society that ran to twenty numbers. The leading essays were written by Irving, his brothers and James Kirke Paulding (1778–1860), all members of a group known as the 'Nine Worthies' or 'Lads of Kilkenny' of 'Cockloft Hall'. Federalist in politics, conservative in social principles and comic in tone, they included one piece by Irving, 'Of the Chronicles of the Renowned and Antient City of Gotham', that supplied New York City with its enduring nickname of Gotham. Characteristically, Irving had borrowed here from a European source: he transferred both the name and a reputation for folly from the original Gotham village in Nottinghamshire, England.

Irving was now famous as an author, wit and man of society, and to consolidate his reputation he published *A History of New York from the Beginning of the World to the End of the Dutch Dynasty* (1809) under the pen name of Diedrich Knickerbocker. Often regarded as the first important work of comic literature written by an American, it initiated the term 'Knickerbocker School' for authors like Irving himself, Paulding, Fitz-Greene Hallek (1790–1867) and Joseph Rodman Drake (1795–1820), who wrote about 'little old New York' in the years before the Civil War. Ostensibly concerned with the Dutch occupation, the book in fact burlesques contemporary historical narratives, satirizes pedantry and literary classics, and offers a comic critique of Jeffersonian democracy. Jefferson himself is satirized as Governor Kieft under whom greedy Yankees attempt 'to get possession of the city of Manhattoes'. And there is an ironic apologia for white dispossession and destruction of Native Americans. The original inhabitants of America, Knickerbocker assures the reader, were 'mere cannibals, detestable monsters, and many of them giants'; 'animals' rather than humans, they 'deserved to be exterminated'. 'The host of zealous and enlightened fathers', in any event, brought many blessings with them for 'these infidel savages', such as 'gin, rum, brandy, and the smallpox'. They also brought them 'the light of religion' and then 'hurried them out of the world, to enjoy its reward!' Irving's style here, and in his earlier essays, is derived from the gently satirical fluencies of English writers like Oliver Goldsmith and Joseph Addison. Five years after the publication of his *History* he went to England to work in the family business there. He remained in Europe for seventeen years. He became friends with Sir Walter Scott, visited Samuel Taylor Coleridge, and in 1820 published *The Sketch Book of Geoffrey Crayon, Gent.*, a collection of essays and sketches that was enormously successful in both England and the United States.

The Sketch Book contains two small masterpieces that initiated the great tradition of the American short story, 'Rip Van Winkle' and 'The Legend of Sleepy Hollow'. Four other sketches are also set in America, but most of the other pieces are descriptive and thoughtful essays on England, where Irving was still living. Both 'Rip Van Winkle' and 'Sleepy Hollow' have origins in German folklore. Irving admits as much in a 'Note' to the first tale where the reader is told that 'the foregoing Tale, one would suspect, had been suggested to Mr Knickerbocker by a little German superstition'. Both also owe a debt, in terms of stylistic influence, to Sir Walter Scott. Nevertheless, both exploit their specifically American settings and create American myths: they explore the social and cultural transformations occurring in America at the time in terms that are at once gently whimsical and perfectly serious. In 'Rip Van Winkle', the lazy, hen-pecked hero of the story ventures into the Catskill Mountains of New York State to discover there some little men in Dutch costume bowling at ninepins. Taking many draughts of some strange beverage they have brewed, he falls into a deep sleep. When he returns to his village, after waking up, he eventually realizes that twenty years have passed, the Revolution has been and gone, and that, 'instead of being a subject of his Majesty George the Third, he was now a free citizen of the United States'. The news naturally takes a long time to sink in; and, at first, when he is surrounded in his homeplace by people whom he does not recognize and who do not recognize him, he begins to doubt his own identity. 'I'm not myself – I'm somebody else,' he complains; 'I'm changed, and I can't tell what's my name, or who I am!' His dilemma is a gently comic response to traumatic change; and it offers a genial reflection in miniature of the sudden, disconcerting process of alteration – and possible reactions to it – experienced by the nation as a whole. A similar transposition of American history into American legend occurs in 'Sleepy Hollow'. This story of how the superstitious hero, Ichabod Crane, was bested by the headless horseman of Brom Bones, an extrovert Dutchman and Crane's rival in love, allows Irving to parody several forms of narrative, among them tall tales, ghost stories and the epic. But it also permits him, once again, to reflect on change and to present a vanishing America, which is the setting for this story, as an endangered pastoral ideal. 'It is in such little retired Dutch valleys,' we are told, as the one where American types like Crane and Bones live,

> that population, manners, and customs remain fixed, while the great torrent of migration and improvement, which is making such incessant changes in other parts of this restless country, sweep by them unobserved. They are like those little nooks

of still water which border a rapid stream; where we may see the straw and bubble riding quietly at anchor, or slowly revolving in their mimic harbour, undisturbed by the passing current.

The tendency towards a more lyrical, romantic strain suggested by Irving's evocation of the sleepy hollow where Ichabod Crane lived became a characteristic of the later work. His next collection, *Bracebridge Hall; or, The Humorists* (1822), was well received, but it mostly consists of sentimental portraits of the England of landed gentry. *Tales of a Traveller* (1824) met with a poor reception; and, discouraged, Irving turned increasingly towards historical subjects. His *History of the Life and Voyages of Christopher Columbus* (1828) and *A Chronicle of the Conquest of Granada* (1829) were both based on careful historical research; so was *Voyages and Discoveries of the Companions of Columbus* (1831). What was described as a 'Spanish Sketch Book', *The Alhambra*, recounting Spanish legends, appeared in 1832. Irving then returned from Europe to America, where he was enthusiastically welcomed, and began travelling in the far West in search of picturesque literary backgrounds. The results of these Western travels were *A Tour of the Prairie*, one of three volumes in *The Crayon Miscellany* (1835), and *Astoria* (1836), an account of the fur-trading empire of John Jacob Astor. Both books evoke the romance of the West but none of its rigours; and the later book idealizes the business tycoon Astor, at whose suggestion it was written. Other books followed: among them, *The Adventures of Captain Bonneville U.S.A.* (1837), *Oliver Goldsmith* (1840), a biography of one of Irving's literary masters, *A Book of the Hudson* (1849) and a monumental *Life of Washington* (1855–9) in five volumes. Irving's literary career was erratic, and he never recovered the wit and fluency of his early style; he also tended, especially in his later work, to bathe the European past in an aura of romance. Nevertheless, in his best work, he was a creator of significant American myths: narratives that gave dramatic substance and shape to the radical changes of the time, and the nervousness and nostalgia those changes often engendered. Perhaps he was so effective in fashioning those myths in particular because the nervousness about the new America, and nostalgia for the old – and, beyond that, for Europe – were something that he himself felt intensely. He was writing himself, and the feelings he typified, into legend.

The making of Western myth

Legend of a very different kind was the work of James Fenimore Cooper (1789–1851). If any single person was the creator of the myth of the American West, and all its spellbinding contradictions, then Cooper was. But he was far more than that. He was the founding father of the American historical novel, exploring the contradictions of American society in a time of profound change. He also helped to develop and popularize such widely diverse literary forms as the sea novel, the novel of manners, political satire and allegory, and the dynastic novel in which over several generations American social practices and principles are subjected to rigorous dramatic analysis. And Cooper did not begin writing and publishing until his thirties. Before that, he had served at sea then left to marry and settle as a country gentleman in New York State. His first novel, *Precaution* (1820), was in fact written after his wife challenged his claim that he could write a better book than the English novel he was reading to her. A conventional novel of manners set in genteel English society, this was followed by a far better work, *The Spy: A Tale of the Neutral Ground* (1821). Set in Revolutionary New York State, on the 'neutral ground' of Westchester County, its hero is Harvey Birch, who is supposed to be a Loyalist spy but is secretly in the service of General Washington. Birch is faithful to the Revolutionary cause but a convoluted plot reveals his emotional ties to some of the Loyalists. What the reader is presented with here, in short, is a character prototype that Cooper had learned from Sir Walter Scott and was to use in later fiction, most notably in his portrait of Natty Bumppo, the hero of the Leatherstocking novels. The hero is himself a 'neutral ground' to the extent that he, his actions and allegiances, provide an opportunity for opposing social forces to be brought into a human relationship with one another. The moral landscape he negotiates is a place of crisis and collision; and that crisis and collision are expressed in personal as well as social terms, as a function of character as well as event. *The Spy* was an immediate success. One reviewer hailed Cooper as 'the first who has deserved the appellation of a distinguished American novel writer'. And it was followed, just two years later, by *The Pilot* (1823), the first in a series of sea stories intended to prove that a former sailor could write a better novel in that genre than the landsman Scott had done in his book, published a year earlier, *The Pirate*. Some of the success of this novel was due to the character of Long Tom Coffin, a daring old sea dog. Even more came, though, because it contrasted Tory ineffectuality with the composure and courage of the hero. The mysterious Pilot of the title is, in the words of the story, 'a Quixote in the behalf of liberal principles', whose status as a natural aristocrat is reflected in his boast: 'I was born without the nobility of twenty generations to corrupt and deaden my soul.'

In the same year as *The Pilot* appeared, the first of the five Leatherstocking Tales, *The Pioneers* (1823), was published. Set in 1793 in Otsego County in the recently settled region of New York State, it introduces the reader to the ageing figure of Natty Bumppo, known here as Leatherstocking. The reader also meets Chingachgook, the friend and comrade of Natty from the Mohican tribe; and, in the course of the story, Chingachgook dies despite Natty's efforts to save him. The other four Leatherstocking Tales came over the next eighteen years. *The Last of the Mohicans* (1826) presents Bumppo, here called Hawkeye, in his maturity and is set in 1757 during the Seven Years' War between the French and the British. In *The Prairie* (1827), Bumppo, known simply as the trapper, has joined the westward movement; he is now in his eighties and, at the end of the novel, he dies. *The Pathfinder* (1840) is set soon after *The Last of the Mohicans*, in the same conflict between the French and Indians and the British colonials. Here, Bumppo is tempted to think of marriage. But, when he learns that the woman in question loves another, he nobly accepts that he cannot have her. Like the many Western heroes for which he was later to serve as prototype, he recognizes that, as he puts it, it is not according to his 'gifts' to love and to marry. The last novel to be written, *The Deerslayer* (1841), is, in fact, the first novel in chronological order of events. It takes the reader back to upstate New York in the 1740s. A young man here, Natty Bumppo begins the action known as Deerslayer. In the course of the story, though, he kills an Indian in a fight that approaches the status of ritual; and, before he dies, the man he has killed gives him a new name, Hawkeye. So the series ends with the initiation of its hero into manhood. It does not quite begin with his death; nevertheless, there is clearly a regressive tendency at work here. The Leatherstocking Tales, as a whole, move back in time, back further into the American past and the youth and innocence of the hero. As they do so, they move ever further away from civilization, in terms of setting and subject, and ever further away from social realism, in terms of approach. *The Pioneers* is set in a settled community where Natty Bumppo, who is a relatively marginal character, can be arrested and jailed for shooting a deer out of season. *The Deerslayer*, by contrast, is set in a place that is several times referred to as a 'wilderness', amidst 'the sleeping thunders of the woods', in a period that, Cooper observes, 'seems remote and obscure' already, 'so distant as seemingly to reach the mists of time'; and it has a hero who is described as a 'legend', 'the beau ideal' that 'constitutes poetry'. At work here, in short, is an Edenic impulse common in American writing that drives the imagination out of the literal and into romance and myth – and out of a world where the individual is defined in relation to society and into one where he or she is more likely to be situated outside it. As the conception of him alters over the course of the five Leatherstocking Tales, Natty Bumppo gravitates more and more towards the condition of an American Adam: in his comradeship with another man, his virginity, as much as in his reliance on action and instinct rather than thought and reasoning – and in his indebtedness, too, not to education or convention but to natural wisdom and natural morality.

Natty Bumppo is more than just an American Adam, however, as his recollection of earlier figures set on 'neutral ground' suggests as well as his anticipation of later Western heroes. And the Leatherstocking Tales are far more than types of the American pastoral, resituating Eden somewhere in the mythic past of the country. They are densely textured historical narratives using contrasts and conflicts both within and between characters to explore the national destiny. *The Prairie* illustrates this. The characteristically convoluted plot involves a series of daring adventures, raids and rescues, during the course of which Bumppo saves his companions from both a prairie fire and a buffalo stampede. Woven through that plot is a close examination of human nature and its implications for human society. The original inhabitants of America, for example, are taken as instances of natural man but, the reader soon discovers, the instances are ambiguous. On the one hand, there are the Pawnees, who are 'strikingly noble', their 'fine stature and admirable proportions' being an outward and visible sign of their possession of such 'Roman' virtues as dignity, decorum and courage. On the other, there are the Sioux, a race who resemble 'demons rather than men' and whose frightening appearance is matched only by their treachery and savagery. Nature, in turn, is represented variously, as benevolent, the source of Natty's natural wisdom (''Tis an eddication!' he is wont to declare, while gazing at his surroundings), and the scene of a desperate inter-necine battle ('Do you see yon birds watching for the offals of the beast they have killed,' Natty asks a companion. 'Therein is a moral which teaches the manner of prairie life'). That reinforces the account of Indians as both Rousseauistic noble savages and imps of the Devil. The issue of whether human beings are good, originally innocent, or evil, steeped in original sin, is sounded here. So is the issue of whether America is an Eden or a wilderness. And both those issues, Cooper realized and intimates, feed into the question of what kind of society was needed, particularly in the New World. This was a question fundamental to the infant republic, and *The Prairie* offers a fascinatingly ambivalent answer.

The ambivalence goes further. The portrait of Natty Bumppo suggests, in many ways, that that government is best which governs least. He does not need any civil laws to guide or restrain him since he is, the reader is told, 'a man endowed with the choicest and perhaps rarest gift of nature, that of distinguishing good from evil'. He knows what is right. Remarkably, this includes knowing about the need for conservation: he is an instinctive ecologist, who laments the inclination he sees all around him 'to strip th' arth of its trees' and rob 'the brutes of their natural food'. But Natty is perhaps a rarity: as his complaints about 'man's wish, and pride, and waste', the destruction of the wilderness he witnesses all around him, intimate. His own comments on civil law are, in fact, conflicting. He is deeply critical sometimes of what he calls 'the wicked troublesome meddling' of society. 'Why, do you know,' he declares, 'that there are regions where the law is so busy as to say, "In this fashion shall you live, in that fashion you shall die . . . !"' At other times, though, he offers a contrary view. 'The law – 'tis bad to have it,' he observes early on in *The Prairie*, 'but I sometimes think it is worse to be entirely without it.' 'Yes – yes,' he adds here, 'the law is needed when such as have not the gifts of strength and wisdom are to be taken care of.' Of all the questions that emerged in the United States in the nineteenth century, the question of what finally was the national heritage, democratic community or individual freedom and advancement, was the most pressing and the most difficult. And on that question even Natty Bumppo stands on neutral ground, despite his status as an icon of freedom. So, even more, does *The Prairie*, since Natty's chief antagonist in the novel, Ishmael Bush, is, as his forename suggests, an outcast from society – and in the worst sense. 'Ishmael Bush,' we are told, 'had passed the whole of a life of more than fifty years on the skirts of society.' There, he has learned to be a predator, following 'the instincts of the beast', and pursuing his own individual advantage without regard to law of any kind, natural or civil. He neatly sums up his own position when he declares of another character, 'he is an enemy . . . hear him! Hear him! He talks of the law'. Violating property rights, ignoring the claims of everyone but himself, he offers a decidedly sardonic reading of human nature and the implications of individualism – and, by extension, a positive case not only for civil laws but for social control and strong government.

At his best, as in *The Prairie*, Cooper explores the basic tensions at work in American culture and history in a way that allows free play to the opposing forces. At the same time, he creates mythic figures, of whom Natty Bumppo is easily the most notable, who offer a focus for debates about the character of American democracy – and also possess the simplicity and stature required of any great epic hero. The first time we see Bumppo in *The Prairie* is typical. He appears to a group of travellers, and the reader, standing in the distance on the great plains with the sun going down behind him. 'The figure was colossal, the attitude musing and melancholy,' the narrator observes, and 'embedded as it was in its setting of garish light, it was impossible to distinguish its just proportions or true character.' Larger than life, romantic and mysterious, Natty Bumppo here anticipates a whole series of Western and American heroes: Captain Ahab in *Moby-Dick*, for instance, the central characters in the Western films of John Ford, or Jay Gatsby in F. Scott Fitzgerald's *The Great Gatsby*. And a similarly heroic closure is given to the story of our hero. At the end of *The Prairie*, Natty dies with his gaze 'fastened on the clouds which hung around the western horizon, reflecting the bright colours and giving form to the glorious tints of an American sunset'. 'The spectators', we are told, of whom the reader is now one, are filled 'with solemn awe' as they watch the old man, supported by friends, struggle to his feet for the last time. 'For a moment he looked about him as if to invite all in his presence to listen'; then, finally, 'with a fine military elevation of the head and with a voice that might be heard in every part of the numerous assembly, he pronounced the word, "Here!"' With that grand, ultimate entry into nature, Cooper may be suggesting the passing of the democratic possibilities Natty Bumppo represents. *The Prairie* certainly has an autumnal mood: it is set firmly in the past, and there are constant references to the way immigration and cultivation, the destruction of the wilderness and the scattering of the Indians have changed the West – and, quite possibly, America – between then and the time of writing. Perhaps; and, if so, the novel is as much a new Western as a traditional one, mapping out the destructive tendencies of the westward movement as well as its place in a heroic tale of national expansion. One further layer of complexity is then added to a narrative that is, in any event, a debate and a mythic drama, a great historical novel and an American epic in prose.

A year before the publication of *The Prairie*, Cooper took his family to Europe. He travelled there, worked as a diplomat, but still found time to write. Books written during this period include *The Red Rover* (1827), a novel of early frontier life *The Wept of Wish-ton-Wish* (1829), and another sea tale called *The Water Witch* (1830). He also completed a historical trilogy, *The Bravo* (1831), *The Heidenmauer* (1832) and *The Headsman* (1833). A year before the final volume of the trilogy was published, he returned to the United States. By now, he was becoming repelled by what he considered to be the absence of public and private virtues in his country, and by the abuses of democracy. In *A Letter to His Countrymen* (1834), *The Monikins* (1835) and *The American Democrat* (1838), he investigated these problems from the standpoint of an aristocratic democrat. In the novels *Homeward Bound* (1838) and *Home as Found* (1838), in turn, he offered fictional explorations of his beliefs. For his attacks on populism, and the politics of Jacksonian democracy, Cooper was vilified in the press. He responded by successfully suing for libel. And his writing continued unabated. In the last ten years of his life, in fact, he produced no fewer than twenty-one books: among them, more novels set all or in part at sea (like *Afloat and Ashore* [1844] and *Miles Wallingford* [1844]), several scholarly and factual works (including a *History of the Navy* [1843]), a number of historical romances (such as *The Oak Openings* [1848]), a utopian social allegory (*The Crater* [1848]), and a novel concerned with the perversion of social justice that is often considered an anticipation of the modern mystery novel (*The Ways of the Hour* [1850]). Perhaps the most notable publication of his last few years, though, was the trilogy known as the Littlepage manuscripts, *Satanstoe* (1845), *The Chainbearer* (1845) and *The Redskins* (1846). These three novels trace the growing tension between the propertied and the propertyless classes in New York State from the colonial period to the 1840s. In the process, they reveal Cooper's continuing interest in adopting and developing different fictional forms, while dramatically interrogating the conflicts at work in American society. Cooper was a great innovator. At his best, as in the Leatherstocking Tales, he was also a great creator of American myths. And through all his fictional innovations, he returned compulsively to issues that were to haunt many later American writers: the different routes a democratic republic might take, the conflict between law and freedom, the clearing and the wilderness, communal ethics and the creed of self-reliance.

Over the three decades when the Leatherstocking series was written, many other attempts were made to translate experience in the West into literature. Notable among these were two novels, *Logan: A Family History* (1822) and *Nick of the Woods; or, The Jibbenainesay* (1837), and an autobiographical narrative first serialized in the *Knickerbocker Magazine* in 1847 and then published in 1849, *The Oregon Trail*. *Logan: A Family History* was one of the several novels and many publications of John Neal (1793–1876). Born into a Quaker family in Maine, Neal was an endlessly energetic writer. His early works included *Keep Cool* (1817), a novel that was also a tract against duelling, two narrative poems titled 'Battle of Niagara' (1818) and 'Goldau, or, the Maniac Harper' (1818), and *Otho* (1819), a romantic tragedy in blank verse. Among his other, later publications were a Revolutionary romance (*Seventy-Six* [1823]), a romantic epistolary novel (*Randolph* [1823]), a romantic novel set in colonial New England (*Brother Jonathan* [1825]), a fictional study of the Salem witchcraft trials (*Rachel Dyer* [1828]), and a picaresque tale about a New Englander abroad (*Authorship* [1830]). Living in England for a while, Neal also wrote a number of articles for *Blackwood's Magazine*, a journal notoriously hostile to American writers. Among the most remarkable of these was a series of five papers on American authors. Marred by errors of fact, and Neal's own prejudices, these papers nevertheless represented the first serious attempt at a history of American literature; and they were eventually published in 1937 under the author's own chosen title, *American Writers*. *Logan: A History* is an essentially romantic account of a noble savage, the Indian chief who gives the book its title. The reverse side of the coin is suggested by *Nick of the Woods*, the work of Robert Montgomery Bird

(1806–54), an equally prolific author whose output included historical drama (*The Gladiator* [1831]), a tragedy dramatizing the assassination of the Spanish conquistador Pizarro (*Oralloosa, Son of the Incas* [1832]), a tragedy set in eighteenth-century Colombia (*The Broker of Bogota* [1834]), two novels concerned with the conquest of Mexico (*Calavar; or, The Knight of the Conquest* [1834]; *The Infidel; or, The Knight of the Conquest* [1835]), a romance of the Revolution (*The Hawks of Hawk-Hollow* [1835]) and a series of travel sketches (*Peter Pilgrim; or, A Rambler's Recollections* [1838]). *Nick of the Woods*, an immensely popular tale in its day and also Bird's best work, has a complicated plot involving Indian raids and massacres, a romantic heroine taken into captivity but eventually rescued, and an eponymous central character who is bent on revenge against the Indians for the slaughter of his family. Throughout all the plot convolutions, however, what remains starkly simple is the portrait of the Indians. As Bird depicts them, they are violent, superstitious and treacherous. They may be savages but they are very far from being noble.

The Oregon Trail is another matter. For a start, it was written by someone, Francis Parkman (1823–93), who went on from writing it to become one of the most distinguished historians of the period. Parkman was one of a generation of American historians who combined devotion to research with a romantic sweep of imagination, and a scholarly interest in the history of America or democratic institutions or both with dramatic flair and a novelistic eye for detail. Apart from Parkman himself, the most notable of these romantic historians were John Lothrop Motley (1814–77), George Bancroft (1800–91) and William Hinckling Prescott (1796–1859). Motley, after writing a novel about the colony of Thomas Morton (*Merry Mount* [1839]), devoted much of his life to historical study of the Netherlands, drawn to this subject by the analogy he perceived with the United States, and the opportunity it offered him to dramatize the triumph of Protestantism and liberty where previously there had been despotism. 'The laws governing all bodies political,' Motley sonorously declared in his book *Historic Progress and American Democracy* (1869), proceeded as 'inexorably as Kepler's law controls the motion of the planets. The law is Progress: the result Democracy.' That was an article of faith not only for Motley but for Bancroft, whose belief in the progressive character of history – and in the duty of the historian to demonstrate the evolution of liberty in historical events – was thoroughly exercised in his major work, a monumental, ten-volume *History of the United States* (1834–76). Prescott concentrated his attention further south, on what was the then neglected field of the conquest of Mexico and Peru. He too, however, mixed historical scholarship with romantic literary forms. In his finest work, the *History of the Conquest of Mexico* (1843), Prescott presents his story in terms of a narrative structure borrowed from the historical novel and, in particular, the fiction of Sir Walter Scott. Within a panoramic portrait of two cultures in collision, the Aztec and the Spanish, Prescott focuses on the conflict between two heroic figures, Montezuma and Cortez. The result is an intervention in both history and literature, a matter of scholarly record and a tragic epic. Parkman also negotiated the borderline between the historical and the literary, in seven works exploring the struggle for domination in the New World published over the period between 1865 and 1892. Surveying, in particular, the conflict between the English and the French for control of colonial America, the series pivoted on a contrast between progress and reaction – represented, respectively, by England and France – seen from the standpoint of an author who once described himself as a conservative republican.

Published before his histories, *The Oregon Trail* is an account of a journey Parkman took along the trail of the title in 1846. His purpose in taking the trip was twofold: to improve his frail health and study Indian life. Skilled in woodcraft and a decent shot, he survived the hardship of the trek, but only just: the strain of travelling eventually led to a complete breakdown in his health, rather than the recovery for which he had hoped. Incapable of writing, he was forced to dictate his story to a cousin and travelling companion. The result has been described as the first account of a literary white man who actually lived by choice for a while among Native Americans. What emerges from this account is, like the other work of Parkman and the romantic historians, an intriguing mix of fact and fiction, matters of record and the stuff of the imagination. It is also, and equally intriguingly, double-edged. As the narrator of *The Oregon Trail*, a Harvard graduate and a member of a prominent Boston family, encounters the landscape and peoples of the West, his tone tends to hover sometimes between condescension and disgust, the style verges on the mandarin. 'The Ogillallah, the Brulé, and the other western bands of the Dahcotah or Sioux, are thorough savages, unchanged by any contact with civilisation,' Parkman tells the reader. 'Not one of them can speak a European tongue, or has ever visited an American settlement.' The white people, the emigrants he meets, also strike the young traveller, very often, as savage, unkempt and unruly. 'I have often perplexed myself to divine the various motives that give impulse to this migration,' Parkman confesses, 'but whatever they may be . . . certain it is that multitudes bitterly repent the journey, and, after they have reached the land of promise, are happy enough to escape from it.' Certainly, it seems to the young narrator that the territories the migrants encounter – drawn, it may be, by their 'desire of shaking off restraints of law and society' – are sometimes landscapes of desolation. 'If a curse had been pronounced upon the land, it could not have worn an aspect more forlorn', Parkman declares of one area he visits on the prairie, where 'all alike glared with an insupportable whiteness under the burning sun'. The only relief he found on this bleak terrain, he recalls, was a solitary 'pine-tree clinging at the edge of a ravine', its 'resinous odors' recalling 'the pine-clad mountains of New England' and a greener, more gracious world.

Yet, for all that, Parkman remembers that he found much to admire, or even cherish, in the West. The two scouts who accompanied him are portrayed in frankly romantic terms. One has the rough charm of the prairie, and an indefatigable 'cheerfulness and gayety', the other a 'natural refinement and delicacy of mind'; the both of them, in their different ways, are true knights of the wild. And the romance of the hunt, and wilderness occupations in general, is fondly recalled: 'I defy the annals of chivalry', Parkman declares at one point, 'to furnish the record of a life more wild and perilous than that of a Rocky Mountain trapper.' Native American life, too, is celebrated for its colour and occasionally chivalric touches. 'If there be anything that deserves to be called romantic in the Indian character,' Parkman explains, 'it is to be sought in . . . friendships . . . common among many of the prairie tribe.' Parkman himself, he discloses, enjoyed just such an intimacy, becoming 'excellent friends' with an Indian he calls 'the Panther': 'a noble-looking fellow', with a 'stately and graceful figure' and 'the very model of a wild prairie-rider'. 'For the most part, a civilised white man can discover very few points of sympathy between his own nature and that of an Indian,' Parkman cautions. But, in this instance, 'there were at least some points of sympathy between him and me' and 'we rode forward together, through rocky passages, deep dells, and little barren plains'. This is the homoerotic romance across the line between white and Indian that Cooper imagined, replayed here in however muted a key. Parkman is framing his recollections within a literary tradition that includes the author of the Leatherstocking Tales and, before him, Sir Walter Scott. And he is not shy about confessing to his model. Observing an Indian village, for instance, with its 'armed warriors', 'naked children', and 'gayly apparelled girls', Parkman suggests that 'it would have formed a noble subject for a painter, and only the pen of Scott could have done it justice in description'. As such remarks intimate, Parkman is drawn to the romance of the West, what he sees as its primitive beauty, its bold colours and simple chivalry, even while he is also repelled by its rawness, its lack of refinement. So he ends up decidedly at odds with himself, when he eventually returns from the trail. 'Many and powerful as were the attractions of the settlements,' Parkman concludes, 'we looked back regretfully to the wilderness behind us.' That was a broken, uncertain note to be sounded in many later stories about going West, negotiating what the traveller sees as the borderline between civilization and savagery. Parkman was playing his part, in *The Oregon Trail*, in inaugurating the frontier as a site of vicarious risk, imaginative adventure: with the West perceived as it was precisely because it was seen through the eyes of the East – as a place destructively, but also seductively, other.

A year after the publication of *The Last of the Mohicans*, in 1827, a very different story about the relationship between white people and Native Americans appeared, and one different in turn from the accounts of Neal, Bird and Parkman: *Hope Leslie* by Catharine Maria Sedgwick (1789–1867). Sedgwick had already produced two best-sellers, *A New England Tale: Sketches of New-England Character and Manners* (1822) and *Redwood* (1824). She was to go on to publish many other books, including *Clarence; or, A Tale of Our Own Times* (1830), set in and around New York City, *The Linwoods; or 'Sixty Years Since' in America* (1835), which portrays the life of New York City during the Revolution, and *Married or Single?* (1857), a contrast between different types of women aimed at showing the valuable activities in which unmarried women might engage. The main figures in these novels tend to be women, and often women of independence and courage. There is, for instance, a character called Aunt Debby in *Redwood* who is described as 'a natural protector of the weak and oppressed'. Aunt Debby, the reader is told, decided to remain single after the Revolution because she was 'so imbued with the independent spirit of the times, that she would not then consent to the surrender of any of her rights'. Similarly, the heroines of both *Redwood* and *A New England Tale* are female orphans who have to make their way in the world. Jane Elton, in *A New England Tale*, suffers a difficult adolescence of restrictions imposed by poverty and Calvinist orthodoxy, before finally achieving the emotional maturity required for the responsibilities of marriage and a family. Ellen Bruce, in *Redwood*, also meets her destiny in marriage. But, in this novel, marriage is part of a larger narrative vision which sees the influence of women as a whole producing an age of virtue, family harmony and love.

Hope Leslie, too, focuses on the destiny of women, but in even more interesting ways than Sedgwick's other novels. There is a white heroine, whose name gives the book its title. There is also a Pequod woman, Magawisca, who saves a white man, Everell Fletcher, from execution at the hands of her father, the chief, in the manner of Pocahontas. Her act involves considerable physical, as well as emotional, courage, since she offers her body to the weapon aimed at Everell's neck and, as a result, loses her arm. 'All paid involuntary homage to the heroic girl, as if she were a superior being,' the reader is told. Hope Leslie herself shows similar heroism when, on not one but two occasions, she frees Indian women from what she considers unjust imprisonment. And Magawisca resumes her status as an evidently 'superior being' towards the end of the narrative, when she is captured by the whites. At her trial for 'brewing conspiracy . . . among the Indian tribes', she is defended by the historical figure of John Eliot, whom Sedgwick identifies as the 'first Protestant missionary to the Indians'. Magawisca, however, insists that she needs no defence, since the tribunal has no authority over her. 'I am your prisoner, and ye may slay me,' she declares, 'but I deny your right to judge me. My people have never passed under the yoke; not one of my race has ever acknowledged your authority.' Clearly, their heroism makes Magawisca and Hope Leslie doubles. Their primary allegiance is to conscience: what Magawisca calls 'the Great Spirit' that 'hath written his laws on the hearts of his original children'. Obeying those laws, they defy those set in power in their respective societies, who are determinately male: Magawisca defies her father, of course, and both she and her white double Hope defy the authority of the Puritan fathers.

What is equally notable about this rewriting of Western tropes is the intimacy that evidently exists in *Hope Leslie* between white and Indian characters. Unlike Cooper, Sedgwick is perfectly willing to contemplate marriage between the two races. Faith Leslie, the sister of Hope, is carried into captivity while still a child; she marries Oneco, the brother of Magawisca; and she then refuses the chance offered her to return to the Puritan community. Sedgwick is also willing to countenance signs of kinship between women of the two races. In one narrative sequence, Hope Leslie resists 'the prejudices of the age' – and, for that matter, the conventions of female behaviour – by liberating an Indian woman called Nelena from prison. Nelena has been condemned as a witch, after she cured a snakebite with the help of herbal medicine; and she repays the debt by arranging for Magawisca to meet

Hope with news of Faith. The two women, Hope and Magawisca, meet secretly in a cemetery where both their mothers are buried, and plot a way for Hope to meet her sister even though this would violate colonial law. The scene where they meet underscores their shared dignity and courage. Even when Hope momentarily balks at the news that her sister is married to an Indian, the sense of mutual respect is quickly restored by Magawisca's response. 'Yes, an Indian, in whose veins runs the blood of the strongest, the fleetest of the children of the forest,' Magawisca proudly insists, 'who never turned their backs on friends or enemies, and whose souls have returned to the Great Spirit as they came from him. Think ye that your blood will be corrupted by mingling with this stream?' The entire scene subtly interweaves intimations of debt and intimacy. The graves of the mothers of the two women lie side by side, the women recall how Magawisca rescued Everell Fletcher and Hope saved Nelena as they talk about the marriage between the brother of one and the sister of the other. It is a celebration of a sisterhood of the spirit and the blood. And its mythic status is confirmed at its conclusion by Hope. 'Mysteriously, mysteriously have our destinies been interwoven', Hope observes to 'the noble figure' of Magawisca as she departs into 'the surrounding darkness'. 'Our mothers brought from a far distance to rest together here – their children connected in indissoluble bonds!'

A word of caution is perhaps necessary here. Sedgwick did not question the prevailing contemporary belief in the Manifest Destiny of the white race. For that matter, she did not seek to challenge the conventional notion that marriage was a woman's proper aim and reward. As for the latter, even *Married or Single?*, written with the stated aim of driving away 'the smile at the name of "old maid"', ends with the heroine being married off in traditional fashion. And, as for the former, even Magawisca admits, at her trial, that, as she puts it, 'the white man cometh – the Indian vanisheth'. Within these constraints, however, Sedgwick did find a place for female integrity and for intimacy between the races. *The Linwoods* offers a neat illustration of this, when the heroine is assisted in rescuing her brother from jail by a free black woman – who tells the jailer, as she ties him up, 'remember, that you were strung up there by a "d-n nigger" – a nigger *woman*!' In effect, she negotiates a position between those women of the time who assigned a special sphere to the exercise of female virtue and those who said a woman could and should be anything she wanted to be, provided she had the talent and dedication. Her female characters, after all, may be directed towards marriage as their appropriate final destiny: but that does not stop them from transgressing the conventional boundaries for women in the name of their own sense of justice. Sedgwick also negotiates, along the way, a different set of meanings for Western myth: one need only compare *Hope Leslie* with the Leatherstocking Tales to measure the difference. It is partly a matter of reversal: male transgression and bonding are replaced by, yet reflected in, their female equivalents. It is partly a matter of rewriting, radical revision: here, the connections between the races are what matter rather than the conflicts – and, whatever else may be present, there is an intensely felt sense of community and continuity. Cooper was a powerful creator of frontier myths but he was not, by any means, the only one: the legends figured in *Hope Leslie* also had a significant impact on how later Americans imagined the movement of their nation west.

The making of Southern myth

However much they differ, though, writers like Cooper and Sedgwick do have common interests and ideas, derived from the basic currency of Western myth: a belief in mobility, a concern with the future, a conviction that, whatever problems it may have, America is still a land of possibility. The counter-myth to this is the myth of the South: preoccupied with place and confinement rather than space and movement, obsessed with the guilt and burden of the past, riddled with doubt, unease and the sense that, at their best, human beings are radically limited and, at their worst, tortured, grotesque or evil. And if Cooper was the founding father of the Western myth in literature, even though he never actually saw the prairie, then, even more queerly, Edgar Allan Poe (1809–49) was the founding father of Southern myth, although he was actually born in Boston and hardly ever used Southern settings in his fiction or his poetry. What makes Poe a founder of Southern myth, typically of him, is not so much a matter of the literal as of the imaginative. 'The Fall of the House of Usher' (1839) is set in an anonymous landscape, or rather dreamscape, but it has all the elements that were later to characterize Southern Gothic: a great house and family falling into decay and ruin, a feverish, introspective hero half in love with death, a pale, ethereal heroine who seems and then is more dead than alive, rumours of incest and guilt – and, above all, the sense that the past haunts the present and that there is evil in the world and it is strong. Typically of Poe, who turned his own life into drama, this Southern dimension is also a matter of self-consciousness: the causes he espoused, the opinions he expressed, the stories he told about himself. 'I am a Virginian,' he wrote in 1842, 'at least I call myself one, for I have resided all my life, until within the last few days, in Richmond.'

Even when Poe had become, to all intents and purposes, an exile from the South, he clung to its conservatism and many of its prejudices. 'I have no faith in human perfectibility,' he wrote to James Russell Lowell in 1844, 'I think that human exertion will have no appreciable effect on humanity. Man is now only more active – not more happy – nor more wise, than he was 6,000 years ago.' Resisting the American, and Western, shibboleth of progress, Poe also never missed an opportunity to poke fun at democracy. 'The sense of high birth is a moral force,' he wrote in 'Marginalia' (1844), 'whose value the democrats, albeit compact of mathematics, are never in condition to calculate . . . "*Pour savoir ce qu'est Dieu,*" says the Baron de Bielfeld, "*il faut être Dieu même.*"' On its uglier side, this adoption of the pose and beliefs of a Southern aristocrat occasionally led Poe into racist stereotyping. An African American character called Toby, for example, in his long story 'The Journal of Julius Rodman' (1840), is said to have 'all the peculiar features of his race: the swollen lips, large white protruding eyes, flat nose, long ears, double head, pot-belly, and bow legs'. On its more positive side, though, it encouraged Poe to promote the cause of Southern literature. 'It is high time that the literary South took its own interests into its own charge,' he insisted in 1836 while editing the *Southern Literary Messenger,* and then followed this up a few months later by announcing boldly: 'we are embarking in the cause of *Southern* literature and (with perfect amity to all sections) wish to claim especially as a friend and co-operator every *Southern* Journal.' And it also encouraged him to attack what he saw as the hegemony of New England and pour comic vitriol on Boston in particular, which he labelled 'Frogpondium'. 'We like Boston,' Poe wrote in 1843 in an essay for the *Broadway Journal,* and then continued with elephantine irony:

> We were born there – and perhaps it is just as well to mention that we are heartily ashamed of the fact. The Bostonians are very well in their way. Their hotels are bad. Their pumpkin pies are delicious. Their poetry is no good . . . But with all these qualities the Bostonians have no soul . . . The Bostonians are well-bred – as *very* dull persons generally are.

Nevertheless, as Poe admits here, he *was* born in Boston. Despite all his aristocratic sneers at the bourgeois dullness and correctness of the town, and his complaints about Southerners 'being ridden to death by New-England', he did not leave there, to be raised by a Richmond merchant John Allan, until he was two. It was from John Allan that, by choice, Poe took his middle name. And it was with the Allans that Poe lived in England from 1815 to 1820. Poe then entered the University of Virginia in 1826, but relations between him and Allan were by now severely strained. Allan wanted Poe to prepare for a legal career. Poe, however, left university for Boston, where he began a literary career with his first volume of poetry, *Tamerlane and Other Poems* (1827). Published anonymously and at his own expense, it went unnoticed. But it clearly announced his poetic intentions: aims and ambitions that were later to be articulated in such seminal essays as 'The Philosophy of Composition' (1846) and 'The Poetic Principle' (1850) and further put into practice in the later volumes, *Poems by E. A. Poe* (1831) and *The Raven and Other Poems* (1845). The poet, Poe wrote in his essays, should be concerned, first and last, with the 'circumscribed Eden' of his own dreams. 'It is the desire of the moth for the star,' Poe says of the poetic impulse in 'The Poetic Principle'. 'Inspired by an ecstatic prescience of the glories beyond the grave,' he goes on, 'we struggle, by multiform combinations among the things and thoughts of Time, to attain a portion of that Loveliness whose very elements, perhaps, appertain to eternity alone.' According to this prescription, the poet's task is to weave a tapestry of talismanic signs and sounds in order to draw, or rather subdue, the reader into sharing the world beyond phenomenal experience. Poems make nothing happen in any practical, immediate sense, Poe suggests. On the contrary, the ideal poem becomes one in which the words efface themselves, disappear as they are read, leaving only a feeling of significant absence, of no-thing.

Clearly, Poe drew elements of this visionary, even cabalistic, notion of poetry from the English Romantic poets, particularly Samuel Taylor Coleridge. What is remarkable, however, is just how far he pushed this notion – so that, in his critical hands, the poet becomes a prophet who has seen the Promised Land and is now trying to lead others there. Or, it could be added, Poe sees the poet as a priest or shaman, using his arts to entice us into a rejection of the here and now – even a kind of magician who is attempting in effect to enchant us, or simply trick us, into forgetting the laws of the ordinary world. Seen from an international perspective, it is easy to understand why Poe became such an influential figure for Charles Baudelaire and the French Symbolist poets, who learned in part from their American cousin to regard the poet as a person with arcane, almost divine knowledge and the poem as a magic document resisting the heresy of paraphrase. And seen from a purely American standpoint, it is handy to remember Franklin's insistence that 'nothing is good or beautiful but in the measure that it is useful'. Quite the contrary, Poe insists. Playing the elegant dandy once again, the Southern aristocrat resisting the demands of a crass, bourgeois culture, he takes the scarlet letter of shame and turns it into a badge of pride: it is the special merit of poetry, he claims, that it is useless.

Just how Poe turned these poetic ideas into practice is briefly suggested in one of his poems, 'Dreamland', where the narrator tells us that he has reached a strange new land 'out of SPACE – out of TIME'. That is the land that all Poe's art occupies or longs for: a fundamentally elusive reality, the reverse of all that our senses can receive or our reason can encompass – something that lies beyond life that we can discover only in sleep, madness or trance, in death especially, and, if we are lucky, in a poem or story. Certain poetic scenes and subjects are favourites with Poe precisely because they reinforce his ultimately visionary aims. Unsurprisingly, life after death is a favourite topic, in poems like 'Annabel Lee' and 'The Sleeper'. So, too, is the theme of a strange, shadowy region beyond the borders of normal consciousness: places such as those described in 'The City in the Sea' or 'Eldorado' which are, in effect, elaborate figures for death. As Poe himself explains in 'The Philosophy of Composition', an account of how he wrote 'The Raven', 'the death . . . of a beautiful woman is unquestionably the most poetical topic in the world' because it enhances the seductive nature of death, transforming annihilation into erotic fulfilment. 'O! nothing earthly', begins 'Al Aaraaf', one of Poe's earliest poems, and that captures his poetic thrust: whatever the apparent subject, the movement is always away from the ordinary, phenomenal world in and down to some other, subterranean level of consciousness and experience. The sights and sounds of a realizable reality may be there in a poem like 'To Helen', but their presence is only fleeting, ephemeral. Poe's scenes are always shadowy and insubstantial, the colours dim, the lighting dusky. In the final instance, the things of the real world are there only to be discarded – as signposts to another country that is, strictly speaking, imperceptible, unrealizable by the waking consciousness.

'Helen, thy beauty is to me, /' 'To Helen' begins, 'Like those Nicéan barks of yore, / That gently o'er a perfumed sea, / The weary, way-worn wanderer bore / To his own native shore.' This is poetry as incantation. Poe uses hypnotic rhythm and recurring, verbal melody and words like 'Nicéan' that suggest more than they state, all to create a sense of mystery, or what a later poet, and disciple of Poe, Arthur Rimbaud, was to call 'a prodigious, and rational disordering of all the senses'. The narrator is transported, by the end of this poem, to 'the regions which / Are Holy-Land!' So, ideally, is the reader. Looking at a poem like this, it is easy to see why Ralph Waldo Emerson attacked Poe as 'the jingle-man'. It is also easy to see why Poe made people like Emerson nervous since he turned the national belief in individualism, the imperial self, in a strange new direction. The motion here is utterly, remorselessly centripetal: away not just from the world of use, getting and spending, but from the entire world outside the self. In dreams, trance, death, Poe intimates, the self fashions its own reality, inviolable and intangible; it draws inward to a world that, to quote 'Al Aaraaf' again, has 'nothing of the dross' outside it, on the material plane. And, if the poet is capable of it, the poem makes a supreme version of that world: self-contained, fixed, perfect, it is a pure or closed field, as autonomous and impalpable as the reality it imitates. It is as if Poe, with typical perversity, had decided to rewrite the dangers that many of his contemporaries saw in the American ethic of selfhood, and the way it opened up the perilous possibility, in particular, of isolation. For, in his work, solipsism becomes the aim: the poet seeks neither to embrace nor to dominate the world but absolute solitude, the sanctuary of the disengaged soul.

Disengagement was not, however, something that Poe could pursue as a practical measure. He had to earn his living, to support himself and then later his wife: in 1836 he married his thirteen-year-old cousin, Virginia. He worked as an editor for various journals, including *Burton's Gentleman's Magazine* and *Graham's Magazine*; he was associated with other journals, such as the *New-York Mirror* and *Godey's Lady's Book*; in 1845, he even became proprietor of the *Broadway Journal*; and he was an apparently indefatigable essayist and reviewer. What the magazines wanted, in particular, was stories; and in 1835 Poe attracted attention with one of his first short stories, 'MS Found in a Bottle', which won first prize in a contest judged by John Pendleton Kennedy (1795–1870) – himself a writer and author of one of the first idyllic fictional accounts of life on the old plantation, *Swallow Barn; or, A Sojourn in the Old Dominion* (1832). This short story was followed by more and more tales appealing to the contemporary taste for violent humour and macabre incident. 'The Murders in the Rue Morgue', 'The Masque of the Red Death', and 'The Imp of the Perverse' were all published in *Graham's Magazine* in 1841–2; while 1843 saw the freelance publication of 'The Tell-Tale Heart', 'The Black Cat', 'The Pit and the Pendulum', and another prize-winning story, 'The Gold Bug'. His first collection of stories, *Tales of the Grotesque and Arabesque*, was published in 1840; it included 'Ligeia', 'Berenice', and 'The Assignation'. In 1845 *Tales* appeared, a book that reprinted previous work selected by Evert Duyckinck (1816–78) – an influential man of letters of the time who, with his brother George (1823–63), was to produce a *Cyclopaedia of American Literature* (1855), the most comprehensive scholarly work of its kind of the period. This later collection contained 'The Pit and the Pendulum' and 'The Tell-Tale Heart' among other notable pieces. In the earlier, in turn, Poe made his attentions as a short story writer clear in a brief Preface. It was true, Poe admitted, that many of his stories were Gothic because they had terror as their 'thesis'. But that terror, he went on, was not of the conventional kind, since it had little to do with the usual Gothic paraphernalia; it was, instead, a terror 'of the soul'.

Whatever else he might have been, Poe was an unusually perceptive (if often also malicious) critic. And he was especially perceptive about his own work. Poe did not invent the Gothic tale, any more than he invented the detective story, science fiction or absurd humour. To each of these genres or approaches, however, he did – as he realized and, in some instances, boasted – make his own vital contribution. In a detective story like 'The Murders in the Rue Morgue', for example, Poe created the detective story as a tale of ratiocination, a mystery that is gradually unravelled and solved. He also created the character of the brilliant amateur who solves a crime that seems beyond the talents of the professionals. In his Gothic stories, he first destabilizes the reader by using unreliable narrators: madmen and liars, initially rational men who have their rationalism thoroughly subverted, men who should by all commonsensical standards be dead. And he then locates the terror within, as something that springs from and bears down upon the inner life. In Poe's stories, the source of mystery and anxiety is something that remains inexplicable. It is the urge to self-betrayal that haunts the narrator of 'The Tell-Tale Heart', or the cruel and indomitable will of the narrator of 'Ligeia', which finally transforms reality into fantasy, his living wife into a dead one. It is the impulse towards self-destruction, and the capacity for sinking into nightmare worlds of his own creation, that the protagonist and narrator of *The Narrative of Arthur Gordon Pym* (1838) reveals at so many moments of his life. For that matter, it is the strange ending of Pym's story. As he hurtles towards a chasm in the seas from which arises 'a shrouded human figure, very far larger in its proportions than any dweller among men . . . the hue of the skin . . . of the perfect whiteness of the snow', he appears to be hurtling towards death. Imaginatively, emotionally, it seems he is dying; and yet, according to other textual detail – and the simple, logical fact that he is narrating the story – he would appear to be alive. Poe tears the Gothic tale out of the rationalist framework it previously inhabited, with accompanying gestures towards common sense, science or explanation. And he makes it a medium for exploring the irrational, even flirting with the anti-rational. As such, he makes it as central and vital to the Romantic tradition as, say, the lyric poem or the dream play.

'The Fall of the House of Usher' shows how Poe makes a fictional art out of inwardness and instability. The narrator, an initially commonsensical man, is confused by his feelings when he first arrives at the home of his childhood friend, Roderick Usher. 'What was it', he asks himself, 'that so unnerved me in the contemplation of the House of Usher?' But he is inclined to dismiss such feelings as 'superstition'; and, even when he is reunited with Usher, his response is 'half of awe', suggesting a suspicion that his host might know things hidden to him, and 'half of pity', suggesting the superiority of the rational man. Gradually, the narrator comes to speak only of 'awe'. He even admits that he feels 'the wild influences' of Usher's 'fantastic yet impressive superstitions' 'creeping upon' him. The scene is set for the final moment, when Roderick's sister Madeline arises from her grave to be reunited with him in death, and the House of Usher sinks into a 'deep and dank tarn'. At this precise moment, Usher turns to the narrator and speaks to him, for the last time, addressing him as '*Madman*'. The reversal is now complete: either because the narrator has succumbed to the 'superstition' of his host, or because his continued rationality argues for his essential insanity, his failure to comprehend a truth that lies beyond reason. Nothing is certain as the tale closes, except that what we have witnessed is an urgent, insistent movement inward: from daylight reality towards darker, ever more subterranean levels, in the house and in the mind of the hero. And as the narrator moves ever further inward, into 'Usher' the house, we the readers move ever further inward into 'Usher' the fiction. The structures of the two journeys correspond. So, for that matter, do the arts of the hero and author: Roderick Usher uses his to transform his guests' minds and expectations, so also does Poe with his imaginative guests. And at the moment of revelation at the end – when the full measure of the solipsistic vision is revealed – both 'Usher' the house and 'Usher' the tale disintegrate, disappear, leaving narrator and reader alone with their thoughts and surmises. In short, the house of Usher is a house of mirrors. Every feature of the story is at once destabilizing and self-reflexive, referring us back to the actual process of creative production, by its author, and reproduction, by its readers. Like so many other tales by Poe, 'The Fall of the House of Usher' stands at the beginning of a long line of Southern narratives that incline towards narcissism and nostalgia, the movement inward and the movement back. It stands at the beginning, also, of an even longer line of fiction, American and European, that disconcerts the reader by jettisoning the mundane in favour of the magical, bare fact in favour of mysterious fantasy – and turning the literal world into a kind of shadow play.

Poe had, perhaps, his own reasons for wanting to turn the world into shadow play, and for associating women with death. His own mother had died when he was only two, which was why he went to live with the Allans; and, in 1847, his young wife Virginia died after a long, debilitating and painful illness. Even during his more successful periods – when, for instance, 'The Raven' was published in 1844 and became an overnight success – he was haunted by feelings of insecurity and inadequacy, reasonless fears that nothing seemed to diminish. In his last few years, he remained prolific: in 1848, he published, among other things, a long philosophical work, *Eureka*, and in 1849 he wrote one of his best-known poems, 'Annabel Lee'. But he was finding it increasingly difficult to place his work. Suffering from periodic attacks of what he called 'brain fever', or temporary mental instability, Poe turned for comfort to a series of relationships with women much older than himself, and to the simpler, chemical release offered by alcohol and opium. Nothing, however, seemed to relieve him; he attempted suicide. Then, in 1849, he disappeared in Baltimore on a journey; he was discovered five days later, in a delirious condition and wearing someone else's clothes. He never recovered enough to explain what he had been doing; he simply died four days after this. It was like one of his own stories; and, bizarre and disconcerting though it was, it seems an appropriate end for a writer who thrived on mystery, viewed life as a masquerade and death as a voyage into another, truer world. As we look at the story of Poe's forty years, we can see certain experiences and obsessions emerging to haunt his writing and aesthetic: death and beauty, alienation and subterfuge, loss and despair. What is perhaps more marked, however, is not this or that particular theme but a guiding impulse: the living and the writing show us someone who by sheer effort of will transforms everything he inhabits, who dissolves the sights and sounds of the world just as he touches them. Poe turned personality into performance, poetry and story into a series of ghostly gestures; in the process, he marked out boundaries for American Romanticism and its succeeding movements that few writers have been able, or even perhaps dared, to cross.

Legends of the Old Southwest

Straddling the borders between the myth of the West and the myth of the South are those heroes and writers who are associated with the humour and legends of the Old Southwest. As for heroes, the notable figures here are Davy Crockett (1786–1836) and Mike Fink (1770?–1823?). Crockett spent a shiftless youth until his political career began when he was thirty. Serving in Congress from 1827 to 1831, and from 1833 to 1835, he was quickly adopted by Whig politicians, opposing the populist hero Andrew Jackson, who saw in Crockett a useful tool for associating their party with backwoods democracy. Davy, who boasted that he relied on 'natural-born sense instead of law learning', was soon turned by skilful politicians into a frontier hero, whose picturesque eccentricities, country humour, tall tales, shrewd native wit and rowdy pioneer spirit were all magnified and celebrated. With the help of a ghost writer, Crockett wrote *A Narrative of the Life of David Crockett, of the State of Tennessee* (1834): a book clearly designed to help him gain or retain political popularity. But soon after that, tales of the legendary frontiersman had begun to spread, by word of mouth, songs and poems, almanacs (known as Crockett Almanacs), and by such publications as *The Lion of the West* (1831) by James Kirke Paulding, *Sketches and Eccentricities of Colonel David Crockett of West Tennessee* (1833) by Mathew St Claire Clarke (1798–1842?) and *An Account of Colonel Crockett's Tour to the North and Down East* (1835). In some of these publications, Crockett may have had a hand; in many, he did not. And when he died at the Alamo in 1836, even more life was given to the legend. Davy Crockett became, more and more, a larger than life figure whose exploits, a mixture of the comic and the legendary, turned him into an embodiment of the rough spirit and even rougher individualism of the frontier. In one story, 'Sunrise in His Pocket', which appeared first in one of the posthumous almanacs, Davy tells a tall tale of how he got the sun moving again after it had 'got jammed between two cakes o' ice'. His solution to the problem was to take 'a fresh twenty-pound bear' he had been carrying on his back, 'and beat the animal agin the ice till the hot ile began to walk out on him at all sides'. Pouring 'about a ton on't over the sun's face', he got the sun loose; then, Crockett says, concluding his brag, 'I lit my pipe by the blaze o' his top-knot, shouldered my bear, an' walked home, introducin' people to the fresh daylight with a piece of sunrise in my pocket'. Simultaneously beautiful and tongue-in-cheek, swaggering and comic, the story captures nicely the rough pride of the hero of these stories and his refusal to take himself too seriously.

As an actual historical figure, less is known of Mike Fink than of Crockett. He was a keelboatman on the Ohio and Mississippi. Before that, he had worked as Crockett had, as an Indian scout; and, when he left the river, he moved west to become a trapper. It was on the river, however, that his violence, humour and energy made him a legend. He evidently helped to foster that legend by telling tales about himself, but it was others who wrote the tales down, among them the newspapermen Thomas Bangs Thorpe (1810–56) and Joseph M. Field (1815–78). The stories about Fink appeared in books, the earliest of which was *The Last of the Boatmen* by Morgan Neville published in 1829. They also appeared in magazines and newspapers, like the *Spirit of the Times*, which specialized in tales of the frontier and sporting sketches, and in almanacs – among them, the Crockett Almanacs, which did not confine themselves to the exploits of Davy. Perhaps the most famous piece of prose associated with Fink is 'Mike Fink's Brag', which achieved circulation around 1835–6. 'I'm a Salt River roarer! I'm a ring-tailed squealer!' Fink announces, in this extended celebration of himself:

> I'm a reg'lar screamer from the ol' Massassip! WHOOP! I'm the very infant that refused his milk before its eyes were open, and called out for a bottle of old Rye! I love the women an' I'm chockful o' fight! I'm half wild horse and half cock-eyed alligator and the rest o' me is crooked snags an' red-hot snappin' turtle . . . I ain't had a fight for two days an' I'm spilein' for exercise. Cock-a-doddle-do!

It captures perfectly the exuberance, the brute humour and animal vitality of the old frontier, and its absolute belief in itself.

Crockett and Fink inhabit an interesting borderland between 'popular' and 'high' culture, the political and the legendary, oral folk tradition and published literature. The first writer to make the legends and humour of the Old Southwest part of the literary tradition was Augustus Baldwin Longstreet (1790–1870). A Georgia lawyer and academic, Longstreet published *Georgia Scenes: Characters, Incidents &c, in the First Half-Century of the Republic* in 1835. In a series of sketches varying from the descriptive to the dramatic, Longstreet presented his readers with illustrations of life in the remoter parts of the state. The sketches were linked by the appearance in nearly all of them of a narrator bearing a suspicious resemblance to the author himself – a kindly, generous but occasionally pompous and patronizing man who tended to treat his subjects as if they were specimens of some strange form of life, with a mixture of curiosity and amusement. A healthy distance was maintained from characters who were presented not so much as individuals as in terms of their common behavioural patterns; and the combined effect of the detachment, the condescension and the generalizing tendency was to create an impression somewhere between folktale and caricature, legend and cartoon. One of the sketches, for example, 'The Fight', describes a country scrap in detail and then ends with a lengthy description of the two fighters' wounds. 'I looked and saw that Bob had entirely lost his left ear,' the narrator recalls, 'and a large piece from his left cheek.' 'Bill presented a hideous spectacle,' he goes on. 'About a third of his nose, at the lower extremity, was bit off, and his face so swelled that it was difficult to discover in it anything of the human visage.' The fighters did not meet after that for two months, we learn. They then made up, with Bill admitting, 'Bobby you've *licked* me a fair fight; but you wouldn't have done it if I hadn't been in the wrong'. The tale acknowledges the notions of rough justice embodied here, but it does not mitigate the brutality. And the narrator concludes by reassuring the, presumably genteel, reader that more refined habits and customs have now arrived. 'Thanks to the Christian religion, to schools, colleges, and benevolent associations,' he explains, 'such scenes of barbarism and cruelty as that which I have been describing are now of rare occurrence, though they may still be occasionally met with in some of the new counties.'

In the Preface to *Georgia Scenes*, Longstreet claimed proudly that he was filling in a 'chasm in history that has always been overlooked'; and 'The Fight' illustrates how he reconciled this claim with the demands of comedy. The tone of the description is humorous but the writer clearly hopes that, by means of his humour, he will show something significant about backwoods character: its simplicity, its rough energy, its notions of justice and its capacity for violence. The simplicity and the exaggeration that create the comic note are there, in effect, because they enable Longstreet to show what is different about people like Bob and Bill, and emphasize that at the expense of any qualities they may share, in a Wordsworthian sense, with the rest of humanity. Longstreet's probable motives for writing in this way were ones he shared with many other Southwestern humorists: among them, Joseph Glover Baldwin (1815–64), author of *The Flush Times of Alabama and Mississippi* (1853), Johnson Jones Hooper (1815–62), who wrote *Some Adventures of Captain Simon Suggs, Late of the Tallapoosa Volunteers* (1845), and Thomas Bangs Thorpe, whose stories about what he called 'a hardy and indomitable race' of frontier people were collected in *The Big Bear of Arkansas; and Other Sketches Illustrative of Character and Incidents in the South-West* (1845). As a professional gentleman and a Whig, Longstreet was inclined to nervousness about the crude habits of frontier life: a life characterized by what Baldwin, in *Flush Times*, called 'vulgarity – ignorance – unmitigated rowdyism . . . bullying insolence' and 'swindling raised to the dignity of the fine arts'. Violent, rowdy and anarchic, that life frightened anyone used to a more stable culture with habits of deference and respect. So, in an eminently understandable way, Longstreet and other Southwestern humorists attempted to distance their frontier surroundings, to place them in a framework that would make them manageable and known. They tried, in effect, to enclose and encode them. One way of doing this was via the humour: by its means, violence was transformed into play, social anarchy into curious spectacle, and fear and anxiety into mild amusement. Another way of doing it was via legend: they also tried to identify the rough, rude world they saw around them with a familiar rural type – the plain farmer, with his straightforward approach to things, his raw integrity and earthy language, and above all his muscular self-reliance. By *this* means, violence could be interpreted as an excess of high spirits and honest energy; apparent moral anarchy was metamorphosed into a reassertion of conventional principles; and the disruption of established social patterns could be regarded as a crucial step on the road to the recovery of a deeply traditional democratic ideal.

These two strategies were, of course, not wholly reconcilable. And if 'The Fight' illustrates the strategy of comedy, then another tale in *Georgia Scenes*, 'The "Charming Creature" as a Wife', illustrates the other approach. In the latter tale, the reader is told how the son of 'a plain, practical, sensible farmer' was ruined by marriage to the only child of a wealthy cotton merchant: a creature infected by what the narrator calls 'town dignity' – which involves an inordinate sense of her own worth, a preference for the glittering social world where she was brought up, and a failure to appreciate the 'order, neatness, and cleanness' of her husband's home and community. There is no doubt where the narrator's sympathies lie here. On every possible occasion, he criticizes or makes fun of the pretensions of the 'charming creature', her idleness and 'irregular hours', and her longing to return to the fashionable world of town. Eventually, she gets her way; the couple leave the simple, rural world she detests, and in their new urban surroundings the husband sinks melodramatically into debt, drunkenness, illness and an early grave. The story then ends with the narrator pointing the moral of his tale: which, unsurprisingly, has to do not only with the pretensions but with the dangers of all those known as 'charming creatures'. It is a rather different moral from the one drawn at the end of 'The Fight'. In that story, all that the nineteenth century associated with the word 'culture' – taste of a certain genteel kind, 'schools, colleges, and benevolent associations' – is held up for approval; it provides a convenient vantage point from which to look down on the 'barbarism and cruelty' of the frontier. In 'The "Charming Creature"', however, that very same culture is mocked – words like 'refinement' and 'fashionable' become terms of abuse – and the idea of the 'natural' becomes the touchstone. Both stories, and the morals that are drawn from them, spring from the same impulse, though: which is to contain the anarchy of the backwoods. In 'The Fight', it is acknowledged as anarchy but then placed in a narrative frame, to be viewed only sometimes and from a distance. In 'The "Charming Creature"', notions of anarchy and the backwoods setting are both changed utterly by the idiom Longstreet adopts, caught safely within the timeless framework of pastoralism. As amusing barbarian or as good, plain farmer, the frontiersman ceases to be a source of anxiety, a rough beast slouching towards the Southwest to be born; he becomes a remembrance of things past rather than the shape of things to come.

As time passed, though, the narrative enclosure in which Longstreet, Baldwin and other Southwestern humorists chose to pen their frontier subjects tended to dissolve. And with dramatic results: the work that certainly represents the culmination of Southwestern humour, *The Adventures of Huckleberry Finn*, shows that. Even before that, the abolition of the conventional narrative frame was a notable feature of the comic stories and tall tales of George Washington Harris (1814–69). Harris began writing about his backwoods hero, Sut Lovingood, as early as 1843, in pieces published in the *Spirit of the Times*. But it was not until after the Civil War, in 1867, that a full-length volume appeared, *Sut Lovingood: Yarns Spun by a Nat'ral Born Durn'd Fool. Warped and Wove For Public Wear*. Sut tells his own tales. And all those tales are guided by his belief that, as he puts it, 'Man was made a-pupus just to eat, drink, an' fur stayin' awake in the yearly part of the nites'. A native of rural Tennessee, Sut is a primitive or natural man: a man who stands on the periphery of conventional society and yet still offers significant comments on it. His life, circumscribed by the animal functions, is a continual drag on our own pretensions, about the nature of our personalities and the efficacy or security of the society we have organized for ourselves. At one point in his narrative, Sut admits that he has 'nara a soul, nuffin but a whisky proof gizzard'; and Harris's habitual strategy, of making us, the readers, share Sut's life and experience the connection between what he is and how he lives, leads us to suspect that in similar conditions we might be forced to say exactly the same.

Harris's intentions and techniques are, in effect, very different from those of Longstreet and the other humorists. They emphasize the difference between the world of the characters and the genteel world of the author and the presumed reader. Harris, by contrast, presents the reader with a kind of test case that paradoxically derives its impact, the sense of relevance to our lives, from the distance it establishes between the literate reader and the illiterate protagonist. Suppose, Harris intimates, we had been brought up in surroundings similar to those of Sut Lovingood: would we be that different from him? Would we not, perhaps, speak the same language, live on the same level; and, if we would, does this not undermine our pretensions – the belief in our dignity as God-given rather than acquired as a matter of special privilege? Sut Lovingood is detached from us, certainly – the use of an almost impenetrable dialect sees to that – but he is detached from us only in the way that a freakish mirror image of ourselves is. We watch him and, in doing so, witness a curious aping and a criticism of our own behaviour.

The criticism is all the more effective because of Harris's capacity for reminding us, in the middle of Sut's various scrapes, that his protagonist does have traces of what we like to call virtue, waiting for the right conditions to bring them to life. He shows pride and independence of judgement, for instance, qualities that lead him to consider himself 'the very best society' and to punish those he feels have insulted him in any way. More telling still is the ability Harris gives him for sensing who his enemies are, regardless of whether they have slighted him or not. They are, he realizes, the preachers and the pedagogues, the politic and educated leaders of society who are there not simply to supply a butt for Sut's fooling, although they certainly do that, but to remind us of the kind of people – people like ourselves, the readers, perhaps – who are indirectly responsible for his condition. For their privileges, the suggestion is, have been bought at his expense; they, and maybe we, are the beneficiaries of a system from which he is excluded and by which he is deprived. The mirror is being held up to the readers as a group, in other words, as well as to the reader as an individual. We see in Sut Lovingood a reflection of possibilities existing in ourselves – and we are forced to acknowledge our complicity in the creation of circumstances that, in Sut's case, have translated possibility into fact. Just in case we should continue to miss the point, denying Sut a germ of sensitivity even after all this, there are moments in the narrative when more energetic hints of his potential are allowed to appear. Instead of a reference to some dormant virtue, the reader is confronted with a passage of lyric beauty – not denying the comic framework but actually growing out of it – that serves as a reminder of all those aspects of Sut Lovingood's character that mostly remain unexercised. In one striking episode, for instance, Sut waxes lyrical about a mealtime. In a long passage, he describes in loving detail a supper that, he recalls, was like 'a rale suckit-rider's supper, whar the 'oman 'ove the hous' wer a rich b'lever'. An evocative catalogue of all the food laid out on the table is followed by a description of the woman who has cooked it all, for Sut and her husband, that combines eroticism and domesticity. 'Es we sot down, the las' glimmers ove the sun crep thru the histed winder,' Sut recollects,

> an' flutter'd on the white tabil-cloth and play'd a silver shine on her smoof black har, es she sot at the head ove the tabil, a-pourin out the coffee, wif her sleeves push'd tight back on her white roun' arm, her full throbbin neck wer bar to the swell ove her shoulders, an' the steam ove the coffee made a movin vail afore her face, es she slowly brush'd hit away wif her lef han', a-smilin an' flashin her talkin eyes lovingly at her hansum husbun.

The occasion being described here is mundane enough, certainly, but what matters is all that Harris allows his protagonist to make out of it. Sut, the reader is forced to recognize, has a sensitivity – a capacity for recognizing the sensuous beauty and the value of a particular experience – which will emerge at the least opportunity, although too often it is left to waste unrecognized. The waste is articulated elsewhere in the narrative, in the scenes of comic violence and degeneracy that illustrate the actual conditions of his existence. Here there is something different: an instinctive insight, and wisdom, that align Sut with the ideal of the natural man. Sut voices a vision, for and of himself, and, at such moments, he is more than just a comic legend. He is one of the first in a long line of American vernacular heroes, who compel the reader to attend because, the sense is, no matter how poor, stupid or peripheral they may appear to be, they and what they have to say deserve attention.

The Making of American Selves

The Transcendentalists

'Our age is retrospective,' wrote Ralph Waldo Emerson (1803–82) at the beginning of perhaps his most famous work, *Nature* (1836). 'It builds the sepulchres of the fathers. It writes biographies, histories, and criticism,' he continued. 'The foregoing generations beheld God and nature face to face, through their eyes. Why should we not also enjoy an original relation to the universe?' An original relation to the universe, one founded on self-reliance and self-respect, is the key to the thought and work of Emerson. It also inspired a number of other writers at the time who saw the liberation of the self as the American imperative. With Emerson, the inspiration came after he resigned his position as a Unitarian minister in 1832. He sailed to Europe, where he met Samuel Taylor Coleridge and William Wordsworth and began a lifelong friendship with Thomas Carlyle. Through them, he became intimately associated with transcendental thought and its sources in German idealism. Later, Emerson also encountered the influence of the sacred books of the East, the traditions of Plato and neo-Platonism, and the line of British philosophy that ran through John Locke, Bishop Berkeley and David Hume. All these influences served to confirm, and enrich, his growing belief in the supreme importance of the individual, the superiority of intuition to intellect (or, as Emerson was to put it, of 'Reason' to 'Understanding'), and the presence of a spiritual power in both nature and the individual human being. 'If we live truly,' Emerson was to write in 'Self-Reliance' (1841), 'we shall see truly.' And he dedicated himself to living and writing the truth as he saw it. He had been keeping a journal since he was a student at Harvard, in which he recorded his daily experiences and impressions, the facts of his life. He was to continue this practice until he died; and the facts he recorded there became the source of the truths he endeavoured to develop in his essays and poems. From these were to be drawn pieces such as the 'Divinity School Address' (1838) and 'The Over-Soul' (1841), in which he rejected institutional forms of religion in favour of his belief that 'God incarnates himself in man'. For Emerson, as for many of the poets and philosophers on whom he drew, nature was a manifestation of the spirit. There was a pervasive spiritual presence, which he called the Over-Soul, from which all things emanate. Each individual, along with all creation, drew their own soul, the divine spark of their inner being, from this source: each was at once a singular self, an utterly unrepeatable, unique being and an integral part of the entire rhythm and pulse of nature. 'The heart in thee is the heart of all,' as Emerson put it in 'The Over-Soul'; 'not a valve, not a wall, not an intersection is there anywhere in nature, but one blood rolls uninterruptedly an endless circulation through all men, as the water of the globe is all one sea and, truly seen, its tide is one.'

Returning to the United States, Emerson began to lecture regularly on the lyceum circuit, to spread his ideas as well as to make a living. He settled in Concord, Massachusetts, in 1835, where he became intimate friends with other writers like

Nathaniel Hawthorne, Henry David Thoreau, Bronson Alcott, and Margaret Fuller. It was here that the movement known as Transcendentalism, gathered around his ideas, took shape; and it was here also, at Emerson's home and elsewhere, that meetings of the Transcendental Club were to be held during the seven or eight years following 1836 – a group, known among its own members as the Symposium or the Hedge Club, that met together occasionally and informally to discuss philosophy, theology and literature. Emerson himself was to become involved in the publication of the Transcendentalist quarterly magazine, *The Dial*, in 1840, assuming the post of editor in 1842, but it was in his lectures and essays that his creed of self-help and self-emancipation was most fully developed and most widely disseminated. Many volumes of essays and poems were to be published by him during the course of his life. They include *Essays* (1841), *Essays: Second Series* (1844), *Poems* (1847), *Representative Men* (1850), *English Traits* (1856), *The Conduct of Life* (1860), *May-Day and Other Pieces* (a second collection of poems [1867]) and *Society and Solitude* (1870). The core of his beliefs, and of the Transcendentalist creed, can, however, be found in a half dozen pieces: 'The American Scholar' (1837), 'Divinity School Address', 'Self-Reliance', 'The Over-Soul', 'The Poet' (1844) – and, above all, *Nature*.

At the heart of *Nature* is an intense commitment to the power and wonder of nature and the individual and to the indelible, intimate character of the connection between the two. The self-reliance that Emerson embraced was not selfishness: since, as he saw it, to be true to the true self was to be true to the self, the spirit present in all human beings, all nature. To obey the promptings of the soul was to obey those of the Over-Soul. 'Every real man must be a nonconformist,' Emerson insisted: but nonconformity meant going against the superficial dictates of society, not pursuing the grosser forms of self-interest and egotism. 'Standing on the bare ground – my head bathed by the blithe air, and uplifted into infinite space, – all mean egotism vanishes,' Emerson declares in the first chapter of *Nature*. 'I become a transparent eyeball; I am nothing; I see all; the currents of the Universal Being circulate through me; I am part or particle of God.' For Emerson here, as for William Blake in *America, A Prophecy* (1793), 'everything that lives is holy, life delights in life'; and to be in communion with oneself, at the deepest level, is to be in touch with what Emerson goes on to call the 'uncontained and immortal beauty' that runs through the veins of everything around us. 'In the tranquil landscape, and especially in the distant line of the horizon,' Emerson suggests, 'man beholds somewhat as beautiful as his own nature,' supplying wonder and instruction, the sense that in descending into his true self he is escaping not only from society but also from his baser, superficial self. Not that Emerson neglects the material life in all this. On the contrary, in *Nature* he begins with commodity before turning to spirit: in the first instance, what Emerson considers in the relationship between human nature and nature is the circumstantial dimension, the uses and practical conquest of our surroundings. 'Beasts, fire, water, stores, and corn serve him,' Emerson observes of man in this context. 'The field is at once his floor, his workyard, his play-ground, his garden, and his bed.' This is the element in Emersonian thought, particularly, that some of his contemporaries and subsequent generations were to distrust. Herman Melville, for example, was reading Emerson when he was composing *Moby-Dick*; and, almost certainly, when he drew his portrait of Captain Ahab, he was offering a critique of that element in Emersonian individualism that assumed power over nature and supplied a rationale for endless growth and expansionism. But, for Emerson, use did not mean exploitation. And, while he admitted that practical use was 'the only use of nature that all men apprehend', he was careful to point out that it was easily the least important. The practical use of nature, as Emerson puts it, 'is a benefit which is temporary and mediate, not ultimate, like its service to the soul'.

The service to the soul offered by nature was, as Emerson saw it, aesthetic, intellectual and, above all, moral. As for the aesthetic, Emerson shared with Coleridge, the English Romantic poets and the German idealist philosophers the belief that each individual can order his or her environment into a harmonious whole. 'There is a property in the horizon which no man has but he whose eye can integrate all the parts, that is, the poet,' Emerson insists in *Nature*. And just as the poet or artist takes a scene and then rearranges it into a harmony of words or colour, so every person, in the act of seeing, can take a scene and rearrange it into harmony in their soul, or mind. Everyone can be a poet of deed, if not of word. As for the intellectual, that service granted to man by nature is summed up in three propositions: '1. Words are signs of natural facts. 2. Particular natural facts are symbols of particular spiritual facts. 3. Nature is the symbol of spirit.' Developing the beliefs of his Puritan forefathers, Emerson was as convinced as they were that every literal fact or event had a spiritual significance. So, in constructing and using an accurate language – that is, a language that cleaves as closely as possible to facts and events – we are sticking closely not only to the literal but also to spiritual truth. When a person or a society uses words that are directly related to the particularities of nature, they are dealing as exactly as possible with the particularities of that spiritual presence that circulates through both nature and human nature. An exact language, in short, is a vital moral instrument. From this, it follows that there is an inevitable connection between the vitality or debility of any language and the health or sickness of the person, or the society, using that language. It is a matter not so much of cause and effect as of correspondence, interdependence; and a measure of the moral decline of anyone or any community is the progressive deterioration of the words being used, as words become less directly and vitally related to natural, and therefore moral, facts. One consequence of this, for Emerson, was the pivotal importance of the poet in any culture. Poets, as he saw it, were 'liberating gods' because they could devise an accurate language. They could establish, or restore, the vital connection between words and facts, and so promote understanding of those truths on which a culture – and the individuals who made it up – depended for their moral survival. This explains why, in his essay on 'The Poet', Emerson said that he waited with impatience for a truly American poet. 'We have yet had no genius in America,' he explained, 'with tyrannous eye, which knew the value of our incomparable materials, and saw, in the barbarism and materialism of the times, another carnival of the same gods whose picture he so much admires in Homer.' For Emerson, poets were crucial to the language and moral life of society; an American poet was needed to enable Americans to speak truly of themselves and their culture.

For Emerson, though, the most fundamental service of nature was moral. 'The Universe is the externization of the soul,' he insisted. Nature is a product and emblem of the spirit, the Over-Soul; the true self or soul of each individual is divinely connected to it, operating according to the same rhythms and laws; so each individual, in beholding and meditating on nature, can intuit those rhythms and learn those laws. 'Every natural process is a version of a moral sentence,' Emerson tells the reader in *Nature*. 'The moral law lies at the centre of nature and radiates to the circumference. It is the pith and marrow of every substance, every relation, and every process. All things with which we deal preach to us.' The style here is characteristic. There is no visible logic to the argument. What Emerson does is to try to possess the idea by attacking it from different directions, to locate the heart or kernel of the matter by inserting various intellectual and verbal probes into its shell. The result is a series of gnomic statements, a rhetorical pattern of repetition with variation. Emerson was not a philosopher but a moralist and a writer of *pensées*; and what the *pensées* or nuggets of thought cluster around here is the notion that nature could and should be our guide, our moral teacher. The fact that Emerson was a moralist rather than a philosopher has one further, interesting consequence in *Nature*. Towards the end, he dismisses the Enlightenment debate over whether the world we perceive is really there or is only the product of our sense impressions. We cannot know, Emerson insists, and it does not matter. What matters is the moral consequences of nature for us. 'Whether nature enjoy a substantial existence without, or is only in the apocalypse of the mind,' he explains, 'it is alike useful and alike venerable to me.' Either way, it can discipline and enlighten the soul.

The belief Emerson retained throughout his life in what he called 'the wonderful congruity which subsists between man and the world' could sometimes have worrying consequences. He was unwilling, for example, seriously to contemplate the existence of evil. What we may take to be evil is simply the result of our partial vision, he argued, our dependence on the superficial claims of the false self. 'The ruin or the blank, that we see when we look at nature, is in our own eye,' he explains in *Nature*. 'The axis of vision is not coincident with the axis of things, and so they appear not transparent but opaque.' Emerson himself distinguished between what he called the Party of Hope and the Party of Memory among his contemporaries: the one committed to the possibilities of the future, the other wedded to the imperfections and failures of the past. And it is quite clear that Emerson saw himself as a member of the Party of Hope. This had questionable aspects for those, like Hawthorne and Melville, of a darker, more sceptical frame of mind. But it also had more unambiguously positive ones. In 'The American Scholar', for instance, which Oliver Wendell Holmes called 'Our intellectual Declaration of

Independence', Emerson exhorted his audience to turn from imitation to originality. 'We have listened too long to the courtly muses of Europe,' he insists. And what the American scholar must do is become 'Man Thinking' in the present, pushing beyond convention and institutions to learn not from books but directly from life. 'Life is our dictionary', Emerson declares, offering the scholar direct rather than mediated access to the real. From this, it follows that everything in life is a source of knowledge, even the humblest, everyday subject or event. 'I am not for the great, the remote, the romantic; what is doing in Italy or Arabia; what is Greek art or Provençal minstrelsy,' he announces. 'I embrace the common, I explore and sit at the feet of the familiar, the low.' From this, it also follows that everyone can be a gatherer of knowledge, a scholar. The sources of knowledge are everywhere and are accessible to anyone who cares to attend. Americans can all be American scholars. Or, as Emerson puts it, 'a nation of men will for the first time exist, because each man believes himself inspired by the Divine Soul which also inspires all men'. There will be a genuine democracy, of men thinking, corresponding to the democracy of facts.

Emerson's belief in individuality led naturally not only to a commitment to democratic equality but to a conviction that life was process. 'Nature is not fixed but fluid,' he said. Change is at the root of existence, change in human beings as well as nature; and so, 'a foolish consistency is the hobgoblin of little minds'. This had vital consequences for Emerson's poetry. 'It is not metres, but a metre-making argument that makes a poem,' he insisted in 'The Poet', 'a thought so passionate and alive, that, like the spirit of a plant or an animal, it has an architecture of its own, and adorns nature with a new thing.' For Emerson, poetry had to be as 'free, peremptory, and clear' as its subject and creator, it had to be original and organic rather than imitative ('Imitation is suicide,' he tells the reader in 'Self-Reliance'); it had, in short, to dramatize the liberated self. As the supreme creative power, illuminating and transforming all that comes in its orbit, the self is placed at the centre of Emerson's poems. The stylistic result is something often close to free verse. As poet, Emerson does accept the preliminary discipline of a particular rhyme and rhythm scheme, but he never lets that scheme inhibit his patterns of speech and thought. He allows himself to vary lines and metres at will, irregularity and disruption are permitted, as long as the basic sense of rhythmic speech – a speech coming directly from the primitive and oracular self – is retained. 'The rhyme of the poet / Modulates the King's affairs /', Emerson declares in 'Merlin' (1847), and then goes on in such a way as to illustrate as well as celebrate the liberating spontaneity of true poetry:

> Balance-loving Nature
> Made all things in pairs
> To every foot its antipode
> Each color with its counter glowed;
> To every tone beat answering tones,
> Higher or graver.

More notable still is the effect of the ethic of self-reliance on the actual, material and moral, landscapes Emerson describes. In poem after poem, the self is shown recreating the world, transforming it into something freshly seen and fully discovered. In 'The Snow-Storm' (1847), for instance, the poetic vision reshapes the scene just as 'the frolic architecture of the snow' is described refashioning familiar objects into fresh and unfamiliar shapes. And in poems like 'Uriel' (1847) and 'Merlin', the poet is translated into an incarnation of God, whose acts of seeing and naming correspond with His original act of making the world. In effect, Emerson puts into practice here the belief he expressed in *Nature* and elsewhere that the poet does in words what everyone can do in action: that is, remake and reorder their surroundings – so achieving what Coleridge in *Biographia Literaria* (1817) called 'a repetition in the finite mind of the eternal act of Creation in the infinite I AM'. Emerson never ceased to believe in what he called the 'infinitude of the private'. Although, in his later work, there is a growing emphasis on the difficulties of knowledge, the limitations imposed by 'fate' and the intimidating vastness of nature, he remained firmly convinced of the authority of the individual. He stayed loyal to the idea that every person had the power to shape and change things: which is one reason why, in the 1850s, he became involved in the movement to abolish slavery. 'Life only avails, not the having lived,' he wrote in 'Self-Reliance'. 'Power ceases in the instant of repose; it resides in the moment of transition from a past to a new state, in the shooting of the gulf, in the darting to an aim.' As Emerson saw it, the permanent principles of the spiritual life were incarnated in the flux and processes of nature and the constantly changing life of the individual. To live according to those laws was to live in the present, with respect for others but without timidity or apology, in the knowledge that the final judge of any person resided in the self.

Those who pursued the Transcendentalist creed included Theodore Parker (1810–60), who managed to remain a Unitarian minister while active in the Transcendental Club, and Bronson Alcott (1799–1888), who tried to establish a cooperative community based on Transcendentalist principles at 'Fruitlands', at Harvard – it failed after only seven months. Emerson did not approve of this cooperative venture. Nor did he like another, more famous communal enterprise that lasted rather longer, from 1841 to 1847. This was Brook Farm, the cooperative community set up under George Ripley (1802–80) nine miles outside Boston. Among those interested in the venture were Nathaniel Hawthorne, who actually lived there and wrote about it in *The Blithedale Romance* (1852), Orestes Brownson (1803–76), Elizabeth Peabody (1804–94), Alcott and Parker, and the person who, apart from Thoreau and Emerson himself, is now the most famous and remembered member of the Transcendental Club, Margaret Fuller (1810–50). Fuller was educated by her father, who subjected her to a rigorous regime: by the age of eight, she was reading Ovid. When her family moved to Cambridge, Massachusetts, in the early 1830s, she met most of those central to the Transcendentalist movement. Forced to support herself when her father died, she took up teaching for a while in Rhode Island. But in 1838 she returned to the Boston area, began working as a translator, edited *The*

Dial for two years, and from 1839 to 1844 ran a series of conversational classes at the home of Elizabeth Peabody. The classes were originally for women. Believing that women had previously been educated for domesticity and adornment, Fuller designed 'Conversations' to guide and draw the class members out, to make them think for and realize the potential within themselves. They were so successful, however, that Fuller was eventually obliged to admit men. Between classes, in 1843, Fuller found time to tour the Midwest. The result of the trip was her first book, *Summer on the Lakes in 1843* (1844), which she described as a 'poetic impression of the country at large'. What is notable about the book is the sympathy its author shows for the plight of the vanished Indians and, even more, the white women of the region. 'They may blacken Indian life as they will,' Fuller writes of her visit to the former site of an ancient Indian village, 'talk of its dirt, its brutality, I will ever believe that the men who chose that dwelling-place were able to feel emotions of noble happiness as they returned to it, and so were the women who received them.' As for the white women, 'the wives of the poorer settlers', Fuller observes that they, 'having more hard work to do than before, very frequently become slatterns'. The wealthier women, in turn, suffer from a mistaken attempt to imitate and inculcate Eastern standards. They struggle to pursue domestic routines and standards of general refinement utterly inappropriate to their surroundings. They 'lament the want of "education" for their daughters, as if the thousand needs which call out their young energies, and the language of nature around, yielded no education'. And, at the first opportunity, they send their daughters to school in some Eastern city, from which the young women return utterly unequipped to deal with 'the wants of the place and time'.

Not long after returning from the West, Fuller went to work for Horace Greeley (1811–72) at the *New-York Tribune*. Greeley, whose main claim to fame now is as the coiner of the phrase 'Go West, Young Man!', had become interested in Fuller after reading *Summer on the Lakes*. And he offered to publish her next book. Fuller obliged by revising and expanding an essay she had written for *The Dial* into what is undoubtedly her most famous work, *Woman in the Nineteenth Century* (1845). The book is written in a rhetorical style similar to that of Emerson and draws its inspiration from the Emersonian and Transcendentalist belief in self-reliance and self-emancipation. 'The gain of creation consists always in the growth of individual minds, which live and aspire,' Fuller declares in the 'Preface'. What gives it its originality and impact is that Fuller, insisting that individualism and liberty are indivisible, applies the idea of self-development to 'the woman question'. The law of freedom, she argues, 'cannot fail of universal recognition'. Linking the cause of female emancipation to the abolition of slavery, she attacks all those who would try to reduce people to property, black or female, or insist that they have to be limited to a particular 'sphere'. It is 'the champions of the enslaved African', Fuller points out, who have made 'the warmest appeal in behalf of Women'. This is partly because many abolitionists are, in fact, women, she explains, and see in the plight of the people whose cause they embrace a reflection of their own plight and problem. But it is also because, at the moment, neither is allowed the power and prerogatives of an adult. 'Now there is no woman,' Fuller remarks bitterly, 'only an overgrown child.'

'What Woman needs,' Fuller writes, 'is not as a woman to act or rule, but as a nature to grow, as an intellect to discern, as a soul to live freely and unimpeded, to unfold such powers as were given her when we left our common home.' But, at present, she is stopped from doing this. 'Every path', Fuller suggests, should be 'laid open to Woman as freely as to Man', and 'as a *right*, not . . . as a concession'. 'If the negro be a soul, if the woman be a soul, apparelled in the flesh, to one master only they are accountable'; and that master is certainly not man. *Woman in the Nineteenth Century* makes wry fun of all those men who would claim that women are too weak and delicate for public duty but 'by no means . . . think it impossible for the negresses to endure field work, even during pregnancy, or the seamstresses to go through their killing labours'. And, characteristic of its author, it places emphasis on education as an enabler, a determining influence that can lead women to 'self-dependence' and 'self-reliance'. The use of Emersonian principles is particularly noticeable here, as Fuller explains how a proper education can allow a woman to 'naturally develope self-respect, and learn self-help'. If a woman wants eventually to confine herself to the domestic sphere, she acknowledges, that is fine – 'we have a high respect for those . . . who create and preserve fair order in houses' – but that should not be the only sphere open to her. On the contrary, everything that is open to men, in education and after, should be open to women. Fuller may admit the existence of 'masculine' and 'feminine' qualities, a series of dualisms gathered around 'Energy and Harmony', 'Power and Beauty', 'Intellect and Love'. What seems like a surrender to gender stereotypes, however, turns out to be precisely the reverse. There may be an 'especially feminine element', Fuller argues, 'but it is no more the order of nature that it should be incarnated pure in any form, than that the masculine energy should exist unmingled with it in any form'. There are no roles that are specific to one gender or the other, because 'male and female represent the two sides of the great radical dualism' that are 'perpetually passing into one another'. Like Emerson, Fuller envisions a world of flux, process, interpenetration where 'fluid hardens to solid, solid rushes to fluid'. So, 'there is no wholly masculine man, no purely feminine woman'.

The imperative of education is one that Fuller sees as primary. She also sees it as one that women will have to pursue for themselves. Men, she argues, have habitually kept women weak and circumscribed; it is hardly to be expected that they will now see the error of their ways and work to make women strong and free. 'At present,' Fuller explains to her readers, 'women are the best helpers of one another.' 'We only ask of men to remove arbitrary barriers', she declares; and it will then be up to women to move towards 'self-subsistence in its two forms of self-reliance and self-impulse'. 'I wish Woman to live, *first* for God's sake,' Fuller insists. 'Then she will not make an imperfect man her god, and thus sink into idolatry.' If she develops properly, finding her true vocation, whatever that may be, then 'she will know how to love, and be worthy of being loved'. What Fuller anticipates, eventually, is a partnership of equals, a time 'when Man and Woman may regard one another as brother and sister, the pillars of one porch, the priests of one worship'. In *Summer on the Lakes*, Fuller writes of how, when contemplating the vastness of the Midwest, she felt elated and proud. 'I think,' she reveals, 'I had never felt so happy that I was born in America.' Now, in *Woman in the Nineteenth Century*, a similarly patriotic feeling inspires her as she contemplates the possibility of a new dispensation, a new and better relation between the sexes, in the New World. 'I have believed and intimated that this hope' for an equal partnership 'would receive an ampler fruition, than ever before, in our own land', she informs the reader. 'And it will do so if this land carry out the principles from which sprang our national life.' In later life, Fuller did not confine herself to the woman question: as a reporter and reviewer, she turned her attention to such diverse issues as the abolition of slavery, capital punishment, the treatment of immigrants and the ill. Nor did she restrict herself to the rights of Americans: by 1847, she had taken up residence in Rome and become involved in the revolutionary movements sweeping across Europe. Nevertheless, it is for her passionate commitment to the liberation of women that she is remembered today, and for her belief that the opportunities for such a liberation were greatest in the country of her birth. For her, the promise of the Declaration of Independence, and the principles of Transcendentalism, really did inspire the conviction that it was in America that the life of woman was likeliest to be 'beautiful, powerful', as she put it, 'in a word, a complete life of its kind'.

'I know of no more encouraging fact,' wrote Henry David Thoreau (1817–62) in *Walden, or Life in the Woods* (1854), 'than the unquestionable ability of man to elevate his life by a conscious endeavour.' That was not only the creed that Thoreau preached in his writings, along with Emerson, Fuller and the other Transcendentalists. It was also the creed that he embraced, and tried to follow, in his life. Elsewhere in *Walden*, Thoreau makes the distinction between 'professors of philosophy' and 'philosophers'. 'There are nowadays professors of philosophy,' he confides to the reader. 'Yet it is admirable to profess because it was once admirable to live.' 'To be a philosopher,' Thoreau suggests, 'is not merely to have subtle thoughts, nor even to found a school, but so to love wisdom as to live according to its dictates, a life of simplicity, independence, magnanimity, and trust.' It might seem unfair to claim that Thoreau is measuring here the difference between Emerson and himself. Emerson tried to live according to the principles he preached. And, in any event, he was of immeasurable help to Thoreau, practically as well as philosophically. Emerson played intellectual master, Thoreau the disciple. But Emerson also provided Thoreau with work and lodging, encouraged him to keep the journal from which his books were made, and, seminally, provided his Walden acres for Thoreau to dwell in even though he did not approve of what Thoreau was doing. Nevertheless, Thoreau did try to live according to the dictates of Transcendentalism to an extent and with an intensity that Emerson never managed. 'I went to the woods,' Thoreau explains in *Walden*,

> because I wished to live deliberately, to front only the essential facts of life, and see
> if I could not learn what it had to teach, and not, when I came to die, discover that

I had not lived. I did not wish to live what was not life, living is so dear; nor did I wish to practice resignation, unless it was quite necessary. I wanted to live deep and suck out all the marrow of life, to live so sturdily and Spartan-like as to put to rout all that was not life, to cut a broad swathe and shove close, to drive life into a corner, and reduce it to its lowest terms, and, if it proved mean, why then to get the whole and genuine meanness of it, and publish its meanness to the world; or if it were sublime, to know it by experience, and to be able to give a true account of it.

The sheer repetition of 'life', 'live' and its variants alerts us to Thoreau's commitment here, his dedication to testing principles in practice and turning ideas into action. So does the energy, the muscularity of the prose. Far more than his teacher, Thoreau wanted to know how it felt to live and see truly: to experience that knowledge in the body, the senses, as well as understand it in the mind. He also wanted the reader to go with him on what he called his excursions into nature, and into himself. He does not simply instruct, as Emerson does, he makes us share the experience; while we read his books, vicariously, imaginatively, we join in his life.

Thoreau pursued a pattern of alternating entry and withdrawal in relation to society. He was educated in the woods near Concord but also at Concord Academy and Harvard. At college, he came under the sway of various teachers – the poet Jones Very instilled in him a lifelong passion for Greek, and for the metaphysical poets – but he was also known as an individualist and a rebel. After graduating, he taught school for a time with his brother John, following the principles of Bronson Alcott. And it was with John that, in 1839, he made a trip on the Concord and Merrimack Rivers. Later, while residing at Walden, he used the journals he had kept during the trip to produce his first book, *A Week on the Concord and Merrimack Rivers* (1849). In it, Thoreau appears for the first time as a living realization of Emerson's American Scholar: in his characteristic role, that is, of 'Man Thinking' on the move. The book also introduces the reader to Thoreau's distinctive style, which is essentially a rhythmic flow of description and apparent digression: a dramatic articulation of what appears to be spontaneous thought and intimate talk. The sudden, unexpected sound of a drum beating on the Merrimack, for instance, stimulates excited reflections on the links between man and the universe, music as 'thought coloured and curved, fluent and flexible', and on the ironic discrepancy between the magical character of the wind's music in the telegraph wires and the mundane nature of the financial news those wires are made to carry. 'I require of every writer', Thoreau was to say in *Walden*, 'a simple and sincere account of his own life'; and simplicity and sincerity were certainly his touchstones. But that should not blind us to the lyricism, the wit and panache of his writings. Like the great Romantics, Thoreau worked hard, and often artfully, to catch the casual rhythms of a mind in process – a mind that *is* process – and the moments of illumination to which its chancy, volatile movements lead.

When his brother John became fatally ill, in 1841, the school Henry had run with him was closed. Henry then lived with Emerson for ten years, serving as a general handyman. During this time, he became an intimate of the members of the

---

Transcendental Club, and contributed work to *The Dial*; he also developed his skills as a surveyor and botanist. A period working as a tutor on Staten Island was followed by a return to Concord; and it was on his return there that he went to live nearby Walden Pond from 4 July 1845 to 6 September 1847. Other Transcendentalists sought a communal life, at Fruitlands or Brook Farm, if they tried to live according to their principles. Characteristically, Thoreau chose to live alone, in a hut he built for himself. It was this sojourn in the woods that, several years later, Thoreau was to recreate in *Walden*, using the journals that, as a matter of habit now, he kept while he was there. Robert Frost was to call *Walden* his 'favourite poem'. Many other descriptions or generic titles have been applied to it: it has been called, among other things, an autobiography, a philosophical narrative, an ecological journal, a spiritual diary. It is, in a way, *sui generis*; it creates its own genre; it is unique. It is also typically American in its intense focus on the first person singular, the 'I' of the narrator and author (and, in fact, its elision of narrator and author); its blend of fact and fiction, personal experience and broader reflection; and its intimacy and immediacy, the sense of a confessional raised to the level of art. *Walden*, in short, is one of the many great American books to which Walt Whitman's remark, 'Who touches this book, touches a man', could act as an epigraph: because, like them, it is the utterly unrepeatable expression of the author, in a particular place and at a particular point in time. Its uniqueness, in the American context, *is* its typicality. It is, in other words, the expression of a culture committed to the idea that every person is being truly representative in being truly singular. And it belongs to a tradition of experiment, the pursuit of the personally unique and new: a tradition for which the cardinal sin is to sound like others – to imitate rather than innovate, and embrace conventional forms.

It was Alexis de Tocqueville who, in his *Democracy in America* (1835–40), observed that, in a democratic society, what the poet takes as his subject is the representative man he knows best: that is, 'himself alone'. He has no need to dwell on gods or princes, 'on legends or on traditions and memories of old days', since these neither embody nor express his culture. In a democracy, everyone does that. Every member of a democratic society enacts its ideals of individualism and equality, or rather should do so; and the poet simply attends to the hero, and the enactment of democratic ideas, with which he is most familiar. He announces the simple and seminal discovery, Tocqueville says, 'I have only to contemplate myself'. That is, of course, the discovery Thoreau makes in *Walden*. As Thoreau puts it, very early on in the book: 'I brag for humanity rather than for myself.' He pursues a universal, democratic possibility in trying to be true to the needs and dictates of his own being. The pursuit is essentially a dramatic one: he does not so much 'brag', in fact, as enact. The style and approach of *Walden* are both energetic and exploratory; the reader is challenged here, as elsewhere in Thoreau's work, by a language that is fluid, witty, vigorous – constantly testing propositions against the evidence and experience, with the help of metaphor, rhythm and pun. At one point, for instance, Thoreau describes the auctioning of the 'effects' or property of a church deacon after his death, 'for his life had not been ineffectual'. 'The evil that men do lives after them', he declares, playing on a famous quotation from the Shakespeare play, *Julius Caesar*. And, in this case, we infer, the 'evil' happened to be the deacon's possessions, and the materialism, the thirst for acquisition they clearly express. Among those possessions was 'a dried tapeworm': a perfect image for suggesting how, devoted to material objects, commodities, a man may measure out his days and suck the blood, the real life, out of them. 'Instead of a *bonfire*, or purifying destruction' of all the detritus the deacon has accumulated, Thoreau reflects, 'there was an *auction*, or increasing of them'. And the witty play on the Latin root word for 'auction' (which literally means to augment, to increase) is followed by an even wittier renovation of a cliché. 'When a man dies,' Thoreau concludes, 'he kicks the dust.' The 'dust' here is plainly the effects spread among the buyers at the auction: the deacon has now scattered the contagion of his own materialism further. He has kicked others into the same slough of getting and spending, and acquiring, as himself. Characteristically, Thoreau uses a complex web of images, allusion, anecdote and wit here to explore and express one of his core beliefs: that everything – education, reform, clothing, shelter and furniture – should be tested by its fitness to living needs and that, correspondingly, anything beyond that is 'dust', superfluous and even destructive waste. He does not *tell* the reader, he *shows* him, or her: Thoreau's theory of organic functionalism, his belief in having only what answers to our immediate necessities, is not so much stated as demonstrated, dramatized through elaborate and excited verbal play.

The dramatic imperative is at work in the overall structure, as well as the verbal texture, of *Walden*. Thoreau spent over two years at Walden Pond. In *Walden*, the sojourn lasts from one spring to the next, the seasonal transit corresponding to the spiritual growth and rebirth of the hero. The first spring is associated with youth and innocence, a spiritual equivalent of 'the heroic ages'. There is clearly beauty and good in this condition, as Thoreau perceives it, but there is also radical limitation. In this stage, in which 'the animal man' is 'chiefly developed', 'the intellect and what is called spiritual man' is left 'slumbering', Thoreau tells us, 'as in an infant'. It is necessary to develop a spiritual nature as well; and this Thoreau does through a gradual process of introspection that is associated with the seasons of autumn and winter. 'I withdrew yet farther into my shell,' Thoreau recalls of the winter, 'and endeavoured to keep a bright fire both within my house and within my breast.' He drew in on himself, just as he drew in on the house and fire he built for himself; and just as, in a sense, the entirety of nature drew in on itself during the cold season. Thoreau deploys a complex web of natural imagery throughout *Walden* to enact the various stages in his self-emancipation. The life of 'quiet desperation' he had led before coming to Walden, for instance, is associated with snakes lying 'torpid' in mud; like them, Thoreau has to slough his old skin, layers of habit, before he can be renewed. And his withdrawal into his shell is compared to the condition of a grub, or chrysalis; out of that comes eventually, in the second spring, the butterfly, a 'beautiful and winged life' that embodies the idea of resurrection, renewal. But the central image of nature, the element in the physical landscape that most fully and vividly corresponds to the spiritual landscape of

Thoreau, is the pond itself. The correspondence, Thoreau points out intermittently throughout *Walden*, is intimate and extensive: making Walden Pond a type of his own spirit, or soul. 'Lying between the earth and the heaven', Thoreau reflects, the pond 'partakes of the color of both'; it is mortal but also partakes of immortality, just as the soul is attached to the Over-Soul. It was created by a divine power, it has origins that go back beyond historical record, it is evidently fathomless, bottomless. It is something that awes Thoreau, and yet with which he feels intimate ('I cannot come nearer to God and Heaven /', he says, 'Than I live to Walden even'); it is also something that he feels compelled to explore, to test the extent of, during winter. Negotiating the depth of Walden Pond, Thoreau is negotiating his own possible deepnesses; contemplating its mysteries, he is also contemplating the mystery of his own individual soul. Walden *is* Thoreau, in the sense that, as he hoped when he 'went to the woods', in discovering and fronting its essential facts he discovers and confronts his own – he learns of himself in learning about nature.

Since nature and human nature are coextensive in *Walden*, it is evidently appropriate that the spiritual rebirth of the hero should be announced by the coming of the second spring. The ice thawing and breaking on Walden Pond is the first movement in the great drama of rebirth that concludes the book in triumph: a triumph deliberately compared to 'the creation of Cosmos out of Chaos and the realization of the Golden Age'. 'Walden was dead,' Thoreau declares, 'and is alive again.' The annual resurrection of nature figures the possible resurrection of human nature, his and ours. It is not just a figure, however: the rhythms of seasonal renewal ground the rhythms of spiritual renewal, they supply a resource and correspondence for the soul. 'Wildness is the preservation of the world', Thoreau insisted in a lecture titled 'Walking, or the Woods' delivered in 1851. More privately, in a journal entry for the same year, he revealed: 'My profession is always to be on the alert to find God in nature – to know his lurking places.' Both remarks spring from the same insight and impulse as the ones enacted throughout *Walden*: a root belief in nature as a material and mystical presence, requiring our respectful attention and conscientious stewardship. To conserve nature, as Thoreau saw it and explains it throughout his writings, is to preserve human nature; to care for it, to cultivate it, is to care for and cultivate the human spirit; to save it is to save ourselves.

'The greater part of what my neighbors call good I believe to be bad,' Thoreau declares defiantly right at the beginning of *Walden*. The defiance found practical expression during his residence at Walden Pond. Refusing to pay poll tax to a government that supported the Mexican War – a war he considered to be merely a land-grabbing scheme for Southern slaveholders – he was imprisoned for a day. The imprisonment briefly interrupted his sojourn in the woods. More importantly, it inspired him to write 'On the Duty of Civil Disobedience' (1849). For Thoreau, there was a higher law which the individual had to obey even when the government of the day violated it. 'The only obligation which I have a right to assume,' Thoreau argues in 'Civil Disobedience', 'is to do at any time what I think right.' If that meant breaking the laws of the day, then so be it: 'under a government which imprisons any unjustly, the true place for a just man is also in prison'. The doctrine of passive resistance was a natural consequence of Thoreau's belief in the ultimate authority of the self. It was to exercise a profound influence, in the next century, on Mahatma Gandhi and Martin Luther King. And, as Thoreau became increasingly involved in the anti-slavery movement in his later years, he became less convinced that resistance had always to be passive. He was profoundly moved by his meeting with John Brown at the home of Emerson in 1857, and celebrated Brown's actions at Harper's Ferry, Virginia, in 1859 – which involved an attempt to incite a slave revolt and ended in several deaths, including that of Brown himself and his two sons. Brown, Thoreau believed, was a man who was carrying out the principles he himself had championed: principles of freedom and equality that, sometimes, it was necessary to fight and die for. Thoreau said as much in three lectures, 'A Plea for Captain John Brown' (1859), 'The Last Days of John Brown' (1859) and 'After the Death of John Brown' (1861).

A few years before his meeting with John Brown, in the period 1849–53, Thoreau made several brief trips, which supplied the material for his posthumously published books, *Excursions* (1863), *The Maine Woods* (1864), *Cape Cod* (1865) and *A Yankee in Canada* (1866). During his final years, he made further journeys to Cape Cod and Maine, then to the Great Lakes, but his increasingly failing health meant that he spent more and more time in and around Concord. Not that he minded this: his reading carried him far and wide, so that he could declare, 'I have travelled a good deal in Concord'. And study and writing kept him busy. He worked on a long ethnological study of the Indians, which was never completed. He continued his journal, indefatigably: by his death, he had written more than two million words, the basis of all his books. And he developed his interest in botanical science, carrying a botanical guide with him and collecting specimens wherever he went on his walks in the vicinity of Concord. That interest formed the basis of a great but unfinished project. He planned to draw a detailed portrait of his immediate 'wildness', the woods and swamps around him. It would be a project at once scientific and sacramental. Thoreau called the work his 'Kalendar', meaning to suggest by this a connection with other periodical registries of natural phenomena. But he also referred to it as '*my* New Testament', since it would be devoted, he confessed, to 'the divine features I detect in Nature'. An immense amount of material was amassed over a few years. Thoreau even began assembling the first draft of what he tentatively called 'Wild Fruits' in the autumn of 1859. Within three years of this, however, he was dead. The 'Wild Fruits' manuscript was left with thousands of pages of other uncompleted projects, and gradually mixed with them as, over many decades, they remained unread.

In 1993, however, and then in 2000, these manuscripts were published as *Faith in a Seed: The Dispersion and Other Late Natural History Writings* and *Wild Fruits: Thoreau's Rediscovered Last Manuscript*. The two books resurrect the voice and vision of Thoreau: reminding readers of why his is a central and living presence in American writing. Of the two, *Wild Fruits* is the more significant, a major work in its own way. It is a record of the ordinary, often hidden, wild plants of the neighbourhood, organized according to the calendar year. Beginning with accounts of 'the winged seeds of the elms' and the 'thousand downy spheres' of the dandelions, and ending with the fruits of winter, Thoreau attends closely to even the humblest plant, obliging us, the readers, to do so too. As we accompany him on his 'excursions', as he continues to call them, we learn about the significance of the everyday. Like an ideal companion, Thoreau mixes learning, passion and wit to convince us that what we are seeing merits, even demands, attention. We learn to call things by their right names. Above all, we learn again the simple lesson all Thoreau's work teaches: that, as *Walden* has it, heaven is 'under our feet as well as over our heads'. In lively detail, *Wild Fruits* discloses the vital thread connecting all forms of life and shows how coexistence is imperative. By unlocking the miraculous in the commonplace, here and elsewhere in his writings, Thoreau reveals its redemptive potential, all that links its survival to ours. Or, as he tersely puts it, at the end of *Wild Fruits*, 'Nature is another name for health'.

Voices of African American identity

Fuller linked the emancipation of women to the emancipation of slaves; Emerson and Thoreau found their commitment to self-emancipation leading them into support of the abolitionist movement and, in Thoreau's case, of abolition by any means necessary. Those who spoke out most powerfully against slavery, however, and the violation of selfhood it involved, were the slaves themselves. Frederick Douglass (1817–95) was born into slavery on a plantation in Maryland. Of his birth, Douglass was later to say that he had 'no accurate knowledge' as to the exact date: slaves were not regarded as important enough as individuals to warrant the recording of such details. Worse still, all he knew of his father was that he was a white man – although he had a shrewd suspicion that it was his 'master'. And although he knew who his mother was, he saw little of her. 'I never saw my mother, to know her as such, more than four or five times in my life,' Douglass recalled, 'and each of these times was very short in duration, and at night.' Douglass was sent to Baltimore, when he was seven or eight. He received no formal education there; in fact, the family he lived with and worked for was adamantly opposed to his learning to read and write. But Douglass quickly saw the importance of learning to read, as a road to freedom. So, first, he bribed young white children to help him; and then, at the age of about twelve, he managed to get hold of *The Columbian Orator*, an anthology of speeches, poems, dialogues and plays. 'Every opportunity I got, I used to read this book,' Douglass remembered. Included in it was an imaginary dialogue between a master and a slave, in which the master rehearsed the traditional pro-slavery argument, 'all of which was disposed of by the slave'. Not for the first time, 'the thought of being *a slave for life* began to bear heavily on my heart', Douglass said later. 'I often found myself regretting my own existence, and wishing myself dead,' he recalled; 'and but for hope of being free, I have no doubt that I should have killed myself, or done something for which I should have been killed.'

Douglass knew that, as a slave, he was not truly a self, an individual, he was property. If he ever had any doubts about this, they were abolished when, as happened from time to time, he was shifted from one master to another, or witnessed the several members of his family being sold off or simply transferred. When his master died, for instance, Douglass was sent for, 'to be valued with the other property', as Douglass sardonically put it. 'We were all ranked together at the valuation,' he recalled. 'Men, women, old and young, married and single, were ranked with horses, sheep and swine.' Douglass, when recollecting his life as a slave, was particularly fierce in his criticism of those arguments in defence of slavery that saw the slave plantation as an extended family, or feudal system, where the slaves were cared for by their 'father', the plantation patriarch. As property, Douglass pointed out, slaves were denied their rights not only as individuals but as members of a family. At an auction or valuation, 'a single word from the white man was enough – against all wishes, prayers, and entreaties – to sunder forever the dearest friends, dearest kindred, and strongest ties known to human beings'. 'If any one thing in my experience, more than another, served to deepen my con-viction of the infernal character of slavery,' he later explained, 'and to fill me with unutterable loathing of slaveholders, it was the base ingratitude to my poor old grandmother.' 'She had served my old master faithfully, from youth to age,' Douglass went on. She had been the source of his wealth; 'she had rocked him in infancy, attended him in childhood, served him through life, and at his death . . . closed his eyes forever'. But she was still a slave and, being old, of 'but little value'. So her new owners, the master's descendants, simply built her a little hut in the woods and then left her there to fend for herself, 'thus virtually turning her out to die!' There was no respect for her selfhood, still less any sense of personal or familial obliga-tion: only the assumption that she was now worthless property. Family ties were being destroyed under the slave system, Douglass insisted; and the notion that white masters and black slaves formed an extended familial or pseudo-familial unity – linked by ties of service and obligation – was an absurdity. All there was, was use, the exploitation of one race by another, and naked, unrestricted power.

Douglass learned to write in a Baltimore shipyard, to which he was hired out and where he learned the trade of caulking. With that, the preliminary education that he saw as 'the pathway from slavery' was complete. He found time to teach his fellow slaves to read and write. With some of them, he planned an escape that proved abortive when one of their own betrayed them. Then finally, in 1838, he escaped to pursue his vision of freedom in the North. Shortly after arriving in the North, he renamed himself: his mother's slave name was Bailey, now he was called Douglass, after a character in *The Lady of the Lake* (1810) by Sir Walter Scott. He also began reading the radical abolitionist newspaper *The Liberator*, published by William Lloyd Garrison. This was his first step towards becoming an abolitionist leader himself and, by 1841, he had begun a career as a black leader and lecturer dedicated to the 'great work' of black liberation. Encouraged by his success on the anti-slavery circuit, Douglass published an account of his life as a slave, *Narrative of the Life of Frederick Douglass, an American Slave* (1845). It was circulated widely, translated into several languages, and quickly helped to establish Douglass as one of the leading spokespeople for his cause. Like other slave narratives, it was primarily addressed to a white audience in the first instance; and it was mediated by white writers – William Lloyd Garrison supplied a Preface and another white abolitionist, Wendell Phillips, provided an introductory Letter. Like them, too, but also like *Walden*, it presents itself as at once a representative autobiography and a testament to the creed of self-emancipation. It shows how its protagonist, who is also its author and narrator, is at once extraordinary and typical – and how he found, or rather made, the means to become himself.

Some of these means have been suggested already, since the preceding summary of Douglass's early life is all taken from the *Narrative*. Ignorance is countered by education. The divisive tactics of the whites are countered by the communal, collective tactics of the blacks, learning to read or planning to escape together. Douglass is particularly forthright, when it comes to outlining the evils of slavery, about sexuality and religion. His master was probably his father, he recalls, and that was not uncommon: 'the slaveholder, in cases not a few, sustains to his slaves the double relation of master and father'. The sexual and social tensions this, and other aspects of slavery, disclose or even generate are subtly negotiated in a narrative that, after all, was written at a time when discussion of such matters was virtually taboo. One slave master, for instance, is described getting a strange kind of satisfaction from whipping a semi-naked slave woman ('the louder she screamed, the harder he whipped'). Another whips a similarly semi-naked slave woman, Douglass's own 'Aunt Hester', out of what is plainly jealousy: she has been discovered 'in company' with a male slave, after the white master has made clear his own interest in her 'graceful proportions'. And any white mistress, Douglass tells the reader, is wracked by resentment and her own jealous feelings in such circumstances. 'She is never better pleased', we learn, than when she sees those whom she suspects to be the 'mulatto children' of her husband 'under the lash' – especially when she suspects her husband of showing those children favours that he withholds from his other 'black slaves'. What adds a further edge of bitterness to all this is the sheer hypocrisy involved: the constant violation of barriers between one race and another that are supposed to be absolute, impenetrable. Like many other, later writers, Douglass saw miscegenation as the suppressed myth of the slave system and an extreme instance of what that system as a whole entailed – the human use of human beings.

The hypocrisy was all the greater, Douglass explains, among the masters who claimed to be religious. 'The religion of the south is a mere covering for the most horrid crimes', he tells the reader; 'of all the slaveholders with which I have ever met, religious slaveholders are the worst' because they are 'the meanest and basest, the most cruel and cowardly'. Among those religious slaveholders whom Douglass encountered was a man called Edward Covey, a notorious 'Negro breaker' to whom he was hired out at the age of sixteen. It was while working for Covey, we learn, that Douglass found the basic means necessary to be himself. The discovery forms a central moment in the *Narrative*. Covey kept his slaves under constant surveillance:

by adopting the habit of creeping up on them unexpectedly, he made them feel that he was 'ever present', that they were ever watched. He submitted everyone to an unremitting regime of 'work, work, work' in all weathers, starving them always and beating them whenever he thought necessary. Nevertheless, he prayed and pretended to be devotional, apparently thinking himself 'equal to deceiving the Almighty'. 'Poor man!' Douglass reflects in a rare moment of pity for Covey, 'such was his disposition, and success at deceiving, I do verily believe that he sometimes deceived himself into the solemn belief that he was a sincere worshipper of the most high God.' Under the brutal hand of Covey, Douglass remembers, 'I was broken in body, soul, and spirit'; 'the dark night of slavery closed in upon me, and behold a man transformed into a brute!' But then came the turning point, introduced by a memorable rhetorical strategy. 'You have seen how a man was made a slave,' Douglass confides to the reader. 'You shall see how a slave was made a man.'

How Douglass is 'made a man' is simple. He stands up for himself. When Covey tries to beat him, he resists; they fight an epic fight 'for nearly two hours'; Covey gets 'entirely the worst end of the bargain' and never tries to beat Douglass again. 'This battle with Mr Covey was the turning-point in my career as a slave,' Douglass says. 'It rekindled the few embers of freedom, and revived within me a sense of my own manhood. It recalled the departed self-confidence, and inspired me again with a determination to be free.' As in *Walden*, the recovery of selfhood is described as a rebirth. 'It was a glorious resurrection from the tomb of slavery,' Douglass recalls, 'to the heaven of freedom.' And just as Thoreau, after his spiritual rebirth, talks about the return of the heroic ages, so Douglass equates his own spiritual rebirth with the restoration of heroism. His emergence as an individual, capable of mental and emotional freedom now and literal freedom not long after, is the consequence of a fight worthy of one of the heroes of ancient legend. And it coincides precisely with his emergence as a man. Douglass was to spend a further four years in slavery after this. In describing those years, he still has plenty to tell the reader about the brutality and hypocrisy of the slave system – and, above all, about how that system dehumanizes not only the slave but also the master. He also has plenty to say about how, nevertheless, slaves make a human space for themselves, through loyalty and love, bravery and friendship. 'We were linked and interlinked with each other,' Douglass recollects of a time he spent with a slave community after his battle with Covey; 'I loved them with a love stronger than any thing I have experienced since.' But Douglass is right to present this moment as central: since it was the moment when he was ready to express his selfhood, his sense of his own worth and dignity, at the expense of his own life if necessary (Covey might have killed him with impunity: a slave could be punished with death for injuring a master). It is also the moment that expresses perfectly a belief held in common with the Transcendentalists – although, of course, Douglass was never a Transcendentalist himself: that a man could raise himself by conscious endeavour, that he could and should struggle to live freely and truly.

After the publication of the *Narrative*, Douglass spent two years promoting the anti-slavery cause in Britain. He returned to the United States, where he purchased his freedom; and then, in 1847, established an anti-slavery journal, first called *The North Star* and later retitled *Frederick Douglass' Paper*. A second journal, *Douglass' Monthly*, began in 1858. Douglass contributed a large number of editorial essays to both these publications. An enlarged autobiography, *My Bondage and My Freedom*, appeared in 1855, and a third autobiographical work, *The Life and Times of Frederick Douglass*, in 1881. In his later life, Douglass was an influential public figure. He was in personal contact with Abraham Lincoln, he organized two black regiments for the Union during the Civil War, and he was in public service for many years, ending this aspect of his career as United States minister to Haiti from 1889 to 1891. But it is for his three autobiographical books that he is a major presence in American literature. They are central texts in the linked traditions of slave narrative and American autobiography. And much of the power and popularity of the *Narrative*, in particular, stems from the way it appropriates the language and symbolism of a white, middle-class tradition while denouncing the evils of slavery and racism and while exploring the trials of Douglass's life. Douglass talks of spiritual death and resurrection, of being reborn. He also talks of a happy coincidence of divine and human purpose that both recalls the histories of the early, white settlers and anticipates many other, later American success stories: the fortunate moments in his early life, Douglass intimates, were all due to 'that kind providence which has ever since attended me' – and to his own efforts, his readiness to work and fight on his own behalf. Above all, perhaps, he talks of the American ideals of self-help and self-realization, and uses the rhetoric of the American dream to distinguish between false and true Americans: between those who would destroy the dream, like the slaveholders, and those who want not only to affirm it but to live it. To that extent, the *Narrative* is a testament to the plurality of America. It is not, in other words, just a central text in this or that particular tradition; it is also an instance of how many great American texts exist at the confluence of cultures – and of how those cultures talk to each other and themselves.

Harriet Jacobs (1813–97) also wrote at the confluence of cultures, but for her those cultures were different. 'I was born a slave,' Jacobs announces at the beginning of her own book, *Incidents in the Life of a Slave Girl: Written by Herself* (1861). That is the classic opening of slave narrative. Jacobs continues, however, in a different vein: 'but I never knew it till six years of happy childhood had passed away'. Her father was a skilled man, a carpenter, Jacobs recalls; and, on condition of paying his mistress two hundred dollars a year, and supporting himself, he was allowed to manage his own trade and affairs. He and she, and her mother and brother, 'lived together in a comfortable home'; and, although they were all slaves, 'I was so fondly shielded', Jacobs tells her readers, that, to begin with, 'I never dreamed that I was a piece of merchandise, trusted to them for safe keeping, and liable to be demanded of them at any moment'. The revelation that she was, indeed, a slave came when she was six. Her mother died; and she learned from the talk around her that this was her condition. The strongest wish of her father had been to purchase the freedom of his children. But he, too, died a year later with his wish unrealized. Aside from her brother, Jacobs's closest relative was now her grandmother, Molly Horniblow, an extraordinary woman whose history had been one of betrayal. Molly was the daughter of a South Carolina planter who, at his death, had left her mother, Molly herself and two other children free. But on their journey from the plantation to live with relatives, all four of them were captured and sold back into slavery. As she grew older, Molly became indispensable to the household into which she was sold, Jacobs explains. Her master and mistress 'could not help seeing it was for their interest to take care of such a valuable piece of property'. However, when the master died, that did not stop the mistress dividing Molly's children up among his heirs. There were five children, and four heirs; and so 'Benjamin, the youngest one, was sold, in order that each heir might have an equal portion of dollars and cents'. Molly still hoped to purchase the freedom of her children; she ran a bakery in her home and had laid up three hundred dollars from the proceeds of her work for that purpose. The mistress, however, borrowed it one day, promising to pay it back, then never did so; and Molly had no legal redress. 'According to Southern laws,' Jacobs caustically points out, 'a slave being property, can *hold* no property.' So there was nothing she could do.

Betrayal of different kinds lies at the heart of *Incidents*. It was an experience her grandmother had had repeatedly, Jacobs reveals; and it was an experience that then happened to her. Her mistress died when she was twelve. She had promised Jacobs's dying mother 'that her children should never suffer for anything'; and, from many 'proofs of attachment' the mistress had shown to Jacobs herself, she could not help 'having some hope' that she would be left free in the will. She was not; she was simply bequeathed to another member of the family. 'My mistress had taught me the precept of God's Word: "Thou shalt love thy neighbor as thyself",' Jacobs remembers bitterly. 'But I was her slave, and I suppose she did not recognise me as her neighbor.' No ties of honour, obligation or intimacy mattered, not even the memory that many of the slaves now sold off were nourished at the same breast as the children of the white family selling them. 'These God-breathing machines are no more, in the sight of their masters, than the cotton they plant, or the horses they tend,' Jacobs reflects. So far, *Incidents* is a familiar if powerful tale: not that different from the *Narrative* of Douglass. And yet there are differences of tenor and tone that perhaps alert the reader to what is coming next. There is, first, more of an emphasis on family ties, blood relationships within the black community, than there is in the Douglass story. In addressing the reader, there is more of an appeal to sentiment, to his or her sympathy, than there is to abstract principles or emotions of anger. Men are a shadowy presence here; even the carpenter father is mentioned only in passing. It is the women who matter: heroic women like Jacobs's mother, great-grandmother and, above all, her grandmother, and evil women who betray promises, borrow money without returning it, and deny the truth of the Bible. This is a tale, in short, that concentrates on the female experience of slavery and, in doing so, appropriates the techniques of the sentimental novel as well as using those of the slave narrative. And at the centre of it is that familiar protagonist of sentimental fiction: the young woman affronting her destiny – and, in due time, faced with a dangerous seducer – the female orphan making her way in the world.

One point that has not been made about *Incidents* is now worth making. The central character in the narrative is not called Harriet Jacobs but Linda Brent. The reasons for this become obvious when Jacobs begins to describe the new household that, as an adolescent slave, she moved into. She became the object of relentless sexual pursuit by her white master, to escape which she became the lover of another white man and bore him two children. In letters to a white friend, Jacobs expressed the discomfort she felt about revealing her life story, and this part in particular. To write a book revealing the sexual exploitation of slave women, she would have to expose her own sexual history and the fact that she was an unmarried mother – a condition not uncommon, but hardly spoken about, let alone approved of, at the time. She solved this problem by creating Linda Brent as an alter ego: in and through the story of Brent she could tell her own story as a sexual victim, move the narrative beyond the limits prescribed by nineteenth-century gentility, and yet remain safely anonymous. Here, especially, *Incidents* becomes a captivating generic mix: a slave narrative still, a sentimental story of female endeavour, a tale of sexual pursuit, attempted seduction and betrayal, and the first-person confession of a 'fallen woman'. 'O, what days and nights of fear and sorrow that man caused me!' Jacobs confides, as she recalls how her master, here called Dr Flint (his actual name was Dr Norcom), tried to make her submit to him. 'Reader, it is not to awaken sympathy for myself that I am telling you truthfully what I suffered in slavery. I do it to kindle a flame of compassion in your hearts for my sisters who are still in bondage, suffering as I once suffered!' The power, and the pathos, of this episode in *Incidents* springs from the direct address to the reader, so common in sentimental fiction, inviting us to participate in the sufferings of the heroine. Even more, it springs from Jacobs's insistence, here and throughout the book, that what she is telling is the truth – and the truth, not just for herself, but for all her 'sisters'. As Jacobs tells in detail how Flint relentlessly pursued her, filling her 'young mind with unclean images', reminding her that she 'belonged' to him, his 'dark shadow' hovering behind her everywhere, she reminds the reader that what she is telling has a general application. Everywhere in the South, she reiterates, there are young slave women, like the narrator herself as an adolescent, with 'no shadow of law to protect [them] from insult, from violence, or even from death'. Everywhere there are white mistresses like Mrs Flint, 'who ought to protect the helpless victim' but instead 'have no other feelings towards her but those of jealousy and rage'. And everywhere, there are masters like Dr Flint, 'fiends who bear the shape of men'.

As Jacobs recalls how she took a white lover, and had two children by him to protect herself against Dr Flint, the tone gravitates towards the confessional. And, true to the confessional, there is the same intimate mode of address. 'And now reader, I come to a period in my unhappy life, which I would gladly forget if I could,' Jacobs declares. 'The remembrance fills me with sorrow and shame. It pains me to tell you of it, but I have promised to tell you the truth.' That emphasis on truth, the assurance that, as Jacobs puts it elsewhere, she is drawing 'no imaginary pictures of southern homes', is vital. Her aim, she plainly states in the Preface to *Incidents*, is 'to arouse the women of the North to a realising sense of the condition of two millions of women at the South'. And, to do that, she is telling a tale that, as she points out persistently, is extraordinary and typical: melodramatic and startling but also plain, unvarnished fact. The story is no less extraordinary when Jacobs recalls how she was determined to see her two children free. They lived at first with her grandmother, in relative comfort. But Jacobs learned, she tells us, that Dr Flint was planning to take them out of the grandmother's care. So, to save them from becoming plantation slaves, she decided to run away. Her hope was that Flint would sell the children if she went away. And the hope proved well founded. Escaping, she hid with various black and white neighbours. Dr Flint then sold the children to their father, who permitted them to stay where they were.

Here, again, in the episode of escape, *Incidents* differs radically from the *Narrative* of Douglass. Jacobs did not flee northwards. Instead, as she discloses to the reader, she hid in a tiny attic in her grandmother's house for seven years. This was what she called her 'loophole of retreat'. 'The air was stifling there', she remembers, 'the darkness total' to begin with: 'but I was not comfortless. I heard the voices of my children'. 'There was joy and there was sadness in that sound,' she confesses. 'It made my tears flow. How I longed to speak to them!' And horrible though it was 'to lie in a cramped position day after day', Jacobs emphasizes, 'I would have chosen this rather than my lot as a slave'. There were, eventually, even more comforts. She succeeded in making a hole 'about an inch long and an inch broad' through which she could see the daylight. Even more important, she could now see the 'two sweet little faces' of her children, and more clearly hear their talk. Occasionally, she could talk to relatives and overhear conversations; regularly, from day to day, she could watch her son and daughter growing up. For Jacobs, liberation comes not in heroic battle, the recovery of manhood and solitary flight but in being still with her family, even if apart from them: enjoying a strange kind of solitude, free from the impositions of her white masters, that nevertheless allows her to see, and sometimes talk with, those whom she loves. It would be wrong to exaggerate the difference between Jacobs and Douglass here; it is certainly not absolute. Douglass, after all, spoke of being 'linked and interlinked' with his fellow slaves. After seven years in hiding, Jacobs eventually fled North – where, in due course, she was reunited with her children and all had their freedom bought. But a difference there is, between these two great slave narratives. Each has its own way of dramatizing the trials of the self and the travails of slavery; each has its own manner of turning autobiography into challenging art.

The Making of Many Americas

'Reader, my story ends with freedom; not, in the usual way, with marriage.' That conclusion to *Incidents*, playing on a conventional ending to sentimental fiction, modestly summarizes the drama of the self that inspired and intrigued so many American writers at this time: that urge towards self-emancipation that the writings of the Transcendentalists and slave narratives certainly shared. But, as Douglass and

Jacobs clearly illustrate, the self could take on quite different shapes and colorations – and emancipation was far more difficult, far more of a challenge, for some. America was becoming even more of a mosaic of different cultures, colliding interests and conflicting voices: for many writers there was not one America but several, often at war with each other. Douglass and Jacobs inevitably register this, since they were born into collision and conflict, the denial of their individual voices and their cultural integrity by that form of social violence known as slavery. So, to a lesser extent, do Emerson, Fuller and Thoreau: all of whom, after all, recognized the challenges to selfhood posed by various forms of injustice – the denial of people as individuals because they were of the 'wrong' race or gender. And so, too, do other writers, deeply aware of the many Americas, the various, often opposing forces that existed in the new republic: among them, the many who wrote in and from the Native American and Mexican American communities, those who engaged in the great debate over slavery, and those who wrote about the condition of women.

Native American writing

Within the Native American tribes, so far as they were able or managed to survive, the oral traditions of folktale, legend and poetry persisted. Inevitably, all these forms betrayed more evidence of the impact of the whites. In one version of the Acoma story of emergence, for example, the legendary twin founders of the culture, who are in this case women, are tempted into what is called 'sin' and 'selfish thoughts' – in one instance by a snake. The fact that they are women simply reflects the matrilineal society of the Acoma and Western Pueblos. Sin, however, was a concept unknown on the American continent before Columbus; and the role of the snake in tempting one of the sisters, more likely than not, is coloured by knowledge of the Bible. For some white observers, the Native American myths were the true American myths. That was why writers like Henry Wadsworth Longfellow chose to appropriate them. It was also why William Channing, writing in the *North American Review* in 1815, went so far as to claim that the 'oral literature of the aborigines' was the only truly national literature, blessed with a common speech that was 'the very language of poetry'. But writing in English by Native Americans inevitably reflected acculturation and the consequences, in particular, of removal and various assimilationist policies. Most of this writing, in fact, came from those whose tribes had been displaced in the East or forced to move to the West. That meant, mainly, the Cherokees in the South, who had acculturated rapidly (although, in the end, it did them no good), and the Six Nations and Ojibwas in the Northeast and around the Great Lakes. Such writing necessarily explored Native American interests and settings, and addressed issues of particular, often pressing importance to the tribes. But it was also likely to be written according to the conventions of the dominant, white culture of the time and, very often, reflected its tastes and habits of mind.

Nowhere is the shaping influence of white culture more evident here than in the poetry written in English by Native Americans. John Rollin Ridge (1827–67), for instance, was a Cherokee. He was actively involved in Indian issues. But his published work is notable, not only for Ridge's insistence that his people had to become 'civilized' – that is, assimilated into white society – in order to survive, but also for his wholesale adoption of white literary forms. In 1854, he published *Life and Adventures of Joaquin Murieta, the Celebrated California Bandit*. The claim made here that it is a true story is simply a bow to one of the literary conventions of the day: it is, in fact, a fairly standard popular romance. As for the poems Ridge produced at various stages in his life, all are marked by a debt to English and American Romantic poetry. Some of these are nature poems, others are autobiographical, still others take as their subject some major public event. All of them, however, are remarkable for their scrupulously exact use of traditional verse forms, and their celebration of the prevailing beliefs of white American society at the time – notably, Progress and Manifest Destiny. So a poem written to commemorate the completion of 'The Atlantic Cable' (1868) begins by declaring: 'Let Earth be glad! for that great work is done, / Which makes, at last the Old and New World one!' 'Let all mankind rejoice!' Ridge goes on, 'for time nor space / Shall check the progress of the human race!' This vision of 'The fair, the bright millenial [*sic*] days to be' leaves no room for doubt. The transatlantic cable is, for Ridge, both a symbol and an instance of the 'knitted unity' to come between all races and nations – of a glorious future time when all 'shall vibrate to the voice of Peace' in a brave new world of improved communication and perfect community.

Not all the work produced by Native Americans at this time conformed to white standards, of course. On the contrary, some tried to register what was different about their people by attempting to record their tales and folklore. Notable among these was Jane Johnston Schoolcraft (1800–41). Born Jane Johnston, to an Ojibwa mother and an Irish trader father, she was educated in Ojibwa lore by the one and in English literature by the other. In 1823, she married the scholar and explorer Henry Rowe Schoolcraft (1793–1864), whose main interest was the American Indian. From then until her death she remained his informant, guide and assistant: interpreting native sources for him and helping him to study the Ojibwa language. Together, the Schoolcrafts began 'The Literary Voyager or Muzzenyegun' in 1826, a magazine containing examples of Ojibwa folklore as well as original poems and essays, many of them by Jane Schoolcraft under assumed names. What is remarkable about the best of this work is how, in the versions of Ojibwa folklore, Jane Schoolcraft deploys her skills in English, her knowledge of English literary techniques and forms, to recreate tales in a way that encourages the (presumably white) reader's interest and sympathy without denying cultural difference, the intrinsic characteristics of the source. A tale like 'The Forsaken Brother' (1827), for instance, is very simple. It tells of how two children, one male and one female, broke their promise to their dying parents by neglecting to look after their younger brother and finally deserting him. What distinguishes it, however, is its unusual blend of morality and magic. The older brother, 'fishing in his canoe in the lake' one day, hears 'the cry of a child'. It is, he realizes, the voice of his little brother, singing out, 'My brother, my brother, / I am now turning into a Wolf'. At the termination of the song, the singer howls like a wolf. The older brother hurries to the shore, sees that his forsaken sibling has indeed turned into a wolf, and tries to catch and soothe him ('My brother, my brother, come to me,' he coos). But it is too late for anything except regrets. The forsaken brother, now a wolf, evades his grasp and disappears from sight. And both his brother and his older sister are left to feed on 'the bitterness of remorse' for the rest of their days.

While some writers worked towards making the folklore of Native Americans available and accessible to an English-speaking audience, others tried to make that audience more aware of Native American history, their rights and, often, how badly they had been treated by the white majority. Among these was the earliest significant Indian writer of the nineteenth century, William Apess (1798 – ?), whose paternal grandmother was a full-blooded Pequot and who claimed descent from Metacomet, the chief known as King Philip among the English. Converted to Methodism when he was fifteen, Apess became a lay preacher. Then, in 1829, his book *A Son of the Forest* appeared, the first autobiography written by a Native American to be published. Apess was raised mainly by whites, and the book is, unsurprisingly, a cultural mix. It is in the tradition of white spiritual autobiography favoured by, say, Jonathan Edwards and John Woolman, but it emphasizes Apess's Indian origins and the basic humanity of the Indian people. To add to the mix, it also insists on the potential of the Indian people for adapting to white culture. This was followed by three further books: *The Experiences of Five Christian Indians of the Pecquod Tribe*, a shorter life history published in 1833 but probably written before *A Son of the Forest*, and two more historical works, *Indian Nullification of the Unconstitutional Laws of Massachusetts, Relative to the Marshpee [Mashpee] Tribe* (1835) and *Eulogy on King Philip* (1836). These three books reveal a more openly critical attitude towards whites and, in particular, a fierce critique of what Apess sees as the brutality and hypocrisy of their general behaviour towards the Indian peoples. 'Now I ask if degradation has not been heaped long enough upon the Indians?' he declaims in the 1833 book. 'I would ask if you would like to be disfranchised from all your rights, merely because your skin is white, and for no other crime?' Jesus, Apess points out to his presumably white readers, came from 'a colored people', the Jews of the East. And, in any event, 'did you ever hear or read of Christ teaching his disciples that they ought to despise one because his skin was different from theirs?' As Apess argues it here, white people could hardly have assumed 'a more efficient way to distress' Indians, to 'murder them by inches', than the one they have adopted. And, in adopting the ways they have, they have not only forgotten that there can be 'as good feelings and principles under a red skin as there can be under a white'; they have also violated the Biblical precept, 'to love your neighbors as yourself'. Nevertheless, Apess writes more in hope than in sorrow or anger. His essential belief, expressed in all his books, is that, with education, the Indian can still rise; with proper observance of Christian principles, the white man can still help him; 'the mantle of prejudice' will be 'torn from every heart', Apess hopes – and 'then shall peace pervade the Union'.

An even more popular Indian autobiography than *A Son of the Forest* was *The Life, History and Travels of Kah-ge-ga-gah-bowh (George Copway), a Young Indian Chief of the Ojibwa Nation*. This was published in 1847, republished as *The Life, Letters and Speeches of Kah-ge-ga-gah-bowh, or G. Copway* in 1850 in New York, and as *Recollections of a Forest Life; or, The Life and Travels of Kah-ge-ga-gah-bowh, or George Copway* in London in the same year. In its different versions, this book had a widespread readership. And it encouraged the author, George Copway (1818–69), in his new career as a writer and lecturer on Indian matters; prior to that, he had served as a Methodist missionary among the Indians. The book is divided into four sections. The first is an account of the Ojibwa culture into which he was born; the second rehearses how his parents were converted to Christianity in 1827 and he himself similarly converted three years later; the third describes his role as a mediator between Indians and whites; and the fourth records the recent history of relations between whites and Ojibwa. 'The Christian will no doubt feel for my poor people, when he hears the story of one brought from that unfortunate race called the Indians,' Copway begins. 'The lover of humanity will be glad to see that once powerful race can be made to enjoy the blessings of life.' What follows is nothing if not conflicted, in ways that are at once intriguing and a typical consequence of the process of acculturation Copway himself had experienced. He celebrates the blessings of white civilization but he also describes how the whites robbed the Indians of their land – and then gave them whisky, so that 'the Ojebwa [*sic*] nation, that unconquered nation, has fallen a prey to the withering influence of intemperance'. He rejoices in his conversion, and the conversion of others to Christianity: 'unchristianised Indians', he says, 'are often like greedy lions after prey'. But he also portrays his early life with the Ojibwa, prior to conversion, as a pastoral idyll. 'I was born in *nature's wide domain*!' he declares, 'I am one of Nature's children.' Invoking the familiar idea of the Indian as a noble savage, Copway also taps that vein of romantic nationalism that sees American nature as superior to European culture: 'I would much more glory in this birthplace, with the broad canopy of heavens above me, and the giant arms of the forest trees for my shelter,' he declares, 'than to be born in palaces of marble, studded with pillars of gold!' That does not stop him, however, from insisting on the adaptability of the Indian to what the opening of his book refers to as 'the blessings of life': that is, the culture, brought to America from Europe, that he elsewhere chooses to scorn.

The autobiography of Copway, in short, is a rich mosaic of inconsistencies, precisely because Copway himself, not unusually, was trying to reconcile different cultures. He was also trying to make his way in a literary world the rules for which were largely dictated by whites. Influential white scholars like Henry Rowe Schoolcraft and Francis Parkman, and equally influential white writers like Washington Irving and James Fenimore Cooper, supplied him with encouragement and support for his later publishing projects. *The Traditional History and Characteristic Sketches of the Ojibway Nation* appeared in England in 1850 and in the United States in 1851, and was far more critical of whites than his autobiography had been. This was followed by *Running Sketches of Men and Places, in England, France,*

Germany, Belgium, and Scotland later in 1851, one of the first travel accounts written by an Indian. But gradually white interest and encouragement waned. The journal Copway tried to establish, *Copway's American Indian*, was inaugurated in July 1851, but lasted only a few months. His influential friends dropped him as his requests for financial and other assistance grew ever more insistent. He was adopted by a group calling themselves 'native Americans' for a while. But, for them, the defining features of the 'native American' were that he or she was neither an immigrant nor Roman Catholic: Copway was simply a convenient tool for their purposes. Gradually, Copway dropped out of literary and political circles, and into obscurity.

The first recorded use of the term 'Native American' as we understand it today, not as the group that briefly adopted Copway interpreted it, was by a Mahican, John Wannuaucon Quinney (1797–1855). In a speech to Congress in 1852, Quinney called himself 'a true Native American'; and the speech as a whole reflects his passionate awareness of the Mahican presence in American history. When he delivered this speech, on Independence Day, he was coming to the end of a long career as a mediator between his tribe and the whites, a lobbyist and a political leader. And Quinney used the occasion to contrast American promise and performance. 'I have been taught in your schools,' Quinney told his audience, 'and been able to read your histories and accounts of Europeans, yourselves and the Red Man.' And what those books had instructed him, he explained, was that 'while your rejoicings today are commemorative of the free birth of this giant nation, they simply convey to my mind, the transfer of a miserable weakness and dependance of my race from one great power to another'. The purpose of the speech was, in fact, threefold. It was, first, to emphasize the total dispossession of his people. Robbed of their land, authority over them simply shifted from white European to white American masters: they had been denied their place in history, since their story did not appear as it should have in the school books American children read every day. Second, it was to redress the balance a little by beginning to tell that story: Quinney rehearsed the tale of his tribe from pre-Columbian days, when prophecies circulated of 'the coming of a strange race, from the sunrise' who would crowd the Indians 'from their fair possessions', right up until the time of telling. The third purpose was to encourage a more substantial redress. Acculturation was necessary, Quinney believed, in response to white American expansionism but, for Indians to achieve this, white Americans had to be willing to accept them as equals. Even the plight of the slave, Quinney suggested, was not as bad as that of the Indian. For, 'while the slave is increasing, and increased by every appliance, the Indian is left to rot and die, behold the humanities of this model *Republic!*' 'For myself and for my tribe, I ask for justice,' Quinney concluded, '– I believe it will sooner or later occur – and may the Great and Good Spirit enable me to die in hope.' Like many other Native American writers writing at this time, Quinney mixed pride in a tribal past with belief in a new American future, defined by the linked blessings of white civilization and Christian conversion. It was not for nothing that he was referred to, among many of his contemporaries, as 'the Last of the Mohicans'.

'Shall red men live, or shall they be swept from the earth?' another Native American writer of the period, Elias Boudinot (1802–39), asked in *Address to the Whites*, delivered and published in 1826. And for Boudinot, just as for Apess, Conway and Quinney, to live meant for the 'red man' to accommodate to and be accepted by the white. Like them, too, his own story was a testament to accommodation. Born a Cherokee, he was sent to a Moravian mission school where he was educated into white values and practices. Initially named Buck Watie, he renamed himself after meeting Elias Boudinot, the president of the American Bible Society, following the Cherokee custom of adopting the name of a benefactor. It was while travelling to solicit donations for a national academy and printing equipment for the Cherokee Nation that Boudinot delivered his *Address*. More even than the address of Quinney or the autobiography of Conway, it is a testament to a future in which Indians assume what Boudinot, at one point, calls 'the mantle of civilization'. 'You here behold an *Indian*,' Boudinot informs his audience; 'my kindred are *Indians*, and my fathers sleeping in the wilderness grave – they too were *Indians*. But I am not as my fathers were – broader means and nobler influences have fallen upon me.' He has improved, Boudinot proudly claims. So, too, may all other Indians; all are 'susceptible of attainments necessary to the formation of polished society'. Boudinot expresses a fundamentally progressive impulse, a belief in the Manifest Destiny of white culture and in the ability of his people to participate in that Destiny. His tribe, in particular, he suggests, have made great strides 'in their movement towards civilization', with 'the invention of letters', 'the translation of the New Testament into Cherokee', and 'the organisation of a Government'. Given time, 'the Cherokee Nation . . . will finally become . . . one of the Garden spots of America', 'the shrill sound of the Savage yet shall die away as the roaring of far distant thunder; and Heaven wrought music will gladden the affrighted wilderness'.

Boudinot was specifically asking for support to accelerate the process of acculturation when he gave his *Address*. That may be one reason why it is, on the whole, a hymn to the values of white culture. It is worth making two further points, however. One is that Boudinot anticipated communication between his people and the whites as a two-way process: the whites would teach the Indians about their cultural practices, and the Indians, in turn, would tell whites about their 'intellectual efforts, . . . their eloquence, . . . their moral, civil, and physical advancement'. The second, more important point follows from the first. Acculturation, for Boudinot and those like him, did not mean absorption. The Cherokees would become 'civilized' but separate: 'not a great, but a faithful ally of the United States'. It would be a partnership of allies and equals: one learning more from the other, perhaps, and adapting more to its ways, but both equally practising 'the common liberties of America' and both integral parts of 'one continuous abode of free, enlightened, and happy people'. Following his *Address*, Boudinot was to become editor of the *Cherokee Phoenix*, the first newspaper produced by American Indians. It served a dual function: to inform local readers about events taking place in their society, and to inform whites elsewhere of the strides towards civilization being made by the Cherokee Nation. He was also to become a translator of English works into Cherokee: a perfect illustration of his hope that his people would acquire the blessings of white culture but maintain their own separate but equal integrity. Boudinot's hopes proved to be without foundation. The Cherokee Nation was forced to remove less than ten years after the *Address* was delivered, along the Trail of Tears; the consequences were, of course, little short of genocide. Ironically, Boudinot was one of those Cherokees who signed the treaty with the federal government, ceding Cherokee land in the East for Indian Territory in the West. He did so in the belief that removal was now the only way the Cherokee Nation could survive. It was a mistaken belief, and he paid for it with his life: he was killed in Indian Territory by members of his tribe, who felt that he had betrayed them by signing the treaty. Boudinot had wondered whether his people would, as he put it, 'become civilized and happy, or sharing the fate of many kindred nations, become extinct'. Of the two alternatives, white society seemed on the whole to prefer the latter. His life and work, consequently, and his death all became poignant testament to the failure of accord: the vision Boudinot cherished, of his 'native country' 'taking her seat with the nations of the earth', never came near to being realized. 'They hang upon your mercy as to a garment,' Boudinot said of his people to his white audience at the conclusion of his *Address*. 'Will you push them from you, or will you save them?' The answer he eventually received to this question was not the one he hoped for and wanted; almost certainly, it was also not the one he expected.

Oral culture of the Hispanic Southwest

Storytelling was not, of course, a monopoly of the Native Americans whose tales the Schoolcrafts helped to record. Apart from those who told tales of Mike Fink, Davy Crockett and other frontier heroes or fools, there was a whole oral culture in the greater Southwest and California, those Mexican lands that prior to 1845 stretched from the Rio Grande northward as far as lower Oregon and Wyoming. This area, known among Mexicans as Mexico de Afuera, or Mexico abroad, was until quite recently the site of a vital storytelling culture. *Cuentos*, or folktales, were usually told at the end of the day as a kind of intimate performance with all the appropriate dramatic gestures, pauses and intonation. And they could take the form of morality tales, tales of magic and enchantment, tales in which animals speak or the dead come alive. In 'La comadre Sebastiana', for instance, the tale is told of a poor woodcutter who steals one of his wife's chickens to eat in the woods. There, in the woods, he is approached first by Jesus and then by the Virgin, both of whom want to share his meal. He refuses them; 'and I'll tell you why', he says. 'I think you neglect the poor. You give everything to the rich and so little to the poor. You don't treat us equally.' This slyly subversive comment on the cosy relationship between the Christian church and the wealthy is followed by a further, equally wry and equally serious, touch. When a third person approaches the poor woodcutter, it turns out to be 'Doña Sebastiana, Death herself'. The woodcutter is happy to share his food with her, because death after all treats everyone equally. Death rewards the poor man with the gift of healing. He will, Death tells the man, be able to heal anyone, even the terminally ill; the one proviso is that, if he should see Doña Sebastiana standing at the head of the bed, he should not cure that sick person because 'he has been called by God'. Eventually, the poor man ignores the proviso. Called to the sick bed of a rich man, he sees Doña Sebastiana at the head of the bed but grabs her and drags her to the foot. He cures the rich man, but, for his disobedience, he has to switch places with him. The story ends with the woodcutter's soul being hurled into Doña Sebastiana's cart 'as it slowly made its way to eternity'.

'La comadre Sebastiana' is an intriguing mix of morality and magic, with a further element of sly social criticism levelled at the church. There are several extant versions of the tale. And there are many more about La Llorona, the 'weeping woman': versions of this story have been found in Mexican American communities all over the United States. Essentially, hers is a story of woman as violator and violated. La Llorona kills her children. Sometimes, she does so because their father and her lover has left her: most often, in these versions, because La Llorona is poor, he is rich, and he has gone off to marry a woman of his own class. Sometimes, she does so because their father and her lover has threatened to take the children from her. Sometimes, she does so because she has been driven insane. La Llorona then commits suicide and roams the streets and countryside, wailing for her loss and terrifying all those who see her. In some versions of her tale, La Llorona is linked with other women with similarly tragic stories: 'Unfaithful Maria', 'the Devil Woman', and 'La Malinche'. The last probably derives from the Indian name for the woman the Spanish called Doña Marina, who acted as interpreter and mistress to Cortés during the first stage of the conquest of Mexico. So the story, strange and supernatural as it is, is threaded into history: the imperial venture that was literally, for many Indian women, accompanied by rape and that was also a larger, metaphorical violation, the rape of a culture and a continent. Both Malinche and La Llorona, in turn, can be linked to another female icon of Mexican American culture discussed earlier, the Virgin of Guadalupe. The individual significance of these three female icons varies, of course, and they are clearly distinct from one another. One contemporary Mexican American writer, Gloria Anzaldúa, for instance, refers to them, respectively, as 'the virgin mother who has abandoned us', 'the raped mother whom we have abandoned', and 'the mother who seeks her lost children and is a combination of the other two'. But all three function as originators and mediators, their stories furnishing a vital element in the Mexican American myth of origins and history. And all three have become captivating cultural icons: not least, in contemporary Chicano literature.

What is especially powerful about these tales from the Hispanic Southwest is what tends to mark out all folktales transmitted via an oral tradition: poetic repetition, narrative spontaneity and fluency, a startling generic mix, and the sense that *this* tale and tale teller form part of a continuity, a vital chain of narrative and human connection. In a story called 'La Llorona, Malinche, and the Unfaithful Maria', for instance, the audience is quickly told the story of three women who killed their children. The first, La Llorona, died; her ring was taken from her dead hand and then passed on to a girl who 'later became known as Malinche'. After drowning all three of her children, she also died, although 'even after she had died, she would cry out, "Ohhhhh, my children, where are they?" ' And the ring was then taken from her finger by a woman 'later known as Unfaithful Maria'. Obeying the instructions of an evil spirit, she killed her three children too. But her fate, we are told, was rather different from that of her predecessors. 'Her head turned into that of a horse'; and, in addition, 'one of her feet was that of a horse, and one was that of a chicken'. After this sudden move into the grotesque, the tale is brought into the present. 'This started back in 1800,' we learn, 'and is still going on today in Mexico.' 'My grandparents told me this story. Then my stepfather,' the anonymous narrator explains. 'Then my grandmother, my father's mother, told me this story of La Llorona who was the first. My mother told me the second story of Malinche. My stepfather told me about the third.' Not only that, we are assured, the stepfather had actually seen Unfaithful Maria. One story shades into another here: so much so that, by the end, Unfaithful Maria is actually referred to as 'La Llorona'. And one storytelling shades into another as well, as earlier versions, earlier moments of tale telling, are invoked. This insistent rhythm of repetition, accumulation is accompanied by a narrative approach that constantly surprises: for all that one episode melts into the next, via the device of the ring, we never quite know where the story will go next or what the exact tone will be. Magic and melodrama, the sentimental and the Gothic, morality and bizarre humour are mixed together to create a mood of enchantment. And, while the audience is reminded of many other occasions of storytelling, and other storytellers, they are intimately involved with this particular one. This, in short and in every respect, is a tale of community.

African American polemic and poetry

The community that aroused most debate in the first half of the nineteenth century was neither the Native American nor the Mexican American one, but the African American community of slaves. And crucial to that debate were not only the slave narratives of writers like Douglass and Jacobs but also the polemic of such African Americans as David Walker (1785–1830) and Henry Highland Garnet (1815–82). Walker was born in North Carolina. His father was a slave but his mother was a free black woman; and so, according to the slave laws of that time, which stipulated that a child would follow the condition of his or her mother, Walker was born free. In 1827, he became an agent for the newly established *Freedom's Journal*. Two years later, he published the work that made him famous, and put a price on his head in the South: *David Walker's Appeal in Four Articles; Together with a Preamble, to the Colored Citizens of the World, but in Particular and Very Expressly, to those of the United States of America.* The elaborately formal title reflected Walker's aim of patterning the structure of his *Appeal* on the Constitution. But, while invoking American political precedent for his argument – and taking time to denounce Thomas Jefferson for suggesting that black people were inferior to whites – Walker also identified himself with the Biblical tradition of the prophet in the wilderness, attacking the hypocrisy of contemporary religious practice and summoning up divine punishment 'in behalf of the oppressed'. 'Are we MEN! – I ask you, O my brethren! are we MEN?' Walker asked his readers. 'Did our creator make us to be slaves to dirt and ashes like ourselves? Are they not dying worms as well as we?' he went on. 'Have they not to make their appearance before the tribunal of heaven, to answer for their deeds done in the body as well as we?' That is the characteristic tone of the *Appeal*. Beginning by pointing out that 'we (the colored people of these United States) are the most degraded, wretched, and abject set of beings that ever lived since the world began', Walker rejects the moderate approach of moral persuasion or an appeal to the religious sentiments of a white audience. Instead, he mocks the hypocrisy of white liberals and of white Christianity, then devotes his energies to making his black audience angry and proud. This militant document is, in effect, the first printed declaration of black nationalism in the United States.

Walker described himself as a 'restless disturber of the peace', and his *Appeal* certainly created a disturbance. It went into three editions in the last two years of his life, each edition increasingly urgent in its denunciation of racial injustice – and increasingly insistent that black people should unite to take action, and be ready to kill or be killed for the cause of freedom. Walker was not thoughtlessly militant. He argued for a programme of African American educational, spiritual and political renewal so that constructive social change would follow black liberation. And his commitment to the black community, and the idea of African Americans freeing themselves, did not prevent him from acknowledging a debt to white abolitionists. He expressed his gratitude, in the *Appeal*, to those white Americans who, as he put it, 'have volunteered their services for our redemption'; 'we . . . thank them from the bottom of our hearts', he explained, 'and have our eyes steadfastly fixed upon them, and their labors of love for God and man'. Nevertheless, Walker not only struck fear into the hearts of white Southerners, he also perturbed some white Northern abolitionists, who found the *Appeal* 'injudicious'. And, given the prevailing political climate of the time, it is easy to see why. Walker affirmed black citizenship in the republic at a time when many white abolitionists were arguing for the return of emancipated slaves to Africa. He insisted on black unity when many others were talking in terms of assimilation. And he made no attempt to be moderate or placatory in tone or gradualist in approach. The white South tried to suppress circulation of the *Appeal*. It may have had a hand in its author's death, since he died in suspicious circumstances; it certainly wanted him dead. But, even after Walker's sudden death, the *Appeal* continued to be reprinted and to circulate widely. 'Our sufferings will come to an *end*, in spite of all the Americans this side of *eternity*,' Walker said: that sounded like, and was indeed, a threat. It was also, though, an affirmation of hope, forged in the belief that African Americans had only to summon up the courage and collective will in order to be free. 'Yea,' Walker asserted, 'I would meet death with avidity far! far! in preference to such *servile submission* to the murderous hands of tyrants': like earlier, white Americans,

Walker asked to be given liberty or death – and he wanted others of his community to ask exactly the same.

Henry Highland Garnet wrote 'A Brief Sketch of the Life and Character of David Walker'. In 1848, with the financial aid of the militant white abolitionist John Brown, he combined his 'Call to Rebellion' speech, as it was known, with Walker's *Appeal* in one pamphlet. That suggests the degree of the connection between the two men, and the sense Garnet in particular had of sharing beliefs and commitments with Walker. Garnet was born a slave in Maryland, but escaped with his family in 1825. He became a Presbyterian minister and, in 1843, he attended the National Negro Convention in Buffalo, New York. There, he delivered his *Address to the Slaves of the United States of America*: his 'Call to Rebellion' speech which, as the popular title indicated, argued for violent resistance if necessary in the slaves' dealings with their masters. Taking up Walker's argument that slaves should be ready to 'kill or be killed' to achieve freedom, Garnet insisted that the condition of slavery made it impossible for slaves to obey the Ten Commandments. 'The diabolical injustice by which your liberties are cloven down, *neither God, nor angels, or just men, command you to suffer for a single moment,*' he told the slaves. '*Therefore it is your solemn and imperative duty to use every means, both moral, intellectual and physical, that promises success.*' Garnet used many of the rhetorical and argumentative strategies of Walker. Like Walker, he asked the slaves, 'are you men? Where is the blood of your fathers?' 'Awake, awake,' he told them, 'millions of voices are calling you! Your dead fathers speak to you from their graves.' Like Walker, too, he insisted that the only choice was '*Liberty* or *death*'. 'Brethren, arise, arise! Strike for your lives and liberties!' he implored the slave community. '*Rather die freemen than live to be slaves. Remember that you are four millions!*'

What Garnet added to the argument and language of the *Appeal* – along with pointing out, fiercely, that no Commandment required a slave to suffer 'diabolical injustice' – was a perspective at once international and peculiarly American. Garnet was a travelled man: he had journeyed in America before giving his 'Call to Rebellion' speech and, later, he was to journey as consul general to Liberia, where he died. He was also widely read and informed. And he used the revolutionary ferment in Europe to support the cause of slave liberation. 'The nations of the old world are moving in the great cause of universal freedom,' he pointed out. Now it was time for African Americans to move in obedience to a similar impulse, since 'no oppressed people have ever secured their liberty without resistance'. They owed it to themselves, Garnet added, not only as a peculiarly oppressed people but as Americans. 'Forget not that ye are native-born American citizens,' he told the slaves whom he addressed, 'and, as such, you are justly entitled to all the rights that are granted to the freest.' And they were Americans who, up until then, had been excluded from the American dream. 'Two hundred and twenty-seven years ago, the first of our injured race were brought to the shores of America,' Garnet exclaimed. But, unlike other immigrants, 'they came not with glad spirits to select their homes in the New World'; 'they came not with their own consent, to find an unmolested enjoyment of the blessings of this fruitful soil'; 'neither did they come flying upon the wings of Liberty, to a land of freedom'. On the contrary, 'they came with broken hearts, from their beloved native land, and were doomed to unrequited toil and deep degradation'. Now it was time to seize what was their right: what others, 'men calling themselves Christians', had gained coming to the shores of America. Garnet's peculiarly effective tactic here was to turn the white dream of American promise against white America, by claiming that it could and should be a black dream as well – and one to be realized, if necessary, by 'resistance, *resistance! resistance!*' When Garnet gave his speech in 1843, it was denounced by Frederick Douglass, who at that time was an advocate of non-violent 'moral suasion'. And it fell short, if only by one vote, of being approved as an official resolution of the Convention. But by the 1850s, Douglass had moved towards agreement with Garnet that freedom was to be seized by any means necessary. By 1863, both men were involved in raising troops for the Union army. Even before that, in 1847, the National Negro Convention endorsed Garnet's militant stand. These were measures of how far, and how quickly, things changed.

Both Walker and Garnet addressed a black audience. On the whole, the authors of the slave narratives addressed a white one; and so did the poet George Moses Horton (1797?–1883?). That was one reason why his comments on slavery tended to be more sporadic and muted, perhaps. Another, far more crucial, is that he lived for most of his life, and for all of his significant career as a poet, as a slave in the South. Born in North Carolina, Horton published his first volume of poetry, *The Hope of Liberty*, in 1829. It was published in North Carolina, with white support and financial aid; it was the first book of poetry by an African American for more than half a century, and the first book of any kind authored by a black Southerner. Most of the twenty-one poems in the volume are conventional variations on the themes of love, death and religion. But three tentatively negotiate the issue of slavery, most notably one entitled 'On Hearing of the Intention of a Gentleman to Purchase the Poet's Freedom'. In this poem, Horton scarcely disguises the confession that he had been 'on the dusky verge of despair' until the chance 'to break the slavish bar' had been opened up to him. The conventions of servile gratitude for a gracious white 'intention' – which, as it happened, was never fulfilled – enables the poet to talk in relatively frank terms about the 'dismal path' of his life as a slave. Horton was never freed before the Civil War, but his master did allow him to hire his time as a professional poet, waiter and handyman, and to publish his work in such abolitionist periodicals as *The Liberator* and *The North Star*. Then, in 1845, Horton published his second volume, *The Poetical Works of George Horton, The Colored Bard of North Carolina*. Again, the poet did not risk offending his white patrons and public by openly attacking slavery. But, again, he did allow himself to comment on the sometimes bitter consequences of being a slave.

A poem called 'Division of an Estate', for example, is remarkable for the sympathy it inspires for its subjects: slaves being sold at auction after the death of their master. There is irony here. The slaves, as property, are rhetorically linked to other property: 'the flocks and herds' of sheep and cattle, the 'bristling swine', howling dogs and 'sad horses' that are left, for a while, 'void of an owner'. And there is also pathos, as the poet asks the reader to behold 'the dark suspense in which poor vassals stand' on the auction block. The mind of each, he points out, 'upon the spine of chance hangs fluctuant', knowing that 'the day of separation is at hand'. Presumably, in this case, the distinction that many white Southerners were willing to make between slavery and the slave trade allowed Horton to emphasize the pathos. It was, at best, a false distinction, since slavery could not have existed without the slave trade: but it gave the poet some room for rhetorical manoeuvre. Horton was, fortunately, never to experience the horrors of the auction block himself. He was freed towards the end of the Civil War, and published a third and final volume called *Naked Genius* just after the fall of the Confederacy. This collection of 133 poems, most of them previously unpublished, continues the themes of his earlier work. In the poems on slavery, however, Horton does move from complaining about the pains and sadness the peculiar institution involves to attacking its fundamental injustice. And in one remarkable piece, 'George Moses Horton, Myself', he offers a fragment of autobiography that explores the difficulties of being both a black slave and a poet. 'My genius from a boy, / Has fluttered like a bird within my heart /', he tells the reader, 'But could not thus confined her powers employ, / Impatient to depart'. 'She like a restless bird, / Would spread her wings, her power to be unfurl'd, /' he concludes, 'And let her songs be loudly heard, / And dart from world to world.' It is an apt summary of the torment he had suffered, both as a man and a poet: a torment that he hardly ever dared openly to confess. And it announces a problem, of being a black writer imprisoned in a predominantly white culture and language, that many later African American poets were to explore.

Abolitionist and pro-slavery writing

Among the white writers who were noted abolitionists were Wendell Phillips (1811–84), Thomas Wentworth Higginson (1823–1911) and, most famously, William Lloyd Garrison (1805–79). Garrison worked with Benjamin Lundy on a periodical titled *The Genius of Universal Emancipation* for several years. But he broke with Lundy and the paper over the position Lundy held, that slaves should be emancipated gradually and removed to Africa. He began to argue for immediate emancipation, without colonization of the freed or compensation for their former masters, and to argue his case he founded *The Liberator* at the beginning of 1831. Inspired by the beliefs of the Great Awakening, Garrison was convinced that the Kingdom of God could be created on earth by men and women actively committed to eradicating evil and injustice. That led him to support the temperance movement, women's rights and, in particular, the abolition of slavery: only by abolition, he argued, could 'the "self-evident truth" maintained in the American Declaration of Independence, "that all men are created equal"', be realized in practice. That was why, he recollected in *William Lloyd Garrison: The Story of His Life* (1885), 'I determined . . . to lift up the standard of emancipation in the eyes of the nation, *within sight of Bunker Hill and in the birthplace of liberty*'. 'I am aware that many object to the severity of my language,' Garrison admitted. But, to them, he posed the question, 'is there not cause for severity? I *will* be as harsh as truth, and as uncompromising as justice'. Besides, he asked, where was the room for thinking, speaking or writing 'with moderation' in such a crisis? 'Tell a man whose house is on fire to give a moderate alarm; tell him to moderately rescue his wife from the hands of the ravisher; tell the mother to gradually extricate her babe from the fire into which it has fallen.' Garrison was fervent in his language. 'I am in earnest –,' he declared, 'I will not equivocate – I will not excuse – I will not retreat a single inch – AND I WILL BE HEARD.' He was, however, in favour of moral persuasion rather than coercion. There was, in fact, a curious gap between the violence of his words and the creed of non-violence he embraced. The violent terms in which he often expressed himself offended some, Garrison admitted. For others, though, like Frederick Douglass, who eventually broke with him over the issue, it was the belief that non-violence could defeat the power of slavery that was the problem.

The editorials and journalistic work of Garrison often possess the rhetorical power of great speeches. In the case of Wendell Phillips, it was his power as a writer and performer of public speeches that secured his place in the abolitionist movement. For twenty-five years, Phillips toured the lyceum circuit. His lectures included diverse topics but the ones for which he became and remained famous were on the subject of slavery. What Phillips was notable for, in particular, was his insistence that black people had a natural right to be free because they were the equal of whites. That might seem an unremarkable argument now but, at that time, there were many scientists ready to argue that African Americans were a separate and inferior race: not only Southerners like Samuel Cartwright, who re-ferred to them as 'the Prognathous Species of Mankind', but Northerners like Louis Agassiz, the eminent biologist. In his speech 'Toussaint L'Ouverture', for instance, eventually published in *Speeches, Lectures, and Letters* (1863), Phillips celebrated the black leader of the revolution against the French in Haiti. In what numerous contemporary audiences found a spellbinding account, Phillips described the courageous life and tragic death of Toussaint. Toussaint was, Phillips suggested, superior to Oliver Cromwell as a soldier and a statesman, superior also to Napo-leon and even to Washington. Talking of 'Negro courage', endurance, wisdom and tolerance in the person of Toussaint, Phillips came quite close to suggesting that black people were not just the equals but the superiors of whites. Certainly, he emphasized that they had had to struggle against greater odds than anyone even to get their story told. 'I am about to tell you the story of a Negro who has left hardly one written line,' Phillips customarily began his oration. 'All the materials for his biography are from the lips of his enemies.' Phillips's aims were immediate: to arouse his audience to support for the abolitionist cause and the possible necessity of direct action – the oration closed, in fact, with the name of John Brown being invoked directly before that of Toussaint L'Ouverture. But in pointing out that he was unearthing a secret history, one that rarely if ever was allowed into white history books, he was curiously anticipating what was to become a resonant theme in much later, African American writing.

Of Thomas Wentworth Higginson little is remembered today, apart from the facts that he trained and commanded a troop of African Americans during the Civil War and acted as a literary mentor to Emily Dickinson. The first supplied the subject for his book, *Army Life in a Black Regiment* (1870); the second led him to co-edit the first published volume of Dickinson's poetry, in 1890. During his life, however, Higginson was one of the most celebrated essayists and speakers in the United States. He was also an active campaigner. He played a vital role in the temperance movement; he fought for labour reforms; he was a founder of the Women's Suffrage Association; he engaged in numerous missions to help fugitive slaves and he gave support and financial aid to John Brown's raid on Harper's Ferry. The involvement in the abolitionist movement, in particular, led him to produce some of his best work: not only, eventually, his account of life in a black regiment but also a series of essays on black rebellions. The essays were written in the 1850s but not published, in the *Atlantic*, until the Civil War began. They are remarkable not least because Higginson, like Phillips, makes the point that he is revealing a secret history. 'The biographies of slaves can hardly be individualised,' Higginson suggests, in his essay on Nat Turner, the leader of the 1831 slave insurrection in Virginia, 'they belong to a class.' That seems questionable, if not downright wrong, given the particularized nature of the slave narratives of, say, Douglass and Jacobs. Higginson is on surer ground, however, when he points out how little is known for a fact about Nat Turner himself. He illustrates this by saying that not much is known about Turner's wife, apart from the fact that she was a slave who belonged to another master. 'But this is much,' Higginson adds, 'for this is equivalent to saying that . . . her husband had no more power to protect her than the man who lies bound upon a plundered vessel's deck has power to protect his wife on board the pirate schooner disappearing into the horizon.' Proceeding with this combination of careful detective work and colourful language, Higginson then goes on to a detailed account of the Turner revolt. Cooler in tone than Phillips, he is also less drawn than Phillips is to the violence of revolution, calling it 'awful work'. He is reluctant, too, to plunge very deep into origins and motivation. Having cited various theories as to the specific origins of the 1831 revolt, he ends simply by saying that 'whether the theories . . . were wise or foolish, the insurrection made its mark'. But while he is by no means attracted to the violence of the revolt, Higginson sees its necessity. And while he allows Nat Turner and his rebellion a degree of mystery, he leaves the reader in no doubt as to the 'extraordinary' character of the man and the exemplary nature of the movement he instigated. 'This poor man, who did not even possess a name, beyond one abrupt monosyllable – for even the name of Turner was the master's property, – still lives,' Higginson ends his essay, 'a memory of terror, and a symbol of wild retribution.' And in the project of naming Nat Turner, and enabling black history to live, Higginson clearly feels he has played his part.

If Garrison was the journalist of the white abolitionist movement, Phillips the orator and Higginson its essayist, then John Greenleaf Whittier (1807–92) was its poet. As his 'Proem' (1849) indicates, Whittier had no vast ambitions. 'O Freedom!

If to me belong / Nor mighty Milton's gift divine, / Nor Marvell's wit and graceful song, /' he declares in that piece, 'Still with a love as deep and strong / As theirs, I lay, like them, my best gifts on thy shrine!' All he wanted to do, in fact, was to denounce those whose preoccupations with their own selfish needs made them oblivious to the needs of others. That meant, above all, the slaveowners: he once said that he placed a 'higher value' on his name appearing on the Anti-Slavery Declaration than on the title page of any book. Beyond that, he also wanted to offer as an imaginative alternative to such selfishness the kind of small and tightly knit community of interests he describes in 'First-Day Thoughts' (1857) and, perhaps his most famous poem, *Snow-Bound* (1866). Whittier was born in Massachusetts to poor Quaker parents, and the Quaker experience remained fundamental to him throughout his life. It was this, in fact, which supplied him with his ideal: of a group of people held together by common values and by the belief that each member of the group is possessed of a certain 'inner light'. During the long narrative of *Snow-Bound*, for instance, the reader receives a strong sense of the particularity and individuality of the characters presented: but he or she receives a strong sense of their 'apartness' as a group as well, and so a sense of their mutuality. Cut off from the rest of the world by a snowstorm, the various members of his family and household that Whittier remembers pass the time in recalling childhood memories; and as the memories accumulate it becomes clear that an act of communion is being realized, comparable to those moments in a Quaker meeting when various of those present recount and share their spiritual experiences with their friends. More than this, the poem itself gradually assumes the status of an act of communion. Since Whittier is describing a particular winter of his childhood, he is also remembering and meditating and, in a way, offering a part of himself to the individual reader; he also is inviting others to share in a separate peace.

Snow-Bound was not, of course, published until after the end of the Civil War. But it was from the experiential basis it describes, a sense of genuine contact and community, that Whittier's poetic assault on slavery was launched. And it was an assault from several directions. 'The Hunters of Men' (1835), for instance, takes the path of bitter humour: a parodic hunting song, it mocks in jaunty rhyme those 'hunters of men' who go 'Right merrily hunting the black man, whose sin / Is the curl of his hair and the hue of his skin'. 'The Farewell of a Virginia Slave Mother to Her Daughters Sold into Southern Bondage' (1838) takes, as its title indicates, the path of melodrama and sentiment: as the mother of the title laments the loss of her daughters, 'Gone, gone, – sold and gone, / In the rice swamp dank and lone' where 'no mother's eye is near them' and 'no mother's ear can hear them'. 'The Slave Ship' (1846), describing the jettisoning of slaves who, having been blinded by sickness, are no longer saleable, takes the direction of Gothic horror. And in 'Massachusetts to Virginia' (1843) Whittier opts for declamation, as he denounces any attempt to return escaped slaves to the slave states. Recalling the war in which 'the Bay State' and 'the Old Dominion' held common cause, and both Massachusetts and Virginia fought for freedom, he ends by proclaiming that there will be 'No slave-hunt in our borders, – no pirate on our strand! / No fetters in the Bay State,

– no slave upon our land!' What Whittier sought in all such poems was to persuade: he used whatever poetic means lay at his disposal to draw the reader into examining his or her conscience. Out of that, he hoped, would develop a clearer sense of personal and communal purpose. To that extent, his anti-slavery pieces are just as clearly targeted as *Snow-Bound* is at making the reader share in the experience of moral re-examination and collective understanding. And they express, just as firmly as the Quaker poems do, his belief that poetry should be no more than a means to a higher, spiritual end.

At the same time as Whittier and his colleagues were arguing for the abolition of slavery, another group in the South were arguing quite the contrary: that slavery was not only an economic necessity but a positive good. As these Southerners saw or claimed to see it, slavery was an integral part of the established, agrarian mode of life enjoyed by all the states below the Mason-Dixon line. These defenders of slavery, and by extension of the social system of the South, included the writer and social philosopher George Fitzhugh (1806–81), the novelist William Gilmore Simms (1806–70), the poet William J. Grayson (1788–1863), the lawyer and writer Henry Hughes (1829–62), the scientific agriculturalist and fanatical secessionist Edmund Ruffin (1794–1865), a professor of political philosophy, Thomas Dew (1802–46), and the politician James Henry Hammond (1807–64). Some of the arguments these defenders of slavery used were drawn from the Bible, purporting to find a theological warrant for the slave system. Others involved supposedly scientific theories concerning the separate, inferior origins of the 'Negro race'. Central to their defence, however, was the contention that Frederick Douglass, among many others, found so offensive – that the South was a feudal society, an extended family in which the master acted as patriarchal head. Everyone, black and white, had their part to play in this family. And to the slave was given the role of child, dependant. Incapable of looking after himself, the slave depended on the plantation patriarch – and, to a lesser extent, the mistress or matriarch of the house – for support and guidance: the security of work and a home, a basic moral education, and care in infancy, sickness and old age.

This defence of slavery as a fundamentally benevolent institution, and of slave society as feudal, hierarchical and harmonious, was articulated in various ways and forms. Fitzhugh wrote several polemical works, among them *Sociology for the South; or, The Failure of Free Society* (1854) and *Cannibals All!; or, Slaves Without Masters* (1857). In these, he argued that the South was 'the most prosperous and happy country in the world' because it embraced a 'protective philosophy, which takes care of the weak while it governs them'. The 'free trade or competitive philosophy' pursued elsewhere was 'silly and suicidal', Fitzhugh claimed, making all men 'slaves to capital'; and the rest of the world would be wise to give it up and to follow the example of the South. Simms published over eighty books. These included *The Yemassee* (1835), a story of Indian warfare set in his home state of South Carolina, and a long series of romances – written between 1834 and 1854 and known as the Border Romances – that are based on the actual history of the South from its settlement to the middle of the nineteenth century. In the Border Romances set during the Revolution, in particular, Simms used the past to foreground contemporary concerns, with the Revolutionaries of the South depicted as heroic cavaliers, fighting for an essentially aristocratic civilization, and the British shown as vulgar surrogates for the Yankees, with nothing to motivate them except 'the love of gain'. So, in the most striking of these works, *The Sword and the Distaff* (1853; revised as *Woodcraft* [1854]), he places his cavalier hero, 'a gentleman and a sportsman' and 'a centre of parish civilisation', against men who think in nothing but crassly utilitarian terms. As one of these foils to the aristocratic hero puts it, talking of the destiny of man, 'He's to go on gitting, and gitting, and gitting to the end of the season, untill Death gits him'. Clearly, this is Fitzhugh's 'competitive philosophy' in vulgar human form; and, equally clearly, the reader is meant to regard the protective paternalism, the aristocratic sense of *noblesse oblige*, embodied in the cavalier heroes, as an infinitely preferable alternative. 'To be national in literature,' Simms once declared, 'one needs to be *sectional*'; and his fictional work, where he celebrated what he called 'the Southern aristocrat – the true nobleman of that region', shows just how much he chose to follow his own advice.

While Simms turned mainly to fiction to defend the South and slave society, Grayson used poetry. In 1856, he published a long poem in heroic couplets, 'The Hireling and the Slave', devoted to the theme that the transplanted African slave enjoyed a far better lot than the supposedly free worker who laboured for bare subsistence. On the one hand, Grayson offered an idyllic portrait of 'Congo's simple child' learning 'each civilising art' under the tutelage of his master; 'schooled by slavery', he was also 'fed, clothed, protected many a patient year'. On the other, he painted a harrowing picture of the place and plight of the hireling, the 'wage slave': 'the worn child compelled in mines to slave', workers 'in reeking masses thrown', the women forced to 'prostitute themselves for bread', a world without security or any sense of community where 'gaunt famine prowls around his pauper prey'. It was a bleak vision of capitalism, framed within a decidedly conservative version of American pastoral. And even when those who argued for slavery took what they regarded as a more forensic, scientific approach, that strange version of pastoralism remained. Both Hughes and Ruffin, for instance, wrote what they saw as learned treatises. Hughes called his *A Treatise on Sociology, Theoretical and Practical* (1854); Ruffin titled his, even more impressively, *The Political Economy of Slavery; or, The Institution Considered in Regard to its Influence on Public Wealth and General Welfare* (1853). Learned they might have been, at least in appearance and general tone. But that did not stop Ruffin from portraying the old plantation as a centre of culture, devoted to 'social and mental occupation' and 'the improvement of mind and manners'. Nor did it prevent Hughes from anticipating the day when slavery, to which he gave the euphemism 'warranteeism', would be accepted everywhere in the United States – and so the sweet benefits of Southern pastoralism would be enjoyed nationwide. 'In the plump flush of full-feeding health', Hughes prophesied, the 'happy warrantees' would one day 'banquet in PLANTATION-REFECTORIES; worship in PLANTATION-CHAPELS; learn in PLANTATION-SCHOOLS'. And, 'at the cool of evening', they would 'chant old songs, tell tales' before retiring to 'PLANTATION-DORMITORIES over whose gates Health and Rest sit smiling at the feet of Wealth and Labour' – then, at daybreak, 'rise . . . to begin again welcome days of jocund toil'. Ludicrous as this all might be, the vision Hughes embraced and prophesied issued from the impulse that animated the central argument for the South and slavery. And it both recollected and anticipated many other, similar visions: many other occasions in American thought and writing on which the slave society of the South was rehabilitated, transformed into a garden paradise.

Of course, Ruffin and Hughes did try to construct an argumentative framework for their visions. So did Dew in his *Review of the Debate in the Virginia Legislature of 1831 and 1832* (1832). So did Hammond, in his speeches in the Senate: most famously, in one delivered in 1858, where he argued that slaves were the 'mud-sill', the material foundation on which 'the civilisation, the refinement' of white Southern culture was built. So, for that matter, did Hammond, Dew, Simms and many others in a seminal document for the cause, a collection of essays published in 1853 called *The Pro-Slavery Argument: As Maintained by the Most Distinguished Writers of the Southern States*. Society was seen, according to this framework, in terms derived immediately from the British political philosopher Edmund Burke and ultimately from Aristotle: that is, as a natural extension of the human personality, a kind of biological unit. Or, as Fitzhugh put it, 'Society is a work of nature, and grows'. Like any organism, society was complex and inegalitarian, a web of different interests and castes. 'All harmonies, whether in the moral or physical world,' declared Simms in a ringing passage in *The Pro-Slavery Argument*, 'arise wholly from the inequality of the tones and aspects; and all things, whether in art or nature, social and political systems, but for this inequality, would give forth monotony and discord.' From this basis – this premise that, as one contributor to *The Pro-Slavery Argument* put it, 'inequality is deeply founded in nature' – the defenders of slavery launched an attack on the entire liberal tradition. Man, they contended, was not born free but – to quote *The Pro-Slavery Argument* again – 'in a state of the most helpless dependence on others . . . to subjection . . . to sin and ignorance'. Nor was he born to equality: that 'much lauded but nowhere accredited dogma of Mr Jefferson' concerning such matters, Hammond was among many others to insist, was 'merely new-fangled philosophy', 'the effusion of a young and ardent mind which riper years might have corrected'.

Out with the Declaration of Independence, also, went the notion of society as a contract between its members. Fitzhugh, for instance, dismissed that notion with the utmost scorn. 'Fathers', Fitzhugh argued, 'do not derive their authority as heads of families, from the consent of wife and children'; and, since the family was simply 'the first and most natural development' of man's social nature, it followed that the leaders of society did not derive *their* authority from the consent of those *they* led. The 'abstract propositions of a Locke, a Jefferson', Fitzhugh among others insisted, were the products of an era when 'the human mind became presumptuous and undertook to form governments upon exact philosophical principles, just as men make clocks, or watches, or mills'; they represented nothing more than an 'ignis fatuus', the airy 'speculations of closet philosophers'. What the pro-slavery polemicists did, in short, was extraordinary. Starting with an organicist notion of society, they attacked the founding principles – drawn from the Enlightenment and a progressive idea of history – on which the American republic had been built. The notions of natural innocence and human perfectibility they countered with their belief in the indelible nature of evil. 'To say that there is evil in any institution,' the first essay in *The Pro-Slavery Argument* declares, 'is only to say that it is human.' To the idea that liberty and equality were natural, universal rights they responded in the spirit of Fitzhugh. 'Liberty and equality,' Fitzhugh loftily declared, 'are new things under the sun.' 'Free competition', Fitzhugh, like others, insisted, was 'but another name for liberty and equality'; that threw 'the whole weight of society on its weakest members'; so 'liberty and equality' were essentially destructive instruments, since they served to 'combine all men in oppressing that part of mankind who most need sympathy, and protection'. Individualism, self-reliance, self-improvement: all that meant, from this perspective, was, to quote Fitzhugh again, 'each man's eagerly pursuing his own selfish welfare unfettered and unrestricted by legal regulation'. All that would result would be a world 'not only destructive to the morals, but to the happiness of society': a jungle of speculative capitalism inhabited by 'cannibals all'. The arguments of those who defended slavery always brought them back to that: the alternatives that, as they saw it, were posed by the social models of the South and the North. A garden or a jungle, an organic society or a brutally competitive one, a world of benevolent paternalism where slaves lived secure in their homeplace or one of oppressive anarchy where wage slaves fought, in a sense consumed, each other for personal gain: these were the maps of the two regions charted by Southerners writing in support of their peculiar institution. And it says much for their rhetorical power, if not for their historical accuracy, that they exercised considerable influence, and perhaps still do. Even those who attacked the South, many of them, tended to see it in terms of feudalism – although, of course, in terms of feudal darkness: 'the South', Wendell Phillips claimed, for instance, 'is the thirteenth and fourteenth centuries'. Those many Southerners, in turn, who defended the vision of the South as a feudal paradise not only paid it lip service. When the time came, they were ready to fight for it, and even pay for it with their blood.

Two women writers who offer intriguing variations on this idea of the pre-Civil War South as a model of paternalism are Caroline Lee Hentz (1800–56) and Mary Boykin Chesnut (1823–86). Hentz was born in the North; however, she moved South, to North Carolina, then later Kentucky, Alabama and Florida. She wrote many novels to support herself and her husband: 'I am compelled to turn my brains to gold and to sell them to the highest bidder', she complained once. But the novel for which she remains best known is *The Planter's Northern Bride* (1854). The interest of the novel lies in the way, in painting an idyllic portrait of life on the old plantation, it replicates the pro-slavery argument in fictional form. In this, it is typical in some ways of plantation novels from *The Valley of Shenandoah* (1824) by George Tucker (1775–1861) and *Swallow Barn* by John Pendleton Kennedy through to many of the romances of William Gilmore Simms. It is typical, too, in other ways, of stories announcing the special status and even Manifest Destiny of the South, like *The Partisan Leader* (1836) by Nathaniel Beverley Tucker (1784–1851) and *The Cavaliers of Virginia* (1834–5) and *The Knights of the Golden Horseshoe* (1845) by William A. Caruthers (1802–46). Above all, though, it is typical of the legion of novels written in response to *Uncle Tom's Cabin* (1852) by Harriet Beecher Stowe. Of Stowe, Hentz once said, 'slavery, as she describes it, is an entirely new institution to us'. She felt she knew the institution far better than the author of *Uncle Tom's Cabin*, having lived in the South; and she was determined to show her readers how. The story contains the usual retinue of characters attending the plantation romance: including young men full of 'magnanimity and chivalry', 'pure and high-toned' young women, and interfering abolitionists who are determined to free the slaves even though those slaves do not want to be freed. But what supplies the argumentative core of the book is the hero, a Southern planter called Mr Moreland, and his faithful personal 'servant', Albert, 'a young mulatto'. Moreland is described as 'intelligent and liberal'; Albert is 'a handsome, golden-skinned youth', 'accustomed to wait on his master and listen to the conversation of refined gentlemen'. As a result of such service, the reader is told, Albert 'had very little of the dialect of the negro, and those familiar with the almost unintelligible jargon which delineations of the sable character put into their lips, could not but be astonished at the propriety of his language and pronunciation'. This relieves Hentz of the burden of writing such dialect herself for a relatively important character with much to say. But it has the further advantage of supplying one small but crucial illustration of the benefits of slavery. The slave system, its defenders were inclined to argue, not only supported and protected the slaves, it helped to educate and refine them; and Albert's distinctive manner of speech supposedly shows just that.

The way that Hentz goes about her business of writing a fictional defence of the South in general, and of slavery in particular, is indicated by the opening chapters of the book. Moreland takes Albert on a trip through New England, secure in the knowledge that Albert is happy in his service and will not try to escape. They visit a village described as 'the very hot-bed of fanaticism', where Moreland explains to a sympathetic Northerner that, in the South, 'we look upon our slaves as friends'. A poignant contrast is drawn, during the conversation with the Northerner, by the sudden appearance in the street where the two men are walking of a destitute young woman, sick and thrown out of work. Inevitably, Moreland reflects on the difference between her plight and the secure position of his slaves – and, more generally, 'between the Northern and Southern laborer, when reduced to a state of sickness and dependence'. He concludes that 'the sick and dying negro, retained under his master's roof, kindly nursed and ministered unto, with no sad, anxious lookings forward into the morrow for the supply of nature's wants, no fears of being cast into the pauper's home . . . had . . . a far happier lot'. The one might have 'the nominal bondage of the slave', certainly: but the other had 'the bondage of poverty, whose iron chains we heard clanking in every region of God's earth'. Whether that may be true or not, Moreland thinks, 'let the thousand toiling operatives of the Northern manufactories tell; let the poor, starving seamstresses, whose pallid faces mingle their chill, wintry gleams with the summer glow and splendour of the Northern cities, tell'. And, as if to underline the contrast between unhappy hireling and happy slave, Albert then reappears, to tell his master with some amusement about his conversation with a few Northerners, whose questions to him reveal that, as Albert puts it, 'they didn't know nothing about us' – or about him, in particular, and his personal contentment. After the conversation between Albert and Moreland, the novel moves back to Moreland's reflections again: as he compares the condition of Southern slaves not only with the wage slaves of the North but with 'the groaning serfs of Russia; the starving sons of Ireland; the squalid operatives of England'. Moreland is now drawn to 'the irresistible conclusion' that 'the enslaved children of Africa' are 'the happiest *subservient* race' to be found 'on the face of the globe'. This alternating rhythm of action and reflection, conversation and polemic, is characteristic not only of *The Planter's Northern Bride* as a whole but also of other plantation and pro-slavery romances of this kind. The narrative illustrates the pro-slavery thesis; the thesis informs and shapes the narrative. The full story is still to unfold but, even in these opening pages, Hentz has established the basic structure. And she has also underscored her fundamental purpose, which is not just to entertain but to instruct: to expose the abolitionist lies told about the treatment of slaves – 'such as being chained, handcuffed, scourged, flayed, and burned alive', as Moreland puts it – and to convince the reader that the peculiar institution of the South is also a humane one.

That, however, was not how Mary Boykin Chesnut saw it. Born in South Carolina, she married into the wealthy Chesnut family. Her husband was an influential politician, with close connections to Jefferson Davis, the president of the Confederacy during the Civil War. Like many at the time, Chesnut kept a diary in which she recorded meetings with national figures, news of the progress of the war, and her everyday experiences and opinions. She then created a book out of the diary and her memories of the past but died before it could be published. This composite work did not appear until 1905, then in a 1949 edition titled *A Diary from Dixie*; and the original, more highly personal diary was not published until 1984. There are many remarkable aspects to the diary: but what perhaps is most remarkable is Chesnut's commentary on slavery. 'I wonder if it be a sin to think slavery a curse to my land,' she muses in an entry for 8 March 1861. 'Men and women are punished when their masters and mistresses are brutes and not when they do wrong – and then we are surrounded by prostitutes.' That last remark picks up a recurrent theme in the diary. Chesnut was acutely aware of the brutal, ironic fact that, while the ruling white patriarchs in the Southern states insisted on their separation from, and even difference as a species to, their black slaves, they did not hesitate to have sexual contact with them. While they drew an absolute boundary between whites and blacks, they crossed the boundary constantly; and the consequences of that were large numbers of children neither 'white' nor 'black' but both. The most vivid example, perhaps, of slavery as a violation of humanity was offered by the white, and usually male, sexual use of their 'property'. And the most striking illustration of the slave system as hypocrisy in action was something Chesnut observed. 'What do you say to this?' she wrote in the entry for 26 August 1861. 'A magnate who runs a hideous black harem and its consequences under the same roof with his lovely white wife and his beautiful accomplished daughters?' 'He holds his head as high and poses as the model of all human virtues to these poor women whom God and the laws have given him,' she went on. 'From the height of his awful majesty he scolds and thunders at them, as if he never did wrong in his life.'

'I hate slavery,' Chesnut confessed. What she hated about it, especially, was the fact that, as she put it, 'our men live all in one house with their wives and concubines, and the mulattoes one sees in every family exactly resemble the white children'. That inspired her sympathy for white women forced to bear daily witness to the infidelity and hypocrisy of their male kin but obliged never to say anything – 'supposed', as Chesnut expressed it, 'never to dream of what is as plain before their eyes as sunlight, and play their part of unsuspecting angels to the letter'. But it did not inspire her to any sympathy for black women who were, after all, the main victims here, subject to constant sexual coercion. 'My countrywomen are as pure as angels, tho' surrounded by another race who are the social evil!' Chesnut lamented. As she saw it, the slave system was to blame for all this 'nastiness', but so were 'facile black women'. Ironically, Chesnut could see through the Southern myth of the extended family far enough to notice that the white 'father' was constantly violating his black 'daughters': but not far enough to absolve those 'daughters' of blame. She was too deeply implicated in myths about black sexuality, and the supposed animalism of the black race, for that. She could appreciate the hypocritical manoeuvre involved in placing white women on a pedestal, as models of 'purity and innocence', and then turning to black women for sexual gratification, the kinds of satisfaction that white women were supposed neither to have nor to give. But she could not understand that both white and black women were being used here, suffering from the manoeuvre, and that, by any human measure, the sufferings of black women were far worse. This is all to say that the diaries of Chesnut offer as much a symptom as a diagnosis of the moral and material brutality of slavery. What she saw was limited, as well as illuminated, by her condition as an intelligent white woman of the privileged class. Her sympathies could only stretch a certain distance. And, at her best moments, she seems to have sensed this. Attending a black religious service, for instance, Chesnut confessed that she was deeply moved by 'the devotional passion of voice and manner' and by the hymns – 'the saddest of all earthly music', she wrote, 'weird and depressing beyond my powers to describe'. She would have liked, in a way, to join in: 'I would very much have liked to shout too', she recalled. But she could not: as she put it, 'it was a little too exciting for me'. The religious passion of the slaves, like their human pain, was something beyond her either fully to understand or to share.

Abolitionism and feminism

The diaries of Mary Boykin Chesnut are her one contribution to American literature, but a substantial one. They illustrate just how much forms of writing often considered to be outside the parameters of literature – among them, the sermon and lecture, the diary and journal – form an integral, in fact central, part of the American tradition: with its emphasis on the regulation and realization of the self. Another writer who became interested in the condition of slaves and the condition of women, Lydia Maria Child (1802–80), was, by contrast with Chesnut, prolific in her output. And her interests led her to become an abolitionist and, for a while, attract public censure. Child first made her mark with a historical novel, *Hobomok* (1824), which dealt with the relationship between a Puritan woman and a Native American man. It offers a vision of interracial union that is closer to Catharine Maria Sedgwick, in its suggestion that such unions are eminently possible, than it is to James Fenimore Cooper. Child founded and edited the first magazine for children in the United States, *Juvenile Miscellany*. She published a second novel in 1825, *The Rebels; or, Boston Before the Revolution*, about the agitation over the Stamp Tax. Then, in 1828, she married David Lee Child, a prominent abolitionist but also an impractical man, whom his wife had very often to support. Partly for financial reasons, Lydia Maria Child began writing practical advice books for women, such as *The Mother's Book* (1831) and *The American Frugal Housewife* (1831). 'Books of this kind have usually been written for the wealthy,' Child wrote in the opening chapter of *The American Frugal Housewife*; 'I have written for the poor.' Along with general maxims on health and housekeeping, and an emphasis on thrift and economy that Benjamin Franklin would have admired, the book strongly advises its women readers to give their daughters a good general education. 'The greatest and most universal error is, teaching girls to exaggerate the importance of getting married,' Child explains, 'and of course to place an undue importance upon the polite attentions of gentlemen.' Child does, certainly, see marriage and the domestic role as the usual, even desirable one for women: but she does not underestimate the importance of other skills and talents, even for women who will only apply them to the domestic sphere.

By 1833, Child had become actively involved in the abolitionist movement. It was that year she published *An Appeal in Favor of That Class of Americans Called Africans*. Later, in 1839, she published her *Anti-Slavery Catechism*, a pamphlet written in the form of questions and answers. What both documents reveal is that Child was a moderate abolitionist, just as she was a moderate feminist, anxious to correct the impression that as an activist, with strong social concerns, she might therefore be an irresponsible and vituperative agitator. Her aim was to persuade what she termed 'our brethren of the South' to reform themselves, to reconstruct the slave system from within. This enabled her to admit that the North did not hold a monopoly on virtue. 'Our prejudice against colored people is even more inveterate than it is in the South,' she said of herself and her fellow Northerners. It also allowed the tactic of irony. 'If the slaves are so well satisfied with their con- dition,' she asked, in response to a common pro-slavery argument, 'why do they make such severe laws against running away?' Child tried to reassure her Southern readers that, as she put it, 'the abolitionists have never . . . endeavoured to connect amalgamation with the subject of abolition'. But her low-keyed, conversational tone, and her presentation of herself as a sensible, humane reformer, were just as obnoxious to Southerners bent on strengthening the slave system as the more openly radical approaches of Walker and Garrison were. She was ostracized by the literary establishment, too; her *Juvenile Miscellany* failed for lack of subscribers; and she turned for work to the abolitionist paper the *National Anti-Slavery Standard*, published in New York City. Here, in the *Standard*, she published a series of 'Letters from New York' that discussed various forms of injustice: slavery, of course, poverty, which she saw as the source of urban crime, an oppressive prison system and the denial of basic rights to women. The tone of the 'Letters' was a curious mixture of the literary and the political. 'To my mind the katydids will forever speak of mobs', one letter begins, before launching into an account of how the first time Child ever heard 'the angular note of that handsome insect' was on the day that she saw a racist attack an abolitionist speaker.

In her later years, after she had resigned from the *Standard*, Child continued to pursue a variety of different careers as a writer and to promote several social causes. A short story, 'Slavery's Pleasant Homes' (1843), explores miscegenation and its brutal consequences in terms that anticipate Mark Twain and William Faulkner. Her last novel, *A Romance of the Republic* (1867), returns to the theme of interracial marriage. Her *Letters from New York* were published in two series, in 1843 and 1845. Her *Appeal for the Indians* (1868) expressed her continuing concern for the people who had been the subject of her first long fiction. And she sustained her commitment to African Americans even after the end of slavery: *The Freedman's Book* (1865), for instance, a collection of pieces by and about black people, was printed and distributed at her expense. For Child, the cause of liberty was an all-embracing one. In particular, she saw a seamless connection between her activism as an abolitionist and her interest in the condition of women. Much the same could be said of many reformers of the time, including the Grimké sisters, Angelina Grimké Weld (1805–79) and Sarah Moore Grimké (1792–1873). Born in South Carolina to a slaveholding family, the sisters shocked their fellow Southerners and relatives by identifying themselves with the abolitionist movement. It was while both were living in Philadelphia that Angelina wrote *An Appeal to the Christian Women of the South* (1836). 'I am going to tell you unwelcome truths,' she told her intended Southern white women readers, 'but I mean to speak those *truths in love*.' Despite the evidently modest, even apologetic beginning, the message of the *Appeal* was radical. Southern white women, Angelina argued, should read about slavery, pray for the truth about slavery to be known, and not only speak out against slavery but also act to eradicate it by freeing their own slaves. They should free their slaves, she added, even if this were illegal, since there was a higher law they had to observe. 'If a law commands me to *sin I will break it*,' Angelina insisted; 'the doctrine of blind obedience . . . to any human power . . . is the doctrine of despotism, and ought to have no place among Republicans and Christians.' To underline her point, that the women of the South could and should act, she cited a list of heroic deeds, from the Bible and contemporary times. Who had performed such deeds? she rhetorically asked, after describing each one of them. Her triumphant answer became a refrain. 'It was a *woman.*' 'The *women of the South can overthrow* this horrible system of oppression and cruelty, licentiousness and wrong,' Angelina concluded. Her 'Sisters in Christ' could and should act. In this *Appeal*, the cause of abolition and the cause of feminism were linked, not least because white Southern women were offered the possibility of affirming their womanhood, and their capacity for significant political action, in and through working towards the end of slavery.

Angelina Grimké also wrote more directly about the feminist cause only a year after the *Appeal*, in her *Letters to Catharine Beecher*. Here, in response to Beecher's argument that women should restrict themselves to the domestic sphere, she insisted that there were no specifically masculine and feminine rights, no such thing as 'men's rights and women's rights' but only '*human* rights'. Humanity was indivisible, the doctrines of liberty and equality had a universal application; and woman should be regarded 'as a companion, a co-worker, an equal' of man, not 'a mere appendage of his being, an instrument of his convenience and pleasure'. Sarah Moore Grimké was lecturing for the anti-slavery movement with her sister at this time; and, while Angelina was writing her *Letters to Catharine Beecher*, Sarah in her turn was preparing her *Letters on the Equality of the Sexes, and the Condition of Women* (1837–8). The *Letters on the Equality of the Sexes* are just as resistant as the *Letters to Catharine Beecher* are to the idea that a woman's place is necessarily in the home. 'We have rested satisfied with the sphere marked out for us by men', Sarah wrote, 'never detecting the fallacy of that reasoning which forbids woman to exercise some of her noblest faculties.' Women were customarily trained 'to attract the notice and win the attentions of men', she observed, 'brought up with the dangerous and absurd idea that *marriage* is a kind of preferment, and that to be able to keep their husband's house, and render his situation comfortable, is the end of her being'. To such notions Sarah offered her own alternative: what was needed, she argued, was for women to be treated as equals, in terms of both educational opportunity and vocation. A 'complete knowledge of household affairs' might be 'an indispensable requisite in a woman's education', not least because most women would continue to find their satisfactions in the home. But even these women required 'mental cultivation' for the proper performance of 'their sacred duties as mothers'. Other women required it for other kinds of work, in which by right they should be paid at the same level as men. And all women, without exception, required it so as to achieve 'that self-respect which conscious equality would engender'; for too long, Sarah insisted, women had been educated 'to regard themselves as inferior creatures'. Like so many others concerned with the condition of American women in the nineteenth century, Sarah saw her 'sisters' as fundamentally powerless and education as a vital source of empowerment. Like some of them, too, including her own sister, she saw that impotence at its most extreme in the female slaves of the South. 'Women are bought and sold in our slave markets,' Sarah wrote indignantly, 'to gratify the brutal lust of those who bear the name of Christians.' They were, she pointed out, completely at the mercy of 'the power which is necessarily vested in the master over his property'. For

Sarah as for Angelina Grimké, then, female emancipation and the abolition of slavery were intimately connected. And, in Sarah's case, that was especially so, since she saw the condition of the female slave as a paradigm, an extreme instance of the condition of all women, the subjection they all shared as the 'property' of white men.

The connection between abolitionism and feminism in the nineteenth century was not, however, always seamless. In 1840, a World Anti-Slavery Convention was held in England, and those present decided on the first day not to seat women delegates. Outraged, William Lloyd Garrison joined female delegates in the gallery. In the same year, the American Anti-Slavery Society split mainly because the followers of Garrison insisted that women could not be excluded from full participation in the work of abolition. Among those sitting with Garrison in the gallery at the World Anti-Slavery Convention was Elizabeth Cady Stanton (1815–1902). She was similarly angered by the treatment of female delegates and decided to organize a convention, as soon as she returned to the United States, wholly devoted to the rights of women. This was the Seneca Falls Convention, which did not, in fact, take place until eight years later, when Stanton and her family moved to Seneca Falls, New York. About three hundred people attended, and a hundred of them – two-thirds of them women – signed a 'Declaration of Sentiments', one of the seminal documents of the century on the condition of women. Modelled, as was observed earlier, on the Declaration of Independence, and beginning by insisting that 'all men and women are created equal', it then went on to point out that 'the history of mankind is a history of repeated injuries and usurpations on the part of man towards woman, having in direct object the establishment of an absolute tyranny over her'. Woman, the 'Declaration' noted, was denied the right to vote and was compelled 'to submit to laws, in the formation of which she had no voice'. Man had 'endeavoured, in every way that he could, to destroy her confidence in her own powers, to lessen her self-respect, and to make her willing to lead a dependent and abject life'. The document was characteristic of its time, in its mix of republican and Christian sentiment: man, for instance, was said to have 'usurped the prerogative of Jehovah himself' by claiming it as his right to arrange for woman 'a sphere of action, when that belongs to her conscience and to her God'. It made no concessions at all, however, to the notion of separate spheres for men and women, or to the usual domestic pieties. And its demands were simple and radical. Women, the 'Declaration' insisted, should have 'immediate admission to all the rights and privileges which belong to them as citizens of the United States'.

If Stanton, along with Margaret Fuller, was the philosopher of the feminist movement in America during the nineteenth century, then Fanny Fern was one of those who translated feminist principles into an enormously successful writing career. Fanny Fern was the pen name of Sara Payson Willis (1811–72). When her first husband died, Willis was left nearly penniless and received only a little, grudging support from her family. Under pressure from her father, she married again but her second husband turned out to be both jealous and oppressive. She left him after two years, and decided to make a living for her children and herself from writing. Her older brother, Nathaniel Parker Willis (1806–67), was a successful poet, journalist and editor, and she appealed to him for help in getting started. The appeal proved fruitless: Nathaniel pronounced her writing vulgar and advised her to make a living in some unobtrusive trade such as shirt-making. Nevertheless, Sara Willis persevered, and she sold her first story in 1851. Soon, she was publishing articles and reviews regularly under her pen name and becoming famous. Her first collection of articles, *Fern Leaves from Fanny's Portfolio*, appeared in 1853 and rapidly became a best-seller. *Little Ferns from Fanny's Little Friends*, a collection of essays for children, followed in the same year; next year, the second series of *Fern Leaves from Fanny's Portfolio* was published. Over the following twenty years, her essays, articles and other writing for various journals, and collections such as *Fresh Leaves* (1857), *Folly as It Flies* (1868) and *Ginger Snaps* (1870), were to establish her as one of the most famous women writers in the nation.

The essays and articles written under the name of Fanny Fern are generally marked by a lively, gossipy style, full of exclamations and rapid asides. There is plenty of sentiment, but there is also plenty of wit. 'Hints to Young Wives', for example, published in 1852, pokes fun at all the manuals that labour under this title. 'Shouldn't I like to make a bonfire of all the "Hints to Young Wives",' Fern declares. 'I have a little neighbor who believes all they tell is the gospel truth, and lives up to it,' she goes on. 'The minute she sees her husband coming up the street, she makes for the door, as if she hadn't another moment to live . . . then chases around (like a cat in a fit) . . . warms his slippers and puts 'em on, and dislocates her wrist carving at table for fear it will tire him.' There are also articles that deal in a more openly serious way with the plight of women. In 'Soliloquy of a House-maid' (1854), for example, Fern adopts the persona of an overstretched house servant to voice the trials and anxieties of working-class women. In 'Critics' (1854) and 'Mrs Adolphus Smith Sporting the "Blue Stocking"' (1854) she takes on the more personal theme of the problems of the woman who wants to be a writer, faced with the prejudice of a male literary establishment and, quite probably, the demands of being a wife and mother as well. 'Independence' (1854) is more humorous in tone but, like many of these pieces, none the less serious in purpose for that. '"FOURTH OF JULY." Well – I don't feel patriotic,' Fern begins. 'I'm glad we are all free; but as a woman – I shouldn't know it.' 'Can I go out at evening without a hat at my side?' she asks. 'Can I stand up in the cars "like a gentleman" without being immediately invited "to sit down"?' 'Can I *even* be President? Bah – you know I can't.' '"Free!" Humph!' And another article, 'The Working-Girls of New York' (1868), makes no concessions to humour as Fern describes what she calls 'the contrast between squalor and splendor' in New York City: with 'the care-worn working-girl' and 'the dainty fashionist' 'jostling on the same pavement'. Fern maintains a tactful balance here, between her recognition of the immense difference between these two female types, as far as their social and economic situations are concerned, and her belief that, as women, their conditions are nevertheless linked. She devotes most of her attention to the desperate lot of the working girls, forced to labour in factories where 'the roar of machinery' is 'like the roar of

Niagara'. But she still suggests that 'the same appalling question' reverberates in the heads of the 'fashionist' and the working woman: *'Is this all life has for me?'* 'A great book is yet unwritten about women,' Fern confides to the reader: one, presumably, that discloses both the differences and the links between rich and poor women she alludes to here. 'Who shall write this bold, frank, truthful book remains to be seen,' she concludes. Meanwhile, 'woman's millennium is yet a great way off', and 'conservatism and indifference gaze through their spectacles at the seething elements of today, and wonder "what ails our women?"'

Fern herself tried her hand at writing, if not a great, then a useful book about women: *Ruth Hall: A Domestic Tale of the Present Time* (1855). 'I present you with my first continuous story,' Fern wrote in her 'Preface: To the Reader'. 'I do not dignify it by the name of "A Novel." I am aware that it is entirely at variance with all set rules for novel-writing.' There was, as always, truth in what she said. Fern drew heavily on her own experiences in the book. Like her creator, Ruth Hall suffers an early widowhood and is forced to make a living for herself. She decides to become a writer, despite the discouragement of her brother, who tells her, 'writing can never be your *forte*; you have no talent that way'. 'I *can* do it,' she tells herself, 'I *feel* it. I will do it.' And, by the end of the story, she has succeeded. Her book of articles has been published, and she is secure in her profession as a journalist and essayist. *Ruth Hall* is not an autobiography, however. Fanny Fern married not long after widowhood, and was to marry again, while Ruth does not. Neither is it a romantic or sentimental novel. Reversing the conventional pattern, the book begins with marriage (to a man who, of course, then dies, leaving Ruth a widow) and ends with the heroine as a successful career woman. It focuses not on the domestic scene but on the literary marketplace in which Ruth must make her way. And the narrative consists, as Fern herself points out in her 'Preface', not of the 'long introductions and descriptions' of the traditional nineteenth-century novel but, rather, of a series of brief episodes and vignettes. 'I . . . have entered unceremoniously and unannounced into people's houses, without stopping to ring the bell,' Fern warns the reader. There is only limited narrative exposition, character analysis and development. What the reader is offered is a succession of brief scenes, snatches of overheard conversation, something remarkably close in many ways to the clipped, disjunctive patterns of the modern novel. *Ruth Hall* is not a modern novel, of course, and there is plenty to remind us of that. The language is very often florid and elaborate: when Ruth posts a letter to her editor, for instance, she is said to have the same hopeful feelings as Noah had when he sent forth a dove from the ark. There are some remarkable plot coincidences, some Dickensian comic characters, and no fewer than three big deathbed scenes. Nevertheless, what Fern describes as her 'primitive mode' of writing does set her at odds with contemporary convention: in tone and narrative rhythm, this is very unlike the standard 'domestic tale of the present time'. What sets it even more at odds is Fern's evident decision to make the story of Ruth Hall a kind of answer to the 'appalling question' she had her 'dainty fashionist' and 'care-worn working-girl' ask themselves in 'The Working-Girls of New York'. By the end of the novel, Ruth has made something of herself, and found that marriage and widowhood are not all life has for her.

Of Sojourner Truth (1793?–1883), someone wrote in 1881 that she 'combined in herself, as an individual, the two most hated elements of humanity. She was black and she was a woman.' For Truth, both elements were a matter of profound pride, and she devoted her life to proclaiming her belief that both were the source of her dignity, her worth as a human being. Much of what is known about Truth is drawn from transcriptions of her speeches, records of her public appearances and her autobiography, the *Narrative of Sojourner Truth* (1850). She never learned to read or write. 'I cannot read a book, but I can read the people,' she declared. What we have are the accounts of her and her orations by others; while the *Narrative*, a contribution to both the slave narrative and the female spiritual autobiography traditions of African American literature, was dictated by Truth to Olive Gilbert, a sympathetic white woman. In 1875, the *Narrative* was reprinted with a supplement called the *Book of Life*, containing personal correspondence, newspaper accounts of her activities and tributes from her friends. This enlarged edition of the autobiography was reprinted several times, in 1878, 1881 and 1884 under the title *Sojourner Truth: A Bondswoman of Olden Time, with a History of Her Labors and Correspondence Drawn from Her 'Book of Life'*. From all this, the reader learns Truth had an 'almost Amazon form, which stood nearly six feet high, head erect, and eyes piercing the upper hair like one in a dream'. Of her appearance and manner, Harriet Beecher Stowe wrote in 1863, 'I do not recollect ever to have been conversant with any one who had more of that silent and subtle power which we call personal presence than this woman'. Her early life, perhaps, had contributed to giving her this presence. She was born into slavery in New York State, as Isabella Baumfree, sold three times before she was twelve, and raped by one of her masters. She had five children from her union with another slave, saw one of her children sold away from her, then fled with another of her children in 1826, so seizing her freedom one year before she was formally emancipated under a New York law passed in 1827. What also contributed to it, though, was her sense of mission. In 1843, she received what she termed a summons from God, commanding her to go out and preach. She changed her name to reflect her new identity, as a traveller dedicated to telling people what is true, and she took to the road. Early in her career as an itinerant preacher, Truth met William Lloyd Garrison and Frederick Douglass. She enthusiastically joined the ranks of the abolitionists, and her commitment to human rights drew her into the growing feminist movement as well. By the late 1850s, she had come to embody a commitment to freedom that both contrasted with and complemented that of Douglass. With Douglass, the cause expressed itself as masculine, individualist, mythic and literary; with Sojourner Truth it was something quite different but equally valuable – female, communal, part of an oral, vernacular tradition.

The most famous speech given by Sojourner Truth expresses this difference. In 1851, during a woman's rights convention in Ohio, she spoke on behalf of the dignity of women in response to attacks from a group of ministers. Her spontaneous oration was reported in the *Anti-Slavery Bugle*. Then, in 1878, a second and more elaborate version of the speech appeared in the *Book of Life* section of the *Narrative*; this was how the president of the convention, Frances Gage, recollected it. The rhetorical question that Gage remembered Sojourner Truth asking again and again in the speech was, 'and a'n't I a woman?' That became the accepted title of the piece. It also vividly expressed Truth's commitment to the related causes of black and female liberation, black and female pride, that she saw as crucial determinants of her identity and that her admirers, similarly, saw embodied in her. 'Look at me! Look at my arm!' Gage remembered Truth as saying. 'I have ploughed and planted, and gathered into barns, and no man could head me! And a'n't I a woman?' 'I could work as much and eat as much as a man – when I could get it,' she went on, 'and bear de lash as well! And a'n't I a woman?' The authenticity of Gage's account has been questioned. Some have suggested that the version printed in the *Anti-Slavery Bugle*, which is simpler and less of a speech in dialect, is closer to what Truth actually said. But the question, and suggestion, may well be misconceived, since it is the essence of the oral tradition – with which Sojourner Truth clearly aligned herself – that there can be no such thing as a single, authentic version. What matter are the fundamental character, style and message of Sojourner Truth as these elements thread their way through the portraits and speeches associated with her. And what is consistent here is the impression of an oracular, prophetic, witty and passionate woman, who actively resists the constraints imposed on her because of her race and gender – and who uses a powerful rhetoric, laced with Biblical allusion and autobiographical references, to assert her rights as an African American and a female. Douglass enshrined his account of how 'a slave was made a man' in a form that was personal, carefully articulated and (in the sense of being written down by him) final. Truth asked the question, 'a'n't I a woman?' in a forum that was communal and in a form that was spontaneous, unpremeditated and (to the extent that it was open to the recollections and revisions of others) fluid. Both are equally memorable; and they share a basic impetus, a commitment to human dignity and natural equality, along with their differences. And both have a crucial, in fact pivotal, place in the traditions of African American and American literature.

African American writing

By contrast to Sojourner Truth, who never wrote down a single one of the speeches for which she is remembered, Frances E. W. Harper (1825–1911) was one of the most prolific, as well as popular, African American writers of the nineteenth century. Over the course of her life, she produced four novels, several collections of poetry, and numerous stories, essays and letters; she also found time to lecture widely on a whole range of reform issues, especially temperance, slavery and racism, and the rights of women. Harper was born in a slaveholding state, Maryland, but to free parents. By the age of three, she was orphaned; by the age of sixteen, she had reportedly published her first, small volume of poetry, *Forest Leaves*, no copy of which is known to have survived; by the age of twenty-four, she had left the

South to settle in a free state, choosing Ohio and then Pennsylvania. The publication of her poem 'Eliza Harris' in 1853 brought her to national attention. One of her many responses to *Uncle Tom's Cabin* by Harriet Beecher Stowe, it described a slave woman escaping across a river covered with ice, carrying 'the child of her love' to 'Liberty's plains'. And it reflected her growing involvement with the anti-slavery movement. That involvement became even more marked a year later, when she inaugurated her career as a public speaker with a speech on 'The Education and Elevation of the Colored Race'. The lecture tour she then embarked on was gruelling. But she managed to produce more poems, and essays, and to publish *Poems on Miscellaneous Subjects* (1854), which effectively began the tradition of African American protest poetry. A good example of such protest poetry is 'The Slave Mother'. There is a striking tension here between the artifice of the form and the realism of the subject. A conventional metrical form, emphatic rhymes and rhythms, elaborate images, and a melodic, repetitive rhetoric, are all put at the service of a devastatingly simple account of how a slave mother has her small son torn from her. 'He is not hers, although she bore / For him a mother's pains; /' the poet observes. 'He is not hers,' she goes on, 'for cruel hands / May rudely tear apart / The only wreath of household love / That binds her breaking heart.'

In 1859, Harper published her first significant fiction, the short stories 'The Two Offers' and 'Our Greatest Want'. 'The Two Offers', the first short story published by a black person in the United States, is concerned with the condition of women. It tells the tale of two cousins, one of whom suffers an unhappy marriage, and the other of whom, learning from her cousin's fate, decides to remain unmarried. Turning from marriage, as one of only several options available to a woman, the second cousin dedicates herself to 'universal love and truth' – in other words, abolitionism and other reform movements. 'Our Greatest Want' deals in more detail with the question of race: suggesting that, while the acquisition of wealth is necessary for African Americans, their development as 'true men and true women' is more important. Both stories are characteristic, in that they are elaborately artificial in tone and sternly moral in tenor: 'true happiness', 'The Two Offers' concludes, 'consists not so much in the fruition of our wishes as in the regulation of desires and the full development and right culture of our whole natures.' And, together, they reflect the overriding commitments of Harper's life and work: to racial and sexual equality. That commitment was also reflected in Harper's first serialized novel, *Minnie's Sacrifice* (1869). This book also developed its author's belief in the redemptive power of women, and black women in particular. Harper participated with many others in the nineteenth century in what has been called the cult of true womanhood, a set of convictions that celebrated the superior piety, domesticity and rectitude of the Christian woman. But she added to this her sense that it was up to black people generally, but black women especially, to 'consecrate their lives to the work of upholding the race'.

Among Harper's many other published works were a free verse narrative, *Moses: A Story of the Nile* (1869), two novels dealing with temperance (*Sowing and Reaping: A Temperance Story* [1876] and *Trial and Triumph* [1888–9]), and a newspaper

---

column, first called *Fancy Etchings* and then *Fancy Sketches*, in which she explored contemporary issues and moral dilemmas through the conversations and activities of various regular characters. Her two most important later works, however, were *Sketches of Southern Life* (1872) and *Iola Leroy; or, Shadows Uplifted* (1892). At the heart of *Sketches* is a series of poems narrated by an Aunt Chloe. Sixty years old, Aunt Chloe tells the reader how she learned to read, take an active interest in politics although she cannot vote, and try to make sure that the men are 'voting clean'. Unlike most of Harper's other poetry, these poems exploit African American oral traditions, as they tell the story of a woman who worked to gain a cabin for herself and her family and to help build schools and churches for the community. They are at once the autobiography of a former slave and a vernacular history of slavery, emancipation and reconstruction. *Iola Leroy* is a novel with a complex plot. The earlier part of it, set in the antebellum period and during the Civil War, assaults the pro-slavery myth of the Old South by describing the fierce desire of the slaves for freedom, then celebrates the bravery of black troops. The later part concentrates on the search of Iola Leroy and her brother for their mother, and the decision of Iola, a very light-skinned African American, not to marry a white man. Instead, she accepts the proposal of an African American and dedicates herself to building up the black community. 'I intend to spend my future among the colored people of the South,' she tells the white man, when she rejects him; 'I don't think that I could best secure my race by forsaking them and marrying you.' *Iola Leroy* in effect reverses the character stereotype of the tragic mulatta and the traditional narrative device of a black person 'passing' for white. Iola is in no sense a victim, and she actively refuses to take on the role of a supposedly 'white' woman married to a white man: 'the best blood in my veins is my African blood,' she declares, 'and I am not ashamed of it.' It also dramatically negotiates a range of issues that were to engage later African American women writers in particular: the separation and longing of mother and daughter, the relationship between the sexes as a cooperative, co-equal one, the search for the right kind of work, role and life for a woman. Harper continued to link the cause of African Americans and the cause of women until the end of her life. 'Today we stand on the threshold of woman's era,' she proclaimed in 'Woman's Political Future' (1894). 'O women of America! . . . It is in your hands . . . to demand justice, simple justice, as the right of every race; to brand with everlasting infamy the lawless and brutal cowardice that lynches, burns, and tortures your own countrymen.' She believed in what she called 'the combined power of an upright manhood and an enlightened womanhood' to change the character of America. And she worked in virtually every literary genre available to her to promote that belief.

Harper made an important contribution to African American writing; she was not, however, the first African American to publish a novel or longer fiction. In March 1853, Frederick Douglass published his novella, *The Heroic Slave*, in his paper *The North Star*. And, in the same year, William Wells Brown (1814?–84) published a full-length novel, *Clotel; or, The President's Daughter*. Douglass's narrative was based on an actual mutiny, on board the slave ship *Creole*, in 1841.

Douglass knew little about the leader of the mutiny, Madison Washington. 'Curiously, earnestly, anxiously, we peer into the dark,' he wrote in his introduction to the story, 'and wish even for the blinding flash, or the light of northern skies to reveal him. But alas! He is still enveloped in darkness.' So, weaving together what he called various 'possibles' and 'probabilities', Douglass used his imagination to create an embodiment of heroic rebellion. Like the slave narrative, *The Heroic Slave* uses white mediation to tell a black story. The hero is Madison Washington, but the narrator is a white Northerner called Listwell. From the start, Listwell listens well (a fairly obvious pun) to the voice of Washington, overhearing him lamenting the terrible contradiction of being a human being and disposable property. 'What, then, is life to me?' Listwell hears Washington saying. 'I am a *slave* . . . How mean a thing am I. That accursed and crawling snake . . . that just glided into its slimy home, is freer and better off than I.' 'But here am I a man, – yes, a *man!*' he insists, '– with thoughts and wishes, with powers and faculties as far as angel's flight above that hated reptile.' 'My resolution is fixed,' Washington concludes, 'I *shall be free.*' In the rest of the story, Listwell continues to listen well to the adventures of the heroic slave: his flight to Canada, his return to rescue his wife, his enslavement again, his leadership of the mutiny. And the reader is clearly being asked to listen well too, and draw the appropriate conclusions.

Like Douglass, William Wells Brown was born a slave, in Kentucky. His father was a white man, his mother a slave woman. He escaped from slavery in 1834, and took the name Wells Brown from a Quaker couple who assisted him in the course of his flight. Moving to Boston, he wrote his autobiography, *Narrative of William W. Brown, an American Slave*. Published in 1847, it was exceeded only in popularity as a slave narrative by the *Narrative* of Douglass, and it established Brown's reputation. It is, however, very different from the *Narrative*, or from *Incidents in the Life of a Slave Girl* by Harriet Jacobs. For that matter, it offers an intriguing variation on the themes played out in such other notable – and, in their own ways, highly individual – slave narratives as *The Narrative of the Uncommon Sufferings and Surprising Deliverance of Briton Hammon, a Negro Man* (1760) by Briton Hammon (?–?), *Life of William Grimes, The Runaway Slave* (1825) by William Grimes (1784–?), *A Narrative of the Adventures and Escape of Moses Roper* (1838) by Moses Roper (1816–?), *Narratives of the Sufferings of Lewis and Milton Clarke* (1846) by Lewis Clarke (1815–97) and Milton Clarke (1817?–?), *Narrative of the Life and Adventures of Henry Bibb, An American Slave* (1849) by Henry Bibb (1815–54), *The Fugitive Blacksmith; or, Events in the History of James W. C. Pennington* (1849) by James W. C. Pennington (1807–70), *Twelve Years a Slave* (1853) by Solomon Northup (1808–63), *Slave Life in Georgia* (1855) by John Brown (1818–?), *The Life of John Thompson, A Fugitive Slave* (1856) by John Thompson (1812–?), *Running a Thousand Miles for Freedom* (1860) by William Craft (1826?–1900) and Ellen Craft (1826–91), *Narrative of the Life of J. D. Green, A Runaway Slave* (1864) by Jacob D. Green (1813–?) and *Life of James Mars, A Slave* (1864) by James Mars (1790–1877?). The contrast with Douglass is particularly striking. Douglass, in his account of his bondage and freedom, uses rhetorical devices, rhythmic speech and the conventions of the conversion narrative to present himself as an exemplary figure, a type of heroic, manly resistance not unlike the protagonist of his novella. Brown, on the other hand, deploys an understated plain style, with little appearance of literary calculation or personal reflection, to depict himself as ordinary, even anti-heroic. He describes how he assisted one master, 'a negro speculator or a "soul-driver"', in preparing slaves for market, making them look younger and fatter than they actually were. He also recalls how, being sent to the jail for a whipping, he tricked a man he met on the way, a freedman, into going to the jail and being whipped instead of him. Brown does not try to excuse or extenuate the part he played as trickster. Rather, he uses his story to explore the contradiction between the survival ethic of the slave and the dominant morality of the day – and the way whites use the morally evasive behaviour they impose on black people to justify their enslavement of them. 'Slavery makes its victims lying and mean,' Brown points out, 'for which vices it afterwards reproaches them, and uses them as arguments to prove that they deserve no better fate.'

Brown travelled to Europe, remaining there until 1854. In 1852, he published *Three Years in Europe*, the first African American travel book, consisting mainly of letters the author had written to friends and newspapers in America. And in 1853, he published *Clotel*. He was later to revise the novel and republish it several times: once in serial form as 'Miralda; or, the Beautiful Quadroon: A Romance of Slavery, Founded on Fact' (1860–1) and twice in novel form, as *Clotelle: A Tale of the Southern States* (1864) and *Clotelle; or, The Colored Heroine – A Tale of the Southern States* (1867). In 1848, Brown had written a piece for a compilation, *The Antislavery Harp*, entitled 'Jefferson's Daughter', based on the well-established rumour that Thomas Jefferson had had a mulatto daughter by his housekeeper, an African American, who was then sold at a New Orleans slave auction. This was evidently the inspiration for *Clotel*, although in none of the different versions is Jefferson ever mentioned by name. What is notable about the novel is how openly, for its day, it explores the related themes of black concubinage, miscegenation and the link between sexual and racial oppression. 'With the growing population in the Southern states, the increase of mulattoes has been very great,' the story begins. 'Society does not frown upon the man who sits with his half-white child upon his knee whilst the mother stands, a slave, behind his chair.' Claiming that 'the real, or clear black, does not amount to more than one in four of the slave population', the narrator then goes on to consider the tragic consequences of this racially and sexually charged situation. Through several generations, black women are shown at the mercy of the arbitrary power and the sexual whims of white men and the jealousy of white women. 'Every married woman at the South', the reader is told, 'looks upon her husband as unfaithful, and regards every negro woman as a rival.' Daughters are sold at slave auction; a black concubine is sent off to a slave trader at the insistence of a jealous white wife; one black woman kills herself rather than suffer further enslavement; another woman is put up for auction with her daughter, on the death of her husband, when it is discovered that, legally, she is black and still a slave.

To an extent, *Clotel* is a symptom of the racial blindness it diagnoses. The narrator observes that there is considerable prejudice 'even among the negroes themselves' about racial coloration. 'The nearer the negro or the mulatto approaches to the white,' he says, 'the more he seems to feel his superiority over those of darker hue.' He then illustrates that prejudice himself: the heroines in this story all tend to be fair-skinned, while the comic characters, the fools, tricksters and villainous collaborators with white oppression all tend to be black. But this is something that Brown may have sensed himself. In its original version, the beloved of the heroine, Clotel, is of lighter complexion just like her. In the revised versions, however, he is described as 'perfectly black'. Clotel is reunited with her white father at the end of the novel; and, 'having all the prejudices against color which characterises his white fellow-countrymen', the father at first expresses his 'dislike' of his son-in-law's complexion. Clotel's reply is forthright and sums up the main intended message of the book. 'I married him because I loved him,' she tells her father. 'Why should the white man be esteemed as better than the black? I find no difference in men on account of their complexion. One of the cardinal principles of Christianity and freedom is the equality and brotherhood of man.' *Clotel* is a romantic novel but it is also a powerful assault on the slave system and, in particular, the fundamental betrayal it represented of humanity and the American dream. It was Brown's only long work of fiction. Brown continued, however, to write and explore other forms. A historical study, *The Black Man, His Antecedents, His Genius, and His Achievements*, appeared in 1862; a second, but first of its kind, *The Negro in the American Rebellion*, followed in 1867, and a third, *The Rising Son; or, The Antecedents and Advancement of the Colored Race*, in 1873. His final work, *My Southern Home*, an account of a trip to the South, was published in 1880. Brown was a firm believer in assimilation, his race becoming part of the promise and project of America; and he was inclined, in his fiction, to appeal to the sentimentalism and moralism of the day. But he mapped out much of the geography of the later African American narrative – the flight to freedom, the bitter fate of denied and mixed identities – and, in the portrait of Clotel, he created a heroine who was not just a victimized tragic mulatta but a combative spokesperson for her race.

For all the trials and tribulations of their careers, writers like Wells and Harper at least saw their work into print. Others were not so fortunate. Among the many African Americans of the period whose work remained unpublished and unread during their lifetime was a woman now known as Hannah Crafts. A manuscript titled *The Bondswoman's Narrative* 'by Hannah Crafts A Fugitive Slave Recently Escaped from North Carolina' lay unpublished for a hundred and fifty years after it was written some time between 1855 and 1860; it eventually appeared in print in 2002. The identity of the author has not yet been firmly established. 'Hannah' is the name she chose for herself as the narrator and protagonist of the novel; 'Crafts' may be a tribute to Ellen and William Craft, who in 1848 made a daring escape from slavery with the fair-skinned Ellen disguised as an invalid white man and William posing as 'his' servant. Still, the evidence suggests that Hannah Crafts, or whatever her name was, was one of a multitude of African Americans, slaves or free, whose voices remained unheard during their lifetime. Many of those voices are likely to remain unheard, except through the collective medium of folk story, song and spiritual. Notable among these are field hands like the ones whose condition of 'degradation, neglect, and ill treatment' Hannah herself notes, with some distaste, during the course of the narrative. Voiceless, outside history, possessed of lives but no biography, they are given no significant part to play, still less a story to tell, in *The Bondswoman's Narrative*. Hannah Crafts, the reader soon learns, is a deeply colour-conscious house slave shaped by a superior education; and she is extraordinarily open about her feelings of dejection, and even horror, when faced with the 'miserable' huts of the field hands, the 'crowds of foul existence' that 'crawled in out of gaps in walls and boards', and the 'vile, foul, filthy' lives lived there. Her highly self-conscious narrative, which mixes together slave narrative, the Gothic and the sentimental conventions, is a story of the enslavement and eventual liberation of one at least given the means to translate her world into written words. As such, it may not give voice or access to the inner lives of those toiling in the fields. But it is, surely, representative of many other documents by and about individual, literate African Americans of this time – stories, memoirs, autobiographies, fictional or semi-fictional recollections – that probably survive, waiting to be published. And if, as seems almost certain, the author here bears a close resemblance to the protagonist, in terms of race and condition, then *The Bondswoman's Narrative* has a pioneering as well as an exemplary status. For it is, in that case, the first novel written by an escaped female slave and possibly the first one ever written by a black woman.

'I am aware of my deficiencies,' Hannah Crafts confesses towards the beginning of *The Bondswoman's Narrative*. 'I am neither clever, nor learned, nor talented.' This, as it turns out, is excessively modest. Hannah 'knew nothing', we learn, of her father and mother; she has, however, enjoyed the tutelage of a kindly old white woman called Aunt Hetty, who has taught her to read and write. Her narrative is scattered with evidence of her reading. There are literary allusions, quotations from the Bible prefacing each chapter, and sometimes outright, unacknowledged borrowings: a description of foggy Washington, 'the Federal City', in the later part of the novel, for instance, leans heavily on the portrait of London Charles Dickens painted in *Bleak House* (1852–3). Establishing the literacy of the narrator, and by implication the immediacy and authenticity of his or her recorded experience, was standard practice in the slave narrative, but here it is more than that. It is part of a strategy of self-portraiture that makes Hannah resemble, among many others, the heroine of a sentimental novel or even, say, Charlotte Brontë's Jane Eyre. Hannah is an orphan, a dispossessed princess, with, she says, 'a silent unobtrusive way of observing things and events' and a desire 'to understand them better than I could' that makes her an ideal storyteller. She is already aware, even as a child, that she has, as she puts it, 'African blood in my veins', which condemns her to a life of 'unremitted unpaid toil'. Intolerable in any circumstances, this is additionally unbearable for her because, Hannah tells us, 'my complexion was almost white'. So, this heroine is not only a princess in exile, she is another blueprint for that central figure in subsequent fiction by and about African Americans, the tragic mulatta. Not only that, the tale she has to tell wastes no time in bringing into play a further classic trope in later stories and novels concerned with the intolerable burden of slavery and racism: that of passing, adopting the fictive role of white, so as to avoid the problems, the penury and oppression attendant on being classed as black.

It is not Hannah herself who passes as white, of course; her condition as a slave is unavoidable despite her fair complexion. It is her mistress. At the beginning of *The Bondswoman's Narrative*, Hannah is a house slave at Lindendale, a place of 'stately majesty' that nevertheless seems to be haunted by a curse. 'I am superstitious, I confess it,' she tells the reader. The walls at Lindendale are lined with ancestral portraits, whose 'steady eyes motionless and void of expression' awe and intimidate her. Like the nervous, trembling, acutely sensitive female observer of classic Gothic fiction – the heroines of Ann Radcliffe, say – Hannah suffers the 'foreboding of some great calamity; a curse of destiny that no circumstances could avert or soften'. And that eerily prophetic feeling grows rawer, more painful, for the reader as well as her, as she recalls the 'legend of Lindendale': the terrible story of an old slave woman who, with her small dog, was gibbeted alive on a linden tree just outside the house and left to die over several days. Before the old woman died, Hannah remembers, she cursed the house, declaring 'I will come here after I am dead to prove its bane'. That curse seems recollected every time the branches of the linden tree creak in the wind. And when the master of the house brings a new bride home, it does not take long for the superstitious Hannah to remark that her new mistress seems 'haunted by a shadow or phantom'. The mistress also has a more tangible phantom shadowing her: an 'old gentleman in black' whose name, Mr Trappe, suggests his dread function. For Mr Trappe brings with him the secret that threatens to entrap and destroy the new mistress. Her mother was a slave, the property of her father; it is only because she was switched in the cradle, exchanged for the dead baby of her father's lawful – and, of course, white – wife, that she now passes for white. 'Call me mistress no longer, thenceforth you shall be to me as a very dear sister,' her mistress tells Hannah, after she has revealed the truth of her origins; 'Oh: to be free, to be free.' Eventually, the 'sisters' seek freedom in flight: into the woods, where they live in a log cabin that seems as haunted as Lindendale, marked by signs of some 'fearful crime' – bloodstains, a skeleton, a hatchet with 'hair yet sticking to the heft'. There they live on wild fruits and berries. But their refuge is temporary. They are found by 'a party of hunters', agents of the sinister Mr Trappe, and then imprisoned in the 'Egyptian' darkness of a dungeon where Hannah finds solace only in a 'blessed dream' of her 'angel mother'. The mistress soon dies, when she learns that she is to be sold by Mr Trappe, privately, to 'a gentleman'. Later, we learn that her husband, the master of Lindendale, commits suicide when he hears from the ubiquitous Mr Trappe the truth about the parentage of his wife. So the curse seems to have run its fearful course.

Characteristically, this opening movement in *The Bondswoman's Narrative* weaves together several different narrative strands and tendencies. Classic Gothic tropes – the haunted mansion, the sinister family portraits, the feverish heroine, the curse

– are enriched by what might be called wilderness Gothic, of the kind favoured by Charles Brockden Brown and, occasionally, Poe: the log cabin that inspires a 'superstitious horror' in the minds of Hannah and her companion in flight is, it turns out, a place where 'it is said a beautiful girl was once murdered'. Sentimental conversations between 'sisters' in suffering are played off against tactics and conventions borrowed from the slave narrative. In her Preface, Hannah tells the reader that she hopes to show how slavery 'blights the happiness of the white as well as the black race'. She does so by exposing the hypocrisies and cruelties and silences to which slavery condemns the oppressors. Mr Trappe damns himself out of his own mouth while offering a sly parody of pro-slavery arguments: 'we are all slaves to something or somebody', he tells Hannah and her companion. He also tries to sell Hannah off, after her mistress has died, by telling a potential buyer that he 'won't find a nicer bit of woman's flesh to be bought for that money in old Virginia'. *The Bondswoman's Narrative* is, in fact, remarkably frank about the sexual abuse of black women, which replenishes the South's 'domestic institution' by breeding more slaves. There is, for example, the tale told of the man who purchases Lindendale after the suicide of the master of the house. 'No Turk in his haram [*sic*] ever luxuriated in deeper sensual enjoyment' than he did, we learn, with the result that 'more than one' of his 'favorites gave birth to children'. He is forced by his jealous wife to sell both favourites and children. However, 'one of the youngest and most beautiful' of his victims seizes a knife and kills her own child rather than have it become part of 'the hedious [*sic*] traffic' in slaves, before killing herself: so, in a macabre way, illustrating Hannah's own belief that marriage and sexual congress should be avoided by the slave community in order 'never to entail slavery on any human being'. The book is also frank about the intimacies that can occur between white mistress and black maid. 'Between the mistress and her slave a freedom exists probably not to be found elsewhere,' Hannah avers, thanks to similarities in their plight as victims. Similarity is not sameness, though, and it does not guarantee fellow feeling, since the weak can be cruel to those even weaker than themselves. So, we read not only of the jealousy but also the brutality of some mistresses: like the one who works three of her female slaves to death. 'I told her 'twasn't right,' her husband declares with consummate hypocrisy, 'and money out of pocket too.'

'What do you think of it? Doctors of Divinity,' Hannah asks at one point in her story. 'Isn't it a strange state to be like them,' the slaves, 'to shuffle up and down . . . in utter darkness as to the meaning of Nature's hieroglyphic symbols'; 'to hear such names as freedom, heaven, hope and happiness and not to have the least idea . . . what the experience of those blessed names might be.' 'The greatest curse of slavery is it's [*sic*] hereditary character,' she explains, as 'an inheritance of toil and misery' is passed from one generation to another. The havoc it wreaks is at once brutal and subtle: denying knowledge to the slaves of those precious documents, the American Constitution and the Bible, that speak of freedom, it also enforces silence and pretence, the obligation 'to say that all is right and good; and true when you know that nothing could be more wrong and unjust'. The Gothic, in particular, serves *The Bondswoman's Narrative* well as Hannah recounts her suffering, since it is just the right form to express the feelings of those without power. Causes and effects are veiled, shrouded in mystery for those, like the slaves, denied access to the workings and meanings of their condition. There are also, too often, instances in which the violence and darkness of the Gothic are only too literally true – the shackles, the dungeon, the gibbet. Gothic tropes, however, continue to mix with the sentimental and the conventions of the slave narrative while Hannah recalls how she had yet 'other toils and trials to endure, other scenes of suffering and anguish to pass through' before achieving her freedom. She even enjoys a brief idyll on an estate called Forget-Me-Not that might have sprung out of the pages of plantation romance. 'Method and regularity . . . prevailed over the estate. The overseer was gentle and kind and the slaves industrious and obedient,' Hannah declares of Forget-Me-Not, 'not through fear of punishment, but because they loved and respected a master and mistress so amiable and good.' But the idyllic soon gives way, once again, to the 'swarm of misery' that, as Hannah reveals, is the common lot of the slave. And the critical moment of choice comes for the bondswoman when, after being removed to another plantation in North Carolina, she is told by her new mistress, a Mrs Wheeler, with whom she had fallen out of favour, that she must go and work in the fields, marry a field hand and live in his cabin. 'With all your pretty airs and your white face,' Mrs Wheeler tells Hannah, 'you are nothing but a slave after all and no better than the blackest wench.' For Hannah, so acutely conscious of the differences of colour and caste within the slave community, and particularly between house slaves and field hands, this change of circumstance turns out to be a shock to her senses as well as her principles. She cannot, she protests, be married to anyone, let alone someone 'whose person, and speech, and manner could not fail to be ever regarded by me with loathing and disgust'. She will not 'be driven in to the fields beneath the eye and lash of the brutal overseer' or be forced to make her home in 'those miserable huts, with their promiscuous crowds of dirty, obscene and degraded objects'. 'I could not, I would not bear it,' she concludes; in such a plight, 'rebellion would be a virtue' and she resolves to flee.

The story of Hannah's flight, like the account of her sojourn in North Carolina – a 'fine plantation' probably based on an actual estate where the author lived and worked as a slave – is less melodramatic, and less inflected with Gothic and sentimental conventions, than previous episodes in the novel. Nevertheless, while Hannah is on the run, disguised as a boy, touches of the sentimental, the Gothic and melodramatic remain. Hannah not only manages to conceal her true gender from a male companion in flight ('he learned to love me . . . as a younger brother', Hannah assures us, so banishing any vulgar thoughts of sexual impropriety), she also has the great good fortune, eventually, to happen upon her beloved Aunt Hetty, the woman who taught her to read and write. Coincidences of this kind are rife in the concluding chapters of *The Bondswoman's Narrative*. Bound north for freedom, on a steamboat, she just chances to overhear a conversation between two gentlemen from which she learns that Mr Trappe finally met his retribution in a violent death. Settled eventually as a free woman, in New Jersey, where she sets up 'a school for colored children', Hannah is even reunited with the guardian angel of her dreams, the mother whom up until that moment she never really knew. 'We met accidentally, where and how it matters not,' she breezily declares. No longer an orphan, she is no longer single either. Her mother now lives with her, Hannah confides to the reader, and so does 'another companion quite as dear – a fond and affectionate husband'. So the novel ends with the heroine no longer a lost princess, having found her kingdom: living happily ever after, we assume, 'in a neat little Cottage' surrounded by friends. '[Y]ou could scarcely believe it,' Hannah reflects, then turns to the 'hand of Providence' by way of explanation. Like the story that precedes it, the final chapter, appropriately titled 'In Freedom', is a highly coloured fiction that is, nevertheless, founded in fact, since there were free black communities in New Jersey of broadly the kind the heroine describes. *The Bondswoman's Narrative* is an elaborate artifice that exposes the real nature of life under slavery, the mental and material shackles forced upon slaves and the brutalities and blindness engendered in oppressors. It is a thing of shreds and patches, perhaps, but that is part of its power as a register of humanity: measuring, as it does, the degree to which the author both resists and surrenders to the vocabularies that are her only means of expression, the values and conventions she has been taught by her white masters and which, however unknowingly or unwillingly, she has internalized. This novel is a major document, and not just because it has floated to the surface, and into publication, many decades after it was written, as one sign or trace of a whole sea of texts as yet unpublished and so largely unread. It is so, also, because it gives us access to the life, the dreams and nightmares of one of the dispossessed. It is not what the narrator describes it as in her Preface, a 'record of plain unvarnished facts'. It is something more and better than that: a revelation of the truth, emotional and imaginative – 'consistent with the writing of a woman', as Hannah herself puts it, and bearing witness to what it might mean to be both female and a slave.

Two other novels by African Americans to appear before the Civil War were *Blake; or, The Huts of America* (partly serialized in 1859, fully serialized in 1861–2, and issued as a book in 1870) and *Our Nig; or, Sketches from the Life of a Free Black, in a Two-Story White House, North. Showing that Slavery's Shadows Fall Even There* (1859). *Blake* was the work of Martin Delany (1812–85), a free black born in what is now West Virginia. In 1852, Delany published *The Condition, Elevation, Emigration, and Destiny of the Colored People of the United States*, which argued for the emigration of blacks to a state of their own creation. *Blake* continued that argument. The hero, Henry Blake, possesses many of the qualities Delany liked to identify with himself. He is 'a black – a pure negro – handsome, manly, and intelligent' and 'a man of good literary attainments'. Born in Cuba, Blake is decoyed into slavery in Mississippi. There, he marries another slave; and, when his wife is sold and sent away from him, he runs away to begin organizing slave insurrections, first in the South and then in Cuba. 'If you want white man to love you, you must fight im!' an Indian whom he meets in the course of his wanderings tells Blake. And, although

Blake does not want the white man to love him, he certainly wants to fight him. 'From plantation to plantation did he go,' the narrator observes of Blake, 'sowing the seeds of future devastation and ruin to the master and redemption to the slave.' For him the site of his ambition, and future redemption, is Africa. There he hopes to 'regenerate' black civilization, on the basis of economic success and entrepreneurial activity. The message of *Blake* is, in fact, at once revolutionary and deeply conventional, in the American grain. 'I am for war – war against whites,' the hero tells his allies, while insisting that they should resist amalgamation, reject life in the United States, and return to their African homeland. But Blake also advises them, 'With money you may effect your escape at almost any time . . . Money alone will carry you . . . to liberty'; and money, he points out, is the reward of enterprise. Delany was a father of black nationalism who did not reject the American way but, rather, hoped to see it pursued by African Americans in Africa. The violence he embraced, and dramatized in his novel, was founded on a simultaneous alienation from and attachment to the land where he was born.

Our Nig is very different. The first published novel by an African American woman, it is also the first in black American literature to examine the life of an ordinary black person in detail. It was originally thought to be the work of a white, and perhaps even male, writer. And it was only recently established that Harriet E. Wilson (1808?–70) was the author, drawing in part on personal experience. The central character, Frado (short for Alfrado and also called 'Our Nig'), is deserted by her white mother after the death of her African American father. She is abandoned in the home of the Bellmonts, where she becomes an indentured servant and is treated cruelly by her white mistress, Mrs Bellmont, who beats her, and by her daughter Mary Bellmont. The white male members of the household try to protect Frado, but they are mostly ineffectual, and Frado has to learn to protect herself. Coming of age at eighteen, she then leaves the Bellmonts and marries an African American who claims to be a runaway slave. She has a child by him, is then deserted and discovers his claim is false, experiences poverty and bad health, the result of years of abuse, and is forcibly separated from her child. As the story of Frado unfolds, some narrative attention is given to events in the Bellmont family, and to the adventures of the Bellmont children as they grow up and marry. In conventional fashion, the subsequent lives of various Bellmonts are even summarized in the closing paragraph of the novel. But the emotional centre throughout is the poor black girl whose nickname – given to her, of course, by whites – provides the book with its main title. And, at the end of the story, the pathos of her plight is emphasized. 'Reposing on God, she has thus far journeyed securely,' the narrator advises us. 'Still an invalid, she asks your sympathy, gentle reader.'

Our Nig is a fascinating hybrid. It is, first, an autobiography, a deeply personal confession and a cry for help. Founded on some of the author's own experiences, it begins with her saying that she is 'forced to some experiment' to maintain her child and herself and ends with a straight appeal to the reader for support. Three testimonials then follow the narrative proper, affirming its literal truth and reinforcing the request for aid. Apparently written by whites to mediate the story for white readers, they are distinctly patronizing in tone (one testimonial, for example, refers to 'our dark-skinned brethren'), and they are quite probably fictional – written by Wilson herself. Not only an autobiography with a fictional addendum, *Our Nig* follows the classic pattern of the slave narrative, so as to show that 'slavery's shadows fall even there', in the North among indentured servants and other victims of racism. There is even a moment of confrontation reminiscent of the *Narrative of Douglass*, when Frado stands up to Mrs Bellmont. 'Stop!' Frado cries, 'strike me, and I'll never work a mite more for you.' 'She did not know, before, that she had the power to ward off assaults,' the narrator confides. 'Her triumph . . . repaid her for much of her former sufferings'; and, after that, there was 'the usual amount of scolding, but fewer whippings'. Along with that, *Our Nig* is a sentimental fiction of sorts. There are numerous moments of pathos involving Frado, courtship and deathbed scenes for the Bellmonts, and a series of appeals to the gentle reader. Some of this sentimentalism is clearly designed to move the audience to sympathy with the plight of the heroine. But some is more complex in effect, since the dynamic of the plot relegates those incidents that, in a conventional sentimental novel, would be central (that is, the familial and love problems of a genteel New England family group) to the margins of the narrative. There they become, more than anything, further evidence of the white capacity for excluding and ignoring blacks – for sidelining black people just as now, in turn, they, the whites, are sidelined. And not only a sentimental novel, *Our Nig* is also a realist one. It focuses not so much on moments of particular brutality (although there are certainly some of them) as on the bitter daily burden of black toil and white indifference and spite. Wilson's book is all of these generic forms, and it is more than the sum of them, as it charts the journey of her heroine towards survival rather than satisfaction, let alone success. In being so, it illustrates the problem so many African American writers have faced, of trying to find a workable genre in which to express and explore themselves: a form that gives them a chance of narrating, properly, their identity. The author's identification of herself as simply 'Our Nig', in the first edition of the book, was, of course, ironic; and it underlined the difficulty of finding a name for herself in a culture that tried to do that work for her – to give her not so much a name as a demeaning label. It is an additional irony that she was to remain unnamed, for over a hundred years, as the author, the maker of her own work: invisibility, the namelessness that is perhaps the central theme in African American writing, was to be the story *of Our Nig*, for a long time, as well as the story *in* it.

The Making of an American Fiction and Poetry

The emergence of American narratives

Our Nig had almost no impact when it was published. The reverse was true of *Uncle Tom's Cabin; or, Life Among the Lowly*. The author of *Uncle Tom's Cabin*, Harriet Beecher Stowe (1811–96), was born in Connecticut. Her father, Lyman

Beecher (1775–1863), was an influential Calvinist preacher, whose sermons and magazine articles were published in a collected edition in the same year as his daughter Harriet's most famous novel. Later, Stowe was to reject his insistence on constant self-searching and a sense of damnation in favour of a gentler gospel, based on a belief in the Christ of the New Testament and on the virtues enshrined in feminine piety and motherhood. But, just as all her brothers went on to become ministers – including the most well known of them, Henry Ward Beecher (1813–87), who also wrote fiction – so Stowe herself remained a fundamentally religious writer, whose art and politics were shaped by her concern for spiritual and moral purity. In 1824, Stowe went to Hartford, where her sister Catharine Beecher (1800–78) – who was to become a distinguished spokesperson for the ideas of female education, the importance of the domestic virtues and a separate sphere for women – had founded a female seminary. She stayed at the seminary, first as a pupil and then as a teacher, until 1832; and in 1834 she collaborated with Catharine on a geography book for children; two years later, she married Calvin Stowe, who was then a professor in her father's theological seminary. Beginning to write sketches and short fiction for mostly evangelical periodicals, Stowe collected some of these in her first book, *The Mayflower: Sketches and Scenes and Characters Among the Descendants of the Puritans* (1843). The pieces included here show the interest in local colour and the didactic purpose that would stay with her throughout her career. But they lack intensity, or passion. That came as she committed herself to the abolitionist cause. Stowe's father, while opposed to slavery, was a gradualist, believing that the slave system could be dismantled in stages. Stowe, however, became convinced of the urgency of the situation, and said so in her first essay on the subject, titled 'Immediate Emancipation' and published in 1845. After the passing of the Fugitive Slave Law in 1850, which required Northerners to help slaveholders recover escaped slaves, Stowe's sister-in-law wrote to her saying that, if she had Stowe's talent, she would write something that would 'make this whole nation feel what an accursed thing slavery is'. Harriet's response was simple and immediate. 'I *will* write something,' she declared, 'I will if I live.' Fired into life by this, and by a vision she had during communion of a slave being beaten to death, she composed the scene in *Uncle Tom's Cabin* in which the hero of her book, Uncle Tom, is killed by Simon Legree.

Uncle Tom's Cabin started out, according to Stowe's intention, as a series of sketches, published in the *National Era*, an anti-slavery magazine, in 1851. Her aim, she told the editor of the magazine, was 'to hold up in the most lifelike and graphic manner possible Slavery'. 'There is no arguing with *pictures*,' she explained, 'and everybody is impressed by them, whether they mean to be or not.' The response was immediate, and so positive that the series, intended originally to last for fourteen weeks, was stretched out eventually to ten months. Then, when the book was published in 1852, it sold 10,000 copies in a few days, 300,000 copies in the first year, and became an international best-seller. No other book had ever sold so well, apart from the Bible. At least twelve unauthorized stage versions of the story were produced. And, when Stowe visited Britain, people gathered at railway stations from London to Scotland just to watch her train pass by in the night. So successful and influential was the book that, in the middle of the civil conflict between the Union and the Confederacy, President Abraham Lincoln was reported to have remarked that Stowe was 'the little lady who wrote the book that made this great war'. The main story, however, is simple. Uncle Tom, a faithful and saintly slave, is sold by his owners, the Shelby family, when they find themselves in financial difficulties. Separated from his wife and children, he is taken South by a slave trader; aboard ship on the Mississippi, he saves the life of Eva St Clare, known as little Eva, and is bought by her father, Angel St Clare, out of gratitude. Tom is happy at the St Clare plantation, growing close to Eva and her black playmate Topsy. But, after two years, Eva dies and then so does St Clare. Tom is sold to the villainous Simon Legree, a cruel and debauched Yankee. The patience and courage of Tom, despite all the brutal treatment meted out to him, bewilder Legree. Two female slaves take advantage of Legree's state of mind, and pretend to escape; and, when Tom refuses to reveal their whereabouts, a furious Legree has him flogged to death. As Tom is dying, 'Mas'r George' Shelby, the son of Tom's original master, arrives, to fulfil his pledge made right at the beginning of the novel, that he would one day redeem the old slave. It is too late for Tom; however, Shelby vows to fight for abolition and, as a first step, he frees the slaves on his own plantation, telling them that they can continue to work for him as 'free men and free women'. Woven in and around this main plot are a number of subsidiary episodes, involving a host of characters. The most important of these episodes concern Eliza Harris, a beautiful 'mixed race' woman, her husband George, who lives as a slave on another plantation, and their son Harry. George is the son of a slave mother and a white father 'from one of the proudest families in Kentucky'. He is said to have inherited 'a set of European features, and a high indomitable spirit' from his father; he has, we are told, 'only a slight mulatto tinge' – and he preaches resistance, defiance. At one point, for instance, he makes what is called 'his declaration of independence': he is 'a free man' by natural right, he insists, and, as such, he has the right to defend his freedom, by violence if necessary. In the course of the story, George and Eliza escape. They stay at a Quaker settlement for a while, with their son Harry. Eventually, they set sail from America. On board ship, both are miraculously reunited with their long-lost mothers. They settle first in France, where George attends university for four years, and then in Africa. 'The desire and yearning of my soul is for an African *nationality*,' George declares. 'I want a people that shall have a tangible, separate existence of its own.' The final gesture of one George, Shelby, in freeing his slaves, is in effect counterpointed by the final gesture of another George, Harris, in seeking to establish what he calls 'a republic formed of picked men, who, by energy and self-educating force, have . . . individually raised themselves above a condition of slavery'. Both appear to be founders of a new order.

'God wrote the book,' Stowe once said of *Uncle Tom's Cabin*, 'I took His dictation.' Stowe was helped not only by divine intervention, though, or her sense of it, but by her reading. There are various forms of discourse at work in the novel that reflect its author's active and informed engagement with the debate over slavery.

Stowe was, for example, well aware of the arguments for and against slavery. At one moment in the St Clare episode, she comprehensively rebuts every facet of the pro-slavery argument; and, at another point, she has a family discuss the Fugitive Slave Law. The story of the flight of George and Eliza Harris clearly recalls slave narratives; the novel as a whole opens with a central situation in plantation fiction, the threatened loss of the old plantation due to debt; and, true to the conventions of sentimental fiction, there are miraculous coincidences, interminable deathbed scenes (notably, the death of little Eva) and the customary address to the gentle reader. Characters out of tall tales and frontier humour are introduced, like a comic black duo called Sam and Andy; two rough slaveholders called Tom Luker and Marks recall the rogues of Southwestern humour; various moments, such as when we are invited to enter Uncle Tom's Cabin for the first time, remind us of Stowe's participation in the local colour tradition; and, along with scenes from provincial life, there are moments of pastoral and anti-pastoral – respectively, the idyllic portrait of the St Clare plantation and the detailed description of the dilapidated estate that Simon Legree owns. But Stowe does not simply imitate, she innovates. So, *this* plantation novel centres, as its subtitle indicates, not on the wealthy plantation owners but on 'life among the lowly'. Its hero is not some impoverished patriarch but a slave who gradually assumes the stature of a Christ figure. And the object of *this* sentimental fiction is, as Stowe declares in her 'Preface', specifically moral and political: 'to awaken sympathy and feeling for the African race, as they exist among us.'

Those whose sympathy Stowe especially hoped to awaken were women: the narrator constantly appeals to the possible experiences of the reader as a wife and mother. In part, this is because she clearly sees the power of sympathy as a useful political instrument and agent of conversion: several characters are, in fact, converted to the anti-slavery cause when they are forced actively to witness suffering. And, in part, it is also because the appeal relates to one of the fundamental arguments of the book. Slavery is shown to be a violation of the American principle of freedom and the higher law of conscience. It is also, of course, identified as the cause of many individual acts of dispossession, division, sexual deviance and mental and material oppression. But what *Uncle Tom's Cabin* concentrates on here are two related issues: slavery as a system that denies and destroys the family, and slavery as an institution that seems to reduce a human being to a thing. Stowe repeatedly returns to incidents in which parents like Uncle Tom are separated from their children, wives like Eliza Harris are separated from their husbands, and slave women are betrayed by the white men who profess to love them. In doing so, she slyly subverts the familial language of the pro-slavery argument; and she appeals to the reader's own experience of familial love to measure the difference between a true family and what is on offer in the South. The emphasis is on the domestic pieties here, understood with special clarity by true Christian women. But it is also on slavery as a sin. Stowe insists, as well, that what is wrong with chattel slavery is that the souls of slaves are placed at the disposal of whoever is able to purchase their bodies: so the soul of the slave is endangered, while the soul of the master is almost certainly consigned to damnation. Of course, a sense of sin is no more a monopoly of Stowe's female readership than an appreciation of the domestic virtues and family ties is. But it is noticeable that Stowe does tend to focus her writerly attention on her white female readers, to appeal to their knowledge and agency. And, given the contemporary cult of true womanhood, that is perhaps neither surprising nor unwise.

To an extent, in fact, *Uncle Tom's Cabin* is a document testifying to female power as well as black possibility: the condition of women as well as that of slaves. Females are consistently better managers than men, in the novel: Mrs Shelby, for instance, is said to have 'a clear, energetic, practical mind, and a force of character every way superior to that of her husband' – the man whose debts lead him into the initial, tragic error of selling Tom. It is the females who offer the most fully realized vision of a redemptive society: in the Quaker settlement where George and Eliza Harris shelter – where everything runs 'so sociably, so quietly, so harmoniously' thanks to the women, who run it on matriarchal and communal lines. And it is the principles identified with the feminine in the novel that we are invited to admire: the organic, creative, supportive, sympathetic impulses associated with Eva St Clare and her 'misty, dreamy' father, Angel (who is said to be more like his mother than his father). The principles identified as masculine are, by contrast, shown to be mechanized, destructive, oppressive, associated with Angel's twin brother Alfred St Clare (who, like his father, believes in 'the *right of the strongest*') and, even more, the brutal Simon Legree. Here, the contrast between Uncle Tom and George Harris is relevant. George resists, invoking the Declaration of Independence, and he is certainly admired for doing so. He is not, however, the emotional centre of the novel. That is supplied by 'the hero of our story', the gentle, unresistant and feminized Uncle Tom, who invokes the Bible and only resists doing wrong – refusing to whip a fellow slave, to betray the whereabouts of two other slaves, and refusing even the chance offered him to kill Simon Legree. George is a political exemplar of a kind, illustrating Stowe's interest in the idea of the removal of emancipated slaves to Africa, where, as she puts it in the 'Preface', 'an enlightened and Christianised community' could be 'drawn from among us'. But Tom is a saint, compared eventually to Christ: ready to be killed, but not to kill. Conversion not revolution is the principal subject and aim of *Uncle Tom's Cabin*; and that project is specifically and consistently associated with the feminine.

The counsel of patience embodied in its hero has earned Stowe's novel opprobrium in many quarters: 'Uncle Tom', after all, has become a term of abuse, a dismissive label stuck on any African American seen to be too servile, too compliant, too foot-scrapingly eager to please the white community. And there is no doubt that *Uncle Tom's Cabin* often resorts to racial stereotypes, typified by the moment when Eva St Clare is compared to her companion Topsy. 'There stood the two children, representatives of the two extremes of society,' the narrator intones. 'The fair, high-bred child, with her golden head, her deep eyes, her spiritual, noble brow, and prince-like movements; and her black, keen, subtle, cringing yet acute neighbor.' 'They stood the representatives of their races,' she goes on, 'the Saxon, born of ages of cultivation, command, education, physical and moral eminence; the Afric, born of ages of oppression, submission, ignorance, toil, and vice!' Reflecting many of the prejudices of her time, Stowe tends to present her black characters as emotional, spiritually alert, loyal and essentially childlike. Only characters with some significant white ancestry, like George Harris, are allowed to deviate from this pattern. She is also inclined to some familiar types and tropes of plantation fiction. There are comic minstrels, comic cooks and tumbling piccaninnies, there are romantic mulattoes who combine the sensitivity of their mothers with the strength of their fathers. There are spoilt servants, who snobbishly identify themselves with the families who own them; there are brutes, like the two black assistants of Legree, Sambo and Quimbo, who offer what is termed 'an apt illustration of the fact that brutish men are lower even than animals'. Stowe extenuates all this, a little, by emphasizing the destructive influence of training in making her black characters what they often are. But training is clearly not everything here; and, in any event, as her description of Topsy shows, she is inclined to slip rather too quickly and easily from comments on education to comments on racial character – from extenuation or explanation to what looks suspiciously like wishing to patronize her black subjects, to generalize in genetic terms and even to blame.

Still, the force of the attack on slavery in *Uncle Tom's Cabin* remains. And, looking at both its form and approach, its imaginative idioms and its dramatic argument, it is easy to see why it made such an enormous impact on contemporary readers. Stowe took the aesthetic weaponry of several popular genres – the plantation romance, sentimental fiction, the slave narrative – and she then used them to show how the slave system violated the most sacred beliefs of her culture – the sanctity of the family and the individual soul. How far she did this knowingly it is impossible to say, and in any case hardly matters. What is clear is that she felt inspired as a writer and moved as the first reader of her work: she wrote the account of the killing of Uncle Tom, she said, with tears streaming down her face. Stowe drew on the wealth of feeling she herself had, concerning the home and family, Christian womanhood and the Christian soul; she then appealed to that same wealth of feeling in her readers. In the process, she wrote what is, by any standards, one of the most important American books. For a while after *Uncle Tom's Cabin*, Stowe continued to write about slavery. In 1853, she wrote *A Key to Uncle Tom's Cabin*, designed to defend the accuracy of her 1852 novel. Then, in 1856, she published *Dred: A Tale of the Dismal Swamp*. This, her second story of slave society, takes a different approach from the first. It tends to concentrate on the demoralising effects of slavery on whites. And this time the character who gives the novel its title is a fugitive and a revolutionary. Modelled on Nat Turner, Dred is said to be the son of another black insurrectionary, Denmark Vesey. He invokes both the Declaration of Independence and the Bible and he preaches defiance, violence: 'I am a free man!' he declares, '"Free by this!" holding out his rifle.' However, even here Stowe does not ignore the destructive consequences of slavery for the slaves themselves. More to the point, she does not allow Dred the last word. He preaches vengeance against the white oppressor. But he is bested in argument by another character,

---

Milly, based on Sojourner Truth, who preaches patience. 'O brethren, dere's a better way,' she tells her fellow sufferers, imploring them to pray to 'de Lord' to give the whites repentance: 'Leave de vengeance to him. Vengeance is mine – I will repay, saith de Lord.'

After *Dred*, Stowe steered away from the subject of slavery. *The Minister's Wooing* (1859), set in New England, uses a romantic plot to explore the limitations of the 'gloomy' doctrine of Calvinism and promote belief in a redemptive Christ and a God of love and mercy. Similar themes, together with an emphasis on the power of female purity, are at work in *Agnes of Sorrento* (1862), set in the Catholic Italy of Savonarola, and *The Pearl of Orr's Island* (1862), another book set in New England which Sarah Orne Jewett credited with inspiring her own career. The local colour element, which had always been there in Stowe's work, grew stronger in her later fiction. *Oldtown Folks* (1869) is set in New England in the post-Revolutionary period and has a narrator modelled on Stowe's own husband. *Oldtown Fireside Stories* (1871) draws on her husband's childhood memories; and *Poganuc People* (1878), her last novel, draws on her own. Stowe remained a prolific writer throughout most of her life. She wrote children's books, travelogues, temperance tracts, practical articles about housekeeping, theological works such as *Bible Heroines* (1878), journalistic sketches on a wide variety of subjects, poems and hymns. And she always remained a writer with a stern moral purpose. Several of her novels, for instance, resemble novels of manners more than anything else, including one called *Pink and White Tyranny* (1871). Even here, however, she was keen to announce her intention to instruct and uplift. 'This story is not to be a novel as the world understands the word,' she wrote in her 'Preface' to *Pink and White Tyranny*, 'it is . . . a story with a moral; and for fear that you shouldn't find out exactly what the moral is . . . we shall tell you in the proper time . . . and send you off edified as if you had been hearing a sermon.' That fierce didactic intention has meant that Stowe has often been granted less than her due as a writer. She is a didactic writer, certainly, but she is also a writer capable of combining adroit use of popular literary models with raw emotional power. Consistently, in much of her fiction and many of her sketches, she is a very good writer indeed; at her best, in *Uncle Tom's Cabin*, she is surely a great one.

'Only this is such a strange and incomprehensible world!' a character called Holgrave declares in *The House of the Seven Gables* (1851), the second full-length fiction of Nathaniel Hawthorne (1804–64). 'The more I look at it, the more it puzzles me; and I begin to suspect that a man's bewilderment is the measure of his wisdom!' Hawthorne was notoriously mistrustful of all speculative schools of thought, or of anyone or any movement that claimed to have solved the mystery and resolved the contradictions of life. That included the two major historical movements associated with his native New England of which he had intimate experience: Puritanism and Transcendentalism. He was someone who managed to make great art not so much out of bewilderment as out of ambiguity, irresolution – a refusal to close off debate or the search for truth. His friend and great contemporary, Herman Melville, spoke admiringly of Hawthorne's ability to 'say no in thunder' to the fixities and definites of life; his great disciple, Henry James, declared that Hawthorne 'had a cat-like faculty of seeing in the dark'. Hawthorne was undoubtedly a moralist, concerned in particular with the moral errors of egotism and pride, separation from what he called 'the magnetic chain of humanity'. But he was a moralist who was acutely aware of just how complex the human character and human relations are, just how subtle and nicely adjusted to the particulars of the case moral judgements consequently have to be – and how moral judgement does not, in any event, preclude imaginative understanding, even sympathy. He was also someone who had inherited from his Puritan ancestors what he termed his 'inveterate love of allegory'. But his alertness to the dualities of experience, his sense that the world was at once intractably material and irresolvably mysterious, meant that, in his hands, allegory passed into symbolism: an object or event assumed multiple possible significances rather than correspondence with one, divinely ordained idea. Finally, Hawthorne was, he confessed in the 'Preface' to *The House of the Seven Gables*, an author of romances rather than novels. 'When a writer calls his work a Romance,' he pointed out, 'it need hardly be observed that he wishes to claim a certain latitude'; he asks to be allowed to deviate, rather more than usual, from the illusion of reality and to cloak his subject in 'some . . . legendary mist'. But, for Hawthorne, that greater imaginative freedom was a means, not an end. His aim, and achievement, was to manoeuvre the romance form so as to unravel the secrets of personality and history: 'the truth of the human heart', as Hawthorne himself put it, and the puzzling question of whether the present is an echo or repetition of the past, a separate world 'disjoined by time', or a mixture somehow of both.

Nathaniel Hawthorne was born in Salem, Massachusetts, to Nathaniel and Elizabeth Clarke Manning Hathorne: the author was later to add the 'w' to his name in a curious, but entirely characteristic, act of disengagement from but deferral to the past – in the sense that he did not drop the family name, but added to it. Both his parents were descended from prominent New England families. On his mother's side, the Mannings had migrated from England in 1679. And on his father's side, Hawthorne's earliest American ancestor, William, had arrived in Massachusetts in 1630. 'The figure of that first ancestor, invested by family tradition with a dim and dusky grandeur, was present to my boyish imagination as far back as I can remember,' Hawthorne was later to say in 'The Custom House', the introductory essay to his greatest novel, *The Scarlet Letter* (1850). 'He was a soldier, legislator, judge; he was a ruler in the Church; he had all the Puritanic traits, both good and evil.' Hawthorne could not help feeling involved with his New England homeplace and ancestry. New England was, in fact, to become the setting for most of his stories; and the burden of the past, the problem of inherited guilt overshadowing the present, was to become a major theme because it was an integral part of his own experience. The sense of guilt was especially strong because John Hathorne, the son of that 'first ancestor', had been a judge at the Salem witchcraft trials. John, Hawthorne wryly confessed, 'made himself so conspicuous in the martyrdom of witches that their blood may fairly be said to have left a stain upon him'. A family tradition even had it that John had been cursed by one of his victims, declaring, 'if you take away my life, God will give you blood to drink'. Hawthorne was later to use that curse as the basis for his second novel. And, long before that, he was inclined to attribute the subsequent decline of the Hathorne family, more than half seriously, to this chilling event.

For decline the Hathorne family certainly did. To make matters worse, Hawthorne's father, a sea captain, died when Hawthorne was only four, leaving his widow to mourn him in a long life of eccentric seclusion. As a boy, he was already acquiring what he would call his 'cursed habit of solitude'. He did go to college for a while, where he began a lifelong friendship with a future poet, Henry Wadsworth Longfellow, and a future president, Franklin Pierce. But, on returning to his mother's house, he spent the next twelve years in what he called his 'chamber under the eaves', reading and writing. Hawthorne's attitude to this solitude was characteristic-ally ambivalent. On the one hand, he could admit, in a letter to Longfellow, that he felt 'carried apart from the main current of life'; 'I have made a captive of myself and put me into a dungeon,' he explained, 'and now I cannot find the key to let myself out.' On the other hand, as he sensed, he was learning his craft. And he was also discovering his subject: since, repeatedly in his fiction, he concentrates on people who seem to be outside of life, set apart by pride, or egotism, or inno-cence, or guilt. The four major characters in *The Scarlet Letter*, for instance, are all like this; each, for quite different reasons, seems to be cut off from ordinary humanity. So, for that matter, are the protagonists in many of his tales. In 'The Minister's Black Veil' (1837), it is Parson Hooper's obsession with guilt that severs him from the human community: viewing the world through the veil of his own guilt, he thinks he sees a black veil on every face around him. In 'Wakefield' (1837), it is the eponymous hero's disengagement. A cold-hearted, selfish, vain, crafty and strange man, Wakefield leaves his wife and home one day and does not return for twenty years; he little realizes that, 'by stepping aside for a moment, a man exposes himself to the fearful risk of losing his place forever', to 'become, as it were, the Outcast of the Universe'. And in 'Ethan Brand' (1851), it is Brand's intellectual egotism, his cold detachment. Seeking to find 'The Unpardonable Sin', he discovers that what he seeks is what he himself has committed: in the course of his search, separating intellect from feeling, he becomes 'no longer a brother man', he realizes, but 'a cold observer, looking on mankind as the subject of his experi-ment, and, at length, converting man and woman to be his puppets, and pulling the wires to such degrees of crime as were demanded from his study'.

In 1828, Hawthorne published his first novel, *Fanshawe: A Tale*, anonymously and at his own expense. An autobiographical work, it went unnoticed. But it did attract the attention of its publisher, Samuel Goodrich, who then published many of Hawthorne's short stories in his periodical, *The Token*. Eventually, these were reprinted in a volume, *Twice-Told Tales*, in 1837, then in a larger version in 1842. In a characteristically modest and self-critical Preface, Hawthorne referred to his tales as having 'the pale tint of flowers blossomed in too retired a shade', and as representing the attempt of 'a secluded man' to 'open an intercourse with the world'. They do, however, include some of his best pieces, such as 'The Maypole of Merrymount', 'Endicott and the Red Cross' and 'The Grey Champion'. And, collectively, they explore the issues that obsessed him: guilt and secrecy, intellectual and moral pride, the convoluted impact of the Puritan past on the New England present. For the next five years, Hawthorne worked as an editor for Goodrich, then became involved briefly in the experiment in communal living at Brook Farm. Used to solitude, however, he found communal living uncongenial: its only positive result for him was the one mentioned earlier – the novel he published in 1852 based on his Brook Farm experience, *The Blithedale Romance*. Married now, to Sophia Peabody, he and his wife moved to Concord, where they lived in the Old Manse, the former home of Ralph Waldo Emerson. There was time for neighbourly visits to Emerson, Henry David Thoreau and Margaret Fuller, for the family – three children were born to Sophia and Nathaniel between 1844 and 1851 – and for writing: in 1846, *Mosses from an Old Manse* appeared, containing such famous stories as 'Young Goodman Brown', 'Rappacini's Daughter' and 'Roger Malvin's Burial'. There was also time, after Hawthorne left a post he had held for three years as customs surveyor, to concentrate on a longer fiction, what would turn out to be his most important work.

The germ of this work, what was to become *The Scarlet Letter*, can be found as far back as 1837. In the story 'Endicott and the Red Cross', the narrator describes a young woman, 'with no mean share of beauty', wearing the letter A on her breast, in token of her adultery. 'Sporting with her infamy,' he goes on, 'the lost and desperate creature had embroidered the fatal token in scarlet cloth, with golden thread' so that 'the capital A might have been thought to mean Admirable, or anything other than Adultress.' Already, the character of Hester Prynne, the heroine of *The Scarlet Letter*, was there in embryo. And gradually, over the years between 1837 and 1849, other hints and anticipations appear in the journals Hawthorne kept. 'A man who does penance,' he wrote in one journal entry, in an idea for a story, 'in what might appear to lookers-on the most glorious and triumphal circumstances of his life.' That was to become the Reverend Arthur Dimmesdale, Hester's secret lover and the father of her illegitimate child, preaching the Election Day Sermon. 'A story of the effects of revenge, in diabolising him who indulges it,' he wrote in another entry. That was to be Roger Chillingworth, Hester's husband and Dimmesdale's persecutor. Ideas for the portrait of Pearl, the daughter of Hester and Dimmesdale, often sprang from Hawthorne's observation of his own daughter, Una. Sometimes, he simply noted something Una had said or done in his journals, and then reproduced it in the speech or action of Pearl. As he wrote the novel, over the course of 1849 and 1850, Hawthorne was simultaneously exhilarated and wary. 'He writes immensely,' Sophia reported in a letter to her mother, 'I am almost frightened.' '*The Scarlet Letter* is positively a hell-fired story,' Hawthorne himself wrote to his publisher; 'it will weary very many people and disgust some.'

The tone or tenor of this 'hell-fired story' is suggested by Hawthorne's general preference for calling his longer fictions romances rather than novels. It is also intimated by a passage in the introductory essay to *The Scarlet Letter*, in which

Hawthorne offers an essentially allegorical account of his own creative process. 'Moonlight in a familiar room', Hawthorne explains in this passage, 'is a medium the most suitable for a romance writer,' because it turns the room into 'a neutral territory, somewhere between the real world and fairyland, where the Actual and the Imaginary may meet.' The ordinary is transfigured, assuming some of the qualities of the legendary. So the four major characters of the story, for example, approach the condition of figures out of folktale. Hester Prynne resembles the Biblical figure of Eve, or the scarlet woman of folklore; Dimmesdale recalls the false priest, Chillingworth the wicked wise man, and Pearl the wise child, a presocial creature who can evidently see things hidden from the adult eye. To the moonlight, in this passage, Hawthorne then adds the figurative presence of the mirror: seen 'deep within its haunted verge', the moonlit room, he observes, gravitates 'one remove further from the actual, and nearer to the imaginative'. What we are being prepared for here is that quality of imaginative removal that also characterizes *The Scarlet Letter*: the action is not only transformed by the beams of the imagination, it is also subtly distanced and framed. The story begins, after all, in the fifth act, after the pivotal event, the adulterous liaison of Hester and Dimmesdale, has taken place. We, the readers, are invited not so much to involve ourselves in a narrative action as to contemplate the consequences of that action. And then those consequences are themselves set at a remove from us, and in a contained series of perspectives, by being presented in a basically pictorial, emblematic way. Each episode is built around a particular object or event: the prison, say, the scaffold, the forest, the Governor's mansion, Hester's embroidery work. The narrator then mediates the episode for the reader, working through the possible meanings of the object or event in a tentative, equivocal way. As he does so, he tries to learn something about the truths of the human heart: which brings us to the third element Hawthorne adds in this passage, to the moonlight and the mirror. In this 'familiar room', Hawthorne tells us, where the writer of romance goes about his business, there is a 'somewhat dim coal fire' casting 'a faint ruddiness' over everything: giving 'as it were, a heart and sensibilities of human tenderness to the forms which fancy summons up'. It is Hawthorne's way of reminding the reader that all his manoeuvres, the imaginative transfiguration and narrative distancing, are there for a distinctly passionate purpose; his aim as a romance writer is nothing less than to search out the secrets of the inner life, to discover and disclose the torments and tensions, those fires that lie hidden within every human being.

The major tensions that Hawthorne searches out in *The Scarlet Letter* are related to his own ambivalent relationship to Puritanism, and his own Puritan ancestors in particular. As he intimates in the introductory essay to his story, he felt haunted by his ancestors yet different from them. He could experience what he calls there 'a sort of home-feeling with the past', but he also suspected that his Puritan founding father might find it 'quite a sufficient retribution for his sins' that one of his descendants had become a writer, 'an idler' and a dabbler in fancy. *The Scarlet Letter* rehearses the central debate in nineteenth-century American literature: between the demands of society and the needs of the individual, communal obligation and self-reliance. The Puritan settlement in which the story is set is a powerful instance of community. Hester Prynne, in turn, is a supreme individualist: 'What we did had a consecration of its own,' she tells her lover. The conflict between the two is also a conflict between the symbolic territories that occur in so many American texts: the clearing and the wilderness, life conducted inside the social domain and life pursued outside it. And the main characteristic of Hawthorne's portrait of this conflict is its doubleness: quite simply, he is tentative, equivocal, drawing out the arguments for and against both law and freedom. As a result, the symbolic territories of *The Scarlet Letter* become complex centres of gravity: clustering around them are all kinds of often conflicting moral implications. The forest, for example, may be a site of freedom, the only place where Hester and Dimmesdale feel at liberty to acknowledge each other. But it is also a moral wilderness, where characters go to indulge in their darkest fantasies – or, as they see it, to commune with the Devil. The settlement may be a place of security, but it is also one of constriction, even repression, its moral boundaries marked out by the prison and the scaffold. Simple allegory becomes rich and puzzling symbol, not only in the mapping of the opposing territories of forest and settlement, clearing and wilderness, but in such crucial, figurative presences as the scarlet letter 'A' that gives the book its title. To the Puritans who force Hester to wear the scarlet letter, it may be an allegorical emblem. In the course of the story, however, it accumulates many meanings other than 'adultress'. It might mean that, of course, and so act as a severe judgement on Hester's individualism; then again, as the narrator indicates, it might signify 'able', 'admirable' or even 'angel'.

The major characters of *The Scarlet Letter*, too, become centres of conflict, the debate become flesh, turned into complex imaginative action. Hester, for example, may be a rebel, modelled on the historical figure of Anne Hutchinson as well as the mythical figure of Eve. But she cannot live outside of society altogether. She is a conflicted figure, unable to find complete satisfaction in either the clearing or the wilderness; and her eventual home, a house on the edge of the forest, in a kind of border territory between the two, is a powerful illustration of this. Dimmesdale is conflicted too, but in a more spiritually corrosive way. 'No man', the narrator observes of him, 'for any considerable period can wear one face to himself and another to the multitude without finally getting bewildered as to which may be true.' Torn between the image he offers to others and the one he presents to himself, his public role as a revered minister and his private one as Hester's lover and Pearl's father, Dimmesdale is fatally weakened for much of the action. In his case, the central conflict of the story finds its issue in severe emotional disjunction. And Chillingworth is there to feed on that weakness, becoming Dimmesdale's 'leech' in more ways than one – apparently his doctor but actually drawing sustenance from Dimmesdale's guilt and his own secret satisfying of the need for revenge. Roger Chillingworth, in turn, is more than just a figure of retribution and a possible projection of Hawthorne's own uneasy feeling that, as a writer, he was just a parasite, an observer of life. 'It is a curious observation and inquiry, whether hatred and love be not the same at bottom,' the narrator comments, after describing how

Chillingworth declined once Dimmesdale died. The link is passion. 'The passionate lover' and 'the no less passionate hater' each sups voraciously on 'the food of his affection'; and the hater, rather more than the lover, reminds us that laws may well be required to curb the individual appetite. Hawthorne was enough of a son of his Puritan forefathers to believe that, as he put it in his journals, 'there is evil lurking in every human heart'. Knowledge of evil, after all, and of her origins, is the means by which Pearl eventually ceases to be a child – a creature of the wilderness, associated with its streams, plants and animals – and starts to become an adult, a woman in the world. And knowledge of evil renders each of the major characters even more vacillating and conflicted, ensuring that the debate between self and society that *The Scarlet Letter* rehearses remains open, for the narrator and for us, his readers.

This, perhaps, is the secret of the mysterious power of Hawthorne's major novel: it is an open text. The story explores many issues. They include, along with the central problem of law and freedom, what the narrator calls the 'dark question' of womanhood. Among many other things, *The Scarlet Letter* considers the condition of woman in and through the story of its heroine, speculating that 'the whole system of society' may have 'to be torn down and built up anew' and woman herself reconstructed, freed from a 'long hereditary habit' – behaviour instilled by social separation and subjection – before women like Hester can assume 'a fair and suitable position'. On none of these issues, however, and least of all on the central one, does the narrator claim to be authoritative or the narrative move towards closure. The subtle manoeuvring of character, the equivocal commentary and symbolism, ensure that meaning is not imposed on the reader. On the contrary, the reader has to collaborate with the narrator, in the construction of possible meanings, every time the book is read. To this extent, for all Hawthorne's profound debt to Puritanism, *The Scarlet Letter* is an extraordinarily modern book: expressing a relativist sense of experience in a form that is more fluid process than finished product. What it offers is not, in the manner of a traditional classic text, an answer issuing out of a belief in some absolute, unalterable truth, but something more like a modern classic – a shifting, disconcerting and almost endless series of questions.

The Scarlet Letter ushered in the most productive period of Hawthorne's life. In the next three years, he was to publish not only the two further novels, *The House of the Seven Gables* and *The Blithedale Romance*, but another collection of stories, *The Snow Image and Other Tales* (1851), and two volumes of stories for children, *A Wonder Book* (1852) and *Tanglewood Tales* (1853). He lived in England for a while, as United States Consul, and then in Rome, returning to America in 1860. The years in Europe supplied him with the material for a novel set in Rome and dealing with the international theme that Henry James was to make his own, *The Marble Faun* (1860). They also resulted in a series of shrewd essays drawn from his observations in England, called *Our Old Home* (1863). But, back in the United States, he found it increasingly difficult to write. Four novels were started and never finished, based on the themes of the elixir of life and an American claimant to an English estate: *Septimius Felton; or, The Elixir of Life* (1872), *The Dolliver Romance* (1876),

Dr Grimshawe's Secret (1882) and *The Ancestral Footstep* (1883). He would begin a scene and then write 'What meaning?' or 'What does this mean?' in the margins. The writer who had once been inspired by the multiplicity of possible meanings that lay beneath the surface of things was stuck, frustrated by an apparent absence of meaning, his evident inability to strike through the surface. The cat-like faculty that Henry James was later to attribute to him had, Hawthorne felt, now deserted him. 'Say to the public', he wrote to his publisher, when he was asked for some stories, 'that Mr Hawthorne's brain is addled at last . . . and that you consider him finally shelved.' It was a sad ending for a great writer. But, of course, it in no way diminishes his achievement. Even the later, unfinished work is far more intriguing than Hawthorne, in his dejection, supposed: the American claimant manuscripts, for example, explore the old theme of past connections to the present in new ways – as the protagonist considers whether to accept his rightful inheritance or reject it. And the earlier work, above all the major stories and *The Scarlet Letter*, forms an indispensable contribution to American literature, as well as to the history of the short story and the novel. Hawthorne was an intensely solitary, introspective man but he put that solitude and introspection to powerful creative use. He was a man tortured by doubt, but, more often than not, he managed to turn that doubt to his advantage, making an art out of uncertainty. At his finest, which was very often, Hawthorne searched honestly and fiercely for the truth, the sources of the moral life, even though he was not often sure his search would be successful. He compelled his readers to share in that search too, and still does. As a result, to read him is to be reminded of his fundamental belief, which he shared with many of his contemporaries and subsequent American writers, that reading is a moral activity.

'He can neither believe, nor be comfortable in his unbelief,' Hawthorne once observed of Herman Melville (1819–91), 'and he is too honest and courageous not to try to do one or the other.' For Melville, human experience was ruled by contraries. 'There is no quality in this world that is not what it is merely by contraries,' Ishmael declares in *Moby-Dick* (1851). 'Nothing exists in itself.' And those contraries were no more evident, he felt, than within each human being, as he or she struggled to find a basis for truth and faith, something that would really make life worth living. Melville could not resign himself to doubt, or to a placid acceptance of the surfaces of things. 'I am intent upon the essence of things,' he has one of his characters, Babbalanja the philosopher, announce in his third novel, *Mardi* (1849), 'the mystery that lies beyond . . . ; that which is beneath the seeming.' That speaks for Melville's own artistic project. What also speaks for that project, however, is an intimation offered by the narrator of Melville's penultimate novel, *Pierre* (1852). 'Far as any geologist has yet gone down in the world,' he tells the reader,

> it is found to consist of nothing but surface stratified on surface. To its axis, the world being nothing but extended superficies. By vast pains we mine into the pyramid; by horrible gropings we come to the central room; with joy we espy the sarcophagus; but we lift the lid – and no body is there! – appallingly vacant as vast is the soul of man!

Melville wanted to probe the visible objects of the world, to discover their animating structure, their significance. But he also sensed that the visible might be all there was – and that that, too, was a masquerade, a trick of the light and human vision. He wanted to read what he called 'the cunning alphabet' of nature so as to interpret its grounds, its meanings. But he also feared that all men could see there was a mirror of their own needs and feelings. He wanted to attend carefully to the phenomenal world, as a possible emanation of the noumenal, the spiritual, to listen for its messages. But he also suspected that there was no message to be heard: that, as one of his narrators put it once, 'Silence is the only Voice of our God'. 'The head rejects,' the reader is told in Melville's long poem, *Clarel* (1876); 'so much more / The heart embraces.' That could stand as an epigraph to all Melville's work because it exists in the tension, the war between meaning and nothingness. It bears constant and eloquent testimony to the impulse most people feel at one time or another: the impulse to believe, that is, even if only in the possibility of belief, however perversely and despite all the evidence.

Melville did not begin with the ambition to become a writer. Nor did he have an extensive schooling. His father died when he was only twelve; and, at the age of fifteen, Melville left school to support his family. Working first as a bank clerk, a teacher and a farm labourer, he then, when he was nineteen, sailed on a merchant ship to Liverpool as a cabin boy: the voyage, later to be described in his fourth novel, *Redburn* (1849), was both romantic and gruelling and gave him a profound love for the sea. Several other voyages followed, including an eighteen-month voyage on the whaler *Acushnet* in the South Seas. When he grew tired of this voyage, in the summer of 1842, he jumped ship at the Marquesas and lived for a month on the islands. Escaping from the locals who were holding him captive in the valley of Typee, he then sailed to Tahiti, where he worked for a time as a field labourer. From Tahiti he sailed on a whaler again: to Honolulu, where he enlisted as an ordinary seaman on the man-of-war *United States*, serving on board for just over a year, until October 1844. Ishmael, in *Moby-Dick*, insists that the whale-ship was the only Yale and Harvard he ever had; and much the same could be said of his creator, who now returned to land, where he was encouraged to write about some of his more exotic experiences at sea. Melville accordingly produced *Typee* (1846) and *Omoo, a Narrative of Adventures in the South Seas* (1847), novels that deal, respectively, with his experiences on the Marquesas and in Tahiti. They were romantic seafaring tales and, as such, proved immensely popular. But, even here, there are anticipations of the later Melville: most notably, in a narrative tendency to negotiate between contraries – youth and maturity, the primitive and the civilized, the land and the sea.

In his next novel, *Mardi: And A Voyage Thither*, Melville grew more ambitious. Based in part on the author's experiences in the Marquesas, *Mardi* is an elaborate allegorical and philosophical narrative. Taji, the hero, visits thinly disguised satirical versions of the United States, Great Britain and other lands. He travels with Babbalanja the philosopher, Yoomy the poet, and others, discussing fundamental issues and problems. He also meets and falls in love with a mysterious white maiden Yillah, rescuing her from sacrifice then taking her to Mardi, the realm of transcendental beauty, where for a while they enjoy intimacy and bliss. When she vanishes suddenly, he goes in search of her. And, after many conversations and distractions, he is still in pursuit of her when the book ends: 'And thus, pursuer and pursued fled, over a vast sea' are its last words. As a narrative of quest, the search for an elusive object of desire, *Mardi* anticipates *Moby-Dick*. What it lacks, however, is any fundamental narrative or imaginative drive. It was also a commercial failure. Melville learned one useful lesson from writing *Mardi*: that, if he wanted to explore deeper issues, he had to wed meaning to action, to twine them together so closely that they became inextricable from and gave strength to each other. The next two novels concentrated on action: first, *Redburn: His First Voyage*, and then *White-Jacket; or, The World in a Man-of-War* (1850) based, like *Redburn*, on Melville's own experience. It was after completing these that Melville turned to the work that was to be his masterpiece and that he was to dedicate, in 'Admiration for His Genius', to the man who had become his friend and neighbour, Nathaniel Hawthorne.

Melville had moved with his wife to Pittsfield, Massachusetts, in 1850, where he soon became acquainted with Hawthorne. Prior to the move there, he had written a highly appreciative review of *Mosses from an Old Manse*, in which he explained how much he admired the author of the stories contained in that volume for the tragic dualism of his vision. Melville was now reading widely, and Hawthorne was to be only one of a multitude of influences that fed into what was first titled 'The Whale' and then *Moby-Dick; or, The Whale*. For the narrative incident, he drew on his own experiences and a host of books on whales and whaling, probably including an article published in *The Knickerbocker Magazine*, 'Mocha Dick; or, The White Whale of the Pacific' by J. N. Reynolds, and a book, *Narrative of the Most Extraordinary and Distressing Shipwreck of the Whale-Ship Essex* by Owen Chase. For the approach and treatment, he drew on the complex symbolic practice of Hawthorne, of course; on epic stories of voyaging from the *Odyssey* to the *Lusiad*, a poem by the Portuguese poet Camoens about Vasco da Gama; and on the work of William Shakespeare. Melville took to rereading Shakespearean tragedy at the time of preparing the story of Captain Ahab's pursuit of the great white whale; and he drew on that experience in a number of ways. There are local resemblances. Ahab addresses the skeleton of a whale, for instance, in a fashion that recalls Hamlet's famous meditation over the skull of Yorick the jester; some conversations between Ahab and his black cabin boy Pip, who has been driven mad by immersion in the sea (but 'man's insanity is heaven's sense', the narrator reminds us), recollect dialogues between King Lear and his Fool; while the sense that Ahab is at once free and the victim of some 'hidden lord and master', a defiantly wilful man and 'Fate's lieutenant', rehearses a paradox at the heart of the portrait of Macbeth. There are stylistic resemblances. Few writers deserve comparison with Shakespeare on this score. But the author of *Moby-Dick* surely does. The language of the novel is extraordinarily variable, but there is a ground bass, as it were, that is richly metaphorical but vividly direct; dense, allusive, packed with neologisms, it

---

manages the seemingly impossible feat of being both deeply philosophical and almost unbearably dramatic. And there is, above all, the conceptual, structural resemblance. 'All mortal greatness is but disease,' Ishmael observes early on in the narrative. That observation, as it happens, is borrowed from an essay by Samuel Taylor Coleridge on Shakespearean tragic heroes. Even without the help of such borrowings, however, it is possible to see that the conception of Captain Ahab is fundamentally tragic. Ahab makes a choice that challenges – the gods, or fate, or human limits, the given conditions of thought and existence. That choice and challenge provoke our fear and pity, alarm and sympathy. And they lead, it seems inevitably, to a catastrophe that compels similarly complex, contradictory emotions: the suffering and death of many, including a hero who appears to exist somehow both above and below ordinary humanity.

The contradictions inherent in the portrait of Ahab spring, of course, from the dualism of Melville's own vision. Together, the narrator and the hero of *Moby-Dick*, Ishmael and Ahab, flesh out that dualism. So does the structural opposition of land and sea, which rehearses in characteristically Melvillean terms a familiar American conflict between clearing and wilderness. The land is the sphere of 'safety, comfort, hearthstone, supper, warm blankets, friends, all that's kind to our mortalities'; the sea, in turn, is the sphere of adventure, action, struggle. The one maps out security, and mediocrity; the other carries intimations of heroism but also the pride, the potential madness involved in striking out from the known. The one inscribes reliance on the community, the other a respect for the self. A densely woven network of reference establishes the difference between these two territories; it also suggests the difficulty, perhaps the impossibility, of either choosing between them or finding an appropriate border area. 'Consider them both, the sea and the land,' the narrator advises, 'and do you not find a strange analogy to something in yourself?' The analogy is ambivalent, however. At one moment, the reader may be urged not to leave the land for 'all the horrors of the half known life' ('God keep thee! Push not off from that isle, thou canst never return!'). At the next, he or she may be told precisely the opposite: that, 'as in landlessness resides the highest truth, shoreless, indefinite as God', nobody should 'worm-like, then, oh! . . . craven crawl to land!' The opposition between land and sea is made all the rawer by Melville's portrait of the ship, the *Pequod*, on which Ahab, Ishmael and their companions voyage. The crew, 'a deportation from all the isles of the sea, all the ends of the earth', are, we are told, a 'joint-stock company' and '*Isolatoes*'. They are together and alone, knit into one shared purpose yet utterly divided in terms of motive and desire. Caught each of them between the land and the sea, the social contract and isolation, they remind us that this is a ship of life, certainly, burdened by a common human problem. But it is also, and more particularly, the ship of America: embarked on an enterprise that is a curious mixture of the mercantile and the moral, imperial conquest and (ir)religious crusade – and precariously balanced between the notions of community and freedom.

All the tensions and irresolutions of *Moby-Dick* circulate, as they do in *The Scarlet Letter*, around what gives the book its title: in this case, the mysterious white whale to which all attention and all the action are eventually drawn. The reason for the mystery of the whale is simple. It 'is' reality. That is, it becomes both the axis and the circumference of experience, and our understanding of it, in the novel. It is nature, and physics, a state of being and of knowing. Each character measures his understanding of the real in the process of trying to understand and explain the whale; it becomes the mirror of his beliefs, like the doubloon that Ahab nails to the mast as a reward for the first man who sights the white whale, to be valued differently by the different crew members. It is both alphabet and message, both the seeming surface of things and what may, or may not, lie beneath them. So, like the scarlet letter 'A' in Hawthorne's story, its determining characteristic is its indeterminacy. How it is seen, what it is seen as being and meaning, depend entirely on who is seeing it. Three characters, in particular, are given the chance to explain what they see at some length. One offers his explanation early on in the novel, even before the voyage in quest of the white whale begins: Father Mapple, whose sermon delivered to a congregation that includes Ishmael in the Whaleman's Chapel – and forming the substance of the ninth chapter – is a declaration of faith, trust in a fundamental benevolence. It is a vision allowed a powerful imaginative apotheosis in a much later chapter entitled 'The Grand Armada'. Here, Ishmael and his fellow crewmen move ever further inward into a school of whales: from the turbulent periphery, where a 'strangely gallied' group circle around in 'a delirious throb', to an inscrutably serene core of 'nursing mothers' and their young. The experience discloses a hope, a possibility of 'that enchanted calm which they say lurks at the heart of every commotion': the belief that there may, after all, be an 'eternal mildness', a still point at the centre of the turning world. Outside of these two moments, however, this is not a vision in which much narrative time or imaginative energy is invested. The visions that matter here, the explanations – or, rather, possible explanations – that count, rehearse the fundamental division around which all Melville's work circulates; and they belong to the two main human figures in the tale, its hero and its teller, Ahab and Ishmael.

For Ahab, Moby-Dick represents everything that represses and denies. Believing only in a fundamental malevolence, he feels towards the white whale something of 'the general rage and hate felt by the whole race from Adam down'. Having lost his leg in a previous encounter with his enemy, he also desires vengeance, not just on the 'dumb brute' that injured him but on the conditions that created that brute, which for him that brute symbolizes – the human circumstances that would frustrate him, deny him his ambitions and desires. Ahab is a complex figure. A tragic hero, carrying the marks of his mortality, the human limitation he would deny – a wooden leg, a scar running down his face and into his clothing that resembles the 'perpendicular seam' made in a tree trunk struck by lightning – he is also a type of the artist, or any visionary intent on the essence of things. 'All visible objects, man, are but as pasteboard masks,' he declares; 'If a man will strike, strike through the mask! How can the prisoner reach outside except by thrusting through the wall? To me, the white whale is that wall, shoved near to me.' Ahab is, in fact, as much embarked on a symbolic project as his creator is, struggling to break through the surface, the seeming to what may lie beneath. An artist, he is also an American: a rebel like Hester Prynne, an enormous egotist like Ralph Waldo Emerson in the sense that he sees the universe as an externalization of his soul, and an imperialist whose belief in his own Manifest Destiny compels him to use all other men like tools and claim dominion over nature. A rich network of allusion and image establishes the several related facets of Ahab's character. He is a 'monomaniac', marked by a 'fatal pride', yet he also has a 'crucifixion in his face'. His 'fixed purpose is laid with iron rails', he insists, just like the railway then marking out the domination of American nature by American culture. But, in his inaccessibility, 'he lived in the world' but 'was still alien to it', Ishmael observes, 'as the last of the Grisly Bears lived in settled Missouri'. His ship sets sail on Christmas Day, initiating the first in a series of references to the story of Christ. Yet the harpoon with which he wishes, finally, to master Moby-Dick he baptizes in the name of the Devil. 'A grand ungodly, god-like man', Ahab projects his overpowering belief in himself, his will to power, on to Moby-Dick, seeing in the great white whale all that prevents a man from becoming a god. And the key to Melville's portrait of him is its dualism: it is as if the author were summoning up his, and possibly our, dark twin.

'Is it by its indefiniteness,' Ishmael asks of 'the whiteness of the whale', 'it shadows forth the heartless voids and immensities of the universe . . . ?' It is Ishmael who describes white as 'a colorless all-color'. It is Ishmael, too, expanding on this, who points out that 'all other earthly hues' are 'but subtle deceits, not actually inherent in substances, but only laid on from without'; produced, every one of them, by 'the great principle of light', which 'for ever remains white or colorless in itself', they are a matter merely of surface, seeming. It is Ishmael, finally, who declares that the whale 'has no face' and is characterized by 'his pyramidical silence'. In short, for the narrator of *Moby-Dick*, the great white whale unveils the probability that the world is nothing but surface stratified on surface – that what is disclosed when we peer intently at our circumstances is neither benevolence nor malevolence but something as appallingly vacant as it is vast, a fundamental indifference. That, though, is not all there is to Ishmael. In the course of the story, he also undergoes a sentimental education. Beginning with a misanthropy so thoroughgoing and dryly ironic that he even mocks his misanthropic behaviour (sometimes, he confesses, 'it requires a strong moral principle to prevent me from . . . methodically knocking people's hats off'), he ends by accepting and embracing his kinship with unaccommodated man, the human folly and weakness he sees all around him. Specifically, he embraces Queequeg, a Polynesian harpooneer, whom initially he finds, even more than most of humanity, repellent. Before embarking on the *Pequod*, he and Queequeg share a bed, out of necessity, in a crowded inn, 'a cosy, loving pair'; they share companionship and each other's religions – with Queequeg joining Ishmael in attending Father Mapple's sermon, and Ishmael participating in Queequeg's ceremonies with his small idol Yojo. Then, on board ship, with a monkey-rope tied between them, Ishmael comes to realize that, as he puts it, 'my own individuality was now merged in a joint-stock company of two'. It is this, Ishmael's return to a specifically human sphere – expressed, in a characteristically American way, in the bonding of two people of the same sex but from different races – that enables him, quite literally, to survive. When all other crew members of the *Pequod* are lost, and the ship itself sunk, after three days of struggle with Moby-Dick; when Ahab is destroyed by becoming one with that which he would destroy, tied by his own ropes to the great white whale; then, Ishmael floats free in what is, in effect, a reproduction of Queequeg's body – a coffin Queequeg has made, and on to which he has copied 'the twisting tattooing' on his own skin. It *is* survival, not triumph. 'Another orphan' of the world, an existential outcast like all humanity, Ishmael lives on because he has resigned himself to the limitations of the sensible, the everyday, the ordinary: to all that is identified, for good and ill, with the land. The difference between his own quietly ironic idiom and the romantic rhetoric of Ahab measures the gap between them: one has opted for a safety that shades into surrender, the other has pursued success only to meet with a kind of suicide. That difference also registers the division Melville felt within himself. *Moby-Dick* negotiates its way between the contraries experienced by its author and by his culture: between head and heart, resignation and rebellion, the sanctions of society and the will of the individual. And, like so many great American books, it remains open, 'the draught of a draught' as its narrator puts it, because it is in active search of what it defines as impossible: resolution, firm belief or comfortable unbelief – in short, nothing less than the truth.

Moby-Dick was not a success when it was first published; and Melville felt himself under some pressure to produce something that would, as he put it, pay 'the bill of the baker'. That, anyway, was his explanation for his next novel, *Pierre; or, The Ambiguities*. This book, he explained while writing it, was 'a rural bowl of milk' rather than 'a bowl of salt water' like his whaling story. It was, he averred, 'very much more calculated to popularity . . . being a regular romance, with a mysterious plot to it, stirring passions at work, and withall, representing a new and elevated aspect of American life'. If Melville really believed this, then he was doomed to disappointment. A dark tale, ending in the suicides of the eponymous hero and his half-sister, *Pierre* carries echoes of Edgar Allan Poe, not only in its macabre tone, violent tenor and rumours of incest but in its self-reflexivity, its variations on the theme that 'the truest book in the world is a lie'. More painfully, for Melville, the book was a critical and commercial disaster. One reviewer was not out of step with most of the others when he called it 'the craziest fiction extant'; and, in the first year of publication, it sold fewer than three hundred copies. *Israel Potter: His Fifty Years of Exile* (1855), a weak historical romance set during the Revolution, was similarly unsuccessful. *The Piazza Tales* (1856) was far more accomplished, containing Melville's major achievements in short fiction, 'Bartleby the Scrivener' and 'Benito Cereno', but it attracted little attention. Melville's audience was evidently not ready for the one tale that tells of a man so convinced of life's futility and fatality that he would 'prefer not to' do anything – or the other that dramatically interrogates the American optimism of its narrator and the European pessimism of its protagonist, Cereno, under the 'shadow' of slavery. Melville did, after this, explore the issues that obsessed him in two other works of prose fiction. *The Confidence-Man: His Masquerade* (1857) offers complex multiple versions of the mythical figure of the trickster; it is at once a bleak portrait of the 'Masquerade' of life and a biting satire on the material and moral trickery of American society. *Billy Budd*, written in the five years before Melville's death and not published until 1924, in turn, reworks the traditional tale of the Handsome Sailor so as to consider the uses of idealism, heroism and innocence in a fallen world. However, to support himself and his family, Melville was increasingly forced to turn to other, non-writing work. And to express himself, he turned more and more to poetry. *Clarel: A Poem and Pilgrimage in the Holy Land*, based on a tour to the Holy Land the author himself had taken, is typically preoccupied with faith and doubt. It was privately financed for publication; so were the poetry collections *John Marr and Other Sailors* (1888) and *Timoleon* (1891). In his shorter poems, published here and in *Battlepieces and Aspects of the War* (1866), Melville is concerned, just as he is in his novels, with the tragic discords of experience; and he expresses those concerns here in a style that is itself often discordant, abrupt. In 'The Portent' (1886), for instance, he presents the militant abolitionist John Brown, the subject of the poem, as an alien and 'weird' Christ figure, whose thwarted aspirations and misdirected zeal become an emblem of the failure visited on all those who try to realize their dreams in the world. The poem, for all its ironic use of the Christ comparison, is not cynical; it does not deny Brown greatness of ambition and courage. As in *Moby-Dick*, though, admiration for, even envy of, such courage is set in tension with the imperative of survival: in its own small way, this poem rehearses again the issue that haunted its creator – the necessity and the absurdity of heroic faith.

Women writers and storytellers

The death of Melville went largely unnoticed by a wider public. Even those who did take note were hardly complimentary. 'He won considerable fame as an author by the publication of a book in 1847 entitled "Typee",' an obituary in the *New York Daily Tribune* observed. 'This was his best work, although he has since written a number of other stories, which were published more for private than public circulation.' It was not until the 1920s that his work began to be appreciated, and his stature as a major American writer was finally confirmed. Conversely, as Melville's star began to wax, the stars of other writers waned. This was notably true of those many women novelists and storytellers of the period whose work had enjoyed a wide contemporary readership. In their case, it is only in the last thirty years that reputations have been rehabilitated. Their writing has now been recognized for the pivotal cultural work it performed: the way it enabled Americans, and in particular American women, to assess their position in society and engage in debates about its prevailing character and possible development. Apart from Stowe, Fern and Harper, those women writers whose reputations suffered for a while in this way include Caroline Kirkland (1801–64), Alice Cary (1820–71),

Elizabeth Stoddard (1823–1902) and Rebecca Harding Davis (1831–1902). Spanning the century in their lives, their work measures the range, diversity and quality of those whom Hawthorne famously, and quite unjustly, dismissed as a 'damned mob of scribbling women'.

Caroline Kirkland was one of the first settlers of Pinckney, Michigan, accompanying her husband there after he had acquired some land. Her ideas of the West, formed by such romantic works as *Atala* (1801) by Vicomte François René de Chateaubriand, were radically altered by the experience. And in 1839, she published a novel, a series of scenes from provincial life on the frontier, *A New Home – Who Will Follow? or, Glimpses of Western Life*, under the pseudonym of 'Mrs Mary Clavers, An Actual Settler'. The book offers a version of the West that eschews romanticism, sensationalism, or even the kind of realism that emphasizes the masculine adventure and challenge of the frontier. Aiming at what she called 'an honest portraiture of rural life in a new country', Kirkland begins by admitting that she has 'never seen a cougar – nor been bitten by a rattlesnake'. The reader must expect no more, she says, than 'a meandering recital of common-place occurrences – mere gossip about everyday people'. What follows is more calculated than that, however, and subtler: a portrait of 'home on the outskirts of civilisation' that focuses on the experience of women as they struggle to make do, and make something out of their daily lives. Kirkland makes wry fun of those with romantic expectations of the West: including a character called Miss Eloise Fisher, a visitor from the East, who writes poetry about the beauty of the woods – although 'she could not walk out much on account of her shoes'. Several of Miss Fisher's sentimental poems are included in the text. Delicious parodies of a nature poetry that identifies the frontier with the pastoral life, they are subverted by their context. For what the narrative concentrates on elsewhere is physical and material hardship: the difficulty of house-keeping in the wilderness, the harshness of work in 'remote and lonely regions', the sheer trouble of travelling anywhere when at any moment one might encounter 'a Michigan mud-hole'. 'We must have a poet of our own,' the narrator, Mrs Clavers, insists; and that poet, it is clear, would be someone quite the opposite of Eloise Fisher. It would be someone, in fact, like the storyteller here, who is not afraid of writing what she calls 'a veracious history of actual occurrences, an unvarnished transcript of real characters, and an impartial record of everyday forms of speech' – but in a manner that carries with it dramatic wit and bite.

Part of that bite comes from the contrast Kirkland draws between men and women on the frontier. The men have their own upwardly and westwardly mobile agenda. They are driven by ambitious dreams and plans: like Mr Clavers, who buys two hundred acres of land and then draws 'the plan of a village' he wants to build 'with a piece of chalk on the bar-room table'. They lead, and the women have to follow: making homes and communities, or at least trying to, before being moved on again. Several women characters in *A New Home* suffer from male physical brutality: the drunkenness of men, for instance, and the consequent fear and despair of their women is a recurrent theme. Other women characters find the rough manners of Western life congenial: like a local schoolteacher who visits Mrs Clavers and, as soon as she arrives, begins to smoke a pipe 'with the greatest gusto, turning ever and anon to spit at the hearth'. But the majority of women in the book, like Mrs Clavers herself, have to negotiate neither brutal treatment nor rough manners but something far more fundamental: the enormity of the gap between how they and their husbands see land and life in the West. For them, the land is a place to settle, life there should be communal; for their men, however, the land is a source of status and power and life in the West is competition – if the game dictates it, then the men, seeing the land as negotiable currency, will readily sell out, pull up stakes. For Kirkland, there is a touch of what she calls 'madness' in this male attitude, but there is nothing the females can do about it. All they can do is try, as best they can, to put up with the hidden emotional costs.

Kirkland published a sequel to *A New Home*, called *Forest Life*, in 1842. She wrote many other sketches and essays, published other volumes such as *Western Clearings* (1845); she became an active editor, and her home in New York City, to which she returned from life on the frontier, became the centre for a network of women writers. But it is for *A New Home* that she deserves a place in American literary history. Similarly, Alice Cary led an active life in several fields. She wrote novels; her poetry was admired by both Poe and Whittier and enjoyed popular success; and, after she moved from her birthplace in Ohio to New York City in 1850, she became a celebrated literary hostess. But, like Kirkland, she deserves recognition for her work in one field in particular: in her case, the short fiction collected in *Clovernook; or, Recollections of Our Neighborhood in the West* (1852), *Clovernook, Second Series* (1853) and *Pictures of Country Life* (1859). What is striking about these sketches and tales is their elusive, carefully selective structure and a rich texture that combines realism of surface detail with intimations of fairy tale. In 'My Grandfather' (1851), for example, the narrator recalls the time when, as she puts it, 'I first made room in my bosom for the consciousness of death'. In a story that is, characteristically, a recollection of childhood in the West, the 'I', the centre of consciousness, moves in a dreamlike state, from the narrative present to the past, adulthood to childhood. She sees her mother, father and brother as they once were: her father, for instance, not the 'scornful old man' he has become, with hair 'thinned and whitened almost to the limit of three score years and ten', but 'fresh and vigorous' and youthful as he once was. She also sees herself as a child, and then becomes that child. And, through the eyes of a child, she witnesses the news being brought about the sickness of her grandfather. She accompanies her mother to her grandfather's house two miles away. Around the closing door of the sick room, she catches a glimpse of his 'pale, livid, and ghostly' face. Timidly creeping into the room, she dares to touch her grandfather's 'damp and cold' hand, only to be told by him, 'Child, you trouble me'; 'those were the last words he ever spoke to me,' the narrator recalls. Finally, she catches another glimpse of her grandfather: this time, of his 'unsmiling corpse' at the funeral. The tale captures the fragmented nature of reality and memory, the shifting, shadowy boundaries between present and past, and the curious way experience can come, especially to children, as a series of hints and guesses, half-suppressed secrets, significant glances and whispered conversations. The grimness of reality is never ignored: the grandfather, for example, is remembered not as a beloved, kindly person but as 'a stern man', whose behaviour was invariably 'uncompromising and unbending'. 'I remember of his making toward me no manifestation of fondness, such as grandchildren usually receive,' the narrator confesses, 'save one, when he gave me a bright red apple.' But the magic, the mystery of things, even the everyday, is not minimized either. 'My Grandfather' works, as all Cary's best short stories do, precisely because it evokes the strangeness of the supposedly ordinary, the familiar – a wonder that is subject only to partial disclosure, and which finds its ideal medium of expression in fragments, gemlike narratives like this one.

Elizabeth Stoddard, born Elizabeth Drew Barstow in a small Massachusetts sea coast town, was a more unconventional person than either Cary or Kirkland. In letters written in 1850, she described herself as being different from other women: intellectual and passionate and self-possessed, someone who saw marriage as a struggle for power and motherhood as a distraction from the destiny she planned for herself. She did get married, however, to a minor poet called Richard Stoddard (1825–1903). And she began to write as well: poetry, short fiction and, from 1854 to 1858, a regular column for the *Daily Alta California*. The short fiction tends to fall into one or other of two categories, formalized sketches like 'Collected by a Valetudinarian' (1870) and tales blending realism and romance such as 'Lemone Versus Huell' (1863). The columns, in turn, reveal Stoddard's resistance to the received wisdom of the day. Stoddard mocked belief in Manifest Destiny, established religion and the notion of a separate domestic sphere for women. She also poked satirical fun at the sentimental novel, with its 'eternal preachment about self-denial'. 'Is goodness, then, incompatible with the enjoyment of the senses?' she asked in one of her columns, and insisted that, on the whole, it was not. It was the 1860s, however, that were to witness her finest work. In 1862, she published her first novel, *The Morgesons*. It impressed Nathaniel Hawthorne, to whom Stoddard sent a copy, and many critics and reviewers including William Dean Howells. But it failed to secure her a reading public. Her two other novels, *Two Men* (1865) and *Temple House* (1867), suffered a similar fate. In the later two books, unlike *The Morgesons*, Stoddard adopted a male protagonist's point of view. All three, though, are characterized by an elliptical narrative style, carried along by rapid transitions of scene, conversations stripped to an explanatory minimum, and a dramatic, aphoristic, densely imagistic idiom. All three, also, reveal a world where social institutions are both repressive and in decay and religious belief is difficult, even impossible; and they show the family as a site of struggle rather than as a source of security, full of strangeness and secrecy, where passion is thwarted, impulse denied.

The Morgesons is exemplary in this respect. Its central character and narrator, Cassandra Morgeson, is clearly modelled on Stoddard herself; and what the book charts is a female quest for empowerment. Described as headstrong, even arrogant, by many of her acquaintances, Cassandra seeks personal autonomy. Born in a small seaport town, between land and sea, she is drawn as her great-grandfather Locke Morgeson was to 'the influence of the sea': to escape, adventure, breaking away from convention and the commonplace. 'The rest of the tribe' of Morgesons, Cassandra caustically observes, 'inherited the character of the landscape.' *The Morgesons* imitates the pattern, the structure of the domestic novel, to the extent that it shows a young woman undergoing a sentimental education that ends in marriage, but it imitates it only to subvert it. Cassandra remains bold and wilful, and an outsider, throughout the novel. She nurtures a dangerous attachment to a married man; she falls in love, later, with a dark, handsome stranger, called Desmond Somers, whom she eventually marries; but she always remains in control, her own woman. Another man who loves her, Desmond's brother Ben, finally admits that Cassandra is too much for him, and chooses to marry her sister Veronica instead. 'You have been my delight and misery ever since I knew you,' Ben tells Cassandra:

> I saw you first, so impetuous, yet self-contained! Incapable of insincerity, devoid of affection and courageously naturally beautiful. Then, to my amazement, I saw that, unlike most women, you understood your instincts; that you dared to define them, and were impious enough to follow them. You debased my ideal, you confused me, also, for I could never affirm that you were wrong; forcing me to consult abstractions, they gave a verdict in your favour, which almost unsexed you in my estimation. I must own that the man who is willing to marry you has more courage than I have.

Cassandra is far more self-confident and sexually emancipated than any sentimental heroine or even, for that matter, Nathaniel Hawthorne's Hester Prynne. In her stern self-reliance, she recalls the definition of true womanhood in *Woman in the Nineteenth Century* by Margaret Fuller. In her passion for life, and her intense dedication to her own needs, she resembles the heroines of those writers whom Stoddard herself especially admired, Charlotte and Emily Brontë. There are, in fact, elements of the Gothic as well as the sentimental novel in *The Morgesons*. There is violence both emotional and literal, a frequent melodramatic heightening of feeling, and the doubling – and, as Ben Somers intimates, the transposing, the crossing over – of males and females. And the ultimate view of life in this feminist *Bildungsroman* is tough, bleak, stoical. 'My audacity shocked,' Cassandra admits, 'my candor was called anything but truthfulness; they named it sarcasm, cunning, coarseness.' A woman 'whose deep, controlled voice vibrated in the ears, like the far-off sounds we hear at night from woods or sea', Cassandra intimidates even her father with her outspokenness, her intellectual courage and her 'sense of mystery'. When her mother dies, Locke Morgeson, the father, soon marries a woman far more manageable and malleable than Cassandra and moves out of the Morgeson family home. With Ben Somers and Veronica gone, Cassandra is left, as she triumphantly observes, 'alone in my own house'; 'I regained an absolute self-possession,' she adds, 'and a sense of occupation I had long been a stranger to.' Walking by her native element, the sea, she casts a cold eye on human existence, accepting its loneliness and challenge: 'Have at thee life!' her senses cry. It is only then, in possession of herself and the Morgeson house (a structure the architecture of which makes it the material embodiment of the family history), that she is willing to take on a loving but equal partnership with Desmond Somers: who returns from a sojourn in Europe, a man quite different from the imposing figure she first met, visibly altered, even defeated – 'I hope I am worthy of you,' he confesses. It is not a comforting ending, any more than Cassandra is a comforting heroine. Writing the closing words of her story from her chamber overlooking the ocean, she tells us there is 'no pity, no compassion' in the 'eternal monotone' of the waves. Nature is indifferent; life is abruptly challenging, casually violent (Ben Somers, for instance, suddenly dies in the last paragraph of the book); there is no sense of a community of faith or custom promising safe harbour. Of the sea, her constant companion and spiritual mentor, Cassandra declares, at the end, 'its beauty wears a relentless aspect to me now'. Much the same could be said of Cassandra herself, and the remarkable novel of which she is the dramatic and narrative centre. *The Morgesons* anticipates later fiction in its ellipses, its disjunctive, allusive idiom. It rehearses and reinvents both the Gothic and the sentimental fiction of its own time, in its curious, subtle mix of romance and realism ('I am *not* realistic – I am *romantic*,' Stoddard once insisted, 'the very bareness and simplicity of my work is a trap for romance'). And it enters vigorously into the contemporary debate about whether there should or should not be separate spheres for women and men. But it is, above all, a book that is far more than the sum of these or any other connections: a novel that, in the spirit of those writers Stoddard most admired like the Brontës and Hawthorne, captures both the mundane and the ineffable – the materiality and the mystery of life.

Rebecca Harding Davis declared that it was her purpose 'to dig into the commonplace, this vulgar American life, and see what is in it'. That purpose was clear enough in her first published work, 'Life in the Iron Mills', which appeared in the *Atlantic Monthly* in 1861. The story was immediately recognized as an important, innovative work, introducing a new subject to American literature: the bleak lives of industrial workers in the mills and factories of the nation. 'Not many even of the inhabitants of a manufacturing town know the vast machinery of system by which the bodies of workmen are governed,' the narrator of the story declares near its beginning. And a major aim of Davis, in 'Life in the Iron Mills', was, quite simply, to end that ignorance: to make readers aware of the oppression and the essential humanity of those workmen. Anticipating one of the major strategies of the Naturalists at the end of the nineteenth century, Davis emphasizes the typicality of her working-class characters, and the way they may be driven into crime by a system that appears to deny them any other possible avenue of escape. The tale begins on a 'cloudy day', with 'smoke everywhere' from the chimneys of the iron mills. As the anonymous narrator observes, from her window, an industrial landscape 'begrimed with smoke', 'fragments of an old story float up' before her. It is one of many possible stories associated with the house in which the narrator lives, she reveals to us, telling of some of the people who lived there some thirty years ago. And it is one of many more stories of this dark city, with its 'myriads of furnace-hands'. 'There is a secret down here, in this nightmare fog,' the narrator declares, 'I want to make it a real thing to you'; and the story will be her way of doing it. The tale 'Life in the Iron Mills' then tells is a simple one. At its centre is a character called Hugh Wolfe, whose activities and fate encapsulate the aspirations and bitter reality of working people. The statue of a woman he has fashioned in his few spare moments expresses his longing for a better life, some possible source of fulfilment: 'She be hungry,' he says of the statue, 'Not hungry for meat.' The prison where he ends up, and where he kills himself, measures the cruel limitations that are his. 'Was it not his right to live . . . a pure life, a good, true-hearted life, full of beauty and kind words?' he asks himself. The answer here is that it may be his right but it is not his destiny.

The power of 'Life in the Iron Mills' stems from the way Davis focuses on a series of vivid images to chart the progress of her tale: the smoke, the house, the statue, the furnace in the iron mill, the prison where Hugh ends his life. It also stems from the use of a narrator who draws the genteel, and presumably ignorant, reader into the tale. The narrative voice is constantly reminding us that Hugh, his cousin Deborah and other industrial workers are people too, who demand our help and sympathy. 'Are pain and jealousy less savage realities down here in this place I am taking you to than in your own house or your own heart,' the narrator asks at one point, '– your heart, which they clutch at sometimes? The note is the same, I fancy, be the octave high or low.' The moralizing tone, the appeal to the sentiments and sympathies of the reader bear comparison with a writer like Harriet Beecher Stowe, and the purpose is similar. Davis's readers are being invited, even compelled, to register the humanity of these wage slaves: to see, through the smoke of their own ignorance, how the increasing hordes of industrial workers are being emotionally and ethically thwarted – denied the right to a decent home and family and the opportunity to lead a morally responsible life. Davis went on to write many more fictions that pursue a similarly reformist agenda. *Waiting for the Verdict* (1868), for instance, deals with the needs of the newly emancipated slaves, while *John Andross* (1874) investigates political corruption. None of her later work, however, had the impact or possesses the imaginative power of her first short story, which made her reputation and marks a turning point in American writing. In 'Life in the Iron Mills', Davis's hope, as her narrator intimates, is to look 'deeper into the heart of things' in a newly industrializing America. And her triumph is that she manages to do just that.

Spirituals and folk songs

Davis was, of course, writing about oppression from a position of some privilege. Among those many writers who spoke, or rather sang, from within their own oppressed condition were those slaves who handed down spirituals from generation to generation. First collected into a book by a black church leader in 1801, spirituals incorporated the secular as well as the divine and were sung not just at times of worship but throughout the day. They offered those who sang them the possibility of restitution from a life of pain: the longing to 'Lay dis body down' is a constant theme. But they also offered release from the deathly definitions of their humanity forged by the slaveholders, and the possibility of resistance to and release from their enslavement. Many spirituals have call and response patterns, with lead singers setting out a line or phrase and the group responding by repeating or playing variations on it. So, the leader might call out, 'Swing low, sweet chariot', and the group singers would respond, 'Comin' for to carry me home'. But not all do; and there are, in any event, wide variations of pace and tone. Some spirituals are dirges, lamentations, like 'City Called Heaven', which begins, 'I am a poor pilgrim of sorrow. / I'm in this wide world alone', or 'Were You There When They Crucified My Lord?':

> Were you there, when they crucified my Lord?
> Were you there, when they crucified my Lord?
> Oh, sometimes, it causes me to tremble, tremble, tremble.
> Were you there, when they crucified my Lord?

Other spirituals are more driving and rapt, like 'God's A-Gonna Trouble the Water', which repeats the title phrase seven times in five short stanzas and the phrase 'Wade in the water, children' no fewer than nine times. And some are jubilant, even ecstatic, like 'That Great Gittin' Up Morning!', a vision of Judgement Day that was perhaps delivered as a ring shout, with the possessed worshippers moving their bodies in time to its percussive rhythms.

Using such rhythms, repetitions, and imagery that anchors the mysteries of religion in the mundane realities of slave life, many of these spirituals express the dream of flying away, leaving the work and worries of the world behind. 'I've got two wings for to veil my face / I've got two wings for to fly away,' declares one. Some look to Christ and to heaven for relief and ease. 'Soon I will be done with the troubles of the world, / Troubles of the world, troubles of the world,' announces another spiritual, 'No more weepin' and a-wailing, / I'm goin' to live with God.' The often colourful accounts of just how easeful this afterlife would be – 'Eatin' hone and drinkin' wine / Marchin' roun de throne / Wid Peter, James, and John' – imply a bitter criticism of the care, labour and injustice that the singers are suffering in the here and now. Most of the spirituals are not about an easeful Jesus, however, but about the God of the Old Testament, His heroes and prophets; and many of them work towards a vision of redemption, even revenge, in this life here on earth. Songs like 'Nobody Knows the Trouble I've Had' tend to elide spiritual trouble with the terrible, troublesome suffering of the slave; 'Steal Away to Jesus' quietly carries the promise of flight in the repeated phrase 'I ain't got long to stay here'; while songs such as 'Deep River' and 'Roll, Jordan, Roll' make an only slightly veiled connection between the journey into the Promised Land, made by the Chosen People, and the deliverance of slaves into their own promised land of freedom, in the Northern states or Canada. Other spirituals are even more open in expressing their dreams of liberation. 'Didn't my Lord deliver Daniel, / And why not every man?' asks one song. 'When Israel was in Egypt's land', the caller would have cried out when singing 'Go Down, Moses'; to which the response would have come, 'Let my people go'. 'Go Down, Moses' was sufficiently frank in its demand for freedom to be banned on most slave plantations. It usually had to be sung out of earshot of the slaveholder. So, quite certainly, did the spiritual called simply 'Oh, Freedom', which repeats the declaration, 'An' befo' I'd be a slave, / I'll be buried in my grave', or 'No More Auction Block':

> No more auction block for me,
> No more, no more,
> No more auction block for me,
> Many thousands gone . . .

'They that walked in darkness sang songs in the olden days,' W. E. B. Du Bois was to write in 1903, '– Sorrow Songs – for they were weary at heart.' As Du Bois saw it, these songs, 'the rhythmic cry of the slave', were 'the singular spiritual heritage of the nation' and 'the most beautiful expression of human experience born this side of the seas'. Even reading them in cold print, without benefit of performance, it is difficult to disagree.

As oral performances, of anonymous authorship and designed to be sung by various communities and generations, spirituals exist in many different versions. 'No More Auction Block', for example, survives in several forms, including one titled 'Many Thousands Go', which begins, 'No more peck o' corn for me, / No more; no more; / No more peck o' corn for me, / Many thousands go'. The same is true of the white folk songs of the period. 'Bury Me Not on the Lone Prairie', for instance, originated as a lament about burial at sea, probably in the 1840s. It was then carried westward and, with the vastness of the open ranges of the West substituted for the vastness of the ocean, became one of the most popular early cowboy songs. The differences between spirituals and white folk songs are at least as important as the connections, however. Spirituals describe dreams of flight and the reality of 'slavery chains forlorn'. White songs, by contrast, are often about wandering in search of wealth or work. 'Did you ever hear of Sweet Betty from Pike, / Who crossed the wide prairies with her lover Ike,' begins one version of 'Sweet Betty from Pike', 'Saying "Good-bye Pike county, farewell for a while, / We'll come back again when we panned out our pile."' In some versions of the song, it is 'the big mountains' Betty crosses to make her fortune. In all versions, she has various adventures, crossing 'the terrible desert' or fighting 'the Injun' or suffering 'Starvation and cholera, hard work and slaughter'. And, in many, she is a powerful figure, a strong woman who scorns her lover when he declares his intention of fleeing 'from the death lurkin' there' in the West back to Pike County. 'You'll go by yourself if you do,' she informs him. Other songs also tell of crossing the American continent in search of a fortune, only to give it up. 'I've wandered all over this country, / Prospecting and digging for gold,' the narrator of a piece called 'Acres of Clams' admits: but then, he confesses, realizing that 'for one who got rich by mining' 'there were hundreds grew poor', he made up his mind 'to try farming'. 'No longer the slave of ambition, / I laugh at the world and its shams, /' he concludes, 'And think of my happy condition, / Surrounded by acres of clams.' And still other songs tell simply of those who travel and work: as migratory labourers, hired hands or on the railroad. 'In eighteen hundred and fifty-four / I traveled the land from shore to shore, /' the narrator of 'Pat Works on the Railway' discloses, 'I traveled the land from shore to shore / To work upon the railway.' 'In eighteen hundred and fifty-five / I found myself more dead than alive, /' he adds, 'I found myself more dead than alive / From working on the railway.'

Sometimes the wanderers of these songs find love. One of the most famous white folk songs of the period, 'Shenandoah', concerns a wandering white trader who falls in love with the daughter of an Indian chief. Sometimes, as in the equally famous song about the daughter of 'a miner, forty-niner', 'Clementine', the subject is death. The tone of such songs can be elegiac, lyrical, as in 'Shenandoah':

> Oh, Shenandoah, I long to hear you –
> Away, you rolling river;
> Oh, Shenandoah, I long to hear you –
> Away, I'm bound away
> 'Cross the wide Missouri

Alternatively, it can be sardonic, even brutal, as in this brief account of the fate of 'my darlin' Clementine' once she has drowned:

> In a churchyard near the canyon,
> Where the myrtle doth entwine,
> There grow roses and other posies
> Fertilised by Clementine.

What most songs have in common, however, is an idiomatic language, images drawn from a common stock of experience available to the community, and simple compulsive rhythms, insistent repetition guaranteed to catch attention and remain stored in the memory. The songs designed for dance as well as singing are, naturally, even more captivating in their rhythms and repetitions. A 'play-party song' such as 'Cindy', for instance, was meant to be danced to without musical accompaniment. The song itself had to get feet tapping, itching to dance: as in the chorus, which simply repeats the line 'Get-a-long home, Cindy, Cindy' three times, followed by the swinging rhythm of the declaration 'I'll marry you some day'. In turn, what were known as 'answering-back songs' were meant to be sung and danced to in a call and response manner by young men and women. In one of the most famous, 'Paper of Pins', for example, each of the many verses sung by the boys plays variations on the theme of offering something by way of a marriage gift. 'I'll give to you a paper of pins, / If you will tell me how our love begins, /' the boys sing in the first verse, 'If you marry, if you marry, / If you marry me.' The girls respond by

---

Spirituals and folk songs   223

declining each offer of 'a paper of pins', 'a pink silk gown', or whatever – until the final offer, and final acceptance. Songs like these depend more even than most on performance: in this case, a communal re-enactment that would almost invariably involve revisions inspired by the moods and interactions of the moment. Only rarely, in any event, did white folk song pass over from the process of popular transmission to the status of self-conscious, literary product. On one famous occasion it did, though. Hearing a band of Union troops singing a popular song in praise of the hero of Harper's Ferry, 'John Brown's Body', the writer and lecturer Julia Ward Howe (1819–1910) rewrote the song, using its melody, rhythms, chorus and fundamental drive, and then had it published. The result was 'The Battle Hymn of the Republic' (1862).

American poetic voices

Another woman poet who achieved at least as much fame during her lifetime as Howe did with 'The Battle Hymn of the Republic' was Lydia Howard Huntley Sigourney (1791–1865). Her work encompassed thousands of periodical publications and more than fifty books of poetry, autobiography, children's literature, advice writing, sketches, history and travel. And her poetry addressed a variety of issues, many of them public ones such as slavery, the treatment of Indians and current events, from a standpoint of compassionate Christianity and devout republicanism. Her most widely anthologized poem, 'Death of an Infant' (1827), is characteristic in its use of familiar language and conventional imagery to offer a consoling portrait of a tragic event. 'Death found a strange beauty in that polish'd brow / And dash'd it out,' the poem begins. 'He touched the veins with ice,' but, 'there beam'd a smile, / So fix'd, so holy, from the cherub brow, / Death gazed and left it there.' The smile on the face of the dead infant offers the consolatory assurance, to the believer, that even the power of death is circumscribed by faith: that smile is 'the signet-ring of Heaven', the poet suggests, and, being so, death 'dar'd not steal' it. Other poems by Sigourney deal with more public issues but always, as in 'Death of an Infant', in a way that consolidates faith and reassures. Any gentle interrogation of individual tragedies, or acts of injustice, is invariably framed within a fundamental acceptance of conventional Christian piety and the benevolence, the rightness of the American way, the domestic and the familial. 'The Indian's Welcome to the Pilgrim Fathers' (1838), for example, explores the irony of a 'red-brow'd chieftain' welcoming those who would eventually supplant him and his kind. The poet invites sympathy for the Indian, 'poor outcast from thy forest wild'. It implicitly asks for better treatment of those who have been 'swept from their native land'. But it does not question either the justice or the necessity of the westward movement, white appropriation and Indian dispossession. Neither does 'The Western Emigrant' (1827). On the contrary, the gentle tear here is shed not for the Native American but for the emigrant family, torn from the cosy comforts of their old, New England home into the vastness of the West. The poem domesticates the westward movement both by focusing on the pains and pieties of an individual family and by offering the reassurance, finally, that 'wheresoe'er our best affections dwell, / And strike a healthful note, is happiness'.

For Sigourney, clearly, poetry was a form of public service. She wrote in a way that would be accessible to her large audience; she wrote of the public and the typical; she wrote of injustice in terms that invited her many readers to anticipate the possibility of quiet reform, amelioration. Her work appeals to the patriotic feelings of her public ('Niagara' [1835]). It assumes, and sometimes even argues, that the arts of the hearth and home, and the measures brought about by friendly persuasion, are the best – that the needle and the pen are mightier than the sword ('The Needle, Pen, and Sword' [1849]). It is not afraid of nostalgia, an affectionate glance at the American past ('In a Shred of Linen' [1849]). Nor is it afraid to remind the reader of how the past lives in the present – how, for instance, 'the Red men' can never be forgotten since 'their memory liveth on your hills, / Their baptism on your shore', the entire landscape is 'indelibly stamped by names of their going' ('Indian Names' [1838]). That Sigourney was no revolutionary, in either her poetic idiom or her argument, is obvious enough. She attacked individual acts of cruelty, against women, for instance ('The Suttee' [1827]), but she remained a firm believer in a separate sphere where women could act as guardian angels. And she expressed that belief in forms that her female audience, in particular, brought up on the popular domestic writing of the day, could readily digest and accommodate. She was, rather, a poet of community: someone whose own best sentiments conveniently coincided with those of her readers – and who used her writing to declare how she, and they, could live up to them.

Two other poets of the period who explored different possibilities of expression for women were Frances Sargent Osgood (1811–50) and Lucy Larcom (1820–93). Osgood, a friend and quite possibly a lover of Edgar Allan Poe, was best known during her lifetime for sentimental pieces such as 'The Lily's Delusion' (1846) and 'The Cocoa-Nut Tree' (1846), or for more didactic works like 'A Flight of Fancy' (1846), which uses an elaborate allegory to explore the relationship between Reason, Conscience and 'the gay little innocent' Fancy. In work that remained unpublished until long after her death, however (in fact, until 1997), Osgood revealed a much bolder spirit, and a much more acid tongue, in writing of the vagaries of love. 'The Lady's Mistake', for instance, deals sardonically with both the falsity of men and the flippancy of women, sometimes, in matters of the heart. In 'Won't you die & be a spirit', the narrator caustically suggests that the best way to keep her lover faithful is to have him die: 'If you only were a spirit / You could *stay*,' she declares. 'The Wraith of the Rose', in turn, a poem carrying the subtitle 'An impromptu written on a visiting card', deals in an extraordinarily frank way with the thoughts of the poet, when her lover comes on a brief visit long after their love affair has ended. 'I wish I'd kept that last fond token, / And not burned your hair!' she confesses; 'I wish we might go back again, / I wish you *could* reclasp the chain, /' she adds a little later, 'I wish – *you hadn't drank champagne, / So freely since we parted!*' These are poems that actively jettison the image of woman as the angel of the house. The speaker here is a smart, knowing, world-weary but passionate creature, speaking in terms that anticipate Dorothy Parker and Edna St Vincent Millay in the next century. Domesticity is introduced here only to be scorned, turned into an acidulous joke. 'I'll wish you all the joys of life, /' concludes the speaker in 'The Wraith of the Rose' to her former lover, 'A pleasant home – a peerless wife, / Whose wishes, Sense shall bridle!'

Lucy Larcom was one of those who contributed work to the *Lowell Offering*, a journal containing the writings of textile mill operators working in Lowell, Massachusetts. From a middle-class background, Larcom became a 'Lowell mill girl' after the death of her father. Her poems in the *Offering* soon attracted attention, and she established a career as a popular poet; a collection, *The Poetical Works of Lucy Larcom*, was eventually published in 1884. Larcom assumed a variety of voices and explored a number of subjects: there are poems on such diverse topics as the seasons ('March'), the city ('The City Lights'), young women ('A Little Old Girl') and old ones ('Flowers of the Fallow'). 'Weaving' shows what she could do at her best. Here, she uses a complex stanzaic form to explore the plight of a white girl working in a textile mill. 'All day she stands before the loom, /' the poet tells us; 'The flying shuttles come and go,' as she dreams of the pastoral scenes, the 'grassy fields' and 'trees in bloom' from which she is separated. 'Fancy's shuttle flieth wide'; and, as it does so, the girl takes up the song for herself, singing of 'the loom of life' on which, she speculates, 'we weave / Our separate shreds'. Eventually, the girl comes to focus on a fate, a 'shred', even more desperate than hers: 'my sisters', as she calls them, who 'toil, with foreheads black', further South. They picked the cotton she weaves, or, as she puts it, 'water with their blood this root / Whereof we gather bounteous fruit!' 'And how much of your wrong is mine, / Dark women slaving in the South?' she asks. 'Of your stolen grapes I quaff the wine; / The bread you starve for fills my mouth.' Making a passionate connection between herself and her black sisters, the mill woman also recognizes that, by these extreme standards at least, she enjoys a condition of relative privilege. The black women of the South suffer in ways that, according to the 'web of destiny', can only terminate in 'the hideous tapestry' of war. The moral of the poem is underscored at its conclusion, couched as 'war's stern message': ' "Woman!" it knelled from heart to heart, / "Thy sister's keeper know thou art!" ' Even without that, however, the moral would be clear. 'Weaving' dramatizes the continuities and differences of oppression in a gently mellifluous, intricately patterned but nevertheless tough way. Using the activity announced in the title – one that Larcom knew only too well – both literally and as a figure, a symbol, it links the fate of an individual to the general, the historical. It not only intimates, it insists on interdependence, the fact that all, white women workers, black women, readers, are part of one web; and it invites sympathy, certainly, but it also contemplates, even demands, action.

For many contemporary readers, the leading American poet of the earlier half of the nineteenth century was William Cullen Bryant (1794–1878). In fact, some of his contemporaries went so far as to honour him as the founding father of American poetry. Certainly, the honour was justified as far as the subjects of

Bryant's poetic landscapes were concerned. Although he was born and raised in Massachusetts and spent most of his adult life as a newspaper editor in New York City, a poem like 'The Prairies' (1834) is sufficient proof of his awareness of the great lands to the West. As its opening lines indicate, it is also evidence of Bryant's realization that all the new regions of America might require the development of new tools of expression. 'These are the gardens of the Desert,' 'The Prairies' begins; 'these / The unshorn fields, boundless and beautiful, / For which the speech of England has no name.' But whatever the native loyalties involved in his choice of subject, and whatever Bryant might say about the irrelevance to that subject of 'the speech of England', when it came to writing rather than talking about poetry, Bryant preferred to imitate English models. The success of his poem 'Inscription for the Entrance to a Wood' (1821), for example, depends on the reader accepting the assumption that he or she and the poet form part of the same polite community. Bryant becomes almost Augustan here in his dependence on large abstractions ('truth', 'guilt'), poetic diction ('school of long experience', 'haunts of nature', 'the marge') and unparticularized description: all used in the evident belief that the poet, although broad and even vague in his gestures, will be understood because he is talking to an audience with interests and values similar to his own. The poem confirms rather than demonstrates or explores. It depends for its effect on the reader giving immediate assent to the context of moral assumptions on which Bryant is operating and then admiring the skill of his poetic manoeuvres.

And within these limitations, Bryant was undoubtedly skilful. 'Thanatopsis' (1821), for instance, a poem that was published in its first version when Bryant was only sixteen, opens in a Wordsworthian vein: 'To him who in the love of Nature holds / Communion with her visible forms, she speaks / A various language.' It then goes on to demonstrate the poet's mastery of the blank verse form, as he alters tone, pace and mood to capture the 'various language' of the natural landscape. Similarly, in 'To a Waterfowl' (1821), Bryant uses an alternating pattern of long and short lines to capture the hovering movement of the bird's flight:

> Whither, midst falling dew,
> While glow the heavens with the last steps of day,
> Far, through their rosy depths, dost thou pursue
> Thy solitary way?

Even here, however, the poet cannot or will not resist the conventional. The bird and its surroundings are described in terms that are heavily reliant on poetic diction ('plashy brink', 'weedy lake', 'rocking billows'); and the description moves remorselessly to the point where the poet can draw the appropriate, cheering moral. 'He who, from zone to zone, / Guides through the boundless sky thy certain flight, /' the poem concludes, 'In the long way that I must tread alone, / Will lead my steps aright.' Most of Bryant's best poetry, like 'To a Waterfowl' and

'Thanatopsis', was written by the time he was forty, and published in two volumes, titled simply *Poems*, appearing in 1821 and 1832. He continued as an active writer and translator, though, right up until the end of his life. Notable among his many later volumes are his translations of the *Iliad* (1870) and the *Odyssey* (1871–2), since they show Bryant's skill with the blank verse line and his ability to assume a simple, epic nobility of tone and style.

A poet who eventually outdistanced even Bryant in terms of popularity among his contemporaries was Henry Wadsworth Longfellow (1807–82). Born in Maine, Longfellow published his first prose work, *Outre-Mer: A Pilgrimage Beyond the Sea*, in 1833–5. A series of travel sketches reminiscent of Irving's *Sketch Book*, this was followed by *Hyperion* (1839), a semi-autobiographical romance, *Voices of the Night* (1839), his first book of poetry, *Ballads and Other Poems* (1841), and *Poems on Slavery* (1842). His fame increased with the publication of a poetic drama, *The Spanish Student* (1843), *The Belfry of Bruges and Other Poems* (1845) and *Kavanagh* (1849), a semi-autobiographical prose tale. Three long poems published at about this time also show Longfellow's ambition to create an American epic poetry by choosing domestic legends and casting them in classical forms. *Evangeline* (1847), written in unrhymed hexameter lines modelled on the Greek and Latin lines of the epic poems of Homer and Virgil, tells the tragic story of the heroine's search for her lover. It is set in Acadie, a province of Canada roughly corresponding to present-day Nova Scotia. *The Courtship of Miles Standish* (1856) is a legend of early New England, also written in unrhymed hexameter. And *The Song of Hiawatha* (1855) tells the story of a Native American hero. Based partly on the work of Henry Rowe Schoolcraft, it uses an accentual, unrhymed metre that Longfellow developed from his reading of the Finnish epic *Kalevala*. Longfellow's popularity was by now such that he felt compelled to resign a professorial post he held at Harvard to concentrate on his writing. The tragic death of his wife, in an accident in 1861, rendered him silent for a while. But many more books then followed, including further volumes of poetry such as *Tales of a Wayside Inn* (published in three parts in 1863, 1872 and 1874), *Ultima Thule* (1880) and *In the Harbor* (1882), and a translation of Dante's *Divine Comedy* (1865–7). During his final years, honours were heaped on him, and not just in his own country. During a tour of Europe, he was given a private audience with Queen Victoria; and, after his death, he became the only American poet to be honoured with a bust in the Poet's Corner of Westminster Abbey.

One of the few of his contemporaries not to admire Longfellow was Edgar Allan Poe, who described him as a plagiarist. The charge might have been unjust, but it did and still does point to a problem. For all his interest in American themes and legends, and his dedication to the idea of an American epic, Longfellow relied on European literary forms and conventions. He did so quite deliberately, because he believed in the value, the centrality of the European American community and its tradition. So convinced was he of its value, in fact, that he inserted a long passage in *Kavanagh* to explain to his audience exactly how he thought the American literature of the future had to depend on European models:

As the blood of all nations is mingled with our own, so will their thoughts and feelings finally mingle in our literature. We shall draw from the Germans tenderness; from the Spaniards, passion; from the French, vivacity – to mingle more and more with our solid English sense.

As this characteristically didactic and generalizing passage suggests, Longfellow's strategy was to assume that, since the European forms had been good enough for the European poets, they were good enough for American poets too. Even if the American poet, as he should, wrote about the American scene, he could and should also borrow from the European tradition, so as to give a sense of authority and universality to his verse. That was what Longfellow tried to do in his longer epic poems. It was, too, what he tried to do in a short piece like 'My Lost Youth' (1858). The poem is about a deeply personal topic, Longfellow's youth in Portland, Maine. But its tone is somehow impersonal, the result mostly of the quotations from and allusions to earlier poems with which the lines are packed. Even the famous refrain, it turns out, is derivative, as Longfellow's use of quotation marks to surround it alerts us: '"A boy's will is the wind's will, / And the thoughts of youth are long, long thoughts."' Like the rest of the poem, it recalls other, earlier poems: in this case, a German translation of a Lapland song.

There is nothing intrinsically wrong with this kind of adaptation, of course, as the work of T. S. Eliot or Ezra Pound indicates. It is just that, whereas in a poem like *The Waste Land* the echoes and allusions are employed for their associative effects, to add to a situation directly apprehended, Longfellow, more often than not, seems to be looking at the subject in and through the associations. That is, he tends to look at life through books: at best, to identify his experiences or those of his typical Americans with something he has read already and, at worst, to reduce character and event to literary stereotype. The kinds of values Longfellow derives from books and then applies in his poetry are equally symptomatic. There is a peculiar sense of self-assurance in most of his poetry: a feeling that everything that really matters, and has been found by earlier writers to matter, occurs within the compass of the respectable fireside. So, in a poem like 'Nature' (1875), the wilderness that awed Herman Melville and mystified Emily Dickinson is characterized as 'a fond mother', whose every aspect can be attributed to a pervasive concern for human welfare. And in 'The Village Blacksmith' (1842), a figure actually outside the sphere of Longfellow's society and sympathy is made acceptable – to the narrator of the poem, that is, and the genteel reader – by being transformed into a rustic gentleman. There are, certainly, more poised and subtler pieces than these. 'The Jewish Cemetery at Newport' (1852) uses the setting announced in the title for a mature, sympathetic meditation on the ancient Jewish experience of suffering and exile; 'Aftermath' (1873) is a quiet reflection on the mixed 'harvesting' of old age, and 'Chaucer' (1873) an exemplary reminder of how old age can be made 'beautiful with song'. But the tendency towards sermonizing remains even in these poems, as do the simply sweet idioms and rhythms and the deference to older, European forms. And there is the inclination, even here, to

---

assume that the poet, the European past and the American present form one domestic circle.

Like Longfellow, Oliver Wendell Holmes (1809–94) chose to identify with a particular group. More modest and pragmatic in his aims and intentions, however, he defined and delimited that group quite closely: to the men and women of sense and taste with whom he came into contact as a distinguished member of Boston society. Holmes is to be seen at his best in his most famous work, *The Autocrat of the Breakfast Table*. First published in the *Atlantic Monthly* in 1857–8 and in book form in 1858, this consists of essays, poems and occasional pieces in the form of table talk in a Boston boarding house. The wit, good sense and moral rigour that characterizes this and later volumes such as *The Professor at the Breakfast Table* (1860) and *The Poet at the Breakfast Table* (1872) is also to be found, in miniature, in poems like 'The Chambered Nautilus' (1858), with its famous concluding instruction to the poet's soul to 'build thee more stately mansions', and 'The Last Leaf' (1836). In the latter poem, Holmes manages to keep a fine balance between sympathy and amusement while describing a decrepit old man, who 'totters o'er the ground / With his cane'. The point of equilibrium is supplied by common sense, which prevents Holmes from becoming either cruel or sentimental. It prevents him, too, from meditating on the larger implications of this emblem of old age or even from analysing the reasons for his refusal to meditate. It would, apparently, be to consider too deeply to consider so. The most Holmes will say is that he hopes people will smile in as kindly and detached a way on him when he is old: 'Let them smile, as I do now, / At the old forsaken bough / Where I cling.' It is a conclusion as just and sensible as it is deliberately limited and limiting.

Whereas Holmes opted for a community consisting of men of sense, however small it might have to be, a contemporary and neighbour of his chose a spiritual isolation which some of his acquaintances interpreted as madness. Jones Very (1813–80) was a lay preacher given to mystical experiences. As a youth, he had been forced to withdraw from Harvard after experiencing a religious frenzy; and throughout his life he had visions which convinced him that his will and God's will were one. The conviction might have turned him into a fanatic or a bigot. Instead, it enabled him to write poetry which, though neglected during his lifetime, some later critics were to call great. It is, certainly, unique. The means of expression is traditional – Very rarely used anything other than the sonnet form – but this belies a poetic stance that is profoundly individualistic. In one of his poems, for instance, ordinary people in the street are transformed into 'The Dead' (1839), whose grotesque and lurid shapes are an outward and visible sign of an inward and spiritual poverty. In another, 'Thy Brother's Blood' (1839), Very claims to see, with the aid of his 'spiritgaze', his 'brother's blood' on the hand of each man he meets: the blood, that is, of guilt and damnation. Very in effect adopts the innocent and often savage eye of the outsider, ignoring the masks people may use to evade self-knowledge. He has no connection with the world he observes and exposes, and in a sense no audience either. For as the poem 'Yourself' (1839) makes clear, Very did not expect his revelations of his inner being and his secret pact with God to be properly understood by those around him. 'He who speaks, or him who's spoken to, /' the poem concludes, 'Must both remain as strangers still to you.' This is poetry that circulates, with all due humility, around the secrecy of the inner life, the way that life is hidden from nearly every gaze apart from the divine – and those blessed with some microscopic portion of divine sight.

Holmes addressing his companions at the breakfast table and Very watching the antics of the 'strangers' surrounding him is a contrast played out in a different key by two other New England poets: James Russell Lowell (1819–91) and Frederick Goddard Tuckerman (1821–73). A member of one of the foremost families in Boston, Lowell succeeded Longfellow as professor of French and Spanish at Harvard. With Holmes, he co-founded the *Atlantic Monthly*, editing it from 1857 to 1861; with Charles Eliot Norton, an eminent scholar and translator, he later edited the *North American Review*. His first volume of poetry, *A Year's Life*, appeared in 1841, his second, *Poems*, three years later. Then, in a single year, 1848, he published *Poems: Second Series*, *A Fable for Critics*, *The Vision of Sir Launfal* and the first series of *The Biglow Papers*. *The Vision* is a verse poem derived from the legends of the Holy Grail. *A Fable for Critics* is a verse satire containing shrewd assessments of the contemporary literary scene and its more distinguished figures. Ralph Waldo Emerson, for instance, is said to have 'A Greek head on right Yankee shoulders, whose range / Has Olympus for one pole, for t'other the Exchange'; which neatly captures Emerson's peculiar blend of idealism and practicality. Edgar Allan Poe, in turn, is said to be 'three fifths . . . genius and two fifths sheer fudge'; while, discoursing on the state of American literature in general, the fictional critic talking to Phoebus Apollo who is credited with these and other opinions complains that, in general, American writers 'steal Englishmen's books and think Englishmen's thought'. 'Plough, sail, forge, build, carve, paint, all things make new, / To your own New-World instincts contrive to be true,' he tells these writers. 'Keep your ears open wide to the Future's first call, / Be whatever you will, but yourselves first of all.' It was a command that Lowell himself sought to obey in his immensely popular *Biglow Papers*, a series of satirical attacks on the slaveholders of the South and their political representatives. Adopting the mask of Hosea Biglow, a crude but honest Yankee farmer, Lowell attempted to fashion an authentically American voice – and to use that voice to direct people into right ways of thinking. Like Holmes, Lowell had a clear sense of his audience. Unlike Holmes, he saw this audience as a potentially large one, which he could instruct and educate. The mission of creating an audience and educating it was sustained in the second series of *Biglow Papers*. If the first series had been written in opposition to the Mexican War – seen by many besides Thoreau as simply a means for the South to expand slavery into new territories – then the second was produced in support of the North during the Civil War. But, although both series were immensely popular, the mission Lowell had undertaken met, really, with only partial success. It was perhaps symptomatic of his difficulties that Lowell felt obliged to assume a rustic persona, in effect to 'lower' himself so as to talk credibly to his readers. And it was a further symptom of those difficulties that, in any event, the voice of the Harvard professor, pointing the moral, kept breaking through the accents of the farmer. Writing a poetry responsive to 'New-World instincts', and creating an audience for that poetry, were not quite as easy as Lowell appears to have believed. The public honours nevertheless accumulated for him, including high political office, first in Spain, and then in Great Britain from 1880 to 1885, as United States Ambassador.

By contrast, Tuckerman never really attempted to cater to or create an audience and never achieved any public honours or recognition. Educated at Harvard, where Jones Very was his tutor, he withdrew before his courses were completed. He returned to take a law degree, was admitted to the bar but never practised. Instead, he devoted most of his adult life to the study of botany and the writing of poetry. He also placed a great emotional investment in his domestic life, until the death of his wife in childbirth in 1857. This loss inspired a series of sonnet sequences, written in the period 1854–60 and 1860–72 and partly published in a privately financed edition in 1860. Hawthorne, Emerson, Longfellow and Alfred Lord Tennyson in England all praised his work. It was reissued in two further editions during his lifetime but, as with the first edition, these later editions were only noticed by a few. The full series of sonnet sequences was not published until the twentieth century; his long poem, *The Cricket*, did not appear in print until 1950; and *The Complete Poems* was only published in 1965. His poems are not, as Tuckerman explains in sonnet I of the first sequence, addressed to anyone. They are, rather, an attempt to give objective life to a subjective complex of emotions. The result is, to some extent, like later poetry, Imagist poetry for instance, in which a sequence of sense impressions is presented as the equivalent of a sequence of emotions. Only to some extent, however: the poetic voice of Tuckerman also bears comparison with the voices of contemporaries, like the later Hawthorne and Melville. It is the voice of a man who feels alienated from nature, from other men, and from God: who senses that there might possibly exist 'signs' in his environment that could lead him away from doubt and into philosophical certainty, but who also suspects that those signs are beyond his deciphering. 'Still craves the spirit: never Nature solves / That yearning which with her first breath began,' declares the poet in one sonnet. 'For Nature daily through her grand design / Breathes contradiction where she seems most clear,' he admits in another. Thrust into a state of extreme isolation, and unable to see beyond appearances, the most that the 'I' of Tuckerman's poetry can do is use those appearances as an alphabet to spell out his own moods. For his fellow New Englander Emerson, the self, the ego, was an assertive presence, illuminating the world and creating the real. For Tuckerman, however, the self was very much on the defence and trying to make what it could of its own defensiveness – its condition of captivity, caught, as the poet put it in one of his sonnets, in what seemed like 'an upper chamber in a darkened house'.

'He is America,' Ezra Pound observed of Walt Whitman (1819–92). 'His crudity is an exceeding great stench, but it *is* America.' Never frightened of being called crude, Whitman would probably have appreciated the comment. And he would have liked being identified with America because that was his aim: to speak as a representative American and turn the New World into words. Whitman certainly had this aim after the day in 1842 when he attended a lecture given by Emerson, in which Emerson prophesied the imminent arrival of an American Homer to celebrate 'the barbarism and materialism of the times'. Whitman saw himself as the fulfilment of that prophecy. He was the man, he felt, with the courage needed to capture the ample geography of the country in lines as bold and wild as its landscape. And in the Preface to the first, 1855 edition of his *Leaves of Grass*, he deliberately echoed Emerson. 'The United States themselves are essentially the greatest poem,' he wrote, thereby alerting the reader to what he was trying to do: to invent a poetic form founded on raw experiment, and a line that swung as freely as the individual voice. There were many influences that helped Whitman to create this form and line. They ranged from Italian opera to the insistent repetitions of the King James Bible, from his interest in the spatial vastnesses of astronomy to his love of American landscape painting with its dedication to and delineation of another kind of space. But the crucial factor was Whitman's sense of himself and the potentials of his craft: for him, poetry was a passionate gesture of identification with his native land.

Like many other American writers, especially of this period, Whitman was largely self-educated. He left school at the age of eleven and learned his trade in the print shop, becoming editor of the *Aurora* in 1842 and then later of the Brooklyn *Daily Eagle*. As he wrote essay after essay about his wanderings through Manhattan, his 'City of . . . walks and joys', he was also serving an apprenticeship for his poetry, with its expansive rhetoric, ambulating lines, and delight in the spectacle of the people. It is in his earliest notebook, written in 1847, that Whitman breaks into something like his characteristic free verse line. Appropriately, for the poet who was to see himself as the bard of American individualism and liberty, this occurs on the subject of slavery. And, after *Leaves of Grass* was published, and enthusiastic-ally welcomed by Emerson ('I greet you at the beginning of a great career,' Emerson wrote to Whitman, after the poet had sent him a complimentary copy of the first edition), Whitman was to devote his poetic life to its revision and expansion. For Whitman, poetry, the American nation, life itself were all a matter of pro-cess, energized by rhythm and change. And *Leaves of Grass* became a process too, responsive to the continuing story of personal and national identity, the poet and his democratic community. A second edition, with several new poems, appeared in 1856. While he was planning a third edition of what he called his 'new Bible' of democracy, Whitman had an unhappy liaison with another man, which became the subject of several poems to be incorporated into that edition, published in 1860. The personal crisis, combined with the poet's own alarm over the threatened dissolution of the republic, casts a shadow over this 1860 version of *Leaves of Grass*, although this is balanced by Whitman's celebration of comradeship and 'adhesive-ness' ('the personal attachment of man to man') and heterosexual or 'amative' love – in, respectively, the 'Calamus' and the 'Children of Adam' sequences. The role Whitman then adopted during the Civil War, as 'wound-dresser' visiting sick or dying soldiers, became the source of poems for *Drum-Taps and Sequel* (1865–6).

The war poems were then appended to the next, 1867 edition of *Leaves of Grass* and incorporated into the main body of the 1871 edition. During the last two decades of his life, poems such as 'Passage to India' and 'Prayer of Columbus' showed Whitman moving away from the material landscapes of America to a more mystical vision of a democratic golden world that might bloom in the future. Along with this new material, the poet revised, reintegrated and rearranged all his poetic work in the 1881 edition of *Leaves of Grass*. He then followed it a year later with what was intended as a prose companion to his poems, entitled *Specimen Days*. Even this was not the end. The final, 'deathbed' edition of *Leaves of Grass* was prepared in the last years of his life, 1891–2. It included two annexes, the 'Sands at Seventy' and 'Good-bye My Fancy' groups of poems. And it ended with a prose piece, 'A Backward Glance O'er Travel'd Roads', in which Whitman attempted to explain both his life and his work.

Along with all the changes in the several editions of *Leaves of Grass*, though, went continuity: a commitment to the principles outlined in the Preface to the very first edition. 'Read these leaves,' Whitman urged in that Preface, 'in the open air of every season of every year of your life, re-examine all you have been told at school or church or in any book, dismiss whatever insults your own soul!' Openness, freedom, above all individualism: Whitman's aim was nothing less than to initiate a poetic tradition in which the one recognition shared is a recognition of difference, one of the few precedents accepted is the rejection of precedent, and truth and beauty are identified with a procedure of constant metamorphosis. The only genuine way in which an American could acknowledge his participation in a common cultural effort, he believed, was by behaving as a supreme individualist. He could pay his greatest respect to the past, Whitman felt, by rebelling from it, and the finest compliment he could to his nation by denying its authority over him. In doing all this, Whitman did not feel that he would be rejecting contact with others: those he lived with, those whom he observed and addressed in his poems. On the contrary, his essential purpose was to identify his ego with the world, and more specifically with the democratic 'en-masse' of America. This identification on which all his poems depend, or, rather, the dialectic from which they derive their energy, is established in the opening lines of 'Song of Myself' (here, as elsewhere, the lines are taken from the version of the poem in the 'deathbed' edition):

> I celebrate myself, and sing myself,
> And what I assume you shall assume
> For every atom belonging to me as good belongs to you.

Two people, Whitman believed, could be separate and somehow synthesized: their paths could be different, and yet they could achieve a kind of transcendent contact. Equally, many people could realize a community while remaining individuals: their lives could be enriched by maintaining a dynamic equilibrium, a dialectical relationship between the needs of the self and the demands of the world. As the opening lines of 'Song of Myself' indicate, it was Whitman's intention to state this again and again. Like many other American writers, he was not afraid of the pedagogical role, and he tried to tell, even teach, his fellow citizens about this dialectical process on which, as he saw it, their lives depended. His aim, though, was not merely to tell and teach but to show. He wanted to dramatize the process of contact: to make his audience aware of the fact that they could be many yet one by compelling them to feel it, to participate in a series of reciprocal relationships in the course of reading his poems.

The most obvious way in which Whitman dramatizes the process of contact has to do with self-presentation. In 'Song of Myself', the poetic 'I' is presented as being capable of sympathetic identification with all kinds of people without any loss of personal identity. 'I am the hounded slave,' Whitman declares at one point; 'I wince at the bite of the dogs, /' he goes on, 'Hell and despair are upon me, crack against crack the marksmen, / I clutch the rails of the fence.' The hunted slave, a lonely woman, a bridegroom, a trapper, a bereaved wife, an 'old artillerist': in the course of the poems, Whitman becomes all these people and many more, and yet still remains 'Walt Whitman . . . of Manhattan the son'. He can, he convinces the reader, empathize, achieve sympathetic identification with others while retaining his own distinctive voice with its dynamic patterns of speech and its predilection for the 'fleshy, sensual' aspects of experience. This is not just 'negative capability', to use John Keats's famous phrase: a loss of the self in the being of another, an act of total immersion or projection. It is, as Whitman presents it, a discovery of the self *in* the other: like many American poets after him, Whitman was firm in his belief that the individual is most himself or herself when honouring and imagining – and, perhaps recreating – the individualism of someone else.

The direct address to his audience with which 'Song of Myself' opens, however, suggests that the relationship Whitman is dramatizing is a triangular one. The 'I' of the poem is there, obviously, the subjects – the slave, the woman, the bridegroom and so on – are there, but so too is the reader, the 'you' to whom the poet turns in the third line of the poem. In a manner that, again, was to become characteristic of American poetry, Whitman invites us, as we read the lines, to participate in the process of sympathetic identification. We are asked to share the experiences and consciousness of the poet, and the beings he presents, while nevertheless remaining the readers – people standing outside this world of words. 'Closer yet I approach you,' Whitman says in another of his poems, 'Crossing Brooklyn Ferry',

> What thought you have of me now, I had as much of you – I laid in
> my stores in advance,
> I consider'd long and seriously of you before you were born.
> Who knows, for all the distance, but I am as good as looking at you
> now, for all you cannot see me?

An intimate contact between the 'I' and 'you' of the poem, the abolition of gaps temporal, spatial and cultural between poet and audience, an encounter between author and reader through the filmy gauze of language: such things are yearned for in these haunting lines, and Whitman's work as a whole – and, perhaps, achieved for a transitory, enchanted moment. At such times, the dilemma of people shut up in the solitude of their own hearts seems to be temporarily forgotten, or rather transcended, because the poem itself has become an act of communion.

Whitman, then, attempts to solve the problems of isolation and audience confronting the American poet, and the debate between individualism and community endemic in American literature and culture, by turning his poem into a gesture of relationship, a bridge between 'I' and 'you'. And it is a relationship that is essentially open, the arc described by this bridge is intended at least to span past, present and future. This comes out strikingly in the closing moments of 'Song of Myself'. 'I bequeath myself to the dirt to grow from the grass I love, / If you want me again look for me under your boot-soles,' Whitman declares; and then later, in the final two lines of the poem, he adds, 'Missing me one place search another, / I stop somewhere waiting for you.' Whitman identifies himself, in these lines, with the 'spear of summer's grass' that, at the beginning of the poem, offered him a medium of mystical insight: a means of achieving a sense of transcendent unity with the given world. The implication is clear: Whitman and his 'Song' will, ideally, act as a source of continuing inspiration and contact for the reader each time he or she reads this poem. They will be an agent of vision and communion quite as inexhaustible as the leaf of grass was for the poet. The poem is transmuted, in effect, into an open field, a process – a journey that the reader is required to take on his or her own terms. Each reading becomes an act of co-production, joint creation, a reinventing or fresh making of the text. And not only of the text. 'The Poet', William Wordsworth insisted in his Preface to the *Lyrical Ballads* (1798), 'is . . . an upholder and preserver, carrying everywhere with him relationship and love.' To which Whitman might well have added that, in an American setting, the reader is as well. Under the pressure of the lessons learned while reading such poems as 'Song of Myself', he or she joins with the poet in the making of community – or, to use Wordsworth's term, 'relationship and love'.

Whitman once referred to *Leaves of Grass* as 'a language experiment'. What is experimented with, in particular, is the possibility of an American epic. Attempts at an epic writing of the nation had, of course, been made before – by, for instance, Cotton Mather and Joel Barlow. It was, however, Whitman who discovered, or rather invented, the form epic would assume in the New World: a form that would be imitated and developed by Ezra Pound, H. D. and William Carlos Williams, among many others, in the twentieth century. The form is, essentially, that of the Romantic epic: as in William Blake's *Jerusalem* (*c*.1797), there is more concern here with spiritual possibility than historical achievement and, as in Wordsworth's *Prelude* (1799, 1805, 1850), the poet himself or herself is at the centre, and the growth and development of the poet's mind supplies the narrative substance. The great American epics, a poem like 'Song of Myself' indicates, would follow the great Romantic epics in being plotless and without a conventional protagonist. Their strategy would be to create a hero rather than celebrate one, and to make rather than record a significant history. They would, in effect, jettison the third-person hero of traditional epic, the prince or aristocratic warrior whose deeds are itemized as a way of articulating and fixing the values of a culture. And, in his place, they would set the poet as a representative, democratic person who discovers his or her identity and values in the course of writing, on their own and on our behalf. The essential form of such epics would have to be open, as open as 'Song of Myself' or the whole 'language experiment' of *Leaves of Grass* is, with the reader exploring for himself or herself the paths the poet has signposted. And, like most great long poems in the Romantic tradition, they would appear to exist in space rather than time, since they would not so much progress in a conventional, linear or logical, way as circle backwards and forwards, supplying workings of form and language in which the audience could bring their own imaginations to bear: each individual member of that audience making connections, establishing priorities and – as any reading of a piece such as 'Song of Myself', 'Crossing Brooklyn Ferry', or an edition of *Leaves of Grass* as a whole clearly requires – collaborating with the poet in the creation of meaning.

Whitman was never nervous about duality. On the contrary, he embraced it. 'Do I contradict myself? /' he asks in 'Song of Myself'. 'Very well then I contradict myself, / (I am large, I contain multitudes.)' For him, the opposites that constitute experience – or, at least, the terms in which most of us think about experience – could all be synthesized in the dialectics of living and the dialectical processes of poetry. Soul and body, good and evil, female and male, and so on: these are all figured, in one short poem, 'The Dalliance of Eagles', as two birds caught for a moment flying and mating – separate and yet united, 'twain yet one'. Whitman was not nervous about appearing clumsy either, as Pound realized. In fact, he boasted of his 'barbaric yawp' in 'Song of Myself', as well as of his capacity for self-contradiction, because he saw it for what it was: an accurate social register of the energy, the plurality and difference of the new republic. Mystic and materialist, moralist and hedonist, individualist and socialist, spiritualist and sensualist, celebrant of heterosexual and homosexual love, 'the poet of the woman the same as the man': as a representative person, a democratic hero, Whitman saw himself, as he put it in 'Song of Myself', as 'an acme of things accomplish'd' as well as 'an encloser of things to be' – and he saw all others, his fellow Americans in particular, as potentially all those things too. At the end of his life, Whitman wrote a poem of quiet intensity, awareness of mystery, called 'A Death Bouquet, Pick'd Noontime, Early January, 1890', in which he described death as 'an invisible breeze after a long and sultry day', setting in 'soothingly, refreshingly, almost vitally'. He also commissioned an absurdly expensive tomb for himself, costing twice as much as the house he was living in and much more than he could afford. Both gestures are characteristic of someone who delighted, as Emerson had hoped the American Homer would, in the 'barbarism' along with the beauty of the times. And to appreciate both, to see both as not only inevitable but necessary acts of conclusion for Whitman, is to begin to understand the poet and the man.

'This is my letter to the World /' begins one poem (no. 441) by Emily Dickinson (1830–86),

---

That never wrote to Me –
The simple News that Nature told –
With tender Majesty
Her Message is committed
To Hands I cannot see –
For love of Her – Sweet – countrymen –
Judge tenderly – of Me

A letter sent without the possibility of response or reply, a message committed to invisible hands: as this poem intimates, Dickinson's condition and subject was isolation. As she put it once, in one of her letters, 'My Business is Circumference'; and the circumference she was talking about was surely that of her lonely self. For her, the self was not the circumscribed Eden it was for Poe. Still less was it a matter of process, a dynamic node or source of energy capable of contact and even confluence with the other, as it was for Whitman. It was, rather, a prisonhouse, from which it was evidently impossible to escape. Her poetic mission, as she saw or sensed it, was to explore the dimensions of her cell: to find out what could be felt or known, what surmised or guessed at, and what could be said and communicated within the constraints of experience and expression that, for her, were the conditions of living. The result is a poetry that manages to be at once passionate and sly, visionary and ironic, as Dickinson tries to push perception and language to the limits while suspecting just how radical, how stringent those limits are. And it is also a voice that not only echoes the doubts of many of her contemporaries, about the possibility of belief and the viability of democracy, truly social living, but also anticipates the scepticism and subversiveness of later, twentieth- and twenty-first-century writers: those for whom any version of reality is just that, a version, a picture or figurative pattern drawn by the prisoner of what he or she sees through the bars of the prison cell.

'I have a brother and sister,' Dickinson wrote in 1862, in response to an inquiry about herself, her family and her work. 'Mother does not care for thought – and father – too busy with his briefs to notice what we do.' 'They are religious – except me –' she added, 'and address an Eclipse, every morning – whom they call their "Father."' The earthly father Dickinson refers to here was Edward Dickinson, an eminent lawyer, politician and judge; he was described by one contemporary as 'a man of the old type, *la vieille roche* of Puritanism'. 'We do not have much poetry, father having made up his mind that its pretty much all *real life*,' Dickinson observed of him in a letter to her brother Austin, away from home at law school. 'Fathers real life and *mine* sometimes come into collision, but as yet escape unhurt!' 'He buys me many Books –' she admitted of Edward Dickinson, in another letter written around ten years later, 'but begs me not to read them – because he fears they joggle the Mind.' Her mind was joggled perhaps a little by attendance at Amherst Academy from 1840 to 1847 and then at Mount Holyoke Female Seminary from 1847 to 1848. Her early years were also certainly filled with the normal social activities of a daughter of a prominent citizen. But gradually she began to withdraw from the world and, by the age of thirty, she had become an almost total recluse: rarely leaving her father's house and garden in Amherst, Massachusetts, dressing completely in white, and conducting most of her many friendships by letter. She never married. She did, however, cultivate intense intellectual companionships with several men in succession, whom she called her tutors. The first was Benjamin F. Newton, a law student in her father's office, who encouraged both her reading and her pursuit of poetry. Religious doubts prompted by his death led her to turn for guidance to the Reverend Charles Wadsworth, whom she called her 'dearest earthly friend' – and whom, for the purposes of her poetry, she transformed into the image of a 'lover' she was never, in fact, to know. After Wadsworth left for San Francisco, Dickinson devoted herself fiercely to her poetry; and she initiated a correspondence with Thomas Wentworth Higginson, whom she knew of only through his contributions to the *Atlantic Monthly*. 'Mr Higginson,' she wrote to him in 1862, 'Are you too deeply occupied to say if my Verse is alive?' And Higginson, although he was too ground in the mill of the conventional to appreciate fully what Dickinson was doing, did encourage her to continue to write. So did other friends and correspondents, including the poet, novelist and essayist Helen Hunt Jackson (1830–85). Dickinson wrote nearly 1,800 poems but publication was another matter. 'Publication – is the Auction / Of the Mind of Man,' she wrote in one piece (no. 709); and only seven of her poems were published during her lifetime, six of them without her consent. Ironically, perhaps, the one that was published with her reluctant permission was one that begins 'Success is counted sweetest / By those who ne'er succeed' (no. 67) and explores a characteristic theme: the possibilities of absence, omission – how an experience denied and imagined may be more intense, more fiercely sweet than the real thing.

The real thing in terms of writing for Dickinson was to collect her poems in packets of about twenty each. When she died, 814 poems bound into forty packets were found in a box in the bottom drawer of her bedroom bureau, together with 333 poems ready for binding and numerous worksheet drafts. Selections from these were published, edited by Higginson and Mabel L. Todd (1856–1932), an author and an Amherst friend of Dickinson's, in 1890 and 1891. Evidently uneasy about what they regarded as the aberrant, eccentric nature of Dickinson's art, however, and possibly nervous about the public reaction, Higginson and Todd altered the poems they published to make them more conventional, more in line with contemporary taste. Further selections, also marred by interventionist and insensitive editing – by Dickinson's niece and others – appeared in 1896, 1914, 1924, 1929, 1930 and 1937. A volume more faithful to the original texts was published in 1945. But it was not until 1955 that a three-volume variorum edition was published, containing all 1,775 known poems. Three volumes of Dickinson's letters then appeared three years later. These were only a small fraction of the letters she actually wrote. As for the letters she received, and which constituted the only way the world wrote to her during her lifetime, she left strict instructions for her sister Lavinia and a woman who worked in the household to destroy them when she was dead. She made no mention of her own letters, or her figurative letters to the world, which it was the luck or fate of Lavinia to discover. That is the reason they survived and, seventy years after her death, could be finally published as she had written them.

'Nature is a stranger yet, /' Dickinson observes in one of her poems ('What mystery pervades a well!', no. 1,400):

> The ones that cite her most
> Have never passed her haunted house,
> Nor simplified her ghost.
>
> To pity those that know her not
> Is helped by the regret
> That those who know her, know her less
> The nearer her they get.

Pushed back from nature, and from the people around her, by their irredeemable otherness, she turns to her internal geography in the belief that it is all she can ever really know. Her self and her feelings tend to encompass the world, and her recognition of this explains the extraordinary intensity with which she describes pleasure, melancholy or despair. The eruption of pain, when it comes, becomes an apocalyptic event ('There's a certain slant of light', no. 258) and exultation, joy, as and when it occurs, seems to irradiate all existence ('I taste a liquor brewed', no. 214). Only *seems* to, however: as Dickinson is only too acutely aware, her self may be her world but that world is in no way co-extensive with reality. This awareness shadows all her work. It explains, for instance, why in some poems she wryly compares her diminutive stature, her literal and metaphorical tininess, with the vast unknowability of nature ('Of bronze and blaze', no. 290). It also explains why, in many other poems addressed or attending to nature, she concentrates on the smaller, more elusive inhabitants of the fields and woods: a small bird or beetle ('A bird came down the walk', no. 328), the cricket ('Further in summer than the birds', no. 1,068), the caterpillar ('How soft a Caterpillar steps –', no. 1,448), a butterfly or bee ('Flowers – Well – if anybody', no. 137; 'Could I but ride indefinite', no. 661; 'The pedigree of Honey', no. 1,627), the hummingbird ('A route of evanescence', no. 1,463), a fly ('Bee! I'm expecting you!', no. 1,035). Each is a 'narrow fellow' for the poet ('A narrow fellow in the grass', no. 986): a creature that supplies a small paradigm of the fickle, freckled character of the human environment, its capacity for surprise, strangeness and mystery.

The elusive, illusive nature of reality, and the radical restraints placed on the self and its perceptions, are registered with particular force not only in the poems about nature but also in those about death and love. Love and death are frequently linked in Dickinson's work: 'Because I could not stop for death' (no. 712), where death takes the form of a gentleman caller – taking a maiden, the narrator of the poem, on a ride that is at once a courtship ritual and a journey to the graveyard – is only one, particularly famous example. And even when they are not, they carry a comparable freight of meaning for the poet because both, for her, mark the possibility of venturing beyond the limits of the self, crossing the threshold into the unknown, into otherness. Death, especially, is an experience that is approached with a mixture of desire and fear because it might, as Dickinson sees it, lead to a 'title divine' ('Title Divine – is Mine!', no. 1,072), the final escape of the self from its confinement into some more expansive, exalted state – or it might simply be a prelude to oblivion. All she can be sure of is the simple fact that she cannot be sure; on this, as on all other matters, the verdict must be left open. The self, Dickinson intimates, is fragile, evanescent, dwarfed by its surroundings; and the worlds it creates, the knowledge it articulates, must – by the very nature of the source – remain arbitrary, temporary and incomplete. So in poem after poem that attends to the experience of dying, the narrator or persona Dickinson habitually adopts, the 'I' and eye of the poetic narrative, approaches the gates of death only to stop short just before she enters, passes through to the other side ('A Clock stopped – ', no. 287; 'I heard a Fly buzz – when I died –', no. 465; 'Our journey had advanced – ', no. 615). The scene then goes blank, and poet, narrator and reader alike are left gazing at the blankness, aware only that they have arrived at the boundaries of human consciousness. To an extent, life on the one hand and love and death on the other are the structural equivalents of the clearing and the wilderness for Dickinson, the one figuring the measured, constructed and known, the other posing the twinned possibilities of adventure and annihilation. This is perhaps why, in those poems that map a literal geography of land and sea, she demonstrates a similar vacillation between fear and desire: the Ishmael-like suspicion that the sea is perilously other ('I started Early – Took my Dog', no. 520) and the Ahab-like conviction that it is seductively, thrillingly so ('Exultation is the going', no. 76). To speak of a literal geography here or elsewhere, though, tends to miss the target. Dickinson thinks feeling and feels thought, and all her best poems are at once, and complexly, literal and figurative. So the poems 'about' the sea, for instance, are also equally poems 'about' the danger and adventure of death and love (the sea is, in fact, associated with Eros and eternity in both no. 520 and no. 76); a poem 'about' death often carries strong erotic undertones ('Death is the supple Suitor', no. 1,445); while a poem 'about' love may pursue the simultaneously thrilling yet unnerving possibility of obliteration, self-abandonment ('Wild Night – Wild Nights!', no. 114). What these poems have in common, apart from their complex layering – a sense of the permeable barriers between different topics, various levels of thought and experience – is their open-endedness: the kind of conclusion in which nothing is concluded that, given Dickinson's situation and stance, is the only one available to her.

The sense of the circumscriptions imposed on the isolated self, and the consequently random, truncated nature of human knowledge, dictates Dickinson's poetic practice. Her poems are not just open-ended but open, and in a way that is interestingly different from, say, Whitman. What Dickinson's work tends to do is underline its own arbitrariness, its dislocated, disjunctive character: a point that is brought out, in particularly high profile, by her disruptive use of rhythm, her frequent recourse to discords and half-rhymes, and her preference for the paratactic over more conventional forms of syntax. Dickinson subverts. She habitually uses the standard hymn stanza form, but then undermines it by lengthening or shortening lines, reversing rhythms, omitting rhymes. She opts for what might seem to be a straightforward declarative style, by placing phrases and clauses paratactically – that is, side by side in an apparently indiscriminate way. But what she is doing, it turns out, is evading the kind of finished effect that is inseparable from more sophisticated kinds of syntactical structure. Experiences, events, expressions are set out on a level verbal landscape, separated only by the minimalist punctuation of the dash; there is no attempt made to draw things into a net of theory, an elaborate verbal plan or hierarchy. She even chooses what might be taken to be conventional subjects – love, death, nature and so on – and may open a meditation on them in an apparently innocent, simple way, with a pretty piece of scene painting ('The pretty Rain from those sweet Eaves', no. 608) or a declaration of faith ('This World is not Conclusion', no. 501). But the scene soon becomes darker, 'Faith slips' into doubt or even despair, as the poem shifts sharply from convention and the innocence assumes an ironic, sceptical edge, the simplicity is exposed as fundamentally deceptive. The poems of Whitman may not end in the accepted sense, but at least they achieve an emotional resolution – the feeling that the ideas and impulses activating them have been granted an adequate shape, appropriately full expression. With Dickinson, even this is denied us. What she slips to us, instead, is the lyric account of a self that is paradoxically both circumscribed and dynamic, engaged in a quest that not only it can never quite complete but the precise nature of which it can never really fathom, never properly know.

One of Dickinson's most famous poems about death, for example, 'I felt a Funeral, in my Brain' (no. 280), ends with these lines:

> And then a Plank in Reason, broke,
> And I dropped down, and down –
> And hit a World, at every plunge,
> And finished knowing – then –

Finished knowing then – and then, what? The closing lines, and indeed the preceding ones, undermine any claims Dickinson may try to make to an understanding of her subject, to an adequate definition and knowledge of the experience that is the poem's occasion. As a result, this is not so much a poem about death in the traditional sense as a poem about the impossibility of ever writing such a poem – and, more generally, about the impossibility of doing much more in any human event than measuring one's own limits. As Dickinson puts it in one of her lyrics, 'I dwell in Possibility – / A fairer House than Prose' (no. 657). The most she can do in this 'House', she intimates, is offer a series of provisional names for the furniture. The names must be provisional because she is, she feels, a prisoner caught within the circumference of her own consciousness: she is, consequently, not describing the world as it is, or even as it might be, but merely constructing a language-system, and by implication a system of values, acceptable to her own individual soul. 'I could not see to see –' ends another of her poems, 'I heard a Fly buzz – when I died'. Others conclude by contemplating the void, the vast gap between life and death, being and possible knowing, the self and the threshold, the crossover into some kind of otherness – as, say, 'Because I could not stop for Death' does, with death and the maiden coming to what appears to be an abrupt end to their journey:

> Since then – 'tis Centuries – and yet
> Feels shorter than the Day
> I first surmised the Horses' Heads
> Were toward Eternity –

Whatever the conclusion, though, the poem remains in a state of radical indeterminacy. So does the poet, the narrator and the reader. Ultimate vision is invariably denied, an adequate vocabulary involving the congruence of word and world is never attained; the need to understand things remains just that – a need.

'I had no Monarch in my life, and cannot rule myself,' Dickinson wrote once to Higginson, 'and when I try to organise – my little Force explodes – and leaves me bare and charred –.' In all her best work, Dickinson walks a fine line between the constraints hinted at here: between rule and chaos, 'prose' and 'possibility', speech and silence. But, as so often, she was being modest to the point of inaccuracy when she suggested that her poetic experiments with her self ended badly. They were explosive, to be sure, but what they did and still do is ignite awareness, compel the reader into a recognition of the magical character of experience. They promote a healthy scepticism, but also curiosity; they invite doubt, caution, but, along with that, awe and wonder, an acute sense of mystery. Here and elsewhere in her letters and poems, Dickinson also unveils a paradox, and one that is not just unique to her. It is a paradox that lies perhaps at the heart of all American writing and, certainly, at the heart of writing of this period, circulating around the idea and practice of a tradition of individualism. Dickinson had 'no Monarch', she told Higginson, nobody to tell her what and how she should write. As someone was to observe of her much later, she consequently wrote as if no one had written before. This made the tenor and texture of her work utterly hers: even the physical look of it on the page tells the reader familiar with it that *this* is the work of Dickinson. But it also established her kinship with so many others: 'isolatoes' like Hawthorne and Melville, say, writers concerned with the honour and dignity due to the self such as Stowe and Stoddard, Douglass and Jacobs, others committed to self-reliance like Emerson, Fuller and Thoreau, and still others like Poe and Whitman who attempted to trace the contours of loneliness. Along with Dickinson, these writers and many others writing between the Revolution and the end of the Civil War, and beyond, defined an area of concern that subsequent American writers were to explore. They established parameters within which others, later, were to undertake their chartings of the country's ample geography, their own stabs at translating the landscapes of

America into literature. Their example was not a restrictive one, of course. It did not, and does not, limit American writers to a narrow set of alternatives beyond which they are forbidden to go. It offers not a prescriptive grammar but a transformational one: a range of options on which each writer might build, structures that are generative, susceptible to change and development, a series of opportunities rather than roles. What Dickinson and her contemporaries sustained and transmitted to their successors, in sum, was a great and continuing tradition founded precisely on the notion that there was and could be 'no Monarch' for the individual: a tradition that has, as at least one of its unacknowledged aims, the forging of the uncreated conscience of a nation.

3

reconstructing the past, reimagining the future
the development of american literature, 1865–1900

Rebuilding a Nation

On 9 April 1865, General Robert E. Lee met General Ulysses S. Grant at Appomattox Court House, a country crossroads in the forest, and handed over his sword. It was one of the great symbolic moments of American history. Within a few weeks, everyone else had surrendered; and by July the Civil War was over. It was and remains the bloodiest war in American history, both in absolute numbers and in the proportion of casualties to the population. About 360,000 Union soldiers and 260,000 Confederates had died on the battlefield or in military hospitals. Slavery was abolished, a Freedman's Bureau had been organized to assist the former slaves, and the Union was restored. The war left an indelible stain on the American consciousness. Even European countries, at this time, had no war to compare with this one. Napoleon invaded Russia in 1812 with a Grand Army of 600,000, cobbled together from the allies of France. It was the largest army assembled in the West up to that time, but it would have been insufficient for the Civil War. The total number of enlistments on the Northern side was 2,778,304, of whom 2,489,836 were whites, 178,975 were African Americans and 3,530 were Native Americans. The figure is slightly misleading, since men sometimes enlisted several times. But the general consensus is that no fewer than two million served on the Union side. Confederate enlistments have been calculated at between 750,000 and 1,223,890. It was the closest thing the world had yet seen to a total war, with more American soldiers lost than the total number killed in the two world wars, Korea and Vietnam. In the South, it left what one traveller in 1875 described as 'a dead civilisation and a broken-down system' and what another, ten years earlier, claimed was 'enough woe and want and ruin and savage' 'to satisfy the most insatiate heart', 'enough of sure humiliation and bitter overthrow' 'to appease the desire of the most vengeful spirit'. In the North, it left a sense of triumph, at the restoration of the nation and the abolition of slavery, but also a sense of tragedy: not least because, even before all hostilities had ceased, only a week after Appomattox, President Abraham Lincoln was dead – killed by a man crying out 'Sic semper tyrannis!', 'Thus always to tyrants', the motto of the state of Virginia.

'A great literature will yet arise out of the era of those four years,' Walt Whitman observed of the Civil War some fourteen years after it had ended. What arose with unparalleled speed, certainly, was a great urban and industrial society dedicated to production, progress and profit. In the early 1860s, the United States as a productive economy extended only as far as the Missouri River. It did not manufacture any steel; and it had an industrial investment of only a half billion dollars. Within twenty years after the Civil War, it had become one of the giants of the international steel industry; the number of factories within its borders had more than doubled; and it had an industrial investment of over four billion dollars. Not only that, it had developed the most extensive railway system in the world, binding East and West together in one vast economic unit. Nearly half the railway mileage in the world was in the United States, and that mileage represented one-sixth of the nation's estimated wealth. America, especially on its eastern seaboard, was being transformed from a country of farms and villages into a country of towns and cities. By 1880, for example, over half the population of the eastern United States lived in towns of more than 4,000 people. Chicago, at the junction of several railway lines, grew from a fur-trapping village of about 350 people in 1830 to a city of half a million people in 1880, then one million by the time of the Chicago World's Fair in 1893. New York City, the largest city in the nation, grew at a similarly phenomenal rate, to a population of three and a half million by 1900. Other Midwestern cities, like Detroit, Milwaukee and Minneapolis, saw their populations double and triple in the decades after the war, while in the West Los Angeles grew from a population of 11,000 in 1880 to five times that number in just twenty years. Certainly, 40 per cent of the population of the United States was still rural by the end of the nineteenth century. But the trend towards urbanization was inexorable and irreversible. And a further symbolic moment, for the American consciousness, came in the early 1890s. The 1890 census revealed that every part of the continental United States had now been organized, most of it already into states. That meant, the historian Frederick Jackson Turner declared, three years later at the Chicago World's Fair, that the frontier was now closed and a new era for America was at hand.

The 1890 census also revealed that the total population of the United States had risen to sixty-three million, and that the foreign-born element in this total numbered nine million. As a proportion of the total, that element did not represent much of an increase on pre-Civil War figures. But it was enough to generate a moral panic, and eventually repressive, anti-immigration legislation, among native whites, because the new immigrants tended to cluster in the cities, as cheap labour for the factories and sweatshops, and were of different ethnic composition from earlier immigrant generations. Before 1860, most immigrants had come from Great Britain, Ireland, Germany and Scandinavia; five million arrived in the four decades prior to the Civil War. The period from then until the end of the century saw no fewer than fourteen million new arrivals, mostly from Poland, Italy, Russia, Austria, Turkey,

Greece and Syria. Catholic or Jewish, many of them non-English speakers, their different manners, customs and beliefs – and, in many instances, different languages – inspired feelings of resentment and distrust, the suspicion that the Anglo-Saxon hegemony was being threatened. Such feelings were, in a sense, a twisted response to a tangible reality: the United States was becoming an even more ethnically mixed, culturally plural nation. Along with these new immigrants arriving mostly on the Eastern seaboard were others arriving mostly on the western: some 264,000 Chinese and a much smaller number of Japanese between 1860 and 1900. Again, the numbers were not necessarily large or out of proportion to earlier waves of immigration. But the Chinese immigrants, in particular, inspired fear, resentment and racial antagonism, with violence against them in the Western states, escalating in the 1870s and 1880s, and repression culminating in the Chinese Exclusion Act of 1882, which outlawed the immigration of all Chinese people apart from a few professionals, students and tourists.

The experience of other minority groups, already in the United States before the Civil War, was mixed, during the latter half of the nineteenth century. With the passing of the 13th Amendment to the Constitution in 1865, four million African Americans were freed. With a decade of reform and Reconstruction, about a quarter of a million received an education, many achieved political office and many more exercised the right to vote. But when federal troops withdrew from the South in 1877, African Americans swiftly lost the franchise. By 1910, all the former Confederate states had radically restricted black voting rights, while even before that a whole raft of laws established segregation in everything from schools to public transport. Where legal means of repression appeared not to work, then violence was used: by the Ku Klux Klan, established in 1866, and other white vigilante groups. And the basic economic situation for African Americans remained unchanged. Sixty per cent of the land in the South was owned by 10 per cent of the white population. Freed black people found themselves forced into sharecropping or tenant farming – by 1900, over 75 per cent of black farmers were tenant farmers. They had, to an extent, merely moved from slavery to serfdom. Mexican Americans were in a more fortunate position. They were not really immigrants, since the United States had merely annexed the territory where most of them already lived. They represented a majority in many of the territories in the Southwest. They could, as a result, maintain their own culture and their own language: their own fierce ethnic pride and independence. For Native Americans, however, the four decades after the Civil War were nothing short of tragic, with the tribes suffering more than they had ever done or were to do in the following years. With whites penetrating into even the remotest corners of the West, the policy of removal was replaced by one of assimilation, the idea being that allotting plots of land to individual Native Americans would draw them into mainstream American society. The new policy was as dismal and disastrous as the old one. It ignored Native American traditions of communal land use, the poor quality of much of the land in question and the lack of operating capital. It also ignored the fact that Native Americans had insufficient knowledge of white law and legal manoeuvring to stop them losing or being tricked out of what was theirs. By 1887, Native Americans had lost all except 150 million of their original three billion acres; and by 1934, when the policy of allotment was finally reversed, all that was left was forty-eight million acres, a miserable 1.5 per cent of what had once been in their hands.

Real power lay elsewhere, for all sections of the population. By 1890, 1 per cent of the entire American population owned over 25 per cent of the nation's wealth. Three years later, a survey revealed that there were over four thousand millionaires in the United States: this at a time when $700 was a reasonable annual income. At one end of the newly emerging economic and social scale was an industrial working class far outnumbering the middle class: by 1915, the poor would in fact constitute 65 per cent of the population. At the other end were those like John D. Rockefeller, Andrew Carnegie and J. Pierpoint Morgan: industrialists and financiers who accumulated vast fortunes and power. Rockefeller gradually acquired control of 90 per cent of the oil industry in the United States. Diversifying, his company Standard Oil had by 1890 become not just the largest oil company in the world but the largest railway company and one of the largest banking concerns. During the same period, Carnegie, who had started working life as a telegraph operator, built up the largest steel manufacturing industry in the world, which he then sold off to a business rival for $500 million. The business rival, Morgan, merged the Carnegie Steel Corporation with other smaller steel companies: the result was the first billion-dollar trust, US Steel, which has dominated its field from its foundation to the present day. Morgan was the spider in a vast web of interlocking directorships, 741 of them in 112 corporations. The web was so intricate, and so tight, that, by the early twentieth century, almost all the leading American capitalists, or 'robber barons' as they were and are sometimes called, were associated with either Morgan or Rockefeller. The emergence of this new breed of capitalism could be seen as the price the United States had to pay for its commitment to economic freedom and its emergence as a global power. It was certainly a high one. By the end of this period, in any event, the development and the rationalization of industrialism by private capital was more or less complete.

Morgan, Rockefeller and their associates sometimes adopted a posture of brazen defiance in response to criticism of their unlimited wealth and power. 'What do *I* care about the law?' Morgan said once to a reporter. 'Ain't I got the money? The public be damned.' 'I cheat my boys every chance I get,' Rockefeller similarly declared, 'I want to make 'em sharp.' But, more often, they subscribed to an emerging ideology which saw their wealth as justified, the reward of pluck and luck. The ideology drew on the Protestant ethic, the belief that wealth was a sign of heavenly favour, and on a popularized version of Darwinian theories of evolution: what was termed 'the survival of the fittest'. That ideology, with its emphasis on success as the inevitable outcome of hard work and sturdy self-reliance, was carried to the public in the popular literature of the day, the exemplary tales for young adults and the new 'dime novels' that first appeared in the 1860s and quickly reached circulation in the millions. Easily the most successful author in this field was Horatio Alger (1834–99), the titles of whose most popular books for boys tell their own story: *Ragged Dick* (1867), *Luck and Pluck* (1869) and *Tattered Tom* (1871). It was also promulgated in the new mass circulation magazines and newspapers. One of the most remarkable features of this period, in fact, along with the general transformation of the economy – and the political corruption that, very often, went with it – was the development of publishing into a vast and multiple industry and, along with that, the growth of a mass readership, eager to consume that industry's products. The spread of education and literacy, the technology of mass production, the access to all markets opened up by the railways: all meant that something like a uniform print culture was possible for the entire nation, and that specialist audiences could also be catered to or even created.

So there was uniformity and diversity. There were new mass circulation publications: not only the dime novels, celebrating cowboy or detective heroes or telling tales of success, but 'story papers' serializing mainly romance and adventure narratives. There were school readers, like the McGuffey readers used in schools between 1836 and 1890 that sang of the virtue of labour and humility ('Work, work, my boy, be not afraid / . . . / And blush not for your humble place'), doing their cultural work by assimilating their young audience to the values of the dominant culture. There was a steady stream of best-sellers, like the forty-five romantic novels of Frank R. Stockton (1834–1902), or *Ben Hur, a Tale of Christ* (1884) by Lew Wallace (1827–1905), which sold over three million copies. But, on the other hand, there were also a vast number of specialist publications, reflecting and reinforcing the existence of many Americas, the continuing fact of cultural plurality. On one level, there were the literary magazines, like the *Atlantic Monthly*, *Harper's Monthly* and *Scribners Monthly*, whose relatively small circulations belied their considerable cultural influence. On another were the more than 1,200 foreign-language periodicals in circulation by 1896, serving mostly the new immigrant groups, the over 150 publications catering to African Americans, and the many other magazines and newspapers circulating among other ethnic groups on a local or larger scale.

Among those who reflected and benefited from both the uniformity and diversity were women writers. The years following the Civil War witnessed an exponential increase in the opportunities available for women, mostly white women but also some others, in education and work outside the menial or domestic sphere. In the South, the challenge of war had required white women to take up more public roles; so did the dearth of men when the war was over, the destruction of a generation in the conflict. In the North and elsewhere, too, the necessities of war, which drew women out of the home in more numbers than ever before, were followed by the demands of the new economy. Women, and especially white women from the middle and lower middle classes, began to enter the new business world as store assistants, telephone and telegraph operators, and clerical workers. For black and white working-class women, it was more a matter of bitter necessity than opportunity: they had to work, in the fields still, or in the factories. The dominant movement, though, was away from the hearth and home, and its accompanying ideology: the notion of the 'true woman', keeper of the domestic pieties,

---

was gradually being replaced by that of the 'new woman', relatively independent and mobile. The change might be regretted by the more traditionally minded, or even by those who saw it as a symptom of a larger change to a culture of insecurity, denial of community. But it was nevertheless acknowledged. And women writers were a part of it. Many of them became writers precisely in response to the new economic opportunities or necessities, because they wanted or needed to find a job. Many of them, like Augusta Jane Evans (1835–1909), Amélie Rives (1863–1945) and Mary Johnston (1870–1936), wrote for the new mass audience and enjoyed a wide readership. Some of them, with less immediate public success in most cases, adopted a tougher, more critical stance towards either the risks women faced in the new dispensation or the restrictions they still suffered from the old. In doing so, they measured a change in writing practice among many American writers during this period, female and male: from depicting the mythic possibilities of America to describing its material inadequacies. They, and those like them, responded to the drastic economic and social alterations occurring in the nation around them by turning ever further from romance to realism, and then later to naturalism.

The Development of Literary Regionalisms

From Adam to outsider

Realism was described by Ambrose Bierce as 'the art of depicting nature as it is seen by toads' and having 'the charm suffusing a landscape painted by a mole, or a story written by a measuring worm'. That definition would have delighted Mark Twain, born Samuel Langhorne Clemens (1835–1910): because of its mordant wit and because all of his work could be seen as a series of negotiations between realism and romance. 'My books are simply autobiographies,' Twain insisted once. True of every American writer, perhaps, the remark seems especially true of him. He relied, frequently and frankly, on personal experience: in accounts of his travels, for instance, like *The Innocents Abroad* (1869), *Roughing It* (1872) and *A Tramp Abroad* (1880). Even those books of his that were the results of strenuous imaginative effort can be read as attempts to resolve his inner divisions, and create some sense of continuity between his present and his past, his critical investment in common sense, pragmatism and progress and his emotional involvement in his childhood and the childhood of his region and nation. The inner divisions and discontinuity were, in fact, inseparable. For all of Twain's best fictional work has to do with what has been called 'the matter of Hannibal': that is, his experiences as a child in the slaveholding state of Missouri and his years as a steamboat pilot on the Mississippi. This was not simply a matter of nostalgia for the good old days before the Civil War, of the kind to be found in other, simpler writers born in the South like, say, Thomas Nelson Page or Richard Malcolm Johnston. Nor was it merely another example of the romantic idealization of youth: although Twain did firmly believe that, youth being 'the only thing worth giving to the race', to look back on one's own childhood was to give oneself 'a cloudy sense of having been a prince, once, in some enchanted far off land, & of being in exile now, & desolate'. It was rather, and more simply, that Twain recognized intuitively that his years as a boy and youth, in the pre-Civil War South, had formed him for good and ill – organized his perceptions, shaped his vocabulary, and defined what he most loved and hated. So to explore those years was to explore the often equivocal nature of his own vision. It was also, and more complexly, that Twain sensed that the gap, the division, he felt between his self and his experiences before and after the war was, in its detail unique of course, but also typical, representative. So to understand that gap, that division, was to begin at least to understand his nation and its times.

Twain moved with his family to the Mississippi River town of Hannibal, Missouri, when he was four. A small town with a population of about a thousand, Hannibal was a former frontier settlement that had become a backwater. Leaving school at the age of twelve, Twain received his real education as a journeyman printer; and, having spent his first eighteen years in the South, he began to travel widely. His travels eventually brought him back to the Mississippi where, in the late 1850s, he trained and was licensed as a riverboat pilot. After his years in Hannibal, this was the most formative period of his life. 'I loved the profession far better than any I have followed since,' Twain was to say later, in *Life on the Mississippi* (1883). 'The reason is plain: a pilot, in those days, was the only unfettered and entirely independent human being that lived in earth.' Piloting taught Twain lessons in freedom that were to be immensely valuable to him later. But when the Civil War began, the riverboats ceased operation; and, after a brief period serving with a group of Confederate volunteers, he travelled west. There, he spent the rest of the war prospecting for silver with his brother and then working with Bret Harte as a journalist in San Francisco. It was while working as a journalist in the West, in 1863, that he adopted the pseudonym Mark Twain. And in 1865, he made that name famous with the tall tale, 'The Celebrated Jumping Frog of Calaveras County'. Brief though it is, the tale is notable not least because it reveals many of the vital ingredients in Twain's art: the rough humour of the Southwest and Western frontier, a recognizable teller of the tale (in this case, a character called Simon Wheeler), above all, a creative use of the vernacular and the sense of a story springing out of an oral tradition, being told directly to us, its audience. Twain now began touring the lecture circuits. His lively personality and quotable remarks made him immensely popular. His lecture tours also reinforced his habit of writing in the vernacular, the American idiom: 'I amend the dialect stuff', he once said, 'by talking and *talking* it till it sounds right.' His first book, *The Celebrated Jumping Frog of Calaveras County and Other Sketches* (1867), appeared just before he set sail on a trip to Europe and the Holy Land. This was followed by his account of that trip, in *Innocents Abroad*, his humorous depiction of his travels west in *Roughing It*, and a satirical portrait of boom times after the Civil War, *The Gilded Age* (1873), written in collaboration with Charles Dudley Warner.

Twain first turned to the matter of Hannibal in a series of articles published in the *Atlantic Monthly* entitled 'Old Times on the Mississippi'. Revised and expanded, with new material added (some of it, as Twain candidly admitted, 'taken from books' by others, 'tho' credit given'), this became *Life on the Mississippi* eight years later. What is remarkable about the essays and the book is how Twain turns autobiography into history. In his account of his own personal development, the author distinguishes between the romantic dreamer he once was, before training as a pilot, who saw the Mississippi merely in terms of its 'grace', 'beauty' and 'poetry', and the sternly empirical realist he became after his training, when he could see the Mississippi in more pragmatic terms – as a tool, to be used and manoeuvred. That same model, contrasting the romance of the past with the realism of afterwards, is then deployed to explain larger social change: with the South of the author's childhood identified with romance and the South of his adult years, after the Civil War, associated with realism – enjoying a sense of 'progress, energy, and prosperity' along with the rest of the nation. The key feature of this contrast, personal and social, between times before the war and times after, is its slippery, equivocal nature. The glamour of the past is dismissed at one moment and then recalled with elegiac regret the next, the pragmatism and progress of the present are welcomed sometimes and at others coolly regretted. No attempt is made to resolve this contradiction. And similar, if not precisely the same, confusions are at work in *The Adventures of Tom Sawyer* (1876), a book clearly based on the author's childhood years in Hannibal, renamed St Petersburg. At the time of writing *Tom Sawyer*, Twain's uncertainty about his purposes was signalled by the fact that he changed his mind over who the book was intended for, adults or children. 'It is *not* a boy's book at all,' he wrote to his friend William Dean Howells, 'It will only be read by adults.' But then he announced, in his Preface, 'my book is intended mainly for the entertainment of boys and girls. I hope that it will not be shunned by men and women on that account.' That uncertainty is then registered in the narrative. There is immediacy in some of the language, but there is distance in much of it, an attempt to sound sophisticated, mature, refined: characters do not spit, for example, they 'expectorate', clothes are 'accoutrements', breezes are 'zephyrs', buildings are 'edifices'. There is the stuff of childhood fantasies (the delicious thrill of overhearing regretful adults mourn your untimely death, bogeymen, the discovery of treasure) and the staple of adult discourse (the tale of Tom and Becky, for instance, is a parody of adult courtship). There is the tendency, on the part of the anonymous narrator, to be ironic and patronizing about the 'simple-hearted' community of St Petersburg and its 'small plain' buildings. And there is also an impulse towards elegy, towards seeing that very same place as 'a Delectable Land, dreamy, reposeful, and inviting'. The only attempt to resolve these contradictions is also the one Twain resorts to in *Life on the Mississippi*: to impose on his material the notions of personal development and social betterment – in other words, the myth of Progress. Tom turns out to be, in the words of his Aunt Polly, not '*bad*, so to say – only mischeevous'. By the end of the story, he has shown his true mettle by assuming the conventional male protective role with Becky and acting as the upholder of social justice. The integrity and sanctity of the community is confirmed, with Tom's revelation of the villainy of Injun Joe and the killing of the villain. And Tom is even ready, it seems, to offer brief lectures on the advantages of respectability: 'we can't let you into the gang if you ain't respectable, you know,' he tells his friend, Huck Finn. That this attempt to resolve the divisions of the narrative is less than successful is evident from the fact that *Tom Sawyer*, like *Life on the Mississippi*, is interesting precisely because of its discontinuity. It is also implicit in the author's intuitively right decision to give equal weight at the end of the story to the voice of the outlaw, Huck, as he tries to resist Tom's persuasions. 'It ain't for me; I ain't used to it,' Huck tells Tom: 'It's awful to be tied up so.'

The voice of Huck, the voice of the outsider, that begins to be heard at the end of *Tom Sawyer* takes over completely in what is without doubt Twain's greatest work, *The Adventures of Huckleberry Finn*, begun in 1876 and published in 1885. Twain began *Huckleberry Finn* simply as a sequel to *Tom Sawyer*, with several narrative threads carried over from the earlier work. Even as he began it, however, he must have realized that this was a very different, more authentic work. For the manuscript shows Twain trying to catch the trick, the exact lilt of Huck's voice. 'You will not know about me', the first try at an opening, is scratched out. So is the second try, 'You do not know about me'. Only at the third attempt does Twain come up with the right, idiomatic but poetic, start: 'You don't know about me.' Like a jazz musician, trying to hit the right beat before swinging into the full melody and the rhythm of the piece, Twain searches for just the right voice, the right pitch and momentum, before moving into the story of his greatest vernacular hero. The intimacy is vital too: in a way that was to become characteristic of American fiction, the protagonist addresses 'you' the reader directly, in terms that appear spontaneous, sincere, unpremeditated. We are drawn into this web of words in a manner that convinces us that we are enjoying an unpremeditated, vital relationship with the hero. The spontaneity is also a function of the narrative structure. Twain once said that he relied on a book to 'write itself', and that is the impression, in the best sense, given by *Huckleberry Finn*. The story has a structure, of course, that of the picaresque narrative (*Don Quixote* [1604–14] was one of Twain's favourite books): but that structure is as paradoxically structureless as the structure of, say, *Moby-Dick* or 'Song of Myself'. The book flows like the Mississippi, at a constantly altering pace, in unanticipated directions; new characters, episodes, incidents pop up without warning, old characters like Jim or Tom Sawyer reappear just when we least expect them to. Like the great works of Melville and Whitman, too, *Huckleberry Finn* remains an open field, describing an open, unstructured and unreconstructed spirit. It does not conclude, in any conventional fashion. Famously, it ends as 'Song of Myself' does and many later American narratives were to do: looking to the open road, with the hero still breaking away – or, as Huck himself has it, ready to 'light out for the Territory ahead of the rest'.

Twain later described *Huckleberry Finn* as 'a book of mine where a sound heart and a deformed conscience come into collision and conscience suffers a defeat'. The central moral dilemma Huck has to face, in this deeply serious, even tragic comedy, is whether or not he should betray his friend, the escaped slave Jim, by revealing Jim's whereabouts to other whites, including Miss Watson, his owner. For much of the narrative, Huck is equivocal. Sometimes, he sees Jim as a slave, as property that should be returned; and sometimes he sees him as a human being and a friend, requiring his sympathy and help. And the vacillation stems from Huck's uncertainty over what takes priority: the laws of society, his social upbringing which, however patchily, has shaped his conscience, or the promptings of his own heart, his instincts and feelings as an individual. The book is about the historical injustice of slavery, of course, and the social inequity of racism, the human use or denial of human beings. But it is also about the same fundamental conflict as the one that fires *The Scarlet Letter* and so many other American narratives into life. Huck must choose between the law and liberty, the sanctions of the community and the perceptions of the individual, civil and natural justice. He chooses the latter, the lessons learned from his own experience, the knowledge of his own rebellious heart. In doing so, Huck reflects his creator's belief at the time in aboriginal innocence, the purity of the asocial – and asocial or presocial creatures like the child. And he also measures the extent of the creative triumph, since Twain manages here a miracle: that rare thing, a sympathetic and credibly virtuous character. The sympathy and credibility stem from the same source: Huck is a grotesque saint, a queer kind of saviour because he does not know he is doing good. His notions of right and wrong, salvation and damnation, have been formed by society. So, when he is doing good he believes that he is doing evil, and vice versa. His belief system is at odds with his right instincts: hence, the terms in which he describes his final decision not to betray Jim. 'All right, then,' Huck declares, 'I'll *go* to hell.'

Twain's strategies for shifting Huck's conflict from the personal to the mythic are several. Easily the most important, though, is his own, almost certainly intuitive, variation on the contrast between the clearing and the wilderness: the riverbank and the river. The riverbank is the fixed element, the clearing, the community. On the riverbank, everyone plays a social role, observes a social function: either without knowing it, like the Grangerford family or the inhabitants of Bricksville, or knowing it and using it to exploit others, like the Duke and Dauphin. Everyone is obsessed with appearances and disguises, and uses language to conceal meaning and feeling from others and themselves. Everyone behaves like an actor, who has certain lines to say, clothes to wear, things to do, rather than as an independent individual. It is a mark of Huck's individuality, incidentally, that, on the riverbank, he is constantly forgetting the role he is playing, who he is supposed to be. Everyone, in short, denies their essential humanity on the riverbank, and the humanity of others: here, Jim is not a human being, he is the lowest form of social function, a slave. What adds to the power of this portrait is that, as with the account of the Puritan settlement in *The Scarlet Letter*, it is simultaneously mythic and historical. This is society, the machinery of the social system, seen from the standpoint of individualism. It is also a very specific society, that of the South before the Civil War. Drawing on the devices of the Southwestern humorists, but exponentially developing them, Twain offers a brilliantly detailed satirical picture of the Old

South: poor whites like Pap Finn and the people of Bricksville, middle-class farmers like the Phelps family, wealthy planters like the Grangerfords – and, of course, the slaves. *Huckleberry Finn* is an unremitting comic assault on the human capacity to substitute 'style' for substance, social illusion for experiential fact. But it is also a satire on one particular kind of social 'style' that Twain knew only too well. It is a tragic account of what, generally, happens when people stop seeing and testing things for themselves, as individual human beings. But it is also a very American tragedy, about a moment in American history when a sense of humanity and individuality was lost, with terrible consequences for the nation.

The river, the fluid element and the medium of escape for Huck and Jim, is, of course, Twain's version of the mythic wilderness. It is a place where Huck can enjoy intimacy with Jim and an almost Edenic harmony with nature. Recasting Huck as an American Adam, Twain shows his hero attending to the moods of the river and its surroundings and, in turn, projecting his own moods in and through those natural surrounds. Huck appears to enjoy a separate peace here on the river, a world apart from rules, codes and clock time, where 'lazying' becomes a positive activity. Free from the postlapsarian compulsion to work, Huck can simply be and wonder: live, meditate and marvel at the miracle of the particular, the minutiae of life. It is in these episodes on the river that the indelible connection between the voice of Huck and his values becomes clear. Huck scrupulously, instinctively tells it as it is. He sees things as they are, free of social pretence or disguise. He describes things as they are, not cloaked in the rhetoric of society. So he can judge things as they are, not as the social system would tell him to judge them. It is also in these episodes that Huck's power as a syncretic figure becomes clear. Huck Finn brings together and synthesizes the warring opposites of Twain's earlier work. Huck is a focus for all his creator's nostalgia, all his yearnings for childhood, the lost days of his youth, the days before the Civil War and the Fall; and he is also, quite clearly, a projection of Twain's more progressive feelings, the belief in human development and perfectibility – he suggests hope for the future as well as love of the past. Again, this is measured in the language of the book, in that it is precisely Huck's 'progressive' attention to the use and function of things that gives his observations such colour and immediacy. His words do not deny the beauty of things: the glory and splendour, say, of a sunrise on the Mississippi River. But neither do they deny that things are there for a purpose. On the contrary, they acknowledge that each particular detail of a scene or moment has a reason for being there, deserves and even demands recording; and they derive their grace and force from that acknowledgement. The language Huck is given, in short, is at once exact and evocative, pragmatic and poetic: it reveals things as they are, in all their miraculous particularity. And Huck himself, the speaker of that language, comes across as a profoundly realistic and romantic figure: a pragmatist and a dreamer, a simple figure and a noble man – a perfect gentle knight, who seems honourable, even chivalric, precisely because he sticks closely to the facts.

Which is not to say that even this book is perfect. As many commentators have observed, the last few chapters do represent a decline – or, to use Hemingway's more dismissive phrase, 'just cheating' – in the sense that Huck is pushed to one side of the action, and Tom Sawyer is permitted to take over and reduce the issue of Jim's slavery to the level of farce. For all Huck's occasional protests at Tom's behaviour, or his famous final declaration of independence, the comedy loses its edge, the moral problems are minimized, and the familiar divisions in Twain's writing begin to reappear. There are many possible reasons for this, but one likely one is that Twain was perhaps beginning to have doubts about the effectiveness and viability of his hero. Certainly, in his next book, *A Connecticut Yankee in King Arthur's Court* (1889), set mainly in Arthurian England, Twain turned to a vernacular hero, Hank Morgan, with a more programmatic, reforming dimension. Hank, 'a Yankee of Yankees', is transported back to the world of King Arthur, and is determined to transform it according to his model of progress and industry. He fails, and, in describing his failure, Twain equally fails to achieve a reconciliation, let alone a synthesis, of his romantic and realistic impulses. *The Tragedy of Pudd'nhead Wilson* (1894) is even darker, the comedy even more biting and desperate. This is partly because Wilson himself – although not the narrator, the presiding genius of the book – is given to caustic comments such as the one supplied as an epigraph to the Conclusion: 'It was wonderful to find America, but it would have been even more wonderful to miss it.' But it is also because the closest thing the story has to an authentic rebel, the slave Roxana, is comprehensively defeated. In any event, she does not tell her own story. Her voice is muted, partly because she is trapped within a narrative that is characterized by closure and ironic pessimism, and partly because, when she is allowed to talk, she never begins to articulate rebellion or resist the racism of her owners. 'Training is everything,' Wilson tells us; and Roxana, together with all the other characters, seems hopelessly trapped in training, the prisonhouse of determinism.

The deepening pessimism of Twain, in his later years, is evident from the story 'The Man That Corrupted Hadleyburg' (1900) and the longer narrative, *The Mysterious Stranger*, which was published posthumously after editorial work by other hands in 1916. 'I believe I can make it tell what I think of Man,' he wrote of the latter work, '. . . and what a shabby poor ridiculous thing he is, and how mistaken he is in his estimate of . . . his place among the animals.' Twain had begun with a gift for comedy and the belief that it could be used to expose the gap between reality and illusion. He ended with the comedy turned bitter, to dark satire and polemic, and with the belief that illusion is all we have, a world of surface and gesture. He had begun with the conviction that there were two forces at war in human nature, feeling and training, and that it was possible to rediscover feeling and restore originality, spontaneity. He ended convinced quite otherwise, that training was all people had, that they could only obey environmental and social conditioning. He had begun with a belief in human nature, its essential innocence, and the rider, the related belief that this innocence could be resurrected in America – that, in short, the American Adam was possible. He ended by calling the human race 'damned' for its irreversible servility to systems and surface, and by regarding the American project as a futile, absurd one: his spokesperson was no longer an American Adam, like Huck, but a cynical outsider who observes humankind with a mixture of desperate laughter and contempt – like Pudd'nhead Wilson or Satan in *The Mysterious Stranger*. On a personal level, Twain continued to enjoy what he termed the 'grace, peace, and benediction' of his family and circle of friends until the end of his life. On the social, he remained an ardent reformer and a brilliantly witty, judiciously savage critic of authority and champion of the underdog: attacking European imperialism in Africa, for instance, and American imperialism in the Spanish–American War. But his sense, most powerfully expressed in *Huckleberry Finn*, that the real could be infused with romance, that it was possible to be true to the facts and to the ideal potentialities of things: that had gone. And his eventual view of life could perhaps be summed up by one other remark culled from what Twain called *Pudd'nhead Wilson's Calendar*: 'We owe Adam a great debt. He first brought death into the world.'

Twain has been called a regionalist, because he was born and raised in the South, lived for a while in the West, and wrote of both. This reflects a general tendency to associate the term 'realist' with those writing in or about the centres of power and the term 'regionalist' with those writing in or about the supposed periphery. Another term commonly used to describe writing of the period like Twain's, local colour, reflects the same tendency. Nevertheless, it is a fact that, during the later nineteenth century, many American writers and readers became interested in the local or regional folkways of the South, West and rural New England, and often, although not always, about earlier times before the war. One reason for this was probably a reaction to the increasing standardization of life, as more and more of American society approximated to an urban and industrial norm and a uniform culture. Another reason for the related interest in older times was a particular instance of a general American tendency to associate the past with innocence, a cultural equivalent of Eden. The nostalgic utopianism that characterizes so many American cultural forms has impelled numerous writers and artists to look back in longing, and to see some moment in the national history as the time the nation crossed the threshold from innocence to experience. In the first half of the nineteenth century, that moment as typified by, say, Washington Irving's 'Rip Van Winkle' was the Revolution; in the twentieth century, it would be the First World War, then later the Vietnam War. In the later half of the nineteenth century, unsurprisingly, the tendency was to associate this version of the Fall with the Civil War. That tendency was memorably illustrated by Henry James, when, looking back at the time of Hawthorne and after, he declared in 1879: 'the Civil War marks an era in the history of the American mind. It introduced into the national consciousness a certain sense . . . of the world being a more complicated place than it had hitherto seemed, the future more treacherous, success more difficult.' 'The good American, in days to come', James added, 'will be a more critical person than his complacent and confident grandfather. He has eaten of the tree of knowledge.'

Among those writers who have been associated with the regionalist impulse was one who worked as a journalist and editor with Mark Twain in the West, Francis Bret Harte (1836–1902). Harte was born in Albany, New York, but moved to California when he was eighteen, where he worked as a prospector, a teacher and a Wells Fargo agent before becoming a journalist. He became editor of *The Californian* and then, in 1868, of the *Overland Monthly*, in which he published the poems and stories that made him famous. Many of the stories were collected in *The Luck of Roaring Camp and Other Stories* (1870). The two most famous, the title story and 'The Outcasts of Poker Flat,' are typical, in that they illustrate Harte's tendency to find innocence flowering in inhospitable frontier circumstances, and miners, gamblers and whores revealing they have hearts of gold. Thomas Luck, in 'The Luck of Roaring Camp', for instance, is an orphan, the son of a prostitute in a California gold-mining settlement who dies after giving birth to him. The tough, blaspheming miners of the settlement, called Roaring Camp, then adopt him; and their spirits are miraculously transformed, as a result, to a touching if awkward sympathy. Next year, when the river rises, Roaring Camp is submerged and one of the miners is drowned with 'The Luck', as he is called, in his arms. Like even the best of Harte's tales, the story flirts dangerously with sentimentality, but it is saved by the wit of the narration and the author's careful attention to detail, the local colour and the coarse texture of life on the frontier. In the same year as his most famous collection of tales appeared, Harte also published his most famous poem, 'Plain Language from Truthful James'. Set, like so much of his work, in a Western mining camp, it tells the story of a wily 'heathen Chinee', who claims not to understand a card game then is revealed as an astute cheat. 'For ways that are dark, / And for tricks that are vain, /' the narrator of the poem, 'truthful James', concludes, 'The heathen Chinee is peculiar, – / Which the same I am free to maintain.' Inadvertently, the poem reveals the racial tensions at work in the supposed freedom of the frontier West and, in particular, the fear and distrust of Chinese immigrants, which was to lead not long after to their virtual exclusion.

'Plain Language from Truthful James' is also a mix of the vernacular and the more formal and rhetorical. What the narrator calls his 'plain' language is not always that; and it is, in any event, set, frozen almost in an elaborate stanzaic pattern, with regular rhymes and repetitive rhythms. In this, it was not untypical of poems of the time about the West. Bayard Taylor (1825–78), for example, wrote poems like 'The Bison Track' (1875) and 'On Leaving California' (1875) that show a similar obedience to poetic traditions, and an equally close observation of the rhetorical roles, while celebrating frontier freedom. And Taylor's poems, in turn, are typical to the extent that they endorse the contemporary belief in Manifest Destiny – the divinely ordained, historically necessary mission of white Americans to settle and civilize the West. 'Thy human children shall restore the grace / Gone with thy fallen pines, /' the poet declares in 'On Leaving California', addressing the 'fair young land' of the frontier directly; 'The wild, barbaric beauty of thy face /

Shall round to classic lines.' 'Hesper, as he trims his silver beam, /' he concludes, 'No happier land shall see, / And Earth shall find her old Arcadian dream / Restored again in thee!' A similar triumphalism, couched in formal rhetoric and carefully moulded verse, is to be found in the work of Joaquin Miller (1841?–1913), who became known during his lifetime as 'the Byron of Oregon'. 'What strength! what strife! what rude unrest! / What shocks! what half-shaped armies met! /' Miller announces in 'Westward Ho!' (1897), a poem that shouts aloud its allegiance to the westward movement in its title as well as every one of its lines; 'A mighty nation moving west, / With all its steely sinews set / Against the living forests.' For Miller, as for Harte and Taylor, there could be no doubts as to the justice as well as the necessity of white settlement. The movement west was, as they saw it, a natural consequence of human evolution and national history, underwritten by both the idea of the survival of the fittest and the example of earlier explorers and settlers. As Miller put it, in his poem about the 'brave Admiral', 'Columbus' (1897): 'He gained a world, he gave that world / Its grandest lesson: "On! Sail on!"'

In the more settled farming regions of the Midwest, the writing tone, in both poetry and prose, tended to be quieter, the narrative vision more narrowly focused on the pieties of family and community. James Whitcomb Riley (1849–1916), for instance, achieved fame and wealth by writing a series of poems in the 'Hoosier' dialect of Indiana. The poems are light and sentimental, concentrating on picturesque figures of pathos, like 'Little Orphan Annie' (1883), or on the simple satisfactions of hearth and home, and the rituals of farming life, as in his most famous piece, 'When the Frost is on the Punkin' (1883). 'When the frost is on the punkin and the fodder's in the shock, / And you hear the kyouck and gubble of the struttin' turkey-cock, /' the latter poem begins, 'O it's then's the times a feller is a-feelin' at his best, / With the risin' sun to greet him from a night of peaceful rest.' Like Riley, Edward Eggleston (1837–1902) was born in Indiana and achieved fame by writing about the simplicity and community of Midwestern life and using the local dialect. He chose fiction as his way of recording and celebrating his small corner of America. But, as his most famous book, *The Hoosier Schoolmaster* (1871), shows, he was similarly inclined to domesticate and sentimentalize. Eggleston took his cue, he said, from the French critic Hippolyte Taine, who insisted, 'the artist of originality will work courageously with the materials he finds in his own environment'. And *The Hoosier Schoolmaster*, based on the experiences of his schoolteacher brother, contains a grain of tough realism in its depiction of the coarseness and bigotry of a group of Indiana farmers, who persecute the hero when a false accusation of theft is made against him. But the tone of the narrative tends towards the pious much of the time, and both the hero and the woman he eventually marries are depicted as improbably ideal and impeccable.

African American and Native American voices

The popularity of poetry and prose that observed regionalist conventions, or what were seen as such at this time, such as the use of dialect, can be measured by the fact that a number of African American and Native American writers associated with lands to the West attempted to write in this mode. The most notable of these were the African American poet Paul Lawrence Dunbar (1872–1906), who was born in Ohio, and the Native American poet, journalist and humorist Alexander Lawrence Posey (1873–1908), who was born in Indian Territory and raised among the Creeks. Dunbar wrote conventional verse, following the standard poetic conventions of the time, but the work that gained him national fame was his poetry written in a stereotypical Negro dialect. *Lyrics from Lowly Life* (1896), the book that brought him to the attention of the reading public, contains pieces like 'A Corn-Song', which offers a dreamily elegiac portrait of life on the old plantation, and 'When De Co'n Pone's Hot', which reveals even in its title just how much Dunbar owed to other dialect poets like Riley. 'Dey is times in life when Nature / Seems to slip a cog an' go, /' 'When De Co'n Pone's Hot' begins, 'Jes' a-rattlin' down creation, / Lak an' ocean's overflow.' Like the Riley poem it clearly alludes to and imitates, it then goes on to rehearse and celebrate the simple pleasures of life down on the family farm. The poetry of Dunbar was popular precisely because, in it, the poet adopted a mask shaped by white culture. In more conventional, formal pieces, as in the poem to 'Harriet Beecher Stowe' (1899), the mask simply involves him in adopting the genteel idiom of that culture. In 'When De Co'n Pone's Hot', the situation is a little more complicated, but the effect is the same. A close imitation of a white dialect poem, it uses a kind of dialect that underwrites a stereotype of black people created by whites; and it belongs to a tradition of minstrel literature devised by white writers. An additional, piquant irony is that Dunbar never knew the Deep South that was the setting for most of his poems. So, when he writes about 'the master' sitting on his 'wide veranda white', his 'dreamy thoughts drowned / In the softly flowing sound' of the black field hands returning from the cornfields, he is writing about something that for him is, in every sense, the result of a white mediation. This is the poet assuming a regionalist mask with a vengeance.

Alexander Posey also wrote poetry that closely observed the poetic conventions of the time. Within the limits of those conventions, however, he was able to pursue themes that reflected his sense of his Native American heritage. His 'Ode to Sequoya' (1899), for example, is an elaborately formal, highly rhetorical poem, with no sense of traditions other than those of white culture in its manner of expression. But what the poem commemorates and celebrates is the inventor of the Cherokee syllabary: 'the people's language', as the poet puts it, which, even when 'the last memorial' of the tribe has been 'swept away' from 'this great continent,' ensures there will remain a record of its 'ancient lore'. Believing that English was an inadequate, inappropriate language for poetry by a Native American, Posey gradually moved away from conventional verse. He first tried to write poems that caught the rhythms and reflected the idioms of his native Creek. 'Hotgun on the Death of Yadeka Harjo' (1908) is an example. In it, the narrator Hotgun, whom Posey elsewhere described as 'a philosopher, carpenter, blacksmith, fiddler, clock-maker, worker in metals and a maker of medicines', recalls the passing away of a famous figure in the Creek Nation, whom he personally knew. The trouble is, it sounds little different from white dialect verse. '"Well so," Hotgun, he say, / "My ol'-time frien', Yadeka Harjo, he / Was died the other day."' Perhaps for this reason, Posey gradually devoted less and less time to poetry. Turning to journalism, he established the first daily newspaper published by a Native American. And, as a substitute for editorials, he began writing the Fus Fixico letters. In these, using the persona of Fus Fixico (Heartless Bird), a full-blooded Creek, Posey commented on local life, customs and politics: satirizing those who profited from the policy of individual land allotment, say, or Native American complicity in the greed and materialism of the times. 'The Injin he sell land and sell land, and the white man he give whiskey and give whiskey and put his arm around the Injin's neck,' we are told in letter number 44 (1904). This is dialect writing with a political purpose, satire that mixes humour with anger: it comes as no surprise to learn that Posey liked the work of Riley and Dunbar, but his favourite poet was Robert Burns. It is also dialect writing that tries, more earnestly and successfully than Posey does in his poetry, to catch the timbre and rhythms of the language he heard spoken among his fellow tribesmen.

Regionalism in New England

'It is difficult to report the great events of New England; expression is so slight, and those few words which escape us in moments of deep feeling look but meagre on the printed page.' The words are those of Sarah Orne Jewett (1849–1909), from the book that secured her place in American literature, *The Country of the Pointed Firs* (1896). As it happens, she made her subject not the 'great events' of her native region but little nameless acts of community, memory or love. But she always tried to capture the speech and silence of New England, the language in which, she said, 'there is some faint survival . . . of the sound of English speech of Chaucer's time', and the avoidance of any 'vain show of conversation' between people habituated to quiet and solitude – who, perhaps, 'spoke very little because they so perfectly understood each other'. Jewett always, too, attempted to mine the deep feelings laconically expressed in this speech and surreptitiously conveyed in this silence. 'Such is the hidden fire of enthusiasm in true New England nature', the reader is told in *The Country of the Pointed Firs*, 'that, once given an outlet, it shines forth with almost volcanic light and heat.' One of the many achievements of her fiction, in fact, is the way Jewett subtly manoeuvres her way between what another, later New Englander, Robert Frost, was to term the fire and ice of the New England soul. This she does, not least, through her adept use of metaphoric and dramatic contrast. The remote farms and fishing towns she writes of are set between the vastnesses of the sea and the woods, 'the unconquerable, immediate forces of Nature'. That is part of the spirit of their inhabitants: when one of the characters speaks, for instance, we are told that it is 'as if one of the gray firs had spoken'. But so is a 'simple kindness that is the soul of chivalry', a domestic affection and a neighbourliness that transforms a 'low-storied and broad-roofed' house, the site of a local reunion, into the likeness of 'a motherly brown hen' gathering together 'the flock that came straying towards it from every direction'. And so, too, is 'love in its simplicity', caught in the voiceless gestures of her New England rural folk: 'so moving', as we learn in *The Country of the Pointed Firs*, 'so tender, so free from their usual fetters of self-consciousness'.

Jewett's subject and setting was also, for most of her life, her home. She was born and raised in Maine, near York, a place that supplied the model for Deephaven, the harbour town of her early stories. Travelling with her father, a doctor, she observed the isolation and decay of the dwindling farms and depopulated towns of the locality. Reading the New England stories of Harriet Beecher Stowe, she began to discover her vocation. Her first stories appeared in the *Atlantic Monthly*; and then a collection, *Deephaven* (1877), established her reputation. This was followed by two novels, and further collections of stories, including *A White Heron* (1886), two books for children, a historical romance and a collection of poems. She formed several important and close friendships with other women: among them Annie Fields (1834–1915), the wife of James T. Fields (1817–81), the publisher and editor of the *Atlantic Monthly*. And she encouraged the young Willa Cather to write as she did, about her own remote homeplace. She travelled occasionally, to Boston in particular to visit Annie Fields, but she always returned to her home territory in Maine. And all her best work focuses on that territory, its life, language and landscape. This is local colour writing, to an extent, but it is also writing that discovers the elemental in the local. *The Country of the Pointed Firs*, for example, uses a device common in stories normally described as regionalist or belonging to the local colour school: the visitor from the city, who is gradually educated in the ways and habits of a remote community – and who encourages the reader to accompany her, to share in this sentimental education. What the unnamed female visitor and narrator of Jewett's book learns, though, is not just the peculiar customs of a particular place. She learns too, and so do we, of the deep feelings beneath the distances, the placid surfaces of communal life. She learns about the problems of women and of ageing – for this is predominantly a community of old people – and about love in a cold climate. Above all, she learns about her and our kinship with these initially strange, distant people, and the further lesson they can offer her, and us, in essential humanity. 'I saw these simple natures clear,' the narrator declares at the end of the story: 'their counterparts are in every village in the world, thank heaven, and the gift to one's life is only in its discernment.'

For the narrator, the growth in understanding is also a 'growth in true friend-ship'. Arriving in the small harbour town of Dunnett Landing, she is gradually included in the lives of the townspeople; in particular, she forms a close bond with Mrs Almira Todd, her landlady, a 'herb-gatherer, and rustic philosopher', Almira's brother William and their mother Mrs Blackett. Her sojourn in Dunnett Landing involves, among other things, a process of healing for her. Long distracted by 'the hurry of life in a large town', she begins to rediscover simplicity, security, coher-ence, to feel 'solid and definite again, instead of a poor, incoherent being'. 'Life was resumed', she explains, 'and anxious living blew away as if it had not been.' She owes this restoration of self and spirit, this growth of knowledge and affection, to many people in Dunnett Landing. There is a woman called the 'Queen's twin', because she was born at the same time as Queen Victoria, who teaches the narrator about true nobility, the grace of natural aristocracy. There is a local woman she hears about called Joanna the hermit, who reveals to her the poles of solitude and companionship between which we all make our lives. There is Esther, the woman whom William Todd loves and eventually marries, who reminds the narrator of how much heroism, passion and glory can be found behind the simplest, quietest, least immediately striking exterior. As she walks with her beloved William, the narrator tells us, Esther 'wore the simple look of sainthood and unfeigned devotion'; 'she might have been Jeanne d'Arc returned to her sheep, touched with age and gray with the ashes of a great remembrance'. Above all, there is Almira Todd. Slowly, the narrator learns about Almira's past: the man she loved but never married ('he's forgot our youthful feelin's, I expect,' Almira confides, 'but a woman's heart is different'), the man she liked and married, and who then died at sea before he could discover where her heart truly lay. She learns about what she calls Almira's 'peculiar wisdom': her habit, for instance, of explaining people by comparing them to natural objects or vice versa ('Grown trees act that way sometimes, same's folks'). What she learns, in sum, is to see and appreciate Almira as an 'absolute, archaic' embodiment of the life and landscape of Dunnett Landing. 'Life was very strong in her,' the narrator observes of Almira, 'as if some force of Nature were personified in this simple-hearted woman and gave her cousinship to the ancient deities . . . She was a great soul.' This sense that Almira Todd and her surrounds belong to each other is never as strong as at the conclusion of the story. Departing from Dunnett Landing at the end of summer, the narrator looks back from the boat carrying her away and sees Almira on the shore. 'Close at hand, Mrs. Todd seemed able and warm-hearted,' the narrator observes, 'but her distant figure looked mateless and appealing, with something self-possessed and mysterious.' As earthy and yet as strange, miraculous as her environment, Almira Todd then vanishes into it: the narrator loses sight of her, finally, as she 'disappeared . . . behind a dark clump of juniper and the pointed firs'.

The note of passing away, departure, on which *The Country of the Pointed Firs* finishes gathers up intimations of sadness and loss that quietly circulate through the entire narrative. This is a book about the ageing of life and communities. Almira Todd vanishes at the end of the story; and, equally, the life she rehearses, in all its homeliness and heroism, its stoicism and subdued passion, its simplicity and mystery – that is vanishing too. Even the narrator, for all her affection for Dunnett Landing, is returning as she must to the city. The subtle beauty of this narrative stems, in part, from Jewett's ability to achieve a balance between emotional contraries. A lively account of a great 'out-of-door feast', for example, is shadowed by the sense of the loneliness, the isolation that is the norm for those gathered there, from various parts of 'that after all thinly settled region'. Moments of union and communion, times of happiness, are caught as they pass, but the eventual stress is always on their passing. 'So we die before our own eyes,' the narrator comments on one such passing; 'so we see some chapters of our lives come to their natural end.' All we have left then, while we live, is the feeling of being 'rich with the treasures of a new remembrance'. What comments like this suggest is that, in her best tales, Jewett manages something quite remarkable: something that other great fiction commonly called regionalist, like that of her disciple Willa Cather, also sometimes manages. She weaves together the great theme of pastoral, that the best days are the first to flee, and a major theme in American thought and writing at the turn of the century, that an older, simpler form of society is dying. Her work is elegiac, singing of old, half-forgotten things, and also strenuously, perceptively social. Jewett, perhaps better than any writer of her time, catches a world as it passes, and then places it, sadly, sympathetically, within the long procession of history, the whole story of human passing. That mood, that inclination, is beautifully encapsulated in a moment when the narrator accompanies her new neighbours and friends along a wide path cutting through a field near the sea: to a place where they are going to have a party. 'We might have been a company of ancient Greeks going to celebrate a victory,' she observes, 'or to worship the god of harvests in the grove above.' 'It was strangely moving to see this and make a part of it,' she goes on:

> The sky, the sea, have watched poor humanity at its rites for so long; we were no more a New England family celebrating its own existence and simple progress; we carried the tokens and inheritance of all such households from which this had descended, and were only the latest of our line.

Another woman writer who devoted herself, at least in the best of her work, to her New England homeplace was Mary Wilkins Freeman (1852–1930). Born in Massachusetts, she spent most of her life there until her marriage in 1902. She began by writing stories for children. During the course of a long career she wrote fourteen novels, three plays and three volumes of poetry, but her finest achievements were the stories she produced for her first two published collections, *A Humble Romance and Other Stories* (1887) and *A New England Nun and Other Stories* (1891). Set in the decaying rural communities of small New England villages and farms, these stories capture the spirit of the people through their dialect. That spirit is often dour: Freeman describes what she calls, in one of her stories, 'A Church Mouse' (1891), 'a hard-working and thrifty' but also 'narrow-minded' group of people whose 'Puritan consciences' often blight their lives. Freeman focuses in particular, as Jewett does, on the lives of women in these small communities. Exploring their interior lives and their relationships, she shows them struggling to assert themselves, and acquire some small portion of what they want, in a community dominated by male power – or, to be more accurate, grumbling male indifference. 'Men is different,' comments one woman in 'Old Woman Magoon' (1909). 'You ain't found out yet we're women-folks. You ain't seen enough of men-folks yet to,' a woman tells her daughter in 'The Revolt of "Mother"' (1891). 'One of these days you'll find out, an' then you'll know we only know what men-folks think we do, so far as any of it goes,' she adds with caustic irony; 'an' how we'd ought to reckon men-folks in with Providence, an' not complain of what they do any more than we do of the weather.' So, in 'The Church Mouse', a homeless, abandoned woman uses her sharp tongue and decisive wit to seize a place for herself in the local meeting-house. The menfolk are first perplexed, then annoyed, but they fail to evict her; and when, eventually, the local women take her side, her new home is secure. In 'The Revolt of "Mother"', as the title suggests, a woman takes similarly decisive action after forty years of accepting that her husband rules the roost. 'I ain't complained,' she points out: but she does so when he begins to build a barn on the site supposedly reserved for their new house. Like the heroine of 'The Church Mouse', she then takes what she will clearly not be given. While her husband is away, she marches her family into the barn and sets up home there: with all the 'genius and audacity of bravery' of General Wolfe, the narrator comments, storming the Heights of Abraham. The husband reluctantly accepts a *fait accompli* when he returns. 'Why mother,' he declares, 'I hadn't no idea you was so set on't as all this comes to.' Whether this is genuine bewilderment or bluster Freeman leaves piquantly unclear. Either way, or perhaps both, it is, we already know, a consequence of male power: he has never had to know, or appear to know, what 'mother' wants, until now. What is clear, however, is that this 'mother' has the same quiet courage, even heroism, as some of Jewett's female characters. 'Nobility of character manifests itself at loop-holes when it is not provided with large doors,' the narrator tells us, in the course of this story. And it is clear that, in taking over the barn, she has acquired power along with territory: she has shown and got what she wants, and also shown and become what she might be.

Regionalism in the South

The writing described as regionalist or local colour after the Civil War was, very often, committed to cultural restitution and recovery, the celebration of a vanishing social order or the commemoration of one that had already vanished. So it is not really surprising that much of this writing came from and concerned the South. Those loyal to the feudal image of slave society could now blame the war for the fact that reality hardly coincided with myth. Those who were more critical were supplied with a perfect subject: the clash between new and old habits of behaviour and belief as the Southern states were assimilated back into the nation. Southerners were drawn to such writing for a whole range of reasons, varying from nostalgic allegiance to the good old days to a more sceptical interest in the legends that had helped justify oppression and engineer civil conflict – and that still held imaginative power and distributed social privilege across the region. So were those from outside the South: not least because they were intrigued by the society they had helped defeat, one that even more than any other prewar social order was now, for good or ill, irretrievably lost. For many writers and readers, this meant that in effect the myth of the feudal South was modulating into the myth of the Lost Cause. The South Carolina poet Henry Timrod (1828–67), for instance, is mainly known for poems that honour the memory of the Confederate dead: those who, as he put it in one of his poems, 'The Unknown Dead' (1872), were 'true martyrs of the fight / Which strikes for freedom and for right'. A Confederate volunteer himself, who was to see his house destroyed by the troops of General Sherman, Timrod chose to see the Civil War, as many Southerners did, as a fight for white Southern 'freedom' and independence rather than as a fight to keep black Southerners in slavery. That made it easier not only to celebrate the heroism of Confederate troops but to revere the cause for which they had fought. 'Sleep sweetly in your humble graves, / Sleep, martyrs of a fallen cause', Timrod declared in his most famous poem, 'Ode: Sung on the Occasion of Decorating the Graves of the Confederate Dead, at Magnolia Cemetery, Charleston, S. C., 1867' (1872). 'Stoop, angels, hither from the skies! /' he concluded, 'There is no holier spot of ground / Than where defeated valor lies, / By mourning beauty crowned!'

A more complex and subtler response to the defeat of the South is to be found in the work of another Southern poet, Sidney Lanier (1842–81), who was born in Georgia. After writing his only novel, *Tiger-Lilies* (1867), Lanier turned to verse, much of which was published only after his death. The verse varies widely in rhythm and movement, reflecting Lanier's interest in prosody: in 1880, he published an influential work on *The Science of English Verse*. It varies just as widely in terms of genre and tone. There are, for example, accomplished polemical, satirical and dialect pieces, such as 'Thar's more in the Man Than Thar is in the Land' (1877) and 'Jones's Private Argument' (1877). There are also major pieces that follow the tradition of, say, 'Tintern Abbey' by William Wordsworth, in combining landscape portraiture with reflection and meditation: like 'Corn' (1877) and 'The Marshes of Glynn' (1877). What links them, above all, is Lanier's belief in the redemptive power of the land: the conviction that the salvation of his region, and indeed his nation, lay in a return to the pieties of hearth and home, the self-reliant smallhold-ing. 'The New South', Lanier wrote in an essay, 'means small farming.' 'The only thing to do', declares a character called Jones, in 'Jones's Private Argument', 'Is, eat no meat that's boughten: / *But tear up every I.O.U. / And plant all corn and swear for true / To quit a-raisin' cotton!*' Lanier was critical of both the dependence on one crop, cotton, that he felt had destroyed the Old South and still weakened the New, and the growth of a more complex, industrial society dependent on trade and capital. 'Trade, Trade, Trade,' Lanier wrote to a friend, 'pah, are we not all sick! A man cannot walk down a green valley of woods, in these days, without unawares getting his mouth and nose and eyes covered with some web or other that Trade has stretched across, to catch some grain or other.' True to this convic-tion, in a poem like 'The Marshes of Glynn', he develops a contrast between the blessings of the rural life and the 'terror and shrinking and dreary unbearable pain' of other forms of existence. Similarly, in 'Corn', he moves from a richly atmospheric description of nature in all its primitive abundance, through a celebration of the culture of the independent farm and 'the happy lot' of 'the home-fond heart', to a critical assault on commercial farming and commerce in general. For Lanier, the choice for the South, and for America, was simple. On the one hand, as he put it in 'Corn', was the 'mild content' of being a 'steadfast dweller on the same spot', the pleasant mediocrity of a family supporting itself on its own land. On the other was a culture governed by the instabilities of exchange: where 'flimsy homes, built on the shifting sand / Of trade, for ever rise and fall / With alternation whimsical'. Despite all the evidence to the contrary, he still believed that the choice had not been made, for his nation as well as his region: and he managed to convince himself that, even now, 'antique sinew' and 'modern art', old aptitudes and new tools, could be combined to recapture the Jeffersonian dream.

Lanier was unusual among those writers concerned with the fate of the South in that he did anticipate a redemptive future. Timrod was, in this instance, more typical in that he dwelled, with an appropriate sense of pathos, on the past and loss. Writers such as Joel Chandler Harris (1848–1908), James Lane Allen (1849–1925) and Thomas Nelson Page (1853–1922) drew a romantic portrait of the antebellum South that presented it as a gracious, feudal civilization, peopled by stereotypes of white male nobility and white female decorum and beauty, humble black retainers notable for their simplicity and devotion to their 'old massa and missis,' and field hands singing melodiously as they worked. There was an element of self-consciousness in all this. In the Preface to one of his novels, *Red Rock* (1898), for instance, Page declared that his story was set 'in the vague region partly in one of the old Southern states and partly in the yet vaguer land of Memory'. But the self-consciousness did not prevent a slide into the nostalgic and stereotypical. On the contrary, what these postwar tales of the prewar South are distinguished for is their formulaic quality and their allegiance to a dreamland of 'old courts and polished halls', verdant lawns and broad acres: where, as Page put it in another of his novels, *On Newfound River* (1891), 'an untitled manorial system' ensured that 'peace and plenty reigned over a smiling land'. Implicit in this elegiac portrait of the 'high times' and 'serene repose' of life in slave society was a critique of progress. Sometimes it was not just implied. In *Gabriel Tolliver* (1902) by Joel Chandler Harris, for example, the reader is pointedly told that 'what is called progress is nothing more nor less than the multiplication of the resources of those who, by means of dicker and barter, are trying all the time to overreach the public and their fellows in one way and another'. And, consistently, the stillness of the Old South is seen through the receding narrative frames of the memorialist, the elegist. 'Dem wuz laughin' times,' declares one of the most famous of these elegists, Harris's Uncle Remus in *Told by Uncle Remus: New Stories of the Old Plantation* (1905), 'an' it looks like dey ain't never comin' back.'

As the character of Uncle Remus indicates, these tales of life in the South entered into dialect through the use of African American characters and narrators. This opened up the chance, at least, of a more critical, interrogative approach to slave society and its postwar residues. Some of that chance was taken up by Harris. Harris, whose Uncle Remus stories drew on African American folk sources, knew only too well why the slaves, with little means of open resistance, had celebrated the success of weak but wily characters like Brer Rabbit over the stronger but slower Brer Fox, Brer Wolfe and Brer Bear. And in such stories as those in *Uncle Remus: His Songs and Sayings* (1880) and *Nights With Uncle Remus* (1883), he drew a contrast that had similar, and similarly hidden, social and ethnic implications. Brer Rabbit is the trickster, who succeeds by playing the part of simpleton, by assuming a deceptive candour and humility. Brer Fox and others are the tricked, whose flaw is precisely their belief in their mastery, their own superior power and wisdom. The best of these tales have a subversive energy that is further informed by the colloquial vigour of the character's speech and the call and response, repetitive narrative structure – which gives the reader the sense of *this* tale being embedded in a much larger, older storytelling tradition. But like Allen, Page and other Southern storytellers who devoted themselves to accounts of life down on the old plantation, Harris could not divorce himself from the romantic, nostalgic impulse. White Southerners of the privileged class remained resolutely noble, in his eyes. African Americans, during and after slavery, had the charm and the endearing craftiness of children: children who, like Brer Rabbit, needed some restraint, some imposed order if they were not to engineer chaos. The fundamental tone and rhythm of these tales were, in fact, registered in two character types particularly popular in these stories: black men or women so involved with old times, so loyal to their memory, that they refused to acknowledge their emancipation – and those who did and who felt themselves lost and anchorless, doomed to a 'shiftless', unprotected life as a result. 'Dem wuz good ole time marster – de bes' Sam ever see!' one such character declares in 'Marse Chan: A Tale of Old Virginia' (1889) by Thomas Nelson Page. He then goes on to celebrate the old, slave South in this way:

> Nigger didn' had nuthin't all to do – jes' had to ten' to de feedin' an' cleanin' de hosses an' doin' what de marster tell 'em to do, an' when dey wuz sick . . . de same doctor came to see 'em what 'ten de white folks . . . Dyer warn' no trouble nor nothin.

It is worth remembering that Page was equally popular outside the South and inside it: he had to be, given the virtual disappearance of the publishing industry in his own region after the Civil War. He, Allen and Harris were describing a lost world that many way beyond the boundaries of their own region found attractive.

Other areas of old Southern life also became the subject of similar narrative indulgence. Southwestern humour, for example, took a nostalgic turn among some writers. So, Richard Malcolm Johnston (1822–98) set his tales, gathered together in *Dukesborough Tales* (1871), in what he called 'the Grim and Rude, but Hearty Old Times in Georgia'. 'It is a grateful solace', he admitted, 'to recall persons whose simplicity has been much changed by subsequent Conditions, chiefly the Confederate War.' The growth of towns and factories, Johnston explained, had served to diminish 'rustic individualities'; changes in labour and employment had 'made life more difficult, and therefore, more earnest'; and his aim was to recover the habits of a simpler, more relaxed and rambunctious world. Other writers of the time found similar simplicity in the remoteness of the Southern mountains. In the later nineteenth century, the Southern Appalachians and the Ozarks were opened up by the mining and tourist industries; and, to many visitors from the lowlands, the Southern highlands offered the appealing vision of the romance of the past preserved in the reality of the present. The folk of the Southern mountains were, one commentator insisted, 'our contemporary ancestors', recalling the character and customs of an earlier America. For Mary Noailles Murfree (1850–1922), what appealed in particular were the breathtaking scenery and simple home surroundings of mountain life, the idiosyncratic, antique language of the mountaineers, and the homely customs and odd, illogical beliefs of mountain society. In eleven volumes of stories, beginning with *In the Tennessee Mountains* (1884), she emphasized the strangeness as well as the simplicity of her highland characters: 'awkward young mountaineers', romantic mountain heroines with eyes like 'limpid mountain streams', weary but defiant and stoical older people – and 'a hospitality that meets a stranger on the threshold of every hut, presses upon him, ungrudgingly, its best'. Murfree approached her fictional subjects with the tendencies of a romantic antiquarian or romantically inclined tourist. Another, immensely popular writer of the time who chose the same subject, John Fox Jr. (1862–1919), took an approach that, if anything, was even more attached to a sentimental vision of the highlands. This he then wedded to the sensational. In books like *A Cumberland Vendetta* (1896), *The Kentuckians* (1898) and *The Trail of the Lonesome Pine* (1908), Fox paid homage to what he saw as the ancient, unsullied character of the mountain blood line and lineage. For him, as he put it in *A Cumberland Vendetta*, the mountaineers were 'a race whose descent . . . was unmixed English; upon whose lips lingered words and forms of speech that Shakespeare had heard and used'. This character was then allowed to demonstrate its primitive nobility in formulaic narratives of violence and adventure: with beautiful mountain girls rescued from the hands of savage villains, and feuds waged with an antique sense of honour amidst the grim beauty of the mountains. For all the talk of the racial purity and antiquity of mountain people, however, neither Murfree nor Fox was ever quite willing to release them from the status of marginal curios, set in another world of literal space and metaphorical time. Heroic status is consistently accorded to lowland characters, or to mountain folk who are either educated into gentility or found to have noble, lowland ancestry – and so felt to deserve it. These stories consequently reveal one animating impulse of regionalism or local colour writing more clearly than most do: which was to visit, briefly and imaginatively, a lost or vanishing America. What was on offer in such writing was a world that was determinately other, definitely different from the society that emerged after the Civil War. And in the tales of Fox and Murfree, that other world was further cordoned off by being denied narrative centrality: the main story, like real life, lay elsewhere.

A more powerful sense of otherness, and the sometimes oppressive strangeness of older Southern cultures, is to be found in the work of two women writers associated with New Orleans, Grace King (1852–1932) and Kate Chopin (1851–1904). King led a curiously ambivalent life. A woman of the privileged class, she experienced poverty after the Civil War and was forced to live in a working-class neighbourhood of New Orleans. A devout defender of the South, she was drawn to feminists in the North and writers interested in imaginatively exploring female disadvantage and oppression: her first published work, *Monsieur Motte* (1888), for instance, shows the influence of *Villette* (1853) by Charlotte Brontë. A bilingual Protestant, she also wrote from the position of an outsider about the Roman Catholic Creoles of New Orleans, and a position that involved both identification with and critical unease about the complex racial and sexual codes she observed. Something of this mix of feelings is to be found in her story 'The Little Convent Girl' (1893), which also shows how often in the South issues of race, gender and identity become entwined. The tale is simple. A young girl travels down by riverboat to New Orleans to join her mother, after spending most of the first twelve years of her life with her father in Cincinnati and in a convent. On arrival in New Orleans, it turns out that her mother is 'colored'. One month later, when the riverboat returns to New Orleans, her mother takes the little convent girl on a 'visit of "How d'ye do"' to the captain. The little convent girl takes the opportunity to jump from the boat into the Mississippi, and disappears under the water. A summary of the story, however, hardly does justice to the sense of mystery, hidden depths, it engenders. There is an element of racism, certainly, running through it, in the account of the 'good-for-nothing lives' of the black roustabouts, with their 'singing of Jim Crow songs, and pacing of Jim Crow steps, and black skins glistening through torn shirts, and white teeth gleaming through red lips'. But there is a subtle understanding here of the dark history of the South, that makes knowledge of self contingent on knowledge of race – and transforms identity, and self-identification, so much for one young woman, when she discovers that she does not come from the privileged race entirely, that she feels life is no longer worth living. About halfway through this story, the riverboat pilot, who befriends the little convent girl, confides to her his theory that 'there was as great a river as the Mississippi flowing directly under it – an underself as a river'. At the end, we are told, the body of the drowned girl may well have been 'carried through to the underground river, to that vast, hidden, dark Mississippi that flows beneath the one we see; for her body was never seen again'. It is a perfect image for the dark, subterranean history of the South: the repressions of knowledge and feeling that contorted, corrupted and eventually undermined an entire society – and here drive one young girl into a sense of abjection and then death.

The fiction of Chopin explores the racial and sexual codes of late nineteenth-century Louisiana with even greater subtlety. Chopin moved to New Orleans following her marriage. After the death of her husband, in 1882, she moved back to St Louis with her six children. Seven years later, she began writing, and, within ten years after that, had published twenty poems, ninety-five short stories, two novels, one play and eight essays. Most of her stories are set in Louisiana and cover all its social classes: aristocratic Creoles, middle- and lower-class Acadians, 'Americans' like Chopin herself, mulattoes and blacks. Her first two collections, *Bayou Folk* (1894) and *A Night in Acadie* (1897), established her reputation as a writer of local colour. That label, however, conceals Chopin's interest, here and throughout her career, in sexual politics and, in particular, the politics of marriage. Her first two published stories, for instance, 'Wiser than a God' (1889) and 'A Point at Issue' (1889), concentrate on what would prove to be her dominating theme: the conflict between social demand and personal need, the social requirement that a woman should centre her life on her husband and a woman's necessary obedience to her own compulsions, the impulse to express and develop her individuality. 'Désirée's Baby' (1892) brings class and race into the equation. Désirée is of 'obscure origin', socially 'nameless'. She marries a man of the patrician class, with a name that is among 'the oldest and proudest in Louisiana', but the marriage is effectively at an end when Désirée gives birth to a child that is 'not white'. Désirée disappears, with her baby; and a bonfire is made of the cradle, and her letters, with the husband presiding. But his supercilious presumption that it is Désirée who has brought the strangeness and the social stigma of mixed blood into the line is shown to be false. It is his own mother, he eventually learns, who 'belongs to the race that is cursed with the brand of slavery'. The story plays with the theme, and in this case the false presumption, of the tragic mulatta in a more ironic, subversive fashion than 'The Little Convent Girl' does. The melodramatic twist, at the end, depends upon the reader sharing the snobbish belief that it is the 'good', old family that is 'pure', and having his prejudices then neatly subverted – along with those of the husband. As Chopin developed, so did this subversive streak. 'A Respectable Woman' (1894) slyly explores the attraction the married woman of the title feels for a friend of her husband. 'A Pair of Silk Stockings' (1896) describes in detail how a woman takes time out from the sterile routines of marriage and domesticity. Buying and putting on a pair of silk stockings, she embarks on a small adventure, a day of indulgence by herself. By the end of the day, and the story 'it was like a dream ended', the reader is told. But, as the woman is transported home, the desire, the longing for release expressed in both day and story, has not been extinguished: she is seized with 'a poignant wish, a powerful longing that the cable car would never stop anywhere, but go on and on with her forever'. Most daring of all, for its time, is 'The Storm' (1898), which uses the upheavals of a stormy day as an occasion and a metaphor for illicit sexual passion. A man and woman, married to others and from different social classes, enjoy an encounter described in unabashedly erotic terms. 'When he touched her breasts they gave themselves up in quivering ecstasy, inviting his lips,' the narrator reveals. 'Her mouth was a fountainhead of delight. And when he possessed her, they seemed to swoon together at the very borderland of life's mystery.' The lyric intensity, the use of wild scenery to depict and celebrate sensuality: these are hallmarks of Chopin's later writing. So is the defiance of the conventional moralism of the day. The lovers remain resolutely unpunished, with each of them returning to 'their intimate conjugal life'. 'So the storm passed,' the tale ends, 'and every one was happy.'

Not surprisingly, stories like 'The Storm' were not published during Chopin's lifetime. *The Awakening* (1899) was, but it provoked enormous criticism. It was banned from the library shelves in St Louis and, following a reprint in 1906, went out of print for over fifty years. It is not difficult to see why. Edna Pontellier, the central character, a wife and a mother of two small boys, awakens to passion and herself. What that awakening involves, eventually, is a suicide that is a triumph of the will and an assertion of her own needs and strength. 'I would give up the unessential; I would give my money, I would give my life for my children,' she tells her friend, Adèle Ratignolle; 'but I wouldn't give myself.' So, in order not to surrender herself, not to lose herself in a conventional marriage or a string of more or less meaningless affairs, she swims out into the sea with no intention of returning. Edna is awoken out of what she later calls the 'life-long, stupid dream' of her life during one summer at Grand Isle. Her husband, Léonce, to whom she has been married for six years, is neither a villain nor a brute, but merely an ordinary husband, a little selfish and insensitive and very conventional. Towards the beginning of the story, Chopin entertains the reader with some sly social comedy, as she reveals just how wedded to respectability Léonce is, to his own comforts and to his notion that Edna is effectively an extension of him. 'You are burnt beyond recognition,' he observes to Edna, after she has been swimming in the sea; and then, to underline his point, looks at her 'as one looks at a valuable piece of property which has suffered some damage'. There is affection between them, certainly, and the kind of reciprocity of understanding that often exists between married couples. But the understanding hinges on an acceptance of Edna's dependent, subsidiary status: easy enough for Léonce, of course, but something that Edna herself begins quietly to question, as she awakens to the 'voice of the sea' she so loves to bathe in and, consequently, to her own spiritual and sensual impulses. Edna loves the sea. For her, it is associated with other instruments of abandon, such as art and nature. For the novel, it is the vital, untamed element, the medium of liberation, the wilderness where one can be oneself. It is everything that is the opposite of social and familial obligation. Marriage, in a sense, and dependence on men, is the equivalent of the structural image of the clearing that underpins so many American texts: it is the cultural space where Edna is required to obey rules that oppress her as a woman and play a role that denies her as an independent human being. Swimming in the sea, 'a feeling of exultation overtook her', the reader is told, 'as if some power of significant import had been given her to control the working of her body and her soul'. And this feeling of power, of her senses and spirit coming alive and her assuming control over her material and moral being, comes to her again when she flirts with Robert Lebrun, the son of the owner of the resort where she and her family are staying.

There is no doubt that Edna falls in love with Robert. There is equally no doubt that, later, she has sexual relations, not with Robert, but with another man, Alcée Arobin, to whom she is attracted but does not love. This, however, is a story not about illicit passion, secret affairs and adultery but about how all these become a means by which Edna begins, as the narrator puts it, 'to realise her potential as a human being'. 'At a very early period,' we are told, Edna 'had apprehended instinctively the dual life – that outward existence which conforms, the inward life which questions.' The romantic involvement with Lebrun, and then the sexual liaison with Arobin, awaken that deeper, inner, questioning part of herself. She realizes for certain now that she could never be one of those 'mother-women' like

Adèle Ratignolle, who 'idolized their children, worshipped their husbands, and esteemed it a holy privilege to efface themselves as individuals and grow wings as ministering angels'. On the contrary, she recognizes, 'it was not a condition of life which fitted her, and she could see in it but an appalling and hopeless ennui'. More to the point, she now sees that she is not a woman who can worship or lose herself in any man, or any other human being; she is too much herself to ever dream of doing that. So when Lebrun finally admits to having had wild hopes that Léonce Pontellier might free her, Edna tells him, 'I am no longer one of Mr. Pontellier's possessions to dispose of or not. I give myself where I choose.' 'If he were to say, "Here Robert, take her and be happy; she is yours,"' she adds, 'I should laugh at you both.' Swimming, romance, erotic experience have awoken her, alerted her to her freedom. So have the simple experience of walking, ambling at will in the city and the more complex, subtler experience of painting – a vocation for which, she is told, she 'must possess the courageous soul'. Awoken, she cannot return to the old life, the days of quiet desperation she remembers and that now, once more, loom before her. And she gives back her life and her self to the sea that had aroused them in the first place, walking back out into the 'soft, close embrace' of the waves naked 'like some new-born creature, opening its eyes in a familiar world that it had never known'.

Throughout *The Awakening*, Chopin negotiates her way between social comedy and sensuous abandon, an attention to the pressure of reality that is commonly associated with the realists and naturalists and a sense of the miraculous potential of things that invites comparison with other great narratives of romance in poetry as well as prose. The subtle manoeuvres of marriage, domestic and sexual politics, the battlefield of the dinner table: all these are scrupulously, and wittily, recorded. And so, too, are the evanescent, ecstatic feelings of Edna Pontellier: as she wanders or has dreams of leaving, observes the flight of birds, listens to music or the voice of the sea, 'never ceasing, whispering, clamouring, murmuring, inviting the soul to wander for a spell in abysses of solitude; to lose itself in mazes of inward contemplation'. As the story draws to a close, and Edna commits herself to the ocean, it is, of course, the sense of the miraculous, the potential for freedom and adventure, that has the major stress. This is a death, certainly, but it is a death that is seen as a liberation and affirmation: an echo and anticipation of all those moments of lighting out or breaking away that supply an open ending, a sense of continuing possibility to so many other American texts. Immersing herself in the sea, Edna realizes now the full import of what she meant, when she said she would give up the unessential, her money and life, but not herself for her children. She recognizes, also, that, despite her love for Robert Lebrun, the day would have come eventually when 'the thought of him would melt out of her existence, leaving her alone'. Her momentary fear, as she looks 'into the distance' of sky and water, is overwhelmed by a deeper impulse that is simultaneously erotic and visionary, expressing the needs of her self both as a body and a spirit; and she expresses that impulse, and meets those needs, by striking out into the sea. Reading *The Awakening*, it is not hard to see why it provoked such hostility among contemporaries: it is, after all, a story of female liberation that grounds existence in the right, the need to be oneself. Its radical character is measured by the fact that Edna's eventual suicide is depicted not as a sacrifice, a surrender, but as a moment of self-affirmation. That character is also very American, though: since what the fate of Edna Pontellier ends by telling us is that the ultimate price of liberty – and a price worth paying – is death.

Like Chopin, George Washington Cable (1844–1925) devoted much of his fiction to his hometown of New Orleans. His earlier stories were published in periodicals between 1873 and 1879 and then gathered together in *Old Creole Days* (1879). Cable is not reluctant to portray the romance and glamour of Louisiana life in these tales: there are coquettish or courageous women, the proud or cunning men of old Spanish-French Creole society, and there are incidents of smuggling and adventure. But he is also careful to register, as accurately as he can, the eccentric characteristics of the Creole dialect. And he explores the shifting character and sinister depths of old Creole society in a way that makes clear his intention of examining the larger society of the South of his own time too. The conflicts between a harsh racial code and a history of miscegenation, between traditional customs and new laws and habits, between the pursuit of aristocratic ease and the economic imperatives of work: all these had relevance not only for the Creole characters Cable described, trying to cope with their new American masters after the Louisiana Purchase of 1803, but for all Southerners after the Civil War. And to explore these, and similar, issues, Cable deployed a range of techniques. 'It is not sight the story-teller needs,' he once wrote, 'but second sight . . . Not actual experience, not actual observation, but the haunted heart: that is what makes the true artist of every sort.' As it happens, Cable was very good at 'sight': seeing and hearing the detail, the minute particulars of everyday social exchange. But he was also extremely good at 'second sight': exploring the haunted margins of society, and exposing its weaknesses and secrets. This made him both a political novelist and a poetic one – or, rather, a writer in the great Southern tradition of using the romantic, the Gothic, even the surreal, to reveal the history, and the repressed story, of the region.

In one tale in *Old Creole Days*, for instance, 'Belles Demoiselles Plantation', Cable describes the efforts of one Colonel De Charleau to provide for his daughters by trading his beloved but heavily mortgaged property. Unfortunately, the property is not only saddled with debt but also situated on an eroding bank of the Mississippi. The bank eventually caves in, and the house then sinks into the river. 'Belles Demoiselles, the realm of maiden beauty, the home of merriment, the house of daring, all in the tremor and glow of pleasure, suddenly sank, with one short, wild wail of terror,' the reader is told, '– sank, sank, down, down, into the merciless, unfathomable flood of the Mississippi.' The vision of the splendid mansion disappearing into the water is a dreamlike echo of the closing moments of 'The Fall of the House of Usher'. But it has a serious political point: the disappearance, the gradual sinking away of Creole ascendancy and power. In another tale, 'Jean-ah Poquelin', a proud French Creole, a former smuggler and slave trader, becomes a recluse in his 'old colonial plantation-house half in ruin'. The house stands 'aloof from civilization', so does old Jean Marie Poquelin. Nevertheless, civilization encroaches in the form of a new road being built through the fetid marshland surrounding them. Cable subtly dramatizes the cultural conflicts of the time in which the tale is situated, as Poquelin struggles to come to terms with a new order and a strange new set of practices. This is 'the first decade of the present century', the narrator tells us; and the old Creole has to deal not only with newfangled notions of Progress and profit but with a 'Yankee' administration and the English language, now that his land is no longer on French territory but American. Poquelin takes his complaint about the incursion of the roadbuilders to the top. He visits the Governor, and the way he addresses him shows how Cable could use his mastery of dialect to expose social and cultural tension. 'I come to you. You is *le Gouverneur*,' Poquelin declares,

> I know not the new laws. I ham a Fr-r-rench-a-man! Fr-rench-a-man have something *aller au contraire* – he comes at his *Gouverneur*. I come at you. If me had not been brought from me king like *bossals* in the hold time, ze king gof-France would-a-show *Monsieur le Gouverneur* to take care his men to make strit in right places. *Mais*, I know; we billong to *Monsieur le Président*.

The speech reveals, in its mixture of languages, just how culturally conflicted Poquelin is, torn between old allegiances and a new set of practices. The old Creole is having to deal with a system the speech and assumptions of which he hardly understands – and for which, quite clearly, he has little sympathy. Much the same could be said of the South in and to which Cable wrote, during a period when the region was facing, and trying to resist, civil and political change. Both the speech and the story in which it is embedded have as much to do with the time in which they were written as with the time in which they are set. Or perhaps it would be more accurate to say that, for Cable, both times were part of one continuing, and often regrettable, history.

Characteristically of Cable, 'Jean-ah Poquelin' becomes darker and more macabre as the narrator turns to violence and the Gothic to reveal the 'haunted heart' of this fictional world. There is mob action against Poquelin. Poquelin dies suddenly, and a secret reason for his wanting to keep the world away is revealed. A ghost that the local community had claimed was haunting his property turns out to be his younger brother, bleached white by leprosy. The brother, accompanied by the one other person left on the estate, 'one old African mute' slave, then disappears 'in the depths of the swamp known as the Leper's Land', never to be seen again. It is difficult not to see the plight of the younger brother as a curse: he became a leper when the two brothers went on a slave-trading mission to Africa. Equally, it is difficult not to see the seclusion into which the two brothers move as, at least in part, a consequence of that curse. They are isolated from the world around them, and the possibility of change and growth, by a scourge and a secret that issue directly from their involvement in slavery. Like so many other characters in Southern fiction, their past is their present; and that past tends to cripple them, to separate them from ordinary humanity – and even from the processes of history. A similar sense of a separation that cripples and confounds is to be observed in Cable's portrait of the Creole families in his 1880 novel *The Grandissimes*. 'I meant to make *The Grandissimes* as truly a political novel as it has ever been called,' Cable declared. And here, again, he uses the medium of a romantic, at times even Gothic, tale to pursue the issues that intrigued him most: pride of caste and class, resistance to necessary change, racial oppression and violence. The plot is a convoluted one, but its central premise is not. *The Grandissimes* hinges on a family feud between two old, proud Creole families: a feud for which the narrator himself finds a romantic analogy in the strife between the Capulets and Montagues in *Romeo and Juliet*. In a move characteristic of fiction generally classed as local colour, the reader is introduced to the warring families, the Grandissimes and the De Grapions, both of Louisiana, by an outsider. Joseph Frowenfeld, a 'young Américain', comes to the city of New Orleans with his family. The rest of his family soon dies of 'the dreaded scourge', but he manages to survive. And he becomes acquainted with both Honoré de Grandissime, banker and head of his family, and the De Grapions, who nursed him during his illness. Slowly, he learns about the tangled history of the two clans, and especially the Grandissimes: he learns, for instance, that Honoré has a brother, 'Honoré Grandissime, free man of color', with the same father but a different mother. He watches and witnesses the habits and eccentricities of the Creoles: their 'preposterous, apathetic, fantastic, suicidal pride', their 'scorn of toil', their belief that 'English is not a language, sir; it is a jargon!' Cable uses his immense skill as a creator of dialect speech to introduce Frowenfeld, and the reader, to the rich plurality of cultures and traditions in old Louisiana. But he also measures the divisions of class and colour that separate the different communities, and, above all, the gap that separates the white race from the black – and, in one notable instance here, brother from brother.

'*The Grandissimes*', Cable was later to say, 'contained as great a protest against the times in which it was written as against the earlier times in which its scenes were set.' That is plain enough. Cable is writing about the Louisiana of old Creole days: the novel begins in 1803. He is also writing about the South of his own time. Families like the Grandissimes, the reader learns, have absented themselves from the 'Américain' system of which, notionally, they have just become a part. They are willing to kill others of their own, Creole kind. Most serious of all, they deny the humanity, the fundamental human rights of a race to which, in very many cases, they are tied in blood and kinship. And all in the name of pride: an absurd belief in caste, class and colour as the determinants of character. 'There is a slavery that no legislation can abolish – the slavery of caste,' Frowenfeld observes:

> That, like all the slaveries on earth, is a double bondage. And what a bondage it is which compels a community, in order to preserve its established tyrannies, to walk behind the rest of the world! What a bondage is that which incites a people to adopt a system of social and civil distinctions, possessing all the enormities and none of the advantages of those systems which Europe is learning to despise! This system,

moreover, is only kept at bay by a flourish of weapons. We have here what you may call an armed aristocracy.

Cable vigorously dissects a pride of caste that is, as he shows it, both destructive and self-destructive. He shows how the very communities and individuals that are severed, separated by this pride are intimately, inextricably bound together. He shows the subtle humiliations that are a consequence of such pride, and the unease and even guilt that sometimes trouble even the proudest. One Grandissime even admits that 'the shadow of the Ethiopian' falls across his family and his society. 'I am *ama-aze* at the length, the blackness of that shadow!' he declares. 'It is the *Némésis* . . . It blanches, my-de'-seh, ow whole civilization.' But Cable also exposes, in detail, the violence that is another consequence of caste pride. A mob of Creoles, enraged by a Yankee shopkeeper's liberal sentiments, attacks and wrecks his shop. An old African American woman is cut down from the tree on which she has nearly been lynched, allowed to run for her life if she can, and then shot and killed as she tries to flee. And a core story tells of an African, Bras-Coupé, 'a prince among his people', who escapes from slavery to the swamps: because, we are told, he would choose 'rather to be hunted like a wild beast among those awful labyrinths, than to be yoked and beaten like a tame one'.

The Grandissimes ends on the promise of peace between the feuding families, with the marriage of Honoré Grandissime to one of the De Grapions. There is even the hope of some broader, social and racial reconciliation, as Honoré has suggested that 'Honoré free man of color' should become a member of the Grandissime mercantile house. But the hope is a faint one. The novel also closes with 'Honoré free man of color' killing one of the haughtier white members of the Grandissime family, who has slighted him precisely because of his racial coloration. Typically of Cable, the reader is left with marriage and murder rather than marriage and music: a sense of conciliation and concord is scarred by the reminder of the deep divisions, the discords that continue to disturb this society. Cable undoubtedly felt an affection for Creole generosity, magnanimity, bravado and glamour; this was tempered, however, by his understanding of what he saw as the disastrous consequences of Creole pride. He was a sympathetic but unremitting critic of the Creole spirit and society; and he used his imaginative analysis of old Creole days to criticize the South of his own time, which he saw as its echo and extension. That criticism, levelled aslant in his fiction and more directly in *The Silent South* (1885), a treatise advocating racial reform, made him increasingly unpopular in his own region. He moved north to Massachusetts in 1885. There, he continued to write novels, like *John March, Southerner* (1894), that dealt with the collision between Northern and Southern morals and manners. Cable was not the first writer from the South to write of his region with a mixture of sentiment and seriousness. But his work resonates with themes and imagery that were to echo in Southern fiction of the twentieth century: brothers divided by the racial barrier, the shadow of slavery, images of the plague and the swamp rehearsing the evil that surrounds and infests an entire society. Cable was one of those writers in whose work the regionalist impulse acquired a sterner, more sceptical dimension. To that extent, he deserves a place with his fellow Southerners, Mark Twain and Kate Chopin; like them, he showed how romance and realism were not necessarily at odds: on the contrary, he could explore the 'dark heart' of his birthplace in and through the glamour of its surfaces.

A writer who knew more than most about the dark heart of racism, North and South, and who, like Cable and Chopin, began his career as a popular 'local colour' writer, was Charles W. Chesnutt (1858–1932). Chesnutt was born in Cleveland, Ohio, to which his parents had recently moved. They had left Fayetteville, North Carolina, to escape the repression experienced by free blacks in the South. After the Civil War, however, the family returned to Fayetteville, and it was there that Chesnutt was educated. Chesnutt first attracted attention as a writer with his story 'The Goophered Grapevine', which appeared in the *Atlantic Monthly* in 1887. This was followed by many other stories set in the South, and in 1899 two collections appeared: *The Conjure Woman and Other Conjure Tales* and *The Wife of His Youth and Other Stories of the Color Line*. At the heart of *The Conjure Woman* is a picture of plantation life in the Old South, presented through the comments and stories of an ex-slave and inhabitant of the region, Uncle Julius McAdoo. Julius's tales were 'naive and simple', Chesnutt was to write of them later. Their subject, he added, was 'alleged incidents of chattel slavery, as the old man had known it and as I had heard of it'; and they 'centered around the professional activities of old Aunt Peggy, the plantation conjure woman, and others of that ilk'. Chesnutt admitted that these stories were written 'primarily to amuse'. But, he added, they 'have each of them a moral, which, while not forced upon the reader, is none the less apparent to those who read thoughtfully'. For example, Chesnutt explained, in one of the tales, 'Mars Jeems's Nightmare', a cruel slavemaster is transformed into a slave for several weeks by the conjure woman so that he might have 'a dose of his own medicine'. The consequence is 'his reformation when he is restored to his normal life'.

'The object of my writings would be not so much the elevation of the colored people as the elevation of the whites,' Chesnutt wrote in 1880, '– for I consider the unjust spirit of caste . . . a barrier to the moral progress of the American people.' His way of doing this, he hoped, would be to 'lead people out' to 'the desired state of feeling' about black people 'while amusing them'. He could use the established literary genres and conventions to persuade white readers out of their prejudices 'imperceptibly, unconsciously, step by step'. So, the stories in *The Conjure Woman* may appear to belong to the traditions of plantation literature and dialect tales typified, on the one hand, by Thomas Nelson Page and, on the other, by Joel Chandler Harris. But they are subtly and significantly different. They introduce the lore of 'conjuration', African American hoodoo beliefs and practices, to a white reading public mostly ignorant of black culture. And they offer a new kind of black storytelling protagonist: Uncle Julius McAdoo shrewdly adapts his recollections of the past to secure his economic survival in the present, sometimes at the expense of his white employer. In effect, *The Conjure Woman* quietly tells the reader about black community and humanity: the cultural forms, the strategies African Americans use to maintain their sense of identity and resist white domination. Conjure figures in these tales as a way to control property and settle disputes; above all, though, it figures as a resource, a form of power available to the powerless in oppressive, intolerable situations. So does storytelling. Julius defends himself against the superior power of the whites – whose surplus capital enables them to buy the McAdoo plantation on which he lives – with the weapon he has in evidently endless supply: the numerous tales he knows about the land that his white masters perceive merely as abstract property.

The story that first brought Chesnutt to public attention, 'The Goophered Grapevine', is exemplary in this respect. The narrator is 'John', who tells us that he decided to buy an old plantation near 'a quaint old town' called Patesville, North Carolina, partly to continue his business of 'grape-culture' but mainly because 'a warmer and more equable climate' than the one available in his native Ohio was recommended for his invalid wife. The tale then revolves around the various anecdotes Uncle Julius McAdoo tells them about this, the McAdoo plantation: all of which focus on evidence to the effect that the plantation, and its grapevines, are 'goophered' or bewitched. 'I wouldn't 'vise you to buy dis yer ole vimyard, 'caze de goopher's on yit,' Julius tells John and his wife Annie, 'an dey aint no tellin' w'en it's gwine ter crap out.' John, however, does not heed the warning. He buys the plantation; and he subsequently discovers, he tells the reader in the conclusion to the tale, that Julius had occupied a cabin there for many years, 'and reaped a respectable revenue from the product of the neglected grapevines'. 'This, doubtless, accounted for his advice to me not to buy,' John infers: but he is sufficiently intrigued by Julius, and his evident quickness of wit, to make up to him 'for anything he lost by the sale of the vineyard' by employing him as a coachman. The whole narrative slyly subverts convention, by showing that the relationship between the races is one of conflict, not the cross-cultural harmony the plantation genre typically evokes. Everything about John identifies him with the white bourgeois ruling class of the years after the Civil War: his genteel speech and Latinate vocabulary, his wife confined to domesticity and refined invalidism, his Sundays spent attending 'the church of our choice' and browsing through the 'contents of a fairly good library'. Above all, there is his belief in enlightened business methods, and 'the opportunities open to Northern capital in the development of Southern industries'. For him, the McAdoo plantation is an investment, a commodity which, like all commodities, should be exploited for maximum profit. This puts him at total odds with a man like Uncle Julius. Uncle Julius instinctively knows this, which is why he tries to get rid of him. His lively, earthy vernacular, his dialect speech creates a dissonance, sets the black character immediately at odds with the white. And the distance between white man and black sounded in their differences of speech, is then elaborated as Julius reveals the true dimensions of himself and his culture in his stories. Julius has his own series of expertises: care of the body administered not by professional men but conjure women, care of the spirit involving not decorous observance of the Sabbath but charms, ghosts and the magical control of natural vitality. He has his own cultural traditions, based on the oral tales he remembers and performs. And he has his own relation to the land where he lives, based not on a system of abstract profit and exchange but on a lived attachment to it, a working with it for limited, immediate, practical gain. For John, places like the McAdoo plantation are part of a colonial economy, where, he confides, 'labor was cheap, and land could be bought for a mere song'. For Julius, they are home, a part of nature and a part of him; and, in his own comically desperate way, he tries to keep his home his. Of course, he fails. As Chesnutt discloses in story after story, real power lies with the dominant white class. But, in failing, he still shows his capacity for resistance: his willingness to assert, however circuitously, his own self and his rights. A tale like 'The Goophered Grapevine' subtly charts the domination of white over black but also the small advantages, the concessions blacks are able to negotiate within the framework of that domination. It shows that social control is never absolute, the oppressed are never simply and entirely the oppressed: they can, and do, declare their own humanity and their own culture.

'I think I have about used up the old Negro who serves as a mouthpiece, and I shall drop him in future stories, as well as much of the dialect,' Chesnutt wrote in 1889. In fact, the other collection of stories he published ten years later had, as its connecting link, not so much a character as a subject: the one indicated by the subtitle, *Other Stories of the Color Line*. Chesnutt was also to claim much later, in 1931, that most of his stories, apart from those in *The Conjure Woman*, 'dealt with the problems of people of mixed bloods'. And many of the tales in *The Wife of His Youth* do dwell on the plight of those who, precisely because of their origins and coloration, seemed to him to exist as a racial battleground: caught between two bitterly divided races and cultures, to neither of which they feel they entirely belong. Some of these tales have a clear didactic intent. One called 'Uncle Wellington's Wives' tells of a middle-aged mulatto who, persuaded by the propaganda about the good life in the North, leaves his wife of many years in the South and sets out to achieve the 'state of ideal equality and happiness' which he believes awaits the black man in Ohio. Forgetting all about the loyal black wife he has abandoned, he marries a white woman and acquires a wellpaying job. However, he soon loses both, and the lesson to be learned from this reversal is underlined for him by a black lawyer friend. 'You turned your back on your own people and married a white woman,' the lawyer tells him. 'You weren't content with being a slave to the white folks once, but you must try it again.' Not all the stories in this collection point the moral as emphatically as this, however, and not all are concerned with the problems of 'mixed blood'. One of the best, 'The Passing of Grandison', neatly reverses the old plantation stereotype of the faithful darky who would never dream of deserting his master, even if prompted by crafty abolitionists to do so. When required to, the Grandison of the title plays up to this stereotype. 'Deed, suh,' he tells his master. 'I wouldn' low none er dem cursed low-down abolitioners ter come nigh me, suh'; 'I sh'd jes' reckon I is better off, suh, dan dem low-down free niggers, suh!' Hearing this, his master finds 'his feudal heart thrilled at such appreciative homage'. However, given the opportunity to escape, Grandison not only seizes it for himself; he takes his wife, his mother and father, his sister and brothers, and his 'Uncle Ike' with him as well. The 'passing of Grandison' and his family shows his protestations of loyalty to have been simply a pose, a ruse. Like his creator, he uses a familiar, comforting generic image of the South as a mask, a means of realizing his own more subversive aims.

Following his two collections of stories, Chesnutt published three novels: *The House Behind the Cedars* (1900), *The Marrow of Tradition* (1901) and *The Colonel's Dream* (1906). *The House Behind the Cedars* is set in the same environs as virtually all his fiction: the South – the fictional town of Patesville, North Carolina, again – 'a few years after the Civil War'. It tells the story of two African Americans, a brother and sister, who pass for white. It is remarkable, because nothing is said about the racial identity of either brother or sister in the earlier chapters. In a novel of passing designed to create sympathy for those whose access to respectability is impeded only by what Chesnutt calls 'a social fiction', the validity of their claim is intimated by 'passing' the characters for white on the reader, for a while, as well. It is also remarkable because the two protagonists deliberately choose passing as a way of pursuing status and success. Passing is presented not as morally duplicitous but as virtually the only means left to an unjustly segregated people to enjoy, as Chesnutt puts it, 'the rights and duties of citizenship'. In *The Marrow of Tradition*, Chesnutt takes a broader canvas. Basing his story on a racial massacre that occurred in North Carolina in 1898, he dramatizes the caste structure of a small town. And he begins from the premise that, although 'the old order has passed away', its traditions remain 'deeply implanted in the consciousness of the two races': with the whites still 'masters, rulers' and the blacks still occupying 'a place the lowest in the social scale'. *The Colonel's Dream*, in turn, describes the attempt of one idealistic white man, blessed with economic power and moral influence, to resist racial intolerance and help a small North Carolina town mired in economic deprivation and social injustice. Chesnutt was, in effect, contributing an African American perspective to three prominent genres of late nineteenth-century social purpose fiction in these three works: the novel of miscegenation and passing, the romance of history and politics, and the 'muckraking' novel written to expose the plight of the deprived. But all three works failed to find a public, and Chesnutt largely gave up writing to devote himself to becoming what he later called 'a moderately successful professional man'. In 1931, in an essay titled 'Post-Bellum-Pre-Harlem', Chesnutt admitted that literary fashion had passed him by. However, he also expressed his pride that African American literature had come far since his own days of writing. For that, as he surely sensed, he had to take some credit. He was a major innovator, not only in the regionalist and local colour tradition, but in several forms. He showed his successors new ways of writing about black folk culture and the emerging black middle class. Above all, he showed them that it was possible to do what, at the outset, he aimed to do: to lead the reader, sometimes 'imperceptibly' and always 'step by step', to a full awareness of 'the unjust spirit of caste'.

The Development of Literary Realism and Naturalism

Capturing the commonplace

'The talent that is robust enough to front the every-day world and catch the charm of its work-worn, care-worn, brave kindly face, need not fear the encounter,' wrote William Dean Howells (1837–1920) in *Criticism and Fiction* (1891). 'The arts must become democratic,' he added, 'and then we shall have the expression of America in art.' For Howells, realism was the appropriate response to the drastic changes taking place in America in the late nineteenth century. And the writer who could achieve that realism could also be described as the creator of a truly democratic, essentially American art that captured the importance and the meaning of the commonplace. 'Commonplace?' declares a character in Howells's 1885 novel *The Rise of Silas Lapham*:

> The commonplace is just that light, impalpable, aerial essence, which they've never got into their confounded books yet. The novelist who could interpret the common feelings of commonplace people would have the answer to 'the riddle of the painful earth' on his tongue.

Howells's fiction was an attempt to define that impalpable essence: to resist the romantic and sentimental, the contrived and the melodramatic, and to register as accurately as possible the way Americans were living. It was, in a sense, a skirmish around the notion of the 'commonplace'. In disclosing the meanings of the apparently ordinary lives of apparently ordinary Americans, Howells was choosing to establish how far from 'commonplace' (using that word in its accepted sense) the 'commonplace' (as a measure and index of realism) actually was. There is a moment in *The Rise of Silas Lapham* when some of the characters take a trip on a boat. 'The greater part of the crowd on board', the narrator observes,

> looked as if they might not only be easily but safely known. There was little style and no distinction among them; they were people who were going down to the beach for the fun or relief of it, and were able to afford it. In face they were commonplace, with nothing but the American poetry of vivid purpose to light them up.

It is that 'vivid purpose' – the challenges it had to meet in a rapidly changing society, its social and moral consequences, the political consequences it engendered – that Howells tried to negotiate in his stories and novels. He was, in his lifelong allegiance to literary realism, pursuing what he saw as the only truly American poetry, to be found in the experience and expressions of average Americans.

Howells was eventually to occupy a position at the centre of literary life in America. As an indefatigable reviewer and critic, and editor in turn of the *Nation*, the *Atlantic Monthly*, *Harper's Monthly Magazine* and *Cosmopolitan*, he was able to affect the lives of three generations of American writers. At the beginning of his career, for example, in 1860, he reviewed *The Marble Faun* by Nathaniel Hawthorne; towards the end, in 1915, he reviewed the first two volumes of poetry by Robert Frost. He was acquainted personally with nearly every significant writer of the time, knowing some of them, like Mark Twain and Henry James, as friends. He advanced the careers of not only Twain and James but women writers like Sarah Orne Jewett, black writers like Charles W. Chesnutt, and ethnic writers like Abraham Cahan. His influence and contemporary eminence eventually earned him the title, 'dean of American letters'. But his own origins were, appropriately for a man dedicated to the 'commonplace', quite humble. He was born in Ohio, received little formal education, and moved from town to town with his family, working for his father, a printer, as a typesetter. Beginning in 1860, he had pieces published in various national magazines. A campaign biography of Abraham Lincoln earned him the reward of the United States Consul in Venice, once Lincoln was elected; and, in 1865, he returned to America to take up the first of several editorial positions. His first published books included two based on his experiences abroad, *Venetian Life* (1866) and *Italian Journeys* (1867). The first of his forty or so novels, *Their Wedding Journey* (1872) and *A Chance Acquaintance* (1873), also made use of his travels. These were followed by two fictions dealing with the contrast between Americans and Europeans, *A Foregone Conclusion* (1874) and *A Lady of Aroostook* (1879). With his first major novel, *A Modern Instance* (1882), Howells moved beyond explorations of manners to the detailed and serious consideration of wider social issues. The novel is structured around the twin themes of divorce and journalism. Howells was the first novelist to focus on journalism, and developed the theme of divorce after attending a performance of a Greek tragedy. During the composition of the book, he called it his 'New Medea', a 'modern instance' of what would happen to a couple whose marriage gradually deteriorates. What is remarkable about it is the way that, in a strategy characteristic of literary realism, it links the personal and the political, the emotional and the social. It is a vivid fictional examination of moral decline in both the home and the workplace. It is also sternly resistant to sentimentalism. No palliative is offered for the waste of the life of the young wife, Marcia Gaylord, as she stiffens into loneliness, or for the decline of the husband, Bartley Hubbard, from ambitious young editor to pariah to a tawdry death in the West at the hands of someone about whom he has published personal details in his newspaper.

The Rise of Silas Lapham also demonstrates what Howells called the 'fidelity to experience and probability of motive' that he felt was an imperative for the American storyteller. More than *A Modern Instance*, it also invites the reader to what he called 'the appreciation of the common'. The central character here, Colonel Silas Lapham, is a Vermont farmer who has risen to wealth through his paint manufacturing business. He is a typical capitalist of the time to the extent that for him business is a sacrament. His paint is not merely 'the best on the market', he declares, but 'the best in God's universe', and he makes this declaration 'with the solemnity of prayer', affirming the holiness of thrift and the profit motive. Lapham moves his family to Boston and begins to build a house on fashionable Beacon Hill: Howells uses the several removals of the family, as other contemporary and later realists were to do, to measure social status and upward mobility. He also encourages his wife and daughters to enter fashionable society. The Lapham family does not fit in well or easily with genteel Boston society. There is no finer piece of social comedy in the novel, in fact, and no clearer index of the shaky position of the newly rich in an older society in American literature than the description of a dinner party held at the house of one high-class family, the Coreys. Unable to negotiate the politics of the dinner table, and finding the conversation beyond his range, Lapham is at first uncomfortably quiet and then, fuelled by the drinks he does not know how to refuse, talks far too much and too loud. One member of the Corey family, however, Tom, falls in love with the older Lapham daughter, Penelope. And although the match between them is delayed for a while, because the younger daughter Irene convinces herself and Penelope that Tom is in love with her, the two are eventually married. Not long after the marriage, they leave for Mexico to escape the rigid social barriers of New England. Lapham, meanwhile, has been threatened with bankruptcy due to some unsuccessful business ventures. A former partner, called Rogers, urges him to save himself by selling some property he knows to be worthless to some British investors. After a struggle with himself, Lapham decides not to make the sale. Economically bankrupt, socially disgraced, he is nevertheless morally restored, and he returns with his family to Vermont.

Structurally, with its movement towards the moral redemption of the protagonist, the moral 'rise' that accompanies his social and financial fall, the story Howells devises here would have tempted other writers towards moralism and sentimentalism. But, like his hero, Howells resists temptation. As Lapham makes his decision not to sell worthless stock, what he is aware of mostly is how deeply unheroic he feels. 'He had a whimsical and sarcastic sense of its being very different from the plays at the theater,' the reader learns. This is a necessary choice for him, but it is not one that is accompanied by any theatrical gestures or even with much sense of satisfaction. 'You've ruined me!' Rogers – who had a share in the anticipated deal – tells Lapham, when he learns of his choice. 'I haven't a cent left in the world! God help my poor wife!' 'This was his reward for standing firm for right and justice to his own destruction,' Lapham muses, as he sees Rogers leave, 'to feel like a thief and murderer.' Lapham has done what he has to do but done so quietly, hesitantly, even regretfully. If there is moral grandeur here, it is no more, and no less, than the grandeur of the commonplace. 'You can paint a man dying for his country,' one character in the novel complains to an artist, 'but you can't express on canvas a man fulfilling the duties of a good citizen.' Howells can. And he leaves us with his 'good citizen', Lapham, averring, with a scrupulous avoidance of heroism or sentimentalism, his humble acceptance of his citizenly duties. 'I don't know as I should always say it paid,' he confesses, reflecting on the choice he made; 'but if I done it, and the thing was to do over again, right in the same way, I guess I should have to do it.'

Earlier on in *The Rise of Silas Lapham*, a character called Mit Kingsbury praises a popular romance she has just read called *Tears, Idle Tears*. The 'dear old-fashioned hero and heroine', she declares, 'keep dying for each other all the way through' and make 'the most wildly and unnecessary sacrifices for each other'. 'You can't put a more popular thing than self-sacrifice into a novel,' another character responds sardonically. 'We do like to see people suffering sublimely.' The whole purpose of Howells's novel is to resist such sentimental notions that self-sacrifice is an intrinsic good. The choice that Lapham makes is not, Howells insists, a wild and unnecessary one. The subplot involving Tom Corey and Penelope Lapham helps to develop this purpose. Penelope is tempted, by consideration for her sister Irene's feelings, to reject Tom when he reveals his love for the older sister. She does not, however, partly persuaded by Irene not to do so. According to what the novel calls the 'economy of pain' and the morality of 'common-sense', it is only right that Penelope and Tom should marry, although a lachrymose tale like *Tears, Idle Tears* would suggest otherwise. The romantic sentimentalism of purposeless self-sacrifice is resisted. So too, at the end of the novel, is the romantic sentimentalism of recon- ciliation. Through the marriage of Tom and Penelope, the 'old' family of the Coreys and the 'new' family of the Laphams are nominally joined, but only nomin- ally. 'It would be easy to point out traits in Penelope's character which finally reconciled all her husband's family and endeared her to them,' the narrator reflects. 'These things continually happen in novels.' Not in this novel, however: 'the dif- ferences remained uneffaced' between 'the Coreys and Tom Corey's wife', which is one reason why the couple leave for Mexico. There is no sense of the old leisure class, with its manners and ease, being united with the new business class, with its vigour and purpose; the two families remain worlds apart. As with so much in the novel, Howells seems to be gesturing towards romantic conventions of motive and incident precisely to indicate just how far from the romantically conventional, just how close to the actual grain of things, his story is.

Three years after publishing *The Rise of Silas Lapham*, Howells himself left Boston for New York. The move, which reflected a gradual transference of cultural power from the old New England establishment to the metropolis, was followed by a change in Howells's choice of subject and method. He was fascinated by the extremes of wealth and poverty he found in the city, and appalled by the brutal treatment of striking workers in Chicago's Haymarket Strike and the Pennsylvania Homestead Strike. Influenced by Tolstoy, whom he began to read in 1885, he gravitated towards socialism and to the belief that he had to adapt his realistic fiction to the problems of the machine age and the city. One result of this was a utopian fiction, *A Traveler from Altruria* (1894). Several hundred utopian fictions appeared between the 1880s and the early 1900s; as writers responded to the radical changes and social injustice of the times by imagining alternatives for America based on economic stability and principles of justice. The most famous and influ- ential of these was *Looking Backward* (1888) by Edward Bellamy (1850–98), which portrayed the United States in the year 2000 as a place where government owner- ship of the means of production and the 'scientific', rational rule of a business class ensured economic equality and happiness for all citizens. In *A Traveler from Altruria* and its sequel, *Through the Eye of the Needle* (1907), Howells envisioned a more socialist utopia, in which all citizens are required to work three hours a day at manual labour in return for food and other goods from government sources. In this completely egalitarian state, property is owned communally, most modern machinery is outlawed, family life is subordinated to civic life, and even style is legislated – with fashion in everything from clothes to architecture being under the supervision of aesthetic commissioners.

Another result of the new direction in Howells's realism was the novel that deserves a place with *A Modern Instance* and *The Rise of Silas Lapham* among his major fiction, *A Hazard of New Fortunes* (1898). The most panoramic of all his works, the novel is set in the magazine world of New York City and explores the conflict between labour and capital on both a personal and a general level. On the personal level, there is, for instance, the conflict between a magazine proprietor, Dryfoos, a millionaire capitalist, and one of his employers, a socialist called Lindau. On the general, there is a vivid account of a strike of streetcar employees, in which Lindau's son is killed. Howells called *A Hazard of New Fortunes*, 'the most vital of my fictions'. That is open to debate. What is not, however, is that it is the one among his major fictions that is most vitally concerned with social injustice – and the one most urgently and immediately directed towards the realization of what he termed 'democracy in literature'. Such a literature, Howells explained, 'wishes to know and to tell the truth'. And that truth was that 'men are more like than unlike one another'. 'Let us make them know one another better,' Howells implored his fellow writers, 'that they may all be humbled and strengthened with a sense of their fraternity.' That catches a note which is there in all Howells's criticism and fiction, with its primary stress on human dignity and connection. For him, as for so many realists, the ordinary was not just inspirational but also what bound humanity together: what was commonplace was what, in the end, was held in common and shared.

Capturing the real thing

Howells never gravitated from realism to naturalism, with its emphasis on the determining influence of heredity and environment and its harrowing depiction of landscapes, social and natural, that are at best indifferent and at worst hostile to humankind. There is a fundamental benevolence, a belief in human worth and social betterment, that is caught in one of the most famous remarks in *Criticism and Fiction*: 'our novelists concern themselves with the more smiling aspects of life, which are the more American.' That remark would have elicited sardonic laughter from Ambrose Bierce (1842–1914?), who was known as 'bitter Bierce' and 'the wickedest man in San Francisco' among his contemporaries, and seemed to revel in both titles. Born in Ohio, Bierce participated in the Civil War. The war disgusted him, prompting him to see soldiers as little more than paid assassins and, when it ended, he moved to California, where he established a reputation as a brilliant and caustic journalist. Living in England for four years from 1872, he returned to California. He then published *Tales of Soldiers and Civilians* in 1891, retitled *In the Midst of Life* in England and in the 1898 American edition. Another collection of stories, *Can Such Things Be?*, followed in 1893. More than half the stories in the first collection, and many in the second, deal with the Civil War; they reflect their author's feelings of revulsion for military life, and his bleak, bitterly comic view of life in general. Some of these stories capture the vicious confusion of battle, just as, say, *Miss Ravenel's Conversion from Secession to Loyalty* (1867) by John William De Forest (1826–1906) does. In 'A Horseman in the Sky', a young Union soldier is forced by circumstances to kill a Confederate officer, who happens to be his father. Others use stream-of-consciousness and suspense endings to explore the subjectivity of time. 'An Occurrence at Owl Creek Bridge', for example, presents the fantasy experienced by a man who is being hanged, in the final seconds of his life. And still others deploy a fluid, almost surrealistic prose style and black humour to dramatize physical and emotional violence. So, in 'Chickamauga', we see a battleground strewn with corpses through the eyes of a child. The child sees but does not understand – although, thanks to an ironic narrator, the reader does – until the end, when he comes across the ruin of his home and the dead body of his mother, 'the greater part of the forehead . . . torn away'. A deaf mute, he then utters 'a series of inarticulate and indescribable cries – something between the chattering of an ape and the gobbling of a turkey – a startling, soulless, unholy sound'. It is the wreckage of a language, used in response to the 'wreck' he sees around him; he has awoken, hopelessly and helplessly, to the horror of life. The same dark light that simultaneously illuminates and shadows these stories also informs Bierce's poems, and the ironic series of definitions – such as the definition of realism quoted earlier – collected in *The Devil's Dictionary* (1911). In 1913, Bierce travelled into war-torn Mexico, to escape American civilization and to seek, he said, 'the good, kind darkness'. He must have found it, for he disappeared. To this day, it is not known when, how or exactly where he died.

At first sight, there are a few connections between William Dean Howells and Henry James (1843–1916). Both saw writing as a serious vocation, and the writing of fiction as a form of artistic endeavour equal to any other. Both were influential, Howells exerting a powerful influence on his contemporaries and James mostly on his successors. Both addressed their work to what they saw as 'the real thing', to use James's phrase: to the strenuous realities of material, mental and moral existence. But the differences between them are clear. Howells, in his very emphasis on the 'commonplace', tended to concentrate on human likeness, typicality, and to give priority, if not a monopoly, to the social context. James, on the other hand, was intensely interested in what he called 'the special case': that is, he chose to focus on how common moral conflicts and shared social concerns were realized in the complexities of individual experience and encountered by the individual conscious-ness. Howells used a variety of fictional techniques, but all of them were character-ized by the directness of the journalist or historian. James, on the contrary, was what Joseph Conrad famously called him, 'the historian of fine consciences'. And to write this history, thoroughly and accurately, he devoted a lifetime to finding and developing the right fictional tools. 'There is, I think, no more nutritive or suggestive truth', James wrote in his Preface to *The Portrait of a Lady* (1881), '. . . than that of the perfect dependence of the "moral" sense of a work of art on the amount of felt life concerned in producing it.' To create that 'felt life', an imaginative experience for the reader, James experimented with narrative structure and texture, developing patterns of character or imagery and moments of epiphany – and, above all, with point of view. 'The house of fiction', James insisted, 'has . . . not one window, but a million – a number of possible windows . . . every one of which has been pierced, or is still pierceable . . . by the need of the individual vision and by the pressure of the individual will.' It mattered hugely, James knew, which window or windows the novelist chose to tell his tale: because, in a variation of the theory of relativity or the indeterminacy or uncertainty principle of Werner Heisenberg (both of which were becoming current at the time James was still writing), what you saw depended on where you stood. James was not a moral relativist, by any means, but he became increasingly a psychological one. His constant experiments with narrative viewpoint, which were perhaps to be his major contribution to the developing aesthetics of the novel, sprang ultimately from the sense he shared with many of his contemporaries in science as well as art that our knowledge of reality is contingent on perspective.

Howells might have been more interested in social justice and the simplicities of realism than James; James might have been more concerned with a kind of secular mysticism of consciousness and the indeterminate, contingent character of the real. But it is to Howells's credit that, as critic and editor, he was among the first to recognize James's talent. 'You showed me the way and opened me the door,' James wrote to Howells in gratitude in 1912; 'you wrote to me, and confessed yourself struck with me – I have never forgotten the beautiful thrill of that.' Credit is due to Howells all the more, perhaps, because as they knew, the two men came from very different backgrounds. James was born in New York City to a wealthy, patrician family, the grandson of an Irish immigrant who had amassed a large fortune. His father, Henry James Sr. (1811–82), acquired a reputation as a moral and social philosopher, developing his own form of liberal Christianity and ideas for social reform in books like *Christianity the Logic of Creation* (1857) and *Substance and Shadow; or Morality and Religion in Their Relation to Life* (1863). Henry James Sr. encouraged intellectual experiment in his sons and gave them the freedom to develop their own systems of morality and discipline. The results were positive. While Henry was to grow up and into a dedication to literature, the eldest son, William James (1842–1910), was to become the foremost American philosopher of his day, developing his ideas about psychology and religion and his view that an idea has meaning only in relation to its consequences in feeling and action in, respectively, *The Principles of Psychology* (1890), *The Varieties of Religious Experience* (1902) and *Pragmatism* (1907). These enlightened principles did not extend to women, however. On the contrary, Henry James Sr. argued that 'Woman' was not truly a person but 'a form of personal affection', whose mission it was to redeem man from his natural egotism and brutality. Such views, not untypical for the time, meant that Alice James (1848–92), the youngest child and only daughter, was denied the formal education given to her brothers. Her family, while respecting her abilities – she was, among other things, an astute critic of both her famous brothers – coddled and, arguably, stifled her. She had several breakdowns during her relatively short life; and her daily journal, which she seems to have intended for publication, only appeared in 1964 as *The Diary of Alice James*.

After being educated by private tutors until the age of twelve, Henry James went to schools in Europe and the United States. Entering Harvard Law School in 1862, he withdrew after the year. Then, with the encouragement of Howells and Charles Eliot Norton (1827–1908), a Harvard professor and translator of Dante, he began to concentrate on writing. Reviews and essays appeared in the *Atlantic Monthly* and the *North American Review*. In 1869, he returned to Europe, his first visit as an adult, first to England and then to Italy, which made a deep impression on him. It was while he was in Europe that his beloved cousin, Mary Temple, died. How exactly this affected his later fiction is open to debate, although the situation of an attractive, lively but doomed or even fatally sick young girl certainly recurs, in such novels as *The Portrait of the Lady* and *The Wings of the Dove* (1902), and in the novella *Daisy Miller* (1878). In any event, James's first novel, *Watch and Ward*, appeared serially in the *Atlantic Monthly* in 1871 (and in volume form in 1878). This was followed by his first collection, *A Passionate Pilgrim and Other Tales* (1875), and *Transatlantic Sketches* (1875), and his first novels of real consequence, *Roderick Hudson* (1876), *The American* (1877) and *The Europeans* (1878). The story 'A Passionate Pilgrim' deals with the reactions of an eager American 'pilgrim' when confronted with the fascinations of the complex European world of art and affairs. And James himself during this period was something of a pilgrim in Europe, which he came to regard as his spiritual fatherland, moving there permanently in 1875. During a year in Paris, he associated with such masters of the art of fiction as Flaubert and Turgenev, who encouraged his interest in what Flaubert called 'le mot juste', the right word, the careful planning of the language and structure of the novel so as to make it an accurate register of reality. After 1876, however, he made his home mainly in London, although he maintained an American home in Massachusetts and, much later, moved to the small town of Rye in Sussex.

James was developing his ideas about his craft, and expressing them in, for instance, his well-known essay on 'The Art of Fiction' (1884). He was also exploring what were to be the dominant themes of this, the first stage of his career as a novelist, which lasted from roughly 1870 until 1890. There is James's interest in the mired complexities of fate and freedom, the possibly determining influences of environment and the potential power, the capacities of the human will: 'don't talk about the will being "destined,"' declares a character in *Roderick Hudson* as a contribution to the debate, 'The will is destiny itself. That's the way to look at it.' There is his concern for the individual consciousness and the terms it must negotiate with society, how it manoeuvres its way through moral and mental complexities. Above all, there is 'the international theme', the series of contrasts James draws between Europe and America. In his book on *Nathaniel Hawthorne* (1879), as was mentioned earlier, James argued that 'the good American' of his own time would be a more complicated, 'more critical person' than the one of the time of his subject. He was thinking, among other things, of his own difference from the author of *The Scarlet Letter*: which was due, he thought, not only to the eruptions of civil conflict but to his exemplary encounter with European culture. There is a residue of 'American' romanticism, as James would see it, in these novels of the first period: stories of young American pilgrims, dark family secrets, oppressive villains. But this is overlaid by habits of realism, empirical rigour and attention to mannerly detail that James, at least, felt he owed to his European masters: to Flaubert or Turgenev, say, rather than to Hawthorne. More seriously and centrally, James was of the passionate belief that, as he put it in his account of Hawthorne, 'it takes a great deal of history to produce a little literature' – and that, despite the Civil War, history 'had left in the United States but so thin and impalpable a deposit that we very soon touch the hard substratum of nature'. What America lacked was what, precisely, Europe had: 'an accumulation of history and custom', 'a complexity of manners and types', all that could 'form a fund of suggestion for a novelist'. James even went so far as to enumerate 'the absent things in American life', the 'items of high civilisation' which, he felt, were nowhere to be found in his place of birth. He was less specific about what was present, apart from insisting that 'a good deal remains'. What was clear, however, and could be succinctly stated is that he felt compelled, as a novelist, to live in Europe and, as an American novelist, to dwell on this contrast. As a result, he offered a series of increasingly sophisticated fictional negotiations between European culture and American nature, European society and the American individual, European experience and American innocence. To an extent, he was transplanting a contrast embedded in American thought, and especially that of the nineteenth century, to the international arena: a contrast articulated in those fundamental divisions of the clearing and the wilderness. But what distinguished this fiction was not merely the transplantation of content but also the transformation of form. 'A novel is a living thing,' James insisted in 'The Art of Fiction', 'all one and continuous, like any other organism and in proportion as it lives will it be found . . . that in each of its parts there is something of each of the other parts.' That belief vividly informed his own practice as a novelist. It stimulated fictions in which, at best, the medium is the message, the 'moral' of the narrative springs from a 'doing' that is subtly intricate and mutually restrained, balanced and brilliantly nuanced.

In *The American*, James explores the contrasts between Europe and America through the story of a protagonist whose name betrays his origins and missions. Christopher Newman is an American who reverses the voyage of his namesake Christopher Columbus and travels from his own, New World to the Old World of France during the Bourbon period. There, he finds his love for a Frenchwoman of the nobility frustrated by her family. James draws a series of sly contrasts between Newman's innocence, candour and ignorance (especially about matters of art and social convention) and the sophistication and cunning of his European hosts. *The Europeans* reverses this voyage, in turn, by bringing Europeans to New England. The transatlantic contrasts multiply and are more complex here, but the fundamental distinctions remain the same. In response to the news, for instance, that one of the European visitors is 'the wife of a Prince', an older American character simply responds, 'We are all princes here'. *Daisy Miller* focuses the international contrast via the story of a charming but ingenuous American girl who is destroyed, first socially and then literally, by her lack of understanding of her new European surroundings. Part of the exemplary subtlety of the story comes from a symbolic pattern it shares with *The American* and *The Europeans*: contrasting American 'brightness', starkness and simplicity with European shadows, secrets and complexities. Part of it comes from the adept use of a narrator, an observer whose developing interest in Daisy, mingled sympathy and criticism, affection and astonishment, and developing feelings and opinions enable the narrative to maintain a delicate balance. Typically, the story offers not so much a judgement of Daisy, and all she comes to represent, as a series of essays towards a critical understanding of both, a knowledge felt along the pulses. It nicely illustrates the remark of T. S. Eliot, meant as a compliment although it hardly sounds like it, that James had a mind so fine no idea could penetrate it.

That is even more finely illustrated by the major work of the first period, and arguably James's greatest novel, *The Portrait of a Lady*. It is, as James put it, the story of 'a certain young woman affronting her destiny'. Isabel Archer, a penniless orphan living in Albany, New York, is taken up by her aunt, Lydia Touchett. She goes to England to stay with her aunt and uncle and their tubercular son Ralph. There, she declines the proposals of both Caspar Goodwood, a rich American, and Lord Warburton, an English aristocrat. Wealthy now, thanks to an inheritance from Mr Touchett arranged for her by Ralph, she then accepts the proposal of an American expatriate, a widower and dilettante living in Florence, Gilbert Osmond. She is introduced to Osmond by another expatriate, Madame Merle, and is impressed by his taste and refinement. Soon after marriage, however, she discovers him to be selfish, sterile and oppressive. She also finds out that Osmond's young daughter, Pansy, is actually the daughter of Madame Merle and that this was the reason for the woman's introducing her to Osmond and promoting the marriage. Despite Osmond forbidding her, Isabel leaves for England when she hears Ralph is dying, and is at his side when he dies. Despite a last attempt from Caspar Goodwood to persuade Isabel to go away with him, though, Isabel determines to return to Osmond. And the novel closes with her accepting her destiny, or perhaps more accurately the consequences of her choices, and preparing to go back to a home that is more like a prison. Stated baldly, the story has strong elements of romance or fairytale, just like *The Scarlet Letter*: the awakening of a sleeping beauty, the three suitors, a villain whose 'egotism lay hidden like a serpent in a bank of flowers', a heroine held captive in 'the house of darkness, the house of dumbness, the house of suffocation', the sick young cousin who observes and admires her from afar before dying, the voyage of an American Adam – or, rather, Eve – and their exile from Paradise. But what distinguishes it, in the reading, is its adherence to the substantial realities of the social life and the subtle realities of the life of the consciousness. Isabel Archer is as much like the heroines of, say, *Middlemarch*

(1871–2) or *Daniel Deronda* (1876) by George Eliot as she is like Hester Prynne: the imaginative manoeuvres of the book represent as much an encounter between the American and the European as its story does. It is both of and about a collision of cultures.

One reason for the subtle but substantial reality of Isabel herself is that James focuses on her. 'Place the centre of the subject in the young woman's own consciousness,' James tells us, in the Preface, he told himself when he was writing the book. 'Stick to *that* – for the centre.' As for the other characters, he explains, his aim was to 'press least hard' on 'the consciousness' of his 'heroine's satellites, especially the male', so as to 'make it an interest contributive only to the greater one'. James wanted to reveal the full implications of the developing consciousness of his protagonist. So the reader experiences a lot through her, and shares the lively animations of her mind on the move, but, in addition, sees her from the outside, through the comments and often critical commentary of the narrator – and through the observations of characters like Ralph Touchett. We understand her sense of herself, her moods and changes, but we also take the measure of 'the whole envelope of circumstances' in which she is implicated. Characteristically of James, the strategy is part of the debate. That phrase, 'the whole envelope of circumstances,' is used by Madame Merle, who has adapted to a European vision sufficiently to believe that self and circumstance, the human being and his or her shell, are indivisible. 'One's self – for other people – is one's expression of one's self,' she insists. Isabel disagrees. Subscribing to the American romance of the self, she believes in freedom as an absolute and the individual as somehow separable from conditions and circumstances. 'Nothing that belongs to me is any measure of me,' she insists; 'everything's on the contrary a limit, a barrier, and a perfectly arbitrary one.' James wryly complicates the debate by intimating that his heroine's profound belief in herself, her 'fixed determination to regard the world as a place of brightness, of free expansion', may itself spring from circumstance. She has grown up in a world, the new world of America, where there have been few forms or authorities, no rigorous or rigidly enforced social practices, to challenge that belief. But that complication is further complicated by the clear admiration that Isabel's 'flame-like spirit' inspires in the narrator, observers such as Ralph Touchett, and the reader. There is candour and honesty here, a fundamental integrity and capacity for wonder as well as innocence, an openness that leaves her vulnerable – and, by some measures at least, humanly incomplete.

With the characters surrounding Isabel, some are quietly developed, the reader comes to know them gradually: sometimes for good, as with Ralph Touchett, and sometimes, as with Osmond and Madame Merle, for ill. Others, like Lydia Touchett, are flatter and deftly summarized when they are introduced. All, however, contribute to our understanding of the heroine and the representative character of her transatlantic encounter. A minor character such as Henrietta Stackpole, for instance, another young American woman abroad, helps the reader place Isabel further; so do the sisters of Lord Warburton, 'the Misses Molyneaux'. Henrietta is self-confidence and independence to the point of bluster: 'Henrietta . . . does smell of the future', Ralph observes, '– it almost knocks one down!' The Misses Molyneux are compliant and decorous to the point of vanishing into their surroundings. The character of Isabel is mapped out using such minor characters as coordinates, in a manner James had learned from another novelist he admired, Jane Austen. And it is mapped out, too, in Isabel's perilous voyage between the possibilities represented by her first two suitors and the alternatives they vigorously embody: America, with its devotion to individual initiative, enterprise and possibility, and Europe, with its adherence to mannerliness, custom and tradition, the rich fabric woven out of the past. Isabel's voyage is a literal one, to begin with, when she leaves New York for England: landscapes that here, as throughout James's fiction, have a symbolic as well as a literal application, with the starkness and simplicity of the one contrasting with the opulence and grandeur of the other. But it becomes an intensely symbolic one: when Ralph Touchett tries, in his words, to put some 'wind in her sails' by arranging for her to receive a bequest from his father.

Isabel, too, tries to put wind in the sails of someone else. She is drawn to Gilbert Osmond precisely because she believes she can help him fulfil the requirements of his imagination. With Goodwood or Warburton, she would, in a sense, be embarking on a ship that has already set sail, committing her destiny to one that had achieved full definition before she appeared; she would, perhaps, be resigning herself to the authority or at least ambience of another. But with Osmond, she believes, it would be she herself who would enable the voyage, create the destiny. 'He was like a sceptical voyager strolling on the beach while he waited for the tide, looking seaward yet not putting to sea,' Isabel observes of the man she eventually marries. 'She would launch his boat for him; she would be his providence; it would be a good thing to love him.' In fact, it is not 'a good thing' at all. Osmond, as it turns out, had just as firm a notion that he would be her providence, when he married Isabel. 'Her mind was to be his', Isabel bitterly reflects after she has come to know her husband, '– attached to his own like a small garden-plot to a deer park.' What all this adumbrates is a theme interwoven with the contrast between Europe and America, and dear to the heart of Hawthorne as much as James: the human use of human beings. The complex interplay of character focused in the figures of voyaging reminds us that to declare oneself may be to deny another. To enable is also to authorize, to will the fate of someone else; there is only a thin membrane separating freedom from power and power from what Hawthorne called 'The Unpardonable Sin'.

James's response to the problem he opens up, as he examines his characters' attempts to negotiate their freedom, is a dual one, and is typical in the sense that it involves what happens in *The Portrait of a Lady* and how it is written. What happens is that Isabel decides to go back to Gilbert Osmond. To run away with Goodwood would suggest that Madame Merle had been right after all, an admission from Isabel that the 'envelope' of her unfortunate circumstances was influential enough to make her evade the consequences of her own actions with a man she never loved. To return involves an acceptance of those consequences, and a fulfil-ment of a promise made earlier to Pansy, Osmond's daughter, that she would

---

come back. It marks her victory over circumstance and over the naive ideal of freedom she had brought with her from America. That ideal had identified freedom with limitless power, the boundless pursuit of her own needs. Pursuing it, she married a man who has sought to extinguish her. Abandoning, or rather refining it, she now sees freedom as conditional on knowledge: being clearsighted enough to choose the right course with reference to all responsibilities and probable consequences. In choosing to go back, Isabel transcends her circumstances by accepting them, keeps her word and keeps faith with herself – accepting her responsibility for her past and future. The choice on which the novel ends depends on a subtle balance between self and circumstance, in that it involves the recognition that expression of the one properly depends on awareness of the other: that freedom is a matter of responsible, realistic self-determination. And that same balance is at work in its narrative texture. James, as he meant to, does not yield to the determining nature of circumstance here, although he admits its irreducible reality. Nor, while emphasizing the power of consciousness, does he present that power as separate and inviolable, somehow superior to the circumstance it encounters. What he does, in his fictional practice, is what he preached in his criticism. He enters into a complex series of negotiations between the 'moral' and the 'felt life', the meaningful structures organizing experience and the contingencies, the fluid processes in which those structures are embedded. He asserts the authority of authorship, the strength of his own individual will as writer, but he also accepts the authority, the reality of the 'living thing', the imaginative experience that constitutes the story. Not only that, he shows that assertion of the one depends precisely on acceptance of the other: that, like any other living organism, the meaning of the novel *is* its being.

James returned to America in 1882, shortly before the death of his mother. His father died in the same year, and then in 1883 his younger brother, Wilky. His sense of attachment to his place of birth was drastically reduced by these deaths. And the second period of his writing career, broadly from the middle of the 1880s to 1900, was marked by an attachment to English settings in much of his fiction. *The Princess Casamassima* (1886), for instance, is set in London and deals with all social classes, exploring the tension between private sensibility and political belief. Other works of this period include *The Bostonians* (1886), a satirical study of the movement for female emancipation in New England ('the situation of women', James explained, 'the decline of the sentiment of sex, and the agitation on their behalf' was the most striking aspect of American life of the time); *The Aspern Papers* (1888), a collection of stories; and *The Spoils of Poynton* (1897). James made a venture into writing plays at this time, which proved disastrous. It came to a humiliating end when his play *Guy Domville* was given a riotous reception on its first night in 1895. The venture did, however, encourage him to develop dramatic techniques for his fiction. If the first period of James's career could be described in terms of moral realism, and the third in terms of psychological realism – although these are, necessarily, labels that do less than full justice to the sophistication of his art – then the second could be called a period of dramatic realism. James used careful manipulation of point of view, elaborate patterning of contrasting episodes and characters, and a focus on dialogue and dramatic scene to achieve here what he always sought: 'the maximum of intensity', to use his own words, 'with the minimum of strain'. The results are powerfully evident in a novel like *What Maisie Knew* (1897) that explores adultery, infidelity and betrayal. The entire story, although written in the third person, is told from the point of view of the perceptive but naive young girl Maisie, who is just six years old when her parents are divorced. The strategy enables James to achieve economy, intensity and irony as he combines and implicitly compares what Maisie sees with what the narrative voice intimates.

Towards the end of his second period, James confirmed his reputation as a writer of short stories with tales many of which were about writers and writing, like 'The Lesson of the Master' (1888), 'The Middle Years' (1893) and 'The Figure in the Carpet' (1896). Again, many of these tales are fired into life by James's ingenious, inspired use of narrative viewpoint. In 'The Turn of the Screw' (1898), for example, the entire narrative depends for its intensity of terror on the fact that everything occurs in the mind of a governess, who desperately needs corroboration that she is not mad in attributing supernatural experiences to her young charges and seeing dead people. The reader is left in doubt, thanks to the possible unreliability of the narrator, as to whether or not she sees ghosts or hallucinations – and as to whether this is a Gothic story of evil or a psychological tale about repression and projection. In its own modest fashion, 'The Turn of the Screw' prepares the way for the emotional and psychological subtleties, the sense the reader has of wandering through the labyrinth of the human mind, that characterize the three major novels of the third and final period of James's career: *The Ambassadors*, written in 1901 and published in 1903, *The Wings of the Dove* and *The Golden Bowl* (1904). In all three, James returns to the international theme. In *The Ambassadors*, for instance, Lambert Strether is sent by a wealthy widow, Mrs Newsome, to persuade her son Chad to return to Massachusetts. Gradually, however, he grows less enthusiastic about his mission, as he becomes more and more receptive to the charms of England and France. Abandoning his aims, and with them the prospect of an advantageous marriage to Mrs Newsome – which is his promised reward, if he fulfils them – he even encourages the liaison between Chad and a charming Frenchwoman, Madame de Vionnet. It would be 'the last infamy', he tells Chad, if he forsook her. 'Live all you can,' Strether declares to another character, when he is provoked by a sense of his own tentative life, 'it's a mistake not to. It doesn't so much matter what you do in particular, so long as you have your life. If you haven't had that what *have* you had?' Nevertheless, Strether remains detached, content to observe rather than participate, eventually returning to his inconsequential life as a widower in Massachusetts. As he searches for the reality of Chad's motives, and the truth of his own relationship to life, living and the conflicting cultures of America and England, there is speculation, meditation, but fundamental irresolution. Europe has its own secrecies – the liaison of Chad and Madame de Vionnet, he eventually discovers, has been an intimate one – just as America has its absurdities. Life is for living, it may be, but not for him. This story of transatlantic encounters acquires some clarity by an elaborate balancing of scene and character: there are four major scenes set in a plainly allegorical garden, for instance, in which knowledge is slowly acquired and, in the course of the action, Chad and Strether change moral places. But it also acquires a certain mystery, even opacity from James's determination to follow the smallest refinement of emotional detail, the slightest nuance of social gesture – and from a style that, in the service of this pursuit, often becomes formidably, impenetrably intricate.

In the last few decades of his life, James devoted much of his time to preparing the New York edition of his works. He made revisions that often reflected his later dedication to a more allusive style. A reference, in the original version of *The Portrait of a Lady*, to the fact that Ralph Touchett had 'simply accepted the situation' of invalid was altered, for instance, to this: 'His serenity was but the array of wild flowers niched in his ruin.' He also wrote eighteen new prefaces for his novels. He travelled widely, and wrote about his travels: in *The American Scene* (1907) and *Italian Hours* (1909). He published two volumes of autobiography, *A Small Boy and Others* (1913) and *Notes of a Son and Brother* (1914); and a third volume, *The Middle Years*, appeared posthumously in 1917. Angered by American reluctance to become involved in the First World War, he became a British citizen in 1915. But, in a sense, as T. S. Eliot was later to put it, it was not the condition of being English to which he – or, at least, part of him – aspired but the condition of being European, 'something which no born European, no person of any European nationality, can become'. James anticipated the direction in which many American writers were to move in the twentieth century: in his concern with the complex fate of being an American in an international culture, his concern with the possibly limited terms of American culture and the fragments that could perhaps be rescued from the ruins of European tradition, in his growing concern with the romance and mystery of the consciousness. He assimilated the romantic tendencies that were part of the pressure of the age into which he was born, the moral rigour that was a continuing characteristic of his part of the nation; he also moved, especially in his later work, towards the Modernist conviction that the truth of art and the truth of life are one and the same. A summative and seminal writer, James stands at the juncture between two centuries, and different moments in American writing. He was also, complexly, his own man. There is no more satisfactory way of summing that complexity up than the one James himself was probably alluding to when he called his last fragment of autobiography 'The Middle Years'. The title is also that of an earlier story, published in 1895, in which a dying writer makes a statement of faith that his creator might well have made for himself. 'We work in the dark – we do what we can – we give what we have,' the writer declares. 'Our doubt is our passion and our passion is our task. The rest is the madness of art.'

Towards naturalism

Of Hamlin Garland (1860–1940), Henry James once declared that he was 'a case of saturation so precious as to have almost the value of genius'. What James presumably meant by this characteristically elliptical remark was that Garland devoted himself to the detailed depiction of one particular area of America: the Midwest where he was born and where he spent his boyhood and youth, as his family moved between farms in Iowa, South Dakota and his native Wisconsin. Garland is sometimes described as regionalist because of this concentration on the life and landscape of the Midwest in his fiction. 'Provincialism (that is to say regionalism) is no bar to a national literature,' Garland declared in *Crumbling Idols* (1894), a collection of essays; 'each locality must produce its own literary record, each special phase of life utter its own voice.' At other times, he has been called a realist or even a propagandist, because of his careful but also socially committed portraits of the poverty and oppression suffered by Midwestern farming families: what Garland himself termed, in his story 'The Return of the Private' (1891), the farmer's 'daily running fight with nature and against the injustice of his fellowmen'. Garland, for his part, called himself a 'veritist'. The 'veritist', he explained, was committed to 'the truthful statement of an individual expression corrected by reference to fact'. 'The veritist sees life in terms of what might be, as well as in terms of what is,' Garland insisted, 'but he writes of what is, and, at his best, suggests what is to be, by contrast.' Sticking closely to the verifiable, the empirical fact, but also catching or alluding to the verities, the realizable values of a life, the veritist is, in essence, a realist and a reformer. That combination of approaches is clearly at work in what is his first and, by a long distance, his finest book, *Main-Travelled Roads* (1891), a collection of stories mostly written before 1890. Along with 'The Return of the Private', it contains such widely anthologized tales and sketches as 'A Branch-Road', 'Up the Coulé' and 'Under the Lion's Paw'. All of these are powerfully informed by Garland's guilt over leaving his family, and particularly his mother, to the barren life of the farm (he departed for Boston in 1884) and by his anger over what he saw when he returned to or remembered that life, with 'its sordidness, dullness, triviality, and its endless drudgeries'.

'Up the Coulé' is typical. Personal in origin, it is based on a return visit that Garland himself made to the parental farm and later described in his autobiographical narrative, *A Son of the Middle Border* (1917). It is, among other things, a comprehensive attack on romantic pastoralism. Howard McLane, a successful dramatist, returns to his boyhood home in Wisconsin for a family reunion, only to have all his romantic preconceptions about homecoming destroyed – along with any residual feelings he may have that rural life is, in any way, idyllic. The village he first sees from the train, and the family farm, are squalid. His brother, Grant, hates him because he has managed to escape and better himself; and his mother, worn down by life and economic circumstance, has become a pathetic shadow of a woman. 'He thought of the infinite tragedy of those lives which the world loves to call "peaceful and pastoral",' the reader is told. And he takes the measure of just how short of the sordid realities of farming life most artistic accounts of it fall. 'The poet who writes of milking the cows does it from the hammock looking on,' Howard reflects; the painter needs to stop looking at this 'sombre landscape' through the 'half-shut eyes' of romance and paint the 'melancholy subject' with 'pitiless fidelity'. The only true art, expressive of this life, would be one that registered its sad facts and its suppressed hopes. Examples are offered here, in the story. There are the paintings of Millet, Howard remembers, which show the 'tragedy' of rural experience 'surrounded by glories', the beauty of nature, sometimes, and human aspiration. There is the violin music he hears at an otherwise rather flat party his family organizes to mark his visit home: music with an 'indefinable inner melancholy', a 'wild, sweet, low-keyed' tune that is an 'unconscious expression of unsatisfied desires'. And there is, of course, the art of the tale itself, which records the grim routines and grinding deprivation of this world while rehearsing, sometimes quietly and at other times with anger, all that is lost or denied in terms of faith, hope, dream or simple human dignity. Certainly, the artistic success here is not total. The skill with the vernacular, and with a style of scrupulous meanness, that Garland shows is sometimes vitiated by sentimentalism of approach, or genteel rhetoric ('Oh, that mystic hour!') that anticipates the weakness of his later work. More fundamentally, there is a potential contradiction at work: a conflict between Garland's populist social agenda, which leads him to attack injustice and inequity, and his evident acceptance of social Darwinism. 'The hawk eats the partridge, the partridge eats the flies and bugs, the bugs eat each other and the hawk, when he in his turn is shot by man,' Howard reflects. 'So, in the world of business, the life of one man seemed to him to be drawn from the life of another man, each success to spring from other failures.' From one standpoint, the deprivation and oppression the farmer suffers are the product of a particular economic system and are remediable. From the other, they are part of the scheme of things, a struggle for survival that is grounded in existence rather than a particular system, and so inevitable. And Garland, not untypical of his time, vacillates between the two. But the raw emotional centre of these stories remains mostly unaffected by these flaws: they are fictions fired by moral indignation rather than logic. For Garland, the 'study of sad lives' was useless unless it led to 'a notion of social betterment', the artist had to combine fact and truth, actuality and aspiration; and, in the best of his work, he did just that.

Garland's remark about the study of sad lives occurred in his review of *McTeague: A Story of San Francisco* (1899). *McTeague* was the first novel of real consequence by Frank Norris (1870–1902), who was one of those writers who gave a new and distinctly darker emphasis to American literature at the end of the century. There were poets among them. These included Trumbull Stickney (1874–1904), whose *Poems* were published posthumously in 1905. Presenting the world as a place of confusion, Stickney claimed to find peace, in poems like 'In Ampezzo', 'In Summer' and 'In a City Garden', only in the past and in the refuge of personal memory. More notable was Edwin Markham (1825–1940), whose finest poem, 'The Man With the Hoe', explored the tragic life of the farmer, 'bowed with the weight of centuries' and 'slave to the wheel of labor'. Like Garland mixing grim realism with reforming zeal, Markham called on 'masters, lords and rulers' to redeem this victim of 'the world's blind greed'. Remarkably, his best work, collected in *The Man With the Hoe and Other Poems* (1899) and *Lincoln and Other Poems* (1901), struck a responsive chord, making him popular and wealthy enough to devote himself to writing. Still more notable, though, than either Stickney or Markham was William Vaughn Moody (1869–1910). Many poets of this time, faced with what they saw as social and moral decline, retreated into fantasy. Madison Cawein (1865–1914) is typical in this respect. Preferring, as he admitted, 'the world of fancy' to the world of reality, and his own Kentucky home, he explored and celebrated his own private dreamland in no fewer than thirty-six volumes of poetry. Moody, however, was determined to explore the dislocation of his times. A poem like his 'Gloucester Moors' (1901), for instance, starts from a sense of disorientation that is at once social, moral and existential. 'Who has given me this sweet, /' Moody asks, 'And given my brother dust to eat?' And the vision of injustice, inequity he sees every-where around him in 'the moiling street' is matched by a feeling of emotional and spiritual instability, the conviction that 'this earth is not the steadfast place' earlier generations had presumed it to be. Doubts are compounded and given a more political slant in his 'On a Soldier Fallen in the Philippines' (1901): an elegy for someone killed in a conflict, the Spanish–American War, that the poet clearly regards as not just useless but obscene. 'Let him never dream that his bullet's scream went wide of its island mark, /' Moody concludes, 'Home to the heart of his darling land where she stumbled and sinned in the dark.' Moody acquired fame during his lifetime from his plays, *A Sabine Woman* (1906) and *The Great Divide* (1909). They deserve a place in American literary history if only because, unlike many dramatists of the period, Moody chose for them distinctly American sub-jects. But it is his verse, collected in *Poems and Plays* (1912), that really takes the measure of his times. It is here that he registers, with far more resonance than most other contemporary poets, the doubt, the sense of vacuum left by the dis-appearance of an earlier America and an older faith and by the spread of evolu-tionism, determinism and relativism – and the suspicion that America had broken faith with its past by moving, in the course of a century, from liberated colony to imperial power.

But the writers who contributed most to this darkening of emphasis and mood were novelists, like Norris. The most notable of these, apart from Norris himself, are Stephen Crane (1871–1900) and Jack London (1876–1916). They also include Theodore Dreiser, whose long career was to make him a contemporary of F. Scott Fitzgerald and Ernest Hemingway and someone, like Edith Wharton and Willa Cather, standing on the cusp between Victorianism and Modernism. And they include Harold Frederic (1856–98), whose best novel, *The Damnation of Theron Ware* (1896), portrays the religious and psychological decline of a Methodist minister while revealing the inadequacy of religious and intellectual fashions from Methodism to Darwinism; Margaret Deland (1857–1945), whose finest novels, *John Ward, Preacher* (1888) and *The Awakening of Helen Richie* (1908), explore moral conflict and growth in the repressive climate of Calvinism; and Henry Fuller (1857–1929), whose book *The Cliff-Dwellers* (1893) takes on a new fictional landscape, the social ambitions of people living in a skyscraper apartment build-ing. Like Norris, both Crane and London – and, for that matter, Dreiser – were naturalists. That is, they subscribed to a darker, supposedly more scientific form of realism, shared with European writers like Émile Zola, that denies human agency: in these fictions, environmental forces control events and the individual is acted upon rather than active, subjected to the determinations of life – the elemental forces running through nature, society and every single human being. 'Men were nothings, mere animalcules, mere ephemerides that fluttered and fell and were forgotten between dawn and dusk,' the central character, Presley, in Norris's 1901 novel *The Octopus* reflects. 'FORCE only existed – FORCE that brought men into the world, FORCE that crowded them out of it to make way for the succeeding generation.' In the fiction of the naturalists, like *The Octopus*, the abiding American myths about individual freedom and heroism are overturned. Human characters are dwarfed, transformed into tiny 'specks' on a vast natural landscape – the ocean, the desert, the plains, the polar wastes – or into frail victims of social circumstance, rising to success or falling to failure more as a matter of accident and event than of ability or will. They are lost in the social landscape, the anonymous, seething mass of the city, or in a natural landscape governed by what Norris termed 'the vast rhythms of the seasons' and the 'eternal symphony of reproduction'. A character in *The Sea-Wolf* (1904) by Jack London puts the same perception rather more brutally. Life is 'unmoral', he insists:

> It is like a yeast, a ferment, a thing that moves and may move for a minute, an hour, a year, or a hundred years, but that in the end will cease to move. The big eat the little that they may continue to move, the strong eat the weak that they may retain their strength. The lucky eat the most and move the longest, that is all.

Sharing intensely in this perception, Frank Norris had more than one term for its realization in fiction. Sometimes he called it 'naturalism with all the guts I can get into it'. More often he called it 'Romance'. 'Realism', Norris argued in 'A Plan for Romantic Fiction' (1903), 'notes only the surface of things'; it 'bows upon the doormat and goes away and says . . . "That is life".' 'To Romance', on the other hand, 'belongs the wide world for range, and the unplumbed depths of the human heart, and the mystery of sex, and the problems of life, and the black unsearched penetralia of the soul of man.' What Norris was after, effectively, was a naturalism that combined the dedication to empirical facts found in realism with the devotion to truth – which for him meant scientific truth – that he claimed to find in romance. In pursuing that kind of naturalism, Norris was prepared to assault conventional taste: to show, for instance, how the brute instincts in human beings were an integral element in them, and played a necessary part in the social struggle. He was also eager to combine a detailed notation of often sordid social detail with an almost poetic celebration of the primal rhythms that, as he saw it, drove through nature and the primal urges that pulsed through man. Admittedly, his earlier work, like the long poem *Yvernelle: A Legend of Feudal France* (1892) and the sea story *Moran of the Lady Letty* (1898), showed a predisposition towards a more conventional kind of romance and, in particular, the influence of Sir Walter Scott.

But his 1899 novel *McTeague* had a naturalistic contemporary setting and revealed a quite different influence, Émile Zola (whom Norris chose to call 'the very head of the Romanticists', using that term, of course, according to his own, enlarged definition of 'Romance'). It tells the story of a man, the McTeague of the title, who descends into primitivism, surrenders to his primal instincts, when his precariously assembled world is brought down by greed and spite. Like one of Norris's later posthumously published novels, *Vandover and the Brute* (1914), it describes the power of the 'lower' instincts – the 'brute' in man which, as Norris had learned from his teachers at the University of California, needed to be acknowledged and harnessed to the development of the 'higher' self. And, in portraying the regression of its hero, it combines vivid realism of social detail – in, say, the account of McTeague's life as a dentist in San Francisco – with an almost Gothic romanticism, designed to search out and expose 'the brute'. At the end of the novel, McTeague is an almost monstrous figure. When the reader last sees him, he is alone in Death Valley, handcuffed to the corpse of the man he has just killed.

Norris's major project was what he called *The Epic of the Wheat*. 'I've got an idea as big as all outdoors,' he triumphantly announced, when he first thought of it. 'There's the chance for the big, epic, dramatic thing in this.' It would, he explained, be in the vein of 'naturalism' but naturalism as he understood it – and so, 'the most romantic thing I've ever done'. 'The Wheat series' he planned was to be a trilogy. There would be first a novel focused on the production of the wheat, and the struggle between farming and railroad interests in California. This was published in 1901 as *The Octopus*: it was, as it turned out, Norris's major novel. The second was to concentrate on the distribution of the wheat and the manipulation of the wheat market in Chicago. That was published posthumously as *The Pit* in 1903. But the third, dealing with consumption and telling of a wheat famine in Europe, was never written: Norris came up with a title for it, *The Wolf*, and little more than that. The epic scale of Norris's ambition, though, is clear from *The Octopus*. The octopus of the title is the railroad – also called a 'Titan' and a 'colossus' – which is the most powerful vested interest in California, and spreads its tentacles all over the state. It controls the movement of prices and interest rates; it owns much of the land and dispossesses the farmers of more; it manipulates the state government and, through its power over the access to information, it ensures that, statewide, no story but its own gets told. In the course of the narrative, the farming and labouring interests are comprehensively defeated. A representative patrician figure, Magnus Derrick, is ruined. A typical labourer and then farmer, Dyke, is forced into criminal activity and imprisoned for life. A farm hand called Hoover, an embodiment of the 'People', is killed in the often violent struggle against the railroad interests, his wife dies and their orphaned daughter is forced into prostitution. On the naturalistic surface, *The Octopus* is the bleakest of epics. What works against the bleakness, however, and gives the novel a strangely affirmatory, even optimistic tone is Norris's belief in 'force', necessity – the sense that, as the final words of this story put it, 'all things, surely inevitably, resistlessly work together for good'.

In effect, the social conflict of *The Octopus* is set in what Norris calls 'a larger view'. It is located in a frame within which, eventually, all human agents are seen as subject to 'primordial energy', part of a 'stupendous drama' of 'creation' and 're-creation', 'the eternal symphony of reproduction'. The narrative rhythm of the book, moving from autumn to autumn, registers this; so do the visual representations of characters, dwarfed by the vastness of the plains, and the structure of individual scenes – which habitually move from close-up into longshot, from 'the minute swarming of the human insect' to 'the great, majestic, silent ocean of the wheat itself', 'wrapped in Nirvanic calm'. But Norris's principal means of creating this vaster perspective of endless, triumphant, primordial struggle are four characters: a writer, Presley, the 'seeing eye' of the novel; Shelgrim, the railroad president, and Behrman, a railroad employee; and a strange character called Vanamee. It is Shelgrim who tells Presley that the railroad company is not in control, still less is he as president. As he explains, in that speech quoted earlier, only 'FORCE' is: on the social level, 'conditions, laws of supply and demand', and on the existential level, 'Nature' in its 'colossal indifference', 'a gigantic engine', 'a vast Cyclopean power'. Behrman illustrates the point in one way. Believing himself to be 'the Master of the Wheat' when the railroad company triumphs, he turns out to be its victim – he is crushed, suffocated to death by 'a sea' of wheat pouring down on him from a chute. And Vanamee illustrates it in another. Losing his lover, Angèle, at harvest time, she returns to him in the visionary shape of Angèle's daughter, at the same time as the recrudescence of the wheat. Her return is seen as a paradigm of the endless cycle of existence, a process involving 'life out of death, eternity rising out of dissolution'. Above all, there is Presley. Modelled on the poet Edwin Markham, Presley begins by searching for his subject in the romance of the Old West. Becoming involved in the cause of the farmers, he then throws away his copies of Milton, Tennyson and Browning to read Mill, Malthus and other social philosophers. He writes a populist poem, 'The Toilers', engages in political debate and violent political agitation. But neither his words nor his actions have much effect. Gradually, he withdraws into the larger view that embraces necessity: the inviolable indifference of nature, the 'mighty world-force' of the wheat, the fact that 'the individual suffers, but the race goes on'. He still believes that, one day, 'the People' will triumph and 'rend those who now preyed upon them'. To that extent, he, and Norris, keep faith with their political commitments: by placing them within an evolutionary framework that sees the often violent processes of evolution leading eventually to the 'good'. But that belief involves a kind of philosophical quietism – or, rather, a relentless, residual optimism that allows Presley to retain hope even in the middle of disaster. *The Octopus* is a characteristic work of American naturalism in its potent mixture of populist political vision and an evolutionary determinism that – in its celebration of force and talk of 'lower' and 'higher' instincts, class and races – teeters dangerously, sometimes, on the borders of fascism. It is also a characteristic work of Norris in its heady mix of fact and surreal fantasy, its seriousness and absurdity, and its extraordinarily cheerful nihilism. This is a book in which nearly all the sympathetic characters are defeated or destroyed, and yet which still manages to end, quite convincingly, on a note of affirmation – even joy.

There is little affirmation, or obvious joy, in the work of Stephen Crane. The tone is more muted, more quietly bleak. In prose and poetry of crystalline clarity and grimly pointed power, Crane pursues his fundamental perceptions that nature is oblivious to human need, that human beings are often relentlessly selfish or blind to circumstance, and that the two moral imperatives are humility and community. The poetry has been sadly, and unjustly, neglected. Crane published two volumes of poems during his lifetime, *The Black Rider* (1895) and *War is Kind* (1900). Stylistically, they show the influence of Emily Dickinson, by whose work Crane was much impressed. In terms of substance, they express a sense of existence that is even more cast in the shadows than that of Dickinson:

> A man adrift on a slim spar
> A horizon smaller than the rim of a bottle
> Tented waves rearing lashy points
> The near whine of froth in circles
> > God is cold.

In his poems, as in his stories, Crane describes a world of darkness, ocean or desert, where a man hugs his heart to himself, 'Because it is bitter /', he declares, 'And because it is my heart', and where the universe blandly dismisses the human demand for recognition. 'A man said to the universe: / "Sir, I exist!"/' one piece declares; '"However," replied the universe, / "The fact has not created in me / A sense of obligation."' That is the entire poem. And it reveals not only the sardonic tone and pellucid idiom of which Crane was master but also a habit of expression that was so drawn towards economy that it often verged on the laconic. Like Hemingway, who admired Crane intensely, Crane knew how to say much in saying little.

It is the prose work, however, that has secured Crane's reputation. Working intermittently as a journalist throughout his short life, Crane covered both the Spanish–American and Greek–Turkish wars. In America, he enjoyed the encouragement of William Dean Howells and Hamlin Garland; and in England, where he settled for a while, he became a friend of Joseph Conrad, Henry James and H. G. Wells. His first novel, *Maggie: A Girl of the Streets* (1893), was not widely noticed when it was first published. Maggie Johnson, the central character, is a victim of poverty and parental abuse. Seduced and abandoned, she tries to survive by becoming a prostitute but eventually drowns herself. Crane wrote of the novel to Garland that 'it tries to show that environment is a tremendous thing in the world and frequently shapes lives regardless'. 'If one proves that theory,' he added, 'one makes room in Heaven for all sorts of souls (notably an occasional street girl) who are not confidently expected to be there by many excellent people.' Set in the Bowery district of New York, *Maggie* in fact combines a trenchant determinism with a sharp, even satiric critique of moralism: the false morality of those 'many excellent people' who would condemn Maggie for those circumstances for which she is not responsible. If human beings cannot determine events, Crane intimates, they can at least free themselves from those systems of judgement that uncritically assume they can. His fictional emphasis bears down not just on the inherent evil of slum life but on the damage done by a false moral environment, an unjust, blandly moralistic perspective on that life. And, in using irony here to measure the gap between human event and human evaluation – 'a girl of the streets' and how 'excellent people' usually tend to see her – he was preparing the way for his finest work, *The Red Badge of Courage* (1895).

The Red Badge of Courage was both a critical and a popular success when it first appeared. In a characteristically pointillist style, Crane captures here the flux and confusion of battle. Unlike Norris, Crane preferred literary impressionism, delicacy of selection and suggestion to saturation. He picks out carefully chosen details, intimations of colour and movement, apparently disconnected images and events. He then places them in juxtaposition. The result is a fictional landscape remarkable for its instability and uncertainty. Many of the scenes are set in a foggy, misty landscape, at night or in the smoke of battle. And they offer a vivid visual equivalent for Crane's view of war and life. 'None of them knew the color of the sky', one of Crane's most famous short stories, 'The Open Boat' (*The Open Boat and Other Stories* [1898]), begins. That is precisely the human fate, and the fate of the soldier: not to know 'the color', the contours or the reality of the environment. Antiheroic, the novel also denies real human agency. For 'the youthful private' whose story this is – and whose name, we eventually learn, is Henry Fleming – war is a disconcerting mix of boredom, ignorance and fear, where long periods of waiting and wondering are punctuated by bursts of action that surprise and disconcert. War is, as Crane describes it, a paradigm of life: not least because it is nasty, brutish, beyond personal control, and has death – in the shape of the loathsome corpse Fleming comes across amidst 'a chapel' made of 'high arching boughs' – at its centre. Characteristically, Crane draws an ironic contrast between the romance and reality of battle, the heroic fate Fleming anticipates for himself and the horrible futility, the fear and the feelings of cowardice he experiences. But he also quietly propels his young protagonist towards a kind of revelation, founded on an understanding of what his true place in war, and the scheme of things, is, and what that should mean for him, in terms of judgement and conduct.

During his first encounter with the enemy, Fleming witnesses a mass retreat of his fellow soldiers. He also receives a head wound from the butt of a gun, when he grabs a deserter to try to find out what is happening. This, and his flight from a second encounter with the enemy, persuade him that he is no more than an insignificant part of a 'vast blue demonstration'. His dreams of glory fade into a sense of absurdity, nihilism and hopelessness. His comrades in arms may admire the 'red badge of courage' on his head, but he knows that it is not his courage but his cowardice and confusion that have helped put it there. Fleming has swung from romanticism to nihilism. Where Crane has him end, though, is with something like a proper human response to the bleak realities of experience. Back with his regiment, after wandering lost for some time, Fleming automatically, instinctively picks up the regimental colours when they fall from the hands of another soldier during a charge forward against the enemy. The description of this event manages a delicate balance between a sense of the fated and the chosen. Fleming 'was aware of the machinery of orders that started the charge', the reader is told; 'the youth was pushed and jostled for a moment before he understood the movement at all, but directly he lunged ahead and began to run'. Equally, the account of the aftermath is poised between pride and guilt, relief and regret. 'He saw that he was good', we learn, but in recalling 'his failure and his achievement', and in particular his moments of cowardice and betrayal, he finds something that 'would become a good part of him' by 'hindering the workings of his egotism'. The muted moral conclusion that Crane and his young protagonist arrive at is neatly imaged in a concluding description of 'a golden ray of sun' breaking for a moment 'through the hosts of leaden rain clouds'. Fleming, the intimation is, is 'tiny but not inconsequent', he can achieve some moral agency in and through an accurate vision of where he stands, as a soldier and a man. He takes the path of realism, understanding and humility of attitude. As a result, 'the red badge of courage' of the title assumes meanings that are both ironic and serious, for him and his creator. It measures the gap between false courage, heroic illusion and reality, but it also rehearses the true courage that Fleming, and any human being, can achieve: the courage of knowing and accepting oneself and situation for what they are.

In *The Red Badge of Courage*, Crane wrote of the way of humility. In his story 'The Open Boat', he wrote of community. Based on his own experience of shipwreck in 1896, when he spent nearly three days in an open boat at sea, the story draws a contrast between the empty, undifferentiated vastness of the ocean and the companionship of the shipwrecked, as they struggle to survive in body and in mind. 'It would be difficult to describe the subtle brotherhood of men that was here established on the seas,' the narrator confides. 'No one said that it was so. No one mentioned it. But it dwelt in the boat, and each man felt it warm him.' Anticipating Hemingway, and after him Albert Camus – and, perhaps, recalling the work of his friend Conrad – Crane proposes the experience of men working together as a prototype of human connectedness, a frail defence against the world in which we find ourselves exiled. Other, later writers were to call this absurdism or existentialism. Crane, typically, preferred a simpler word. 'Most of my prose writings', he declared, 'have been toward the goal partially described by that misunderstood and abused word, realism.' That word would not have been rejected, either, by Jack London, who, like Norris and Crane, saw reality as a naturalistic struggle for existence, dominated by what he termed – in one of his most famous stories, *The Call of the Wild* (1903) – the 'law of club and fang'. For London, even more ruthlessly than for Crane or even perhaps Norris, life was a battle for power. 'The ultimate unit of matter and the ultimate unit of force were the same,' the reader is informed in *The Iron Heel* (1908). 'Power will be the arbiter,' the hero of that novel declares. 'It is a struggle of classes. Just as your class dragged down the old feudal nobility, so shall it be dragged down by my class, the working class.'

Ernest Everhard, the hero of *The Iron Heel*, is addressing his remarks to a member of The Oligarchy, a defensive, proto-fascist conglomeration of major trusts and their private militias. The story is set in the years 1911–32 and is supposedly a transcription of a manuscript written at the time by Avis Cunningham, the wife of Everhard and fellow revolutionary, and edited seven hundred years later by Anthony Meredith, who lives in what is called the fourth century of the Brotherhood of Man. It describes a violent revolutionary struggle against the iron heel of totalitarian capitalism that ends disastrously: Everhard is killed, Avis is apparently executed, and the revolution is crushed. The descriptive frame, however, offers not just hope but the fulfilment of the hero's prophecy, since the reader is told that the iron heel was finally overthrown some three hundred years after the events related in what is called the 'Everhard Manuscript'. Like *The Octopus*, *The Iron Heel* places the specifics of political defeat within a visionary framework that proposes eventual redemption, the triumph of the people emerging out of a potentially endless struggle for power. Like *The Octopus*, too, it offers the reader a powerful mix of socialist message and proto-fascist feeling. Everhard, for instance, proclaims himself a revolutionary socialist and is certainly portrayed as such. But we are also told that 'he was a superman, a blond beast such as Nietzsche has described'; 'in addition,' the narrative adds, perhaps a little too late, 'he was aflame with democracy.' Nearly all London's fiction betrays a similar fissure between a kind of idealistic socialism and a general view of existence that is vigorously amoral. A commitment to the political and economic jostles with celebration of the primitive, the morally indifferent power of nature and the beauty of blond, clean-limbed heroes: Wolf Larsen in *The Sea-Wolf*, for instance, is lovingly described as being of 'Scandinavian stock', 'the man type, the masculine, and almost a god in his perfectness'. This reflects London's overwhelming commitment to the will to power, in man, society and nature. Even self-inflicted death can become an expression of that will, in his work. In *Martin Eden* (1909), for example, London's most autobiographical novel, the hero commits suicide by forcing himself to stay below the surface of the ocean, despite the struggle his body makes to persuade him otherwise. Suicide becomes, in these terms, a triumph of the will.

Martin Eden, Wolf Larsen and Ernest Everhard are all men of genius from humble surroundings. Each has a touch of the rebel, the Antichrist in him: Larsen, a 'mighty spirit', who insists he would prefer 'suffering in freedom to all the happiness of servility', is even compared to John Milton's portrait of Lucifer. Clearly, there was a sense in which London was presenting an idealized portrait of himself, and his rise from a humble background, in these portraits. Born illegitimate, London grew up on the waterfront of Oakland, received only intermittent schooling, and for much of his youth lived on the wrong side of the law. After a spell in prison, he worked at sea. Returning to land, he discovered communism. Enrolling in the University of California briefly, he left to join the Klondike gold rush. Then, returning to Oakland in 1898, he began to write about his experiences. Stories appeared in

Overland Monthly in the West and the *Atlantic Monthly* in the East. His first and second novels were published in 1902; and a year later the third, *The Call of the Wild*, catapulted him to fame. The 'hero' of the story is a dog, Buck, who is kidnapped from his comfortable existence on a California estate and sold into service as a sledge dog in the Klondike. Eventually, abandoning human society and companionship altogether, Buck becomes leader of a pack of wolves. He has returned to nature, the primitive, aboriginal condition of existence. 'Suddenly jerked from the heart of civilisation and flung into the heart of things primordial', all social veneer is stripped away and he is restored to the fundamentals of existence and the 'primordial beast' lurking within him. Buck is clearly a means for London to expose and explore the primitive bases in all nature, including the human. His story is a story of regression but, unlike *McTeague* or *Vandover and the Brute*, a triumphant one. Moving from the warm, 'ordered', 'civilised' 'Southland', where he lives the life of 'a sated aristocrat', he encounters the cold vastness of the 'Northland', nature in all its blank neutrality and indifference to human and animal welfare. He grows strong from the encounter: with the reader last seeing him in all his primal beauty – 'leaping gigantic above his fellows, his great throat a-bellow as he sings a song of the younger world, which is the song of the pack'. A comparison with earlier American texts inscribing a return to nature and the natural, like *Walden* and *The Adventures of Huckleberry Finn*, is perhaps instructive. Thoreau and Twain, in their separate ways, saw nature as a fundamentally moral agency: the source of a humanly sympathetic, ethically sound life. Man, in their work, returns to nature as a means of moral instruction and regeneration. For London, however, nature is what Wolf Larsen calls it in *The Sea-Wolf*, 'unmoral': it is pure precisely because it is primitive, existing apart from human judgement. His characters, human or otherwise, return to it and learn there a truth that is determinately unhuman: that life is a matter of neither emotion nor ethics but 'the call of the wild', 'ruthless struggle'.

That truth is also learned in *The Sea-Wolf*: a novel that deserves a place with *The Call of the Wild*, *The Iron Heel* and *Martin Eden* as one of London's major works. Here, it is a man who is suddenly removed from civilized society. In the fog on San Francisco Bay, two ferry boats collide and Humphrey Van Weyden, the narrator, is thrown overboard. He is saved by a sealing schooner, the *Ghost*, whose captain, Wolf Larsen, presses him into service. The character of Van Weyden is suggested by his interests. He is a critic who has written an essay on Poe and is planning another essay entitled 'The Necessity for Freedom: A Plea for the Artist'. Clearly, London intends the reader to regard Van Weyden as not only effete but suffering from a dangerous delusion: that human beings are capable of free will, determining their own fate. The accident that propels Van Weyden out of society is plainly symbolic of the chance rhythms that govern all human existence. The fog, too, is a symbol. It is, the reader is told, 'like the gray shadow of infinite mystery brooding over the whirling speck of earth'. 'Men, mere motes of light and sparkle' simply ride 'their steeds of wood and steel through the heart of the mystery': at the mercy of forces beyond their control, as Van Weyden is when he is cast overboard. Van

Weyden is first consigned to the water, the 'mighty rhythm' of which offers a paradigm of the mighty rhythms ruling all things. He is then drawn into a new life on a ship the name of which suggests an afterlife, another form of existence, where he is given 'new' clothes, a new name 'Hump', and a new job as a cabin boy. In his 'new and elemental environment' in which, he reveals, 'force, nothing but force obtained', Van Weyden receives an education into the realities of power from Larsen. The lesson is learned from Larsen's instruction and example and, not least, from the sheer brute magnificence of his appearance: in terms of physique he is, we are told, like one of 'our tree-dwelling prototypes' while he has a voice 'as rough and harsh and frank as the sea itself'. Gradually, Van Weyden changes. 'It seemed to me that my innocence of the realities of life had been complete indeed,' he now confesses, 'I was no longer Humphrey Van Weyden. I was Hump.' His muscles grow strong and hard; and his mind grows accustomed to the daily fact of brutality.

London did try to temper the harsh message of *The Sea-Wolf* by introducing another castaway, a woman called Maude Brewster. A poet and a 'delicate, ethereal creature', Maude is clearly intended to embody a more humane philosophy: to offer Van Weyden, and the reader, an alternative to the predatory principles of Larsen. But the episodes involving Maude are easily the weakest element in the book. Inadvertently, by their very weakness, they reveal where London's fundamental sympathies lay. The imaginative commitment of *The Sea-Wolf* is to the character who is, in many ways, a version or projection of its author, or at least of how he would have liked to see himself. And that is especially the case in its closing pages. At the end of the novel, Larsen is deserted by his crew. Suffering from cerebral cancer, he first goes blind and then dies on a deserted island. Struggling to survive against his creeping paralysis, his will and his disbelief in immortality never falter: as the very last word he ever writes, a defiant 'B-O-S-H', indicates. He ends as he began in the novel, by saying no, in thunder, to convention, custom and conscience and by demonstrating his core belief in willpower and struggle. He dies, as so many of London's human characters do, the sacrificial death of a hero who embraces his dying as a necessary part of the 'yeast', the 'ferment' of existence. It comes as little of a surprise to learn that, after a turbulent forty years of living and writing (not only fiction, but vivid accounts of poverty like *The People of the Abyss* [1903] and social treatises such as *The War of the Classes* [1904]), London committed suicide. His body worn down by the strenuous life he had gloried in, and by alcoholism, his mind worn out by disillusionment and depression – the things he had seen and endured, the discrepancy between his own success and the suffering he still saw around him – he performed one last act of the will. For London, life was struggle. While he could, he engaged in the struggle with intense enthusiasm; when he felt he could no longer, he embraced the inevitable. Like his hero Martin Eden, in effect, he ended by affirming his own bleak belief that life is a thing that moves and then moves no more – and his power over at least one 'thing' that moved, himself.

The Development of Women's Writing

Writing by African American women

The world of the naturalists is, on the whole, a determinately male one, defined by power and struggle. In the work of Norris and London, in particular, there is a distinctively and additionally masculine strain: marked by barely concealed homoerotic feelings and loving admiration for those men who have understood and perhaps embody the principle of force. In the work of a number of women writers of the later nineteenth century, there may be a similar interest in the allocation and distribution of power. However, it tends to express itself in different forms, less conspicuously wedded to the notion of life as war. The forms in which women writers expressed themselves during this period were several, and usually involved a continuity with writing before the Civil War. Some of the forms they took up and developed, such as spiritual autobiography, Gothic and polemic, had not been the special preserve of earlier women writers. Some, like domestic realism, had. But there was a marked tendency to use these forms to explore, as Kate Chopin did, the condition and vocation of women, their relationship to the changing worlds of home and work. And there was an equally marked tendency to look, as Mary Wilkins Freeman did, at how women could get the attention of society, and men in particular, how they could acquire a voice that mattered and get themselves heard. Such tendencies are, quite naturally, to be found with especial force in the work of those who came from, and saw themselves as representing, the most powerless, underprivileged community of women, African Americans: among them Julia A. J. Foote (1827–1900) and Pauline Elizabeth Hopkins (1859–1930). Foote, the daughter of former slaves, was born in New York State and, while still only ten, began work as a domestic servant for whites. At the age of fifteen, she converted to an African Episcopal church in New York and began to devote herself to evangelical work. What she preached, above all, was the doctrine of sanctification: the belief that a Christian could be completely liberated from sin and empowered to lead a life of spiritual perfection. And her conviction that she herself had been sanctified made her sure that her destiny was to be a preacher: something that brought her into conflict with church leaders, and the general customs and prejudices of the day.

This, and other notable events in Foote's life, are recounted in her autobiography, *A Brand Plucked from the Fire* (1879). To an extent, the book goes back to a tradition of spiritual autobiography that finds its American roots in the earliest writings of the Puritans. But it also reflects a growing commitment to the idea of spiritual androgyny, to be found in similar texts by black and white women of the time. Foote details her problems, when the minister of her church in Boston denied her access to the pulpit and threatened to throw her out of his congregation. She also describes how she took her case to higher church authorities; how, when she received no help from them, she embarked on a professional preaching career;

how she was involved in the holiness revivals that swept across the Midwest in the 1870s; and how she became the first woman ordained a deacon and the second woman to become an elder in her church. As she does so, she insists on her spiritual equality with men, and the spiritual equality of women in general. Women have 'suffered persecution and death in the name of the Lord Jesus', she points out; 'The conduct of holy women is recorded in scripture', and 'in the early ages of Christianity many women were happy and glorious in martyrdom'. Citing the Bible, to the effect that 'there is neither male nor female in Christ Jesus', Foote makes an eloquent case for spiritual parity that is, in her humble opinion, further proven by her witness and testimony. Her conversion, her experience of the Holy Spirit and her successful pursuit of the vocation of preacher are all, she infers, evidence that she, and indeed all women, stand equal in the sight of the Lord. And, she clearly indicates, that should make them equal in the sight of society and its institutions as well.

Unlike Foote, Pauline E. Hopkins worked in many forms and genres, and was the most productive African American woman writer of her generation. Born in Maine and raised in Boston, where she was encouraged to develop her considerable literary talents, she won a prize for an essay on *The Evils of Intemperance and Their Remedy* (the prize was presented by the earlier African American writer, William Wells Brown) at the age of fifteen. At the age of twenty, she composed and produced a musical drama dealing with the underground railroad. And some years later, in 1900, she became involved as literary editor and major contributor with the *Colored American Magazine*, one of a number of important black periodicals of the time that included imaginative writing, journalism, scholarship and political commentary. Hopkins published a large body of work in the *Colored American*, including short stories, biographical articles and historical sketches. What has secured her reputation, however, are her four novels, three of which were serialized in the *Colored American* and one of which, *Contending Forces: A Romance of Negro Life North and South* (1900), was published by the press that issued the magazine, the Colored Co-operative Publishing Company. These novels are remarkable for the use of established popular genres to explore the themes of race and gender. In *Winona, A Tale of Negro Life in the South and Southwest* (1902), for instance, a love story about a beautiful, tragic mulatta becomes a means of exploring the contentious issues of slavery and racial and sexual oppression. And in *Of One Blood; or, the Hidden Self* (1903), Hopkins produces an early example of black science fiction writing, using an imaginary underground African city as an imaginative site for exploring the racial mixing of blacks and whites. Most notable of all, in *Contending Forces*, Hopkins takes on a wide canvas and the mainstream literary genres of domestic and historical romance. The setting ranges from Bermuda in the 1790s to Boston in the late nineteenth century. Thrilling episodes, involving endangered heroines and lecherous villains, are juxtaposed with scenes of domestic bliss. Tragic misunderstandings and melodramatic coincidences are mingled with scenes of marriage and motherhood. And, throughout all this, Hopkins presses upon the issues of racial injustice and sexual oppression, as her black women are violated, and her black men characters brutalized and killed, by the dominant whites.

At the centre of *Contending Forces* is a character called Sappho Clark. Sold into prostitution by her white uncle at the age of fourteen, she has a son who was conceived during the period when she was effectively a sexual slave. To a degree, she is the conventional romance heroine, the tragic mulatta. Perhaps exploiting the prejudices of the time, but more probably reflecting them, Hopkins even attributes to Sappho the conventional beauty of the white heroine. Sappho is 'tall and fair', the reader learns, 'with hair of a golden cast, aquiline nose, rosebud mouth, soft brown eyes veiled by long, dark lashes which swept her cheek'. So far, so conventional: Hopkins is not above subscribing to racial stereotype. Particularly, she is not above stereotyping lower-class black characters, who seem to have a virtual monopoly on dialect, 'wild vivacity', a tendency towards easy morality, and the provision of comic relief. But Sappho is more than meets the eye. For a start, Sappho is not her real name. She has adopted it to disguise her identity, and it is a clear allusion to the ancient Greek poet who created a school of women's poetry and music on the island of Lesbos. The portrait of Sappho Clark, beneath its conventional veneer, has a definite political agenda. Her personal story exposes what Hopkins, in her Preface to the book, refers to as a history of 'lynching and concubinage', a series of 'monstrous outbreaks' of injustice 'under a government founded upon the greatest and brightest of principles for the elevation of mankind'. Her character and stoicism, in turn, are meant to inspire admiration, and so contribute to what Hopkins saw as the ultimate aim of the book: 'in an humble way', as the author puts it, 'to raise the stigma of degradation from my race'. And Sappho's declarations of independence – her insistence, for example, that she actively enjoys working outside the home for pay – add to our sense that this is a book that uses literary stereotypes, of race and gender, only to resist and subvert social ones. The domestic scenes and the eventual destiny of Sappho bring this out with particular force. While Sappho is at a boarding house, she shares in gatherings of women at sewing circles and tea parties. What at first appears a commonplace of domestic fiction, however, turns out to be much more than that. The domestic sphere was an important site of resistance, at this time, for African American women; and the black women's club movement of the 1890s, which Hopkins is effectively describing in these scenes, became a powerful collective force for change, fighting for integration and sexual equality and against racial prejudice and sexual abuse. The 'sewing circle', as Hopkins presents it, is a political forum, whose members celebrate their solidarity as women and blacks – while discussing such pressing issues as 'the place which the virtuous woman occupies in upbuilding the race'. The reader is given a rare insight into the lives of African American bourgeois women here. More to the point, he or she is also in at the beginnings of a seminal political movement, permitted to witness meetings that both confirm the dignity and community of African American women and interrogate the elaborate machinery of legal instruments and social prejudice that keeps them down. There is a pungent realism of attitude at work in these domestic scenes, and implicitly throughout the book: 'The great cause of the evolution of true womanhood', the narrator quietly reminds us, would be greatly assisted by 'money, the sinews of living and social standing'. 'It is an incontrovertible truth', one member of the sewing circles acidly observes, 'that there is no such thing as an unmixed black on the American continent.' At her best, Hopkins uses romance to communicate that realism and to express hope for the future founded upon it. That is nowhere more clearly illustrated than in the fate of Sappho. Falling in love with the son of her landlady, Will Smith, she fears that her past will prevent their union and, for a while, runs away. But she is finally reunited with Will, who recognizes that she is not to blame for her life as a prostitute and is happy to marry her. The resolution may seem, and indeed is, romantic, even sentimental. But it presses home the point that woman is the victim, the innocent here. In acknowledging this, and acting on the acknowledgement, Will is a romantic hero making a realistic judgement of what can happen to women, especially poor, black women, in a society dominated by men. He is doing what his creator set out to do: as she put it in her Preface to *Contending Forces*, 'pleading for justice of heart and mind'.

Writing and the condition of women

Pauline Hopkins tried to write for a living but, much of the time, had to support herself by working as a stenographer. Writing was also the means that Louisa M. Alcott (1832–88) sought to support not only herself but her mother and sisters. Her father, Bronson Alcott, was more interested in pursuing his utopian ideals than bread-winning – indeed, he tended to regard working for money as inconsistent with his Transcendentalist ideals. And Louisa Alcott, who never married, having experienced debt and dependency as a child was determined to avoid them as an adult; she was determined to save her family from them too. She completed her first book, *Flower Babies*, when she was only sixteen, although it was not published until 1855. Working as an army nurse during the Civil War, she used this experience as the basis for *Hospital Sketches* (1863). During the remainder of her life, she produced over three hundred titles. What she is mainly remembered for, however, are her domestic novels written for children. The best known of these is *Little Women: or, Meg, Jo, and Amy*. This novel was originally published in two parts: the first, *Little Women*, appeared in 1868, the second part, *Good Wives*, was published the following year, and in 1871 the two came out as a single volume, *Little Women and Good Wives*. Alcott drew on her own life and family experiences in writing these and other domestic tales: Jo March, for instance, one of the 'little women', is based on Alcott herself. But the March family live in genteel poverty, whereas the Alcotts, when Louisa was young, often suffered a fiercer deprivation. With the spectacular commercial success of *Little Women*, however, the financial security of Alcott and her relatives was assured. She continued to write domestic tales. But, before and after the publication of *Little Women*, she also continued to try her hand at other forms. Between 1863 and 1869, for instance, she published anonymous and pseudonymous Gothic romances and thrilling tales with titles like 'Pauline's

Passion and Punishment'; these were eventually collected and published in 1975 as *Behind a Mask*. She wrote, under her own name, *Moods* (1864), a grimly realistic account of adultery and divorce as alternatives to unhappy marriage, and *Transcendental Wild Oats* (1873), a satirical treatment of Fruitlands, the utopian community founded by her father. 'Tired', as she put it, 'of providing moral pap for the young', she also produced a tale influenced by Goethe called *A Modern Mephistopheles* (1877), in which an innocent young woman resists seduction by the diabolic genius with whom her poet husband has made a Faustian pact. And, in 1873, she published what is perhaps her most interesting book, an autobiographical fiction that covers nearly twenty years in the life of its heroine, *Work: A Story of Experience*.

Work begins with Christie, its heroine who is twenty-one, declaring her independence of her guardian, Uncle Enos. It ends with her, at the age of forty, discovering her vocation as a spokesperson for the rights of women. Christie is resolved, as she puts it, 'not to be a slave to anybody'. And, in pursuing that resolution, she takes jobs ranging from sewing to acting. She is also helped and inspired by the companionship and the stories of female friends, the women she meets after her declaration of independence: among them, a runaway slave and many fellow women workers. The episode in which Christie becomes an actress is typical of the narrative as a whole, in its cunning mix of realism and melodrama, empirical detail and romantic allusion. 'Feeling that she had all the world before her where to choose', like Eve after she is expelled from the Garden of Eden, our heroine meets two boarders at her lodging house, 'an old lady and her pretty daughter'. They are both 'actresses at a respectable theatre', and they help Christie to acquire the role of 'Queen of the Amazons' in a 'new spectacle'. Christie is spurred on to take a role that clearly expresses her own sense of her power as a female by the thought that Uncle Enos would disapprove. 'Uncle Enos', she reflects, 'considered "play-actin" as the sum of all iniquity'; and, in becoming an actor, 'a delicious sense of freedom pervaded her soul, and the old defiant spirit seemed to rise up within her'. Christie has 'no talent except that which may develop in any girl possessing the lively fancy, sympathetic nature, and ambitious spirit which make such girls naturally dramatic'. But she soon rises in the theatrical ranks. As she does so, however, she becomes aware that she is growing, as a result of her success, 'selfish, frivolous, and vain'. She has 'reached the height of earthly bliss', she reflects; she may become 'a fine actress perhaps, but how good a woman?' Play-acting has served its purpose, in further liberating and developing her; and she quits it, after an appropriately melodramatic episode in which she forgets herself and risks injury to save a fellow actress from an accident onstage. She has shown her mettle as a true woman, caring selflessly for another woman, and it is time to move on. By the close of the story, Christie has a daughter, and is joined with her and other females in what is termed a 'loving league of sisters'. Devoted now to the cause of women, she is roughly the same age as her creator was when she published this novel; and it is hard not to see her sense of her own empowerment as something shared with Alcott. *Work* is a celebration of female liberation and labour of many kinds: including the liberation experienced in and from the labour of writing.

Harriet Spofford (1835–1921) also wrote to support herself and her family. Her reputation was established when the *Atlantic Monthly* published her short story, 'In a Cellar', in 1859. She went on to write poetry, articles and several novels. The longer fiction includes *Sir Rohan's Ghost* (1860), a Gothic story of a man who tries to kill his mistress and is later plagued by her daughter, and *Azarian: An Episode* (1864), a more poetic tale concerning an artistic Bostonian called Constant Azarian who is too self-absorbed to appreciate the devotion of the idealistic Ruth Yetton. Born in New England, and moving to Washington, DC, after marriage, Spofford also wrote of her New England friendships in *A Little Book of Friendships* (1916) and the local colour of the capital city in *Old Washington* (1906). Notable among her non-fictional work is her book *Art Decoration Applied to Furniture* (1878), where she develops her belief that style in dress and furnishings reflects the people who wear and acquire them. That belief informs what is undoubtedly her best work, her short stories, collected in such volumes as *The Amber Gods and Other Stories* (1863), *New-England Legends* (1871) and *The Elder's People* (1920). In the title tale of her first, 1863 collection, for instance, the two major, female characters are defined by the jewellery they wear. The passionate Yon wears 'pagan' amber ornaments, while the placid and patient Lu wears 'light' and 'limpid' aqua-marina. What also informs the best of these stories is a firm commitment to female power and community. In 'A Village Dressmaker', for example, the dressmaker Susanna gives the wedding gown she made for herself to Rowena Mayhew, who is marrying the man they have both loved. And she is happy to do so because, as her two maiden aunts recognize, she has acknowledged necessity and, at the same time, she has helped another woman. That tale is from Spofford's final, 1920 collection, which is a detailed, realistic account of New England life. Some of the earlier stories are more strangely, hauntingly romantic but they still explore the terms in which women can express and assert themselves: through companionship, say, or through the quilts and clothes they make or the way in which they dress themselves.

One particularly remarkable earlier story is 'Circumstance' (1863). In this, an unnamed woman returns home through 'those eastern wilds of Maine in that epoch frequently making neighbours and mile synonymous'. In the gathering dark, she appears to see a winding-sheet and hear a melancholy voice. But the woman is tough: she has been brought up on the frontier and 'dealing with hard fact does not engender a flimsy mind'. Besides, she is determined to get back to her husband and child. Further on, however, she encounters 'a swift shadow, like the fabulous flying-dragon'. It turns out to be 'that wild beast . . . known by hunters as the Indian Devil': a panther, which leaps upon her and begins to gnaw at her arm. The woman cries out; the beast is suddenly still; and the woman realizes that she can keep the beast from harming her, at least for the moment, by breaking the silence of the forest. So she sings, all the songs she knows, all through the night. 'Still she chanted on' is a refrain in this strange, dreamlike tale. Eventually, as dawn comes, the woman loses her voice, and is only saved by the timely arrival of her husband, who shoots the panther. Returning home, she and her family then find that, in their absence, their home is a 'smoking ruin', destroyed by Indians. There is desolation but there is also a sense of hope. 'The world was all before them,' the tale concludes, 'where to choose.' Like Alcott, Spofford recalls the description of Adam and Eve leaving Eden, in the concluding lines of *Paradise Lost* (1667) by John Milton, to inscribe her emancipatory theme. Her heroine has saved herself by finding her voice; she has tamed the beast by rehearsing her own will to live in song. Her chant, like the dramatic performances of Christie in *Work*, is her art: her way of surviving and asserting herself. Thanks to that art, she has the world before her and can begin again. And 'Circumstance' itself, of course, like the novel *Work* for Alcott, is Spofford's art: it is the author's way of announcing not only the power of female action but the power, and necessity, of female narrative.

Elizabeth Stuart Phelps (1844–1911) was less convinced that women would be allowed the time for their art. At least, in her best work she was. The daughter of a popular author, whose name she took as her own, she continued her mother's interest in religious fiction by writing *The Gates Ajar* (1868). This was not so much a novel as a series of conversations by fictional characters about the beauties of heaven. It was immensely popular, particularly with women readers, and was followed by a number of books, the 'Gates' series, exploring the same theme. But Phelps also wrote *Hedged In* (1870), a novel that attacks the hypocrisy of society in its treatment of women who transgress conventional moral standards. This was followed by other novels that focus on the condition of women, and, in particular, on women and work: among them, *The Silent Partner* (1871), a story of New England mill girls, and *Dr Zay* (1882), an account of a successful woman physician. Of these novels, the most memorable is *The Story of Avis* (1887). At the beginning of this novel, the talented heroine, Avis Phelps, returns home to New England after training as an artist in Europe for four years. She is courted by Philip Ostrander, who has been wounded in the Civil War; and, while she is aware of the risk to her career as an artist involved, she marries him. She soon realizes her mistake. The care of her husband (who eventually becomes too much of an invalid to continue work), and then her son Van and daughter Wait, leave her little time for her art. In particular, she finds her work on her major project, a painting of the sphinx, constantly frustrated. Phelps uses a mixture of irony, incantation and allusion here, to measure the losses of her heroine's life. There is irony, for instance, in Phelps's account of Philip's obliviousness to his wife's needs, his quiet satisfaction in the way he has helped her into being 'so comfortable a housekeeper' as he perceives her to be. There is incantation in the way the narrative describes how Avis is ground in the mill of domesticity. One such description repeats the ironic phrase, 'it was not much', while going through the details of Avis's daily routine, then concludes: 'It was not much, but let us not forget that it is under the friction of such atoms, that women far simpler, and so for that yoke, far stronger, than Avis, had yielded their lives as a burden too heavy to be borne.' And there is an adept use of allusion, as Avis looks at her painting of the sphinx and seems to see 'meanings' in its enigmatic expression, 'questionings . . . to which her imagination had found no controlling reply'. The riddle of the sphinx, for Avis, is how to be both a woman and an artist. It is a riddle she never manages to resolve for herself. Unlike 'other women – content to stitch and sing, to sweep and smile', she never completes her masterwork to her own satisfaction. All she can hope for, at the end of the novel, is that her daughter will not repeat her mistake. Her husband dead, and her son, Avis moves back into her father's house, where she will give Wait, she hopes, the training necessary not to waste her talent as she has.

A similar concern with the waste to which most women's lives are subject informs nearly all the writings of Charlotte Perkins Gilman (1860–1935). Regarded as the leading intellectual in the women's movement around the turn of the century, Gilman was mainly known during her lifetime for her non-fictional work. In *Women and Economics* (1898), she argued that the economic dependence of women on men hindered the happiness of all. Blending history, sociology, psychology and anthropology in her analysis of the present and the past, Gilman suggested that 'women's work' and women themselves should be separated from the domestic sphere. The work would then be done by trained and paid professionals, and women would be free to follow the vocation of their choice in the public sphere. The programme Gilman developed here was based on the abolition of the sexual division of labour; as she saw it, only child-rearing should remain the special preserve of women. This programme was publicized in extensive lecture tours she undertook in the United States and elsewhere. And it was developed in other works of non-fiction. *Concerning Children* (1900) and *The Home* (1904), for instance, proposed further changes to liberate women to lead more productive lives; while *Man Made World* (1911) and *His Religion and Hers* (1927) anticipated a major role for women in international affairs and the church. Gilman explored similar or related themes in her fiction, which received less attention from her contemporaries. Late in her career, for example, she wrote three utopian novels that offered feminist solutions to social problems: *Moving the Mountain* (1911), *Herland* (1915) and *With Her in Ourland* (1916). *Herland*, the best of these, is typical of all three. It describes a society of women without men, governed by principles of nurturing and caring in which children are raised by the community and cherished as the most important collective resource. Like her non-fiction, it resists any division of labour based on gender, or any definitions of behaviour founded on a distinction between 'masculine' and 'feminine' traits. And it works actively against any map of being that charts its territory in terms of gender – that portrays any area of life as determinately female or male.

From 1910 until 1916, Gilman edited a magazine, *The Forerunner*, consisting entirely of her own fiction and articles on women's issues. Over her lifetime, she also wrote more than two hundred stories, most of them for her magazine. Of these, easily the most famous is 'The Yellow Wall-Paper' (1892). Gilman based the story on her own experience of a 'rest cure': a regimen of bed rest and confinement that almost drove her, she said later, to 'utter mental ruin'. In it, an unnamed woman records her strange experiences when she and her husband, 'John', go to live in 'ancestral halls' for the summer. Her husband is a physician, she tells us, so is her brother; and so, although she does not believe she is sick, when they tell her she has 'a slight hysterical tendency', she feels helpless to refute them. 'What is one to do?' she asks. At their new house for the summer, John chooses the room where she is to stay to deal with her 'nervous condition'. She would have preferred another room, 'but John would not hear of it'. And the room where she is to spend most of her time she soon begins to dislike, because it is covered with a wallpaper the colour of which is 'repellent, almost revolting, a smouldering unclean yellow, strangely faded by the slow-turning sunlight'. John, who is, his wife says, 'practical in the extreme', does not take her complaints about the wallpaper seriously. Alone in her room, though, discouraged from writing or any other labour, she becomes obsessed with it. She first sees eyes staring from the wallpaper. Then she begins to see a 'shape' behind the pattern. There is a 'front pattern' and a 'back pattern', she believes; the front pattern is like bars, and the shape is that of 'a woman stooping down and creeping about behind'. As her obsession with the paper grows, she can see the front pattern move as, she believes, 'the woman behind shakes it!' 'I think that woman gets out in daytime!' the narrator confesses; 'I can see her . . . creeping all around the garden', 'when I creep by daylight'.

The narrator, it is clear, is starting to see the shape in the paper as a double, a secret sharer in her own imprisonment. And as that intensifies, she tears at the yellow wallpaper that constitutes her jail as well as that of her *doppelgänger*, in a desperate effort to liberate herself and her reflection, the pair of them. In her own eyes, that effort meets with success. The story ends with the narrator declaring to her husband – who has had to break down the door with an axe to get into the room – 'I've pulled off most of the paper, so you can't put me back!' She has broken down and broken out. Under the coercive pressure of her husband, and other physicians, she has become what they prescribed her to be. They have resisted taking her, and her needs, seriously; unsympathetic and unimaginative, their best intentions have made her a prisoner. She has taken the only way out she sees or senses: through the 'bars' of the wallpaper and into insanity. The power of this story stems from its mix of the surreal and the simple, the Gothic and the realistic. The narrator records her extraordinary experiences in an ordinary style, the style of a journal, because each strange event she describes is utterly real to her. The subtlety of the story, in turn, issues from the way the author frames the narrator: allowing us to see what she does not see, just how much her manacles are mind-forged and man-forged. 'John says' is a constant, deferential refrain in the tale. Even when John denies precisely what the narrator most wants, she is reluctant to resist him. She writes her journal, this story, in secret, for instance, because she knows he does not like her to write. 'He hates me to write a word,' she confesses, 'but I *must* say what I feel and think in some way – it is such a relief!' Subject to the prevailing pieties about the superior wisdom of men and the necessary subordina-tion of women, she is forced into guilt or denial. She can only write herself on the secret paper of her journal or the wallpaper. Gilman shows us all this, while never permitting us to waver in our sympathy for the narrator, or to feel the grip of her own rapt imagination upon our own. We know her strange experiences, because we share them, but we also know the motives, the reasons for them; we are compelled to see them as necessary, inevitable delusions. 'The Yellow Wall-Paper' is one of the most impressive accounts in American literature of male suppression and female subjection, and the tortured consequences to which both can lead. It is also, as Gilman surely intended, a revelation of what the denial of human need can bring about for anyone – of how humanity, if it is repressed, will always have its revenge.

The Development of Many Americas

Things fall apart

Henry Adams (1838–1918) was also interested in the rights and the condition of women. In 1876, he delivered an influential lecture on 'The Primitive Rights of Women'. His first novel, *Democracy* (1880), explores not only political life in Washington but the contemporary situation of American women; so does his second novel, *Esther* (1884). In his two most celebrated and important works, *Mont-Saint-Michel and Chartres* (privately printed in 1904, published in 1913) and *The Education of Henry Adams* (privately printed in 1907, published in 1918), he was to explore his theory of feminine force and, in particular, the unifying cultural power embodied in the figure of the Virgin. Adams was descended from one of the most powerful dynasties in American history. The grandson of the sixth president of the United States, and the great-grandson of the second president, he served as private secretary to his father, the American diplomatic representative in London, during the Civil War. He taught history at Harvard, where he had also been educated, from 1870 to 1877; edited the *North American Review* during the same period; and wrote numerous histories and political essays. His most important contribution to formal history was his *History of the United States During the Administration of Thomas Jefferson and James Madison* (1889–91), a book that follows the development of political life in the United States up to the arrival of John Monroe as the fifth president. Adams employed Germanic scholarly methods here. He also hoped to locate a key to the American past that could be used predictively to apply to the American future. He failed, however, to find one that satisfied him: although, as the chapter on 'American Ideals' clearly indicates, he did see American history as a tragic decline from the noble principles of the founding fathers – and, in particular, Thomas Jefferson's belief in human perfectibility – to more materialistic aims. Adams was intellectually drawn to discoveries in contemporary science and, especially, to the discovery that physical matter contained its own potential for disintegration. So was his younger brother, Brooke Adams (1848–1927), who, in his most distinguished work, *The Law of Civilization and Decay* (1893), argued from scientific analogy that any established order always contains the elements of its own decline, since it will eventually be overcome by economic forces that lead to the establishment of another order. For Henry Adams, as for Brooke, science proved that nature was without system. 'The kinetic theory of gas is an assertion of ultimate chaos,' Henry Adams wrote. 'In plain words, Chaos was the law of nature; Order was the dream of man.' In his attempts to impose order on the flux of his experience, man was, as he saw it, like a spider snaring the forces of nature that 'dance like flies before the net' of its web. That perception of disorder and entropy was to feed into later American writing; and it was memorably expressed and investigated in his two major works of personal and cultural exploration.

The first of these, *Mont-Saint-Michel and Chartres*, is subtitled *A Study of Thirteenth-Century Unity*. The book is structured as a tour of medieval France, with the author acting as an expert guide. Along the route, the two most significant points of interest, for our guide, are the fortress abbey of Mont-Saint-Michel and the cathedral at Chartres. And, as Adams takes the reader around them, he considers the dominant cultural power of the Middle Ages: the Catholic faith, which informed all aesthetic and intellectual endeavour as well as spiritual and ethical thought. In particular, he sees the force, the power of 'the Queen Mother', the Virgin, as 'absolute' during this period; adoration of the Virgin, he suggests, created a unifying ideal for the medieval sensibility, an ideal that composed life and art into a fluent harmony of sex, love, energy and benevolence. This notion of what Adams calls, at one point, 'the purity, the beauty, the grace, and the infinite loftiness of Mary's nature' is not so much a matter of faith, for Adams himself, as one of comparative cultural inquiry. He clearly sees faith in the Virgin, during the Middle Ages, as an agent of order, that 'dream of man': a cohesive cultural force and, as such, in marked contrast to the disintegrative, dispersive and essentially destructive tendencies of his own contemporary culture. That contrast is developed in his second major work, *The Education of Henry Adams*: the contrast is even registered in its subtitle, *A Study of Twentieth Century Multiplicity*.

The *Education* has the form of an autobiography. Among other things, Adams describes here his experiences as both student and teacher at Harvard, his impressions of England when he lived there during the Civil War, and the impact the theories of Charles Darwin had upon him. But it is no more an autobiography than *Mont-Saint-Michel* is a guidebook or a travel journal. Adams remains silent about his marriage, his wife and her eventual suicide; and he distances author from subject by describing himself in the third person. The core of the *Education*, like that of *Mont-Saint-Michel*, is intellectual and speculative: Adams is considering himself as a unique but also representative man, typical of his time, and he is using his experiences as a source of meditation, a means of considering what it is like to be alive at the turn of the twentieth century. That strategy comes out, with particularly memorable intensity, in the chapter titled 'The Dynamo and the Virgin'. Here, Adams picks up his earlier meditations on the Virgin. 'Symbol or energy, the Virgin had acted as the greatest force the Western world ever felt,' Adams argues, 'and had drawn man's activities to herself more strongly than any other power, natural or supernatural, had ever done.' 'She was the goddess because of her force,' he suggests; 'she was reproduction – the greatest and most mysterious of all energies.' As such, her absence from American thought and culture has a particular poignancy.

'American art, like the American language, and American education', is 'as far as possible sexless', Adams avers, because 'this energy' embodied in her is 'unknown to the American mind'. 'An American Virgin would never dare command,' Adams concludes; 'an American Venus would never dare exist.'

These speculations on the absence of the female principle from American life, as a source of power and unity, occur during Adams's account of his visit to the Paris exhibition of 1900. Entering 'the great hall of dynamos' there, in the company of aeronautics pioneer Samuel P. Langley, Adams began, he says, 'to feel the forty-foot dynamos as a moral force, much as the early Christians felt the Cross'. Langley was enthusiastic about the power of the modern motors, although he confessed himself worried about the anarchic potential of newly discovered forces. Adams, however, declares that those motors were unequivocally a 'nightmare' for him; he had, he tells the reader, 'his historical neck broken by the sudden irruption of forces totally new'. 'Woman had once been supreme' as an agent of social, cultural and intellectual unity. Now, as image and instrument of his place and time, Adams speculates, there was and is only 'this huge wheel, revolving ... at some vertiginous speed': reducing matter and mind to nothing more or less than a 'sequence of force'. 'He had entered a supersensual world', Adams says of himself, at this moment in the hall of motors, 'in which he could measure nothing except by chance collisions of movement imperceptible to his senses, perhaps even imperceptible to his instruments, but perceptible to each other, and to some known ray at the end of the scale.' For Adams, this experience was representative, like all the others recounted in the *Education*; and it was also seminal. All, he felt now, was a delirium of change. For the centripetal cultural energies of a female age, at once gentler and more energetically powerful, had been substituted the centrifugal forces focused and figured in the dynamo. A sense of being in the world, with substance, meaning and power, Adams believed and argued here, had been replaced by a feeling of merely surviving in a world over which we have marginal control and of which we enjoy minimal knowledge. Adams can be faulted on particular issues. His reverence for the past, American or medieval, can be excessively uncritical. There may be some intellectual imposture in his utopian notion of the age of ascendancy for Catholicism; there is certainly some posturing in his accounts of his spiritual trials. But his two major works are masterly innovations, extravagantly humble, daringly speculative, gathering together ideas and personalities in a web of speculation. Not only that, here and elsewhere in his writings, Adams takes the measure of his times and the diminutive role to which, in his view, man as well as woman in the late nineteenth and early twentieth centuries had been relegated. His language has the wit, grace and decorum of an earlier age of letters, the one to which his great-grandfather belonged. His forms and feelings, however, place him decidedly at the forefront of his own times, as he reflects on a world in process with a mixture of awe and panic. What Adams offers the reader, in short, is an elegant measuring of the vortex, a portrait of constant dispersion and dissolution that is at once dizzying and clearly focused – as precise and yet as disturbing as a late impressionist painting.

When Henry Adams wrote of multiplicity, there is no doubt that what he primarily had in mind was the disappearance of any tenable idea of order, a system of belief that would enable personal stability and cultural coherence. But inseparable from that was the sense Adams and others like him had that the Anglo-American model of civilization, embodied in such leaders of the early republic as his own great-grandfather, no longer enjoyed a monopoly on civic power. It was being challenged, more than ever, by other models. The voices of other Americans, describing other visions of America, were demanding to be heard. These included those other Americans who had been there before the whites, or those whose lands had been appropriated by the United States. They also included those who had come over, or had been brought over as slaves, before the Civil War, and those who had entered the country afterwards seeking opportunity or just survival. What these voices spoke of was their need for recognition as human beings and citizens; what they raged against was injustice. Sometimes, they celebrated resistance, individual or communal. At other times, they anticipated an America that embraced difference, that drew strength from its plural character – that saw multiplicity, in short, as a source of hope rather than fear.

Voices of resistance

In the Mexican American communities of the Southwest, the most popular and compelling form for expressing racial and cultural pride and resistance to white domination during this period was the *corrido*. The *corrido* is derived from the Spanish word for 'to run', and it describes the rapid pace of those narrative ballads whose roots can be traced to the romances of medieval Spain. *Corridos* first appeared, as a distinct ballad form, in Mexico during the middle of the nineteenth century. Soon afterwards they emerged in the American Southwest, assuming immense popularity and currency in the forty or fifty years after the Civil War. *Corridos* flourished, in particular, in circumstances of cultural conflict, as an expression of a people living in a border territory. Their composers were generally anonymous, and they were transmitted by word of mouth to commemorate significant events or local heroes or to celebrate prototypical situations in the family and the community. Unsurprisingly, many *corridos* focused on the conflict between Mexican Americans and Anglo-Americans. Some, for instance, celebrated the superior prowess of Mexican Americans as fighters or lovers, farmers or ranchers. In a *corrido* called 'Kiansas' (or 'Kansas'), describing a cattle drive from Texas to Kansas, the Mexican American cowboys are celebrated as superior to the other cowboys in every respect, tougher, more fearless and more accomplished. Others spoke and sang of more open, violent conflict. In 'Gregorio Cortez', a rancher shoots 'the Major Sheriff' to defend his brother. Knowing that he will never receive justice in a Texas court, he flees for the Mexican border, but then gives himself up when he learns that his people are being persecuted and killed by the authorities because of him. The ballad presents Gregorio Cortez as 'godlike' and heroic: 'the Americans', we learn, 'were whiter than a poppy / from the fear they had of Cortez and his pistol.' He is presented, in effect, as an emblem of resistance to Anglo domination. So, for that matter, is the eponymous hero of 'Jacinto Treviño', who faces the Texas Rangers down when they come to arrest him. 'Come on, you cowardly *rinches*, you're not playing games with a child, /' he tells them, 'You wanted to meet your father? I am Jacinto Treviño!' And his courage inspires awe, we are told, even among his enemies: 'The chief of the *rinches* said, even though he was an American, / "Ah, what a brave man is Jacinto; you can see he is a Mexican!"'

Racial pride and resistance of a different kind was expressed, during this period, in the speeches and songs of Native Americans who were also trying to counter white domination. Among the speeches, perhaps the most famous was the one given by Standing Bear (1829–1908), a member of the Ponca tribe, in 1881, when he persuaded the whites not to remove him and his people to Indian Territory. The speech, transcribed and translated by a native speaker, is a powerfully simple protest against racial injustice. Spare and stoical in a way characteristic of Native American oratory, it is also a vivid rehearsal of communal identity. 'You have driven me from the East to this place,' Standing Bear declares, 'and I have been here two thousand years or more.' Standing Bear, as he describes himself, *is* his people, the individual is one with the community. And it is in the name of his people that he declares: 'My friends, if you took me away from this land it would be very hard for me. I wish to die in this land. I wish to be an old man here.' Standing Bear successfully used persuasion, the traditional powers of Native American oratory. Others anticipated revenge and redemption. 'The spirit host is advancing, they say,' the 'Ghost Dance Songs' declare:

> They are coming with the buffalo, they say.
> They are coming with the new earth, they say,
> They are coming with the new earth, they say.

The Ghost Dance originated when the Paiute prophet Wovoka had an apocalyptic vision. He saw the Crow coming to bring the whirlwind and the earthquake to 'the whole earth' and destroy the white invaders. The slaughtered buffalo and Indian people, the 'ghosts', would then, he prophesied, return to reclaim their land, which had belonged to them at the beginning. This vision, and the hypnotic dance and song that expressed it, spread rapidly among Native American tribes from the West coast to the Midwest. It became the first genuinely intertribal experience: a dream of a time when the enemies of the tribes would be overthrown and Indians would be restored to their rightful inheritance. 'A nation is coming, a nation is coming,' the 'Ghost Dance Songs' announce; 'the whites are crazy', '*I' yehe!* We have rendered them desolate – *Eye' ae' yuhe'yu!*' The song, the dance, a vision at once elegiac and apocalyptic, a mixture of memory and prophecy: all expressed powerful, communal feelings of loss and hope, betrayal and vengeance. And all created a moral panic among the whites. White fear about the Ghost Dance was, in fact, to lead directly to the massacre of 150 Indian men, women and children at Wounded Knee in the Badlands of Dakota. With that, the dream of Wovoka was dead.

For other American voices of the time, the vision of the future involved neither resistance nor revenge, however, but restoration of natural rights and reform. These included the Cuban immigrant essayist, journalist and activist José Martí (1853–95), the African American writer and scholar Anna Julia Cooper (1858?– 1964) and the Native American historian and folklorist Charles Alexander Eastman (1858–1939). Martí described his vision in 'Our America', an essay published in 1891. 'The government must originate in the country,' he argued in this essay. For him, that meant that European models of government had to be jettisoned. So had other European models, for instance those of education and knowledge. 'The European university must bow to the American university,' Martí suggested. 'The history of America, from the Incas to the present, must be taught in clear detail and to the letter, even if the archons of Greece are overlooked. Our Greece must take priority over the Greece which is not ours.' Identifying the United States as 'Anglo-Saxon America', Martí pleaded for 'Our America': a multicultural, multi-racial community founded on the aboriginal uniqueness of the New World, separate from Europe and sustained by the mutual knowledge and respect of all its members. 'The youth of America' should create a new nation, not imitate an old one, he insisted: 'the pressing need of Our America is to show itself as it is, one in spirit and intent, swift conqueror of a suffocating past.' In such a new and plural republic, 'there can be no racial animosity, because there are no races', 'the soul, equal and eternal, emanates from bodies of various shapes and colors'. Martí was well aware of the forces that threatened the realization of his vision, and, in particular, the residual forces of colonialism which he identified as 'the tiger'. 'The tiger lurks behind every tree,' he warned, 'the colony lives on in the republic.' But he believed fiercely in that vision of an America that recognized its indigenous roots and its multiple identity: an America, in short, that was not 'theirs' but 'ours'.

The aims of Anna Julia Cooper were rather more modest, or at least moderately stated. In her book *A Voice from the South* (1892), she declared that she wanted to break the silence, to give voice to the 'hitherto voiceless Black Woman of America'. And she wanted to do this, she explained, because 'the fundamental agency under God in the regeneration, the re-training of the race, as well as the ground work and starting point for its progress upward, must be the *black woman*'. 'Only the BLACK WOMAN', Cooper suggested, 'can say "when and where I enter, in the quiet, undisputed dignity of my womanhood . . . then and there the whole *Negro race enters with me*".' Cooper subscribed to the contemporary belief in 'true womanhood', woman as the conscience of society. 'The American woman is responsible for American manners,' she wrote; 'our country's manners and morals are under our tutoring.' But she also insisted that the black woman, in particular, had a pivotal role to play in the regeneration of American society: because, as a black person as well as a woman, she knew with special intensity what was wrong and needed to be put right. For her, freedom was indivisible. 'The cause of freedom', as she put it, 'is not the cause of a race or a sect, a party or a class – it is the cause of human kind.'

And that the black woman, doubly denied her freedom, was in a special position to know. 'When all the weak shall have received their due consideration,' she asserted, 'then woman will have her "rights", and the Indian will have his rights, and the Negro will have his rights, and all the strong will have learned at last to deal justly.' Cooper was a devout believer in equality but not integration. 'The dark man', she wrote, 'wants . . . merely to live his own life'; 'the social equality which means forced or unbidden association would be as much . . . strenuously opposed by the circle in which I move as by the most hide-bound Southerner in the land.' And she argued from the standpoint of gentle feeling and faith rather than from that of politics or principle. All 'our fair land' had to learn, she suggested, was 'the secret of universal courtesy' which was 'after all nothing but the art, the science, the religion of regarding one's neighbor as one's self'. Within these constraints, though, which were partly ones she shared with her times, Cooper offered a quiet plea for what she called 'courteous contact, which is naught but the practical application of the principle of benevolence'. In anticipating a time when, as she put it, 'race, color, sex, condition, are realized to be the accidents, not the substance of life', she aimed to give voice to the voiceless – not just black women, finally, but 'every man or woman who has writhed silently under a mighty wrong'.

Although he too hoped for a time when his people would be assimilated into a broader, more benevolent form of American society, Charles Alexander Eastman was more troubled and conflicted than Cooper. A member of the Sioux tribe, he was educated in white schools; and living, after that, on the margins of both societies, he was never really comfortable in either. Although Eastman accepted the assimilationist ideas of his white educators, his early work is marked by nostalgia for the simplicities of tribal life. His account of the years before he was sent to school, *Indian Boyhood* (1902), was immensely popular. This was soon followed by several books on Sioux history and folklore, including *Old Indian Days* (1907) and *Wigwam Evenings* (1909). Later work signalled Eastman's own sense that he was occupying the border between two cultures, trying to bring them closer together. In *The Indian Today: The Past and the Future of the American Indian* (1915), he considered the past and possible contributions of his people to American society as a whole. In the autobiographical work *From the Deep Woods to Civilization* (1916), he presented his own career as exemplary, charting the route to assimilation. And in *The Soul of the Indian: An Interpretation* (1911), he tried to interpret Indian culture for his white readers: to make them understand the system of religious beliefs that were in place when the early settlers arrived in America. The portrait Eastman paints here of Indian 'worship of the "Great Mystery"' is intensely idealized and clearly designed to invite sympathy. 'The native American', the reader is told, was an 'untutored sage', in 'sympathy and spiritual communion with his brothers of the animal kingdom'. 'Being a natural man, the Indian was intensely poetical', Eastman explains, and his worship of his Maker was 'silent, solitary, free from all self-seeking'. 'He would deem it sacrilege to build a house for Him who may be met face to face in the mysterious, shadowy aisles of the primeval forest, or on the sunlit bosom of the virgin prairies'; his innate nobility of soul found an appropriate place of worship in the 'cathedral' of nature where in 'solitary communion with the Unseen' he could express his instinctive 'consciousness of the divine'. 'The spirit of Christianity and of our ancient religion is essentially the same,' Eastman suggests. What stands out in marked contrast to both is the Christianity of his own day, which, with its brute materialism, its 'professionalism of the pulpit' and 'lust for money', has lost touch with the primitive purity of its origins. Eastman hoped to draw the two cultures between which he existed closer together, by making connections such as this. To remind white readers of the crass failures in their own society, and the residual nobility of the Indian, also played a part in this project. His hope, and that project, were both sorely tested by his witnessing the carnage left after the massacre at Wounded Knee: an experience he recalls in *From the Deep Woods to Civilization*. But neither was ever really abandoned. Even in his last years, Eastman was still writing books like *Indian Heroes and Great Chieftains* (1918), aimed at youthful readers now. He still believed, perhaps desperately, that Indians could assimilate and that whites would welcome them, once they recognized the noble traditions and powerful potential they brought with them into American society.

A similar predicament, a sense of belonging neither in the white world fully nor in the Indian, haunted Gertrude Bonnin or Zitkala-Sa (Red Bird) (1876–1938). The daughter of a white man, of whom little is known, and a Sioux woman, Bonnin left the reservation to attend a Quaker school in Indiana, 'the land of red apples' as she called it. She returned to the reservation but found herself culturally without anchorage: 'neither a wild Indian nor a tame one', as she described herself in an autobiographical essay, 'The Schooldays of an Indian Girl', published in the *Atlantic Monthly* in 1900. Feeling herself separate from her mother but also outraged by mistreatment of her people by white America, she began to write articles de-nouncing racial injustice and describing her own sense of cultural disorientation. In 'The Schooldays of an Indian Girl', she recalls how she knew 'but one language' until she was eight, 'and that was my mother's native tongue'. She then travelled east 'on the iron horse' to learn another. 'I want to see the wonderful Eastern land,' she told her mother before she left; and her mother, while she feared her daughter would 'suffer keenly in this experiment', accepted her departure as necessary for her education. Disillusionment, as Bonnin remembers it, soon set in. On the journey east she soon found herself watched by the 'scornful and curious eyes' of the other, white passengers. At school, shortly after her arrival there, she was forced to have her 'thick braids' cut off, even though her mother had taught her that only cowards or mourners have short hair. It is a powerful paradigm of the humiliation and confusion she experienced, as she was rudely introduced to the manners and beliefs of the white world. Bonnin found herself lost, unmoored in the old Indian world of the West, whenever she returned there, she tells the reader. But she was equally adrift and lonely in what she had believed would be the new 'wonderful land' of the East. It was not a wonderful land at all, but a bleak one inhabited by 'a cold race whose hearts were frozen hard with prejudice'. Bonnin never lost this sense of being a stranger in two strange lands, an alien living between cultures. Her aim, like Eastman's, was somehow to mediate between them: by explaining to whites the Indian need for justice, by revealing to anyone the power and necessity of the Indian traditions. So, in 1901, she published *Old Indian Legends*. 'I have tried', she wrote in the introduction to this book, 'to transplant the native spirit of these tales – root and all – into the English language, since America in the last few centuries has acquired a second tongue.' And twenty years later, she produced a larger, revised work, *American Indian Stories*, in which she used both fiction and auto-biography to pursue her project of transplanting one culture, translating one language, into another. The first Native American woman to write her own story without assistance, Bonnin stood not only between Indian and white societies but between the oral culture of the Indian past and the literate culture that would dominate its future. As her work on Indian legend suggests, she firmly believed that the political rights of future generations would be on shallow ground if they were not securely rooted in the remembrance and reverent rehearsal of the older, oral traditions. To that extent, she was trying to build a bridge between separate generations as well as divided cultures.

Mary Austin (1868–1934) was born into a typical Midwestern family in Illinois. But like José Martí, she saw it as her mission to turn American culture away from the Anglo-American traditions of the East coast and towards the Native American and Indian traditions of the Southwest. Like Gertrude Bonnin and Charles Eastman, she saw herself as a mediator between cultures. She collected, preserved and encouraged the continuation of American Indian and Hispanic folk arts; she published studies of American Indian songs in *The American Rhythm* (1923); and collected Indian songs and original poems in *Children Sing in the Far West* (1928). Like many regionalists of the time, she saw place as a profound determinant of character. Moving to California at the age of eighteen, living after that in New Mexico (where she continued her study of the Indians), she wrote continually and lovingly about life and landscape in the West: a region that 'if it had a history', she said, 'nobody could recount it' – and where the 'plants had no names' that her 'Middlewestern botany could supply'. And like many writers of the period, especially female ones, she wrote about the condition of women and how to change it. 'There was something you could do about unsatisfactory conditions besides being heroic or a martyr to them,' Austin observed, 'something more satisfactory than enduring or complaining, and that was getting out to hunt for a remedy.' And Austin hunted for a remedy in fiction, factual analysis and autobiography. Her novel *A Woman of Genius* (1912), for instance, describes how a woman escapes from her restricted life through art; *Love and the Soul Maker* (1914) is a discussion of modern problems of love, marriage and divorce; while *The Young Woman Citizen* (1918) is a handbook of politics for the newly enfranchised woman voter. Her two major books reflect the range of her commitments and her interest, in particular, in the liberatory impact of the West and the necessary liberation of women. *The Land of Little Rain* (1903) is an evocative account of the beauties and the mystery of Western desert life. It was one of the earlier books to suggest that the true story of the West resided in its wilderness condition, its challenge to all notions of human domination, rather than in ideas of rugged individualism, empire and conquest. Responsive to her own feelings expressed here, Austin herself became an activist for environmental causes. *Earth Horizon* (1932), in turn, her other major work, is an autobiography with a revolutionary form. Austin records how she felt herself 'marked' by a sense of destiny, special mission. She remembers how she was mocked and criticized by her family for her 'individual divergences' from the norms of female behaviour. She rehearses her annoyance with the notion that 'the crown of a woman's life' should be 'the privilege of being the utterly giving and devoted wife of one man'. And to register the tensions inherent in this conflict between the demands of society and her own needs, or what she terms 'tradition and realism', she distinguishes between her socially ordained self and her true self in an innovative way. Her true self, which finds fulfilment for instance in intimate contact with the Western landscape, is 'I' or 'I-Mary'; the false self that others would wish to impose upon her is 'she', 'you', or simply 'Mary'. Austin sees her story as special, but also typical. She constantly reminds the reader that other women felt and fought as she did. 'Mary wasn't by any means the only girl of that period', she declares, 'insisting on going on her own way against the traditions, and refusing to come to a bad end on account of it.' Like an earlier writer with whom she has much in common, Thoreau, she brags for humanity as well as for herself. And she argues for another America in which 'I-Mary' might be comfortable: where the centres of power and place have radically shifted.

The immigrant encounter

From the land of little rain to the South Side of Chicago is an enormous leap, in terms of landscape, life and language. But that in itself suggests just how many Americas were contending, arguing to be heard at this time. Chicago's South Side, and in particular the Irish working-class neighbourhood of Bridgeport, was where Finley Peter Dunne (1867–1936) located his most famous creation, Mr Dooley, an Irish saloon keeper, who was never reluctant to voice his opinions on life, current events and the social scene. Dunne, a journalist and editor of the Chicago *Evening Post*, wrote a series of monologues for his paper. They were rich in dialect, a genuine and on the whole successful attempt to catch Irish vernacular in print; and the monologues delivered by Dooley became a Chicago tradition. About three hundred Dooley pieces appeared between 1893 and 1900 in Chicago newspapers. In these, Dooley came across to the reader as a man of shrewd native wit, and the place where he lived became a solidly realized social fabric. Dooley himself rarely, if ever, descends into the caricature of a stage Irishman: his fatalism, his dark side that views the world as irredeemably fallen (something he shared with his creator), as well as the sheer energy of his speech, prevent that. And Bridgeport itself never becomes mere background or local colour. It is rich with life and a sense of urban neighbourliness, a genuinely working-class, ethnic community. The range of subject and tone in the Chicago pieces is impressive. Dooley talks eloquently and elegiacally of his passage to America ('The Wanderers' [1895]); he offers comic accounts of the clash between the old and the new in Irish American culture ('The Piano in the Parlor' [1895]). He also comments, with wry humour, on public events. And it was his satirical observations on the Spanish–American War – a 'splendid little war', he ironically called it – that brought him to national attention. Following this, in 1900, Dunne moved to New York, where Dooley quickly became the most popular figure in American journalism. The satirical bent became stronger, as Dooley's inherently sceptical mind addressed the notable events of the day. In response to proposals to restrict immigration, for example, Dooley declared that, 'as a pilgrim father that missed th' first boats', he had to raise his 'claryon voice against th' invasion iv this fair land be th' paupers an' annychists iv effete Europe'. 'You bet I must –', he added, 'because I'm here first.' American foreign policy Dooley defined as 'Hands acrost th'sea an' into somewan else's pocket'. The majority of the law he described in these terms: 'America follows th'flag, but th' Supreme Court follows th'illiction returns.' The Dooley pieces were published as a series: *Mr. Dooley in Peace and War* (1898) was the first, *Mr. Dooley on Making a Will* (1919) the last. Together they represent not just a major contribution to realism and the vernacular in literature but the voice of yet another America.

The dilemma that the newer immigrant communities faced, over whether to assimilate or resist assimilation to the norms of the dominant American culture, lies at the heart of the writings of Abraham Cahan (1860–1951). Having emigrated to the United States from Russia, Cahan founded the *Jewish Daily Forward*, which became a mass circulation market leader in the Yiddish Press. His first novel, *Yekl, a Tale of the New York Ghetto* (1896), won him national prominence and the support of William Dean Howells. It tells the story of an immigrant who transforms himself from 'Yekl' to 'Jake', compromising his religion and traditions, his dress and behaviour, so as to become an 'American'. Three years after his arrival in the New World, his wife Gitl follows him. On first seeing her at the Immigration Bureau of Ellis Island, Jake feels himself ashamed of her 'uncouth and un-American appearance'. A 'bonnetless, wigged, dowdyish little greenhorn', she looks like 'a squaw', he thinks, and dresses 'like an Italian woman'. Such allusions to other 'un-American' cultures slyly spread the frame of reference here. 'Jake the Yankee', as our hero describes himself, is now part of the mainstream; he does not wish to be associated with any kind of marginalized culture. Eventually, Jake leaves Gitl for an Americanized Jewish woman called Mamie. The novel ends with Jake, now divorced, setting off to remarry. But the irony is that, by this stage, Gitl herself is becoming assimilated too, as Jake observes with some irritation. Not only that, as he prepares to marry Mamie, he feels, 'instead of a conqueror', like 'the victim of an ignominious defeat'. He has lost more than he has gained by becoming what he defines as an American. Similar feelings of loss haunt many of the characters in *The Imported Bridegroom and Other Stories of the New York Ghetto* (1898), a collection of tales, and Cahan's other major novel, *The Rise of David Levinsky* (1917). In the novel, a rich but deeply dissatisfied garment manufacturer looks back at his rise from poverty in Russia and in the ghettos of New York. It is another variation on the theme of the price of success and Americanization. In later years, Cahan wrote five volumes of memoirs, *Leaves from my Life* (1926–31); he also became a powerful voice in Yiddish and national journals. But it is his fiction that has left a mark. If, as Toni Morrison has claimed, American literature of the twentieth century was shaped by its encounter with the immigrant, then Cahan clearly stands near the beginning of that trend. He was among the first to rewrite the story of what it might mean to be an American.

A more clearly optimistic version of the encounter with the immigrant is offered in the work of Mary Antin (1881–1949). Born in the Jewish Pale, the area of Russia where Jews were permitted to live, Antin arrived in America when she was thirteen. While still young she wrote *From Plotz to Boston* (1899), an impressionistic account of the emigration of her family. And in 1912, she extended her early book to make *The Promised Land*, a fuller account of the hardships of European Jews and the freedom and opportunity they discovered in America. Loosely structured around the Book of Exodus, from which its title is drawn, *The Promised Land* tells of the rebirth of its author in the New World. In America, Antin tells the reader, she was granted new clothes, substituting 'real American machine-made garments' for her 'hateful homemade European costumes'. She was given a new name to replace her 'impossible Hebrew' one, Mary for Maryashe, and allowed to 'wear' the 'dignified title' of her surname 'even . . . on week days'. Above all, she was offered a new life, the core and agent of which was education. For Antin, 'the essence of American opportunity' was, she explains, that 'education was free'. At school, she learned the new language, the knowledge, that would enable her to become an American, a free, self-reliant citizen. 'The apex of my civic pride and personal contentment', she recalls, 'was reached on the bright September morning when I entered the public school.' That moment when she entered school for the first time, accompanied by her siblings and led by her father, is rehearsed in reverent detail. It is, as Antin portrays it, the crossing of a threshold: the proud father sees it as 'an act of consecration', and even the children are excited as they walk towards 'the Elysian fields of liberal learning'. As the father handed over the certificates that enabled his children to begin their schooling, it was as if 'he took possession of America', Antin remembers: he and his family were now finally moving from an oppressive, almost medieval past into a future bright with promise. 'I am wearily aware that I am speaking in extreme figures, in superlatives', Antin confesses, but these were her thoughts at the time, 'typical of the attitude of the intelligent immigrant child toward American institutions.' And, 'what the child thinks and feels', she adds, 'is a reflection of the hopes, desires, and purposes of the parents who brought him overseas'. Antin never lost her belief in the immigrant dream, as her later work *They Who Knock at Our Gates* (1914) also testifies. For her, passage to America was genuinely passage into another, finer level of experience in which all Americans could and should share.

Probably no writer is further from this optimistic view of the passage to America, the immigrant encounter and the condition of the poor, than Upton Sinclair (1878–1968). Born to a prominent but impoverished family in Maryland and educated in New York City, Sinclair wrote six novels before publishing the book that made him famous, *The Jungle*. *The Jungle* first appeared serially in *Appeal to Reason*, a weekly socialist journal, and then was released in book form in 1906. Sinclair had joined the Socialist Party of America in 1904; and, in the same year, he had spent seven weeks living among the men and women who laboured in the stockyards of Chicago. A powerful study of the inhuman living and working conditions of the workers, and the unsanitary methods of production in the stockyards, *The Jungle* clearly reflected Sinclair's commitment to socialism. 'It will open countless ears that have been deaf to Socialism,' Jack London enthused after he had read the novel. 'It will make thousands of converts to our cause.' However, Finley Peter Dunne was nearer the mark when he had Mr Dooley observe that, since Sinclair's book came out, 'th' President, like th' rest iv us, has become a viggytaran'. *The Jungle* was enormously successful. On its release date, such was the anticipation caused by its earlier serialization in *The Appeal to Reason*, the story of its publication was splashed on the front pages of newspapers from coast to coast. So impressed was the then president, Theodore Roosevelt, on reading an advance copy that he invited Sinclair to the White House to discuss the issues it raised. And, in the next several decades, it was translated into forty-seven languages in thirty-nine countries: making Sinclair equally famous abroad and at home. It did not, however, promote the cause of socialism so much as it did that of food hygiene. Sinclair's major purpose in writing *The Jungle* had been to attack 'wage slavery', the oppression of the workers in a place he called Packingtown. Scarcely a dozen pages in the book were devoted to the gruesome details of meat production. It was these, however, that hit a nerve, leading directly to the passing of the Beef Inspection Act and the first Pure Food and Drug Act. Sinclair himself perceived the irony and summed it up nicely. 'I aimed at the public's heart,' he said, 'and by accident I hit it in the stomach.'

As the portrait of another America than the commonly accepted and celebrated one, *The Jungle* is the most vivid and lasting example of what was called, at the time, the muckraking movement. The term, devised by Roosevelt, described those writers who, around the turn of the twentieth century, devoted themselves to the exposure of corruption in politics and business. Several leading periodicals of the time lent their pages to the muckrakers, among them *McClure's*, *Collier's* and *Cosmopolitan*. And among the most influential and popular muckraking writers were Ida Tarbell (1857–1944), Lincoln Steffens (1866–1936) and David Graham Phillips (1867–1911). Tarbell was the author of a two-volume exposé, *The History of the Standard Oil Company* (1904). Steffens, seen as the leader of the movement, wrote articles collected in *The Shame of the Cities* (1904), *The Struggle for Self-Government* (1906) and *Upbuilders* (1909). In his *Autobiography* (1931), he also recorded his evolution from sensational reporting to the belief in a fundamental relation between the various forms of corruption he discovered. Phillips, for his part, carried muckraking into fiction. *The Great God Success* (1901), for instance, investigates American myth and American practice, the idea of success and the pursuit of fraud; *The Cost* (1904) and *The Deluge* (1905) expose the manipulation of the stock market; and *The Fashionable Adventures of Joshua Craig* (1909), *The*

Conflict (1911) and *George Helm* (1912) deal respectively with national, municipal and state corruption. A prolific writer, Sinclair was to produce more than a hundred works, many of which could be seen as part of the muckraking movement. Among his pamphlets and social studies were *The Profits of Religion* (1918), which described the church as a capitalist tool designed to oppress the poor, *The Brass Check* (1919), on journalism, *The Goslings* (1924), on education, and *Money Writes!* (1927), on art and literature. Among his muckraking novels were *King Coal* (1917), *Oil!* (1927), *Boston* (1928) and *Mountain City* (1930). His fiction also includes a monumental series of eleven novels, beginning with *World's End* (1940) and ending with *The Return of Larry Budd* (1953), which describes the adventures of the illegitimate son of a munitions tycoon who travels the world and becomes involved in international political intrigues. But Sinclair never surpassed the book that made him famous and stands as a monument to the muckraking movement. *The Jungle* is an exposure of poverty and oppression; it is also a darker vision of the immigrant encounter, and another America, than that imagined by nearly all his contemporaries.

The Jungle is the story of Jurgis Rudkus, a Lithuanian peasant, and a group of his relatives and friends, all immigrants, who live, work and die in the stockyard industry. At the beginning of the book, Jurgis is young, energetic and optimistic. He is fascinated by stories of America, 'where a friend of his had gotten rich'. America, he reflects, is a place where a man might earn 'three roubles a day', which would make him wealthy. In addition, 'in that country, rich or poor, a man was free, it was said'; 'he might do as he pleased and count himself as good as any other man'. So, Jurgis resolves to go to this 'place of which lovers and young people dreamed' because, 'if he could only manage to get the price of a passage', he believes, 'he could count his troubles at an end'. Taking various members of his family with him, including his new wife Ona, he sets out for Chicago. 'It was in the stockyard that his friend had gotten rich,' we learn, 'and so to Chicago the party was bound. They knew that one word, Chicago – and that was all they needed to know, at least until they reached the city.' Sinclair carefully delineates how hope turns to confusion, and then eventually to despair. Arriving 'in the midst of deafening confusion', the noise and bustle of the big city, Jurgis and his companions are 'utterly lost'. With few words of English, it takes some time for them to find their way to the stockyards, Packingtown. And what they find, as they approach them, is that the atmosphere grows 'darker all the time', and there is 'an elemental odor, raw and crude' in the air. The vision is one of hell. There is an 'endless vista of ugly and dirty little wooden buildings': the tenements in which, Jurgis will discover, people are crowded sometimes 'thirteen or fourteen to a room'. There are larger buildings from which smoke billows, 'thick, ugly, black as night'; 'it might have come from the centre of the world, this smoke'; in fact, it comes from the slaughterhouses. Worst of all, there is a sound as elemental as the odour blanketing Packingtown, 'a sound made up of ten thousand little sounds'. 'It was only by an effort that one could realize it was made by animals,' the reader is told, 'that it was the distant lowing of ten thousand cattle, the distant grunting of ten thousand swine' being prepared for or experiencing the process of slaughter.

Lodged in Packingtown, in one of the tenement houses, Jurgis and his companions soon discover that America is the land of high prices as well as high wages. Here, 'the poor man', he reflects, 'was almost as poor as in any other corner of the earth'. Each part of the stockyards is 'a separate little inferno'. And, instead of the land of plenty he had anticipated, Jurgis encounters an economic jungle. 'Here in this huge city, with its stores of heaped-up wealth,' Jurgis gradually realizes, 'human creatures might be hunted down and destroyed by the wild-beast powers of nature, just as truly as they were in the days of the cave men!' The realization comes to him as he and his fellow immigrants encounter virtually every evil to be found in American industry, politics and society. With poor English, they are easily exploited by those in power: the packers and their foremen, the police, the political bosses, the real-estate dealers, and all the rest of the 'upper-class'. Jurgis has to pay graft to get and keep his job. The real-estate man cheats him by selling him a house on the instalment plan with hidden clauses the Lithuanian cannot read, and which eventually cause him to lose his home. He is mercilessly speeded up on the job and suffers injuries. He and his family are afflicted by terrible diseases. He is laid off and blacklisted, then goes to prison for smashing the face of a brutal boss. One by one, Jurgis and his group are crushed. Older men are thrown on the scrap heap to starve; women turn to prostitution to survive; Ona, attended in childbirth by an ignorant midwife, dies for lack of proper care; Jurgis and Ona's infant son is drowned in one of the vile pools of green water surrounding their shack. The catalogue of suffering is remorseless. Sinclair does not spare the squeamish reader and his narrative approach is the reverse of subtle. Each episode is packed with what seems like redundant detail, to emphasize the point and ensure an air of authenticity. Each character, even Jurgis, is drawn in plain, strong terms rather than in delicate nuances, since the focus is on action and argument rather than personality. Each moment, in this account of the hero's wanderings through the jungle of capitalism, is unashamedly melodramatic and didactic. Yet the accumulative power of the novel is undeniable. Like many other, major works of realism or naturalism, *The Jungle* achieves its impact from its sheer remorselessness, using the technique of the sledgehammer rather than the rapier. By the end of the story, the reader feels that he or she has suffered the burden of Jurgis's life with him. And, characteristically, Sinclair turns despair into hope in the final chapters. Broken, Jurgis discovers socialism, which mends him and makes him a 'new man'. He is 'delivered from the thralldom of despair', we learn; and he is privileged to witness widespread socialist gains in the elections of 1904. The final words of the novel, 'CHICAGO WILL BE OURS!', anticipating the day when socialism will prevail in the city, look to the triumphs of the future rather than the tragedies of the past.

Other immigrant groups might be exploited, in the way Jurgis Rudkus was; Chinese immigrants fared even worse. They were exploited, abhorred and attacked; then, under the terms of an act of government in 1882, almost all further Chinese immigration was banned. It was in this climate that two of the earliest Asian American writers began their work. Edith and Winnifred Eaton were the daughters of a Chinese mother and an English father. It was a measure of the complex racism of the times that, when she began to write, Winnifred Eaton (1875–1954) assumed a Japanese pseudonym. As her sister, Edith, was to observe, Americans had 'a much higher regard for the Japanese than for the Chinese'. So, she explained, 'several half Chinese young men and women, thinking to advance themselves, both in a social and business sense, pass as Japanese'. Edith was not referring to Winnifred when she said this: the observation occurs in her autobiographical essay, 'Leaves from the Mental Portfolio of an Eurasian' (1909). But, under the name of Onoto Watanna, Winnifred certainly found success. She wrote hundreds of stories and seventeen best-selling novels, most of them set in Japan. In some of the stories, such as 'Two Converts' (1901) and 'The Loves of Sakura Jiro and the Three Headed Maid' (1903), she explores the situation of the emigrant with verve and sly wit, emphasizing in particular the confusions involved in belonging to two cultures. But neither the tales nor the novels ever really challenge racial stereotypes, or for that matter sexual stereotypes. The Japanese men are invariably noble and heroic, the Japanese women shy, delicate and charming. There is interracial romance, but it is continually set within the terms of accepted romantic convention. That is, romance occurs between English or American men and Japanese women, never the reverse. Her fiction made Winnifred Eaton popular at the time, and reasonably wealthy. It also provided a ticket to Hollywood: from 1924 to 1931, she was chief scenarist at Universal Studios.

Edith Maud Eaton (1865–1914), on the other hand, adopted a Chinese pseudonym, Sui Sin Far, and wrote specifically about Chinese people and the Chinese experience in America. Born in England, she spent her early childhood in Canada. She travelled back and forth across the United States between 1898 and 1912, supporting herself with her journalism. And her stories and articles soon began appearing in popular and important national magazines like *Overland*, *Century* and *Good Housekeeping*. 'Leaves from the Mental Portfolio of an Eurasian' illustrates the position from which she wrote. A tireless campaigner for social and racial justice, Eaton describes in this piece how she gradually came not only to accept but proudly to embrace the Chinese part of her identity. She also explains how she encountered racial prejudice on both sides of her inheritance – although, given white power and dominance, white prejudice against the Chinese has, she insists, far more pervasive and destructive consequences. 'Fundamentally, I muse, all people are the same,' she observes; 'My mother's race is as prejudiced as my father's. Only when the whole world becomes as one family will human beings be able to see clearly and hear distinctly.' 'Some day,' she adds, 'a great part of the world will be Eurasian.' That was the positive side of her predicament. In her better moods, Eaton could see her dual inheritance, and her 'Chinese instinct' in particular, as something that made her 'a pioneer'; 'and a pioneer', she reflected, 'should glory in her suffering'. The more problematical side was not just the slights and humiliations she tells us she experienced when she refused to 'pass' as white or Japanese, although, given her appearance, she could have. It was her sense that she inhabited a neutral territory, a cultural hinterland. 'So I roam backward and forward across the continent,' Eaton concludes her little autobiography. 'When I am East, my heart is West. When I am West, my heart is East. Before long I hope to be in China. As my life began in my father's country it may end in my mother's.' 'I have no nationality', she admits, but her consolation is that she is not 'anxious to claim any'. It is also that she is still her own person – and 'individuality is more than nationality' – and that, with her equivocal cultural status she may, after all, supply a 'connecting link' between cultures, giving, as she puts it, 'my right hand to the Occidentals and my left to the Orientals'.

The achievement of the stories Eaton wrote for the magazines, and collected in *Mrs. Spring Fragrance* (1912), is that they negotiate the cultural hinterland inhabited by their author with wit, passion and pathos. With their shifting narrative perspectives, fragmented structures and rapid changes of mood, as well as with their preference for allusion and intimation rather than emphatic statement, these tales tell us what it is like to be a person of multiple identities in a racist society. The ironically titled 'In the Land of the Free', for instance, describes the plight of a Chinese couple who have their son taken from them by immigration officers. The couple have lived in America for many years, the man is a successful merchant in San Francisco. But, when his wife became pregnant, he tries to explain to the impatient officers, he realized that he wanted his son 'to be born in our country'. And she returned to China to give birth. After considerable delay and expense, the couple finally acquire the papers permitting their son to stay. When they go to collect their son, however, he does not want to leave with them. 'The Little One shrank' from his mother, we are told, 'and tried to hide himself in the folds of the white woman's skirt', one of the mission nurses who has been taking care of him. '"Go 'way, go 'way", he bade his mother': he has already begun to be a person with 'no nationality'. 'Mrs. Spring Fragrance', the title story in Eaton's collection, adopts a more gently humorous approach, as it explores cultural difference. Through the tale of misunderstandings resolved between a Chinese American couple, Mrs Spring Fragrance and her husband, Eaton measures the distance between Chinese and American attitudes to marriage. She quietly reveals, however, how both forms of marriage can involve love and how, as one Chinese character regretfully observes, 'the old order is passing away, and the new order is taking its place, even with us who are Chinese'. The slippery narrative frame here alerts us to a world in which experience is changing as well as fragmented, and people are consequently caught between different times as well as different cultures.

A story like '"Its Wavering Image"', in turn, is more keenly autobiographical. It tells of 'a half-white, half-Chinese girl' called Pan who lives in the Chinatown district of San Francisco. She meets a young white journalist called Mark Carson, her 'first white friend'. 'It was only after the coming of Mark Carson', we learn, 'that the mystery of her nature began to trouble her.' 'Born a Bohemian', as indeed Eaton was, 'exempt from the conventional restrictions imposed upon either the white or Chinese woman', Pan introduces Carson to Chinatown, the neighbourhood, family and friends. Slowly, affection grows between them. As it does so, Carson sings to her a song about the 'wavering image' of the moon in the water, a 'symbol of love'. He also tells her that she has to decide what she will be, 'Chinese or white', adding, for her benefit, 'you do not belong here. You are white – white'. Pan resists his persuasions. 'I was born here,' she reflects, 'and the Chinese people look upon me as their own.' Carson leaves for two months and, while he is away, an article by him titled 'Its Wavering Image' appears in the newspaper. It is based on all he has learned with the help of Pan during their times together. Pan sees it as a betrayal of confidence, the trust that she and her Chinese friends and relatives had placed in Carson. She 'would rather that her own body and soul had been exposed', we learn, 'than that things, sacred and secret to those who loved her, should be cruelly unveiled and ruthlessly spread before the ridiculing and uncomprehending foreigner'. We do not learn what those things are; that is typical of Eaton's delicate, allusive art. But they are enough to make Pan rebuff a plainly bewildered Carson on his return. Appearing before him in a Chinese costume, rather than the American dress she had habitually worn in his company, she now insists, 'I am a Chinese woman'. 'I would not be a white woman for all the world,' she adds, in answer to his protests. 'You are a white man. And *what* is a promise to a white man!' The strength of this story derives from its imagining a clash of cultures that is none the less definite for being delicately stated, none the less clear for being a matter of intimation rather than analysis. Its pathos, and quiet wit, stem, in turn, from our sense that Pan has not resolved her predicament by her act of will. She may say, and even think, that she is 'a Chinese woman' but, as the story intimates, she is rather more complicated, more conflicted than that. In tales like this, Eaton used her own divided self to explore the divided state of Chinese Americans; she caught the wavering image of yet another America in the fragile web of her writing. To that extent, she not only added another chapter to the story of immigrant encounter; she prepared the way for other, later writers, particularly Asian American ones, who have found themselves in exile in two different lands – living between two countries, two cultures, and not really at home in either.

4

making it new

the emergence of modern american literature, 1900–1945

Changing National Identities

Attending the World's Columbian Exposition in Chicago in 1893, Henry Adams had found himself in a state of what he termed 'helpless reflection'. 'Chicago', Adams recalled in his autobiography, *The Education of Henry Adams*, 'asked in 1893 for the first time the question of whether the American people knew where they were driving'; and 'Adams answered, for one, that he did not know.' What was more, 'he decided that the American people probably knew no more than he did'. However, he went on, both for his own sake and other people's, he felt that he would try at least to find out. And a crucial moment of discovery occurred seven years later, when visiting the Great Exposition in Paris. Standing in the Gallery of Machines at the Great Exposition, he felt, while looking at all the machinery whirring and humming around him, that 'in . . . seven years man had translated himself into a new universe which had no common scale of measurement with the old'. The old signs and scales, the old means of production, had been demolished; and along with them, the old modes of feeling too. 'The child born in 1900', Adams suggested,

> would . . . be born into a new world which would not be a unity but a multiple. Adams tried to imagine it, and an education that would fit it. He found himself in a land where no one had ever penetrated before; where order was an accidental relation obnoxious to nature; artificial compulsion imposed on motion; against which every free energy of the universe revolted; and which, being merely occasional, resolved back into anarchy at last.

Instead of unity, there would be proliferation and change, what Adams christened 'the law of the multiverse'; in place of systems there were only 'charts of energy collisions'. Such alterations, Adams had believed, would affect all cultures, but particularly those strongly committed to the new 'anarchical' forces – and, above all, a 'twenty-million-horse-power-society' like America. Just because the American had embraced the 'occult mechanism' of the new age so fiercely, he or she would be especially susceptible to the consequences – whatever, as it turned out, those consequences might be. The American might become part of a new evolutionary cycle or part of a new, radically dehumanizing system; he, or she, might become 'the child of new forces', energetic and liberating, or might equally be transformed into 'the chance sport of nature', reduced to one more helpless atom in a random universe. Adams was not sure, although on the whole his patrician habits of thought inclined him towards the latter, gloomier series of possibilities. However, one thing he was perfectly certain about, the process of accelerating technological change would lead to an alteration of consciousness, vitally affecting every American's structure of perception, the way they thought about themselves and the world – and new forms of education, new epistemological and aesthetic structures would be needed to grasp the conditions of contemporary life, to register and at least try to understand the 'multiverse'.

Henry Adams's apocalyptic prophecies about the direction of American history have proved only too accurate. The material culture (which is to say, towns, factories and so on) radically altered over the first half of the twentieth century; and, at almost the same time, the non-material culture (that is, belief, customs and institutions) altered too, in ways that were quite unprecedented and far-reaching. By the second decade of the twentieth century, the United States had become the most powerful industrialized nation in the world, outstripping Britain and Germany in terms of industrial production. Accompanying this growth of industry, there was a rapid expansion of urban centres. The ten largest cities in the United States in 1910 – New York, Chicago, Philadelphia, St Louis, Boston, Cleveland, Baltimore, Pittsburgh, Detroit and Buffalo – had experienced an almost threefold increase in population in the previous thirty years; while, over the same period, new cities like Los Angeles, Minneapolis and Seattle had sprung into existence. Perhaps the main agencies for disseminating urban lifestyles, however, were the smaller cities. In the last decade of the nineteenth century and the first one or two of the twentieth, thousands of quiet little townships with their few services for the surrounding farming population were transformed into small urban centres, each with its own paved streets, bank, cinema, department store, hospital, shops, factories and warehouses. There was a radical alteration in the material landscape, as more and more people crowded into the towns: the national census indicated that by 1920 the urban population exceeded the rural population – and it is quite likely that this change of balance had in fact occurred five or six years earlier. America was no longer a nation of happy farmers, even if it had ever been; and, regardless of where they lived, Americans found themselves a part of the emergent technological culture. The telephone ceased to be a curiosity and became a commonplace: by 1915, the ratio of telephones to population was one to ten. And the radio, along with other agencies of mass communication, began imposing its own imagery of the new normalcy on the nation at large. In 1926, the National Broadcasting Company, and the following year the Columbia Broadcasting Company, confirmed this trend, when they hooked together hundreds of local radio stations in two giant national networks. So, along with the changes in the material landscape – as America evolved from entrepreneurial to corporate capitalism, and from the ideal of the business buccaneer to that of the business executive – came change in the non-material systems of belief and behaviour. Along with alterations in the national economy came alterations in the national consciousness.

Some of these alterations in consciousness can be traced back to the new systems of thought that encouraged, and in some cases enabled, social change at the turn of the century. Darwinism, for instance, with its new view of human nature and society, was one of the first movements to threaten the non-material fabric of American culture, not only because it challenged the religious inheritance of places like New England, the fundamentalist South and the Catholic Southwest but because it called into question the humanist legacy of nineteenth-century intellectual America. Marxism placed a large question mark over the liberal orthodoxies of mainstream American culture. Freudianism helped to demolish the notion of unitary personality, the solidarity of the social and moral self – what D. H. Lawrence scornfully referred to as the old stable *ego* of the character, and, in its place, substituted a duality, the idea of two levels in the mind which might be not only discrete but at odds. In turn, the relativity theory of Albert Einstein offered nothing less than a new view of reality, since it implied a multiple perspective on the universe. There is no absolute view, the theory suggested, no 'God's view' of events in the universe. The relationships of before and after, and simultaneous with, depend on the observer's position in relation to events; things are determined by the viewpoint of the spectator and our knowledge of reality is inevitably contingent. Either as a matter of influence, or as part of the intellectual currency of the time, theories of relativity or indeterminacy such as these – or, for that matter, the ideas of Darwin, Marx and Freud – had an enormous impact. They contributed to a growing sense of what Adams had termed the 'multiverse', even or especially among a larger public who knew of such theories only in popularized, and probably simplified, forms. But perhaps nothing symbolizes the change in the direction of American thought, feeling and energy in the early decades of the twentieth century as something far more everyday and commonplace than theories of relativity, evolution, class conflict and the unconscious. And that is, the automobile.

In 1925, a woman in Muncie, Indiana, remembered that, as she put it, 'in the nineties we were all much more together'. 'People brought chairs and cushions out of the house and sat on the lawn evenings,' she recalled. 'We put cushions on the porch steps to take care of the unlimited overflow of neighbors that dropped by. We'd sit out so all evening.' The citizens of Muncie were different now, she lamented: assaulted by advertising urging them to buy cars and 'Increase Your Weekend Touring Radius'. 'A man who works six days a week', a banker was quoted as saying in one such advertisement, 'and spends the seventh on his own doorstep certainly will not pick up the extra dimes in the great thoroughfares of life.' Mobility had completely supplanted stability. In 1891, on 4 July, a Muncie merchant had noted in his diary that the town was 'full of people' celebrating Independence Day:

by contrast, some twenty-nine years later, two observers found the streets deserted – all the town had apparently left for the day and taken to the road. Some of those in authority might occasionally denounce the Model-T Ford, as one judge memorably did, by describing it as 'a house of prostitution on wheels'. But one million models of the 'Tin Lizzie' were sold each year, and there were 26,500,000 vehicles on the road by 1929. Others might lament, as that Muncie woman did, the passing of the old folkways. But those ways were irrecoverable now: cars, along with radios, vacuum cleaners, record players and other consumer goods, had become the foundation stones of the new economy – and the precipitants of a new consciousness. Listening to network radio shows, seduced by the imagery of advertising and the cinema, encouraged to ride out of familiar locations in search of the unfamiliar or for the sheer experience of movement, Americans became part of a distinctively modern, discontinuous culture: a culture that was, and is, not specifically tied down to any individual locality, state or region – or, indeed, to any particular nation.

Such changes in culture and consciousness were accelerated by the experience of the First World War. The United States emerged from involvement in global conflict with an altered economic relationship with the rest of the world: from a debtor nation it had been transformed into a creditor nation, with loans to Europe worth thirteen billion dollars. For a while, under the leadership of Woodrow Wilson, it tried to assume the status of a moral and cultural creditor as well: in 1918, while war was still being waged, Wilson formulated his Fourteen Points, which outlined the need for a peaceful world and provided a 'guarantee' of continued peace through a 'general assembly of nations'. It was this League of Nations that was rejected by Congress in 1919, after which American foreign policy seemed to move decisively towards isolationism. But while it is true that the United States did tend to withdraw from active political involvement in world affairs – at least, involvement to the extent that Wilson had hoped for – it was too deeply implicated now, economically and culturally, in what happened outside its borders ever to recapture the isolation, the sheer sense of apartness, that it had experienced in the previous century. Mass immigration from Europe and elsewhere, a mass communication system and a system of culture that ultimately denied national boundaries: all these, among other things, ensured that America was involved with the rest of the world regardless of whether or not its political leaders wanted it to be.

The most immediate and obvious sign of this withering away of cultural boundaries between the United States and the rest of the world, and in particular Europe, was the expatriate movement. After the First World War was over, hundreds of writers or would-be writers invaded Europe in a literary migration that has had no equal either before or since. A favourable rate of exchange was perhaps the immediate precipitant. Other motivating factors included a possible desire to escape from provincialism and puritanism and, as one expatriate, Gertrude Stein, put it, to be 'all alone with English and myself'. But whatever the reason, these writers soon found themselves involved with other, European novelists and poets who shared their hunger for new modes of thought and expression and absorbed into literary and artistic movements that ignored the existence of national boundaries.

The revolt against earlier norms of belief and behaviour was not, people like Ernest Hemingway and Hart Crane discovered, a purely American prerogative; the anxious need to have the emergent culture, and the new sensations it engendered, adequately explained, was not the monopoly of either side of the Atlantic. So, while remaining American writers, they began to participate in the international experiments of Symbolism, Surrealism and Dadaism; the resources of language they carried with them from the New World were added to, and enriched, by their encounter with the Old. Whether they ventured to Europe only for a while, or stayed most of their lives, or whether, for that matter, they stayed firmly within the boundaries of the United States, very many American writers became involved in literary movements or tendencies that denied the traditional categories of history and geography. Above all, they became involved in what has become known as Modernism. Modernism, the major and most widespread response to what Adams had seen as the 'multiverse', can be defined in terms of its feelings: principally, of cultural exile and alienation. It can be defined in terms of its forms, which incline towards the innovative, the disjunctive, associative and experimental. It can be defined in terms of its more specific stylistic features: a willingness to disrupt traditional syntax and form, to mix together modes or levels of writing that had traditionally been kept separate, and to risk possible incoherence so as to challenge preconceived notions of order, stability and value. But perhaps the most fundamental definition stems from the historical perception shared by so many different writers of this period, American or otherwise, that things had altered beyond established means of recognition. As Virginia Woolf put it, in 1912 human nature changed; or, as D. H. Lawrence preferred it, in 1915 the old world ended. And the aim of Modernism was to place questions of form and structure, aesthetic vision, uppermost so as to achieve or move towards newer, more appropriate means of recognition – to enable writer and reader to begin to see things properly, truly, again.

'Some people', a reporter for the *New York Sun* commented in the 1920s, 'think that women are the cause of modernism, whatever that is.' For many observers, as this comment suggests, there was a connection between modernism as a process of social transformation, Modernism as a cultural movement, and feminism, the emergence of the 'new woman'. Whatever the truth of this, the change in the position of women during this period was remarkable. In 1920 the Nineteenth Amendment giving American women the right to vote was adopted. At the same time, the spread of scientific, reasonably reliable methods of birth control was enabling women to exercise some, limited, control over their lives. The fall in the birth rate was dramatic. In 1800, white women bore on average seven children; in 1860, that figure was down to 5.21; but by 1920 it had fallen dramatically further, to an average per person of 3.17. Opportunities for education grew during this period, especially at higher level; women were making many of the new professions their own; and it was women who mainly led the successful campaign to establish female suffrage, just as they were to lead an equally successful campaign to prohibit the sale of alcohol, a prohibition that lasted from 1920 to 1933. Admittedly, the new professions women began to enter, like social work, nursing and librarianship, tended to be ones with low pay and social status; to that extent, they were like older, more established jobs, such as teaching, that had traditionally been a female prerogative. And the more lucrative professions, like medicine and the law, were still mostly closed to women for half a century. So, for that matter, were positions in business and finance, and in the skilled trades. But American women had a higher profile in public life and a greater freedom of choice in their personal lives than they had ever had before. And with the vote in their hands, some eighty years after the Seneca Falls convention, they had some degree of real political power.

Or, rather, white women of the middling classes had. Women of other ethnic groups, and white working women, like their male counterparts, continued to be mostly marginalized and dispossessed. Some 40 per cent of working women, especially African Americans, were still engaged in household labour. For that matter, while the 'new woman' or the 'flapper' might excite the public imagination with ideas of female freedom or female sexuality, most Americans still tended to believe that a woman's proper place was in the home – and that the sexuality of anyone, but particularly the female kind, needed to be kept under lock and key. This was also the period of the Committee for the Suppression of Vice and a Motion Picture Production Code that prevented the depiction of a man and a woman, even husband and wife, together in bed. It was also the period when the editor of the *Little Review* – one of the little magazines that proliferated at this time, as an outlet for Modernism and other literary experiment – was fined one hundred dollars for publishing part of *Ulysses* (1922) by James Joyce. American culture, for all its general gravitation towards the social forms of modernity and the artistic forms of Modernism, was still a complex of different, conflicting interests, more a collision of cultures than a monolith. Labour fought with triumphalist and eventually triumphant capitalism: the Industrial Workers of the World, a union embracing all working people, was founded in 1905: Eugene Debs captured nearly a million votes as the socialist candidate for president in 1920; there were major if ultimately unsuccessful strikes in the coal and rail industries in 1922. Traditionalism fought with the new thought: in 1925, a young schoolteacher named Scopes was put on trial in Tennessee for teaching Darwinian theories of evolution. And various ethnic and immigrant groups, the other Americans, demanded attention, wanted their claims to an American identity to be heard.

In the 1920s, in particular, immigration to the United States reached new levels, comparable to those of the 1880s and provoking another moral panic: new immigration quotas were consequently implemented in 1924. Many of these newcomers ended up living in the cities. All of them supplied writers with a different twist on the Modernist theme of exile: these were strangers in a strange land in a different, more mundane and material sense than that often felt and meant by the major Modernist writers. And it often provoked those who wrote about them to favour the realism of social record to literary experiment. Native Americans continued to suffer their own forms of cultural dislocation. Subjected first to removal to reservations, then to the social experiment of the Allottment Act – which gave separate allottments of land to individuals who were then, very often, tricked out of them

– they suffered their own peculiar extremes of exile. Stripped of their tribal names, their land, their place in an ancient community, their predicament encouraged writers to socialism too, sometimes, but also to forms that mixed folk and native materials with other traditions. Wandering between cultures, like other ethnic groups and notably Hispanic and Asian American, they often inspired works that wandered between cultures too – that pursued the question of mixed identity, a conflicted history through a mixture of languages and literary forms. That was also the case with many African American writers of the period. W. E. B. Du Bois, in *The Souls of Black Folk* (1903), suggested that the black person in America was burdened with 'a double-consciousness . . . two souls, two thoughts, two unreconciled strivings, two warring ideals in one dark body'. The African American is, after all, American *and* African; and the question was, and is, which is the more important? Should the primary impulse be towards absorption into the dominant culture or assertion of a separate national identity? Is assimilationism the priority, or black nationalism? To that, at the time, were added further traumas, other forms of exile or strangeness demanding writerly recognition. For this was the era of the Great Migration, when thousands of African Americans left the rural South for such urban centres as Detroit, Chicago and New York. And it was also an era of intensified racial violence: in 1900, for instance, at the dawn of the new century, there were 115 recorded lynchings, all but nine of them of blacks.

Caught between the pulse of the new and the rhythms of the old, as well as experiencing a 'double-consciousness', African American writers of this period are usually included under the heading of the Harlem Renaissance. Many wrote in Harlem, but not all; there were other centres of writing activity for African Americans located around the country; and another term sometimes used to describe these writers is less topographically specific, the New Negro Movement. It is taken from the work of Alain Locke, an influential black critic, whose essay on the New Negro and anthology of that title were both published in 1925. Whatever the preferred title for this new generation of black writers, what is notable about them is how they explored different literary forms to express the condition of African Americans in their times. Facing a racial experience the determining feature of which was that it was mixed and conflicted, they were prepared individually to confront and collectively to debate the question of just how their experience should be turned into literature. There were three particularly pressing aspects to that question. First, there was the matter of the balance between politics and art, the bargain to be struck between political message and aesthetic form. Second was the issue of the relative claims of literary experiment and verisimilitude: whether the black experience could best be caught in innovative structures, traditional forms or more socially conscious, strictly realist ones. Third, there was the problem of the racial inheritance, its relevance or otherwise. There was a rich vein of African and African American cultural tradition available for the writer to tap. In the African American traditions of the past, for instance, there were the conventions of folktale, slave narrative and spiritual; and in those of the present there were, say, the rhythmic forms of blues, gospel and jazz. The issue here was how, if at all, to use these resources to register the shape and meaning of the contemporary experience, to transform African American worlds into words. There was, of course, no settled answer to any of these aspects of the question; the writers of this time found multiple means for giving voice to the New Negro. And in their differences with each other, just as much as in their distances from white writers, they revealed just how much American literature continued to resist a monolithic reading – even the one supplied by Modernism.

Nor was double consciousness the monopoly of African Americans or those who became known, during this period, at the height of resistance to mass immigration, as 'hyphenated Americans'. Dualism of a different kind was a characteristic feature of the dominant culture in America as, caught between optimism and nostalgia, celebration of the new and regret for the old, many Americans found themselves compelled towards the horizons of tomorrow but also drawn towards the golden landscapes of yesterday. The flight of Charles Lindbergh across the Atlantic in 1927, for instance, provoked quite different responses. On the one hand, Lindbergh became in the popular mind the living embodiment of the pioneer spirit, the 'Spirit of St. Louis', the young, independent and individualistic American, unaffected by public institutions and pressures. On the other, his achievement was also seen as a witness to the miracle of technology, what was possible with the help of teamwork, organization and commitment to the production economy. The same groups or individuals could and did respond to Lindbergh's achievement as an anticipation of future technological miracles and as an affirmation of the values of the past. Committed to the power, leisure and wealth of the new, urban world, they could nevertheless feel irresistibly drawn towards what they saw as the simpler, purer values of the old. 'We live in a new creation,' one politician of the time observed. 'Literally, the old things have passed away and all things have become new.' The conviction of newness and uniqueness mattered to Americans of this period, profoundly affecting their thought and language; and while part of them was inspired by it, an equal part was clearly frightened. The compulsions that led, in literature, to the innovation and experiment of Modernism were countered by an impulse to look back with yearning to times that seemed simpler, morally more certain and socially more stable – to the quietude and contentment of a more pastoral age.

This yearning or nostalgia for apparently simpler and better times assumed many forms. In 1920, the newly elected President Warren Harding caught some of the mood when he told his fellow Americans that theirs was a period for 'not heroics but healing; not nostrums but normality; not resolution but restoration'. In the same year, the passing of the Eighteenth Amendment prohibiting the sale of alcohol showed how the progressive and nostalgic impulses could sometimes work together to support each other. Some of those advocating this amendment, certainly, were progressives who believed that it was as legitimate to preserve a person from the consumption of alcohol as it was to protect him or her against unhealthy or dangerous factory conditions. But many came from rural, Protestant districts and wanted to enshrine fundamentalist beliefs in law: for them, it was a symbolic reform, which gave institutional legitimacy to the norms and values of the old

America. 'The Old America', as one Southern newspaper of the time put it, 'the America of Jackson and of Lincoln', was also what those who objected to the influx of immigrants claimed they wanted to recover. At its worst here, fear of the new led not only to the trial of someone teaching evolution but to the Ku Klux Klan, which experienced a startling growth in numbers after the First World War. 'When the Klan first appeared,' its leader Hiram Wesley Evans declared in 1925, 'those who maintained the old standards did so only in the face of constant ridicule' and 'the Nordic American' was 'a stranger in large parts of the land his fathers gave him.' So, he argued, Americans had had to turn to organizations like the Klan, in the belief that nothing else could save them other than 'a return of power into the hands of the everyday, not highly cultured, not overtly intellectualized, but entirely unspoiled and not de-Americanized average citizen of the old stock'.

These nostalgic impulses that found convoluted, and sometimes corrupted, expression in such things as the Scopes trial, prohibition or immigration quotas also helped varieties of artistic traditionalism during this period. There was a new interest in the recovery of the past among both writers and critics of many different cultural groups. Observers of the cultural scene, like Van Wyck Brooks (1886–1963) and Matthew Josephson (1899–1978), began constructing the idea of an American literary tradition. And writers began imaginative exploration of what one of them, Willa Cather, termed 'the precious, the incommunicable past'. While Cather explored the uses of the Western past, others such as John Crowe Ransom and Allen Tate considered the uses of the Southern past; and still others, like Jean Toomer and Mourning Dove, turned, respectively, to the African American and Native American past as an imaginative resource and a source of material. What these writers sought was, inevitably, different. Cather was intrigued, for instance, by the power of memory, and the grip the imagined past of the West, and of America, has on the present. Other Western writers turned to the Western past as a way of returning to the earth and 'the real'. Southern writers, like Ransom, Tate and their colleagues in the Fugitive and Agrarian movements, were drawn to the idea of a fundamentally rooted, traditional and rural society as a bulwark, a means of resistance to urban anonymity and social change. Toomer and Mourning Dove were more inclined to find in the folkways and art of the past a healing agency or a way of restoring their own people. What all such writers had in common, however, was the belief that a return to and recovery of the past was not only possible but imperative: that an act of remembrance was vital to the restoration of personal and social health. This passage from Cather's novel *My Ántonia* (1918) captures something of that belief. The words are attributed to Jim Burden, the narrator, but they clearly express Cather's own views, and the impulses that fired so many of these backward-looking works into life:

> While I was in the very act of yearning towards the new forms . . . brought up before me, my mind plunged away from me, and I suddenly found myself thinking of the places and people of my own infinitesimal past. They stood out strengthened and simplified now. They were all I had for answer to the new appeal.

'The past is never dead. It's not even past,' observes a character in one of William Faulkner's novels: which is another way of expressing this obsession with yesterday, the desire to reinvent past times. Other ways, many of them, were offered by writers of this era as they sought sure anchorage, moral and perhaps formal.

The cultural history of the United States in the first half of the twentieth century is not, of course, simply the story of the encounter between different Americas – and the conflict or tension between optimism and nostalgia, the pull towards the future and the backward glance towards the past, the urge to experiment and the search for more traditionalist norms. Other forces were at work. And Americans were inevitably and profoundly affected, in particular, by what seemed to be the crisis of capitalism: when, on one Friday in 1929, the Wall Street Crash occurred. Within four years after the Crash, per capita income had dropped 100 per cent and unemployment, which had been remarkably low in the 1920s, had risen from 500,000 to thirteen million. Many of those who were unemployed had no economic assistance of any kind, and were forced to wander the country in search of work. They rode freight trains from one state to another, risking injury or even death, and erected shanty towns, ironically called 'Hoovervilles' after the then President Hoover. Farmers unable to meet mortgage payments were evicted from their hold-ings; beggars, street-corner orators demanding revolution, breadlines and soup kitchens all became commonplace. Those in employment fared little better: in 1932, the average wage in several major industries ranged between 20 and 30 cents an hour and the average income of Americans in general dropped back to what it had been at the beginning of three decades of technological revolution. Over all this chaos, Hoover presided with little sense of what to do: the measures he offered to alleviate or alter things were too little, too late. Farm relief, federal loans for business, public works, all these measures were tried half-heartedly because they went against Hoover's own cherished philosophy of 'rugged individualism'. He believed that the slump was a short-term affair that would gradually correct itself. Others, including the vast majority of the American public, tended to disagree. Hoover had been elected as 'the Great Engineer' in 1928; in 1932 he was defeated by Franklin Delano Roosevelt in a landslide. Even in his own home state of Iowa, Hoover was picketed during the election by two thousand men holding placards that said it all: 'In Hoover We Trusted, Now We Are Busted'.

If the Crash and the Depression that followed it was a significant economic event, though, it was an even more significant cultural and psychological one, as those placards carried in Iowa indicated. For what it generated was a crisis in confidence: the ingrained American belief in the rewards due to hard work, the central importance of self-help, the inevitability of progress – all were called into question by an occurrence for which the word 'panic' seemed precisely right because it was at once devastating in terms of the human suffering it caused and unpredict-able, more or less totally unexpected. When the Crash came, most bankers and financiers not only were unprepared for it, they tried at first to deny its implica-tions and seemed oblivious to the sheer scale of the collapse. And, as it worsened, many were inclined to treat it not as a cultural event, susceptible to analysis and explanation, but as a natural one: a natural disaster, like an earthquake or typhoon, for which little preparation was possible and which had to be endured for a while. The simple and terrible fact was that a failure of language occurred: Americans, to begin with, lacked the vocabulary, political, economic or imaginative, adequately to confront and possibly to deal with what had happened. Even the most realistic of the popular cinematic forms at this time, the gangster movie, was concerned as much with compensatory fantasy as it was with hard facts. For while it acknowledged that the urban-industrial surroundings, the cities of America, had become oppressive, bewildering and even terrifying places, it offered a series of dynamic, rebellious and above all individualistic protagonists who seemed to have achieved mastery over the urban jungle. Morally, these heroes might be subject to a disapproval that required them to be killed in the final reel. On another, subliminal level, however, they offered their audiences another version of the dream of freedom, the independence and mobility of the outsider – suitably darkened to reflect the darker times.

'I like the Americans because they are healthy and optimistic,' the novelist Franz Kafka once remarked, adding, when he was asked what he knew about America, 'I always admired Walt Whitman.' The Crash and Depression may have provoked people in the United States to bewilderment and anger and compensatory fantasies of power: but the economic situation could never quite extinguish that belief in possibility, in reinventing the self and society however shattered, of which Kafka was thinking – and for which, as Kafka realized, one of the most memorable spokesmen in earlier writing had been the author of *Leaves of Grass*. The election of 1932 foregrounded this belief: insisting that Americans had nothing to fear but fear itself, the newly elected president helped to restore popular confidence at least a little. In the first hundred days of the administration – the first hundred days of what he called the New Deal – Roosevelt pushed Congress into passing a mass of legislation designed to restore some health to a radically sick economy. In the following years came other measures. The three Agricultural Adjustment Acts of 1933, 1936 and 1938 were attempts to maintain farm prices by artificially created scarcity; the Social Security Act of 1935 was an important welfare-state measure, providing for a system of old-age retirement payments and unemployment pay; the Works Progress (later Work Projects) Administration (WPA) was established to implement relief work on a vast scale and by 1939 had provided employment for eight and a half million people in a whole variety of occupations. It is possible to argue over the practical efficacy of all this legislation – and to suggest, for instance, that it took the demand created by the Second World War to restore the economy and full employment. What is unarguable, though, is that Roosevelt helped restore Americans' belief in their power to manage things, the solubility of the problems with which they were confronted. In an ideological sense, this meant that most Americans never completely lost confidence in the system, the virtues of capitalism and free enterprise. And in a more specifically moral sense, this involved a recovery of the 'can do' philosophy, the conviction that everything is manageable, given hard work, pluck and luck, and the exercise of the independent, individual will.

In the arts, this crisis of confidence and gradual recovery was reflected in many forms. There was, for instance, a renewed sense of the social responsibility of the artist: a sense that tempted both modernists and traditionalists along many different, cunning corridors of history and inspired a renewed interest in the possibilities of literary realism and naturalism. Ezra Pound, for instance, was to see a solution to contemporary problems in the politicization of poetry and the aestheticizing of politics and, eventually, in commitment to fascism. Others, like William Carlos Williams, tried to take the measure of the times in hard, spare distillations of the urban scene. While many of the traditionalists, notably those in the South, became even more intent on celebrating the values of an earlier, inherited American culture – a system at once prior to and superior to the contemporary confusions of capitalism – as a means of staving off what they saw as the otherwise inevitable triumph of socialist revolution. There were 'proletarian novels' – books, that is, written by working-class people – such as *The Disinherited* (1933) by Jack Conroy (1899–1980). There were novels of protest like *The Land of Plenty* (1934) by Robert Cantwell (1908–78), *The Grapes of Wrath* (1939) by John Steinbeck, or three novels dealing with a strike that took place in the textile mills of North Carolina: *To Make My Bread* (1932) by Grace Lumpkin (1893–1980), *Call Home the Heart* (1932) by Fielding Burke (Olive Tilford Dargan) (1869–1968) and *Beyond Desire* (1932) by Sherwood Anderson. There was fiction exploring the plight of dispossessed urban minorities, such as *Call It Sleep* (1934) by Henry Roth (1906–2000) or *Native Son* (1940) by Richard Wright. Writers like F. Scott Fitzgerald, William Faulkner and Ernest Hemingway tried to secrete an awareness of contemporary problems into their narratives: Fitzgerald did so in *Tender is the Night* (1934) and Faulkner and Hemingway in, respectively, *The Wild Palms* (1939) and *To Have and Have Not* (1937). Others turned directly to the techniques of journalism or documentary to make their point: as, say, James Agee (1909–55) did in his account of three poor Southern tenant-farming families, *Let Us Now Praise Famous Men* (1941). A sense of apocalypse or annunciation, which had always come relatively easily to American writers, now became even more pronounced. Apocalypse, for example, feelings of nightmare and catastrophe, are all clearly there in books like *The Day of the Locust* (1939) by Nathanael West, while Hart Crane's epic poem *The Bridge* (1930) is, to some extent, one long annunciatory act.

There is no simple way of summing up the artistic response to crisis: crisis in general, that is, or the specific crisis encountered by the American people between the two World Wars. It certainly encouraged a different cultural milieu. Writers on the right, like Allen Tate, wrote enthusiastically of the imminent 'destruction of the middle class-capitalist hegemony, and the restoration . . . of traditional society'. Writers on the left, like Jack Conroy, wrote of the general need for socialism and a classless society, and the need for the contemporary writer, in particular, to pursue 'social understanding, which is the life of revolutionary prose'. Communist Party intellectuals, in turn, like Michael Gold, developed theories of 'proletarian realism' based on Marxist theories, or what they termed 'the higher sphere of dialectical development of character'. Accompanying such enthusiasm, there was fear of what might happen if crisis did not engender the right kind of change: although, naturally, writers disagreed about what they feared just as much as they did about what they desired. Those to the right, like the Southerner John Peale Bishop, wrote of the urgent imperative to resist 'some American form of communism'; otherwise, he lamented, 'with us Western civilization ends'. Those inclining to the left, on the other hand, like Lillian Hellman and Dorothy Parker – as well as Ernest Hemingway in *For Whom the Bell Tolls* (1940) – turned, with an equal sense of urgency, to writing about the fight against fascism. The American Writers' Congress of 1935 supplied a platform to debate such issues. So did a number of journals whose titles express their commitments and the urgencies of the times: on the right, periodicals like *American Review*, on the left, *Partisan Review* and *New Masses*. And, in a radical departure from the traditional American belief that the artist, like every good citizen, should be self-reliant, even the government intervened in the debate, to the extent that government agencies were actually established to employ people in the creative arts. Among the most notable of these agencies was the Federal Theatre Project, sponsored by the Works Project Administration, which was a national organization of theatre groups that re-employed thousands of theatrical workers – by 1937, it was playing to weekly audiences of 350,000. Other projects included the financing of photographic accounts of the rural working class, popular America and American folk customs; the employment of painters under the Federal Arts Project to decorate banks, post offices and schools with murals developing themes of labour, agriculture and history; and the federal support of books and films intended to reveal the essential nature of the United States, its human and natural resources, to its people. Impossible as it is to summarize, though, perhaps something of all this can be caught by saying that, in reaction to crisis, American writers rediscovered their social and prophetic function; they were reawakened to their responsibility as citizens, members of a multiple community. It was a responsibility that few of them had ever really forgotten, least of all those who came from and wrote about peoples who had been dispossessed long before that Friday in October 1929. But it was one that they took on with renewed enthusiasm, as they delved into that most fundamental and frequent of themes in American writing: the relation between promise and performance, America as an idea and America as a complex, changing and conflicted society – the dream of one America and the fact that there are many.

Between Victorianism and Modernism

The problem of race

As the twentieth century began, many Americans saw race as the most pressing issue they faced. Certainly, this was true of those African American writers who initiated debate about the 'color line' as W. E. B. Du Bois (1868–1963) termed it: Du Bois himself, Booker T. Washington (1856–1915) and James Weldon Johnson

(1871–1938). Washington was born in Virginia, the son of a slave mother and a white father. 'My life had its beginning in the midst of the most miserable, desolate, and discouraging surroundings,' he was later to say in his autobiography, *Up From Slavery* (1901). His early years, he recalled, 'were not very different from those of thousands of other slaves'. He lived in a 'little cabin', had no schooling whatever while he remained in bondage, and what information he received 'by what was termed the grape-vine telegraph'. Of his ancestry he knew 'almost nothing', he explained; of his mother he knew little, and of his father, even less – indeed, he did not 'even know his name'. Yet, despite that, Washington was curiously ambivalent about slavery in his adult years. Thanks to their 'kindly and generous nature', Washington declared, slaves felt 'tenderness and sympathy' towards their masters. 'The slaves would have laid down their lives', he insisted, for 'the women and children who were left on the plantations when the white males went to war.' Not only that, 'there are many instances of Negroes tenderly caring for their former masters and mistresses who for some reason have become poor and dependent since the war'. Washington left his readers and audiences in no doubt that slaves wanted freedom: 'I have never seen one who did not want to be free,' he pointed out in *Up From Slavery*, 'or one who would return to slavery.' Yet he tended to emphasize its positive, ameliorative or less offensive features, as the white Southern apologists had once done. Frederick Douglass, whose biography Washington wrote and published in 1906, saw the slave system as hell. So did the authors of other slave narratives. For Washington, however, it was educative, helping to prepare African Americans for the role they had to assume after the Civil War. Thanks to 'the school of American slavery', he averred, 'Negroes . . . are in a stronger and more hopeful condition, materially, intellectually, morally, and religiously, than is true of an equal number of black people in any other portion of the globe'.

Eventually, after the Civil War, Washington went to school. Entering Hampton Normal Agricultural Institute in Virginia in 1872, he felt, he said, that he was starting 'a new life' and 'had reached the promised land'. There he met and won the favour of one of many whites who were to assist him with his career: the college president, Samuel Armstrong, whom Washington referred to in *Up From Slavery* as 'a great man', typical of 'that Christlike body of men and women who went into Negro schools at the close of the war . . . to assist in lifting up my race'. It was Armstrong who recommended that Washington should found the Tuskegee Institute, a school for black teachers funded by the Alabama legislature. Washington moved to Tuskegee in 1881. From then until his death, he divided his time between developing the Institute, pursuing his career as a national black leader, and pub-licizing his programme of education and advancement for his people. In a few years, he had assumed national prominence as a thinker, educator and public orator. He organized the National Negro Business League in Boston in 1901; his Institute received endorsement and support from such influential figures as the millionaire Andrew Carnegie; and, after he gave an address at the opening of the Cotton States and International Exposition in Atlanta in 1895, he received a letter of congratulation from the then president, Grover Cleveland, who also visited the

Institute. The Atlanta address, which Cleveland declared to Washington could not 'fail to delight and encourage all who wish well for your race', was a brief summation of its author's ideas on black education and progress. In it, Washington emphasized the importance of a vocational, utilitarian education for African Americans. 'It is at the bottom of life we must begin,' he declared; 'we shall prosper in proportion as we learn to dignify and glorify common labour and put brains and skill into the common occupations of life.' 'Cast down your bucket where you are,' was the repeated refrain of the speech. Blacks should learn to 'cast it down in agriculture, mechanics, in commerce, in domestic service, and in the professions'. Whites should learn to cast it down 'among those people who have, without strikes and labour wars, tilled your fields, cleared your forests, builded your railroads and cities, and brought treasures from the bowels of the earth'. There should be mutual trust and aid.

Mutual but separate: Washington insisted that 'in all things that are purely social' blacks and whites could be 'separate as the fingers, yet one as the hand in all things essential to mutual progress'. He saw 'the agitations of questions of social equality' as 'the extremest folly'. Progress would come for African Americans as and when it was earned by hard work, diligence and thrift: as it had for him, he pointed out, because he had been 'determined to succeed'. The core text here, for explaining Washington's gospel of progress and his own career as exemplary, a demonstration of that gospel, was *Up From Slavery*. It is a slave narrative of a kind, at the beginning. But it more clearly resembles the *Autobiography* of Benjamin Franklin, as it describes the rise of its hero from humble beginnings to fame and fortune – and prescribes the same resolution and route for other men and women like him. Washington even recalls Franklin in specific episodes. His account of his arrival in Richmond, Virginia, to enrol in Hampton Normal Agricultural Institute, penniless, anonymous and painfully hungry, echoes Franklin's description of his own first entry into Philadelphia. And he models the narrative on the archetypal American success story that Franklin initiated: our representative man rises to prominence thanks to hard work, thrift and diligence and then, relentlessly optimistic, divulges the secret, the agenda he followed that enabled him to rise and will now enable his reader to rise as well. It is hardly surprising that *Up From Slavery* was an enormous success, becoming the most famous book by an African American for half a century after its publication. For it formulates a myth of black effort and achievement that slotted neatly into the prevailing white myths of the time. It was a book that white readers could find appealing, because it was unthreatening, even eager to please: 'I believe it is the duty of the Negro . . . to deport himself modestly in regard to political claims,' Washington concluded on the crucial issue of enfranchisement, 'depending upon the slow but sure influences that proceed from property, intelligence, and high character for the full recognition of his political rights.' It was also one that many black readers could find attractive because it offered a measure of hope, however limited.

Not all black readers, however: in *The Souls of Black Folk* (1903), W. E. B. Du Bois offered a comprehensive criticism of Washington's modest stance on black disenfranchisement as well as his emphasis on 'formation of character', vocational instruction at the expense of liberal education. Du Bois began his critique by damning Washington with faint praise. 'Today,' he declared, 'Mr. Washington is certainly the most distinguished Southerner since Jefferson Davis,' the leader of the Confederacy during the Civil War, 'and the one with the largest personal following.' That sly linking of a self-proclaimed leader of the black community with the leader of the white slaveholding community at war led into the recognition that 'Mr. Washington represents in Negro thought the old attitude of adjustment and submission'. His programme, Du Bois pointed out, 'practically accepts the alleged inferiority of the Negro'. It was a 'gospel of Work and Money' founded on a 'triple paradox': by which Du Bois meant that, as he saw it, Washington was asking black people to sacrifice the three things they most urgently needed. These three, as Du Bois succinctly summarized them, were 'the right to vote', 'civic equality' and 'the education of youth according to ability'. Washington, Du Bois argued, tended to shift responsibility for the racial problem from white people 'to the Negro's shoulders'; whereas 'in fact the burden belongs to the nation'. 'So far as Mr. Washington preaches Thrift, Patience, and Industrial Training for the masses, we must hold up his hands and strive with him,' he concluded. 'But as far as Mr. Washington apologizes for injustice . . . , does not rightly value the privilege and duty of voting, belittles the emasculating effects of caste distinction, and opposes the higher training . . . of our brighter minds', then, Du Bois insisted, he and those like him had to be 'unceasingly and firmly' opposed.

Du Bois had been born in Massachusetts and educated at Fisk and Harvard universities. He had had little personal experience of the social and political exclusion of blacks until he went south to Fisk in 1885. 'I suddenly came to a region where the world was split into white and black halves,' he wrote later, 'and where the darker half was held back by race prejudice and legal bonds.' In the first stages of his career, he devoted himself to the scholarly study of the status and condition of black people in the United States. His books during this period included *The Suppression of the African Slave Trade to the United States of America* (1896) and *The Philadelphia Negro: A Social Study* (1899). But Du Bois wanted to reach a wider audience. For him, racial prejudice was a national issue and an intensely urgent one. As he put it, 'the problem of the twentieth century is the problem of race'. And he wanted to make as many people as he could, black and white, aware of it. So he began to experiment with different forms, various ways of communicating with the general public. These included general studies of black people in the United States, such as *The Negro* (1915), *The Gift of Black Folk* (1935) and *Black Reconstruction* (1935). They included essays, poems, short stories, plays and sketches, many of which were published in two magazines he edited, *The Moon* and *The Horizon*. They included a novel, *Dark Princess* (1928), and an autobiographical work, *Dusk of Dawn* (1945), which Du Bois described as 'the autobiography of a concept of race'. Du Bois's activism led him to help found the National Association for the Advancement of Colored People (NAACP) in 1909, and to edit its magazine, *Crisis*, from 1910 until 1934. But his major and most influential work was the one in which he launched his attack on Booker T. Washington – which, unsurprisingly, initiated the most bitter phase of the conflict between the two black leaders – *The Souls of Black Folk*.

The Souls of Black Folk uses song, sketch and story to explore the condition of black people in terms that are at once brilliantly intuitive and piercingly analytical. In the first chapter, for instance, Du Bois begins with two epigraphs: one from a spiritual (or what Du Bois himself called a 'sorrow song'), 'Nobody Knows the Trouble I've Seen', the other from a poem by Arthur Symons about loss. He then moves into a restlessly imaginative exploration of what he calls 'our spiritual strivings'. The chapter is a secular transposition of the theme of the spiritual: an account of the trouble involved not in being hidden from 'the Lord' but in being hidden from oneself. It is also a black transposition of the theme of the poem by Symons: a meditation not on lost love but on lost identity, a lack of connection with oneself and with others. All this issues from Du Bois's seminal account, alluded to earlier, of the 'double-consciousness' of 'the Negro'. When he was young, Du Bois recalls, a 'shadow' suddenly swept across him. It dawned upon him that he was different from others: 'or like, mayhap, in heart and life and longing, but shut out from their world by a vast veil'. In this, he suggests, he was and is like all others of his race. He, and they, have been 'born with a veil, and gifted with second-sight in this American world': a world that yields them 'no true self-consciousness', but only lets them see themselves 'through the revelation of the other world'. 'It is a peculiar sensation, this double-consciousness,' Du Bois confides, 'this sense of always looking at one's self through the eyes of others.' The African American 'ever feels his two-ness, – an American, a Negro: two souls, two thoughts, two unreconciled strivings; two warring ideals in one dark body, whose dogged strength alone keeps it from being torn asunder'. For Du Bois, 'the history of the American Negro is the history of this strife'. It gives him or her, certainly, a special knowledge, the 'second-sight' of the secret sharer. But it also leads to a potentially disabling ambivalence: 'the contradiction of double aims' as an African and an American. The African American longs 'to merge his double self into a better and truer self', a merging in which 'he wishes neither of the older selves to be lost'. That, however, still remains a consummation devoutly to be wished. Despite the end of slavery, the shadow still falls across every black man and woman in America. Du Bois weaves together autobiography and analysis, meditation and incantation, in this seminal account of African American dualism, the veil of invisibility thwarting identity and true community. Gathering together intimations dimly perceived and expressed in earlier works by black Americans, it was to exercise a profound influence on later writing. Ironically, Du Bois seemed in later life to gravitate towards one side of his own 'double-consciousness'. In 1934, he was expelled from the NAACP for advocating the use of segregation as a means of drawing blacks together into a cohesive group during the Depression. And in 1963, just a year before his death, he became a citizen of Ghana.

The notion of the 'double-consciousness' of the African American found an immediate echo in the work of James Weldon Johnson. In his first novel, *The*

Autobiography of an Ex-Coloured Man (1912), the protagonist suggests that 'every coloured man' in the United States has, 'in proportion to his intellectuality, a sort of dual personality'. 'He is forced to take his outlook on things, not from the viewpoint of a citizen, or a man, or even a human being,' he explains, 'but from the viewpoint of a *coloured* man.' 'There is one phase of him', the protagonist adds, 'which is disclosed only in the freemasonry of his own race.' This gives the African American a certain insight, what Du Bois had termed 'the gift of second-sight': 'I believe', the 'ex-coloured man' declares, 'that the coloured people of this country know and understand the white people better than the white people know and understand them.' But it can also be a source of deep confusion: in the course of his life, as he tells it, Johnson's 'ex-coloured' hero crosses the racial barrier no fewer than four times because, being to all appearances white, he can effectively act out his own ambivalence. Unlike his protagonist, Johnson had no doubts about his identity or aims. For all of his career as a writer, he sought what he described as 'a form that will express the racial spirit'. And he sought in more than one form. While practising law in Florida, for instance, he collaborated with his brother in writing popular songs and spirituals. One of these, 'Lift Every Voice and Sing' (1900), became known as the black national anthem. Later, while teaching creative literature at Fisk University, he published a black history of New York City, *Black Manhattan* (1930). And later still, he published an account of his political activities as US consul in Nicaragua and Venezuela from 1906 to 1912, *Along this Way* (1933), and a summary of his role as a major figure in the NAACP, *Negro Americans What Now?* (1934).

It is for his poetry and fiction, however, that Johnson deserves a place as a pivotal figure in African American writing at the dawn of the twentieth century. Pursuing his quest to express the racial spirit in verse, he wrote poems addressed to the anonymous authors of blues and spirituals ('O Black and Unknown Bards' [1908]) or written in imitation of black musical forms ('Sence You Went Away' [1900]). The most powerful poetic realization of this quest, however, was *God's Trombones: Seven Negro Sermons in Verse* (1927), a series of poems in which Johnson attempted to recreate the passion and power of black sermons using polyrhythmic cadences, vivid diction and a technique of intensification by repetition. The most powerful prose realization, in turn, and his most influential work, was *The Autobiography of an Ex-Coloured Man*. Published anonymously at first, it was reissued under Johnson's own name in 1927, at the height of the Harlem Renaissance, to become a model for later novelists ranging from Zora Neale Hurston to Richard Wright and Ralph Ellison. Born to a black mother and a white father, a 'tall man' whom he sees only twice during his life, the narrator begins by telling the reader that he is about to divulge the 'great secret' of his life, the one he has guarded more carefully than any of his 'earthly possessions'. The secret, of course, is that he is 'coloured'. So much of a secret was this, apparently, that his early years were spent without him knowing it either. It was only at school he learned that he was himself what he had become accustomed to call 'a nigger'. At first, rushing back from school, he had been reluctant to believe it. Gazing at himself in the mirror in his 'little room,' what he saw, he confides, hardly warranted the belief. 'I noticed the ivory whiteness of my skin,' he recalls, 'the beauty of my mouth, the size and liquid darkness of my eyes, and the long, black lashes that fringed and shaded them produced an effect that was strangely fascinating even to me.' It is only when his mother confirms the truth – while adding, 'your father was one of the greatest men in the country, the best blood in the South is in you' – that he is forced to accept it.

As the description of his youthful, beautiful image in the bedroom mirror suggests, the 'ex-coloured man' is something of a narcissist. Gradually, the reader learns that he is an egoist, too, inclined to celebrate his talents and his success. Working in a cigar factory in Jacksonville, he claims that 'his talent for language' enables him to speak 'better Spanish than many of the Cuban workmen' there. As a gambler and occasional musician in a New York nightclub, he tells us that he acquired a reputation for both his gambling and his music: indeed, he explains, 'I developed into a remarkable player of rag-time' and 'gained the title of "the professor"'. Travelling in Europe, more as a companion than the servant of a millionaire friend, the 'ex-coloured man', by his account of it, was admired for his taste and musical talent wherever he went. And returning to America, he describes with lipsmacking relish how he began 'to contract the money fever' and how his successful deals and investments gave him an almost erotic thrill. 'What an interesting and absorbing game is money-making!' is his conclusion. *The Autobiography of an Ex-Coloured Man* was once considered the first instance in African American fiction of a first-person narrator, although that title perhaps belongs to *The Bondswoman's Narrative* now and Harriet Wilson had employed the first person in the opening chapters of *Our Nig*. It stands, in any event, as a bridge between nineteenth- and twentieth-century black literature; and that is a considerable achievement in itself. But to that achievement can be added several others. It dramatizes the dualism Du Bois had discovered and spoken of in *The Souls of Black Folk*. It captures the inner rituals of the black community, what is called here 'the freemasonry of the race', in a way that had rarely been done before. It uses a picaresque form, a narrative of wandering around and beyond America, to enact a search for black identity. Above all, it presents us with a flawed hero. The subjects of earlier black autobiographies had tended towards the sensitive, the sympathetic, even the noble. The 'ex-coloured man' is not that at all: on the contrary, he is proud and rendered unattractive by his pride. And pride comes here before a fall. In the end, he has to recognize his error: that, as he puts it, 'I have sold my birthright for a mess of pottage'. Sometimes, he reflects bitterly in the final chapter, 'it seems to be that I have never really been a Negro, that I have been only a privileged spectator of their inner life'. At other times, he adds, 'I feel that I have been a coward and a deserter, and I am possessed by a strong longing for my mother's people'. But such feelings come too late. Trapped in the white world now, with two children who are to all appearances white, the 'ex-coloured man' cannot escape; and he can only reveal his 'secret' covertly, anonymously, in the pages of this book. It is a remarkable conclusion to a story that plays subtle variations on the themes of black duality and invisibility – and that makes its points about race not by lecturing or heroics but by something new in African American writing, a sadly contracted, alien hero.

Building bridges: Women writers

At the same time as African American writers like Washington, Du Bois and Johnson were carving out new territory in black literature, a number of women writers were building a bridge between the preoccupations of the nineteenth century and those of the twentieth. These included three major novelists: Edith Wharton (1862–1937), Ellen Glasgow (1873–1945) and Willa Cather (1873–1947). What is remarkable about at least two of these writers, Glasgow and Cather, is the degree to which they relied on a network of mutual support among women authors. Cather, it was mentioned earlier, received help and advice, and an example of what to write and how to write about it, from Sarah Orne Jewett. Glasgow belonged to a loose group of fellow women writers that included, at different times, Mary Johnston, Charlotte Perkins Gilman, Rebecca Harding Davis and Marjorie Kinnan Rawlings (1896–1953), who wrote about what she called 'the firmly entrenched outpost of the vanishing frontier' in such novels as *The Yearling* (1938). Wharton was different to the extent that she drew example and encouragement from her long-time friend Henry James rather than other women authors. All three, however, dedicated themselves to the imaginative exploration of one or two particular regions or areas of the United States. For Wharton, this was New York, for Glasgow the South, and for Cather it was the West and Southwest. And all three were preoccupied with the social and moral transformations they saw occurring in their particular corner of the nation, and the clash between past and present, the old habits and customs and the new, that those transformations engendered. In their hands, this concentration on a particular place was not an act of provincialism but of pressure and focus: they treated the societies they examined, their practices and myths, as a paradigm of what was happening in the nation at large, and perhaps beyond. They were profoundly interested in change, and the tension between change and ingrained habits of belief and behaviour – all that is gathered under the categories of tradition, convention and memory – and the imaginative sites they chose were their way of exploring that subject.

Wharton was born Edith Jones into a wealthy New York family. In 1885, she married Edward Wharton, a man considerably older than her from her family's circle of acquaintances. The marriage, never a happy one, ended in divorce. Wharton was in love for some time with another man, Walter Berry, an expatriate. Berry, however, made it clear that he did not want marriage, and she never married again. The themes of frustrated love and unhappy marriage became common ones in Wharton's fiction. Her first book, however, was a non-fictional work, *The Decoration of Houses* (1897). It anticipated at least some of the interests and strategies of her later novels to the extent that it explored status and snobbery in old New York, and furnishings in particular and taste in general as an index to character. Her first full-length novel, *The Valley of Decision* (1902), was set in eighteenth-century Italy. But then followed subjects closer to home. As a wife and hostess at this time, Wharton belonged to New York society. As a novelist, however, she analysed its customs with irony. Her New York novels, which are her best work, present a changing society and an internecine conflict between an old, patrician upper-middle class rather like her own and a newly rich upper-middle class for whom traditional ideas of culture were losing their sanctity. They also consider, in particular, the position of women in New York society, torn, as Lily Bart, the heroine of her first major novel, *The House of Mirth* (1905), is, between personal desire and social law – the need to fulfil the requirements of the imagination and the need to make a good marriage. *The House of Mirth* was a popular success, but it shocked many contemporary readers because of its inwardness, realism and inclination towards tragedy: in the end, Lily Bart dies from an overdose of a sedative. In 1911, Wharton turned from a New York setting to explore the themes of thwarted love and failed marriage in a rural New England setting, in *Ethan Frome*. But in both *The Reef* (1912) and the moral satirical novel *The Custom of the Country* (1913), she returned to her fictional investigation of the habits and hypocrisies of the New York social world.

By now, Wharton had become an expatriate, living in Paris, and divorced. During the First World War, she worked tirelessly for combatants and refugees. After it, she wrote of the conflict in two novels, *The Marne* (1918) and *A Son at the Front* (1923). She also established a house in Paris that became a gathering place for many younger writers. She had exhausted herself with her welfare activities during the war. But she recovered her powers sufficiently to write more fiction looking back to her early years in New York. She also completed an autobiography, *A Backward Glance* (1934), and a book on *The Writing of Fiction* (1925). The book on writing fiction acknowledges her debt to James. But, together with her later novels and stories, it measures both the connection and the subtle differences between them. Like James, and the early James in particular, Wharton was committed to the solid, detailed presentation of a social scene, emotional subtleties and social nuances. Like James, too, she believed that the novelist should have a fine ear for the different shades of conversation and a fierce concern for moral issues. But Wharton remained more concerned than James ever was with the concrete detail of furnishings and dress, as a measure of character and taste, and much more intensely interested in the various gradations of social status. And, as she developed, she also paid more attention than she did in her earlier work to careful planning – in this she was following James, of course – to the selection of what she called 'crucial moments', epiphanies or significant revelations, to balance or harmony of structure, and to irony. Writing about these strategies, Wharton worked them into the fabric of her later fiction. They are there, for instance, in her best-known collection of tales, *Xingu and Other Stories* (1916). For that matter, they are there in her finest novel, *The Age of Innocence*, published in 1920.

Set in 1870, *The Age of Innocence* tells the story of Newland Archer, a lawyer, and his involvement with two women: May Welland, who becomes his wife, and her cousin Ellen Olenska, the wife of a Polish count. Having left her abusive husband, Ellen appears in New York society, where her unconventional behaviour causes ripples of concern and displeasure. Attracted by her exoticism, her difference from the social norms of old New York, Newland falls in love with her, but the constraints of society and his impending marriage to May keep them apart. Still, his interest in Ellen continues after his marriage. This prompts May to disclose to her cousin that she is pregnant; Ellen then leaves New York to live alone in Paris. It is not only external constraints and May's manoeuvrings – which, characteristically, have a childlike, almost innocent slyness about them – that frustrate Newland and Ellen. They are also separated by the very things that attract them to each other. Newland is drawn to Ellen because of her candour, openness, sensitivity and grace: qualities that are proven by her resistance to the idea of any hole-in-the-corner affair, by her pointing out realistically to Newland that there is no world elsewhere or 'other place' that they can flee to, and, above all, by her departure when she learns May is pregnant. Ellen, in turn, is attracted to Newland by his fineness of spirit and his making her realize that, as she puts it, 'under the dullness' of New York life 'there are things so fine and sensitive and delicate that even those I cared for in my other life look cheap in comparison'. He belongs in New York, she realizes, with its dull veneer and its finely tuned spirit; and he proves this finer side by renouncing her and accepting what he sees as his 'obligations'. The paradox of a love of such a kind, one so intense that it both draws them together and sets them apart, is caught in Ellen's simple declaration to Newland: 'I can't love you unless I give you up.' That statement takes the measure of a society founded on notions of duty, the many shades of which are caught in Wharton's detailed portrait of old New York. It is also a register of Wharton's own, fundamentally bleak view of existence: that repression just might render the emotional life more intense, that an experience unrealized but imagined might be 'more real' than one simply lived through, and that the denials practised in a closed society breed the suffering which in the long run breeds character.

That view, together with Wharton's acknowledgement of the passing of old New York society, is subtly underlined in the closing pages of *The Age of Innocence*. Thirty years have passed. Newland, now a widower, visits Paris with his son. The son, Dallas, is about to marry a woman who is just as much of a social outsider as Ellen Olenska once was. But there is no problem for him in this, because the 'little world' Newland had grown up in, 'and whose standards had bent and bound him', has faded away. Dallas belongs to a looser social dispensation, a freer, less constrained but arguably less civilized order of things. Reflecting on his marriage, Newland observes that there was 'good in the old ways'. His 'long years together' with May, he concludes, 'had shown him that it did not matter so much if marriage was a dull duty, as long as it kept the dignity of a duty; lapsing from that, it became a mere battle of ugly appetites'. These stark, stoical reflections continue as Dallas confides to his father that May had known of his love for Ellen. Dying, May had told her son that she knew her children were safe with Newland because, Dallas recalls her saying, 'once when she asked you to, you'd given up the thing you most wanted'. 'She never asked me,' Newland declares, startled by this sudden revelation of just how much fineness of observation and feeling circulated below the dull, tranquil surfaces of his married life. 'No . . . you never did ask each other anything, did you?' Dallas wryly responds. 'And you never told each other anything. You just sat and watched each other and guessed what was going on underneath.' To Dallas, this is further proof that his parents belonged to 'a deaf-and-dumb' generation: although, he admits, 'I back your generation for knowing more about each other's private thoughts than we ever have time to find out about our own'. For Newland, it is a demonstration of the rightness of his – and, for that matter, May's and Ellen's – choice. Following the logic of that choice, made thirty years ago, Newland now makes another one. 'The difference is that these young people take it for granted that they're going to get whatever they want,' Newland comments to himself on Dallas and his contemporaries, 'and that we almost always took it for granted that we shouldn't. Only, I wonder – the things one's so certain of in advance: can it ever make one's heart beat so wildly?' Dallas is going to visit Ellen in her Paris apartment. Newland, however, decides not to go in with him. He sits on a bench outside the apartment block, and then returns to his hotel. 'It's more real to me here than if I went up,' he suddenly hears himself saying, as he sits outside. That comment is perfectly in tune with the feeling which has determined his life, that a life denied is a life fulfilled. It was a feeling that shaped an old New York society, now vanished, the portrait of which forms the substance of the book. And it is a feeling that Wharton, looking back with a mixture of affection, compassion and irony, seems now, with whatever reservations, to share.

As a Southern writer, Ellen Glasgow bridged the gap between the hopefulness of the Reconstruction era and the traditionalism of what became known as the Southern renaissance. As a woman writer, she divided her attention between affectionately satirical accounts of the Southern cult of white womanhood, in novels like *Virginia* (1913), and heroic portraits of women redeeming themselves through stoical endurance of suffering and stubborn labour in the soil, in such books as *Barren Ground* (1925) and *Vein of Iron* (1935). Glasgow herself, born into a wealthy family in Richmond, Virginia, was imaginatively torn between her mother, a 'perfect flower of Southern culture' as her daughter called her, with a mixture of awe and irony, and her father, a successful businessman who was, Glasgow recalled, 'stalwart, unbending, rock-ribbed with Calvinism'. 'Everything in me, mental or physical, I owe to my mother,' Glasgow insisted in her autobiography, *The Woman Within* (1954). And, certainly, Glasgow learned from her mother about ancestral pride, the burden of the past and tradition, and the sad story of Southern decline. But, whether she was willing to admit it or not, she learned a lot from her father too: a determination to succeed, a pursuit of authority (in this case, the authority of authorship) and, above all, an interest in that 'vein of iron' that enabled individuals to survive and allowed Southern and American society to evolve from the old to the new. 'It is possible that from that union of opposites', Glasgow admitted, of her mother and father, 'I derived a perpetual conflict of types.' And that was surely true. Her fiction revolves around antinomies that were caught in her own personal version of the family romance: the female emblem of the Old South and the male emblem of the New South, the romance of the past and the reality of the present, the fluid, yielding 'feminine' and the rigid, authoritative 'masculine'. The perspective in her fiction varies, but it does so because of the different strategies she deploys for examining those 'types' – and the way she tends to vacillate, in terms of sympathy, between them.

The stance from which Glasgow started her career was a simple one. This was to work from the premise that the old feudal order was decaying, in the South and elsewhere, and that the 'plain man' was 'building the structure of the future' that would replace it. From that premise, she developed two fictional strategies to explain its implications. One was the strategy of comedy: a satirical inventory of the weaknesses of the 'aristocratical' person, the aim being to show how 'stationary and antiquated' he was. The other was more in the heroic line. It required Glasgow to concentrate her attention on the poorer white and the qualities, latent in his character, that appeared to guarantee eventual success – and this as a prelude to the presentation of his actual success story. The result was to create two different types of novel. Glasgow herself liked to refer to them as 'novels of history' or 'of the town', on the one hand, and 'novels of the country', on the other. Among the books in the first mode, along with *Virginia*, were *Life and Gabriella* (1913), *The Romantic Comedians* (1926), *They Stooped to Folly* (1929) and *The Sheltered Life* (1932). Among those in the second, together with *Barren Ground* and *Vein of Iron*, were *The Voice of the People* (1900), *The Romance of a Plain Man* (1909), *The Miller of Old Church* (1911) and *One Man in His Time* (1922). For all the differences between the two veins of writing, though, the same optimism managed to shine through them both and betray their common authorship; satire and heroic tale were equally shaped by the conviction that the small farm was about to secure the state.

Among the satirical novels, the most accomplished are what Glasgow called the Queenborough trilogy, after the district of Richmond in which they are set: *The Romantic Comedians*, *They Stooped to Folly* and *The Sheltered Life*. In each of these, the reader is presented with persuasive examples of different women whose lives and personalities have been repressed and distorted by the story of them a man wants to tell. The point is a fundamentally social one and is often made more or less explicit. Here, for instance, is Virginius Littlepage, the main character in *They Stooped to Folly*, meditating on the women in his life and the changes in sexual mores he has witnessed:

> If only women had been satisfied to remain protected, how much pleasanter the world, even the changing modern world, might be today! If only they had been satisfied to wait in patience, not to seek after happiness! For it seemed to him . . . that there could be nothing nobler in women than the beauty of long waiting and wifely forbearance . . . the true feminine character had never flowered more perfectly than in the sheltered garden of Southern tradition.

The misrecognition of women by Virginius and those like him, Glasgow intimates, has a specific social origin. It is of a recognizably local kind, nurtured by 'the sheltered garden of Southern tradition'; and the implication, here and throughout the novel, is that the ironic conflicts contained in such an attitude have been as responsible for the collapse of an entire class as the more obviously material facts of defeat and economic ruin.

Glasgow once declared that 'what the South needs now is – blood and irony'. Irony there is, in plenty, in the Queenborough trilogy. The blood is shed, spent imaginatively, in the heroic novels, where the reader encounters men and women of such nerve and resolve that, we are told, their 'secret self' 'could not yield, could not bend, could not be broken' even under enormous pressure. Of the novels of this kind, the most powerful is *Barren Ground*, which Glasgow called 'the truest novel ever written'. It tells the story of Dorinda Oakley. Forsaken by the man she loves, suffering poverty and injury, she fights back. She restores the family farm, which because of all its barren ground has fallen into decay. She shelters the man she once loved when he returns, degenerated and desperate. But she no longer loves him; and, having been married once, to a man whom she liked rather than loved who has now passed away, she plans never to marry again. She is, she reflects, thankful 'to have finished with all that'. 'The storm and the hag-ridden dreams of the night were over,' the reader is told, towards the conclusion of the novel,

> and the land which had forgotten was waiting to take her back to its heart, Endurance. Fortitude. The spirit of the land was flowing out again toward life. This was the permanent self, she knew. This was what remained after the years had taken their bloom.

'I'm through with soft things', Dorinda tells local people who complain that she is 'hard as stone'. 'Yes, I'm hard,' she triumphantly declares. She is also 'barren': although she nurtures other people's children, and restores fertility to the family farm, she has no offspring of her own. *Barren Ground* has been praised as an intense account of personal and social redemption: a woman discovering her true vocation, a representative figure anticipating a new social and economic order. It has also been criticized for its drive towards emotional denial and a tough, even repressed heroine who appears to excite too much sympathy in her creator. These are, surely, different sides of the same coin. In this, her most successful fictional account of personal and social change, Glasgow has her central character gravitate from what is perceived to be the 'female' principle to what is seen to be the 'male' one. From the soft, yielding and passive to the stalwart, unbending and rock-ribbed: to adopt the vocabulary only partly hidden in these and other narratives celebrating the 'vein of iron' in human character, Dorinda affirms her 'secret self' and, in the process, becomes a man.

'I was a radical when everyone else was a conservative,' Glasgow declared in her autobiography, written towards the end of her life, 'and now I am a conservative when others appear to be radical.' That comment certainly located a change that took place in her thinking. Her last full-length novel, *In This Our Life* (1941), measures the change. Its central character, Asa Timberlake, an older person like Glasgow herself, is a gentleman of the old school and he is allowed to offer a largely negative judgement on his children, grandchildren – and also on contemporary life. The 'elegance, grace, dignity and beauty' of 'the old days' have vanished, the reader is told, there has been a 'general breaking-up in the pattern of life'. 'Nobody . . . had any patience, nowadays, with the graces of living,' Asa laments. 'Acceleration, not beauty, was the strange god of our modern worship.' Whatever she might like to think, however, Glasgow was no more exceptional in this, her old age, than she had been in her youth. Her earlier books shared the optimism of those writers, at the turn of the century, who saw the general social changes that were taking place as potentially liberating, not least for women. Her last few works, in turn, belong to that vein of writing, from the South and elsewhere, that sought in the past and tradition a refuge from, and possible corrective to, the upheavals of capitalism and modernity. Glasgow's work is, in any event, conflicted: offering what a later Southern writer, Allen Tate, rather testily referred to as a 'mixed thesis of old South and Progress'. Even in the satirical novels, there is affection for the old ways that, after all, her own mother represented. Even in the heroic fiction, there is the only partially repressed sense that success has its price: requiring that people become like her father, hard, stubborn and unbending. Those conflicts, though, only complicate Glasgow's evolution from 'radical' to 'conservative': the change in tendency, from progressivism to conservatism, is still there. And both the conflict and the change declare Glasgow very much as an author of her times: someone writing of fundamental social alterations that affected her, especially, because she had been brought up in a place where and period when the terms 'writing', 'career' and 'woman' were just about mutually exclusive.

Like Glasgow, Willa Cather was born in Virginia. Only her last novel, *Sapphira and the Slave Girl* (1940), is set there, however. In 1883, when she was only ten, she moved with her family to Nebraska. Webster County, where they settled, was still on the frontier and there her father farmed for a year. But then, to Cather's regret, the family moved into the small town of Red Cloud. Cather was an unconventional child, a tomboy inclined to dress in boys' clothes, and she found the small town atmosphere stifling. To escape it, she went to Lincoln, to the University of Nebraska, and then to Pittsburgh, where she worked as a journalist and then a teacher. She also found the time to write: a book of poems was published in 1903 and then a collection of short stories, *The Troll Garden*, appeared two years later, showing the influence of Henry James. Derivative though they were, they nevertheless impressed S. S. McClure (1857–1949), the proprietor of *McClure's Magazine*, one of the leading periodicals of the day. He offered her a job on his magazine; and in 1903 she moved to New York, which was to be her home, apart from travels and expeditions, for the rest of her life. She continued as a journalist until 1912, when she decided to devote herself to writing fiction. She had been inspired to do so, in part, by her meeting with Sarah Orne Jewett four years earlier. They became close friends, not least because Jewett offered Cather the positive example of someone writing about her own homeplace, the local as focus for the universal. That example did not show in her first novel, *Alexander's Bridge* (1912), which was another, rather poor, imitation of James. In her second novel, though, *O Pioneers!* (1913), Cather found her subject: the West, its life and landscape, its place in American history, the American character and imagination. She also found, again with the help of Jewett, a way of writing, a narrative structure that was right for her, that was not Jamesian elaboration but what Cather herself termed the 'novel démeublé'. The novel, she decided, should be without obvious artifice, free from the clutter of well-made, highly wrought fiction. The writer's best material, Cather felt, was there in the novelist, already moulded. 'If he tries to meddle with its vague outline, to twist it into some categorical shape,' she said, 'above all if he tries to adapt or modify its mood, he destroys its value.' In working with such material, the writer should 'have little to do with literary devices', he had 'to depend more and more on something else'. What that 'something else' was Cather caught in an image that was characteristically earthy and evocative: 'the thing by which our feet find the road home on a dark night, accounting of themselves for roots and stones which we had never noticed by day'.

Cather, as that remark suggests, had come home to her subject, her source of inspiration. And, although based in New York, she often returned to her imaginative homesite to stimulate her imagination. *O Pioneers!* was written after a trip to the Southwest; and, after visiting the Southwest again in 1915, she produced *The Song of the Lark* (1915), which is partly set in the ancient cliff-dwellings of Arizona. Then, in 1916, on a trip back to Red Cloud, Cather visited a Bohemian woman, Anna Pavelka, whom she had known and admired in her youth. She found Anna serene and happy, and surrounded by children; it seemed to Cather that Anna's story ran close to the central stream of life in Nebraska and the West; and she decided to write about her. The result was her masterpiece, *My Ántonia*, published two years later. The novel is divided into five sections. In the first, the narrator Jim Burden recalls his early life in the Nebraskan countryside, his relationship with the Shimerda family and the daughter in that family, Ántonia Shimerda in particular. The second records how Burden moves into the small town of Black Hawk, clearly modelled on Red Cloud, and renews his acquaintance with Ántonia, who is now one of the 'hired girls' working for a local family. In the third section, Jim, as Cather once did, moves to the university in the state capital of Lincoln, where he forms a close friendship with another Bohemian girl, Lena Lingard. The brief fourth section tells the story of Ántonia's betrayal by Larry Donovan, from one of the 'native' or non-immigrant families. And, in the fifth, Burden remembers how, on a return west, he saw Ántonia again after many years, happily married now to a Czech called Cuzak and surrounded by children. Apparently, while she was writing *My Ántonia*, Cather told an old friend that she wanted her 'new heroine' to be 'like a rare object in the middle of a table, which one may examine from all sides'. This, however, is misleading. Ántonia is not seen from all sides; the reader is offered only the dimmest conception of certain moments of her life, such as her time as a hired girl; and there are numerous intriguing gaps and omissions – her seducer Larry Donovan, for example, remains in the shadows. What is seen from all sides is not Ántonia herself but the memory of Ántonia carried by the appropriately named Jim Burden. It is not for nothing that, in the short, fictional 'Introduction' to *My Ántonia*, another, anonymous narrator remembers being presented with the manuscript of this book by Burden; and, as Burden handed it over, (s)he recalls, he carefully added 'My' to 'Ántonia' in the title. This, the memory, becomes a thing complete in itself: which is why the reader is never worried by the missing pieces in Ántonia's own story.

The entire novel is, in fact, about memory, the determining impact of the past: the past of the narrator, the past of other characters who are constantly rehearsing their memories, 'the precious, incommunicable past' of America that is a crucial part of the national heritage – and is vanishing. By extension, it is about the past of all peoples and nations, and its function in the present: the past as influence (we are all, Cather intimates, what our past has made us) and as intense focus of commemoration, nostalgia (we find it difficult, Cather suggests, to surrender a past that seems the more 'precious' the more it becomes 'incommunicable', separate from ourselves and those around us). The imaginative thrust of *My Ántonia* is, powerfully, backward. Presented as a memory, the novel begins in autumn: the dominant mood tends towards the elegiac and the heroic, a preference for legend, the imaginative transfiguration of the past, over history. This is American pastoral: a point that Cather makes perfectly clear when she has Jim Burden read the first version of pastoral, the *Georgics* of Virgil, with their powerful refrain that the best days are the first to flee ('*Optima dies . . . prima fugit*') and their creator's proud claim that he will 'be the first . . . to bring the Muse into my country'. Considering a woman like Ántonia, Burden sees a connection between her and the poetry of Virgil. As a focus for his personal memories and a kind of racial memory for America, its formative past, 'she was a rich mine of life', he concludes, 'like the founders of early races'. She embodies the past: as a resource that may be lost for a while but, as in that last, magnificent section when Burden finds Ántonia restored to her old vital self, may be returned to and recovered. What gives the book its tension is that, while the imaginative thrust is backward, its narrative movement is forward: in the story of his life, Burden rehearses the present and future of America, from country to small town to large town to city (by the end of the book he is based, like Cather, in New York). But what gives *My Ántonia* its beauty, its power, is this rhythm of return and recovery. The entire book, the reader is made to realize, is about just such a journey back into memory as Burden has made here: a resurrection of the past, not to seek refuge but to restore, to revitalize the present. We are made to see yesterday as Burden finally sees Ántonia, in its plenitude and its potential for today and tomorrow.

A complex pastoral, *My Ántonia* mixes its meditations on American history and myth with a telling exploration of gender. This is a book in which a woman writes about a man writing about a woman. Playing on the ironic possibilities opened up by this, Cather quietly juxtaposes Burden's mythologizing of Ántonia with the mundane labour of her life: the role of the woman in the making of Western myth and her role, more fundamentally, in the making of the West. This is a book, also, that pulls no punches in its account of the tensions between 'natives' and 'immigrants', the 'cramped' atmosphere of the provincial small town, and the gradual transformation of the American landscape under the pressure of agribusiness. Cather never allowed her tenderness for the uses of the past, or her tactful appreciation of the power of Western legend, to undermine her sense of just how small, plain and mean life in the West could sometimes be. Her finest books, consequently, maintain a fine balance between romance and realism, elegy and analytical insight, the tale of the virgin land as an epic and as an economic one. Along with *My Ántonia* and *O Pioneers!*, those books include *A Lost Lady* (1923), *The Professor's House* (1923), *Death Comes for the Archbishop* (1927) and *Shadows on the Rock* (1931). Generally, the later fiction is sparer, leaner, a little more inclined towards the occasional allegorical detail and the moment of epiphany. Occasionally, it also dips further back into the past than *My Ántonia*. *Death Comes for the Archbishop*, based on the careers of two actual French missionaries, is set in the New Mexico territory in the middle of the nineteenth century; *Shadows on the Rock* moves further back and afar, into the seventeenth century and the French Canadian frontier. But the determining rhythm of these later narratives remains the same as the one rehearsed in the story of Ántonia Shimerda. And there is the same densely woven texture of remembrance, personal, familial and cultural: a shared sense that what matters to people is what they carry from their predecessors, engraved on their hearts and minds and pulsing through their blood. Cather may not have been the first to bring 'the Muse' into the country of her formative years. She was and is, however, among the finest. It is difficult, maybe impossible, to think of anyone who has told a truer tale of the American West, its vast landscapes and little rural communities, its mixing of many races and cultures – and its strange, sometimes dreamlike blend of progress and return, the forward vision and the backward glance, desire and memory.

Critiques of American provincial life

'Too much detail', Cather once observed, 'is apt, like any form of extravagance, to become slightly vulgar.' Theodore Dreiser (1871–1945) would scarcely have agreed. Of man Dreiser once declared, 'his feet are in the trap of circumstance; his eyes are on an illusion'. And in order to capture his vision, of a world governed by the forces of determinism, blind chance and change, and human beings moved by a need for personal affirmation, a desire they can neither articulate nor suppress, he forged a style that is simultaneously cluttered and opulent. There is a wealth of circumstantial detail, an accumulation of notes about the surfaces of social life and behaviour that sometimes appears indiscriminate, unselective, even elephantine. At the same time, there is a constant striving towards the ornately poetic: a pursuit of the ineffable that is as awkward and perhaps as unsuccessful as that of his characters. All Dreiser's major protagonists suffer from a need that their lives should assume dramatic form; and they suffer not so much because they cannot fulfil this need as because they do not really understand it. Wealth, worldly success, sexual gratification are the only aims they can know or name, but none of these reassures them or curbs their restlessness. They grapple for money, they wound themselves trying to climb to fame and fortune, yet they remain outcasts, existential orphans, sullen and bewildered: always hopeful for some sign that will release them from their craving for a state of grace or, at least, illumination. In his emphasis on humanity as the naturalistic victim of circumstance, Dreiser bears a close resemblance to such early contemporaries as Stephen Crane and Frank Norris. It was Norris, in fact, who recommended that Dreiser's first novel, *Sister Carrie* (1900), should be accepted for publication. 'As I see him,' Dreiser once declared, 'the utterly infinitesimal individual weaves among mysteries a floss-like and utterly meaningless course – if course it be. I catch no meaning from what I have seen, and pass quite as I came, confused and dismayed.' In his interest in human yearning, however, the need for some principle of value to overcome the meanness, the littleness of life – and the tendency to confuse the fulfilment of that need with the accumulation of material power – Dreiser more nearly resembles his later contemporaries, like F. Scott Fitzgerald. His other major book besides *Sister Carrie, An American Tragedy* (1925), was actually published in the same year as *The Great Gatsby*, although Dreiser had been preparing for it for nearly twenty years. And, in its own stubborn, clumsy and dreamy way, it charts, just as Fitzgerald's novel does, the strange energies that can flow from the ingrained American belief that the absolute can be found, immaculately preserved, at the very top of the ladder of success.

Dreiser was born, the ninth child of German-speaking parents, in Terre Haute, Indiana. He was profoundly affected by the poverty of his upbringing, by the harsh bigotry of his father and by the character of his mother, whom he later called 'a dreamy, poetic, impractical soul'. After briefly attending university, he became a reporter, working in Chicago, St Louis and Pittsburgh before moving to New York City in 1894. Dreiser's experiences as a journalist, the habit of a careful notation of detail, fed into his writing of *Sister Carrie*. So did his interest in 'the exploration of the familiar' in the documentary photography of Alfred Stieglitz (1864–1966), who stalked the streets of New York with a hand-held 'detective' camera, as well as in the 'Ashcan School' of painters, 'New York Realists' like Robert Henri (1865–1929) and John Sloan (1871–1951), who specialized in bold, rough renderings of low-life scenes. Arriving in Chicago in 1890, Dreiser had fallen in love with its boom and bustle: what he was later to call, in his novel *The Titan* (1914), 'this singing flame of a city, this all-America, this poet in chaps and buckskin, this rude, raw Titan, this Burns of a city!' And in *Sister Carrie*, which begins in Chicago and ends in New York, Dreiser recorded his impression of cities that, like life itself, glitter, beckon, seduce and destroy without reference to notions of justice and desert. The result was and remains a novel remarkably free from moralizing. Carrie Meeber, a Midwestern country girl, moves to Chicago, becomes the mistress of a salesman, Charles Drouet, then the mistress of a middle-aged, married restaurant manager, George Hurstwood. Hurstwood embezzles money; they flee to New York, where Hurstwood gradually sinks into failure, becoming a drunken beggar on Skid

Row. Carrie, meanwhile, becomes a chorus girl, deserts Hurstwood, and, although she fails to find the happiness of which she dreams, not only survives but is launched on a successful career. With a natural buoyancy, like a cork bobbing on water, Carrie is ambitious and, like so many of Dreiser's outcasts and waifs, given to moral expediency. When, for instance, her 'average little conscience' questions her about what she is doing, the reply is simple: 'the voice of want made answer for her'. 'Not evil,' Dreiser suggests, 'but longing for that which is better, more directs the steps of the erring.' By the end of the novel, Carrie is still longing, destined to know 'neither surfeit nor content' as she sits dreamily in her rocking chair. But that, Dreiser intimates, is the human condition, not a punishment for the errant protagonist. Unlike the morally aberrant heroines of other, roughly contemporary novels, like Chopin's *The Awakening*, Crane's *Maggie* or Wharton's *The Custom of the Country*, Carrie does not die or lose her looks, starve or become pregnant. She has vague regrets but no anguished repentance, and retribution does not overtake her. When *Sister Carrie* was first published, this absence of a conventional moral code led the publisher, despite Norris's enthusiasm for the book, to provide it with only limited publicity and distribution. The positive critical response to an English edition in 1901 led to its reissue in the United States in 1907. Even then, though, it was more of a scandal than a success; or, as Dreiser himself put it later, 'the outraged protests far outnumbered the plaudits'.

Continuing to work as a journalist, Dreiser took ten years to publish his next novel, *Jennie Gerhardt* (1911). The heroine of this book is another orphan in the world, a 'fallen woman' who refuses to believe that it is 'all blind chance', insisting that 'there must be something', 'some guiding intelligence'. She has, however, a sterner sense of duty than Carrie Meeber, which prompts her, among other things, to adopt two orphaned children when her own child dies. Despite her finer sensibility, however, she is not rewarded any more than Carrie is punished: she remains an outcast, an outsider at the funeral of her former lover with which the book ends. And, despite its more traditional moral tenor, this novel too was attacked for its candour and unconventional subject matter. No such moralism inhibits what Dreiser called his 'Trilogy of Desire': *The Financier* (1912), *The Titan* and *The Stoic* (published posthumously in 1947). The 'survival of the fittest' ideas that he had gathered from Herbert Spencer and T. M. Huxley led Dreiser not only to sympathize with the weak and victimized but also to place a heavy emotional investment in the Nietzschean business superman of this trilogy. Based on the character of the business magnate Charles T. Yerkes, Frank Cowperwood, the hero of all three novels, is a man with a simple motto: 'I satisfy myself.' The tone of the trilogy is set early on in *The Financier*, when the ten-year-old Cowperwood, already a 'natural leader' of his brothers and schoolmates, sees a glass tank at the local fishmarket. In it are a lobster and a squid; and, every day he passes by, Cowperwood notices that the lobster has devoured just as much as it needs for its nourishment. 'That's the way it has to be I guess,' Cowperwood comments to himself; 'That squid wasn't quick enough.' Having 'figured it out' to his own satisfaction, Cowperwood resolves to be quick enough, and to be like an animal that can 'adapt itself to conditions'.

He rises to power in terms that are both economic and erotic. Sandwiched between triumphant accounts of his success as a businessman and a financier are similarly triumphal and sympathetic stories of his sexual conquests: he is, as Dreiser lovingly puts it, 'a real man' in the sense that he is a very superior animal. For all his successes, though, Cowperwood remains as fundamentally unsatisfied as every other Dreiser protagonist: 'for him', the reader is told, 'was no ultimate peace, no real understanding, but only hunger and thirst and wonder'. And he, too, is eventually defeated by the 'trap of circumstance', when, at the end of *The Titan*, his business plans are defeated. There is no moral to this, his fall, Dreiser intimates, any more than there is to his rise. The time has come, quite simply, for the pendulum to swing against him. There is a constant rhythm, an incessant swinging back and forth 'wherein the mass subdues the individual, or the individual the mass', and it is now time for power to return to 'the mass'.

'He is even as a wisp in the wind,' Dreiser observed of man in *Sister Carrie*, 'moved by every breath of passion, acting now by his will and now by instincts, erring with one, only to retrieve by the other, falling by one, only to rise by the other – a creature of incalculable variability.' Dreiser's own variability took him towards socialism, his faith in which he expressed in such later works of non-fiction as *Dreiser Looks at Russia* (1928) and *Tragic America* (1931). And his sense of the variability of all human creatures, his conviction that people were wisps in the wind, subject to rhythms they could hardly understand or articulate, led him to perceive a fundamental connection between the 'giants', as he called them, and the 'pygmies' of the world, the Cowperwoods and the Carries. Despite their obvious differences, both Cowperwood and Carrie are described as innocents and soldiers of fortune, destined to make their way in a world they never made, to fight in the name of aspirations they can feel but cannot name – and, in the long run, to lose. That destiny also belongs to Clyde Griffiths, the protagonist of *An American Tragedy*. This novel, inspired by an actual murder case that occurred in 1906, tells the story of how Clyde falls in love with Sondra Finchley, a rich girl who represents the elegance and wealth to which he has always aspired. A poor boy himself, he hopes to marry Sondra. What stands in his way is that another woman, Roberta Alden, just as poor as him, is carrying his child. She demands that Clyde marry her; Clyde plans to murder Roberta and takes her boating to fulfil his plans. He lacks the resolution to carry it through but, when the boat accidentally overturns, Clyde swims away, leaving Roberta to drown. Dreiser is at pains to make Clyde a minimalist case. His very ordinariness dictates his typicality, his status both as an expression of an American possibility and as an embodiment of our collective human smallness amidst what is called 'the vast skepticism and apathy of life'. An elaborate scheme of incremental repetition and a welter of incidental detail work to reveal Clyde as the image and prisoner of a culture, hungering with its hunger, empty with its emptiness. As the narrative shifts too, between agonizing close-up and a distanced perspective that reduces Clyde to insect size, the reader may share his cramped conditions and shabby dreams and aspirations but he or she is also compelled to see the protagonist as yet another orphan, like ourselves, drifting

---

on the great stream of circumstance. Clyde is not tragic in any traditional sense; that is the irony of the title. He has almost no assertive will or compelling idea; the pivotal event of his life, the death of Roberta, is an accident; in his passivity, rootlessness and alienation even from himself, he is no more, and no less, than another man, and, in particular, another American. With a compelling mixture of sympathy and criticism, Dreiser moves Clyde, in the first half of An American Tragedy, towards a moment in his life that, while an accident, seems inevitable, the sum of all his failures of will and understanding. Then, in the second half, he shows in relentless detail how the trap of circumstance closes more tightly and literally on his protagonist, as he faces indictments, trial, conviction and execution. The result overall is a book that, like Sister Carrie, captures both the real conditions of life, as Dreiser saw them, and what he termed 'the restless heart of man', the necessity and the pathos of things. It is a tragedy not in the traditional sense but because it registers what its author called 'the essential tragedy of life', that human- ity is 'a waif and an interloper in Nature'. And it is an American tragedy because, like other, later tragedies of this kind, it gives us a protagonist who is the victim not just of circumstance but of his own circumscribed dreams – the trifles of desire laid out for him by his culture.

While his rejection of conventional morality earned Dreiser the disapproval of many readers and reviewers of the time, he was stoutly defended by such leading cultural commentators as H. L. Mencken (1880–1956). Mencken was chiefly not- able for founding the detective magazine the Black Mask in 1920 and the influential periodical the American Mercury in 1924 with the playwright George Jean Nathan (1882–1958), for writing a study of the English language in the United States titled The American Language (1919), and for producing numerous caustic essays collected in six volumes called Prejudices (1919–27). He delighted in attacking middle-class America, or what he termed the 'booboisie'; and the defence of Dreiser gave him the opportunity to do so. So, for that matter, did his support and encouragement of other writers of the day who sometimes aroused antagonism: notably James Branch Cabell (1879–1958), Sinclair Lewis (1885–1951) and Sherwood Anderson (1876–1941). Cabell, Lewis and Anderson are all sometimes associated with what has been called 'the revolt from the village': that reaction against small-town values which characterized many American writers early in the twentieth century. That, however, masks many differences. Cabell, for instance, from Richmond, Virginia, was a friend of Ellen Glasgow, whom he claimed to know 'more thoroughly and more comprehendingly' than 'any human being during the last twenty years of her living'. Like her, he wrote romances of contemporary Virginia like The Cords of Vanity (1920) and satires on the romantic idealism of the South such as The Rivet in Grandfather's Neck (1915). His most striking work, however, involved the cre- ation of a mythical French province Poictesme, whose history from 1234 to 1750 he chronicled in a series of allegorical novels that comment obliquely on American life. Cabell went into some detail about the life and liberal morality of the people of Poictesme; and one novel in the series, Jurgen (1919), was suppressed for supposed immorality. But the case against the book, not for the first or only time in literary history, aroused public interest and curiosity; and for most of the 1920s he enjoyed considerable fame and popularity.

The fame of Sinclair Lewis spread even wider: in 1930, he became the first American author to win the Nobel Prize for literature. Lewis, however, chose the path of satire, a critique of provincial American life, and the middle class in particular, that became the more tempered the older he grew. His first successful novel, *Main Street* (1920), tells the story of Carol Kennicott, the young wife of the local doctor in the small town of Gopher Prairie. For her, Gopher and its main street are the epitome of the dullness, the mediocrity of American provincialism. What characterizes the town she lives in, she reflects, is 'an unimaginatively standardized background, a sluggishness of speech and manners, a rigid ruling of the spirit by the desire to appear respectable'. Rebelling against what she sees, she tries to raise the cultural level of the town. Lewis carefully places Carol between a series of other characters who help the reader measure her position and opinions. On the one hand is a conformist of the best sort like her husband Will Kennicott. His work as a country doctor requires courage and skill, as Carol discovers when she accompanies him on one of his calls. However, he is successful in Gopher Prairie, his wife realizes, not just because of his virtues and skill but because of his orthodoxy. He accepts the prevailing views of the town as normal and natural. His knowledge of the value of his work may make him successful in his own eyes, but it is thanks to his unquestioning acceptance of Gopher Prairie views that he is acceptable there. On the other hand, there are malcontents like Guy Pollock, the local lawyer, who explains what he hates about Gopher Prairie to Carol, and what he calls 'the Village Virus'. 'The Village Virus is the germ which . . . infects ambitious people who stay too long in the provinces,' he tells her. 'You'll find it epidemic among lawyers and doctors and ministers and college-bred merchants – all those people who have had a glimpse of the world that thinks and laughs, but have returned to the swamp.' Unable to settle for the placid complacency of her husband or cynical, bitter defeatism of Guy Pollock, Carol tries to turn her 'active hatred' to positive use, attempting to wake her neighbours up out of what she defines as 'the quiet contentment of the quiet dead'. When this fails, she flees to Washington. There, she discovers the pleasure of being 'no longer half of a marriage but the whole of a human being'. But she also learns tolerance for Gopher Prairie. Returning to the small town finally, she admits the dashing of her hopes for reform but reassures herself that, at least, she clings to her own opinions. 'I do not admit that Gopher Prairie is greater or more generous than Europe!' she stoutly maintains. 'I may not have fought the good fight, but I have kept the faith.' So the pattern that characterizes all Lewis's satires of American provincialism is established: the impulse to escape the restrictions of class or routine leads to flight, but the flight meets with only partial success and is followed by a necessary compromise with convention. In the end the critique is muted, not least because the last word is given to Will Kennicott who, for all his stolidity, is portrayed as honest, hard-working, kindly and thrifty. The worst qualities of the American middle class, such as materialism, smugness and hypocrisy, are castigated in *Main Street*. The better qualities, however, those embodied in Will Kennicott, are those in which the narrative seeks moral investment: Carol is captured, eventually, by the 'Village Virus', but so perhaps is Lewis.

In *Babbitt* (1922), Lewis continued his critique of the American provincial. This time, the setting is Zenith City, boasting three or four hundred thousand inhabitants and towers that 'aspired above the morning mist'. But the satirical thrust remains much the same. The central character, George F. Babbitt, is a hollow man, defined by the objects that surround him, his possessions, and determined, in every detail, by the conventions of middle-class dress and behaviour and the dull aim of material success. It was in writing *Babbitt* that Lewis established what was to be his characteristic method of work: which was to choose a social area, usually a subclass within the middle class, and then research it by mingling with the kind of people he would write about armed with notebooks. Only after completing this research would he compile what he called a 'plan', with every scene of the projected novel sketched out. And in *Babbitt* the plan is clear enough: to take the reader systematically through the various elements that comprise the protagonist's social life and community. Babbitt is a typical Lewis hero, someone who can neither give himself wholly over to the business of being a businessman nor commit himself fully to the more difficult business of being a man. He has dreams of escaping, which for him are expressed in the feebly romantic visions of a 'fairy child' that come to him at random moments, such as when he awakens from sleep. He even makes gestures towards escape. He goes away on a hunting trip with a friend, in an episode which reads almost like a parody of the 'buddy theme' and the impulse to break away that circulate through much American writing. He has an affair, he expresses vaguely liberal opinions for a while, he even takes up with a fast set of local bohemians. But, like Carol Kennicott, he is eventually absorbed back into the provincial. Defined, once again, by a world of convention and commodity, all he can hope is that his son Ted will not surrender like him. 'Don't be scared of the family,' he tells Ted; 'No, nor all of Zenith. Nor of yourself, the way I've been. Go ahead, old man! The world is yours!'

What is striking about *Babbitt* is that its satirical account of middle-class boosterism and provinciality hovers close to the affectionate. Lewis seems half in love with the thing he mocks. More to the point, there are no values in the book beyond those of the protagonist; and all he has to offer, by way of resistance to the normality of Zenith City, is feeble dreams, sad moments of escape, and, for a while, a bohemian lifestyle that turns out to be as conventional and internally competitive as that of the boosters. By the time Lewis came to write *Dodsworth* (1929), a novel about a retired automobile manufacturer travelling in Europe, the muted, compromised criticism of the middle class that characterized his earlier novels had taken a further turn. The central character, Samuel Dodsworth, is almost wholly admirable. A man who embodies all the solid, practical virtues of the provincial middle class, it is he who truly values not only American sense but European sensibility. Not only that, he is both a scholar of a kind and an artist, we are told: 'an authority on automobile designing' and someone who 'had been influenced by his vision, a quarter of a century ago, of long, clean, streamlines!' By contrast, his wife Fran is Carol Kennicott or the 'fairy child' of the earlier novels seen through a glass darkly. It is she at whom the satire is levelled because of her levity and pretentiousness, her failure to appreciate all that is best about her husband and her homeplace. Lewis continued to write novels committed to the idea of social and political change: such as *Asa Vickers* (1933), about a Midwestern girl who becomes a social worker, and *It Can't Happen Here* (1935), a warning about the possibility of fascism in the United States. But, by now, he had returned to a reassertion of those very middle-class, middle-brow and middle-western standards he had begun by satirizing. Hardly a radical in his youth, he was certainly not a conservative in his later years: one of his last novels, for instance, *Kingsblood Royal* (1947), deals critically with race relations, while another, *The God-Seeker* (1949), explores the problems of Native Americans. To that extent, his is not the same story as that of Ellen Glasgow. But, in his own way, he reacted as she did to radically changing times by returning to values he had once vigorously resisted: as a result, a novelist who began as a pathfinder ended up seeming curiously old-fashioned.

Lewis has been called one of the worst writers in modern American literature, yet someone without whose books that literature cannot be imagined, not least because he opened up a new world, that of the middle-class Midwest, to American literature. By contrast, Sherwood Anderson was a deliberate stylist. But he, too, focused his best work on the provincial life of the West. And without that work, too, modern American literature is difficult to imagine. 'He was the father of my generation of writers,' William Faulkner was to observe. Storytellers as otherwise different as Faulkner himself, Ernest Hemingway, F. Scott Fitzgerald, Jean Toomer and Erskine Caldwell were indebted to Anderson because he introduced new methods of storytelling, in terms of style and narrative focus, and new ways of structuring stories into a cycle. Anderson came late to writing. Born in Camden, Ohio, he spent the first two decades of his life in small towns of northern Ohio, in particular Clyde, which became the setting for his finest work, *Winesburg, Ohio* (1919). He participated in the Spanish–American War, took up a career in advertising, then founded a paint business. Then, in 1912, as he tells it in his autobiography, *A Story Teller's Story* (1924), he dramatically left family and business and went to pursue a literary career in Chicago. Anderson soon became acquainted with writers and critics of the Chicago Renaissance. Chicago was experiencing a sudden expansion of cultural activity at the time. This was in part a consequence of the city being established as the unofficial capital of the Midwest; as the economic and political importance of the city grew, so did its interest in arts and culture. In quick succession, a new university and a new symphony orchestra were founded, both of them destined to gain an international reputation. It acquired its own small theatre and its own bohemian quarters. Local poets like Carl Sandburg, Vachel Lindsay and Edgar Lee Masters began to publish work, much of it in *Poetry: A Magazine of Verse*, a prominent little magazine that the poet Harriet Monroe (1860–1936) had founded in Chicago in 1912. And among these influential figures Anderson now met, along with Sandburg, were Floyd Dell (1887–1969), whose first novel, *Moon-Calf* (1920), was to distil the disillusionment of the postwar generation, and Ben Hecht, a playwright who was to score enormous success with *The Front Page*, a drama co-written with Charles MacArthur about Chicago news-papermen. Anderson's first book, *Windy McPherson's Son* (1916), described a man who grew up to make a great deal of money but felt little consequent satisfaction. This was followed by *Marching Men* (1917), a novel about coal miners in Pennsylvania that revealed the tyranny Anderson saw inherent in modern capitalism, and *Mid-American Chants* (1918), a volume of unrhymed verse. Then came *Winesburg, Ohio*. Sharing the radical instincts of 'muckraking' journalists, Anderson first arranged for extracts from the book to appear in three 'insurgent' magazines, the *Seven Arts*, the *New Masses* and the *Little Review*. With the public appetite whetted, he then published the volume which he hoped would restore primitive American virtues, reassert what he called 'the strangeness and wonder of man' and reveal the value of instinct – the superiority of the hidden emotional underbelly of life to its materialist, commonplace and conventional surfaces.

Anderson dedicated *Winesburg, Ohio* to his mother: 'whose keen observations on the life about her', he explained, 'first awoke in me the hunger to see beneath the surface of lives'. Set in the small town of the title, the stories in the book acquire further unity through the character of George Willard, a reporter for the local newspaper who has literary ambitions, to whom all the characters gravitate at one time or another. And they gain further unity still from the 'hunger' which becomes both narrative source and subject. *Winesburg, Ohio*, the reader is told, is 'The Book of the Grotesque'. Initially, the word grotesque appears to mean some incongruity or other that characterizes all the people the narrator has met. But then, curiously, he suggests that grotesqueness is the product of truth or truths. 'It was his notion', we learn, 'that the moment one of the people took one of the truths to himself, called it his truth, and tried to live by it, he became a grotesque and the truth he embraced became a falsehood.' The different characters whose stories are told in this volume all hunger for something, some 'truth' to live by and communicate. Snatching up 'the truth of virginity and the truth of passion, the truth of wealth and of poverty', they take their singular truth, their partial reading of reality, as the complete text of the world. Winesburg is a town full of people who have overdeveloped one 'truthful' aspect of themselves until it has achieved a disproportion that amounts to falsehood. One character called Joe Welling, who likes to talk, has become obsessive and compulsive in his speech. Another, Jesse Bentley, a religious man, has come to see himself as the Abraham of his time, ready not only to lead his people out of Canaan but to sacrifice children. Still another, Alice Hindman, has become obsessed by what she regards as the lack of fulfilment of spinsterhood. She runs naked through the streets at night, the rain on her skin offering the nearest thing she knows to the touch of a lover. Such people long to be and belong: to know the love that would give them identity and communality. They long also to communicate their longing, to George Willard in particular; to speak the needs that their 'strained, eager' voices and strange behaviour can only articulate in a distorted fashion. They are alienated, not only from others but from themselves; and it is this that distresses and disfigures them. What they want, Anderson intimates, is all that is at odds with the piety and provinciality of life in small-town America. No wonder, then, that when the book first appeared Hart Crane called it an important chapter in 'the Bible of American consciousness'.

The style in which Anderson tells the stories of the people of Winesburg, or the story of Hugh McVey, the Midwestern protagonist of his best novel, *Poor White* (1920), is often described as naturalistic. It is, however, more than that. Quiet and modest in tone, idiomatic in diction, attentive to the minute surface details of gesture and behaviour, Anderson's style also makes a virtue of its own awkwardness. It is hesitant, moving forward stealthily as if words were hazards; it is repetitive, circling back and forth as if words had to be probed, gently teased to disclose their meanings; it vacillates between the simple and the slightly odd, the clarity of the vernacular and quaintness of something translated from another language. This amounts to saying that style is a measure of subject here. The style is a relatively easy one to parody: and, in fact, Ernest Hemingway and William Faulkner both did so – in, respectively, *The Torrents of Spring* (1926) and *Sherwood Anderson & Other Famous Creoles* (1926) – in order, partly, to disengage themselves from Anderson's influence. But at its best, as in *Winesburg, Ohio*, that style enacts the problem of communication while solving it: it dramatizes the hunger to speak of what lies beneath the surface of life, in this case to the reader, and it describes a hunger satisfied. In short, it acknowledges both the difficulty and the possibility of telling the truth. It is this acknowledgement, rather than any particular stylistic traits, that was Anderson's principal gift to writers like Hemingway and Faulkner, who were to offer, in their work, far more intense but nevertheless related explorations of both the problems and the potential of language. And as with style, so with narrative structure: what Anderson offered here, to the storytellers who followed him, was a fundamental breakaway from plot into mood and meaning. Individually, the stories in *Winesburg, Ohio* break with the tradition of tightly plotted, linear narrative, in order to tell and retell moments glowing with possible significance. Collectively, they work as a cycle, a group of tales that, to use Anderson's phrase, 'belong together' thanks to their intimations, their latent meaning. Anderson was never to write so well again as he did in his book about Winesburg, although there were some fine collections of stories like *The Triumph of the Egg* (1921) and *Death in the Woods* (1933), and novels that made a considerable impact at the time of publication, such as *Many Marriages* (1923) and *Dark Laughter* (1925). But with that book, and many of his other tales, he made a difference to American writing: he showed both how minimalist and how momentous a style could be, and how stories could brim with quietly revealed meaning.

Poetry and the search for form

The twentieth century was to witness an explosion of poetry in America. The Modernist experiment was to be sustained through such poetic movements as Imagism, Vorticism and Objectivism. The traditionalist search for a past and precedent was to be maintained, not just by the Fugitive group but in other ventures into formalism. There was to be a fresh outburst of poetry of politics or prophecy, poetry with a mystical aim and poetry of minimalist experiment and pragmatic measure. African American and Native American poets, in particular, were to tap the rhythmic sources of their culture. And very many poets, identified with no particular movement, were to manoeuvre their way between the different positions and pressures that characterized American poetry at this time, in search of that quality of prime importance to the American poet: a distinctive individual voice. Bridging the gap between all these later tendencies and the verse, innovative or otherwise, of an earlier period are several poets whose work reflects the search for form, and forms of belief, that distinguishes so much of the writing around the turn of the twentieth century. With poets like Edwin Arlington Robinson (1865–1935), Robert Frost (1874–1963) and Robinson Jeffers (1887–1962) in particular, the reader is confronted with work that negotiates between the solidity and the subversion of the moral self and poetic structure, the pursuit of form, discipline, and the impulse towards fragmentation, doubt. Distinctions of this kind are always slippery. Frost, after all, was born only five years before Wallace Stevens, Jeffers just two years before Ezra Pound. But change assumes a different pace and coloration with different places and temperaments, no cultural transformation is monolithic; and it is surely the case that Robinson, Frost and Jeffers adopted more of the older habits of thought and writerly practices than many of those roughly contemporary with them. Their work, with its intense seriousness of moral purpose and questioning, rather than collapsing traditional measures, shades into the old modes of writing just as much as into the new.

Nothing perhaps illustrates the transitional status of Edwin Arlington Robinson more than his own description of himself, as someone 'content with the old-fashioned way to be new'. Robinson's first and last love was what he called 'the music of English verse'. As he explained to a friend, he was 'a classicist in poetic composition' who believed that 'the accepted media for masters of the past' should 'continue to be used for the future'. However, he was far from being one of the 'little sonnet-men' as he contemptuously referred to them, mere imitators of English fashion and forms. On the contrary, he was deliberately local: many of his poems are set in Tilbury Town, a fictive place based on his boyhood home of Gardiner, Maine. And he was a genuine original, obsessed with certain personal themes: human isolation, the tormented introversions of the personality, the doubts and frustrations of lonely people inhabiting a world from which God appears to have hidden His face. Few poets have ever understood loneliness better than Robinson: perhaps because he suffered from it severely himself. The early death of his mother, and then of his father in ghastly circumstances, helped make life 'a living hell' for him, Robinson said, while he was young. In his adult years, Robinson was to enjoy considerable success. His early work, published in such volumes as *The Children of Night* (1897), earned him the support of Theodore Roosevelt. His 1910 collection, *The Town Down the River*, was popular enough to allow him to devote himself to writing. His later work, like *The Man Against the Sky* (1916), won him critical acclaim. His trilogy of poems based on the Arthurian legend, published between 1917 and 1927, *Merlin*, *Lancelot* and *Tristram*, enjoyed a wide readership; and his *Collected Poems* (1921) was awarded a Pulitzer Prize. Yet he struggled against depression and alcoholism all his life. And his perennial subject became what he termed 'the slow tragedy of haunted men' – those whose 'eyes are lit with a young light', illusions that at once cripple and save them – and 'The strange and unremembered light that is in dreams' – the obsessive effort to make sense of experience when there is perhaps no sense to be made. 'The world is not "a prison-house"', Robinson insisted, 'but a kind of spiritual kindergarten, where millions of infants are trying to spell "God" with the wrong blocks.' Robinson saw himself and his poetic characters as notable members of that kindergarten: people whose minds and language, their 'words', can never quite encompass the truth about the universe, the 'Word', but who nevertheless keep on trying.

The bleakness of Robinson's vision, particularly in his early work, comes out in poems like 'The House on the Hill' and 'Richard Cory'. In 'The House on the Hill', the bleakness issues from the sense that, now that the house in question is in 'ruin and decay' and its inhabitants are departed, any comment seems a superfluous gesture. The opening lines announce this perception:

> They are all gone away,
> The House is shut and still,
> There is nothing more to say.

To try to attach words to vacancy, to clothe transience and loneliness in language, is a futile gesture, the poem suggests. More remarks are added to the opening ones: but the constant repetition of the first three lines, in varying sequence, gives the impression that nothing more is really being said. Perhaps there is indeed 'nothing more to say'. Nevertheless, Robinson keeps on trying to say more; and in 'Richard Cory' he explores the anonymous surfaces of life in another way – by suggesting, however cryptically, the contrast between those surfaces and the evident hell that lies beneath them. The character who gives the poem its title is described in admiring detail, from the perspective of his poorer neighbours. 'He was a gentleman from sole to crown, /' the reader is told; 'Clean favoured, . . . imperially slim' and 'rich – yes, richer than a king.' Comments like these hardly prepare us for the horror of the final stanza:

> So on we worked, and waited for the light,
> And went without the meat, and carved the bread;
> And Richard Cory, one calm summer night,
> Went home and put a bullet through his head.

The irony of these lines, and the poem as a whole, depends on the contrast between the serenity of Cory's appearance and the violence of his death; its melancholy, upon our recognizing that Cory – for all his privileges – is as acutely isolated and spiritually starved as anyone else. 'There is more in every person's soul than we think,' Robinson observed once; 'Even the happy mortals we term ordinary . . . act their own mental tragedies and live a far deeper and wider life than we are inclined to believe possible in the light of our prejudices.' This is precisely the lesson that the 'we' of the poem, Cory's neighbours in Tilbury Town, never learn: the night on which Cory shoots himself remains 'calm' in their view, and the use of that word only underlines the distance between him and them.

Quiet desperation, the agony that Richard Cory's neighbours failed to notice, is a distinguishing feature of many of Robinson's characters. The despair may come, apparently, from emotional poverty ('Aaron Stark'), the pain of loss and bereavement ('Reuben Bright', 'Luke Havergal'), or the treadmill of life ('The Clerks'): whatever, it is palpably there in an awkward gesture, a stuttered phrase, a violent moment as in 'Richard Cory' or, as in 'The House on the Hill', the sense that behind the stark, simple words lies an unimaginable burden of pain. Many of Robinson's poems, in fact, derive their power from reticence, a positive refusal to expand or elaborate. In 'How Annandale Went Out', for example, the reader only gradually realizes that 'Annandale' is the name of a man who has been reduced by some incurable disease, or accident, to the vegetable state, and that the narrator is a doctor who has evidently been merciful enough to relieve him of his life. Such is the cryptic indirection, the emotional austerity of lines like 'They called it Annandale – and I was there / To flourish, to find words, and to attend' that the meaning is not immediately clear. New Englanders, Robinson observed, are not like 'those / Who boil elsewhere with such a lyric yeast', at least not on the surface. Their dramas, whatever they may be, are enacted within. So the power of many of his poems stems from the reader recognizing just how much emotional pressure there is behind the spare diction, the poignant contrast between the enormity of feeling implied and the bare, stripped manner of implication. In effect, the reader is often asked to conjecture, just as so many of Robinson's narrators conjecture about the lives of those who have gone or those they hardly know except as inhabitants of the same town. The poem becomes an act of commemoration, in which the speaker recalls and rehearses a life with the discomforting sense that he can only offer some provisional notes towards understanding it. 'We cannot have them here with us', admits the narrator of his departed friends in 'Calverly's', '/ To say where their light lives are gone.' He cannot say what has happened to them, what their lives were and the fates are; and because he cannot say – and because there is nothing and no way to find out – he cannot know what his own fate is, or its meaning. He can only know that he himself once spent time at an inn called 'Calverly's', that the others were there and are now gone, and that he will follow them in due course. He cannot say what this means or if, in fact, it means anything.

In rehearsing the mute, inglorious lives of the inhabitants of Tilbury Town, Robinson was, he knew, rebelling against the orthodoxies of the pastoral tradition: that body of writing, particularly strong in the United States, that locates happiness, a kind of Edenic innocence and peace, in the rural world and village life. His sonnet addressed to the English poet George Crabbe ('George Crabbe') establishes his allegiances. Like Crabbe, he implies, he is concerned with the loneliness of country people, the austerity and sheer poverty of their existence; and he tries to write about these things 'In books that are as altars where we kneel / To consecrate the flicker, not the flame'. The image measures the scope of Robinson's ambitions and the way he tries to place himself in terms of his Romantic predecessors. The flame is a traditional Romantic image for the transfiguring power of the imagination. Crabbe's work, and by implication his own, may not have this, Robinson admits: but traces of that flame, one or two 'flickers' of imaginative possibility, are discernible there nevertheless. A character like Miniver Cheevy, in Robinson's poem of that name, illustrates the point; for, while Miniver might not be capable of transforming his environment in the way a Romantic hero would be, he is not entirely determined by it either. Miniver, we are told:

> sighed for what was not
> And dreamed, and rested from his labours
> He dreamed of Thebes and Camelot
> And Priam's neighbours . . .

Lines like these, combining irony with a touch of sympathetic melancholy, at first invite us to see no resemblance between the dreamer and his dreams and then gradually, through their very poignancy, qualify this, just a little, by hinting that a 'flicker' of the heroic impulse is to be found in a man like Miniver – even though it may be too feeble ever to burst into 'flame'. At worst, Miniver Cheevy is dimly aware of the barrenness of his circumstances and finds refuge in what Robinson elsewhere calls 'the . . . / Perennial inspiration of his lies'; at best, he can perhaps dream better possibilities – his mind is actively engaged in a quest for meaning.

In his later years, Robinson tended to concentrate on the more positive implications of impulses like Miniver's, the human capacity for dreaming dreams of a better life. Something of this is suggested by the short poem 'Mr Flood's Party', published eleven years after 'Miniver Cheevy'. Like 'Miniver Cheevy', it describes a pathetic figure who retreats from an intolerable present into dreams of the past; it, too, mixes irony with sympathy. But, whereas in the earlier poem the sympathy is relatively slight, peripheral and qualified, in 'Mr Flood's Party' it is central to our understanding of the protagonist. When, for instance, about midway through the poem Robinson compares Mr Flood to 'Roland's ghost winding a silent horn', the comparison seems at once incongruous and just. In some ways, Mr Flood is quite unlike the bravest of Charlemagne's officers who, after most of his friends had gone, died blowing on his horn for help. Mr Flood's horn, after all, is not a horn at all but a jug full of liquor, and he is not so much a bold young adventurer as a tired old man. In other ways, though, the knight and the drunkard turn out to be very much alike. Both, for example, present types of endurance, as men who recall the past while preparing to meet their former companions in another world. Comic Mr Flood may be, but there is a touch of the hero to him as well: more than a touch, perhaps, when, towards the end of the poem, Robinson describes him 'amid

---

the silver loneliness / Of night' lifting up his voice and singing 'Until the whole harmonious landscape rang'. By now, the jug has assumed a symbolic status roughly analogous to the jar in Wallace Stevens's poem 'Anecdote of the Jar': belonging to a world where 'most things break', it has nevertheless become the node around which the scene is momentarily harmonized. More important, Mr Flood's inebriated state now smacks of the divine drunkenness of the poet: the man who comes close to liberating himself, and metamorphosing his environment, with the help of his vivid imagination.

It was in a series of longer poetic narratives, however, rather than in short pieces like 'Mr Flood's Party' that the later Robinson moved towards affirmation: poems such as the Arthurian trilogy *Merlin, Lancelot* and *Tristram*. 'The Man Against the Sky', written at about the midpoint in Robinson's career, indicates the change; in a reflective poem over three hundred lines long, the poet sketches out the mature philosophical attitude implicit in later and even longer works. The opening lines establish the basic image, of a man making the upward climb over the hill of life to death, in a way that suggests both the man's diminutiveness and his possible grandeur. This image then leads the poet to speculate on the various attitudes of people as they face death. Representing different philosophies of life as well as death, they describe a scale of increasing negation, from faith to doubt to denial, and seem, too, roughly chronological, moving from primitive religious belief to contemporary materialism. Having pushed the argument this far, the poet then develops it a little further. We no longer believe in the 'two fond old enormities' of heaven and hell, he acknowledges, but that is no reason for assuming that life is meaningless and death an annihilation. Perhaps there is an order in the universe. Admittedly, we can never know whether there is or not because we are limited by the confines of the self. But it is surely better to believe that there is such an order, since life is otherwise reduced to 'a blind atomic pilgrimage', a pointless trek; better, and more reasonable. For our own continued will to survive, Robinson argues, and to perpetuate the race suggests that we have some intuitive conviction implanted in us, something that tells us that life is worth living. We persist; and that, together with any further glimpses of the truth we may receive by means of dreams, hints and guesses, is the best possible evidence we can have of the existence of purpose. 'Where was he going, this man against the sky', the poet asks, and then answers:

> You know not, nor do I.
> But this we know, if we know anything:
> That we may laugh and fight and sing
> And of our transience here make offering
> To an orient Word that will not be erased,
> Or, save in incommunicable gleams,
> Too permanent for dreams,
> Be found or known.

The argument is characteristically tentative, but clear. Perhaps, the suggestion is, the simple human will to live, and to look for meaning, provides a basis for belief.

Despite their isolation, and the acute limitations imposed on them, people continue to search for value; they remain dreamers. And perhaps their dreams, together with the instinct to continue, bring them closer to the truth than they can ever know. The world may well be 'a spiritual kindergarten', Robinson concedes, but it can offer occasional lessons, moments of illumination however dim and inadequate. We, its members, may not be able to spell the 'orient Word' with the few words available to us: but the failure to spell it does not disprove its existence – it may still be lurking there, somewhere.

Like Robinson, Robert Frost was drawn towards traditional forms. 'I had as soon write free verse', he once declared, 'as play tennis without a net.' For him, traditional metres were a necessary discipline, something against which he could play off the urgencies of his own speaking voice, the chance movements of his emotions, the catch and tilt of his breath. Like Robinson, too, Frost acquired fame but never shed what he referred to as his 'daily gloominess'. His first volume of poetry, *A Boy's Will* (1912), was published in England, where he lived for a while and became acquainted with both Ezra Pound, who helped Frost to get his work in *Poetry*, and the 'Georgian' group of poets that included Edward Thomas. *North of Boston* (1914), his second collection, became a best-seller; *Mountain Interval* (1916), the third collection, attracted national attention; and his *Collected Poems* (1930) won national prizes. By 1955, he had so many honorary degrees that he could have his doctoral hoods sewn together to make a quilt for his bed. And by the 1960s, he was sufficiently famous to be invited to read a poem at the inauguration of President Kennedy and to represent the United States on a goodwill mission to Russia. Yet Frost, through all this, was haunted by personal misfortune. Two children died in infancy, a son committed suicide, and one of his daughters was committed to a mental institution. And not just at moments of crisis such as these, Frost sprinkled his journals with remarks such as: 'one of the hardest disciplines is having to learn the meaningless', or, more simply, 'nature is chaos'.

'I've wanted to write down certain brute throat noises', Frost said, 'so that no one could miss them in my sentences.' Those noises, he felt, acquired additional pungency and point from being placed in tension with established rhythms and rhymes: what he was after, in effect, was a creative tension between musicality and the cadences of everyday conversation, a casual but crafty play of speech and song. That play, as it emerges in his poems, is not just a matter of voice, however, but of vision. By means of it, he explores the paradox implicit in one of his most famous lines: 'The fact is the sweetest dream that labour knows.' 'Stopping by Woods on a Snowy Evening' illustrates this. Its opening stanza establishes the ambivalent tone of the poem and the imaginative tension that constitutes its debate:

> Whose woods these are I think I know,
> His house is in the village though;
> He will not see me stopping here
> To watch his woods fill up with snow.

The duality of the narrator's response to the woods is caught in the contrast between the relaxed, conversational idiom of the first three lines and the dream-like descriptive detail and hypnotic verbal music of the last. Clearing and wilderness, law and freedom, civilization and nature, fact and dream: these oppositions reverberate throughout American writing. And they are registered here in Frost's own quietly ironic contrast between the road along which the narrator travels, connecting marketplace to marketplace, promoting community and culture, and the white silence of the woods, where none of the ordinary limitations of the world seems to apply. In a minor key, they are caught also in the implicit comparison between the owner of these woods, who apparently regards them purely as a financial investment (he lives in the village), and the narrator who sees them, at least potentially, as a spiritual one.

This contrast between what might be termed, rather reductively perhaps, 'realistic' and 'romantic' attitudes is then sustained through the next two stanzas: the commonsensical response is now playfully attributed to the narrator's horse which, like any practical being, wants to get on down the road to food and shelter. The narrator himself, however, continues to be lured by the mysteries of the forest just as the Romantic poets were lured by the mysteries of otherness, sleep and death. And, as before, the contrast is a product of tone and texture as much as dramatic intimation: the poem communicates its debate in how it says things as much as in what it says. So, the harsh gutturals and abrupt movement of lines like 'He gives his harness bells a shake / To ask if there is some mistake' give verbal shape to the matter-of-fact attitude attributed to the horse, just as the soothing sibilants and gently rocking motion of the lines that follow this ('The only other sound's the sweep / Of easy wind and downy flake') offer a tonal equivalent of the strange, seductive world into which the narrator is tempted to move. 'Everything that is written', Frost once said, 'is as good as it is dramatic'; and in a poem like this the words of the poem become actors in the drama.

The final stanza of 'Stopping by Woods' does not resolve its tensions; on the contrary, it rehearses them in particularly memorable language.

> The woods are lovely, dark and deep,
> But I have promises to keep,
> And miles to go before I sleep,
> And miles to go before I sleep.

Having paid tribute to the dangerous seductiveness of the woods, the narrator seems to be trying to shake himself back into commonsense reality by invoking his 'promises' or mundane responsibilities. The last line is repeated, however; and while at first it seems little more than a literal reference to the journey he has to complete (and so a way of telling himself to continue on down the road), the repetition gives it particular resonance. This could, after all, be a metaphorical reference to the brief span of human life and the compulsion this puts the narrator under to take risks and explore the truth while he can. Only a few 'miles' to go before 'I sleep' in death: such a chilling *memento mori* perhaps justifies stopping by the woods in the first place and considering the spiritual quest implicit in the vision they offer. Perhaps: the point is that neither narrator nor reader can be sure. 'The poem is the act of having the thought,' Frost insisted; it is process rather than product, it invites us to share in the experiences of seeing, feeling and thinking, not simply to look at their results. So the most a piece like 'Stopping by Woods' will offer – and it is a great deal – is an *imaginative* resolution of its tensions: the sense that its conflicts and irresolutions have been given appropriate dramatic expression, revelation and equipoise.

'It begins in delight and ends in wisdom,' said Frost in his remarkable definition of 'the figure a poem makes':

> The figure is the same for love ... It begins in delight, assumes direction with the first line laid, it runs a course of lucky events, and ends in clarification of life – not necessarily a great clarification, such as sects and cults are founded on, but in a momentary stay against confusion.

The incessant coupling of opposites, the felicitous, serious play that ends in 'a momentary stay against confusion', is precisely what characterizes Frost's work. It makes all his best lyrics, like 'Stopping by Woods', essentially dramatic in that they enact internal conflicts, savage dualisms of thought and feeling. In turn, it makes all of his best dramatic poems, like 'The Death of the Hired Man' and 'West-Running Brook', essentially lyrical in that they reproduce, in beautifully individualized form, those same conflicts, turning them into intimate human communication. In 'The Death of the Hired Man', for example, the event that gives the poem its title is merely the occasion for a loving argument between husband and wife that brings out their differences of speech and approach. The husband's voice is abrupt, with many stops and few connectives, full of imperatives and wilful declarations, turning aside for brusque rhetorical or cross-examining questions. The seal of his tone is set by his caustic description of home: 'Home is the place where, when you have to go there, / They have to take you in.' His character, clearly, is that of the maker of good bargains, the shrewd calculator of motives, the uncompromising champion of harsh truth. The wife is very different, as her definition of home suggests: 'I should have called it / Something you somehow haven't to deserve.' Far more hesitant, her speech has breaks of another kind from her husband's: of someone reaching for the right word, more sympathetic and imaginative, using emotion and a kind of lyric responsiveness to soften the hard edges of fact. Very different in character, and in their reactions to the hired man who returns to them after a long absence looking for work, they are nevertheless in intimate touch with each other; and they are drawn even closer together by the hired man's sudden death. They never entirely agree; their differences are no more resolved than the differences in 'Stopping by Woods' are. But, like 'Stopping by Woods', they suggest the possible coexistence of these differences, a marriage or, to use Frost's own phrase, 'happy-sad blend' of realism and romance.

Another, simpler way of describing the circuitous, serpentine character of Frost's work is to say that he is the supreme example of the sceptic in modern American poetry: the person who mistrusts categorical answers, utopian solutions, and who, for reasons he thoroughly articulates, cannot or will not make up his mind. In 'For Once, Then, Something', for instance, he plays on the traditional idea of looking down into a well in search of the truth. The narrator, we are told, once peered into the subterranean darkness and, for a moment, saw 'a something white, uncertain': but then a ripple in the water 'Blurred it, blotted it out'. 'What was that whiteness?' the narrator asks himself, and can find an answer only in his own indecision: 'Truth? A pebble of quartz? For once, then, something.' 'Something' might be everything or nothing. Having wound, in slow, meditative hendecasyllabics, through the mysteries of exploration, the poem ends in a series of questions that only underline the difficulties of knowing. A comparison with an earlier New England poet, Emily Dickinson, is relevant here, for in 'What mystery pervades a well!' Dickinson pursues exactly the same theme. Dickinson, however, concludes that 'nature is a stranger yet': she is at least sure that she has seen nothing, or at least very little, and so measured the dimensions of what she called her 'magic prison'. For Frost, even this radically limited degree of certainty is impossible. He cannot gauge the size or nature of his cell; he cannot be certain whether the 'something' he has seen is trivial or significant. Dickinson at least knows that she cannot know: Frost, by comparison, cannot know even this. The limits to perception, the nature and scope of knowing and naming, the accessibility of truth: all these things remain hidden from him, and so he falls back on the ultimate weapon of the impotent and irresolute, irony.

Irony is by no means Frost's only weapon, though. As his autobiographical poem, 'The Oven Bird' makes clear, he is a poet struggling to find 'what to make of a diminished thing'. Transcendence is not available for him in the way it was for earlier writers like Emerson and Whitman. Consequently, he must do what he can with what has been called 'a minimal case'. This sometimes involves ironic meditations on the human pursuit of knowledge, as it does in 'For Once, Then, Something' or 'Neither Out Far Nor In Deep'. But just as often it precipitates tentative inquiry into the mysteries that hover on the edges of experience, the possible sources of fear and wonder. The more unnerving results of such an inquiry emerge in poems like 'Out, Out –' and 'Design'. 'Out, Out –' begins with what seems like a gently nostalgic piece of rural portrait-painting:

> The buzz saw snarled and rattled in the yard
> And made dust and dropped stove-length sticks of wood,
> Sweet-scented stuff when the breeze drew across it . . .

From this, the poet moves slowly, in an almost relaxed fashion, into an account of an apparently minor accident: we are told, in quietly serio-comic terms, how one of the workers, a young boy, cut his hand on the buzz saw. Things grow more serious when the possibility emerges that the boy might lose his hand. Just the same, we are hardly prepared for the final lines:

And then – the watcher at his pulse took fright.
No one believed. They listened at his heart.
Little – less – nothing! – and that ended it.
No more to build on there. And they, since they
Were not the one dead, turned to their affairs.

This is death stripped of any sense of occasion, denied preparation or ceremony. Unanticipated, greeted with incomprehension, stilted phrases and awkward reactions, and followed by numbness, together with the indelible feeling that the dead are gone while the living must continue, this is death as the terrifying, universal and in some sense inconsequential fact that it is – and as very few writers have been willing to acknowledge it.

Fear and dread lurk close to the surface of a poem like this, certainly: but, in other poems, Frost's playfulness, his willingness to entertain all kinds of doubts and possibilities, leads him in the contrary direction – not to transcendence of facts, perhaps, but to a wondering, joyful apprehension of their potential, to the sense that nature might after all be whispering secret, sympathetic messages to us. 'The Most of It' belongs in this second group. It presents us with a situation familiar enough in Romantic literature, and one that American writers like Cooper, Emerson and Whitman were particularly fond of exploring: the protagonist – the 'he' of the poem – stands looking across a lake towards some distant hills, seeking comfort and instruction from nature. In accordance with the tradition, Frost's protagonist cries out to the hills, seeking what the poet calls 'counter-love, original response': some sign that nature sympathizes and that he has not 'kept the universe alone'. But, in this case at least, there is no clear reaction. All he seems to get back is the 'mocking echo' of his own voice, confirming him in his isolation. Or does he? This, after all, is the concluding description of the echo:

As a great buck it powerfully appeared,
Pushing the crumpled water up ahead,
And landed pouring like a waterfall.
And stumbled through the rocks with horny tread,
And forced the underbush – and that was all.

If a symbol is, in Jung's phrase, 'the best possible expression of a relatively *unknown* fact', then this is the purest of symbols. Perhaps all the protagonist apprehends is the echo of his voice. However, that echo is described with such dramatic bite, such vitality, that perhaps he apprehends more: perhaps he has glimpsed, if not the Emersonian Over-Soul, then at least some of the strange, animistic forces that give life dimension and energy, that transform 'fact' into 'dream'. He, and we, cannot be sure, and it is the achievement of the poem that we cannot be: that we are left, in short, with a feeling of mystery.

Although Frost was born in San Francisco, he spent most of his life in New England. Like Robinson, his poetry is indelibly marked by the vocal habits of that region and an ingrained regional tendency to fluctuate between irony, melancholy and wonder. Robinson Jeffers was born in Pittsburgh and studied in Europe. After he married, however, he went to live on the sparsely populated coast of California, where he built a granite house and tower on cliffs facing the sea. Jeffers found his poetic voice with *Tamar and Other Poems* (1924). Reaction to the volume, published privately, was enthusiastic, and a commercial edition with new poems added, *Roan Stallion, Tamar, and Other Poems*, was published in 1925. Many other volumes followed, among them *The Women at Point Sur* (1927), *Give Your Heart to the Hawks and Other Poems* (1933) and *Hungerfield, and Other Poems* (1954). Together, they established Jeffers as the supreme poet of the Far West of his time: a man whose work both imitates and celebrates the vast, elemental tendencies of the Western landscape and the sea beyond. Jeffers declared that his aim was to 'uncentre the human mind from itself'. He wanted his verse to break away from all the versions of experience which emphasized its exclusively human properties, and to rediscover our relationship with the foundations of nature. Humankind, Jeffers insisted, must acknowledge the superior value of the instinctive life, of natural action and self-expression. Humanity must try to imitate the rocks in their coldness and endurance, the hawks in their isolation, and all physical nature in its surrender to the wild, primeval level of being. This necessarily meant a repudiation of all humanistic philosophies in favour of what the poet liked to call 'Inhumanism'. It meant, he admitted, 'a shifting of emphasis and significance from man to notman' with a consequent loss of those values which, for centuries, we have learned to cherish – among them, reason and self-restraint, urbanity and decorum. But, Jeffers hastened to add, it also meant the discovery of an older liberty, aligning us with the people of ancient cultures; and it involved, too, an escape from the involuted self-consciousness, the entanglements and dark internecine conflicts, which make our modern world such a painful one.

A poem like 'Divinely Superfluous Beauty' illustrates the means by which Jeffers tried to express his philosophy of Inhumanism. It opens with a vision of the spontaneous energy running through all things, 'The storm-dances of gulls, the barking game of seals', and then concludes with the wish to be identified with this energy, to become one with all that is 'divinely superfluous'. 'The incredible beauty of joy / Stars with fire the joining of lips,' declares the poet:

> O let our loves too
> Be joined, there is not a maiden
> Burns and thirsts for love
> More than my blood for you, by the shore of
> seals while the wings
> Weave like a web in the air
> Divinely superfluous beauty.

As in all of Jeffers's shorter poems, the impact of these lines depends upon perspective: human life is seen from an immense distance, as it were, placed within the larger dimensions of earth, sea and sky. The poet-philosopher who speaks here helps to place the subject as well, for his voice, primitive and oracular, seems to align him with the older freedoms he is celebrating. This is largely the result of the style Jeffers developed, in which the tones of colloquial speech are recreated without weakening formal control of the line. Of great flexibility, hovering somewhere between free verse and iambic pentameter, the rhythms are precise and emphatic without being regular. Together with the unelaborate syntax, and comparatively simple diction, they help to give poems like this a feeling of rugged exactitude: to communicate what Jeffers himself termed 'power and reality . . . , substance and sense'.

If Jeffers was unlike Robinson or Frost in terms of his fundamental vision and voice – categorical where they were uncertain, rapt and bardic while they played in a quieter, more enigmatic key – he was nevertheless like them in his obsession with the past and his attachment to place. With Jeffers, though, the past that signified was not immediate, a matter of conscious memory and cultural history, but ancient, prehistorical, not so much a human as a subhuman inheritance. Traditionalist he might be, in the sense of looking backward for his allegiances, but he was one for whom the crucial traditions were beyond the scope of consciousness and community – incorporating the sense that, as he put it once, 'the universe is one being, all its parts are different expressions of the same energy'. It was only in 'the Monterey Mountains', he insisted, that he had ever found 'people living . . . essentially as they did in the Idyls or Sagas, or in Homer's Ithaca. Here was life purged of its ephemeral accretions. Here was the contemporary life that was also permanent life.' In addition, the position of California, facing what he called 'the final Pacific', convinced him that here was 'the world's end'. With the conquest of the American continent, Jeffers believed, the westward movement of civilization was completed. Human history was effectively over; although, of course, cosmic history would continue.

Among the many poems that explore Jeffers's own peculiar version of frontier legend, the mythology of the West, are 'The Torch-Bearer's Race' and 'Continent's End'. In the latter, the poet stands on the Californian coastline, watching the Pacific. As he watches, and meditates, it occurs to him that the sea represents a form of life much older than human history, a form from which human beings, in the progressive stages of their development, have moved ever further away. But perhaps the finest of Jeffers's pieces in which California is a visible, palpable presence is the longer narrative poem 'Roan Stallion'. Jeffers was frequently drawn towards longer forms. Most of his published volumes include one or two long narrative or dramatic poems. Among his dramatic pieces are adaptations of Greek legend, like 'The Tower beyond Tragedy', 'At the Fall of an Age' and *Medea* (1947), as well as his idiosyncratic version of the story of Jesus, 'Dear Judas'; while, over thirty years, he wrote fifteen narrative poems all located in California in the twentieth century. Not alone among these narratives, 'Roan Stallion' has its origins in local character and experience: at least some of its events, Jeffers later claimed, were 'part of . . . actual history'. Starting from there, however, the poem soon assumes the dimensions of myth: like so much of Jeffers's work, it belongs at once to a particular people and place and to a world of elemental human experience. Its central action suggests these larger dimensions; when the heroine rides a stallion by moonlight to a hilltop, and there falls upon the ground prostrating herself beneath its hooves. The stallion, the poet tells us:

> backed at first; but later
>   plucked the grass that grew by her shoulder.
> The small dark head under his nostrils: a small round
>   stone that smelt human, black hair growing from it;
> The skull shut the light in: it was not possible
>   for any eyes
> To know what throbbed and shone under the sutures
>   of the skull, . . . a shell full of lightning . . .

After this moment of brooding excitement, the poem quickly rises to a strange, mystical experience of union:

> The atom bounds-breaking,
> Nucleus to sun, electrons to planets, without recognition
> Not praying, self-equalling, the whole to whole,
>   the microcosm
> Not entering nor accepting entrance, more equally,
>   more utterly, more incredibly conjugate
> With the other extreme and greatness; passionately
>   perceptive of identity . . .

Reading lines like this in context, we cannot help being reminded of one of the most consistent of ancient legends, in which a god comes to a woman in the shape of a beast and there is sexual contact between them. This, in turn, encourages us to see the entire narrative as a symbolic one, with several different levels of meaning. One level is registered in the heroine's name, California, and the fact that she is one-quarter Indian, one-quarter Spanish and one-half Anglo-Saxon. On this level, the poem is clearly a myth of the American West: California represents a new land and a new breed of people, and her moment of communion with the horse figures the close contact with nature that land and those people enjoy – 'life', to recall Jeffers's description of the Monterey mountains, 'purged of its ephemeral accretions'. On another level, 'Roan Stallion' is a kind of racial myth which has as its subject myths and the mythologizing process in general. Jeffers presents us with a legendary union between a mortal woman and a god in the shape of a beast, and then proceeds to explain why, since the beginning of time, people have created such legends. After the passage just quoted, for instance, the poet connects the central incident of the poem to other mythical annunciations, and then connects every one of these in turn with what he calls:

> ... the phantom rulers of humanity
> That without being are yet more real than what they
> are born of, and without shape, shape that which
> makes them.

All of these legends, he is saying, exist because we need them. They serve to remind us of the power and the glory latent in us, which we share with the elements, and which can only find a partial expression in the lives that we lead, the societies we build.

This leads to the third, and most significant, level of meaning in the poem. Above all, 'Roan Stallion', like all of Jeffers's work, is about the gospel of Inhumanism. The stallion, according to this reading, figures the power of nature just as the creatures in 'Divinely Superfluous Beauty' do; and, in surrendering to it, the woman momentarily identifies herself with that power, just as Jeffers always longed to. The identification is not easy, as the poet's description of the mystical experience at the heart of the poem indicates. A rapprochement between woman and nature begins to occur at the beginning of the lines quoted just now, suggested by the comparison of California's 'small dark head' to a 'small round stone'. But, at first, there is a gulf if only because the head is full of the 'lightning' of self-consciousness. More effort is required to bridge that gulf and turn rapprochement into union: 'lightning' in this sense could also refer to the power generated in the struggle to escape self-consciousness. And, at the lines beginning 'The atom bounds-breaking', the gulf is finally bridged. 'Humanity is the mould to break away from,' Jeffers insists elsewhere in the poem, 'the crust to break through, ... / The atom to be split.' Suddenly, in an experience that transcends and illuminates all that surrounds it, the atom *is* split and man assumes the status of 'not-man'. 'I think one of the most common intentions in tragic stories', Jeffers said, 'is to build up the strain for the sake of the explosion of its release – like winding up a ballista.' If this is true, then 'Roan Stallion' is certainly a tragic story. Its heroine may only be able to achieve union with inhuman nature for a while: at the end of the poem, in fact, she betrays the beast-god by shooting him. But, for a brief enchanted moment, she does experience that union, and in doing so provides narrator and reader alike with a very special version of tragic catharsis.

Towards the end of Jeffers's life, however, there was a distinct shift of emphasis away from the tragic and towards the mystical. The sense of an inescapable conflict between nature and human nature became of less concern; and the poet concentrated more than ever before on the possibility of union. Of course, union as an idea (as in 'Divinely Superfluous Beauty') or a momentary experience (as in 'Roan Stallion') is often present in his earlier work: but there it is normally qualified by a recognition of the needs and limits of the human character. In the work of Jeffers's last years, by contrast, this recognition tends to lose its power, and the poet is consequently left freer to contemplate those occasions when, as he put it once, there is 'no passion but peace'. In 'The Eye', for instance, the poet finds refuge from the horrors of the Second World War in a feeling of identification with 'the staring unsleeping / Eye of the earth': the poem is a perfect illustration of Jeffers's claim that Inhumanism is 'neither misanthropic nor pessimistic' but 'a means of maintaining sanity in slippery times', because it fosters 'reasonable detachment as a rule of conduct'. In 'My Burial Place', in turn, Jeffers anticipates the moment at which the union between himself and nature will be complete, when his body will be compounded into dust. 'Now comes for me the time to engage / My burial place', he insists:

> put me in a beautiful place far off from men
> No cemetery, no necropolis,
>
>   . . .
>
> But if the human animal were precious
> As the quick deer or that hunter in the night the lonely puma
> I should be pleased to lie in one grave with 'em.

Like Robinson and Frost, Jeffers contemplates mortality here, in severe and immaculate lines that register how absurd and petty the human animal is, and how everything is dwarfed by the enigmatic beauty, the intrinsic perfection, of nature. More starkly even than they do, he also reminds the reader that words are nothing but a temporary bridge erected over a vacuum. He recalls his audience to the thought that all human ceremonies are shadow play: no more than fragile defences against the time when, as we inevitably must, we shed our humanity, returning to the earth, our origins.

The Inventions of Modernism

Imagism, Vorticism and Objectivism

'The *point de repère* usually and conveniently taken as the starting point of modern poetry', declared T. S. Eliot, 'is the group denominated "imagists" in London around 1910.' Actually, the beginnings of the Imagist movement can be traced to an earlier date than this, and to the feeling common among young writers in the first few years of the twentieth century that poets were for the most part playing for safety and sentimentality. In reaction to this, a group began to gather in London dedicated, among other things, to the aim of reproducing 'the peculiar quality of feeling which is induced by the flat spaces and wide horizons of the virgin-prairie' – and to the belief that 'poetic ideas are best expressed by the rendering of concrete objects'. They were joined, in April 1909, by the young expatriate Ezra Pound, whose own ideas about poetry had been outlined in a letter to William Carlos Williams six months earlier: '1. To Paint the thing as I see it. 2. Beauty. 3. Freedom from didacticism. 4. It is only good manners if you repeat a few other men to at least do it better or more briefly.' In 1911, Pound then renewed acquaintance with Hilda Doolittle, newly arrived from the United States and calling herself H. D. By now, Pound was looking around for good poetry to send to Harriet Monroe in Chicago and found it both in the work of H. D. and in that of a young British writer, Richard Aldington. Pound then, in 1912, informed them, apparently to their surprise, that they were Imagists. The next step was to produce an anthology, which duly appeared in 1914. The anthology was poorly received, and Pound himself moved on to Vorticism, a stricter form of Imagism that emphasized the dynamic nature of the image. 'The image is not an idea,' he declared while campaigning on behalf of Vorticism: 'It is a radiant node or cluster . . . a VORTEX, from which, and through which, and into which ideas are constantly rushing.' With Pound abandoning Imagism, the way was left clear for Amy Lowell (1874–1925), descendant of a distinguished New England family, to assume control of the movement. Under her auspices, two more anthologies were published in 1916 and 1917. After that, Lowell declared, there were to be no more collections since the movement had 'done its work'. As far as Pound was concerned, the announcement came none too soon. For him, Imagism had already become 'Amy-gisme', an excuse for mediocrity. This was, incidentally, unfair to Lowell, who was an accomplished poet in a variety of forms. She could write intense emotional vignettes in the Imagist vein, like 'Wakefulness' (1919), 'polyphonic prose' (that is, writing that is prose in its typography and poetic in its density), and longer poems such as the piece addressed to 'The Sisters' (1925), the 'strange trio' of her fellow female poets Sappho, Elizabeth Barrett Browning and Emily Dickinson. Above all, in her collection *Pictures of the Floating World* (1919), she could produce a series of stories and longer love poems, woman to woman, that are notable for both their passion and their discipline. But what mattered about Imagism, as Pound sensed and indeed Lowell acknowledged in her assumption of its ending, was not so much the movement itself as the beliefs it articulated. It provided a focus: not, like Harriet Monroe's little magazine *Poetry*, a practical focus but an ideological one. It crystallized tendencies, certain notions about the nature of poetic experiment, which had been developing in a piecemeal fashion over the previous decade – to organize, define and so promote them as to supply a convenient basis for Modernism.

The character of these tendencies can be glimpsed by the three 'rules' for Imagists that one member of the group, F. S. Flint, drew up in an essay published in *Poetry* in 1913. The rules were:

1. Direct treatment of the 'thing' whether subjective or objective.
2. To use absolutely no word that did [*sic*] not contribute to the presentation.
3. As regarding the rhythm: to compose in sequence of the musical phrase not in sequence of the metronome.

'The point of Imagisme', Pound wrote in 1914, 'is that it does not use images as ornaments. The image itself is the speech. The image is the word beyond formulated argument.' That remark, corresponding to the first of Flint's rules, suggests the primary Imagist objective: to avoid rhetoric and moralizing, to stick closely to the object or experience being described. The image, as what Pound elsewhere called 'an intellectual and emotional complex in an instant of time', could do all the work of suggestion, evocation; and the poet, or any writer, need hardly ever, if at all, move into explicit generalization. That slotted in neatly with the second

Imagist 'rule': which Pound, in 1917, summed up by advising, 'Use no superfluous word, no adjective which does not reveal something'. This advice was perhaps what Amy Lowell had in mind when she said that the Imagist principles 'are not new; they have fallen into desuetude. They are the essentials of all great poetry.' Be that as it may, this 'ridding the field of verbiage' became one of the central activities in modern American poetry. 'Cut and cut again wherever you write', William Carlos Williams was to suggest to his fellow poet Denise Levertov, '– while you leave by your art no trace of your cutting – and the final utterance will remain packed with what you have to say.'

And then there was the third 'rule' promulgated by Flint and expanded on by Pound when he declared: 'Rhythm MUST have meaning. It can't be merely a careless dash off, with no grip and no real hold to the words and sense, a tumty tum tumty tum tum ta.' The free verse of the Imagists was one aspect of their work to which contemporary critics took special exception. One reviewer, for example, claimed to see no difference between Amy Lowell's free verse and the prose of the British novelist George Meredith: to which Lowell replied, 'there is no difference. Whether a thing is written as prose or verse is immaterial.' Pound did not put things quite as categorically as Lowell. As he saw it, poetry should be at least *as well written as prose*', but there was a difference: because in poetry, he believed, words are infused with something more than their prose meaning. 'To break the iamb, that was the first heave', as he put it in his *Cantos*: the poet should first shake off the tyranny of predetermined verse forms. Having done this, his or her aim should be to produce movements and melodies intrinsic to the occasion: tough, sinuous, sharply etched rhythms that described the contours of an individual experience – a hidden but clearly audible music that captured the pace, poise and tone of the personal voice. In this sense, Imagism – and the many Modernist poets who pursued a necessary organic rhythm – took their cue not only from the innovations of an obvious experimentalist in free verse like Walt Whitman but from idiosyncratic rhythmists like Poe and Dickinson. And to this extent, the Imagist belief in a flexible verse form (which was in turn the symptom of a broader commitment to an open, unpremeditated structure) was to find expression both in the language experiments of e. e. cummings and Marianne Moore and in the less extreme but no less original musical shapes of Hart Crane.

Among the poems included in the 1915 Imagist anthology was 'Oread' by H. D. (1886–1961). Cited by Pound as the supreme example of an Imagist poem, it is besides a perfect illustration of what has been referred to as the 'accurate mystery' of H. D.'s work:

> Whirl up, sea –
> Whirl your pointed pines,
> Splash your great pines
> On our rocks,
> Hurl your green pine over us,
> Cover us with your pools of fir.

Perhaps the first thing that strikes a reader about a poem like this is the absence of certain familiar elements. There are no similes, no symbols, no generalized reflections or didacticism, no rhymes, no regular metre, no narrative. One might well ask what there is, then; and the answer would be a great deal. There is a pellucid clarity of diction, and a rhythm that is organic, intrinsic to the mood of the poem; there is a vivid economy of language, in which each word seems to have been carefully chiselled out of other contexts; and there is a subtle technique of intensification by repetition – no phrase is remarkable in itself, perhaps, but there is a sense of rapt incantation, an enthralled dwelling on particular cadences that gives a hermetic quality, a prophetic power, to the whole. It is the entire poem that is experienced, not a striking line, a felicitous comparison or an ingenious rhyme; the poem has become the unit of meaning and not the word, so each single word can remain stark, simple and unpretentious. In 'Oread', the image that constitutes the poem becomes not merely a medium for describing a sensation but the sensation itself. The sea *is* the pinewood, the pinewood *is* the sea, the wind surrounds and inhabits both; and the Greek mountain-nymph of the title comprehends and becomes identified with all three elements. There is a dynamic and unified complex, an ecstatic fusion of natural and human energies; and the image represents the point of fusion, 'the precise instant' (to quote a remark of Pound's) 'when a thing outward and objective transforms itself, or darts into a thing inward and subjective'.

'Oread' is typical of H. D.'s work in many ways. 'I would be lonely', she once admitted, while living at the heart of literary London, 'but for the intensity of my . . . inner life.' And this became the subject of her work, from the early Imagist verse to the later, more oracular poems: the secret existence that cast her, in the midst of company, into permanent but willing exile, the ecstatic sense of inhabiting a borderline between land and ocean, outer world and inner, time and eternity. The earlier work (of which, of course, 'Oread' is an example) is what she is, perhaps, most well known for. Here, greatly influenced by classical Greek poetry, H. D. speaks in a taut and suggestive manner, omitting everything that is inessential, structurally or emotionally unimportant. But the later poems, although less well known, are just as notable, since they represent a far more open, and frequently moving, attempt to discover what H. D. called 'the finite definition / of the infinite'. In making this attempt, she drew on Greek and Egyptian mythology, her own Moravian heritage, astrology, psychoanalysis and numerology, and then fashioned out of those diverse sources a poetry that is at once crystalline and prophetic: a tough, muscular and yet mystical verse to which she gave the title 'spiritual realism'.

All through her life, H. D. retained an intense belief in the religious possibilities of art – or, to be more exact, in the mystical nature of the creative process, the act of turning experience into words. 'Writing . . . trains one to a sort of yogi or majic [*sic*] power,' she insisted; 'it is a sort of contemplation, it is living on another plane.' In her eyes, poetry tended to become an equivalent of prayer. Her great war trilogy makes this especially clear. Written in London during the Second World War, the three books that comprise the trilogy – *The Walls Do Not Fall* (1944), *Tribute to the Angels* (1945) and *The Flowering of the Rod* (1946) – represent a search for 'ancient wisdom', the still, generative centre at the heart of the contemporary turbulence. *'We are voyagers,'* she declares:

> *discoverers*
> *of the not-known*
> *the unrecorded;*
> *we have no map;*
> *possibly we will reach heaven,*
> *haven.*

Firm in the belief that 'every concrete object / has abstract value', she attempts to fashion the mystery of personality, to recreate her own identity – in a sense, to write herself by reinventing her life in the process of remembering and rehearsing it. The activity hauntingly recalls Whitman's in 'Song of Myself', as, indeed, does H. D.'s firm denial of egocentricity: 'my mind (yours)', she insists, '/ your way of thought (mine)'. Each individual imagination has its 'intricate map', we are told, but each map charts the same 'eternal realities'; as in all great American epics, to sing and celebrate oneself is also to sing and celebrate others.

H. D.'s trilogy is an American epic, then, but it is also an Imagist epic: it does not, even in its form, represent a departure from her poetic beginnings. The reason is simple. Like Whitman, H. D. dispenses with narrative; far more than Whitman, however, she depends on what Pound called the ideogrammic method – which involves, essentially, a rapid association of images. Images are, in H. D.'s own words, 'superimposed on one another like a stack of photographic negatives': one image or perception leads into another and the reader's imagination is actively engaged, making the connections, discovering the point of intersection. Instead of a story, in which events occur in time, or a process of logical argument, there is a juxtaposing or overlaying of different images or impressions; and their interaction, the energy that passes between them, constitutes the 'argument' of the poem. In her trilogy, H. D. characteristically uses an image to describe this Imagistic technique – of the many colours which, at their point of intersecting, become one colour:

> And the point in the spectrum
> where all lights become one,
> is white and white is not no-colour
> as we were told as children
> but all-colour;
> where the flames mingle
> and the wings meet, where we gain
> the arc of perfection, we are satisfied, we are happy,
> we begin again . . .

In this sense, H. D.'s trilogy stands, along with Pound's *Cantos* and William Carlos Williams's long poem *Paterson*, as a major work of the Imagist genius and a Modernist epic.

As H. D.'s work suggests, Imagism – or, to be more exact, the impulses that brought Imagism into existence – could lead off in a number of different directions. One of these was Objectivism, associated in particular with William Carlos Williams, George Oppen, Louis Zukofsky and Charles Reznikoff. In February 1931, *Poetry* brought out a special Objectivist issue edited by Zukofsky, who specified as required reading Pound's *xxx Cantos*, Williams's *Spring and All*, Eliot's *The Waste Land* and 'Marina', e. e. cummings's *Is 5*, Marianne Moore's *Observations* and Wallace Stevens's *Harmonium*. A press was founded, financed by George Oppen, and in 1932 under the name of 'To Publishers' it brought out *An 'Objectivists' Anthology*. Edited by Zukofsky, it included work by Williams, Oppen, Reznikoff, Carl Rakosi (1903–) and Kenneth Rexroth. Pound was represented by his 'Yittischer Charleston' and Eliot by 'Marina'. Shortly after this, 'To Publishers' became the Objectivist Press, under the general editorship of Zukofsky and Williams. The main differences between Imagism and Objectivism were a greater emphasis on the formal structure of the poem, its physical contours, and a more intense interest in its musical properties, the aural dimension as compared with the visual. But it seems fairly obvious that Objectivism grew dialectically out of Imagism – not in opposition to it but in fruitful tension with it, not least because both movements shared the core Modernist beliefs: precision, exactitude, experience rendered rather than stated, the imperatives of organic rhythm and form.

The poet associated with Objectivism in whom the concern with music, sound, is at its strongest is Louis Zukofsky (1904–78). 'The order of all poetry', he insisted, 'is to approach a state of music wherein the ideas present themselves sensuously and intelligently and are of no predatory intention.' For him, and in his work, meaning is subordinated to sound. In his literary essays, for instance, he has spoken of his own poetry as a 'process of active literary omission', involving a conscious rejection of crude metaphor and symbolism and an exploitation of typography in order to demonstrate 'how the voice should sound'. The individual word becomes an object, its sound and look more important than its meaning, and the poem becomes a score: a score investigating the possibility that the order and movement of sound in a poem might themselves create a flux and reflux of emotions underlying the literal significance of the words. All of this may make Zukofsky's work seem intolerably abstract. In fact, as even a brief glance at *All: The Collected Shorter Poems* (1966) will testify, the opposite is true. A poem like 'Ferry', for instance, uses a vivid verbal structure to make the reader share the experience, feel the cold night, the water, the fog, the silence punctuated by the sound of the siren – as these lines from it suggest:

> Gleams, a green lamp
> In the fog:
> Murmur, in almost
> A dialogue
>
> Siren and signal
> Siren to signal

Other poems, such as 'During the Passaic Strike of 1926', can convey fierce political passion through the use of hissing sibilants and harsh gutturals, and others, like 'To my baby Paul', employ gentle labials and soft consonants melting into one another to suggest delicate but deep personal emotions. Many use typography as well as verbal pattern to recreate a particular moment: in 'Ferry', for instance, Zukofsky deploys the blank spaces between each verse paragraph to intimate, or suggest, the foggy emptiness within which the lights and sounds of the ferry are forced to operate – and, perhaps, the vacuum that we must all try to negotiate with our signs and signals.

Nor was Zukofsky just a composer of vignettes. In 1927, he began writing a long poem entitled 'A'. 'A' 1–12 was published in 1959, 'A' 13–21 in 1969, and 'A' 22 & 23 in 1977, shortly before his death. Zukofsky described the poem as an autobiography. 'The words are my life,' he explained: 'The form of the poem is organic – that is, involved in history and a life that has found by contrast to history something like perfection in the music of J. S. Bach.' The poem opens, in fact, with memories of a performance of Bach's St Matthew Passion; and then, with characteristic frugality of speech, precision of cadence and warmth of feeling, Zukofsky considers the injustices and inequalities of contemporary America, personal memories and affections, and aesthetic experience. Bach jostles alongside Henry Ford; the Chinese and Chinese poetry are celebrated for their clarity and brevity of utterance; and, despite the size of the work, there is the feeling that each word has been chosen, and each line chiselled, with scrupulous care. Zukofsky's aim, essentially, is to evolve something shapely, rhythmic and structured out of experience: something with its own intrinsic life, its own capacity for change and surprise. One critic has called it a continuous day-book. Perhaps it would be more accurate to call it an Objectivist epic: which, like other great epics in the American tradition, was and is destined never to end.

A poet who was perhaps more aware of growing out of the Imagist movement, as well as the Objectivist, was George Oppen (1908–84). 'What I felt I was doing was beginning from imagism as a position of honesty,' he said once. 'The first question at that time in poetry was simply the question of honesty, of sincerity.' 'At that time' was the time of writing the poems in his first book, *Discrete Series*, which was published in 1934. These early poems are remarkable for their attention to the word as the primary unit of meaning and to the relationships between words and images and things. They slow down the mind, concentrating it on words and things one at a time and so quicken it, eventually, into a new sense of the relations between them. A poem like 'Bad Times' is exemplary, in this respect:

> Bad times:
> The cars pass
> By the elevated posts
> And the movie sign.
> A man sells post-cards.

Oppen's language is stark, stripped ('What I couldn't write I scratched out,' he said; 'I wrote what I could be sure of'), but in its starkness it positively requires us to be alert. This is a *constructed* world, Oppen suggests, in which a word of great value ('elevated') has been so devalued as to be associated only with posts, and where 'cars pass' as if their mechanism had taken over the city completely. The only human activity involves dehumanization: a man is reduced to a marketing activity, less important than a 'post' (the repetition of the word is intentional) or a machine.

Oppen did not publish a second collection until 1962. During the intervening years, he was involved in political activity, becoming a member of the Communist Party in 1935. The second collection, *The Materials*, shows how Oppen gradually extended his 'position of honesty' from the instant of perception to sometimes complex processes of thought. The result is philosophical poetry that retains what Oppen himself has termed 'the imagist intensity of vision', that explores the sometimes problematical relationship between language, thought and things. 'Psalm', for instance, presents us with an intensely realized vision of deer in a forest that nevertheless subtly reminds us of their otherness:

> Their eyes
> Effortless, the soft lips
> Nuzzle and the alien small teeth
> Tear at the grass.

Nature is a stranger yet, here as it is in Dickinson; and this portrait of an 'alien small' world is juxtaposed with the words naming it:

> The small nouns
> Crying faith
> In this in which the wild deer
> Startle, and stare out.

'This in which' the deer occur is at once 'the small beauty of the forest' and the poem made out of 'small nouns': two utterly separate objects that are, all the same, vitally attached. Oppen's allegiance is to them both, to the language human beings have made and the world they have not made but share with other creatures; and it is to the relationship between the two – the bridge built between world and language, earth and 'household', out of seeing and speaking.

Two other, noteworthy poets who show the different directions in which the Imagist intensity of vision could lead are Charles Reznikoff (1894–1976) and Lorine Niedecker (1903–70). In Reznikoff's case, a general indebtedness to Pound was combined with an almost uninterrupted residence in New York to produce what has been called 'urban imagism': a poetry that alerts the reader to the loneliness, the small ironies and amusements, and the numbness of the immigrant in the urban tenement. In the best of his earlier, shorter poems, eventually collected together in *By the Waters of Manhattan: Selected Verse* (1962), Reznikoff refuses to moralize, the social comment is all the more powerful for being implicit. At some point in the 1950s, Reznikoff dedicated himself to a larger enterprise: a four-volume history of the United States between 1885 and 1915, written in free verse, and consisting entirely of the testimony, the cases Reznikoff had encountered in law books. He chose the period because he believed that a social and psychic crisis in the nation had occurred then; he was driven by the characteristically American assumption that every life is worth remembering, the testimony of every person is worth attending to in and for its own sake. The result is *Testimony* (1978–9), an American epic that draws its energy from its omnivorousness: the poet's refusal to exclude anything from his unselective eye, his attitude of wonder. Unlike Reznikoff, Niedecker was born and spent most of her life in rural surroundings, in the region of the lakes in Wisconsin. Like him, however, the sense of place has clearly and indelibly imprinted itself on her poetry. Her work, gathered together in *My Life by Water – Collected Poems 1936–68* (1970), communicates the vastness of American geography, the simple fact of wide open spaces and the feelings of loneliness and exile that fact can instil. Faced with that vastness, though, Niedecker herself looks back at it without flinching – with a steady, determined optimism issuing from the recognition that loneliness is not to be feared and is, in any case, never total. There is room for human intimacy, the pleasures and affections of family life, as the characteristically titled – and characteristically terse and idiomatic – 'You are my friend' illustrates:

> Remember my little granite pail?
> The handle of it was blue.
> Think what's got away in my life –
> Was enough to carry me thru.

If the work of Niedecker marks out one extreme to which the impulses expressed in Imagism could move, that of John Gould Fletcher (1886–1950) and Conrad Aiken (1889–1973) marks out another. One function of the image might be to plumb the depths and register the vagaries of the unconscious through the agency of figurative language. Fletcher clearly believed this. An associate of Pound and Lowell, he used an impressionistic free verse in his early years, in collections such as his best-known, *Irradiations: And and Spray* (1915), blending intoxicating colours with a prodigality of imagery in an attempt to capture the wanderings of his sensibility. In his later years, in volumes like *South Star* (1941), he turned back to being a regionalist and to more traditional forms. But this was not before, along with Lowell, he invented 'polyphonic prose' as an even more capacious medium than free verse, designed, like the stream-of-consciousness fiction of the time, to accommodate all the haphazard movements of the subconscious. Aiken, similarly, was convinced that poetry could and should be, as he put it, 'the vanguard of man's consciousness'. Profoundly influenced by Freud – who, he said, had reformulated 'that perennially fascinating problem of personal identity' for his time – he committed himself to what he termed a 'quest for the knowable'. 'Know thyself', Aiken argued, had always been 'the theme' of all significant intellectual activity. Now Freud had revealed how images, 'magic words', could supply access to that knowledge: opening up a road for 'the only religion that was any longer tenable or viable, a poetic compression of man's position in the universe, and of his potentialities . . . through self-knowledge and love'. Pursuing these aims, Aiken devised a poetic form that reflected his deep love of music: in which lines, words and images come together and separate with a gentle fluidity, like a stream following the poet's consciousness. The *Preludes*, published in two books (1931), represent one step in this direction. Another is represented by his most ambitious work, *The Divine Pilgrim*, which was not published until 1949 although its constituent poems were written between 1915 and 1925. In *The Divine Pilgrim*, as in his other poems, Aiken conducts no systematic quest, only a circuitously conducted inquiry: an inquiry that is not so much stated as demonstrated, alluded to in numerous, indirect ways. As in a tone-poem by Richard Strauss or Schoenberg, themes are offered that conflict, resolve themselves into harmony or disharmony. And, as in so many American poems, there is no ultimate conclusion. Our first duty, Aiken intimates, is to ask the question, 'Who am I?'; and that is our last duty as well.

Making it new in poetry

Of all the writers of this period, none revealed a greater commitment to the imperatives of poetic Modernism – a greater belief in the need, as he put it, to 'make it new' – than Ezra Pound (1885–1972). Pound's commitment to poetry was total: to poetry as a craft, as a moral and spiritual resource, and eventually as a means of salvaging culture, redeeming history. 'It is tremendously important that great poetry be written,' he declared once, 'it makes no jot of difference who writes it'; and this disinterested belief in the poem – a belief that, not coincidentally, he shared with his great American predecessor, Whitman – was proved by his dedicated support of other poets. 'Il miglior fabbro', Eliot called him, borrowing the phrase from Dante, 'the better artist', in recognition of Pound's help in transforming *The Waste Land* into the dense, allusive and elliptical poem that we have today. Pound was the great evangelist for poetry, and he was also the great assimilator: absorbing and, in the best sense, imitating the work of other imaginations so as to make it available for his own audiences. Starting from the premise that the state of art in a culture, and the state of poetry and language in particular, is a gauge or symptom of its health, he attempted to mediate the achievements of other, earlier periods – to offer the best that had been thought and said in the past as an example and agent of recovery for the present. This was not an antiquarian enterprise; Pound was not simply trying to write 'like' earlier poets, to borrow their idiom. His aim, rather, was to reclaim the *principles* implicit in the work of other people: principles that were expressed, and could only be expressed (for Pound was an Aristotelian, not a Platonist), in specific, material terms, according to the language

---

and conditions of an individual culture. 'Poetry is a sort of inspired mathematics,' Pound said, 'which gives us equations . . . for human emotions. If one has a mind which inclines to magic rather than science, one will prefer to speak of these equations as spells or incantations.' Human emotions, for Pound, remained the same, but the equations or spells used to uncover them altered with time and place. Each poet, in this sense, had to contrive his own mathematics or magic; no matter how much he might derive from others, he had ultimately to forge his own style – a voice that was more than just the sum of the myriad voices he echoed.

Pound's early poetry, in *A Lume Spento* (1908), *Personae* (1912) and *Exultations* (1912), is saturated in the kind of *fin-de-siècle* romanticism he was later to abjure. There are the familiar poetic subjects: songs in praise of a lady ('Praise of Ysolt', 'Ballatetta'), songs concerning the poet's craft ('Mesmerism', 'And Thus In Nineveh'), love and friendship ('The House of Splendour', 'The Altar'), death ('For E. McC.'), the transience of beauty and the permanence of art ('Na Audiart'). Not unrelated to these, there are some of the subjects that Pound was to make peculiarly his own: the pain of exile ('In Durance'), metamorphosis ('The Tree'), the 'delightful psychic experience', the ecstatic moment that is none the less perfect for being just that, a moment ('Erat Hora'). There are elaborate conceits, images that call attention to their own bravura, poetic inversions, self-conscious archaisms of word and phrasing. What saves these poems, however, is Pound's consummate sense of rhythm. From first to last, Pound was blessed with the gift of what he called 'melopoeia': 'wherein the words are charged, over and above their meaning, with some musical property, which directs the bearing or trend of that meaning'. Most of these early poems are written according to an established metrical pattern, and Pound turns the form into an instrument on which he can play his own music: an apparently inevitable medium for his own speaking or singing voice.

The other important aspect of this earlier poetry is Pound's use of antiquity. Many of these poems are imitations of earlier verse or adopt the voice of an earlier poet; and, even when this is not the case, Pound very often speaks from behind an assumed character, a mask. The reasons for this return us to the heart of his beliefs. Pound, after all, saw the poem as an objective verbal equation for an emotional, and basically incommunicable, experience. Imagism or Vorticism was, he felt, one way of finding such an equation; and the use of personae was another. The poet, he argued, cannot relate a delightful psychic experience by speaking out directly in the first person: he must 'screen himself' and speak indirectly through 'an impersonal and objective story'. The story, and in particular the stories of myth and earlier literature, can supply the modern poet with luminous details which he can arrange to adumbrate certain moods or perceptions of his own; they can provide him with the means not only of expressing his own ecstatic encounter with fundamental principles but also of relating that encounter to the common stock of human experience. A poem like 'The Seafarer' illustrates how Pound turned these ideas into action. A translation of an Anglo-Saxon poem, it does two things. First, it communicates a sense of the past in all its past-ness: the use of the Anglo-Saxon alliterative verse form, the stylistic tessellation, the gnomic phrasing excite a sense of strangeness, as if the narrator were calling to the reader across the chasms of history. But, secondly, it explores certain common human feelings that Pound himself experienced with peculiar intensity: feelings of exile, distance, loss, separation not only from the world of the 'Burgher' but from other, more comforting domesticities that can never be known to the poet-wanderer – feelings, too, of nostalgic stoicism that have little to do with the Christian elements in the original but have been highlighted by Pound, not least through the vigorous, muscular quality of the language. The eventual result of all this is a perfect example of what Pound called 'criticism in new composition'. Pound captures here something of what he termed the 'permanent basis in humanity': the common principles, the moral order that survives through the flux of experience. At the same time, however, he honours the thing as it was: the particular historical shapes, the very specific human and physical ways in which such forms necessarily manifest themselves.

'The Seafarer' appeared in *Ripostes* published in 1912; and, apart from Pound's subtle use of antiquity, this collection is remarkable because it reveals the poet's discarding of metrically regular unrhymed verse in favour of free verse. A poem like 'The Return' shows this; and it also illustrates Pound's growing ability to write pieces that are not necessarily 'about' anything in any traditional sense but are, rather, equations for a mood or an emotion. As Pound's work grew in authority, he retained this understanding of the possibilities of rhythm and image but coupled it with a growing distinctiveness of voice and a greater alertness to the problems of modern culture. A poem like 'The Garden', for instance, published in *Lustra* (1916), shows Pound becoming distinctly 'modern', using unromantic similes drawn from contemporary life. More to the point, it shows him developing his own language: a combination of the mandarin and the demotic, the passionate, the satirical and the vividly self-critical that serves to express both his own deracination and the precarious, polyglot character of the society through which he moves.

So, in effect, Pound gradually added to his gift of 'melopoeia' the two other necessary constituents of good poetry, as he saw it: 'phanopoeia', which he described as 'a casting of images upon the visual imagination', and 'logopoeia', 'the dance of the intellect among words'. As far as 'phanopoeia' is concerned, Pound was helped not only by his formulation of 'do's' and 'dont's' for Imagists but also by his interest in Japanese and Chinese poetry. His haiku 'In a Station of the Metro' illustrates the Japanese influence and how it helped Pound pursue brevity and imagistic indirection. And the poems collected in *Cathay* (1915) reveal the importance of Chinese verse for him. They were written after he had read the work of a distinguished Chinese scholar, Ernest Fenollosa. Fenollosa pointed out that the Chinese language is made up of characters, each simple character representing a 'particular', an image. Each complex character is then made by combining simple characters, and, in this sense, Chinese remains anchored in concrete, perceptual reality; it can never lose itself in vague abstraction. Not surprisingly, Pound with his hatred of abstract discourse jumped at this; and, without knowing a word of the language, he began working on a set of versions from the Chinese which, as

Eliot has said, have made him 'the inventor of Chinese poetry for our time'. These are poems remarkable for their utter limpidity of diction, the parallelism of line and rhythm, and the technique of intensification by repetition whereby no phrase or image is memorable in itself but instead the sad, slow dwelling on a dying cadence makes for the memorableness of mood. The emotion generated by each piece is a matter of voice rather than statement. What each says, its drama, is a product of movement and metaphor; typically of Pound, the medium of a poem *is* its meaning.

Taken together, the poems in *Cathay* are not just a reinvention of a particular language and culture, however, and more than new chapters in the story of Imagism. Their pervasive themes are loneliness, loss, exile: absence from home and from loved ones through some accident, it may be, from human choice or historical necessity. Which is as much to say that the voice of 'The Seafarer' is recalled, albeit in a different key; although Pound himself hardly begins to acknowledge it, these pieces offer further impersonal and objective stories through which the poet can express his feelings of uprootedness and isolation. In its own quiet way, each voice in *Cathay* is a mask, a persona: just as, for that matter, the multiple voices in another, very different poem are – *Hugh Selwyn Mauberley*, published in 1920. *Mauberley* has been variously described as Pound's departing address to England and his farewell to aestheticism. But it could be more accurately described as a packed, allusive and notably modernistic look both at his own plight and at the plight of modern culture. In effect, the dance of the intellect in *Mauberley* is at once lively and complicated. Writing in the aftermath of the Great War (which is very much a presence in the poem), Pound analyses the plight of modern society in and through an investigation of the plight of its writers: who are tempted, he suggests, either to give in to society's claims, offering it 'an image / Of its accelerated grimace', or to withdraw from it completely into 'the obscure reveries / Of the inward gaze'. Going back into the previous century, focusing powerfully on recent symptoms of cultural decline, moving like quicksilver between different personae and poetic forms, he offers us the poetic equivalent of Henry Adams's *Education*: an ironic, self-critical, third-person account of a multiple, modern personality that is also a radical dissection of the miscellaneousness of modern culture – its restlessness, its variety and its lack of a centre. There are no answers in *Mauberley*, except in the sense that the poem itself is an answer, suggesting a way out from the constricting alternatives of surrender or solipsism, a mask other than those of the protagonist or aesthete. Instead, the reader is offered a kaleidoscopic series of questions: a creative analysis that follows Pound's customary route from the state of the language to the state of the culture.

In its own way, this route is also the route of the *Cantos*, which Pound began very early in his career, since before the Vorticist period (the first four appeared in *Quia Pauper Amavi* [1919]), and was still writing shortly before his death (*The Cantos of Ezra Pound (I–CXVII)* was published in 1970). Only here the route is a far more complex and labyrinthine one, because Pound is openly concerned not just with contemporary cultural decay but with the possible sources of cultural renewal. The *Cantos* are Pound's epic. Following in the tradition of Whitman, he attempts to tell the 'tale of the tribe' in and through the story of an epic hero or wanderer who is, first and last, the poet himself. In doing so, however, his poetic imagination ranges a good deal further than Whitman's, to embrace multifarious examples of humanity, multiple ideas of order. There is a quest at the basis of the *Cantos* which, as Pound suggests from time to time, can be likened to Odysseus's ten-year quest in search of his home. The difference – and it is a crucial one – is that this quest is unending, involving as it does the human being's perpetual search for civilization, his or her constant attempts to rediscover the springs of skill or delight. The content of the *Cantos* stretches out far and wide, in pursuit of appropriate models of language, thought and conduct, taking in, among many others, the Provençal and early Italian poets, founders of modes of government and codes of behaviour like Confucius and Jefferson, and some of the examples of primitive religious feeling recorded in Ovid's *Metamorphoses*. And as it does so, Pound constantly reminds us of his Imagist background, just as H. D. does in *Trilogy*: by relying not on an argument or a narrative in the traditional sense but on a series of instances and images that take fire from their placing – that quicken the reader's mind into a new sense of awareness by virtue of rhythm, phrasing and juxtaposition.

It is not difficult to see how the *Cantos* grew out of Pound's earlier work. The imagistic form of discourse, the linking of ethics, politics and aesthetics, the found-ing of correct principles on correct language, and, not least, the belief that poetry can offer a verbal equation for those moments when, metaphorically at least, the human encounters the divine: all these are as basic to his poetic beginnings as they are to the tale of his tribe. Nor is it difficult to see the connections with American epic: a language experiment more radical than anything Whitman ever dreamed of, the *Cantos* set within their open-ended structure a poet who is at once a repre-sentative person, a prince and a pedagogue, a voyager and a visionary, who tells us about good citizenship and offers us its appropriately heroic model. Whether the *Cantos* are a great single poem or a series of magnificent fragments is open to debate. Pound himself seems to have been undecided: 'I am not a demigod / I cannot make it cohere,' he admitted in Canto CXVI, but then added, 'it coheres all right / even if my notes do not cohere.' How much the *Cantos* are damaged by Pound's espousal of fascism, which led him to be arrested at the close of the Second World War (he was declared unfit to stand trial on the grounds of insan-ity): that, too, is a deeply serious question. What is indisputable is that, if there is coherence, it is of a different kind than that to be found in traditional epics, and that, even if there is not – and even if Pound held some opinions that were nothing short of obscene – there is still poetry here that is the fruit of a lifetime's experi-ence, and lines that are among the finest in the language.

Pound was an expatriate. He left the United States in 1908 and, apart from the thirteen years he was in confinement after being declared insane, he spent most of his life in England, France and Italy. Despite that, he remained a definitively American poet. Responding to history in a self-evidently personal and eclectic way, he insisted, like so many American writers on inventing a tradition for himself – a mythology that was his alone, a personal 'Kulchur' – out of the wealth of historical possibilities available to him. The case of T. S. Eliot (1888–1965) is more complex, and raises the whole question of literary nationalism and nationality – what it means to call a writer American or British or whatever, especially at times of increasing internationalism in art or communication or modes of production. Born in St Louis, Missouri, Eliot was descended on both sides of his family from early English settlers in New England. Andrew Eliot emigrated from the village of East Coker in 1667, and T. S. Eliot's maternal ancestor Isaac Stevens was one of the original settlers in the Massachusetts Bay Colony in 1630. The memory of that place from which the Eliot family had departed, over two hundred years before the poet's birth, was to inform 'East Coker' (1940), the second of the *Four Quartets* (1943): where Eliot, realizing that 'In the beginning is my end', returns in imagination to the home of his ancestors. It was natural that a writer for whom the immanence of the past in the present was an obsessive theme should register his English and American Puritan origins in his lines and his consciousness; and equally natural, perhaps, that his Midwestern upbringing should appear so often, though through a glass darkly, in his work. 'A writer's art must be racial,' Eliot wrote in 1917, '– which means, in plain words, that it must be based on the accumulated sensations of the first twenty-one years.' And what we know of his childhood shows that it became the source of insistent images in his poetry. Close to the family house in St Louis, for instance, was a school founded by Eliot's grandfather and attended by his sisters, and he preserved a vivid memory of it throughout his life. It had 'a high brick wall', he later recalled, and 'concealed our back garden from the schoolyard'; from the garden he could listen to the children playing in the yard, and after school hours he could play in the empty schoolyard himself and even venture into the school. In this, we have the source for the laughter of hidden children that recurs in Eliot's poetry. In 'Burnt Norton' (1935), the first of the *Four Quartets*, for example, there are these lines: 'Go said the bird, for the leaves were full of children, / Hidden excitedly, containing laughter.' As one critic has put it, 'this . . . symbol of the laughter . . . of children heard playing was not only a symbol of the happiness that the childless Eliot was never to know, but a memory of childish loneliness, hearing the "others" . . . and longing to be "one of them"'.

When Eliot was just nine, his father built a summer home for the family by the sea at Gloucester, Massachusetts; and here the boy was to spend his summer vacations. So another source of vivid imagery and mythic allusion was initiated. Memories of the sea pervade his poetry. In *Ash Wednesday* (1936), for instance, the reader is offered a glimpse 'from the wide window toward the granite shore' of 'The white sails' that 'still fly seaward, seaward flying / Unbroken wings'; while Eliot's expertise at sailing, acquired during these summer visits, is invoked in the brief, memorable reference, towards the end of *The Waste Land* (1920), to the boat that 'responded / Gaily, to the hand expert with sail and oar'. Mingled imagery of fog and water was, in any case, something that Eliot could associate with his childhood homeplace for the spring, autumn and winter months. St Louis itself, with its mists and 'the sunsets and the dooryards and the sprinkled streets', seems to be the setting for 'The Love Song of J. Alfred Prufrock' (1915). And Eliot's recollections of the 'strong brown god' of the Mississippi River, which flows by the city, were to be captured in the third of the *Four Quartets*, 'The Dry Salvages' (1942). 'I think I was fortunate to have been born here', Eliot declared of St Louis, 'rather than in Boston, or New York, or London.' Certainly, his birthplace added to the sense of the complexity of his fate, the mixed nature of his background: particularly since he himself tended to see St Louis not so much as a Midwestern town as a Southern one. 'Some day I want to write an essay about the point of view of an American who wasn't an American,' he said in 1928, 'and who . . . felt himself to be more a Frenchman than an American and more an Englishman than a Frenchman and yet felt that the U.S.A. up to a hundred years ago was a family extension.'

Southerner, Northerner – and, surely, Midwesterner – by birth and background, Eliot transmogrified himself into 'a Frenchman' and 'an Englishman' by a subtle and yet strenuous act of will. After a thorough reading of poets like Jules Laforgue, Arthur Rimbaud and Paul Verlaine, and a year studying at the Sorbonne, he succeeded in assimilating the achievements of French Symbolism into English-speaking poetry. 'Prufrock', for example, his first major poem, employs the Laforgian dramatic monologue, unfolding the fragmentary consciousness of its narrator (whose name, it turns out, is borrowed from a firm of furniture wholesalers in St Louis) in a way that locates him as a name plus a voice rather than as a character. Like so many poems derived from the Symbolist experience, the poem offers us not a verifiable description of the world, nor the depiction of a 'real' character, but a zone of consciousness which each of us, as readers, has to pass through for himself or herself. The scene is, perhaps, initially American but it, and the narrator who dissolves into it, are presented in those radically disintegrative, dream-like terms that characterize many of the best French poets of the late nineteenth century. The name and voice are, in this sense, unlocated: the 'one-night cheap hotels / And sawdust restaurants' that are recalled could be part of any unreal city, Paris or London as much as (or perhaps even more than) St Louis.

After his stay in Paris, from which he returned 'perceptibly Europeanised' according to Conrad Aiken, Eliot spent three more years in the United States before embarking for England in the summer of 1914. Apart from a brief trip back a year later, he did not revisit the United States until 1932; and, although Eliot was to continue these visits almost annually from the late 1940s until his death in 1965, he came to look on England as his home. This was confirmed in 1927 when, in the same year that he announced his conversion to Anglo-Catholicism, Eliot became a British citizen. Gradually, he assimilated a particular concept of the English tradition: his dress, speech and manners all became impeccably English, although, if anything, excessive in their perfection. He was, he declared, 'classicist in literature, royalist in politics, and anglo-catholic in religion'. Almost from the beginning, he had been convinced of the necessity of a literary tradition: something that, as he put it in his essay 'Tradition and the Individual Talent' (1934), 'compels a man to write not merely with his own generation in his bones, but with a feeling that the whole of literature of Europe from Homer . . . has a simultaneous existence and composes a simultaneous order'. Slowly, this idea of a specifically literary tradition enlarged so as to acquire social, political and theological implications. The individual was to shuffle off the constraints of the self, was to find perfect freedom in service to his culture, just as the poet, he had once said, was to 'escape from personality' in obedience to the demands of an impersonal art. How Eliot himself did this, as individual and poet, is the story of his career. He moved from *The Waste Land*, where he uses a cunning mixture of Symbolist, Imagist and dramatic strategies to expose the rootless, sterile nature of his own immediate culture, through the spiritual voyagings of *Ash Wednesday* to the more achieved, if still tentative, spiritual wisdom of the *Four Quartets*. And in the course of this career he raised, in a particularly sharp way, the problem of his and others' literary nationalism.

The problem can be stated simply, although as with most literary expatriates the simplicity of the statement conceals a host of difficulties. Eliot 'became' an Englishman and an English poet: but he did so in a fashion that is characteristically American, that betrays his origins in the New World. His earlier poetry demonstrates that concern with the isolated self, the lonely 'I' which is perhaps *the* predominant theme in American writing. Only it demonstrates it in what was to become known as a distinctively Eliotic way: refracted through a fragmented persona, the self being dissolved into a series of objective correlatives. At its most obvious – in, for example, the opening line of 'Prufrock', 'Let us go then, you and I' – 'I' becomes 'you and I' to dramatize the narcissism of isolation; and the narcissistic ego translates the blank stare of reality into, alternatively, a mirror of its own concerns or a threat to its purity, or even its existence.

And in a very real sense, *The Waste Land* continues this lonely drama of the self. Of course, any genuinely imaginative reading of Eliot's most famous poem is likely to yield larger cultural inferences. Like the *Cantos*, *The Waste Land* uses a form of the ideogrammic method, dense patterns of imagery and a disjunctive narrative sequence, a radical juxtaposition of different perspectives and languages, to solicit an active response, a collaboration in the creation of meanings; and the meanings so created will probably include commentary on the decay of contemporary civilization. It is, however, worth recording Eliot's own comment here. 'To me,' he declared of *The Waste Land*, 'it was only the relief of a personal and wholly insignificant grouse against life; it is just a piece of rhythmic grumbling.' 'I wrote *The Waste Land* simply to relieve my own feelings,' Eliot said elsewhere; and there can be little doubt that a sense of sterility is so powerful in the poem precisely because its ultimate source is personal. At its inception, *The Waste Land* was a poem of the lonely self: a cry from the heart of a man who had been haunted since childhood by the 'hidden laughter of children', whose own marriage was childless, and who, at the time of writing, was acutely troubled by feelings of sexual unhappiness. Characteristically, Eliot then transformed this cry into a dramatic, imagistic, objective work of art that each reader could and still can experience and interpret according to his or her own terms of reference, personal *and* cultural.

The search for otherness, some order that denies and disciplines the lonely self that cries out in *The Waste Land*, is at the heart of Eliot's later poetry. Consider, for instance, these lines from *Ash Wednesday*:

> And the weak spirit quickens to rebel
> For the bent golden-rod and the lost sea smell
> Quickens to recover
> The cry of quail and the whirling plover . . .
> And the blind eye creates
> The empty forms between the ivory gates
> And smell renews the salt savour of the sandy earth

This passage occurs towards the end of the poem, when the narrator has come to believe what he has only sensed up until then: that the only way he can redeem himself is to surrender himself, that the only means of finding his being is to lose it. Only the blind eye sees the true forms of liberation, the intimation is; only the spirit that rebels against its own devouring inwardness can begin to tap the sources of salvation and creativity. There is repetition in these lines, and parallelism, of a kind that hauntingly recalls Whitman, and a sense of natural bounty, the fruits of earth, sea and sky, that is reminiscent of both Whitman and many other American poets. But the formal echoes of these other poets only emphasize the utter difference of tone and sensibility. If anything, the Whitman style is adopted here in order to deny the cogency and truth of all that Whitman said; memories of the American Adamic mode are evoked only so as to be slyly mocked and rejected.

As his career developed, Eliot grew sufficiently sure of his grounding in another, and established, tradition to be able to measure himself openly against the Whitman line. In these lines from 'East Coker', for instance, the opposition is scarcely veiled at all. There is not only an echo of Whitman's phrasing but also a recall of the earlier poet's metrical arrangement of syntax – and both seem to be there openly so as to establish moral, emotional and imaginative distance:

> You say I am repeating
> Something I have said before. I shall say it again.
> Shall I say it again? In order to arrive there,
> To arrive where you are, to get from where you are not,
> You must go by a way wherein there is no ecstasy.
> In order to arrive at what you do not know
> You must go by a way which is the way of ignorance.
> In order to possess what you do not possess
> You must go by the way of dispossession.
> In order to arrive at what you are not
> You must go through the way in which you are not.

Whereas Whitman would absorb everything into the image of himself, Eliot organizes everything – and denies the presence, or at least knowledge, of himself – so as to catch a hint, or a glimpse, of otherness. The 'I' in this passage is not, as it is in Whitman and so much American writing, the active and reactive core of the poem, its vital centre and source of creative energy. It is, at its best, a linguistic convenience, a way of locating the initial source of these perceptions and, at worst, a kind of spiritual undertow that those following the 'way of dispossession' must resist. Here, a wholly personal style takes on a grand impersonality: the language and line of Whitman are used against themselves. And here, too, the illusion of personality is raised for a moment only to be dismissed as just that, an illusion: the words 'you' and 'I' become floating signifiers, which can never be anchored in any meaningful, moral reality.

Whitman does not represent all of American poetry, of course. And the principle of definition by rejection has to be acknowledged at some point: writers, like other people, are defined by the things they reject (or try to reject) as much as by anything else – and, in this sense, Americanism seems to have been as important to Eliot as, say, Catholicism was to James Joyce. Still, the basic point remains the same: Eliot was and was not an American writer precisely because the confluence of cultures required him, he believed, to make a deliberate choice. He was an American by birth and an Englishman by force of will. Brought up in St Louis, where the South meets the Midwest, deeply affected by the introspective inheritance of New England, he became a European, and more specifically an English, poet. Yet, while doing all this, he retained the marks of his American upbringing, as he had to, on his imagination and memory. Commonly identified with the British tradition as he is now, all he wrote can nevertheless be seen in terms of a fierce, irreconcilable conflict with his birthplace – and what he believed were the limited terms of American culture. There is no easy definition of Eliot, as there cannot be of any writers of clearly mixed nationality like him. But not just of such writers: others, many of whom never even left their native shores, have found themselves caught in the borderlands between several homes and histories, required to make sense of the various traditions they have inherited. Eliot was and is maybe unusual only to the extent that, in crossing such cultural boundaries with such calculation and determination, he helps to emphasize a common experience. To be an American has always been a complex fate. And to be an American writer has, nearly always, been a matter of living in the encounter between different cultures, trying to dramatize and resolve the differences. Eliot simply experienced difference in a more knowing fashion than most; and, knowing this as a difference of nationalisms, felt compelled to alter allegiance – to reshape his national identity. Reversing the common process by which so many have made themselves Americans and American writers, Eliot also repeated or reflected a dominant strain in American writing – the intimation of duality of consciousness, a mix of cultures. Curiously, Eliot was never more of an American than when he was reinventing himself as an Englishman – and never more of an American writer than when he took that reinvention as his shaping narrative, his story.

Not that William Carlos Williams (1883–1963) would have agreed. When *The Waste Land* was first published, Williams recalled in his *Autobiography* (1951),

'I felt that it had set me back twenty years'. 'I'm sure it did,' he added. 'Critically, Eliot returned us to the classroom just at the moment when I felt we were on the point of an escape to . . . a new art form . . . rooted in the locality which should give it fruit.' What Williams was disconcerted by was Eliot's academicism: his commitment to a complexly allusive, highly wrought poetics that dismissed the pleasures of the local, the pressures of the particular and personal. Allied to this, what frightened Williams was what he saw as Eliot's fiercely articulated yearning for otherness: for more traditional forms of culture, and stricter, more prescriptive codes of being, than anything his American inheritance could supply. Formally and intellectually, Williams believed, *The Waste Land* implied a rejection of its creator's birthplace. Inscribed in its subtext was a denial of the New World, both as a fact and as a possibility, an imaginative space. And, for him, this was anathema. Born in Rutherford, New Jersey, he spent time elsewhere in the United States and in Europe, studying medicine and meeting poets, but he eventually returned to his birthplace to work as a doctor there. And that movement back, not just to America but to one special American locality, expresses his allegiances. For Williams was, above all, a poet of the local, concerned with the specifics of a specific place. In Williams's work, there are, to quote a famous injunction of his, 'no ideas but in things'. Attention is concentrated on the individual object or emotion or event, caught at a particular moment in time and a particular point in space. The object does not stand for anything; it is not a symbol, nor is there even a great deal of figurative language. Instead, the reader is asked to attend to the thing in itself: its *haecceity* or 'this-ness' – what makes the object or moment *this* and no other. Our yearning towards the abstract, what might be, is quietly checked in Williams's poems; and, instead, we are reminded of the homely beauty of the actual, what *is*.

Williams, then, is the great populist in American poetry, for whom the world is a democracy of objects. There are no hierarchies, no one thing is more important than another, each is to be valued for itself. And there are no allegories: no one thing is to be used as a tool, a vehicle to refer to another thing – it does not mean, it simply exists. Whether it is a woman lamenting the loss of her husband as in 'The Widow's Lament in Springtime' (1921), a natural object as in 'Sea-Trout and Butterfish' (1917), a strange moment of happiness as in 'The Revelation' (1917), a street scene as in 'Proletarian Portrait' (1917), or an instance of intimacy as in 'This Is Just To Say' (1934), whatever it may be, Williams's purpose remains the same: to emphasize or identify with the thing, not just to describe it but to imitate it in words, to allow it to express itself, to give it verbal shape, a voice. And the immediate consequence of this is, not surprisingly, a commitment to free verse: rhythms that follow the shape of the object and that respond to the exigencies of a specific occasion. 'I must tell you,' begins Williams in 'Young Sycamore' (1934): the address is characteristically urgent and intimate, as if the poet were speaking under the pressure of immediate experience. And, having grabbed our attention, he then directs it to the object, the young sycamore of the title, whose contours are caught in the curve, pitch and sway of the free verse line. The poem, like so much of Williams's poetry, is packed with tactile references: in a sense, the poet is trying to 'touch' the tree and make us touch it – to achieve contact (an important word for Williams) and, for a moment, live the life of another thing. And similarly, typically, it is packed with verbs and verbals. Williams, like Whitman, sees life as process, constant motion. As in a painting by Van Gogh, there is a sense of the tree as animate life, thrusting towards the sky and continuing to grow long after the artist's imitation of it is finished. Not that, in principle, it is ever definitively finished. Many of Williams's poems do not really end, they stop short without a full stop or even any punctuation mark. Sometimes, as in 'Young Sycamore', the sentence that constitutes the poem is also left syntactically incomplete. What the reader is left with, as a result, is a sense of possibility; as in a poem by Whitman or Dickinson, there is, finally, the quiet reminder that everything must remain open, in a world governed by change.

'The poem is made of things – on a field,' declared Williams. A statement like this helps explain his patience and care with language. There is reverence for the individuality of words in his poems, as well as of objects. And it alerts us to the intense *inner* activity of his verse. Like a series of particles on a magnetic field, the words in Williams's poems insist on their status as separate entities, engaged in an active relationship with their context. Individualism of word, object and person: it is a very American concept, and Williams was, in fact, among the most self-consciously American of modern poets. This was not a matter of narrow nationalism. It was simply because of his firm belief in the particular and local. 'Place is the only reality,' he insisted: 'the true core of the individual. We live in one place at one time, but . . . only if we make ourselves sufficiently aware of it, do we join with others in other places.' To be an individualist meant, for Williams, to attend to one's individual locality: not to turn away from even its most alienating or inhibiting features but to try to understand and achieve communion with it. The aim, Williams argued, was not to 'run out – / after the rabbits' as Pound and Eliot did, deserting American nature in search of European culture. It was to stay as and where one was, as Poe and Whitman had: to 'return to the ground' in order truly to know the 'new locality' of America, the particulars of the here and now – which, in Williams's own case, meant his hometown of Rutherford, New Jersey.

There was a potentially debilitating side to this approach to poetry, of which Williams himself was well aware. Poems might resolve themselves into a series of isolated instances, fragments that could not develop beyond the pressure of the immediate moment nor comment beyond the demands of the singular experience. One should not exaggerate this danger, of course. Even a poem written during Williams's 'Objectivist period' like 'Young Sycamore' is hardly imprisoned in its occasion; and it is shaped by feelings of tenderness and generosity that suggest an appropriate stance towards reality. Nevertheless, Williams clearly did begin to feel that he wanted more opportunity to comment and a chance, too, to develop his poems beyond the moment, eliciting and perhaps quietly stating principles that had only been implicit in the earlier work. Sometimes, in his later poetry, the desire to comment on issues is just that, comment. 'Asphodel, That Greeny Flower'

(1955) illustrates this. Addressed to the poet's wife, it weaves a lyric meditation out of the flower of its title: a meditation on love, empathy and memory and on the human being's destructive and creative capacities – 'the bomb' and the 'grace of the imagination'. Certainly, the bright, particular asphodel supplies the occasion for all this: the poet never strays very far from it, or from the sphere of domestic affection. But there is a degree of generalization springing from the occasion, and the experience of affection, that the younger Williams would probably never have allowed himself:

> What power has love but forgiveness?
>   In other words
>   by its intervention
>   what has been done
>   can be undone.

There are other ways in which these later poems begin to comment and expand, though. One, also illustrated by 'Asphodel, That Greeny Flower', or, for that matter, by the opening poem in *Spring and All* (1923), 'By the road to the contagious hospital', is symbolism, or something very close to it. The poet concentrates upon a particular thing – a flower or, in the case of the *Spring and All* poem, a day in early spring – and by the sheer intensity of his concentration, the degree of imaginative responsiveness he brings to bear, that thing begins to assume additional meanings, new dimensions. By the end of 'By the road to the contagious hospital', for example, the poet and reader are still gazing at something specific and mundane: the 'waste of broad, muddy fields' that Williams saw on his way to work at the hospital. The descriptive detail is such, however, that many other things have been suggested: the babies in the hospital wards who, like plants, 'enter the new world naked / cold, uncertain of all', the quickening of the individual imagination ('One by one objects are defined – / It quickens: clarity, outline of leaf'), the revival of all life, material and moral, caught up in the 'contagion' of spring. 'That is the poet's business,' Williams insisted; 'Not to talk in vague categories but to write particularly, as a physician works upon a patient, upon the thing before him, in the particular to discover the universal.' The particularity is still there in such poems, as it was in earlier work, but the universality is just a little less implicit, a fraction closer to the surface. It is a small difference, perhaps, but a significant one.

The third and probably the crucial way in which Williams allowed his later poetry to expand had to do with his growing concern with structure. 'It is a design', concludes 'The Orchestra', published in *The Desert Music* (1954), and that precisely is what many of the later poems are. They are, in the first instance, aural designs that permit radical variations of rhythm within coherent and often quite complex musical patterns and, in the second, imaginative designs, verbal tapestries or mosaics that allow within their framework for significant combinations of detail. As far as imaginative design is concerned, the exemplary instance is Williams's epic poem *Paterson*. Like so many American epics, *Paterson* is unfinished: Book One was published in 1946, and Williams was still working on Book Six at the time of his death in 1963. Long before he died, though, Williams had anticipated this. There would never be an end to the poem, he explained, because it had to remain open to the world of growth and change. This was something his epic shared with all his work, and so too was its general approach; for, in its own way, *Paterson* is as much concerned with a reverent investigation of the particular as Williams's other poems are. The basic particulars in this case are Paterson the town, an imaginative space or place not unrelated to Rutherford, New Jersey, and Paterson the man who is, like other protagonists in American epic, at once the poet himself and all people, all democratic individualists. The two identities of Paterson are, in any case, related, since from the very beginning of his career Williams had insisted that personality was inextricable from place – that the human being and his or her activities were 'an extension of nature's processes . . . transfused with the same forces which transfuse the earth'. 'A man himself is a city,' declared Williams in his 'Author's Note' to the poem, 'beginning, seeking, achieving and concluding his life in ways which the various aspects of a city may embody – if imaginatively conceived.' To descend into locality, in this case Paterson, was consequently also to descend into character; to investigate the city, with the help of the imagination, was necessarily to investigate the man.

The notion of 'design', however, is not so much a matter of subject as of form, the terms in which this investigation is conducted. 'To make a start, / out of particulars,' *Paterson* begins:

> and make them general, rolling
> up the sum . . .
>   . . . rolling up out of chaos,
> a nine months' wonder, the city
> the man, an identity . . .
> Rolling up, rolling up heavy with
> numbers.

In his later years, Williams was attracted by the example of the Bayeux tapestry and the paintings of Pieter Brueghel, because in such works, he felt, great mosaics of life were constructed out of a multitude of cherished particulars. *Paterson*, as he saw it, was to be a verbal equivalent of such visual adventures. During the course of his epic, Williams uses verse, prose, drama, dialogue, excerpts from books, letters, interviews, anecdotes, history and fable. Every experience recorded, every event or person recreated, is studied closely, permitted the dignity of close attention. Yet out of this conglomerate of individual moments and objects, Williams manages to fashion a total pattern of meaning, a vision of life that draws its energy and its coherence from the poet's reverence for simple things, the pleasures, pains and the dreams of ordinary people. 'This is a POEM!' Williams insists cheerfully at one point in Book Four. *Paterson* is that, although it should perhaps be added that it is a poem set firmly within the twin traditions of American epic and Imagist method. 'Unless there is / a new mind there cannot be a new line,' says Williams elsewhere, in Book Two, 'the old will go on / repeating itself with recurring deadliness.' *Paterson* is a testament to that, as well: Williams's lifelong belief in the necessity of personal experiment. Perhaps the final emphasis, though, should be on something else characteristic of the poet that this great personal epic of his reveals: which is, quite simply, his sympathy, his capacity for imaginative understanding. More than any other American poet of the twentieth century, Williams was possessed of what Keats called 'negative capability', the ability to bridge the gap between the perceiving subject and the perceived object. For some reason, he was able to feel a sense of kinship with any particular thing, to appreciate and to imitate its particularity: which makes him, after his great predecessor Whitman, the finest American celebrant of the democratic impulse.

Of Wallace Stevens (1879–1955) Williams once wrote: 'He was the well-dressed one, diffident about letting his hair down. Precise when we were sloppy. But we all knew, liked, admired him. He really was felt to be part of the gang.' The 'gang' included Marianne Moore and e. e. cummings; and, after graduating from Harvard, Stevens moved to New York City and got to know them well. As Williams indicates, however, Stevens was different. Born in Pennsylvania, his father was a lawyer; he first studied and then practised law in New York; then, in 1916, he moved to Connecticut to work for the Hartford Accident and Indemnity Company, becoming vice-president of the company in 1934. He was a lawyer, a successful businessman, but he was also a poet. Four of his poems appeared in *Poetry* as early as 1914. His first collection, *Harmonium*, was published in 1923; and although its relative lack of success discouraged Stevens from further publication for some time, twelve years later a second collection, *Ideas of Order*, did appear. This was quickly followed by a succession of volumes, among them *The Man With the Blue Guitar and Other Poems* (1937), *Notes Toward a Supreme Fiction* (1942) and *Esthétique du Mal* (1944); a *Collected Poems* was published in 1954 and *Opus Posthumous* two years after his death. What the poems collected in these volumes offer is a series of meditations on the nature of reality, its relationship to human knowledge, human need, human belief and human art. Like many great artists in different fields during the earlier twentieth century – like Joyce, for instance, or Picasso or Stravinsky – Stevens was fascinated by the interplay between the mind and the world, particularly as that interplay was expressed and explored in the different languages of literature, music and the visual arts. He was obsessed with what he called, in 'The Idea of Order at Key West' (1935), the 'blessed rage for order': the human desire for form and a sense of meaning recovered, however temporarily, from the essential chaos of life. And he made that, the struggle between word and world, mind and its surroundings, the irrepressible search for belief and the irreducible concrete reality of things, the source, subject and inspiration of his work.

Another way of putting this is to say that Stevens believed, as did the great Romantic poets, in the power of the imagination. Reality, Stevens felt, is not something given to us, which our minds receive passively, but is on the contrary something made, the product of an interchange between our minds and our given circumstances. Our consciousnesses are not simply blank pieces of paper on which the world writes its messages, not just mirrors that reflect our environment; rather, they are lamps, active, creative things which illuminate that environment, helping to give it form and perspective and so making it adequate, even if only temporarily, to ordinary human desires. 'The imagination', declared Stevens, echoing William Blake and Samuel Taylor Coleridge, 'is the power of the mind over the possibilities of things'; 'like light, it adds nothing, except itself.' In a way, Stevens argued, our world is always an imagined one because our senses start to arrange things almost as soon as they perceive them, and whenever we think about experience we begin to structure it according to some law – such as the scientific law of cause and effect. We start to 'read' and interpret the world in the same manner that, instinctively, we read and interpret a written text. For Stevens, however, the supreme example of this shaping, structuring capacity was the artistic imagination: those acts of the mind whereby people attempt quite consciously to give significance to life – to devise some moral or aesthetic order, however fragile or provisional, which can give coherence and a sense of purpose to things. This kind of order was what Stevens called a 'supreme fiction', and for him, as for Coleridge, the prime creator of such fictions was the poet. The poet, according to Stevens, strives for a 'precise equilibrium' between the mind and its environment at any given moment in time; and then creates a fiction which is at once true to our experience of the world and true to his or her need for value and meaning.

It is worth emphasizing the fact that, as Stevens perceived it, the imaginative faculty does not so much impose designs *on* the world as discover designs inherent *in* it. And it is also worth adding that he saw the act of the imagination as a continuous, theoretically unending one: that he insisted on the primacy of change. We are always altering, Stevens believed, our given circumstances alter too, and the fictive world created out of the synthesis or union of the two must invariably respond to this. We must be reassessing our personal needs and given circumstances continually so as to devise new ideas which do full justice to the dynamic nature of both mind and world; and the poet, in turn, must be writing new poems, new fictions, all the time so as to pay his or her tribute to the metamorphic nature of things. Stevens's analogue for this process was the seasons, with winter seen as the bare, icy reality void of all fictive covering ('The Snow Man' [1923]); spring as the moment when the imagination and the world meet together, 'embrace / and forth the particulars of rapture come' (*Notes Toward a Supreme Fiction*, II, iv); summer as the period of fruition when the marriage between the desires of the mind and the things of the world is complete and harmonious ('Credences of Summer' [1947]); and autumn as the moment when the fiction no longer suffices because the imagination that created it, and the world it was created for, have altered, requiring new fictions, fresh identities and relationships ('The Death of a Soldier' [1923]). As this rather bare outline indicates, perhaps, the imagery of sexual congress and conflict mingles with that of natural growth and decay to describe what Stevens, in one of his poems, termed the imagination's 'ancient cycle'. Mind and world, 'flesh and air', male and female: life is seen as a marriage of opposites ('Life is Motion' [1923]). Joy, or a sense of meaning, is the offspring of this marriage (*Notes*, I, iii). And what Stevens called 'poverty' or 'the malady of the quotidien' ('The Ordinary Women' [1923], 'The Man Whose Pharynx Was Bad' [1923]) – a sense of melancholy and futility – comes when the marriage fails; when, for example, the world is too much with us and the mind becomes a passive instrument ('Depression Before Spring' [1923]) – or, alternatively, when the mind escapes from the pressures of the world altogether and withdraws into solipsism and daydreaming (*Esthétique du Mal*, xv).

'A poet looks at the world as a man looks at a woman.' This, from *The Necessary Angel: Essays on Reality and the Imagination* (1956), offers a variation on the sexual metaphor; and it is also a reminder of just how seductive, for Stevens, was the figure of the poet. For Stevens was no less of a Romantic in this, his tendency to see the fabulator, the maker of poems, as a latter-day prophet: someone who creates the myths that give meaning to people's lives and so enables them to survive – and who offers an example to his audience, by showing them how to devise their own myths as well as listen to his. The poet's function, Stevens insisted, 'is to help people live their lives'. In effect, he returned the poet to his ancient role of bard or mythmaker, offering purpose and a sense of meaning to his tribe. And to this he added another, more peculiarly Romantic and American dimension: which was that of the hero. For the poet, Stevens suggested, is his own hero because his mind, his representative imagination, is the catalyst of events. Instead of a third-person protagonist, the poet, the 'I' of the poem, occupies the centre of the stage; there, as Stevens puts it in 'Of Modern Poetry' (1942), 'like an insatiable actor, slowly and / with meditation', he speaks words and acts out a drama to which

> an invisible audience listens
> Not to the play, but to itself, expressed
> In an emotion as of two people, as of two
> Emotions becoming one.

Just what, in detail, the poet/actor spoke of, and what his audience attended to, was explained elsewhere in Stevens's work. 'Poetry', he declared in 'The Man With the Blue Guitar' (1937), '. . . must take the place / Of empty heaven and its hymns.' Like so many of his great nineteenth-century predecessors – and, in particular, like his mentor, the philosopher George Santayana (1863–1952) – Stevens was convinced that the old religious myths had crumbled into irrelevance. So poetry had to act now as an agent of redemption. The poet had to replace the priest. Art had to replace the liturgy of the church. Imaginative belief – 'belief . . . in a fiction, which you know to be a fiction' – had to replace religious faith. And a possible earthly paradise, created here and now out of the marriage between mind and world, had to replace the vision of a heavenly paradise, situated in some great hereafter. 'The great poems of heaven and hell have been written,' said Stevens, 'and the great poem of earth remains to be written.' The opposition this announces

---

is at once the motive and the subject of much of his work. It is, for example, central to 'Sunday Morning', one of the finest pieces in *Harmonium*. In it the poet conducts a meditation through a woman whose mind is the scene, which has as its focus the choice between two alternatives. One alternative is the vision of paradise proposed to us by the Christian faith, 'The holy hush of ancient sacrifice': a vision founded upon the belief that since this is a universe of death, never answering to our desires, then we must look for our satisfactions in another dimension. The other alternative is the vision of an earthly paradise. The universe, the poet admits, may well be a universe of death when looked at in its pristine state: but it can perhaps be transformed into a living, constantly changing 'mundo' with the help of the active imagination. It is, of course, the second alternative that is ultimately preferred. Believing that 'The greatest poverty is not to live / In a physical world', the poet ends his meditation with a hymn to the earth: as 'At evening, casual flocks of pigeons make / Ambiguous undulations as they sink, / Downward to darkness, on extended wings'. Beautifully poised between motion and rest, the perfect still-ness of an artefact, a thing of the mind, and the movement, the restlessness and changeableness (and the odour of death) which belongs to the things of this world, the closing lines illustrate why Stevens is commonly regarded as one of the modern masters in blank verse.

The particular spot of earth that Stevens hymned in 'Sunday Morning' and elsewhere was almost exclusively American: an important point because, as Stevens put it in one of his very last poems, 'a mythology reflects its region'. 'The gods of China', he insisted in 'A Mythology Reflects its Region' (1957), 'are always Chinese': that is, the world the imagination embraces is always a specific, local one, and the fictions created out of that embrace must bear the stamp of their locality. 'One turns with something like ferocity toward a land that one loves', he said in an essay in *Opus Posthumous*, '. . . to demand that it surrender, reveal, that in itself which one loves.' As Stevens saw it, this marriage between a particular person and place, was 'a vital affair, not an affair of the heart . . . , but an affair of the whole being, a fundamental affair of life'. It was not simply a matter of idiom and gesture, in other words, but of identity and vision. Of course, the paraphernalia of American culture is there in Stevens's poems – things like coffee, saxophones and large sombreros – and, like Whitman, Stevens uses a rich, polyglot language that shows he has fallen in love with American names. But these things matter less, as a mark of origin, than the fact that Stevens chose as his starting point what he called in 'The Sail of Ulysses' (1957) 'human loneliness / A part of space and solitude'. Like every great American poet, in fact, he began with the isolated consciousness – Whitman's 'essential Me' – and then progressed from there to the new dimensions, the moments of self-assertion or communion, which that consciousness struggles gamely to create.

Here, however, we are confronted with a crucial paradox in Stevens's work. Like other American writers, Stevens began with the isolated self, the separate mind and its world. Unlike most of them, however, he then moved in two quite different directions. One direction is centripetal and recalls that arch-egotist and solipsist, Edgar Allan Poe. The self, Stevens insists, devises its own world, which the poem then imitates in that it is closed and autonomous, a durable integration of experience. The other recalls Emily Dickinson. For Stevens can be quite as insistent that the self is limited, transient, and that the worlds or works it creates must carry the imprint of their creator in being tentative, provisional and unfinished. In some respects, Stevens's poems resemble Poe's. 'Pure' or closed poems in a way, they are as self-sufficient and intangible as the realms of experience they describe; they seem to exist in their own special dimension or, as Stevens himself put it in *Notes*, 'beyond the compass of change / Perceived in a final atmosphere'. In other respects, though, they edge out tentatively towards the boundaries of experience just as Dickinson's poetry does. 'Impure' or open poems of a kind, they tend to emphasize their own arbitrariness, to offer themselves up to reinvention – and so remind us that they are (to quote 'The Man With the Blue Guitar') 'inconstant objects of inconstant cause / In a universe of inconstancy'.

Just how Stevens manages to walk this tightrope between open and closed structures is illustrated by poems like 'Anecdote of the Jar' (1923) or 'Thirteen Ways of Looking at a Blackbird' (1923). Both pieces work through repetition and echo, a series of significant if often subterranean connections. This repetitive pattern becomes far more elaborate in some of the longer, more sustained pieces, with the result that poems like, say, 'The Idea of Order at Key West' resemble mosaics, in which the poet seems to be trying to construct his own personal version of the imaginative fictions he celebrates. Complex designs of word, sound and image, they offer the reader a special world, in this case a verbal one, which may be abstracted from and so depend upon our given surroundings – but which has its own innate structure and system of cross-reference. Both 'Anecdote of the Jar' and 'Thirteen Ways' adopt a serio-comic, slyly evasive tone too. Here as in, say, 'Bantams in Pinewoods' (1923) or 'Le Monocle de Mon Oncle' (1923), the poet uses wit and irony to qualify and complicate matters, and so prevent the reader from coming to too simple or final a conclusion. And both are written in such a way as to seem complete and incomplete: so imitating in their form, as well as describing in their content, the continuing act of the imagination, by which worlds are created that are sufficient in themselves and yet subject to alteration. The section that concludes 'Thirteen Ways', for instance, describes a moment of absolute stillness: a scene, in which 'It was snowing / And it was going to snow', where the blackbird has become a still point. Everything appears to be at rest, complete and sufficient within itself: until the reader remembers that, for Stevens, winter, the season of snow, was a beginning as well as an end. The section concludes 'Thirteen Ways', certainly. But by reminding us of the process of decreation – what Stevens called, in one of his letters, 'getting rid of the paint to get at the world itself' – it also acts as a prelude to further imaginative activity, an opening to poems as yet to be written.

It would be wrong, however, to dwell on 'Thirteen Ways' as if it summed up the whole of Stevens's work, even in its paradoxes and ambiguities. No one poem could do that. One reason is that the later poetry is, on the whole, less spry and balletic than the earlier – more meditative and austere, more discursive and openly philosophical. And another is that Stevens rarely allowed himself to be contained by a particular idiom even within the space of one poem. Each of his pieces is complexly layered, moving almost casually and without warning between high rhetoric and the colloquial, book-words, foreign borrowings and native slang. As a result, each seems unique, with its own particular rhythms and adjustments – its own special way of turning the world into words. One of the finest of Stevens's later poems, for example, *Notes Toward a Supreme Fiction*, explores his familiar subject: 'The imagination, the one reality / In this imagined world'. But it creates its own separate 'mundo', full of noise, colour and movement; and, rather than any argumentative structure, it is this 'mundo', strange, illogical and quite unpredictable, which enables the reader to see the world in a new light. It ends, as 'Sunday Morning' does, with a hymn to the earth, the 'fat girl' as Stevens calls her. Her changeableness, her extraordinary vitality and variety, he concludes, can be caught for a moment in a single, crystalline image. With that image, 'my green, my fluent mundo', he says, 'will have stopped revolving except in crystal'. The revolving crystal is, of course, an image of an image: a fictional embodiment of the kind of imaginative fiction that can at once recover the world about us, in all its plenitude, and raise it to a higher power, a superior dimension of reality. It summarizes in the only way possible for Stevens (that is, in an imaginative way) what was for him the central fact of life and the continuing concern of his work: the ability of the mind to achieve a kind of redemption – by working *with* the world to abstract something of value out of that world, and so, as Stevens himself put it once, build a bridge between fact and miracle.

Marianne Moore (1887–1972) knew both Stevens and Williams well and commented acutely on their work. Of Williams, for example, she observed that he was a poet supremely 'able to fix the atmosphere of a moment'. But she was very much her own woman and her own poet. 'We must', she once declared, 'have the courage of our peculiarities'; and she showed that courage herself. She was always willing to be different and to embody that difference in poetry. Born in Missouri and brought up in Pennsylvania, Moore published her first poems in 1915. Three years later, she moved to New York City and remained there for the rest of her life. Her first volume, *Poems*, was published in London in 1921 without her knowledge by two friends, one of them being H. D. Several other collections followed, among them *Observations* (1924), *Selected Poems* (1935) and *What Are Years?* (1941); and her *Collected Poems* (1951) was followed by three further collections and a *Complete Poems* five years before her death. All of her work demonstrates that stubborn determination to be oneself that she saw as the core of personality and poetry. She was willing to risk eccentricity, if it meant the creation of her own measure, and the results were original and inimitable. Just as in life she had her own vivid, odd presence, instantly recognizable because of the black cape and black tricorn hat she habitually wore, so, in her own work, she had her own distinctive, unique voice, as this opening stanza from her poem 'The Steeple-Jack' (1935) illustrates:

Dürer would have seen a reason for living
　　　in a town like this, with eight stranded whales
to look at; with the sweet air coming into your house
on a fine day, from water etched
　　　with waves as formal as the scales
on a fish.

The peculiar quality of lines like these, poised as they are between the controlled and the spontaneous, largely results from Moore's use of the medieval device of 'rime-breaking'. The formal outlines are severe: the stanzas based on syllable count, the lines so arranged on the page as to repeat specific and often quite complicated patterns. But these strict proportions are rendered much less strict by making the stanza, instead of the line, the basic unit. Rhymes are sparse, enjambement the rule, and the sense of run-on lines is increased by ending lines with unimportant words and hyphenations. There is a frequent use of internal rhyme, too, to break up the apparently formal pattern; and the pattern itself, which depends on such extreme differences in line length (there are, for example, nine syllables in line five of this and every other stanza, only three syllables in line six), seems to participate in the liveliness of the material quite as much as to organize it or set it off. The mixed feelings of order and spontaneity generated by this complex verse structure are then underlined by Moore's special way with images and words. The descriptive detail is extraordinarily, almost gratuitously, specific ('eight stranded whales'), asking us to look closely at the object. Moore, like Williams, tried to capture the exact contours of things in a painterly, microscopic manner, but not because, like Williams, she wished to be appropriated by them or live their life. On the contrary, her firm belief was that, by observing an object lovingly, she could discover significance *in* it which extended *beyond* it. Precision liberated the imagination, she felt; the discipline of close observation was, for her, a means of imaginative release.

　　There is a peculiar correspondence between Moore's voice and her vision: for the patterns of her verse embody and reinforce our sense of a world where spontaneity and order are not at odds and where the marriage between them results in spiritual poise. All Moore's poems start from a belief in discipline, the acceptance of boundaries. This acceptance was necessary, she felt, for two reasons. In the first place, the mind could discover a safeguard against danger by accepting limitations. A good deal of Moore's poetry is about armour, protection, places to hide; and it is so probably because Moore saw life in terms of risk, the threats our environment confronts us with, the menace likely to overcome us if ever we should lose control. The second reason is more significant, however: Moore also clearly believed that, in accepting limitations, the mind discovers fulfilment. Freedom and happiness, she felt, are to be found only in the service of forms, in an acknowledgement of the needs and restrictions of our natures, the scope of our particular world. For Moore, as she puts it in 'To a Snail' (1935), 'Contractility is a virtue / as modesty is a virtue' and just as 'compression is the first grace of style': as poets, and as people, we need discipline – formal, moral, intellectual or whatever – in order to realize our best possibilities. Something of this is suggested in 'The Steeple-Jack' by the character who gives the poem its title. From 'the pitch / of the church', the poet tells us:

> a man in scarlet lets
> down a rope, as a spider spins thread;
> he might be part of a novel, but on the sidewalk a
> sign says C.V. Poole, Steeple Jack,
> in black and white: and one in red
> and white says
>
> Danger.

The steeple-jack may be dressed in a flamboyant colour, stand high above the town; he may even seem to be 'part of a novel'. But, after all, he is not a hero, epic or exotic. He is an ordinary man, performing his duties with the minimum of fuss and wasted effort: devoted to his craft and doing his best to avoid all the dangers he can during the course of his day. Within the limited space marked out by his signs, his words, he has created an area of freedom; he has devised his own humble example of the spiritual – and, as it happens, physical – poise.

On the subject of poetry, Moore declared, in a poem simply called 'Poetry' (1935), 'I, too, dislike it: there are things that are important beyond all this fiddle'. But, then, she added this:

> Reading it, however, with a perfect contempt for it,
> one discovers in
> it after all, a place for the genuine.

For Moore, as she goes on to explain, 'genuine' poetry is the absolute of the 'high-sounding'; it is 'useful' just as Whitman believed it was – in the sense, that is, that all things necessary to the perpetuation of life are. Everything is the stuff of poetry, even 'business documents and / school-books'. 'All these phenomena are important', she says; only 'half poets' make the mistake of thinking otherwise. So Moore can make her poetry out of the world of nature ('The Pangolin' [1941]) and of art ('No Swan So Fine' [1935]), out of the activities of everyday life ('When I Buy Pictures' [1935]) and individual moments of meditation ('What Are Years?' [1941]), out of places ('England' [1935]), institutions ('Marriage [1935]) or people ('The Student' [1941]). What matters is the *how* of poetry: how a thing is perceived, how it is felt, experienced, imagined.

The range of Moore's work shows how closely she followed her own prescription for 'genuine' poetry. Each of her best pieces constitutes an act of imaginary possession, in which she perceives an object carefully, and with reverence, and then attempts to absorb it – to grasp its significance in her mind. There is no imperialism of the intellect here. The essential properties of the object are not denied; on the contrary, it is precisely because the poet acknowledges them that she can then go on, in language that is all sinew, severe and pure, to discover ulterior meaning. Many of her poems concerned with inanimate objects, such as 'An Egyptian Pulled Glass Bottle in the Shape of the Fish' (1935), are what William Carlos Williams called 'anthologies of transit . . . moving rapidly from one thing to the next' and thereby giving 'the impression of a passage through . . . of . . . swiftness impaling beauty'. They depend, in effect, on their deftness of vision and lightness of touch, their absolute refusal to moralize in the conventional way. In turn, her animal poems are notable for the refusal to anthropomorphize. In 'The Frigate Pelican' (1935), for example, Moore first insists on the bird's remoteness from humankind, 'a less / limber animal'. It has been difficult, we are told, to find 'the proper word' for this creature; furthermore, it is impossible to equate it with human standards of morality, because it lives in a way that we might well regard as makeshift and ruthless – by bullying other birds, the 'industrious crude-winged species', and forcing them to surrender what they have caught. Only when Moore has established this difference does she then go on to make the moral discovery. 'The unconfiding frigate bird', the poet tells us, 'hides / in the height and in the majestic / display of his art.' The creature may exist apart from human concerns but in the very act of doing so he seems to offer what John Crowe Ransom called 'an exemplum of rightness and beauty': his capacity for going his own way can, after all, be translated into *strictly human terms*. He has the courage of his own peculiarities: he follows the dictates, the truths and limitations, of his nature. So, paradoxically, the bird is 'like' the good man in being so 'unlike' him: like the good man and, Moore might have added, like the good poet too.

'Ecstasy affords / the occasion and expediency determines the form': Moore's memorable formulation could serve as an epitaph to her work. For that matter, it could serve as an epitaph to the work of a number of other writers who, like Moore, used formal structures to channel and so intensify feeling. Elinor Wylie (1885–1928), for instance, was a distinguished practitioner of the classical lyric, using it to create an art that was, to use her own words, 'elaborate, neat, enamelled, elegant, perhaps exquisite'. 'Avoid the reeking herd' begins one of her poems; and this expresses one of the major impulses in her poetry – the longing to escape a malicious, stupid world, where 'The rumbling of the market-carts / The pounding of men's feet' bruise the soul, and to seek out some private realm where it may be possible to 'Live like that stoic bird / The eagle of the rock'. The realm may be a pastoral one ('Wild Peaches' [1932]); it may be one of pure artifice ('The Fairy Goldsmith' [1932]), or of sleep and death ('The Coast Guard's Nephew' [1932]). Whatever form it assumes, it is shaped by the rapt, hermetic nature of Wylie's vision, her peculiar ability to mingle sensuousness and spirituality. In some of her later work, Wylie became, at times, more frankly sexual (as in 'One Person', a series of autobiographical sonnets addressed to a lover [1943]) and, at other times, more openly visionary (as in 'Chimera Sleeping' [1943], where the poet talks of pursuing a 'foreknown and holy ghost' that dissolves as she pursues it). Even these later poems, though, have that quality of dreamy sensuality, erotic mysticism that characterizes her earlier poetry – and that sense of dark passions lurking beneath a bright, brittle surface that Wylie herself was probably thinking of when she declared, 'All that I / Could ever ask / Wears . . . / . . . a thin gold mask'.

Several of Wylie's poems are addressed to 'that archangel' Percy Bysshe Shelley; he is the subject of one of her novels; and members of her family tried to promote the legend that Wylie was a sort of female Shelley of the twentieth century. If Shelley's presence does indeed hover behind Wylie's writing, then Lord Byron, in turn, is a ghostly presence in the work of another skilful manipulator of classic lyric forms, Edna St Vincent Millay (1892–1950). Like Byron, Millay combined a lively iconoclasm, a positive desire to offend bourgeois sensibilities and mock bourgeois morality, with an astute understanding of traditional forms and metres. For a while, during the 1920s, she became the lyric voice for the lost generation. In poems that sang gaily of going 'back and forth all night on the ferry' or cavalierly acknowledged the death of a love affair ('Unremembered as old rain / Dries the sheer libation'), she attacked conventional notions of virtue – and, in particular, feminine virtue – with impudence, irreverence and wit. 'What lips my lips have kissed, and where, and why, / I have forgotten', she announced, and elsewhere in perhaps her most famous lines from 'First Fig' (1920):

> My candle burns at both ends;
> It will not last the night;
> But ah, my foes, and oh, my friends –
> It gives a lovely light!

Several of her poems, such as 'Thursday' (1923), recall the bravura, the insouciance and the sly grace of the Cavalier poets:

> And if I loved you Wednesday,
> Well, what is that to you?
> I do not love you Thursday –
> So much is true.

While her rejection of utilitarian structures, standard measurements of use and value, in a poem like 'Second Fig' (1920), echoes that first American bohemian, Poe:

> Safe upon the solid rock the ugly houses stand:
> Come and see my shining palace built upon the sand!

As the 1920s faded, the work Millay produced showed her branching out towards political commitment ('Justice Denied in Massachusetts' [1928]) and, on the other hand, classical themes ('Oh, Sleep Forever in the Latmian Cave' [1931]). But she began losing much of her audience, like that other, greater poet of the Jazz Age, Fitzgerald. It is, in any case, for the earlier work that she will be remembered – and,

more especially, for her ability to capture both the rebelliousness and the romanticism of what Fitzgerald called 'the greatest, gaudiest spree in history'.

Three other poets whose work demonstrates a vivid contrast between the intensely
personal, subjective nature of their themes and the extraordinarily polished, objective
character of the poetic forms they use are Josephine Miles (1911–85), Louise Bogan
(1897–1970) and Léonie Adams (1899–1988). The forms used by these three,
however, are less obviously lyrical and romantic than the ones favoured by Wylie
and Millay: they belonged to what Yvor Winters termed the 'reactionary generation' – poets, like Winters himself, who chose a strict impersonality of voice as well
as tight disciplines of structure and metre. Of these, Josephine Miles is probably
the least impressive. A teacher of English interested in the systematic use of literary
language, she tends towards highly wrought intellectualism, a poetry that at its best
is strenuous, witty and abstruse. The closing lines of a poem called 'Grandfather'
(1960) are typical:

> And I think, Pater and my fine fathers,
> Your rich prose taught and taught us at its knee,
> And still thunders its cloud we argue we under,
> Yet now we argue barest daylight in the expanse of green.

The interplay of concrete and abstract diction here, the ironic pun ('Pater',
'fathers') and veiled allusion to Andrew Marvell's 'green thoughts in a green shade',
the urgent rhythms and cunning use of repetition and verbal echo: all make for
a verse that is as tense, nervously mobile and as unnerving as anything written
by Allen Tate.

Louise Bogan is also a supreme technician, concerned with what she called 'the
strong things of life'. In her case, though, clarity of image, exactitude of phrase and
rhythm, and a measured, lucid diction make for poems that derive their emotional
power from the poet's positive refusal to invite an easy, emotional response. 'Portrait'
(1923), for instance, describes a woman who has 'no need to fear the fall / of
harvest', and no need either to 'hold to pain's effrontery / Her body's bulwark'.
The reader is not told why, exactly. All the poet offers us (and it is a great deal) are
lines that capture the larger paradoxes of life – its ebb and flow, losses and gains,
passion and its ambiguous rewards. Elsewhere, Bogan uses other, similarly effective
distancing techniques. In 'The Dream' (1954), for instance, the nightmare of a
'terrible horse' is used to dramatize and objectify the attraction, and the fear, of
desire. In 'Stanzas' (1968), the dying away of desire itself is expressed in jewelled
yet implicitly sensual imagery ('No longer burn the hands that seized / Small
wreaths from branches scarcely green'): there is a personal inspiration here, certainly,
but the hieratic treatment turns it into something separate from the poet, rounded
and crystalline. In turn, 'Simple Autumnal' (1923) begins with an evocative portrait
of autumn ('The measured blood beats out the year's delay'), and then modulates
into a subtle evocation of grief's longing, and failure, to find in the season a
consoling mirror of its mood. 'Full season's come, yet filled trees keep the sky, /'

---

she concludes, 'And never scent the ground where they must lie.' Characteristically, Bogan makes 'grief in its prime' all the more moving by her rejection of the pathetic fallacy, because of the contrast she draws between 'sorrow' longing for fallen leaves to reflect its mood and the stubborn indifference of the 'filled trees' to such pressures.

The setting and theme that Bogan deals with so astutely in 'Simple Autumnal' are ones that Léonie Adams made peculiarly her own. Adams's early poems are a little precious, perhaps, with their deliberate archaisms and invocations to 'Beauty'. Yet even here the preciousness is tempered and qualified by a harsh sense of what she calls 'the old cheating of the sun': the recognition that even the most beautiful of days must pass, even the most intense of experiences wither away. This harsher element grew as she and her poetry matured. Poems like 'Grapes Making' (1925) or 'Sundown' (1929) are exquisitely shaped, vividly sensuous portraits of rural America that, however, derive much of their colour and poignancy from the recollection that 'The careless autumn mornings come, / The grapes drop glimmering to the shears'. 'The faint leaf vanishes to light', Adams declares in 'Grapes Making': sunset, late summer and early autumn are her favourite occasions, moments when everything in nature seems to be waiting, hushed with expectancy, for the ebb tide, the falling away of things. She is like Emily Dickinson and Robert Frost in this, her interest in what Dickinson called the 'spectral canticle' of late summer and Frost, 'that other fall we name the fall'. However, she is unlike them in that premonitions of mortality are rarely dwelt upon in her work, and the immediate, personal note struck even more rarely. Transience, or rather awareness of it, is always there shaping her verbal landscapes, but it is all the more powerful for remaining in the background, an admonitory presence. Like Moore, Adams clearly believed that, as Moore herself put it, 'The deepest feeling always shows itself in silence; / not in silence, but restraint'.

'To be nobody-but-yourself in a world that is doing its best, night and day, to make you everybody else – means to fight the hardest battle which any human being can fight.' Marianne Moore would undoubtedly have approved of this remark made by e. e. cummings (1894–1962). Perhaps she knew of it, since the two were friends and not only liked but admired each other. But whereas Moore's individualism led her towards a firm (if idiosyncratic) belief in discipline, measure, cummings's individualism led him towards a kind of imaginative anarchism. To be 'nobody-but-yourself', he felt, you had to achieve liberation from the 'unworld', the mind-forged manacles of society and culture. You would then become 'incorrigibly and actually alive', experiencing everything with a 'unique dimension of intensity'; and you could begin to discover a world in which love transcends time, natural spontaneity prevails over the demands of habit and convention, and the dreams of each particular person are the supreme reality.

According to cummings, freedom was not easy: especially, freedom in poetry. 'As for expressing nobody-but-yourself in words,' he declared, 'that means working just a little harder than anybody who isn't a poet can possibly imagine.' His aim was to create a unique, and where necessary eccentric, voice to express his unique, and sometimes eccentric, personality; and, in order to fulfil this aim, he armed himself with a whole battery of technical effects – free verse or, on occasion, a highly original development of traditional verse forms, irregular typography, startling imagery, word coinages and syntactical or grammatical distortions.

Like Twain and Whitman, cummings chooses 'roughs and little children' for his heroes: outsiders who, according to the Romantic and American notions of things, have achieved absolute selfhood. Among the roughs is Buffalo Bill, a typically Western hero associated with the careless energy of the frontier: 'he was a handsome man', cummings tells us, in 'Buffalo Bill's / defunct' (1920), who used to 'break onetwothreefourfivepigeonsjustlikethat'. And among the other exceptional individuals and supreme individualists is cummings's own father, celebrated in one of his most famous poems, 'my father moved through dooms of love' (1954). cummings has also written frequently about love: in part because, as he sees it, love offers access to that dimension of intensity needed to be 'incorrigibly and actually alive'. And his best love poems are precisely those that combine intense personal feeling with intelligence and verbal felicity. In 'since feeling is first' (1926), for instance, the poet wittily mocks the rules and regulations of language, the very disciplines he is using: 'who pays any attention / to the syntax of things', he insists, 'will never wholly kiss' the woman he is addressing. Similarly, in 'somewhere i have never travelled, gladly beyond' (1958), cummings alters the conventional word order and employs a delicate mixture of adverbs, repetition and nicely placed parentheses to create a gently ruminative tone. We are obliged to pause while we read this poem, and so experience that attitude of patient meditation which is, apparently, one of the special blessings of love.

Closely related to cummings's poetry of love are his erotic poems. cummings's erotic verse is at its best when it is at its funniest, as in 'she being Brand / – new' (1940). In fact, a lot of his poetry generally is at its best in this vein. He is probably the finest American comic poet of the twentieth century because his comedy issues from serious commitments: a dedication to Eros, the intensities of physical love, and a hatred of 'manunkind' – those people who reject such intensities in favour of stock reactions, the language and instincts of the crowd. Ogden Nash is probably as skilful as cummings when it comes to satirizing particular social types or writing nonsense verse; Don Marquis (1878–1937) is almost as adept in the use of verbal and typographical oddities to disturb and amuse the reader. Only cummings, however, can successfully fuse swingeing comic polemic and verbal jugglery, trenchant satire and typographical play. 'next to of course god america;' (1926), for instance, is a brilliant parody of patriotic cant that makes a powerful point about people who prefer to lose their identity in some anonymous nationalistic mass rather than discover an identity for themselves.

At its most extreme, cummings's commitment to individualism and anarchic experiment can lead to difficulties of interpretation. One highly idiosyncratic piece, for instance, begins in this way:

a –

float on some

?

i call twilight

(1953)

Its subject is the moon, which is transformed as it is described into a symbol of the dream world of the liberated individual; and an appropriate quality of enigma is given to this symbol by the poet's radical innovations of technique. Here, for instance, he replaces the second syllable of 'something' with a question mark, the implication being that 'thing' is too solid and mundane a word to use in describing the shifting, delicate presence of the twilight. And, elsewhere, he uses a punctuation mark, the second half of a parenthesis, for its visual effect: because it traces the gentle curve of the moon. cummings sometimes referred to his work as 'poempictures', which perhaps alerts us to its visual quality: the impact of the typography on the blank white page can be a primary part of its meaning. At its best, though, cummings's writing blends the visual dimension with the aural: as in this passage, which concludes a poem about death, 'enter no (silence is the blood whose flesh' (1963), written towards the end of the poet's life:

> O, come, terrible anonymity, enfold
> phantom me with the murdering minus of cold
>
> . . .
>
> gently
>
> (very whiteness: absolute peace
> never imaginable mystery)
>
> descend

Beautifully cadenced, these lines dramatize the gradual relaxation of consciousness, the slipping away of life. Left syntactically and grammatically unfinished, they also imply that the descent into death is rich in possibilities. Characteristically, cummings responded to death, with fear certainly, but also with wonder: to be enfolded in 'terrible anonymity', he felt, was a unique experience that nevertheless deserved comparison with other, unique moments of intensity in life.

It would be an exaggeration to say that, in his later poems, cummings was edging towards mysticism; it was more a sense of death as an adventure, a possible entry into new forms of experience. Other Modernist poets were, however, driven towards the mystical impulse, most notably, Muriel Rukeyser (1913–80), Laura (Riding) Jackson (1901–91) and Hart Crane (1899–1932). Much of Rukeyser's early work is determinedly Modernist, using a free verse line, allusive imagery, disruptive syntax and grammar, and an associative structure to capture something of the rapid, disjunctive movements of modern life. Even here, however, the concerns that were to dominate her poetry are quite clear: power and its betrayal, the immense possibilities latent in the human being, human 'dynamics of desire', and their denial by a society that 'makes thin the imagination and the bone'. The title poem from her first volume, for instance, 'Theory of Flight' (1935), contrasts Whitman's dreams of rapid movements through space now translated into a reality (Rukeyser was a student pilot at the time) with the world left on the ground: where 'our superiors, the voting men' sit 'around the committee-table', voting to disavow 'the eyes, and sex, and brain', the powers of perception, reproduction and knowledge – and voting death, too, to all those who would liberate such powers, including poets and visionaries like Blake and Whitman. 'Now, in our time,' wrote Rukeyser, in the introduction to one of her volumes, *Orpheus* (1949), 'many of the sources of power are obscured ... or vulgarized ... I have hoped to indicate some of the valid sources of power.' The piece with which she chose to begin her *Selected Poems* (1951), 'This Place in the Ways', makes the point in another way. 'I set out once again', she says, 'From where I began: / Belief in the love of the world, / Woman, spirit, and man.' 'I find love and rage', she adds: 'Rage for the world as it is / But for what it may be / More love now than last year.' As these lines indicate, Rukeyser moved towards a greater clarity of diction, a more openly affirmative stance and an incantatory (and, on occasion, even declamatory) tone in order to unravel 'The strength of the mystery'. A poem like 'Boy with His Hair Cut Short' (1938) reveals her rage. The subject is simple enough: set in Chicago during the 1930s, it describes a boy having his hair cut by his sister in the hope that this might help him find a job. However, Rukeyser's elliptical style here, harsh diction and suggestive imagery turn this into a vision of a shadow world where the machine rules ('The arrow's electric red always reaches its mark / successful neon!') and the human spirit is cowed. Brutally contemporary though the scene is ('Sunday shuts down on a twentieth-century evening. / The El passes. Twilight and bulb define / the brown room'), the ritual of hair-cutting cannot but recall the Biblical tale of Samson losing his strength with his hair: this is a society, evidently, that requires impotence as a sign of obedience. And, elsewhere, Rukeyser uses symbolic and mythic reference more openly on the grounds that, as she puts it, 'The fear of symbol is linked with the fear of poetry in our culture. It is poetry's enemy, part of a great emotional wound.' This is particularly true of those poems more immediately concerned with 'love of the world' and the search for 'valid sources of power'. In her long poem *Orpheus*, for instance, she uses the ancient Greek story of the death and resurrection of the poet-hero ('he has died the birth of the God') to celebrate the cycle of life and the creative spirit: 'There is only life', the poem tells us, and 'To live is to create'. In the poem-sequence 'Ajanta' (1973), on the other hand, she uses another, Eastern tradition. The frescoes painted on the walls of the Ajanta caves in India become the occasion for celebrating 'The real world where everything is complete', where 'There are no shadows ... / ... no source of distortion' – and for lamenting this unreal world we now inhabit, 'World, not yet one ... / ... / A world of the shadow and alone'.

Laura (Riding) Jackson began from a very different base to Rukeyser and moved, eventually, in a very different direction, even though she too was guided by the visionary impulse. She was an honorary member of the Fugitive group for a while, sharing with them a strong commitment to poetic discipline and, with Tate in particular, a certain chilly intensity. However, she was hardly interested in their verbal variety and dexterity, and had visionary, even absolutist poetic aims. 'A poem', Laura (Riding) Jackson says in the Preface to her 1938 *Collected Poems*, 'is an uncovering of truth of so fundamental and general a kind that no other name besides poetry is adequate except truth.' Inspired by a passionate search for what she called 'an ultimate of perfect truth', she rejected metaphorical language, verbal ambiguity or anything that, as she saw it, failed to illuminate the object or idea.

'A most improbable one it takes / To tell what is so', she declares in 'The Way It Is'; and this idea of the difficulty, perhaps the impossibility, of telling 'what is so' recurs throughout her poetry, even while she is trying to tell it. Sometimes it results in a desperate resort to paradox ('One self, one manyness'), oxymoron or simple self-contradiction ('The strangeness is not strange'), as if the poet were trying to cancel definitions out as she uses them. Sometimes, and not unrelated to this, she narrows her focus down to one very specific example of the difficulties of telling, as in 'Beyond', where she insists: 'Pain is impossible to describe / Pain is the impossibility of describing / Describing what is impossible to describe.' (Riding) Jackson wanted to 'describe' a reality that is as immediate and yet intangible, as searingly present but incommunicable as, from the experience of all of us, we know pain to be. In the end, she felt that poetry could not help, because, as she put it, 'truth begins where poetry ends'. 'My kind of seriousness,' she said, 'in my looking to poetry for the rescue of human life from the indignities it was capable of visiting upon itself, led me to an eventual turning away from it as failing my kind of seriousness.' Her desire that poetry should tell the truth about 'the human reality . . . the reality of All, of which we are exponents': this, she believed, had been frustrated. The reason was simple: the currency in which poetry dealt was counterfeit. Far from providing 'for practical attainment of that rightness of word that *is* truth', it led only to 'a temporising less-than-truth (. . . eked out with illusions of truth produced by physical word-effects)'. So she turned her attention to a work of linguistics which would, she hoped, provide 'a single terminology of truth'. It was to be 'a work that would help dissipate the confusion existing in the knowledge of word-meanings': something in which, she insisted, 'all probity of word must start'. 'I was religious in my devotion to poetry,' she said. 'But in saying this,' she added, 'I am thinking of religion as it is . . . a will to know and to make known, the ultimate knowledge'; and that – or rather, the equivalent of that – poetry had singularly failed to be.

Unlike (Riding) Jackson, Hart Crane never lost his belief in the religious possibilities of poetry. It became and remained for him a means of absolute vision: 'the articulation', as he put it, 'of contemporary human consciousness *sub specie aeternitas*'. Poems could and should, he felt, carry their author and readers alike 'toward a state of consciousness', an 'innocence' or 'absolute beauty': a condition in which 'there may be discoverable new forms, certain spiritual illuminations'. Crane may have been driven towards this pursuit of what he termed 'a more ecstatic goal' by the pain and tragedy of his life. As a child, he suffered from what he later described as 'the curse of sundered parenthood': his parents separated, his mother was admitted to a sanatorium, and he went to live with his grandparents.

As an adult, he enjoyed some success as a poet: his first volume, *White Buildings*, appeared in 1926 and was reasonably well received, and his most famous poem, *The Bridge*, was published privately in 1929 and then in a general edition in 1930. But he had to cope with being a homosexual at a time when homosexuality was against the law. As he grew older, he was increasingly dogged by a sense of failure, alcoholic dependency and a breakdown in personal relationships. While still only thirty-two, Crane disappeared from the ship returning him from Mexico to New York; and it is probable that he committed suicide by leaping into the sea. It is perhaps no wonder, then, that he sought in his work not so much escape as a means of mystical redemption. Each of his poems, Crane hoped, would supply the reader with 'a single new word, never before spoken, and impossible to enunciate but self-evident in the consciousness henceforward'. Each, in supplying an access to purer vision, would create a language rather than just use one.

'As a poet,' Crane declared, 'I may very probably be more interested in the so-called illogical impingements of the connotations of words on the consciousness (and their combinations and interplay in metaphor on this basis) than I am interested in the preservation of their logically rigid signification.' He saw each word, almost, as a cumulus of possibilities and latent associations many, but not all, of which could be fired into life by their verbal surrounds – by the words, and combinations of words, with which they were juxtaposed. The overtones of his language, consequently, tend to matter more than its strictly denotative meaning: what echoes in our minds forms an important part of what is being said. This is as true of the earlier poetry as it is of the later. But in the earlier, as in, say, 'Chaplinesque', the positive overtones – the feelings of redemptive possibility generated by the words – tend to be tentative and partial. These gradually disappeared, as Crane went in search of what he called 'the metaphysics of absolute knowledge'. The immediate cause of this alteration was a personal experience. Crane apparently enjoyed a moment of vision, or mystical seizure, which opened fresh possibilities in himself and convinced him that 'we must somehow touch the clearest veins of eternity flowing through the crowds around us'. 'Did I tell you of that thrilling experience this last winter in the dentist's chair,' Crane asked a friend:

> when under the influence of aether . . . my mind spiralled to a kind of seventh heaven and egoistic dance among the seven spheres – and something kept saying to me – 'You have the higher consciousness'? . . . I felt the two worlds . . . Today I have made a good start on . . . 'Faustus and Helen'.

As Crane indicates here, his long poem 'For the Marriage of Faustus and Helen' grew directly out of his mystical experience and, in a sense, tried to recover it, to make it and the knowledge it supplied available to every one of his readers. Faustus, Crane explained, is 'the symbol of . . . the poetic and imaginative man of all times', Helen the symbol of an abstract 'sense of beauty'; and the marriage between them is seen not as an event really, but as a continuing possibility – the moment of communion between the soul and the spirit of essential Beauty which illuminates all existence afterwards.

The poetry that followed 'Faustus and Helen' includes 'At Melville's Tomb', a hymn of praise to the prophetic author of *Moby-Dick*, and 'Royal Palm', an evocative description of the 'green rustlings' of a palm tree that is also a symbolic account of the imagination climbing to discovery of the absolute, 'launched above / Mortality – ascending emerald-bright'. But perhaps the most powerful and moving expression of Crane's visionary impulse in his lyric poetry is to be found in 'Voyages'. A series of six poems written over three years, these are, as Crane explained at the time he was writing them, 'love poems' and 'sea poems' too: the sea appears in them as a threat to the poet-lover and as a rival, as a partner, an enemy, and eventually as a source of comfort and vision. One reason for the constant presence of the sea in the sequence is that the person to whom they are addressed was a sailor living temporarily in New York; another, that the poet and his lover stayed together in an apartment overlooking the harbour; and still another, that the sea was always a suggestive image for Crane. Like Whitman and Melville, he used the sea to describe both the cruelty of this 'broken' world and the mysterious 'answers' that ultimately might make the world whole again.

Apart from 'Voyages', Crane's greatest achievement of his visionary years was his attempt at what he termed a 'Myth of America', *The Bridge*. 'I am concerned with the future of America,' Crane wrote, 'not because I think America has any so-called par value as a state . . . It is only because I feel persuaded that there are destined to be discovered certain as yet undefined spiritual qualities . . . not to be developed so completely elsewhere.' It is the old problem of the American dream the poet poses, in a series of eight poems that follow the westward thrust of the bridge into the body of the continent. The movement is one in time as well as space; and as Crane moves across the continent he continually presents the reader with the same question. How, he asks, can the ideal possibilities of people be liberated so as to recover the kingdom of heaven on earth? How can an arc or bridge be constructed between the world in which we live and the world of the imagination, so that the life of the individual may assume a fresh nobility and the forms of the community approximate to the divine? Having asked the question, he also tries to answer it. For Crane is no less visionary in that he sees himself as an agent of liberation, formulating in his work the new relationship between consciousness and reality which will make the changes he requires possible. *The Bridge*, like so much of Crane's verse, offers a series of visionary acts intended to alter our minds – to propose to us what Crane called 'a new hierarchy of faith' – as a preliminary to altering our surroundings. In 'Proem: To Brooklyn Bridge', for example, the opening poem in the sequence, the poet beseeches Brooklyn Bridge to act as a mediator between the actual and the ideal:

> Sleepless as the river under thee
> Vaulting the sea, the prairies' dreaming sod,
> Unto us lowliest sometimes sweep, descend
> And of the curveship lend a myth to God.

The poet is appealing to the bridge as a figure, of course, rather than a given object. He has transformed the *actual* bridge into an *ideal*, liberating symbol: uniting river and sea, land and sky in one revelatory 'myth', a single inviolate curve that leaps upward towards the absolute. In doing so, he has offered one small illustration of how the two dimensions, the mundane and the visionary, can be related – and how, consequently, his prayers can be answered.

'Unless poetry can absorb the machine,' Crane said, '. . . then poetry has failed of its full contemporary function.' In choosing Brooklyn Bridge for his 'myth', Crane was making a deliberate attempt to 'absorb the machine': to find a source of creativity in the industrial age. Traversing the same stretch of river, Whitman had used Brooklyn Ferry, with its perpetual ebb and flow of passengers, to symbolize what he called the 'eternal float of solution', the 'simple, compact, well-join'd scheme' to which all passing things belong. Crane had at his disposal a comparable, and yet significantly more contemporary, image: the bridge, which is a part of the technological age and yet somehow seems to 'condense eternity'. 'Thy cables breathe the North Atlantic still,' exclaims the poet, 'And we have seen night lifted in thine arms.' Elliptical and allusive in texture, associative and even disjunctive in structure, *The Bridge* is clearly much more of a *modern* epic than 'Song of Myself', 'Crossing Brooklyn Ferry' or *Leaves of Grass* as a whole. Yet it is, finally, in that great tradition initiated by Whitman: in that it is, above all, an *American* epic, concerned with spiritual possibility rather than historical achievement, creating a hero or heroic consciousness instead of simply celebrating one. Whitman, Crane once observed, 'was able to co-ordinate those forces in America which seem most intractable, fusing them into a universal vision which takes on additional significance as time goes on'. The same is surely true of Crane. Like all other major attempts at American epic, *The Bridge* is responsive to the material pressures of the nation and its promise – which, for Crane, means its mystical potential. And it remains open, requiring the reader to complete it – by continuing the spiritual journey begun by the poet. It embarks on the road of visionary discovery in the hope that, one day, other visionaries and other Americans will follow.

Making it new in prose

As Gertrude Stein (1874–1946) was dying, she asked those with her, 'What is the answer?' There was no reply and, after a short pause, she laughed and added, 'Then what is the question?' Those last words were characteristic of a writer who was committed to experiment and inquiry, and in particular to asking fundamental questions about the relationship between language and reality. 'Beginning again and again is a natural thing,' she wrote in *Composition as Explanation* (1926). As she saw it, innovation was necessary because it was the 'business of art' to live in 'the complete and actual present'. The enemies were traditional narrative – with its reliance on habit and continuity rather than instantaneousness – and memory. 'It is very curious,' she declared in *What Are Masterpieces* (1940), 'you begin to write something and suddenly you remember something and if you continue to

---

remember your writing gets very confused.' To see the thing as it is, the thing-in-itself rather than the thing in history, was her aim: and that meant clearing away the grime of old emotions and associations. 'After all,' she suggested in *Picasso* (1938), 'the natural way to count is not that one and one make two but go on counting one and one and one . . . One and one and one and one and one.' Applied to prose, this would mean no 'assembling', no comparison, no increasing density of significance; it would mean a style that, literally, was not additive. Language could and should become a recreation of each perception ('now and now and now'), 'composition' rather than 'description'. It should involve, fundamentally, repetition, with small additions and modifications catching the differences as well as the similarities between each separate moment. For Stein, this project, not only to live in the actual present but 'to completely express that actual present' (as she put it in her *Lectures in America* [1935]), was an aesthetic imperative but also, critically, an American one. This was because Americans were, supremely, of the present. 'It has always seemed to me a rare privilege, this, of being an American, a real American, one whose tradition it has taken scarcely sixty years to create,' she confessed in *The Making of Americans* (1906–8, published in 1925). 'We need only realise our parents, remember our grandparents and know ourselves and our history is complete.' 'If you are an American,' she added in *Narration* (1935), 'gradually you find that really it is not necessary not really necessary that anything that everything has a beginning a middle and an ending.' You return to 'the simplicity of something always happening', the purity of what is existing now and for itself and, as Whitman did, Stein suggests, to a language that evokes the sheer quality of the here and now, existing things.

Whitman was singled out as exemplary here: 'he wanted really wanted to express the thing', Stein insisted in *Lectures in America*. So too were the Modernist visual experiments of Picasso and the contemporary cinema. Picasso, Stein suggested, was trying to look at things as if for the first time: like a child who sees only vivid fragments – one side of its mother's face, for example – and has not yet learned to infer the whole. 'He was right,' she insisted, 'one sees what one sees, the rest is a reconstruction from memory and painters have nothing to do with reconstruction.' Nor do any artists, including writers like herself, she felt: what she found in Picasso was what she wanted in her own work, 'things seen without association but simply as things seen'. And she also found it in the cinema. 'The cinema has offered a solution of this thing,' she explains in *Lectures in America*: the thing, that is, of simulating people, objects, emotions 'as they are existing' and without having recourse to 'remembering'. 'By a continuously moving picture of any one there is no memory of any other thing and there is that thing existing,' she goes on. Just as life never repeats itself, so the cinema does not quite repeat itself and prose should not really repeat itself: there are minute differences in each successive moment, frame or phrase making up a sequence that presents itself as a flowing continuity, a continually developing present complete and actual at any given moment. Now and now and now – one and one and one: what Stein pursues in her work is an experience of wonder at the constant newness of things. By the use of partly repetitive statements, each making a limited advance, she presents us with an uninterrupted series of instantaneous visions, so that we can grasp living moments in precise, ordered forms. Reading her prose is sometimes like holding a strip of movie film and looking at each frame separately. There is stillness, newness, difference in each frame or phrase but there is also the impulse towards process, motion – registered, in Stein's work, in particular, in her preference for verbs and participles over nouns and adjectives, and her minimal use of punctuation. The present and process: that was a very American coupling, as well as a Modernist one, as Stein knew well. 'It is something strictly American to conceive a space that is filled with moving,' she observed in *Lectures in America*, 'a space of time that is filled always with moving.'

Stein herself left America in 1903. Having spent her early years in Vienna and Paris as well as the United States, she moved back to Paris where she lived until her death, except for the years of Nazi occupation, when she moved to the south. A lesbian, she lived with another expatriate American, Alice B. Toklas, from 1907. A friend of such painters as Picasso, Matisse and Braque, she established a salon in the 1920s that became a gathering place for both European artists and American expatriates like Hemingway, Anderson and Fitzgerald. Her first published work, *Three Lives: Stories of the Good Anna, Melanctha, and the Gentle Lena* (1904–5, published 1909), shows some of the influence of naturalism. But already the hallmarks of Stein's mature style are there, especially in the second section concerning the black woman Melanctha. Melanctha is defined by her excited involvement in the present moment. One of her lovers tells her, 'you never can remember'; her explanation is 'it's because I am always knowing what it is I am wanting, when I get it'. And to capture her character's strange combination of 'ignorance and power and desire', Stein uses a style marked by repetition that moves ever forward in a rhythmic pattern with an emphasis placed on the verb. Nouns being names, Stein observed in *Lectures in America*, 'things once they are named the name does not go on doing anything to them and so why write in nouns'. With poetry, however, she held a different theory of language. Although nouns did not carry prose forward, Stein argued, 'you can love a name and if you love a name then saying that name any number of times only makes you love it more'. And poetry is 'really loving the name of anything', she said. So in *Tender Buttons* (1914), her prose and poetry meditation on 'Objects: food: rooms', she sometimes dwells upon nouns: repeating one as if, each time it is repeated, a bit of inertia and impercipience is shaken loose off it and the reality is freshly brought to our minds. That strategy is at work in what is perhaps her most famous phrase: 'a rose is a rose is a rose is a rose'. 'I caressed completely caressed and addressed the noun' here, she later explained, so as to take the reader away from the common word and towards the rare reality. It was her way of pursuing a strategy common in American writing: to reassert the presence of the miraculous in the commonplace and so replace habit with wonder.

Altogether, Stein produced over five hundred titles: novels, poems, plays, articles, memoirs and portraits of the famous. These included *The Geographical History of America* (1935), *Ida: A Novel* (1940), a relatively straightforward account of a contemporary American woman, and *The Mother of Us All* (1945–6), a portrait of the nineteenth-century American leader Susan B. Anthony. One of her best-known works from her later period is *The Autobiography of Alice B. Toklas* (1933), a fictionalized account of her own life from the point of view of her companion and partner. In the *Autobiography* Stein, through the persona of Toklas, tells of their travels and their life 'in the heart of an art movement': their acquaintance with a wide variety of artists and intellectuals from Picasso to Pound, from T. S. Eliot to Djuna Barnes. Stein had a high opinion of her own work that has not always been shared. She claimed that only three writers of her time were being true to the writerly imperatives she outlined: Proust, Joyce and herself. And in *The Geographical History of America*, she makes it clear that, in her opinion, she is doing the major literary thinking of her period. There is a curiously airless quality about some of her pronouncements, such as her repeated contention, in the *Geographical History*, that 'human nature has nothing to do with it', 'nothing to do with master-pieces'. Perhaps this is because she tended to confuse two separate issues: she wished to look at reality as though for the first time; she then thought it necessary to write about this reality without using words that contained compelling evidence of previous realities witnessed, previous attempts at a direct encounter with the world. No matter the debate over her achievement, though, and the problems or contradictions latent in her approach, there is no doubt that she was a major innovator, one of the leading figures in American literary Modernism. Ernest Hemingway confessed that he was grateful to Stein 'for everything I learned from her about the abstract relationship of words'. Many other writers said, or could have said the same. There may, perhaps, be doubts about the literary solutions, the aesthetic answers she came up with, but there can be no doubt that she always asked the right questions.

Three Modernist writers who asked questions, in particular, about the condition of being a woman were Katherine Anne Porter (1890–1980), Elizabeth Madox Roberts (1881–1941) and Djuna Barnes (1892–1982). Porter, born in Texas, worked on a newspaper in Colorado before spending many years in Mexico and Europe. It was the experience of foreign cultures that supplied the catalyst for her first collection of stories, *Flowering Judas and Other Stories* (1930). Several of these stories are set in Mexico and, whatever the setting, they explore the theme that was to dominate her writing: a woman's search for independence and the conflict between this and, on the one hand, the pressures of custom and tradition, and, on the other, her own desire for love and the conventional security of home and family. That theme is dramatized with particular subtlety and passion in *Pale Horse, Pale Rider* (1939), a volume consisting of three short novels, and also in the stories collected under the title, 'The Old Order', in *Collected Stories* (1965). Miranda Rhea, the central character in 'The Old Order' and two of the narratives in the 1939 collection, is semi-autobiographical. Growing up in the South, she has to learn simultaneously about the limitations inherent in the codes and traditions transmitted to her by her family and about the scope of her responsibilities. Eventually, these two levels of her story, the examination of impersonal myth and the issue of personal development, become inseparable, since the static and disciplined world into which Miranda is born is seen to be typical of the Old South and of childhood; while Miranda's gradual freeing of herself from her environment and the forms of behaviour it dictates is, Porter intimates, as much the consequence of its general decay as of her own increasing maturity. Becoming an adult, she becomes less of a conventional Southerner; forsaking childhood and childish things, she forsakes along with them the codes and ceremonies of the old plantation. The lessons learned by Miranda in growing up are consolidated and confirmed in a story like 'Pale Horse, Pale Rider'. Set during the First World War, it is nominally about her love for a soldier who dies in an epidemic. More fundamentally, it is about Miranda learning to rely on nobody but herself because, in the final analysis, everyone is alone. Experiencing near fatal illness, she sinks 'through deeps under deeps of darkness' in a kind of delirium: until she reaches one 'minute fiercely burning particle of being that knew itself alone, that relied upon nothing beyond itself for strength'. It is her self, her individual consciousness and her stubborn will to live: 'Trust me, the hard unwinking angry point of light said. Trust me. I stay.' That trust in an independent consciousness is the core value in Porter's stories; and it is expressed not only in what Porter says but how she says it. Her finest pieces demonstrate that agility and luminosity of mind apparently so essential to travellers along what she called 'the downward path to wisdom'. All her characters need to guide them through their lives is shown to be there in the controlling intelligence of the narrative; in this sense, as in so many instances of Modernism, the medium of Porter's work *is* its meaning.

The volume of Porter's work is small. It includes one novel, *Ship of Fools* (1962), which was well received when it was first published, but it is her little over two dozen short stories and novellas that represent her real achievement. By contrast, Elizabeth Madox Roberts produced several volumes of poetry and no fewer than nine novels. It is, however, on two books, *The Time of Man* (1926) and *The Great Meadow* (1930), that her reputation rests. In a sense, *The Great Meadow* is a historical novel: set in the early nineteenth century, it deals with the settlement of Kentucky. Only in a sense, however: what it is really about is an act of creation. 'Life is from within,' Roberts declared; and what she shows here is her central character, a young woman called Diony Hall, making her own errand into the wilderness to build there a world and identity for herself, to create something adequate to her needs and commensurate with her capacity for wonder. In *The Time of Man* there is, again, a feminine central consciousness shaping the subject. This time, the consciousness is that of a poor white woman living in the twentieth century, Ellen Chesser. Born to a family of tenant farmers, her life of wandering and 'a-walken' from one small patch of hired land to another is described in harsh detail. Nothing is spared or excluded from the report: but the book is much more than a tough account of life among the rural poor. 'I began to think of the wandering tenant farmer of our regions as offering a symbol for an Odyssey of Man,' Roberts said, as she described how she came to write her most famous novel. And what *The Time of Man* does is precisely to give Ellen's life as a 'wanderer buffeted about by the fates and the weathers' an epic dimension, to make the reader believe in the possibility of heroism. There is a constant tension in the novel between its documentary level, which tells us of what is, and what might be called the level of dream or desire, which intimates to us just what might be. Roberts's strategy for realizing this other level is quite simple: she makes us share in the consciousness of Ellen Chesser and her imagining of 'some better country' where her mental and material needs might be met. The reader is invited to witness the act of the mind: the continuing attempts to build an ideal, a possibility, out of the ruins of the actual. Ellen manages not just to survive life but to change it, since her need for a better condition of things is perceived as an agent of transformation as well as an act of transcendence. The agrarian dream – the dream, that is, of a world in which each moment of farm life becomes meaningful – enables her to keep on going, it may be, but it also furnishes the simplest of her routines with a quality of ritual; it breathes life, and the sense of an almost sacramental significance, into even the most ordinary and everyday of tasks. Roberts is not subscribing here to the kind of idealism that would deny the pressure of the actual; among other things, *The Time of Man* is a vividly naturalistic fiction. But she is imputing as much power to the mind, and again in this case the female mind, as to matter in the creation of the real. As a result, her heroine can use her idea of the good life actively to improve her condition; somehow, thanks to the sheer energy of her needing and thinking, she can achieve real moments of redemption.

Whereas Roberts set much of her work in her native Kentucky, Djuna Barnes went much further afield, in fact and in her imagination. Born in the state of New York, she worked in New York City before moving to Paris where, enjoying the company of other expatriates, she wrote novels, plays, short stories and poems. While still in New York, she was associated with the experimental theatre company the Provincetown Players, who produced three of her one-act plays. Her first publication was a collection of poems, *The Book of Repulsive Women* (1915); her stories and short plays were collected in *A Book* (1923); and her first published novel was *Ryder* (1929), a satiric chronicle of family history. But her major work is *Nightwood* (1936), an intensely poetic novel that T. S. Eliot described as having 'a quality of horror and doom very nearly related to that of Elizabethan tragedy'. Focusing on the relationships of a group of expatriates in Paris and Berlin, *Nightwood* transforms its author's affair with a sculptor, Thelma Wood, into a study of relationships between women. Thelma becomes one of the main characters, Robin Vote, a 'somnambule' and figure of the night. Other characters include Nora Flood, an American who becomes Robin's lover and who is the emotional centre of the book, Jenny Petherbridge, a cultural parasite who takes Robin away from Nora, Felix Volkbein, a German Jew in search of a history and a family whom Robin marries, and Doctor Matthew O'Connor, an Irish American unlicensed gynaecologist and student of night, war and contemporary culture whose alcoholic, melancholic and apocalyptic meditations help give *Nightwood* its unique, Modernist shape. Barnes was inclined to see her century as a carnival or circus; she was absorbed in figures of the night, shadowy exiles and grotesques; and she depicted characters crippled by weaknesses of the body and the spirit, struggling to redeem themselves from an intense sense of doom. The final scene clearly reflects her dark vision and the word play she used to communicate it. Robin lies on the floor of a chapel in the woods, a dog beside her; and 'dog', we are invited to recall, is the inverse of 'god'. Unlike Roberts's heroines, she has not found redemption or peace; she remains, as she was, a creature of the night.

Of all American writers concerned with the inventions of Modernism, F. Scott Fitzgerald (1896–1940) was the most autobiographical. Finding in the compulsions of his life the contours of his fiction, he sustained for his generation the great American romance of the self. It was a romance, however, that was alive to the dissonances and disjunctions of the modern age and that was refracted through Fitzgerald's own sense of the porous, plural nature of his personality. 'Sometimes,' Fitzgerald once said, 'I don't know whether I'm real or whether I'm a character in one of my own novels.' And there is no doubt that the protagonists of books like *This Side of Paradise* (1920), *The Great Gatsby* (1926), *Tender is the Night* (1934) and *The Last Tycoon* (1941) bear an extraordinary resemblance to their creator. In each case, there is the same commitment to flamboyant excess, combined with a very personal kind of idealism; in each case, too, there is a testing, a trying out taking place – of the dreams of power, possibility and wealth that have fuelled America and individual Americans and of how those dreams can be negotiated in a world dedicated to consumption, a surfeit of commodities. 'There never was a good biography of a good novelist,' Fitzgerald observed in his notebooks. 'There couldn't be. He is too many people.' And, as usual, when he was being most perceptive, that comment sprang from observation of himself. Fitzgerald was, as he once put it, 'a cynical idealist'. He could manoeuvre his way through the dreams and realities that captivated him and his fellow Americans and moderns: he could measure both the necessity and the impossibility of idealism, the 'green light' in the distance that heroes like Jay Gatsby stretch out towards and never quite reach. Easily as much as any American writer, and more than most, Fitzgerald demonstrates the paradox that to talk of oneself may also be to talk of one's times, the character of a culture – and that self-revelation, ultimately, can be a revelation of humanity.

Born in Minnesota, Fitzgerald entered the army in 1917; and it was while stationed in Alabama that he met Zelda Sayre, an aspiring writer like him and a woman renowned for her daring, gaiety and beauty. 'I fell in love with her on September 7th,' Fitzgerald recorded, with characteristic precision of sentiment. They were eventually married in 1920, the year his first collection of stories, *Flappers and Philosophers*, and his first novel, *This Side of Paradise*, were published. Both were an immediate success. America was going on what Fitzgerald later called 'the greatest, gaudiest spree in history' with 'a new generation dedicated more than the last to the fear of poverty and the worship of success'. It was Fitzgerald who christened it 'the Jazz Age'; his *Tales of the Jazz Age* was published in 1922. 'I wanted to be the historian of that generation,' Fitzgerald explained, 'and at first I could only see it as it saw itself.' That is not strictly true and does less than justice to his earlier work. Amory Blaine, the protagonist in *This Side of Paradise*, is presented with glancing irony along with entranced sympathy, as a representative of the age: as the working title for the novel, 'The Romantic Egotist', clearly indicates. And *Tales of the Jazz Age* includes 'The Diamond as Big as the Ritz', one of the most corrosive contemporary accounts of the confusions of capitalism. But it is true that, for this earlier work, Fitzgerald won fame, fortune and the title of 'the poet laureate of the Jazz Age', all of which enabled him and Zelda to lead a life of boisterous consumption. For a while, the couple lived in New York City, their glamorous lifestyle supported by a steady production of short stories from Fitzgerald, many of them of stunning mediocrity. Then, in 1924, they moved to France, where they could live more cheaply. Two years after their removal there, two more books were published: a third collection of stories, *All the Sad Young Men*, and Fitzgerald's third and probably finest novel, *The Great Gatsby*.

In writing *The Great Gatsby*, Fitzgerald set out, as he put it, to 'make something *new* – something extraordinary and beautiful and simple and intricately patterned'. And, to achieve this, the first and most important choice he made was to drop the third-person narrator of his two previous novels, *This Side of Paradise* and *The Beautiful and Damned* (1922). Instead of an omniscient viewpoint, there is a fictional narrator, Nick Carraway, a man who is only slightly involved in the action but who is profoundly affected by it. To some extent, Nick is quite like the protagonist Jay Gatsby. Like so many representative figures of the 1920s, including Fitzgerald himself, both are young people from the Midwest trying to prove themselves in the East. The East, and in particular its cities, have become for them a new frontier, a neutral space in which their dreams of wealth, measureless power and mobility may perhaps be realized. Both Nick and Gatsby, too, have a love affair with a charismatic woman that ends in disillusion: Gatsby with Daisy Buchanan (a character modelled in part on Zelda Sayre) and Nick with a glamorous golf professional called Jordan Baker. This creates a bond of sympathy between the two men. Part of the immense charm of this novel is inherent in its tone, of elegiac romance. Nick is looking back on an action already completed that, as we know from the beginning, ended in disaster, some 'foul dust' that 'floated in the wake' of Gatsby's dreams; he is also recording how he grew to sympathize with, like and admire Jay Gatsby – on one memorable level, this is the story of a love affair between two men. Liking, or even loving, does not mean approval, however; and it does not inhibit criticism. Nick has had 'advantages' that Jay Gatsby, born to poverty as James Gatz, has not had. He has a reserve, a common sense and even an incurable honesty that make him quite different from the subject of his meditations. That helps to create distance, enables him to criticize Gatsby and the high romanticism he embodies, and it makes his commentary vividly plural; Nick is, as he himself puts it, 'within and without, simultaneously enchanted and repelled' by the hero he describes. The use of Nick Carraway as a narrator, in effect, enables Fitzgerald to maintain a balance for the first time in his career between the two sides of his character. The idealist, the romantic who believed in possibility and perfectibility, and the pragmatist, the realist, convinced that life is circumscribed, nasty, brutish and short: these opposing tendencies are both allowed their full play, the drama of the narration *is* the tension between them. 'The test of a first-rate intelligence', Fitzgerald was later to say in his autobiographical essay 'The Crack-Up' (*The Crack-Up* [1945]) 'is the ability to hold two opposed ideas in the mind at the same time, and still retain the ability to function.' That is precisely what he does in *The Great Gatsby*, thanks to the use of Nick Carraway as a narrator: by his own stringent standards, the book is the product not only of a refined sensibility and a strenuous act of imaginative sympathy but also of 'a first-rate intelligence'.

What this first-rate intelligence is applied to is a story about the reinvention of the self: the poor boy James Gatz who renamed and recreated himself as Jay Gatsby, and who sees a woman as the crown, centre and confirmation of this process. Daisy Buchanan is the dream girl whose voice, sounding like both music and money, measures the contradictions of the dream, its heady mix of mystery and the material, moral perfection and economic power. Gatsby had known Daisy when he was younger, Nick and the reader learn, before she was married to Tom Buchanan. Tom, incidentally, is a man born into wealth and former football hero, whose sense of anti-climax since his days of sporting glory has tempted him to embrace racist ideas for explanation and excitement, to convince himself that he is not stale and past it; Fitzgerald is a brilliant analyst of the political through the personal and his story, lightly and even comically sketched, is a brief history of what tempts people into fascism. But Gatsby now wants to win Daisy back: to 'repeat the past', as Nick characterizes it, and 'fix everything just the way it was before'. The erotic mingles with the elevated in this strange but somehow typically American desire to remould the present and future in the shape of an imagined past: looking backward and forward, Gatsby embodies a national leaning toward not just the confusion of the ethical with the economic but a peculiar form of nostalgic utopianism. Quickly, subtly, the dream Gatsby cherishes begins to fray at the edges. The narrative moves forward on an alternating rhythm of action and meditation, a series of parties or similar social occasions around which the moments of meditative commentary are woven; and Gatsby's parties – which he approaches with the air of an artist, since they are momentary realizations of his dream of order, glamour and perfection – deteriorate ever more quickly into sterility and violence. Daisy becomes less and less amenable and malleable, less open to Gatsby's desire to idealize or, it may be, use her (part of the subtle ambivalence of the novel is that it can, and does, include the possibilities of both idealism and use). Quite apart from anything else, she refuses to declare that she has never loved her husband, something that may seem perfectly reasonable but that Gatsby takes as proof of her contaminating contact with a world other than his own.

Economical but also elegant, precisely visual but also patiently ruminative, *The Great Gatsby* rapidly moves towards catastrophe. It is a catastrophe that draws together many of the pivotal images of the book. The initial setting for this concluding sequence is the Valley of Ashes, a wasteland that is and embodies the foul dust floating in the wake of Gatsby's dreams, not least because it reminds the reader that success is measured against failure, power and wealth are defined by their opposites, there is no victory in a competitive ethos without a victim. Among the victims in this valley, presided over by the eyes of Dr T. J. Eckleburg – an enormous advertisement that somehow sees the realities Gatsby is blinded to – is Myrtle Wilson, a resident of the place and the mistress of Tom Buchanan. Her victim status is only confirmed when she runs out in front of a car being driven by Daisy and is immediately killed. Wilson, Myrtle's husband, makes the easy mistake of thinking Gatsby is responsible for his wife's death. Tom and Daisy, when he asks them where Gatsby lives, do not disabuse him. So, although it is Wilson who actually kills Gatsby at the end of the story, the Buchanans are morally responsible too. They retreat 'back into their money, or their vast carelessness, or whatever it was that kept them going'. And, with Gatsby destroyed with the tacit connivance of the 'very rich' he has always admired, his dream shattered thanks to the quiet agency of the woman he wanted to dwell at its centre, the story is almost over.

Almost, but not quite. At the funeral of Gatsby, Nick meets Henry C. Gatz, the father of the man who tried to reinvent himself. What he learns about, among other things, is the scheme of self-improvement that Gatsby drew up when he was still James Gatz and only a boy. The scheme is written on the fly-leaf of a copy of 'Hopalong Cassidy'. And, although it is an anticipation of the later ambitions of the hero, it is also clearly a parody of the manual of self-help that Benjamin Franklin drew up. By extension, it is a parody of all those other manuals of self-help that have thrived in American writing ever since. It does not take too much ingenuity to see that a link is being forged between Gatsby's response to life and the frontier philosophy of individualism. The link is confirmed when Nick confesses that he now sees the story of Gatsby as 'a story of the West after all'; in a sense, Gatsby and the Western hero are one. But this is not only a story of the West, Nick intimates, it is also a story of America. That is powerfully articulated in the closing moments of the story, when Gatsby's belief in 'the green light, the orgiastic future that year by year recedes before us', is connected to 'the last and greatest of all human dreams' that 'flowered once for Dutch sailors' eyes' as they encountered the 'fresh green breast of the new world'. Gatsby believed in an ideal of Edenic innocence and perfection, Nick has disclosed. So did America. Gatsby tried to make the future an imitation of some mythic past. So did America. Gatsby tried to transform his life into an ideal, the great good life of the imagination, that strangely mixed the mystic and the material. So, the reader infers, did America. Gatsby's dream is, in effect, the American dream; and Fitzgerald is ultimately exploring a nation and a national consciousness here as well as a single and singular man.

But who are the 'we' in the famous ending sentence of the novel: 'So we beat on, boats against the current, borne back ceaselessly into the past'? Americans, certainly, dreaming of the West in particular, but also surely anyone who tries to search for meaning, realize an ideal, or just make sense of their life: which includes just about everyone. Even the brutely material Tom Buchanan tries to grope for an explanation, something to help him feel that his life is not just decline and waste. What he finds, to help him explain things, may be not only absurd but obscene:

but it shows that even he, in his own blundering way, is trying to make sense of things. Within the confines of the story, though, the person who matters here, along with Gatsby, is the teller of the tale. Nick is the crucial other member of the 'we', the company of those driven by the desire to shape experience into some meaningful pattern, some radiant revelation. All the while, the reader is reminded, it is Nick's consciousness that is recalling and rehearsing the past in *The Great Gatsby*, trying to understand it, to discover its shape and meaning. Nick replicates in his telling of the tale what, fundamentally, Gatsby is doing in the tale being told: there is a shared need for order here, a pursuit of meaning that is definitively human. To that extent, Gatsby's project is Nick's; the form of the book dramatizes its theme. And both form and theme point to a paradox that is basic to Fitzgerald's life and writing. As Fitzgerald saw it, 'we' must try to pursue the ideal; in this sense, 'we' are and must be romantics, and on this capacity depends our survival as moral beings. But 'we' must always remember that the ideal will remain ceaselessly beyond our reach; in this sense, 'we' are and must be realists, and on this capacity depends our simple continuation and our grasp on sense. No matter how hard 'we' try to reach out to the green light, it will continue to elude us: but 'we' must keep on trying. That is the paradox that fires Fitzgerald's work into life. Or, as Fitzgerald himself succinctly put it, in 'The Crack-Up': 'one should . . . be able to see that things are hopeless and yet be determined to make them otherwise'.

The moral resilience which that remark discloses was to be sorely tested over the remaining years of Fitzgerald's life. In 1930, Zelda had the first of a series of nervous breakdowns; she was confined to a sanatorium periodically, both in Europe and in the United States, until she died in 1948. Pressed for money, suffering from alcoholism, Fitzgerald found employment in Hollywood on several occasions. He worked on a number of screenplays, but only completed one, *Three Comrades* (1938), and he was eventually dismissed because of his drinking – a story that Budd Schulberg (1914–) tells, thinly disguised as fiction, in his novel *The Disenchanted* (1958). Fitzgerald's fourth novel, *Tender is the Night*, was well received by reviewers. The title is taken from 'Ode to a Nightingale' by John Keats. It alerts the reader to the fact that a familiar romantic pattern is at work here, in which someone, a poet or a lover perhaps, tries to create an ideal world, immune to time and change, but, if he succeeds, only does so for a brief enchanted moment. What it does not alert the reader to is that this, a much more autobiographical novel, also represents an attempt at social commentary. Fitzgerald is much more openly critical here, for instance, of the lassitude and carelessness of the very rich, and the immense social and economic machinery that is required to enable them to live their lives as conspicuous consumers. Impressive as *Tender is the Night* is, though, it did not sell well when it was first published. Neither did *Taps at Reveille*, a collection of short stories that appeared in 1935. For a while, after his disastrous encounter with Hollywood, Fitzgerald stopped writing. But then, helped by the columnist Sheila Graham with whom he formed a new liaison, he returned to fiction again, writing a series of tales about a Hollywood scriptwriter, *The Pat Hobby Stories*, and a novel about another romantic egotist, this time a Hollywood producer, *The Last Tycoon*. *The Last Tycoon* was unfinished when Fitzgerald died suddenly of a heart attack. It was published in its incomplete form a year after his death; and the stories about Pat Hobby did not appear until 1962. At the time of his death, Fitzgerald's reputation had just about reached its nadir. He was generally dismissed as a writer of the 'lost decade' of the 1920s (to use Fitzgerald's own phrase), who had become irrelevant with its passing. What was not realized then, but what is now, is that Fitzgerald was, certainly, the poet laureate of the Jazz Age but that his way of writing about that age, and its aftermath, laid bare fundamental issues – about American and modern society and how 'we' define ourselves as human beings. He was no doubt a romantic, but a romantic with a firm grip on reality, a cold, knowing eye. For Fitzgerald, the personal was the political; he saw the quality of private experience as a gauge of society, a way of understanding history. That is why his fiction is an intimate disclosure of its author and his times and of ourselves, the 'we' of his audience, as well.

'Christ, Man,' wrote John Dos Passos (1896–1971) to Fitzgerald, after he had read 'The Crack-Up', 'how do you find time in the middle of the general conflagration to worry about all that stuff?' Dos Passos was clearly baffled by Fitzgerald's preoccupation 'with all that stuff' about the meaning of his personal experience. For him, what mattered was the 'general conflagration', the crisis of capitalism, in the 1930s; and he directed all his energies, and his skills as a Modernist innovator, to depicting that conflagration in his greatest work, *U.S.A.* (1930–6). Prior to writing the three books that constitute the *U.S.A.* trilogy, *The 42nd Parallel* (1930), *1919* (1932) and *The Big Money* (1936), Dos Passos had written several novels, essays and poems. His first two novels, *One Man's Initiation: 1917* (1920) and *Three Soldiers* (1921), are typical of their time in that, like so many works reflecting postwar disillusionment, they reveal the horror with which sensitive and idealistic young men confront war and an alien society. *Three Soldiers*, in particular, anticipates Dos Passos's later work. Describing the related careers of three American soldiers during the First World War, it deploys what was to become its author's habitual strategy: the characters are not so much individuals as representative social types. Not only that, it explores his habitual theme, the subject that dominates nearly all his work: that is, the conflict between humanity and system, between a consciousness struggling to maintain its autonomy and the crushing, reductive power of a social machine – sometimes identified as the army, sometimes called the law, the corporation or the city, but always identified with the impersonal mechanisms of the modern world. The narrative form of *Three Soldiers* is, however, relatively conventional. Its Modernism is a matter of theme – its preoccupation with social exile, alienation – rather than technique. With *Manhattan Transfer* (1925) all that changed. By now, Dos Passos believed that, if he was to recreate the new, urban America in prose, he would have to pursue a new mode of apprehension, a new form of fiction that was as far removed from the old as the city was from the farm. Set, as its title implies, in the city of New York, *Manhattan Transfer* moves rapidly between numerous characters who have in common only their status as New Yorkers. They come together, if at all, only by chance and impersonally;

sometimes, they simply pass each other in the street and the author then switches from the story of one to the story of the other. Each chapter begins with passages of almost poetic prose, consisting of observations of city life, slogans, snatches of dialogue, advertisements or newspaper headlines. These passages make it even clearer that this is a collective novel about New York City – about its superficiality, its surfaces, its immorality and crushing mechanization – rather than any individual. Dos Passos learned this disjunctive, disconnected narrative technique, in part, from abstract impressionist painters, with their interest in the power and perplexity of the present moment, and from film directors like Eisenstein and D. W. Griffith, with their development of rapid cutting, montage. But it was, fundamentally, his own invention, his own way of translating into prose what he saw as the delirium and danger of modern life.

That came to full fruition in *U.S.A.*, where, as Dos Passos puts it in a brief Preface to the trilogy, the author was intent on producing a new language. 'Mostly *U.S.A.* is the speech of the people,' Dos Passos declares. And that speech is meant to capture the discontinuous movement of city life, the noise, pace and claustrophobia of modernity, the sense of many different messages, images and impressions all bombarding the consciousness at the same time. *U.S.A.* is, definitively, of and about modern America. To be exact, it covers the period from 1900 to 1930, the period which, Dos Passos felt, witnessed the emergence of modern American society. Beginning roughly with the Spanish–American War of 1898 and ending with the Wall Street Crash and its aftermath, it dramatizes the lives of a large array of characters. Although several of these characters appear in all three novels, their activities do not constitute a unified plot. As in Dos Passos's earlier novels, they are types rather than fully developed individuals and, rather than agents, they are subjects; things happen to them, they do not so much have lives as destinies; acts, emotions, ideas suddenly settle within them, then disappear, without their having much to say in the matter. It is almost as if Dos Passos is anticipating the existentialist belief that experience precedes essence: that existence is, in fact, no more than the discontinuous flow of experience. But, unlike the existentialist, he has another, social point to make. All the people in these three books are evacuated of character, choice and individuality precisely because they are social victims. They are destroyed by a society that has become totalizing in its opposition to human freedom; they are subjects because they are totally subjected beings. And this, Dos Passos insists, is the social tragedy of our times.

Interspersed between Dos Passos's panoramic account of his many characters are other sections, using techniques specifically invented for *U.S.A.*, that add to its message and impact. One is called 'Newsreel'. It is a mixture of newspaper headlines and advertising slogans, snatches of political speeches and popular songs, all drawn from the moment in social history that is being recorded in the main narrative. The Newsreel is a verbal collage, a folk poem for industrial society, rehearsing in particular the war between capital and labour. And, just as it makes poems out of the public experience of America, so Dos Passos's second technical invention, 'The Camera Eye', makes poetry out of the private feelings of the author

---

Making it new in prose   441

at the time. In a charged, lyrical prose Dos Passos recalls how he saw and reacted to the major historical events that bear down on the lives of his characters. Along with these two kinds of narrative intervention, there is also a series of sections titled 'Biography'. These are brief, socially charged accounts of major public figures of the time, such as Henry Ford, Frank Lloyd Wright and Rudolph Valentino. All three innovations – Newsreel, Camera Eye, Biography – are, first of all, devices for highlighting the general social significance of an individual's experience. The Newsreel gives us the crude public image of that experience. The Camera Eye supplies the author's own immediate sense of socially important events. The Biography gives us the individual experience of a socially significant public figure. Dos Passos does not stop there, however, since he is not simply trying to show the reader that the public life is inseparable from the private, as if they were equals. He is, in addition, trying to suggest that – in an urban environment such as that of *U.S.A.* – the public life acts to dominate and control the private. He is repeating the point made in his portrait of his evacuated characters: that modern society overwhelms the individual. So, the Newsreels present the reader with all the images that bombard the consciousness in the city; they simulate an urban world that is indigestible, indecipherable and so uncontrollable. The Camera Eye sections show us a mind struggling gamely, but with a sure sense of defeat, to deal with its new surroundings; tellingly, it is a mind reduced to the status of a recording instrument, reflecting rather than managing and directing events. The Biography series, in turn, shows us people reduced to a media stereotype or social role: here, the person becomes the public image as we watch. What Newsreel, Camera Eye and Biography tell the reader, in short, is what all the characters in *U.S.A.* also do: that America has become a total institution, a prisonhouse for the mind as well as the body. While proclaiming allegiance to the principles of individualism and freedom, 'the speech of the people' reveals the subtext that Americans have become little more than cogs in a machine.

During the 1920s and 1930s, Dos Passos aligned himself politically with the left. He became disillusioned with communism, however, and broke completely with his left-wing friends and allies at the time of the Spanish Civil War. His later fiction, such as the trilogy *District of Columbia* (1939–49) and the novel *Midcentury* (1961), continue his stylistic innovations but show an increasingly conservative political stance. He was always, first and last, an individualist, concerned with the threat to the individual posed first, as he saw it, by capitalism and then, in his later work, by communism. To that extent, he belonged in the American Adamic tradition, with its commitment to the primacy of the individual, the supreme importance of the single, separate self. Consistently, Ernest Hemingway (1898–1961) belonged to that tradition too. For Hemingway, as for many earlier American writers – for Thoreau, for instance, for Cooper and Twain – the essential condition of life is solitary, and the interesting, the only really serious business is the management of that solitude. In this respect the first story, 'Indian Camp', in his first book, *In Our Time* (1925), is exemplary. Young Nick Adams, the protagonist, witnesses a birth and a death. The birth is exceptionally agonizing, with the mother, an Indian woman, being cut open by Nick's father and being sewn up with a fishing line. And the death too is peculiarly awful, the husband in the bunk above, listening to the woman in her agony, and cutting his throat. 'Why did he kill himself, Daddy?' Nick asks. 'I don't know, Nick,' comes the reply. 'He couldn't stand things, I guess.' Although this is the only significant, foreground suicide in Hemingway's fiction, the terms have been set. 'Things' will remain to the last hurtful and horrible, to be stood with as much dignity and courage as possible. For the moment, though, these things of horror are too much for Nick to dwell on. He must bury them far down in his mind and rest secure in the shelter of the father. 'In the early morning on the lake sitting in the stern of the boat with his father rowing,' the story concludes, 'he felt quite sure that he would never die.'

Such are the good times of boyhood in Hemingway: not mother and home but out in the open with father, recreating a frontier idyll. So, in the second story in *In Our Time*, to escape his wife's nervous chatter, Nick's father goes out for a walk. 'I want to go with you,' Nick declares; 'all right,' his father responds, 'come on, then.' Soon, when Nick is older, in the later stories 'The End of Something' and 'The Three-Day Blow', father will be replaced as companion by his friend Bill. But only the counters have altered, not the game. As the title of his second collection of stories, *Men Without Women* (1927), plainly indicates, the best times of all, because the least complicated, the least hurtful and the most inwardly peaceful, are had by men or boys together, preferably in some wide space of land or sea, away from the noise, pace and excitement of cities: Jake Barnes, the hero of *The Sun Also Rises* (1926), fishing with his companions Bill Gorton and Harris; Thomas Hudson and his three sons in *Islands in the Stream* (1970); and from *In Our Time*, in 'Cross-Country Snow', Nick and his friend George skiing in Switzerland one last time before Nick commits himself to the trap of marriage and fatherhood. 'Once a man's married, he's absolutely bitched,' is Bill's drunken wisdom in 'The Three-Day Blow': bitched by responsibilities, bitched by domesticity, but above all bitched by the pain locked in with a love that, one way or another, may easily be broken or lost. And a man's world, although safer from certain kinds of anxiety or threat, is for Hemingway only relatively so. A man will lose his wife but he will also lose his father, not just in death but in disillusionment. Near the end of *In Our Time*, an exemplary father dies, not Nick's but the jockey, 'My Old Man', with whom, around the race-courses of France and Italy, the young narrator has had a perfect time out, with no mother or woman in sight. When his father falls in a steeple-chase and is killed, the son is left to bear not just his grief but also the discovery that his father had been crooked. It is more than a life that has been lost. As he overhears the name of his father being besmirched, it seems to the boy 'like when they get started, they don't leave a guy nothing'.

'It was all a nothing,' observes the lonely protagonist of 'A Clean Well-Lighted Place' (*Winner Take Nothing* [1933]), 'and man was a nothing too.' In the face of palpable nothing, meaninglessness, there are, finally, only the imperatives of conduct and communion with one's own solitariness. 'I did not care what it was all about,' Jake confides in *The Sun Also Rises*. 'All I wanted to know was how to live in it.' One way to 'live in it', in some of Hemingway's novels, has a political slant. *To Have and Have Not* (1937) is an emphatic protest against corruption, political hypocrisy and the immorality of gross inequality. *For Whom the Bell Tolls* (1941) commemorates three days of a guerrilla action in the Spanish Civil War and celebrates the republican fight against fascism. 'I suppose I am an anarchist,' Hemingway had written to Dos Passos in 1932; and the novel, like *To Have and Have Not*, shows a lonely individualist fighting while he can, not for a political programme but for the simple humanist principles of justice and, above all, liberty. But a more fundamental way to 'live in it' is to live alone. In 'Big Two-Hearted River', the story that concludes *In Our Time*, Nick starts out from the site of a burned-out town in Michigan. 'There was no town, nothing but the rails and the burned-over country,' the reader is told. 'Even the surface had been burned off the ground.' The disaster that has annihilated the town aptly crowns the world of violence and slaughter revealed in the vignettes that have interleaved the stories of *In Our Time*. For Hemingway, wounded in the First World War, life *was* war, nasty, brutal and arbitrary; and that is a lesson Nick has now learned. Putting this stuff of nightmares behind him, Nick heads away from the road for the woods and the river. Far from other human sound, he fishes, pitches a tent, builds a fire, prepares himself food and drink. 'He was there, in the good place,' the reader is told. 'He was in his home where he had made it.' It is a familiar American moment, this sealing of a solitary compact with nature. It is also a familiar concluding moment in Hemingway's work: a man alone, trying to come to terms with the stark facts of life, and of death – sometimes the death of a loved one, as in *A Farewell to Arms* (1929), other times, as in 'The Snows of Kilimanjaro' (1938), his own inevitable and imminent dying. And what seals the compact, and confirms the starkness, is, always, the pellucid clarity of expression, the rigorous, simple economy of the terms in which Hemingway's lonely heroes are rendered to us. 'A writer's job is to tell the truth,' Hemingway observed. And he told that truth in a style that was a verbal equivalent of the grace under pressure shown by his finest protagonists: concrete, contained, cleaving to the hard facts of life, only disclosing its deeper urgencies in its repetitions and repressions – in what its rhythms implied and what it did not say.

Hemingway called this verbal art the art of omission. 'You could omit anything if you knew that you omitted,' Hemingway reflected in *A Moveable Feast* (1964), his memoir of his years in Paris after the First World War; 'and the omitted part would strengthen the story and make people feel something more than they understood.' He had begun to develop this art as a newspaperman: the copyroom of the *Kansas City Star*, where he worked before the First World War, was as much his Yale and Harvard as it was for Mark Twain, or the whaling-ship was for Herman Melville. 'Pure objective writing is the only true form of storytelling,' his closest companion on the *Star* told him. Hemingway never forgot that advice; and he never forgot the importance of his newspaper training to him, either. 'I was learning to write in those days,' he recalled in *Death in the Afternoon* (1932), 'and I found the greatest difficulty . . . was to put down what really happened in action, what the actual things were which produced the emotions that you experienced.' The 'real thing', Hemingway remembered, was 'something I was working very hard to try to get', first in Kansas, and then in Paris, where he received encouragement in his pursuit of concrete fact, and an example of how to do it, from Ezra Pound and, even more, Gertrude Stein. The experience of the First World War was also vital here. Like so many of his generation, Hemingway learned from that war not just a distrust but a hatred of abstraction, the high-sounding generalizations used as an excuse, or justification, for mass slaughter. 'I was always embarrassed by the words sacred, glorious, and sacrifice and the expression, in vain,' says the protagonist Frederic Henry in *A Farewell to Arms*, set, of course, in the Great War: 'the things that were glorious had no glory and the stockyards were like the stockyards of Chicago.' 'There were many words that you could not stand to hear and finally only the names of places had dignity.' Like Frederic Henry, Hemingway came to feel that 'abstract words such as glory, honour, courage, or hallow were obscene'; the simple words, those that carried the smallest burden of stock attitudes, were the safest ones. What the individual, and the writer, had to respond to were things and experiences themselves, not ideas about them; and the closer he or she stuck to them, the less risk there would be of losing what was truly felt under a mass of evasions and abstractions. The real thing the person or writer must pursue, Hemingway felt, is the truth of the individual, immediate experience and emotion. That truth is discovered by the Hemingway hero – just as it is by Huckleberry Finn – in *seeing* and *responding to* things for himself. And it is expressed by Hemingway – just as it is for Huck's creator, Mark Twain – in *describing* things for oneself, things as they are, not mediated by convention or abstraction. The style, in fact, is a measure of a commitment; it is the proper reaction to the world translated into words.

What Hemingway was after, in terms of words and action, is caught in perhaps his most successful novel, *The Sun Also Rises*, the seminal treatment of the 'lost generation' and its disillusionment in the aftermath of the First World War. The story is slight. The book describes a few weeks of spring in Paris, during which we watch the hero Jake Barnes living his customary life. He then goes on a fishing trip in Spain and attends a fiesta in Pamplona. Running through this small slice of his life is a minimal plot, concerned largely with the relationship between Jake and an Englishwoman, Brett Ashley. Brett is the woman with whom Jake has been in love off and on for some time. But when the novel ends, Jake and Brett are exactly where they were at the start. The novel finishes where it began; the characters walk around in a circle, not getting anywhere but just surviving. This is a world full of people with nothing to do and no place, apparently, to go. The characters – typically, for Hemingway, and for many stories of the postwar period – are situated in another country, an alien place; and they seem cut off from all sense of purpose, communal identity or historical direction. Their common situation is, as one of them succinctly puts it, 'miserable' – existentially, that is, rather than economically. Few of Hemingway's characters have to worry about where the next meal is coming from; on the contrary, they tend to eat rather well, food being one of the 'real things', the basic sensory pleasures of life. They live under constant stress, the pressure of living in a world without meaning, and their challenge is to show grace under that pressure. In a sense, this is a novel of manners: each character is judged according to how clearly he or she sees the truth – and, if they see it, how well or badly they behave.

The first question asked, implicitly, of all the characters in *The Sun Also Rises* is, is he or she 'one of us'? That is, is the character one of those who have learned to see what their true circumstances are, and what they truly feel? Those who have learned this seem to recognize each other and so constitute a kind of secret society. They are 'aficionados' of life, because they understand the perils of existence just as the good bullfighter, and the good bullfight spectator, understand the perils of the bullring. Being 'one of us', however, is not enough. There is also the question of how you behave. Some behave well, like Jake; some behave badly, sometimes, like Brett Ashley. Some never get the opportunity to behave well or badly because, like the least attractive character in the book, Robert Cohn, they never see what life is really like or know what they truly feel. They never recognize what the rules of the game are, and so never get to be a player. What the good player in life should do, how he or she should behave, is illustrated in the description of the perfect bullfighter, Romero – one of Brett's several lovers – as he confronts the charging bull. 'Romero never made any contortions, always it was straight and pure and natural in line,' Jake tells the reader; he never tries to concoct 'a faked look of danger'. He had 'the old thing', Jake concludes, 'the holding of his purity of line through a maximum of exposure'. Romero confronts 'the real thing', the challenge of life, with immediacy and intuitive simplicity. He responds to things as they are, without posture or pretence; and, in responding this way, he achieves a certain pure nobility. It is a neat example of how, in Hemingway's work, realism assumes a heroic quality, even an aura of romance. The noblest character is, invariably, the one who sticks closest to the facts.

That is especially true of Jake Barnes, who holds his purity of line as both the narrator and the protagonist. As narrator, Jake tries to tell us what he truly sees and feels, in a prose that is alert to the particular. As a protagonist, Jake tries for a similar clarity, simplicity and honesty; and, for the most part, he succeeds. What Jake has to see and deal with, above all, is his own impotence. He is incapable of sexual intercourse, because of a wound sustained in the First World War. This impotence is not a symbol. For Hemingway, life had no meaning independent of immediate experience, so symbolism was impossible for him. It is a fact: an instance of the cruel tricks life plays and the pressures everyone must, somehow and someday, confront. For Jake and Brett, love seeks its natural expression and issue in sex, sensory fulfilment. But this is impossible. And for Jake, as for Hemingway, to the extent that love, or any emotion, is not felt in sensory terms, translated into concrete experience, it is incomplete, even unreal. This is the trial Jake must face, the fundamental challenge thrown down to him in life: that his love can never be a 'real thing', it must remain thwarted, a loss and waste. Sometimes, Jake begins to crack under this pressure. 'It is really awfully easy to be hard-boiled about everything in the daytime,' he observes, 'but at night it is another thing.' He finds himself sleepless; and, his mind 'jumping around', he even starts quietly to cry. But, fundamentally, Jake weathers the storm. The end of the novel shows that, despite the temptation to pity himself, to dream of what might have been, to indulge in fantasy or fakery, he can see and stand things as they really are. He can be straight and pure and natural in his response to even the worst his life has to offer. Brett invites him to indulge, to escape from truth into daydream: 'Oh Jake,' she tells him, 'we could have had such a damned good time together.' His reply is simple, and supplies the last words in *The Sun Also Rises*: 'Yes, isn't it pretty to think so?' It is the perfect response for the Hemingway hero, because it is so simple and so stoical: so tersely, terribly rejecting the 'pretty', the fanciful, and, in doing so, registering the volcanic feelings that have to be contained in order to prevent mental and moral confusion. Jake is wounded, an exile in a world without pity: but so are all men and women, Hemingway intimates. He is also a hero: just as, potentially, we all are if we have the courage to face things and ourselves. Purity of line is what Jake sticks to, in the face of nothing; he regards it as his job, his duty to tell the truth. So, of course, does Hemingway; and, at his best, he does so; he sees and calls things by their right names.

'I am telling the same story over and over,' William Faulkner (1897–1962) admitted once, 'which is myself and the world.' That remark catches one of the major compulsions in his fiction: Faulkner was prone to interpret any writing, including his own, as a revelation of the writer's secret life, as his or her dark twin. By extension, he was inclined to see that writing as shadowed by the repressed myths, the secret stories of his culture. Repetition was rediscovery, as Faulkner saw it: his was an art not of omission like Hemingway's but of reinvention, circling back and circling back again, to the life that had been lived and missed, the emotions that had been felt but not yet understood. Shaped by the oral traditions of the South, which were still alive when he was young, and by the refracted techniques of Modernism, to which he was introduced as a young man, Faulkner was drawn to write in a way that was as old as storytelling and, at the time, as new as the cinema and Cubism. It was as if he, and his characters, in T. S. Eliot's famous phrase, had had the experience but missed the meaning; and telling became an almost obsessive reaction to this, a way of responding to the hope that perhaps by the indirections of the fictive impulse he could find directions out. That the hope was partial was implicit in the activity of telling the story 'over and over': Faulkner, like so many of his protagonists and narrators, kept coming back, and then coming back again, to events that seemed to resist understanding, to brim with undisclosed meaning. There would always be blockage between the commemorating writer and the commemorated experience, as Faulkner's compulsive use of the metaphor of a window indicated: the window on which a name is inscribed, for instance, in *Requiem for a Nun* (1951), or the window through which Quentin Compson gazes at his native South, as he travels home from Massachusetts, in *The Sound and the Fury* (1929). Writing, for Faulkner, was consequently described as a transparency and an obstacle, offering communication and discovery to the inquiring gaze of writer and reader but also impeding him, sealing him off from full sensory impact.

'You know,' Faulkner said once in one of his typically revelatory asides, 'sometimes I think there must be a sort of pollen of ideas floating in the air, which fertilizes similarly minds here and there which have not had direct contact.' In his case, that 'pollen of ideas' was primarily Southern in origin. He was born, brought up and spent most of his life in Mississippi; and most of his fiction is set in his apocryphal county of Yoknapatawpha, based on his home county of Lafayette. Not only that, every exploration of identity in his fiction tends to become an exploration of family, community and culture. 'No man is himself,' Faulkner insisted. 'He is the sum of his past.' And, while he was thinking in particular of his own self haunted by his ancestors, when he said this, he was also thinking of that interpenetration of past and present that is, perhaps, the dominant theme in Southern society and its cultural forms – and of his own determining conviction that any identity anywhere is indelibly stamped by history. A society, Faulkner believed and said, was 'the indigenous dream of any given collection of men having something in common, be it only geography or climate'. It was a material institution and also a moral, or immoral, force. 'Tell about the South,' asks a Canadian character, Shreve, in *Absalom, Absalom!* (1936). '*What's it like there. What do they do there. Why do they live there. Why do they live at all.*' In a sense, Faulkner never stopped 'telling', since his novels constitute an imaginative recovery of the South, an attempt to know it as a region. Those novels not only tell, however, they show. Much of their power derives from the fact that, in drawing us a map of his imaginary county, Faulkner is also charting a spiritual geography that is, in the first instance, his but could be ours as well. The dreams and obsessions which so startle and fascinate Shreve – with place, with the past, with evil, with the serpentine connections between history and identity – all these are the novelist's, and not just an aspect of described behaviour. And as the reader is drawn into the telling, attends to the myriad voices of every story, he or she becomes an active member of the debate. The consequence is that when, for example, Quentin Compson is described in *Absalom, Absalom!* as 'a barracks filled with stubborn backlooking ghosts', each reader feels the description could equally well apply to the story itself, to Faulkner the master storyteller, and to us his apprentices. Each reading of the story is its meaning; each reader is caught up in the rhythm of repetition, the compulsion not only to remember but to reinvent.

Faulkner began his creative life as a poet and artist. He published poems and drawings in student magazines in his hometown of Oxford, Mississippi; his first book, *The Marble Faun* (1924), was a collection of verse that showed the influence of an earlier generation of British and French poets, like Swinburne and Mallarmé. His first two novels, *Soldier's Pay* (1925) and *Mosquitoes* (1927), are conventional in many ways: the one a tale of postwar disillusionment, the other a satirical novel of ideas. *Soldier's Pay*, written in New Orleans, does, however, anticipate some familiar Faulkner trademarks; the absent centre or central figure who is both there and not there (in this case, because he has been traumatized by war), the small-town setting, the black characters acting as a shadowy and admonitory chorus, the present shadowed by the past. And *Mosquitoes*, set in and around New Orleans, carries traces of its author's obsession with the link, if any, between words and doing, language and experience – and with the question, issuing from that, of whether writing and speech, by their very nature, are doomed to fail. *Sartoris* (1929), his third novel, is the first to be set in his fictional county of Yoknapatawpha (although it was not given this name until *As I Lay Dying* [1930]). 'Beginning with *Sartoris*,' Faulkner later recalled, 'I discovered that my own little postage stamp of native soil was worth writing about, and that by sublimating the actual into the apocryphal I would have complete liberty to use whatever talent I might have to its absolute top.' *Sartoris* was originally written as *Flags in the Dust*; it was rejected and only published, under its new title, in an edited version. Any other writer might have been discouraged by this, to the point of silence. Faulkner, on the contrary, wrote a series of major Modernist novels over the next seven years: *The Sound and the Fury, As I Lay Dying, Sanctuary* (1931), *Light in August* (1932) and *Absalom, Absalom!* These were, eventually, to secure his reputation, if not immediately his future. Although highly regarded, by other writers in particular, he was frequently in financial trouble. Selling stories to the magazines like the *Saturday Evening Post* helped a little; working periodically in Hollywood, where his more notable credits included *To Have and Have Not* (1945) and *The Big Sleep* (1946), helped even more. The restoration of Faulkner's reputation, and his financial health, began with the publication of *The Portable Faulkner* in 1946; it was consolidated by the award of the Nobel Prize in 1950. By this time, Faulkner had produced fiction reflecting his concerns about the mobility and anonymity of modern life (*Pylon* [1935]; *The Wild Palms* [1939]) and his passionate interest in racial prejudice and social injustice in the South (*Go Down, Moses* [1942]; *Intruder in the Dust* [1948]). He had also written *The Hamlet* (1940), a deeply serious comedy focusing on social transformation in his region. This was to become the first book in a trilogy dealing with the rise to power of a poor white entrepreneur called Flem Snopes, and his eventual fall; the other two were *The Town* (1957) and *The Mansion* (1959). Generally, the later work betrays an inclination towards a more open, direct address of social and political issues, and a search for some grounds for hope, for the belief that humankind would not only endure but prevail. This was true not only of the later fiction set in Yoknapatawpha, like *Requiem for a Nun*, but also of his monumental *A Fable* (1954), set in the First World War, which uses the story of Christ to dramatize its message of peace. There is, certainly, a clear continuity between this later work and the earlier. Faulkner, for example, never ceased to be driven by the sense that identity is community and history, that we are who we are because of our place and past. And he never ceased, either, to forge a prose animated by the rhythms of the human voice, talking and telling things obsessively even if only to itself. But there is also change, transformation. It can be summed up by saying that Faulkner gravitated, slowly, away from the private to the public, away from the intimacies of the inward vision towards the intensities of the outward. Or, to put it more simply, he turned from Modernism to Modernity.

Making it new in prose

'*Maybe nothing ever happens once and is finished,*' reflects Quentin Compson in *Absalom, Absalom!*. Many lives are woven into one life in Faulkner, many texts into one text – a text that seems to be without circumference or closure. Repetition and revision are the norms of consciousness and narrative here. That makes it difficult, even dangerous, to separate the life of one text from the others. The inimitable texture of each individual text, and the translation of the author from Modernism to Modernity, prevents any one story or novel from acting properly as a mirror, reflective of Faulkner's art as a whole. But some measure of that art, at least, can be taken from the fourth and among the finest of the novels Faulkner produced, *The Sound and the Fury*; it was the one most intimately related to his own experience ('I am Quentin in *The Sound and the Fury*,' he once admitted), and his personal favourite because it was, he declared, his 'most splendid failure'. The novel is concerned with the lives and fates of the Compson family, who seem to condense into their experience the entire history of their region. Four generations of Compsons appear; and the most important of these is the third generation, the brothers Quentin, Jason and Benjy and their sister Candace, known in the family as Caddy. Three of the four sections into which the narration is divided are consigned to the voices of the Compson brothers; the fourth is told in the third person and circles around the activities of Dilsey Gibson, the cook and maid-of-all-work in the Compson house. The present time of *The Sound and the Fury* is distilled into four days, three of them occurring over the Easter weekend, 1928, the Quentin section being devoted to a day in 1910 when he chooses to commit suicide. There is, however, a constant narrative impulse to repeat and rehearse the past, to be carried back on the old ineradicable rhythms of memory. The memories are many but the determining ones for the Compson brothers are of the woman who was at the centre of their childhood world, and who is now lost to them literally and emotionally: their sister, Caddy Compson.

Caddy is the source and inspiration of what became and remained the novel closest to Faulkner's own heart. *The Sound and the Fury* began, he explained, with the 'mental picture . . . of the muddy seat of a little girl's drawers in a pear tree where she could see through a window where her grandmother's funeral was taking place' – while her three brothers gazed at her from down below. She is also the subject of a book that, as this brief explanation suggests, carries linked intimations of sex and death. 'To me she was the beautiful one, she was my heart's darling,' Faulkner said of Caddy later. 'That's what I wrote the book about,' he added, 'and I used the tools which seemed to me the proper tools to try to tell, try to draw the picture of Caddy.' Trying to tell of Caddy, to extract what he called 'some ultimate distillation' from her story, is the fundamental project of the book. And yet she seems somehow to exist apart from it or beyond it, to escape from Faulkner and all the other storytellers. To some extent, this is because she is the absent presence that haunts so many of Faulkner's other novels: a figure like, say, Addie Bundren in *As I Lay Dying*, or Thomas Sutpen in *Absalom, Absalom!*, who obsesses the other characters but very rarely speaks with his or her own voice. Even more important, though, is the fact that she is female, and so by definition someone who tends to exist for her creator outside the parameters of language: Faulkner has adopted here the archetypal male image of a woman who is at once mother, sister, daughter and lover, Eve and Lilith, virgin and whore, to describe what Wallace Stevens once referred to as 'the inconceivable idea of the sun' – that is, the other, the world outside the self. And while she is there to the extent that she is the focal point, the eventual object of each narrator's meditations, she is not there in the sense that she remains elusive, intangible – as transparent as the water, or as invisible as the odours of the trees and honeysuckle, with which she is constantly associated. It is as if, just as the narrator tries to focus her in his camera lens, she slips away, leaving little more than the memory of her name and image.

Not that Faulkner ever stops trying to bring her into focus – for himself, for his characters and, of course, for us. Each section of the book, in fact, represents a different strategy, another attempt to know her. Essentially, the difference in each section is a matter of rhetoric, in the sense that, each time the tale is told, another language is devised and a different series of relationships established between author, narrator, subject and reader. When Benjy occupies our attention right at the start, for instance, we soon become aware of a radical inwardness. Profoundly autistic, Benjy lives in a closed world where the gap between self and other, being and naming, cannot be bridged because it is never known or acknowledged. The realm outside himself remains as foreign to him as its currency of language does, and Faulkner is creating an impossible language here, giving voice to the voiceless. The second section, devoted to Quentin, collapses distance in another way. 'I am Quentin,' we may remember Faulkner said. And, as we read, we may feel ourselves drawn into a world that seems almost impenetrably private. Quentin, for his part, tries to abolish the gap between Caddy and himself – although, of course, not being mentally handicapped he is less successful at this than Benjy. And he sometimes tends to confess to or address the reader, or try to address him, and sometimes to forget him. Whether addressing the reader or not, however, his language remains intensely claustrophobic and liable to disintegration. Quentin cannot quite subdue the object to the word; he seems always to be trying to place things in conventional verbal structures, only to find those structures slide away or dissolve into uncontrolled stream of consciousness. Equally, he cannot quite construct a coherent story for himself because, in losing his sister Caddy, he has lost what Henry James would call the 'germ' of his narrative – the person, that is, who made sense of all the disparate elements of life for him by providing them with an emotional centre.

With Jason, in the third section of The Sound and the Fury, distance enters. Faulkner is clearly out of sympathy with this Compson brother, even if he is amused by him (he once said that Jason was the character of his that he disliked most). Jason, in turn, while clearly obsessed with Caddy, never claims any intimacy with her. And the reader is kept at some remove by the specifically public mode of speech Jason uses, full of swagger, exaggeration and saloon-bar prejudice. Attempting, with some desperation, to lay claim to common sense and reason – even when, as he is most of the time, he is being driven by perverse impulse and panic

---

– Jason seems separated from just about everything, not least himself. The final section of the novel offers release, of a kind, from all this. The closed circle of the interior monologue is broken now, the sense of the concrete world is firm, the visible outline of things finely and even harshly etched, the rhythms exact, evocative and sure. Verbally, we are in a more open field where otherness is addressed; emotionally we are released from a vicious pattern of repetition compulsion, in which absorption in the self leads somehow to destruction of the self. And yet, and yet . . . : the language remains intricately figurative, insistently artificial. The emphasis throughout, in the closing pages, is on appearance and impression, on what seems to be the case rather than what is. We are still not being told the whole truth, the implication is, there remain limits to what we can know; despite every effort, even the last section of the novel does not entirely succeed in naming Caddy. So it is not entirely surprising that, like the three Compson brothers before her, Dilsey Gibson, who dominates this section, is eventually tempted to discard language altogether. Benjy resorted, as he had to, to a howl, Quentin to suicide, Jason to impotent, speechless rage: all to express their inarticulacy in the face of the other, their impotences as they stood in the eye of the storm, the sound and the fury of time and change. And Dilsey, responding to a more positive yet passionate impulse, becomes part of the congregation at an Easter Day service – where, we are told, 'there was not even a voice but instead their hearts were speaking to one another in chanting measures beyond the need for words'. In ways that are, certainly, very different, all four characters place a question mark over their attempts to turn experience into speech. And they do so, not least, by turning aside from words, seeking deliverance and redress in a non-verbal world – a world of pure silence or pure, unintelligible sound.

The closing words of *The Sound and the Fury* appear to bring the wheel full circle. As Benjy Compson sits in a wagon watching the elements of his small world flow past him, 'each in its ordered place', it is as if everything has now been settled and arranged. Until, that is, the reader recalls that *this* order is one founded on denial, exclusion, a howl of resistance to strangeness. The ending, it turns out, is no ending at all; it represents, at most, a continuation of the process of speech – the human project of putting things each in its ordered place – and an invitation to us, the reader, to continue that process too. We are reminded, as we are at the close of so many of Faulkner's stories, that no system is ever complete or completely adequate. Something is always missed out it seems, some aspect of reality must invariably remain unseen. Since this is so, no book, not even one like this that uses a multiplicity of speech systems – a plurality of perspectives, like a Cubist painting – can ever truly be said to be finished. Language can be a necessary tool for understanding and dealing with the world, the only way we can hope to know Caddy; yet perversely, Faulkner suggests, it is as much a function of ignorance as of knowledge. It implies absence, loss, as well as fulfilment. Sometimes, Faulkner admitted, he felt that experience, life 'out there', existed beyond the compass of words: a feeling that would prompt him to claim that all he really liked was 'silence. Silence and horses. And trees.' But at other times he seemed to believe that he should try to inscribe his own scratchings on the surface of the earth, that he should at least attempt the impossible and tell the story over again, the story of himself and the world, using all the tools, all the different voices and idioms available to him. As Faulkner himself put it once, 'Sometimes I think of doing what Rimbaud did – yet I will certainly keep on writing as long as I live.' So he did keep on writing: his final novel, *The Reivers* (1962), was published only a month before he died. To the end, he produced stories that said what he suggested every artist was trying, in the last analysis, to say: '*I was here.*' And they said it for others beside himself: others, that is, including the reader.

Making it new in drama

Modernism came late to American drama. So, for that matter, did realism, experimentalism and even, with the notable exception of *The Contrast* by Royall Tyler, Americanism. There was, in fact, plenty of theatrical activity in the first hundred years of the American republic but little really indigenous drama. Even a touring group that called itself the 'American Company' and stimulated interest in the theatre in Virginia, South Carolina, and New York in the early nineteenth century was actually British in origin. Not only that, it mainly performed English plays; it did stage *The Prince of Parthia* (1763) by the American Thomas Godfrey (1736–63), but this, as its title intimates, was derivative, a blank-verse tragedy that carried no traces of its American authorship. The first professional playwright in the United States, William Dunlap (1766–1839), specialized in adapting European plays for American audiences. Despite some success with plays like *The Father; or, American Shandyism* (1789) and *The Stranger* (1798), his theatre failed and he went into bankruptcy; and his most notable work is probably his *The History of the American Theatre* (1832), a first-hand record of his experiences and the first account of the American stage. Popular plays of the time invested their mostly European but sometimes American settings with sweet sentiment and melodrama. James Nelson Barker (1784–1858), for example, produced the first dramatic version of the Pocahontas legend in *The Indian Princess* (1808); it is a highly sentimental one, at that. Similarly, the tone of the once immensely popular *Clari, or the Maid of Milan* (1823) by John Howard Payne (1791–1852) can be gathered from the fact that it introduced 'Home Sweet Home' as a song to be sung by its heroine.

It was not until the last quarter of the nineteenth century that realism of a kind came into vogue and American settings became more common. Character drama began to make its appearance with *Margaret Fleming* (1890) by James Horne (1839–1901), a work that showed the influence of Ibsen in its portrait of a woman reconciling herself to the infidelity of her husband and assuming responsibility for his illegitimate child when its mother died. Focus on character, and the frailties of character in particular, is also a distinctive feature of *The Easiest Way* (1909) by Eugene Walter (1874–1941) and *The Girl with Green Eyes* (1902) by Clyde Fitch (1865–1909). These were both popular plays that exploited the growing interest in the psychological. Equally popular were those dramas that concerned themselves with psychological aberrations and extremes, such as *The Witching Hour* (1908) by Augustus Thomas (1857–1934) and *The Faith Healer* by William Vaughn Moody. Psychological interest, in turn, began to be assimilated into social reality. In *The Great Divide* (1906) by Moody, for instance, a young woman from New England, a modern product of inherited Puritan traditions and inhibitions, overcomes her conditioning when she realizes she is in love with a free spirit, an individualist from the 'Wild West'. And a number of plays addressed social issues more directly. *Paul Kauvar* (1887) by Steele Mackaye (1842–94), for instance, explores the growing tensions between capital and labour; *The Lion and the Mouse* (1905) by Charles Klein (1876–1915) examines the power of monopolies; and *The Nigger* (1909) by Edward Sheldon (1886–1946) investigates the racial issue as it tells the story of a Southern political figure who learns, to his dismay, that he is not a pure 'Anglo-Saxon'. All these and similar plays written at the turn of the twentieth century show a greater disposition towards empirically accurate notation of American character and culture. But they are invariably compromised by the theatrical habits of the time that favoured circumlocution and cliché, jocularity, sentiment, pseudo-refinement – and the inevitable happy ending. Whatever their engagement with social and psychological detail, they tended to remain stuck in convention; as a result, they were not so much realistic as pseudo-realistic.

In the 1920s, David Belasco (1859–1931) tried to develop a drama of social concern using naturalistic settings. The use of ordinary domestic and street scenes, however, could not disguise the sentimentality of his scripts. His enduring contribution to the theatre was probably the romanticized Orient of *Madame Butterfly* (1904), written in collaboration with John L. Long (1861–1927). This was to achieve greater fame when it formed the basis for the Puccini opera, just as *Porgy* (1927) by DuBose Heyward (1885–1940), adapted from his own novel (1925) with the help of his wife Dorothy, was to become far more famous as the source for *Porgy and Bess* (1935) by George Gershwin (1898–1937). Both *Porgy*, produced by the Theatre Guild of New York, and *Madame Butterfly* enjoyed considerable success in their own right; but they could not really match the success of the comedies of manners written by Philip Barry (1896–1949), S. W. Behrman (1893–1973) and Robert Sherwood (1896–1955). Barry and Behrman were both characteristically divided in their aims. The urbane Barry wavered between his comic élan and a striving for spiritual drama consonant with his early Catholic background; Behrman tended to vacillate between sophistication and social conscience. So, in his comedies *Holiday* (1928), *Paris Bound* (1929), *The Animal Kingdom* (1932) and *The Philadelphia Story* (1939), Barry slyly undermines conventional worship of wealth and social status as well as puritanical moralism, whether of the left or the right, while he moves his characters towards an acceptance of the need for common sense, humility and tolerance. Behrman, in turn, gravitated from comedies with a serious and sometimes political edge, like *The Second Man* (1927) and *Biography* (1932), to plays openly concerned with politics, such as his anti-fascist play *Rain from Heaven* (1934), or openly concerned with the problem of writing political drama, such as the highly autobiographical *No Time for Comedy* (1938). Few other contemporary playwrights matched the comic deftness of Barry and Behrman. Robert Sherwood did so, however, in *Reunion in Vienna* (1931). So did Howard Lindsay (1889–1968) and Russel Crouse (1893–1968) in *Life with Father* (1939). And Crouse and Sherwood did not confine themselves to comedy. Typical of many journeyman playwrights of the time, Crouse turned his hand successfully to political satire (*State of the Nation* [1945]), melodrama (*The Great Sebastians* [1956]) and the musical (*Call Me Madam* [1950]); while Sherwood was equally successful with romance (*Waterloo Bridge* [1930]), the melodramatic thriller (*The Petrified Forest* [1935]) and social drama (*Idiot's Delight* [1936]).

Sherwood spent many years working as a scriptwriter in Hollywood, and several of his plays were turned into successful films. With the arrival of talking pictures, after *The Jazz Singer* (1927) proved the popularity of sound, the opportunities for playwrights to sell both their plays and their scriptwriting skills suddenly and dramatically grew. An exemplary figure here is Ben Hecht (1895–1964). In the early 1920s, Hecht began writing novels, but he did not achieve national prominence until he turned to playwriting a few years later. He scored a huge success with *The Front Page* (1928), a smart, satirical, wisecracking comedy about Chicago journalists co-written with Charles MacArthur (1895–1956), and he and MacArthur then consolidated that success with another comedy, *Twentieth Century* (1932). After that, Hecht continued to write drama and fiction; however, he became better known as a screenwriter. Still collaborating with MacArthur, he was responsible for the screenplays of such films as *Wuthering Heights* (1939), *Spellbound* (1945) and *Notorious* (1946). *The Front Page*, too, was made into a successful film, as was *Twentieth Century*. Similarly, Garson Kanin (1912–99) scored his first success with a political farce, *Born Yesterday* (1946), before going on to Hollywood. And George S. Kaufman (1889–1961) turned Hollywood into a source of comedy in *Once in a Lifetime* (1930), co-written with Moss Hart (1904–61) – with whom he also wrote such notable plays as *You Can't Take It With You* (1936) and *The Man Who Came To Dinner* (1939). Not all dramatists turned to Hollywood, as subject or source of income, to the extent that Hecht, MacArthur and Kanin did. Kaufman, for instance, devoted nearly all his career to writing plays or musicals on many other subjects, and with collaborators ranging from Richard Rogers and Lorenz Hart to short story writer Ring Lardner, then, later, the Gershwins. But Hollywood did open up new chances, new material, and a new way of transcribing reality for many of them: quite probably, it even began to alter the way they saw the task of playwriting, by opening up the possibility of more cinematic forms.

Certainly, theatrical experiment became more common in this period, sometimes inspired by the cinema and sometimes by other forces, such as German expressionist drama. The first play of Elmer Rice (1892–1967), *On Trial* (1914), for example, employs the technique of the motion picture 'cutback' to present scenes that are described by trial witnesses. With his works for the Morningside Players, a little theatre group, published in *Morningside Plays* (1917), he then scored a second success in experimental drama with *The Adding Machine* (1923). Here, he used the expressionist techniques of fantasy and symbolism to satirize the reduction of individuals, in the machine age, to 'waste product'. Rice continued to experiment with different styles. His other most distinguished play, *Street Scene* (1929), for instance, may be more geared towards empirical realism in its presentation of slum life. But it still uses a panoply of sound effects to enhance audience involvement and get its message across. Thornton Wilder (1897–1975) borrowed from an entirely different theatrical tradition in *Our Town* (1938). Born in Wisconsin, but raised in China, Wilder dispensed with scenery in his most famous play, and used the Chinese theatrical convention of the property man as narrator to portray life in a small town in New England. Wilder also achieved fame with his novel *The Bridge of San Luis Rey* (1927), about a South American bridge disaster and the ironic way providence directs disparate lives to one end. And he experimented with several different dramatic forms: including comedy (*The Merchant of Yonkers* [1938]), a play inspired by Joyce's *Finnegan's Wake* (1939) (*The Skin of Our Teeth* [1942]), and a tragedy inspired by Euripedes's *Alcestis* (*A Life in the Sun* [1955]). The theatrical experiments of Maxwell Anderson (1888–1959) were similarly various. After achieving success with a bluntly realistic war play, *What Price Glory?* (1924), he wrote, among many other things, a series of blank-verse dramas in which the innocent and idealistic tend to be defeated by the political, the economic and the mundane. *Elizabeth the Queen* (1930) is concerned with the love of Elizabeth I of England for the Earl of Essex. *Night Over Taos* (1932) dramatizes the end of the feudal era in New Mexico in 1847 ('This is what death's for –' declaims the leading character towards the end; 'To rid the earth of old fashions'). And *Winterset* (1935), also in verse, is set in contemporary America and was clearly suggested by the trial and execution of the anarchists Sacco and Vanzetti – which, as a gross miscarriage of justice, became a *cause célèbre* for the left during the 1930s.

Night Over Taos was produced by the Group Theatre, *Winterset* was rejected by the Group. That is a measure of what the most influential American production company of the 1930s was after. Its aims were social as well as artistic. Although it was never a doctrinaire political theatre, the Group did see itself as a community of artists working to say something significant and useful about society. It did tend to favour a particular series of styles that could be handily described as left-wing symbolism; and it did prefer optimism and hope over pessimism and despair. Which is, perhaps, why *Night Over Taos*, with its resonant theme of the old giving way to the new, found favour and support, while *Winterset*, in which the two leading characters choose to die rather than live in a corrupt world, did not. The Group Theatre grew out of the Theatre Guild of New York, the leading drama company of the 1920s. It was in operation from 1931 to 1941, at first under the direction of Harold Clurman (1901–80), Lee Strasberg (1901–82) and Cheryl Crawford (1902–86), and then, from 1937, under Clurman alone. It has been described as the most successful failure in the history of American theatre. Except for a couple of years when one of its plays, *Golden Boy* (1937) by Clifford Odets (1906–63), scored a big success, it was always in financial difficulties. Nevertheless, in the ten seasons it existed, it managed to get twenty-two new productions on stage. There were occasional revivals, tours, second companies and experimental evenings, but the main job of the Group as a production company was how to get something of dramatic and social value into performance each spring – and, in the process, keep the Group alive. Its first production was *The House of Connelly* (1931) by Paul Green (1894–1981), a searing account of an old Southern family that is a combination of Greek tragedy and regional folk play. Its last was *Retreat to Pleasure* (1940) by Irwin Shaw (1913–84). In between it produced plays in a wide variety of styles. *Gentlewoman* (1934) by John Howard Lawson (1895–1977), for instance, is a drawing-room play of ideas; *Johnny Johnson* (1936) by Paul Green and the German composer Kurt Weill (1900–50) is a musical satire; *Waiting for Lefty* (1935) by Odets, a play about a taxi-drivers' strike, is made up of naturalistic cameos set in a non-realist frame; *My Heart's in the Highlands* (1939) by William Saroyan (1908–81) is a sweet, wide-eyed, stylized fable. All of them are driven, though, by an optimistic energy, sometimes angry, sometimes rapt, sometimes plaintive: a desire to find some grounds for affirmation and belief. 'We'll never lose our faith and hope and trust in all mankind,' *Johnny Johnson* concludes. 'The world is at its morning . . . and *no man fights alone!*' declares a character in *Paradise Lost* (1935) by Odets. Two other characters in another play by Odets, *Night Music* (1940), sum up the positive feelings with which these plays are charged. 'Where there is life there is hope, in my humble opinion,' observes one; 'Only the living can cry out against life.' The other's comment, or cry, is much simpler: '*Make this America for us!*'

Of all the dramatists associated with the Group Theatre, Odets is at once the most significant and the most symptomatic. He was a member of the company from the beginning, an actor in many of the earlier productions. When he finally convinced the directors that he was a playwright, his name became almost synonymous with the Group. They produced seven of his plays, where no other dramatist had more than two: *Waiting for Lefty, Awake and Sing!* (1935), *Till the Day I Die* (1935), about the struggle of the German communists at the beginning of the Hitler regime, *Paradise Lost, Golden Boy*, about a young Italian American violinist whose desire for wealth leads him into boxing and then into death, *Rocket to the Moon* (1938) and *Night Music*. Odets continued his career after the Group broke up. Among his later plays are *The Big Knife* (1948), which explores power and corruption in the film industry, and *The Country Girl* (1950), a backstage drama about an alcoholic actor's return to theatre life. But the plays written for the Group Theatre represent his major achievement. They are marked by a language that captures a particular urban rhythm and that utilizes a tough, oblique way of speaking, a hardboiled mask for sentiment. Like a skilful cartoonist, Odets exaggerates, subtly, exploits milieu-oriented metaphor ('I wouldn't trade you for two pitchers and an outfielder'), uses repetition and the clichés of everyday speech ('So go fight City Hall!'). The result is a stylized language that feels realistic, while avoiding the flatness of most real speech or the fixed exaggerations of dialect. It is the perfect tool for his purpose: which is to capture the humour, the gloomy fatality and the burning beliefs of the ordinary people who are his subjects – the urban lower middle class from which Odets himself came.

So in *Awake and Sing!*, perhaps his finest play, we are introduced to a series of characters who, Odets tells us, 'share a fundamental activity: a struggle for life amidst petty conditions'. They are the Berger family, living in the Bronx – where Odets was born – trying to get along and get by, caught between the ugliness of their given circumstances and their sometimes cheap dreams of something better. *Awake and Sing!* is a play of enormous vitality, not least because it captures this family warts and all: their arguments and cruelty, their moments of kindness and affection, the web of apparently aimless conversation that holds them together and embodies their shared life. At the centre of the drama is a typical Odets protagonist: Ralph Berger, the son, a young man on the edge of life and about to make his discovery, right or wrong, of where he is going. Ralph wants, he says, 'a chance to get to first base'. He is given plenty of advice by others – some bad and some good. The good advice is given to him by his grandfather Jacob, a socialist who believes in a revolution that should be both political and personal. 'Wake up!' he tells Ralph. 'Be something. Make your life something good . . . take the world in your two hands and make it new.' Jacob later quotes the verse from Isaiah that gives the play its title: 'Awake and sing, ye that dwell in the dust; and the earth shall cast out the dead.' And, by the end, Ralph has taken the advice to heart. 'I'm one week old!' he announces. 'I want the whole city to hear it – fresh blood, arms. We got 'em. We're glad we're living.' It is a typical ending, for Odets and for the Group Theatre: Ralph has experienced a personal awakening that is coincident with awaking to the realities of his and others' social condition. Sometimes the affirmation on which these plays close came out of conviction or convention, emotional need or dramatic requirement, rather than out of the material of the play. But it was just about always there: there was invariably the sense that out of the ashes of the old – the decaying social system on which, of necessity, the drama was focused – a new dispensation, and a new state of being, should and could emerge.

'Most modern plays', Eugene O'Neill (1888–1953) once declared, 'are concerned with the relation between man and man, but that does not interest me at all. I am interested only in the relationship between man and God.' That is not strictly true, for two reasons. The first is that, in many of his plays, like *Lazarus Laughed* (1927) and *Marco Millions* (1928), even *The Hairy Ape* (1922), he does move towards the condition of social drama to the extent that he explores the contemporary emphasis on acquisition and material standards or the plight of those at the bottom of the social and economic ladder. And, in all of them, he is drawn into intensely poetic, often erotic accounts of the tentacular relationships to be found, say, in families (*Mourning Becomes Electra* [1931], *Long Day's Journey into Night* [1956]), among confined groups at sea, say, or in a bar (*Bound East for Cardiff* [1916], *The Iceman Cometh* [1946]) or in local communities and neighbourhoods (*All God's Chillun Got Wings* [1924]). The second is that it was not so much God as the absence of God that preoccupied O'Neill. 'The playwright today must dig at the roots of the sickness of today as he feels it,' O'Neill wrote in a letter, '– the death of the old God and the failure of science and materialism to give any satisfying new one for the surviving primitive religious instinct to find a meaning for life in and to comfort its fears of death with.' O'Neill was born into a generation that included Joyce, Eliot and Stevens, profoundly concerned with the death of the old grounds for belief. He was deeply affected by European expressionism (the expressionism of Strindberg especially), with modern psychology as an instrument to analyse human nature, and by a Nietzschean philosophy which reinforced a characteristically American tendency to explore heroic individuals and their search for self-realization. The fundamental problem O'Neill dramatizes and develops in all his work is that of the relation of the human being to something, anything, outside himself; something to which he can belong, something in which he can ground his life so that it can have more shape, a sense of purpose, something that saves him from feeling lonely, lost, an existential exile – or, as one of O'Neill's characters puts it (in *Long Day's Journey into Night*), 'a stranger in a strange land'. *The Hairy Ape* is exemplary in this respect. The character who gives the play its title is the leader of the stokers on a transatlantic liner. He is content with his lot, stupid and brutal though it is, as long as he believes that he is essential to the ship and the voyage of the ship has a meaning. 'I belong,' is his recurrent, triumphant cry. When, however, he loses that belief, when he comes to realize that the system he serves is unaware of his existence and that, consequently, he has no function in or proper under-standing of it: then he falls into the curse of consciousness, bewilderment and despair. He ceases to think of himself as a man, a meaningful creature, and despises himself as a 'hairy ape'. He feels, and is, abandoned in a world that is both brutally material and bafflingly mysterious – one that, like the world experienced in fog, in darkness or in an alcoholic haze (all common situations and figures in O'Neill's plays), is abruptly at hand but unseen.

The younger son of a popular actor, O'Neill began writing drama when he was confined in a sanatorium. During this period of enforced rest and reflection, he produced a series of one-act plays based on his life at sea and among the outcasts in many places: he had been, at various times, a prospector for gold, a merchant seaman and a beachcomber. His first play, *The Web* (1913–14), was followed by nine others. Gaining further dramatic experience with George Peirce Baker's 47 Workshop at Harvard in 1914–15, he then spent a winter in Greenwich Village, New York. Then, in 1916, his involvement with the Provincetown Players brought him, and the company, to the attention of the New York public, initially with a series of plays about the *SS Glencairn* and its crew, among them *Bound East for Cardiff* and *The Moon of the Caribees* (1918). With the production of his *Beyond the Horizon* in 1920, O'Neill was acknowledged as the leading American playwright of his day. For a while, from 1923 to 1927, he helped manage the Greenwich Village Theatre; he was also a director of the Provincetown Players and a founder of the Theatre Guild, which produced his later plays. But he devoted more and more of his time to writing, in a variety of styles, to express and explore his view of life. Plays that gravitated towards naturalism included *Chris Christopherson* (1920), rewritten as *Anna Christie* (1921), *All God's Chillun Got Wings* and *Desire Under the Elms* (1924). As such plays revealed, O'Neill was not afraid to explore difficult and, for their time, even controversial subjects. Anna Christie is a prostitute, *All*

God's Chillun is concerned with interracial marriage, in *Desire Under the Elms* a woman bears a child by her stepson only to kill the child when her husband, learning that it is not his son, repudiates and disinherits him. A similar daring, a willingness to test the boundaries, and extend them, is also a feature of O'Neill's more experimental and expressionist work. Only now the boundaries that are tested are as much a matter of dramatic form as social norm. In *The Hairy Ape*, for example, the fall of the central character into consciousness, exile and death is charted in eight scenes that, as O'Neill explains at the beginning, 'should by no means be naturalistic'. The play concludes at the zoo, where 'the hairy ape' goes to see a gorilla, the only creature with whom he can now feel kinship; then, when he liberates the beast, to help him wreak destruction on a world he never made, it responds by crushing him to death. A similarly stunning, symbolic and almost surreal conclusion marks *The Emperor Jones* (1920), which is remarkable among plays of the time not least because a black character dominates the stage in the central role. To the incessant thumping of a tomtom, Brutus Jones, an ex-convict who has presided as autocratic 'emperor' for two years over a West Indian island, tries to flee his former domain after an uprising. He returns in mind and vision to earlier phases of his own life and the history of his race – the prison chain gang, a slave auction, a slave ship and so on – before being hunted down and killed by the people over whom he has presided.

O'Neill's interest in experiment drew him towards the use of symbolic masks for the actors in *The Great God Brown* (1926), a play that fuses symbolism, poetry and the affirmation of a pagan idealism in an ironic critique of the materialism of the modern world. It also led him to experiment with a dramatic form of stream of consciousness in *Strange Interlude* (1928), where conventional dialogue is juxtaposed with stylized internal monologue to reveal the inner lives of the characters. The more romantic impulse in O'Neill, that straining towards affirmation, some source of hope, that is typical of so many of O'Neill's characters is given freer play in *The Fountain* (1925), which is dominated by a celebration of what is called here 'the Eternal Becoming which is Beauty'. The comic impulse, in turn, is more evident in *Ah, Wilderness* (1933), a gently humorous, nostalgic portrait of New England life that draws on O'Neill's memories of his own family. More generally typical, though, of his use of drama as a means of exploring human abandonment, the human fate of spiritual orphanhood, wandering and homelessness, are *Dynamo* (1929), *Days Without End* (1934) and the trilogy *Mourning Becomes Electra*. In *Dynamo*, the electrical device of the title becomes a divine symbol, in an uncanny echo of Henry Adams; it replaces the old God but destroys its worshippers. In *Days Without End*, the hero is irresistibly, desperately drawn towards Catholicism to heal his existential despair. And in *Mourning Becomes Electra*, the *Oresteia* of Aeschylus is retold as a story of the Civil War, with the classical sense of fate replaced by an emphasis on character conceived of in Freudian terms. The essential elements of the ancient Greek story of the curse on the house of Atreus are retained here in this story of a New England family called the Mannons: a woman in love with her father, a man in love with his mother, the wife who kills her husband as an act of vengeance, the son who kills similarly in vengeance and is consumed by the 'furies'. These elements, however, are redrawn and reset in modern terms, theatrical and conceptual: the chorus, for example, is replaced by choric characters and the 'furies' that pursue the son, leading him in this case to commit suicide, come from within, his own devouring sense of guilt. More to the point, there is no final tragic recognition, no sense of an ultimate purpose or resolution. At the end of *Mourning Becomes Electra*, the surviving member of the Mannon family, the daughter Lavinia Mannon, simply shuts herself up in the house, to live with the ghosts of her father, mother and brother. 'Love isn't permitted to me,' she confesses; 'The dead are too strong!' She is imprisoned in the past, not liberated by it; there is for her, and the audience, no final tragic insight into the meaning of suffering, because it seems to have no meaning; no end to the pain is promised, just further pain.

After the failure of *Days Without End*, O'Neill maintained a long theatrical silence, during which he suffered severe mental and physical ill health. The silence was broken by *The Iceman Cometh*, his first new play to be produced after a gap of twelve years. Set in a run-down New York bar, it is a tragi-comic exploration of O'Neill's obsessive theme, the need for meaning expressed here as the human need for a saving illusion: as one of the bar-room regulars puts it, 'the lie of the pipe dream is what gives life'. Other plays written after this were, many of them, produced after O'Neill died. *A Touch of the Poet* and *More Stately Mansions*, part of a projected cycle of eleven plays entitled 'A Tale of Possessors Self-Dispossessed' tracing the fortunes of an American family from the eighteenth to the twentieth centuries, were first staged in, respectively, 1958 and 1962. *Hughie*, the single play in another projected series, was first performed in 1958. Above all, *Long Day's Journey into Night*, which has a claim to the title of O'Neill's finest work, appeared in the theatre three years after his death, in 1956. Set over the course of one long day in August 1912, *Long Day's Journey into Night* tells the story of the Tyrone family: James Tyrone, a former matinee idol, his wife Mary, a nervous, sickly woman addicted to morphine, their older son Jamie, a hard-drinking cynic, and their younger son Edmund, who has literary aspirations and suffers from tuberculosis. O'Neill was clearly drawing on his own life, and the life of his family, when he wrote this play. Edmund, for example, is an exercise in self-portraiture. But he was drawing on this for a deeper purpose. What is on offer here is a study of lives in disintegration, people without something to give coherence, shape and significance to their lives. They have lost that something, anything, that might have convinced them once that life made sense; that is, even if they ever had it. As a result, they are left astray and anxious. They look back, perhaps, with a sense of longing and loss; they look around them in pain and confusion, stumbling uncertainly through their lives like people in a fog seeking release, relief from their vacillation and division – their sense of separation even from themselves – in numbness and dreams. 'It was a great mistake, my being born a man. I would have been much more successful as a sea-gull or a fish,' Edmund wryly observes, and, in doing so, speaks for all the Tyrone family. 'As it is, I will always be a stranger who never feels at home,' he explains, 'who does not want and is not really wanted, who can never belong, who must always be a little in love with death!'

'Stammering is the native eloquence of us fog people,' Edmund says, shortly after this. The Tyrones are divided, disintegrated people. Lacking belief, grounding, they lack a sense of community, stability. They are at odds with themselves and each other; and this is expressed in the words they use, their reflections and conversations, which are characterized by a continual oscillation, an ebb-and-flow movement in which one statement will cancel out another. So Mary Tyrone can fluctuate between longing to be alone, despairing of being alone, then longing to be alone again, all within a space of a single speech. She can call herself a 'sentimental fool' for dwelling on her childhood dreams of becoming a nun or a concert pianist, or her 'schoolgirl' romance with 'a matinee idol' that led to marriage. Then she can and does lapse back into those dreams again. Every member of the family vacillates, with alarming speed, between expressions of hatred and love, self-justification and self-recrimination, despair and hope, pride, guilt and remorse. That comes out, with particular power, in the episode when Jamie warns his younger brother against himself. 'I'd like to see you become the greatest success in the world. But you'd better be on your guard,' he tells Edmund. 'Because I'll do my damnedest to make you fail. Can't help it. I hate myself. Got to take my revenge. On everyone else. Especially you.' There is no continuity here because there is nothing, no grounds for it, no foundations in faith or conviction. The characters are aimless, without anchor in anything except their dreams of what they might have been (a nun, a concert pianist, a great Shakespearean actor) or what they might be (a great writer, a success), and no forms of emotional rescue other than those offered by various narcotics – drugs, alcohol, poetry, the blanketing numbness of the fog. What they all long for, secretly, intuitively, is described when Edmund recalls his life as a seaman. At sea once, he remembers, he felt that he had 'dissolved in the sea', 'became beauty and rhythm, became moonlight and the ship and the high dim-starred sky!' On the beach once, he 'became the sun, the hot sand, green seaweed anchored to a rock, swaying in the tide'. 'For a second you see', he explains, '– and seeing the secret, are the secret. For a second there is meaning!' 'I belonged', he insists, 'within something greater than my own life, or the life of Man, to Life itself! To God, if you want to put it that way.' But such moments of union, of belonging, are rare here. 'The hand lets the veil fall', Edmund concludes bitterly, 'and you are alone, lost in the fog again, and you stumble on toward nowhere, for no good reason!' That is the condition of the Tyrones, and the human condition in O'Neill's plays. The secret of joy, losing oneself in 'a fulfilment beyond men's lousy, pitiful, greedy fears and hopes and dreams', is professed, if at all, only for a fleeting moment. Before and after, there is only waste and exile.

O'Neill is essentially a religious writer without a religion. The power and pain of his best work is a measure of that paradox. *Long Day's Journey into Night* achieves a tragic pathos precisely because it requires the audience both to see and to share in the disintegration of the Tyrones: to recognize that they are 'fog people', stammering for something they can never possess, but also to share their need, feel compelled by their 'native eloquence'. What is especially remarkable about this portrait of a family being borne towards extinction is how intricately O'Neill weaves the familial web. Like Faulkner, he believed that, as he has one of the characters say here, 'the past is the present'; like Faulkner, too, he uses that belief to present the family as an elaborate network of blame and dependence, in which the family members both resist and rely on each other – feel isolated and betrayed, yet also feel an intense need to be with one another for personal survival, mutual support. The Tyrones are constantly accusing one another, blaming one another for what they did or were not able to do, for the damage done to their own lives. They are also, constantly, relying on one another: not just for advice or assistance, nor even just for conversation or comfort, but to bolster their image of themselves through the rehearsal of shared memories and illusions – by seeing themselves as they would like to be, in the mirror of the past or the gaze of a husband or wife, a father or mother, a son or a brother. This sense that the fates of the different members of the Tyrone family are all intimately bound together – and that we, the audience, are intimately bound to them – as they journey inexorably into night is never stronger than in the closing moments of the play. Mary Tyrone appears, trailing her wedding gown and utterly immersed in her memories of the past. 'What is it I'm looking for?' she asks her family. 'I know it's something I lost.' 'I remember when I had it I was never lonely or afraid,' she recalls. 'I can't have lost it for ever. I would die if I thought that. Because then there would be no hope.' Slowly, in details, it comes back to her. It is her dreams, her illusions, the moments when she was surprised by joy. 'Then in the spring something happened to me,' she concludes. 'Yes I remember. I fell in love with James Tyrone and was so happy for a time.' Her family can only watch and wonder, as they see themselves in her: their own cry for meaning that has become a crying for the past and a crying out against life. It is a seminal moment in American theatre. An American family of ordinary means inspires the awe, the fear and pity, that used to be reserved for the special few, in traditional drama. It is also a key moment in American literary Modernism. The insignificant life becomes here the significance of literature. What matters is that, in the old terms, nothing matters; what this means is the loss of, and yet our need for, meaning; what we know, O'Neill tells us, is that we must live in the absence of what we need fully to be and to know.

Traditionalism, Politics and Prophecy

The uses of traditionalism

Not everyone during this period went after the strange gods of Modernism. On the contrary, responding to that yearning for the past to be found in writers as otherwise different as Wharton and Cather, Robinson and Frost, and that preoccupation with cultural loss notable in writers as otherwise complexly modern as Pound,

Faulkner and O'Neill, many writers sought refuge and support in traditionalism. Following the example, sometimes, of these and similar writers, notably Eliot, they sought to allay some of their anxiety about the immediate moment by discovering possible redemption in yesterday. The present might be confused, their belief was, modernity might create fracture and division, but with the help of traditionalist codes or forms that confusion might be alleviated, the fractures might be healed, and they might find balm for their own divided minds. Of those who pursued this belief, actively and with passion, none were so influential as those gathered in the South, initially around what was termed the Fugitive movement. 'A Fugitive', one of their number, Allen Tate, was to explain later, 'was quite simply a Poet: the Wanderer, . . . the Outcast, the man who carries the secret wisdom of the world.' Meeting in Nashville, Tennessee, from 1915 on, the Fugitive group was composed of Southerners, many of them associated with Vanderbilt University. However, when the first edition of the magazine that gave them their name, *The Fugitive*, appeared in 1921, it was not the regional affiliation that was emphasized, nor even the sense of existential exile described by Tate. 'THE FUGITIVE flees from nothing faster than from high-caste Brahmins of the Old South,' the opening statement declared. The common theme was alienation from a particular tradition: 'a tradition', as the editors of the magazine put it, 'that may be called a tradition only when looked at through the haze of a generous imagination.' The Fugitives saw themselves fleeing, in fact, from Southern romanticism, nostalgia for the region's past. And they saw themselves fleeing, too, from the dehumanizing environment that they witnessed all around them – in Nashville, in the modern South, and in the United States. Something of both their distaste for regional atavism and the disdain they felt for modern, urban culture was reflected in the pseudonyms the leading members of the group adopted for the first two issues. Tate called himself Henry Feathertop, John Crowe Ransom was Roger Prim, and Donald Davidson Robert Gallivant. Names like these suggested a coterie of elegant dandies who, like Poe, had little affection for utilitarian culture or for the sentimentality of the moonlight and magnolias school of writing. And even when the pseudonyms were dropped, the sense of distance remained: for the Fugitives, it seemed, to be conscious of their age meant to be conscious of their isolation from it.

The Fugitive magazine lasted for three years, during which others joined the group, notably Robert Penn Warren and Laura Riding. It never sold more than five hundred copies, and the actual quality of the poetry published in it was not especially high. There are, in fact, few poems produced by Fugitive writers during the Fugitive period, apart from those of Ransom, which can be called major. Yet this little magazine is of real importance in the story of twentieth-century American writing, and for several reasons that suggest a resemblance with Imagism. Like the Imagist movement, the Fugitives supplied a nursing-ground for a number of exceptional writers. Like the Imagists, they developed together certain ideas about writing that were to be crucial both to them individually and to many other American writers during the century, whether directly influenced by them or not. Like the Imagists, they progressed to other, related movements, aesthetic, social and political, that were to have a significant impact on the reading of literature and culture. That, however, is about as far as the connection between the Fugitives and the Imagists goes. In most other ways, in terms of precisely what they believed and practised, they offer a profound contrast to each other: a difference that, to some extent, measures the poles between which American literature moved in the first half of the twentieth century. Whether seen as contrast, conflict or dialectic, that difference maps out much of the territory inhabited by American writing, especially during the period from the beginning of the First World War to the end of the Second. It was somewhere within that territory that most American writers of the time operated.

It was Allen Tate, in fact, who, when he was trying to explain what was special about the Fugitive group, used their difference from Imagism as a means of definition. 'I would call the Fugitives', he declared, 'an intensive and historical group as opposed to the eclectic and cosmopolitan groups that flourished in the East.' As far as literature was concerned, the Imagists were experimental and internationalist. They believed in making it new, and they saw themselves as part of a larger, cosmopolitan cultural community. The Fugitives, by contrast, were traditionalists and regionalists. With the occasional exception of Tate, who liked to pose as the Modernist gadfly of the group (although, as his prose and poetry show, he was not much of a Modernist in practice), they subscribed to the traditional forms, metres and diction. And, with the exception only of Riding, they belonged to the South: they were born in the South, raised in the South and – for all their attacks on the nostalgic habits of their region – they saw themselves primarily in terms of their 'Southern-ness'. Nor does the contrast end there. The Imagists were, for the most part, optimists, rationalists, creatures of the Enlightenment: believing in the innocence and perfectibility of the individual, the possibility of progress, and the improvement or even perfecting of an entire society. The Fugitives were very different. Classical humanists or, alternatively, typical products of the Bible Belt, they believed in the reality of evil: inherited and tested forms and principles were necessary, they felt, to support the individual in his weakness, to focus his vision and prevent him from wandering. Perhaps the Imagists could be called a movement, in the loose sense. Innovative, enthusiastic, revolutionary in impulse, and alive with the unexpressed possibilities and the mobility of the present, they helped lay the foundations for Modernism. If so, the Fugitives should be called a school. Disciplined, cautious, deliberate, and aware above all of an immense debt to the past, they served the forces of reaction and acted as a nucleus, a catalyst for traditionalism.

The impulse towards traditionalism assumed a more regional character among those who had made up the Fugitive group after their magazine ceased publication. Moving away from the South, as many of them did, it became a faraway country for them: an attractive alternative to the urban, cosmopolitan centres, where they were now living – a place perhaps idealized by memory and distance. Then came the Scopes trial in Tennessee, popularly known as 'the monkey trial'. The attacks on the benighted backward population of the South, and the Bible Belt in general, that accompanied reports on the trial prompted people like Tate and Ransom to draw together again to defend their homeplace. With allies old and new, they began to argue the case not only for traditionalism but for regionalism. The result was the formation in 1926 of a loose but mutually supportive association of individuals who shared concerns that were distinctively Southern; they were eventually to be known as the Agrarians. Along with former Fugitives, they included Andrew Nelson Lytle (1902–99) and Stark Young (1881–1963). Lytle was later to produce major traditionalist, mainly historical fiction, such as *The Long Night* (1936) and *The Velvet Horn* (1957), novels set around the time of the Civil War, a historical biography, *Bedford Forrest* (1931), and a family chronicle *A Wake for the Living* (1975). Young published, among many other works, one of the most popular romances of the time, *So Red the Rose* (1934), set in Mississippi before and during the Civil War. Responding to the shared impulse to look backwards to the inherited forms of the South, Ransom wrote *God Without Thunder: An Unorthodox Defence of Orthodoxy* (1930). In it, he dismissed what he saw as the contemporary deification of science; and he defended fundamentalist belief in the mysterious God of the Old Testament as a necessary corrective to human pride. Tate, in turn, declaring that he had 'attacked the South for the last time', began a search for spiritual roots that led almost immediately to his major poem, 'Ode to the Confederate Dead' (1928, 1937), and then, later, his novel *The Fathers* (1938). And, working together, the Agrarians produced *I'll Take My Stand: The South and the Agrarian Tradition* (1930) by 'Twelve Southerners'. The approaches and arguments of the essays in this volume necessarily reflected the individual training and interests of the contributors. But they were all characterized by three things: a hatred of contemporary society in all its aspects, a commitment to the heritage of the South and, related to this, a conviction that the best kind of social order is one 'in which agriculture is the leading vocation, whether for wealth, for pleasure, or for prestige'.

The Agrarian reformulation of those pastoral and regionalist impulses recurrent in American writing is important to the literary and cultural history of the nation. As a social programme, however, it had just about no impact. Gradually, the individual Agrarians drifted away to pursue other interests. Several of them, however, continued to share a residual commitment not only to the South, the past and the rural community but to the promotion of a close, critical reading of literature, which was to become known as the New Criticism. As author of *The New Criticism* (1941), Ransom gave the new critical movement its name; as a prolific essayist, as *Essays of Four Decades* (1969) and *The House of Fiction* (written with Caroline Gordon [1895–1981] [1950]) both attest, Tate gave it intellectual muscle; as the authors of the immensely popular and influential *Understanding Poetry* (1938) and *Understanding Fiction* (1943), Warren and the critic Cleanth Brooks (1906–94) were largely responsible for making the New Criticism the standard practice in American schools and colleges for three or four decades after the Second World War. There are many things that could be said about the New Criticism. It encouraged close reading of a text, separated from discussion of historical, biographical or other contexts. It steered attention towards certain specific literary practices, such as the use of symbol, wit and irony. It was promoted by other eminent critics and writers of the time, many of them from the North and some of them liberal. In its Southern manifestation, though, the New Criticism did have the additional advantage of allowing former Fugitives and Agrarians to retain some of their cherished principles. What people like Ransom and Tate were seeking for in works of literature, as New Critics, was, it turned out, what they had once sought for in social and historical institutions: a harmonious system, an organism in which there was a place for everything and everything was in its place – and which, ideally, was part of an identifiable tradition, referring back to systems of a similar kind. This put them at odds with the tradition of American writing and criticism typified by, say, Whitman in the nineteenth century, and in the twentieth by William Carlos Williams, since their idea of literary form was that it should be closed rather than open, and orthodox and inherited rather than imitative and experimental. And it permitted them to find some sort of redress, in the balance and wholeness of art, for what they saw now as the irredeemably unbalanced and fractured world of modernity. As Ransom himself put it, 'the arts are expiations, but they are beautiful. They seem worth the vile welter through which homeless spirits must wade between times, with sensibilities subject to ravage as they are.' The old active faith in traditionalism had been shattered irretrievably but, in this way, parts of it could be reclaimed, even if only by indirection and stealth. It could become the grounds for a new reading of literature and culture and, consequently, help reshape consciousness; it could act as compensation, emotional and intellectual, for the irreversible thrust of America towards the modern.

Of all the writers nurtured by the Fugitive movement, John Crowe Ransom (1888–1974) is among the most interesting, as his poetry, gathered together principally in *Chills and Fever* (1924), *Two Gentlemen in Bonds* (1927) and then in *Selected Poems* (1945; 1963; 1969), attests. He is also among those most firmly committed to the belief that only a traditional society, through its myths and ceremonies, can promote human wholeness. Contemporary society, on the contrary, the one Ransom saw all around him in America, left people divided, dissociated, their personalities fragmented or underdeveloped. The desperation of many of Ransom's poetic characters springs from the fact that they cannot achieve unity of being. They are like the narrator of 'Winter Remembered' who, separated from his beloved, comes to typify the sense of fragmentation, estrangement and sheer vacuum which all those who have failed to attain wholeness of being must experience. Lonely old spinsters ('Emily Hardcastle, Spinster'), young scholars ('Persistent Explorer'), old eccentrics ('Captain Carpenter'), thwarted lovers ('Parting at Dawn', 'The Equilibrists'), abstract idealists and optimists ('Man Without Sense of Direction'): they all illustrate that 'old illusion of grandeur' which Ransom explores in one of his later poems, 'Painted Head' – the belief, that is, that the mind can exist apart, 'play truant from the body bush'. This, certainly, is one of Ransom's favourite themes: that 'cry of Absence, Absence in the heart' which charts out a more general situation of emptiness and loss. Others are death and the world of the child, which are often treated together: as in 'Dead Boy', 'Bells for John Whiteside's Daughter' and 'Blue Girls'. 'Death is the greatest subject for poetry,' Ransom insisted, '... there's no recourse from death, except that we learn to face it.' As such, it provides modern humankind in particular with a timely reminder of its limitations: the most powerful example possible of all that the reason cannot encompass or control. And when that subject is the death of a child, then, for Ransom, a further dimension is added: because, in a fragmented society such as our own, only the child's world is whole. Only this world does not suffer from dissociation, Ransom believed, and a consequent feeling of spiritual absence; and even so it presents a less than satisfying possibility because – as the very facts of transience and mortality indicate – it is innocent, limited and frail.

Ransom's aim is not simply to describe such characters and situations, however. He tries to place them, most often with the help of a singular quality of language and tone. 'Winter Remembered', for instance, ends with these lines:

> Dear love, these fingers that had known your touch,
> And tied our separate forces first together
> Were ten poor idiot fingers not worth much,
> Ten frozen parsnips hanging in the weather.

This mundane image, contrasting sharply with the romantic framework of the preceding lines, brings together the conflicting figures of heat and cold that characterize the rest of the poem: the parsnips, normally capable of experiencing warmth and growth, have been frozen into lifelessness just as, in a way, the narrator and his limbs have. The peculiar tone or attitude engendered by this comparison is typical of Ransom, and has been variously described as a kind of acid gaiety, a wrinkled laughter or detached wit. Perhaps the best description is Ransom's own, though. For when he refers in his essays to that 'irony' which, by combining the dream of the ideal with the dismay of the actual, becomes 'the rarest of the states of mind, because ... the most inclusive', he is implicitly describing the strategy of his own work. In such lines, in fact, the poet himself seems to step forward, to establish the kind of 'mellow wisdom' (to use Ransom's own phrase) of which the narrator-lover himself is incapable: the ironic inclusiveness of vision that somehow eludes most people in an un-traditional world.

Not that it is always left to the style to perform this positive function in Ransom's poetry: just occasionally he is more explicit. This is the case with one of the few poems where he is directly concerned with the Southern tradition, 'Antique Harvesters'. Set on the banks of the Mississippi, the poem presents Ransom's native region as a place where wholeness of being is still available. This is not, it should be emphasized, because the poet indulges in that easy nostalgia that the Fugitives criticized. On the contrary, it is because he invites us into the mythmaking process. He observes the river, the land, the harvesters, the old men who watch them, and 'the hunters, keepers of a rite' who ride by. And, as he does so, he gradually and consciously associates all these things with the notions of ceremony and chivalry, the belief in a usable past and an inheritable pattern of living. What seemed at first little more than 'A meager hill of kernels, a runnel of juice' is transformed during the course of the poem into a spiritual resource, a setting that evidently furnishes roots and identity; and that process of transformation, whereby an anonymous and apparently unpromising environment becomes a heroic land, is as much a matter for the reader's attention as the purported subject is. The earth becomes 'our Lady'; the hunters become 'archetypes of chivalry', the hunted fox a 'lovely ritualist'; the harvesters become *antique* harvesters, participating in time-honoured ceremonies and expressing through their work a religious devotion to the land. Yet all this is done without any rejecting or minimizing of the original facts in the case of the farm labourer, or in the case of any person destined to work and then die. 'Antique Harvesters' is, in fact, not so much a portrait from life as a minor historical myth, in which the process of creation, the act of making a landscape and then attaching to it the idea of unity of consciousness, is the intent of the poem – and constitutes a vital part of its *content* too.

In some ways Allen Tate (1889–1979) bears a haunting resemblance to Ransom. He was similarly preoccupied with the radical discontinuities of modern existence; and he also longed for a traditional society in which moral unity was the norm. But there were profound differences too. The volume of Ransom's creative work is relatively small; after 1927, he committed only four new poems to print, concentrating instead on public affairs and aesthetics and founding and editing the *Kenyon Review*. Apart from a year in England as a Rhodes scholar in 1913, he spent his life in America, teaching first at Vanderbilt and then at Kenyon College, Ohio. And the whole tone and texture of his poetry was highly wrought but resistant to the specific forms of experiment associated with Modernism. Tate, on the other hand, was prolific. From *The Golden Mean and Other Poems* (1928) to *The Swimmers* (1971), he produced a steady stream of verse over six decades, brought together in *Collected Poems* (1977). He wrote interpretative biographies of Stonewall Jackson (1928) and Jefferson Davis (1929) and several volumes of comment and criticism, from *Reactionary Essays on Poetry and Ideas* (1936) to *Memoirs and Opinions* (1975). He also produced one major novel, *The Fathers*. Set in Virginia before and during the Civil War, it tells the story of two families, the Buchans of Pleasant Hill and the Poseys of Georgetown. Major Lewis Buchan, patriarch of the one family, is the consummate Southern aristocrat. George Posey, his son-in-law, is the modern man, steeped in Southern tradition but restless and outside it. Young Lacey Buchan, son of Lewis and just coming into manhood, narrates a sequence of events that tear his father and brother-in-law apart and his family asunder. These events are coincident with and inseparable from events on a larger canvas: where the South experiences comprehensive defeat and division. The personal is the political here, and vice versa. This is an intensely emotional novel that explores social conflict and dissolution through war in and between families. And through war within a single personality, since Lacey Buchan is himself divided in his loyalties between the old and the new, drawn in love and veneration towards both his 'fathers', Major Buchan and George Posey. As Tate observed, many years after writing *The Fathers*, the novel has two heroes: 'Major Buchan, the classical hero, whose *hubris* destroys him' and 'George Posey . . . a modern romantic hero'. It is torn between two characters, and the dispensations they symbolize, just as much as its narrator is. The triumph of the novel, in fact, is that Tate, despite his intense attachment to traditionalism and the South, is able to keep a sufficiently critical purchase on his subject, and sufficient distance from his own instinctive loyalties, to create real balance and tension. The old Southern way of life, epitomized by Major Buchan, is destroyed by its own inherent flaws as much as, or more than, anything else. The new order of things, embodied in Posey, is a compelling mix, or confusion, of the dangerous and the desirable, violence and energy. Which is why, perhaps, the very last words in the story express Lacey's yearnings towards his brother-in-law: 'I love him', he says, 'more than I love any man.'

Tate was different from Ransom, too, in that he was affected by the poetic experiments of Eliot and Crane. He even defended *The Waste Land* against Ransom's dismissive criticisms. This is reflected in the tone, and sometimes the structure, of Tate's own poetry. Freer forms alternate with logical patterns. Logical connectives are omitted, sentences inverted and scenes changed rapidly. The distance between Tate and Ransom is measured with particular force in Tate's most famous poem, 'Ode to the Confederate Dead'. In some ways, 'Ode' operates within the same series of assumptions as 'Antique Harvesters'. It, too, is a profoundly traditionalist poem which attempts to create a myth, an ideal version of the past, as a corrective to the present. It, too, is a poem that dramatizes the mythologizing process, the creation of an idea, a complex of possibilities, out of historical fact. The narrator, a man who characterizes the modern failure to live according to principle, stands by the monuments raised to those killed fighting for the South during the Civil War; and as he describes their lives, or rather what he imagines their lives to have been, the description is transmuted into celebration. The past is reinvented, just as place, landscape is in 'Antique Harvesters'; the soldiers being remembered are transformed into a heroic alternative to the plight of the person remembering them. The voice of 'Antique Harvesters', however, is the voice of all Ransom's poems: accomplished, witty, serene – the voice of someone who can, apparently, fathom and perform his nature. The voice of 'Ode', by contrast, is uncertain, feverish, disoriented – the voice of the 'locked-in ego' as Tate puts it elsewhere, of a man unable to liberate himself from a sense of his own impotence and frag- mentation. The narrator of Ransom's poems remains triumphantly detached: some- times helping to gauge the failure of his subjects and sometimes, as in 'Antique Harvesters', helping to endow his subjects' achievements with articulate shape. The narrator of the 'Ode', however, is like the narrator of most of Tate's poetry and fiction: a person obsessed with his failure to attain unity of being, whose introversions, tortured idiom, clotted imagery and convoluted syntax register what Tate has called 'the modern squirrel cage of our sensibility, the extreme introspec- tion of our time'.

Tate's search for a traditional order, with its associated idea of wholeness of being, eventually led him away from the South and into religious faith. From the first, he had been a little sceptical about the claims of his region: even at its finest, before the Civil War, it was, he declared, 'a feudal society without a feudal religion' and to that extent was fatally incomplete. And he gradually turned, for the promise of moral unity, to the Roman Catholic church. Out of the actual process of conversion came poems like 'Seasons of the Soul', a powerful and often pained sequence that ends with a prayer to a mysterious 'mother of silences' who, recalling both the 'Lady of Silences' in Eliot's 'Ash Wednesday' and Baudelaire's 'maîtresse de maîtresses', seems to combine intimations of the spiritual and the sensual, the Virgin Mary and the carnal knowledge that concludes in death. After the conversion, in turn, came poems like 'The Swimmers'. Relaxed, fluent, idiomatic, although capable of allusion and even moments of apocalypse, such poems reveal a new willingness to submit to the material rather than force it into a new mould – and, in particular, to submit to the sanctions of memory and the compulsions of personality. Tate was neither the first nor the last writer to feel that ultimate salvation for the traditionalist was to be found in religion. This, in turn, enabled him to relax his tone and recall the more personal details of his past life, 'the shrill companions' of his youth, and to rehearse intimate experience, moments of affection.

The paths of the two other notable Fugitive writers, Donald Davidson (1893–1968) and Robert Penn Warren (1905–89), were different from those of Ransom and Tate, and different, in turn, from each other. Davidson's is the simpler case. Uppermost in the minds of the Fugitive group, Davidson later claimed, 'was a feeling of intense disgust with the spiritual disorder of modern life'. 'We wanted a life which through its own conditions . . . would engender . . . order, leisure, character, stability,' he explained. 'What history told us of the South drove us straight to its traditions.' Partially true of other Fugitive writers, this is almost entirely true of Davidson himself. Disgust with the present precipitated a turning in on the past. Revulsion from the 'mechanical age', and the myriad random impressions with which 'the modern brain' is assaulted, led Davidson to celebrate the security and the splendour of the Southern tradition, in poems gathered together in such volumes as *The Tall Men* (1927), *Lee in the Mountains and Other Poems* (1938) and *The Long Street* (1961), and in prose works one collection of which carries the characteristic title *Still Rebels, Still Yankees, and Other Essays* (1957). If Davidson developed at all, it was only to the extent that his opinions hardened into prejudices, so that he became more of a reactionary than a traditionalist. Warren, on the other hand, changed in the course of an enormously productive career. Unlike Davidson, too, who confined himself mostly to poetry and essays, Warren was a genuine and wide-ranging man of letters. His literary criticism, identifying him as one of the founders of the New Criticism, won him enormous influence: along with *Understanding Poetry* and *Understanding Fiction*, critical works written on his own include *Homage to Theodore Dreiser* (1971), *John Greenleaf Whittier* (1971) and the studies collected in *New and Selected Essays* (1989). An early biographical study exploring the dangers of idealism, *John Brown: The Making of a Martyr* (1929), betrays the conservative stance that aligned the younger Warren with the Agrarians. Even here, though, he took a more interrogative stance than most of his colleagues: his essay in *I'll Take My Stand* may be a defence of segregation, but at least it is honest enough to confront the racial issue. Two later works of social and historical meditation, *Segregation: The Inner Conflict in the South* (1956) and *Who Speaks for the Negro?* (1965), measure Warren's progress towards a more liberal position and a dispassionate advocacy of civil rights. *The Legacy of the Civil War* (1956), in turn, reveals its author's lifelong interest in history as a subject and a moral discipline and his particular concern with how the war has shaped American society and sensibilities. As one of the speakers in Warren's long dramatic poem *Brother to Dragons: A Tale in Verse and Voices* (1953; revised edn, 1979) puts it: 'without the fact of the past, no matter how terrible, / We cannot dream the future'.

As a poet and novelist, above all, Warren has been constantly concerned with the indelible fact of the past: the necessity to return to the place where 'the father waits for the son' because, without that return, no genuine progress, no meaningful development, personal or social, is possible. 'History', says Warren in one of his later poems, 'Shoes in Rain Jungle' (1966), 'is what you can't / Resign from'; nor should you try, since what the fact of the past can develop is a healthy awareness of human limits – a sense of the sheer 'massiveness of experience' bearing down on the human personality and drastically circumscribing the capacity for action. Looking at what has gone before, people can learn from their mistakes and also begin to understand the nature of the fallible human community to which they belong. That is not the entire story, though: as Warren indicates, there is the dream of the future as well as the fact of the past. 'Of the brute creation' people may be, but they are also, potentially, 'a little lower than the angels'. Consequently, while they require an adequate definition of terror to remind them of their monstrous origins, they need at the same time to find some way of 'accommodating flesh to idea' so as 'to be able to frame a definition of joy'. Tradition, the stored wisdom of the past, is certainly crucial in suggesting appropriate values, principles by which to live. But values, according to Warren, are actually formulated by individuals out of the experience of living and, even as they develop, qualify and enrich that experience. Past and future, fact and idea, father and son, the traditionalist sense of what has been and the utopian feeling for what might be: the process is a dialectical one and there is no end to the growth and discovery of the self, other than that offered to each of us individually by death.

Much of Warren's finest poetry and fiction is concerned with the failure to realize this dialectic. His poetry, from *Eleven Poems on the Same Theme* (1942) through such seminal volumes as *Promises* (1957) and *Audubon: A Vision* (1969) to *New and Selected Poems* (1985), has returned again and again, in lyric, narrative and meditative modes, to what one poem, 'I Am Dreaming of a White Christmas: The Natural History of a Vision' (1974), calls the 'process whereby pain of the past in its pastness / May be converted into the future tense / Of joy'. Like Ransom, Warren has his own gallery of betrayed idealists, and many of his poems offer secular versions of the Fall. At its worst, this fall into experience provokes nihilism, surrender to the brute materiality of things: the so-called 'realist' is, in Warren's eyes at least, no more adequate – that is, just as blind to the dialectic of past and future – as the idealist is. But, at its best, it leads on to a kind of redemption, expressed sometimes in terms of a rediscovery of the father. Seeing his father properly, the narrator/protagonist of Warren's poems begins to see himself; accepting and embracing him, warts and all, he starts to accept his own limitations and embrace the human community. 'Man can return to his lost unity,' Warren has insisted in one of his essays, 'Knowledge and the Image of Man', 'and . . . if the foliage and flower of the innocent garden are now somewhat browned by a late season, all is the more precious for the fact, for what is now achieved has been achieved by a growth of moral awareness.'

The figure of the garden or clearing – 'browned by a late season', perhaps, yet not without a sense of serenity – recurs throughout Warren's work, and it brings together the two patterns of the fall followed by redemption and the return to the father. For it is at once the familiar home of Adam and the old homestead, somewhere in western Kentucky, to which Warren and his protagonists, born in just such a place, dream of returning. Quite apart from that, it also offers a reminder of that equipoise so vital to Warren's work, since it is neither utterly savage nor completely subdued. Just as the human personality, according to Warren, operates best in the space between fact and idea, tradition and opportunity, so the various clearings he describes exist in a border territory between forest and town, the energies of wilderness and the structures of civilization. They are not necessarily cultivated spots. For example, the place where the protagonist in *Audubon: A Vision* has his first mystical experience is simply an open space created by nature. They are always, though, both outer landscapes and inner ones: they are products partly of history and Warren's own experience and partly of myth, his fictive powers.

Given that Warren is so committed, in principle, to the notion of change, it is hardly surprising that his writing bears witness to some remarkable alterations of language and tone – and even, to a certain extent, of vision. In his poetry, for example, the early work tended towards the highly wrought and frigidly impersonal: crabbed, allusive and sometimes rather too knowingly ironic, it seemed to be borrowing a manner – from Ransom and Tate, in particular – instead of shaping one in response to personal needs. The later work, by contrast, was more expansive and open: a richer, more variable idiom was combined with fluent, muscular rhythms to create a sense of energetic composure, disciplined ease. At the same time, the preoccupation with failure or chilly forms of redemption that characterized the early writing gave way to an interest in existential humanity, the possible sources of courage and awe. Above all, Warren began to seek the springs of well-being more fiercely than ever before: to search for an identity forged out of a passionate and positive engagement with the world. 'Tell me a story of deep delight,' *Audubon* concludes, and that line articulates the impulse that prised the poet loose from his earlier habits. Traditionalist Warren remained, but a traditionalist seeking poetic narratives that released the glory of life – or, as he put it once, enabled him to 'frame a definition of joy'.

The development in the fiction was less marked, but there was still a general tendency noticeable over the course of Warren's ten novels, from *Night Rider*

(1939) to *A Place to Come To* (1977), to move from the more highly wrought to the more expansive and openly personal. *Night Rider*, for instance, a novel exploring its author's characteristic moral concerns with reference to a struggle between tobacco growers and manufacturers in early twentieth-century Kentucky, is a carefully articulated work of symbolic naturalism. Each episode in it, each character, is rendered in naturalistic detail but each is clearly balanced against some meaningful opposite and, equally clearly, resonates with meaning. *A Place to Come To* is no less concerned with exploring Warren's familiar preoccupations. Presented as the reminiscences of a sixty-year-old classics scholar starting with his youth in Alabama, it is, however, not only more relaxed in tone but creates the illusion of being less premeditated. And it is an engaging mix of anecdote and autobiography, meditation and tall tale. Consistently, however, in all his fiction Warren returns to the themes that dominate his other work. There, on one side of the dialectic, is a rich gallery of dreamers and idealists. There are political fanatics like Professor Ball in *Night Rider* and Percival Skrogg in *World Enough and Time* (1950), religious visionaries like Ashby Wyndham in *At Heaven's Gate* (1943), romantic dreamers like Adam Rosenzweig in *Wilderness* (1961), those driven by some purely erotic illusion such as Nick Pappy in *The Cave* (1959) and Leroy Lancaster in *Meet Me in the Green Glen* (1971), and those who simply retreat from human engagement into the role of observer like Yasha Jones in *Flood* (1964) and Jed Tewkesbury in *A Place to Come To*. And there, on the other side, are the realists, those who sacrifice moral principle to material interests. They include some of Warren's finest fictional creations: the financier Bogan Murdock in *At Heaven's Gate*, the politician Willie Stark in *All the King's Men* (1946) and Murray Guilfort in *Meet Me in the Green Glen*. Products of what is called, at the end of *All the King's Men*, 'the terrible division of our age', they are no less hollow – without guiding principles, and so no less deficient in their creator's eyes – than those who live in the ice-cold world of ideas or intellectual detachment. And it becomes the project of the novels, just as it is of the poetry, to explore those divisions and to express the possibility of resolution. Each novel is, to use Warren's own term, an 'adventure in selfhood' in which the protagonist struggles to heal those divisions – and sometimes succeeds in doing so, as in the poetry, by finding a place to come to where his father, literally or metaphorically awaits him: a homeplace where, as Warren puts it, he can 'return to his lost unity'.

All the King's Men, Warren's most famous and accomplished novel, shows precisely how he gave these fundamental ideas fictional life. At its centre is a division typical for Warren between an idealist and an opportunist: Adam Stanton, whose forename suggests his prelapsarian innocence, and Willie Stark, whose equally eponymous surname indicates just how far he is committed to stark fact. The protagonist and narrator, Jack Burden, is the man who must face and heal this division by coming to terms with the burden of his past, specifically in the shape of his father, and so enjoy the chance of a purely secular redemption. All this makes *All the King's Men* sound schematic. Like all Warren's fiction, the novel does veer towards the heavily freighted, a narrative so loaded with significance that it threatens to sink its surface naturalism. Like the best of it, though, it is rescued by its personal specificity and social density – and because Warren obeys his own injunction to immerse himself in history. The personal detail comes from Jack Burden, who is both man acting and man narrating. Burden in the narrative present, radically altered by experience, is recalling Burden in the narrative past, and the particular experiences that altered him, crucially. He is intimately, passionately involved in the story he is telling and, through him, Warren makes sure that the reader is too. As for the immersion in society and history: that comes from the understanding of place the novel reveals, the peculiar, polyglot culture of early twentieth-century Louisiana with its mix of populist enthusiasm and easygoing cynicism, its romanticism and its money-grabbing. Something of this culture is caught in the rich variety of idioms Warren deploys, from the hardboiled to the dreamlike and lyrical. But even more to the point here is Warren's reimagining of a pivotal moment in Louisiana history. The character of Willie Stark is clearly based on Huey Long, the populist politician elected governor in 1928 who ran the state as if it were his own personal fiefdom, and who, just before being assassinated, was preparing to run for president on a 'Share Our Wealth' programme that made the New Deal look positively conservative. What Warren does is to take this story, the facts in the case of Long, and set it in the kind of dialectical relationship with the shaping idea of *All the King's Men* that creates a new form and meaning for both. He does not distort history in revising it, at least in terms of its essential pattern. What he does is to place it in such a context as will demonstrate its direct and effective relationship to other experience. The present is changed by the past, in the sense that Warren has found in a specific set of circumstances a means of dramatizing the 'terrible division' of his age. And the past is changed by the present, since the 'odds and ends' of history, as Jack Burden calls them, have been woven into a pattern that makes them coherent, 'all of one piece' with each other and with the lives of those remembering. *All the King's Men* is consequently an apt realization of Warren's project: to remain true to the imperatives of the past and the needs of the present and future. It is also that rare thing, a philosophical novel that makes its discoveries in the welter of politics and social conflict. And it is a genuinely historical fiction in a dual sense: because it tries to come to terms with the stark facts of historical experience, and because it tries to formulate an idea of history.

Ransom, Tate, Warren: together these three major figures chart the various possibilities of traditionalism, and in particular Southern traditionalism. But they are not alone in doing this, even within the context of their region. Another, unjustly neglected figure suggests other possibilities: John Peale Bishop (1892–1944). Born in West Virginia, a close friend to F. Scott Fitzgerald and the writer, critic and editor Edmund Wilson (1895–1972), Bishop thought of himself as a Southerner to the end of his life. More than any other writer, too, Bishop reveals the neo-classical strain in the Southern tradition. The feeling in his poems and essays, gathered together in *Collected Poems* (1948) and *Collected Essays* (1948), and in his one novel, *Act of Darkness* (1935), is consistently stoical; the sense of humour is fierce, the form of expression laconic, chiselled. Many Southerners, especially in the eighteenth century, liked to mould themselves on republican Rome; and Bishop developed this tendency, perceiving himself as a patrician republican confronted with the corruption of empire. He saw a parallel between the decline of Rome and the decadence of the United States; and he felt the necessity of withdrawing into the exercise of private virtue. Convinced of the necessity of order, personal and public, he was totally committed to the ideas of duty and ceremony. And ceremony was lost in America, Bishop felt: the pursuit of the future excluded any honouring of the past. In works like 'Experience in the West' (1935), he hauntingly reversed the westward myth since, for him, it was precisely the tragedy of America that it supplanted culture with nature. Striding apart from the human community, the pioneer had made for himself a world without 'soul': that is, without those dimensions and resonances that only ritual and ceremony could offer. Other writers have celebrated the openness of America, its substitution of geography for history: in Bishop's opinion, however, that was something to be lamented. As he saw it, there was a seamless, sad connection between the literal wilderness, that 'green savage clime' into which Americans had gone centuries ago, and the moral wilderness that was the America of his own time.

Bishop was roughly a contemporary of the Fugitives but other, later Southern writers continued to testify to the vitality and variety of traditionalism. Most notable here, and very different from each other, are Wendell Berry (1934–) and James Dickey (1923–99). Poet, essayist and novelist, Berry has developed what might be termed the ecological tendency in traditionalist writing. The titles of some of his collections of essays testify to his allegiances: *The Unforeseen Wilderness* (1971), *A Continuous Harmony* (1972), *The Gift of Good Land* (1981). His novels *Nathan Coulter* (1960), about a boy growing up in tobacco-farming land, *A Place on Earth* (1967) and *The Memory of Old Jack* (1974), in which a ninety-two-year-old farmer recalls his earlier days, reveal an attachment to one dear, particular place that blossoms out into a recognition of kinship with nature. So do the poems, in collections like *The Broken Ground* (1964) and *Travelling at Home* (1988). Always, the animating conviction is that 'slowly we return to earth'. And always the enemies are those familiar *bêtes noires* of the traditionalist, mechanism and abstraction – a world in which people are turned into products in the name of certain insubstantial theories concerning nature, human nature and power. Dickey is as preoccupied with nature and the past as Berry is, but his preoccupations take very different forms. For his major interest is in the primeval bases of existence – that storehouse of energies and imagery, the series of remembered and recurring experiences which belong almost entirely to the sub-rational levels of life. Hunting, or more generally the expedition into the wilderness, supplies the framework for much of Dickey's work: for his most famous novel, *Deliverance* (1970), and for many of the poems in his numerous volumes from *Into the Stone* (1960) to *The Early Motion* (1980) and *The Central Motion* (1983). Its incidents are frequently his subjects, its rituals supply him with a language, and its code prescribes the nature and scope of his perceptions. It is, in effect, during and by means of the hunt, the errand into the wilderness, that many of Dickey's narrators achieve contact with the subliminal dimensions of experience – go down into the ground, as it were, to commune with the inhuman. For writers like Ransom or Tate that may be a single past, identified with a singular historical figure or culture. For Dickey, however, there is not one 'father' but many 'fathers': many pasts, battalions of the dead who exist within us whether we like it or not – and who speak not only to us but through us.

Outside the South, the convictions to which the Fugitives gave such spirited expression animated many writers, among them Yvor Winters (1900–68), J. V. Cunningham (1911–65) and Richard Eberhart (1904–). A distinguished critic as well as a poet, Winters published his *Collected Poems* in 1952. And his poetry pursued the same priorities as his criticism. To achieve 'the final certitude of speech', Winters believed, the writer had to reflect and select. He had to use a rigorously disciplined form, containing concise and rationally controlled reflections on experiences of moral significance. At first his own pursuit of precision led Winters towards Imagism: poems that mixed Imagist instantaneity with his own special brand of rational reflection. He soon felt, however, that Imagism lacked intellectual backbone and convincing structure: so he moved away from it towards more traditional forms, through which he could comment lucidly and concisely on experience. 'The fine indignant sprawl', he wrote in 'On Teaching the Young', '/ Confuses all.' Far better was 'corrosion and distrust': a healthy scepticism, a keen eye for cant and a willingness to refine and refine again so as to produce something 'small but good'. Cunningham, whom Winters admired, was if anything even more drawn towards compressed, close-woven forms of speech. Some of his best work consists of epigrams. All of it tends towards the laconic or lapidary, the language pure to the point of austerity, the verse movements precise and poised. His seven volumes were brought together in *The Collected Poems and Epigrams* (1971); and, throughout that volume, there is a characteristic blend of wit and sadness, metrical severity and verbal subtlety. His is a voice that resists the urge towards transcendence, and offers no solace, no comfort other than that supplied by clear understanding. Sometimes he makes his traditionalist leanings very clear. A reference, for instance, to 'Ambitious boys / Whose big lines swell / With spiritual noise' in 'For My Contemporaries' is an unambiguously sardonic comment on the influence of Whitman on American writing. More often, however, his belief that the best work is done 'By caution under custom's guide' emerges from the tone and texture of his verse. *To What Strangers, What Welcomes* (1964), for example, is a set of poems on the familiar theme of travelling westward. Cunningham makes it unfamiliar and his own, however, by adopting an approach of classical restraint towards this subject, and attaching his account of 'the vacancies of need', the emptiness of landscape he encounters in the West, to the traditional theme of *lacrimae rerum*. In spare and severe lines, he manages to suggest some of the contradictory feelings that issue from being 'lost in this place' called the open road of the American West, the luminosity and the exile, and something too of the melancholy attendant on the mere condition of being alive.

The wit and sadness, and the preoccupation with mortality, that characterize so many traditionalist writers are also typical of Eberhart, the author of more than thirty volumes of poetry, among them *A Bravery of Earth* (1930), *Selected Poems 1930–65* (1965), *The Long Reach: New and Uncollected Poems, 1948–84* (1984) and *Collected Poems 1930–1986* (1988), and someone who has been important both in his own right and as an influence on others. 'We are / Betrayed by time, which made us mortal,' Eberhart declares in 'Anima'; and nearly all his work starts from this recognition. The structure of the world is 'hard'; we all fall from 'the pitch that is near madness', the 'violent, vivid' and 'immaculate' state of childhood, 'into a realm of complexity . . . / Where nothing is possible but necessity'; and only a willingness to see things 'in a hard intellectual light' can restore the 'moral grandeur of man'. These beliefs feed into Eberhart's writing, so that even his simpler poems become striking for their intellectual dexterity and rigour: ideas or experiences are introduced in a straightforward, even ingenuous, fashion and then cunningly extended, in ways that often rely on allusion or verbal or metaphoric tension for their impact. Eberhart's aim is not only to see things clearly, however, but to see them with 'the supreme authority of the imagination' as his guide. Consequently, an acknowledgement of what is never inhibits an awareness of what might be. 'The light beyond compare is the light I saw,' he says in one of his finest pieces, 'The Incomparable Light'. 'I saw it in childhood . . . / I glimpsed it in the turbulence of growing up'; now, he adds, 'It is this strange light I come back to, / Agent of truth, protean, a radical of time'. In effect, Eberhart sees no contradiction between the 'hard' light of the intellect and the 'strange' light of the imagination: on the contrary, the one is for him the precondition of the other. He uses wit and dexterity not as a substitute for vision but as a means of liberating it, of discovering what he calls 'The truth of the positive hour': which, for him, consists of 'love / Concrete, specific', 'the grace to imagine the unimaginable' that 'Elevates man to an angelic state', 'the heart's lonely rapture', and the 'Inescapable brotherhood of the living'. 'What shall I say to Walt Whitman tonight?' asks Eberhart in his 'Centennial for Whitman', and admits he has little time for Whitman's 'loose form', 'positive acclamation' or 'frenetic belief'. But he does, he declares, meet with the founding father of American poetry in his 'Knowledge of the changeless in birth and death', his glimmering sense of a process whereby 'Death is but a door' into other forms of living. He does, as Eberhart concludes, 'speak to him in the universe of birth and death'. There could hardly be a more measured, and so more honest, tribute from a traditionalist to one who was above all an experimentalist. And it shows how, in the hands of some American writers at least, traditionalism became a means, if not of transcendence, then of crossing the boundaries of the familiar into new thresholds, new discoveries.

Populism and radicalism

Of those who did, contrary to Eberhart, think that a looser form and fierce if not frenetic belief were appropriate responses to a time of change and challenge, none was more committed than Carl Sandburg (1878–1967). The son of Swedish immigrants, Sandburg left school at the age of thirteen. Travelling through the West and taking a variety of jobs, he worked on a newspaper in Chicago, then as secretary to the socialist mayor of Milwaukee, then returned to Chicago again in 1913. There, one year later, some of his poems were published in *Poetry*, the magazine founded and edited by Harriet Monroe. Shortly after, *Chicago Poems* (1916) and *Cornhuskers* (1918) established him as a major poet of the Midwest and Chicago renaissance. His poem 'Chicago' (1916) announced the nature of his vision. 'Hog Butcher for the World / Tool Maker, Stacker of wheat, /' it began, 'Stormy, husky, brawling, / City of the Big Shoulders.' 'I turn once more to those who sneer at this my city,' Sandburg proudly declared, '. . . and say to them / Come and show me another city with lifted head singing so proud to be alive and coarse and strong and cunning.' 'Chicago', like so many of Sandburg's poems, is at once a description of the newly emergent economic centre of the Middle West and a celebration of the common people, its inhabitants. Its direct, unanalytical populism is reflected in the style, in which a rhetorical and flexible line, an idiomatic language and bold rhythms, all become part of the attempt to create a poetic equivalent of folk speech. Chicago, in turn, seems to be transformed into a folk hero, along the lines of Paul Bunyan or Mike Fink; and at certain points the narrator seems something of a folk hero too, responding to everything as he does with an equal feeling of wonder, a reverence for its power and particularity. This is a simple poem, perhaps, but it is also a remarkable one, because its celebration of the Middle West and America in general is a matter not only of vision but of voice. It is a song both in praise and in imitation of American energy, the sense of strength and possibility that an almost unlimited amount of living space can bring.

Sandburg's response to America was not uncritical, however. He could be hard, when he turned from celebration of the innate energies of the people to an attack on those who would suppress such energies or divert them to their own ends. In 'A Fence' (1916), for instance, the fence that a rich man builds around 'his stone house on the lake front' is identified with the barriers behind which he and his special interests prefer to hide. Other poems, such as 'New Feet' (1916) and 'Gone' (1916), suggest not so much the critical side of Sandburg as a sadder, more ironic one, as he captures the anonymity of urban life rather than (as in 'Chicago') its vitality. Nor does Sandburg confine himself to the city scene; on the contrary, some of his finest poems, like 'Sunset from Omaha Hotel Window' (1918) and 'More Country People' (1918), are concerned with the signs, sounds and the people of the prairies. All of his work, though, whatever its subject, tone or treatment, is shot through with his democratic populist values; and none more so than two monumental works, his biography of Abraham Lincoln, begun in 1919 and not finished until 1939, and his reworking of folk song and idiom in *The People, Yes*, a long poem that appeared in 1936. In the biography, Lincoln appears as an embodiment of the American dream; while, in the poem, Sandburg declares his faith in the democratic experiment. 'The people will live on,' Sandburg insists, towards the end of the poem, 'The people is a polychrome, / a spectrum and a prism.' 'In the night', he concludes, 'and overhead', 'a shovel of stars for keeps, the people march! / "Where to? What next?"' Using a frequently apocalyptic tone and an incantatory rhythm and language, Sandburg presents 'the people' as an indomitable force, dormant now but about to assert its rightful supremacy. This is American epic at its most straightforward: plotless, concentrating more on natural potential than on cultural attainment, and ending on a note of hope. At its centre is what Sandburg calls 'a polychrome, / a spectrum and a prism': a mysterious, multifarious figure who is at once everybody and nobody in particular – nobody, that is, apart from that representative of his nation the writer knows best, himself.

'Oh, the great poem has yet to be written . . . Jeffersonian democracy as an art is a thing to be desired.' The words are those of another poet associated with Chicago, Vachel Lindsay (1879–1931). Like Sandburg, Lindsay was devoted to Abraham Lincoln: 'The prairie-lawyer' he called him, 'master of us all'. He was equally devoted to Andrew Jackson (a man for whom, as he saw it, 'Every friend was an equal'), and to William Jennings Bryan. Bryan, in particular, was a charismatic figure for him: the Democratic presidential candidate of 1896 who, for a time, made it seem possible that the farming interests of the West might yet prevail over the cities and factories of 'the dour East'. Lindsay was, in fact, raised in Illinois during the period of agrarian and populist revolt against the emergent urban-industrial economy; and it left an indelible mark on him. So, too, did the walking tour of the United States that he undertook in 1912, without occupation or even prospects. Out of both experiences grew a determination to create an 'American' rhythm, related to the sounds of galloping herds and shrieking motors, black music and what he called 'vaudevilles' and 'circuses'. And out of this, in turn, came poems like 'General William Booth Enters Into Heaven' (1913) (which reveals his millennialism, his commitment to the social gospel of the underprivileged), 'In Praise of Johnny Appleseed' (1913) (the mythical American hero for whom, Lindsay suggests, 'the real frontier was his sunburnt breast') and, perhaps his most famous work, 'Bryan, Bryan, Bryan, Bryan' (1913). The two collections that brought Lindsay fame were *General William Booth Enters Into Heaven and Other Poems* (1913) and *The Congo and Other Poems* (1914). The title piece of the second volume is a celebration of black Americans and is relatively atypical of Lindsay's work in its use of syncopated rhythms. It is, however, otherwise characteristic of all his poetry in that it is heavily rhetorical, with a proliferation of heavy accents, emphatic rhymes and verbal melodies, repetition and chanting rhymes. Lindsay's is really a poetry meant to be spoken: the later years of Lindsay's life were devoted to an exhausting programme of public performances, which had as its aim nothing less than what he termed 'an Art Revolution'. 'We must make this', he insisted, 'a *Republic of Letters*'; and, in order to establish such a republic, he hoped that at least ninety-nine other poets would follow in his wake. 'When I quit,' he said, 'I want the 99 to be *well started, singing.*' Predictably, his hopes remained unrealized; less predictably, and more tragically, he committed suicide. Whatever may be thought of his work and aims, though, he remains a curiously noble figure, someone who took the populist fervour, the pedagogical and proselytizing impulses implicit in the American tradition to their logical and not entirely absurd extreme.

A third memorable writer associated with the Chicago Renaissance was a populist in a different sense, in that he wanted to record the real lives of people as they were lived in the Middle West, without heroic disguise or romantic decoration. Edgar Lee Masters (1868–1950) aimed, he said, to write 'a sort of Divine Comedy' of small-town life: its minor tragedies, its melancholy and its frustrations. Like Sandburg and Lindsay, he received the encouragement of Harriet Monroe; and it was still quite early on in his career when the major fruit of his labours appeared, *Spoon River Anthology* (1915). Using a loose verse form and spare, dry language, Masters presents the reader with a series of self-spoken epitaphs. The tone is sometimes elegiac, very occasionally lyrical and affirmative: but the major impression left by the book is one of waste. Men, women and children reveal what happened to them and what happened was, for the most part, shame and disappointment. 'Why, a moral truth is a hollow tooth / Which must be propped with gold,' declares 'Sersmith the Dentist' at the conclusion of his epitaph; and the gaunt, bitter tone of this is characteristic. Gradually, the poems overlap to produce a composite picture of Spoon River: a picture that recalls Tilbury Town, Winesburg, Ohio, but without the passion and the mystery, or Robinson's and Sherwood Anderson's sense that perhaps something more lies beneath the monotonous surface. Masters is largely forgotten now, except as an example of that reaction against small-town values which characterized so many American writers early on in the twentieth century. Perhaps it would be more useful, though, to remember him as someone who attempted to honour the stoicism of ordinary men and women, their laconic idioms and the harsh rhythms of their existence, and who, in this sense at least, achieved one of the aims of American populist writing – of speaking not only to the people (Masters was immensely popular for a time) but for them.

Implicit in the work of Sandburg, Lindsay and even Masters is a kind of radicalism: the kind that Whitman gave voice to when he declared that 'our American republic' was 'experimental . . . in the deepest sense'. It was left to some other writers, however, to give free rein to this radical feeling: with them, the populist strain was sometimes still evident but, even when it was, it was absorbed into a larger structure of feeling that anticipated political, social and perhaps moral change. Responding in part to the horrors of the Depression, in part to the wider economic pressures the United States was experiencing between the two World Wars, these writers were politically engaged. Notions of commitment and relevance lay fairly close to the surface in much of their work. In short, they wanted America altered, and they said so in no uncertain terms. Among the poets were many who used a documentary mode. Alfred Hayes (1911–85), for example, took on the voice of a young, unemployed man in a poem titled 'In a Coffee Pot' (1936) to capture the boredom and despair of those denied a chance by society. And in 'Up-State Depression Summer' (1936), Genevieve Taggard (1894–1948) offered a succinct, laconic but almost novelistic account of a farm family going under to dispossession and destitution. Others employed surrealism or expressionism or other non-naturalistic means to get their message across. In 'Papermill' (1931), for instance, Joseph Kalar (1906–72) wrote in a kind of Depression Gothic style to describe the 'chill empty rooms' of a disused and abandoned factory. Similarly, in 'Season of Death' (1935), Edwin Rolfe (1909–54) fused realism and the supernatural in his portrait of 'the sixth winter' of economic ruin, with the dead and the dying haunting each 'darkened street'. Kay Boyle (1903–93) used a rich variety of poetic modes in 'A Communication to Nancy Cunard' (1937) to explore the plight of nine young black men in Scotsboro, Alabama, who were tried and convicted for rape on false testimony. Tillie Olsen (1913–), used the long line and incremental repetition of Whitman to describe the exploitation of Mexican American women in the Southwest in 'I Want You Women Up North to Know' (1934). Taggard used the tradition of spirituals in the poem-sequence 'To the Negro People' (1939–41), her tribute to the oppression and the courage of African Americans. There are poems about the sufferings of working people ('Asbestos' [1928] by Rolfe), the persecution of those who tried to represent them ('Stone Face' [1935] by Lula Ridge [1871–1941]). There are poems about the Spanish Civil War, which is seen generally as Hemingway saw it, as a dress rehearsal for a worldwide struggle against fascism ('Elegeia' [1948] by Rolfe; 'To the Veterans of the Abraham Lincoln Brigade' [1941] by Taggard). There are poems that respond to contemporary waves of anti-immigrant feeling by insisting 'the alien is the nation' ('Ode in Time of Crisis' [1940] by Taggard), and those that see economic crisis and social deprivation as a useful breeding ground for revolution: 'Good bye Christ, good morning Revolution!' concludes a piece called 'Goodbye Christ' by Langston Hughes. To be politically engaged, even an activist, did not prescribe one style or subject for these writers: something that is clear from the work of the four most accomplished radical poets of the period, Kenneth Rexroth (1905–82), Archibald MacLeish (1892–1982), Kenneth Fearing (1902–61) and Kenneth Patchen (1911–72).

With Rexroth, the nature of his political commitment is clear from the conclusion to a poem called 'New Objectives, New Cadres', one of the many gathered together in *The Collected Shorter Poems* (1967) (*The Collected Longer Poems* was published a year later, to be followed by several other volumes, including *The Morning Star: Poems and Translations* [1979]). The narrator describes an 'arch dialectic satyriast' and activist and lecturer 'drawing pointless incisive diagrams' for an audience of 'miners and social workers'. 'We do not need his confessions /', the narrative voice observes: 'The future is more fecund than Molly Bloom – / The problem is to control history, / We already understand it.' This has many of the trademarks of Rexroth's poetry, and indeed of his prose in *An Autobiographical Novel* (1966) and his critical essay collections, *The Bird in the Bush* (1959) and *Assays* (1961): a cool, sardonic and yet passionate tone, a fierce commitment to the community of ordinary people and an equally fierce hatred of intellectuals ('spectacled men', as he calls them in another poem), the sense of a spirit as flinty and tenacious as the Western landscape where the writer made his home. There is nothing strained or artificial about such lines. 'Poetry', Rexroth insisted, 'is the living speech of the people', elsewhere adding, 'I have spent my life trying to write the way I talk.' Consequently, he disdained elaborate and elevated rhetoric in favour of clarity of speech, a poised syntax and simple, lucid images. As one of his mentors, William Carlos Williams, observed of Rexroth, 'he is no writer in the sense of a word-man. For him words are sticks and stones to build a house – but it's a good house.'

Another way of putting it is to say that writing, for Rexroth, was not so much an imitation of life as a state of being alive. 'Poetry', he suggested, 'is vision, the pure act of sensual communion and contemplation'; it is 'the very link of significant life itself, of the individual to his society, of the individual to his human and nonhuman environment.' What he means by this is suggested by his 'Requiem for the Spanish Dead', where Rexroth links himself standing in the Sierras to those people in the Spanish mountains who are 'clutched with cold and huddled together' in fear as the fascist enemy fly overhead. The solitary poet with his beliefs and the many men and women suffering and dying for those beliefs in other parts of the world – and, in particular, the Spanish Republicans – are woven together into an imagined community. They, in turn, are linked to others: some 'emigrants on the corner' of a street in the poet's hometown of San Francisco, 'holding / A wake for their oldest child' in which 'Voice after voice adds itself to the singing'. There is interpersonal, imaginative connection between these scattered human subjects: the poet alone in the Sierras then 'Alone on a hilltop in San Francisco', those in war offering up a sacrifice in the name of human community, those at the wake struggling to find a ritual to redeem pain. Such connection is also quietly placed as part of a greater continuity between human and non-human worlds, as the poet evokes the shared surroundings of each and all: the mountains and hilltops, sea and sky, and the constellations that seem almost to be 'Marching in order' to the songs sung by the mourners. Occasions of contact like the ones he describes are tiny and temporary, Rexroth intimates, yet that only makes them all the more precious: because they *are* cherished for a moment, before being absorbed into what he elsewhere calls 'the tragic unity of the creative process'. And 'Requiem for the Spanish Dead' is part of that process. The poet's intimate forms of communication, the reader is led to believe, make him a part of the ceremony. In this sense, the poem not only describes a sacrament, it also performs one; it functions, however briefly, as a moment of union.

As Rexroth saw it, this, the sacramental nature of poetry, had a peculiar significance for his contemporaries. 'The conviction that "nobody wants me, nobody needs me . . ." is coming to pervade all levels of modern society,' he said. So the problem was how 'in the face of a collapsing system of values . . . to refound a spiritual family': how to heal the divisions that capitalism engendered, how to reclaim the humanity and restore the connection with nature that the city and the factory denied. Poetry was part of the solution since it promoted 'the realization . . . of universal responsibility'. 'A kelson of the creation is love,' Whitman had proclaimed; Rexroth agreed, and agreed too with Whitman that poets had a crucial role to play in the publication of this truth. They were indispensable, in fact, to the rediscovery of community. Sometimes, the community Rexroth celebrates and dramatizes is with one particular person, as in 'A Letter to William Carlos Williams' or 'Delia Rexroth'; sometimes it is with many people, past and present, as in 'Autumn in California' or 'Wednesdays of Holy Week, 1940'; sometimes, as in 'The Signature of All Things', it is with all created life, 'streaming / In the electrolysis of love'. Always, though, it involves a devoted attention to the particulars of the object, and a faithful recreation of the voice of the subject: Rexroth's phrasing is organically determined by his own speaking and breathing, so a powerful sense of Rexroth the individual emerges from his work – humorous, honest, irascible, passionate, proud. William Carlos Williams called him 'a moralist with his hand at the trigger ready to fire at the turn of a hair'. To which could be added that he was also a poetic prophet whose prophecies were shaped by an indestructible optimism, an abiding hope.

A similar, if less persuasive, optimism characterizes another poet for whom the social role, the idea of the writer as agent of cultural change, was crucially import-ant: Archibald MacLeish. MacLeish's early work, written mostly while he was in Europe, is preoccupied with the plight of the artist and is full of unassimilated influences: notably Eliot, Pound and the French Symbolists. On his return to the United States, however, at about the time of the Depression, he became increas-ingly interested in social issues and began to work towards a poetic diction closer to common speech. A series of poems followed examining the problems and pos-sibilities of his native country (*New Found Land* [1930]). These were followed, in turn, by an epic poem describing the attempted conquest of the Mexican Aztecs by the Spanish Cortés (*Conquistador* [1932]) and by other poems satirizing the excesses of American capitalism (*Frescoes for Mr. Rockefeller's City* [1933]) or chastizing American writers for their withdrawal from what MacLeish saw as their social responsibilities (*The Irresponsibles* [1940]). 'Instead of studying American life,' MacLeish declared of the writers of the 1920s, 'literature denounced it. Instead of working to understand American life, literature repudiated it.' His clearly stated aim was to reverse this trend: 'This is my own land,' he announced in 'American Letter' (*Collected Poems, 1917–52* [1952]). 'It is a strange thing – to be an Amer-ican.' For MacLeish, as for so many of his predecessors, this strangeness, the special quality of his native land, resided in the idea of America rather than the historical fact: the New World as a place of freedom and solitude, a site of possibility. 'America is neither a land nor a people, /' he insisted in 'American Letter', 'America is West and the wind blowing / America is a great word and the snow.' These lines repeating a common theme illustrate a significant weakness in MacLeish's poetry. His most famous poetic statement comes from 'Ars Poetica', 'A poem should not mean / But be'; and its fame perhaps prevents us from registering that it *is* a statement. Paradoxically, it invites us to interpret its meaning even while it insists that a poem should not 'mean'. What is missing from much of his work, in fact, is indicated by his occasional successes. His fine poem 'You, Andrew Marvell', for instance, begins with an evocative description of the sunset, the 'always rising of the night', that carries with it intimations of mortality ('To feel . . . / The earthy chill of dusk'). At first, this looks like a meditation on personal death, inspired

forms, he gravitated between haunting lyrics of personal emotion ('The Character of Love') and vitriolic social comment ('Nice Day for a Lynching'), sharp vignettes of city life ('Do the Dead Know What Time It Is?') and fierce jeremiads directed at 'falsity, the smug contempt' of 'drugstore-culture' in America ('O Fiery River'). Sometimes, the social comment has a slightly automatic quality to it: the targets are too easy, the conclusions a little too pat. For instance, a poem with the eye-catching title 'The Eve of St. Agony or, The Middleclass Was Sitting on its Fat' ends with the glib cry 'Hey! Fatty, don't look now but that's a Revolution breathing down your neck'. More characteristic are poems like 'Street Corner College' and 'The Fox', or *Memoirs of a Shy Pornographer*. *Memoirs* is a biting satire. Styled 'an amusement' by its author and told by a Candide-like innocent called Alfred Budd of Bivalve, New Jersey, it holds a grotesque distorting mirror up to American society. In 'Street Corner College', Patchen adopts an entirely different voice to speak for the adolescent boys found on the corner of any city street. The poem is a mixture of the abrupt, abrasive language of urban life ('Watching the girls go by; / Betting on slow horses; drinking cheap gin') and a strange, surreal idiom ('solitude is a dirty knife at our throats'). Out of all this comes a powerful feeling of sympathy for such people: the contrast between their jazzy, streetwise exterior and their jumpy inner selves, their vitality dimmed by the perception that they are 'Sleep-walkers in a terrible land'. They are the dispossessed, the poet intimates: on the bottom rung of a society they cannot begin to comprehend, destined when war comes to die for a culture that has given them nothing – not even the courage to be themselves. 'The Fox' uses a more lyrical mode to arrive at equally stark conclusions. It opens with an evocative description of a snowscape, 'white falling in white air', into which the figure of a wounded, bleeding fox is introduced. Slowly, incrementally, the poem then builds to the final lines. 'Because she [the fox] can't afford to die / Killing the young in her belly,' the poet says, 'I don't know what to say of a soldier's dying / Because there are no proportions to death.' In this bleak landscape of red and white, hunters and hunted, victimizers and victims, no one death is worse or better than another, nothing is morally quantifiable. No comparison need apply; all there is, is the simple, recurring fact of exploitation.

Although Patchen produced notable prose works, his energies, like those of Rexroth and Fearing, were mostly devoted to poetry. There were, however, many radicals who turned to fictional or non-fictional prose to examine the contemporary crisis and to express their convictions. Among the most distinguished of these were Randolph Bourne (1886–1918), Michael Gold (1893–1967) and Albert Maltz (1908–85). Bourne established his reputation as an essayist in the *New Republic* and other magazines. His work reveals an interest in education (*The Gary Schools* [1916], *Education and Living* [1917]), and a firm commitment to the development of a socially responsible fiction (*The History of a Literary Radical* [1920]). As America entered the First World War, he also became an increasingly eloquent but also increasingly isolated advocate for pacifism and non-intervention (*Untimely Papers* [1919]). A theoretical piece entitled 'The State' (1919) was left unfinished, leaving many to speculate about his possible political influence had he lived longer to complete it and other similar pieces. However, his essay on an ethnically diverse American culture, 'Trans-National America' (1916), shows both his perception and his prescience. In it, Bourne attacked the idea of 'the melting-pot', which, he said, reflected 'English-American conservatism' and 'washed out into a tasteless, colorless fluid of uniformity'. Instead, he anticipated 'a new and more adventurous ideal', 'a federation of cultures' in which each immigrant community could retain the 'distinctiveness of their native cultures' and so be 'more valuable and interesting to each other for being different'. America, he argued, was destined to be 'the first international nation', 'not a nationality but a trans-nationality, a weaving back and forth . . . of many threads of all sizes and colors'. And in this 'transnational' mosaic, each American would enjoy a 'dual citizenship': a cosmopolitan double consciousness which, unlike the dual consciousness described by Du Bois, would be a privilege and a possibility rather than a burden. To this 'novel international nation', a 'future America' woven out of the 'threads of living and potent cultures', Bourne gave the name 'the Beloved Community'. It was a powerful expression of the belief in a multicultural community that has sustained many American writers. And, as Bourne saw it, it offered a way out, liberation from the social divisions and 'Anglo-Saxon predominance' characteristic of the society around him.

Michael Gold was born Yitzhak Granich to Jewish immigrants on the Lower East Side of New York City. The major themes of his work are derived from that background. Yitzhak was anglicized to Isaac; then, in adolescence, evidently dreaming dreams of glory of the kind that persuaded Fitzgerald's James Gatz to rename himself Jay Gatsby, he took the name Irwin. It was in 1919–20 that he became Michael Gold, in honour of a Jewish veteran of the Civil War who, he said, had fought to 'free the slaves'. And already, embittered by the failure of his father's business and aroused by a demonstration he witnessed in Union Square in 1914, the commitment suggested by this final name change had prompted him to write. As a youth, Gold recalled, he had 'no politics . . . except hunger', but now he gravitated to the political left and a lifelong involvement with the Communist Party. His first piece was published in 1914 in *The Masses*, the radical magazine edited by Max Eastman (1883–1969) and Floyd Dell. It was, typically, a poem about three anarchists who had died in a bomb explosion. Not long after, he was to publish a more important piece, an essay entitled 'Toward Proletarian Art' arguing for a literature by workers rather than bourgeois leftists, about workers and for workers. If any single work was responsible for initiating the proletarian movement in American literature, then this was. Moving to Greenwich Village from the Lower East Side, Gold became involved in the leftist literary circles centred around Eugene O'Neill and John Reed (1887–1920), the writer and activist whose most important work was an eyewitness account of the Russian Revolution, *Ten Days That Shook the World* (1919). He left the United States for a while to avoid the draft: but, on returning in 1920, he became editor of *The Liberator*, the successor to the suppressed *Masses*. Then, when *The Liberator* became wholly political, he helped found *The New Masses*, becoming editor-in-chief of the new magazine in 1928. His fiery columns, notable for their polemical Communist views and their espousal of the cause of proletarian literature, were to be collected in *The Mike Gold Reader* (1954) and *Mike Gold: A Literary Anthology* (1972).

Throughout the 1920s, Gold had been working on a fictionalized autobiography. It was published in 1930 as *Jews Without Money*, just at the right time for such a fiercely political novel, and was an immediate success. Based on the author's early life in a Jewish ghetto, it describes in detail the deprivation and degradation of poverty. It also offers a ferocious arraignment of capitalism: a system in which 'kindness is a form of suicide'. The father of a family is overwhelmed by the depression and dispossession he sees all around him. 'People are turning into wolves!' he despairs. 'They will soon eat each other!' It is the mother, Katie Gold, who is the cornerstone of the family and the heroic centre of the book. 'I have time and strength for everything,' she boasts, and her endless funds of optimism and energy make that boast a reality. Standing up to the landlords and other class enemies, struggling to survive and support her family, she offers a paradigm for the revolution of the proletariat. She also offers an example to her son, the protagonist. The story ends with his conversion to the cause of Communist revolution. Witnessing the demonstration at Union Square in 1914, and knocked down by a policeman, he experiences an epiphany in which he realizes that the 'worker's Revolution' is 'the true Messiah': '*O Revolution, that forced me to think, to struggle and to live,*' the novel concludes, '*O great Beginning!*' Stylistically, *Jews Without Money* moves between expansive, exclamatory prose like this, which recalls the fact that Whitman was the American writer Gold admired most, and a more journalistic idiom, with short, punchy sentences, paragraphs and chapters, snappy vignettes and dramatic moments. And thematically it blends its revolutionary message, just as the plays of Odets do (Gold, in fact, also wrote several one-act plays for the Provincetown Players), with a vivid account of Jewish family life, its conflicts and squabbles, its moments of pettiness, pathos or self-pity – and, too, its warmth, courage and affection. Gold remained a loyal Communist throughout his life, despite the manifest brutality of Stalinism. He became a daily columnist for the mass circulation Communist newspaper the *Daily Worker* in 1933; and, in 1941, he published the anti-Trotskyite *The Hollow Men*, a collection of his newspaper articles attacking the political errors of such former allies as Sherwood Anderson, Ernest Hemingway and Archibald MacLeish. He is perhaps the archetypal twentieth-century American literary radical. He is, however, also a writer who had an instinctive understanding not just of the generalized plight of the workers but of the needs and passions of individuals, specific members of the dispossessed. As Gold himself realized – when, in 1935, he described his novel as a useful response to the 'anti-Semitic demagogues' sweeping to power at the time – a work like *Jews Without Money* is a vivid testament to community, the sense of kinship among its subjects. To that extent, its revolutionary spirit is inseparable from its humanity of feeling.

That is also true of the fiction of Albert Maltz, who, he once said, wanted to write proletarian literature that did not betray 'the great humanistic tradition of culture' by serving 'an individual political purpose'. That aim got him into some trouble. When, for instance, he questioned whether art was to be used as a weapon in the class war in 'What Shall We Ask of Writers?' (1946), he was so severely criticized by his political allies that he felt compelled to publish a retraction in *The New Masses*. Then, only a year later, trouble came from the other end of the political spectrum. As a Hollywood screenwriter now, with such movies to his credit as *This Gun for Hire* (1942), he was investigated by the House Un-American Activities Committee as part of its inquiry into Communist infiltration in the motion picture industry. Refusing to answer the Committee's questions as to whether he was a member of the Communist Party, he was fined and sentenced to a year's imprisonment in 1950. Blacklisted and so unable to go back to work in Hollywood, he moved to Mexico on his release and remained there until 1962. Despite all that, Maltz produced a considerable body of work that, at its best, is at once radical and humane, focusing on the individual struggle for fulfilment in oppressive circumstances. His characters remain resolutely human, often pathetically decent, despite the inhumanity of the system against which they are forced to struggle. Maltz wrote several plays to begin with, for the newly formed Theatre Union, among them *Black Pit* (1935). But it is his stories and novels that represent his main achievement. His short story 'Man on a Road', published in *The New Masses* in 1935, initiated a Congressional investigation into the dangers of silicosis among miners. Another story, 'The Happiest Man on Earth', published three years later, is an account of how some people are forced to take work that will kill them, and others are forced to give them that work, because, in a land of competition and depression, there is no alternative. It is all the more moving because it is so laconic and ironic; its protagonist actually feels, and says he is, 'the happiest man on the whole earth' when he finally persuades his brother-in-law to let him have a job – transporting nitroglycerine. These and similar tales were collected in *The Way Things Are* (1938). Two years after the collection came out, Maltz published his first novel, focusing on the struggle between automobile workers and an oppressive management, *The Underground Stream*. Several other longer works of fiction then followed, despite other distractions and problems. They included *The Cross and the Arrow* (1944), the story of a German factory worker who has the courage to turn against his own country; *The Journey of Simon McKeever* (1949), a novel of the open road whose originality stems from the fact that its hero has escaped from an old people's home to pursue a perennial American dream; and *A Long Day in a Short Life* (1957), a starkly realistic account of prison life based on the writer's own experience. Together, these longer fictions and the earlier short stories make up a body of work that is remarkable for its variety as well as its vitality. At its best, that work is animated by its author's convictions rather than overwhelmed by them; it is charged with his idealistic intensity of vision and does seem, genuinely, to be part of 'a great humanistic tradition'.

Like so many writers of the time who concerned themselves with the condition of the poor, Maltz has sometimes been dismissed as a producer of social protest. That ignores the fact that such writers might have felt drawn to portray, and maybe protest, the social conditions around them but they did so in different forms. Those forms range from the energetic rewriting of Southwestern humour for social purposes in *Tobacco Road* (1932) and *God's Little Acre* (1933) by Erskine Caldwell (1903–87) to a more literally realistic fiction like the Studs Lonigan trilogy (*Young Lonigan* [1932], *The Young Manhood of Studs Lonigan* [1934], *Judgement Day* [1935]) by James T. Farnell (1904–79), which doggedly charts the representative life and death of a young urban Irishman. It also includes the strange supernaturalism of the stories of poor mountain people in *The Hawk's Done Gone* (1941) by Mildred Haun (1911–66) and accounts of similarly poor but heroic mountain folk in *Mountain Path* (1936) and *The Dollmaker* (1954) by Harriette S. Arnow (1908–84) that are an extraordinary blend of realism and romantic lyricism. What blanket references to social protest also manage to conceal is that, for many, commitment was sustained, remaining an inspiration throughout their career and inspiring a rich variety of activity and expression. Among these was Lillian Smith (1897–1966), the leading Southern white liberal of the mid-twentieth century, who devoted her life to lifting self-deception in the South about race, class, gender and sexuality. Born into an upper-class family in the Deep South, Smith emerged into public debate in opposition to the Agrarians. She produced a small literary magazine, *Pseudopodia*, later changed to *North Georgia Review* and then *South Today*, which she co-edited with Paula Snelling. Then, in 1945, she produced her most famous book, *Strange Fruit*. At once the love story of a mulatto girl and a powerful critique of racial prejudice, it became a best-seller. Her other novel, *One Hour*, appeared sixteen years later; it is about the response of a Southern town to the hysterical accusation of immorality that a young girl makes against an older man. But her notable work, apart from *Strange Fruit*, is her journalism, her works on civil rights, *Now is the Time* (1955) and *Our Faces, Our Words* (1964), and, above all, her autobiographical critique of Southern culture, *Killers of the Dream* (1949). 'By the time we were five years old,' Smith recalls in *Killers of the Dream*, 'we had learned . . . that masturbation is wrong and segregation is right.' 'We believed certain acts were so wrong that they must never be committed,' she adds later, 'and then we committed them and denied to ourselves that we had done so.' Which, Smith explains, issued for her and Southerners like her in a 'split' mind, 'a two-level existence'. That is characteristic of Smith at her best throughout her varied career. She recognized that her society's concepts of race invariably interacted with those of gender, sexuality and class. And although she rarely considered class apart from race, issues of gender and sexuality are persistent in her work. Her writing was controversial precisely because it explored the interrelatedness of her culture's attitudes towards race and sexuality and the ways in which the South's institutions perpetuated a dehumanizing existence for all its people – male and female, white and black, rich and poor.

Three other writers whose concern with social issues was woven like a thread through the varied tapestry of their careers are Lillian Hellman (1905–84), Mary McCarthy (1912–89) and Meridel Le Sueur (1900–96). Hellman came to public attention with a series of successful plays. Her first, *The Children's Hour* (1934), shows the havoc caused by a malicious girl's invention of a lesbian relationship between her two teachers. *The Little Foxes* (1939) concerns the struggle of a reactionary Southern family to retain wealth and power despite internal feuds and the encroachments of modern society. *Watch on the Rhine* (1941) and *The Searching Wind* (1944) are two openly political dramas, dealing with the fight against Nazism. Other, later plays include *Toys in the Attic* (1964), which deals with the theme of miscegenation. 'I am a moral writer,' Hellman once wrote; and, in her drama, she used the conventions of the well-made play to compel her mainly middle-class audience to confront questions of justice, social equality and personal responsibility. The crises her characters face are, invariably, ones that force them to choose between the imperatives of conscience and the demands of society. Hellman was eventually made to make that choice herself when, in 1952, because of her political activities, she was called to testify before the House Un-American Activities Committee. Courageously, she told the Committee that, while she was willing to speak about her own activism, she would not say anything about the activities of others. 'I cannot and will not cut my conscience to fit this year's fashions,' she told the Committee. For this, although she was not jailed as many of her friends and her companion Dashiell Hammett were, she found herself blacklisted. However, she responded by launching a new career as a writer of autobiographical memoirs. *An Unfinished Woman* (1969) and *Pentimento* (1973) are largely concerned with her childhood experiences and early personal and political involvements. In *Scoundrel Time* (1976), however, she returned to the period when, as she put it, thanks to the Un-American Activities Committee, 'truth made you a traitor as it often does in a time of scoundrels'. The book replays the familiar theme of Hellman's drama, a crisis of choice, a moral challenge that, as she shows, many American intellectuals and radicals of the time failed. And it emphasizes, just as that drama does, the dangers of American innocence in the face of evil and injustice, whether that evil come from fascism in Germany or Spain, childish malice or familial pride, or 'high-powered operators' like the members of the Un-American Activities Committee. 'We are a people who do not want to keep much of the past in our heads,' Hellman observes in *Scoundrel Time*. 'It is considered unhealthy in America to remember mistakes, neurotic to think about them, psychotic to dwell upon them.' Hellman shows, however, that it is necessary to look backwards honestly in order to be able to go forwards. If America does not acknowledge its errors, it will simply go on repeating them; if Americans do not accept their responsibilities as individuals and citizens, then they will get the kind of scoundrels to rule them they deserve.

A similar concern with moral and social responsibility lies at the heart of all Mary McCarthy's work. McCarthy began her career by writing reviews for the *New Republic*, the *Nation* and the *Partisan Review*, whose editor Philip Rahv (1908–73) was for a while her partner. In 1938, however, McCarthy left Rahv to marry the critic and novelist Edmund Wilson; and, at Wilson's urging, she began to write fiction. That fiction has often been quite close to the autobiographical bone. *The Company She Keeps* (1942), for instance, is a witty portrait of a bohemian, intellectual young woman; while *The Groves of Academe* (1952), a satirical portrait of faculty life at a liberal college for women, is based on McCarthy's experiences of teaching at Bard and Sarah Lawrence colleges. Her most famous novel, *The Group* (1963), in turn, springs from its author's experiences as a student at Vassar in the early 1930s. Beginning with the inauguration of Franklin Roosevelt and ending with that of Harry Truman, *The Group* follows the lives of eight Vassar women. McCarthy commented that the book was 'about the idea of progress really, seen in the female sphere'; and what it reveals, fundamentally, is a lack of progress, thanks to the damaging norms of masculine aggression and feminine passivity. Despite their optimism about the possibilities of modern life, these Vassar women find that they depend on men for economic and social survival much as their mothers did. Among McCarthy's other novels are *Birds of America* (1971), which explores both the contemporary gap between the generations and the cultural collision between Europe and America, and *Cannibals and Missionaries* (1979), which confronts the moral and social issue of terrorism. But at least as important as her fiction is her political commentary, in works like *Vietnam* (1967), *Hanoi* (1968) and *The Mask of State: Watergate Portrait* (1974), her travel books with their accompanying social comment, such as *Venice Observed* (1956), her critical work and journalism collected in *Occasional Prose* (1985) and other volumes, and her autobiographical writing. Of the autobiographical work, *Memories of a Catholic Girlhood* (1957) is the most significant and characteristic. After she was orphaned at the age of six, McCarthy was sent to Catholic schools by relatives; and *Memories* describes how, at convent school, she felt herself to be 'an outsider'. 'I did not fit into the convent pattern,' she recalls, and, in order to give the appearance at least of fitting in, she was forced to pretend. 'I was a walking mass of lies,' she remembers, 'pretending to be a Catholic and going to confession while really I had lost my faith', and accepting a nickname given to her by the other girls, 'Cye McCarthy', when she really did not know what the name meant and hated it. 'I loathed myself,' she recollects, when 'I had to identify myself' as 'Cye'; 'and yet I subscribed to the name totally, making myself over into a sort of hearty to go with it – the kind of girl I hated.' Finally, however, she resisted. Leaving convent school for 'public high school', McCarthy gave up her nickname, along with her Catholicism and, with them both, her 'false personality'. 'I got my own name back,' McCarthy informs the reader; she 'sloughed off' the mask she had been forced to wear, the spurious title she had been forced to accept, and the pretence she had been forced to live. And she became herself. It is the perfect illustration in miniature of the prevailing theme in McCarthy's work, and the one she summed up quite simply when she said that it is necessary 'to choose the self you want'.

Meridel Le Sueur is less well known than McCarthy, Hellman or even Smith. Nevertheless, she is an important radical voice in American writing, speaking in particular for the social and mythic possibilities of women. The work that Le Sueur wrote and began to publish during the 1920s explored subject matter and established themes that she pursued throughout her work. Central to these explorations in the early writing is the figure of a 'raw green girl', lonely, curious, seeking. Sometimes this figure is connected, as in a story called 'Persephone' (1927), to a mythic formulation of experience: the separation from the mother, the plunge into the darkness of the underground, the woman (or the earth) as wounded, invaded and raped. In time, although not in the early work, the further implications of the myth of Persephone and her mother Demeter would be explored too: the rebirth from the darkness and the return to the mother and the world of women. In the later work, the young and wandering Persephone, orphaned and 'lost to the realm of her nativity', not only returns to the mother but is herself transformed into Demeter. This is the case, for example, with the title poem of a volume Le Sueur published in 1975, 'Rites of Ancient Ripening', which, like much of the later writing, mixes ancient Greek myth with the legends of American Indian cultures to create a sense of continuity, a continuous harmony between the human body and the body of the earth. In 'Rites of Ancient Ripening', it is, in fact, the Demeter-mother-earth figure who speaks. 'Luminous with age', she is anticipating death but death will be a renewal, since her body will nourish and fertilize the earth. 'The rites of ancient ripening / Make my flesh plume,' she declares. 'And summer winds stir in my smoked bowl. / Do not look for me till I return'. That sense of affirmation is there too, sometimes, in the earlier work, although divorced from the Persephone myth or any other legend. In 'Annunciation' (1935), for instance, the bleak world of a pregnant woman is transformed by her 'inward blossoming'. The pear tree outside her tenement porch, producing its fruit even in the 'darkest time' just like her, becomes a symbol for rebirth and the continuity of life. Le Sueur had herself decided to have a child in 1927 as a deliberate affirmation of life in a world that she felt had become 'dead' and 'closed' thanks to social injustice and oppression. And 'Annunciation', which she began in the year of her pregnancy, in the form of notes to her unborn child, communicates a profoundly personal as well as deeply passionate sense of 'the bud of a new flower within the time of the old'. Conducting 'a kind of conversation' with her unborn baby, the young woman of the story feels a deep sense of kinship with the flowering she perceives around her. 'I feel like a tree,' she declares, 'in a trance of wonder.' 'The alley below and all the houses are to me like an orchard abloom, shaking and trembling'; the pear tree outside her window participates like her in this 'slow time of making', 'the leaves are the lips of the tree speaking in the wind as they move like so many tongues'. What woman and tree share is what the speaker in 'Rites of Ancient Ripening' experiences, the secret of life, renewal: resistance to death and the deathlike institutions of society. Creativity, the blossoming of the earth, the human body and human speech and writing, is set in fierce opposition to a time of darkness, and in a 'strange and beautiful' way, as the young woman reflects, it is triumphant.

'People are ready to flower and they cannot.' That comment in 'Annunciation' suggests just how closely the political and the personal, the social and the mythic, are interwoven in Le Sueur's work. She is perpetually concerned with how 'the body repeats the landscape' ('The Ancient People and the Newly Come' [1976]) and how, in recognizing the imperatives of the body, it is possible to resist and triumph over a 'society built upon a huge hypocrisy, a cut-throat competition which sets one man against another' ('I Was Marching' [1934]). That recognition, Le Sueur intimates, is easier for women, since 'they don't read the news', she says, 'they very often make it. They pick up at its source, in the human body, in the making of the body, and the feeding and nurturing of it day in and day out' ('Women Know a Lot of Things' [1937]). Their history has very often been 'suppressed within the history of man', she believed: which is why the recognition of renewal, continuity and communality, is hidden from American society and one reason why she chose to concentrate on female experience. But, 'the cause of women will be the cause of all toiling humanity', she insists; and her notion is of everyone eventually being born into 'a complete new body', biological and spiritual, personal and social, with men and women enjoying 'a polarity of equals', 'a dialectic of equal opposites'. Le Sueur explored these notions in her short stories, her novel *The Girl* (written in 1939, published in 1978), based on tales of women she had known, her history of the Midwest based on folk materials, *North Star Country* (1945), and her autobiographical pieces, some of which were collected in *Salute to Spring* (1940). She also explored them in her journalism, some of which is also found in *Salute to Spring*. 'Written on the Breadlines' (1932), for example, describes 'the suffering of endless labor without dream', in a Depression where 'like every commodity now the body is difficult to sell'. 'I Was Marching', perhaps Le Sueur's most famous piece of reportage, recalls her involvement in the Minneapolis trucker's strike in 1934. 'In these terrible happenings you cannot be neutral now,' Le Sueur observes of that strike; and, as she charts the stages of her participation in the collective effort, she presents a sense of fusing with a larger reality. 'For the first time in my life,' she concludes 'I Was Marching', 'I feel most alive and yet . . . not . . . separate.' Mixing political comment and narrative cunning, the report is a startling anticipation of later New Journalism; it is also animated, as all her work is, by a belief in what she later described as the 'circular' and the 'continuous' – the repetition of each life in every other, the sourcing of all bodies in the one.

For a while, during the Cold War period, Le Sueur fell out of fashion and suffered harassment for her political views. She still wrote, however: notably a piece based on a period when she travelled across America by bus. 'The Dark of the Time' (1956), as it is called, describes a people 'in the dark of capitalism', experiencing the bewilderment attendant on postwar anxiety and racial tension. 'The source of American culture lies in the historic movement of our people,' Le Sueur concludes this essay, 'and the artist must become voice, messenger, awakener, sparking the inflammable silence, reflecting back the courage and the beauty.' It is the perennial American idea of the writer as a prophetic voice of the people. And in her later work, as she came back into some degree of recognition from the 1970s on, she attempted to be just that. Apart from reflecting a renewed interest in Native American culture (Le Sueur began around this time to live among American Indians and work for Indian land rights), this later writing rejects linear narrative and conventional form – which are seen as the products of an overly purposive, appropriative view of the world – in favour of structures founded on the circular and the cyclical, repetition and reclamation. So the poetry recalls the line of Whitman, or Native American chant, and other works like 'The Origins of Corn' (1976) are a multidimensional, multilayered blend of prose and poetry, in which words, figures, images return again and again recalling the fruits of the earth and the body they celebrate. For all the alterations of form, though, and the expansion of source and subjects, Le Sueur's central concerns remained the same: women and the land, their centuries of parallel suffering and exploitation, the hope of rebirth and renewal offered by both. 'Let us all return,' she once wrote, and that impulse of returning, to origins, the grounds of being, pulses through all her work. It is what makes it at once true to the realities of the lives of ordinary working-class women, their struggle for survival, and responsive to other, mythic pressures – so that each woman she describes in her fiction, journalism and poetry seems alive with the lives of others, of other places and generations, and with the 'ancient ripening' of the earth.

Prophetic voices

'I believe that we are lost here in America,' wrote Thomas Wolfe (1900–38) once, 'but I believe we shall be found. And this belief . . . is not only our hope, but America's everlasting, living dream.' That remark captures the abiding romanticism of Wolfe's work, its concern with loss and prophecy, and its search for a self-realization that is co-extensive with the discovery of national identity. It also captures its dualism. All Wolfe's writing weaves its way between an intricate pattern of opposites: the rural past and the urban future, rootedness and escape, the 'lonely austerity and mystery of the dark earth' where Wolfe and his protagonists grow up and 'the powerful movement of the train' carrying them away from that place to ever wider horizons. 'It seemed to him', observes Wolfe of his hero Eugene Gant in *Of Time and the River* (1935), 'that these two terrific negatives of speed and stillness, the hustling and projectile movement of the train and the calm silence of the everlasting earth, were poles of a single unity – a unity coherent with his destiny, whose source was somehow in himself.' Wolfe claimed 'the enormous space and energy of America as a whole' as his subject. He also described his first novel, *Look Homeward, Angel* (1929), as 'the story of a powerful creative element trying to work its way toward an essential isolation, a creative solitude, a secret life'. There was no contradiction here for him, however, because, like Whitman and so many other American writers, he saw the story of the nation as the story of his individual self – for he was Eugene Gant, he was the 'powerful creative element', the source and subject of his fiction. And in working out his own perplexities, in prose that moves back and forth between lofty romanticism and literal prosaicism, rhetoric and reportage, he was trying to confront, and if possible resolve, the problem of the nation, as it vacillated between loss and hope, its historical failure and its 'everlasting, living dream'.

Wolfe was born and raised in the mountain town of Asheville, North Carolina, the place that became the 'Old Catawba' of his fiction. As he became Eugene Gant in his first two novels, so his father, a powerful stonecutter from the North, became the prototype of Eugene's father Oliver. And his mother, in turn, a member of a puritanical mountain family, became the prototype of Eugene's mother, Eliza Gant, a woman who, like Wolfe's own mother, combines the 'visionary fanaticism' of her ancestors with a 'hard monied sense' that leads her, among other things, to move out of the family home to open a boarding-house. Leaving home himself, Wolfe entered the University of North Carolina in 1920, where he wrote and acted in several plays. Then, after studying at Harvard and writing more drama, he travelled abroad for a while before returning to teach literature at New York University. With the publication of *Look Homeward, Angel*, he was able to give up teaching and devote himself to his writing, since it was an immediate success. A vast, sprawling book, like all Wolfe's major novels, it follows the contours of the author's early life closely. Eugene Gant grows up in a household torn between restlessness and rootedness. His father has a love of rhetoric, craft and a demonic passion for adventure; his mother is wedded to her ancestry, place, making money and finding security; and they quarrel constantly. Eugene reads voraciously, attends school, then state college, where, while he continues to feel 'different' and lonely, he is beginning to fulfil his desire for 'getting away', getting on and finding a place in the world. The pilgrimage Eugene is embarked on, in search of 'the lost lane-end into heaven, a stone, a leaf, an unfound door', is continued in *Of Time and the River*, which covers experiences at Harvard and abroad and his teaching in New York City. Together, the two narratives move outwards in a series of concentric circles – from provincial hometown to state college to cosmopolitan centres and the wide world beyond – just as Wolfe's own life did. And, as they do, they chart that urge towards movement, that restless desire to break away that, like Le Sueur, Wolfe saw as the source of American culture. What Wolfe adds to this, however, like, say, Cather, is a backward glance, a centripetal impulse that is a matter of emotion rather than action. Neither Gant nor America can properly escape, Wolfe suggests, since they are 'acted upon by all the accumulated impact' of their ancestral experience. They can no more deny this than Gant can rid himself of a mysterious 'tetter of itch' that appears on the nape of his neck one day – a blemish his creator identifies as the outward and visible 'sign of kinship' with his ancestors in the mountains. For Gant, as for Wolfe, as for America, the past is a part of their blood. They cannot go home again, to the old, lost times, but they can never entirely leave them either.

You Can't Go Home Again (1940) is, in fact, the title of a novel by Wolfe that was published posthumously. It is the sequel to *The Web and the Rock* (1939), which also appeared after Wolfe died suddenly at the age of thirty-eight. In these two books, which were edited from material that Wolfe left behind at his death, the hero is called George Webber. He is, however, indistinguishable in character from Eugene Gant, and he continues Wolfe's project of turning his life into a national epic and himself into a representative man. The title of the first novel symbolizes the problem of its protagonist and recalls the dualism of all Wolfe's writing. George Webber is caught between the web of environment, experience, ancestry and the rock, the original strength, adventure and beauty of the vision of his father. He concludes that 'you can't go home again' but, even as he departs from his hometown, he suffers the same conflict as his fictive predecessor, Eugene

Gant: a 'tension of the nerves' so painful as to make him 'grit . . . the teeth and harden . . . the jaws'. George continues his pilgrimage in the second novel, as he discovers, among other things, the unpleasant changes that progress and property have brought to his own hometown and the horrors attendant on the rise of fascism in Germany. And, like Wolfe again, he is torn between a sense of loss and hope. He recognizes that a corrupt society destroys the individual, but he still believes that 'the true fulfilment of our spirit, of our people, of our mighty and immortal land is yet to come'. So Wolfe remained true, throughout his life, to that nostalgic utopianism so characteristic of American thought that scores a corrupt present by measuring it against what has been irretrievably lost and what might still, perhaps, be gained. Yesterday is gone, leaving only its failures, its corrupted residues, today is a tale of waste and want, but there is still tomorrow; there is still the future, which might become a bright mirror of a more mythic past.

A similar vein of prophecy is at work in the fiction of John Steinbeck (1902–68), although, in this case, prophecy is more closely wedded to political vision. Born in California, Steinbeck studied marine biology at university: a subject that may have later helped shape his interest in humanity as a kind of collective biological organism, and his belief in the mass movement of that mass humanity as the fundamental condition of life. His first book, published in 1929, was a romantic tale about buccaneering; his second, *The Pastures of Heaven* (1932), a collection of stories about people in a farm community; and his third, *To a God Unknown* (1933), a novel about a farmer whose religion is a pagan belief in fertility and who sacrifices himself on a primitive altar to bring an end to drought. It was *Tortilla Flat* (1935), however, a vivid portrait of life among the poor in Monterey, that brought Steinbeck to prominence. And it was *In Dubious Battle* (1936), the story of a strike among migratory workers in the California fruit orchards, that brought a new political edge to his work. With *Of Mice and Men* (1937), Steinbeck firmly established himself as the novelist of the rural poor, dispossessed farmers and destitute farm labourers and migratory workers. It is the tale of two itinerant farm workers, drawn into a brotherhood of suffering with each other, who yearn to find some sort of home. With the Depression wreaking economic havoc and drought turning vast swathes of agricultural land into a Dust Bowl, farmers and their families were reduced to absolute poverty, forced out of their homes and buildings; they needed desperately to find another, better place where they could settle and survive. As they travelled across America, as so many did in this time in search of work, they also needed to find a voice, someone to make the nation aware of their suffering. And they found it in Steinbeck, particularly with the publication of his most famous and influential novel, *The Grapes of Wrath*, in 1939.

The origins of *The Grapes of Wrath* lie, typically for the time, in a series of newspaper articles Steinbeck wrote about migratory labourers. Published in 1936, they were reprinted as a pamphlet, *Their Blood is Strong*, with an epilogue added, in 1938. It was then that Steinbeck decided to turn fact into fiction to gain maximum impact: to tell a story that would enable his readers to experience the suffering he had seen. So he invented the Joad family, Oklahoma farmers who are driven off their land by soil erosion, and who drive to California hoping to take advantage of what they imagine to be a land of plenty. The migration of the Joad family is punctuated by interchapters, written in gravely intense lyrical prose, that generalize the experience of the family, and force us to see what happens to them as representative, a type of what was happening to all the rural poor of the time. Steinbeck plays cunningly with different mythical structures, too, to add resonance and representativeness to his story. The journey of the Joads recalls many other earlier, epic migrations: notably, the Biblical journey to the Promised Land and the westward movement that helped shape the history of the American nation. What the Joad family find when they reach California, however, is no land of promise. For these western adventurers, there is no realization of a dream of freedom. There is only further injustice and inequity, more poverty and pain. Tom Joad, the older son in the Joad family and the epic hero, joins with Jim Casy, a minister turned labour organizer, to try to build resistance to the exploitation of the 'Okies', as they are dismissively called, and other migrant labourers. Casy is killed; Tom kills to avenge his death; those few members of the Joad family who have survived try to hide Tom. But then Tom leaves, telling his mother, 'I'll be ever'where – wherever you look. Wherever they's a fight so hungry people can eat, I'll be there.' 'Maybe', he tells Ma Joad, 'a fella ain't got a soul of his own, but on'y a piece of a big one.' 'God, I'm talkin like Casy,' he reflects, on saying this; 'Comes to thinkin' about him so much. Seems like I can see him sometimes.' Casy has died but the spirit of Casy, his belief in collective identity and action, lives on in Tom. Not only that, the intimation is, it will soon be 'ever'where', just as the spirit of Jesus Christ (whose initials are recalled in Casy's own name) spread everywhere after his death. That spirit is evidently at work in the last, symbolic moment of *The Grapes of Wrath* when Rose of Sharon, Tom's sister, who has just given birth to a stillborn child, nurses an anonymous starving man with the milk intended for her baby. She has recognized, as Tom has, her involvement in a collective being, a communal identity larger than her own immediate family; and she has realized, instinctively, that her giving of herself to that communality is the source of renewal.

As its title indicates, as well as its narrative drive, *The Grapes of Wrath* is an angry but also a fundamentally optimistic book. Recalling 'The Battle-Hymn of the Republic' with its prophecy of truth marching to victory, and recollecting an earlier triumph over another kind of oppression, that title announces what the book will say: that the oppressors will be conquered, with a crusade to end poverty, virtual serfdom, succeeding in the twentieth century, just as the crusade to end slavery triumphed in the nineteenth. Steinbeck acknowledges the power of the oppressors and catalogues, in remorseless detail, the destitution and defeats of their victims: people like the Joads who, in the present system, seem to have nowhere to turn. But he also anticipates the trampling under of that power. Weaving together the literal and the legendary, the details of history and possibilities of myth, he outlines not only what America is but also what it might be. And what it might be is registered not just in the conversion of people like Casy, Tom and Rose of Sharon, not just in the quizzical comments of other characters, as they grope towards some form of political consciousness, and not just in the transformation of the religion of Christ on the cross into a religion of man on the move. It is there, also, in the sheer sweep of Steinbeck's prose as he describes the vastness of the American continent. In terms of narrative fact, the westward movement of *The Grapes of Wrath* may meet with closure. But, as far as narrative feeling is concerned, there remains something else: the conviction that there is still space, and time, to find a true West. The betrayal of the American dream may be what gives the novel its quality of barely controlled rage. But the belief in the continuing presence of that dream, as a source of renewal, is what gives it also a prophetic fervour. Steinbeck was never to write anything nearly as powerful or influential as his story of the Joads: although there were to be many further novels about the poor (*Cannery Row* [1945]), about family troubles and tensions (*East of Eden* [1952]) and a book about Steinbeck's own journeying across America (*Travels with Charley* [1962]). *The Grapes of Wrath* stands, though, as a worthy equivalent in the twentieth century of *Uncle Tom's Cabin* in the nineteenth: a work founded on the conviction that things should and could change which, thanks to its author's mixing of the documentary and the visionary, argument and sentiment, managed to ensure that many others were equally convinced.

Community and Identity

Immigrant writing

'Where is America?' asks the narrator of 'America and I' (1923), a short story by Anzia Yezierska (1885–1970). 'Is there an America? What is this wilderness in which I'm lost?' The teller of the tale is, she informs the reader, an immigrant who has fled from 'the airless oppression of Russia' to what she believes will be 'the Promised Land'. 'From the other end of the earth from where I came,' she says, 'America was a land of living hope, woven of dreams, aflame with longing and desire.' That dream, which mirrors the dream Steinbeck's migrants carry in their hearts as they cross the American continent, begins to be challenged when she arrives in the New World. 'I was in America, among the Americans, but not of them,' she recalls. Working first as a servant and then in a sweatshop, she cannot find what she calls '*my America*, where I could work for love and not for a living'. Still, 'the feeling that America must be somewhere, somehow' survives. It encourages her to learn the language and become 'a trained worker'. She goes to her factory teacher, then to the local Vocational Guidance Centre. 'What *do* you want?' she is asked; to which she replies, 'I want America to want me'. 'You have to *show* that you have something special for America before America has need of you,' she is told. 'America is no Utopia. First you must become efficient in earning a living before you can indulge in your poetic dreams.' That lesson learned, and 'stripped of all illusions', she begins to read American history. There she discovers, she tells the reader, that 'the great difference between the first Pilgrims and me was that they expected to make America, build America, create their own world of liberty. I wanted to find it ready made.' 'Then came a light – a great revelation!' the narrator reveals. 'I saw America – a big idea – a deathless hope – a world still in the making.' She realizes, at last, that 'it was the glory of America that it was not yet finished' and that she, 'the last comer', could have 'her share to give, small or great, in the making of America, like those Pilgrims who came in the *Mayflower*'. So, she concludes, she began to play her part in the creation of 'the America that is every day coming to be'. And she began 'to build a bridge of understanding between the American-born' and herself by opening up her life and the lives of her people to them. 'In only writing about the Ghetto I found America.'

The story speaks for many immigrants of the time, who wanted to play their part in the creation of what Randolph Bourne had called a 'trans-national America'. It also speaks for those immigrant writers who wanted to write that America into existence, by sharing their world with 'the American-born' and making it play a part in the process of a developing national identity. Of those writers Yezierska, who emigrated with her family from Russian Poland when she was fifteen, was an important one, not least because she was the only immigrant Jewish woman from Eastern Europe of her generation to produce a body of fiction in English. Her family settled in the Lower East Side of New York; and all her writing expresses the feelings of characters leading underprivileged lives, marginalized by mainstream American society, but still ready and eager to become 'Americans of tomorrow'. 'As one of the dumb, voiceless ones I speak,' 'America and I' begins. 'One of the millions beating, beating out their hearts at your gates for a breath of understanding.' And that cry articulates the motive and material of her fiction. Yezierska was considerably better educated and more widely experienced than most of her ghetto characters and narrators: she was close to John Dewey (1859–1952), the philosopher and educator, for several years; she worked in Hollywood in the 1920s and for the Federal Writers' Project in the 1930s; she reviewed for the *New York Times* and lectured in the 1950s. Nevertheless, her emotional experiences as an immigrant were her inspiration. They were the source of her stories, many of them collected in *Hungry Hearts* (1920) and *Children of Loneliness* (1923), and several novels, including *Salome of the Tenements* (1922) and *Bread Givers* (1925); and they formed the basis of her fictionalized autobiography, *Red Ribbon on a White Horse* (1950). Her narrators and characters range from feisty immigrant girls making their way in the world, thanks to a combination of hard work and native wit, to older women, isolated, disenfranchised, frustrated by years of domestic life and demeaning labour. Always, though, there is the same vision shaping them as there is in the creation of the characters of Wolfe and Steinbeck, of an America still ripe with promise. And the voice is, invariably, the same one that sounds in 'America and I', and many other immigrant fictions of the time, which declares that the full story of America has yet to be told – and that this is someone who will help tell it.

That hopeful message does not shape all immigrant writing of the period. It is not there, for instance, in the fiction of Pietro Di Donato (1911–92), a self-taught son of Italian immigrants who described the lives of exploited workers in a rich, lyrical prose that imported the rhythms of his ancestral home into the language of his adoptive one. Di Donato was haunted by the central, personal experience of his young life that came to express for him the full measure of suffering, the crucifixion suffered by the poor. When he was only eleven, his father was killed in a terrible accident on a construction job; and he was suddenly forced to take over his father's role of bricklayer and financial support for his family. Laid off from work in the 1930s, Di Donato found, he said, 'the leisure to think' and to read 'the immortal minds of all countries'. 'That gave me freedom,' he remembered. He began to write a short story, 'Christ in Concrete', based on the death of his father. Published in 1937, it supplied the germ of a novel, also called *Christ in Concrete*, which appeared two years later. Centred on a man like his father, an immigrant caught between two worlds and in captivity to his job, it was greeted with acclaim. Success rendered Di Donato silent for nearly twenty years; and his later books, two novels and two biographies, never achieved the same reception or a wide readership. But the story of the life of his father, the 'Christ in concrete', remains a central event in immigrant writing of the time; and the account of his untimely death, in particular, tells a very different story, of the fate of the poor from the Old World in the New, from the one told in 'America and I'.

On the night before Good Friday, Geremio enjoys 'the crowning point of his life'. He buys a house. 'Twenty years he had helped to mold the New World,' he reflects. 'And now he was to have a house of his own!' 'Tomorrow is a day for great things,' he tells his wife, '. . . and the day on which our Lord died for us.' But, although it is Good Friday, it is not a day of rest for Geremio on the building site where he works. Di Donato describes in pulsating, rhythmic prose how the 'job loomed up damp, shivery gray. Its giant members waiting.' 'The great Good Job, he did not love,' Geremio thinks bitterly, as he buckles down to it with his fellow workers, also Italian American. And his pleas to the 'padrone', the contractor, that the underpinning should not be left unsafe, 'just for the sake of a little profit', fall on deaf ears. 'Lissenyawopbastard,' the contractor, who is of course an Anglo-American, tells him, 'If you don't like it, you know what you can do!' With terrible, tragic inevitability, the building then collapses. 'The floor vomited', the reader learns, and 'the strongly shaped body' of Geremio 'thudded as a worthless sack among the giant debris'. Other workers die at once. Geremio, though, is left trapped beneath a huge hopper gushing grey concrete from its mouth. And, despite the efforts of rescuers, he suffers a slow, agonizing death, as he is drowned, crushed in the concrete. Entombed in the 'icy wet' concrete, with his brain in the end only 'miraculously alive', Geremio rages over the waste of his life, in oppressive labour and now in death. 'I've never known the freedom I wanted in my heart,' he thinks. 'There has been a terrible mistake! A cruel crime! The world is not right!' 'I say you can't take my life!' he calls voicelessly to those who have oppressed him, stolen his life in a double sense. Then, to his now dead friends and fellow workers: 'Men! Do you hear me? We must follow the desires within us for the world has been taken from us: we who made the world!' But the life, and the world, that have never been his, in a sense, are now literally, ineluctably taken from him as 'the concrete slowly contracted and squeezed his skull out of shape'. The death of Geremio is tragic in the true meaning of that word, since he has achieved a recognition at the instant of dying. He knows now that 'the world is not right', where the blame lies and what is needed to right it. The feeling of 'queer', 'fathomless' dissatisfaction he often felt during his life has crystallized into an understanding of shared identity and injustice, and the need for shared action: a knowledge which, reading his story, we are now asked to assume. In *Christ in Concrete*, story and novel, the author gives voice to the socially silenced. That is what 'America and I' does too. What the voice tells us is very different, though; its message is redemptive but also intensely, passionately radical.

Significant immigration into the United States from Asia began in 1849, when Chinese men began to arrive in order to escape internal conflicts. This early immigration was mainly to California, where Chinese immigrants joined the 'Forty-Niners' during the gold rush. The initial surge of movement resulted in the Chinese term for the United States, 'Gold Mountain', a name that is still in use today, despite the fact that immigrants soon turned to many other kinds of work: helping to build the transcontinental railroad in the 1860s, then turning to various, mainly low-paid jobs in the service industries, manufacturing and agriculture. These early immigrants were mostly male. And, owing to the difficult conditions and prejudice they encountered, many considered themselves *huagiao*, 'overseas Chinese', who intended to return to China. Early Chinese American literary production was, in any event, mainly limited to a few autobiographies and oral testimonies. Much of this literature was influenced by Chinese literary traditions, which incorporated elements from oral culture, and was often imitative of Chinese literary forms. An example of such writing is the poetry, originally written in Chinese, which was carved on the walls of the immigration station on Angel Island in San Francisco Bay, through which all new immigrants to the United States had to pass between 1910 and 1940. This poetry, composed by some of those 175,000 Chinese who came during this period, while they awaited interrogation and, in some cases, deportation, is variable in quality. But it vividly documents the despair and difficulties of the newly arrived immigrants; and, at its best, it has that quality of fiercely understated emotion that Pound so admired in Chinese poetry. 'I boarded the steamship for America. / Time flew like a shooting arrow', declares one, 'Already, a cool autumn has passed.' 'Still I am at the beginning of the road. / I have yet to be interrogated. / My heart is nervous with anticipation.' Some anticipate revenge, recalling that 'The dragon of water is humiliated by ants; / The fierce tiger who is caged is baited by the child'. Others compare themselves to famous literary or heroic figures in Chinese legend and history who have faced similar adversity. Still others, simply, quietly lament their fate: 'Leaving behind my brush and removing my sword, I came to America /', begins one. 'Who was to know two streams of tears would flow upon arriving here?' 'There are tens of thousands of poems composed on these walls,' comments one anonymous contributor to this rich gallery of immigrant experience; 'They are all cries of complaint and sadness.' 'The day I am rid of this prison and attain success,' he or she goes on, 'I must remember that this chapter once existed.' Storing up memories for themselves, and for fellow detainees who followed after them, these composers of mostly unsigned and undated pieces were also, however unawares, bringing a new note into immigrant writing. Using China as their formal source, and America as their subject, they were introducing a new sensibility into the American literary tradition, that of the Chinese American.

Of course, something of that sensibility had already been registered in the published writing of Sui Sin Far. Something more of it was caught in the work of Jade Snow Wong (1922–). In her autobiographical *Fifth Chinese Daughter* (1945), she described her experience of growing up in America as the daughter of traditional and strict Chinese parents. What her parents wanted, Wong recalls, was filial obedience, piety and adherence to the Chinese understanding of the female role. And, while Wong herself was not totally resistant to these expectations, she did find it difficult to reconcile them with her attempts, and her need, to assimilate into American society. As Wong describes it, she never really resolved this dilemma. Part of her was drawn to traditional Chinese life: to its emphasis on the family, the imperatives of heritage, to inherited customs and rituals. And part of her was eager, even desperate, for acceptance into white society and ready to adopt white habits of thought and belief. The ambivalence of her position, her sense of herself, was caught not only in her book but also in how Wong came to write it. She was encouraged to write her story by a white publisher, who wanted the voice of this second-generation immigrant, and by extension the voice of Chinese Americans, to be heard. But the part played by the publisher was interventionist, to say the least: Wong was advised what to include, her manuscript was extensively edited to make it supposedly more palatable to white audiences, and two-thirds of it were cut. In terms of its literary production, as well as its content, *Fifth Chinese Daughter* is a formative document, confirming what was to be a presiding theme of Chinese American, as of so much immigrant, literature – the condition, and sometimes the curse, of living more than one history.

Japanese people began emigrating to the United States in significant numbers in the 1880s, Koreans at the end of the nineteenth century, and Filipinos from about 1900. Although the majority of immigrants from these Asian American groups tended to be single men, quite a few were married and brought their wives with them: with the result that a second generation born in the United States – called *nisei* among the Japanese – appeared earlier than it did among the Chinese. Here, the formative writers in the earlier part of the twentieth century, respective to the different cultural groups, were Etsu Sugimoto (1873–1950), Younghill Kang (1903–72) and Carlos Bulosan (1917–56). Etsu Sugimoto wrote what was possibly the first of a substantial amount of *nisei* writing that appeared in the 1920s and 1930s, an autobiographical novel titled *A Daughter of the Samurai* (1925). True to the rich mixture of cultural influences at work in these texts, the book juxtaposes the American life of its author with portraits of Japan that are both actual and fictional. Sugimoto has been called an ambassador of goodwill, writing to promote understanding and appreciation of Japanese Americans; and she combines a mostly favourable portrait of Japanese life with a gracious, complimentary account of America. Delicately blending the real and the imagined, and the ancient Eastern world and the newer Western one, she does allow herself criticism, however veiled, of the feudal traditions of Japan, particularly in relation to the treatment of women. But the general tenor of the narrative is positive, as she tries to build a bridge between cultures, and between the generations among her own special community.

Younghill Kang was born in Korea, educated first in the Confucian tradition and then in Christian mission schools, and emigrated to the United States in 1921. Unlike Sugimoto, who tended to see herself as a guest in the United States, Kang desperately desired acceptance and to make America his home. Describing himself as self-educated, Kang read English and American classic literature voraciously, and attended classes at Harvard and Boston universities while working to support himself. With the help of his American wife, he began writing in English in 1928; then, while he was teaching at New York University, he became friends with Thomas Wolfe. Wolfe read some of the book Kang was working on at the time, and took it to his own editor. It was published in 1931 as *The Grass Roof*. A novel about the life of a young man in Korea, up to the point of his departure for America, it had plainly autobiographical roots. Well received, it was followed by *East Goes West* (1937), the story of the life of a Korean in America. But, while the portrait of Korea as a 'planet of death' in *The Grass Roof* had been applauded, Kang's account of American prejudice and Korean problems in America hit a less responsive chord. In his second novel, Kang subtly drew distinctions between different immigrants: the ones who try to behave like 'a typical New Yorker', the 'very strong nationalist' who remains 'an exile only in body, not in soul' and wants to get back to 'Korean land' where he can raise '100 per cent Korean children'. He quietly, humorously sketched Korean bemusement with American habits and tastes and, less humor-ously, American indifference to the humanity of the Koreans they employ. Above all, he described the fundamental yearning of his protagonist for a proper, perman-ent place in American life: the need to move from the status and perspective of visitor to that of citizen. Ironically, Kang never really achieved such a place himself: he was never offered a stable teaching position, or a satisfactory permanent job of any kind. Always a visiting lecturer or travelling speaker, he was forced to wander the country and to supplement his meagre earnings with translations, writing for children and book reviews. Nevertheless, he managed to produce work that voices a shared impulse among many Asian American writers: to criticize America, certainly, but also to claim it as their own.

Carlos Bulosan also emigrated to America while he was a young man. In 1930, he left his birthplace in the Philippines, after an impoverished childhood and a struggle to save enough money for his passage. He worked in the United States as an itinerant labourer and union activist. Eventually, he became one of the best-known Filipino writers in the United States, writing poetry, short stories and essays about Filipino American life between the 1930s and the 1950s. His fame grew during and after the Second World War, when he produced such works as *Letter from America* (1942), *The Voice of Bataan* (1944), *Laughter of My Father* (1944) and *The Dark People* (1944). But it is for his autobiographical narrative, *America is in the Heart* (1943), that he is best known; and it is on this work that his reputation rests. Divided into four parts, the book opens in 1918 with the young Carlos sharing the extreme economic hardship and suffering of his family. Aware of the gross inequities of Filipino society, American cultural imperialism in the Philippines and the need for 'radical social change', Carlos embarks for the United States. Part two then sees him arrive in Seattle. Travelling around, eking out a meagre existence in a series of seasonal jobs, he comes into contact with the Filipino labour movement. Forced into a ghettoized existence, he also becomes aware of just how hostile and racist a society America is. 'I almost died within myself,' Bulosan recalls, 'I died many deaths in those surroundings where man was indistinguishable from beast.' The second part of *America is in the Heart* ends, though, with a clear articulation of hope from another character, who tells Carlos, 'America is a prophecy of a new society of men'. And part three documents Carlos's transformation into a radicalized union activist, working for the Filipino labour and the New Tide movements. The short, final section, in turn, shows Bulosan achieving some literary success. Reading *The Grass Roof*, he reflects, 'Why could I not succeed as Younghill Kang had?' This spurs him on to write his own story: an act which he sees as his means of fighting for a better life in America. 'The time had come, I felt, for me to utilize my experiences in written form,' Bulosan explains; 'I had something to live for now, and to fight the world with.' Writing also becomes his means of feeling he belongs. 'It came to me that no man – no one at all – could destroy my faith in America again,' he concludes his narrative. 'It was something that grew out of the sacrifices and loneliness of my friends, of my brothers . . . I know that no man could destroy my faith in America that had sprung from all our hopes and aspirations, *ever*.' Bulosan was to die, thirteen years after the publication of *America is in the Heart*, without ever changing his original nationality. But in writing this book, he firmly laid claim to his place, his presence in the American tradition. As Bulosan put it, 'America is not merely a land or an institution. America is in the heart of men that died for freedom; it is also in the eyes of men that are building a new world.' Of that America, he was a full and distinguished citizen.

Native American voices

Among Native American writers, the first flourishing of literature written in English came in the 1920s and 1930s. Prior to that, the only notable fictions were *The Life and Adventures of Joaquin Murieta, the Celebrated California Bandit* (1854) by John Rollin Ridge and *O-gî-mäw-kwe Mit-i-gwä-kî: Queen of the Woods* (1899) by Simon Pokagon (1830–99). The authorship of the latter has been disputed; but the book by Ridge, a sensationalist novel dramatizing the violent actions of a Mexican bandit who raided the California gold fields in the early 1850s, was almost certainly the first novel by a Native American author to be published. Of the several Native American writers who began exploring the plight of their people in fiction, during the earlier part of the twentieth century, the most renowned were

Thomas S. Whitecloud (1914–72), John Joseph Matthews (1894–1979), D'Arcy McNickle (1904–77) and Mourning Dove (1888–1976). Necessarily, they focused on different tribal traditions, geographies and histories, and different aspects of the Native American experience. What they had in common, however, were certain fundamental concerns relating to the crisis in their culture. Whatever their approach, all of them were preoccupied with the debate over personal and tribal identity in the face of land loss, radical social and cultural change, and, not least, the pressure from white society to assimilate and acculturate Native Americans. The struggle of Native peoples to reconcile their ancient tribal traditions with the material and moral forces of American modernity became a dominant, determining theme in their fiction, explored, very often, through the plight of an Indian of mixed race who, as Thomas S. Whitecloud observes of his narrator and protagonist in 'Blue Winds Dancing' (1938), 'don't seem to fit in anywhere'. It is a struggle that only rarely meets with a successful outcome. The portrait of Archilde, the young male protagonist of *The Surrounded* (1936) by D'Arcy McNickle, being shackled and taken away by white law officers concludes the novel with an image of resistance and criminalization that is repeated in other works of Native American fiction of the time. Seldom do the leading characters in these stories find a way home.

In 'Blue Winds Dancing', the hero does so, however. 'Blue Winds Dancing' is the only significant published work of a man, himself of mixed ancestry, who found success in a number of quite different fields. Thomas St Germain Whitecloud was born to a white mother and a Chippewa father in New York City. When his parents divorced, Whitecloud stayed with his mother, but his childhood was spent on the reservation as well as in white society. And, although he encountered difficult times while growing up, he managed to fulfil his ambition of training to become a doctor. His medical duties were then to take up a significant part of his time, but he engaged in various civic activities, as a county coroner and a deputy sheriff; he travelled extensively in the United States and served as a battalion surgeon in Europe during the Second World War; and he wrote and lectured extensively. As a student, Whitecloud had contemplated a writing career for a while. Some of the essays and tales he completed he sent, while he was still young, to Hamlin Garland, for criticism and encouragement. And, while he never realized his aim of becoming a full-time writer, his story 'Blue Winds Dancing' remains a powerful, and clearly semi-autobiographical, account of a man caught between a conflict of cultures. The narrative is simple. A man of Indian origin dreams of home. 'I am weary of trying to keep up this bluff of being civilized,' he says. He sees the geese going southward. 'They were going home,' he observes. 'Now I try to study, but against the pages I see them again, driving southward. Going home.' 'I hear again the ring of axes in deep woods, the crunch of snow beneath my feet,' he adds. 'I feel again the smooth velvet of ghost-birch bark. I hear the rhythm of the drums.' So he leaves his white school, to return to his people, who, he reflects, 'have many things that civilization has taken from the whites'. On the road, he meets many 'outcasts' from white society, both like and unlike himself, people living on 'the relief and the WPA'. And he is fearful that, once returned to the reservation, he will not fit in. 'Am I Indian, or am I white?' he asks himself. His question is answered for him when, finally, he is back on the land of his people, where he sees the blue winds dancing and hears the drums beat. 'It is like the pulse beat of the world,' the reader is told. He is back where he belongs. 'I am one with my people and we are all a part of something universal,' he declares triumphantly. And the last three words of the story seal the triumph: 'I am home.'

The fiction of D'Arcy McNickle is similarly autobiographical in origin and, in being concerned with reaffirming traditional, indigenous values, equally at odds with the popular contemporary belief that Indians should be assimilated into the dominant Anglo-American culture. McNickle also strove, in this fiction, with even more perseverance than Whitecloud, to resist the conventions of the Western narrative, popular images of Native American life, and what he called 'the sentimental and inept efforts that have been made on behalf of the Indian in the past'. The precise racial origins of McNickle are a matter of debate. There is no doubt, however, that he identified himself as a Native American, and that his family history was inextricably interwoven with the histories of the Cree, Métis and Salish (Flathead) tribes. After his parents were divorced, McNickle was sent, as many other Native American children in the same situation were, to a federal boarding school in Oregon. He was to write about this experience in several of his books, including two novels, since it illustrated, for him, the fundamental conflict that Native American peoples had faced ever since the arrival of the Europeans: between the indigenous culture and the modern, the old pieties and the new habits and beliefs that whites were trying assiduously to impose on those whom they had conquered. Torn as he himself was between Indian traditions and white education, McNickle continued his studies in Montana and in England. He then became an influential academic and activist, writing books on Native American history (*They Came Here First* [1949], *Indian Man: A Life of Oliver La Farge* [1972], *Native American Tribalism: Indian Survival and Renewals* [1973]), numerous stories (*The Hawk is Hungry and Other Stories* [1992]), and three novels (*The Surrounded* [1936], *Runner in the Sun: A Story of the Indian Maize* [1954], *Wind From An Enemy Sky* [1978]). He was also appointed the first director of the Newberry Library's Center for the History of the American Indian, helped found the Department of Anthropology at the University of Saskatchewan, and became a founding member of the Congress of American Indians. What his many activities have in common is pride in Native American traditions and a persistent belief in the right of Native Americans to self-determination, to be left alone to pursue their future in their own way. His fiction, in particular, combines a critique of Anglo-Americans and their myopic attempts to impose their values with a detailed portrait of Native American resistance. In *The Surrounded*, for instance, all the major Native American characters renounce their Catholicism and return to the life they lived before the missionaries arrived. The account of Anglo-American ethnocentrism is often humorous; the portrayal of Native people trying to resist 're-education' is, however, deeply serious, passionate and sometimes tragic. As McNickle insists, time and again, in his work, what Native Americans want is a basic human right. But it is a right that is often denied them. And, in trying to assert it, they may be branded by white society as criminals.

Like Whitecloud and McNickle, John Joseph Matthews was of mixed-blood status, having both white and Osage origins. For him, too, the conflict between tribal and dominant cultures was an intense personal experience, felt in the pulses and the blood. Born in the Indian Territory later to become Oklahoma, he was intensely aware of the alterations taking place in reservation life. And, after a youth full of incident and wandering that included study in America and England and work as a flight instructor during the First World War, he devoted his life to public service and to writing. His first book, *Wah'kon-tah: The Osage and the White Man's Road*, was published in 1929 and was immensely successful; his only novel, *Sundown*, appeared five years later. As the title suggests, *Sundown* is coloured by the melancholy reflection that the old tribal life is passing away in Oklahoma. Founded in the experiences of its author, the novel tells the story of young Challenge 'Chal' Windzer, the son of a progressive, optimistic man who believes Chal will become strong and talented enough to deal with change and an uncertain future. Chal starts off well. Educated at the University of Oklahoma, he is then involved in the early days of aviation. But, after the First World War, he is unable to find a place in his community or a satisfying vocation; and he succumbs to the seductive attractions of white society, notably alcohol. Returning to the reservation, he tells his mother that he will make something of himself. 'I'm goin' to Harvard law school, and take law,' he boasts, '– I'm gonna be a great orator.' But his mother remains unconvinced; she knows, instinctively, that there is little hope for him. This account of the personal failure of the protagonist is framed by a narrative of social decline, as the tribe, in general, succumbs to the corruptions of white society. 'The black derricks crept further west,' the reader is told. And those oil derricks represent the terrible consequences of instant wealth brought by the exploitation of resources on the reservation. The tribe becomes rich for a while and then, as the oil money begins to run out, falls into poverty, cultural dereliction and despair. As 'the all-powerful life that had come with the creeping black derricks' begins 'to recede to the east', the Native peoples try to convince themselves that the good times, 'the fever brightness of the Great Frenzy', will one day return. But that hope is as clearly without foundation as Chal's boastful dream of the future. Both the protagonist and his tribe have lost touch with the old, indigenous culture and found no true place in the new. They are people who do not seem to belong anywhere.

While Matthews, along with McNickle and Whitecloud, concerned himself with the dilemma of living in the collision of cultures, Mourning Dove was more interested in trying to recover and reaffirm the culture of her ancestors. Born in Idaho, and descended from an ancient line of warrior-chiefs, her paternal grandfather was Irish. Her maternal grandmother, however, with whom she lived for much of her adolescence, taught Mourning Dove about the oral traditions of her people, the Okanogans. Mourning Dove received little in the way of a formal education from white society but, from the stories her grandmother told her, she developed a lively and informed interest in her indigenous culture. And one early result of that interest was *Cogewea, the Half-Blood: A Depiction of the Great Montana Cattle Range* (1927), the first novel written by an American Indian woman. The book was produced in collaboration with a white friend and mentor, Lucullus McWhorter, a scholar of Indian traditions who had been adopted into the Yakima tribe. McWhorter was well aware of the expectations of white readers, and the book bears the marks of his intervention: such as a sometimes stilted lyricism and a self-conscious use of slang, poetic epigraphs and detailed notes on the traditions of the Okanogans. Still, despite this, and despite its conventional romance plot, *Cogewea* offers an intimate portrait of tribal life. It also anticipates the direction the later work of Mourning Dove was to take: towards a retelling of the stories of the Native peoples that is at once conscientious and quietly passionate, scholarly and personal.

The book that Mourning Dove published six years after *Cogewea*, *Coyote Stories*, was, as it happened, also produced with the help of McWhorter. Heister Dean Guie, another white colleague, received credit on its title page for illustrating and editing the stories; Chief Standing Bear, the author of two popular autobiographies at the time, provided a foreword; and both Guie and McWhorter insisted on standardized spelling and verification of the details *Coyote Stories* contained about Okanogan beliefs, since they did not regard Mourning Dove as an authority. Nevertheless, this second publication bears much more clearly the marks of Mourning Dove's own personality and is stamped with the authority of her knowledge. To that extent, this collection of folk tales is much more unambiguously her own work. 'The Animal People were here first – before there were any real people,' Mourning Dove announces in her Preface. 'Coyote was the most important', she explains, 'because, after he was put to work by the Spirit Chief, he did more than any of the others to make the world a good place to live.' Before rehearsing a series of stories that have Coyote as their protagonist, she then goes on to explain her own involvement: how she was told them as part of the heritage of her family and her tribe, and how she learned from them of the subtle connections between her people and the vitality and the mystery of their natural surroundings. Coyote emerges from these stories as a sharer in both the vitality and the mystery. A comically cunning but vulnerable trickster, he is also, thanks to the Spirit Chief, a being of divine power. He comes out, too, as the source and origin of the traditions of 'the New People, the Indians': 'You are to be chief of the tribes,' the Spirit Chief tells him. Showing how such rituals as the sweat-house, a mystic shrine for physical and spiritual cleansing, emerged, thanks to the activities of its protagonist, *Coyote Stories* is at once a series of lively tales and a passionate affirmation of tribal identity. The Native American past lives in the present, Mourning Dove intimates, a source of personal and communal power. And, as long as acts of narrative restoration like this continue, it can survive on into the future.

The literature of the New Negro movement and beyond

Among those other Americans who had, for many years, formed part of the nation, the African Americans, a pivotal event in literature was the publication of *The New*

Negro in 1925. Conceived and edited by Alain Locke (1886–1954), it grew out of a special issue of the *Survey Graphic* magazine in March of that year devoted to the district of Harlem in Manhattan. And it served as a catalyst for a growing sense of confidence that black America was on the verge of a second Emancipation: the consequence, this time, not of government action but of the will and the achievements of the people, and, in particular, the artists and intellectuals. Migration from the South into such urban centres as New York, Chicago and Detroit, the opening up of new economic and cultural opportunities, the challenge of continued racism and racial violence (the summer of 1919, for instance, was marked by some of the bloodiest anti-black riots in American history): all this served as a stimulus, and a challenge, to those who wanted to make the voice of African Americans heard. The term 'the New Negro' was not coined by Locke, nor did it appear for the first time in print in his anthology. It had been in use since at least the late 1890s. Nevertheless, it was this book that gained it currency, as the term of choice to describe a new sense of racial pride, personal and cultural selfhood. *The New Negro* was the first major literary attempt to revise the collective portrait of black America painted by W. E. B. Du Bois in *The Souls of Black Folks*. Others, perhaps, had an equal claim to be seen as promoters of the new movement in black cultural self-consciousness. Notably, Jessie Fauset (1882–1961) encouraged and published many of the new black writers while she edited Du Bois's *Crisis* magazine and wrote four novels, depicting the experience of black women, that all insisted on the need to accept the African American inheritance rather than escape it: *There is Confusion* (1924), *Plum Bun* (1929), *The Chinaberry Tree* (1931) and *Comedy: American Style* (1936). But it was Locke who, through his landmark anthology and his energetic championing of the intellectual achievement of African Americans in the 1920s, received most of the credit. As a result, he became known as the father of the New Negro and the dean of the Harlem Renaissance.

Liberal and cosmopolitan in his outlook, Locke made sure that *The New Negro* included men and women, blacks and whites, the older and younger generations among its contributors. 'In the very process of being transplanted, the Negro is becoming transformed,' Locke declared in his introductory essay. And, in order to chart this transformation – 'a spiritual coming of age', as he called it – he felt free, perhaps even obliged, to draw on a variety of perspectives. The variety has certain limitations, though. Some of these seem entirely right. For instance, given that Locke's main purpose is to declare the growth of a 'common consciousness' among African Americans and to show that, as he puts it, 'the American mind must reckon with a fundamentally changed Negro', it seems natural that he should limit the number of white contributors to three. Others, however, are more questionable. There are only six black female contributors to *The New Negro*, among them Zora Neale Hurston, and only two contribute essays – only one of which, in turn, Jessie Fauset writing on drama, is concerned with what Locke saw as his core project, 'the first fruits of the Negro Renaissance'. These limits aside, the list of contributors to the collection is impressive. It includes Countee Cullen and Langston Hughes, Arna Bontemps and Claude McKay, Jean Toomer and, from an older generation, James Weldon Johnson and W. E. B. Du Bois. Divided into two sections, 'The Negro Renaissance' and 'The New Negro in a New World', the first and more important section gathers together essays on African American art and literature with generous selections of African American fiction, poetry and drama. The second, in turn, contains reflections on broader social issues and on the connection between the Harlem Renaissance and similar movements in other parts of the United States. And it concludes with an essay by Du Bois tracing the global implications of the New Negro movement, and, in particular, its relationship to colonialism and the struggle for freedom in Africa. All this is followed by an extensive bibliography, compiled by Arthur A. Schomburg (1874–1938), documenting the significant books and other studies written by and about African Americans and, to a lesser extent, Africa. And it is supplemented by a series of illustrations that emphasize racial pride by playing variations on the theme that black is beautiful. These were considered bold at a time when even politically conscious magazines often contained advertisements for creams to facilitate the lightening of skin colour. There are, inevitably, omissions and weaknesses in the volume. The blues is mentioned only in passing. Jazz is accorded respectful attention but is scorned because, as one essayist puts it, 'at present it vulgarizes, with more wholesome growth in the future, it may on the contrary truly democratize'. But, on the whole, *The New Negro* performed the remit Locke had set for himself here: to announce, as he put it, 'a dramatic flowering of a new race-spirit . . . among American Negroes', and to capture the optimism that accompanied that flowering – a burgeoning sense of communal energy, collective cultural power and joy.

A very different perspective on the Harlem Renaissance, however, is offered in *Infants of the Spring* (1932), a satirical roman-à-clef by Wallace Thurman (1902– 34). Thurman was a talented poet, playwright, editor and literary critic as well as a novelist. Joining with Hughes, Hurston and a handful of other young black writers and artists in 1926, he helped to publish *Fire!!*, the most iconoclastic magazine black America had ever produced. Its many scandalized critics extinguished *Fire!!* after only one issue. But, undaunted, Thurman went on to experience success in 1929 with his play *Harlem*, which ran for over ninety performances at the Apollo Theatre, and to write three notable novels: *The Blacker the Berry* (1929), an exploration of a subject taboo in most earlier African American fiction, intraracial colour prejudice and the self-hatred engendered by it, *The Interne* (co-authored with A. L. Forman [1929]) and *Infants of the Spring*. Thurman was a scathing critic of the bourgeois attitudes that, he believed, motivated the Harlem Renaissance old guards like Locke and Du Bois, arguing that they proclaimed aesthetic and intellectual freedom while seeking white approval with slanted portraits of African Americans. And his aim, he declared, was to create black characters 'who still retained some individual race qualities and who were not totally white American in every respect save skin colour': an aim he shared, in his opinion, with many of the younger generation of black writers, including the co-editors of *Fire!!* In *Infants of the Spring*, Alain Locke is satirized in the character of Dr A. L. Parkes, the pompous, self-appointed leader of a literary salon given to vapid prophecies about a new racial millennium. Hurston becomes Sweetie May, 'a short story writer, more noted for her ribald wit and personal effervescence than for any actual literary work'. While Countee Cullen is transformed into De Witt Clinton, 'acclaimed as the most handsome Negro in Harlem by a certain group of whites'. In his account of what he terms the 'niggerati', a self-absorbed, self-congratulatory coterie more concerned with promoting themselves than furthering the interests of their race, Thurman spares few of his contemporaries, or even himself. Only Jean Toomer is said to have 'elements of greatness'. Even Langston Hughes, depicted as Tony Crews, is damned with faint praise: 'his work was interesting and unusual,' the reader is told, 'it was also spotty.' 'I don't expect to be a great writer,' declares the protagonist of *Infants of the Spring*, Raymond Taylor, who becomes Thurman's own fictional surrogate, mirror and mouthpiece. 'I don't think the Negro race can produce one now, any more than can America.'

Satirized by Thurman, celebrated by Locke, the New Negro movement of the 1920s and beyond did nevertheless help to produce a host of writers. Many of them were good, and some of them were surely great. Among the novelists and short storytellers, these writers included Rudolph Fisher (1897–1934), the author of the first African American detective novel, *The Conjure Man Dies* (1932), whose collected short stories, *City of Refuge*, was published in 1987, and Walter White (1893–1955), the author of an authoritative study of lynching, *Rope and Faggot: The Biography of Judge Lynch* (1929), as well as two notable novels, *Fire in the Flint* (1924) and *Flight* (1926), concerned, respectively, with racial violence and crossing the colour line. They also included two utterly different figures, George Schuyler (1895–1977) and Claude McKay (1890–1948). Schuyler is a curious figure. Starting as a socialist, he became a convinced anti-Communist whose political position was measured by the title of his 1966 autobiography, *Black and Conservative*. From almost the beginning, however, he argued that there was essentially no difference between black and white Americans. 'The Aframerican is merely a lampblacked Anglo-Saxon,' he wrote in his 1926 essay 'The Negro Art-Hokum'. And he deployed his considerable gifts for satire and polemic to ridicule and attack what he termed the 'colorphobia' of both white and black Americans. In his satirical novel *Black No More* (1931), for instance, Schuyler imagined a situation in which a black doctor invents a formula that makes blacks white. As blacks become white, as a result, whites work strenuously to become black so they can retain their dearly cherished difference and separation. In his later years, because of his attacks on black leaders, Schuyler was dismissed as someone who had simply sold out to the white establishment. He is perhaps more accurately seen, though, as an unreconstructed isolationist. 'I have always said and written just what I thought without apologies to anyone,' he once wrote. 'I shall continue to pursue this somewhat lonely and iconoclastic course.'

Claude McKay, besides being different, is a far more considerable figure. Born in Jamaica, McKay became known as 'the *enfant terrible* of the Harlem Renaissance' after the publication of his most famous poem, 'If We Must Die' (1919), established him as a militant. In the poem, written in response to the race riots that erupted in Chicago and other cities, McKay advocated violent resistance to violence. 'If we must die, O let us nobly die,' he declared. 'Like men we'll face the murderous, cowardly pack, / Pressed to the wall, dying, but fighting back!' Other poems attacked lynching ('The Lynching' [1920]), and slavery and its heritage ('In Bondage' [1920]), or revealed an intense love–hate relationship with his adoptive home. 'Although she feeds me bread of bitterness, / And sinks into my throat her tiger's tooth, /' McKay wrote in 'America' (1921), 'Stealing my breath of life, I will confess / I love this cultured hell that tests my youth!' But, as his collection of poems, *Harlem Shadows* (1922), reveals, McKay was also inclined towards more sensuous, romantic and even nostalgic modes. He celebrated the vibrant, sensual life of Harlem ('The Harlem Dances' [1917]), the lush vegetation of his birthplace ('I Shall Return' [1920]), and the emotional and earthier pleasures of love ('Flower of Love' [1953], 'A Red Flower' [1953]). And the mixture of racial concern and sensuous impulse comes out, with especial clarity and intensity, in his three novels: *Home to Harlem* (1928), *Banjo* (1929) and *Banana Bottom* (1937).

In *Home to Harlem*, for example, the portrait of the hero Jake Brown was controversial at the time, especially in the eyes of African American reviewers. Jake is a freewheeling, high-living ex-soldier returning to the 'mad riotous joy' of Harlem after the First World War. Back in 'the contagious fever' of 'chocolate Harlem! . . . dark-eyed Harlem!' he gets caught up in the 'haunting rhythm' of the world surrounding him. And he abandons himself to 'pure voluptuous jazzing': a life of dancing and sex, gambling and city ambling, drink and drugs. Some critics of this, McKay's most successful novel, argued that Jake was merely a stereotype of black vagrancy, reproducing an image of the streets and nightclubs of Harlem already made popular in *Nigger Heaven* (1926) by the white writer Carl Van Vechten (1880–1966). That, however, ignored what McKay presented as the positive side of Jake's character: his freedom from pretence, his vigorous assertion of his own manhood, and his instinctive distrust of the seductions of white society. It also ignored the importance of another major character, an alienated Haitian intellectual called Ray, who is both attracted to and disturbed by the hedonism of Jake – and who consistently expresses his impatience with what he calls 'the contented hogs in the pigpen of Harlem'. Registering the bleaker side of his surroundings, their 'brutality, gang rowdyism, promiscuous thickness', Ray does not want to become a 'Harlem nigger', he reflects. Instead, he has 'dreams of making something with words'. 'Could he create out of the fertile reality around him?' he asks himself. For him, Harlem may be a possible source and subject, but it can never be a home. And, at the end of the novel, he decides to leave it and all it represents. The narrative manoeuvres its way between the figures of Jake and Ray, who clearly express the two sides of their creator, the sensuous and the reflective, the romantic hedonist and the dispassionate activist, the man who feels at home in Harlem and the one who feels at home nowhere. McKay was to continue the story of Jake and Ray in his two later novels. These were never as successful. Nor was his autobiography, *A Long Way from Home* (1937), or his sociological study, *Harlem: Negro Metropolis* (1940), or his memoir, *My Green Hills of Jamaica* (completed in 1946, published in 1979). And his later commitment to what was widely perceived as an unprogressive political programme – he became a vociferous critic of Communism and converted to Catholicism – made him increasingly isolated. He remains, however, one of the most significant figures of the Renaissance, as well as one of the most symptomatic.

So, for that matter, do two African American women writers of the period who, like McKay, suffered neglect during their later years only to be rediscovered after their deaths: Zora Neale Hurston (1891–1960) and Nella Larsen (1891–1964). Hurston was born, as she tells the reader in her autobiography *Dust Tracks on a Road* (1942), in Alabama. Her family then moved, while she was still an infant, to Eatonville, Florida, the first incorporated black community in America. Her father was a preacher, and three times mayor of Eatonville. Her mother, a former school-teacher, advised Zora to 'jump at the sun. You might not land on the sun, but at least you'll get off the ground.' But the idyll of her childhood ended when her mother died in 1904. No longer 'Eatonville's Zora', she remembered, she 'became a little colored girl'; and her life turned into 'a series of wanderings', involving various menial jobs, until she became a student at Howard University in Washington. At Howard, she began to write. Some of her work attracted the attention of major figures in the Harlem Renaissance, including Locke, who published one of her stories in *The New Negro*: and in 1925 she moved to New York, where she began to study anthropology at Barnard College. This revitalized her interest in the black folklore of the South. So, in 1927, reversing the tide of the Great Migration, she returned to the South, with the help of a scholarship, to research that folklore. The result of her research was *Mules and Men* (1935), a collection of tales, songs, games and hoodoo practices that presented African American folklore as a lived culture. In a way that was innovative at the time, but later common practice among ethnographers, Hurston placed folklore texts in their communal context so as to demonstrate the process of their creation.

Another result of Hurston's fieldwork was her first novel, *Jonah's Gourd Vine* (1934). Based to an extent on the lives of her parents, the novel tells the story of a poet-preacher who defines himself through his art. At its centre is a sermon Hurston transcribed from her field notes. It is fired by its author's lifelong conviction that individuals and communities voice themselves into being, that they achieve identity and continuity through the telling of themselves. Something else Hurston had learned from her research was also pivotal to her second novel, and her master-piece, *Their Eyes Were Watching God* (1937). Women, she had noticed, were denied access to the pulpit and the porch, the privileged sites of storytelling, and, to that extent, denied the chance of self-definition. Her aim, here and elsewhere in her work, became especially to revise and adapt vernacular forms to give voice to women, to create a genuinely democratic oral culture, or, as she put it, 'words walking without masters'. 'Two things everybody's got tuh do for theyselves,' the central character of *Their Eyes Were Watching God*, Janie Crawford, concludes. 'They got tuh go tuh God, and they got tuh find out about livin' fuh theyselves.' The conclusion is hard earned. Janie has to win the right to see and speak about living for herself. She has to resist the demeaning definitions her society would impose on her, as a black person and a woman. She has to defy the instructions of one of her husbands not to engage in 'porch talk'. She has to claim her own voice, and in the process her own self and rightful place in the vocal community. Raised by her grandmother Nancy, an ex-slave who has suffered most of the abuses heaped on black women in slavery, she is told by the old woman, 'De nigger woman is de mule uh de world so fur as Ah can see'. But Janie holds on to her dignity, and her desire to realize herself, through two loveless marriages. And in her third marriage, to an itinerant labourer and gambler much younger than her, Tea Cake Woods, she finds love, laughter and the opportunity to be and speak for herself. The marriage ends tragically, with the violent death of Tea Cake. Janie, however, a 'born orator', has now claimed her birthright. With Tea Cake, she has learned the expressive codes of her culture; she has been given the chance to speak herself into being. She returns to her hometown of Eatonville, at the end of the novel, a single and singular woman, where she can now participate in the 'porch talk', the 'big stories' and 'big arguments' of the community. She has come home to her true speech, and her true self.

The triumph of *Their Eyes Were Watching God* is that its language is the literary equivalent of the oral performances Hurston studied as an ethnographer. Vernacular voices speak in and through the narrative, informing its dialogue and narration. Hurston evokes a community in the act of making and remaking itself; and she links that to the endless, restless activity of talk. She shows how a small group of people ground themselves, begin to make sense of their trials and changes, through the manoeuvrings of speech and ceremony. She discloses how one remarkable woman fulfils the promise of her life by insisting on her own right to participate in the speaking and the ceremonials. And she opens up the chance to the reader as well, of finding ground and definition, by inviting us into the process of debate. In a review of *Their Eyes Were Watching God* when it was first published, Richard Wright dismissed the book, because, he said, 'it carries no theme, no message, no thought', just a 'minstrel technique' to make white folks laugh. That was profoundly wrong, however. The vocal medium of the narrative has nothing to do with minstrelsy. It is expressive of a self, and a society, in full, rightful possession of themselves. As a result, that medium *is* the message.

In the years immediately following *Their Eyes Were Watching God*, Hurston published another novel, *Moses, Man of the Mountain* (1939), exploring the story of Moses as recorded in the Bible and African oral traditions. She also produced another collection of folklore, *Tell My Horse* (1938). But the quality and quantity of her work began to wane. A novel about white life in Florida published in 1948, *Seraph on the Sewanee*, did nothing to prevent her sinking from public notice. What little attention she did receive, in the last decade or so of her life, was mostly unwelcome. In 1954, for instance, she earned some notoriety for attacking the Supreme Court ruling on school desegregation. She had long been a critic of civil rights organizations; she argued that the struggle for integration was founded on a belief in black inferiority and would threaten the historic black institutions of learning. But her arguments brought her only opprobrium among the African American community. By the time Hurston died, in poverty in a Florida welfare home, all her books were out of print. Her rediscovery came at the hands of a later generation of African American women writers. Notably, Alice Walker, going 'in search of our mother's gardens', found in Hurston a literary foremother. So did Toni Morrison and Sherley Anne Williams. She is now appropriately seen not only as a crucial figure in the literature of 'the New Negro' but as a vital link in the chain of African American writing – and, especially, in the tradition of African American writing by women – that emphasizes the power of continuity and community, locality and vocal intimacy, the simple sense of a shared dignity and common ground.

With some justification, Nella Larsen has been called the mystery woman of the Harlem Renaissance. Part of the mystery was of her own making, because Larsen was inclined to create a personal myth about herself: claiming, for instance, that she was born in the Virgin Islands whereas, in fact, her birthplace was Chicago. Born Nellie Walker and reared in a visibly white, Danish immigrant family, she was a lonely child whose dark skin separated her from her parents and a sibling. Leaving Fisk University Normal High School, a black institution, without a diploma, she trained as a nurse, entered the African American middle class when she married a black research physicist, then found a job at the New York Public Library. It was this job that introduced her to the coterie of writers emerging in Harlem. And, within a few years, she had produced her only two novels, *Quicksand* (1928) and *Passing* (1929). *Quicksand* was hailed by W. E. B. Du Bois as 'the best piece of fiction' by an African American since Charles Chesnutt. With *Passing*, Larsen became one of the first African American women to win a Guggenheim Fellowship for literature, which enabled her to spend a year researching further novels in Europe. But no more books were to appear. Larsen had been shattered by accusations of plagiarism in one of her short stories, published in 1930, and the infidelity of her husband. Writing projects were planned and announced but never completed or published. The writing stopped. Larsen was forced to return to nursing to support herself, and lived the final years of her life in greater obscurity even than Hurston. Her two remarkable long fictions, which were rediscovered after her death, are, however, very different from *Their Eyes Were Watching God*. Her location is, for the most part, a more bourgeois, educated, confined world than the one Hurston wrote about; her major characters, intelligent, sophisticated women of mixed race, are caught up in troublesome confusions of race, gender and class as they try to negotiate their way through a complex social milieu. And the recognizably Modernist, disjunctive and episodic structure of her narratives creates a multiple subjective space for those characters as they search for a means of realizing identity, of marking themselves out and achieving personal fulfilment in a world that seems intent on division and erasure – defining them in terms of a series of rigid divisions and denying them as individuals.

Quicksand, for instance, tells the story of Helga Crane. The daughter of a Danish American mother and an African American father, her mixed heritage irretrievably complicates her search for security and self-realization. 'What did she want?' she asks herself. She does not know. She is consumed by a sense of 'outsidedness', of being 'different' wherever she goes and having 'no home'. And, in quest of something, some source of satisfaction, she moves from the South to New York to Copenhagen, then back to America again, always wondering 'why couldn't she be happy, content somewhere?' 'She hadn't belonged there' in Harlem, she reflects. Among the Danes, 'she wasn't one of them either'. Continually, she is seized by a restlessness that leads to vacillation of feeling, emotional fissure. Wherever she goes, she may be convinced for a moment that she has found 'a place for herself, that she was really living'. But the conviction soon wears off. All she is left with, then, is what she calls 'this knowledge, this certainty of the division of her life into two parts'. And those divisions are never resolved. All that happens, at the end of the novel, is that Helga falls victim, for a while, to the 'desire to believe', a 'seductive repentance' that leads her to a conversion experience and marriage to a preacher. Journeying back with him to the South, she sinks into 'asphyxiation', the 'quagmire' of marriage to a man she now hates, constant childbearing and domestic routine – and the sense that the faith to which she had once surrendered is a destructive illusion. Recovering from the miscarriage of her fourth child, Helga persuades herself that she will escape from the quicksands of her life 'later. When she got up. By and By.' The final words of the novel put paid to that illusion, however, at least for the reader. 'Hardly had she left her bed and become able to walk again without pain,' we are told, '. . . when she began to have her fifth child.'

Passing uses a very different narrative line to explore similar mired complexities of gender, race and class. In this case, there are two protagonists. Both are African American women who could pass for white. One of them, Clare Kendry, does so and is married to someone who is not only white but a racist. The other, Irene Redfield, only does so occasionally as a matter of social convenience – when visiting a white restaurant, say. She is married to a prominent African American physician, devotes herself to various good causes, and has established her identity as a respectable wife and doting mother. Through the story of the separate but inextricably linked lives of these two women, former childhood friends, Larsen explores the multiple forms that social repression and self-deception can assume. 'She was caught between two allegiances,' Irene observes of herself at one point in the novel. That links her not only with her old friend but with the heroine of *Quicksand*. Like Clare and Helga Crane, she suffers from what is called here 'the burden of race', which tells her different stories about herself. Like them, too, she is compelled to make her way in a social world that seems to depend upon masks and masquerade, the dissolution of character into category. At the end of this subtle, circuitous novel, Clare is killed when she falls from a window; and there is a hint that Irene, who is there beside her when she dies, may have pushed her. Linked in life, the two women are also linked at this moment of death: Irene, it may be, is attempting the futile gesture of resolving her divisions by ridding herself of her *doppelgänger*, the secret sharer of her plight. Just as *Quicksand* manoeuvres the traditional theme of the tragic mulatta into a poignant, pioneering portrayal of a modern woman

---

– and, in the process, offers one of the first serious studies of those aspiring to the African American middle class – so *Passing* rewrites the story of crossing the colour line in psychological terms. Both are major novels of racial and sexual identity, in the Modernist vein.

The work of Jean Toomer (1894–1976) can also be seen as a bridge between the New Negro movement and Modernism. A contributor during the 1920s to such black journals as *Opportunity* and *Crisis*, as well as *The New Negro*, Toomer published as well in such experimental magazines as *Broom* and the *Little Review*. One of the few writers to receive positive comment in *Infants of the Spring*, Wallace Thurman's satirical portrait of the Harlem Renaissance, he also received encouragement and support from such luminaries of the Greenwich Village avant-garde as Waldo Frank (1888–1967), whose own work included social criticism (*Our America* [1919]), expressionist drama (*New Year's Eve* [1929]) and a variety of novels in different modes (among them *City Block* [1922], *Holiday* [1923] and *The Bridegroom Cometh* [1939]). Toomer saw himself as a confluence of different races and influences. 'In my body were many bloods, some dark blood, all blended in the fire of six or more generations,' he recollected. 'I was then, either a new type of man or the very oldest. In any case, I was inescapably myself.' What that self was, he believed, apart from unique, was American. 'From my own point of view I am naturally and inevitably an American,' Toomer wrote in a letter to *The Liberator* magazine. 'I have strived for a spiritual fusion analogous to the fact of racial intermingling. Without denying a single element in me, with no desire to subdue one to the other, I have sought to let them all function as complements.' Born Nathan Pinchback Toomer, he was, in fact, the grandson of a part-black acting governor of Louisiana during Reconstruction. A mixture of several races and nationalities, an individual who could be identified as an Indian or a dark-skinned European, Toomer spent his childhood in his birthplace of Washington, DC; attended various colleges without proceeding to a degree; then, in 1921, he took a job as superintendent of a black rural school in Georgia. This, his first trip to the South, was seminal. It was, he said just a few years later, 'the starting point of almost anything of worth I have done'. 'My growing need for artistic expression pulled me deeper into the Negro group' in Georgia, he explained. 'I heard folk-songs come from the lips of Negro peasants. I saw the rich dark beauty that I had heard many false accents about, and of which till then, I was somewhat sceptical.' In short, Toomer was captivated by the Southern landscape and the impact of African Americans on Southern culture. And, returning to Washington, DC, he began to write what was to become the third section of his masterpiece, *Cane* (1923). Within a year of his return, he had completed the experimental work that is at once a record of his discovery of his Southern inheritance, an act of homage to a folk culture that he believed was doomed to extinction, and an exploration of the forces that he saw as responsible for extinguishing that culture and for the spiritual fragmentation of modern times. With the help of Frank, who wrote the foreword, the book found a publisher. It sold poorly at the time, although it was warmly praised by critics and other writers such as Hurston and Langston

Hughes. But it is recognized as one of the pivotal African American works of the period.

Confluence is as much a characteristic of *Cane* as it is of its creator. A highly innovative hybrid of prose and poetry, the book is divided into three sections. The first section is set in the South, in Georgia, and it concentrates on women, especially women whose thoughts, desires and behaviour set them at odds with the expectations of society. There is Karinthia who 'ripened too soon', experiencing her sexual awakening at the age of twelve. There is Becky, a woman destroyed by the bigotry of both black and white people. There are Carma, destroyed by male expectations, and Fern, a woman transfixed and worshipped by men who do not understand her. And there is Louise, who is loved by two men, one black and one white; when the two men fight over her, and the white man is stabbed, the black man is burned to death by a lynch mob. Punctuating their stories are poems written in a similarly rapt, incantatory style, marked by repetition and recurrent images of dusk, pines, cane and fire. The overall effect is haunting: this is a South that comes across to the reader as a dreamscape and a very real place of racial prejudice and violence, a romantic nightworld and a vibrant folk culture. Not the least of the achievements here is the way, like Larsen, Toomer weaves together intricate misunderstandings of race, sex and gender: the misrecognition of women as well as the mistreatment of black people, male and female. A similarly rich tapestry of different but interconnected themes characterizes the second section. Here, the scene drifts to the North, to Washington, DC. It begins with a lyric account of black settlement in the city, marked by more syncopated rhythms and harsher imagery of hard surfaces and nervous movement. It continues with a surreal portrait of Rhobert, a man sinking under the weight of his own poverty ('His house is a dead thing that weighs him down'). Following this, a series of intercalated poems and prose passages explores the dreams and the disintegrative impact of city life. Here, as in the first section, are men who rationalize their physical desires into idealized abstractions or cower in drink, daydreaming or sex to hide their fears and avoid commitment. Here, too, are women transfixed into virgins by men who do not understand them, wailing futilely against society or neuroticized by the tensions between their subconscious physical desires and their conscious conformity to the restrictive emotional codes that society imposes. This is a more brutally material, more deeply insecure world than the one evoked in the first section – all sense of folk culture and community has evaporated – but here, too, finally, is a society marked by racial conflict rather than confluence, without even the balm of custom to alleviate its more bigoted practices.

The final section of *Cane* was the first to be written, and it clearly has a more autobiographical base than the others. It describes how an educated African American from the North, called Ralph Kabnis, visits the South. Written partly in the form of a story, and partly in dramatic form, it shows him witnessing racial prejudice and violence, measuring the decline of the old ways and trades, and wondering if he could become the 'face' of the South and sing its songs. Frustrated in his search for a way of life, he ends by experiencing a dark night of the soul: a party in a cellar, full of drinking and sex, that offers him not even a moment of relief. Unlike Larsen, however, Toomer is not content to leave the reader on this dying fall. The third section, and *Cane* as a whole, ends with Kabnis crawling out of the cellar as the sun rises. 'Gold-glowing child,' he observes, 'it steps into the sky and sends a birth-song slanting down gray dust streets and sleepy windows of the southern town.' The hint of a new beginning, the hope of renewal, is slight perhaps, but it is still there. And it helps make the closing moments of *Cane* as much of a confluence, an innovative mix, as the rest of this extraordinary book: poised as it is on the cusp between darkness and light, despair and possible redemption. Toomer was never to write so well again. His later work bears the influence of the mystic Georgei I. Gurdjieff. Little of it could find a publisher. And what little has been published – noble as it sometimes is in its expression of Toomer's lifelong desire to transcend what he saw as the narrow divisions of race – is turgid and didactic to the point of tedium. The reputation of Jean Toomer rests on just one work. But, with that, it is secure. It is one of the many great American experiments.

Unlike Toomer, another significant figure in the New Negro movement, Arna Bontemps (1902–73), dedicated himself to the recovery of a specifically black history and culture. Born in Louisiana and raised in California, he accepted a teaching position in Harlem at the height of the Harlem Renaissance. Later, he was to work at Fisk University and the University of Illinois. Over the course of a long career, he was to author many works in different genres, portraying the lives, past and present, of African Americans. Collaborating with Langston Hughes, he produced, among many other books, several anthologies, *The Poetry of the Negro* (1949), *The Book of Negro Folklore* (1959) and *American Negro Poetry* (1963). Working as a ghost-writer with the blues musician and composer W. C. Handy, he wrote *Father of the Blues* (1941). With the proletarian radical writer Jack Conroy, he wrote a number of books for children, among them a tall tale entitled *The Fast Sooner Hound* (1942). The books he produced by himself were equally various. They included more than a dozen tales of the South, eventually collected in *The Old South: 'A Summer Tragedy' and Other Stories of the Thirties* (1973); a novel about a black jockey, *God Sends Sunday* (1931), that was turned into a successful musical, *St. Louis Woman* (1946), by Countee Cullen; poetry that, during the 1920s, was to win him several prizes in contest with other New Negro poets; and a history of the black race since Egyptian civilization, *The Story of the Negro* (1948). His two most distinguished works, however, express his lifelong commitment to the cause of black freedom through the retelling of two major slave revolts. One of them, *Drums at Dusk* (1939), describes the celebrated eighteenth-century black revolution on the island of Santo Domingo, led by Toussaint L'Ouverture. The other, and his finest work, transforms a slave revolt that took place in Virginia in 1800, led by Gabriel Prosser, into fiction. It is called *Black Thunder* (1936).

Bontemps began *Black Thunder* after he had come across a rich and apparently forgotten collection of narratives by former slaves at Fisk University. Using the few contemporary resources available to him, he then wrote the novel while living in the black urban community of Watts. When it was published, it was greeted with acclaim by a number of radical writers, some of them black like Langston Hughes and Margaret Walker, and some of them, like Jack Conroy, white. Reading the book now, it is easy to see why the book touched a nerve and granted Bontemps entry into radical literary circles. For it fuses historical facts and imaginative changes into a story of the struggle of liberation that reflected on both the scene of the fiction and the scene of writing. 'The times were hopeful,' a character reflects during the course of the narrative. The 'times' are, of course, those of slave society during the 1800s, disrupted as they were by the libertarian spirit of the new republic, egalitarian ideas imported from revolutionary France, and, not least, religious doubts – expressed by the Quakers and some Methodists, among others – about controlling the destiny, and the soul, of another man. But they are also those of the 1930s, when many artists and intellectuals believed in the imminent triumph of radical socialism brought about by revolution. To that extent, Bontemps was clearly think-ing of the environment he was writing in, as much as the one he was writing about, when he allowed one character – a white lawyer from Philadelphia – to observe that 'the revolution of the American proletariat would soon be something more than an idle dream'. 'Soon,' he muses, 'the poor, the despised of the earth would join hands around the globe: there would be no more serfs, no more planters, no more classes, no more dreams, no more slaves, only men.'

At the centre of the action is Gabriel Prosser, the instigator of the abortive revolt. He is described as 'a man of destiny'; he is not, however, allowed to dominate. No single character or voice is. Liberally using interior monologue, Bontemps explores a variety of consciousnesses, with multiple points of view. There are those, like Gabriel and a free black called Mingo, who are dedicated to the cause of freedom. There are other African American characters, like one called 'Old Ben', who vacillate, torn between defiance and dejection, the desire for liberty and simple cowardice or sentimentality. There is also one character, called Pharoah, based like so many of the others on an actual historical figure, who betrays the revolt and, when it is over, testifies against the others. Equally, among the white characters, the slave masters and drivers vary from the brutal to the paternalistic, and those who sympathize with the revolt number among them those who invoke 'the Rights of Man' and those who quote the Bible, immigrant French radicals, American liberals and Quakers. Each voice and view is allowed its opportunity; as, in a strategy that might be called cinematic, Bontemps rapidly cuts from one to another. And that strategy is crucial not only to the form but also to the meaning, the political conscience of the novel. The prevailing idea, deriving from the radical socialist aesthetics of the 1930s, is of the reality and power of mass consciousness. Bontemps is clearly expressing here the sense, the conviction, that change arises from the bottom up. What is known as Gabriel's revolt, he intimates, was not ultimately a one-man show, any more than any process or event in history is. It was not down to any one individual imposing his will on others and altering the course of events. Gabriel is a strong character, certainly, but he is strong (we are invited to believe) because he is the living symbol of the will of the people, black and white, to be free. And that will is never more firmly expressed than when

Gabriel goes to his death with pride and defiance, telling each of his comrades to 'die like a free man'. In doing so, he exemplifies most clearly the spirit of African American slaves, but he stands also for a more universal impulse towards liberty. 'Don't you want to be free?' That question is asked at least three times in the novel. First and last, the question is addressed to the black masses, past and present: which is why, perhaps, Langston Hughes took it as the title of the first play he wrote for the Harlem Suitcase Theatre in 1938. In between, though, it is addressed to all those suffering oppression, black and white, male and female, in America – and, for that matter, beyond.

Langston Hughes (1902–67) was the most eminent poet associated with what he later called 'the years of Manhattan's black Renaissance', 'when the Negro was in vogue'. He was not just a poet. He wrote novels (*Not Without Laughter* [1930], *Tambourines to Glory* [1958]), plays (collected in *Five Plays* [1963]), short stories (*The Ways of White Folks* [1934], *Laughing to Keep From Crying* [1952], *Something in Common* [1963]) and autobiography (*The Big Sea* [1940], *I Wonder as I Wander* [1956]). He wrote numerous essays on social, historical and musical subjects, and edited collections of black folklore, poetry and stories. In the latter part of his life he devoted his energies to writing the 'Simple Stories', involving an apparently slow, even dull-witted black character who always manages to outwit his antagonists (*Simple Speaks His Mind* [1950], *Simple Takes a Wife* [1953], *Simple Stakes a Claim* [1957], *Simple's Uncle Sam* [1965]). But it is for his poetry that he is likely to be remembered. His first collection of poems, *The Weary Blues*, was published in 1926, with the support of Carl Van Vechten. Other collections that appeared over the next forty years include *Fine Clothes to the Jew* (1927), *Harlem* (1942), *Montage of a Dream Deferred* (1951) and *Ask Your Mama* (1961). And all of it is marked by a powerful commitment to the notion of a separate and distinctive black identity, a sense of the shared presence of African Americans, that Hughes announced in his seminal essay 'The Negro Artist and the Racial Mountain' (1926). 'To my mind, it is the duty of the young Negro artist', Hughes wrote in this essay, 'to change through the force of his art that old whispering "I want to be white" hidden in the aspirations of his people, to "Why should I want to be white? I am a Negro – and beautiful".' This does not mean, Hughes said, that the black writer should simply idealize black life. 'We know we are beautiful,' he observed, 'And ugly too.' But it did mean that black writers should devote themselves to uncovering the power and glory of African American traditions, the 'heritage of rhythm and warmth' and 'incongruous humour that, so often, as in Blues, becomes ironic laughter mixed with tears'.

True to this formula, Hughes made black people his subject, especially 'low-down folks, the so-called common element'. His poetry shows him more interested in the ordinary men and women of the fields and streets, and in particular of Harlem, than in the black bourgeoisie – who, on the few occasions when they do appear in his work, are ''buked and scorned'. Like Whitman, Hughes's aim is clearly identification, imaginative empathy, with these people. He is, above all, a dramatic poet, speaking through a multiplicity of voices – a young schoolchild, perhaps ('Theme for English B'), a smart and sassy older woman ('Madam's Past History') or a dying man ('Sylvester's Dying Bed') – so as to capture the multiple layers, the pace, drive and variety, of black American life. Like Whitman, too, although in a much more specific sense, Hughes is a socially committed poet. 'The major aims of my work', he declared, 'have been to interpret and comment upon Negro life, and its relations to the problems of Democracy.' This commitment is most evident in the work that permits itself overt social comment: some of the poems written within a Marxist frame in the 1930s, say ('Christ in Alabama'), or, more generally, his bitter attacks on 'The lazy, laughing South / With blood on its mouth'. But it is just as powerful a shaping force in works dramatizing the petty frustrations and particular oppressions of individual black people ('Ballad of the Landlord'), their dreams of liberation ('Dream Variations') or their stony endurance ('Life is Fine'). 'I've been scarred and battered /', admits the narrator of one poem, 'Still Here', then adds, 'But I don't care! / *I'm still here!*'; and his one voice, defiant, resolute, even hopeful, speaks for a thousand others.

'Most of my . . . poems are racial in theme,' Hughes said; 'In many of them I try to grasp and hold some of the meanings and rhythms of jazz.' The latter remark suggests another, crucial way in which consciousness of the black tradition enters into his work. Hughes may have learned a great deal about free verse from Sandburg, Lindsay and, above all, Whitman: but he learned even more from African American music, and what he called its 'conflicting changes, sudden nuances, sharp and impudent interjections, broken rhythms . . . punctuated by . . . riffs, runs, breaks, and distortions'. 'Jazz is a heartbeat,' Hughes argued, 'its heartbeat is yours.' By 'jazz' Hughes nearly always meant black musical culture in general: jazz, as he saw it, was a vast sea 'that washes up all kinds of fish and shells and spume with a steady old beat, or off-beat'. That sea was the source of spirituals, work songs, field hollers and shouts, as it was of blues, gospel, ragtime and rock and roll. 'A few more years', he observes, 'and Rock and Roll will no doubt be washed back half forgotten into the sea of jazz.' In the meantime, it too could play its part in fostering an art of subversion: for the essence of jazz, Hughes believed, was that it was open-ended and improvisational and as such challenged the closed structures of the dominant white culture. Whether it assumed the shape of, say, jive or be-bop – offering 'a revolt against weariness in a white world, a world of subway trains and work, work, work' – or of blues – suggesting 'pain swallowed in a smile', resistance to the apparently irresistible – jazz for Hughes constituted an act of rebellion. Hughes's exploitation of black music takes many forms. Sometimes he uses the classic, three-line blues form ('Seven Moments in Love'); sometimes, as in 'Still Here', he employs fragments of blues themes and vocabulary; sometimes, as in 'The Weary Blues', he mixes classic with other forms. Elsewhere, as in a poem titled 'The Cat and the Saxophone', he tries to imitate the energy, the frenetic excitement of instrumental jazz. And in one of his most impressive works, *Montage of a Dream Deferred*, Hughes employs the free associations and abrupt rhythms of boogie-woogie and 'street poetry', rapping and jive-talk ('Oop-pop-a-da! / Skee! Daddle-de-do! / Be-bop!'), to create a verbal portrait of Harlem. His use of black religious music is less frequent and pervasive, but a poem like 'Fire' shows how he could turn to it to dramatize the spiritual side of his culture. 'Fire, / Fire, Lord! / Fire gonna burn my soul!' the poems begins, 'I ain't been good, / I ain't been clean – / I been stinkin' low-down, mean.' Spirituals or street poetry, be-bop or blues: whatever form Hughes utilizes, he demonstrates an intimate knowledge of its intricacies – 'The rhythm of life', he said, '/ Is a jazz rhythm', and this, in turn, is the rhythm of his poetry.

While emphasizing his commitment to black community and culture, though, Hughes was always willing to acknowledge his debt to certain white writers and, in particular, the author of *Leaves of Grass*. He saw no contradiction here, because what Whitman offered him above all was the example of self-emancipation and self-discovery. As Claude McKay observed of poets like Whitman: 'I could feel their race, their class, their roots in the soil, growing into plants, spreading and forming the backgrounds against which they were silhouetted.' 'I could not feel their reality without that,' McKay added. 'So likewise I could not realize myself writing without conviction.' The ways Hughes plays his variations on this American theme, singing his own 'Song of Myself', is suggested by two of his finest poems, 'I, Too' and 'The Negro Speaks of Rivers'. 'I, Too' involves a fairly clear echo of Whitman. 'I, too, sing America,' it begins:

> I am the darker brother.
> They send me to eat in the kitchen . . .
>
> . . .
>
> Tomorrow,
> I'll sit at the table
> When company comes . . .
>
> . . .
>
> They'll see how beautiful I am
> And be ashamed, –
>
> I, too, am America.

The poem plays beautifully on two themes. The first is the ancient, legendary theme of dispossession: the 'darker brother' is banished from the table of communion for a while but, growing strong, proud, confident of his beauty, he prepares to reclaim his rightful inheritance. And the second is the more recent American theme of the poet as democratic hero, the representative of his culture: not, however, in this case as it is but as it might and should be. Even more firmly and fiercely than Whitman, Hughes seems to declare, 'I project the history of the future'.

'The Negro Speaks of Rivers' is more concerned with the past than the future, the heritage that is the black American's special privilege and strength. 'I've known rivers,' its narrator reveals, 'I've known rivers ancient as the world and older than the flow of human blood in human veins. / My soul has grown deep like the rivers.' The poem then goes on to describe some of the rivers with which 'the Negro', or rather his spirit and his race, has been associated – the Euphrates, Congo, Nile and the Mississippi – before returning, like the river, to its beginnings: 'My soul has grown deep like the rivers.' As with Whitman in some of his more elegiac works ('Out of the Cradle Endlessly Rocking', for instance), Hughes uses a sonorous, flowing line here to create a sense of meditation, and incremental repetition ('I bathed . . . I built . . . I looked . . . I heard') to suggest the tones of the prophet, the tongue of the seer. The vision unfolded is at once accurately historical and elemental, mythical: since the rivers, as they are named in order, recall some of the civilizations the black race has helped build, while rehearsing the ancient idea that the same deep forces run through the body of the earth and the bodies of men and women. Knowing the rise and fall of cultures, black people have known the tale of time; they have seen once proud civilizations pass away and will doubtless see others follow in due course. Participating in the flow of waters 'ancient as the world', however, they also know something of the story of eternity: through their veins and those of the world course the same ceaseless currents, endowing them with both strength, the capacity to endure, and a kind of magic and majesty. 'Consider me, /' one of Hughes's other dramatic voices asks (in a poem actually entitled 'Consider Me'), 'Descended also / From the / Mystery.' Hughes's poems are always asking the reader to consider this, the mysterious essence of black life, as well as its jazzy surfaces. As in the best black music there is energy, sensuality, humour, certainly, but also that unique quality, soul.

Other poets roughly contemporary with Hughes shared a similar desire to voice the separateness of black culture. Notable among these were Sterling A. Brown (1901–89) and Gwendolyn Bennett (1902–81). Born in Texas, Bennett became a close friend and associate of Hughes and Hurston, Thurman and Countee Cullen when she moved to New York City. She collaborated with them on *Fire!!*, wrote poetry that was published in *Crisis*, *Opportunity* and other magazines, and became involved in the Federal Writers' Project. Her poetry is lyrical and intensely personal, and often preoccupied with the primary facts of love ('Advice' [1927]) and death ('Lines Written at the Grave of Alexander Dumas' [1927]). But a poem like 'Heritage' (1923) makes clear her fundamental commitment to composing a determinately black verse. 'I want to hear the chanting / Around a heathen fire / Of a strange black race,' she declares here. 'I want to feel the surging / Of my sad people's soul / Hidden by a minstrel smile.' In turn, 'To Usward' (1924) reveals a sense of solidarity with other black writers who shared a similar commitment. A celebration of all those who have 'songs to sing' – and, in particular, songs 'Of jungle heat and fires' and 'Negro lullabies' – it was written in honour of Jessie Fauset, on the publication of *There is Confusion*, a novel that uses the theme of the 'tragic mulatta' to explore the problems of black women. Unlike Bennett, Brown enjoyed widespread recognition during his lifetime. An influential scholar and anthologist, he helped shape perception of African American literature and subjects through such works as *Negro Poetry and Drama* (1938), *The Negro in American Fiction* (1938) and *The Negro Caravan* (1944). Editor of Negro Affairs for the

Federal Writers' Project from 1938 to 1940, and a researcher for the classic study of race, *An American Dilemma* (1944) by Gunnar Myrdal, he produced an extensive body of poetry, published in *Southern Road* (1932), *The Last Ride of Wild Bill* (1957) and *Collected Poems* (1980).

'I wanted to get an understanding of people, to acquire an accuracy in the portrayal of their lives,' Brown explained of his poetry, adding that there was 'a flavour, a color, a pungency of speech' in black language that offered him, he felt, the best way of getting at this understanding. So, like Hughes, Brown exploited African American idioms and cultural forms, wedding them with the free verse patterns of Whitman, Sandburg and Lindsay to evoke a sense of the extraordinary nature of supposedly ordinary black people – some of them known to the wider public, and some of them not. 'When de Saints Go Ma'ching Home' (1927), for example, celebrates the black blues guitarist Big Boy Davis using African American vernacular and jazzy rhythms to reproduce the reality and rhythms of his life. 'Ma Rainey' (1931) is a loving recreation both of the blues singer of the title and of the black community and culture she embodied and voiced. 'Strong Men' (1931), in turn, tells of all the anonymous ancestors who were enslaved 'to give a few gentlemen ease' and helped build the roads and lay the tracks for America, although they received no credit for it. Typically, it interlaces the long line of Whitman and Sandburg with echoes of black folk songs and spirituals to create a vision of the black past that now gives the black present strength. Other poems show a similarly rich confluence of traditions being used to get at an understanding of the black people who were Brown's ancestors and contemporaries. In 'Slim in Hell' (1932), for example, Brown draws on the tradition of the tall tale, stories about 'the colored man in heaven' and the myth of Orpheus to describe a suspiciously familiar version of the infernal regions. 'De place was Dixie / Dat I took for Hell,' Slim declares. To which Saint Peter responds, in exasperation, 'Where'n hell dja think Hell *was* / Anyhow?' Other poems use an elegiac or satirical mode, to consider, say, the example of those black heroes who fought for freedom ('Remembering Nat Turner' [1929]) or the triumphalist tone and terrible consequences of white racism ('Song of Triumph' [1980]). Always perceptible in his work is his fundamental belief in the tonic nature of black speech, its remedial and redemptive qualities: the way it could be used, he felt, to resist white oppression and restore black dignity. And driving it, continually, is the conviction he shared with others, like Hughes, that, as Brown himself put it once, 'art is a handmaiden to social policy'.

Not everyone shared that conviction, however. George Schuyler characteristic-ally insisted that 'the Aframerican' was 'subject to the same economic and social forces' that shaped 'the actions and thoughts of the white American'. 'It is sheer nonsense', he declared, 'to talk about "racial differences".' Few would have put it as categorically as that, perhaps. But there is a sense in which poets like William Stanley Braithwaite (1878–1962), Anne Spencer (1882–1975) and, above all, Countee Cullen (1903–46) found themselves inclining in the same direction. Braithwaite, for instance, remained committed throughout his life to the idea that poetry should be an expression of spiritual truth and beauty beyond the claims of politics or race.

Wary of any work he saw as polemical or didactic, he favoured traditional, lyrical voices in his influential annual *Anthology of Magazine Verse*, which began in 1913. In his criticism, he championed poets like Frost and Robinson, Dunbar and Cullen. And in his own poetry, published in *Lyrics of Love and Life* (1904), *House of Falling Leaves* (1908) and *Selected Poems* (1948), he showed the influence of such favourite writers as Keats and Wordsworth. Spencer, born Annie Bethel Scales, similarly preferred non-racial themes and traditional lyric forms. She could find, she confessed, 'no civilised articulation' for the things she hated, such as racial prejudice. So, using elaborate rhythmic patterns, highly wrought language and densely woven imagery, she explored the personal but also universal subjects of life and time ('Substitution' [1927]), love and peace ('For Jim, Easter Eve' [1949]), nature and beauty ('Lines to a Nasturtium' [1926]).

Countee Cullen is a slightly more complicated case. Publishing his most important collection of poems, *Color* (1925), when he was still young, he quickly became a significant figure in the New Negro movement. As literary editor of *Opportunity*, one of the two most important black periodicals of the 1920s, he also exercised considerable influence. Cullen did explore race in some of his work. A poem like 'Incident' (1924), for instance, recalls the first time when he was called 'nigger', when he 'was eight and very small'. 'From the Dark Tower' (1924) expresses the hope that black people 'shall not always plant while others reap'. The title piece in *The Black Christ, and Other Poems* (1929) recounts the lynching of a black youth for a crime he did not commit. Most interesting of all perhaps, 'Scottsboro, Too, Is Worth Its Song' (1934), subtitled '*A poem to American poets*', asks why no poets have written about one of the most notorious examples of racial injustice to occur in the 1930s. Cullen, however, was inclined to place his poems about his African American heritage in a kind of ghetto: in each of his first three collections, there is a section specifically entitled 'Color'. And even these poems, although *about* that heritage, are not determinately *of* it. 'What is Africa to me', begins one piece actually called 'Heritage' (1925): 'One *three centuries removed* / *From the scenes his fathers loved*, / *Spicy grove, cinnamon tree*, / *What is Africa to me?*' Cullen wanted, he said, to be 'a poet, not a Negro poet', adding elsewhere, 'the individual diversifying ego transcends the synthesising hue'. So, for the actual forms and language of his verse, he chose as his models poets like Keats and was largely content to follow Romantic convention. Sometimes the pain involved in his struggle always to sound non-racial, and usually to concentrate on non-racial subjects, breaks through the discreet surfaces of his work. 'My color shrouds me,' he admits in 'Heritage'; and in 'Yet Do I Marvel' (1925), he laments, 'Yet do I marvel at this curious thing: / To make a poet black and bid him sing!' But, as a rule, he refused to think or write in terms of a distinctive ethnic heritage. In response 'To Certain Critics' (1925) who had apparently questioned this refusal, he was quite adamant: 'never shall the clan / I', he insisted, 'Confine my singing to its ways / Beyond the ways of man'. For Cullen, evidently, his identity as black could and had to be cordoned off from the rest of his being and experience; and, in any event, it was more or less incompatible with his role as poet.

In the transitional generation of African American poets following Hughes and Cullen, the most articulate spokesmen for Cullen's position were Melvin B. Tolson (1898–1966) and Robert Hayden (1913–80). Tolson, whose first significant poem, 'Dark Symphony', was published in 1939 and first collection, *Rendezvous with America*, appeared in 1944, certainly identified himself as 'a black poet', with an equal emphasis on both those terms. He wrote of Africa (*Libretto for the Republic of Liberia* [1953]) and absorbed some of the bluesy, oral quality of African American storytelling. However, 'as a black poet', Tolson insisted, he had absorbed the 'Great Ideas of the Great White World' and had roots 'in Africa, Europe, and America'. And as poet, it is clear, he came under the spell, the almost exclusive determination, first of Whitman and then of writers like Eliot and Tate. The result of that spell, or debt, and the polyglot sense of his own identity, was poems like *Harlem Gallery: Book 1, The Curator* (1965). Designed as the first in a series of five volumes representing stages in the African American diaspora, *Harlem Gallery* is determinedly Eliotic: a dense, intricate exercise in literary allusion and cultural reference, linguistically precise, stylistically complex. In a preface to this long epic poem, another, white poet Karl Shapiro claims that Hayden 'writes and thinks in Negro'. But other, black writers, associated with the Black Aesthetic movement, were surely closer to the mark – if unfair about his motives – when they accused Tolson of writing just for a white audience. In *Harlem Gallery*, the other four books of which were never completed, Hayden writes and thinks in a Modernist vein that remains, for the most part, racially uninflected. This is a poem about Harlem, not of it.

Robert Hayden claimed, in a manner similar to Cullen then later Tolson, that he was 'opposed to the chauvinistic and doctrinaire'. He saw 'no reason why a Negro poet should be limited to "racial utterance"', he said, or why his writing should be 'judged by standards different from those applied to the work of other poets'. However, like Cullen and Tolson again, that did not stop him from exploring racial themes. 'The Black Spear', for example, written in 1942 and published in part in *Selected Poems* (1966), is a memorable attempt to explore the African American presence in American history. Writing in response to the invitation in *John Brown's Body* (1928) by Stephen Vincent Benét (1898–1943) for a black writer to produce the seminal 'black epic', Hayden used material he had unearthed while working for the Federal Writers' Project here to produce a montage of visions and voices. Despite that, Hayden was essentially a traditional poet, uninclined to reinvent black traditions or rehearse the particularities of black life. As his *Collected Poems* (1985) shows, his work – published over forty years, beginning with *Heart-Shape in the Dust* (1940) – is written mostly in formal metres. Even when he uses free verse, it is a free verse that is markedly iambic. And his subjects include the perennial ones of personal memory ('Those Winter Sundays') and the conflict between the impulses towards life and death ('The Swimmer'). He can, certainly, dramatize the sufferings of black people with clarity and power ('Night. Death. Mississippi') and their 'dream of the beautiful, needful thing – known as freedom' ('Frederick Douglass'). But, even here, he is not slow to relate 'the news from Selma to Saigon', or to see a connection between the black victims of American history and the victims of history generally, of whatever complexion. 'From the corpse woodpiles, from the ashes / and staring pits of Dachau, / Buchenwald they come – /' he says in 'From the Corpse Woodpiles, From the Ashes', 'From Johannesburg, from Seoul, / Their struggles are all horizons, / Their deaths encircle me.' There is little place here for the perception of a distinctive inheritance of suffering, or its transcendence.

Opposed to this position, in turn, in this transitional generation is Gwendolyn Brooks (1917–2000). Born in Kansas, but 'a Chicagoan' as she called herself in terms of upbringing, sentiment and commitment, Brooks published her first collection, *A Street in Bronzeville*, in 1945. Prior to that, she had published more than a hundred poems in her weekly column in the *Chicago Defender*. Following that, she published numerous collections: among them, *Annie Allen* (1949), *Maud Martha* (1953), *Bronzeville Boys and Girls* (1956) and *In the Mecca* (1968). In her early work, admittedly, she was rather like Tolson. For, while her main subject was black life, her style was mannered, academic and sometimes difficult. Much of this poetry is traditional, with regular stanzas and rhyme schemes, archaic diction and inverted syntax. Even at its best, such writing often offers a disconcerting contrast between form and content, the elegant phrases and cadences and the violent, vivid experiences being described. Gradually, however, as Brooks absorbed herself more in the lives of urban blacks, particularly of the South Side of Chicago, her style became looser, more idiomatic, incorporating such diverse influences as free verse, black vernacular and the blues. A catalyst for change, in particular, was her association with the Black Arts movement in the 1960s. With the encouragement of younger poets, and especially those like Haki R. Madhubuti (Don Lee) involved in the Organization of Black American Culture in Chicago, Brooks developed a more unequivocal, committed stance. She became one of the most visible articulators of 'the black aesthetic'. This reinforced her lifelong interest in social issues, in street life and supposedly insignificant, everyday characters like Annie Allen trying out her hat in a milliner's shop or De Witt Williams 'on his way to Lincoln Cemetery' or Satin-Legs Smith trying to decide what sharp suit to wear on Sundays. It honed her style, making it flintier, edgier. And it prompted her to be more challenging, provocative: because, as she put it in 1967, 'Art hurts. Art urges voyages.'

'It is my privilege', Brooks said, 'to present Negroes not as curios but as people.' Like Hughes, she often adopts the voice of the poor and dispossessed ('the mother'), but she can just as easily assume that of the more articulate and self-conscious ('Negro Hero'). There is little sense of victimization in her work, even though many of her subjects are social victims: these are people who manage to get by, who have achieved the dignity of survival. There is, however, an almost overwhelming sense of injustice, inequality and anger in poems like 'Riot', and a sharp perception of the gap between black and white that sometimes leads, as in say 'The Lovers of the Poor', to crafty satire at the expense of white liberals. A hard, stony idiom, taut syntax and primitive, urgent rhythms are all harnessed to the recreation of black street life: a recreation that combines sympathy for the oppressed with a sardonic appreciation of the sources of their oppression. 'We Real Cool' is exemplary in this respect. Taking up the voice of some black streetwise kids, Brooks catches their nervous self-confidence, their edgy slickness and smartness, and the forces simmering just below the surface of their lives threatening any moment to boil over and destroy them. 'We real cool. We / Left school,' begins this jazzy litany of disaffection, recording all the habits and routines these kids adopt to assure themselves that, if nothing else, they can enjoy the security of the disaffected. 'We / Jazz June /', it concludes; 'We / Die soon.' There can be few tougher, truer accounts of what it feels like to be young, poor and black in America.

Like so many African American writers of this and later periods – like so many American writers generally – Brooks was influenced by African American musical forms, and in particular by the blues. The blues has been described by Ralph Ellison as 'an autobiographical chronicle of personal catastrophe expressed lyrically'. Other writers, James Baldwin for example, have tended to see it not so much as a personal experience as a communal or species experience: a sound expressive of the 'bleeding, . . . cracked-open heart' to be heard everywhere in black life. Either way, it articulates what Ellison has called 'an impulse to keep the painful detail and episodes of a brutal existence alive in one's aching consciousness' and 'to transcend it, not by the consolation of philosophy but by squeezing from it a near-tragic, near-comic lyricism'. And, as a form, it emerged at the turn of the twentieth century. Its grounding influences were many. Socially and historically, those influences included the conditions of Southern farms and plantations where black singing flourished, the experience of a nominal freedom that brought with it continued racial discrimination and little economic success, and, later, the impact of the Great Migration northwards. Culturally and musically, they included the harmonic and structural devices and vocal techniques from work songs and spirituals. Like those earlier forms, blues involved a compulsively rhythmic sound that relied on patterns of call and response. Unlike some of them, however, it was decidedly secular in tone; unlike all of them, the blues was usually sung not by a chorus but by a single voice accompanied by one or more instruments. The creation, like other, older African American musics, of a people often unable to read or write, the blues was passed on orally. When songwriter and bandleader W. C. Handy (1873–1958), often called 'the father of the blues', began to transcribe the blues songs he heard, and compose some of his own, those songs existed in a variety of stanzaic forms. The text of a blues stanza might consist of one line repeated twice (AA), one line repeated twice or three times with a rhyming line to complete the thought expressed in the first line (AAB, AAAB), one line followed by a rhyming line sung twice (ABB), or a number of other patterns. What characterized all blues forms, however, was a fluid sense of measure and the feeling, the impulse, described by Baldwin and Ellison. As the blues began to be recorded in the 1920s, the AAB pattern tended to become the predominant form. Not only that, with the original performance context in the community removed, the traditional, often non-thematic or associative texts were replaced by more deliberately thematic ones. There was more trace of an author determining the tone and content of the song, although different performers still allowed themselves plenty of room for manoeuvre, even reinvention.

Sometimes blues songs are about just that, the blues. 'Good, mornin', blues,' begins a song composed by Jimmy Rushing (1907–72) then sung and reinvented by Huddie ('Leadbelly') Ledbetter (1885–1949), 'Blues, how do you do?' Even here, though, the reasons for the blues usually emerge as the familiar ones: loving 'someone, when that someone don't love you' ('Down-Hearted Blues' by Albert Hunter [1897–1984] and Louis Armstrong [1897–1972]), love and loss when, for instance, 'mah baby, he done lef' dis town' ('St. Louis Blues' by W. C. Handy), the pain of having 'to keep moving' – because, perhaps, as a song by Robert Johnson (1912–38) puts it, 'there's a hellhound on my trail'. The blues describes a world of mean women and hard-hearted men. 'My man don't love me / Treats me oh so mean, /' declares one song, 'Fine and Mellow', made famous by Billie Holiday (1915–59), 'He's the lowest man / That I've ever seen.' 'Now she's the meanest woman that I've ever seen, /' echoes a song credited to Ishmon Bracey (1901–70), 'And when I asked for water give me gasoline.' Sometimes the songs refer to specific historical events and places. 'Backwater Blues' by Bessie Smith (1895–1937) deals with a famous Mississippi flood of the 1920s. 'Beale Street Blues' by W. C. Handy celebrates the main black street in Memphis, Tennessee. There are many blues texts about the great migration north. 'I left my babe in Mississippi picking cotton down on her knees, /' begins one associated with Tommy McLennan, 'She says, "If you get to Chicago, please write me a letter if you please".' 'Going to Chicago, sorry that I can't take you, /' begins another, 'There's nothing in Chicago that a monkey woman can do.' Other times the songs celebrate the strength and sexual needs of women ('I need plenty grease in my frying pan 'cause I don't want my meat to burn') or men ('Yeah, you know I'm a hoochie coochie man / Every-body knows I'm here'). There are even some songs, such as 'Prove It On Me Blues' by Ma Rainey (1886–1939), that celebrate love, or lust, between women ('I went out last night with a crowd of my friends, / They must've been women, 'cause I don't like no men'). More often, though, the blues sadly, passionately recalls what one song names 'trouble in mind' ('Trouble in Mind' by Richard M. Jones [1889–1945]), and another 'trouble in my mind' ('In the House Blues' by Bessie Smith). More often, too, that trouble is historicized only in the sense that it springs from the history of a people: experiences that are determinately racial in origin, even though the feelings they engender can and do go on to touch many others of other races. 'Don't the moon look lonesome shining through the trees?' asks one blues song, 'Sent for You Yesterday' by Jimmy Rushing (1903–72). 'How long, how long, has that evenin' train been gone?' asks another, 'How Long Blues' by Leroy Cass (1905–35): 'Heard the whistle blowin', couldn't see no train, / 'Way down in my heart I had an achin' pain.' Questions, declarations like these commemorate ex-periences that are at once deeply personal and communal. And they have offered a wealthy resource, of structure and rhythm, theme and tone, to many writers – most of them African American, but by no means all.

Among those who were affected by the blues, and black cultural and musical forms, were some other African American writers of the transitional generation writing mostly in prose: Dorothy West (1907–98), Ann Petry (1911–97), Margaret

Walker (1915–98) and Richard Wright (1908–60). West began her career as a friend of the leading figures of the Harlem Renaissance. Then, in the years of the Depression, she began the literary quarterly *Challenge*. The magazine failed in 1937, after three years, but, undeterred, West then began *New Challenge*. A co-editor was Richard Wright, and Wright published here his influential 'Blueprint for Negro Writing' (1937), in which he declared his independence from bourgeois literary forms. A Marxist conception of reality and society, he argued, offered 'the maximum degree of freedom in thought and feeling . . . for the Negro writer'. West herself became uneasy about the association of *New Challenge* with a strict Communist Party line. Nevertheless, under her editorship the magazine encouraged and published pieces that explored the terrible conditions of the black working class. Many of West's own short stories were published in the *New York Daily News*. Her most notable single achievement, however, was her novel, *The Living is Easy* (1948), a dramatic investigation of the insularity, snobbery and shallowness of the black bourgeoisie of New England, whom West called the 'genteel poor'. At the centre of the story is a powerful female character, Cleo Judson, an unscrupulous, scheming woman who brings ruin on herself and those members of her family who allow themselves to fall under her control. A strong black female character of a very different kind stands at the centre of Ann Petry's most memorable work, *The Street* (1946), which was the first novel by an African American woman to sell more than a million copies. Lutie Johnson, as she is called, fights desperately to make a decent living for herself and her son on the mean streets of the inner city. She knows that her body is a spectacle to the men who have economic power over her, that she is the object of male sexual desire and exploitation. And, using a mixture of naturalism and dream, Petry shows Lutie struggling with that knowledge – and the problem of being a woman as well as poor and black. In other novels, Petry turned her attention to the hypocrisies of rural New England (*Country Place* [1947]) and to the tragic relationship between a black man and a white woman (*The Narrows* [1953]). But the driving concern of most of her work was what she called a desire to show black people as 'a sturdy, indestructible, wonderful part of America, woven into its heart and into its soul'.

Margaret Walker had a career that extended from the last days of the Harlem Renaissance in the 1930s to the Black Arts movement of the 1960s. Born in Alabama, the daughter of a minister, Walker moved to Chicago, where she became a member of the Works Progress Administration, studied at the University of Chicago, and became a member of the Southside Writers Group led by Richard Wright. Walker was later to end her friendship and collaboration with Wright, describing her reasons for doing so in *Richard Wright: Daemonic Genius* (1986). Before that, however, they enjoyed what Walker called a 'rare and once-in-a-lifetime association'. Wright read and advised Walker on her poetry. And, even after Wright moved to New York in the 1930s, Walker helped Wright with the research for his novel *Native Son*, sending him newspaper clippings about Robert Nixon, a young black man accused of rape in Chicago who partly inspired Wright's portrait of Bigger Thomas, the novel's protagonist. Even before Walker's first book of poetry, *For My People*, was published in 1942, she had won national attention for her work: the title poem, for example, had been published in Chicago five years earlier. And with its publication her reputation was secured. 'For My People', in particular, was acclaimed as a significant piece for African Americans. Deploying the long line of Whitman here, and the cadences learned from her preacher father and the rhythms of the new American poetry encountered in Chicago, Walker sang, as she put it, 'for my people everywhere'. Mixing piety with prophecy, she also combined commemoration of the black past with lively anticipation of the future. 'Let a new earth arise,' she concluded the poem, 'Let the martial songs be written, let the dirges disappear. Let a race of men now rise and take control.'

Despite the success of *For My People*, Walker did not publish anything else for over twenty years. Her novel, *Jubilee*, appeared in 1966. Based, Walker explained, on the tales of her great-grandmother told to her by her grandmother, it tells the story of Vyry, the child of a white plantation owner and his black mistress. To the extent that the book is built around the seminal events of Southern history – the days of the old slave order, the Civil War and Reconstruction – *Jubilee* replicates the structure of the traditional plantation romance. To the extent that it tells of one powerful woman in particular, committed to her own passionate needs and set of values, it recollects one famous version of plantation romance in particular, *Gone With the Wind* by Margaret Mitchell. But this is a radical rewriting of plantation romance, and the myths of black and white womanhood underwritten by Mitchell's novel. In her revisionist account of the Southern past, Walker exposes the rigid barriers of race, gender and class that scarred slave society and were perpetuated after the Civil War. And the dramatic setpieces here tend to be incidents of racial violence and oppression rather than the traditional tableaux of, say, the banquet, the wedding party and the hunt ball. At the centre of all this is an intelligent, energetic young woman. Unlike Scarlett O'Hara, however, this young woman is born black and a slave. Dreaming 'confused dreams in which she struggled to be free', Vyry has to deal with a confinement, chains that are all too literal and brutal; but her will and determination are never defeated. Neither is her belief not only in herself but in human nature. 'I don't believe the world is full of peoples what hates everybody,' Vyry declares towards the end of *Jubilee*. 'I know lots of times folks doesn't know other folks,' she adds, 'and they gits to thinking crazy things, but when you gits up to people and gits to know them, you finds out they's got kind hearts and tender feelings just like everybody does.' This is a book that preaches not so much revolution as the imperative of black resistance and the possibility of white redemption. As such, it helped to initiate a new tradition in tales about the South.

Like Margaret Walker, Richard Wright was born in the South, in Natchez, Mississippi. His childhood was spent in poverty. His formal education ended when he left junior high school. Worse still, as he reveals in the first of his two autobiographical volumes, *Black Boy* (1945), he was denied a sense of his own humanity and identity as he grew up. 'Not only had the southern whites not known me,' he explained in retrospect, 'but, more important still, as I had lived in the South I had not had the chance to learn who I was.' Moving to Memphis in 1925, he survived by working at a variety of odd jobs. Away from work, he began to read voraciously, people like H. L. Mencken, Theodore Dreiser, Sinclair Lewis and Sherwood Anderson. 'These writers seemed to me to feel that America could be shaped nearer to the hearts of those who lived in it,' Wright declared in *Black Boy*. 'And it was out of the novels and stories and articles, out of the emotional impact of imaginative construction of heroic or tragic deeds, that I felt touching my face a tinge of warmth from an unseen light.' Following that light, and full of hope, Wright travelled north to Chicago in 1927. 'I dreamed of going north and writing books, novels,' Wright remembered. 'The North symbolised for me all that I had not felt and seen; it had no relation whatever to what actually existed,' Like so many others involved in the Great Migration, Wright had his dreams of a better life shattered, encountering only new forms of racial oppression and economic deprivation when he went northwards. He did, however, find comradeship in the John Reed Club and in the Communist Party, which he joined in 1936. That comradeship was short-lived, perhaps. Within a year, he had broken with the party because of its attempts to control his intellectual and creative freedom. But he did continue to work with others, black and white, of similar social and political commitment. 'The ideological unity of Negro writers and the alliance of that unity with all the progressive ideas of our day', he wrote in 'Blueprint for Negro Writing', 'is the primary prerequisite for collective work.' So, as well as editing *New Challenge* with Dorothy West, he wrote proletarian poetry for *New Masses* and *Partisan Review*; he served as a correspondent for the *Daily Worker*; and well up to the publication of *Twelve Million Black Voices* (1941), an illustrated folk history of African Americans, he tried to work out the relationship between the techniques of fiction and the tenets of Marxism.

For Wright, the best way of working out that relationship was in his own fiction. Even before moving to New York City in 1937, he had written most of his novel *Lawd Today*, which was published posthumously in 1963. And in 1938 his first book, *Uncle Tom's Children*, was published. A set of four novellas set in the Jim Crow South, the book casts an ironic light on its own title by showing a series of protagonists becoming increasingly rebellious – less and less accommodating to white demands – as they find the collective means to resist. 'I wanted to try to build a bridge of words between me and the world outside, that world which was so distant and elusive that it seemed unreal,' Wright recalled in the second volume of his autobiography, *American Hunger* (1977). And bricks for that bridge were discovered not only in certain systems of thought he found congenial, particularly the Marxist analysis of society and the Freudian system of psychology, but in literary naturalism. 'All my life had shaped me for realism, the naturalism of the modern novel,' he wrote. Of the African American folk tradition he was less certain. In *Black Boy*, he was to talk of 'the cultural barrenness of black people', 'the essential bleakness of black life in America', which he attributed to the fact that, as he put it, 'Negroes had never been allowed to catch the full spirit of Western civilisation, . . . they lived somehow in it but not of it'. For him, identity was a social construct, cultural not natural: it had to be 'won, struggled, and suffered for'. And, just as he had been denied the chance to learn who he was while he stayed in the South, so, he felt, African Americans had been denied a similar knowledge. The cruellest blow white society dealt them was to exclude them from a sense of fully being in the world. Still, that did not stop Wright from believing, with fierce pride, that he had made a self, made himself. Together, *Black Boy* and *American Hunger* constitute one of the great retellings of the American myth of personal reinvention, the making of an identity. And it did not stop him, either, from responding with sensitivity to the speech and sounds of black culture. In his fiction, in particular, Wright's feeling for the pain and pathos of black life – his sense that living for blacks, in a world they never made, is 'like living in a dream, the reality of which might change at any moment' – gives to his work the resonance, the melancholy residue, of the blues.

Despite the success of *Uncle Tom's Children*, Wright was uneasy about its potential for sentiment. It was, he suspected, a little too like the work the title of which it parodically echoed, *Uncle Tom's Cabin*: one that 'even bankers' daughters could read and weep and feel good about'. So, he resolved that his next fiction would be so 'hard and deep' that readers 'would have to face it without the consolation of tears'. The result was his most important book, *Native Son* (1940). Set in the black ghetto of the South Side of Chicago, it presents a protagonist who would deny any attempt to see him as a figure of pathos. Bigger Thomas kills two women, one white and one black. The first killing is an accident but, recalling the pivotal murder in *An American Tragedy* by Theodore Dreiser, it is seen as an accident waiting to happen. It issues out of the fear that is the emotional condition of Bigger's life; it is seen as the product not of will but of circumstance and the desperate violence it engenders. And the second, more deliberate killing follows from this. Waiting in prison for his trial, Bigger feels for the first time a sense of freedom: because, he believes, he has broken out of the prison of himself. Previously, there had been 'two worlds' for him, 'something the *world* gave him and some-thing he *himself* had; something spread out in *front* of him and something spread out in *back*'. 'Never in all his life,' he senses, 'with this black skin of his, had the two worlds, thought and feeling, will and mind, aspiration and satisfaction, been together; never had he felt a sense of wholeness.' Now, he begins to feel it. So, despite the attempts of his Communist lawyer Max to move him from a sense of identity built on 'hate', 'resistance and defiance', to one founded on 'hope', a recognition of others similarly suffering, he cannot do so. He cannot deny what he sees as the logic of his actions, the imperative of violence. He lacks the social consciousness, the capacity for articulation, that Max requires of him. All he can say, and it is much, is, 'what I killed for, I am!'

Native Son is a story that brilliantly combines intense involvement with inter-rogation. The reader shares the fear, the pulsating terror of the protagonist, can understand the reasons why Bigger revels in his violence but can also see exactly how and why he is in error. It also mixes naturalism with the Gothic, even surreal. The irreality of Bigger's life, on the shadowy edges of white society, lends a dreamlike quality to many of his experiences. The constant terror he feels, surrounded by circumstances that vacillate between the threatening and the baffling, makes the streets he travels through seem both naturalistically mean and supernaturally eerie. And Chicago, as Bigger moves through its dark tenements frightened by the whiteness of the snow, takes on the qualities not only of the gritty urban landscapes described by Dreiser or James T. Farrell but of the unreal cities of Hawthorne, Melville and, above all, Poe. Standing at the narrative centre, although by no means limiting the narrative perspective, is a character who gradually assumes multiple dimensions, several shades of meaning. Bigger is 'a scared colored boy from Mississippi', as his lawyer calls him. He is a modern instance, a product of certain racial, social and economic practices. He is a historical paradigm, in that Wright clearly asks us to connect the paths of 'hate' and 'hope' to the larger, historic possibilities of fascism and socialism, the black nationalist movement and internationalism. He is even a classic American hero, to the extent that the 'two worlds' between which he is divided recall the two that have divided many other American protagonists, black and white – and which have been traditionally figured as the wilderness and the clearing. All of which is by way of saying that *Native Son* is as rich in meaning as it is in terms of narrative medium. A fiction burning with a fierce sense of racial and social injustice, it is also a major historical novel and a narrative fully and provocatively in the American grain. Bigger may finally lack the 'words', the capacity properly to articulate and so understand his plight. Utterly the reverse is true of his creator who, in finding precisely the right words, wrote one of the most complex yet coherent works about the indelible connection between where and who we are – our being in the world and our knowledge of ourselves.

Following the publication of *Native Son*, Wright left the United States for Mexico. Then, in 1946, he moved to Paris, where he spent the rest of his life. In Paris, he became associated with Jean-Paul Sartre, Albert Camus and Simone de Beauvoir. They may have influenced his gravitation towards forms of existentialism noticeable in his 1953 novel *The Outsider*, about the search of a self-conscious black intellectual for identity. Other fiction followed: *Savage Holiday* (1954) and *The Long Dream* (1958). So did works of non-fiction that placed social oppression in a global context, linking racism in America to colonialism in Africa and Asia: *Black Power* (1954), *The Color Curtain* (1956) and *White Man Listen!* (1957). The move towards black nationalism in many of these later works was to attract the Black Aesthetic writers of the 1960s, who claimed Wright as a favoured ancestor. What they valued in these works, and in another way in *Native Son*, was what they saw as Wright's militancy: his willingness, even eagerness, to use art as a weapon. That militancy was and is undeniably there. 'A Negro writer', Wright had written as early as 1937 in 'Blueprint for Negro Writing', 'must learn to view the life of a Negro living in New York's Harlem or Chicago's South Side with the consciousness that one-sixth of the earth's surface belongs to the working class.' This meant, he explained, that 'a Negro writer must create in his readers' minds a relationship between a Negro woman hoeing cotton in the South and the men who loll in

the wilderness; there was an emphasis on action, Progress and the blessings of Manifest Destiny; and the settings were appropriately epic, with vast, wild, open spaces. The dime novel operated at the level of fantasy, where conflicts that could not be resolved in the real world could find appropriate resolution. It celebrated the self-reliance, natural nobility and individuality of a modern American whose daring actions confirmed the inevitable onward march of his nation. When the writer Edward Judson (1823–86), known by his pseudonym Ned Buntline, discovered William F. Cody in Nebraska in 1869 and later that year dramatized him as 'Buffalo Bill, the King of the Border Men', a story published serially in the *New York Weekly*, the Western dime novel had found its most influential icon. Prentiss Ingraham (1843–1904) followed Buntline with more than a hundred 'Buffalo Bill' novels, nine of them written in 1892 alone. This tidal wave of fiction, working together with Buffalo Bill's own immensely popular 'Wild West Show', helped confirm the formulaic character of the Western and a dominant literary identity for the West and the Western hero – the one a place of sublime landscapes and splendid adventure, the other a splendid adventurer. And, in the first half of the twentieth century, three novels in particular were to underwrite the romance of the West, and, in the process, acquire enormous popularity. They were *The Virginian* (1902) by Owen Wister (1860–1938), *Riders of the Purple Sage* (1912) by Zane Grey (1872–1939) and *Shane* (1949) by Jack Schaefer (1907–91).

Owen Wister, who was born in Pennsylvania, wrote *The Virginian* after he had travelled to Wyoming to improve his health. This rejuvenating experience encouraged him to construct a moral geography in which the East represented custom and culture and the West energy and individualism. Wister, himself a member of the Eastern elite, was torn between these opposites – which clearly mirrored the opposing elements in the historical American dialectic of wilderness and civilization. And in his portrait of the Virginian he created a synthesis, to illustrate the claim made in the novel that 'the creature we call a *gentleman* lies deep in the hearts of thousands that are born without chance to master the outward graces of the type'. The mythic status of the Virginian is emphasized by the fact that he is given no name: he is purely and simply, as the subtitle puts it, 'a horseman of the plains'. Although nominally a cowboy, he is rarely seen doing cowboy work. The narrative revolves around incidents intended to prove his courage and nobility, and a romantic plot in which his innate gentility enables him to woo and win a young, cultured schoolteacher from Vermont. The narrator, who arrives from the East in the opening chapter, supplies a suitably heroic perspective, as he records, in awe and wonder, the epic stature and skills of this man who is at once a rugged individualist and a perfect gentle knight. And, in the closing sequence, this hero of the West is also seen to be a hero of America. 'With a strong grip on many enterprises', he marries the schoolteacher and becomes an entrepreneur, so contributing his vitality, energy and natural morality to the onward march of Progress. 'If this book be anything more than an American story,' Wister declared in the Preface, 'it is an expression of American faith.' It was an expression of faith that touched many readers. It sold more than 50,000 copies in just two months and helped determine the character of the mainstream Western hero, as a romantic individualist, and of the mainstream Western story, as an epic of freedom, Progress and Manifest Destiny.

A more prolific writer than Wister, Zane Grey also grew up in comfortable circumstances in the East and became an enthusiast of the West after a restorative trip there, to the Grand Canyon. In his fiction, the Western wilderness becomes a force that leads to redemption. The typical plot involves a jaded and perhaps frail member of Eastern society travelling westward and there experiencing renewal. He is revitalized and reoriented towards a new set of values that bear a close resemblance to social Darwinism, the ethic of the survival of the fittest. So, in *Riders of the Purple Sage*, which rivals *The Virginian* for popularity among classic Westerns, the man whom the wilderness makes strong and independent is Bern Venters. Many things happen to him, as he experiences the rugged wildness of canyon country and encounters various adventures. But everything is summed up by one simple statement: Venters 'had gone away a boy', from the East, the reader is told, '– he had returned a man'. A man is what the eponymous hero of *Shane* already is, when he appears right at the beginning of the story. 'He rode into our valley in the summer of '89,' the opening sentence declares. Immediately, he is given the mythic status of a man who does not even have to be named, set in the epic vastness of the West (he can be seen from 'several miles away', we are told two sentences later), and associated with an elegiac moment, the closing days of the frontier. There is the same awe in the narrative voice as there is in *The Virginian*: this time because the narrator is recalling a period when he was 'a kid . . . , barely topping the backboard of father's old chuck-wagon'. And the story itself unfolds with the simplicity and inevitability of myth, as the narrator recalls how Shane defended his family, and the surrounding homesteaders, against the greed and violence of a cattle baron. Shane seems not so much a knight as a natural saint, as he uses his strength and his skills to protect the settlers and, in the end, kill those who would drive them off their land. At the end, having completed his mission, he rides off wounded into exile, never to be seen again. He has made the valley safe for Progress.

The mass production and circulation of popular myths of America took another step in 1895, when a magazine publisher called Frank A. Munsey decided to revamp one of his publications, *Argosy*, in two distinct ways. He turned it into a publication devoted to fiction and designed for adult readers; and he decided to have it printed on rough wood-pulp paper, which was much less expensive than the smooth paper stock standard for periodicals at the time. The conversion to wood pulp enabled Munsey to print and distribute a greater number of copies of *Argosy* and his other magazines. And the rewards were immediate. By 1900, *Argosy* had a circulation of more than 80,000 a month; by 1910, it was up to 250,000. Rivals soon brought out pulp magazines of their own; and the pulps generally became the medium for popular fiction, including Westerns. One pulp periodical in particular, *Western Story*, was the main descendant of Western dime novels when they died out in the 1920s. It did much to confirm the character of the Western and the Western hero, not least because its editors demanded stories with predictable plots and stereotypical characters. Other pulp magazines devoted to the Western genre arose and flourished. Popular 'slick' periodicals, such as the *Saturday Evening Post*, featured Western fiction. And writers like Grey and Max Brand (1892–1944), the author of a prodigious number of cowboy stories (such as *Destry Rides Again* [1930]), ensured that the general popularity of the Western, as a myth of American progress, continued to be sustained. Illustrating that popularity is the extraordinary career of Louis L'Amour (1910?–88), a self-taught scholar of Western history from North Dakota. During the course of a long career, he produced two hundred novels and fourteen books of short stories, all on the West. By the time of his death, those works had sold no fewer than 182,000,000 copies.

Among the other genres popular in dime novels were detective stories. From the 1870s on, stories of street life in New York City, Philadelphia and elsewhere came into fashion, and soon afterwards the mass-audience tale of detection emerged. 'Old Sleuth, the Detective' was published in *Fireside Companion* in 1872 and was soon followed by many other fictional investigators. Not all of them were men; successful series featured such female sleuths as Round Kate and the Western Lady Detective. But the most popular of them was Nick Carter, whose career spanning two decades of publication began in 1886 in *New York Weekly*. These dime-novel detectives offered little in the way of character complexity or development; they were, for the most part, narrative ciphers, convenient vehicles for carrying a plot full of action and adventure to its inevitable conclusion. Contrivances though they were, however, they signalled the beginning of the transference of the hero from the wide open spaces of the West to the cavernous streets of the city. Following on from them, the detective in American twentieth-century fiction would slowly supplant the cowboy as a mythic embodiment of national values: an urban individualist whose commitment to his own code was more internalized, more a matter of manoeuvring his way within the labyrinth of society rather than outside it. From 1915, prototypical detective stories also began to appear in the pulp magazines, the first being a conversion of a dime novel thriller, *Nick Carter*, which, in addition to the eponymous hero, featured tales about other sleuths. In this genre, as in the others, pulps soon replaced dime novels and story-paper weeklies as the staple source of cheap fiction. So, by the late 1920s, dime novels and weeklies were virtually extinct. Prior to that, in 1920, H. L. Mencken and George Jean Nathan had founded a pulp monthly called *The Black Mask*. Their aim in starting what Mencken dismissively referred to as 'a lousy magazine' was to subsidize another periodical they owned, the *Smart Set*, a 'magazine of cleverness' that was in constant financial trouble. The magazine began by publishing traditional drawing-room mysteries, with mannered characters modelled after English stereotypes. After Mencken and Nathan sold it, however, at a tidy profit, it became the medium for a new kind of detective tale, involving hardbitten detectives and tough-minded stories, and reflecting the gritty realities of post-First World War America. Many writers were to experiment with writing in this vein for *The Black Mask*, before it began to decline in the 1940s, supplanted by its numerous imitators like *Black Aces*, *Dime Detective*, *Detective Tales* and *New Detective*. They included Carroll

John Daly (1889–1958) and Erle Stanley Gardner (1889–1970). But easily the most important were Dashiell Hammett (1894–1961) and, later in the history of the magazine, Raymond Chandler (1888–1959).

Dashiell Hammett had worked as a private detective for the Pinkerton Agency in San Francisco, shortly before serving in the army in the First World War. That experience served him well in his stories for *The Black Mask*, set in a sharp and credibly drawn northern California landscape. Beginning in 1923, they featured a character called the Continental Op, the toughest and shrewdest investigator in an outfit called the Continental Detective Agency. Altogether, the Op was to appear in two dozen *Black Mask* stories, and in the serialized versions of the novels *The Dain Curse* (1929) and *Red Harvest* (1929). His other, hugely influential heroes were the mildly inebriated husband and wife team of Nick and Nora Charles, in *The Thin Man* (1934), and the protagonist in what is perhaps the single most important private-eye novel, *The Maltese Falcon* (1930), Sam Spade. Raymond Chandler wrote of Hammett and his followers that they were responsible for 'taking murder out of the library and putting it back on the streets where it belonged'. Of Hammett, in particular, he observed that he 'wrote at first (and almost to the end) for people with a sharp, aggressive attitude to life'. Such people, Chandler added, 'were not afraid of the seamy side of things; they lived there. Violence did not dismay them; it was right down their street.' Hammett created heroes who were not merely cool, tough, cynical; they confronted the conditions surrounding them with a full knowledge of their latent violence and their pervasive, inherent corruption. Favouring a rapid tempo and economy of expression, Hammett nevertheless wove elaborate patterns of intrigue and deceit. His novels became narrative labyrinths, replicating the literal labyrinths of the city streets and the social labyrinth of urban power, in which it became just about impossible to know whom to trust – other than oneself. Pursuing the fabulous jewel-encrusted black bird that supplies the title of *The Maltese Falcon*, 'the stuff that dreams are made of', Sam Spade discovers what in a sense he has always known: that there is little he can rely on, apart from his own nerve and work – and the simple code that tells him, 'when a man's partner is killed he's supposed to do something about it', even if he did not like him.

What fires the work of Hammett into life, above all, is what came to be known as his 'hardboiled style'. The style of all his fiction is hard, brittle, unadorned. The emphasis is on dialogue, the vernacular and basic colloquial rhythms. Hammett did not invent the style, of course. In the short term, it was an offshoot of the styles deployed by Ernest Hemingway, Sherwood Anderson and Ring Lardner. In the longer term, its antecedents could be traced back to that concern for American speech shown by Mark Twain or even Walt Whitman. What he did add to it, though, was what another detective storywriter, Ellery Queen (the pseudonym of Frederic Dannay [1908–82] and Manfred Lee [1905–71]), called 'romantic realism'. Placing his stories against a stark backdrop, Hammett peopled them with protagonists who combined cynicism with a strange kind of commitment: to their own sense of things, not a vision perhaps but a stern sense of vocation. The longtime partner of Hammett, Lillian Hellman, said that he was the kind of person who had a 'reserve so deep that we all know we cannot touch it with charm or jokes or favors. It comes out as something more than dignity and shows on the face.' The poet Richard Wilbur, she recalled, said that 'as you came toward Hammett to shake his hand in the first meeting, you wanted him to approve of you'. That is precisely the reaction that, despite their toughness, even bitterness and occasional brutality, the detective heroes of Hammett tend to inspire. The style, as it were, underwrites this. Just as the hero is the one true thing in a deeply duplicitous world, so the style, spare to the point of verbal starvation, is a true coinage that defines more complex styles as counterfeit. Surrounded by masks and metaphors, it is the man and the speech closest to silence that we trust.

The fiction of Hammett brims, then, with undisclosed romanticism. In the work of Raymond Chandler, that romanticism is more or less disclosed. Many of the familiar elements of the hardboiled detective story, as perfected by Hammett, are still there: the setting in an urban labyrinth (it was Chandler, after all, who coined the phrase 'mean streets'), the sense of a conspiratorial network of evil, the terse dialogue, rapid narrative tempo and flashes of violence. What is relatively new with Chandler, however, is a more highly wrought style and more open concern with a code of honour. Chandler was born in Chicago, educated in England, and only began writing fiction at the age of forty-five. When he began writing, he mixed the hardboiled with other idioms, which he saw at least as the product of his European education. 'All the best American writing', Chandler argued, 'has been done by cosmopolitans. They found freedom of expression, richness of vocabulary' in the United States. 'But they had to have European taste to use the material.' That taste, in his case, led to a vivid use of metaphor and allusion, sharp street language and a trenchant use of wisecracks. It also led to evocative scene-setting: creating the sense of a neon-lit jungle. Chandler helped originate what later became known as a noir world: rainswept streets, dark, empty buildings, shadows and fog punctuated by the occasional streetlamp, light from the window of a lonely room or an all-night café. This is the world in which Chandler's solitary detective makes his way. Usually, as in *The Big Sleep* (1939), *Farewell My Lovely* (1940) and *The Long Goodbye* (1953), that hero is Philip Marlowe. Marlowe, more than most detectives of his kind, is a man of honour, committed to justice and principle, a righter of wrongs as well as an agent of the law. As Chandler was well aware, he bears little resemblance to any real private detectives; 'the real-life private eye', Chandler observed, 'is a sleazy little drudge' with 'about as much moral stature as a stop and go sign'. In the mean streets, but morally not of them, Marlowe is more like the familiar figure of the American Adam, redrawn and resituated in California. Surrounding him are vicious villains, corrupt cops, avaricious businessmen and politicians, and usually decadent women. Somehow, he manages to keep his integrity in the midst of all this. He is as much alone as the mythic cowboy in the vastness of the West is: that is the source of his pride, as well as his strange pathos.

Not all writers associated with the hardboiled school concentrated on stories with detectives at their centre, however. Particularly as the Depression set in, many turned their attention to the lives of apparently average people caught up in a cycle of deprivation – turning to sex or violence or both in a desperate attempt to break that cycle. Or, perhaps mindful of the way the boom times of the 1920s had suddenly been turned upside down, they showed ordinary men and women spiralling down into nightmare worlds, victims of chance and coincidence – a malign fate, a malevolent system or an unknown, malicious individual. Among such writers was Cornell Woolrich (1903–68). Author of many novels and short stories, including *The Bride Wore Black* (1944) and 'Rear Window' (1941), his bleak view of life is summed up in just one phrase he coined, 'First You Dream, Then You Die'. There was also David Goodis (1917–56) and Horace McCoy (1897–1955). Goodis wrote a series of fictions, beginning in 1939 and including the novel *Dark Passage* (1946), that have as their guiding impulse a sense of dislocation. 'That's fine piano,' a character in one of his novels, *Down There* (1956), thinks, hearing music. 'Who's playing that? He opened his eyes. He saw his fingers caressing the keyboard.' McCoy, in turn, describes a world of seedy hotels, cheap dance halls, rundown movie theatres and precinct station backrooms, all inhabited by drifters, loners, the victims and the corrupt. In his first and most notable novel, *They Shoot Horses, Don't They?* (1935), for instance, the narrator is a man awaiting his own execution. He tells the story of how he came to kill his marathon dance partner, at her insistence. 'They shoot horses, don't they?' he remembers her saying to him, in order to persuade him. She feels like an animal for which the world has no use, no place or vocation. The only logical next step, then, is a swift and efficient death.

At the core of these hardboiled or noir novels is a myth of success with no social world to sustain it. That is especially true of the fiction of one hardboiled writer in particular, James M. Cain (1892–1977), who for a while, in the 1930s and 1940s, was the most notorious writer in the United States. Cain started his career by writing editorials for the New York *World* under the supervision of the critic and commentator Walter Lippman (1889–1974). He then became magazine editor of the *New Yorker*. In 1934, he published his first novel, *The Postman Always Rings Twice*. It tells the story of Cora Papadakis and a drifter Frank Chambers, lovers who murder Cora's wealthy husband for his money, making it look like an accident. Cora then dies in a car crash, and ironically Frank is convicted of murder for her death when it was in fact an accident. Other novels followed, notably *Double Indemnity* (1936), in which again an unmarried man and a married woman plan and execute the husband's 'accidental' death, this time for the insurance money. They established Cain as a master of what became known as hardboiled eroticism: with sex, presented with a frankness unusual for the time, seen as a primary motive, the instinct driving people to escape from their mean, petty, sometimes impoverished lives. However, Cain himself insisted that he made 'no conscious effort to be tough, or hard-boiled, or grim'. 'I merely try to write as the character would write,' he said, 'and I never forget that the average man . . . has acquired a vividness of speech that goes beyond anything I could invent.' In this sense, his work, like that of McCoy, Goodis, Woolrich and others, is a version of the American demotic tradition in literature. In prose rhythms that imitate those of ordinary American speech, in an idiom that is as hard and elemental as the everyday vernacular of the street, he shows 'the average man' and woman caught up in the dullness of their lives and dreams of leaving: destroyed by the very passions – adultery, incest, hatred, greed, lust or whatever – that, however perversely, they see as their avenues of escape.

Humorous writing

Far removed from the cold eye that many hardboiled novelists like Cain cast on American society were the more affectionate, even accepting perspectives of contemporary humorists. 'The humorous story is American,' Mark Twain declared, explaining that what he meant by this was that American writers had devised and perfected the kind of storytelling humour that depended on how something was said rather than what was said. True or not, Twain himself was capable of corrosive satire: humour that went beyond the wry pleasure of recognition to sardonic, even bitter exposure of social and moral corruption. Few humorists between the two World Wars ever ventured that far. Clarence Shepard Day (1874–1935), for instance, produced a series of popular books, *God and My Father* (1932), *Life With Father* (1935) and *Life With Mother* (1937), that depicted a quaint, indignantly conservative character whose habits of thought had passed out of fashion. Public life was certainly infested with 'chuckle-headed talk and rascality in business and politics': that was admitted. But the clear implication was that to expect otherwise, or to want to alter the way things were, was to become like 'father': an absurdly quixotic figure, a charming but anachronistic eccentric, whose tirades could only be a source of amusement rather than instruction. Similarly, and in their different ways, Robert Benchley (1889–1945) and Ogden Nash (1902–71) appeared to follow the dictum that small is beautiful – or, at least, beautifully, and modestly, humorous. The character Benchley portrays in such books as *From Bad to Worse* (1934), *My Ten Years in a Quandary* (1936) and *Inside Benchley* (1942) is always thwarted from doing the little, simplest things: like leaving a party, smoking a cigarette or wearing a white suit. The resulting comic cameos neatly capture the frustrations of modern urban existence but also make them seem tolerable, even attractive: a source of amusement, ingratiating entertainment, rather than anxiety. Ogden Nash, in turn, knocks language out of shape and into a wisecrack. His comic verse is pointed by rhythms that become funnier the more strained and tortuous they are. His swiftly epigrammatic verse seems somehow designed to obey the injunction that another humorist, S. J. Perelman (1904–79), used as the title for one of his books, *Keep it Crisp* (1946).

Perelman himself tended to obey his own injunction. As a contributor to the *New Yorker* for over forty years, he wrote many short satirical pieces, collected in volumes with titles like *Parlor, Bedlam and Bath* (1930), *Crazy Like a Fox* (1944), *The Ill-Tempered Clavichord* (1953) and *Chicken Inspector No 23* (1966). They often took the form of fantastic dramas which, with a surreal style and a feeling for the slapstick possibilities of language, lampooned advertising, the movies, the mass media and popular fiction. And one of their virtues was, nearly always, their brevity. Ring Lardner (1885–1933) also excelled in the kind of short sketch or story that was more than half in love with the thing it satirized. With Lardner, however, there was something more: a remarkable ear for American speech and an extraordinary capacity for catching on paper what Marianne Moore called the accuracy of the vernacular. Lardner was an established sports journalist before he began writing a series of letters in the disguise of 'Jack Keefe', a newcomer to a professional baseball team. Published first in the Chicago *Tribune*, they brought him fame as an explorer of semi-literate idiom and an exposer of demotic vanity, incompetence and self-deception. They were published in 1914 as *You Know Me, Al: A Busher's Letters*. Other subsequent volumes included *Bib Ballads* (1915), a collection of verse, *The Big Town* (1921), a humorous novel and the collections *How to Write Short Stories* (1924) and *The Love Nest* (1926). Americans of all walks of life appear in his writing, their personalities defined by their utterances. And, although that writing appears to obey the conventional limits of contemporary American humour, it is in fact unusually mordant, even cynical. The songwriters, barbers, stenographers and others to whom Lardner gives voice are reduced to their essential banality or dullness, cruelty, violence or stupidity. The sardonic surfaces of his fiction only partially conceal a deeply pessimistic viewpoint, as Lardner allows his 'average' characters to condemn themselves out of their own, forever open mouths.

Apart from Lardner, the two most renowned humorous writers in the first half of the twentieth century were James Thurber (1894–1961) and Dorothy Parker (1893–1967). Thurber was a regular contributor to the *New Yorker* for many years, as both a cartoonist and a writer. His sketches and stories were collected in such volumes as *The Owl in the Attic, and Other Perplexities* (1931), *The Seal in My Bedroom, and Other Predicaments* (1932) and *My World – and Welcome to It!* (1942). With E. B. White (1899–1985) he wrote *Is Sex Necessary?* (1929), satirizing pseudo-scientific sex manuals. With Elliot Nugent (1899–1980), he produced a successful dramatic comedy, *The Male Animal* (1940). Of his own prose and drawings Thurber said, 'the little wheels of their invention are set in motion by the damp hand of melancholy'. This was in keeping with his view that, as he put it, 'humor is the best that lies closest to the familiar, to that part of the familiar which is humiliating, distressing, even tragic'. The strange and whimsical characters Thurber describes, some of them animals and many of them people, respond to upsets, incredible accidents, with a sad persistence. They all seem repressed and misshapen, subject to malignant circumstances that somehow they survive, even combat. 'Humor is a kind of emotional chaos told about calmly and quietly in retrospect,' Thurber observed. The chaotic times on which Thurber's own humour, in particular, forces attention stretch 'from the year Lindbergh flew the Atlantic to the year coffee was rationed': that is, the period between the two World Wars. And the victims of chaos who receive his special attention are all his sad middle-aged men, caught by the dreariness of their lives, custom and predatory women – and quietly dreaming of escape into a world of adventure, where they can perform feats of daring that range from the quaintly romantic to the comically bizarre.

The humour of Dorothy Parker was considerably more acerbic. Her writing career began as a dramatic and literary critic in her native New York City; and she soon acquired an almost legendary reputation for her malicious and sardonic wisecracks. She once described the actress Katharine Hepburn, for instance, as 'running the whole gamut of emotions from A to B'. Then, in 1926, she published her first book of poems, *Enough Rope*. A best-seller, it was followed by two other books of verse and, in 1936, by her collected poems, *Not So Deep As a Well*. The poems show that Parker was just as sceptical about relations between the sexes as Thurber was. Only, whereas Thurber tended to show feckless husbands at the mercy of tyrannical wives, Parker was more cynically evenhanded. She simply dismissed the possibility of romantic fulfilment for either sex. 'By the time you swear you're his, / Shivering and sighing,' she declares in 'Unfortunate Coincidence', 'And he vows his passion is / Infinite, undying –/', then, she concludes, 'Lady, make a note of this: / One of you is lying.' Parker pursued similar caustic variations on the frustrations of love and the futility of idealism in her prose work. The short stories and sketches collected in *Laments for the Living* (1930), for example, and in *After Such Pleasures* (1933) and *Here Lies* (1939) are marked by their wry wit, their economy and polish, but, above all, by their refusal to take any prisoners. And she could be just as devastating in conversation as she was in print: on hearing that ex-President Calvin Coolidge – famously inactive while in office – had died, she responded, 'How could they tell?' Parker could be tough on herself. 'I am just a little Jewish girl, trying to be cute,' she once observed. She could write successfully in many different genres. Apart from poetry, stories and sketches, reviews and criticism, she collaborated with Elmer Rice on the play *Close Harmony* (1929) and with Arnaud d'Usseau on *Ladies of the Corridor* (1953); and she also produced articles, columns and reportage for many different magazines and newspapers. She was even aware of the limits of humour, or at least her own brand of it. 'I know now that there are things that never have been funny, and never will be,' she wrote in *New Masses* in 1937, after witnessing the Spanish Civil War firsthand. 'And I know that ridicule may be a shield, but it is not a weapon.' But it was with her epigrammatic wit, which usually instilled fear in those around her, that she made her mark – a wit that moved between the cool, the clever and the cynical and could even turn her own death into a wisecrack: 'Excuse my dust', was the epitaph she prepared for herself.

Fiction and popular culture

Margaret Mitchell (1900–49) would never qualify as a humorist. The closest she came to humour, outside of *Gone With the Wind* (1936), was her sardonic comment that 'long ago' she gave up thinking about her long romantic tale set in Georgia during the Civil War and Reconstruction as her book. 'It's Atlanta's, in the view of Atlantians,' she said, 'the movie is Atlanta's film.' That says something about the phenomenal success of her novel. An instant best-seller, it set a sales record of 50,000 copies in one day and one and a half million during the first year of publication. At least twenty-five million more have been sold since then. It has been translated into twenty-seven languages and published successfully in thirty-seven countries. In turn, the film of the book, which had its premiere in 1939, has been seen by more people than the entire population of the United States, with gross earnings estimated at over three hundred million dollars. Some of the lines from both book and film ('Tomorrow is another day', 'My dear, I don't give a damn') have passed into popular currency and been subject to endless repetition and parody. No wonder the citizens of Atlanta, in Mitchell's view, wanted to claim *Gone With the Wind* as their own. And no wonder Mitchell was to complain, 'alas, where has my quiet peaceful life gone?' after publication of the one book she ever wrote. Despite her subsequent efforts to protect her family and herself from the treadmill of publicity and the gaze of adoring fans, she became a kind of public property. The book that brought all this about is a fundamentally simple tale that, in the tradition of plantation and Civil War romance, tells the story of the South entirely from the point of view of the middle-class planters. More specifically, it is the tale of Scarlett O'Hara and how, under the pressures of war and hardship, she grows from a girl to a woman, a belle to a matriarchal figure who has developed a 'shell of hardness'. Many of the familiar, stereotypical characters of Southern plantation romance are on display here. There is the world-weary plantation Hamlet, played here by Ashley Wilkes, the roguish, dangerous plantation Hotspur, a role taken here by Rhett Butler. There are, inevitably, a 'Mammy', various 'Uncle Tom' figures who faithfully serve and save their white masters, a vicious white over-seer, melodious field hands and women like Scarlett's friend, the gentle Melanie Hamilton, who fulfil Southern expectations of what it means to be 'a very great lady'. What ignites *Gone With the Wind*, however, is its heroine. Here, with Scarlett O'Hara, Mitchell revisits a familiar character type, the strong woman – particularly popular in the 1930s, when such characters were often seen as potential redeemers of a barren land – and gives that character type new complexity and depth, not least through subtle inflections of gender.

Like the heroine of many popular female narratives, from romance through the prototypical early feminist novel to soap opera, Scarlett O'Hara is an initially unexceptional girl who is forced into an exceptional maturity. As the opening line of the novel has it, she is 'not beautiful, but men seldom realised it' thanks to her wiles. Nor is she educated, or even a reader ('I don't read novels,' she declares); she does, however, have 'sharp intelligence' – and, as it turns out, determination and guile. Like the central character in many a female narrative, in her love trials she is torn between respectability and risk, in the respective figures of Ashley and Rhett. However, while she possesses some of the stereotypical 'feminine' characteristics, such as a lack of interest in war and politics, what makes her remarkable is her possession too of supposedly 'masculine' traits. As she develops, during the course of the narrative, she shows herself to be tough, ruthless, competitive. She is com-mitted to the land, her property, and money as a means to keep that land. What is more, she is quite unsentimental: marrying men she does not love and giving birth to three children she uniformly finds a nuisance – as Rhett observes, 'a cat's a better mother than you'. According to the conventions of Southern society, Scarlett is very often a scandal: dancing in widow's weeds, driving a hard bargain, leasing convict labour and cavorting after the war with Yankees. Like the central character of the classic historical novel, too, she herself becomes a site of struggle between the old order and the new. Or, as the narrative puts it, 'her mind pulled two ways', between nostalgia for the past and the necessities of the present and future. At the end of the novel, Scarlett does turn back, to Tara, her homeplace. She also turns back, in intention, to a man who is himself, he says, seeking to recapture some of the 'honour and security, roots that go deep' of the old, antebellum days, in that she determines to try to win back Rhett. But even this apparent victory for the backward glance, the past, is more ambivalent than at first appears and suggests the richly layered nature of the heroine of *Gone With the Wind*. In going back, Scarlett is perhaps going forward, trying for a synthesis of the new aims and the old values: a balance between past and future registered in her famous closing remark, 'Tomorrow, I'll think of some way to get him back. After all, tomorrow is another day.'

What is striking, and regrettable, about this most popular of American romances is that it combines this relatively sophisticated representation of gender, the role of women, with a presentation of race, and in particular the African American race, that is regressive to the point of being obscene. The opening references to 'darkies' 'pop-eyed with fear' over some scary matter, and the 'laughter of negro voices' as the hands return from the fields, set the initial tone. African American characters are, at best, comic, choric commentators, at worst ignorant and mischievous, or they are turned into anonymous, helpless and occasionally shiftless shadows. All this, the traditional stuff of antebellum romance, is bad enough. What is worse is what happens when the narrative turns to the Civil War and, even more, Reconstruction. There are scattered references now to 'drunken blacks', 'illiterate negroes in high office' who 'conducted themselves as creatures of small intelligence might naturally be expected to do' when faced with political responsibility. 'Like monkeys or small children turned loose', the freed slaves, and especially the men, are seen as a threat: to white society in general, and to white women in particular. The 'peril to white women', the reader is told, created 'the tragic necessity' of the Ku Klux Klan. And Rhett Butler himself is jailed for killing an African American who 'insulted' a white woman. 'He was uppity to a lady,' Rhett explains, 'and what could a gentleman do?' Scarlett O'Hara herself is attacked by a 'ragged' white man and black man, whose 'rank odour' she can smell as he tears off her basque. She is rescued, however, by 'Big Sam', an Uncle Tom figure who declares, after rescuing her, 'Ah hope Ah done kill de black babboon'. 'Ah done had nuff freedom,' Sam adds, 'Tara mah home': a sentiment later echoed by Scarlett's 'Mammy', when she declares 'Ah's gwine home' to Tara. The deep racial flaw of *Gone With the Wind* is a matter of omission as much as anything else. The humanity of black men is a conspicuous, constitutive absence in the novel. So, too, are the humanity and sexuality of black women, since the only black women who receive any attention are asexual. Miscegenation here, apart from occasional references to 'the enormous increase in mulatto babies since the Yankee soldiers settled in town', is a matter of forced relations between black male rapists and pure white women. Mitchell shows absolutely no sense of what writers like Charles Chesnutt, William Faulkner and Toni Morrison have understood: that the use of black women by white men – with its equation of sex and power, its interrogation of the colour line and its revelation of a secret history – is the repressed myth of the South and, maybe, of America. Her book is an inescapable fact of American literary history; it represents a confluence of narrative traditions; and it has at its centre one of the most memorable heroines in American fiction. But that fact is an ugly one, in some ways. And the book shows how romance may have its dark side, may even depend on or feed off that dark side to survive. To that extent, *Gone With the Wind* is far more frightening than its author intended, because it is a symptom rather than a diagnosis of historical failure. Recalling an American dream, Mitchell inadvertently exposes an American nightmare. In the process her novel illustrates the famous remark of Walter Benjamin that there is no document of civilization that is not at the same time a document of barbarism.

Despite the enormous success of the film of her book, Mitchell had very little interest in Hollywood or visiting there. In fact, she rarely strayed outside Atlanta. Unlike her, though, one thing many of the humorists and hardboiled writers did have in common was precisely their experience of the film capital of the world. Together with novelists like Faulkner and Fitzgerald, and playwrights like Hecht and Odets, Cain and McCoy, Benchley and Parker were among those lured west to write film scripts. And, while they were there or afterwards, some writers at least felt compelled to write about the experience. Fitzgerald did so, of course, in *The Last Tycoon*. McCoy did so in *I Should Have Stayed Home* (1938), the title of which suggests just how much this was a novel about failure in the dream factory. Even Faulkner, who despised a place where he said 'they worship death,' had to write about it: 'Hollywood which is no longer Hollywood,' the narrator observes in *The Wild Palms* (originally titled *If I Forget Thee, Jerusalem*), 'but is stippled by a billion feet of burning colored gas across the face of the American earth.' Of those who came to Hollywood, however, and registered the impact of popular culture generally in their writing, no author was more perceptive than Nathanael West (1903–40). Born Nathan Wallenstein Weinstein in New York City, West lived in Paris for two years, where he completed his first novel, *The Dream Life of Balso Snell* (1931). A surrealist fantasy about the wandering of its eponymous hero within the Trojan horse – where, among others, he meets a naked man in a bowler hat who is writing a history of Saint Puce, a flea who lived in Christ's armpit – it was completely ignored. It did, however, prove useful for its author: West's apprenticeship to surrealism undoubtedly freed him from the constraints of naturalism. His later work presents and is preoccupied with a border territory, situated somewhere between the actual and the absurd, the naturalistic and nightmare. This is, West intimates, the world in which we live now: mediated for us by the strange dreams, the visions of ourselves that our culture throws up for us and marked by excess, a seemingly endless surfeit of commodities. The subsequent fiction of West, written after he returned to the United States in the early 1930s, sprang from his confrontation with America at its most meaningless. Something of that is registered in his third book, *A Cool Million: The Dismantling of Lemuel Pitkin* (1934), a brutally comic attack on the American myth of success, the rise of the self-made man from rags to riches. But the works in which West explored and exploited the absurd – as the essential narrative of life and entire story of America – were his second, and fourth and final ones: *Miss Lonelyhearts* (1933), written just after he returned from Europe, and *The Day of the Locust* (1939), written while he was working as a scriptwriter in Hollywood – and published just a year before his sudden death.

The hero of *Miss Lonelyhearts* is – Miss Lonelyhearts. The reader never learns his real name. He is the agony aunt on the New York *Post-Dispatch*, which tells its customers: 'Are-you-in-trouble? – Do-you-need-advice? – Write-to-Miss-Lonelyhearts-and-she-will-help-you.' The trouble is, the people who write to Miss Lonelyhearts really do need help. He is appalled and obsessed by their sufferings. 'For the first time in his life,' as he explains to his girlfriend Betty, he is forced 'to examine the values by which he lives.' And, finding nothing, he realizes that his taking on of the agony column as a kind of joke has backfired: 'he is the victim of the joke and not its perpetrator'. The nothingness Miss Lonelyhearts finds can, however, be described, and is. Life, Miss Lonelyhearts knows, has always been meaningless. 'Man has a tropism for order,' he reflects, 'the physical world has a tropism for disorder, entropy.' 'Every order has within it the germ of destruction. All order is doomed' and everything is running down. What is different, now, is the absence of a saving illusion. 'Men have always fought their misery with dreams,' Miss Lonelyhearts tells himself at one point. 'Although dreams were once powerful, they have been made puerile by the movies, radio, and newspapers. Among many betrayals, this one is the worst.' And Miss Lonelyhearts is among those who feel most fiercely betrayed. In his agony, the sense of his own futility, Miss Lonelyhearts momentarily becomes the persecutor of the wretched, whose suffering he cannot extenuate or explain. Twisting the arm of a poor old man in a public toilet, 'he was twisting the arm of the sick and miserable, broken and betrayed, inarticulate and impotent'. He is really twisting his own arm because, as he senses, he is 'capable of dreaming the Christ dream', passionately embracing a saving fiction. He is, in fact, a Christ figure himself, even if an absurd and impotent one. And this is underlined in the story by his editor Shrike, who plays the part here of Satan. Shrike, named after a bird of prey, is a man of inexhaustible cynicism. Like Miss Lonelyhearts, he has lost belief but appears to revel in that condition. And, offering Miss Lonelyhearts the kingdoms of the earth, he mocks all possible faiths – religion, art, nature or whatever: anything that might give some significance to life. The climax, a darkly comic one, comes when Miss Lonelyhearts has a religious experience. Succumbing to the temptation of the 'Christ dream', he is convinced he has become one with God. Driven by that conviction, he holds out his arms Christlike to the crippled husband of a woman who has written to him for advice, whom he has met and with whom he has had sexual relations. He is persuaded that, when he has embraced him, the crippled man will be made whole, and that, in running to help him, he is running to all the wretched of the earth 'to succour them with love'. But the crippled husband fights to escape from his embrace. In the struggle that follows, the gun the man is carrying suddenly goes off, and Miss Lonelyhearts is killed. Miss Lonelyhearts's bid to become a saviour, a redeemer, ends in a black, bleak farce.

When writing *Miss Lonelyhearts*, West gave it the provisional title 'a novel in the form of a cartoon strip'. That suggests the tone of this book, which turns a potentially tragic theme into a comedy of the absurd. Beneath the surface of the narrative, West makes sly, allusive play with all manner of myths, all kinds of stories that other, earlier cultures have used to endow their (as West sees it) fundamentally meaningless lives with a sense of meaning. Along with being a mock Christ, for instance, Miss Lonelyhearts is a mock Oedipus, a mock quester and a mock hero of vegetation myth. On the surface, however, what the reader is presented with is precisely that: a world of surfaces. The characters are, intentionally, ciphers, caricatures, identified by one or two exaggerated features. Each short, sharp chapter is a comic routine, a cartoon strip the nature of which is announced by its title: 'Miss Lonelyhearts in the dismal swamp', 'Miss Lonelyhearts and the cripple', and so on. Within each routine, too, each character seems to be doing no more than playing a game, telling a story or adopting a role to give himself or herself the illusion of human presence. 'There was something clearly mechanical about her pantomime,' we are told of one character; while of Miss Lonelyhearts it is said that his 'gestures' are 'too appropriate, like those of an old-fashioned actor'. With characters reduced to objects – parts of their own bodies, say, or 'machines for making jokes' – or a label – and one that, in the case of the protagonist, is not even accurate in terms of gender – objects are magnified, take on a life of their own. So, on one day, we learn, the 'inanimate things' over which Miss Lonelyhearts 'had tried to obtain control took the field against him. When he touched something, it spilled or rolled to the floor. The collar button disappeared under the bed, the point of the pencil broke, the handle of the razor fell off, the window shade refused to stay down.' This is a world in which things, evidently, are more animated than people: where character is commodified and commodities assume character, and an often malevolent one at that. It is also a world stripped of meaning: where there is a play of surfaces, and nothing else (apart, that is, from the old, redemptive myths that the narrative allusively mocks). In its self-evident artifice, *Miss Lonelyhearts* effectively reminds the reader what its protagonist learns, and then forgets: that nothing can explain things – least of all, a story like the one we are reading. To that extent, West was writing here on the borderline between Modernism and postmodernism: negotiating a move from art as explanation, a source of redemption or redress, to art as game, a verbal playfield. *Miss Lonelyhearts* anticipates many books written several decades later that play with the premise that everything, including the book before us, is insignificant, a play of signs – in a word, a fiction.

For West, the difference with popular culture was not that it was superficial: in a depthless world, as he saw it, such comparative terms were impossible. All was depthless, a veneer. The difference was that, in its pursuit of the appearance of depth, the appropriation of meaning, it succeeded in being only, as Miss Lonelyhearts put it, 'puerile'. That puerility is the subject of *The Day of the Locust*. The novel opens with a brief impression of a film set. The central character, Tod Hackett, a painter working at a film studio, looks out of his office window to see an eighteenth-century battle in progress. The armies disappear behind 'half a Mississippi steamboat'. It is all absurdly artificial. But the reader then accompanies Tod through Los Angeles, past 'Mexican ranch houses, Samoan huts, Mediterranean villas, Egyptian and Japanese temples, Swiss chalets, Tudor cottages, and every possible combination of these styles that lined the slopes of the canyon'. So, it is clear, what is depicted in the studio is no more unreal than what lies outside. This is a place where 'the need for beauty and romance' has issued in 'the truly monstrous', and nothing is what it seems. Its inhabitants are those who hang about the studios, waiting for a break: cowboys who have never roped a steer, young women who have become imprisoned in the masks and masquerades they have assumed in the hope of becoming stars. They are also the nameless crowd, the spectators: the retired, middle class and middle-aged, who have travelled to southern California at the end of years of 'dull, heavy labour' in the Middle West, in search of 'the land of sunshine and oranges', the dream world described to them in the movies and magazines. Once there, they have become overwhelmed by a sense of tedium and betrayal. 'The sun is a joke. Oranges can't titillate their jaded palates. Nothing can ever be violent enough to make taut their slack minds and bodies.' In an ironic inversion of American myth, these are people who have bought into a commodified version of paradise, a cheap vision of the West, only to find how counterfeit the dreams sold to them are. And the discovery prompts them to violence, of the kind that their own jaded appetites, fed to saturation by the popular media, had led them to expect would be waiting for them to watch and enjoy in California. At the end of *The Day of the Locust*, the hopeless hordes of Midwesterners who have poured locust-like into California now pour into Hollywood to gaze at the celebrities arriving at a movie premiere. There, the crowd becomes a mob, goes berserk; and Tod, crushed almost to death, sees in a kind of vision the canvas he has been working on, 'The Burning of Los Angeles', as if it were completed. It is an appropriately apocalyptic note on which to end a story that announces the selling and subversion of the American dream. The America West describes is one that has lost touch with the real. All it has left is boredom and fear, the resignation of the crowd and the rage of the mob: the both of them signs of a culture that has no sustaining connection with the past – and no adequate means of imagining its future.

5

negotiating the american century

american literature since 1945

Towards a Transnational Nation

Americans ended the decade of the 1930s in an inward-looking mood, concerned with economic issues, unemployment and the need to heal internal ideological divisions. By the close of the Second World War, however, that mood had changed. The United States had become a global superpower, committed to the international arena. In the new era of postwar, postcolonial politics, it had come to stand for the 'American' way of capitalism, individualism and the open market: opposed in every respect to the 'Russian' or 'Communist' way of collectivism and the organized economy. A war machine that had managed to treble munitions production in 1941 continued, if in a slightly lower gear. The cessation of conflict did not mean an end to arms production, now that the United States discovered a new threat in international socialism, and the next decade or so saw the rapid expansion of what one president was to term 'the military-industrial complex': a compact between military interests, eager to acquire ever newer and more powerful armaments, and industrial interests, just as eager to produce them, that was to prove satisfactory and very profitable to both. At the same time, the manufacturing industries catering to more peaceful demands began to expand rapidly. Construction boomed; the demand for the consumer durables of modern mass society – cars, television sets, refrigerators – grew among people suddenly released from the constraints of war; and unemployment only rose a little above the all-time low of 1.2 per cent created by a war economy. The only nation to emerge from the Second World War with its manufacturing plant intact and its economy strengthened, America presented itself to the rest of the world – and, in particular, to Europe – as an economic miracle. In 1949, the per capita income of the United States was twice that of Britain, three times that of France, five times that of Germany and seven times that of Russia. It had only 6 per cent of the world's population: yet it consumed 40 per cent of the world's energy, 60 per cent of its automobiles, 80 per cent of its refrigerators and nearly 100 per cent of its televisions. This, evidently, was the

---

society of abundance, appearing to prove the claim of an earlier president, Calvin Coolidge, that the business of America was business.

The business of America was also, perhaps, to dictate the terms of modern culture, at least to its Western allies, and to other parts of the globe where it claimed a right of intervention and control. As the 1940s passed into the 1950s, America seemed to set the style in everything, from high art to advanced technology to popular culture. In Eisenhower, the president from 1952 to 1960, Americans also had someone at the head of state whose main aim seemed to be to preserve this economic abundance and cultural hegemony through a strategy of masterly inactivity. Gone were the frenetic commitments of the New Deal; and in their place was an administration that appeared intent on stopping things happening – on maintaining equilibrium by vetoing any legislation that seemed likely to promote radical change. To some commentators, it looked like a case of the bland leading the bland. Like Ronald Reagan thirty years later, Eisenhower made a dramatic exhibition of not working too hard; as he apparently saw it, his job as president was to leave Americans alone to go about their business, and to discourage the state from any interference in the day-to-day life of the individual. If self-help was to be encouraged, then citizens had to be left to themselves: to work hard and then to enjoy the material comforts thereby earned. 'These are the tranquillized *Fifties*,' observed the poet Robert Lowell; and for many Americans they were – a period when, after several decades of crisis, it was evidently possible to enjoy the fruits of their labour and exploitation of the earth's natural resources without any fear that, some day, those resources might run out. Many intellectuals and artists – although by no means all of them – participated in this era of consensus. This was the period of so-called 'value-free' sociology; much of the liberal intelligentsia acted on the assumption that it was possible to exercise the critical function untouched by social or political problems; and many writers withdrew from active involvement in issues of public concern or ideology into formalism, abstraction or mythmaking. One notable dissenter, Irving Howe (1920–93), complained about this in an essay appropriately entitled 'This Age of Conformity' (1952). 'Far from creating and subsidising unrest,' Howe observed, 'capitalism in its most recent stage has found an honoured place for the intellectuals; and the intellectuals, far from thinking of themselves as a desperate "opposition", have been enjoying a return to the bosom of the nation.' He concluded: 'We have all, even the handful who still try to retain a glower of criticism, become responsible and moderate. And tame.'

No consensus, however, is quite as complete as it seems, just as no society – not even the most totalitarian one – is without its areas of dissent. Abundance breeds its own anxieties, not least the fear of losing the comforts one enjoys; in many ways, the calm society is the one most susceptible to sudden, radical fits of panic. This uneasiness that hovered beneath the bland surfaces of the times found its outlet in many forms. In popular culture, for instance, it was expressed in a series of 'invaders from space' movies that uncovered a dark vein of public paranoia about the possible arrival of hostile forces, aliens who would rob Americans of their comforts and complacency. In literature, related insecurities issued in a preoccupation with evil, the possible eruption of weariness, guilt and remorse, into the rhythms of routine experience. In this respect, there was an almost willed dimension to the formalism of so many writers of the 1950s: it was as if, like their fellow Americans (although, obviously, in a far more self-conscious and articulate way), they were trying to contain their anxiety by channelling it into socially established and accepted structures. And in the political life of the period, in turn, perhaps the most significant expression of this fear of invasion, subversion or even destruction by covert agencies was the phenomenon known as McCarthyism. Joseph McCarthy was a young senator from Wisconsin who had a self-appointed mission to wage war on anything he saw as Communist subversion. Exploiting his position on the Un-American Activities Committee, playing on popular anxieties about the growing power of Russia and the possible presence of an 'enemy within', he embarked on a modern-day witch-hunt, the result of which was that many people were sacked from their jobs and blacklisted on the mere suspicion of belonging to the Communist Party. Guilt was established by smear; loss of job followed on false witness; and a cast of characters that included Hollywood scriptwriters, intellectuals and academics suddenly found themselves the subject of vicious public abuse. McCarthy declared that he was engaged in a battle that could not be ended 'except in victory or death for this civilization'; and, during the period when he flourished, he managed to convince many Americans that the preservation of their material wealth and social health depended upon his rooting out enemies of the people wherever he could find or invent them.

One crucial fear that McCarthy exploited was the fear of the betrayal of atomic secrets. America had unleashed strange and terrible forces when it dropped atom bombs on Hiroshima and Nagasaki. The bomb cast its shadow over the immediate postwar decades, just as it has done ever since; and the discovery that certain people in the United States, Canada and Britain had passed atomic secrets to the Russians, who could now explode nuclear weapons of their own, clearly exacerbated public anxieties about hidden enemies and conspiracies, and made it that much easier for McCarthy and his committee to flourish. Fear of the potential nuclear capability of the enemy, allied to this suspicion of a powerful enemy within, also increased the tensions of what Winston Churchill christened 'the Cold War': that policy of brinkmanship between the United States and Russia, their respective satellite states and allies, that was based on the premise that the two superpowers were engaged in a life-or-death struggle for global supremacy. Eisenhower's secretary of state, John Foster Dulles, talked of 'the liberation of captive peoples' and the possibility of turning back the Communist tide. His vice-president, Richard Nixon, who had first come to public attention while serving on the Un-American Activities Committee, announced that there would be no relaxation in the drive to root suspected subversives out of public service. And even Eisenhower himself, despite his evident mildness of manner, promised the American electorate, 'We will find out the pinks, we will find the Communists, we will find the disloyal'. The Red scare of the Eisenhower years was more than just a useful weapon in the hands of certain ambitious politicians, helping to generate policies of confrontation and containment. It was a clear symptom of the uneasiness, the nightmarish fears that haunted Americans at the time, despite their apparent satisfaction with themselves. There was abundance and some complacency, certainly, but there was also a scarcely repressed imagination of disaster fuelled by the threat of nuclear war.

By the late 1950s, this threat – and, more specifically, the bomb that embodied it – had become a potent symbol for the destructive potential of the new society: the dark side of those forces that had created apparently limitless wealth. Everywhere in the culture there were signs of revolt, as the fears and phobias that had been lurking just below the 'tranquillized' surfaces of middle America began to bubble to the top. There was a renewed spirit of rebelliousness, opposition to a social and economic order that had produced abundance, admittedly, but had also produced the possibility of global death. In music, the emergence of rock and roll, derived mainly from black musical forms, signalled a reluctance to accept the consensual mores, and the blandness, of white middle-class America: which is why, until they were absorbed into the mainstream, performers like Elvis Presley were perceived by political and religious leaders as such a potent threat, offering a gesture of defiance to 'civilized standards'. In the movies, similarly, new heroes appeared dramatizing an oppositional stance to the dominant culture: James Dean, in films like *Rebel Without a Cause* (1955), and Marlon Brando in, say, *The Wild One* (1953), seemed living monuments to the new spirit of alienation. And in literature, too, there were analogous developments. Two key fictional texts of the period were *The Catcher in the Rye* by J. D. Salinger and *On the Road* by Jack Kerouac. Radically dissimilar as these two books were, they had in common heroes at odds with modern urban-technological life: outsiders who moved between fragile mysticism and outright disaffiliation in their search for an alternative to the orthodox culture. They were willing, in effect, to say no, in thunder, just as earlier American heroes had been. This was also true of many writers of the period, who bore witness to a gradual slipping away from the formalism and abstraction – and, to some extent, the conformism – of the postwar years and towards renewed feelings of freedom, individualism and commitment. Recovering the impulse towards the personal, sometimes to the point of the confessional, and the urge towards an individual, perhaps even idiosyncratic beat, they gave voice to a growing sense of resistance to the social norms. Reinventing the old American allegiance to the rebellious self, and weaving together personal and historical traumas, they sought in their line and language for a road to liberation, a way of realizing their fundamental estrangement. No cultural development is seamless, of course, and it would be wrong to suggest that the story of the first two decades after the Second World War is one simply of abundance and anxiety merging into revolt and repudiation of fixed forms. But, in terms of a general bias of direction or tendency, this was the way that many American writers moved, along with their fellow Americans, as they saw one president, Eisenhower, who seemed 'pretty much for mother, home, and heaven', succeeded by another, Kennedy, who preferred to talk in terms of 'a new generation of Americans' 'tempered by war, disciplined by a hard and bitter peace' – 'unwilling to witness or permit the slow undoing of those human rights to which this nation has always been committed, and to which we are committed today at home and around the world'.

President John F. Kennedy spoke in these terms at his Inauguration in January 1961. He had won the election by only the narrowest of margins. But, once elected, he brought with him to office the expectation of great change, an optimism and confidence about the character of the United States and its role in the world that many Americans were eager to share. His words were ambiguous, to say the least. Did they anticipate the elimination of poverty and inequality or a renewed aggressiveness in foreign policy – or perhaps both? Despite this, or maybe even because of it, they struck a responsive chord in the heart of the nation. 'We stand today on the edge of a new frontier,' Kennedy declared, 'a frontier of unknown opportunities and perils. . . . I am asking each of you to be pioneers on that New Frontier.' The appeal to the apparently timeless myth of the West, pioneering and conquest, was echoed in the words of Robert Frost at the Inaugural. Frost had been invited to the ceremony as America's unofficial poet laureate, and as an emblem of Kennedy's belief that he could, among many other things, preside over a revitalization of the nation's cultural life. Eighty-six years old now, he recited from memory his poem 'The Gift Outright': 'This land was ours before we were the land's, /' the poem begins. 'She was our land more than a hundred years / Before we were her people.' Going on to 'the land vaguely realising westward, / But still unstoried, artless, unenhanced', the poem, just like the speech, captures a dominant feeling of the time. It captures the confidence, the ambition, the sense of potential and the arrogance of a 'new generation of Americans', and weds all this to the ideology of a long-vanished frontier.

The America to and of which both poet and president spoke was a constellation of many new attitudes and forces: a nation of 180 million people, a growing number of whom were white suburbanites living in quiet comfort on the edge of the older, urban areas, buying their goods in out-of-town shopping malls and working in white-collar service-sector industries. Nine out of ten families, by this time, owned a television, and six out of ten of them a car. The gross national product seemed to move inexorably upward, from $285 billion in 1950 to $503 billion in 1960, and so too did the population index: during the 1950s, the population had risen by 18.5 per cent. Most of this increase was due to the rapid rise in the birth rate and a prolonged life expectancy rather than to immigration; and the result was that nearly half of the population was either under eighteen or over sixty-five, too young or too old to participate in the economic life of the nation. To those excluded by youth or age from full participation in the nation's growing wealth could be added those excluded by race or situation: fruitpickers in California, say, black sharecroppers in the South, and the different ethnic groups comprising the urban poor. While the income of middle-class Americans of working age continued to improve, that of the bottom 20 per cent showed hardly any advance at all. There was conspicuous abundance, certainly, but there was equally conspicuous poverty: the rhetoric of the president possibly acknowledged this but it tended to be forgotten amidst the general euphoria, the sense of irresistible expansion and movement forwards towards a 'New Frontier'. And it was only in the later 1960s that the seeds of discontent and dissension sowed by this conspicuous contrast between haves and have-nots began to be harvested.

In the meantime, in the early 1960s, optimism and the promise of adventure were in the air. Responding to the sense of new frontiers to be conquered, many artists of the period, of every kind, were notable for their willingness to experiment, to confront and even challenge cultural and social norms. A decade is, of course, an artificial measure and, in this respect as in most others, 'the Sixties' had really begun in the middle to late 1950s: when the popular arts were revivified by a new sense of energy and power, and a lively avant-garde embarked on challenging conventional norms and forms. Happenings, festivals, multimedia performances became commonplace events. Readings of poetry and prose, often to jazz accompaniment, attracted dedicated audiences. There was a sense of risk, of venturing beyond the formalism, the preoccupation with craftsmanship of earlier decades. Writing became more open, rawer, alert to the possibility of change and the inclusion of random factors. There was a renewed emphasis on chance, difference, impermanency, a new willingness to see the new artistic object as a shifting, discontinuous, part of the flux and variety of things. Modernism was, in effect, shading into postmodernism, with its resistance to finality or closure, to distinctions between 'high' and 'low' culture, to grand explanations and master narratives – and to the belief that there is one, major or monolithic truth to be apprehended in art. With its preference for suspended judgements, its disbelief in hierarchies, mistrust of solutions, denouements and completions, the postmodernist impulse was a characteristic product of these times. It encouraged forms of writing that thrived on the edge, that denied the authoritative in favour of the arbitrary and posited a random, unstructured world as well as an equally random, unstructured art. This was a different kind of new frontier, perhaps, from the one Kennedy anticipated. But it tapped a similar excitement: 'this country might have / been a pio / neer land, once,' declared the black poet Sonia Sanchez, 'and it still is.'

If one growing tendency of American writing of the 1960s and later was towards postmodernism, another was towards the political. Nowhere was this more notable than among African American writers, like Sanchez. The Black Arts movement, in particular, reacted to calls for 'black power' and a new feeling of racial pride captured in the slogan 'black is beautiful'. Its attempt to define a 'black aesthetic', what it meant to be a specifically black writer, encouraged analogous developments among other ethnic minorities and among women of all races. In conferences and workshops, like the Second Black Writers' Conference at Fisk University in 1967, critics and writers worked with the issues of how literature might properly express and promote political causes. 'The Black Arts and the Black Power concept', Larry Neal (1937–81) wrote at the beginning of his essay 'The Black Arts Movement' (1968), 'both relate broadly to the African American's desire for self-determination and nationhood. Both concepts are nationalistic.' And, just as African American writers became intent on explaining and expressing their solidarity with their black brothers and sisters – the urban poor and dispossessed, the people of the newly independent African nations – so women writers, many of them, expressed a commitment to new forms of feminism. 'We can no longer ignore that voice within women that says, "I want something more than my husband and my children and my home",' wrote Betty Friedan (1921–) in *The Feminine Mystique* (1963). Following on from her, there was an exponential increase in writing about experiences and issues that vitally affected women – women's sexuality, the 'feminine' role, childbirth, domestic politics, lesbianism – and a steady development of feminist criticism and theory, social history and aesthetics. Not long after *The Feminine Mystique* was published, in 1965, Luis Valdez (1940–) combined Mexican American literature with political purpose when he joined with the farmworkers' union, led by César Chavez, to form El Theatre Campesino. This theatre company mixed traditional Spanish and Mexican dramatic forms with agit-prop techniques to create dramatic sketches in support of union issues. The publication of *House Made of Dawn* by N. Scott Momaday in 1968, heralding the emergence of a major movement in Native American writing, coincided with an upsurge in Indian protest: the symbolic seizing of Alcatraz and later armed conflict on reservations that helped generate revisionist histories like *Bury My Heart at Wounded Knee* (1971) by Dee Brown (1908–). Asian Americans, too, gradually asserted their presence, first male writers such as Louis Chu (*Eat a Bowl of Tea*) and then later female writers like Chuang Hua (*Crossings*). In these works, a similar confluence of the personal and political was perceptible: the lives of Chinese men, who have left their wives to search for a better existence in America (*Eat a Bowl of Tea*), the lives of women struggling with the racial and cultural constraints imposed on them by an ancient culture (*Crossings*).

The impulse towards more openly political forms of writing, and the postmodern inclination towards the absurd, both received a push from events that took place not long after President Kennedy took office. Indeed, if his Inauguration acted as a catalyst for the optimism of the early 1960s, then his assassination in Dallas in November 1963 served as a focus for energies of another kind. The belief in the possibility of radical change persisted but it was now continued within a harsher, more abrasive and confrontational sense of the social realities. The divisions and discontent that had always been there – in a society still painfully split between rich and poor, white and black, suburbanite and ghetto-dweller – now came to the surface; the violence that brought the president's life to an end was echoed in the national life, at home and abroad. Of course, there was and is an honoured tradition of protest in American life, ever since the Puritan settlement, and a spirit of unease had been particularly notable in the culture since the late 1950s, symbolized by popular heroes like James Dean and poetic heroes like Allen Ginsberg. But now the protest became more widespread and exacerbated, and the uneasiness burgeoned into open revolt. The civil rights movement, for example, grew more militant. Instead of merely boycotting segregated businesses and services, black and white activists began to use them, challenging the authorities to enforce iniquitous segregationist laws. Confrontations occurred in several Southern townships, between civil rights workers and white authorities: in Little Rock, Arkansas, for instance, in

Selma, Alabama, and Oxford, Mississippi. In August 1963, there was a massive demonstration in Washington, DC, involving over a quarter of a million people, who heard Martin Luther King, the movement's inspired leader, talk of his dream of a multiracial society. The demonstration was notably and triumphantly peaceful: but, in this respect, it marked the end of an era. Within a few years, King himself had been assassinated, and the ghettos of Los Angeles, Detroit, New York, Washington and many other cities were aflame. During the late 1960s, it seemed as if rioting in the streets of the cities had become an annual event, as black people expressed their anger with a social and economic order that tended to deprive them of their basic rights. At the same time, the nation's universities were the scene of almost equally violent confrontations, as students expressed their resistance to local university authorities and the power of the state.

For university students, as for many other protest groups of the time, the central issue was the Vietnam War. In the summer of 1964, President Lyndon Johnson persuaded Congress to give him almost unlimited powers to wage war against what was perceived as the Communist threat from North Vietnam. American troops were committed to a massive land war against an indigenous guerrilla movement; the American military was involved in saturation bombing and what was euphemistically known as 'defoliation' – that is, destruction of the forests, the vegetation and plant life of a country situated about 12,000 miles from Washington; and American policy was, effectively, to bleed the nation's human and economic resources in support of what was little more than a puppet government in South Vietnam. By 1967, millions of Americans were beginning to feel that the war was not only useless but obscene, and took to the streets in protest: these included novelists like Norman Mailer and poets like Robert Lowell and Allen Ginsberg. Simultaneously with this, in response to what looked like the obscenity of the official culture, a vigorous alternative culture developed. Much of this alternative culture was specifically political in its direction. Young men burned their draft cards; and, when the Democratic Party met in Chicago in 1968 to nominate their candidate for president, young people upstaged the proceedings by engaging in pitched battles with the police in the streets. But much of it, too, had to do with styles of life and styles of art. Hair was worn unconventionally long, skirts unconventionally short; hallucinogenic drugs, psychedelic art, hugely amplified rock concerts all became part of an instinctive strategy for challenging standard versions of social reality, accepted notions of behaviour and gender. The analytical mode was supplanted by the expressive, the intellectual by the imaginative; artists as a whole went even further towards embracing a sense of the provisional, a fluid, unstructured reality; and artistic eclecticism became the norm, as writers in general hit upon unexpected aesthetic mixtures – mingling fantasy and commitment, myth and social protest, high and popular art.

One of the paradoxes of the year 1968 was that it witnessed alternative culture at its zenith *and* the election of Richard Nixon, self-proclaimed spokesman for the 'silent majority' of white middle-class Americans, to the office of president. To the extent that 'the Sixties' have become a convenient label for a particular frame of mind – radical, experimental, subversive and even confrontational – they did not end in 1970 any more than they began in 1960. Many aspects of the alternative culture survived well into the next decade; and some, like the feminist and ecological movements, effectively became part of the cultural mainstream. Nevertheless, the election of such an un-alternative, un-radical president as Nixon, and his re-election in 1972, did signal a shift in the national mood that was gradually confirmed in the 1970s and beyond. The Vietnam War was brought to an ignominious end, removing one of the major sources of confrontation and revolt. Black Americans remained economically dispossessed, but the civil rights movement did increase their electoral power, and so gave them the opportunity of expressing their dissatisfaction through the ballot-box rather than by taking to the streets. The children of the postwar 'baby boom', who had fuelled the fires of apparent revolution, began to enter the workforce and take on the responsibilities of jobs, homes and families. And, while the United States continued to prosper – the gross national product had risen to $974 billion in 1970 – there were worrying signs of possible economic crisis. Inflation was worse than in most Western European countries; the balance of payments deficit began to grow to frightening proportions; while the dollar steadily lost its purchasing power. As the economic situation grew harsher, especially after the oil crisis of the early 1970s, more and more Americans narrowed their horizons, devoting their attention and energies to the accumulation and preservation of personal wealth. One commentator christened the 1970s 'the me decade'; another referred to the culture of narcissism. And these significant tendencies did not alter with the resignation of Nixon. First Gerald Ford, and then later Jimmy Carter and Ronald Reagan, offered distinct alternatives to the radicalism of the 1960s. With Carter, for instance, there was a new emphasis on the limits to growth and power and a new, introspective moralism: 'Your strength', he told the American public at his Inauguration in 1977, 'can compensate for my weakness, and your wisdom can minimize my mistakes.' The rhetoric of Reagan might have sounded similar, at times, to that of Kennedy: when, for instance, he talked about building a shining city upon a hill or declared that the best years of America were yet to come. But this rhetoric occurred within structures of belief and assumptions that were quite different from those of the assassinated president. For Reagan, the crucial appeal was to the past, the mythical American past of stable, familial and to an extent pastoral values that, as he saw it, it was the duty of Americans to recover; and to this predominantly backward-looking impulse was added a strong sense of personal responsibility, a feeling that each American should look after himself or herself, which found little room for accommodating the communal vision of an earlier decade.

Reagan might have appealed to the past. Later, in the 1990s, Bill Clinton might have tried to claim some of the spirit of the 1960s for himself, with his talk of being part of a raw, new postwar generation, his declaration of belief in a place called Hope, and, not least, his use of an old movie showing him, as a boy, shaking hands with John Kennedy. The two President George Bushes, father and son, might suggest in turn a warier, more combative and conservative America. What all these presidents have in common, however, is what they have presided over: a dissolution of the old social and cultural markers. Many of the great nation-states have disintegrated, notably, that sinister other of Cold War America, the Union of Soviet Socialist Republics. Along with them the great narratives, the metanarratives used once to explain historical movement, have lost plausibility. The myth of Plymouth Rock, for example, of America as the exclusive domain for Europeans seeking religious and political freedom has far less resonance in a world characterized by transnational drift and an American nation that is more than ever multicultural. So does the classic iconography of the United States as a melting pot, in which all cultures, all nationalities, are resolving into one. Which brings in the most significant series of markers that have now disappeared. American popular culture has become internationally dominant. In the global marketplace, it is America that is the biggest item on sale. In a postcolonial world, our imaginations have been colonized by the United States. At the same time, and crucially, the United States itself has been internationalized. It has become not a melting pot but a mosaic of different cultures, what one American writer, Ishmael Reed, has called 'the first universal nation'.

'The world is here,' Reed declared in an essay called, appropriately enough, 'America: The Multinational Society' (1988). And the world is there, in the United States, for these seminal reasons. In the first place, particular ethnic groups that have been there for centuries have gained in presence and prominence. The National Census of 1990, for instance, reported 1,959,234 Native Americans living in a total population of over 248 million Americans. This figure was an almost fourfold increase on the number of 523,591 Native Americans reported in the 1960 Census, which in turn built upon the population nadir of around 250,000 in 1900. The huge rise in the Native American population was attributable to a consistently high birth rate, and improved medical care, but also to the increased number of people who claimed Native American ancestry. Whether or not, as some cultural commentators have claimed, ethnicity is a matter of consciousness rather than cultural difference, it is clear that the consciousness of ethnicity has secured the status and significance of certain ethnic groups in the United States. Many more Americans are proud, eager, to define themselves as Native American. Many Mexican Americans, in turn, have lived in a cultural borderlands for two centuries, what they call *la frontera*, thanks to Spanish conquest and then American annexation. In his novel *Becky and Her Friends* (1990), for example, the Mexican American novelist Rolando Hinojosa records of one of his characters that she 'was born a Spanish subject in 1814; at age ten she was a Mexican citizen; by the summer of 1836, she was a Texan. Later, in 1845, an American when Texas was annexed that December 21st.' And their numbers have steadily grown, thanks not only to natural increase but to waves of immigration, especially during and after the Second World War. Along with certain other ethnic groups, notably those from Cuba, Dominica and Puerto Rico, Mexican Americans have effected a sea change in American culture and transformed the demographic destiny of the nation. So much so that, in 1997, the Census Bureau calculated that by 2050 Hispanics would account for nearly one in four of the American population: 96 million in a total of 393 million.

'American literature, especially in the twentieth century, and notably in the last twenty years,' Toni Morrison wrote in 1992, 'has been shaped by its encounter with the immigrant.' Which leads to the second seminal reason why the United States has become 'the first universal nation'. Along with immigrants from the Hispanic world, those from the third world generally have been changing the character and destiny of the United States, especially after legislation in the 1960s first abolished national-origin quotas (which tended to favour Northern Europeans) and then expanded immigration from countries such as China and India. Almost nine million legal immigrants came to America during the 1980s, along with two million undocumented immigrants. They accounted for 29 per cent of the population growth from 226.5 million to 248.7 million during the decade. From 1990 to 1997, another seven and a half million foreign-born individuals entered the United States legally, accounting for 29.2 per cent of the population. By the middle of the twenty-first century, it has been calculated, 'non-white' and third world ethnic groups will outnumber whites in the United States. And the 'average' American resident will trace his or her ancestry to Asia, Africa, some part of the Hispanic world, the Pacific Islands, Arabia – almost anywhere but white Europe. Revealing the central dynamic of Western, and in some sense global, life today, which is marked by the powerful shaping force of shifting, multicultural populations, America has witnessed the disappearance of the boundary between the 'centre' and the 'margins'. And with white Americans moving, it seems, inexorably into a minority, it has lost any claim it may have had, or any pretence of one, to a Eurocentric character and an exclusive destiny.

The consequences of all this for literature in America are debatable. Given that writers are responding on some level to their own unique encounters with history, they are in any event not easy, perhaps impossible, to summarize. For some, there has been a notable shift away from public affairs and commitment and towards introspection, the cult of the personal. Writers, quite a few of them, have turned away from immediate history, the pressures of the times, and devoted their imaginations to the vagaries of consciousness, the deeper forms of myth, ritual and fantasy, the imagery figured and the language articulated by the isolated mind. For others, particularly many women writers and writers from 'ethnic' or 'non-white' cultures, the engagement with history remains pressing, even painful: although the terms in which that engagement is expressed may vary from the literal, the direct, as in the New Journalism and forms of social realism, to the resonantly abstract, the figurative or the archaic. Writers may devote themselves, say, to the interrogation and alteration of verbal structures, in the belief that what we see and think is shaped by such structures; our social life being grounded in language, in order to change society it is language that must be changed. Or they may respond to what Clifford Geertz has called 'the international hodgepodge of postmodern culture' by creating an art of palpable discontinuity, yoking together wildly incongruous elements, mixing voices and genres, pursuing the inconsistent, the divergent and indeterminate. They may be inclined to the use of fabulation, magic or dreams in the conviction that consciousness shapes history – or the simpler assumption that only a literature of the strange, the fantastic, can begin to recover the strangeness of contemporary America. Or they may turn to the oral or other traditions of one of the ancient cultures that inform American history: not to legitimate that culture (the time for that, if there ever was one, has long gone), but to explore the meanings of those traditions for all American society.

What surely all these, and other, forms of writing in contemporary America share is their condition: their presence in a permeable space where nations and cultures meet. This is the space that writers in America now inhabit and struggle to represent. It is a liminal space, the space of postmodernity or radicalized modernity, marked by dissolution and dispersal, mobility and fragmentation, the heterogeneous and the hybrid – all on a global scale. Representing different cultures, living between them, and responding to their diverse origins and experiences, all these writers effectively challenge the notion of a common heritage and fixed boundaries. In doing so, of course, they challenge the assumptions so central to the grand narrative of the American state. The country they discover and describe in their work does not have the older, absolute contours of the American Eden. It is a place with fluid boundaries, where rival, overlapping and ultimately interdependent cultural histories meet, conflict and perhaps converge. American writers are still, as much as ever, concerned with the possibles and variables of American life, the material and mental contours of the American landscape, the imperatives of American history, and the inspiration of the American dream. But the possibles of American life have multiplied; the contours of the American landscape have assumed a more elusive, enigmatic character; the imperatives of American history are more plural, more polyglot than ever before; and the American dream now is inspired by what seems a process of accelerated transformation, insistent reinvention. Responding to these changes, American writers have changed. What has happened may be measured in a small but significant shifting of words: American writing is now writing in America. The point is simple but fundamental. Nationality, at the scene of writing, is less determined and determining than it ever was previously, more open to other stories and histories. The scene of writing is one that is now genuinely transnational.

Formalists and Confessionals

From the mythological eye to the lonely 'I' in poetry

In the period immediately following the Second World War, American writers looked back – in anger, in regret, in grief, in relief or in one or more of many other series of emotions – on a conflict that had threatened to engulf humankind. Among these were the numerous poets who wrote of their own involvement in conflicts for which – as one of them, Randall Jarrell, put it – 'The soldier sells his family and his days'. 'It is I who have killed, /' declared Karl Shapiro (1913–2000), 'It is I whose enjoyment of horror is fulfilled', and, for a while, this sense of having participated in a great historical crisis nurtured a poetry that was notable for its engagement, its direct address to public issues and events. In 1945, for instance, two substantial collections of war poems were published, *The War Poets* edited by the influential anthologist Oscar Williams (1900–64) and *War and the Poet* edited by Richard Eberhart. Not long after this, Louis Simpson (1923–), in poetry included in *The Arrivistes: Poems 1940–9* (1949), produced work that spoke sardonically of 'war-heroes, . . . wounded war-heroes', 'packaged and sent home in parts', and that tried, too, to capture the tension, the actual experience of war. Shapiro, for his part, in early collections like *Person, Place and Thing* (1942), produced plangent memorials for the unknown soldier ('Elegy for a Dead Soldier'), bitter accounts of a war machine in which 'Trains lead to ships and ships to death or trains' ('Troop Train'), and vivid descriptions of the life of an ordinary conscript during battles ('Full Moon: New Guinea') and on the return home ('Homecoming'). 'Lord, I have seen too much', begins one of Shapiro's poems; and that remark suggests the documentary accuracy, tinged with a bitter knowingness, a sense of having *seen* what life is really like at its worst, that characterizes many of these pieces.

But if documentary accuracy was the primary aim of most of these poets, this did not necessarily preclude other ambitions. In particular, many writers were keen to see the war in mythological terms. 'Lord, I have seen too much', for example, ends with the poet-combatant comparing himself to Adam 'driven from Eden to the East to dwell'; and the legend of the Fall became a favourite way of adding a further resonance to global conflict. This was especially true of Randall Jarrell (1914–65), whose volumes of poetry began with *Blood for a Stranger* (1942) and whose *Complete Poems* were published in 1969. Innocence, and its destruction, obsessed him; and the war became for Jarrell a powerful symbol of loss, a reversal of the westward myth in that his combatants invariably 'fall to the East' (as Shapiro puts it), from innocence to suffering and experience. This does not mean that his war poems are lacking in documentary detail. On the contrary, they give a vivid, particularized portrait of the life of pilots and gunners ('Eighth Air Force'), life aboard aircraft carriers ('Pilots, Man Your Planes'), in prisoner-of-war camps ('Stalag Luft'), in barracks, camp and field ('Transient Barracks', 'A Lullaby', 'Mail Call'). What is remarkable, however, is Jarrell's capacity for capturing the dual nature of the experience of war. As he presents it, war makes life more 'real' – in the sense that it brings people closer to the pressures of history and the physical acts of living and dying – and more 'unreal' – in that it cuts them off from everyday routine, propelling them into an unfamiliar realm, a world of potential nightmare. 'The soldiers are all haunted by their lives', Jarrell remarks in one piece; and it is this feeling of moving through experience half-asleep and half-awake, together with imagery of a monstrous birth, of a fall in which innocence is violated, that distinguishes his most famous war poem, 'The Death of the Ball Turret Gunner'.

The work of Randall Jarrell in fact indicates the direction in which American poetry was to go within ten years of the end of the war: towards mythology, the use of dream and archetype. His poems are, certainly, intimate and idiomatic. 'What can be more tedious', he asked, 'than a man whose every sentence is a balanced epigram without wit, profundity and taste?' Particularly in his later pieces, where he turns from a taut, often strained voice to a richly varied use of iambics, he manages to capture the lively play of his speech and mind. In all his poems, however, and especially the earlier ones, the lively texture is complicated by the use of legends, dreams and fairytale. 'All this I dreamed in my great ragged bed . . . / Or so I dreamed', he says in one piece; in another, he refers to a young girl reading in a library as 'An object among dreams'. Frequently, the dream convention or the structure of fairytale enables him to edge between the real and the surreal; soldiers mingle with figures from the Gospels in his work, ordinary people rub shoulders with angels, devils, corn kings or characters from the Brothers Grimm. 'Behind everything', Jarrell insists, 'there is always / The unknown unwanted life'; and his extraordinary capacity for combining what he called 'the plain / Flat object-language of a child' with the vocabulary of dream registers this. The plain surfaces of a world where, so often, 'we miss our lives' and the 'inconceivable enchantment' beneath: they are both there, in the amphibious medium of his writing, recalling us constantly to his own sense that 'Living is more dangerous than anything'.

Writing in 1952, W. H. Auden commented on this interest in legends and archetypes that seemed to characterize a new generation of poets. Auden's remarks were written as a preface to the first volume of W. S. Merwin (1927–), *A Mask for Janus* (1952); and Merwin, at least in his earlier work, illustrates this mythologizing tendency even more clearly than Jarrell. With Jarrell, the impulse towards the legendary is tempered by his use of peculiarly fluent, even flat forms of speech and his professed commitment to the lives and dreams of ordinary people, their losses, their courage and their longing for change. In the early poetry of Merwin, however, the landscape is stylized and anonymous (there are, in fact, no references to the United States in the 1950s); the language is elevated and often archaic; and the tone is distanced, hieratic. The opening of 'Dictum: For a Masque of Deluge' is typical: 'There will be the cough before the silence, then / Expectation; and the hush of portent / Must be welcomed by diffident music.' Exploiting traditional metres, populated by archetypal figures and ancient myths, this is a poetry that absolutely refuses any accommodation to the contemporary. Its subjects are the perennial ones of birth, death and renewal, departure and return, and it deals with them in terms of allegory and parable, a vocabulary as old as the human race.

If the early poetry of Merwin reveals a characteristic feature of American poetry at the beginning of the 1950s, then the work of Richard Wilbur (1921–) illustrates analogous ones. 'Most American poets of my generation', Wilbur has said, 'were taught to admire the English Metaphysical poets . . . and such contemporary masters of irony as John Crowe Ransom . . . Poetry could not be honest, we thought, unless it began by acknowledging the full discordancy of modern life . . . I still believe that to be a true view of poetry.' For Wilbur, the appropriate way of acknowledging discordancy in verse is to accommodate it within an elaborate formal structure. The poet, he argues, has to convert 'events' into 'experiences', and he does this through a skilful application of form; the poet's forms supply a context, while his ironic, quizzical yet steady voice draws disparate elements together, relates them and holds them in equilibrium. The precision, the sense of control supplied by a traditional framework, is necessary: but so also are lightness of touch, wit, irony and ambiguity, so as to prevent a hardening of the poetic arteries – to preserve nuances of feeling, the flash and play of this 'maculate, cracked, askew / Gay-pocked and potsherd world'. 'The strength of the genie', Wilbur declared, 'comes of his being confined in a bottle'; and, in saying this, he was speaking for many poets of his generation, with their belief in 'Beauty joined to energy', the magical, liberating possibilities of form.

'Poems are not addressed to anybody in particular,' Wilbur declared; 'The poem . . . is a conflict with disorder, not a message from one person to another.' To make a crude but serviceable distinction: he committed himself, early on in his career, to the idea of the poem as object rather than vehicle of communication, an object with its own 'strictness of form'. Having made that commitment, he has stuck to it, from the early poems gathered in *The Beautiful Changes and Other Poems* (1967), through *The Poems of Richard Wilbur* (1963), to later collections such as *The Mind-Reader* (1976) and *Mayflies: New Poems and Translations* (2000). Others of roughly his generation have done so too: among them, Stanley Kunitz, Weldon Kees, Reed Whittemore, Howard Nemerov, Anthony Hecht, Edgar Bowers, Donald Justice, X. J. Kennedy – and above all, in her own inimitable way, Elizabeth Bishop. After the early 1950s, however, many American poets actively rejected formalism, and the mythologizing tendency, and went in search of other gods, new ways of turning the world into words. Some of those ways will be considered later. The main one worth mentioning here is the movement towards autobiography: poetry became, once again, not a flight from personality but a dramatization, a reinvention of the personal. The first person, 'I', was restored to the centre of the poem. Recovering one of the major impulses, probably the major one, in the American tradition, poets began placing themselves squarely at the centre of the poem. The poet's private self became both subject and speaker, just as it had in 'Song of Myself'; the growth of the poet's mind informed the narrative or supplied whatever coherence there might be; and the poet addressed the reader directly, with an often unnerving intimacy, as if that reader were confessor, therapist, friend or even lover. These lines, taken from very different poems, illustrate the change – or, to be more exact, the rediscovery of what Whitman meant when he said, 'Who touches this book touches a man':

> I'm writing this poem for someone to see when
>   I'm not looking. This is an open book.
>   (Karl Shapiro, 'I'm writing this poem for someone to see')

From the mythological eye to the lonely 'I' in poetry   567

I am taking part in a great experiment –
whether writers can live peacefully in the suburbs
and not be bored to death.
>   (Louis Simpson, 'Sacred Objects')

I was stamped out like a Plymouth fender
into this world.
First came the crib
with its glacial bars.
>   (Anne Sexton, 'Rowing')

I'm Everett Leroi Jones, 30 yrs. old.
A black nigger in the universe.
>   (Imamu Amiri Baraka [Leroi Jones], 'Numbers, Letters')

I must write for myself . . .
I look at my face in the glass and see
a halfborn woman . . .
>   (Adrienne Rich, 'Upper Broadway')

I haven't read one book about
A book or memorized one plot.
Or found a mind I did not doubt.
I learned one date. And then forgot.
>   (W. D. Snodgrass, 'April Inventory')

I have no priest for now
Who
will forgive me then. Will you?
>   (John Logan, 'Three Moves')

I am busy tired mad lonely & old.
O this has been a long long night of wrest.
>   (John Berryman, 'Damned')

I am only thirty.
And like a cat I have nine times to die.
>   (Sylvia Plath, 'Lady Lazarus')

I myself am hell,
– nobody's here.

>   (Robert Lowell, 'Skunk Hour')

'Be guilty of yourself in the full looking glass', a poet of a slightly earlier generation, Delmore Schwartz, had said; and that injunction, to see and know the truth about oneself no matter how painful or embarrassing it might be, is clearly the enterprise, the heart of these poems.

This rediscovery of the personal in American poetry assumed many forms – as various, finally, as the poets involved. At one extreme are poets who attempted to plunge into the unconscious: in the work of Robert Bly (1926–) (whose best collection is *The Light Around the Body* [1967]), Robert Kelly (1935–) (some of whose best work is in *Finding the Measure* [1968]), Galway Kinnell (1923–) (whose *Selected Poems* appeared in 1982) and James Wright (1927–80) (*Collected Poems* [1971]), for example, the poet dives down beneath the level of rational discourse, using subliminal imagery and a logic of association to illuminate the darker areas of the self, the seabed of personal feeling, dream and intuition. In Robert Bly's case, exploration of the subrational has led him towards 'tiny poems', in imitation of the Chinese, and prose poems that are, as he puts it, 'an exercise in moving against "plural consciousness"'. His aim is to uncover the 'dense energy that pools in the abdomen', as he has it in a poem titled 'When the Wheel Does Not Move': the fierce, mystical forces that unite him, at the deepest level, with the looser, livelier forms of the natural world. Kelly and Kinnell dip perhaps even further down. 'My wife is not my wife,' Kelly insists in one of his poems, called 'Jealousy', '/ *wife* is the name of a / process, an energy moving, / not an identity, / nothing in this world is / mine but my action.' To articulate the process, the activity that constitutes identity, Kelly has devised a poetry that is a haunting mixture of dream, chant and ritual: his poems are an attempt to translate the interpenetration of things into intelligible (although not necessarily paraphraseable) signs and sounds. 'The organism / of the macrocosm,' as he puts it in 'prefix', 'the organism of language, / the organism of *I* combine in ceaseless naturing / to propagate a fourth, / the poem, / from their trinity.' Kinnell began from a rather different base from Kelly, in that his earlier poems were informed by a traditional Christian sensibility. But, while retaining a sacramental dimension, his later work burrows ferociously into the self, away from the traditional sources of religious authority – and away, too, from conventional notions of personality. 'If you could keep going deeper and deeper, /' he wrote in 1978, 'you'd finally not be a person . . . you'd be an / animal; and if you kept going deeper and / deeper, you'd be . . . / ultimately perhaps a stone. And if a stone / could read poetry would speak for it.'

The poems that issue from this conviction show Kinnell trying to strip away formal, verbal and even surface emotional constructs, anything that might dissipate or impede the poet's continuing exploration of his deepest self and experience. 'How many nights', he asks in 'Another Night in the Ruins', 'must it take / one such as me to learn / . . . / that for a man / as he goes up in flames, his one work / is / to open himself, to *be* / the flames?' Short, chanting lines, a simple, declarative syntax, emphatic rhythms, bleak imagery and insistent repetition: all turn the poet into a kind of shaman, who describes strange apocalyptic experiences in which he throws off the 'sticky infusion' of speech and becomes one with the natural world ('The Bear') or participates in the primal experiences of birth ('Under the Maud Moon') and death ('How Many Nights'). The tone of James Wright's work is quieter, less prophetic than this: but, he too, attempts to unravel from his own unconscious the secret sources of despair and joy. Of another poet whom he

---

admired, Georg Trakl, Wright said this: 'In Trakl, a series of images makes a series of events. Because these events appear out of their "natural" order, without the connection we have learned to expect from reading the newspapers, doors silently open to unused parts of the brain.' This describes the procedures of many of Wright's own poems, which evolve quietly through layers of images until they surface with the quick thrust of a striking final image or epiphany. For instance, in 'Lying in a Hammock at William Duffy's Farm in Pine Island, Minnesota', Wright carefully annotates his surroundings. 'Over my head', he begins, 'I see the bronze butterfly / Asleep on the black trunk / Blowing like a leaf in green shadow.' The vision of the butterfly suggests a being wholly at one with the world: entrusted, pliable, possessed of the stillness of a plant or even a mineral ('bronze'). This feeling persists into the following lines through the subtle harmonizing of time and space ('the distances of afternoon') and the sense of cowbells, heard from far off, as the musical measure of both. It is growing late, however, and as 'evening darkens' a succession of images tolls the poet back to his sole self. The last two lines complete the series and confirm the discovery: 'A chicken hawk floats over, looking for home. / I have wasted my life.' The hawk, presumably, will find its home; it possesses the ease, the buoyancy and assurance, that characterize the other natural objects in this landscape. But the poet will not. He can see in the things of this world only a vivid, subliminal reminder of ruin, his failure truly to live. Surprising though this last line may seem, it has been carefully prepared for by the hidden agenda of the poem; the images that constitute the argument, strange and emotionally precise as they are, have opened the doors to this revelation.

While writers such as Wright and Kinnell have tried to register the movements of the subconscious, others have dramatized the personal in more discursive, conscious forms. These include poets like Richard Hugo (1923–82), Karl Shapiro and Louis Simpson, who explore the self's discovery of the outer world and its reaction to it, and, rather more significant, those like John Logan (1923–87), Adrienne Rich (1929–), Anne Sexton (1923–74) and W. D. Snodgrass (1926–) who incorporate elements of their personal histories in their poems. In the poetry of Richard Hugo, collected in 1984, the personal dimension is founded on the relationship between the private self of the poet and the bleak, lonesome world he describes. The setting he favours is the Far West – not the Far West of legend, however, but a far more inhospitable, emptier place. Looking at one decaying township in Montana, he asks himself, 'Isn't this your life?'; and his own poetic voice, sombre and laconic, seems to answer him in the affirmative. Yet he can also learn from his surroundings; their strength of spirit, 'rage' and endurance, have stamped their mark on him. 'To live good, keep your life and the scene,' he concludes in 'Montgomery Hollow', '/ Cow, brook, hay: these are the names of coins': the currency of the West has, in fact, saved him from moral bankruptcy, helped him pay his dues to himself and the world. Hugo's poetic stance has hardly shifted over the years: by contrast, Shapiro and Simpson began (as we have seen) as poets of public event, and only gradually changed their interests and allegiances. As the personal element in their poetry grew, so its shape and tone altered too. 'Sabotage the stylistic approach,' Shapiro commanded in 'Lower the standard: that's my motto', '. . . Get off the Culture Wagon. Learn how to walk the way you want.' Attacking 'the un-American-activity of the sonnet', writing pieces with titles like 'Anti-Poem', he adopted a long, flowing line somewhere between free verse and prose poetry. With this, he has explored himself and his surroundings (in volumes like *Poems of a Jew* [1958]) with sometimes embarrassing frankness: 'When I say the Hail Mary I get an erection,' he admits in 'Priests and Freudians will understand', adding wryly, 'Doesn't that prove the existence of God?' The alteration in Simpson's work (as a collection like *At the End of the Open Road: Poems* [1963] indicates) has been less radical: his verse, while becoming freer, has retained an iambic base. But he, too, wants to know what it is like to be him at this moment in history, 'an American muse / installed amid the kitchen ware'. Like Whitman, he is concerned with the representative status of his self, his Americanness; unlike Whitman, his landscapes are often suburban. 'Where are you Walt?' Simpson asks in 'Walt Whitman at Bear Mountain', observing sardonically, '/ The Open Road goes to the used-car lot': that observation measures the distance, as well as the kinship, between its author and the person addressed, the first, finest poet of national identity.

Of the four poets just mentioned who insert their own histories directly into their narratives, John Logan (whose several collections include *The Bridge of Change: Poems 1974–9* [1980]) is the most apparently casual. His poems seem simple, informal: 'Three moves in six months,' begins one, 'and I remain the same.' But, in fact, they are carefully organized, to allow for a subtle orchestration of theme and tone. In the poem just quoted, for instance, 'Three Moves', he graduates from startling colloquialism ('You're all fucked up') to moments of lyricism and grace: 'These foolish ducks lack a sense of guilt / and so all their multi-thousand-mile range / is too short for the hope of change.' And although, as these lines imply, Logan himself suffers from 'a sense of guilt' from which the animal kingdom is blessedly free, he can occasionally participate in the vitality, the innocence of the natural world around him. 'There is a freshness / nothing can destroy in us –', he says in 'Spring of the Thief'; 'Perhaps that / *Freshness* is the changed name of God.' The voice of W. D. Snodgrass, and his stance towards nature, is at once more controlled and intense. His finest work is 'Heart's Needle' (1959), a series of poems which have as their subject his daughter and his loss of her through marital breakdown. 'Child of my winter,' begins the first poem, 'born / When the new fallen soldiers froze / In Asia's steep ravines and fouled the snows.' Cynthia, the poet's child, was born during the Korean War and she is, he gently suggests, the fruit of his own 'cold war': the static, frozen winter campaign that is getting nowhere is also Snodgrass's marriage. The allusions to the war, and descriptions of the season, are there not because of any intrinsic interest they may possess, historical, geographical or whatever, but because they image the poet's inner world, his personal feelings. 'We need the landscape to repeat us,' Snodgrass observes later: the measured, musical quality of his verse, and his frequent attention to objects and narrative, disguise an obsessive inwardness, a ferocious preoccupation with the subjective.

'My poems . . . keep right on singing the same old song': the words could belong to Snodgrass, but in fact they were spoken by Anne Sexton, whose first two collections, *To Bedlam and Part Way Back* (1960) and *All My Pretty Ones* (1962), established both her reputation and her intensely personal stance. Even those pieces by Sexton that appear not to be concerned with herself usually turn out to be subjective, to have to do with her predicament as a woman. 'The Farmer's Wife', for instance, begins as a description of someone in rural Illinois, caught up in 'that old pantomime of love', and then concludes with lines that suddenly switch the focus from farmer and wife to the poet and her lover. Elsewhere, when the narrative mask is dropped, the tone can be painfully raw and open, and given a further edge by elaborate rhyme schemes or tight stanzaic forms. 'All My Pretty Ones' is a good illustration of this. Addressed to the poet's father, the contrast between the passion and intimacy of the address and the strictness of the given measure only exacerbates the situation, intensifies the feeling of the poem. It is as if the disciplines of the poetic form, which Sexton confronts in a half-yielding, half-rebellious fashion, were part of the paternal inheritance, something else that the father she both loves and hates has left her to deal with. However, she was not only concerned with the pain of being daughter, wife, mother, lover. She also sang, as she put it, 'in celebration of the woman I am'. Long before it was fashionable to do so, she wrote in praise of her distinctive identity, not just as an American poet, but as an American *female* poet. 'As the African says,' she declares in 'Rowing', 'This is my tale which I have told'; and for her this tale was, finally, a source of pride.

A similar pride in the condition of being a woman characterizes the poetry of Adrienne Rich. Rich's early work in *A Change of World* (1951) and *The Diamond Cutters* (1955) is decorous, formal, restrained. But even here there is a sense of the subversive impulses that lie just below the smooth surfaces of life. In 'Aunt Jennifer's Tigers', for example, the character who gives the poem its title seems to be crushed beneath patriarchal authority: 'The massive weight of Uncle's wedding band / Sits heavily upon Aunt Jennifer's hand.' However, the tigers she has embroidered 'across a screen' suggest her indomitable spirit. Even after her death, 'The tigers in the panel that she made / Will go on prancing, proud and unafraid'. 'Sleek chivalric' and poised as they are, these animals nevertheless emblematize certain rebellious energies, turbulent emotions that will not be contained: polite on the surface, passionate beneath, Aunt Jennifer's art is, at this stage, Adrienne Rich's art. Gradually, though, Rich came to feel that she could 'no longer go to write a poem with a neat handful of materials and express these materials according to a prior plan'. 'Instead of poems *about* experience,' she argued, 'I am getting poems that *are* experiences.' A work like 'Diving into the Wreck', the title poem in her 1973 collection, measures the change. In it, the poet tells of a journey under the sea, during which she has to discard all the conventional supports, the crutches on which she has leaned in the upper world. 'I came to explore the wreck, /' she says: 'The words are purposes. / The words are maps.' And she describes what she calls 'the thing I came for: / the wreck and not the story of the wreck / the thing itself and not the myth'. Diving deep into the innermost recesses of her being, exploring the 'wreck' of her own life, Rich feels compelled to jettison inherited techniques and fictions. A more open, vulnerable and tentative art is required, she feels, in order to map the geography of her self: a feeling that is signalled in this poem not only by its argument but by its directness of speech, its stark imagery and idiomatic rhythms, above all by the urgency of its tone. The map, as it happens, is not just for her own use. 'We are confronted', Rich has declared in the Preface to *On Lies, Secrets and Silence: Selected Poems 1966–1978* (1979), 'with . . . the failure of patriarchal politics.' 'To be a woman at this time', she goes on, 'is to know extraordinary forms of anger, joy and impatience, love and hope.' 'Poetry, words on paper, are necessary but not enough,' she insists; 'we need to touch the living who share . . . our determination that the sexual myths underlying the human condition can and shall be . . . changed.' In Rich's later work, in fact, the confrontation with herself is inseparable from her broader, feminist purposes; her work has become intimate, confessional, but it is an intimacy harnessed to the service of the community, the invention of a new social order.

From formalism to freedom in poetry

The example of Adrienne Rich is interesting and symptomatic in several ways. In the first place, her later poetry shows how ready American poets have become to take risks. 'I have been increasingly willing', she has said, 'to let the unconscious offer its material, to listen to more than the voice of a single idea.' This does not mean that she offers the reader unmediated psychic experience: as she is aware ('the words are maps'), such a thing is impossible and probably undesirable as well. Her aim, on the contrary, is like that of many of her contemporaries: to surrender to her material and then, in the act of writing, try to re-enact its complex rhythms – to turn activity, physical, emotional, or whatever, into speech and breath. In the second, she illustrates the particular triumph of the better poets of the personal. Her best work – 'Diving into the Wreck', for instance, or 'The Will to Change' – is squeezed out of her own intimate experience, it can be painfully straightforward and frank, but it can also be surreal and political. Personal experience, after all, includes dream and history: the fantasies of the inner life and also the facts of that larger world of war, work and income tax to which every one of us, whether we like it or not, is subject. Rich's poetry acknowledges this. It absorbs the data of private events, the dramas of the public stage, and the fears and desires encountered in sleep. It incorporates the conscious and subconscious levels, intimate confession and the historical imagination; as such, it bears comparison with the work of the finest poets of the personal mode over the past forty years – Theodore Roethke, John Berryman, Robert Lowell and Sylvia Plath. Finally, Rich is representative in a richer, broader sense, in that she was far from alone in terms of her stylistic development from formal to freer verse forms. Not everyone ceased to be a formalist. Nor did those who changed their poetic voice necessarily do so as Rich – or, for that matter, Shapiro and Simpson – did, as part of a commitment to a more confessional mode. But, whether interested in personal confession or not, many poets turned at about the same time Rich did (that is, in the late 1950s or early 1960s) towards a more open and idiomatic poetry – in search of what one poet, Alan Dugan, has called 'words wrung out of intense experience and not constructed'.

Among the poets who show this alteration is Donald Hall (1928–) (the range of whose work is shown in *The Alligator Bride: Poems New and Selected* [1969]), who moved from traditional forms, as in 'My Son, My Executioner', to the more fluent and relaxed measures of poems like 'The Town of Hill' and 'Maple Syrup'. More important, there is Robert Bly, who began by writing short, quiet, carefully constructed portraits of rural life and landscapes in the West before graduating to a more sensuous, various and insinuating music – as in 'Looking into a Face'. 'I have risen to a body / Not yet born, /' Bly declares here, 'Existing like a light around the body / Through which the body moves like a shining moon.' Bly's later poetry of the apocalypse, experiences at once mystical and erotic, in fact gains its impact from his mastery of very free verse forms. The feeling of an experience that is simultaneously luminous and unknown – present but as yet undisclosed to the rational sense – is caught not only in the imagery of light and incantatory repetition but in the stealthy yet passionate movement of the verse. A similar transfiguration of restless life into mobile language is noticeable in the later work of W. S. Merwin. His earlier poetry – as some lines from 'Dictum: For a Masque of Deluge', quoted earlier, illustrate – is formal and mythological, with the poet concealed behind the text paring his fingernails. From this Merwin moved, in collections like *The Moving Target* (1963) and *The Carrier of Ladders* (1970), to more contemporary, sometimes personal subjects, though mostly written in fairly regular iambics ('Pool Room in the Lion's Club', 'Grandmother Dying'), and then on, in turn, to the angular, radically disruptive rhythms of 'Morning': 'The first morning / I woke in surprise to your body / for I had been dreaming it / as I do.' This is certainly not confessional verse, but it does represent a startling departure from Merwin's earlier work. 'We are words on a journey,' Merwin insists in one of his later poems, 'An Encampment at Morning', '/ not the inscriptions of settled people', and that remark alone serves to illustrate the change: an interest in the more obviously permanent forms of human vision and voice has been replaced by a pursuit of the mobile and temporary – of life as it passes, in all its rapid, disjunctive rhythms.

The change from formal to freer verse forms has not, however, always been a happy one. The earlier poems of Delmore Schwartz (1913–66), collected in *In Dreams Begin Responsibilities* (1938), were predominantly iambic, and the relative strictness of the forms he employed seems to have exercised a useful discipline. Some of these poems represent Schwartz as the engaged observer. Other pieces are more like an open wound: 'Shy, pale, and quite abstracted', Schwartz is confronted by the ineluctable, ugly fact of himself. 'I am I', one poem concludes; and to know who that 'I' is, Schwartz finds it necessary to deal with the accumulated debts of his past. 'The past is inevitable', he insists, and what the 'ghost in the mirror' – that is, the image of our past – tells us is that guilt is inseparable from the fact of living. 'Guilt is nameless', Schwartz says, '/ Because its name is death'; we are all burdened

by 'the guilt of time' and so 'the child must carry / His father on his back'. There are many things to be said about this poetry but perhaps the most important thing is that it is, above all, a poetry of agony and transformation: in 'Someone is Harshly Coughing as Before', for instance, a man heard coughing in an upstairs apartment is transformed, in quick succession, into Christ (who has 'caught cold again'), 'poor Keats', and the archetypal vision of the victim, 'Longing for Eden, afraid of the coming war'. The formal and emotional dangers of this kind of verse are perhaps obvious: the transformations could easily become chaotic and unconvincing, while the sense of agony could degenerate into a maudlin, occasionally generalized self-pity. In his early work, though, Schwartz usually manages to skirt such dangers thanks to his adept handling of traditional forms; 'the subject of poetry', he said, 'is experience not truth', and he turns his own obsessive truths into imaginative experience with the help of inherited metres and conventional structures. In 'O City, City', for example, he uses the framework of the sonnet to focus a contrast between the quiet desperation of 'six million souls' in New York (established in the octave) and his own longing for a world of purity and passion, where 'in the white bed all things are made' (described in the sestet). It is a simple device, but it works beautifully. Unfortunately, in his later work, Schwartz adopts a long, rambling line, attempting to assimilate prose rather than speech rhythms. At best, the verse that results is like higher conversation ('An adolescent girl holds a bouquet of flowers / As if she gazed and sought her unknown, hoped-for, dreaded destiny'). At its worst, and this is more frequent, it is slack and banal.

As American poets gravitated, during this period, towards more flexible verse forms, they also, many of them, went in search of a more idiomatic vocabulary. 'When you make a poem,' William Stafford wrote in 1966, 'you merely speak or write the language of every day.' 'Rather than giving poets the undeserved honour of telling us how . . . special poetry is,' he went on, 'everyone should realise his own fair share of the joint risk and opportunity present in language.' This is a theme that recurs in the remarks of many postwar American poets. 'I'm sick of wit and eloquence in neat form,' Alan Dugan announced; while David Ignatow insisted that he is 'antipoetic' – 'nothing', he said, 'should be taken for more than it says to you on the surface'. The ideal, in effect, seems to be a virtual transparency of idiom. For John Ciardi, for instance, there was nothing worse than what he termed 'the signatory way of writing': that is, language that is foregrounded, calling attention to the distinctive 'signature' or style of its inventor. What he dreamed of, Ciardi said, is 'an act of language so entirely responsive to the poetic experience' that his 'habituated way of speaking' would be 'shattered and leave only the essential language called into being by the aesthetic experience itself'. The perfect poem would then be one that, as Ciardi put it, 'seem[s] to declare not "X spoke these words in his unique way" but rather "man spoke these words of himself"'. This is a desire not, as it may appear at first sight, for impersonality or anonymity but for a language so simple and apparently inevitable that it seems to be the only possible way of expressing the subject. It is, in sum, another version of that commitment to authenticity – the precise application of word to event without superfluous gesture or ornament – that characterized so many earlier American poets from Whitman to Oppen and Williams.

Oppen and Williams were, of course, very different poets; and it has to be said that the search for authentic language among recent writers has had some strikingly diverse consequences. With Alan Dugan (1923–), whose *New and Collected Poems* appeared in 1983, the result has been a tough, brittle, determinedly populist style. 'Here the world is', he declares in 'Prayer', '/ enjoyable with whiskey, women, ultimate weapons, and class'; and he does his best to express that world as it is, together with all the detritus of contemporary life. John Ciardi (1916–85) also clearly likes the radicality of the colloquial, the voice of the plain-speaking, rough-and-tumble man who tolerates no nonsense, verbal or otherwise. The opening line of 'In Place of a Curse' is typical, in its candour and bluff wit: 'At the next vacancy for God, if I am elected'. Ciardi frequently tries to shock the reader into attention in this way, whereas the poems of William Stafford (1914–93) (included in *Stories That Could Be True: New and Collected Poems* [1978]) tend to open quietly ('Our car was fierce enough', 'They call it regional, this relevance – / the deepest place we have') and then move towards some muted discovery of a small truth, a partial explanation of things. 'The signals we give – yes or no, or maybe – / should be clear,' Stafford says at the conclusion to 'A Ritual to Read to Each Other', adding, 'the darkness around us is deep'. Clarity of language, verbal modesty, is for him, it seems, a stay against oblivion, something to illuminate or at least hold back the surrounding dark.

David Ignatow (1914–97) is just as verbally modest as Stafford, as his *New and Collected Poems 1970–1985* (1987) amply illustrates, but not in entirely the same way. An avowed imitator of Williams's formal experiments, and concerned primarily with urban life, Ignatow said that he had two main purposes: to remind other poets that 'there is world outside' in the streets, and to reveal to people in general 'the terrible deficiencies in man'. 'Whitman spent his life boosting the good side,' he claimed; 'My life will be spent pointing out the bad' – although pointing it out, he adds, 'from the standpoint of forgiveness and peace'. The quarrel with Whitman, and by implication with the moral dimension of Williams's work, runs through Ignatow's poetry, generating a poignant contrast between method and message. The limpidity of diction and movement that those earlier writers had used to celebrate human innocence is now harnessed to a haunting vision of guilt. A similar combination of verbal clarity and visionary sadness is notable in the work of Philip Levine (1928–). 'I was born / in the wrong year and in the wrong place,' Levine has written; and many of his poems are in fact concerned with his childhood, spent in the Middle West during the Depression. The bleak cityscape of Detroit, the lonely farmlands of Illinois and Ohio, the sad, wasted lives of family and friends condemned to drudgery in factories and 'burned fields': all this is recounted with the strength and simplicity of idiom of Edgar Lee Masters, but without Masters's abiding feeling of waste. 'You / can pledge your single life, the earth / will eat it all,' admits Levine. Nevertheless, his characters are marked by their courage in the face of the inevitable. In 'Animals are Passing from our Lives' (1968), for instance, Levine assumes the voice of a pig on its way to be slaughtered. 'The boy / who drives me along', says the pig, 'believes / that any moment I'll fall / . . . / or squeal / and shit.' 'No,' he swears defiantly, 'not this pig.' The jaunty obstinacy of this, framed as it is by the ultimate absurdity of such a gesture, allows for both humour and moral complexity. We are all going to the slaughterhouse, Levine intimates. Any defiance we show along the way is, *practically* speaking, useless, even ridiculous; still, it has its own, odd nobility – it is not *morally* insignificant.

'Dispossess me of belief / between life and me obtrude / no symbolic forms': this request, made by another postwar poet, A. R. Ammons (1926–2001), repeats the aims of Levine and Ignatow, but in a different key. It also exposes a further, crucial way in which American verse has removed itself from formalism: by dispensing not only with conventional metres and 'signatory' language but also with the 'symbolic forms' of narrative closure. Revitalizing the earlier American interest in 'organic form', Ammons was one among many contemporary writers who want the radiant energy they perceive at the heart of the natural world to become the energy of the poem, 'spiralling from the centre' to inform every line. A poem like 'Corsons's Inlet', the title piece of his 1965 collection, dramatizes the details of this commitment. It opens in a characteristic way: 'I went for a walk over the dunes again this morning to the sea.' Few human beings appear in Ammons's work, apart from the omnipresent 'I': who is there, however, not to impress but to observe. Ammons was preoccupied with what he calls the 'amness', the intrinsic identity of things – which includes himself, of course, but also 'stars and paperclips' – and, in order to know this 'amness', he has to pay attention, 'losing the self' when necessary 'to the victory / of stones and trees'. In this instance, he tells us, the walk on which he embarks liberates him – from himself, as usual – and 'from the perpendiculars, / straight lines / of thought / into the hues, . . . flowing bends and blends of sight'. In particular, it releases him into knowledge of the inlet mentioned in the title. Watching its fluid, changing shape and the microscopic lives that animate it, Ammons perceives in it not a symbol but an example of what an appropriate form should be. 'In nature there are few sharp lines', the poet comments, and what he sees here is 'an order held / in constant change: a congregation / rich with entropy'. The inlet opens up to him 'the possibility of rule as the sum of rulelessness': a form of knowing in which there is 'no forcing of . . . thought / no propaganda', and a form of expression, an aesthetic shape, that is vital and kinetic, a ' "field" of action / with moving incalculable centre'.

The notion of the 'field' was one that Williams cherished ('the poem is made of things – on a field') and that Charles Olson developed. What such a notion resists, at all costs, is what Ammons calls 'lines' and 'boundaries': demarcations that exclude, hierarchies that prioritize, definitions that impose the illusion of fixity on the flux of experience. There are, Ammons suggests, 'no / . . . changeless shapes': the poet-seer must invent structures that imitate the metamorphic character of things. The organisms he creates must respond to life as particularity and process; they must be dynamic, unique to each occasion; above all, they must be *open*. 'There is no finality of vision,' Ammons concludes (with deliberate inconclusiveness), '. . . I have perceived nothing completely, / . . . tomorrow a new walk is a new walk.' Echoing a whole series of great American texts, Ammons also speaks here for another generation of poets, who respond to 'The wonderful workings of the world' with their own persistent workings and reworkings of the imagination. 'ecology is my word,' Ammons affirms in another, longer poem published in 1965, 'Tape for the Turn of the Year', '. . . come / in there: / you will find yourself / in a firm country: / centres and peripheries / in motion.' 'My other word is *provisional*,' he continues, '. . . you may guess / the meanings from *ecology* / . . . / the center-arising / form / adapts, tests the / peripheries, draws in / . . . / responds to inner and outer / change.' Those lines could act as an epigraph to many volumes of American verse published during the 1960s and later, in which the poet tries to insert himself in the processes of life, and, in turn, the reader is asked to insert himself or herself in the processes of the work.

The emphasis Ammons places on ecology in his 'Tape for the Turn of the Year' brings into focus one aspect of postwar American poetry that unites formalist poets, confessional poets and others: that is, a willingness to attend to social and political issues, and to the historical experience of the late twentieth and early twenty-first centuries. On one, deep level, such attention is unavoidable: we are historical beings and our participation in sociopolitical processes must necessarily feed into everything we do. Sylvia Plath clearly had this in mind when she said, 'the issues of the time which preoccupy me . . . are the incalculable genetic effects of fallout and . . . the terrifying . . . marriage of big business and the military in America'; however, she went on, 'my poems do not turn out to be about Hiroshima, but about a child forming itself finger by finger in the dark. They are not about the terrors of mass extinction, but about the blackness of the moon over a yew tree in a neighbourhood graveyard.' As it happens, this is not the whole truth about Plath's own work: her poems sometimes address social problems (notably, the position of women), and she is not afraid to link her personal intimations of disaster to the holocaust of world war and the apocalypse now threatened by nuclear weaponry. But, as a general point, it is still worth making: it is one thing to have a historical consciousness – and this nobody, not even the most abstracted writer, can avoid – and quite another to be historically involved, to have the imagination of commitment. One form of such commitment has already been touched on with reference to the work of Sexton and Rich: that is, the willingness of many poets to confront the questions of sexual identity and sexual politics. This is not, incidentally, a willingness confined to women poets. Robert Bly, among others, has seemed ready to blame the failure of American culture on its denial of what he sees as the inner-directed feminine principle ('the mother of solitude') in favour of the outer-directed masculine one ('the father of rocks'). Later, in *Iron John* (1990), he developed his ideas into a best-selling series of instructions on becoming a whole man. Other kinds of commitment have been generated among poets speaking in and for 'ethnic' and 'minority' communities and cultures. There are, of course, many others. Two further issues, in particular, have haunted postwar poets and in one case at least continue to do so: the experience in

Vietnam, which introduced America to defeat, and the possible destruction of the world by nuclear war.

The war in Vietnam stimulated an enormous amount of poetry, much of it of doubtful quality. A representative collection is *Where is Vietnam? American Poets Respond*, which was published in 1967. For the most part, the poems published here and elsewhere rely on simple invective ('All your strength, America, is in your bombs!') or on equally simple documentation:

> On Thursday a Vietcong flag was noticed flying
> Above the village of Man Quang in South Vietnam.
> Therefore Skyraider fighter-bombers were sent in,
> Destroying the village school and other 'structures'.

With the first kind of poetry, anger tends to lose its edge in generalized, unfocused condemnation (American poets have, on the whole, been remarkably unsuccessful with satire and polemic). With the second, apart from the occasional gesture, very little seems to be added or gained by turning the experience into verse: in the passage just quoted, for instance, except for the parody of the neutral dehumanized tone of war communiqués ('structures') and the ordering of the data within a fairly rudimentary rhythmic pattern, the writer does nothing more than act the good journalist by handing us a series of received facts. It is worth adding perhaps that the poem from which these lines are taken, 'School Day in Man Quang' by Denis Knight, has a footnote: 'This incident was reported from Saigon . . . by the Special Correspondent of the London *Times*.' This, presumably, is meant to stress the factual nature of the piece. However, it also serves to remind us that this poem, like the vast majority of those written about Vietnam, is by a non-combatant. The best poems of the Second World War were produced by people like Jarrell, Shapiro and Simpson, who actually participated in it and, for the most part, saw it as nasty, brutish, but necessary. By contrast, many of the best poems about Vietnam have been by those who were not there but had an *imaginative* involvement in it, and were committed to doing all they could to stop it. 'All wars are useless to the dead,' Adrienne Rich insisted. 'Why are they dying?' Robert Bly asked. 'I here declare the end of the War,' announced Allen Ginsberg. Such pronouncements are typical. American poets felt that they had to participate; they were gripped by what they read about, what they saw on television, what they felt was happening in the streets and to the youth of their country. They also had the firm conviction – as poems like 'The Asians Dying' by W. S. Merwin and 'The Altar in the Street' by Denise Levertov suggest – that the war could be ended with the help of the language of poetry.

There were two types of poetic language that were particularly successful, if not in stopping the war, then at least in giving an adequate definition of its horror. The first is illustrated by the Vietnam poems of Robert Bly, collected in such volumes as *The Light Around the Body* and *Counting Small-Boned Bodies* (1979). Some of these poems, like 'The Teeth-Mother Naked at Last', are jeremiads, fierce prophecies of 'the end of the Republic' thanks to an increasingly authoritarian government. Others show him adopting the mask of some member of that business-dominated, power-oriented society which brought the war into being ('Counting Small-Boned Bodies'), or translating the obscene realities of war into a crazy, nightmarish surrealism, as in 'War and Silence': 'The bombers spread out, temperature steady / A Negro's ear sleeping in an automatic tyre / Pieces of timber float by saying nothing.' In all of these pieces, however, Bly relates the contemporary political crisis to a more general crisis of belief. Like Ginsberg, say, or Robert Duncan, he seeks an explanation for and answer to public events in terms that are, ultimately, mystical, erotic and apocalyptic. The other strategy, adopted by Robert Lowell and a few other poets – Adrienne Rich, for instance – is subtly different and, arguably, even more compelling. In poems like 'Waking Early Sunday Morning', published in *Near the Ocean* (1967), Lowell links the godless militarism of his society and the bloody, futile conflict in Southeast Asia to the sense of his own spiritual dereliction: 'Pity the planet, all joy gone / from this sweet volcanic cone; / peace to our children when they fall / in small war on the heels of small / war /', Lowell concludes this poem, 'until the end of time / to police the earth, a ghost / orbiting forever lost / in our monotonous sublime.'

The final lines of 'Waking Early Sunday Morning', with their vision of the earth as 'a ghost / orbiting forever lost', recall another way in which American poets have felt compelled to think the unthinkable. After Auschwitz no lyric poetry could be written, Adorno insisted. Similarly, many writers have felt that no language is adequate before the possibility of global annihilation: the mind, perhaps, cannot encompass the destruction of mind, speech cannot speak of its own extinction. Still, poems have been written not only after Auschwitz but about it; and poets have tried to tell about the potential death of the earth. They suffer from the imagination of disaster and the struggle to give verbal shape to their imaginings in the hope that, this way, disaster may be forestalled. The quiet voice of William Stafford, in 'At the Bomb Testing Site', suggests one possible manoeuvre, to allow the obscene phenomenon to speak for itself. He simply describes a 'panting lizard' in the desert near a testing site that 'waited for history, its elbows tense'. Nothing seems to happen in the poem, and it concludes with these lines: 'Ready for a change, the elbows waited. / The hands gripped in the desert.' It is what Stafford called 'the sleeping resources in language' that carry the message here: the sense of doom that occurs, as it were, in the spaces between the words. The unknown is presented as just that; the unspeakable becomes the only partially spoken; under a nuclear cloud, Stafford intimates, all we have is unnamed, unnameable dread. Galway Kinnell also uses the perspective of a primitive creature in his 'Vapour Trail Reflected in a Frog Pond', only in his case the frogs' eyes that keep 'The old watch' create a point of view that eerily resembles the Inhumanist vision of Robinson Jeffers. These prehistoric creatures, with 'their / thick eyes' that 'puff and foreclose by the moon', make the vapour trail of an aircraft, and the power it emblematizes, seem not only insane but inane: a passing cloud puffed by a race who have jettisoned the self-containment of the other animals in favour of self-absorption and self-destruction.

'The bomb speaks,' said William Carlos Williams in one of his last poems, 'Asphodel, That Greeny Flower', '. . . the bomb has entered our lives / to destroy us.' Against the 'mere picture of the exploding bomb' he set the powers of love and the imagination: which, he said, were 'of a piece' since they both required a dedication to life, its beauties and possibilities. This is a theme on which James Merrill plays his own variations in his trilogy *The Changing Light at Sandover* (1982), where he tells us of conjured spirits who inform him, 'NO SOULS CAME FROM HIROSHIMA U KNOW'. Merrill, in effect, uses prophecy and magic to release his vision. The spirits he has met, he says, are 'HOPING AGAINST HOPE THAT MAN WILL LOVE HIS MIND & HIS LANGUAGE'; if man does not, then the 'WORLD WILL BE UNDONE' and 'HEAVEN ITSELF' will 'TURN TO ONE GRINNING SKULL'. If Merrill claims that he has become a medium for absolute truth, in order to voice his sense of the potential for mass destruction – and the redeeming power of love and language – then Sylvia Plath adopts similarly vatic tones in a poem like 'Nick and the Candlestick'. Here, the poet sets her fear of 'the incalculable effects of nuclear fallout' against her care for her as yet unborn child. 'Let the stars / Plummet to their dark address,' she declares: 'You are the one / Solid the spaces lean on, envious. / You are the baby in the barn.' Lines like these illustrate, again, how the poetry of the personal can become the poetry of prophecy. Universal annihilation and individual fertility are placed side by side: the poem is about both history and the body, the bomb and the womb, and manages to be at once oracular and intimate. In a very different sense, some of this is also true of a formalist piece on the nuclear threat, 'Advice to a Prophet' by Richard Wilbur. Wilbur adopts the modest pose of advising rather than being the prophet but the result is, in its own way, just as resonant – and just as personal. 'When you come . . . to the streets of our city,' Wilbur advises, 'Speak of the world's own change.' 'We could believe, /' he goes on, 'If you told us so, that the white-tailed deer will slip / Into perfect shade, grown perfectly shy, / That lark avoid the reaches of our eye.' The beautiful objects of this world will be lost, Wilbur intimates, which means, too, the loss of ourselves. Unable to see or speak them, we shall also be unable to see and speak our own being; we, and our words, will 'slip / Into perfect shade'. 'Ask us, ask us,' Wilbur repeats through the poem, 'Ask us, prophet, how we shall call / Our natures forth when that live tongue is all / Dispelled.' Formalists and confessionals alike retain their belief in the power of speech – the language that summons us to knowledge of our lives – even in the face of absolute silence.

The uses of formalism

There are many ways of being a formalist poet. One way is illustrated by the subtle, serious wit of Richard Wilbur. Another, by the passionate, metaphysical sensibility of Stanley Kunitz (1905–), whose *Collected Poems* appeared in 2000. In a poem like 'Foreign Affairs', for instance, Kunitz develops the conceit of lovers as 'two countries girded for war' to examine the intricacies, and erotic heat, of a relationship. The poem is at once cerebral and sensuous, turning what could have been little more than an intellectual *tour de force* into a sensitive analysis of the way 'fated and contagious selves' can somehow be 'separated by desire'. It represents, as it were, a peculiarly intense, mentally energetic kind of formalism, whereas the reverence for form that characterizes, say, the work of Howard Nemerov (1920–91) is calmer, more reflective, expressive of Nemerov's belief that a poem should mean as well as be: even great poems, he suggests, unlike the things of nature 'tell . . . rather than exemplify / What they believe themselves to be about'. Nemerov's 'Gulls' is characteristic in this respect. Carefully structured, written in a slightly formal, even abstract language, the poem nevertheless accommodates some powerful visual effects ('they glide / Mysterious upon a morning sea / Ghostly with mist'). It begins with an unsentimental vision of the birds – 'I know them at their worst,' the poet tells us – and gradually emblematizes them, teases out moral inferences from their activities: 'Courage is always brutal,' Nemerov insists, 'for it is / The bitter truth fastens the soul to God.' 'Bless the song that sings / Of mortal courage,' he concludes, 'bless it with your form / Compassed in calm amid the cloud-white storm.' What Nemerov wants, evidently, as his *Collected Poems* (1977) shows, is a poetry that has the poise and assurance, and the bravery before the facts of life, possessed by the gulls; and in poems like this one, or 'Storm Window' and 'Death and the Maiden', he manages to achieve that aim.

Still other varieties of formalism, different in turn from those of Wilbur, Kunitz and Nemerov, are illustrated by the idiomatic, often bizarre wittiness of Reed Whittemore (1919–) ('I wish I might somehow / Bring into light the eloquence, say, of a doorknob'), the incisive, sardonic tones of Weldon Kees (1914–55) ('Sleep is too short a death') and the patent concern with getting it right, trying to put things properly, that characterizes the work of Donald Justice (1925–) ('I do not think the ending can be right'). At one extreme, perhaps, is the dispassionate, distanced reflectiveness of Edgar Bowers (1924–2000) ('The enormous sundry platitude of death / Is for these bones, bees, trees, and leaves the same') or the equally dispassionate elegance of X. J. Kennedy (1929–) ('She sifts in sunlight down the stairs / With nothing on. Nor on her mind'). At the other is the poetry of Anthony Hecht (1923–) (*Collected Earlier Poems* (1990]), whose measured, sometimes ironic voice (learned, in part, from his former teacher, John Crowe Ransom) becomes a medium for passionate explorations of autobiography and history, the fear and darkness at the heart of things: 'We move now to outside a German wood. / Three men are there commanded to dig a hole, /' the reader is told in Hecht's 'More Light! More Light!'; 'In which two Jews are ordered to lie down / And be buried alive by a third, who is a Pole.' In recent time, however, perhaps the most memorable lesson in the uses of formalism has been given by Elizabeth Bishop (1911–79), whose *Complete Poems: 1927–1979* was published in 1983. Of her good friend Marianne Moore, Bishop once said, 'The exact way in which anything was done, or made, was poetry to her'. Precisely the same could be said of Bishop herself: 'all her poems', Randall Jarrell once suggested, 'have written underneath, *I have seen it.*' Bishop's aim is to attend carefully to the ordinary objects around her; and then, through that gesture of attention, to catch glimpses of what she calls 'the always-more-successful surrealism of everyday life'. The more closely she observes something, the more it seems to become arrested in time, translated for a moment into a world of stillness and dream. This resembles Moore's habit of using close attention as a means of imaginative release. However, Bishop's poetic voice is quite unlike Moore's. Strongly musical rhythms, unexpected but inevitably recurring rhymes, wit and clarity of idiom, above all a use of inherited formal structures that is characterized by its elegance and tact: all help to create a poetry that balances itself between mellow speech and music, the lucidity of considered thought and the half-heard melodies appropriate to a more sensuous, magical vision.

The dreamlike sharpness of sight and the alertness of tone that typify Bishop's best pieces are illustrated by a poem like 'The Map'. The subject is a favourite one: like so many American poets, Bishop is interested in space, geography rather than history, and she uses maps as both a figure and a medium for imaginative exploration. As the opening lines indicate, the poem has a fairly tight yet unobstructive formal structure, enhanced by delicate tonalities and repetitions: 'Land lies in water; it is shadowed green /', the poem begins. 'Shadows, or are they shallows, at its edges / showing the line of long sea-weeded ledges / where weeds hang to the simple blue from green.' The picture Bishop paints is at once precise and surreal, in the sense that it is through a careful enumeration of the details of the map that she begins to unlock the mysteries of the land and water, shadows or shallows, that it encloses. As the poet's imaginative voyage continues, so her feeling for potential magic grows. Sometimes, the tone is languorous, even sensual: 'Labrador's yellow,' she murmurs, 'where the moony Eskimo / has oiled it. We can stroke these lovely bays.' At other moments, Bishop allows her wit to play around the given particulars: 'These peninsulas take the water between thumb and finger', she observes mischievously, '/ like women feeling for the smoothness of yard-goods.' Neither the play of fancy nor the feeling for mystery is unrestricted, however: both are firmly yet quietly anchored to an awareness of the actual, the formal constraints of map and poem. The contours of the map are constantly kept before our eyes, and the poet never strays too far from the original structure, the dominant rhythms and idiom. The closing four lines, in fact, return us to the frame established in the opening four, an emphatic rhyme scheme contained within a simple, bell-like repetition: 'Are they assigned, or can the countries pick their colors? /' the poem asks. '– What suits the character or the native waters best. / Topography displays no favorites; North's as near as West. / More delicate than the historians' are the map-makers' colors.' By this stage, the arts of the map and the poem describing the map have become almost indistinguishable. A democratic eye that discloses the wonder nestling in everything, a lively imagination that denies limits, spatial or otherwise, in its efforts to retain the world for the mind: these qualities, Bishop intimates, characterize both the map-maker and the poet, as they attend to the sights we see, the signs we create.

The map for Bishop is like a poem because, above all, it is a symbolic journey, an excursion that is perhaps promising and perhaps not. Her poetry is full of travel, literal and otherwise. There are poems about travellers ('Crusoe in England'), poems that recall things seen while travelling ('Arrival at Santos'), poems that ask the question, 'Should we have stayed at home and thought of here?' One of her pieces has as its epigraph a quotation from *Landscape into Art* (1979) by Kenneth Clark, 'embroidered nature . . . tapestried landscape'; and this suggests the peculiar ability she possesses to mingle landscapes literal with landscapes imagined, or to find the sources of art and inspiration in the most unpromising and apparently mundane of surroundings – in a 'Filling Station', for instance:

> Somebody
> arranges the row of cans
> so that they softly say:
> ESSO-SO-SO-SO
> to high-strung automobiles.
> Somebody loves us all.

Typically, as here, the revelations her poetic journeys achieve are joyful but also sad: with the sadness of rootlessness, perhaps, and isolation. Bishop's watching eye and musing voice are kept at one remove, as it were, in this case unable to determine who the 'somebody' might be – the arrangement is perceived, but not its shadowy creator. Whether peering through a map at the 'long sea-weeded ledges' it signifies, or looking at a landscape with the suspicion that there is something 'retreating, always retreating behind it', the quality of distance is always there, enabling wonder, certainly, but also loss. As some of Bishop's personae learn, the solitude that is a prerequisite of attentiveness, and so imaginative discovery, promotes absence: to look and see is, after all, to stand apart.

One of Bishop's poems, 'In the Waiting Room', actually describes how the poet learned about this apart-ness. While sitting in a dentist's waiting room, she recalls, 'I said to myself: three days / and you'll be seven years old'. 'I felt: you are an *I*,' she goes on, 'you are an *Elizabeth*': 'I knew that nothing stranger / had ever happened, that nothing / stranger could ever happen.' The position realized here is the site of most of her work, whether she is attending to objects, people or events. Her explorer's eye transforms ordinary creatures into extraordinary characters, the stuff of artifice and legend: a sandpiper, for instance, is metamorphosed into a fanatical investigator, 'final, awkward / . . . a student of Blake' in the sense that it evidently searches for the world in a grain of sand. The aim is not to be merely fanciful or whimsical, even in more openly bizarre poems such as 'The Man-Moth'. On the contrary, what Bishop is after is a deeper realism. She is trying to reveal things that may be most available to the unhabituated eye: to uncover, perhaps, the peculiar strategies we and other animals use to confront and defy the forces that govern us ('The Armadillo'), or the strange communications that can occur between the different dimensions of life, the earth and the sea, waking and sleeping. One such communication is described in 'The Fish', where the poet remembers how oil that 'had spread a rainbow / around the rusted engine' of a fishing vessel led to sudden revelation. 'Everything / was rainbow, rainbow, rainbow!' the poet exclaims and, in that moment of illumination, 'victory filled up / the little rented boat'. Such insights are as bright, particular and as fleeting as a mingling of oil, water and light: objects, as Bishop shows them, brim with meaning that is vividly but only temporarily disclosed. In one of her most famous poems, 'At the Fishhouses', Bishop uses another image to convey the shock and the ephemerality of the revelatory experience: not a rainbow this time, but the drinking of 'Cold dark deep and absolutely clear water' – so cold, in fact, that it seems to 'burn your tongue'. 'It is like what we imagine knowledge to be, /' she declares of such a draught, 'dark, salt, clear, moving, utterly free, / drawn from the cold hard mouth / of the world . . . / . . . and since / our knowledge is historical, flowing, and flown.' It is surely not stretching a point to say that it is exactly this kind of knowledge that Bishop realizes in her own work: where truth slips in, as it were, through the cold peculiarities of fact and then quietly slips away again.

Another poet who at least began as a formalist of sorts was Theodore Roethke (1908–63). His first volume of poetry, *Open House* (1941), used traditional verse structures and depended on the then fashionable mode of tough intellectualism. The opening lines of the first, and title, poem show that this was no ordinary formalist, however. 'My secrets cry aloud, /' Roethke declared. 'I have no need for tongue. / My heart keeps open house, / My doors are widely swung.' Here, in a language that is stripped and bare, and rhythms that are driving and insistent, Roethke announced his intention of using himself as the material of his art. His major preoccupation was to be with the evolution and identity of the self: and these tight, epigrammatic verses cry that aloud. 'I'm naked to the bone,' Roethke declares later in this poem, 'Myself is what I wear': that is almost, but not quite, true. He is still, after all, dressed in the uniform of an inherited poetics. But beginning with his second volume, *The Lost Son and Other Poems* (1948), this too was to be discarded in the search for the subrational, prehistorical roots of being. 'Cuttings (later)' bears witness to the change: 'I can hear, underground, that sucking and sobbing, / In my veins, in my bones I feel it, – /' Roethke confesses here – 'The small waters seeping upward, / The tight grains parting at last.'

Much of his verse after the first volume, Roethke explained, 'begins in the mire, as if man is [sic] no more than a shape writhing from the rock': a being, the birth and growth of whose consciousness can be fruitfully compared to the birth and growth of plants, trees and all organic matter. There is a new rooting of poetry in sensuous experience here, the 'greenhouse' world or natural landscape of the poet's childhood (Roethke's father was a florist, joint owner of over twenty-five acres of greenhouses). Along with this, there is a new search for some dynamic concept of correspondence between the human and vegetable worlds. Roethke felt that he had to begin at the beginning, with primitive things: to journey into the interior of the natural order, and into himself as part of that order. This required, in turn, a more primitive voice. 'If we concern ourselves with more primitive effects in poetry,' Roethke argued, 'we come inevitably to the consideration . . . of verse that is closer to prose . . . The writer must keep his eye on the object, and his rhythm must move as his mind moves.' So, in the poem just quoted, Roethke uses the free verse line, long, elaborately alliterated, with a preponderance of heavy stresses, open vowels and participles, to create an effect of enormous effort and evolutionary struggle; instead of imposing order on experience (*all* experience, conscious, subconscious and preconscious), he tries to discover the order latent in it. This ties in with an alteration of idiom. 'Approach these poems as a child would,' Roethke instructed, 'naively, with your whole being awake, your faculties loose and alert.' As he dwelt on primeval life, so he naturally gravitated towards a more subliminal language: the intuitions of folklore, fairytale and myth, shapes that lurk 'Deep in the brain, far back'.

Of growing up in the Midwest Roethke once said, 'sometimes one gets the feeling that not even the animals have been there before, but the marsh, the mire, the void is always there . . . It is America.' Roethke's poetry is a poetry of the self, certainly, but it is also very much a poetry of the West, in that it is concerned with the frontiers of existence, the ultimate, inchoate sources of being. This is particularly noticeable in some of the later work, where the poet lights out, beyond childhood and the natural world, for the unknown territory of racial memory: a journey backward into unindividuated experience that then in turn becomes part of a general, evolutionary process forward. Talking of the poems that made up his third volume, *Praise to the End!* (1951), for instance, Roethke said, 'Each . . . is complete in itself; yet each is a stage in a . . . struggle out of the slime'. 'The method is cyclic,' he continued; 'I believe that to go forward as a spiritual man it is necessary to go back . . . There is a perpetual slipping-back, then going-forward; but there is some "progress".' Acting on this belief, Roethke modelled such poems as 'Where Knock is Open Wide' and 'Unfold! Unfold!' on an archetypal pattern: in which the heroic protagonist – in this case, the poet – travels into a nightworld, suffering perhaps a dark night of the soul, conquers the dangers he meets there, and then returns to lead a fuller, more inclusive life in the daylight realm of ordinary existence. Ancient and familiar as the tale may be, however, what gives it an air of unfamiliarity is Roethke's way of telling it. He compresses language and syntax into abrupt, dreamlike units. At its most extreme, when the frontiers of individual consciousness are crossed and 'the dead speak' (that is, the inhabitants of the collective unconscious utter their communications), Roethke presents us with what he calls a 'whelm of proverbs', a speech as primitive as folk-saying, as subhuman, almost, as an animal cry. Along with such mutterings of a rudimentary sensibility, Roethke telescopes imagery and symbols and employs rhythms that are primeval, even oracular in their effect. All this he does because, instead of simply reporting the journey to the frontiers of being as many other writers have done, he is trying to recreate it. He is inviting the reader to share in the departure to the interior and the return. If the reader accepts this invitation, then he or she can also share in the moments of revelation, that knowledge of the correspondences of life, on which each of these pieces ends.

'Often I think of myself as riding –', observes the narrator of one of Roethke's later poems, '/ Alone, on a bus through western country.' 'All journeys, I think, are the same,' she says a little later; 'The movement is forward, after a few wavers.' The narrator here is an old woman, modelled partly on the poet's mother; and the poem from which these observations are taken, 'Meditations of an Old Woman' (1958), illustrates two ways in which the poet, even as he grew older, continued to change and grow. One way involved an intensified interest in the people around him. Having established a true sense of himself in poems like 'Unfold! Unfold!', Roethke turned outward to affirm his relationship with others: by adopting their voice and vision for a while, perhaps, as in 'Meditations' or 'The Dying Man' (1958), by celebrating the 'slow world' of erotic fulfilment where the lovers 'breathe in unison', or by a gently particularistic portrait of an individual – his father, it might be, 'Who lived above a potting shed for years', or 'a woman, lovely in her bones'. The other way in which Roethke moved was towards a creative analysis of ultimate questions: about God, Eternity – above all, about 'Death's possibilities' and their significance for the living. 'Old men should be explorers?' Roethke asked, echoing Eliot, '/ I'll be an Indian'; and he lived up to this promise in poems that sing of any person, like himself, who 'beats his wings / Against the immense immeasurable emptiness of things'. As the old woman meditates, she considers the imminence of her death ('What's left is light as seed'), and the disappointments of her past ('I have gone into the waste lonely places / Behind the eye'): but she remembers positive moments as well, when she achieved growth by realizing a harmonious relationship with all that is. Such moments more than make up for others, she believes: they are blessed with a special perfection of their own, a sense of ecstasy that no deity can ever supply. 'In such times,' she says, 'lacking a god / I am still happy.' It seems appropriate that even this poem, the product of 'an old crone's knowing', should end on a note of affirmation and possibility. For Roethke, as the work gathered in his *Collected Poems* (1966) shows, life was a continual wayfaring, an expedition into the grounds of being that offered joy or wonder as a reward. It was a process of constant beginnings, 'many arrivals': whereby, the poet felt – to quote from one of his most famous pieces, 'The Waking' – 'I learn by going where I have to go'.

Confessional poetry

'Alas, I can only tell my own story.' The words could be those of many American poets; in fact they were written by Robert Lowell (1911–77), and could be said to sum up his work. Despite the touch of regretfulness noticeable in this remark, Lowell did seriously believe that his story needed to be told; and for this his good friend Elizabeth Bishop envied him. 'I feel that I could write in as much detail about my uncle Artie, say,' she wrote to Lowell: '– but what would be the significance? Nothing at all . . . whereas all you have to do is put down the names!' For Bishop, the source of this good fortune lay in the sheer splendour of Lowell's background, the fact that he was descended from two distinguished New England families. But two other things were quite as important: Lowell's characteristically American tendency to see himself as a representative of his culture, and his willingness, or rather his determination, to assume the role of scapegoat – to challenge and confront (or say 'No, in thunder' as Herman Melville put it), and to expose himself, for the purposes of revelation and discovery, to the major pressures of his times.

In his early work, collected in *Lord Weary's Castle* (1946), Lowell's painful awareness of self, together with his anxiety over a world that seemed to him to be corrupted by egotism, led him towards a consciously Catholic poetry. Poems like 'The Holy Innocents' and 'The Quaker Graveyard in Nantucket' juxtapose the self-absorption of the isolated individual with the selflessness of true faith. The introspective and fragmentary nature of the New England and American traditions is contrasted with the serenity and coherence of the Roman Catholic order. The short poem 'Children of Light' illustrates this position. It is divided into two, densely imagistic passages, which offer the reader two historical examples of the crime of Cain, or violence committed against the brotherhood of man: first, the depredations of the early Puritan settlers, and then the horrors of the Second World War. The Puritans, Lowell argues, were 'Pilgrims unhoused by Geneva's night'. They were deprived of the support of Catholicism, a system of beliefs founded on the community rather than the individual; and their imperialism of the self led them to slaughter the Indians ('Our fathers . . . / . . . fenced their gardens with the Redman's bones') and claim absolute possession of the land. The Second World War is the product of similar single-mindedness, prompting destruction even of the natural abundance of the earth in the pursuit of personal power; it also illustrates the primary truth that inwardness finds its issue, eventually, in the disruption of both the private and the public life. 'And here the pivoting searchlights probe to shock / The riotous glass houses built on rock, /' the poet concludes, in appalled response to global conflict: 'And candles gutter by an empty altar, / And light is where the landless blood of Cain / Is burning, burning the unburied grain.' Lines like these suggest the characteristic voice of this early poetry: learned partly from Allen Tate, it is notable for its cold passion, its icy bitterness and despair. The language is packed and feverish, the syntax often contorted, the imagery disruptive: all is barely kept in control by the formal patterns of the verse. Like an unwilling disciple, the poet seems to be trying to force himself into accepting the rigours of inherited form and faith; he has to will his speech and his spirit into submission. For all the fierceness of his initial conversion, in fact, Lowell was too much and irrevocably a part of New England – too solitary, introspective and individualist – to be comfortable as a Catholic or, indeed, stay a Catholic for very long; and it was only his rage for order that made him try for a while to compel himself into submission.

'It may be', Lowell wrote once, 'that some people have turned to my poems because of the very things that are wrong with me. I mean the difficulty I have with ordinary living.' By the time he wrote this, Lowell had had several nervous breakdowns and left the Catholic church. More to the point, perhaps, this difficulty he had with 'ordinary living' had helped turn his poetry in a new direction: for in the hope, apparently, that he might resolve his problems, he had begun writing, first in prose and then in poetry, about his life and family. In part, Lowell was prompted to take this change of course by his reading of other poets, notably William Carlos Williams: but in part it seemed a natural course for him to take, not only because of its possible therapeutic function but also because it enabled him to pursue his search for a satisfactory voice and place. In the event, in the poems that were eventually published in *Life Studies* (1959), Lowell discovered not just a medium for expressing his immense, devouring inwardness but a way of fulfilling his desire for spiritual anchorage as well: something that, besides offering him the opportunity for emotional release, described a fleeting sense of stability and order.

As the reader compares the poems in *Life Studies* – like 'My Last Afternoon with Uncle Devereux Winslow' or 'Memories of West Street and Lepke' – with the earlier work, the contrast could hardly be more striking. Gone is the Catholicism; in its place is a different, more muted and ironic kind of belief, in the imaginative and moral power of faithful speech. Gone, too, are the tortuous language and elaborate arrangements of line and rhythm; in *their* place are lines that are limpid and flexible, a syntax and idiom that play cunning variations on the colloquial, and rhymes that when they do occur are invariably unexpected and elusive. The poet, it seems, no longer begins with a predetermined structure for his material, but instead tries to discover structure of a kind, and immutability, in the actual processes of remembering and articulating. The only order now tolerated, the reader surmises, is the order of literature; the poem recreating the experience becomes the one acceptable means of refining and shaping it.

The success of *Life Studies* helped turn Lowell into a public figure, the most visible American poet of his generation. And it was partly in response to this enhanced status that he began taking a public stand on some of the major issues of the day, such as the war in Vietnam. At the same time, his poetry, while remaining profoundly personal, addressed problems of history and culture: in his own way, like Whitman he tried to consider what it was like to be an American at mid-century. 'Waking Early Sunday Morning', discussed earlier, gives one illustration of how Lowell wedded his intense inwardness of impulse to historical event and contemporary crisis. Another is offered by 'For the Union Dead', the title poem in his 1964 collection. In this poem, the civic disorder of the present is contrasted with two alternative ideas of order. One is the public order of the past: old New England, conceived of in consciously mythological terms and figured in the statue of a Colonel Shaw, who commanded a black regiment during the Civil War. Shaw, the poet suggests, had 'an angry wrenlike vigilance, / a greyhound's gentle tautness' and rejoiced 'in man's lovely, / peculiar power to choose life and die'. He found perfect freedom in service to civic values, the values of a culture: the disciplines he accepted enabled him to live, and even to die, with grace and purpose. But, Lowell suggests, those disciplines are unavailable now. All that is offered by the present culture is anarchism and enslavement. 'Everywhere', declares the poet, 'giant finned cars move forward like fish / a savage servility / slides by on grease.' In seeking to aggrandize themselves, people have lost themselves: the pursuit of power has generated the greatest betrayals of all – of humanity and of community. So the only possible order for the present and future is a personal one, registered here in the architecture of the poem. Shaw's statue, a monument to public principle, has to be replaced by acts of private judgement which, like this poem, may then furnish others with the vision and vocabulary necessary to change their own lives.

For many of the last years of his life, Lowell concentrated on a series of unrhymed and irregular sonnets, collected in books like *Notebook 1967–1968* (1969, augmented edition 1970), *The Dolphin* (1973) and *History* (1973). Talking about these sonnets, Lowell explained that they were 'written as one poem, intuitive in arrangement, but not a pile or sequence of related material'. They were, he added, 'less an almanac than the story of my life'. As a whole, they are further proof of their creator's belief in the power and efficacy of literature: in an almost manic way, the poet seems intent on metamorphosing all his life into art, in endowing his every experience, however trivial, with some sort of structure and durability. They are also proof of his Americanness; for, taken together, they constitute another epic of the self. Less openly responsive to the problems of political society than the *Cantos*, less deliberately preoccupied with the future of America than 'Song of Myself', *Notebook* and the succeeding volumes nevertheless share with those poems a concern with the life-in-progress of the protean poet, as representative of his time and place. Journeying over the blasted terrain of his own life, Lowell is also travelling over the wasteland of his culture; measuring his personal feelings he is, too, taking the measure of larger events. Writing now becomes an existential act, a means of establishing presence: as Lowell puts it in one piece, 'Reading Myself', in *Notebook*, the poem, the made work, 'proves its maker is alive'. By definition, it is also an act that must go on and on: 'this open book', the poet says, is his 'open coffin'. An epic of personal identity, an epic that effectively *creates* identity, must remain unfinished, available to change. Lowell was continually composing new sonnets and revising old ones, then scattering the results through different volumes: because, like Whitman, Pound and others, what he was after was not so much a poem as a poetic process – something that denied coherence, in the traditional sense, and closure.

After the sonnets, Lowell published only one further volume, *Day by Day* (1977). The poems here, which show him returning to freer, more varied verse forms, are elegiac, penitential and autumnal, as if the poet were trying to resolve ancient quarrels and prepare himself for death. With storybook neatness, in fact, Lowell did die very shortly after the book was published: his life and his life's work were completed at almost exactly the same time. In reading these final poems, the reader is likely to be reminded again just how much faith in the self provided the bedrock value, the positive thrust, in all Lowell's writing: at times challenged, as in his earlier poetry, occasionally questioned or qualified, as in the later, but always, incontestably there. 'Sometimes everything I write', the poet admits at the end of *Day by Day*, '... seems a snapshot, / ... / ... paralysed by fact.' 'Yet,' he continues, 'why not say what happened?' 'We are poor passing facts /', he concludes, 'warned by that to give / each figure in the photograph / his living name.' 'I desire of every writer', Thoreau once said, 'a simple and sincere account of his own life.' 'Simple' and 'sincere' are not, perhaps, words that we normally associate with a poet as subtle and ironic as Lowell; but in his own way he tried to fulfil Thoreau's demand – by confronting his experience, pursuing the goal of self-discovery and attempting to achieve some sense of order, however fragile and evanescent, through the activities of memory and reinvention. Like other great American poets, Lowell learned how to translate the poor passing facts of autobiography into what he called 'the grace of accuracy'. Consequently, his story becomes history: he told true tales of his life which have, in turn, become true tales for all of us.

'Really we had the same life,' Lowell wrote in his elegy for John Berryman (1914–72), 'the generic one / our generation offered.' Lowell recognized in Berryman a fellow explorer of dangerous psychological territory: 'I feel I know what you have worked through,' he declared, 'you / know what I have worked through . . . / . . . / John, we used the language as if we made it.' What is more, he learned from Berryman: *Notebook*, he acknowledged, bore the imprint of Berryman's *The Dream Songs* (1969) – of which Lowell said, in an admiring review, 'All is risk and variety here. This great Pierrot's universe is more tearful and funny than we can easily bear.' But *The Dream Songs* was by no means Berryman's first work: like Lowell again, 'cagey John' (as he was later to call himself) began under the burden of alien influences, particularly Yeats and Auden. 'I didn't so much want to resemble [Yeats] as to *be* him,' Berryman later admitted, 'and for several fumbling years I wrote . . . with no voice of my own.' 'Yeats . . . saved me from the then crushing influence of . . . Pound and . . . Eliot,' he added, 'but he could not teach me to sound like myself.' On the whole, his earlier poetry is constricted by its formal quality, attentiveness to established models. *Berryman's Sonnets*, for instance, written in the 1940s although not published until 1968, starts from an intensely personal base, an adulterous love affair the poet had with an unspecified woman. But everything is distanced by the use of the strict Petrarchan form, archaic language and a conventional argument that leads us through love and loss to transference of affection from woman to muse ('my lady came not / . . . I sat down & wrote'). Only now and then do we get glimpses of the vain, sad, drunken, lustful, comic and pathetic 'I' that dominates and distinguishes the later work.

'I want a verse fresh as a bubble breaks,' Berryman declared in one of his sonnets; and the fresh style came in *Homage to Mistress Bradstreet* (1956), which the poet called a 'drowning' in the past. In this long poem of fifty-seven stanzas, the 'benevolent phantom' of the seventeenth-century poet Anne Bradstreet is conjured from the grave; she speaks, through the voice Berryman gives to her, of her emigration to New England and her hard life there; in a moment of intense communion, at once spiritual and erotic, the two poets from different centuries engage with each other; then Bradstreet succumbs to the pull of the past, and she and Berryman are once more imprisoned in their own times. 'Narrative!' Berryman recalled himself thinking while he was writing the poem, 'Let's have narrative . . . and no fragmentation!' Along with the fundamental coherence of narrative, he was also aiming, he said, at poetic forms 'at once flexible and grave, intense and quiet, able to deal with matter both high and low'. He did not choose Anne Bradstreet, Berryman claimed, she chose him; and she did so, 'almost from the beginning, as a woman, not much as a poetess'. It is not the author of 'bald / abstract didactic rime' he encounters, in other words, but a passionate rebel who resists the conventions of youth and age, the restrictions of her environment and culture, the limitations of her body and the apparent will of God. In each case, though, rebellion is followed by surrender: 'My heart rose,' as she puts it, 'but I did submit.' This pattern of defiance followed by submission, or reconciliation, is caught in each individual stanza, with its halting ebb-and-flow released in a long, last line; and it is the pattern of the poem as a whole – almost certainly because Berryman himself saw it as the basic rhythm of life. 'We dream of honour, and we get along,' he was to say later: existence is a series of small, proud assertions made within the shadow of death, little victories in the face of ultimate defeat. Undoubtedly, *Homage* is a work of the historical imagination, in that Berryman recreates the past, makes it alive in and for the present. But it is also a personal poem to the extent that it enables him to realize his own voice by making the dead speak and tell their story.

'Man is entirely alone / may be,' Berryman remarks just over midway through *Homage*, then adds, 'I am a man of griefs & fits / trying to be my friend.' This anticipates the tone and vision of Berryman's major work, the *Dream Songs*, the first of which were published in 1964 and the last few of which he was still writing just before his death by suicide in 1972. 'I am obliged to perform in great darkness / operations of great delicacy / on my self,' Berryman admits in one of these songs, and this suggests their essential thrust. Like *Notebook*, they document, in the manner of a journal or a diary, the chaotic growth of a poet's mind: the processes of his life, in all their absurdity, fear, pain and wonder. Unlike *Notebook*, however, the story is told with the help of a character, a person called Henry, who is 'at odds wif de world and its god'. Along with his creator, Henry is many things: transient, criminal, troubled and gone, wilful, lustful, tired, ridiculous, stricken. In the course of the poem, he dies ('I am breaking up', 'Henry's parts were fleeing') and then comes back to life ('others collected and dug Henry up'); and he is aided and abetted, particularly in the earlier songs, by another character called Tambo who speaks in a thick, stage-Negro dialect. If Henry, and by extension Berryman, is 'a divided soul', then Tambo helps to dramatize that division. Tambo talks to Henry like the end man in a minstrel show, calling him 'Mister Bones' or 'Brother Bones' ('Am I a bad man? Am I a good man? / – Hard to say, Brother Bones. Maybe you both, / like most of we'). And, as he does so, the reader is irresistibly reminded of earlier dialogues of self and soul, or mind and body: but with the suspicion that these dialogues have been transposed here into a more contemporary, fragmented and disjunctive key. The shifts of mood are kaleidoscopic: boredom ('Life, friends, is boring') slides into happiness ('moments of supreme joy jerk / him on'), then into guilt ('There sat down, once, a thing on Henry's heart'), then into stoic endurance ('We suffer on, a day, a day, a day'). Within this loose, baggy monster, Berryman can incorporate pain at the death of friends ('The high ones die, die. They die'), references to his casual lecheries or heavy drinking ('a little more whiskey please'), irritation with whatever power rules the world ('I'm cross with god'), and horror at the lunacies of the twentieth century ('This world is gradually becoming a place / where I do not care to be any more'). Certain themes or obsessions recur, such as the suicide of his father then, later, the pleasures of his new marriage and the birth and growth of his child, but no particular theme is allowed to dominate. 'These songs are not meant to be understood, you understand,' warns Berryman, '/ They are only meant to terrify and comfort.' They are '*crazy* sounds', intended to give tongue to life as it passes: hell-bent on resisting any notions of 'ultimate structure' (although 'assistant professors' will 'become associates' trying to find one, Berryman wryly observes), or any suggestion of a stable, unitary self.

At one point in *Dream Songs*, Berryman quotes Gottfried Benn: 'We are using our own skins for wallpaper and we cannot win.' Elsewhere, he refers to his verse as 'Henry's pelt put on sundry walls'. Both remarks invite us to see the poem as raw and immediate, made up, as it were, out of pieces of the poet. The flow of the bloodstream becomes a flow of language which, while the poet lasts, cannot stop: so the poem ends, appropriately, on a note of anticipation – its last words, 'my heavy daughter', looking forwards towards a future burdened with promise. It is worth emphasizing, however, that the intimacy of these songs is the product of craft. The calculated use of personae, a lively and varied idiom, a powerfully forced syntax and dense imagery, and a fairly tight formal structure: all these things enable the poet to displace and dramatize the play of feeling, translating the 'data' that is 'abundantly his' into objective imaginative experience. The tragedy of most of Berryman's last poems, in *Love & Fame* (1970; revised edition 1972) and *Delusions* (1972), is that he forgot this. 'I wiped out all the disguises,' he said of these poems, '. . . the subject was . . . solely and simply myself.' Their tone varies from the brashly self-confident ('I make a high salary & royalties & fees') to the desperate ('I'm vomiting. / I broke down today in the slow movement of K365'). There are some rather repellent litanies of sexual conquests ('shagging with a rangy gay thin girl / (Miss Vaughan) I tore a section of the draperies down'), statements of belief that range from the convincing ('Man is a huddle of need') to the banal ('Nobody *knows anything*'). And, as a whole, these poems chart a progress from skirt-chasing and self-promotion to humble religious faith ('I do not understand; but I believe'). The problem is that whether Berryman is declaring 'I fell in love with a girl, / O and a gash', or admitting, 'I fell in love with you, Father', the poetic result remains the same: the rhythms are lumpen, the imagery thin, the idiom casual to the point of sloppiness. 'I am not writing autobiography-in-verse,' Berryman insists: unfortunately, he is at least trying to, and very little is added to the meanings or measure of his autobiography by the use of verse. This is not so much confessional poetry, in fact, as pure confession: moving, sometimes, in the way that the confidences of any stranger might be, but not something in which we can begin to share.

'I've been very excited by what is the new breakthrough that came with, say, Robert Lowell's *Life Studies*,' said Sylvia Plath (1932–63), 'This intense breakthrough into very serious, very personal emotional experience, which I feel has been partly taboo.' 'Peculiar and private taboo subjects I feel have been explored in recent American poetry', she went on, '– I think particularly of the poetess Anne

Sexton . . . her poems are wonderfully craftsmanlike . . . and yet they have a kind of emotional and psychological depth which I think is something perhaps quite new and exciting.' Plath's excitement grew, of course, from a sense of kinship. Even her earlier poems are marked by extremism of feeling and melodic cunningness of expression. But it was in the poems published after Plath's suicide, in *Ariel* (1966), that the impulse towards oblivion, and the pain that generated that impulse, were rendered in inimitably brutal ways: in terms, at once daring and deliberate, that compel the reader to participate in the poet's despair. The suffering at the heart of her work has received ample attention; however, the craft that draws us into that suffering is sometimes ignored. Fortunately, Plath did not ignore it. 'I think my poems come immediately out of the . . . experience I have,' she admitted, '. . . but I believe that one should be able to control and manipulate experience, even the most terrifying . . . with an informed and intelligent mind.' Her later poetry is a poetry of the edge, certainly, that takes greater risks, moves further towards the precipice than most conventional verse: but it is also a poetry that depends for its success on the mastery of her craftsmanship, her ability to fabricate larger, historical meanings and imaginative myth out of personal horror. And it is a poetry, as well, that draws knowingly on honoured traditions: the Puritan habit of meditation upon last things, the American compulsion to confront the abyss of the self – above all, the burning conviction felt by poets as otherwise different as Poe and Dickinson that the imagining of death is the determining, definitive experience of life.

A poem like 'Tulips' is a good illustration of Plath's passion and her craft. Its origins lie in personal experience: a time when the poet was taken into hospital and was sent flowers as a gift. The opening four stanzas recover her feelings of peace and release on entering the hospital ward. 'Look how white everything is, how quiet, how snowed-in, /' she exclaims. 'I am learning peacefulness, lying by myself quietly / As the light lies on these white walls, this bed, these hands, / I am nobody.' The almost sacramental terms in which Plath describes herself here turn this experience into a mysterious initiation, a dying away from the world. 'I have given my name and my day-clothes up to the nurses,' Plath says, '/ And my history to the anaesthetist and my body to the surgeons.' Everything that gives her identity, that imprisons her in existence, has been surrendered; and she sinks into a condition of utter emptiness, openness, that is associated at certain times with immersion in water – a return to the foetal state and the matrix of being. The only initial resistance to this movement comes from a photograph of her husband and children she has by her bedside, reminding her, evidently, of the hell of other people, who cast 'little smiling hooks' to fish her up out of the sea.

In the next four stanzas, the tulips – mentioned briefly in the first line and then forgotten – enter the scene with a vengeance. 'The tulips are too red in the first place, they hurt me,' Plath declares. They are all that is the opposite of the white, silent world of the hospital, carrying associations of noise and pressure, 'sudden tongues and . . . colour'. They draw Plath back to life, the conditioning forces that constitute existence. She feels herself 'watched', identified by 'the eyes of the tulips':

their gaze commits her to a particular status or role. What is more, this contradict-ory impulse drawing her back into the world and identification 'corresponds' to something in herself: it comes from within her, just as the earlier impulse towards liberation did. This probably explains why the conflict of the poem remains unre-solved: the ninth and final stanza of the poem simply and beautifully juxtaposes images of imprisonment and escape, the blood of life and the salt sea of death. 'And I am aware of my heart,' Plath concludes: 'it opens and closes / Its bowl of red blooms out of sheer love for me.' 'The water I taste is warm and salt, like the sea,' she adds, '/ And comes from a country far away as health.' The alternatives are familiar ones in American writing: either to live in the world and accept the identity it prescribes, or to flee into a state of absolute freedom. What is less familiar is that, here as elsewhere, Plath associates these two alternatives, tradition-ally figured in the clearing and the wilderness, with the absolute conditions of being and not-being. Fixity, in these terms, is life; flight is immolation; freedom is the immediate metaphor of the hospital and the ultimate metamorphosis of death.

'Dying / Is an art, like everything else,' Plath remarks in 'Lady Lazarus', '/ I do it exceptionally well.' Her poetry is artfully shaped, setting stark and elevated imagery of the sea, fire, moon, whiteness and silence – all suggestive of the purifying, peaceful nature of oblivion – against figures of domesticity and violence – the pleasures and the pains of living in the world. Everything is incorporated within a habit of intense personal meditation, conversation with the self: 'I've got to . . . speak them to myself,' Plath said of these later poems; 'Whatever lucidity they may have comes from the fact that I say them aloud.' The poems concerning the affections that tie us to this world, like 'Morning Song' (about the birth of her daughter), are notable for their wry tenderness and wonder; those that describe the false self the world requires us to construct, such as 'The Applicant', are, on the other hand, marked by a corrosive wit; while the pieces that concentrate on the ambiguous nature of death ('Death & Co.') or the perfecting of the self in the experience of dying ('Fever 103', 'Edge') are more rapt and bardic, singed by the fire of pro-phecy. What characterizes all this work, however, despite evident differences of tone, is the sheer seductiveness of Plath's voice: she conjures up the roots of her own violence, and the reader is caught in the spell.

The artful way in which Plath immerses the reader in her experience is illus-trated by 'Daddy', a poem that in addition measures the distance between her use of the confessional mode and, say, Lowell's. 'Daddy', Plath said, 'is spoken by a girl with an Electra complex.' More to the point, it is based on her own ambivalent relationship with her father (who died when she was still young), her tendency to recreate aspects of that relationship in later, adult relationships, her attempts at suicide, and her desperate need to come to terms with all these things. The secret of the poem lies in its tension. There is the tension of the narrator's attitude to her father and other men, between fear and desire, resentment and tenderness. There is tension beyond this, the poet intimates, in all human connections: the victim both detests and adores the victimizer, and so is at once repelled and attracted by the brutal drama of life. Above all, there is tension in the poem's tone. The banal horrors of personal and general history that Plath recalls are rendered in terms of fairytale and folk story; while the verse form is as insistently jaunty as that of the nursery rhymes it invokes. This manic gaiety of tone, at odds with the bleak content, has a curiously hypnotic effect on the reader, who feels almost caught by a contagion, compelled to surrender to the irresistible litany of love and hate. Nor do the closing lines bring any release. 'Daddy, daddy, you bastard, I'm through,' Plath concludes: but the impression is more that she is 'through' in the sense of being over and done with than 'through' to and with her father. Like scratching a wound, the speaking of her relationship seems only to have exacerbated the pain. 'Maybe it's an irrelevant accident that she actually carried out the death she predicted,' Lowell observed of Plath, '. . . but somehow the death is part of the imaginative risk.' This captures perfectly the difference between the two poets. There is an art of reconciliation and an art of resistance. There are confessional poets who discover peace, therapeutic release in the disciplines of writing, and those, equally disciplined, whose writing only pushes them further towards the edge. If Lowell is an example of the former, then Plath is clearly an illustration of the latter: in the interests of her art she committed herself, ventured to the point where there was nothing left but the precipice and little, if any, chance of a return.

New formalists, new confessionals

Since the deaths of Plath, Berryman and Lowell, new generations have been busy redrawing the map of American poetry. Among these generations are some notable formalists, poets who necessarily derive their inspiration from personal experience but use a variety of means to distance things and disengage their work from autobiography. The personal stimulus and the desire for disengagement are particularly remarkable in the work of Charles Wright (1935–) (a selection of which is to be found in *Country Music* [1982]). 'I write poems to untie myself, to do penance and disappear / Through the upper right-hand corner of things,' he declares in one poem, 'Revision'; other typical lines are, 'I am weary of daily things', 'I'm going away now, goodbye'. If the first person enters Wright's poetry, it does so only to be erased. His poetry is poetry of an 'I' yearning for transcendence, and its own obliteration. It is a poetry of spiritual hunger rather than fulfilment: expressed sometimes directly, as in 'Next' ('I want to be bruised by God . . . / . . . / I want to be entered and picked clean'), and sometimes, as in 'Spider Crystal Ascension', through symbolism of, say, a chrysalis turning into a mayfly or the Milky Way ('The spider, juiced crystal and Milky Way . . . / . . . looks down, waiting for us to ascend'). The structures Wright chooses – the three-stanza form of 'Tattoos', for instance, or the twelve- and fourteen-line forms of *China Trace* (1977) and 'Skins' – are clearly a part of this larger project: seeking the still point of the turning world, he commits himself to spatial forms, a frozen moment, arrested motion. 'I'm talking about stillness,' Wright says in a poem called 'Morandi'; and that stillness is something he tries to imitate in his remote and severe lines.

Ambiguous but subtly different kinds of distancing are to be found in the work of Amy Clampitt (1920–94) and Louise Glück (1943–). Clampitt has a habit of weaving the phenomenal world into an artful piece of embroidery. In 'The King-fisher', for example, the title poem of her 1983 collection, the calculated play of imagery, a strict and quite complex stanzaic form, winding syntactical shapes and a feeling for words as distinctly odd artefacts: all help transmute the story of a love affair into a tapestry, rich and strange – or, as Clampitt herself puts it, into 'an illuminated manuscript in which all the handiwork happens to be verbal'. With Glück, the effect is not so much of a mosaic as of ritual. Glück's poems (in collections like *Firstborn* [1969], *The House on the Marshland* [1976], *The Triumph of Achilles* [1985] and *The Wild Iris* [1992]) deal with themes that are intensely personal in origin: family life ('Poem', 'Still Life'), motherhood and children ('All Hallows', 'The Drowned Children'), a lost sister ('Descending Figure'), love between a man and a woman ('Happiness'). But everything is rendered in an oblique, impersonal manner, seen as if through the wrong end of a telescope. The actors in these human dramas are usually anonymous; there is a timeless quality to their actions; and the terms in which they are rescued for our attention possess the stark inevitability of fable. This is the realm of divination, or myth: an oracular voice tells us of events that are dreamily repetitive, foreknown yet mysterious because they are attached at all times to certain rites of passage, the primal and traumatic experiences of birth, growing up and death.

Along with these new departures in formalism, however, poetry of the personal has continued unabated. In several instances, recent writers have developed the tradition of relating identity to landscape. John Haines (1924–), for instance, connects the wintry surroundings of Alaska, and the Middle West 'with its trodden snow / and black Siberian trees', to harsh visions of himself and his culture; in such collections as *Winter News* (1966) and *News from the Glacier* (1982), the natural world is seen in terms of internecine conflict ('Here too are life's victims,' he exclaims), and so too is America ('There are too many . . . / . . . / columns of brutal strangers'). His aim, evidently, is to identify himself with these conflicts: to participate in a struggle that is at once elemental and political. The tone of this involvement is sometimes celebratory ('I believe in this stalled magnificence'), sometimes meditative ('I walked among them, / I listened and understood') and occasionally angry ('There will be many poems written in the shape of a grenade'). Whatever, it constantly recalls that great poet of participation, Whitman: for Haines shares with the Good Gray Poet not only a populist impulse and a feel for organic rhythms but also a radicalism that is both personal and political – a commitment to revolution in the self along with revolution in the state. Similar echoes of Whitman, tracing a correspondence between inner and outer worlds, are to be found in the work of Robert Pinsky (1940–), a poet who tries to capture what he calls the 'mothlike' life, the 'thin / Halting qualities of the soul' hovering behind 'The glazed surface of the world'. Pinsky's voice, quieter than Haines's, may sound ordinary, but that is precisely the point: like Whitman, he is obsessed with the heroism of the ordinary – or even of the apparently banal. So, in volumes that

---

include *Sadness and Happiness* (1975), *The Want Bone* (1990) and *Jersey Rain* (2000), he describes 'the tyranny of the word visible', and in particular the suburban landscapes of New Jersey, and hints at the 'unique / Soul' beneath this, the 'hideous, sudden stare of self' that can be glimpsed by the sympathetic imagination. American life is marked for him by its doubleness: there is 'cash, tennis, fine electronics', certainly, but there is 'music, . . . yearning, suffering' as well. A favourite setting, the seashore, implies this duality of perspective. Set between the mysterious ocean and 'vast, uncouth houses', Pinsky and his characters inhabit a border area. They want the shock of vision and they want simply to make a living: they work 'For truth and for money' – two very different yet related 'stays / Against boredom, discomfort, death and old age'.

Dave Smith (1942–) also secretes the poetry of the personal in the poetry of place: 'Grandfather,' he declares in one poem, 'Cumberland Station', 'I wish I had the guts to tell you this is a place I hope / I never have to go through again.' Only in this case the place is Southern: the 'anonymous fishing village' where he lives, perhaps, the woods and rivers ('The Last Morning'), a disused railway ('Cumberland Station'), or a Civil War cemetery ('Fredericksburg'). His poetry, gathered in collections like *Goshawk, Antelope* (1970), *The Roundhouse Voices* (1985) and *Wick of Memory* (2000), is saturated in locality, focusing in particular on what most art, in its pursuit of an 'entirely eloquent peace', 'fails to see': the disinherited, those victimized by society and often excluded from its frames of reference. And through this plenitude of landscape moves the poet himself, trying to 'hold . . . obscure syllables / one instant'. He, it seems, is given presence by the 'eye', the observation of extrinsic detail. Another way of putting this would be to say that, for all his interest in the personal, Smith – like Haines and Pinsky – chooses to refract personality, to clothe the naked self in the warm details of circumstantiality.

Something very similar could be said about such otherwise different poets as Maxine Kumin (1925–), Carolyn Kizer (1925–), Jay Wright (1935–) and Charles Simic (1938–). It is also true of many poets of a later generation, like Ai (1947–), Carol Frost (1948–), Yusef Komunyakaa (1947–), Naomi Shihab Nye (1952–) and Elizabeth Spires (1952–). Kumin has explored the darker side of suburban living in many of the pieces included in her *Selected Poems 1960–1990* (1997). Kizer has found an edge and a new range for her poetry in feminism ('We are the custodians of the world's best-kept secret: /' she announces in one of the poems in *Calm, Cool and Collected* (2000), 'Merely the private lives of one half of humanity'). In such volumes as *Dimensions of History* (1976) and *Boleros* (1991), Wright has linked his own life as an African American to the histories of Africa, America and Europe in the belief that all cultures share a common mythic ground. And Simic, whose *Selected Early Poems* appeared in 1999, has found an outlet for his absurdist vision – founded in his childhood in wartime Yugoslavia where 'Hitler and Stalin fought over my soul, my destiny', as he puts it – in becoming what he calls 'a realist *and* a surrealist, always drawn between the two'. Likewise, in the later generation, Ai, born Florence Anthony and, as she describes herself, 'one-half Japanese, one-eighth Choctaw, one-fourth black, and one-sixteenth Irish', has used dramatic verse monologues to explore the roots of American violence. 'The history of my family', she has said, 'is itself a history of America'; and the titles of her collections – among them *Cruelty* (1973), *Sin* (1986), *Greed* (1993) and *Vice* (1999) – show what she believes American history to be. Frost (a selection of whose work is to be found in *Love and Scorn; New and Selected Poems* [2000]) subdues the verse of self within what she describes as 'the harmony and breaking down of such harmony that is the passing world'. Komunyakaa links his African American heritage to the traditions of European and American romanticism, or what he terms 'my impossible white wife', while Nye, whose *Selected Poems* was published in 1995, refracts her meditations on the 'secrets of dying' through the contemplation of simple objects, minute particulars. And Spires, a disciple of Bishop, in volumes like *Globe* (1981) and *Worldling* (1995), sets the particulars of experience in the pattern of circumstance, the rhythms of process since, as she puts it, 'only when we are "in the process" do we lose our sense of time rapidly passing and, for a little while, escape death'. For all these poets, forms, cultural or mythical, literal or visionary, become a means of connecting the personal by what Kizer calls 'invisible wires' to the lives of others, living and dead. So, in a poem by Kumin called 'Woodchucks', the mundane task of ridding a garden of a pest can lead to a meditation on the Holocaust. And, for Jay Wright, in 'The Homecoming Singer', the experience of returning home can inspire a celebration of the way all people in all cultures return 'home', to the common ground of archetypal experience.

The difference with other practising poets wedded to a more confessional mode is, perhaps, a difference of inclination. It is, nevertheless, a radical one. There is still a poetry of the primal scream: speech that, in obedience to one of the most fundamental American impulses, springs immediately out of the depths of the self – and finds its vital life there. Poets of one generation, born just before the Second World War, who sustain this allegiance to the innermost recesses of identity include Audre Lorde (1934–97), Diane Di Prima (1934–), Lucille Clifton (1936–), Diane Wakoski (1937–), and Frank Bidart (1939–). From another, later generation, they number, among them, Sharon Olds (1942–), Olga Broumas (1949–), Kimiko Hahn (1955–) and Li-Young Lee (1957–). Lorde insisted that she wrote to fulfil her responsibility 'to see the truth as I felt it, and to attempt to speak it with as much precision and beauty as possible'. That truth, above all, involved the necessity of her power and survival as a woman, an African American, and a lesbian. And it compelled her not only to write poetry, but also to create what she called 'biomythography': to tell the story of herself and 'the women who helped give me substance', as she put it, in *Zami: A New Spelling of My Name* (1982) and *Our Dead Behind Us* (1986). Di Prima, in such collections as *Revolutionary Letters* (1969), links bright, particular accounts of her life to an unabashedly optimistic vision of the political future ('America is not even begun yet / This continent is in seed'). Wakoski, by comparison, is more exclusively confessional, favouring what she terms 'the completely personal expression' in books like *The Collected Greed* (1984). So, too, is the African American poet Clifton, whose *Blessing the Boats: New and Selected Poems 1988–2000* appeared in 2000. She has written spare, unsentimental and often wry poems, about, for instance, her aborted baby ('the lost baby poem'), her 'big hips' ('homage to my hips'), and the loss of her uterus and one of her breasts in operations ('poem to my uterus', 'lumpectomy eve', 'scar'). The distances between the three of them, or with Lorde, however, are minimal or peripheral. Like Bidart, whose work is ignited by the pleasures and the pains of being a homosexual ('I feel too much, I can't stand what I feel', he declares in 'Happy Birthday', from *The Book of the Body* [1977]), they write, fundamentally, a poetry of the first person singular.

That stress on the singular presence is just as strong in the work of the later generation. The subject of the poetry of Sharon Olds, for instance, is the body: her body, in particular, the space it inhabits, the subjectivity it determines, and the violations of both that subjectivity and that space. For Olds, the body supplies a defining sense of self against the psychological abuse of the father; it becomes, like language, a way of escape from domesticity and dysfunction. And collections like *The Father* (1992) and *Blood, Tin, Straw* (1999) show her proclaiming the power and privacy of the body, pursuing her selfhood in poems that explore formerly taboo subjects with blunt, sometimes vulgar language. Broumas, too, is preoccupied with the body in its various configurations. *Rave: Poems 1975–1999* (1999) contains work that is just as frank and provocative as Olds's is. Unashamed in her celebration of lust, and her explanation of the politics of desire, Broumas conflates flesh and landscape: their common salts lending an ecstatic, feminist slant to her accounts of coming together with other women. Hahn and Lee are, maybe, less confrontational. Hahn, as a collection like *The Unbearable Heart* (1995) illustrates, uses the storytelling traditions of her Asian American community to realize a degree of indirection. That same community, and a sense of family, are at the heart of the poems of Lee, to be found in collections like *Book of My Nights* (2001). But the bedrock of this poetry, too, remains the self, telling its story, treasuring its subjectivity. 'I can only speak for myself,' admits Hahn in a poem called 'The Izu Dancer'. This could be said by any and for any one and all of these later generations of confessional writers. So, too, could an equally simple, seminal declaration made by Lee – 'You must sing to be found,' he has said, 'when found, you must sing.'

Public and Private Histories

Documentary and dream in prose

'Our history has moved on two rivers,' Norman Mailer (1923–) wrote in *The Presidential Papers* (1963), 'one visible, the other underground; there has been the history of politics which is concrete, practical . . . and there is the subterranean river of untapped, ferocious, lonely and romantic desires, that concentration of ecstasy and violence which is the dream life of the nation.' That may sound like a reformulation of a perennial American dialectic: the clearing and the wilderness, fixity and fluidity, the structures of society and the subversive impulses of the self.

If it is, then it was certainly given additional impetus in many prose texts in the three decades or so after the Second World War, when writers struggled to negotiate what they saw as an increasingly baffling and bizarre world. On the one hand, there were those who subscribed to forms of realism to try to catch the grainy, visible contours of American life. And, at its most extreme, the devotion to the concrete led to styles of scrupulous meanness, the New Journalism and dirty realism. As one dirty realist put it, 'in these overwritten times . . . it is enough to write the facts in a clear hand: it is a mistake to embellish or improve upon the fantastic actuality'. On the other hand were those who submitted themselves to the secret, subterranean life of America, who believed that only literary forms that man-oeuvred their way above, below, beyond realism could cope with the nation's fantastic actuality. So, Vladimir Nabokov described himself and his contemporaries as being 'faced by the task of inventing America'; and his own work, he said, was 'a subjective specific affair' 'set in a dream America'. Fabulators, fantasists, beat writers and surrealists, some of them appropriated the language of popular culture. Some of them viewed language itself as their subject, since it circumscribed their world, constituted all that was the case for them as Americans. Some of them drew on forms and genres that could perhaps feed the hidden streams of the national life into literature: automatic, instinctive writing, say, the cut-up method, collage, or the strangeness of Gothic or science fiction. As Mailer himself intimated, these two strategies were not mutually exclusive. Since both rivers carried into American history, both streamed into American circumstance and consciousness, they could, in turn, both percolate in American writing, shaping the character of individual texts by creating a dialectic. At one extreme, it may be, were the creators of the non-fiction novel, wedded to fact; at the other were the creators of fictive space, lexical playfields, married to the elusive, desirable substance of dream. But in between were the many American writers who saw it as their project to weave their way between these extremes, to work in territory bordering both: to show, in short, the interdependence of the 'two rivers'.

For Mailer himself, the American history that mattered for him personally began with the Second World War. That war inspired a powerful vein of fiction. Some of it was written in what Gore Vidal (1925–), commenting on his own war story *Williwaw* (1946), called 'the national manner . . . a simple calculated style'. Apart from *Williwaw*, such novels included *From Here to Eternity* (1951), a grimly realistic story of army life in Hawaii on the eve of the attack on Pearl Harbor, by James Jones (1921–77), and *The Gallery* (1947) by John Horne Burns (1916–53). But Vidal himself, as his remark suggests, did not remain long within the con-straints of realist simplicity. His later work shows him using a mixture of realism and satire, sardonic comment and acerbic wit, sometimes surreal fantasy and always irony, to explore such disparate subjects as homosexuality (*The City and the Pillar* [1948]), politics ancient (*Julian* [1964], *Creation* [1981]) and modern (*Washington D.C.* [1967], *Hollywood* [1990]) or both (*Two Sisters* [1970], *Live from Golgotha* [1992]), transsexuality and the media (*Myra Breckinridge* [1968], *Myron* [1974]), and the heroes and villains of American life and society (*Burr* [1973], *1876* [1976],

Lincoln [1984]). And two of the most notable novels to come out of the war exploited the techniques of the absurd to capture the bleak, bitter absurdities of that conflict: *Catch-22* (1961) by Joseph Heller (1923–99) and *Slaughterhouse-Five; or The Children's Crusade* (1969) by Kurt Vonnegut (1922–). *Catch-22* shows its protagonist, Yossarian, as the victim of a mad, conspiratorial military and political complex, caught in a closed system (the military, the war machine, society), from which his simple desire to escape proves his sanity and so his fitness to go on serving it. And *Slaughterhouse-Five* circulates around the firebombing of Dresden, which as a prisoner of war Vonnegut had witnessed. The Heller novel uses a disjointed narrative technique, nightmare sequences and bleak humour to depict a world gone crazy. The Vonnegut novel goes further. Mixing science fiction with satire, comedy with a bleak determinism, it shows its protagonist, Billy Pilgrim, inhabiting zones of time and space. Haunted by a punitive air raid that burned to death more people than died at Hiroshima, Billy plods through dull middle age in suburban America while simultaneously alive and comfortable on the distant planet of Tralfamadore. The time-warp technique allows Vonnegut simultaneously to offer ironic commentary on our inhumanity and the opportunity for destruction provided by twentieth-century technology, to satirize middle America and the bourgeois standards of suburbia, and to explore human inconsequence and impotence. 'Among the things Billy Pilgrim could not change', the reader is told, 'were the past, the present, and the future.' Vonnegut has written many other fictions that move between satirical humour and surreal fantasy: among them, *Player Piano* (1952), *The Sirens of Titan* (1959), *Cat's Cradle* (1963), *Breakfast of Champions* (1973) and *Bluebeard* (1987). Heller also wrote several other novels, including *Something Happened* (1974) and a sequel to *Catch-22, Closing Time* (1994). Neither of them, however, equalled their absurd comedies set in and around the nightmare of war. In *Catch-22* and *Slaughterhouse-Five*, human beings grapple to find meaning in the meaningless, and fail; and the conflict that haunts them defies both reason and morality – it seems illogical as well as obscene.

Mailer wrote his own war novel *The Naked and the Dead* (1948), he said, as 'a parable about the movement of man through history'. His book, he explained, explored 'the outrageous proposition of cause and effect . . . in a sick society'. It found 'man corrupted, confused to the point of helplessness', but it also found that 'there are limits beyond which he cannot be pushed'. And it showed that 'even in this corruption and sickness' man had 'yearnings for a better world'. The parable is executed remorselessly in terms of flesh and blood, depicting the capture of the island of Anopopei from the Japanese. There are two levels to the action. There is the actual fighting of the reconnaissance platoon under Sergeant Croft, which gives us the view on the ground of the combatant soldier. And there is the strategic view of the operation as conceived by General Cummings. Connecting these two levels is the middle-class liberal, Lieutenant Hearn, who will not agree with Cummings's fascist beliefs, is humiliated by him and is eventually killed by the agency of Croft. There is a bleak irony at work throughout the narrative; we are in the realm of the absurd. The island is captured. But that is thanks not to the strategy of Cummings but to the actions of the incompetent Major Dalleson. The capture of the island serves no useful purpose. And what prevails in the end is the desperate obstinacy of oppressed men, who reach the point where they can be oppressed no further. The ultimate irony is the way in which the members of the platoon turn. Pushed by Croft almost to the top of Mount Anaka, they stumble into a nest of hornets, from which they flee in terror down the mountainside. Discarding their weapons as they go, they suddenly understand that 'if they threw away enough possessions, they would not be able to continue the patrol'.

The eight men of the reconnaissance platoon are clearly meant to be a representative cross-section of American society. They are drawn from different places and ethnic groups. Their backgrounds and prewar lives, however, represented in inter-chapters that Mailer calls 'The Time-Machine', have a grim similarity about them. These are the wretched of the earth, conceived in terms that recall the fiction of Dos Passos. The energy of the book does not lie here, really, but arises from the portraits of the two men of power. Croft is the natural fascist, a sadist who kills for the thrill of killing. Cummings, in turn, is the intellectual fascist, who not only enacts but expresses his beliefs. 'The only morality of the future', he tells Hearn, 'is a power morality, and a man who cannot find his adjustment to it is doomed.' 'There is one thing about power,' Cummings adds. 'It can flow only from the top down.' So, with its rigid hierarchies and distinctions, 'you can consider the Army as a preview of the future'. That remark made by Cummings was seminal for Mailer, since much of his work – extraordinary in its range and volume as it is – can be seen as an exploration of power: its different manifestations and modes of operation, how it expresses itself in men, women and society. His second novel, *Barbary Shore* (1951), set mostly in a run-down boarding-house in Brooklyn, is about power and politics. His third novel, *The Deer Park* (1955), set around Hollywood, is more about power and sex. A later book, in turn, *Why Are We in Vietnam?* (1967), is about precisely those national fantasies of power that prompted America into its imperialist venture in Southeast Asia. Narrated by a character called D. J., who claims to work for a Texas radio station, much of it is taken up with the account of a larger-than-life hunting trip: which recalls other, legendary hunting trips in the fiction of Cooper, Hemingway and Faulkner. And all of it is written in a wild, surreal idiom that replicates the patter of American disc jockeys. What the book circulates around, in fact, both in its use of American mythic material and in its play with the nervy, syncopated language of the American media, is power on a national level – and, given the emergence of the American empire, on an international level as well.

What *Why Are We in Vietnam?* also suggests, perhaps, is the willingness of its author to incorporate fact and dream, the documentary and the demonic modes, in his imaginative investigation of power. It may be a war novel of a kind, but that is a very different kind from *The Naked and the Dead*, which, for all Mailer's talk of it as a parable, is clearly in the tradition of American naturalism. In an essay titled 'The White Negro' (1957), Mailer wrote that no matter how terrifying the twentieth century was, it was exciting 'for its tendency to reduce all life to its ultimate alternatives'. These alternatives have been, for him, a matter of writerly practice as much as existential choice: his work has moved on two rivers, at least, as it has attempted to explore the two rivers of American history. A master storyteller in the realist and naturalist vein, Mailer has also excelled at the New Journalism, a form he helped to create, which takes actual events and submits them to imaginative transformation. *Armies of the Night*, for instance, which is subtitled 'History as a Novel, The Novel as History', has as its subject a 1967 protest march on the Pentagon. *Miami and the Siege of Chicago* (1969) deals with the Republican and Democratic conventions of 1968; *The Prisoner of Sex* (1971) is Mailer's encounter with feminism; *Marilyn: A Biography* (1973) is a study of the life and meaning of Marilyn Monroe; and *The Executioner's Song* (1979) is at once an account of the events surrounding the execution of the convicted killer Gary Gilmore and an investigation into the roots of American violence. An essay like 'The White Negro', in turn, shows Mailer becoming part of the beat movement, calling on his contemporaries to resist corporate America and pursue a radical, more spontaneous alternative. *Of Women and Their Elegance* (1980) returns to Marilyn Monroe, whom Mailer sees as both an American icon and an embodiment of the power and potential corruptibility of sex; but this time in the form of fantasy, an 'imaginary memoir' of the star. And *Ancient Evenings* (1983), set in ancient Egypt, has a protagonist who is reborn three times, as he rises from a peasant childhood to become an adviser to the pharaohs. The power explored here is that of the body and the body politic, certainly, but it is also the power of mystery and magic – among other things, what the protagonist calls the magical 'power to father oneself'. Throughout his 1965 novel *An American Dream*, Mailer has his hero Rojack negotiating the edge between an America of hard facts and power politics and a nightworld America of strange, subrational or supernatural experience. It is an edge that this novel itself inhabits, as Mailer negotiates his way between a harsh, empirical idiom and one that gestures towards strangeness – a dreamplace or subterranean jungle where, as Rojack observes, 'universes wheeled in a dream'. 'I was caught' between those two Americas, Rojack admits: which clearly correspond to the two rivers of American history described by his creator. All his career, Mailer has been similarly caught. Out of that capture, though, he has produced fiction and non-fiction that goes much further than most in uncovering that mysterious dialectic of power that – for him, as for many others – constitutes the story of his nation.

There are a number of other novelists who have attempted a comparable negotiation in the forms and themes of their writing. John O'Hara (1905–70), from his acidic first novel *Appointment in Samarra* (1936) to the attenuated realism of *Ten North Frederick* (1955) and *From the Terrace* (1958), has investigated the interconnections of money, sex and social position. John B. Marquand (1893–1960) explored class, and often the struggle between inherited conformity and personal desire in novels like *Point of No Return* (1949). So does Louis Auchincloss (1917–) in such books as *Powers of Attorney* (1963), *The Dark Lady* (1977) and *Her Infinite Variety* (2000). There is a waspish, satirical quality to many of Auchincloss's fictional dissections of middle Americans. And that bent towards satire, a mordant moralism, is even stronger in the fiction of John Cheever (1912–82). *The Wapshot Chronicle* (1957), for example, his most famous work, is an account at once wistful and comic of a wealthy but declining Massachusetts family. *The Stories of John Cheever* (1978) contains many pieces that ask the question why, as Cheever himself puts it, 'in this most prosperous, equitable, and accomplished world – where even the cleaning women practice the Chopin preludes in their spare time – everyone should seem to be disappointed'. In turn, his last book, *Oh What a Paradise It Seems* (1982), continues the theme of the American dream, and the mystery of its unfulfilment. But this time, by focusing on an ageing man who is rejuvenated by an unusual romance, Cheever informs his usual vein of comic melancholy with a feeling of hope, some promise for the future. The comic note is stronger in the work of Peter De Vries (1910–93), many of whose works, like *The Mackerel Plaza* (1958), expose the superficiality of the American suburbs. Richard Condon (1915–96) is more coolly clinical in his analysis of Cold War paranoia (*The Manchurian Candidate* [1960]), the technique of mass murder (*An Infinity of Mirrors* [1966]), the greed of American big business (*Mile High* [1969]), the corruptions of American politics (*The Vertical Smile* [1971]) and the arrogance of American empire (*The Star-Spangled Crunch* [1974]). Nelson Algren (1908–81) and William Gaddis (1922–98) offer another severe contrast, a further illustration of the different formal possibilities for rewriting contemporary America. In novels like *The Man With the Golden Arm* (1948) and *A Walk on the Wild Side* (1956), Algren uses a hardbitten prose style to narrate the lives of an American underclass, a world of dealers and dope, poker and prostitution. Gaddis, on the other hand, employs a richly parodic idiom, a protean narrative manner that insists on its own fictiveness, to play with such themes as art and illusion (*The Recognitions* [1955]), the hypocrisies of corporate empire (*J R* [1975]), ambition, loss and the hunger for apocalypse in a world of competition (*Carpenter's Gothic* [1985]) and the complex figurations that make up the maze of American law (*A Frolic of His Own* [1994]).

A contrast of a different kind is offered by Paul Bowles (1910–99) and William Styron (1925–). Bowles became an expatriate in the 1940s, and his work is generally set in Morocco where he lived most of his life. *The Sheltering Sky* (1949), for instance, *Let it Come Down* (1952) and *The Spider's House* (1955) are all set in North Africa. Their nominal scene, however, is less important than the interior world of his characters: which is a world of nothingness. Many of them are rich American exiles and most of them have reached – to use the phrase that concludes *The Sheltering Sky* – 'the end of the line'. In his own cosmopolitan way, as he exposes the horror of nothing, Bowles exploits one vein of writing often associated with the South. Styron, who has spent most of his life in the United States – first in Virginia, then in Connecticut – has exploited others. His first novel, *Lie Down in Darkness* (1951), revealing the tragic life and suicide of a girl whose rich Southern family was unable to supply either her or themselves with love and security, is almost an exercise in Faulknerian tropes and themes, while his fourth, *The Confessions of Nat Turner* (1967), concerning the life of the eponymous hero, the leader of an 1831 slave revolt, is a radical rewriting of plantation romance. It is also, as Styron explains in an 'Author's Note', 'a meditation on history'. So, for that matter, are his 1953 novella *The Long March* (1957) and his 1979 novel *Sophie's Choice*, which deals with the historical event that has cast its shadow over all subsequent Western history, the Holocaust. If Styron, despite his imaginative adventuring into other parts of the world, seems peculiarly Southern in his pre-occupation with guilt, the indelible nature of evil, then others roughly contemporary with him seem notably Western or Midwestern: among them, William Eastlake (1917–97) and William H. Gass (1924–). Eastlake made the West, especially New Mexico, his fictional terrain, in stories about fraternal rivalry (*Go in Beauty* [1956]) and friendship between a white man and a Navajo (*Portrait of an Artist with Twenty-Six Horses* [1963]), while Gass imaginatively settled in the Midwest. *Omensetter's Luck* (1966) is a densely written story of a symbolically significant man who settles in an Ohio River town; *In the Heart of the Heart of the Country* (1968) takes us, in turn, in a series of stories, into a landscape of bleached lostness where objects assume a discreet pathos, buildings have a strangely vacant air about them – and characters are, as it were, absent presences. 'Where their consciousness has gone I can't say,' observes the narrator of the title story; 'It's not in the eyes.'

Among other writers whose work tended to cut through Western mythology during the immediate postwar period were Vardis Fisher (1895–1968), whose tetralogy published just before the war became *Orphans in Gethsemane* (1966); Walter Van Tilburg Clark (1909–71), author of *The Ox-Bow Incident* (1940); and Frederick Manfred (1912–94), whose trilogy *The Primitive* (1949), *The Brother* (1950) and *The Giant* (1951) concentrates on what he calls 'Siouxland'. But those who have most effectively wedded a grainier, unsentimental portrait of the actual West to a sympathetic understanding of its potential as myth are Frank Waters (1902–95), Wallace Stegner (1909–93) and, from a later generation, Larry McMurtry (1936–). In *The Man Who Killed the Deer* (1942), Waters offers a harsh account of the conflict between white and Pueblo Indian laws, as he tells the tale of a young man experiencing an initiation into a non-white, non-dualistic view of life: a view that sees the land in terms of union and stewardship rather than possession and conquest. 'So little by little the richness and the wonder and the mystery of life stole upon him.' The landscape acts upon character in this novel, until the two merge. Other books by Waters explore similar rites of immersion and illumina-tion, among the underclass of a Mexican border town (*The Yogi of Cockroach Court* [1948]) and with a young woman living in New Mexico (*The Woman at Otoni Crossing* [1966]). Stegner once said that he was seeking 'a usable continuity between past and present'. That search is perhaps most noticeable in *Angle of Repose* (1971), in which the narrator, a retired historian, sets out to write his grandparents' – and, in particular, his grandmother's – story chronicling their days carving a life for themselves in the West. The book subtly disposes of what the narrator calls 'several dubious assumptions about the early West', pointing out, for instance, that 'large parts of it were owned by Eastern and foreign capital and run by iron-fisted bosses'. But it also fiercely interrogates a new West that has lost touch with its past. 'I get glimpses of lives close to mine, related to mine in ways I recognize but don't completely correspond,' says the narrator as he browses through his grandparents' papers. 'I'd like to live in their clothes for while.' He does so; and his act of research, remembering, becomes an act of recovery. He discovers, precisely, the usable continuity between his present and his past, and the 'angle of repose' where the lives of his ancestors came to rest in him. McMurtry has moved between very different modes. His work includes novels honouring the land and the earlier generations who were its stewards (*Horseman, Pass By* [1961], *Leaving Cheyenne* [1963]), books satirizing small-town life or urban displacement (*The Last Picture Show* [1966], *Cadillac Jack* [1982], *Texasville* [1987]), and fiction that casts a cold but not entirely unromantic eye on such traditional Western themes as the trail drive (*Lonesome Dove* [1981]) and Billy the Kid (*Anything for Billy* [1988]). Significantly, these books on old Western themes came after McMurtry himself called for writers in his home state of Texas 'to turn from the antique myths of the rural past and to seek plots and characters and literary inspiration in modern Texas's urban, industrial present'. Which suggests how equivocal writers of the West can be about the myths enshrined in its past – or, more positively, with what care and self-consciousness they tend to manoeuvre their way between Western myth and Western reality.

A novelist who has negotiated his way with particular subtlety between past and present, the legends and facts, in this case of the Midwest, is Wright Morris (1910–98). He was born in Nebraska, and his acutely crafted fiction observes characters often in oblique fashion as they try to come to terms with others, with the past of their family and community and with the history and pastoral legends informing the places where they live. Morris said that his aim in many of his books was 'to salvage what I considered threatened, and to hold fast what was vanishing'. He pursued this aim in novels that, typically, concentrate on one situation diversely affecting the people involved in it (*My Uncle Dudley* [1942], *The Field of Vision* [1956], *Ceremony in Lone Tree* [1960]) or show characters searching for a meaningful life (*The Ways of Love* [1952]) or loving relationships (*The Huge Season* [1960]). He did so too in books like *The Home Place* (1948) that combine sharp but sensitive verbal and visual description. In *The Home Place*, for instance, a tender account of conflict between generations, and the vanishing of a more considered and authorized way of life, is contained not only in the story of a writer and his family returning to their home town in Nebraska. It is there also in the photographs of landscape, people, objects that have acquired dignity from the people who have used them: all of which, taken by Morris himself, intersperse the text and suggest how close the story is to the autobiographical bone. Typically, Morris avoids prolonged dialogue and moments of intense action in his novels. His characters are marked by their refusal to speak at length: 'Cora . . . welcomed silence', we are told of one leading figure at the beginning of *Plain Song* (1980). Moments of conventional crisis are less crucial to them than moments of gradual illumination, quiet or even mute understanding – which are usually the gifts of maturity. 'Already,' we learn of a character in *Fire Sermon* (1971), 'he was old enough to gaze in wonder at life.' What they achieve, if they are lucky, is immersion in the land, and the habits and rituals it instils. So, for one of the protagonists in *Plain Song*, 'voices, bird calls, a movement of the leaves, the first hint of coolness of the air' become 'not separately observed sensations but commingled parts of her own nature'. 'Her soul', the reader is told, 'experienced a sense of liberation in its loss of self.' The older characters in Morris's work, those of an earlier generation, are more likely to be luckier in this way. For the younger, the later generations – when, say, they return to the 'home folks' – there is the feeling, simply, of being 'withdrawn from the scene', as if they were looking at it 'through a window, or within the frame of a painting'. 'Abstinence, frugality, and independence – the home-grown, made-on-the-farm trinity,' reflects the writer, the protagonist in *The Home Place*. 'Not the land of plenty, the old age pension, or the full dinner pail. Independence, not abundance, is the heart of . . . America' – or, at least, of the old America to which he has tried to return. But it is, he recognizes, a heart that beats less fiercely, less insistently in his own generation. And for most of the time, like so many of Morris's protagonists, he can only gaze at what he and America have lost with a sense of longing.

Contested identities in prose

The first novel of E. L. Doctorow (1931–), *Welcome to Hard Times* (1960), was a Western of sorts. But it was also a violent demythologizing of the romance of the West, which, in a manner to become typical of its author, explored the need for community in an atomized, fragmented, destructively individualistic culture. Doctorow has consistently used, expanded or even subverted established generic forms to investigate an American paradox: the elaborate circuitries of wealth and influence that connect one thing to another in American society and its funda-mental lack of cohesiveness, the lack of any real bonds between people other than those of manipulation and use. In *The Book of Daniel* (1971), based on the case of Julius and Ethel Rosenberg, who were put to death as convicted spies in 1953, Doctorow used the form of the political novel to consider divisions that are social, familial and generational – a matter of the gap between old and new left as well as left and right, sons and parents, immigrant and non-immigrant cultures, Jewish people and gentiles. For *Ragtime* (1975), an account of three fictional families at the beginning of the twentieth century intertwined with such actual historical figures as Henry Ford, Scott Joplin, Emma Goldman and Harry Houdini, he turned to a form of the historical novel that recalled *U.S.A.* by John Dos Passos. The historical sense and social comment of Doctorow's novel, however, are edged with a sense of absurdity. *Loon Lake* (1980) is more the novel as hybrid, a mix of styles and perspectives. *World's Fair* (1985) is a mixture of memoir and scrapbook, and thinly disguised autobiography. In *Billy Bathgate* (1989) and *The Waterworks* (1994), Doctorow uses the generic conventions of the gangster novel and the Gothic novel to explore different historical moments in the life of New York City. Doctorow is a tireless and accomplished experimenter in the forms of the novel. Consistently, though, he has stretched those forms to accommodate and test his vision of a society that is not so much a community as a conspiracy: a system of vested interests that maintains itself by ubiquitous and often almost invisible forms of control.

'We have two lives,' observes a character in *The Natural* (1952), the first novel of Bernard Malamud (1914–86), 'the life we learn with and the life we live after that. Suffering is what brings us toward happiness.' All the novels of Malamud offer variations on the theme sounded here. They are set in different times and places and have very different nominal subjects. *The Natural*, for example, deals with baseball as a realm of American heroism and myth. *The Assistant* (1957), Malamud's second novel, is about an Italian American called Frank Alpine who becomes an assistant to a New York Jewish shopkeeper. His third, *A New Life* (1961), tells the tale of a Jewish professor of English who goes to teach in an Oregon 'cow college'. Among his later novels, *The Fixer* (1967), based on actual events that occurred in 1913, describes how a Russian Jew is falsely accused of and imprisoned for murder. *Pictures of Fidelman* (1969) tells of a middle-aged Bronx resident who goes to Italy to be an artist; *Dubin's Lives* (1974) is about the marriage and love affairs of a famous author; *God's Grace* (1982) is a pseudo-Biblical tale about a man who is the sole survivor of a nuclear war and begins a new civilization among apes. Some of the novels are comic or satirical, others sadder, wrier or more intensely serious. All, however, are parables: fables that are, on one level, dense with historical specificity and personal detail and, on another, placeless, timeless. And what these fables narrate is a painful progress from immaturity to maturity: the process by which an individual can truly become a hero by entering into the lives of others – and, quite often, manages to do so.

Each of Malamud's stories tends to begin with the hero travelling somewhere in quest of a new life. He is, to begin with, equipped with distinct personal abilities of some kind – on the pitch, say, in the shop, in the classroom or the studio – but he has no faith in anything except the urgency of his appetites. Gradually, though, he learns that to be born as a real human being, a real hero, is to be born into history. Everything else fades before the experienced fact of involuntary involvement in the lives of other people. This discovery is either preceded or accompanied by a ritual slaying or replacing or dispossessing of a symbolic father-figure of fading powers – never an actual parent. In turn, the promise of a coming of age is signalled by the fact that the protagonist has to decide whether or not to assume the symbolic role of father. He has, in effect, to show his awareness and acceptance of his responsibilities as a human being by agreeing to be the father, in name or office, of children not his own. If he fails or refuses this test, then his suffering has been for nothing, his life has no meaning; like the hero of *The Natural*, he is really no hero at all. If he accepts his burden, however, the role of father, then he finds his true freedom: which is not gratification of self but service to others. 'It came to her that he had changed,' a character observes of Frank Alpine, after he has accepted just such a burden towards the end of *The Assistant*. 'It's true, he's not the same man,' she says to herself. 'It was a strange thing about people – they could look the same and be different. He had been one thing, low, dirty, but because of something in himself . . . he had changed into somebody else.' Hovering between realism and wry fable, history and parable, Malamud's fiction takes the measure of this 'strange thing', this process of transformation whereby a man can become 'no longer what he had been'. 'If I must suffer let it be for something,' the protagonist of *The Fixer* decides. With just such an act of choice, his heroes enter into a genuinely new life. Suffering is inevitable for them, it seems, it is their uninvited, unavoidable history; it is what they do with their suffering that counts.

'It's obvious to everyone that the stature of characters in modern novels is smaller than it once was,' Saul Bellow (1915–) once wrote, 'and this diminution powerfully concerns those who value experience.' 'I do not believe that human capacity to feel or do can really have dwindled or that the quality of humanity has degenerated,' he went on. 'I rather think that people appear smaller because society has become so immense.' This catches something of the concern that lies at the heart of Bellow's own novels, which navigate the two rivers of American history in their own agonized yet corrosively comic way. Bellow is scornful of those writers who believe that, as he puts it, 'fiction cannot leave current events without withering away'. Yet he is also of the conviction that no novel can satisfy without what he calls 'a firm sense of the common world'. He is equally contemptuous of those who believe it should be 'the intent of the writer to pull us into an all-sufficient consciousness which he, the writer, governs absolutely'. But he also clearly believes that the novelist can and should be a historian of the consciousness: especially at a time when the apparatus of society threatens, as he sees it, to overwhelm both consciousness and conscience. His aim, throughout his career, has been to steer between two kinds of novel: the novel of information, with its exclusive interest in externals, things, process and documentation, and the novel of sensibility written out of the assumption that 'the important humanity of the novel must be the writer's own'. He has tried to assimilate and understand his times without surrendering to the hideous facts mongered by the mass media – what is called, in his 1970 novel *Mr Sammler's Planet*, 'the anarchy of the streets'. He has tried, in short, to be a historian of civilization as well as consciousness.

No novel by Bellow is exactly exemplary, because a key feature of his achievement is his ability to dramatize his concerns in a variety of fictional forms. His two earliest novels gravitate towards the condition of nightmare and the leading character as victim. His second novel, actually called *The Victim* (1947), is about the agonizing, equivocal relation between a Jew and Gentile, who, despite their radical differences, seem 'dependent for the food of spiritual life' upon each other. His first, *Dangling Man* (1944), shows us a man caught precisely between the life around him and the life within him, as he waits for induction into the army. With his third novel, *The Adventures of Augie March* (1953), Bellow adopted a picaresque, far more extrovert form; as he was also to do for his fifth book, *Henderson the Rain King* (1950). 'The great pleasure of the book', Bellow recalled of *Augie March*, 'was that it came easily. All I had to do was to be there with the buckets, to catch it. That's why the form is loose.' 'I am an American,' Augie announces on the first page of the book, 'Chicago born . . . and go at things as I have taught myself, free-style.' Adventuring through several countries, Bellow's larger-than-life mythic hero pursues, just as his other protagonists do, a search for identity. 'I have always tried to become what I am,' he insists. And his story is a quest to discover what the right relationship between his self and his society should be: what will enable him to realize what he calls the 'universal eligibility to be noble'. Typically of this extroverted novel, the extremes he has to manoeuvre between are dramatized in two characters, his brothers. The one, his older brother, has become a social success but at the expense of brutalizing, even destroying, himself. The other, his younger brother, is pure of spirit, sweet, simple-minded and helpless – and terrified of leaving the enclosure of the self, just as much as he is of venturing outside the walls of the asylum in which he is confined. 'I know this double power,' another character tells Augie, 'that if you make a move you may lose, but if you sit still you will decay.' Faced with this double power, Augie's solution is to run and dodge: to slip between the fixities and definites of the social world and the swamplike inertia of the isolated self – and to find freedom in movement, the provisional and the possible. 'Look at me going everywhere!' Augie declares at the end of the novel. 'Why, I am a sort of Columbus of those near-at-hand . . . this immediate *terra incognita* that spreads out in every gaze.' It is a characteristically American conclusion, as Bellow knows only too well, and signals by making the last word of the book 'America'. Augie brags for humanity as much as for himself, in expressing the belief, the hope that somehow, somewhere, the double poser can be solved, civilization and consciousness can be squared.

The novel that competes with *Augie March* as, arguably, Bellow's finest, *Herzog* (1964), signals a return to a more introspective, meditative form. Moses Herzog, the narrator, is possessed, as he is only too aware, of a representative modern mind, 'inconstant, divided, vacillating'. He is caught between the isolated ambit of consciousness, a place of retreat for the formulation of ideal patterns, and the teeming surfaces of society, where those patterns seem to be bombarded out of existence by a welter of details. '*The human soul is amphibian*,' Herzog reflects, '*and I have touched its sides.*' And his own amphibious nature compels him to vacillate, hysterically but it seems helplessly. He feels driven out of the world by the wasteland of information, the petty distractions that surround him there, as well as those he calls 'Reality-Instructors' who would shape him in his own image – his second wife, his mistress, his brother. Yet he senses that to immerse himself in the fluid elements of his own lonely consciousness can be equally destructive and irresponsible. It might also be impossible since, as he observes at one point, 'public life drives out private life. The more political our society becomes (in the broadest sense of "political" – the obsessions, the compulsions of collectivity) the more individuality seems lost.' He is torn, a man dangling between pride and humility, self-assertion and self-mockery, assertion of his power and confession of his impotence. He makes forays, skirmishes into the streets, then withdraws. He writes 'letters' to establish contacts with the world outside, but he does not complete or read them. No more than Augie March, or Bellow's other protagonists, does he heal this gap, this fissure in himself, as well as between himself and his world. But, just as much as they, he remains convinced of the possibility of healing, the chance of resolution. '*The dream of man's heart, however much we may distrust and resent it,*' Herzog reflects, '*is that life may complete itself in significant pattern. Some incomprehensible way. Before death.*' That dream stays with him. He refuses to accept that all facts are 'nasty', or that the 'intensity', the occasional 'idiot joy' within him 'doesn't . . . mean anything'. And he closes the story with a sense of peace and promise, which seems to exist outside language. 'At this time he had no messages for anyone,' the novel concludes. 'Nothing. Not a single word.' The conclusion is beautifully, meaningfully equivocal. Since Herzog is our source of information here, as throughout the narrative, we cannot be sure whether the peace and promise he has found is an assured discovery or a pious hope. What we can be sure of, however, is that his creator, Bellow, has taken us on one of the most revelatory explorations into a problem that has haunted America, and so many American writers. And taken us, then, into the prospect of a solution, a resolution that lies beyond words.

No subsequent novel of Bellow's has perhaps matched the achievement of *Herzog* or *Augie March*. In their own fiercely ruminative manner, however, they have considered the same overwhelming question. His 1970 novel *Mr Sammler's Planet* acquires additional urgency, as it considers the possibility of 'the collapse of civilization' and the barbarous destruction of consciousness, from the fact that its protagonist, in his seventies, is a survivor of the Holocaust. *Humboldt's Gift* (1975), his next novel, presents a story of personal and social crisis through the account of the relationship of an ambitious young writer and a visionary poet, Von Humboldt Fleisher, modelled on Delmore Schwartz. *The Dean's December* (1982) places its clearly autobiographical central character between two social orders, the decaying Communism of Eastern Europe and the anarchic capitalism of the United States, that seem equally repellent. Collectivism and individualism both lead here to violation of the spirit. And there is, it appears, no alternative, no third way. What is notable about these later books, and about Bellow's 1987 novel *More Die of Heartbreak*, is their darkening of tenor and tone, their reluctance to admit much hope, much sense that '*the dream of man's life*' may somehow be accomplished. What the historian of civilization tends to see now is its failure, the decline of Western society into barbarism. What the historian of consciousness records is its impotence, the inability of the individual to do much more than gaze, in anger or despair, at the spectacle of the streets. What remains for Bellow, however, as he pursues both these histories, is a ferocious belief in the integrity of knowledge: the imperative of looking without flinching into the heart of things – and the ineluctable nature of the truth we can find there. As Mr Sammler puts it, despite all the vagaries of consciousness and violence of civilization, 'we know *what is what*'. There is a primitive, creaturely understanding of what is right, what is humanly necessary, that anyone, in the process of death, 'summoned to the biggest of the black', will surely feel. 'In his inmost heart, each man knows,' Mr Sammler insists; 'we all know, God, that we know, that we know, we know, we know.' That knowledge is something all Bellow's protagonists possess, at some juncture. It is also what his fiction, even at its darkest, manages to teach.

By the end of *Herzog*, the narrator has reached a point where, he tells us, he felt 'a deep, dizzy eagerness to *begin*'. At the end of *Portnoy's Complaint* (1969) by Philip Roth (1933–), to conclude the manic monologue that constitutes the book, the narrator Alexander Portnoy's psychiatrist is permitted the final word: 'Now vee may perhaps to begin. Yes?' One condition for beginning, or being able to think about doing so, is some measure of liberation from the past. Herzog perhaps achieves this by the conclusion of Bellow's novel. But Alexander Portnoy still seems to be drowning in his own subjectivity: a subjectivity which, like that of so many of Roth's protagonists, seems to be determined by other people, the larger narrative of his family, his community and his culture. In an earlier Roth novel, *Letting Go* (1962), Gabe Wallach, one of the major characters, reveals some of the psychologically crippling effects of being raised in the family nest, or trap. He tells his girlfriend that he can never escape from that trap, be 'off the hook', until, as he puts it, 'I make some sense of the larger hook I'm on'. Within the terms of the story, he never does. Similarly, in Roth's first novel, *Goodbye, Columbus* (1959), the protagonist Neil Klugman stands staring at his reflection in a library window, after the painful end of an affair. 'I was only that substance,' he reflects, 'that face that I saw in front of me.' 'The outside of me gave up little information about the inside of me,' Klugman says; he wanted 'to go behind that image and catch whatever it was that looked through those eyes'. However, as he 'looked hard' at his own image, he recalls, and his 'gaze pushed through it', all he ended up seeing was 'a broken wall of books, imperfectly shelved'. The project of all Roth's fiction could be said to be precisely this: to gaze at the image of an American like himself, to discover what lies beneath. What, it asks, is the mysterious self, the subjectivity that stares back, that captivates me? There is no simple answer to this question, of course. But as Roth's protagonists and narrators manoeuvre their way between the outside and the inside – what Portnoy calls the 'hundreds of thousands of little rules laid down by none other than None Other' and 'Nothing but self! Locked up in *me*!' – they incline towards the inclination Neil Klugman offers as he looks in the library window. Perhaps selfhood is a fiction, a product of the past and the dreaming imagination: all that is written and recorded in books. For that matter, perhaps nationhood is as well.

The earlier novels explore this enigma of subjectivity through a series of protagonists who share Roth's own Jewish upbringing, and who find it hard, if not impossible, to escape from the narrative of the Jewish family and culture. Portnoy, for instance, is locked in a past that is circumscribed by his mother and orthodox 'boundaries and restrictions', the 'None Other' of traditional Jewish law. He seeks relief, in obsessive masturbation, and in an equally obsessive, masturbatory monologue. But the forms of relief, sexual and verbal, that he finds for himself only reveal his entrapment: endlessly, it seems, he circles around the past and the guilt it instils. Constantly, like so many of Roth's entrapped Jewish males, he looks with longing at the 'goyim' and their world. 'These people are the *Americans*,' he declares; 'these blond-haired Christians are the legitimate residents and owners of this place.' They occupy 'centre-field' rather than the margins of society; and they seem to him to possess a freedom from the past, a mobility and unreflective, unconstrained subjectivity that he can only look at with envy. This perception of 'the *Americans*', as Portnoy calls them, is a mirage, of course: the product of his yearning, his own dreaming imagination longing to escape from the stories of his culture. And, in many of his later novels, Roth has explored both that mirage and the use of writing to reflect selfhood and nationhood. Much of the finest of this later fiction considers the fate of a writer, Nathan Zuckerman, very much like Roth, so that the book itself becomes a mirror – or, perhaps more accurately, becomes a means of gazing through the library window at other books: *The Ghost Writer* (1979), *Zuckerman Unbound* (1981), *The Anatomy Lesson* (1983), *Zuckerman Bound* (1985), *The Counterlife* (1986), *The Facts* (1988). Some of it has a writer called Philip (*Deception* [1990]) or Philip Roth (*Operation Shylock: A Confession* [1993]) as a protagonist. And all of it is concerned, in the last analysis, not just with personal identity but with the identity of America. That is never clearer than in Roth's 1997 novel *American Pastoral*, where Zuckerman, in trying to tell the story of a man he sees as an archetypal American hero – occupying what Portnoy would have called the 'centre-field' – finds himself telling the story of his nation. 'I dreamed a realistic chronicle,' Zuckerman explains. But, as that paradoxical remark intimates, what he ends up with is fiction, myth: the pastoral story Americans have invented for themselves of their aboriginal innocence – their longing for freedom, a pure subjective space, and their feelings of dereliction and dismay when they do not have it. In an earlier novel, *The Counterlife*, Zuckerman had described the womb as 'the pastoral landscape par excellence'; and that suggests the take on American versions of pastoralism here. *American Pastoral* is a meditation on the yearning, the looking backward that maybe determines any attempt to understand and narrate ourselves. It is also, and more specifically, about the special American inflection given to this, which claims the United States as what Zuckerman calls 'desire's homeland', a state of primal, prelapsarian grace.

Grace, or the possibility of it, is one of the concerns of John Updike (1932–), whose 1963 novel *The Centaur* has an epigraph from Karl Barth. 'Heaven is the creation inconceivable to man, earth the creation conceivable to him,' Barth observes here. 'He himself is the creature on the boundary between heaven and earth.' All Updike's major characters inhabit this boundary: between heaven and earth, between the intensity of life and the inevitability of death, between dreams of freedom and the comforts of a compromised, suburban environment. 'I feel to be a person is to be in a situation of tension,' Updike once explained. 'A truly adjusted person is not a person at all.' So characters like George Caldwell (*The Centaur*), Harry Angstrom (*Rabbit, Run* [1960], *Rabbit Redux* [1971], *Rabbit is Rich* [1981], *Rabbit at Rest* [1990]), Piet Hanoma (*Couples* [1968]), Henry Bech (*Bech: A Book* [1970], *Bech is Back* [1982]) and Roger Lambert (*Roger's Version* [1986]) all perform and pursue their maladjustments in what is called, in *Couples*, 'a universe of timing': enacting the beauty, and the terror, of their own duality. So, in *The Centaur*, George Caldwell, an ageing schoolteacher, is having to come to terms with his own decline and imminent death. 'I'm a walking junk-heap,' he declares, announcing an obsession with waste, human and universal, that runs through Updike's fiction. In *Couples*, for instance, Piet Hanoma similarly suffers from a 'dizzying impression of waste' and a 'sense of unconnection among phenomena and of feeling'. As a teacher of evolution, Caldwell can reflect on a time 'when consciousness was a mere pollen drifting in darkness' and on his own annihilation: from nothing and to nothing. His mind is preoccupied with the wasting of nature. 'I hate Nature. It reminds me of death,' he insists bitterly. All things, cars, houses, people, landscapes, fall apart, revert to zero. 'Things never fail to fail,' Caldwell tells himself.

Against this entropic vision, this dread of the void, is set the possibility of love. 'A man in love ceases to fear death,' Updike observed in one of his essays. 'Our fundamental anxiety is that we do not exist – or will cease to exist. Only in being loved do we find external corroboration of the supremely high valuation each ego secretly assigns itself.' There is also what Updike has called the 'brainless celebration of the fact of existence': like the carnival celebrations that conclude his first novel, *The Poorhouse Fair* (1959). And there are the comforts of the customary, routine and structure. Piet Hanoma, in *Couples*, for instance, comes from a family of builders and is a dedicated carpenter. Grappling with materials helps him to fend off a sense of the void. 'He needed to touch a tool. Grab the earth,' the reader is told. 'All houses, all things that endured, pleased Piet'; they give him a self-stabilizing pragmatism, a feeling of 'space secured'. And yet such is the duality, the constant vacillation of Updike's characters, they can also feel like a prison sometimes. The void is terrifying but maybe liberating; the structures of houses, the suburbs, suburban routine may be comforting but they can also be claustrophobic. Updike always returns to the fundamental intimation that structures waste away too, they are part of 'the world's downward skid'. 'I think books should have secrets, like people do,' Updike has said. And the secret his own books disclose is the imminence of the void, the dread fear of death and the dim possibility of grace: another dimension that gives depth and resonance to what might seem to be the fleeting contingencies of his suburban settings. One way he alerts the reader to this extra dimension is through sly allusion to myth, folktale and fairytale. The myth of Chiron lurks beneath the surface of *The Centaur*, for example, to give the story what Updike called a 'counterpoint of identity'. The magic of the story of Peter Rabbit underlies the Rabbit series. And the tale of Tristan and Iseult informs and enriches Updike's 1994 novel about love and criminality, *Brazil*. Another way is through a playful mixing of genres or temporal planes. In *The Witches of Eastwick* (1984), three mischievous suburban divorcees enjoy sexual adventures with Satan. In *Memories of the Ford Administration* (1992), parallel narratives invite us into the times of twentieth-century President Gerald Ford and nineteenth-century President James Buchanan. But the most productive way of all, for Updike, is through the severe elegance of his prose, which weaves a sinuous path between the demotic and the exalted, the documentary and the magical, as it details the dense tissue of appearances that make up the contemporary American suburb while also intimating the existence of another world, to be perceived dimly through this tissue, that is a world not only of death but also of mystery, a saving revelation.

At the end of the first book in the Rabbit tetralogy, *Rabbit, Run*, the protagonist of all four novels, Harry Angstrom, finds himself confronted with a 'dense pack of impossible alternatives'. Standing in the streets, he imagines a road leading back into the heart of the city, to his responsibilities as a husband, father and family provider. It will take him back to both his wife and his mistress, to his job, to the pleasures and pressures of the suburbs, and to a home town where his nickname, Rabbit, reminds him of his days of glory as a local basketball champion. 'The other way', he reflects, leads 'to where the city ends.' 'He tries to picture how it will end, with an empty baseball field, a dark factory, and then over a brook into a dirt road, he doesn't know.' As he imagines the end to this other road, this other pathway, as 'a huge vacant field of cinders', 'his heart', we are told, 'goes hollow'. The field of cinders or the suburban net: it appears to him to be death either way. Searching around for a light to guide him in the darkness, Harry can find none. There is no light in a nearby church window; 'unlit', there is only 'a dark circle in a stone facade'. 'Funny', Harry tells himself, 'how what makes you move is so simple and the field you must move in is so crowded.' He cannot make a choice, as he stands poised between the two routes. All he can do is manoeuvre, engage in simple motion. As the final words of the novel put it, 'he runs. Ah: runs. Runs.' Norman Mailer, never a great admirer of Updike, complained, 'Updike does not know how to finish' when he reviewed *Rabbit, Run*. But this is a little unfair. Indecision, evasion of this kind, after all, has a long history in American writing. As the American hero or heroine lights out, it is often hard to tell whether they are engaged in quest or vagrancy – or whether, indeed, there is a fundamental difference. And it is perfectly clear that, by traditional standards, the conclusion they offer concludes nothing at all. What is more, it is precisely running of one kind or another that becomes the tactic of so many characters in recent American fiction, as they find themselves poised between what Updike calls two roads, and Mailer himself the two rivers of American history. Dodging, weaving, manoeuvring, balancing: these are agencies of existential deferral, means of living between the two roads or rivers. Weaving together, wavering between documentary and dream, protean monologue and picaresque, public history and pastoral, the demotic and the magical: these, in turn, are devices of stylistic deferral, means of writing between, allowing the novel to inhabit a border territory. With his vacillating heroes and variety of styles, Updike is closer to many of his contemporaries than Mailer allows or than perhaps he himself knows. And, like them, he sees death as the only conclusive moment. Before that, life is process, running, a series of beginnings.

Of the many other novelists who have attempted to navigate the two rivers of American history, among the most accomplished is Don DeLillo (1936–). Although not formally a postmodern novelist, DeLillo is fascinated by the condition of postmodernity. *White Noise* (1984), for instance, is an ironic comedy about the mass replication of images in modern America and the anxiety technology engenders in its characters' precarious sense of identity. With a paranoid professor of Hitler studies at a Midwestern college as its central character, *White Noise* addresses the media and, more subtly, the idea of mediation as it occurs in a wide range of disguises. DeLillo is concerned here, and elsewhere in his fiction, not just with the power of the media to invade consciousness but with the idea that all contemporary American experience is crucially informed by modes of representation which determine consciousness at every level. And not just contemporary American experience: *Mao II* (1991), for example, explores the impact of mass culture on a global level. What place is left for the individual, the novel asks, in the face of the totalizing ideologies of the media? Perhaps 'the future belongs to crowds'. In the fictional world of DeLillo, characters negotiate their ironic or pathetic way through a culture defined by its consumption: not so much of the actual as of the imaginary, the promissory image offered to them on the television screen. DeLillo is, in a way, the novelist as anthropologist, sifting through American lives as signifiers of their culture to see what place there is, if any, for the notion of the individual or the authentic. The anthropological character of his fiction is never more noticeable than in his 1997 novel *Underworld*, which plots the course of American history from 1951 to 1992. It pivots, in particular, on the technology of waste. 'Waste is the secret history, the underhistory,' one character declares, 'the way archaeologists dig out the history of early cultures.' Future historians, the reader infers, might interpret twentieth-century America in terms of the story of its waste products, the relics or aftermath of consumption. And that, at any rate, is DeLillo's narrative project here: to gather and study the discarded remnants of American culture, weaving historical memory and imaginative recall together to produce a secret history, an underworld narrative.

What distinguishes so many of the characters of DeLillo is their subjection to the anonymizing processes of the market and certain feelings generated by that subjection – a vague anxiety, or anomie, and an even vaguer sense of dissatisfaction, yearning. These are precisely the distinguishing features of protagonists in a number of other late twentieth-century novels: notably, *The Moviegoer* (1961) by Walker Percy (1916–99), *Cabot Wright Begins* (1964) by James Purdy (1923–), *Ironweed* (1983) by William Kennedy (1928–), *The Universal Baseball Association, Inc., J. Henry Waugh, Prop.* (1968) by Robert Coover (1932–), *The Sportswriter* (1986) and *Independence Day* (1995) by Richard Ford (1944–), the 'New York Trilogy' (*City of Glass* [1985], *Ghost* [1986], *The Locked Room* [1987]) of Paul Auster (1947–), *Bright Lights, Big City* (1984) by Jay McInerney (1955–), *Straight Cut* (1986) by Madison Smartt Bell (1957–) and *Less than Zero* (1985) by Bret Easton Ellis (1965–). Nominally, all these novels and their protagonists are very different. *The Moviegoer*, for instance, is suffused with Percy's own special brand of ironic existentialism and urgent faith. Over a third of *Cabot Wright Begins* is spent discussing the problems connected with writing a book, the biography of Cabot Wright: which announces its theme, the fabrication of reality. The novels by Coover and Kennedy both turn to the game of baseball to explore the journeys of Americans in and out of the literal and the imaginary. The stories of McInerney and Ellis are initiation tales, set in bleak modern landscapes, of two young men trapped in their own alienation. The 'New York Trilogy' pursues similar forms of entrapment in a series of postmodern detective stories set in a dystopic New York City. Bell and Ford, in turn, write about dangling men, leading outwardly comfortable lives (in the movies, journalism, insurance) but wryly ill at ease, at odds with themselves and the world – and sunk in a desperation that is, inevitably, quiet. What connects all these fictions, however, is a dread of inconsequence. Their protagonists all share what one of them, Frank Bascombe in *Independence Day*, calls a fear of 'the cold, unwelcome, born-in-America realisation that we're just like the other schmo, wishing his wishes, lusting his lusts, quaking over his idiot frights and fantasies, all of us popped out from the same unchinkable mold'. What is more, most of them also share the feeling that, maybe, the fear has been realized: that they have indeed been 'tucked ever more deeply', as Bascombe puts it, 'more anonymously, into the weave of culture'. And that culture is itself anonymous, an accumulation of insignificances. It could be anywhere; it might be in the city or the suburbs, east or west, south or north. It is, above all, not just ordinary but blank.

Nothing could be further from all this than the world of Cormac McCarthy (1933–), whose work is marked with an indelible sense not so much of blankness or evil (although both are certainly there) as of homelessness. Some commentators have referred to the elemental and equivocal activity of human settlement as the essential subject of McCarthy's fiction. Others, perhaps more accurately, have called his novels a series of meditations on the unhomelike nature of our environment, the scary disconnection of the human from the non-human that both Freud and Heidegger called the *unheimlich*. And still others have been vexed by the question of just how to place him. There is an argument, for instance, for seeing McCarthy as a Southern writer – or, to be more accurate, one of those many white male writers who have been busy recently rewriting Southern subjects and themes: among them Peter Taylor (1917–94), Harry Crews, Barry Hannah, Robert Olen Butler and Larry Brown. The literal geography of his first four novels (*The Orchard Keeper* [1965], *Outer Dark* [1968], *Child of God* [1973], *Suttree* [1979]) is, after all, scrupulously confined to one Southern place within a hundred-mile radius of Maryville, Tennessee. And they could be said to participate in one of the oldest debates in Southern writing, between pastoralism and the anti-pastoral. There is, however, equally an argument for situating McCarthy among those other white male writers who have been busy deconstructing Western myth and telling tales of a newer, truer West: among them, Edward Abbey (1927–89), William Gibson (1944–), Frederick Barthelme (1943–), Tim O'Brien and Rick Bass (1950–). McCarthy's 1985 novel *Blood Meridian* marks the beginning of his departure from the South into Western settings: a departure confirmed by his 'Border Trilogy', *All the Pretty Horses* (1992), *The Crossing* (1994) and *Cities of the Plain* (1998). And all four later novels are characterized not only by an inversion of traditional Western stories about crisis and redemption – there is violence here but no visible sign of regeneration through it – but also by a sense of the bleakness of Western space. The unobstructed extension of the landscape triggers here not the conventional feelings of freedom and possibility but intimations of empty immensity, the denial of human value and distinction. There is even an argument for associating McCarthy with those writers who work through verbal experiment, the exploration of different styles: like Stanley Elkin, Harold Brodkey (1930–96), Walter Abish, Russell Banks (1940–) or David Foster Wallace (1962–). Reading his work is, quite often, like strolling through a museum of English prose styles: with, say, sentences imitating Hemingway's gift for simple words and connectives modulating into recollection of the old, ineradicable rhythms of Faulknerian speech. There are echoes of Melville and Eliot here, but also of Erskine Caldwell and the rough-and-ready folktales of the frontier. The great tradition of Greek tragedy is present, in the shadows, but so too is the fiction of Zane Grey.

Perhaps the most useful way of looking at all McCarthy's work is precisely this: in terms of a confluence of styles – and in the context of his own preoccupation with homelessness, orphanhood and wandering. McCarthy (and he is not untypical of his contemporaries even in this) is a literary hybrid. And he is so because he is reflecting the mixed, plural medium which, as he sees it, everyone inhabits now, and perhaps always has: the border territory that is our place of being in the world, made only the more starkly remarkable to us all by the collapse of those cultural barriers that used to give us shelter – the illusions of belonging to one stable community and set of traditions. The landscape of all McCarthy's novels is a liminal, constantly changing one, in which different human cultures encounter one another's otherness, and appropriate it through language. His characters cross and recross that landscape, dissolving and reconfiguring what might have once seemed a series of static oppositions: civilized and savage, past and present, South and West, town and wilderness, and, in the Border trilogy, the United States and Mexico. What is at stake here is at once metaphysical – or, more to the point, an argument against metaphysics – and social. McCarthy is intent on melting down the structures of perception, to reveal to us what one of his characters in *Blood Meridian* calls 'a world without measure or bound'. He is also clearly fired into imaginative life by his own experience and knowledge of the fluid social geography of the contemporary: his recognition that, as another character of his, in *Outer Dark*, comments, 'lots of people on the road these days'. 'Where is your country?' the protagonist of *All the Pretty Horses*, John Grady Cole, is asked. 'I don't know,' Cole confesses, 'I don't know where it is.' Homelessness is the source as well as the subject of McCarthy's work, because at the heart of it lies an uncanny sense of the 'dark parody of progress' (as *Blood Meridian* calls it) that *is* our lives, now more than ever: the restless wandering, the displacement, cultural and topographical, that turn every day into a crossing of borders.

Crossing borders: Some women prose writers

A fiction writer from the South who has believed, on the contrary, very firmly in place is Eudora Welty (1909–2001). 'Feelings are bound up in place,' Welty insisted in her essay on 'Place in Fiction' (1962). 'It is by knowing where you started that you grow able to judge where you are.' For Welty, that place is the

---

Southern region of the United States and her home state of Mississippi in particular. Some of her short stories are set elsewhere, in London, Italy or Greece. But most of those collected in, for instance, *A Curtain of Green* (1941), *The Golden Apples* (1949) and *The Bride of Innesfallen* (1955) are situated in and around the South. So, too, are such novels as *The Robber Bridegroom* (1942), *Delta Wedding* (1946), *Losing Battles* (1970) and *The Optimist's Daughter* (1972). The tone and tenor of her fiction is remarkably various. So, *The Robber Bridegroom*, set in the Natchez Trace region of Mississippi in the late eighteenth century, based loosely on a Brothers Grimm fairytale, mixes the actual and the extraordinary to the point where the line between the two becomes virtually indistinguishable. Not 'a *historical* historical novel', as Welty points out, it nevertheless captures what is called at one point in the narrative 'the dream of time passing'. It explores the ways in which we try to understand the past and accommodate it to the present, to attach memory to locality. And it shows how, strictly speaking, landscape and history are both *fictions*, spun out of certain given facts of space and time; and, in being so, are simultaneously 'out there' and 'in here', a function of matter but also of mind. *Delta Wedding*, the novel that followed *The Robber Bridegroom*, is a magical but also slyly mocking plantation novel. It is set on a Mississippi plantation in 1923, a year Welty chose from an almanac as being one in which there were no wars or natural disasters to disrupt the normal pattern of domestic life. The narrative is uneventful in the conventional sense: the uneventfulness allowing Welty, she has said, 'to concentrate on the people without any undue influences, to write a story that showed life that went on on a small scale of its own'. Beneath the surface of events, however, or rather the lack of them, a very different story is being told, of 'many little lives lived privately': people living alone, leading lives of extraordinary solitude and even mystery. 'More different and further apart than the stars' from each other in most ways, any communality they share is partial, any order or ceremony they achieve seems fleeting, provisional. It is as if, for all the warmth of family and company, they inhabit what the narrator calls at one point 'a nameless forest'.

What these two novels share, despite all their differences, is what they share with all Welty's fiction. There is, first, an understanding of place as fact and feeling: 'location pertains to feeling', Welty has said, 'feeling profoundly pertains to place'. There is, second, a sense of the dialectics of living and notably of historical experience as a matter of record and myth, memory and reinvention. There is, third, a conviction that it is through language, especially, that the human animal realizes identity and community. And there is, finally, an animating belief that, as Welty herself put it once, 'ambiguity is a fact of life'. 'All things are double', the reader is told in *The Robber Bridegroom*: so what is needed, in writing as well as living, is 'the power to look both ways and to see a thing from all sides'. All these habits of mind and imagination come together in all Welty's best stories, whether they are comic, like 'Why I Live at the P.O.', lyrical, like 'A Still Moment', tragic, like 'Death of a Travelling Salesman', or Gothic and grotesque, like 'Petrified Man'. For that matter, they come together in a novel very different from either *The Robber Bridegroom* or *Delta Wedding*: *Losing Battles*, a comedy that, with sympathy and humour, describes people waging a disgracefully unequal struggle with circumstances who remain hopeful despite everything – and who, above all, use old tales and talking as a stay against confusion.

'I wanted', Welty has said of *Losing Battles*, 'to get a year in which I could show people at the rock bottom of their lives.' So, instead of the wealthy Delta family in good economic times described in *Delta Wedding*, she focused on some poor farmers from the hill country during the Depression. 'I wanted', Welty has also explained, 'to see if I could do something that was new for me: translating every thought and feeling into speech.' 'Can't conversation ever cease?' asks one character, an outsider, towards the end of *Losing Battles*, and the reader can see what he means. The novel is centred in a family reunion, and the Beechams and Renfros who make up the bulk of it never seem to stop talking. There are tall tales, family legends, personal memories, folk humour, religious myth, stories of magic and mystery; and everyone seems to possess his or her own storytelling technique. Always accompanying the main text, the talk requiring the reunion's attention, there is a subtext of comment, criticism and anecdote, like that background of anonymous voices, inherited folk speech and wisdom, that gives resonance to traditional ballads and epic. There is a constant sense, in fact, that each tale and conversation, however trivial, belongs to a larger body of speech, a continuum of storytelling: stories knit into one another, one anecdote recalls another in the series, and tales are told which we learn have been told many times before. 'A reunion', Welty has observed, 'is everybody remembering together.' 'There's someone to remember a man's whole life', she added, 'every bit of the way along.' That suggests why the Beechams and Renfros talk. It enables them to escape from their loneliness; it gives them a feeling of identification with a particular place and past (a place and past that, of course, their talk helps to create); and it seems to certify experience for them, to make it manageable and real. In turn, their language gives them a sense of being and a feeling of belonging; to put it crudely, they feel they are there because they say they are and other people say so too. Yet all the while they are saying so, they are, as always in Welty's fiction, warning about the other side of things: the mystery of personality, the secret phases of experience, the accidental moments in life – the things that no language or code, no model of reality, can ever accommodate. An accomplished photographer, Welty was fond of using photography as a paradigm of the human project to name and know experience: to use stories, like her own, and ceremonies, like those of the Beechams and Renfros, to get a purchase on ourselves and our world. Just as we click the shutter, Welty intimates, the object will disappear, leaving 'never the essence, only a sum of parts'. Writing is a pursuit of the real, but the real will always elude us. It is, as Welty memorably put it in her 1972 novel *The Optimist's Daughter*, like 'a child who is hiding in the dark while others hunt him, waiting to be found'.

'Ours is the century of unreason,' Welty declared once, 'the stamp of our behavior is violence and isolation: non-meaning is looked upon with some solemnity.' Flannery O'Connor (1925–64) would have agreed with some of this, but not all. What troubled her was not lack of reason but absence of faith. 'The two circumstances that have given character to my writing', O'Connor admitted in her collection of essays, *Mystery and Manners* (1969), 'have been those of being Southern and being Catholic'; and it was the mixture of these two, in the crucible of her own eccentric personality, that helped produce the strangely intoxicating atmosphere of her work – at once brutal and farcical, like somebody else's bad dream. A devout if highly unorthodox Roman Catholic in a predominantly Protestant region, O'Connor interpreted experience according to her own reading of Christian eschatology – a reading that was, on her admission, tough, uncompromising and without any of 'the hazy compassion' that 'excuses all human weakness' on the ground that 'human weakness is human'. 'For me,' she declared, 'the meaning of life is centred in our Redemption by Christ'; and to this she might well have added that she neither saw humankind as worthy of being redeemed, nor considered Redemption itself as anything other than a painful act of divorce from this world. With rare exceptions, the world she explores in her work – in her novels *Wise Blood* (1952) and *The Violent Bear It Away* (1960) and in her stories gathered in *A Good Man is Hard to Find* (1955) and *Everything That Rises Must Converge* (1965) – is one of corrosion and decay. It is a world invested with evil, apparently forsaken by God and saved only in the last analysis by His incalculable grace. It is a netherworld, in fact, a place of nightmare that is comic because absurd, and (as in early Christian allegory) the one path by which its inhabitants can travel beyond it is that of renunciation, penance and extreme suffering.

O'Connor herself was inclined to talk in a distinctly equivocal way about the relationship between the two circumstances that shaped her life, her region and her faith. Sometimes, she suggested, it was her 'contact with mystery' that saved her from being stereotypically Southern and 'just doing badly what has already been done to completion'. In the Bible Belt, after all, Roman Catholics were and still are in a distinct, occasionally distrusted, minority. Other times, she argued, there was a perfect confluence, or at least congruity. 'To know oneself', she said once, 'is to know one's region.' And her region, in particular, enabled her to know herself as a Catholic writer precisely because it was 'a good place for Catholic literature'. It had, she pointed out, 'a sacramental view of life'; belief there could 'still be made believable and in relation to a large part of society'; and, 'the Bible being generally known and revered in the section', it provided the writer with 'that broad mythical base to refer to that he needs to extend his meaning in depth'. Whatever the truth here – and it probably has something to do with a creative tension between her education in Southern manners and her absorption in Catholic mystery – there is no doubt that, out of this potent mixture, O'Connor produced a fictional world the significance of which lies precisely in its apparent aberrations, its Gothic deviance from the norm. Her South is in many ways the same one other writers have been interested in – a wasteland, savage and empty, full of decaying towns and villages, crisscrossed by endless tobacco roads. And, like Twain, she borrows from the Southwestern humorists, showing a bizarre comic inventiveness, in describing it. Her characters – the protagonist Haze Motes in *Wise Blood*, for example – are not so much human beings as grotesque parodies of humanity. As O'Connor herself has suggested, they are 'literal in the same sense that a child's drawing is literal': people seen with an untamed and alien eye. Where she parts company with most other writers, however, is in what she intends by all this, and in the subtle changes wrought in her work by this difference of intention.

O'Connor herself explained that difference by saying that 'the novelist with Christian concerns will find in modern life distortions which are repugnant to him'. His or her audience, though, will find those distortions 'natural'. So such a novelist has to make his or her vision 'apparent by shock'. 'To the hard of hearing you shout,' she said, 'and for the almost-blind you draw large and startling figures.' Her figures are grotesque, in other words, because she wants us to see them as spiritual primitives. In order to describe to us a society that is unnatural by her own Christian standards – and to make us feel its unnaturalness – she creates a fictional world that is unnatural by almost any accepted standards at all. O'Connor's characters are distorted in some way, social or physical, mental or material, because their distortions are intended to mirror their guilt, original sin and the spiritual poverty of the times and places they inhabit. That is only half the story, though. From close up, these characters may seem stubbornly foolish and perverse, ignorant witnesses to the power of evil. But ultimately against their will, they reveal the workings of eternal redemption as well. They are the children of God, O'Connor believes, as well as the children of Adam; and through their lives shines dimly the possibility that they may, after all, be saved. So an extra twist of irony is added to everything that happens in O'Connor's stories. Absurd as her people are, their absurdity serves, as much as it does anything else, as a measure of God's mercy in caring for them. Corrupt and violent as their behaviour may be, its very corruption can act as a proof, a way of suggesting the scope of His extraordinary forgiveness and love. As, for instance, O'Connor shows us Haze Motes preaching 'the Church Without Christ' and declaring 'Nothing matters but that Jesus was a liar', she practises a comedy of savage paradox. Motes, after all, relies on belief for the power of his blasphemy: Christ-haunted, he perversely admits the sway over him of the very faith he struggles to deny. Every incident in *Wise Blood*, and all O'Connor's fiction, acquires a double edge because it reminds us, at one and the same time, that humanity is worthless and yet the favoured of God – negligible but the instrument of Divine Will. The irremediable wickedness of humanity and the undeniable grace of God are opposites that meet head on in her writing, and it is in the humour, finally, that they find their issue, or appropriate point of release. What we are offered on the surface is a broken world, the truth of a fractured picture. But the finely edged character of O'Connor's approach offers an 'act of seeing' (to use her own phrase) that goes beyond that surface, turning what would otherwise be a comedy of the absurd into the laughter of the saints.

A writer whose fictional world was as strange yet instantly recognizable as O'Connor's was Carson McCullers (1917–67). 'I have my own reality', McCullers said once towards the end of her life, 'of language and voices and foliage.' And it was this reality, her ghostly private world, that she tried to reproduce in her stories (collected in *The Mortgaged Heart* [1971]), her novella *The Ballad of the Sad Café* (1951) and her four novels, *The Heart is a Lonely Hunter* (1940), *Reflections in a Golden Eye* (1941), *The Member of the Wedding* (1946) and *Clock Without Hands* (1961). She gave it many names, over the years, and placed it consistently in the South. Southern though its geographical location might be, however, it was like no South anybody had ever seen before. It was another country altogether, created out of all that the author had found haunting, soft and lonely in her childhood surroundings in Georgia. It also evolved out of her own experience of melancholy, isolation and occasional if often illusory happiness. 'Everything that happens in my fiction has happened to me,' she confessed in her unfinished autobiography (*Illumination and Night Glare* [2000]). Her life, she believed, was composed of 'illumination', moments of miraculous insight, and 'night glare', long periods of dejection, depression, frustration – feelings of enclosure within herself. So are the lives of her characters. The people she writes about may seem or feel strange or freakish: because they belong to a marginal group, maybe, because of their awkward age, because of their anomalous desires, aberrant behaviour or grotesque appearance. But in their freakishness they chart the coordinates of all our lives; their strangeness simply brings to the surface the secret sense of strangeness all of us share in what McCullers sometimes called our 'lonesomeness'. So, for example, *The Ballad of the Sad Café* revolves around a *danse macabre* of frustrated love, thwarted communication. 'There are the lover and the beloved,' the narrator tells us, 'but these two come from different countries.' Similarly, *The Member of the Wedding* is an initiation novel in which the lonely, sensitive, twelve-year-old protagonist, Frankie Adams, is initiated into the simple ineradicable fact of human isolation: the perception that she can, finally, be 'a member of nothing'. At the heart of McCullers's work lies the perception Frankie comes to, just as the protagonist of *Clock Without Hands*, J. J. Malone, does when he learns that he has a few months to live. Each of us, as Malone feels it, is 'surrounded by a zone of loneliness'; each of us lives and dies unaccompanied by anyone else; which is why, when we contemplate McCullers's awkward and aberrant characters, we exchange what she called 'a little glance of grief and lonely recognition'.

Whereas McCullers published only four novels in her short life, and O'Connor only two, Joyce Carol Oates (1938–) has produced more than twenty. In addition, she has written hundreds of shorter works, including short stories and critical and cultural essays, and several of her plays have been produced off Broadway. Often classified as a realist writer, she is certainly a social critic concerned in particular with the violence of contemporary American culture. But she is equally drawn towards the Gothic, and towards testing the limits of classical myth, popular tales and fairy stories, and established literary conventions. Many of her novels are set in 'Eden County', based on the area of New York State where she was born. In her early fiction, *With Shuddering Fall* (1964) and *A Garden of Earthly Delights* (1967), she focuses her attention on rural America with its migrants, social strays, ragged prophets and automobile wrecking yards. In *Expensive People* (1968), by contrast, she moved to a satirical meditation on suburbia; and in *Them* (1969) she explored the often brutal lives of the urban poor. Other, later fiction has shown a continued willingness to experiment with subjects and forms. *Wonderland* (1971), a novel about the gaps between generations, is structured around the stories of Lewis Carroll. *Childwold* (1976) is a lyrical portrait of the artist as a young woman. *Unholy Loves* (1979), *Solstice* (1985) and *Maya: A Life* (1986) cast a cold eye on the American professional classes. *You Must Remember This* (1987) commemorates the conspiratorial obsessions of the 1950s, while *Because it is Bitter, and Because it is My Heart* (1991) dramatizes the explosive nature of American race relations. Common to most of her fiction, however, whatever its form or focus, is a preoccupation with crisis. She shows people at risk: apparently ordinary characters whose lives are vulnerable to threats from society or their inner selves or, more likely, both. In Oates's much anthologized short story 'Where Are You Going, Where Have You Been?' (1970), for instance, the central character, Connie, is an all American girl, fatally at ease with the blandness of her adolescent life. She becomes the helpless victim of a caller, realistically presented yet somehow demonic, whom she mistakes for a friend. Her sense of security, it is intimated, is a dangerous illusion. The stories and novels of Oates are full of such characters. Some, like Connie, find violence erupting from their surroundings; others, frustrated by the barren or grotesque nature of their lives and social circumstances, erupt into violence themselves. With all of them, there is the sense that they are the victims of forces beyond their control or comprehension. Whatever many of them may believe to the contrary, they are dwellers in a dark and destructive element.

Violence also threatens the lives of the characters in the stories of Grace Paley (1922–). In this case, however, the characters seem to find the energy to resist, or at least survive. In tale after tale in her several collections (*The Little Disturbances of Man* [1959], *Enormous Changes at the Last Minute* [1974], *Later the Same Day* [1985]), the reader is presented with irrepressibly energetic children, feisty women and tough-minded men. Supposedly ordinary working-class people, mostly inhabiting the cheaper, rougher districts of New York City, they show an extraordinary capacity to weather economic deprivation, social oppression or familial violence. And Paley explores their irrepressible hunger for life, their courage in the face of ageing and loss – and, not least, their willingness to take risks to encourage change within their lifetimes – in a prose that is equally extraordinary. At once quirky and lyrical, ironic and poetic, her style becomes a measure of how far from average 'average' people are, as each one of them confronts 'the expensive moment' when, driven 'by conscience or passion or even only love of one's own agemates', they try to make their lives count. Nothing, perhaps, could be further from this than the fiction of Alison Lurie (1926–) and Anne Tyler (1941–). In novels like *Love and Friendship* (1962), *The War Between the Tates* (1974) and *Foreign Affairs* (1984), Lurie has marked with quiet satire the lives of academics and authors: the politics of the family and the campus, the contacts and conflicts between American and English society. Tyler has ranged more widely, in such novels as *Earthly Possessions* (1977), *Dinner at the Homesick Restaurant* (1982), *The Accidental Tourist* (1985) and *Breathing Lessons* (1988). But certain preoccupations tend to recur: families and the separations they suffer through death and through the isolation of one member from another, the need to live more than a life of quiet desperation and the desolate fact of truly living, taking a risk. What these writers have in common is worth emphasizing, though, for all their differences. It is something shared with other recent and notable women writers, among them Ann Beattie (1947–), Gail Godwin (1937–) and Josephine Humphreys (1944–). 'On an afternoon two years ago,' the narrator of *Rich in Love* (1988) by Josephine Humphreys declares, as she prepares the reader for the story she is going to tell, 'my life veered from its day-in day-out course and became for a short while the kind of life that can be told as a story – that is, one in which events appear to have meaning.' That hits the note all these writers share. All of them reveal, with gentle intensity, those moments in life – usually experienced by a group or community, perhaps a family – when the familiar suddenly becomes strange. The contours of the everyday are disrupted, by bereavement perhaps or betrayal; and the characters, often female, are forced to question the assumptions of their lives, to review and revise accepted notions about their own nature and those dear to them – and to make a choice about where they stand, even if only quietly to themselves.

One of the most remarkable groups of recent women writers to examine communities, and especially families, in crisis comes from the South. The group includes Bobbie Ann Mason (1940–), Lee Smith (1944–), Ellen Gilchrist (1935–), Dorothy Allison (1950–), Jayne Anne Phillips (1952–) and, from an earlier generation, Ellen Douglas (1921–). Mason is the author of a number of remarkable short stories (*Shiloh and Other Stories* [1982]) that show, she says, how she was 'haunted by the people I went to school with'. Working in local dime stores or wrecking yards, perhaps, or living in rural trailer parks and frequenting shopping malls, her characters register not only the changes in their own lives but also larger transformations in their culture. Or, as one feisty young woman character tells her father, 'Times are different now, Papa. We're just as good as the men.' In novels like *In Country* (1985), *Spence & Lilla* (1988) and *Feather Crowns* (1993), Mason has continued her sensitive exploration of such people, as they weave their way between a vanished past, a slippery present and an uncertain future. *In Country*, for instance, shows us a young woman trying to come to terms with the death of her father in the Vietnam War. As she makes her way through 'contemporary state-of-the-art U.S.A.', she struggles to set up a channel, a current of sympathy between the dead and the living, that will enable her to settle accounts with her present, and her past, and move on. In her early stories in *Black Tickets* (1980), Phillips is similarly concerned with people trying to make sense of their aimless lives, their world of broken families, truck stops, strip joints, people on the move. And to do so, they seem never to cease talking, about their lives and world, to others or themselves. More ambitiously, in her novels *Machine Dreams* (1984), *Shelter* (1994) and *Motherkind* (2000), she has woven voices together to tell stories of death and desire, the subterranean ties that bind one person to others, personality to history. In *Machine Dreams*, for instance, she uses voices talking to one another (particularly mother to daughter), talking to themselves (particularly in dream and memory) and talking through letters to tell the tale of an entire, disintegrating family from the Depression to 1972.

'Granny would lean back in her chair and start reeling out story and memory,' recalls the protagonist in *Bastard Out of Carolina* (1992) by Dorothy Allison. That suggests something else that many of the more recent white women writers from the South share. The tales they tell are often rehearsed in oral telling, or they seem to emerge in a style that recalls the spoken rather than the written word. Lee Smith, for instance, has an uncanny ear for voices and an unusual range. In her appropriately titled *Oral History* (1983), the reader hears first the voice of a college student, who hopes to capture her own mountain past in an oral history project. Her slightly genteel, academic voice is then slyly subverted by the lyricism and longings of other voices, the people of the mountains, who suggest both the exuberance and the enclosure of mountain life. Nor are the voices written into life by Smith, or any of these authors, confined to just one or two kinds of communities. Smith herself catches the vocal timbre of the small town (*Fancy Strut* [1973]) and the rural community (*Family Linen* [1985]), sensitive young women (*Black Mountain Breakdown* [1986]) and indomitable older ones (*Fair and Tender Ladies* [1988]). The voices that inhabit the work of Gilchrist tend to be more educated, conventionally articulate: but they carry, in their idiom, what the protagonist of *The Annunciation* (1983) calls the 'cargo' of other, remembered voices that she 'must carry with her always'. And in *Cavedweller* (1998) by Allison, the interplay between present and recollected voices is even more on the surface, as, like so many protagonists in these stories, the leading character returns to her home town to try to come to terms with the past – the 'caves' beneath the surfaces of her life that need to be seen and understood. Unsurprisingly, too, the clash of voices often encountered in these books by white Southern women has a racial inflection. In what is probably her finest novel, *Can't Quit You Baby* (1988), for instance, Ellen Douglas tells the story of two women – one rich, white and pampered, the other poor, black and world-weary – who share a Mississippi kitchen for fifteen years. And as the two women, the mistress of the house and the housekeeper, talk, bicker, argue and tell stories, the reader learns of a prolonged encounter that is too complex to be described in terms of simple love and hatred. It is a matter of being tied irrevocably together by what they and their two races have done and said to each other, and by a strange kind of mutual need.

'I am crawling through the tunnel of myself,' observes a character in *The Benefactor* (1963) by Susan Sontag (1933–). Sontag has written in various genres and forms: essays cultural, critical and political (*Styles of Radical Will* [1969], *On Photography* [1977], *Under the Sign of Saturn* [1980], *AIDS and Its Metaphors* [1988]), drama (*Alice in Bed, A Play* [1993]), short stories and longer fiction (*I, etcetera* [1978], *Death Kit* [1967], *The Volcano Lover, A Romance* [1992]). All of her works, however, could be said to be concerned with varieties of alienation and mediation: the pressing, often claustrophobic, relationship between reality and what she calls in one of her books 'the circle of my consciousness'. Her writings, fictional and non-fictional, could in fact be described in the terms she herself used for the work of Samuel Beckett: as 'delicate dramas of the withdrawn consciousness – pared down to essentials, cut off, often represented as physically immobilised'. In this, she is not alone. A number of other recent women writers have been concerned with the predicament of the trapped sensibility, often female. The problem is there in such otherwise different books as *Final Payments* (1978) by Mary Gordon (1949–) and the immensely popular novels *The Women's Room* (1977) by Marilyn French (1929–) and *Fear of Flying* (1973) by Erica Jong (1942–). More seriously and powerfully, it is present in the work of Joan Didion (1934–). Didion is an enormously accomplished writer of non-fiction that explores American dreams and, more often, American nightmares: that recent history of ecstasy and violence that Mailer spoke of, and that has led so often to political disaster or cultural breakdown (*Slouching Towards Bethlehem* [1968], *The White Album* [1979], *After Henry* [1992]). And in novels like *Play It As It Lays* (1970) and *The Last Thing He Wanted* (1996), she has taken alienation to a kind of logical conclusion. In spare, lyrical prose that works as much through its absences, the spaces between the words, as through the words themselves, she presents the reader with a world of vacancy, where the protagonists find it difficult, if not impossible, to escape from emotional numbness, other characters approximate to objects, things to be manipulated, and experience is casually random, violent and without meaning. As the protagonist of *Play It As It Lays*, Maria Wyeth, watches an unknown woman walk across a supermarket parking lot in the 'vacant sunlight' of California, she feels that she is 'watching the dead still centre of the world, the quintessential intersection of nothing': a heart of emptiness, a void, rather than a heart of darkness. The fragmented structure, as well as the laconic style, of Didion's stories catches that emptiness, and the lives of drift and insignificance characters like Maria lead. Which is a comment, clearly, on the vacancy, the blandness of American culture – and on a society that, for Didion, resembles 'an inchoate army on the move' – and a barbed aside on the condition of women in particular. 'It occurred to Maria', we are told, 'that whatever arrangements were made, they worked less well for women.'

For some characters in recent novels by women, the way to escape from these conditions is precisely to go way out west: not to the coast, necessarily, but to the wide open spaces that lie between that coast and the Mississippi River. So, the protagonist in *The Bean Trees* (1989), then later *Pigs in Heaven* (1993), by Barbara Kingsolver (1955–) flees westward to Arizona, from the poverty and pressures of her life in Kentucky. There, she builds a new life for herself and a new kind of 'home' and 'family' with friends and the abandoned child she takes up with her on the journey. In *Heading West* (1981) by Doris Betts (1931–), the main character is taken from a life in the East that she feels 'could be summarized in two words: Unsatisfactory Conditions' to a more real, more elemental existence, also in Arizona. 'I've been sensible all my life,' she reflects; now she surrenders to the authenticity of rocks and rivers, the superiority of archaeology to history. What, however, is remarkable about the fiction of Jane Smiley (1949–) and E. Annie Proulx (1935–) is that it refuses to accommodate the West to these notions of liberatory flight. The women and men in the stories of Smiley, for instance, are caught up in the conflicts of family life, condemned to see in themselves 'the fusing and mixing of their parents' and to scrabble for material success or mere survival, even though the places where they work out their fates are vast and open – where 'prairie settlers always saw a sea or an ocean of grass'. So in *A Thousand Acres* (1991), Smiley rewrites the story of King Lear and his daughters, transporting it to a farm in Iowa. The book is at once a subtle but radical transformation of the Shakespearean tragedy, a visionary version of the politics of the family, particularly fathers and daughters, and an unravelling of some familiar Western tropes. Life in the West, Smiley intimates, can be as embroiled in the past, disputes over blood and earth, as anywhere else: in the world of *A Thousand Acres*, we are told, 'acreage and financing were facts of life as basic as name and gender'.

The politics of the family have been a shaping force in the world of E. Annie Proulx, too, whatever setting she has chosen. In *The Shipping News* (1993), for example, set in Newfoundland, she satirizes what some American politicians like to refer to lovingly as family values. Violence and abusive sex are all in the family here. So, too, is lovelessness: so much so that the main character feels at an early age that 'he had been given to the wrong family, that somewhere his real people . . . longed for him'. Nevertheless, while the book does not by any means idealize the family, it does suggest that coming to know one's family, even distant family, is a way to know oneself. The verdict on the family in *Close Range* (1999), a series of stories set in the West, is more corrosive. And equally corrosive is the verdict on the West. Here, families disintegrate, relationships rarely last for more than 'two hours', and the culture itself seems to be given over to the abstractions of money and image. In one story, 'The Mud Below', a character called Diamond Felts tries to pursue a model of cowboy masculinity and courage that he finds seductive by joining a rodeo. He is motivated, it turns out, by the refusal of his father to accept him: 'Not your father,' his father tells Diamond, 'and never was.' But his adventure ends in a disastrous accident. Even before that, the brutal reply of his mother when Diamond asks her who his father was, 'Nobody', lets us know how much this is a tale about two kinds of failed paternity. There is the failure of the literal father, of course, but there is also the failure of the founding fathers of Western myth. Casting a cold eye on that myth, Proulx sees it as a mask and a masquerade: a concealment of the real, historically, that has been converted into a commodity. Proulx is, of course, not alone in this, nor is she in the conviction that the two rivers of American history have become fatally mixed and muddied. Or, as the caustic epigraph to *Close Range* has it, 'Reality never been of much use out here'.

Beats, Prophets and Aesthetes

Rediscovering the American voice: The Black Mountain writers

In 1950, Charles Olson (1910–70) began his essay on 'Projective Verse' in this way:

(projectile   (percussive   (prospective

vs.

The NON-Projective

With these words, he declared war on both the formalists and the confessionals; and he announced the emergence of new and powerful forces in postwar American poetry. 'Closed' verse, the structures and metred writing 'which print bred', was to be jettisoned, Olson declared: so too was 'the private-soul-at-any-public-wall', the lyricism and introspection of the strictly personal approach. What was required was an 'open' poetry. A poem, he announced, was 'a high-energy construct', the function of which was to transfer energy 'from where the poet got it' in experience 'to the reader'. This transfer could be achieved by means of 'FIELD COMPOSITION': 'FORM IS NEVER MORE THAN AN EXTENSION OF CONTENT,' Olson insisted, writing the words large (as he often did) to register the importance of what he was saying. And in his view the ideal form would consist of a steady, dense stream of perceptions: 'ONE PERCEPTION', as he put it, 'MUST IMMEDIATELY AND DIRECTLY LEAD TO A FURTHER PERCEPTION' so the poem could become more 'the act of the instant' than 'the act of thought about the instant'. The 'smallest particle' in this form, or rather field, would be the syllable, 'the king and pin of versification': the poet should always pay attention to the sound of the syllables as they unrolled from the mind and appealed to the ear. 'It is by their syllables that words juxtapose in beauty,' Olson said; and these syllables, energetically constructed, should in turn rule and hold together the lines, which constituted 'the larger forms' of the poem. 'The line comes . . . from the breath, from the breathing of the man who writes,' Olson argued, 'at the moment he writes'; it was therefore unique to the poet and the occasion. Breath reified experience by creating an awareness of bodily 'depth sensibility': the poet responded to the flow and pressure of things, he registered this in his diaphragm, and he then compelled his readers, by sharing his breathing rhythms, to feel the same pressures and participate in the flow of the moment.

'I have had to learn the simplest things / last,' Olson wrote in one of his poems, 'Maximus, to himself' (1953), 'Which made for difficulties.' The problem, as he saw it, was not that truth was intrinsically difficult: on the contrary, earlier civilizations like the Mayan had acted upon it with instinctive ease. It was that habits of mind and language that had been entrenched for centuries had to be *un*learned: man had become 'estranged / from that which was most familiar', and he had to turn his consciousness against itself in order to cure the estrangement. The process of unlearning, and then making a new start, began with books like *Call Me Ishmael* (1947), Olson's extraordinary critical work on Melville which opens with the ringing assertion, 'I take SPACE to be the central fact to man born in America . . . I spell it large because it comes large here': a belief that was to be developed in his preoccupation with spatial rather than linear forms as well in his later, direct explorations of 'American space' (where there is 'nothing but what is', Olson claimed, 'no end and no beginning'). It was also initiated in some of the earlier poems published in the 1940s, which celebrate the movement of nature in 'Full circle' and attack the tendency to perceive life and literature in closed terms ('The closed parenthesis reads: the dead bury the dead, / and it is not very interesting'). However, it was in the work published after this, through the 1950s and beyond, that his sense of poems as performative moral acts was fully exercised, in shorter pieces like 'The Kingfishers' (1949), 'In Cold Hell, In Thicket' (1950), 'The Lordly and Isolate Satyrs' (1956), 'As the Dead Prey Upon Us' (1956) and 'Variations Done for Gerald Van de Wiele' (1956), as well as in the *Maximus Poems* (1983), written over several decades, which represent Olson's own version of the American epic. A poem such as 'The Kingfishers' powerfully expresses Olson's belief in serial, open forms. 'Not one death but many, /' it begins, 'not accumulation but change, the feed-back proves, the feed-back is the law / Into the same river no man steps twice.' But it not only expresses it in the literal sense, it also enacts it: working on the assumption that nothing can be said exactly and finally, Olson uses repetition, parenthesis and apposition. 'To be in different states without a change', the poet suggests, '/ is not a possibility'; and so recurring figures metamorphose according to the altered conditions in which they are placed. As they change, the line changes, too, in lively responsiveness: rapid, energetic, constantly varying in pace, it denies any attempt to receive the discourse and experience of the poem as anything other than a continuous flow. Nor does the flow end with the nominal end of the poem: as the last line, 'I hunt among stones', indicates, it is simply stepped aside from, not staunched. The poet remains committed to the activities of attention and discovery.

Undoubtedly, though, Olson's major poetic achievement is the *Maximus Poems*. The Maximus who gives these poems their title is an 'Isolated person in Gloucester, Massachusetts', the poet's home town, who addresses 'you / you islands / of men and girls': that is, his fellow citizens and readers. A 'Root person in root place', he is, like Williams's Paterson, a huge, omniscient version of his creator. The poet is the hero here, as he normally is in the American epic, and this poet is notable as an observer, correspondent (many of the poems are described as 'letters'), social critic, historian, pedagogue and prophet. The poems that constitute his serial epic vary in stance and tone. The ones in *Maximus IV, V, VI*, for example, published in 1968, are more clearly mythic, more openly preoccupied with convincing their audience that 'the world / is an eternal event' than are the pieces in *The Maximus Poems*, published eight years earlier. Nevertheless, certain themes recur, supplying a stable centre to this constantly shifting work. Olson's aim is a specific reading of the history of Gloucester, and the surrounding area by land and sea, that will enable a revelation of truth: one particular 'city' will then become the 'City', an 'image of creation and of human life for the rest of the life of the species'. The opening lines of the first poem announce the quest: 'the thing you're after / may be around the bend'. The voyage of discovery is, in effect, in search of the near, the familiar: 'facts' or particulars which must be dealt with 'by ear', spontaneously and as if for the first time. Such a goal is not easy, Olson suggested, at a time when 'cheapness shit is / upon the world' and everything is measured 'by quantity and machine'. Nothing valid is easy, even love, when 'pejorocracy is here', the degradations of capitalism and consumerism – and where the familiar has been contaminated by the 'greased slide' of 'mu-sick', the evasions of modern mass culture. But it is still possible to live *in* the world, achieving the recognition that 'There are no hierarchies, no infinite, no such many as mass, there are only / eyes in all heads, / to be looked out of'. It is still possible, in fact, to resist the myopic barbarism of 'Tell-A-Vision' and 'the several cankers of profit-making' so as to pay reverent attention to the real ('The real / is always worth the act of / lifting it'), to realize contact with particular places and moments ('there is no other issue than the moment'), and to build a new community or 'polis' based upon humility, curiosity and care.

Like many other American epics, the *Maximus Poems* juxtapose America as it is – where 'The true troubadours / are CBS' and 'The best / is soap' – with America as it might be. 'The newness / the first men knew', the poet informs us, 'was almost / from the start dirtied / by second comers.' But 'we are only / as we find out we are', and perhaps Americans can 'find' a new identity and society; Gloucester itself, we are told, is a place 'where polis / still thrives', and it may be that enough will be found there to promote a 'new start'. Certainly, Olson hoped so and worked hard, in both his art and his life, to realize that hope: he had something of the evangelical fervour of Pound, which came out in particular during the years he taught at Black Mountain College in North Carolina. Among his colleagues and pupils there were a number of poets who shared at least some of his aims. They and a few others found an outlet for their work in *Origin* and then later *Black Mountain Review* (1954–7). As a result they have become associated as a group, a loose constellation of people who, for a while at least, found in Olson a guide, example and father-figure. These poets include Jonathan Williams (1929–), whose Jargon Press became an important publisher of *avant-garde* writing, and Denise Levertov (1923–97), an Englishwoman who emigrated to America – where, she claimed, she found 'new rhythms of life and speech', and was transformed into 'an American poet'. 'These poems decry and exalt', Williams has said of his work, in *An Ear in Bartram's Tree: Selected Poems 1957–67* (1969); and he has added elsewhere that 'being a mountaineer', he has 'a garrulous landscape nature' and yet at times can be 'as laconic . . . as a pebble'. Whether sprawling or succinct, though, satiric or lyrical, his poems are marked by their radical innovations of language and line ('Credo'), their affection for the Appalachian Mountains and English rural landscapes ('Re-flections from Appalachia', 'Two Pastorals for Samuel Palmer at Shoreham, Kent') and by a constant desire to see 'not with / but *thru* / the eye!' – to couple percep-tion with vision. Levertov has a similar obsession with seeing, pairing this with the use of open forms and idiomatic language. But for her, as she admits in 'The Third Dimension' (1956), 'Honesty / isn't so simple'. She tends to be more deliberate, painstaking, more hesitant in her unravelling of theme. The poetic 'I' here is quieter, more tentative. It involves, as she puts it in 'Beyond the End' (1953), 'a gritting of teeth' in order 'to go / just that much further, beyond the end / beyond whatever end: to begin, to be, to defy'.

Two other poets whose work has registered the impact of the Black Mountain experience are Paul Blackburn (1926–71) and John Wieners (1934–). Wieners studied at the college briefly, Blackburn published work in *Origin* and the *Review*;

and both poets acknowledged the influence of Olson – which would in any event be clear from their use of the poem as an open field, their preoccupation with 'breath' and typographical experiment. It is there, however, that the resemblance ends. Blackburn is much the more expansive, outgoing of the two. His poem 'The Continuity' (1953), for example, begins as an overheard conversation ('The brick-layer tells the busdriver / and I have nothing to do but listen'), moves into a skilful imitation of street speech ('Th' holdup at the liquor store, d'ja hear?'), and then concludes with a celebration of community. 'A dollar forty- / two that I spent . . .', the poet says, '/ is now in a man's pocket going down Broadway.' 'Thus far the transmission is oral,' he adds, referring to the conversation he has just heard: exchanges, financial, conversational, literary, are all a way of maintaining 'the continuity'. They are all acts of communion, no matter how small, and that includes this poem. The work of John Wieners – who came to prominence with *The Hotel Wentley Poems* (1958) – could not be more opposed to this idea of communality: he has even referred to public poetry reading as 'a shallow *act*'. For him, an audience is a dangerous thing, a 'wild horde who press in / to get a peek at the bloody hero' and seem not only to violate but to feed off his privacy. Intense, edgy, his poetry withdraws from nightmare landscapes ('America, you boil over / The cauldron scalds') and presses in upon his inner life, where, however, he discovers other kinds of horror. For him, in effect, the poem is not an act of communion but an authentic cry of pain: or, as he puts it in 'A Poem for Painters' (1958), 'a man's / struggle to stay with / what is his own, what / lives within him to do'.

Apart from Olson, however, the most important poets connected with the Black Mountain group are Robert Creeley (1926–), Ed Dorn (1929–99) and Robert Duncan (1919–88). In the case of Creeley (whose *Collected Poems* [1982] has been followed by many other volumes), an interest in open forms and the belief that 'words are things too' has combined with two quite disparate but in a way complementary influences. There is, first, his involvement with the free-flowing experiments of Abstract Expressionism and modern jazz. 'To me,' Creeley has said, 'life is interesting insofar as it lacks intentional "control"'; and it is clear that the example of painters like Jackson Pollock and musicians like Charlie Parker and Miles Davis has encouraged him to see the artist as someone immersed in the work he creates, experiencing its energy, involved in its movement, and limited in terms of how he expresses himself only 'by the nature of the activity'. Along with this, there is what Creeley has termed his 'New England temper'. New England has given Creeley many things, including a tendency to be 'hung up', to suffer from pain ('I can / feel my eye breaking') and tension ('I think I grow tensions / like flowers'). Above all, though, what it has given him is two things, one to do with perception, the other with expression. 'Locate *I*,' declares Creeley in one of his poems; elsewhere, he insists, 'position is where you / put it, where it is'. He is fascinated, in effect, by the perceptual position of the speaker, how the poem grows out of the active relationship between the perceiver and perceived. The preoccupation with the limits of vision that earlier New Englanders demonstrated is consequently translated into cool, Modernist terms, the aim being not an 'ego-centred' verse but precisely its opposite, words that reveal how our eyes and minds 'are not separate . . . from all other life-forms'. At the same time, New England habits have, Creeley says, given him a 'sense of speech as a laconic, ironic, compressed way of saying something to someone', the inclination 'to say as little as possible as often as possible'. So the forms of his saying have become, as he believes they should, an extension of content. His purpose is 'a realisation, a reification of what is': 'a process of discovery' that turns out to be a matter of vocabulary as well as vision. 'What's the point of doing what we already know?' Creeley has asked, and his writing continually illustrates this belief in experiment. His poems evolve on both a sequential grammatical level and a cumulative linear level; each line reaffirms or modifies the sense of the sentence and the total argument, each word exists in contrapuntal tension with all the others. There is risk here, in fact, a taste for the edgy and subversive, of a kind that would be equally familiar to Thelonious Monk and Emily Dickinson.

Given the habit 'I' or self-consciousness has of getting in the way of revelation, Creeley tries to strip poetry of its more obtrusive, interfering devices: easy generalizations, abstractions and colourful comparisons are eschewed in favour of patient attentiveness, a tendency to approach things and words as if they were small bombs set to explode unless carefully handled. To capture the 'intense instant', what is needed is caution, perhaps ('The Innocence'), surprise ('Like They Say'), spontaneity ('To Bobbie'): above all, a willingness to follow the peculiar shape and movement of an experience, however unpredictable it may be. This last point is nicely dramatized in 'I Know a Man', where the unnamed narrator talks to his friend 'John' about what they might do, or where they might drive, to escape 'the darkness' that surrounds them. John's reply is short and to the point: 'drive, he sd, for / christ's sake, look / out where yr going.' As Creeley has observed, 'you can drive to the store with absolute predetermination to get the bread and return home'. Alternatively, 'you can take a drive, as they say . . . where the driving permits you certain information you can't anticipate'. To plan is one thing: it has its advantages, but it inhibits discovery, 'the delight of thought as a possibility of forms'. To take a chance is quite another, and it is clearly what John and his creator prefer: to go off in an unpremeditated way and simply to watch, to 'look out' where one is going. 'I want to range in the world as I can imagine the world', Creeley has said, 'and as I can find possibility in the world.' This he has done in sparse, brittle poems that use their silences just as effectively as their speech and that ('true / Puritan' as the poet is, he admits) present the cardinal sin as cowardice, a reluctance to resist the several forces that would imprison us in habit – the fear of the challenge thrown out to us by the as yet unseen and unarticulated.

If Creeley's work represents a peculiarly Eastern, and more specifically New England, form of 'open' verse, then the poetry of Ed Dorn draws much of its point, wit and power from his attachment to the American West. This is not simply because some of his poems, like 'The Rick of Green Wood' (1956), are situated in Western landscapes or, like 'Vaquero' (1957) or Slinger (1975), play with popular mythic versions of the frontier. It is also because Dorn adopts a poetic voice that in its expansiveness, cool knowingness, ease and wry humour seems to belong to wide open spaces. Additionally, it is because he adopts an alert political stance that depends on an understanding of the different possibilities of American 'know-how', mobility and energy: the same forces that could be positive, humane and liberating – and have been, sometimes, in his own personal history and the story of the West – have also, he realizes, generated the 'North Atlantic Turbine' of mass production, conscienceless power and the destruction of people and the planet for profit. 'From near the beginning,' Dorn has said, 'I have known my work to be theoretical in nature and poetic by virtue of its inherent tone.' He is not afraid of speculation and direct, unmetaphorical speech; however, he is saved from simple didacticism by his 'tone', which is the combined product of rapid transitions of thought, subtle tonalities of rhythm and phrasing, and an astute use of personae, irony ('a thing I've always admired'), comedy and sarcasm.

Apart from political works such as 'The Sundering U.P. Tracks' (1967) or 'The Stripping of the River' (1967), Dorn wrote many lyrical poems: explorations of human sentiment, like 'The Air of June Sings' (1955), that demonstrate, with especial clarity, what Creeley has called Dorn's '*Elizabethan* care for the sound of syllables'. In the later part of his career, he favoured epigrams, tight aphoristic pieces which he labelled 'dispatches'. Light and essential enough, Dorn hoped, to be accepted 'in the spirit / of the Pony Express', they carried his commitment to alertness of perception and precision of speech to a new extreme. In between, he produced *Slinger*, a long, anti-heroic poem of the American West that enacts its significances through radical variations of idiom, surreal imagery, puns, per-sonifications and jokes. Constantly allusive, packed with a range of characters that includes – besides the eponymous Slinger – a madam of a brothel, a refugee from a university and Howard Hughes, it explores questions of thought and culture (Lévi-Strauss is invoked, both the anthropologist and the jeans manufacturer) and the use and abuse of power, money, words and weaponry, in 'cosmological america'. As far as his 'personal presence' in the poem is concerned, Dorn said, 'It's omnipresent, absolutely omnipresent', then added, 'Actually I'm absolutely uncommitted except to what's happening'. In its own way, in fact, *Slinger* is an-other version of the American epic, a song of the self in which the self becomes dispersed, problematic, part of the matter for attention. Asked what the meaning of the poem's actions are, at one stage, Slinger laughs. 'Mean? / Refugee, you got some strange / obsessions,' he declares; 'you want to know / what something *means* after you've / seen it, after you've been there.' That makes the point. Meaning and identity inhere in the actual processes, the activities of the lines; like Olson and Creeley, Dorn seems to be recalling what Williams meant when he said 'the poet thinks with his poem'.

'I like to wander about in my work writing so rapidly that I might overlook manipulations and design': that remark of Robert Duncan's suggests that he, too, saw the poem as a process, of being and knowing. However, another remark of his illustrates the mystical strain that helps to distinguish him from his Black Mountain colleagues: 'Poetry is the very life of the soul: the body's discovery that it can dream.' With a background as a romantic and theosophist, Duncan said that he experienced from the first an 'intense yearning, the desire for something else'. 'I knew the fullest pain of longing', he declared, '. . . to be out of my being and enter the Other.' Consumed with a desire for 'identification with the universe', he was still quite young when he recognized in poetry his 'sole and ruling vocation'; 'only in this act', he felt, could his 'inner nature unfold'. His feeling for verse and its constituent language was, in fact, prophetic, cabalistic. Language, he believed, we drink in with our mother's milk, possessed by its rhythmic vibrations; we acquire it 'without / any rule for love of it / "imitating our nurses"' and hardly aware of its 'vacant energies below meaning'. Poems spring from this nurture, and from our dim recognition of the 'metaphorical ground in life'. A metaphor, Duncan claimed, 'is not a literary device but an actual meaning . . . leading us to realise the coinherrence of being in being': it reveals correspondences in that world of forms 'in which . . . spirit is manifest', and it offers glimpses of 'the wholeness of what we are that we will never know'. Language, rhythm, metaphor: all these, then, Duncan began by seeing as a means of transcendence, an access to revelation. What the Black Mountain experience added to this was the liberating influence of open forms. Duncan took the notion of the poem as field and coloured it with his own original impulses, so that it became, for him, the idea of the poem as a 'Memory-field' in which 'all parts . . . co-operate, co-exist' in mystical union. Past and future are folded together in the 'one fabric' of his verse, with the result that what the reader sees, ideally, is 'no first strand or second strand' but the 'truth of that form', the timeless 'design' as a whole.

'There is a natural mystery to poetry,' Duncan wrote in 1960. In his poems, beginning with early collections such as *Heavenly City, Earthly City* (1949), *The Opening of the Field* (1960) and *Roots and Branches* (1964) and ending with *Ground Work II: In the Dark* (1987), he tried to announce that mystery. His frequently anthologized piece, 'Often I Am Permitted to Return to A Meadow' (1964), is characteristic. Using plangent repetition of word and phrase, subtle verbal melody and a serpentine syntax that seems to fall back on itself, Duncan creates a verse that is, in equal portions, magic, ritual and incantation. Above all, there is the image of an 'eternal pasture' here, which gradually accumulates associations that are pagan ('ring a round of roses'), Platonic ('light / wherefrom the shadows that are forms fall') and Christian ('likenesses of the First Beloved / whose flowers are flames to the Lady'). Like the figures of H. D. (a poet whom Duncan admired), this image is at once precise and resonant, exact and strange; and while it is possible to gather some of its reverberations (omens and celebrations that are at once sacred and sensual, the holy place that links 'being' and 'Other'), it is precisely the point that it should remain unparaphraseable, a 'releasing / word' that releases us simply into a dim awareness of the 'god-step at the margins of thought'. The last line of the poem, 'everlasting omen of what is', in a way takes us no further than the first. Yet that, surely, is because Duncan is intent on making us feel that we have been in the 'meadow' he describes. Like a suddenly remembered dream, an experience of *déjà vu* or a half-recovered melody, its appeal depends on the suspicion that it has always been there below 'the currents of language' – and still is, even if we cannot quite grasp it.

Restoring the American vision: The San Francisco renaissance

Duncan gradually moved, he claimed, from 'the concept of a dramatic form to a concept of musical form in poetry'. This does not tell the whole truth, if only because his poetry written after his initial involvement with the Black Mountain group *is* capable of dramatic statement: it incorporates vigorous attacks on 'The malignant stupidity of statesmen', vivid accounts of homosexual experiences ('my Other is not a woman but a man') and careful descriptions of how 'The poem / feeds upon thought, feeling, and impulse'. As a broad brushstroke portrait of the impact that Olson and others had on him, though, it is reasonably helpful – and handy, since it brings into focus a second group of poets who reacted, in their own way, against the formalist and confessional establishments. The 'dramatic form' Duncan refers to is the one he favoured when he emerged as a leading poet in the late 1940s, as part of what has become known as the San Francisco Renaissance. For the San Francisco poets, drama and performance were primary. As one of them, Lawrence Ferlinghetti (1919–), put it in 1955, 'the kind of poetry which has been making the most noise here . . . is what should be called street poetry'. 'It amounts to getting poetry back into the street where it once was,' he added, 'out of the classroom, out of the speech department, and – in fact – off the printed page. The printed word has made poetry so silent.' Ferlinghetti was speaking for a more demotic, populist poetry than the kind preferred by many of the San Franciscans – including Duncan, even in his early years – but he still spoke for more than himself. Immediacy, drama, above all language and a line shaped by the *voice*, in conversation or declamation: these were the priorities of a group of otherwise different poets who wanted to liberate poetry from the academy.

Ferlinghetti's own poems illustrate this interest in oral impact: many of them were, in fact, conceived of as 'oral messages' and have been performed to a jazz accompaniment. The line is long and flowing, often using Williams's 'variable foot' to govern the pace; the language is strongly idiomatic; the imagery colourful to the point of theatricality. As Ferlinghetti sees him, in 'A Coney Island of the Mind' (1958), the poet is at once a performer, 'a charleychaplin man', and a pedagogue, a 'super realist' who is willing to risk absurdity as he strives not only to entertain but also to instruct. 'Balancing . . . / above a sea of faces', he uses all the tricks at his disposal, 'entrechats' and 'high theatrics', to perceive and communicate 'taut truth'. 'Only the dead are disengaged,' Ferlinghetti has insisted and his poetry, while indulging in slapstick and corny jokes, is seriously engaged with the issues of the day: the 'engines / that devour America', the absurdities of institutional life, the humourless collectives called nation-states. The energy of his voice, in fact, expresses the coherence of his vision, which is that of the anarchic individualist who waits hopefully for 'the final withering away / of all governments' – and the day when 'lovers and weepers / . . . lie down together / in a new rebirth of wonder'.

Someone else from the San Francisco area who used roaming verse forms and a declamatory style was Brother Antoninus, a writer who, after his departure from the Dominican Order in 1970, published under the name of William Everson (1912–94). Like Ferlinghetti, Everson also favoured such devices as incremental repetition and a paratactic syntax. In his case, though, the poetry that resulted has a rugged, flinty quality to it, an austere intensity. None of his work has the flat speech rhythms that characterize so much late twentieth-century verse. On the contrary, it fluctuates between a long, wavering line that can approach the stillness of a moment of contemplation and a line that tightens together into an abrupt, insistent rhythmic unit. Whether recording the harsh landscapes of the West Coast and the 'wild but earnest' forms of life that inhabit them or rehearsing more immediately personal experiences of love, religious faith and doubt, his work is notable for a diction that ranges between the brutally simple and the lofty, imagery that can be at once primitive and apocalyptic, frequently incantatory rhythms and a general tone that recalls the work of Robinson Jeffers (a poet to whom Everson professed an allegiance). 'A Canticle to the Waterbirds' (1950) is exemplary, in many ways. It opens with an invocation to the birds, inviting them to 'make a praise up to the Lord'. The Lord they are asked to praise is no gentle Jesus, however, but the creator and overseer of a 'mighty fastness', 'indeterminate realms' of rock, sea and sky. And the praise they are asked to give is not so much in the saying as the being. What Everson celebrates, in fact, is the capacity these birds possess for living in the Now; they have none of the human taint of self-consciousness, no compulsion to look before or after. They act with purity, simplicity and instinctive courage, as part of the processes of creation. To live beyond evasions and inwardness: this is the lesson taught by the waterbirds. For that matter, it is the lesson taught by Everson's tough yet oracular poetry, which represents a sustained assault on the idea of a separate self – and which is insistently reminding us of the 'strict conformity that creaturehood entails, / . . . the prime commitment all things share'.

'I would like to make poems out of real objects,' another poet associated with the San Francisco area, Jack Spicer (1925–65), declared in 'Letter to Lorca' (1957); 'The poem is a collage of the real.' This sounds like Ferlinghetti and Everson, in their commitment to what Williams called 'things – on a field'; and Spicer does certainly share with those poets an interest in the irreducible reality of objects as well as a preference for open-ended structures and a flexible line – in effect, the poem as process. Just as Ferlinghetti and Everson are not entirely alike, however, Spicer is different from both of them in that his commitment (as the phrase 'collage of the real' intimates) is to a more surreal medium; the materials of his work seem to come from the subconscious, even though the organizing of those materials is achieved by a conscious poetic intelligence. His 'Imaginary Elegies' (1957), for instance, begin by asking if poetry can mean that much if all it deals with is visible phenomena, 'like a camera', rendering them 'alive in sight only for a second'. Then, working through a complex association of imagery, Spicer answers his own question simply by dramatizing his own sense of the potentials of poetry. 'This much I've learned,' Spicer says, '. . . / Time does not finish a poem': because

American Literature since 1945

a poem is a fluid, changing medium that actively imitates the equally fluid, changing stream of life. It is a matter not of perception but of correspondence; 'Poet, / be like God', Spicer commands, that is create 'not . . . an image or a picture but . . . something alive – caught forever in the structure of words'. This alertness to poetry as active translation, a carrying across of 'real objects' called things into other 'real objects' called words, also characterizes the writing of another poet from the Bay Area, Philip Lamantia (1927–). Lamantia has claimed that he 'broke with surrealism in 1946': but it is clear that, like Spicer, he retains the essential surrealist quality of revealing the inner life via explosive patterns of imagery. So, his work, gathered in volumes like *Erotic Poems* (1946), *Eustasis* (1959) and *Meadowland West* (1986), uses disjunctive rhythms and an ecstatic tone, as well as kaleidoscopic images to create feelings of dread or rapture – sometimes religious, and sometimes inspired by drugs.

A similar extremism is to be found in the work of two other poets more loosely associated with the Bay Area, Philip Whalen (1923–) and Michael McClure (1932–). 'This poetry', Whalen said of his writing in 1959, 'is a picture or graph of a mind moving', and his poem 'The Same Old Jazz' (1957) shows what he means. For him, as he insists in this piece, there is 'A one-to-one relationship' between inner and outer, 'The world inside my head and the cat outside the window'. His aim is to dramatize that relationship, to write a kind of Abstract Expressionist diary in which abrupt, syncopated rhythms, a pacy idiom and images that are continually deliquescing into other images are all harnessed to the recreation of experience as a mixed-media event. Something that McClure says of his own work could, in fact, be applied to Whalen's poetry: 'I am the body, the animal, the poem / is a gesture of mine.' With McClure, however, the 'gesture' is a much more unnerving one because he chooses to confront and challenge the reader and, when-ever necessary, uses violence as a means of revelation. 'The poem . . . is black and white,' says McClure in 'Hymn to St. Geryon' (1959), 'I PICK IT UP BY THE TAIL AND HIT / YOU OVER THE HEAD WITH IT.' What McClure wants, he has said, is to 'BREAK UP THE FORMS AND FEEL THINGS', to 'Kick in the walls', literary, social and psychological – and that includes the conventional 'walls' or barriers between writer and reader. This is, perhaps, Thoreau's and Whitman's notion of self-emancipation through writing carried about as far as it can go: 'my viewpoint is ego-centric,' McClure has admitted; 'The poem is as much of me as an arm.' But while favouring 'the direct emotional statement from the body', like those earlier writers McClure is also intent on addressing and embracing the body, or identity, of his audience. 'Self-dramatisation is part of a means to belief and Spirit,' he claims; and 'hopefully . . . the reader' will learn about this by challenge and model – from the emancipation enacted by the 'loose chaos of words / on the page'.

Liberation is also an impulse at the heart of the work of Gary Snyder (1930–), who was born in San Francisco and has worked as a logger, forester and farmer in the Northwest. 'As much as the books I've read the jobs I've done have been significant in shaping me,' Snyder said in his book of essays, *Earth House Hold* (1969); 'My sense of body and language and the knowledge that . . . sensitivity and awareness are not limited to educated people.' Most of his poems (gathered in such collections as *A Range of Poems* [1966], *Turtle Island* [1974], *No Nature* [1992] and *Mountains and Rivers without End* [1996]) are direct and simple, characterized by an elemental reverence for existence and salvaging poetry from the most primitive human experiences. Unmarked by the normal tensions of language, they depend on lucidity and specificity, open forms and the 'rhythms of physical work . . . and life' for their impact. The simplicity of Snyder's work is not simplification, however. It derives in part from his devotion to Zen Buddhism; and it reflects his need to fill the 'Intricate layers of emptiness' where 'Human tenderness scuttles / Down dry endless cycles' with the peace of enlightenment, purification and quiet. Zen encourages the active appreciation of the natural world as an agent of vision, transcendence and elimination of the self; and its art of deft brushstrokes dispenses with calculated technique and structured reasoning in favour of immediate, spontaneous attention to living things. 'A poet faces two directions,' Snyder suggests, 'one is the world of people and language and society, and the other is the non-human, non-verbal world . . . the inner world, as it is itself, before language . . . custom, . . . culture.' Zen has helped Snyder to bridge the gap between these two worlds, to achieve 'a new sense' via a passionate encounter with objects; it has enabled him to find 'the way of activity', positive silence through the movements of body and speech.

'I hold the most archaic values on earth,' Snyder insists; 'They go back to the Paleolithic.' 'I try to hold history and the wilderness in mind,' he has added, 'that my poems may approach the true nature of our times.' For him, identification with 'that other totally alien, non-human' can be experienced in tilling the soil, shaping word or stone, 'the lust and ecstasy of the dance', or 'the power-vision in solitude'. And it has led him on naturally to a hatred of human assumptions of power and 'the ancient, meaningless / Abstractions of the educated mind'. His work celebrates such primary rituals as hunting and feasting ('Eating each other's seed / eating / ah, each other') and the mysteries of sex and birth ('How rare to be a human being!'): but, with its commitment to participation in nature rather than possession of it, it is equally capable of polemic, an unremitting radicalism of consciousness – something that is especially noticeable when Snyder directs his attention to the ecology and the 'Men who hire men to cut groves / Kill snakes, build cities, pave fields'. It is at this point, in particular, that Eastern and Western strains in his writing meet and marry. Snyder has learned about 'the buddha-nature', the intrinsic vitality lurking in all things, not just from Zen but from poets like Whitman; just as his habit of meditation rather than appropriation has been borrowed from Thoreau as well as the Buddhist tradition, and his belief in renewal springs from the spirit of the frontier as much as from oriental notions of the eternal cycle. In his eyes, enlightenment remains perpetually available, a fresh start can always be made. As Thoreau said at the end of *Walden* – and Snyder borrows the line for one of his poems – 'The sun is but a morning-star': each day represents a new opportunity to recover the nobility of life, another chance to turn aside from use to wonder.

Snyder, Ferlinghetti and many of the other San Francisco poets were also involved in the activities of another group that rose to prominence and notoriety in the 1950s, commonly known as 'the beat generation'. The term 'beat generation' seems to have been coined by one of the most famous members of the group, Jack Kerouac; and it has several relevant connotations. In a musical sense, the word 'beat' suggests keeping the beat, being in the groove or harmony with others. More specifically, it implies the jazz beat: beat poetry is, as one of the group has termed it, 'typewriter-jazz', aimed at catching the abrupt, syncopated rhythms, the improvisational dash and bravura of jazz, bebop and swing. In a social, psychological and vaguely political sense, 'beat' connotes the 'beaten' condition of the outsider, who is down perhaps but certainly not out. Like so many Romantic and American writers, the beats cherished the stance of the alienated, the dispossessed and even the nominally insane: those who look at normal, 'square' society from the periphery and reject its discipline and codes. As Allen Ginsberg put it, echoing a whole line of poets from Blake to Whitman and Dickinson, 'The madman is holy as you my soul are holy'. Finally, in a spiritual sense, 'beat' is related to 'beatitude' and describes the innocence, blessedness and raptness of what Ginsberg called 'angel-headed hipsters burning for the ancient heavenly connection': the pursuit of 'visionary consciousness' through music or meditation, drugs, mantras or poems. 'The only poetic tradition is the voice out of the burning bush', insisted Ginsberg, and that sums up an impulse shared by most of the beat generation. They were, undoubtedly, a remarkable social phenomenon, part of a decade that seemed suddenly to have invented adolescence and rebellion. More important, though, they were and are part of a great tradition that identifies imaginative writing with prophecy.

The beat generation was initially associated with New York, but it first attracted the interest of a larger public when, in 1956, Ginsberg, Kerouac and Gregory Corso joined Ferlinghetti, Snyder, Whalen and others in public reading appearances in the coffeehouses and colleges of San Francisco. And national fame was almost guaranteed with the confiscation of copies of Ginsberg's *Howl* by the San Francisco police in the same year, on the grounds that, as the Collector of Customs put it, 'The words and the sense of the writing are obscene'. *Howl*, Ginsberg's first published book of poems (although by no means his first stab at poetry), then sold over 50,000 copies within a relatively brief period of time. Along with Kerouac's *On the Road*, it became what Kenneth Rexroth, something of a father-figure for some of the beats, called 'the confession of faith of the generation that is going to be running the world in 1965 and 1975 – if it is still there to run'. For a while, the figure of the beat or the beatnik even attracted national media attention, although he (and it was usually a 'he' rather than a 'she') tended to be considered only to be mocked and dismissed. *Time* magazine, for instance, referred to the beat as 'a rebel without a cause who shirks responsibility on the grounds that he has the H-bomb jitters'. The liberal establishment was hostile, too: the critic and journalist Norman Podhoretz (1930–), for example, declared, 'No new territory is being staked out by these writers', while Diana Trilling (1905–96) sniffily observed, 'there is no more menace in "Howl" or *On the Road* than there is in the Scarsdale P.T.A.'. What such commentators seemed to object to was that, while the beat generation was anti-establishment, it was not involved with the kind of programmatic leftism that characterized many of the writers of the 1930s. Rather, it was committed to what critic Norman O. Brown (1913–2002) termed 'metapolitics': the politics of Blake, that is, in which psychological or spiritual freedom is the only sure warrant for political freedom.

There was, perhaps, no surer exponent of 'metapolitics' than the greatest poet of the beat generation, Allen Ginsberg (1926–97). When he took part in a demonstration against American involvement in Vietnam, for instance, he carried a placard that declared simply, 'War is black magic'. With him, as he said, poetry was 'a catalyst to visionary states of mind'; and he was assisted in his pursuit of a visionary goal by a mystical experience he had while still quite young. As he described it, he was reading Blake's poem 'Ah, Sun-Flower!' when he heard Blake's voice reciting the lines; it seemed to him, listening, as if 'God had a human voice'. He then had, he said, 'the consciousness of being alive unto myself, alive myself unto the creator'; more than that, he became convinced that he was 'the son of the Creator – who loved me . . . or who responded to my desire'. At first, Ginsberg attempted to insert his prophetic vision into what he later termed 'overwritten coy stanzas, a little after Marvell, a little after Wyatt'. This came to an end when William Carlos Williams commented, 'In this mode, perfection is basic, and these are not perfect'. Ginsberg needed, he now saw, to do what Williams and before him Whitman had done, 'to adapt . . . poetry rhythms out of . . . actual talk rhythms'; and he now recognized Whitman's long line as an appropriate precedent, a possible vehicle for what he called 'my romantic – inspiration – Hebraic-Melvillian bardic breath'. 'My breath is long,' Ginsberg declared, 'that's the Measure, one physical-mental inspiration of thought contained in the elastic of breath.' *His* breath, *his* speech was to be the organizer of the line, a perception to which he was helped not only by Whitman and Williams but also by the advice of Jack Kerouac. A jazz musician, Kerouac observed, and especially a saxophone player when improvising, is 'drawing breath and blowing a phrase . . . till he runs out of breath, and when he does, his sentence, his statement's been made'. This sense of drawing in the breath, in a way that reminds the reader at once of Charlie Parker and a prophet of the Old Testament, is what is perhaps most noticeable about the famous opening lines of *Howl* (1956):

> I saw the best minds of my generation destroyed
>   by madness, starving hysterical naked,
> dragging themselves through negro streets at dawn
>   looking for an angry fix . . .
>
>   . . .
>
> who poverty and tatters and hollow-eyed and high
>   sat up smoking in the supernatural darkness
>   of cold-water flats floating across the tops
>   of cities contemplating jazz . . .

Having established the basic beat in the opening lines, Ginsberg then relied, he said, on the word 'who' to retain it, to supply 'a base to keep the measure, return to and take off from again onto another stream of invention'. It offered a theme on which he could improvise, a rhythm he could twist and turn in response to what he once termed 'the actual movie of the mind'.

'Mind is shapely': that remark of Ginsberg's suggests how much a piece like *Howl* is committed to the discontinuities of consciousness and its sudden revelations. What he was after, he suggested, was 'the poem *discovered* in the mind and in the process of writing it out on the page'. For all their discontinuities, though, Ginsberg's poems do have paraphraseable arguments – or, if not that exactly, certain structures of feeling and assumption that are more immediately assimilable than those that animate earlier exercises in the ideogrammic method, like the *Cantos* and *Paterson*. *Howl*, for instance, is a grimly serious and yet comically surreal account of the betrayal of a generation. The first part explores the denial of the visionary impulse by forces like 'the narcotic tobacco haze of Capitalism' and celebrates its continuance in such subversive elements as 'angel-headed hipsters', 'saintly motorcyclists' and 'the madman bum and angel beat in Time'. In the second part, the poet denounces 'Moloch the loveless', the god of power and 'pure machinery', in a way that recalls earlier prophets like Isaiah. It suggests what another poet, Richard Eberhart, meant when he said the poem was 'profoundly Jewish in temper'; and it demonstrates Ginsberg's peculiar ability to combine the disjunctures of Modernism with melancholy, an ancient sense of apocalypse. Finally, the third part concentrates on the destiny of one man, Carl Solomon, whom the poet identifies with as an archetype of suffering. Fired by this identification, Ginsberg then projects an imaginary liberation for them both, where they 'wake up electrified out of coma' to their 'own souls' airplanes roaring over the roof'. That jubilant remark illustrates the mixture of religious intensity and wry realism which is one of Ginsberg's most memorable gifts. Poems like *Howl*, 'In Back of the Real' (1956) or 'A Supermarket in California' (1956) work precisely because they walk a tightrope between acknowledgement of the grubby particulars of everyday life and proclamations of the immanent presence of the ideal. Even moments of annunciation, statements of vision and purpose, can be tempered with a wise and sufficient irony – a measured appreciation of what, in 'Sunflower Sutra' (1956), the poet calls the 'skin of grime' covering 'all beautiful golden sunflowers inside'. And this is because, as Ginsberg saw it, the two, skin and sunflower, were inseparable. For him that 'battered old thing' known as the soul announced itself through the 'dread bleak dusty' apparitions of the body; the joy of the spirit was incarnated in the sadness of the flesh.

'It occurs to me that I am America, / I am talking to myself again.' These lines are another example of Ginsberg's capacity for being intimate and prophetic, comic and serious, at one and the same time. And they also express his very American desire to celebrate and sing himself as representative man: to present his poems as what he called 'a complete statement of Person'. As part of this statement, Ginsberg wrote some extraordinarily powerful accounts of personal grief, like 'Kaddish'

(1961), his fugue-like elegy to his mother. He also produced poems of passionate sexual encounter, such as 'Love Poem on Theme by Whitman' (1956), and other pieces, including 'The Reply' (1956), that describe his experience of drugs in terms that recall earlier, prophetic accounts of wrestling with God. In the 1960s, in particular, Ginsberg made his wanderings over America and the globe his subject: in poems that were, as he put it, 'not exactly poems nor not poems: journal notations put together conveniently, a mental turn-on'. Often spoken into a tape-recorder rather than composed on the page, they carried his commitment to 'mind-flow', 'jumps of perception from one thing to another', to a new extreme. 'All contemporary history', Ginsberg said, 'whatever floated into one's personal field of consciousness and contact' was drawn together here, 'like weave a basket, basket-weaving'. Some of these poems of the late 1960s and early 1970s reveal a greater commitment to the specifics of history; nevertheless, they do so from the standpoint of Ginsberg's root concerns. In 'Wichita Vortex Sutra' (1972), for instance, the poet denounced the Vietnam War. But 'The war is language', he insisted: that is, the Vietnam conflict was product and symptom of something deeper – the 'Black magic language' or 'formulas for reality' with which corporate America blinded itself. Ginsberg's answer to this problem was to construct a model of 'language known / in the back of the mind': a true vocabulary, enabling true vision, of the kind once sculpted by Whitman and Pound and now constituted by this poem as a whole. Like the *Cantos*, in effect, 'Wichita Vortex Sutra' situates moral and political failure in words and proposes itself as 'the right magic / Formula' for recovering the good of body, spirit and the body politic. 'I lift up my voice aloud,' announces Ginsberg, '/ Make mantra of American language now, / pronounce the words beginning my own millennium, / I here declare the end of the War!' A new language will promote a new vision and a new society: it is a noble aim and one that has haunted American writing ever since what Ginsberg refers to as 'the prophecy of the Good Gray Poet'.

In his later years, as *Death and Fame: Poems 1993–97* (1998) indicates, Ginsberg gravitated closer to Buddhism. The idea of 'an awakened emptiness' or 'no Self' that was always lurking in his earlier work now assumed more importance, promoting what the poet himself termed 'a less attached, less apocalyptic view'. He was trying hard, he said, to 'Avoid that mountain of ego vision!'; 'not even great Whitman's universal self', he claimed, suited him any longer. One side result of this was that the Blake epiphany interested him less than it had done. Another was that many of his poems in later collections directed gentle mockery at his own egotism, or surveyed the nightmares of contemporary history and his own story with a sense of acceptance, even distance. His poem about the death of his father, 'Don't Grow Old', included in *Collected Poems 1947–1985* (1986), charts the alteration: unlike 'Kaddish' it responds to loss not with rage but with a grave, melancholy quietude. 'What's to be done about Death?' Ginsberg asks, and then softly, with sad resignation, answers his own question: '/ Nothing, nothing.' This is not to say that such poems are unfeeling: but they place human emotion within the measureless scope of 'a relatively heavenly emptiness' and they aim to 'set surpassing example of sanity as measure for late generations'. Nor is it to ignore the continuities that underpin the evident change. The long line remains in evidence; so do humour, fits of exuberance, lust or anger, and the impulse to transmute verse into vision. Behind the Buddhist mask, in fact, the authentic American rebel was still at work; the voice of the prophet was still there, demanding to be heard.

Among the other beat poets, the most memorable is probably Gregory Corso (1930–2001). The writings of Peter Orlovsky (1933–) are too slight to constitute a distinctive body of work; and although Jack Kerouac wrote some interesting poems, like his variations on black musical forms 'Mexico City Blues' (1955), it was, as Ginsberg suggested, in his 'inspired prose' that he created 'really a new poetry'. Corso, on the other hand, evolved a distinct identity out of his poems, or perhaps it would be more accurate to say, identities. 'Should I get married? Should I be good?' begins one of his most famous pieces, 'Marriage' (1959), which then presents him trying out possible marriages, inventing potential selves, only to discard each one of them in turn. Jokey at times, at others wildly surreal, the poet is like Whitman's 'essential Me': standing apart from the game of life, and the roles and rules it prescribes, refusing to commit himself to a fixed, definite status. The rapidity of Corso's verse line is, in this sense, part of his message, as are his subversive humour and unpredictable alterations of pace and tone: the poet will not, it seems, be tied down by any of the institutions or forms that we use to organize life, whether they involve metre, stability of mood, or marriage. Chameleonlike, his is the voice of fluidity and change, the American as underground or confidence man. In his own way, in fact, Corso has tried to do what the novelist Ken Kesey has attempted in prose: 'to go with the flow', as Kesey puts it, to 'exist in the moment itself – Now!' – and to do this by means of mockery of other people's 'movies', conventional notions of the serious and the significant.

Reinventing the American self: The New York poets

Another, rather different vision of alternative America surfaces in the work of a group whose main connections have been with the visual arts, both 'high' and 'popular': the New York poets, among them Frank O'Hara, Kenneth Koch, Ted Berrigan and John Ashbery. 'Poetry was declining,' wrote the leading member of this group, Frank O'Hara (1926–66), in one of his poem-painting collaborations with the painter Larry Rivers, '/ Painting advancing / we were complaining / it was '50.' O'Hara felt at odds with most of the poetry that was being written in America in the 1950s. He deeply disliked the confessional poets, complaining that Lowell's 'confessional manner' let him 'get away with things that are just plain bad': 'but you're supposed to be interested', he added, 'because he's supposed to be so upset.' Ginsberg was a personal friend, but O'Hara studiously avoided the beat poet's revolutionary fervour and prophetic assumptions: politics and metaphysics were not among his immediate interests: 'I don't believe in god,' he said, '. . . You just go on your nerve.' As for the Black Mountain group, O'Hara was wary of what he saw as their programmatic approach. Of Olson he remarked, with a characteristic blend of sympathy and acumen, 'I don't think that he is willing to be as delicate as his sensibility may be emotionally and he's extremely conscious . . . of saying the important utterance'. He was less generous towards Creeley and Levertov, however, observing that they 'pared down the diction' to the point that what came through was 'the experience of their paring it down' rather than 'the experience that is the subject'. All these poets had too palpable designs on the reader, he believed: at some point, no matter how circuitous the route, they began to spin off beyond the hard material surfaces and processes of their purported subject. 'The objective in writing is to reveal,' O'Hara insisted; 'It is not to teach, to advertise, not to see, not even to communicate . . . but to reveal.' Too often this objective was ignored: succumbing to the 'symbols of an over-symbolic society', writers assumed an aesthetics of transcendence rather than what should be the case – an aesthetics of immediacy, of presence.

'I am needed by things', O'Hara declared, 'as the sky must be above the earth.' His aim was to defamiliarize the ordinary, even what he felt was the 'sheer ugliness in America': and, in order to do this, he wanted to be as attentive as possible to the world around him. It was the artist's 'duty to be attentive', he felt: so the artists he cherished were those like his friend Larry Rivers who, as he put it, 'taught me to be more keenly interested while I'm still alive'. 'Perhaps this is the most important thing art can say,' he suggested, and as a way of saying this himself – a means of assuring recognition of the lively details of the now – he pursued a poetic structure that was changing, shifting, quirky, quick and immediate. His literary mentors were people like Whitman, with whom O'Hara shared a belief in the multiple nature of identity ('Grace / to be born and live as variously as possible'), and Williams, whose commitment to seeing and mobility O'Hara appreciated ('How I hate . . . / . . . all things that don't change'). There was also Pound, whom he called 'the father of modern poetry in English'. More to the point, O'Hara clearly learned much from the Surrealists and Dadaists, who taught him how to capture the simultaneity of the instant. On a strictly literary level, in fact, O'Hara's development could be charted through his *Selected Poems* (1974), from his early experiments in what might be termed 'straight Surrealism' ('Chez Jane') and, rather different, his imitations of American writers such as Williams ('Les Étiquettes Jaunes') to the mature poetry of the late 1950s where the two modes are wedded. The result of this union – between a surreal understanding of the elusive, metamorphic nature of things and a toughly empirical American idiom – is poetry that can shift, with astonishing speed, from flat literalism to fantasy and then back again. But to talk in strictly literary terms about O'Hara or the other New York poets is only to tell half the story. 'After all,' O'Hara mischievously remarked, 'only Whitman and Crane and Williams, of the American poets, are better than the movies.' He, and his friends, were interested in an art fired into life by the moment; and that meant certain kinds of poetry, undoubtedly, but also all forms of dance, the *motion* picture and *action* painting.

'We . . . divided our time between the literary bar, the San Remo, and the artists' bar, the Cedar Tavern,' O'Hara later said of his early days together with Ashbery and Koch, '... the painters were the only generous audience for our poetry.' A rapport was quickly established between the poets and painters as diverse as Jasper Johns, Larry Rivers, Robert Rauschenberg, Grace Hartigan and Willem de Kooning. All of them shared the excitement of New York City: which was, as they saw it, a model of simultaneity, the place where more was happening at one moment than anywhere else in the world. By comparison, the rest of the country, and especially the countryside, seemed stale: 'I can't even enjoy a blade of grass', O'Hara claimed, 'unless I know there's a subway handy, or a record store or some other sign that people do not totally *regret* life.' The shared excitement issued in collaborative work, poem-paintings and mixed-media performances, and in mutual appreciation: O'Hara was and Ashbery still is a distinguished art critic, while O'Hara was also a curator at the Museum of Modern Art. Above all, it generated a common aesthetic, one that perceived the surface of the poem or painting as a field on which the physical energies of the artist could operate, without mediation of metaphor or symbol. 'Now please tell me', wrote O'Hara in a letter to Larry Rivers, in which he enclosed some of his work, 'if you think these poems are filled with disgusting self pity ... if the surface isn't "kept up" ... or if they don't have "push" and "pull".' That request signals his priorities, those imperatives of artistic creation that he shared with other members of the New York group. The surface is to be 'kept up': that is the first imperative. The artwork should not be 'reflective, or self-conscious', there should be nothing *behind* it. A successful relation of verbal imagery or visual planes should create a lively, depthless microcosm of the artist's world, as empirically verifiable as a street map yet also surreal, fantastic – since it involves mind as well as scene, the *active* engagement of the artist with subject matter and materials. In turn, the audience responding to the work should 'travel over the complicated surface exhaustively': that is the second imperative. The audience, in effect, should be no more self-indulgent than the artist is, and no more detached: they should give themselves up to the lively play of figuration, the 'marvellous burgeoning into life', that constitutes the work, continually refreshing their instinctive sense of what it 'says'. 'The best of the current sculpture', O'Hara insisted, 'didn't make me feel I wanted to *have* one, they made me feel I wanted to *be* one.' And it is precisely this surrendering of the self to surface, not interpreting but participating, that he aimed for in his own work. If the poem or painting creates presence, he believed, and if the audience is as attentive to presence as the artist has been, then the process of identification is complete.

O'Hara's own term for this aesthetic he shared with other poets and painters was 'Personism'. He even wrote his own 'manifesto' for this 'Personism'. Characteristically, this is both an act of comic bravado (he had an instinctive distrust of programmes of any kind and this, in part, is a witty parody of them) and a serious statement of intention. 'Personism', the poet tells us, 'puts the poem squarely between the poet and the person ... The poem is at last between two persons instead of two pages.' True to this credo, there is a quality of intimate conversation to much of O'Hara's poetry – of talk 'between two persons' that is at once familiar and fantastic. 'It is 12.10 in New York and I am wondering / if I will finish this in time to meet Norman for lunch /', is a typical opening ('Adieu to Norman, Bon Jour to Joan and Jean-Paul'); 'ah lunch! I think I am going crazy / what with my terrible hangover and the weekend coming up.' The voice talking here, however, is not a confessional but a responsive one, eager to attend to the continuum of things and ready for immersion in the processes it contemplates. O'Hara does not reflect in a traditional way nor try to extrapolate significances. Instead, he swims in the medium of his feeling and being, inviting us to come into momentary awareness of things just as he does. He traces, say, the disjunctive movements of his sensibility ('In Memory of my Feelings', 'Ode (to Joseph Le Sueur) on the Arrow that Flieth by Day'). Or he compels us into attention to the total environment of the city: its noises ('a faint stirring of that singing seems to come to me in heavy traffic'), its shifting qualities of light ('the cool graced light / is pushed off the enormous glass piers'), its discontinuities, surprises and the 'strange quiet excitement' it can generate. As he does so, he alerts us to his own instinctive belief that 'the 'slightest loss of attention leads to death'. Life in these terms has an immanent rather than transcendent value: it is, as O'Hara himself put it once, 'just what it is and just what happens'. 'I'm not going to cry all the time, / nor shall I laugh all the time,' O'Hara announces in 'My Heart', '/ I don't prefer one strain to another.' 'I want my face to be shaven,' he continues, 'and my heart – / you can't plan on the heart, but / the better part of it, my poetry, is open.'

How does O'Hara achieve this 'openness', and so dodge the habitual? On a larger scale, he does so by opting for a range of tone and form. There are his 'I do this, I do that' poems, like 'Joe's Jacket', 'Personal Poem' and 'Lana Turner has Collapsed!'; and there are also more intensely surreal pieces, such as 'Second Avenue', Whitmanesque odes like 'To the Film Industry in Crisis', and powerfully erotic lyrics of homosexual love, the most striking of which perhaps is 'You are Gorgeous and I'm Coming'. On the more local level of the individual poem, O'Hara's discomposing mix of literalism and surrealism works with other strategies to strip away the veneer of habituation. His lineation, for instance, with its ambivalent positioning of words, constant breaks and compulsive enjambement, generates tension, a sense of breakneck speed. At the same time, an elaborate system of syntactical ambiguity, based on non-sequiturs, pseudo-connectives, ellipses and dangling, incomplete sentences, helps turn the poem into an instantaneous performance, denied conventional divisions of beginning, middle and end. Like a Cubist or Abstract Expressionist painter, O'Hara scrambles his representational clues, preferring complex effects of simultaneity, the clash of surfaces, to the illusions of depth and coherence. There are constant temporal and spatial dissolves too; the poet shifts rapidly from one place to another without the usual semantic props, such as 'when', 'after' or 'before'. Everything, as a result, is absorbed into an undifferentiated stream of activity, the flow of the now – as in these lines from 'Rhapsody', where an elevator ride in Manhattan becomes a trip to heaven becomes a voyage into a Hollywood jungle:

515 Madison Avenue
door to heaven? Portal
stopped realities and eternal licentiousness
or at least the jungle of impossible eagerness
your marble is bronze and your lianas elevator cables
swinging from the myth of ascending
I would join . . .

'O'Hara's poetry has no programme', John Ashbery has insisted, 'and therefore cannot be joined.' This is perfectly true. Nevertheless, many poets have felt an affinity with him, and shared at least some of his purposes. Their personal affection for him has been expressed in the numerous elegies that appeared after his death, the most notable of which, perhaps, are 'Strawberries in Mexico' (1969) by Ron Padgett (1942–), 'Buried at Springs' (1969) by James Schuyler (1923–91), and 'Frank O'Hara' (1967) by Ted Berrigan (1934–83). And the sense of aesthetic kinship is evident not only from what members of the New York group have said about O'Hara but also from particular poetic habits. The attention to surface, the unexpected line breaks and gamey, casual idiom, the switchback movement between the literal and surreal, an almost voyeuristic attention to empirical detail and an expressionist involvement in the poem as field of action: all, or at least some, of these characteristics help to mark out writers like Schuyler, Berrigan, Barbara Guest, Kenneth Koch and Ashbery himself. But of course such writers are not possessed of a corporate mind and, as Ashbery points out, were not following a formulated programme; so, inevitably, very clear differences have emerged between them. The poetry of Barbara Guest (1920–), for instance, whose *Selected Poems* appeared in 1995, is edged with delicacy of feeling and a frail exoticism: 'In the golden air, the risky autumn / leaves on the piazza, shadows by the door /', begins her poem 'Piazzas', 'on your chair the red berry / after the dragon fly summer.' Schuyler similarly recomposes landscape in a painterly manner, finding new shapes and patterns, but he possesses an intrinsic reverence for nature that is rare among the group. These lines taken from his elegy to O'Hara are a poignant illustration not only of tenderness but also of the difference of sensibility between their author and their subject (who once claimed that 'One need never leave the confines of New York to get all the greenery one wishes'):

Delicate day, setting the bright
of a young spruce against the cold
of an old one with unripe cones
each exuding at its tip
gum, pungent, clear as a tear . . .

Some of the poems of Ted Berrigan are embarrassingly derivative of O'Hara: 'Today I woke up / bright and early,' 'Today in Ann Arbor' (1969) begins, '/ Then I went back to sleep / I had a nice dream.' What is more, they imitate O'Hara's reverence for detail while missing his extraordinary modulations of tone, his split-second dissolves and syntactic displacements; as a result, the mood is slack, tending towards a simple empiricism, a catalogue of particulars that do not really add up. At its best, though, Berrigan's work has a memorable clarity that issues from his willingness to put the 'I'/eye of the poet at the centre of things: as he says of New York, 'it's only here you can turn around 360 degrees / And everything is clear from the centre / To every point along the circle of the horizon'. This clarity can sometimes be the clarity of consciousness (he can create hallucinatory effects out of the condition of 'Sleep half sleep half silence'), the clarity of American speech (many of his poems, like those of Williams, are vignettes of urban life and idiom), or forthright clarity of feeling. So, in 'Last Poem' (to be found in *New and Selected Poems, 1958–79* [1980]), the epitaph he composed for himself, Berrigan declares simply, 'Love, & work, / Were my great happiness, that other people die the source / Of my great, terrible, & inarticulate one grief'. 'In my time,' he adds, 'I grew tall & huge of frame, obviously possessed / Of a disconnected head, I had a perfect heart. The end / Came quickly & completely without pain.' Kenneth Koch (1925–2002) is less immediately serious than this: 'I think I have three souls,' he announced in 'Alive for an Instant' (1975), '/ One for love one for poetry and one for acting out my insane self.' His poems are alive with wild, surreal comedy, rambunctious rhythms and verbal inventiveness; it is as if they were written by a Kafka with a slapstick sense of humour. His aim, he said, was to 'recreate the excitement', the spontaneity and exuberance, he found in French poetry; and the main objects of his aesthetic loathing were what he called the 'castrati of poetry', 'Young poets from the universities' who wrote 'elegant poems' in 'stale pale skunky pentameters'. At the heart of his writing is an absurdist sense that poets and readers alike are victims of 'an absolute and total misunderstanding (but not fatal)'; and the result is that nearly everything he wrote, from parodies of other poets ('Variations on a Theme by William Carlos Williams' [1962]) through surrealistic love poems ('To You' [1958]) to autobiography ('Alive for an Instant' [1962]), is edged with a verbal grin that is simultaneously playful and grim.

Apart from O'Hara, however, the most significant poet associated with the New York group is John Ashbery (1927–). Ashbery has written in a variety of genres. *A Nest of Ninnies* (1969), written with James Schuyler, is a novel satirizing the vacuous lives of two suburban families. *The Heroes* (1952), *The Compromise* (1956) and *The Philosopher* (1956) are plays that exploit, and sometimes travesty, conventional forms from classical myth to detective story drama. The international edition of the *New York Herald Tribune* became the outlet for his extensive art criticism. But it is for his poetry that he has become well known. Ashbery published his first book of poems, *Turandot and Other Poems*, in 1953. Other notable volumes include *Some Trees* (1956), *The Tennis Court Oath* (1962), *Rivers and Mountains* (1966), *Self-Portrait in a Convex Mirror* (1975), *A Wave* (1984), *Flow Chart* (1991) and *Girls on the Run: A Poem* (1999). Ashbery first encountered O'Hara at Harvard, and when O'Hara moved to Manhattan in 1951 the two met regularly. 'Frank got me interested in contemporary music,' Ashbery has recalled. 'American painting seemed the most exciting art around,' he added, 'and most of my feeling for Rothko and Pollock came through Frank.' The enthusiasms the two poets shared generated at least some similar tendencies in their poetry. There is the same commitment to the work as personal idiom, for instance, the discontinuous activities of individual experience: 'I know that I braid too much my own / snapped-off perceptions as they come to me /', admits Ashbery in 'The One Thing That Can Save America', 'They are private and always will be.' There is, too, a similar estrangement from simple mimesis, a shared belief that poetry does not reflect reality, it constitutes it: which leads, in turn, to a relentless opposition to systematics ('there's no excuse / For always deducing the general from particulars'), consistency ('I often change my mind about my poetry,' he has said) and the illusion of meaning. 'What does it mean??????????????' he asks of one of his poems, during the course of writing it; and the fourteen question marks slyly subvert the assumptions, the need for cause and explanation, that lie behind the question. 'Most of my poems are about the experience of experience,' Ashbery has remarked, in one of his rare moments of elucidation, '. . . and the particular experience is of lesser interest to me than the way it filters through me.' 'I believe this is the way in which it happens with most people,' he declares, 'and I'm trying to record a kind of generalized transcript of what's really going on in our minds all day long.' According to these terms, if the poem is a verbal graph of the consciousness, then the poet is a transparent medium through which the experiences of the day flow; and the words of the poem, in turn, constitute the notations, the signs that cease to apply as quickly and imperceptibly as the experiences they signify, and the moment of consciousness that acted as signifier.

Another way of putting all this, and signalling the difference between Ashbery and O'Hara, is to say that Ashbery's is a poetry of absence. Ashbery has said as much himself. 'The carnivorous / way of these lines is to devour their own nature,' he confides in 'Grand Galop', 'leaving / Nothing but a bitter impression of absence, which as we know involves presence.' 'Nevertheless,' he adds, 'these are fundamental absences, struggling to get up and be off themselves.' There are various influences at work here, to which O'Hara was more or less immune: among them Poe, with his belief in a poetry that disappears as it is read, and Stevens, with his interest in epistemology, the mind's baffling encounter with the objects it contemplates. Also, the example of Gertrude Stein is not to be discounted, since what Stein called 'counting one by one' to create 'a continually moving picture' – with 'no memory', no 'assembling' or 'relating', no increasing density of significance – is what Ashbery does. His poetry deflates our expectation of sense, or presence, by offering us always the playful, fluid zone of deferred sense, suspended meaning. 'Someday I'll explain,' he promises jokily in 'Ode to Bill', 'Not today though.' The 'I' that shadows his writing consequently resembles Sartre's existential man, in whom, as Sartre puts it, 'acts, emotions, and ideas suddenly settle . . . and then disappear'. 'You cannot say he submits to them,' Sartre points out; 'He experiences them. There seems to be no law governing their appearance.'

Ashbery's earliest published poems, such as 'Some Trees', are mainly concerned with the operations of the sleeping consciousness, and are activated by the belief that the function of the poet is, as he puts it, to 'give fullness / To the dream'. These were followed by his experimenting, at roughly the same time as O'Hara, in 'straight surrealism'. In poems like 'Europe' and 'They Dream Only of America', fractured images, jumbles of non-sequiturs and techniques of verbal collage are used to dramatize the humiliating and reifying aspects of modern life. But it has been from the later 1960s on that Ashbery has hit his real stride, with poems such as 'The Skaters', 'Self-Portrait in a Convex Mirror', 'A Wave' and the 216-page poem that constitutes *A Flow Chart*, as well as prose pieces like 'The System'. No one work is entirely characteristic of his mature writing, since each new one tends to constitute an act of renewal. What is common with them all, however, as Ashbery tries to realize what he calls 'the quirky things that happen to me', are certain stylistic features. An irresolute syntax, the casual use of slang, cliché and apparent redundancies, false starts and backtracking, free associations, occasional opacity of phrasing and the equally occasional hard, focused image: all these are the verbal weapons of a mind in process – or, rather, a mind that *is* process, a medium in which disparate objects meet and merge. The long, serpentine verse paragraphs Ashbery favours hold the different elements in close physical contiguity, as if the writer were trying to create a multidimensional space, a 'seamless web' in which everything could be folded into everything else. This is a poetry which insists that structures are always virtual, always to-be-known or, more exactly, always to-be-inferred. And this is a poet who insists on the disjunctive nature of history and personality. Historical experience, evidently, is a 'tangle of impossible resolutions and irresolutions', which happen outside the neat demarcations of sagas and story-tellers. 'The sagas purposely ignore how better it was the next day', Ashbery observes, '/ the feeling in between the chapters', and it is clear he does not want to imitate them. Personality, in turn, is stripped of conclusive choices: 'I cannot decide in what direction to walk,' the poet admits in 'Grand Galop', adding happily, '/ But this doesn't matter to me.' Lacking such determinants, the coordination of a particular road taken, it too becomes shadowy, as shifting and irresolute as the language that enacts its absence, its baffling and blank contingency.

'All was strange': the closing remark in 'A Wave' sounds a theme that resonates through Ashbery's poetry and the work of other contemporary American poets, not all of them necessarily identified with the New York group. The metamorphoses of consciousness, the absolute ravishment of the senses by the radiant surfaces of the world, are, for instance, the primary intuitions of a writer who is in many respects hauntingly different from Ashbery or O'Hara, James Merrill (1926–95). Merrill is commonly associated with the disciples of the New Critical school and, in a strictly formal sense, there is some truth to this association: much of his work, a useful selection of which is to be found in *From the First Nine* (1982), is characterized by a delicate, ironic verbal wit, formal prosody, careful crafting of syntax and metaphor, and a baroque sense of decor. He betrays traces of the confessional tendency too, in that some of his poems deal with painful autobiographical material: his tangled erotic involvement with his mother, say ('The Broken Home', 'Emerald'), his fiercely Oedipal relationship with his father ('Scenes from Childhood'), or the pleasures and pains of being a homosexual ('Days of 1964', 'Mornings in a New House'). That said, however, it has to be added that Merrill begins and ends where Ashbery and O'Hara do: with what Merrill himself, in 'Transfigured Bird', calls 'the eggshell of appearance'. There may be a perilous abyss beneath *this* surface, perhaps, but what Merrill senses always is the inevitability and necessity of masks, screens, fictions. In fact, the eye that attempts to peer beneath the 'glassen surface' of things is for him a kind of predator – a monster. Life, in Merrill's view, is 'fiction in disguise'. As poets and as people, our function is to skim over the surfaces that constitute our known world 'with an assurance of safety – the thoughtful ease of someone skating upon a sheet of ice . . . formed above a black torrent'. This may be 'a form of flight', Merrill admits, 'but it is also a form of healing': the surfaces we stay poised above are 'protecting' ones, sheltering us from waste and anxiety, unconditional surrender to the void.

If Merrill's lyric poems aestheticize autobiography, reflecting what he calls 'the dull need to make some kind of house / Out of the life lived, and out of the love spent', then his epic trilogy *The Changing Light at Sandover* (1982) expresses a larger desire to create an aesthetic for survival. Written in a variety of poetic forms, the trilogy was the result, Merrill claimed, of a communion with spirits: into it he poured his beliefs and fears, spread among passages of revelation that were spelled out to him on an ouija board. 'The design of the book swept me along,' he said: this is an epic as formless and personal, as locked into process and possibility, as all other American epics. It can sometimes be as absurd or narcissistic as, say, 'Song of Myself': as, for instance, when the poet tries to argue that homosexuals are the ultimate triumph of evolution, the true creators of poetry and music, 'THOSE 2 PRINCIPAL LIGHTS OF GOD BIOLOGY'. Equally, it can be as obscure as the *Cantos* or the *Maximus Poems* occasionally are, as prosaic as passages in *Paterson* or *Notebook*, as fragmented and bewildering as *The Bridge* or *The Dream Songs*. Along with these and other experiments in this genre, though, it is also possessed of a fierce energy, the animating conviction that there is still time to choose between the apocalypse and the millennium. On the one hand, Merrill points out, there is the danger of global destruction wrought by 'ANIMAL SOULS', the passive victims of technology and their own destructive impulses. On the other, there is the opportunity of a new life, a paradise on earth springing from the liberation of the imaginative intelligence and its discovery of a redemptive fiction. 'Stevens imagined the imagination / And God are one,' Merrill observes: 'the imagination, also / As that which presses back, in parlous times / Against "the pressure of reality".' Merrill was clearly in agreement with this: the words and artefacts fashioned by feeling were for him, as for so many other American writers, an access to a saving knowledge of our predicament. They are as necessary, he implies, as breath and bread; and in this sense the true opposite of poetry is not prose or science but annihilation.

In prose, resistance to orthodox culture took various forms, even among those predominantly white male writers who formed the major part of the beat movement. Just how various these forms could be, within the ranks of those associated with the beats, is suggested by the contrast between Jack Kerouac (1922–69) and William Burroughs (1914–97). Outside the movement, a similar contrast is registered by other major figures of literary dissent: Henry Miller (1891–1980), J. D. Salinger (1919–), Charles Bukowski (1920–94), Richard Brautigan (1935–84) and Ken Kesey (1935–2001). Dissent has not, of course, been the monopoly of these writers. On the contrary, dissent and its literary corollary, experiment, could be said to be *the* American way. What these writers have had in common, however (and it was sometimes all they had in common), is a primary, pivotal interest in the aesthetics and politics of rebellion. There has been a thin, sometimes invisible, line between their own lives and the lives of their protagonists, disaffiliated from mainstream culture, driven or directed by their own choice to the social margins. And there has been a similarly narrow line between the status of their work as imaginative document and as social handbook. Their writing, with its search for an alternative to what Kerouac once called 'the whorey smell' of orthodox America, has influenced several generations not just to imagine but to try out different lives, to create a separate territory for themselves. The consequences of that attempt have been various social movements: while Kerouac inspired the beats, Burroughs has clearly influenced both the beat and the psychedelic movements, and Kesey and Brautigan, in turn, have helped to shape hippie and other, later forms of alternative culture. Which is, in its own way, another honourable American tradition, from the time of the Puritan preachers and writers through to the Transcendentalists. Behind the hippie commune, after all, hovers the shadow of earlier attempts to live the lives of the visible saints; behind the lonely, mobile heroes of Kerouac, Kesey and even Salinger lie many other romantic egotists, bragging or yearning for humanity as much as for themselves.

Jack Kerouac was born Jean-Louis Kerouac in Massachusetts. After a Catholic upbringing, he roamed about the United States, taking various odd jobs, and worked as a merchant seaman before writing the first of his semi-autobiographical novels, *The Town and the City* (1950), about a family in his home town of Lowell. *On the Road* followed in 1957. It established Kerouac as the novelist of the beats, just as *Howl* identified Ginsberg as their poet. Several books that followed were similarly documents of beat consciousness, although they also reflected their author's growing interest in the discovery of truth or 'dharma' through Zen Buddhism: *The Subterraneans* (1958), *The Dharma Bums* (1958), *Tristessa* (1960), *Big Sur* (1962) and *Desolation Angels* (1965). Other books, still beat in sensibility, were evocations of Kerouac's childhood: *Doctor Sax* (1959), *Maggie Cassidy* (1959) and *Visions of Gerard* (1963). Still others described his search for his Breton ancestors (*Satori in Paris* [1966]), his travels (*Lonesome Traveller* [1960]) and his recollections of his life and his friends and, in particular, of Neal Cassady, his travelling companion (*Visions of Cody* [1972]). What is common to all these books, and to his poems collected in *Mexico City Blues* (1959), is an urgent, rhythmic style that works through repetition and an excited, evocative tone to create a feeling of spontaneity and intimacy. Kerouac pushed to an intense extreme the insight of Whitman: that, ideally, who touches the book touches the man. He was also clearly inspired, as Whitman was, by the sheer vastness, the space of the American continent: it is no accident that the final paragraph of *On the Road* has the narrator contemplating that space. 'So in America when the sun goes down,' he declares, '... I ... sense all that raw land that rolls in one unbelievable huge bulge over to the West Coast, and all that road going, all the people dreaming in the immensity of it.'

On the Road, more energetically than any of Kerouac's other novels, brings American self and American space together, in a celebration of the vastness, the potential, of both. The protagonist and narrator is Sal Paradise. Clearly a self-portrait of the author, Paradise is a struggling writer in his mid-twenties. He tells of his encounters with Dean Moriarty, a teenager whose soul is 'wrapped up in a fast car, a coast to reach, and a woman at the end of the road'. During the next five years they travel from coast to coast, either with each other or to each other. Five trips are described, during the course of which Dean meets and deserts different wives and lovers. Sal has a brief affair with one of Dean's partners and sells his novel to a publisher. Nothing substantial, in terms of plot, seems to have happened by the end, although, having been abandoned by him in Mexico, Sal continues to 'think of Old Dean Moriarty, the father we never found'. Plenty occurs, of course, but events possess the fluidity of a stream, say, rather than the fixity of narrative form. Things happen, and then our heroes move on to encounter something else, something new in the experiential and fictional process. Like those heroes, the reader is initiated into a contact with the now, life as present and process. Style and structure similarly invite us to freewheel through the open spaces of personality and geography. This lends a curiously amoral dimension to the fictional space Kerouac describes: the narrative is interested not so much in evaluation as in experience (which is one reason why Dean's casual, even brutal, treatment of women receives less criticism than it deserves). And the experience that interests author and narrator here, above all, is the love, loneliness and longing they feel, in equal measure, as they contemplate the apparently boundless territories they travel over, in fact or imagination. What the book charts, finally, is what is called at one point 'all the wilderness of America', at once liberating and terrifying: a world that stretches out as far as the eye can see and, within, far beyond what the mind can know.

Just as Sal Paradise is Kerouac in fictional disguise, so Dean Moriarty is Kerouac's friend, Neal Cassady. Another character in *On the Road*, Carlo Marx, is Allen Ginsberg. And another, Bull Lee, is William Burroughs. 'Bull Lee' is described as a teacher who 'had every right to teach because he spent all his time learning'. 'The things he learned were what he considered to be and called "the facts of life"'; and he learned them, Paradise explains, by dragging 'his long, thin body around the entire United States and most of Europe and North Africa'. He learned them by studying Shakespeare ('the "Immortal Bard" he called him') and the Mayan Codices. He learned them by 'experimenting with narcoanalysis'. 'Now his final study', we are told, 'was the drug habit.' Kerouac captures here some of the obsessive themes and pursuits of Burroughs's life – the voracious curiosity and experimentation, for instance – but by no means all: which is hardly surprising, given that Kerouac died young while Burroughs, after being involved with the beats, lived most of a long life as an expatriate, in Paris, Tangiers and elsewhere. What Kerouac misses, in particular, is the formative influence on Burroughs of two circumstances in particular: his experiences as a drug addict (although, admittedly, Kerouac begins to touch on this) and as a homosexual in the claustrophobic moral climate of Cold War America. Among the first books Burroughs wrote, in fact, were two dealing precisely with these two circumstances: *Junkie*, published under the pseudonym of William Lee in 1953, and *Queer*, which was written in 1953 but not published until thirty-two years later. Starting from his own experiences with drug addiction – in which the body is 'fixed' by an alien power that enters and takes it over – Burroughs began to develop a whole mythology of need and control. 'The algebra of need', as Burroughs calls it, means that need creates subservience, allowing malign forces of all kinds to enter and exploit the individual consciousness. 'The face of "evil"', the reader is told at the beginning of *The Naked Lunch* (Paris, 1959; New York, 1962), 'is always the face of total need.' And his experience as a homosexual, in a homophobic postwar culture that identified gay people with other repressed enemies of the state like Communists, allowed him to recognize how forms of control could be exercised in the body politic and the American body politic in particular. For Burroughs, the malign forces bent on absorbing or exploiting the unique identity of the individual are omnipresent, waiting to do their parasitic work: 'I can feel the heat closing in,' the narrative of *The Naked Lunch* begins, 'feel them out there making their moves.' 'The US drag closes around us like no other drag in the world . . . there is no other drag like the US drag,' the reader is told later on in the same book; 'You can't see it, you don't know where it comes from.'

Undoubtedly, Burroughs's most powerful fictional exploration of the algebra of need, the virus of control that enters bodies and bodies politic, and the dream of being freed from all conditioning forces is *The Naked Lunch*. An intense rendering not only of the horrors of addiction but also of the cultural illusions for which addiction functions as a metaphor, the book has no narrative continuity and no sustained point of view. Its separate episodes are not interrelated; they simply coexist in a particular field of force, brought together by the mind of William Burroughs, which then abandons them. And its title means just what it says: 'a frozen moment when everyone sees what is on the end of every fork'. To produce such frozen moments, when we can see the ugly object inside the egg, the worm inside a piece of fruit – both of which are images for the corruptions inside civilization – is the project of the narrative. This Burroughs pursues creating a series of wastelands, dark cities and barren landscapes that hover somewhere between cartoon and nightmare, the surreal and science fiction. They are populated by such

strange creatures as Dr Benway, 'a manipulator and co-ordinator of symbol systems', Dr Shafer, the Lobotomy Kid who produces 'The Complete All American
De-anxietized man', and various victims whose consciousness and humanity are
gradually cancelled – 'finally the brain must have died', we are told of one of them,
'because the eyes *went out*'. 'Which ride are you on?' the reader is asked at one
point, 'Fro-Zen Hydrolic? Or do you want to take a look around with Honest Bill?'
The reference to Fro-Zen Hydrolic is part of an image series which compares the
spine of the junkie to a frozen hydraulic jack when his metabolism has nearly
reached zero. Most people, the narrative intimates, collude with or surrender to a
system, a power that reduces them to a similar state of inertia, a comparable
deathly coldness. What that narrative offers, as an alternative to this, is a chance to
'look around with Honest Bill': to become alert not only to the ways human
identity is devoured and dissolved in the modern world but to the possibility of
resistance, even release. The reader, Burroughs insisted, could cut into *The Naked
Lunch* at any point: so as to enjoy the spontaneity and independence of constituting his or her own system. It offers this too through a play of different language
habits. No verbal code, no code or construction of reality prevails, as Burroughs
moves towards what he was eventually to call his goal: 'the writing of silence'.

That phrase suggests the predicament Burroughs faced, with increasing intensity.
If he started his work out of a sense of vulnerability to drug addiction and social
stigmatization – two powerful ways in which the alien can enter and take over the
body – his emphasis gradually shifted to word addiction, language as an ultimate
form of control. 'They are rebuilding The City . . . in Four Letter Words . . .
Vibrating Air Hammers The Code Write' is an entry in Burroughs's next work
after *The Naked Lunch*, *The Exterminator* (1960), written with Brion Gysin. '*Rub
out the word forever*' is the call in a later novel, *Nova Express* (1964). Both remarks
register the tension at the heart of his work: he was using language against itself.
Intent on liberating the consciousness from all forms of control, the weapon he
had at his disposal for this purpose was, as he saw it, the original and ultimate
controlling agent. 'WHAT SCARED YOU INTO TIME?' Burroughs wrote once to Allen
Ginsberg; 'I WILL TELL YOU, THE WORD.' Burroughs's response to this dilemma,
this question of how to achieve 'the writing of silence' and so liberate the self from
all systems, and from verbal ones in particular, took several forms. Like Pound, he
became interested in other cultures and vocabularies that resist the abstractions
and oppositions of Western language and thought. In his case, as *The Yage Letters*
(1963) indicates, this drove him more towards the Mayan codices. He also became
convinced, as *The Ticket that Exploded* (1967) suggests, that, while human beings
are vulnerable to damaging instructions fed into them as on to a tape-recorder, the
tape can be wiped clean; the ticket of entry into contemporary reality can be
exploded or impounded. 'Why not take over the ticket?' we are asked. And one,
seminal way of taking over the ticket, a logical development of earlier verbal
experiments in *The Naked Lunch*, is what Burroughs called the cut-up method.
Which is just that. Words and phrases are cut up into fragments and rearranged at
random so as to create not propositions or declarative statements but suggestive

word series. 'The Word Lines keep thee in Slots,' the reader is told in *The Exterminator*, 'Cut the Word Lines with scissors or switch blade as preferred The Word Lines keep you in time . . . Cut in lines . . . Make out line to Space.' How successful Burroughs was in his 'blocks of association', using language to destroy language, is a matter for debate. What is clear, however, is that he was responding to a need, felt by the beats and many earlier American writers, to shuffle off all constraints on the self. 'Words, at least the way we use them, can stand in the way of what I call non-body experience,' Burroughs said (using words, of course). That answers to an imperative as old, at least, as the dream of America: to escape from the constraints of society, history, language or whatever, to lose even the constrictions of a particular identity in a condition of absolute space, a fluid territory that lies somewhere ahead.

The freedom, the resistance to orthodoxy embraced by Henry Miller and Charles Bukowski is simpler. And the nature of that freedom is suggested by the fact that both men wrote a kind of fictive autobiography. Miller was a traveller, living in various areas of the United States and for ten years as an expatriate in Europe. Among his many works, the best known is *Tropic of Cancer*, which was published in France in 1934 but not in the United States until 1961. 'This is not a book,' Miller declares at the beginning. 'No, this is a prolonged insult, a gob of spit in the face of Art, a kick in the pants to God, Man, Destiny, Time, Love, Beauty . . . what you will.' 'I am going to sing for you,' Miller insists, 'a little off key perhaps, but I will sing.' What he sings of here, in a literal sense, is his life as an expatriate in Paris: his adventures in art, his sexual relations, his quasi-philosophical and aesthetic musings, all animated by his belief that 'more obscene than anything is inertia'. What he sings of, here and elsewhere, more generally, is his conviction that (as he puts it in *Tropic of Capricorn* [France, 1939; US, 1962]) 'there is only one great adventure and that is inward towards the self'. 'The aim of life is to live,' Miller insisted in *Black Spring* (France, 1939; US, 1962), 'and to live means to be aware, joyously, drunkenly, serenely, divinely aware.' 'In this state of godlike awareness one sings,' he added, 'in this realm the world exists as a poem.' Drawing on a realm of influences, including Eastern religion, Walt Whitman and D. H. Lawrence, Miller presents himself in his work as a man alive in just this way: 'a pre-Socratic being', as he puts it, 'a creature part goat, part Titan'. And he presents the world around him, Western society and in particular America, as one 'rotting away, dying piecemeal', a denial of all that is truly life. *The Air-Conditioned Nightmare* (1945) and its sequel, *Remember to Remember* (1947), sum up his feelings about the American scene, which he describes in terms of a prison or a cancer ward, a place isolated from real health and life. And works like *Sexus* (1949), *Plexus* (1953) and *Nexus* (1960), *The Rosy Crucifixion* as Miller called this trilogy, continue his fictive autobiography in a form that is, as usual, deliberately formless, obedient only to what Miller saw as the sprawling, insistent rhythms of existence, and the self.

'I AM. That covers all experience, all wisdom, all truth,' Miller wrote in *Remember to Remember*. Charles Bukowski might have said something similar, although he would have said it in a much more laconic, downbeat way. The son of an American soldier and a German woman, Bukowski grew up in Los Angeles, worked mainly in unskilled jobs and only began to write when he was thirty-five. Bukowski shared a number of impulses with Miller: a distrust of art and the artistic establishment, a commitment to living his own life outside the norms of American society (in 1962, *Outsider* magazine named him 'Outsider of the Year' as a reward), a related commitment to recording that commitment in forms that hovered somewhere between the imagined and the literal, the fictive and the autobiographical. But Bukowski as he was and how he perceived himself – in, say, the fictive persona of Henry Chinaski – was much more the tough, lowbrow outsider, hard-living and hard-drinking, floating casually through a world of sex and violence: in short, a drifter rather than, like Miller, a seeker. Bukowski produced his first book of poems, *Flower, Fish and Bestial Wail*, in 1960. Like most of his work, it was published by a small press and reached out to an underground rather than a mainstream audience. It was followed by more than thirty poetic collections, ending with *The Last Night of Earth, Poems*, in 1992. His stories appeared in several collections, such as *Erections, Ejaculations, Exhibitions and General Tales of Ordinary Madness* (1972), as well as in little magazines. And novels like *Notes of a Dirty Old Man* (1969), *Post Office* (1971), *Women* (1978) and *Ham on Rye* (1982) turned his life on the seedy edge of things into hardboiled narratives that, characteristically, combine the eye of the camera, with its disposition for empirical detail, with the inner eye of the fabulist, alert to the nightmare of the streets. There are no large gestures in Bukowski's work. Using an off-hand, free-flowing line or sentence and an off-hand, casual idiom, he simply records things as they pass in a cryptic, even sardonic way. And what passes before him, most of the time, is the other America: life among the underclass, the bums, the dropouts, the dispossessed who cast a shadow over the national dream of success. This commitment to the writer as recording instrument does not, however, inhibit judgement. Bukowski is a frustrated moralist, in a way. 'I am not aiming high,' he says in one of his poems, '/ I am only trying to keep myself alive / just a little longer.' But the sheer difficulty of survival, for him and for the street people that surround him, is a measure clearly of the failure of the society from which he and they are excluded. Slyly, Bukowski reminds us of what another writer, Kenneth Rexroth, called 'the unfulfilled promise of "Song of Myself" and *Huckleberry Finn*'.

A writer who has made the unfulfilment of that promise his primary subject is J. D. Salinger. Salinger began writing stories for magazines, which he has not chosen to collect, before the Second World War. His first book, however, and his most famous, was a novel, *The Catcher in the Rye*, published in 1951. Its opening words, 'If you really want to know about it, the first thing you'll probably want to know is where I was born', introduce us to Holden Caulfield. They also introduce us, in an intimate, immediate way that is characteristic of so much American writing, to the troubles and contradictions of Holden's life. Holden is an unhappy teenager who runs away from boarding school. Lonely, quixotic, compassionate, he is plagued by the 'phoniness' of his environment. And in the book, he tells the story of his flight to New York and his eventual nervous breakdown. It turns out, in the end, that he is recalling all this from a sanatorium. The title of the novel refers to his desire to preserve innocence: not his own – that, he senses, is already lost – but the innocence of those still to grow up. He keeps picturing 'little kids playing some game' in 'this big field of rye and all', he tells his sister Phoebe. 'Nobody big' is around, except him; he is 'standing on the edge of some crazy cliff'. 'What I have to do,' he explains to Phoebe, 'I have to catch everybody if they start to go over the cliff.' He has, in short, to stop them from experiencing a fall that recalls both the mythical fall of Adam and Eve into knowledge and the universal fall from innocence into experience, from childhood into adulthood. Images of falling and flight pervade *The Catcher in the Rye*. Holden dreams of heading west or lighting out for the country; he cherishes anywhere that time seems to stand still. Equally, he fears any kind of fall, for himself and others; at one point, he even finds it difficult, frightening, to step down from the pavement on to the street. The novel is a triumph in the vernacular and confessional mode, drawing the reader into the narrator's deep resistance to the world that surrounds him and, he feels, threatens to stifle him. It also offers us a hero who, in his sadly contracted way, reminds us of the many other rebels and dreamers, grotesque saints and would-be saviours, that populate American fiction.

In particular, Holden recalls Huckleberry Finn in some ways. Like Huck, Holden is an outsider who dislikes system and distrusts authority; like Huck, too, he has to make his way through a world of hypocrisy and deceit that seems to threaten him at every turn. For that matter, like Mark Twain, Salinger catches an American idiom, the trick and lilt of his narrator's voice, to draw the reader into a rapport with the protagonist. And, also like Twain, one of the main weapons in his fictional armoury is a humour that depends on the telling, the quirky, comic way his hero describes the venality and stupidity of the people he meets. The differences between the two books, however, are at least as important as the connections; and these have much more to do with the simple facts that Holden is a little older, much richer than Huck and moves in an urban environment – an America where there is no longer any territory, no frontier to which the hero can flee. Huck has an innocent eye. Holden is more knowing, more judgemental and more deeply implicated – whether he likes it or not – in the 'phoney' circumstances he describes. He plays the social game when he has to, quite successfully; he is aware of himself, and his image, in a way that Huck clearly is not. Above all, the clarity and candour that characterize Huck, who is, in the last analysis, a truthteller, are replaced by a deep unease, uncertainty. Holden is confused; and, as his apparently spontaneous recollections of a crisis in his life make clear, he is not entirely sure what the truth about himself and his world is. This is all to say that the power of *The Catcher in the Rye* is also its problem. Holden is telling us his story from a sanatorium, which is not, perhaps, a cause for concern – about the veracity of what he says, that is – since, as many American books show us, much madness can be divinest sense. But he does also lie, he confesses to us that, often, he can spin yarns, inflate facts and be economical with the truth. In sum, he *tells* us that he is an unreliable narrator. So the novel moves on to slippery ground. How are we to see Holden? As authentic American rebel? As a troubled adolescent? As the only person close to sanity in an insane world? Or the reverse? There is no real way of knowing, of being certain. That slipperiness, though, is in turn part of its attraction, and its modernity. *The Catcher in the Rye* draws us into a sometimes painfully close relationship with a narrator, who is simultaneously confessional and defensive, longing to reveal himself but fearful of dropping the mask – and not, perhaps, sure what that self is. So, we feel, we know Holden and we do not know him: he is an intimate and a mystery. This is the American rebel transplanted into a new, shifting and distinctly modern landscape.

After *The Catcher in the Rye*, Salinger produced several collections of stories (*Nine Stories* [1953], *Franny and Zooey* [1961], *Raise High the Roof Beam, Carpenters and Seymour: An Introduction* [1963]). Many of them concerned the Glass family and, in particular, the lonely, brilliant, eccentric individualists Franny, Zooey, Seymour and Buddy Glass. In the early 1960s, however, he retired to his rural home, withdrew from the literary scene and stopped publishing his work. Richard Brautigan did not withdraw in this way but, before committing suicide in 1984, he gradually slipped from public view. Although he continued publishing into the early 1980s, his most successful work had appeared a decade or so earlier: *A Confederate General from Big Sur* (1964), *Trout Fishing in America* (1963), *In Watermelon Sugar* (1968) and *The Abortion: An Historical Romance* (1971). *Trout Fishing in America* is characteristic. It describes the search of the narrator for a morning of good fishing in a crystal-clear stream. His search takes him through a variety of American landscapes: city parks in San Francisco, forests in Oregon, a Filipino laundry, a wrecking yard that sells used trout streams by the foot. Surreal and anarchic, whimsical and nostalgic, the narrative is at once a critique of a culture that has betrayed its early promise – where the dream of trout fishing has become a purchaseable commodity, a matter of exchange – and a celebration of continuing possibility, the defiant, anarchic, unbowed spirit of the individual. 'I ended up by being my own trout,' the narrator tells us: which is a typically quirky way of saying what he says elsewhere in a more straightforward fashion – America is, after all, 'only a place in the mind'. This is the book as fictional play, a typographical game eschewing plot or structure of any ordinary kind, using surprise and spontaneity to make its central point. The point is a simple, seminal and very American one: we can be whatever we want to be, do whatever we want to do, whatever the destructive element that surrounds us. To that extent, thanks to the liberating imagination, trout fishing in America is still possible.

A similarly anarchic optimism characterizes the work of Ken Kesey. Born in Colorado and brought up in Oregon, Kesey worked for a while as a ward attendant in a mental hospital. This provided him with the material for his first and easily his finest book, *One Flew Over the Cuckoo's Nest* (1962). The novel is set in a psychiatric ward that is dominated by a character called the Big Nurse, who appears to have limitless power over the inmates. Controlling her charges by subtle pressures and, wherever necessary, more aggressive measures such as electric shock treatment, she embodies the principles of behaviourism. Forcing them to adjust to a prescribed norm, she also suggests forces at work in society generally. For she is constantly referred to by the narrator as an agent of 'The Combine'. Society is run by some secret force, the implication is, which tries to manipulate all its members. And of that force the Big Nurse is a servant and a symptom, although by no means the only one. Then into the ward comes an authentic American rebel, Randle McMurphy, who offers the inmates the example and the chance of independence. Swaggering, bold and with an incorrigible sense of humour, McMurphy has his greatest triumph when he sneaks everyone out on a yachting trip. 'Exultation', wrote Emily Dickinson, 'is the going / Of an inland soul to sea'; and an entire tradition of lighting out from the shore, and the prisonhouse of society, is recaptured in this moment. Soon after this, however, McMurphy – who is increasingly seen as an enemy to the institution, whom it must repress to survive – has a lobotomy performed on him, reducing him to a vegetable, passive and compliant. And unwilling to see him like this, finding it unbearable, his best friend in the institution, an ex-reservation Indian named Bromden, smothers McMurphy and so takes his life. The smothering is described in sexual terms, because it is an act of love. It is also an act of devotion by a disciple. For, like some of the inmates, Bromden has grown immeasurably under the influence of McMurphy. So much so that, after killing his mentor, Bromden breaks out of the mental institution to go on the road and maybe return to his tribe. McMurphy may be dead but, evidently, the spirit of rebellion that he embodied still survives.

If McMurphy is the hero of *One Flew Over the Cuckoo's Nest*, then Bromden supplies its vision. A giant, schizophrenic Indian who has pretended to be deaf and dumb to remain as far from the centre of activity as possible, he is the narrator. He is an outsider, an innocent eye, in a way, like Huck Finn: but what he sees is far stranger, far more surreal. It may not be literally true but it is symbolically so because, to quote Emily Dickinson again, 'Much madness is divinest sense'. The eye of Bromden sees the inner truth. He sees the Big Nurse as a nightmare figure, a mammalian monster and a machine, who can make the clocks go fast or slow. She is compared at one point to a cartoon character called the Spider Lady, who drew her victims into an electrified web. McMurphy, in turn, is likened to heroes such as Superman. He is an urban cowboy, plain-speaking, hard-living, a gambler and a risk-taker. Kesey said that he was addicted to comic books, which he calls 'the honest American myths'. And here that addiction turns the story into a vivid mix of naturalism and carnival. Celebrating a kind of anarchic individualism, *One Flew Over the Cuckoo's Nest* has its own anarchic energy. This retelling of the combat between the self and the system is unique precisely because it carries a comic-book edge: which adds a further touch of subversion. The compelling tropes of what has been called the American drama of beset manhood are all there: the rebel in action and the rebel in vision, the bond between two men, the woman as a threatening instrument of the system, the liberation in the wilderness, the sacrifice of the mentor, the survival of the disciple, and the final lighting out for the territory. But they are all set in their own transgressive space, an area of vulgar power and possibility that mocks claims to authoritativeness and authority of any kind – including those of high culture. Kesey was to go on to chart that transgressive space in other fiction and essays (*Sometimes a Great Notion* [1964], *Kesey's Garage Sale* [1973], *Demon Box* [1986], *The Further Enquiry* [1990]). He was also to attempt to create it for himself and others: travelling in his 'Magic Bus' around America with his companions, whom he called 'the Merry Pranksters', organizing psychedelic events and light shows – all of which Tom Wolfe wryly recorded in his book *The Electric Kool-Aid Acid Test* (1968). But *One Flew Over the Cuckoo's Nest* remains his most powerful mapping of transgression, his most memorable expression of the belief that lost freedom can and must be recovered. 'I been away a long time' are the last words of Bromden as he lights out for a past that is also his future. It stands not only as a supremely serious comic book but also as a major document in the American literature of resistance and rebellion.

The Art and Politics of Race

Defining a new black aesthetic

Nobody has had to resist more in American society, and rebel more as far as the institutional structures of the nation are concerned, than African Americans. On the level of what Norman Mailer would call the 'visible' river of public events, there has been the trauma of the assassinations of Malcolm X and Martin Luther King, the 'Second American Revolution' of the civil rights movement and its aftermath, the emergence within the framework of party politics of leaders like Jesse Jackson and, outside of it, of the followers of Elijah Muhammed and the Black Muslim movement, the controversies and crises surrounding the cases of Rodney King and O. J. Simpson. And much more. On the level of the 'subterranean' river, there has been the slow, painful, but triumphant growth of black pride. Black pride and the black aesthetic were promoted, in the first instance after the Second World War, by the Black Arts movement. Following that movement, there has been an exponential increase in significant writing by African American women. African American women suffered, many of them felt, from the double jeopardy of racism in the women's liberation movement and sexism in black liberation movements. That sexism led Eldridge Cleaver (1935–98), for instance, to equate black pride with sexual manhood and, in his best-known book, *Soul on Ice* (1968), to describe the rape of white women as 'an insurrectionary act'. The remedy, as Toni Cade (1939–95) argued in her Preface to *The Black Woman* (1970), a seminal anthology of short stories and essays, was for black women to start 'turning toward each other'. This is what African American women writers proceeded to do. Toni Cade turned to her own ancestors first, adding her grandmother's name, Bambara, to her own. That name was to appear on her short story collection *Gorilla, My Love* (1972), about a young black woman who is trying to survive in the city – and whose sassy straight talk expresses what Bambara herself called 'a certain way of being in the world'. 'I say', the young woman declares, 'just like the hussy my daughter always say I am.' Her words, catching the rhythms of African American folk speech and the 'games, chants, jingles' of the streets, are her way of improvising and affirming herself; they speak resistance, and her sense of relation to other black women, into life.

Audre Lorde was to pursue a similar path to Bambara, in her accounts of what she called the 'strong triad of grandmother mother daughter', the 'mattering core' of strong black females who gave her her sense of presence. So, as we shall see later, have many other African American women novelists. So, too, has a writer whose work is part autobiography, part picaresque fiction and part social history, Maya Angelou (1928–). In the first volume of her series of autobiographical fictions, *I Know Why the Caged Bird Sings* (1970), Angelou confers an exemplary status upon the experiences of the narrator, whose childhood is spent shuttling between rural and urban America, smalltown America, San Francisco and St Louis. Exemplary, too, is what she learned: the two major strands of the African American tradition, both of them inherited from women. From her grandmother, the narrator tells us, she absorbed the religious influences, the gospel tradition of African Americans. From her mother, in turn, she received 'the blues tradition'. Both elements of the black vernacular inform the account of this exceptional yet exemplary woman, and her meetings with other remarkable black women: among them, a friend who teaches her to speak again, to rediscover the beauty of the 'human voice', after the shock of rape has left her temporarily dumb. They also inform the later, extraordinary volumes in this series, *Gather Together in My Name* (1974), *Singin' and Swingin' and Gettin' Merry Like Christmas* (1976), *The Heart of a Woman* (1981) and *All God's Children Need Travelling Shoes* (1987).

'The black man is the future of the world,' wrote the man who has been described as the father of the Black Arts movement, Imamu Amiri Baraka (1934–). 'Let Black people understand that / they are the lovers and the sons of lovers', Baraka has declared, '/ and warriors and sons of warriors. Are poems / poets & all the loveliness here in the world.' 'We are unfair, and unfair,' he says elsewhere, in a poem titled 'Black Art', '/ we are black magicians, black art / & we make in black labs of the heart / . . . / . . . we own / the night.' Appropriating the mythic power that Western symbolism habitually imputes to blackness, black writers have been in the vanguard of those aiming to turn those symbols inside out, so as to make them a source of pride for black people and a source of fear and wonder for whites. Absorbing black cultural influences as ancient as Islam and as modern as the music of John Coltrane, they have pushed Langston Hughes's commitment to cultural separateness to a fresh extreme. As far as forms and performances are concerned, this has involved the frequent adoption of the 'preacher style' of public speaking, endemic to the African and African American traditions, where the poet/leader recites at a rapt, rapid pace and the audience/chorus dance, shout and sing in response to the nervous fire of his words and the contagious nature of his rhythms. And as far as concerns content, this has had as one consequence a new assertiveness of tone and aggression of gesture: a renewed eagerness to see poetry as, to use the words of one black poet, D. L. Graham (1944–), 'survival motion set to music' – or, to borrow a phrase from another, Carl Wendell Himes, Jr (1946–), 'magic . . . spells, to raise up / return, destroy, and create'.

'The black artist's role in America is to aid in the destruction of America as he knows it.' The author of this remark is Imamu Amiri Baraka and it powerfully summarizes a presiding aim that he has shared with many other black writers of this period: another one, Ron Karenga (1945–), for example, has put it this way: 'all our art must contribute to revolutionary change and if it does not, it is invalid.' To such remarks, however, it is worth adding a gloss. Not all black poets feel this way. Some even seem content to follow the path of Countee Cullen, by producing work that is virtually indistinguishable from the white tradition. David Henderson (1950–), for instance, writes poems like 'Sketches of Harlem' (1967) that resemble those of the white street poets of New York; while, in a different key, the woman poet G. C. Oden (1951–) chooses to be closer in much of her writing to Louise Bogan ('The Carousel' [1967]) or Elizabeth Bishop ('A Private Letter to Brazil' [1967]) than to other black writers, male or female. Even the poets who have committed themselves to a specifically black revolutionary art cannot be entirely separated from the white tradition. Rebellion is hardly a black monopoly, after all; and much of the most trenchant white American writing has also been pre-occupied with the gap between performance and promise: America as the writer 'knows it' – which invites destruction – and America as he or she dreams of it – which begs to be realized, first in words and then in deeds. A gloss of this kind may be necessary, then, but it should not take away from the vital fact: at its best, recent black poetry *is* different. The difference can even be measured in terms of Baraka's own progress, as he moved from imitation of white forms, however innovative or subversive, to the formulation of a purely black aesthetic.

Baraka established his reputation under his given name of Leroi Jones. His first published work was a play, *A Good Girl is Hard to Find* (1958). Two other plays soon followed, *The Baptism* (1964) and *The Toilet* (1964), mostly concerned with issues of personal identity. Before them, *Preface to a Twenty Volume Suicide Note* (1961) appeared, a collection of personal and often domestic poems. In the earlier stages of his career, while he was still known as Leroi Jones, Baraka was clearly influenced by those white American poets who, like him, saw themselves as alien-ated from the cultural mainstream. There are several poems that recall the work of Frank O'Hara: in 'Epistróphe', for instance, Baraka uses the random, chancey rhythms of casual speech and imagery assembled by a mobile vision to capture the oddity of a familiar vista, 'what you see (here in New York)'. The figure of Charles Olson, in turn, hovers behind 'How You Sound??', Baraka's announcement of his aesthetic published in 1959. '"How You SOUND??" is what we recent fellows are up to,' he declared: 'There must not be any preconceived *design* for what the *poem* ought to be.' 'The only "recognisable tradition" a poet need follow is himself,' he added, '& with that, say, all those things out of tradition he can use . . . to broaden his *own* voice with.' Baraka's principal involvement at this time, however, was not with the Black Mountain poets (although some of his earlier poems, such as 'In

Memory of Radio', do resemble projectivist poetry) but with the beats. There have been a number of black writers associated with the beat generation. Among them is Bob Kaufman (1925–86), who used the long, sweeping line favoured by Ginsberg to announce that 'no man is our master' and address the possibility of universal brotherhood 'On this shore'. There is also Ted Joans (1928–2003), whose claim, 'Jazz is my religion', is catchily illustrated by poems like 'Voice in the Crowd' that imitate the abrupt, syncopated movement and startling dissonances of Ornette Coleman. But Baraka was, at least for a while, the most innovative and accomplished of the black beat poets, blending influences as disparate as European Surrealism and Dadaism, the jazz poetry of Vachel Lindsay and Langston Hughes, the African American oral tradition and the music of Charlie Parker. With these he fashioned poetry that, in marked contrast to his later work, was determinedly autobiographical, preoccupied with sex and death and shaped by existential despair.

An alteration in Baraka's voice and vision came in the 1960s, when, like many black nationalists, he dispensed with his white 'slave name' Leroi Jones and adopted a title more in keeping with his new self and his new mission. His work became correspondingly more radical and more involved with issues of racial and national identity. The plays *Dutchman* (1964), *The Slave* (1964) and *Slave Ship: a Historical Pageant* (1967) all deal with relations between black and white people. As works of 'revolutionary theatre', they demonstrate Baraka's awareness of himself as a leader of a black arts movement that seeks to use drama as a weapon against American racism. The episodic novel *The System of Dante's Hell* (1965) equates the black slums of Newark, New Jersey, with the Inferno. The various essays of *Home: Social Essays* (1966), originally published in a number of liberal and leftist journals, trace his artistic transformation from black beat poet to father of the Black Arts movement. And the poems in *The Dead Lecturer* (1964) represent Baraka's poetic farewell to the beats. Marked by an ever-increasing preoccupation with racial issues, these lyrics crystallize his commitment to revolutionary action and his disavowal of what he saw as the political decadence of his former compatriots. Other volumes of poetry followed: *Black Magic: Collected Poetry 1961–1967* (1969), *It's Nation Time* (1970) and *In Our Terribleness* (1970). Other work, such as *Blues People: Negro Music in White America* (1963), showed his growing involvement in the African American tradition, or, like the work published in *Four Black Revolutionary Plays* (1969), showed him reaching out to, and trying to teach, a largely unlettered audience. Around 1974, Baraka announced a further development in his political ideology and aesthetic, with a formal commitment to a Marxist-Leninist perspective, anticipating the overthrow, by blacks and whites alike, of oppressive capitalist systems. Plays such as *S-1* (1974) and *The Motion of History* (1977) testify to the change. And works like *Hard Facts* (1975), *Poetry for the Advanced* (1979) and *Daggers and Javelins* (1984) demonstrate his efforts to reconcile the more positive and useful aspects of black nationalism with what he saw as the scientific accuracy of Marxism. Later publications show that effort continuing, among them, *Eulogies* (1996), *Funk Love: New Poems, 1984–1995* (1996) and *The Autobiography of Leroi Jones/Amiri Baraka* (1997). As an organizer and activist, he has continued, ever since the 1960s, to influence immeasurably the direction of African American thought and writing.

As a writer, in particular, though, Baraka's main contribution has been to encourage a generation to be unapologetic, even proud and aggressive, about their African American heritage. Particularly in the writing of the 1960s and early 1970s, he introduced a prophetic, apocalyptic dimension into black writing, a sense of mission, the violent redemption of the sins of the past in the revolutionary future. 'We want poems that kill,' he announced in 'Black Art', 'Assassin poems. Poems that shoot / guns.' 'Let there be no love poems written /', he added, 'until love can exist freely and / clearly.' What Baraka anticipated was nothing less than a 'jihad' or holy war of believers against unbelievers, black against white ('Come up, black dada / nihilismus. Rape the white girls / Rape the fathers. Cut the mothers' throats'). From this holocaust, this ritual bloodletting of all that is false and dead – that is, specifically, white Christian civilization – little would survive. But creation would nevertheless follow destruction. Primal innocence and energy would be restored; and a new nation would emerge out of the union between black power in America and anti-colonialist movements in Africa. 'It's nation time eye ime,' Baraka sang triumphantly in the poem of that title: 'it's nation ti eye ime / chant with bells and drum / its nation time.' In a way, this was the American dream in bright new pan-African robes: liberation from the present tyranny, the poet hoped, would be accompanied by a recovery of the perfection of the past and its restitution for an imagined future. There was no place for whites here, certainly: 'white people', we are told, '. . . are full of, and made of / shit'. But, ironically, Baraka still reflected the millennial tendencies of a culture he was determined to reject.

As for that determination itself, Baraka's conscious need to reject Western culture: that was all real enough. Apart from certain crucial aspects of that culture, notably Marxism and socialism, it still remains one of his dominating motives. He could not entirely unlearn his American education, or excise those portions of himself that had been shaped by traditional or apolitical white culture, but he tried hard to do so. 'When I die, / the consciousness I carry I will to / black people,' he wrote in 'Leroy'. 'May they pick me apart and take the / useful parts . . . And leave / the bitter bullshit rotten white parts / alone.' The process of excision was, in effect, to be continued after his death: the few, lingering traces of white identity were to be left to decay while the rest, 'the sweet meat' of the black self, was to achieve a strictly carnal resurrection, growing in and through the bodies of others. As far as active practice was concerned, this insistence on 'Black feeling, Black mind, Black judgement' led Baraka not only to political involvement but also to the promotion of black community theatre. With his help, the Black Arts Repertory Theatre/School was opened in Harlem in 1965, to become of critical importance in the development of the Black Arts movement. And, following its demise, Baraka set up the Spirit House in Newark, with its troupe of actors called the Spirit House Movers. On the level of theory, in turn, it was Baraka above all who formulated, and gave definitive expression to, the idea of a Black Aesthetic. 'I think of the artist as a moralist,' Baraka declared, in his Preface to *Black Magic*, 'demanding a

---

cleaner vision of the world.' 'We are spiritual,' he went on, '. . . we must see ourselves again, as black men, as the strength of the planet, and rise to rebuild . . . what is actually good.' Even the rage that has characterized so much of his work has been defended by him in terms of his moralist/nationalist aesthetics. 'What I'm after is a sense of clarity,' he claimed in *Black Music* (1967), 'if it sounds like anger, maybe that's good in a sense.'

Anger has not, of course, been Baraka's only mode, even in the more purely nationalist writing of the 1960s and 1970s. His work is also punctuated by cries for help ('calling all black people come in, black people, come on / in'), friendly persuasion ('I want you to understand the world / as I have come to understand it'); above all, by respect for the energy of black people – something that he has identified with the ultimate agent of creativity ('God . . . is energy') and as an instrument of change, to be mobilized by force if necessary. 'We are beautiful people with african imaginations / full of masks and dances and swelling chants,' Baraka declares in 'Ka' Ba', '/ with african eyes, and noses, and arms / though we sprawl in grey chains in a place / full of winters, when what we want is sun.' There is pride here and faith in collective identity, the belief that black people 'are all beautiful'. Seeking to harness the 'ancient images' and 'magic' of the African inheritance to his cause, Baraka couples this with the verve he finds in all black cultural forms, from the speeches of Malcolm X to the music of Muddy Waters. 'What will be / the sacred words?' he asks. His aim, which he still sees himself as sharing with other black writers, is to unravel a new language and rhythm, 'sacred words' that will liberate him, his work and, in the process, the hearts and minds of all his 'black family'. 'We have been captured, / brothers,' he proclaims, 'And we labour / to make our getaway.' A new song that will generate a new self and, eventually, a new society: it is an ambition at least as old as *Leaves of Grass*, but it has been rendered almost unrecognizable. For this is a song in the service of, if necessary, violent revolution: the revolt not only of Baraka's 'black family' – although they matter to him, especially – but of all those similarly oppressed.

The Black Arts movement was, in particular, a movement that inspired poets, and among those poets who received inspiration from it, and sometimes also from Amiri Baraka, were Mari Evans (1927–), Sonia Sanchez (1934–), Nikki Giovanni (1943–), Don L. Lee/Haki R. Madhubuti (1942–) and David Nelson (1944–). These writers have shared with Baraka the belief that, as Sonia Sanchez puts it, in some lines from 'Right on: white america' (1969) quoted earlier, 'this country might have / been a pion / eer land once, / and it still is'. By way of explanation, Sanchez then adds pointedly: 'check out / the falling gun / shells / on our blk / tomorrow.' In other words, they have rejected the white American dream: 'The white man's heaven is the Black man's hell,' we are told in *The Black Bird* (1969), a play by the poet and playwright Marvin X (1944–). But they are also trying to restore the pioneer values of liberation and mobility, once so fundamental to that dream, in and for their own people. This has necessarily involved them in a commitment to revolutionary struggle. 'change up,' Don L. Lee/Haki R. Madhubuti commands, 'let's go for ourselves / . . . / change-up and yr children will look at u differently / than we looked at our parents.' The aim is to achieve an irreversible shift of power: 'I'm / gonna make it a crime to be anything BUT black,' Mari Evans has announced in 'Vive Noir!' (1968), 'gonna make white / a twenty-four hour / lifetime / J.O.B.' Formally, this has aligned them with all those trying to 'write black', to realize a verbal approximation of the frantic energy, the hip rhythms, of black speech and music: 'to be black', as Lee/Madhubuti puts it in one poem ('But He Was Cool' [1970]), 'is / to be / very – hot.' This is a literature of exhortation, primarily, which, rather than dwell on personal suffering, insists on the abolition of communal suffering. 'Don't Cry, Scream', Lee/Madhubuti tells his audience in the poem of that name (1971), and then obeys his own instructions, in a wild typographical imitation of modern jazz:

> scream – eeeeeeeeeeeee – ing
> SCREAM – EEEeeeeeeeeeee – ing   loud &
> SCREAM – EEEEEEEEEEEEEEEE – ing   long with
>   feeling

The need to scream, to shout and fight rather than lament, has led some of these poets at least to jettison those aspects of black culture which, they believe, might impede the revolutionary momentum. Among those aspects, the most notable are the music and spirit of the blues which, as the black scholar and theorist Moulana Karenga (1941–) explains in 'Black Art: Mute Matter Given Force and Function' (1968), are 'not functional . . . because they do not commit us to the struggle of today and tomorrow'. Blues are 'a very beautiful, musical, and psychological achievement of our people', Karenga admits, but 'they keep us in the past' and 'whatever we do we cannot remain in the past'. So no more blues, Sonia Sanchez insists in 'Liberation Poem' (1970), 'blues ain't culture / they sounds of oppression / against the white man's shit'. 'We ain't blue, we are black', Lee/Madhubuti argues in 'Don't Cry, Scream', and clearly David Nelson would agree with him: 'Blues was for making and enduring and suffering / We need a new BLACK thing,' he declares in 'No Time for Blues Now' (1970). This 'new BLACK thing' will be the opposite of the old, a 'music for the senses' that is 'fast an' happy an' mad!!!!!' Reversing the vicious cycle of oppression, it will be what Baraka in *Black Music* has called a 'song above horror', alive with 'black rhythm energy' and alert above all to the necessity to 'change-up'. It will also be, though, like the blues a song for performance. Along with the beats, as well as the poets of the San Francisco and Black Mountain groups, many of the more recent black poets have relied as much on the spoken word as the written. Writing also to be immediately accessible and to nurture feelings of community, they have moved towards a poetry of and for the street that is determinedly populist, rejecting conventional distinctions between 'high' and 'popular' culture. So the four-man group known as The Last Poets (both the originals and the subsequent groups of that name) have exploited ghetto culture, rapping and hip-hop to get the message across to their Harlem neighbours. And some of the recordings of David Nelson, Nikki Giovanni and, more recently,

---

Gil Scott-Heron (1949–) have become popular hits on a national scale. The 1970 recorded poem of Scott-Heron, 'The Revolution Will Not Be Televised', for instance, shows just how much black poetry of the last thirty-five years or so stands at the crossroads between different African American musical and rhetorical forms. Using percussive rhythm, repetition, a driving beat and an urgent streetwise idiom to make its point that 'The revolution will be no re-run, brothers. / The revolution will be LIVE', it recollects and reinvents such otherwise different African American forms as jump-rope rhymes and game chants, sermons and scat singing, rhythm and blues and gospel.

Although not rap music as such, 'The Revolution Will Not Be Televised' vitally influenced the themes and forms of rap: a form that is characterized by deft rhymes and an insistently percussive verse performed against a background of sounds 'sampled' from snatches of previously recorded music. The sampling, together with the element of performance, even self-mockery often to be found in rap, gives it a distinctly postmodernist edge. Then, again, that element of wry self-mockery, verbal strutting, is as old as the trickster toasts and badman boasts of folk heroes like Stackolee and Brer Rabbit. And in its verbal fire and ice, its thundering drumlines and rapid firings of chanted sound, it takes up a black heritage of sound and song that goes back to before the day Africans saw the first slave ship. Some rap preaches the same revolutionary message as the poetry and prose of Baraka. Some, less open in its message of revolt, rehearses with grim humour the moral and social hell of the ghetto: 'It's like a jungle sometimes,' 'The Message' (1982) begins, 'it makes me wonder / How I keep from going under.' And then there is 'gangsta rap', which simply offers raw and raucous testimony to the life of the streets: a life, it seems, with no exits, grim, violent, even vicious. Like the badmen boasting and tricksters toasting in early black folktales, the gangsta rappers use sharp talk and shock, making no apologies for their obsession with what they see as the basic necessities of life – money and sex – as they struggle to survive in the black underclass. From the poetry of the Black Arts movement through the recorded work of Giovanni and Scott-Heron to rap and gangsta rap, there is a sustained emphasis on dance, voice and fight. Moving, strutting your stuff to keep from falling over the edge, speaking, chanting, singing to make your presence known, squaring up to the common enemy and making the folks around you square up too. Some of this work, especially gangsta rap, is not only subversive but offensive too: but it always throws up the same serious issues about black disempowerment and drift, and the urgent, booming need for change.

The women among more recent African American poets have also urged the need for another kind of change: the need to combat not just the racism of white culture but the latent sexism of the black. Even revolutionary poets like Baraka have tended to talk in generic terms about 'the black man' and to identify black women with the sexual and reproductive functions. And sometimes, as in some gangsta rap, the sexism is nowhere near being latent. 'i wish I knew how it would feel / to be free,' says Nikki Giovanni in 'Woman Poem' (1983), and then goes on to link her historical imprisonment as a black with her cultural imprisonment as a woman. 'its a sex object if you're pretty / and no love / or love and no sex if you're fat,' she observes; 'get back fat black woman be a mother / grandmother strong thing but not a woman.' This sense of the redoubled oppression of black women, on the grounds of gender as well as race, has led Sonia Sanchez to celebrate her attachment to others like herself. 'I cried', Sanchez declares in 'Just Don't Never Give Up on Love' (1984), 'For myself . . . For all the women who have ever stretched their bodies out anticipating civilization and finding ruins.' It has encouraged Mari Evans, in turn, to celebrate the simple fact of her own black womanhood. 'I am a black woman /', she announces in the poem with that title (1970), 'tall as a cypress / strong / beyond all definition'; 'look on me and be / screwed.' For Jone Jordan (1936–), the edge to her experience as a woman is more devastating and traumatic. A victim of rape, she has seen in the violence she has suffered a connection with other forms of violence, more general and historical, perpetrated in Africa and America. '*It all violates self-determination*': all forms of racial oppression rupture personhood, personal and political space. And in 'Poem About My Rights' (1989), she explores and insists upon the ineluctable link between her own past and, say, 'South Africa / penetrating into Namibia penetrating into / Angola'. 'I am the history of rape,' she confides, '/ I am the history of the rejection of who I am / I am the history of the terrorised incarceration of / my self.' The connection between herself and history does not stop there, however, with the simple, sad acknowledgement of the evil done to her as a black woman and the evil done to black people in many parts of the world. '*I am not wrong. Wrong is not my name,*' she insists, 'My name is my own my own.' She will fight back, so setting an example to others similarly violated. 'From now on,' she tells all her oppressors, past and present, 'my resistance / my simple and daily and nightly self-determination / may very well cost you your life.'

The violence which seeps into Jordan's work is, unsurprisingly, there in the work of many other African American poets. It is part of the suppressed history of the race that Lucille Clifton invokes in her poem 'at the cemetery, walnut grove plantation, south carolina, 1989' (1991). It makes Audre Lorde insist, in 'Power' (1978), that, *pace* W. B. Yeats, the difference between poetry and rhetoric is not the difference between the argument with oneself and others but 'being / ready to kill /yourself / instead of your children'. That violence is also the determining feature, perhaps, in the work of two other remarkable African American poets of this period, Etheridge Knight (1931–91) and Michael Harper (1938–). Both Knight and Harper, like so many other black writers, allow the rhythms of African American musical traditions to pulse through their work. So, in 'A Poem for Myself (Or Blues for a Mississippi Black Boy)' (1980), Knight exploits blues forms to tell a story of black wandering from Mississippi to Detroit, Chicago, New York, then back to Mississippi. And in 'Ilu, the Talking Drum' (1980), he takes the black American life experience in a full circle from Africa to the South then back to an Africa of the spirit using an African rhythmic structure to imitate the voice of an African drum. The titles of several of Harper's collections betray his own very similar allegiances: *Dear John Coltrane* (1970), *Song: I Want a Witness* (1972),

Healing Song for the Inner Ear (1985). Exploring his connection to jazz artists like Coltrane and Charlie Parker, insisting on human and cultural continuity ('A man is another man's face,' he has written), his work is oriented to performance: 'blacks have to *testify*,' he proclaims in 'Song: *I Want a Witness*', '/ and *testify* and *testify*.' For Harper, however, the violence he records is a matter of family loss and racial history: the death of an infant son ('Nightmare Begins Responsibility' [1975]) or of a brother ('Camp Story' [1985]), the suffering inflicted upon Native Americans by 'mad Puritans' ('History as Apple Tree' [1977]), the assassinations of Malcolm X and Martin Luther King ('Here Where Coltrane Is' [1977]). For Knight, the violence was closer to the bone. 'I died in Korea from a shrapnel wound and narcotics resurrected me,' he once confessed. 'I died in 1960 from a prison sentence and poetry brought me back to life.' Many of Knight's poems were written in prison – his first collection was, in fact, simply called *Poems from Prison* (1968) – and they detail the loneliness, the bitter frustration of prison life. They work through a violence of language and verve of movement learned from the black oral tradition: 'the brown / hills and red gullies of mississippi send out their electric / messages, galvanizing my genes,' he declares, characteristically, in 'The Idea of Ancestry' (1968). But they also work through the way Knight links himself, in his isolation and pain, to others in his family, his race and the American underclass, to a communality of suffering. And they work, not least, through their resilience, their refusal to let any violence cow or corrupt the spirit. 'Going back to Mississippi,' 'A Poem for Myself' concludes, '/ This time for good – / Gonna be free in Mississippi / Or dead in the Mississippi mud.'

Violence, though, is no more the single defining feature of recent African American poetry than any specific definition of race – of what it means to be an African American – is. What is remarkable about so much of this work, in fact, is the multiple forms in which African Americanism can enter into this poetry. With Rita Dove (1952–), for instance, there is a marked inclination towards multiculturalism. The settings of her spare, enigmatic poems range from Ohio to Germany to Israel; and in just one volume slaves, mythological and Biblical characters, and the ancestors and immediate family of the poet all jostle side by side. 'I am profoundly fascinated by the ways in which language can change our perceptions,' she has said. Some of her work addresses that subject head on, by exploring how a single word or image can permit a voyage into strange seas of thought ('Ö' [1980]), or how a poem can provide 'a little room for thinking', a chance and space to dream ('Daystar' [1986]). Some of it approaches the liberating potential of language in a sidewise fashion, as it were, by considering, perhaps, how earlier generations of African Americans nurtured the 'crazy feeling' that they could change their lives in the words they spoke, the songs they sang ('Kentucky, 1833' [1980]). Dove is continually trying to speak the unspoken, to give voice to the voiceless. That includes those dimensions of experience and history that have been suppressed, or sidelined, most often for reasons of gender or of race. So, in a poem called 'Arrow' (1989), she quietly subverts those literary positions that reduce black people to marginal caricatures and women to convenient symbols of the elusive, the ineffable. And in her long poem sequence *Thomas and Beulah* (1987), she resurrects the rarely acknowledged contribution of working-class blacks to American life by telling the story of the courtship, marriage and subsequent life of her own grandparents.

The perspective of Wanda Coleman (1946–) is very different, but just as racially inflected in its own way. So, in turn, is that of Nathaniel Mackey (1947–). An electrifying reader and performer of her own work, Coleman has said that her 'one desire' is 'through writing' to 'control, destroy, and create social institutions'. 'I want to wield the power that belongs to the pen,' she has declared. Using nervy rhythms, a stark idiom and an elliptical line, she has done just that, in poems that recall racial violence ('Emmett Till' [1990]), the violence done to women, black women in particular ('American Sonnet (10)' [1993]), and the constant threat, the fear that eats away at the soul in the urban ghetto ('Today I Am a Homicide in the North of the City' [1990]). Mackey has other priorities, although many of them are also marked by his African Americanism. 'Music includes so much,' he has suggested, 'it's social, it's religious, it's metaphysical, it's aesthetic, it's expressive, it's creative, it's destructive.' The music that specifically 'just covers so much' for him is modern jazz. Combined in poems like 'Falso Brilliante' (1985) and 'Song of the Andoumboulou' (1994) are the influence, the idiom of jazz pioneers like Charlie Parker and Thelonious Monk and the experiments in breath and line of such projectivist poets as Charles Olson and Robert Duncan. Jazz is important, too, to Yusef Komunyakaa, as a poem like 'February in Sydney' (1989) indicates, since it uses memories of the jazz musician Dexter Gordon as the source, the base line, for a sort of free-form meditation. But with Komunyakaa there are other, racially tinged experiences at work in the poetry, too: his boyhood in rural Louisiana ('Sunday Afternoons' [1992]), his years as a soldier and war correspondent in Vietnam ('Facing It' [1988]) and, sometimes, a strange, surreal mixture of the two ('Banking Potatoes' [1993]).

With Ntozake Shange (1948–), African Americanism has led to a studied rejection of literary convention. Born Paulette Williams, in 1971 she assumed an African name that announced her new priorities: Ntozake translates as 'she who comes with her own things', and Shange as 'who walks like a lion'. Living up to that name, six years later she produced a choreopoem, a mesh of poetry, music and drama, called *for colored girls who have considered suicide / when the rainbow is enuf*. Shange has explained that *for colored girls* is about 'our struggle to become all that is forbidden, all that is forfeited by our gender, all that we have forgotten'. In it, seven women wearing the colours of the rainbow plus brown, the colour of the earth, perform twenty poems that trace their development from youth to maturity. The poems focus on the lack of understanding between men and women, the misrecognition of women and the pain of unfulfilment, unrequited love. Marked by the idioms and inflections of the African American oral tradition, they reject conventional grammar and spelling, the standard English that Shange sees as re-flective of the hierarchies inherent in mainstream society. So do her later poems, collected in *Nappy Edges* (1978) and *Ridin' the Moon in Texas: Word Paintings*

(1987) and plays like *Spell #7* (1980). For Essex Hemphill (1957–95), on the other hand, it was not so much literary as social convention that was rejected. Certainly, the style he favoured was far from conventional. Using an edgy, rapping line, he could be blunt in confronting the reader with what he called 'the ass-splitting truth'. But it was resistance to the myths of black masculinity that supplied his driving motive. In wanting to assert his identity as both an African and a homosexual, he renounced the silence that, he felt, had been imposed on black gays. 'I speak for thousands,' Hemphill declared. 'Their ordinary kisses . . . are scrubbed away by the propaganda makers of the race,' he went on, 'the "Talented Tenth", who would just as soon have us believe Black people can fly, rather than that Black men have been longing to kiss one another, and have done so for centuries.' So in *Ceremonies* (1992), a collection of poetry and prose, Hemphill constructed an alternative to what he called 'watered-down versions of Black life' and the stereotypes of the sad, doomed gay. He anticipated a new erotic dispensation, in which men transformed institutions to fit their needs: where, as he put it, 'Every time we kiss / we confirm the new world coming'. Like so many other more recent African American writers, Hemphill gave a fresh spin to the literature of protest and resistance, as well as to the myth of the promised land. And he did it as they have done, by insisting on internal resistances, differences within the African American community as well as differences from white America.

Defining a new black identity in prose

As far as prose is concerned, a seminal event in the history of African American writing since the Second World War was the publication, in 1952, of *Invisible Man*. The author was Ralph Ellison (1914–94). Born in Oklahoma and the grandson of slaves, Ellison was named Ralph Waldo after Emerson. Educated in a segregated school system, he then went south to Alabama to attend the black college of Tuskegee. In the South, in particular, Ellison recollected in his second collection of essays, *Going to the Territory* (1986), he found all 'the signs and symbols that marked the dividing lines of segregation'. But he also found time to read modern poetry. 'Somehow in my uninstructed reading of Eliot and Pound,' he remembered, 'I had recognized a relationship between modern poetry and jazz music.' 'Indeed,' he added, 'such reading and wondering prepared me not simply to meet Richard Wright but to seek him out.' It was in New York City that Ellison met Wright, who was then editor of the *New Challenge*. And it was while he was there that he wrote his first short story, and also worked in the black community gathering and recording folk material that was to become an integral part of his fiction. The early work Ellison produced reflected the influence of Wright and naturalism. But Ellison slowly developed his own style, a cunning mix of realism, surrealism, symbolism, folklore and myth. 'I was to dream of a prose which was flexible and swift, confronting the inequalities and brutalities of our society forthright,' Ellison explained in his first book of essays, *Shadow and Act* (1964), 'but yet thrusting forth its images of hope, human fraternity and individual self-realisation.' 'It would use the riches of our speech,' he added, 'the idiomatic expression and the rhetorical flourishes from past periods which are still alive among us.' That dream, of a language as diverse as American culture and African American life, was realized in *Invisible Man*, arguably the most profound and compelling novel about identity to be published during this period.

Set in the 1930s, *Invisible Man* describes the experiences of its anonymous black protagonist and narrator as he wanders through America, struggling to come to terms with the dilemma Ellison summed up in one of his essays: 'the nature of our society is such that we are prevented from knowing who we are'. He is 'invisible', he discovers, his black skin renders him nameless and anonymous in white society. And, like so many heroes in American fiction, black and white, he is torn between unsatisfactory alternatives, corresponding, in their own distinctly Modernist, racially inflected way, to the mythic opposition of the clearing and the wilderness. He can either, he learns, surrender to the various demeaning and degrading roles prescribed for him by society, or he can escape into a fluid, formless territory, a subterranean world that seems to exist outside history, where, instead of a repressed, constricted self, he seems to have no self, no coherent identity at all. Each stage in the journey of the invisible man, usually marked by a site and a speech, sees him trying on a new role, a fresh change of clothes and identity. He begins as a 'darky', subjected to ritual humiliations and the level of a beast: forms of subjection that Ellison pointedly compares to those suffered by women. This is in the South, and still in the Southern states he is then offered the chance to become the 'college boy', following the Booker T. Washington road to success in a segregated institution. Journeying to New York City, he takes on the role of worker at a factory called the Liberty Paint Company, whose principal product is a kind of whitewash. Here, as elsewhere in the book, Ellison moves smoothly between a variety of very different stylistic modes as he describes a workplace that is, quite clearly, a paradigm and parody of American society. Following his factory experience, the invisible man takes on a new role, by joining a group called the Brotherhood in New York. The Brotherhood is a thinly described version of the Communist Party, and the protagonist has now become an activist. This role is no more satisfactory than the others, though, as the continued imagery of games, blueprint, plans, repression and castration suggest. The invisible man is still required to deny a crucial part of himself as an individual, a man, and, above all, a black man. And, at the climax of the narrative, following a race riot in Harlem, he retreats to an underground sewer, which he furnishes and lives in while, he tells us, he writes this book. He is now in a 'border area' where he can understand his invisibility and ask us, the readers, the question that ends the book: 'Who knows but that, on the lower frequencies, I speak for you?'

What *Invisible Man* offers as a solution to the unsatisfactory alternatives of the clearing and the wilderness, a restrictive system and pure chaos, is what the protagonist realizes. He lives on the edge, a borderland where he can negotiate his way between the contingencies of history and the compulsions of himself, the fixities and definites of society and the formless desires of the individual. So,

---

stylistically, does Ellison. Just as the hero manages to extricate himself from a series of fixed environments, so the author shows a comparable suppleness by avoiding getting trapped in one idiom, one language. The style of *Invisible Man* mixes several verbal forms and influences into one multicultural whole. The structure, in turn, offers a crafty variation on a number of narrative forms. This is a picaresque novel, to an extent, its wanderings allowing both author and hero to explore the pluralities of American culture and identity. It is also a novel in the great tradition of American monologue: a tradition of anecdote and tall tale, sermon and auto-biography, journals and songs of the self. It is the novel as epic and the novel as myth; it follows Ellison's own succinct definition of myth, 'a narrative linked with a rite' that 'celebrates a god's death, travels through the underworld, and eventual rebirth'. It also, in its spellbinding mixture of naturalism and nightmare, recollects other great novels that have explored American society and, in particular, the American racial divide: *Absalom, Absalom!*, say, or *Native Son*. Speaking of himself and his fellow novelists, Ellison observed once that their task was 'always to challenge the apparent forms of reality' and 'to struggle with it until it reveals its mad, vari-implicated chaos, its false faces, and on until it surrenders its insight, its truth'. It is a task that Ellison took on boldly and amply fulfilled in *Invisible Man*; the result is that, 'on the lower frequencies', the book has spoken and still speaks for more people, of any race, than its author could ever have imagined.

Ellison died without completing another novel. Apart from *Invisible Man*, two collections of his essays were published in his lifetime. When he died, he left behind six unpublished short stories and an uncompleted novel. These appeared in, respectively, 1996 and 1999: *Flying Home and Other Stories* and *Juneteenth*. By contrast, the productivity of a comparable figure in African American prose writing, James Baldwin (1924–87), was immense. Principally known as a novelist and essayist, he was also a playwright, scriptwriter, poet, director and film-maker. His novels and essays, and his play *The Amen Corner* (1955), revolve in particular around the themes of racial and sexual identity. 'The question of colour, especially in this country,' Baldwin wrote in *Nobody Knows My Name: Notes of a Native Son* (1961), 'operates to hide the great question of the self. That is precisely why what we like to call "the Negro problem" is so tenacious in American life.' And to the question of colour, as a determinant of identity, he added the question of sexuality, since most of his intimate relationships were homosexual – and at a time when homosexuality was still criminalized. To these questions, in turn, he added the questions of family and religion. Born in Harlem when his mother was single, Baldwin suffered at the hands of his stepfather as he grew up. The stepfather, David Baldwin, an itinerant preacher, insisted that James was ugly and bore the mark of the Devil: the writer was later to use this, and the shame such abuse of religious and parental power engendered, as the material for his first novel. Isolated and alienated, Baldwin joined the church of a black woman evangelist he encountered. 'Whose little boy are you?' he remembered her asking in *The Fire Next Time* (1962). The question so evoked a sense of belonging in the fourteen-year-old youth that he simply replied, 'Why yours'. For a while, Baldwin served as a 'young minister' in the Pentecostal church. His earliest stories even reflect a religious influence. But in 1944 he moved to Greenwich Village, then began to shuffle off his church associations and to work on a novel, provisionally titled 'Crying Holy' and then 'In My Father's House'. It was published in 1953 as *Go Tell It on the Mountain*; it immediately established Baldwin's reputation and is probably his most accomplished novel.

Essentially, *Go Tell It on the Mountain* is an initiation novel. Its protagonist, John Grimes, whom we first meet on 'the morning of his fourteenth birthday', is modelled in part on the young James Baldwin. Other members of the fictional family recall other members of the Baldwin family. In particular, John's stepfather Gabriel is a recollection of David Baldwin. The book is divided into three sections. Told from John Grimes's perspective, the first section, 'The Seventh Day', establishes John's marginal position in the family. Denied by his stepfather, dismissed for his unmanliness, ugliness and intellect, his situation is at once intensely personal and profoundly symbolic. As the rejected son, he embodies what Baldwin sees as the historical experience of the African American. Dispossessed of his birthright, despised not least for his nascent homosexuality, he is like the 'darker brother' in the poem by Langston Hughes, 'I, Too': the generic racial figure who is excluded from the American family, the table of communion. 'What shall I do?' John asks himself. The possible answers to that question are two: and they are investigated both in his own story and in that of his family. He can either see himself as others see him and lapse into hatred and rejection of himself. The consequences of that are shame, guilt, fear or, perhaps, compensatory fantasy, all of which John succumbs to for a while. Or he can struggle to accept and realize himself: to pursue the kind of self-realization that Baldwin was thinking of, on a larger, historical scale, when he wrote, 'the American Negro can no longer, nor will he ever again, be controlled by the white American image of him'.

The second section of *Go Tell It on the Mountain* concentrates on John's aunt, stepfather and mother, and offers variations on the theme of self-denial. Images of dirt, darkness, grime (the pun on the family name is clearly intentional) evoke what is to be denied, cleared away, got rid of; the dominant emotional pattern here is one of retreat, repression, since all three older people choose to suppress and evade their true feelings, to hide their true selves behind masks. What is additionally remarkable about this second section is how Baldwin links the story of individuals to history. Informing what we hear about the three characters is the substance of the African American experience, from slavery to the Great Migration. Enlivening every word we hear are the rhythms of African American speech and song. That sense of another, racial dimension, deepening and enriching the personal fate, then feeds into the final section, 'The Threshing-Floor', which recounts the struggle of John for his own self, his own soul. In a complex religious experience, John moves from a sense of damnation to one of salvation: a process that is co-extensive with a movement from rejection to acceptance of himself, from disgust to delight. What he accepts is not only himself, the core of his being, but also his community: 'the multitude' of other African Americans who have suffered, encountered denial and shame, just as he has done. The acceptance is expressed through speech and sound: sound that, we are told, 'had filled John's life . . . from the moment he had first drawn breath'. It is the sound of the blues, the sound of sermons, the sound of all the rhythms of African American life, through which an entire race has found a way to express itself, to face and transform its pain. The achievement of *Go Tell It on the Mountain* is that, as an initiation novel, it works on so many levels. It records the initiation of a boy into knowledge of his own sexuality, the initiation of a black boy into realization of his own racial inheritance and identity, and the initiation of a young person into a recognition of his own humanity and presence in the community. Not only that, it registers another, parallel initiation: that of the author, Baldwin himself, into an understanding that would subsequently shape his career, that only in accepting himself could he express himself, only in embracing the cultural forms, the 'sound' available to him as an African American, could he encounter and possibly transcend his own suffering and that of his race.

While he was still working on *Go Tell It on the Mountain*, in 1948, Baldwin moved to France. He was to spend the rest of his life travelling between Europe and the United States, living in France and Switzerland but never leaving the United States imaginatively. His second novel, *Giovanni's Room* (1956), openly explores homosexuality, in the story of a young white American expatriate in Paris. *Another Country* (1962), his third novel, uses New York, Paris and elsewhere as settings for several characters trying to explore issues of racial and sexual identity. Other, later novels similarly pursue problems of race and sexuality: among them, *Tell Me How Long the Train's Been Gone* (1968), *If Beale Street Could Talk* (1974) and *Just Above My Head* (1979). His first book of essays, *Notes of a Native Son* (1955), was followed by several others: notably, *The Fire Next Time*, in which Baldwin insisted that America could never truly be a nation until it had solved the colour problem. If it did not solve it, he warned, America would not only never become a nation, it would face apocalypse, 'the fire next time'. His play *The Amen Corner* was, in turn, followed by another three: *Blues for Mr Charlie* (1964), *One Day, When I was Lost* (1973) and *A Deed from the King of Spain* (1974). Right up until his final book of essays, *The Price of the Ticket* (1985), Baldwin continued to be committed to what he called 'the necessity of Americans to achieve an identity' and the questions of systematic racism and injustice – the active denial of black identity by white America – that this necessarily raised. 'There is an illusion about America, a myth about America to which we are clinging which has nothing to do with the lives we lead,' he once wrote. Baldwin made the gap between the illusory and the real, on a personal, racial and national level, his subject: insisting always, as he did so, that the only way for individuals, races or nations to survive was to face the truth.

For many years, and especially during the 1950s and early 1960s, Baldwin was a political activist. He marched, talked and worked with a number of civil rights leaders, including the two most famous, whose speeches and other writings give them a place in American literary history, Malcolm X (1925–65) and Martin Luther

King (1929–68). Born Malcolm Little, and later also known as el-Hajj Malik el-Shabazz, Malcolm spent his earliest years in Michigan. After his father died, probably at the hands of a white racist group, and his mother was placed in a mental institution, Malcolm moved to Boston to live with his half-sister. He became involved in the nightlife and underworld of Boston, then later Harlem; and in 1946 he was arrested and imprisoned for armed robbery. During his prison years, he experienced a conversion to the Nation of Islam. Upon his release, he changed his name to Malcolm X, the X signifying the unknown name of his African ancestors and their culture that had been erased during slavery. Becoming a minister for the Nation of Islam, which preached the idea that whites are devils, he helped build it into a significant force in urban black life. However, in 1963, he split from the leader of the Nation of Islam, the Honorable Elijah Muhammed, and he began to move from the mainly spiritual philosophy of the Nation to a more political black nationalism. About this time, too, he began to collaborate with the author Alex Haley (1921–92), whose later main claim to fame was a chronicle of his own ancestry, *Roots* (1976), on *The Autobiography of Malcolm X*. The *Autobiography* was published in 1965, the same year that Malcolm X was assassinated.

As an orator, especially in his last few years, Malcolm X was renowned for his quick wit, fast talk, nervy syncopated rhythms, and for his erudition. 'I don't see any American dream,' he declared in his speech 'The Ballot or the Bullet' (1964), 'I see an American nightmare.' 'I see America through the eyes of the victim,' he added. And he enforced that vision, insisting that what he wanted was not so much 'civil rights' as 'human rights', using a punchy combination of argument and assertion, sharp, memorable images and phrases, street language and rhythmic repetition. 'When you're under someone else's control,' he insisted, 'you're segregated'; 'it's time for Negroes to defend themselves.' What he was after was power for the black community, by any means necessary including violence. 'This is the day of the guerrilla,' he argued; and, craftily recalling a famous slogan of the War of Independence, prophesied that 'It'll be liberty or it'll be death'. The *Autobiography* has the same oracular, oral power as the speeches. Here, in a way typical of both American and African American autobiography, Malcolm X presents his own experience as exemplary. He shows, for instance, how the demeaning label of 'nigger' applied to him, when he was young, even by white liberals, betrayed a general tendency to erase the humanity of African Americans. 'What I am trying to say', he explains, is that 'it has historically been the case with white people, in their regard for black people, that even though we might be *with* them, we weren't considered *of* them.' 'Thus,' he concludes, 'they never really did see *me*.' In opposition to this erasure, Malcolm X asserts his own presence, the reality of the many identities he realized during his life: the hustler, the criminal, the spiritual leader, the political activist and so on. He also uses the autobiographical models of the spiritual narrative, the record of a conversion experience and the success story of a self-made man to inform, enliven and generalize this personal account. What he achieved in his relatively short life was considerable, making him a charismatic figure and a catalyst for political activity. And what he achieved in this, his account of that life, is just as remarkable: whatever else it is, and that is much, it is one of the great American autobiographies.

Unlike Malcolm X, Martin Luther King, Jr embraced a gospel of non-violence in the quest for racial equality. Like Malcolm X, he was the son of a minister. King grew up immersed in the doctrine of Christian love and in the music and rhetoric of the Baptist church. Both were to affect him profoundly, as was his extensive reading of theological and literary texts as a college student and afterwards. King became a minister of a Baptist church in Montgomery, Alabama, in 1954. Soon after that, in 1955, he gave his first civil rights address. Between then and his assassination in 1968, he travelled the nation giving approximately two thousand speeches and sermons: among them 'I Have a Dream' (1963), the climactic speech at a massive civil rights demonstration in Washington, and 'I've Been to the Mountaintop', the speech he gave in Memphis the night before he was killed. 'I Have a Dream' illustrates King's characteristic rhetorical strategy, learned from the many sermons he had both heard and given, of using memorable images, verbal play, literary allusions and Biblical borrowings to communicate his message. As the insistent use of the phrase which gives that speech its title shows, it also indicates his love of incremental repetition: using a repeated phrase ('I have a dream') to build one statement, one sentence, on another. It is a device at least as old as the King James Version of the Bible, as American as the poems of Langston Hughes and Whitman, and it gives to many of his speeches and sermons the irresistible force of a tidal wave. 'I've Been to the Mountaintop', in turn, reviving the old slave identification of themselves with the Biblical Hebrews, trapped in Egyptian bondage, shows how skilfully, and passionately, King could update the religion and world view of slavery, making all this relevant to a new struggle for freedom. At the close of the speech, King boldly compares himself to Moses. 'I've seen the promised land,' he told his audience, 'I may not get there with you. But I want you to know tonight, that we, as a people, will get to the promised land.' King was hardly to know that his death, a few hours after delivering this speech, was to give his words an additional resonance, an eerily prophetic ring. But, as the speech indicates, he did know exactly how to weave different traditions of thought and language, many of them black and some of them white, into a series of intricate, intense variations on the theme, the message that concludes 'I Have a Dream': 'Let freedom ring'.

Born in Chattanooga, Tennessee, and raised in Buffalo, New York, Ishmael Reed (1938–) interviewed Malcolm X for a local Buffalo radio programme, as a result of which the programme series was cancelled. Moving to New York City in 1962, he helped found the *East Village Other*, one of the first and best-known alternative newspapers. He also became involved in the formation of the Black Arts movement. However, his participation in that movement was always both participatory and adversarial. A complex, combative thinker, Reed acknowledges that the black element reveals the permeable nature of American experience and identity. But he also insists on the permeable nature of blackness. He has made it his aim, as a poet, playwright, essayist and, above all, a novelist, to live between cultures and dramatize the exchanges between them. And he has done so not only in his own writing but also in editing works like *MultiAmerica: Essays on Cultural Wars and Cultural Peace* (1997) and in founding the Before Columbus Foundation in 1976, a multi-ethnic organization dedicated to promoting a pan-cultural view of America. Reed is not afraid of controversy. The first of his major novels, *The Free-Lance Pallbearers* (1967), for instance, represents a subversive departure from the autobiographical style of earlier African American narratives. It also offers a parody of *Invisible Man*, for many critics the masterwork of African American fiction. Nor is he frightened of going against the grain of any prevailing critical or creative fashion. The sheer slipperiness of his works has, in fact, led to him being given many wildly different labels. He has been called a revolutionary and a reactionary (a judgement of his position that he satirized in his poem 'The Reactionary Poet' [1978]), a satirist and a postmodernist. Perhaps it would be more accurate to see him as someone who uses tradition to illuminate and reinvigorate tradition, combining continuity and the spontaneous, the impromptu, in a cultural dynamic that Amiri Baraka described as 'the changing room'.

In some of his best work, for example, Reed has taken up a common theme of African American writing, the return to the past, to origins and the revolt against the present, and given it a new, multicultural twist. Reed has insisted, often, that his abiding interest lies in the connection between then and now, the dead and the living. 'Necromancers used to lie in the guts of the dead or in tombs to receive visions of the future,' he said once; 'that is prophecy.' And, he added, 'the black writer lies in the guts of old America, making readings about the future'. With Reed, what he tries to resurrect goes back to what he calls 'the genius of Afro satire'. This he excavates, and then explores, in his fiction, so as to catch a sense of reality that is protean, spontaneous and at odds with any definition of culture in singular terms. 'Nowhere is there an account or portrait of Christ laughing,' he tells the reader in his 1972 novel *Mumbo Jumbo*. 'Like the Marxists who secularised his doctrine, he is always stern, serious and as gloomy as a prison guard.' In order to restore the laughter, and with it a sense of risk, the tricky, tricksy complexity of things, Reed has elaborated what he describes as his 'Voodoo aesthetic', the determining feature of which is its roots in plurality, a mutually reflective, uncoercive 'crisscross' of cultural forms. Monoculturalism, or what Reed has termed 'Atomism', lies at the heart of Western thought: politically, people may be 'left', 'right' or 'middle', but, he argues, 'they are all together on the sacredness of Western civilisation and its mission'. His task, simply and radically, is to 'humble Judeo-Christian culture', with its presumptions to a monopoly on the truth, and to affirm instead not African American culture as such (that would simply mean substituting one monolith with another) but the multiplicity of cultures: to replace the cultural subordination of 'Western civilisation' with the idea of a multiculture.

What all this means, for novels as otherwise diverse as *Mumbo Jumbo*, *Flight to Canada* (1976), *The Terrible Twos* (1982) and *The Terrible Threes* (1989), is serious fun and a teasing, passionate waywardness. Voodoo, Reed has said, 'teaches that past is present'; and each of these novels, and others, offers that lesson in a sly, subversive, jokily – and sometimes horrifically – disjunctive way. The resistance here is to the narrow functional forms favoured by what one of Reed's characters in *Mumbo Jumbo* dismisses as the 'neo-social realist gang'. More particularly, it is to any traditional kind of African American narrative that, as Reed himself has put it, 'limits and enslaves us' by confining black experience to a singular, linear model. The writer metamorphoses into the voodoo-man or magician, the trickster god weaving backwards and forwards in time and between different levels of narration. And the writing turns on a syncretic, densely textured and multilayered vision of reality – with the clear enemy, the target, being the idea of a master narrative, the overdetermined. In *Flight to Canada*, for instance, Reed picks up the old form of the slave narrative and then, through a transformation of style, changes a remembrance of servitude into an act of liberation. A flight from slavery is enacted twice in the book: the first time in a poem called 'Flight to Canada' written by a character called Quicksill, and the second time in Quicksill's escape to Canada. But a flight from slavery also *is* the book. 'For him, freedom was the writing,' it is said of Quicksill. And freedom is the writing of *Flight to Canada* the novel as well as 'Flight to Canada' the poem, as Reed deploys self-reflexiveness, parody, deliberate anachronism and constant crisscrossing between different histories and cultures to manoeuvre himself out of the straightjacket of social realism. According to some critics, at least, the traditional slave narrative was constrained by its moral earnestness, its patient accumulation of detail. It was a clear illustration of what some black commentators in particular have seen as the political uses to which the abolitionists put black literacy: with a prescriptive and painstaking verisimilitude denying blacks the possession of their own story, or the possibility of breaking out of monocultural forms. *Flight to Canada*, on the other hand, with its punning title, its mixing of an antebellum setting with casual references to the *dreck* of contemporary culture, and its irreverent humour ('Go to the theatre,' a slaveowner advises Abraham Lincoln; 'Get some culture') slips off all these shackles. The Civil War is spliced with the civil rights wars of the 1960s, with the image of Lincoln's assassination, for example, being constantly replayed in slow motion on the late night news. Edgar Allan Poe, the Marquis de Sade and Captain Kidd mingle with such props of the modern age as television, jumbo jets and *Time* magazine. And a slaveowner declares himself doubly outraged at his runaway slaves because, as he puts it, 'they furtively pilfered themselves'. Through meaningful mischief such as this (slaves are property but also, for the purposes of moral censure, people), through shrewd mixings and the sudden splicing of stories, Reed slips the reader the message that freedom springs from confluence not control, an easygoing commerce between cultures. Reed refuses to be slave to his narrative, *Flight to Canada* or elsewhere. In the process, he resites the act of connection between living and dead in an altered demography. This a return to origin, a flight into and out of the past that occurs within a fictional version of the uncertainty principle: an America that seems to follow no set rules, other than those of diversity, chance and change.

Two African American writers whose return to origins is less slippery are Ernest Gaines (1933–) and Albert Murray (1916–). 'I go to San Francisco but I cannot stay away from here,' Gaines has observed. 'Here' is Louisiana, where Gaines spent his childhood and most of his youth. Born to a black sharecropping family in the Point Coupe parish, Gaines was working in the fields by the time he was nine and, after his parents separated and his father disappeared, he was brought up by a crippled but indomitable great aunt, Miss Augusteen Jefferson, who, Gaines was to say later, 'did not walk a day in her life but who taught me the importance of standing'. Then, in his fifteenth year, he joined his mother in northern California, which has been his main residence ever since. He returns regularly to Louisiana, however. More to the point, his collection of stories, *Bloodline* (1968), and all his novels are set in the fictional parish of St Raphael, based on the parish in which he was born. Return to the homeplace is a shaping impulse in Gaines's fiction, from his first novel *Catherine Carmier* (1964) through *In My Father's House* (1978) to *A Lesson Before Dying* (1993). So is Gaines's desire to resurrect what he sees as a missing history. Covering a period as far back as the 1860s, but concentrating as Gaines himself has said on the era 'between the thirties and the late seventies', his works tell the story of cultural confluence and social conflict between whites, Cajuns and blacks, but they focus on the group whose past has, the author feels, been ignored or actively suppressed, the 'peasants', 'the blacks of the fields'. Certain themes recur throughout – manhood and, in particular, what is called in *In My Father's House* 'the gap' between black fathers and their sons, womanhood as the arbiter of value and guarantee of continuity in the Southern black community, the moment of trial, testing, when a person has the 'chance to stand' (to borrow a phrase from Gaines's 1983 novel *A Gathering of Old Men*) and so assert his courage and define himself. But the determining factor in all of Gaines's fiction is not so much this theme or that but voice. 'I come from a long line of storytellers,' Gaines has said. His fiction, he has admitted, works best when he 'can get into the person of some other character and let him carry the story'. So in *The Autobiography of Miss Jean Pittman* (1971), the title character, based on Gaines's great aunt, recovers her past and that of her people in a heroic act of tale telling. In *A Gathering of Old Men*, the old men testify to past weakness and announce their newly found courage in a series of overlapping monologues. And in *A Lesson Before Dying*, a young black man condemned to death seizes the chance to be in touch with his own humanity by bearing witness to it in his diary. In each case, and others, voice becomes a means to empowerment for Gaines's characters – and, by implication, for the black community to which they belong. The silence is broken, the suppressed history released, in an act that involves both a recovery of folk idioms, the rhythms of the past, and resistance to the present; talking here has a clear social dimension – in terms of the speech author, narrator and character employ, the personal *is* the political.

With Albert Murray, what has been returned to is not so much voice, the oral tradition, as the blues idiom. Like Gaines, Murray has drawn on a number of European and white American influences, but the most powerful shaping factor has been his African Americanism: in this case, the general, nurturing aspects of the African American community described in his essay collection *South to a Very*

Old Place (1971), and the specific cultural forms celebrated in such books as *The Hero and the Blues* (1973) and *Stomping the Blues* (1976). For Murray, the blues idiom works like classical tragedy. It supplies a stylistic code for dramatizing the most terrible, painful situations; and it offers a strategy for living with, even triumphing over, them, surviving with dignity and grace. As with any developed aesthetic form, the blues idiom enables the artist to transform the grit of raw experience into significant art, to celebrate human possibility, 'in spite of the fact that human existence is so often mostly a low-down dirty shame'. Murray has realized his belief in the formal and moral potential of the blues in his fictional trilogy, *Train Whistle Guitar* (1974), *The Spyglass Tree* (1991) and *The Seven League Boots* (1996). The three novels trace the growth of their protagonist and narrator, Scooter, from his childhood in smalltown Alabama to his maturity as a bass player in a touring jazz band. Along the way, he learns lessons about living and testifying from his family, friends and neighbours: from the man, for instance, who plays guitar 'as if he were also an engineer telling tall tales on a train whistle'. Above all, he learns individual worth and communal responsibility; he discovers that the best life is in an instinctive, rhythmic exchange between self and others – something like the relationship between musicians, the jazz soloist and the supporting band.

Two African American male writers of an earlier generation who have had a significant impact in the period since the Second World War are John O. Killens (1916–87) and John A. Williams (1925–). Killens published his first novel, *Youngblood* (1954), during the early years of the civil rights struggle. Bearing the stamp of its times, it describes the lives of four characters in the segregationist South who fight against oppression. His 1967 novel *'Sippi* also addresses the struggle for racial equality. In *The Cotillion; or, One Good Bull is Worth Half the Herd* (1971), however, he moved away from racial protest to satire, exploring the conflicting claims of Afrocentrism and Eurocentrism specifically within the black community. A more prolific writer than Killens, John A. Williams has produced eleven novels, six non-fiction books, one play and many essays. His main claim to fame, however, is *The Man Who Cried I Am* (1967). Structurally complex, *The Man* has a double chronology. On one level, it recounts one day in the life of its protagonist, a writer called Max Reddick. Terminally ill, Reddick discovers an international agenda for annihilating all people of African origin; the day ends with his murder. On another level, the novel moves through the entire experience of Reddick, with special reference to his encounters with American racism. The net effect of this chronology and the structural complexity is to problematize the notion of history. History is written out not in linear terms, as a monolith, but as myriad – changing, contingent, related to states of being, habits of narration. It is seen, in short, as inextricable from power, its truth dependent on whose story manages to get told. This was a perception to be taken up, structurally and theoretically, by a number of other African American writers, some of whom have acknowledged Williams's influence; among them Charles R. Johnson, John Edgar Wideman and Toni Morrison.

John Edgar Wideman (1941–) began as a self-conscious Modernist. It was only after a long writing hiatus, in the late 1970s, that he learned, as he put it, 'a new language to talk about my experience'. The result of this was his 'Homewood Trilogy' (*Damballah* [1981], *Hiding Place* [1981], *Sent for You Yesterday* [1983]), set in his birthplace, Pennsylvania's Homewood community, reconstructing the family history and reclaiming and recording the central role played by his great-great-great grandmother, a runaway slave, in founding an African American version of the city upon a hill. Aware now of what he has called the 'pervasive process of the paradigm of race', Wideman sees himself as a 'seer/writer' who uses his narrative powers to access racial memories, to struggle against forgetting, to 'break out, to knock down the walls' that separate African Americans from their past. And that project has led him into non-fiction, notably meditations on grave family tragedies involving his brother and son (*Brothers and Keepers* [1981], *Fatheralong: A Meditation on Fathers and Sons* [1994]), as well as into documentary fiction in *Philadelphia Fire* (1990), his novel concerning the bombing by the city of Philadelphia of a house occupied by a militant African American organization in 1985. For Charles R. Johnson (1948–), by contrast, the racial paradigm has always been there in his complex, allusive work. In each of his novels, an educated African American male comes to the discovery of himself through an understanding of the nature and definition of freedom. In each novel, also, Johnson explores and subverts traditional genres as he investigates the relationship between meaning and being, history and knowledge. So, in *Middle Passage* (1990), Johnson draws on such diverse sources as the sea story and the slave narrative, *Moby-Dick*, *Arthur Gordon Pym* and *Invisible Man*, to tell the story of a newly freed slave, Rutherford Calhoun. To escape debts and an impending marriage, Rutherford jumps aboard the first ship leaving New Orleans, the *Republic*, a slave ship en route to collect members of a legendary tribe. What follows, told in the form of a ship's log, fluctuates between historical naturalism, magic and myth as Rutherford tells how he came to mediate between the tribe and his shipmates, and to learn a new paradigm – a new prism through which to look at himself and his relation to the world.

The determining influence of race on a writer like Johnson is suggested by the fact that his first novel, *Oxherding Tale* (1982), draws on the *Narrative* of Frederick Douglass, while his third, *Dreamer* (1999), draws on the life of Martin Luther King. For James Alan McPherson (1943–), race is less of a determinant, however: or, at least, race in exclusive, oppositional terms. In his short story collections *Hue and Cry* (1969) and *Elbow Room* (1977), McPherson has explored his vision of an America whose citizens would be, as he has put it, 'a synthesis of high and low, black and white, city and country, provincial and universal'. Racially inflected though the stories are – dealing, that is, with specific problems of racial prejudice and injustice – their bias is towards more general issues of diversity and identity: how the complex character of any community or identity can be denied by any failure of the imagination. With Leon Forrest (1937–97) and David Bradley (1950–), the canvas is wider in a formal sense and more targeted thematically.

Forrest, for instance, created his own sprawling fictional world of Forest County, based on his homeplace of Cook County, Illinois, in his trilogy *There is a Tree More Ancient than Eden* (1973), *The Bloodworth Orphans* (1977) and *Two Wings Veil My Face* (1984). Stylistically dense and innovative, the three novels are linked not just by their shared location but by interlocking genealogies and the developing consciousness of a protagonist who grows to maturity during the course of them. Not only that, they are connected by their common concern with orphanhood. Like Hughes, Ellison, Baldwin and so many other African American writers, Forrest sees his race as the orphans of the nation, seeking the place, the parentage they have been consistently denied. A sense of orphanhood leads inevitably into the search for a past, which is the subject of *The Chaneysville Incident* (1981), the second and major novel of David Bradley. The incident the title refers to is a collective suicide. According to local legend, the protagonist John Washington learns, his forebear and thirteen slaves killed themselves at Chaneysville, Pennsylvania, on the Underground Railroad route. Determined to discover the truth about this, John, a history professor, undertakes assiduous research. The research remains abortive, at first. It is only when John's wife, white and the descendant of slaveholders, joins him and questions his motives that the gaps in the story begin to be imaginatively bridged. The slaves evidently chose death in preference to threatened recapture and a return to bondage. Out of respect, a white miller then buried them: an act of empathy between the races that is repeated in the restored relationship between John and his wife. Complexly mixing black and white narrative forms, *The Chaneysville Incident* bears witness to the chance of racial reconciliation in both the past and the present; and it does so through the use of a familiar trope in African American texts, the speaking of a silenced history. By forging the link between history and storytelling, too, it inscribes the belief that finding a past and a voice are indissolubly linked enterprises. And to this it adds a rider: to find a voice is to find oneself, as an individual, a race and a nation.

Defining a new black identity in drama

An African American dramatist who believed equally in possibility, the chance to be and express oneself, was Lorraine Hansberry (1930–65). Accused by some critics of confining herself to the conventions of the well-made play, and verisimilitude, Hansberry replied by insisting that what she was after was 'genuine realism'. This she carefully distinguished from naturalism. 'Naturalism tends to take the world as it is,' she explained; 'but . . . I think that the artist who is creating the realistic work imposes on it not only what is but what is *possible* . . . because that is part of reality too.' Hansberry believed firmly that people could, as she put it, 'impose the reasons for life on life'; and she was profoundly sceptical about any intellectual or artistic tendency that seemed to her to deny hope or the opportunity for social change. When she died, for instance, one of the unpublished plays she left satirized *Waiting for Godot* (1956) by Samuel Beckett and what she felt was the spiritual bankruptcy of absurdism. Born and brought up in Chicago, the child of middle-class parents who dared to move into a white neighbourhood and faced the threat of violence as a result, Hansberry decided to become a writer after seeing a performance of *Juno and the Paycock* (1925) by Sean O'Casey. She wanted to capture the authentic voice of the African American working class. After associating with various prominent figures in the cultural life of Harlem and working on *Freedom*, a newspaper founded by the singer and activist Paul Robeson (1898–1976), she began working on a play set in the South Side of Chicago. Originally titled 'The Crystal Stair', after a line from a poem by Langston Hughes, it was eventually named after another line from a Hughes poem called 'Harlem'. 'What happens to a dream deferred?' Hughes had asked. 'Does it dry up / Like a raisin in the sun? . . . / Or does it explode?' Hansberry called her play, a dramatization of dreams deferred that threaten to explode, *A Raisin in the Sun* (1959).

A Raisin in the Sun has been compared to *Native Son*. Set in a black Chicagoan working-class environment, it explores, as Richard Wright's novel does, frustrations and struggles that are determined by the primary fact of race. It even opens in the same explosive way, with the sound of an alarm clock that seems to herald crisis and to call on the audience to pay attention. While Hansberry investigates many of the same issues as Wright, though – the relation of material wealth to human dignity, the crippling consequences of poverty and racial prejudice, the conflict between separation and assimilation – she does so in a different key, a more hopeful register. The dramatic premise is simple. An insurance benefit of ten thousand dollars paid on the death of the father of the household becomes the source of conflict within the Younger family, as Mama Lena Younger, the widow, beneficiary and matriarch, argues with her son, Walter Younger Jr, over its use. Not only does the premise allow Hansberry to unravel the tensions within the family, tensions that are clearly symptomatic of differences within the African American community as a whole, it enables her to suggest the intimacy of their shared experience – and their ultimate solidarity in the face of white prejudice and oppression. In the end, resisting white threats and attempts at bribery, Walter Younger Jr goes along with his mother's desire to move from their cramped apartment into a white neighbourhood. 'We come from people who had a lot of pride,' Walter tells a white man who tries to dissuade the Younger family from becoming his neighbours. 'We have decided to move into our house because my father – my father – he earned it.' 'He finally come into his manhood today, didn't he?' Mama Lena proudly observes of her son. 'Kind of like a rainbow after the rain.' Working together, despite their disputes and differences, they end the play preparing for the move that will change their lives, perhaps for good, perhaps for ill, probably both. The dream is no longer deferred.

Hansberry never wrote a play to equal *A Raisin in the Sun*. Another work, *The Sign in Sidney Brustein's Window* (1964), about the vacillation of a Jewish intellectual between disenchantment and commitment, was produced with only moderate success. Other work, which showed her edging towards feminist issues and the discovery of her own lesbianism, was never produced or published during her lifetime. By contrast, another African American woman playwright, Adrienne

Kennedy (1931–), has been enormously prolific and has seen her work produced by numerous different companies in the United States and Europe. More than a dozen plays have been published, together with several autobiographical works of non-fiction and a novella. A number of pieces have been commissioned by drama companies, ranging from the Juilliard School in New York to the Royal Court in London. She even worked with John Lennon on a dramatic version of his writing. 'I see my writing as a growth of images. I think all my plays come out of dreams I had two or three years before,' Kennedy has said. Her dramatic style is, in fact, a vivid mix of expressionism, surrealism and African ritual. She uses non-linear plots, dream imagery, split characters who exist in trancelike states, and fragmented formats. Characters may be played by more than one actor, one character may mutate into another, masks and music may be used. What she creates is a mosaic woven around figures whose sense of identity seems to be floating, fluid, permeable. In her first professionally produced play, *Funnyhouse of a Negro* (1964), for instance, she deployed her experience as an African American female, her travels in Europe and her knowledge of the classics to dramatize the ambiguities of a people, like her own, created out of the clash between European and American cultures. In *The Owl Answers* (1965), her personal favourite among her plays, she touches on the quest for identity of a black woman in a world dominated by whites, using composite characters who transform back and forth into different parts of themselves. In *A Movie Star Has to Star in Black and White* (1976), she maps out overlapping dramatic spaces, of family scene and movie scene, as she describes the dilemma of her central character, caught between daylight and dream, her role as a wife and mother and her being as a writer. Kennedy's many other plays include *Son: A Poem for Malcolm X Inspired by His Murder* (1968), *An Evening With Dead Essex* (1973) and *The Alexander Plays* (1992). Mixing influences as different as Wagner, Tennessee Williams and James Baldwin, characters out of myth and movies, fantasy and history, autobiography and theology, all of them are marked by an intense concern with issues of identification and attachment. 'There was always great confusion in my own mind where I belonged, if anywhere,' Kennedy has admitted; and she has turned that confusion into complex drama.

Both Ed Bullins (1935–) and August Wilson (1945–) are also seminal figures in the story of African American drama since the war. Bullins was brought up in a tough Philadelphia neighbourhood and knows the violence of the ghetto at firsthand: he was nearly stabbed to death as a youth. The gritty existence his characters lead, in a street world that Bullins describes as 'natural' rather than naturalistic, reflects the influence of that environment. After a spell in the navy, and travelling around America, he settled in San Francisco. There he joined other African American writers to form Black Arts West, a militant cultural and political organization, and to direct the Black House Theatre. Other writers committed, like him, to drama as an agent of cultural and political change included Ben Caldwell (1937–) and Ron Milner (1938–). The writer who influenced him most, however, was Amiri Baraka. In his play *Dutchman* in particular, Baraka had used elements of myth, mixing absurdist conventions and realistic strategies with a brittle colloquialism to tell a fast-paced tale of a fatal encounter between a provocative white woman and a naive, middle-class black man. The woman, called Lula, turns from flirtation to taunts as she attacks the black man, Clay, for playing the role which the dominant white society has handed him. Clay finally replies with all the force of racial hatred that he has repressed in order to survive, claiming that for a black man repression and conformity are necessary because murder is the only alternative. Furious at losing control of the situation, Lula fatally stabs Clay. She then orders the other riders on the subway train where she and Clay have met and where all the action occurs to remove his body. As they are doing so, the play ends with another black man entering the subway car and Lula begins her act all over again. The claustrophobic physical setting, the sense of irresistible force and motion, and, not least, the constant references to Adam and Eve, fairytales and the Flying Dutchman all suggest the synthesis of styles and approaches at work in this powerful tale of racial tension and sexual repression. Clearly affected by this, and other plays by Baraka, Bullins has created his own special mix of streetwise dialogue and sophisticated dramatology, the vernacular and the mythic, in the more than fifty plays he has written, starting with *Clara's Old Man* (1965) and *Goin' a Buffalo* (1968).

Goin' a Buffalo, for instance, is about a group of characters, prostitutes and pimps, living on the edge in Los Angeles. 'This play is about some black people,' Bullins tells us in the initial stage directions. For these people, money, drugs and sex circumscribe their lives. They are caught, it seems, in enclosed spaces that reflect their captive, constrained status in society; and they are bewildered by the gap, or rather chasm, that opens out between the promise of America and the realities, the sheer violence of their everyday existence. For them, Buffalo, on the other side of the American continent, beckons as an escape, a chance to realize the unrealizable dream of freedom and a fresh start. The dream, however, dissolves in conflict, manipulation and deception. Bullins later chose to include *Goin' a Buffalo* in his Twentieth-Century Cycle, a proposed series of twenty plays on the African American experience, that deals not so much with race relations as with the everyday lives of African Americans. Other, subsequent plays in the series include *In the Wine Time* (1968), *Home Boy* (1976) and *Boy x Man* (1995). All the plays in the series so far, together with those outside it, carry his familiar trademarks. 'Each individual in the crowd', Bullins has written, 'should have his sense of reality confronted, his consciousness assaulted.' So, his plays consistently startle in their immediacy, their raw power of language and action, their concentration on the psychosocial anger of African American culture. The 'natural' style Bullins says he follows is a product of craft, calculation. Music, particularly rhythm and blues and jazz, is used to frame the actions and focus feeling. Symbolism, such as the symbols of boxes, enclosures, that run through *Goin' a Buffalo*, establishes meaning. Language, a stripped, rhythmic vernacular, discloses only what the characters want to disclose: there is no obvious attempt made to impose a meaning, impart a message. This is an art that resists overt ideology – Bullins left the Black House Theatre when he felt that there was too much pressure on him to produce simply agitprop plays – but that nevertheless explores the many avenues by which drama can issue out of and return to black life, carrying with it in the process a series of potentially revolutionary ideas. As such, it represents, perhaps, the finest realization of the black aesthetic on the stage.

While Bullins has been central to the story of alternative theatre, success on the mainstream stage has tended to elude him. By contrast, August Wilson has enjoyed considerable mainstream success. His *Ma Rainey's Black Bottom* (1982), *Fences* (1983), *Joe Turner's Come and Gone* (1984), *The Piano Lesson* (1986), *Two Trains Running* (1992) and *Seven Guitars* (1995) were all produced on Broadway, for the most part to critical and commercial acclaim. Born on 'The Hill', a racially mixed area of Pittsburgh, Pennsylvania, to a black mother and a white father he seldom saw, Wilson encountered racial prejudice early. He also encountered two formative cultural influences: black talk and black music. In a cigar store in Pittsburgh, he has recalled, he would stand around when he was young listening to old men telling tales and swapping stories. Later, listening to the records of the blues singer Bessie Smith, he became determined to capture black cultural and historical experience in his writing. One of his first publications was, in fact, a poem called 'Bessie'. Beginning to write plays in the 1970s, *Ma Rainey's Black Bottom* established his reputation. Set in 1920s Chicago, it describes the economic exploitation of black musicians by white record companies and the ways in which victims of racism are compelled to direct their rage at each other rather than at those who caused their oppression. It is also a memorable combination of the vernacular, violence and humour. So is *Fences*, which concerns the struggles of a working-class family in the 1950s to find security. Here, Wilson also uses myth to tell the story of Troy Maxson, a garbageman, ex-convict and former Negro Baseball League player, who cannot believe that his son will be allowed to benefit from the football scholarship he has been offered.

Joe Turner's Come and Gone is set some forty years earlier than *Fences*, in a Pittsburgh boarding house in 1911. Focusing on the personal and cultural aftermath of both slavery and the Great Migration, it explores the lives of characters who are in danger of being cut off from their roots. *The Piano Lesson*, in turn, is placed in 1937, in Pittsburgh: concentrating on a conflict between a brother and a sister, over who has the right to own a family heirloom, the piano of the title, it dramatizes the debate between African American and mainstream cultural values. *Two Trains Running* moves forward several decades, to the late 1960s – to a coffee shop where regulars discuss their troubled relation to the times – and *Seven Guitars* then moves back to the 1940s. Wilson has declared that, as a playwright, he wants to 'tell a history that has never been told'. His major plays reflect this. For him, they are all part of a major project: a cycle of ten plays, each of them intended to investigate a central issue facing African Americans in a different decade of the twentieth century. He is aiming at nothing less than raising the collective awareness, rewriting the history of every decade so that black life becomes a more acknowledged part of the theatrical history – and, for that matter, the general history – of America. In 1991, Wilson recalled that his plan, to bring a silenced past into dramatic speech, began with 'a typewritten yellow-labelled record titled "Nobody in Town Can Bake a Sweet Jellyroll Like Mine" by someone called Bessie Smith'. 'It was the beginning', he explained, 'of my consciousness that I was a representative of a culture and the carrier of some very valuable antecedents.' He has continued to pursue that plan ever since, in plays that work precisely as the 'yellow-labelled record' did: by bringing a whole culture, and its past, to life, with rhythmic flair and passion.

Telling impossible stories: Recent African American fiction

If any novelist can be said to have a project similar to that of August Wilson in drama, it is surely Toni Morrison (1931–). 'For me, in doing novels about African Americans,' she has declared, 'I was trying to move away from the unstated but overwhelming and dominant context that was white history and to move it into another one.' Her work can, in fact, be seen as an attempt to write several con- centric histories of the American experience from a distinctively African American perspective. A series of fictional interventions in American historiography, her novels draw what she has called, in *Playing in the Dark: Whiteness and the Literary Imagination* (1992), 'the overwhelming presence of black people in the United States' from the margins of the imagination to the centre of American literature and history. What has been distinctive about the history of the United States, Morrison has argued, is 'its claim to freedom' and 'the presence of the unfree within the heart of the democratic experiment'. This was, and remains, 'a nation of people who *decided* that their world view would combine agendas for individual freedom *and* mechanisms for devastating racial oppression'. As such, it 'presents a singular landscape for a writer'. And her aim in mapping that landscape has been twofold. On the one hand, she has charted a specifically *black* history, giving voice to the silence: pointing to the culpability for it of white America's 'failure' to apportion human rights equally, while simultaneously celebrating that history's achievements and identifying its own failings. On the other, she maps out a general history of America from the readjusted perspective, the angle of black experience. As Morrison has noted in *Playing in the Dark*, 'Africanism is inextricable from the definition of Americanness – from its origins on through its integrated or disintegrating twentieth-century self'. The history of black America, over the last two hundred years and perhaps more, *is* the history of America, as she sees it. So what she is pursuing, reclaiming in imaginative terms, is a history of the whole American experience.

'The crucial difference for me is not the difference between fact and fiction,' Morrison once admitted, 'but the distinction between fact and truth. Because facts can exist without human intelligence, but truth cannot.' That search for truth began with her first novel, *The Bluest Eye* (1970). It has a simple premise. A narrator, Claudia McTeer, tells the story of Pecola Breedlove, a black girl whose hunger for love is manifested in a desire for blue eyes that eventually drives her to insanity. What complicates things is both structural and social. Morrison has said that one of her goals as a writer is 'to have the reader work *with* the writer in the construction of the book'. And here she uses a number of narrative devices to realize that goal. The novel opens, for example, with a parodic passage from a Dick and Jane school primer that presents an ideal, inevitably white family: the kind of cultural intervention that seems calculated to create false consciousness. Working with the writer here, and elsewhere in the novel, the reader gradually unravels a tale of personal and social disintegration. Pecola, it seems, is driven inward, by the norms of white society (the bluest eye, the ideal family), to shame, the destruction and division of the self. Claudia, the narrator, finds herself directed outward, to anger against white society: finding a convenient scapegoat, a focus for anger, for instance, in the 'white baby dolls' she cuts up and destroys. *The Bluest Eye* deconstructs the image of the white community as the site of normality and perfection. It also exposes the realities of life in an impoverished African American community, whose abject socioeconomic status is exacerbated by the politics of race. Those politics point, in particular, to internalized racism, manacles that are mind-forged as well as devastatingly material. As Morrison has put it in an Afterword to a recent, reprinted edition of the novel, 'the trauma of racism is, for the racist and victim, the severe fragmentation of the self'.

Co-extensive with Morrison's concern with the psychosocial consequences of racism is her interest in what she calls 'silence and evasion': the shadows and absences, the gaps and omissions in American history. In her second novel, *Sula* (1973), for example, she shows how a black community evolves and shapes itself, with its own cultural resources and elaborate social structure. She rescues it from a kind of historical anonymity. Through the lives of the two main characters, Sula Peace and Nel Wright, in turn, she opens up the area of intimate friendship between African American women. Also, through a poignant account of the rifts and disputes between Sula and Nel, she charts differences, the diverse paths and possibilities available to females as part of or apart from communal tradition. Morrison's third novel, *Song of Solomon* (1977), sustains her commitment to what is called here 'names that had a meaning': the evolution of a distinctive black identity and community through the habit of language. A complex tapestry of memory and myth, *Song of Solomon* tells the story of a young man, Milkman Dead, who comes to know himself through a return to origins. He is captivated by the legends surrounding his family, from slave times. He learns, in particular, from the stories of men who flew to freedom and the realities of women who remained to foster and to nurture. Just as the novel does, he returns to the past and, through that, discovers how to live in the present. *Tar Baby* (1981) also pursues themes of ancestry and identity, how African Americans come to name and know themselves. It does this primarily through the contrast between two characters, Jadine Childs, a model, and William (Son) Green, an outcast and wanderer. Jadine, brought up with the help of white patrons, has been assimilated into white culture; Son remains outside it, in resistance to it. Drawn to each other, they seem to be trying to 'rescue' each other, the one from assimilation, the other from separation. 'One had a past, the other a future and each bore the culture to save the race in his hands,' the reader is told. 'Mama-spoiled black man, will you mature with me?

Culture-bearing black woman, whose culture are you bearing?' The love affair between them is aborted. Neither fundamentally changes. And although the perspective on Jadine is less than sympathetic ('she has forgotten her ancient properties,' one oracular black character observes of her), the identity crisis posed by the conflict between her and Son is never really resolved. Morrison adopts her usual strategy, of leaving the narrative debate open.

With her fifth and most important novel so far, *Beloved* (1987), Morrison took the core of a real story she had encountered while working as a senior editor at Random House. It was recorded in *The Black Book* (1974), an eclectic collection of material relating to more than three hundred years of African American history. And it concerned a fugitive slave called Margaret Garner who killed her daughter, then tried to kill her other children and herself rather than be returned to slavery. Morrison took this as the nucleus, the germ of her story about Sethe Suggs, who killed her own young daughter, Beloved, when faced with the same threat. Circling backwards and forwards in time, before and after the Civil War, the novel discloses how Sethe and other characters – especially her daughter Denver and her lover Paul D – struggle with a past that cannot yet must be remembered, that cannot yet must be named. In other words, it pivots around the central contradiction in African American, and for that matter American, history: living with impossible memories. There is the need to remember and tell and the desire to forget; there are memories here with an inexhaustible, monstrous power to erupt and overwhelm the mind that must somehow be commemorated yet laid aside if life is to continue. It is a contradiction caught in a phrase repeated in the concluding section of the narrative: 'it was not a story to pass on' (where 'pass on' could mean either 'pass over' or 'pass on to others'). It is one caught, too, in the scandalous nature of the act, the killing that haunts Sethe. In that sense, the mother/daughter relationship that Morrison characteristically focuses on here is at once a denial of the institution of slavery and a measure of its power.

Beloved is an extraordinary mix of narrative genres. It has elements of realism, the Gothic and African American folklore. It is a slave narrative that internalizes slavery and its consequences. It is a historical novel that insists on history as story, active rehearsal and reinvention of the past. It weaves its way between the vernacular and a charged lyricism, the material and the magical, as it emphasizes the centrality of the black, and in particular black female, experience. It also forces the reader to collaborate with the author, narrator and characters in the construction of meaning: the energetic refiguring of a past that is seen as a necessary precondition of the present – determining (and so to be resurrected) yet different (and so to be laid to rest). This involvement of the reader in the exhumation of a secret that is also the narrative's secret – the unspeakable heart of the story that remains intimated rather than spoken – is the main grounds for the emotional intensity of *Beloved*. This is a novel that reorients history, American history in particular, to the lived experience of black people. It is also a passionate novel that sets up a vital, unbreakable circuit between historical events and emotional consequences, and then connects up that circuit to any one, black or white, or whatever, who reads it. We the readers are caught as the main characters of *Beloved* are in the 'look', the gaze that seeks to reduce the black subject to the position of otherness. We share with these characters the rigours of the disciplined body – the denial of the ownership of one's own flesh. We also participate in the strenuous, successful effort to resist all this: the right to one's own body and consciousness, the responsibility for them in the past, present and future. Above all, we share in the project of naming. 'Did a whiteman saying make it so?' Paul D asks himself at one point. The immediate answer turns out to be 'yes'; the ultimate answer is 'no'. The novel and its characters turn out, after all, to offer another form of 'saying', a more authentic way of seeing and telling the personal and historical past. That is why the last word of *Beloved* is, precisely, 'Beloved'; because the whole aim of the story, and its protagonist, has been to name the unnameable. That way, we know by now, African Americans, and all Americans, can come to terms with a past that should be told, that will not be told (the paradox is irresolvable) – and then, perhaps, be able to continue.

After *Beloved*, Morrison published two books that, with it, form part of a loosely connected trilogy, *Jazz* (1992) and *Paradise* (1998). Morrison has said that the three novels are about 'various kinds of love': the love of a mother for her child, romantic love and 'the love of God and love for fellow human beings'. The three might equally be described as charting the history of African Americans. *Jazz*, set in Harlem in 1926, was inspired by Morrison reading in a book she was editing, *The Harlem Book of the Dead*, about a young woman who, as she lay dying, refused to identify her lover as the person who has shot her. What distinguishes the novel more than its plot, however, is Morrison's innovative way of telling it. Imitating the improvisational techniques of jazz music, she presents us with a narrative that constantly revisits events and a narrator who frankly confesses her fallibility. 'I have been careless and stupid,' the narrator declares at one point, 'and it infuriates me to discover (again) how unreliable I am.' History is consequently presented as a process of constant telling and retelling, with the openings for chance, the impromptu and mistake that that implies. And, at the end, the responsibility for that process is passed on to us, the readers. 'Make me, remake me,' the narrator tells us. 'You are free to do it and I am free to let you because look, look. Look where your hands are. Now.' *Paradise* is set in 1976. In describing the intimate contact between two communities, though, one a black township and the other a refuge for women, it circles as far back as 1755. It also supplies another example of Morrison's characteristic strategy of giving voice to the silence while initiating its own forms of silence. That is, it brings those traditionally exiled to the margins, for reasons of race, gender or both, to the centre of the stage; it allows them to name themselves and narrate their history. But it quietly intimates its own lack of authority, the blanks and absences detectable in its own account, and the responsibility that this imposes on the reader.

In *Beloved*, for example, the reader never knows who the young girl who returns to Sethe during the course of the story is. Is she the ghost of the two-year-old daughter Sethe killed twenty years earlier? Does she recall Sethe's nameless mother, since some of her dreams and narrations seem to recall the horrors of the Middle

Passage? Is she a myriad figure, a composite of all the women ever dragged into slavery? Or is she a very singular young woman who has been driven mad by her enslavement? We cannot know, for sure: all we can do is allow these possibilities to feed into our own retelling of an intolerable, impossible past, our own project of naming the unnameable. Nor, for that matter, can we be certain what happens at the end of *Paradise*. The pivotal act of this novel is the shooting, and apparent killing, of the women at the refuge by nine men from the township. *Paradise* closes, however, with the 'marvellous' disappearance of the bodies of the women and the reappearance, then, of four of them. One of the several, unresolved puzzles of *this* story is, therefore, what they return *as*, ghosts or human beings who somehow survived the attack. But just as *Beloved*, for all its push beyond realism, leaves no doubt as to the monstrous *fact* of slavery and its central place in the story of America (indeed, using magic, mystery, as a measure of that monstrosity), so *Paradise* leaves no doubt about the *necessity* for the reappearance of women like these, in some form or another, for the survival of the republic. *Paradise* is a book about the failures of American democracy (hence its setting in the bicentennial). It is about the strengths and fatal flaws in the black community (hence its complicity in the shootings). It is about the core meaning of the African American story to American history (hence the narrative connections forged with key events since 1776). And it is also a book about the failure of patriarchy. Morrison has resisted the description of herself as a feminist. She is right to do so because *Paradise*, like all her novels, is so much more than a polemical statement of a position. But, in its own way, it registers a fundamentally optimistic belief in the recovery of the American republic – a belief that all her work tends to share – and, in this case, at the hands of women. The beguiling mystery at the end of *Paradise* is centred, just as the mystery at the heart of *Beloved* is, by a powerful analysis of history, past disasters and possible future directions. Any doubts about that surely dissolve in the meditations of one female character as she considers the possibility of reappearance, the return of the women shot by the men of the township. 'When will they return?' she asks herself. 'When will they reappear . . . to rip up and stomp down this prison calling itself a town?' 'She hoped with all her heart that the women were out there,' the meditation concludes, 'darkly burnished, biding their time, brass-metaling their nails, filing their incisors – but out there. Which is to say she hoped for a miracle.'

Apart from the occasional excursion into drama (*Dreaming Emmett* [1986]) and critical and social theory (*Playing in the Dark, En-Gendering Power: Essays on Anita Hill, Clarence Thomas, and the Construction of Social Reality* [1992]), Morrison has focused on the writing of novels. By contrast, Alice Walker (1944–) has written six novels, on which her reputation rests, but she has also produced five volumes of poetry, two collections of short stories, three volumes of essays and four children's books. All her work, in different genres, is dedicated to what she has come to call 'womanism'. This she defines in *In Search of Our Mothers' Gardens* (1987) as a form of black feminism that 'appreciates and prefers women's culture, women's flexibility . . . and women's strength'. Womanism, according to Walker, is not narrowly exclusive. On the contrary, it is 'committed to survival and wholeness of entire people, male and female'. Still, she tends to concentrate on the evolution of female wholeness: the development of identity and community among black women 'in the face', as she puts it, 'of the Great White Western Commercial of white and male supremacy'. In her non-fiction, this has led her to search out and celebrate her connection with other African American women, particularly writers. *In Search of Our Mothers' Gardens*, for instance, is at once a memoir and a series of observations on African American women's culture. It establishes a specifically womanist tradition, a series of role models from the silent and unheralded (mothers whose gardens or hand-crafted quilts are their art) to the writer who has been the 'queen bee' for Walker, Zora Neale Hurston. Searching for foremothers, Walker has helped to establish the pivotal importance of works by African American women. She has also helped to promote that work: for instance, by co-founding a publishing outlet, the Wild Tree Press, and by editing *I Love Myself When I Am Laughing* (1979), a seminal selection of Hurston's prose.

In fiction, Walker inaugurated her career with *The Third Life of Grange Copeland* (1970), a realistic novel describing three generations of a family whose history is marred by racial oppression and sexual violence. It is notable, in particular, for its stark account of a repetitive cycle of abuse, wife beating and sexual exploitation, within the black family and community. *Meridian* (1976), Walker's second novel, concentrates on the civil rights movement and the fight for social change. It is, however, centred on the experience of women. Its central character, Meridian Hill, lives in the North but returns to the South to help in a voter registration drive. Meridian, the reader learns, is '*held* by something in the past', a 'something' that includes, above all, her mother and a church that is both her mother's church and – whether she likes it or not – her mother church. 'Her mother's life was sacrifice,' Meridian reflects. And her main feeling, when she thinks about her, is guilt: guilt over abandoning her own child and so betraying 'maternal history', and guilt over involving herself in politics. Meridian never comes to personal terms with her mother but, by returning to her mother's history and ancestry, she does experience a symbolic rapprochement. 'Mama, I *love* you. Let me go,' Meridian is able to whisper to the figure of her mother she sees in a dream. She has made peace with her, and can move on. Meridian is also able to make her peace and come to terms with the church, and in a less purely symbolic way. For the church she encounters in the South is one transformed by the civil rights revolution. From it, she learns a new song: 'it is the song of the people, transformed by the experience of each generation, that holds them together'. It offers a new form of personal and sociopolitical revolution; and it enables Meridian to connect her present to her past. Her return to origins has initiated change, but change that is contiguous with the earlier experiences of her community. In that way, she has come back to her own history only to transcend it, and become a whole woman.

Change, a purely secular salvation involving the discovery of identity and community, is also at the heart of *The Color Purple* (1983). At the centre of this novel is Celie, the victim of racial and sexual oppression. Raped by the man she believes to be her father, she is battered and abused in a loveless marriage. Nevertheless, she gradually learns 'how to do it', how to grow into being and companionship. Her mentors here are three women. One, called Sofia, teaches her by example the lesson of resistance to white and male oppression. Another, her sister Nettie, offers her a more complex lesson, primarily through her letters. A missionary, who goes to work in Africa, Nettie discloses to Celie the ancient, cultural and spiritual dimensions of the African American tradition: the proud inheritance they share. Through her encounters with white colonists and developers, she also quietly links the story of racial oppression in America to a larger history of imperial adventure and conquest. The third mentor Celie encounters is a blues singer, Shug Avery. The first person for whom Celie feels a definite physical attraction, Shug teaches Celie about her body, she offers her the possibility of sexual pleasure. She also unpacks the cultural forms, specific to America, that she and Celie share as African Americans: the sensual promise of jazz, the tragic melancholy of blues. And, like Sofia and Nettie, she leads by example. She is a powerful illustration of selfhood, a person who positively fills the space she occupies. More than anyone, Shug encourages Celie to believe in herself. Everything, Shug suggests, is holy. Everything is worthy of respect and wonder. The divine is to be found not in 'the old white man' worshipped in church, in this place or that, but in everything. Even the color purple. Even, and especially, Celie. It is a profoundly American sentiment, this belief in a democracy of being, a divinity that informs every individual. And it allows Celie to flower from absence into presence: to become herself.

That process of becoming herself is co-extensive with learning a language; Celie learns 'how to do it' by learning how to say it. *The Color Purple* is an epistolary novel. Most of the letters are written by Celie. And they measure her growth, not just as a person but into being a person. Language, finding the right words, and being, finding a real self, are inseparable here. At first, the words written by Celie seem to come, as it were, from nowhere. They are a series of shapes to fill a lack; they seem existentially sourceless, because Celie has never been allowed properly to exist – never been given the opportunity to be and know herself. Gradually, though, Celie learns the right words. She develops a language, vibrant and vital, that is a medium of selfhood. As she does so, her letters cease being letters to 'God' – sent from nobody to nowhere – and become letters to her sister Nettie. By implication, they are letters to all her sisters, as she edges towards that discovery of communality, the divine in everything, on which her own belief in herself depends. Since writing *The Color Purple*, Walker has written several books that push at the formal boundaries of fiction while developing themes and revisiting characters first encountered in this seminal 1983 novel. *The Temple of My Familiar* (1989), for instance, explores a wide variety of subjects from a womanist perspective. It reintroduces Shug Avery; it introduces us to the granddaughter of Celie; and it is, perhaps, not so much a novel as a collection of loosely related tales, a sermon, and a stream of dreams and memories, bound together by the belief that 'all daily stories are in fact ancient and ancient ones current . . . There is nothing new under the sun.' In turn, *Possessing the Secret of Joy* (1992) picks up the issue of female circumcision, touched on in *The Color Purple* as a symptom of male cultural violence; and *By the Light of My Father's Smile* (1998) explores the thin, permeable boundaries between different ethnic traditions, and between life and death. No subsequent book, however, has matched either *The Color Purple* or *Meridian* as an account of human wholeness, the discovery of being. And none has matched *The Color Purple*, in particular, in its revelatory use of form. *The Color Purple* is not just a story of personal growth that happens to be written as a series of letters. It achieves its meaning precisely by being an epistolary novel: by returning to one of the oldest forms of prose fiction and using that as the source, the key to the opening up of the self. Celie writes herself into existence, into contact with herself and communion with others. And those others include the readers, since the letters are ultimately addressed to us.

Like Toni Morrison, whom she has acknowledged as an influence, Gloria Naylor (1950–) achieved critical success with her first novel, *The Women of Brewster Place* (1982). Consisting of the interrelated tales of seven African American women, all of whom end up in a dead-end street in a northern ghetto, it focuses in particular on male insensitivity and violence. The women range in age from their twenties to their fifties but, like so many of the characters of Alice Walker, they all suffer at the hands of men from their own families and community. With her second novel, *Linden Hills* (1985), Naylor moved from the ghetto to a middle-class community. Set in the 1980s, the novel traces the journey of a young African American poet, in the company of a fellow poet, through an exclusive black neighbourhood, looking for odd jobs. The resemblance of the two to Virgil and Dante, and of Linden Hills itself to the Dantean Inferno, becomes inescapable. This is a place, it seems, that lost souls inhabit; it is full of those who have sold out, to the dream of success. It is also a place that shares its general geography with Brewster Place: Naylor shares, not only with Morrison but also with Faulkner, an interest in the determining impact of setting and the intention of creating her own fictional map. Her third and fourth novels, *Mama Day* (1988) and *Bailey's Cafe* (1992), extend that map. In *Mama Day*, Naylor superimposes the two settings of Willow Springs – an island off the coast of South Carolina and Georgia – and New York City. In *Bailey's Cafe*, she centres the action on a New York City restaurant of that name. These two novels also substantially enlarge her formal range. With *Mama Day*, for instance, Naylor has said that her aim was to analyse the nature of belief. Reiterating the existence of an ancient African American folk tradition here, she allows the consciousness of the island to narrate some of the novel; she dramatizes exchanges between the living and the dead; and, in effect, she invites the reader to participate in that willing suspension of disbelief that magic, religion and fiction all share. *Bailey's Cafe* is different to the extent that it is written in the form of a jazz suite. But it also combines the grimly material and the strangely mythic. The all-night café is a kind of way station for the lost souls who wander in there, and lurking behind it is a realm of fantasy: a dock on the water that is evidently capable of meeting the desperate hopes, the dreams of these lost souls by miraculously transforming reality. In 1998, Naylor published *The Men of Brewster Place*, which returns to the men whose violence and indifference made the lives of the women of her first novel miserable. It also grants them a voice. The novel is, perhaps, less formally daring than some of her earlier work but it shows the same imaginative compulsion to map out the mundane facts, the magical dreams and monstrous nightmares that belong to one particular place.

Friendship between women is a common theme in the fiction of Naylor, Walker and Morrison, and also in the novels of Terry McMillan (1951–) and Sherley Anne Williams (1944–99). McMillan has been called the Frank Yerby (1916–91) of her generation. This seems to miss the point. Like Yerby, McMillan has achieved crossover appeal, in the sense that novels like *Waiting to Exhale* (1992) and *How Stella Got Her Groove Back* (1996) have attracted a large popular audience. But Yerby made a conscious decision to move from protest writing to popular novels like *The Foxes of Harrow* (1946). True, he never gave up protest fiction completely; and his romances set in the South offer a revisionist view of its history and a harsh critique of its racism. But he remained, above all, a genre writer; and it was not until 1969, in *Speak Now*, that he introduced his first black protagonist. McMillan, on the other hand, has concentrated on serious fictive treatments of contemporary issues, notably race and gender, and on the experiences of African American women. *Waiting to Exhale*, for example, chronicles the lives of four intelligent, unattached females; while *How Stella Got Her Groove Back* tells the story of a middle-aged mother and divorcee struggling to make her way in the world. Without being programmatic, both novels address the various roles and possibilities open to women of colour in a system still dominated by white males; and they are remarkably resistant to pat solutions. *Dessa Rose* (1986) by Sherley Anne Williams also concentrates on the experience of women. A neo-slave narrative, it recounts the experiences of a woman born into slavery, her struggle for freedom and, in particular, her friendship with a white woman, Ruth Rufel, on whose plantation she stays and works when she becomes a runaway. Williams said that she based the novel on 'two historical incidents'. One involved an uprising on a coffle, a group of slaves chained together, led by a black woman; the other, occurring a year after this, in 1834, involved a white woman who gave sanctuary to runaway slaves on her isolated farm. 'How sad, I thought then, that these two women never met,' she recalled, and she allowed them to do so in her novel. Gradually, Dessa and Ruth form a bond, an intimate friendship that is nevertheless hedged around by inevitable differences of experience and race. And, eventually, they part: one goes east, the other west. Williams also confessed that she had been appalled by *The Confessions of Nat Turner* by William Styron, which she saw as a travesty, a distortion of the story of slave revolt, and wrote *Dessa Rose* as a corrective, a critical response. What she produced, as a result, was remarkable. This is a novel that allows the silenced voice of the female slave to speak, not only through its imaginative reclamation of history but also through its musical form. For, in its fundamental narrative rhythm, the telling of a solitary woman's experience of love denied, bondage, revolt, wandering, freedom and love restored, *Dessa Rose* imitates the structure of blues: repeating and varying a few central, soulful themes.

Paule Marshall (1929–) and Jamaica Kincaid (1949–) approach the experiences of people of colour, especially women, from a different perspective, because of their West Indian background. Kincaid was, in fact, born in Antigua, leaving there for the United States when she was sixteen. Marshall was born in the United States, in Brooklyn; the influence on her of her West Indian background, however, has been profound. The daughter of second-generation Barbadian immigrants, Marshall grew up listening to the tales and talking of her mother and her female West Indian friends, whom she has described in her non-fiction as the 'poets in the kitchen'. Her first novel, *Brown Girl, Brownstones*, was also a first in several different ways when it appeared in 1959. It was one of the first novels, since the time of Claude McKay, to explore the link between African American people and their West Indian counterparts. It was one of the first to delve into the inner life of a young black female protagonist. It was also one of the first to explore in detail the relationship between a black mother and daughter. Selina Boyce, the protagonist in *Brown Girl, Brownstones*, is the daughter of first-generation Barbadian immigrants. She is brought up in the brownstone buildings of Brooklyn, in an area that, as the novel opens in 1939, is experiencing a sea change in terms of its inhabitants. The whites are moving out or 'discreetly dying', and West Indian immigrants are moving in. The brownstones constitute an anchor in this sea of racial change; and, as Selina grows up there, listening to the kitchen talk of her mother Silla and her friends, and witnessing the reveries of her father Deighton in his upstairs sun room, she finds herself torn. Her mother, a powerful figure, longs to assimilate, to 'buy house' as she puts it and buy into the American dream. Her father, a feckless romantic whom Selina adores, dreams of returning to Barbados. 'He's always half-studying some foolishness,' Silla complains. Doting on her father, wrestling with the overwhelming force and influence of her mother, Selina also has to contend with the prejudice of the white people she encounters: in whose eyes, like 'a well-lighted mirror', she sees 'with a sharp and shattering clarity – the full meaning of her black skin'. Marshall pointedly refuses to resolve the process of cultural and national adaptation Selina engages in as she grows up. At the end of *Brown Girl, Brownstones*, Selina is still faced with the task of coming to terms with her equivocal feelings about her mother and (now dead) father and the mixed, polyglot character of her inheritance. She plans, however, to leave Brooklyn for the 'islands': not, it seems, to imitate the return to origins dreamed of by her father but to retrace the diasporic wanderings of her mother. Silla had arrived by ship from the Caribbean to the New World, 'watching the city rise glittering with promise from the sea'. 'I'm truly your child,' Selina now tells Silla; and she takes up the burden, not of abandoning her American identity – that would be impossible – but of discovering the other cultural fragments required for self-definition.

The wandering quest Selina takes up at the end of *Brown Girl, Brownstones* has become a hallmark of Marshall's fiction. It characterizes the four novellas collected in *Soul Clap Hands and Sing* (1961) and her later novels *The Chosen Place, the Timeless People* (1969), *Praisesong for the Widow* (1987) and *Daughters* (1991). Involving, very often, a reverse Middle Passage, it dramatizes a search for and reconciliation of the self with an African diasporic historical past. In its own way, it also marks the longer fiction of Jamaica Kincaid: *Annie John* (1985), *Lucy* (1990) and *The Autobiography of My Mother* (1996). *Annie John* charts the growth of an angry, alienated and exceptionally bright girl, who wryly refers to herself and her friends as 'descendants of slaves', from the ages of ten to seventeen. Growing up in Antigua, she is about to embark for England at the end of the novel, to study nursing: not because she loves that country, or desires that particular career, but because she needs to reject all boundaries of family and island. In *Lucy*, a similarly acerbic character, now aged nineteen, arrives in the United States from Antigua in 1967, just after the island has received its independence from Great Britain. Working as an au pair for a white family in New York City, she finds herself, as she puts it, wrapped 'in the mantle of a servant'. But her position, her origins in what she calls 'the fringes of the world', and, not least, her keenly ironic intelligence enable her to cast a cold eye over the generic American household she enters (Kincaid stresses the point by supplying no family name). Observing a supposedly ideal American family from close up, she becomes a witness to its destructive tensions and divisions. Eventually, she leaves her job as au pair; her commitment to her fashioning of herself, she feels, requires her to reject that life, just as, earlier, she had felt compelled to abandon an 'ancestral past' rooted in the 'foul deed' of slavery. Selfhood is now seen as a process, the self as contingent, constantly negotiable; and Lucy prepares to pursue that process in the fluid, multicultural terrain of New York City, the ultimate metropolis. *Lucy* ends with Lucy beginning to write her story in her diary, opening with her full name, Lucy Josephine Potter. It is an apt expression of her newfound desire to take possession of her own being, to trace its evolution as she passes through different contexts, different cultures. 'I understood that I was inventing myself,' she asserts. That is her task, and her need, as she now sees it. Which is a task that links her, as Kincaid must know, with many other travellers to and sojourners in the New World. Even in her resistance to the orthodoxies of America, and cultural orthodoxies of any particular kind, Lucy is making a very American choice.

Realism and its Discontents

Confronting the real, stretching the realistic in drama

The New York City in which Lucy decides to make her way is not just the ultimate metropolis. For many years it has been the theatrical capital of America. Until around the end of the 1950s, it was even more localized than that. One street in particular, Broadway, was synonymous with the American theatre; and that street, together with the side streets intersecting it, dominated the theatrical activity of the nation. The fifteen years following the Second World War were, arguably, the high point of the Broadway theatre. During this period, not only were the late and posthumous plays of Eugene O'Neill produced there. The greatest plays of the two other greatest American playwrights, Arthur Miller and Tennessee Williams, appeared on Broadway. Influential directors like Elia Kazan (1909–) practised their craft in distinguished productions. The Method school of acting was introduced and developed. Not only that, the major achievements of the Broadway musical appeared. Prior to the 1940s, the most notable musical was probably *Show Boat* (1927) because it took up serious themes, including miscegenation, without trivializing or sentimentalizing them. The music was by Jerome Kern (1895–1945). The lyrics were by Oscar Hammerstein (1895–1960), whose career charts the rise of the musical in the 1940s and 1950s. After working with Kern, then Lorenz Hart (1895–1943), Hammerstein teamed up with Richard Rodgers (1902–79). The result was *Oklahoma!* (1943), the first musical to use dance as an integral part of the plot and a powerful celebration of the mainstream values of the American West. It was followed by other successes: *Carousel* (1945), *South Pacific* (1949), *The King and I* (1951), *Flower Drum Song* (1958) and *The Sound of Music* (1959). Even after Hammerstein's death, the success continued for his collaborator, Rodgers, when he teamed up with Stephen Sondheim (1930–) and also went on to write musicals by himself. Besides working with Kern, Hart and Rodgers, Hammerstein collaborated with George S. Kaufman (1889–1961) and Moss Hart. The most remarkable outcome of this collaboration was *Pal Joey* (1940), based on a series of sketches by John O'Hara about a seedy nightclub operator. Between them, Hammerstein, Rodgers and the various people they teamed up with from time to time turned the musical into a characteristically American art form, a medium for serious entertainment and, sometimes, for revealing the nation to itself.

As far as drama is concerned, what is remarkable about the work produced when Broadway was at its height is its roots in domestic realism. This was not, however, a limitation, since the finest American dramatists of the period used realism as a means of exploring fundamental issues. Method acting helped to expand the potential of realism here. With its emphasis on exploring the subtext, the emotional drama lurking beneath the most mundane situations and talk, it encouraged emotional adventure. The function and capacity of domestic realism could be expanded, as a result, to reveal the dread – the fear of, and occasional triumph over, disaster – that hovered below the surfaces of the everyday. As it happens, the careers and styles of Arthur Miller and Tennessee Williams are exemplary. Those careers reveal certain parallels. Both playwrights followed initial failure with a second play that established a reputation and particular dramatic territory. Both produced, in a third play, the finest of their career. Both went on to write some of the finest plays of the 1950s, and ended the period of their greatest achievement in the early 1960s. Their styles, however, reveal radical differences. Miller, for instance, used realism to explore wider moral and political issues, whereas Williams was more interested in deploying it to explore emotional and psychological forces. Miller concentrated on the ordinary person put under extraordinary pressure by his or her society, to be destroyed or survive. Williams, on the other hand, focused on misfits: extraordinary people trying to bear up against the ordinary pressures of life. For Miller, the orbit of attention was formed by what he called 'the Common Man'. 'It matters not at all whether a modern play concerns itself with a grocer or a president,' he once declared, 'if the intensity of the hero's commitment to his cause is less than the maximum possible.' To pursue this, he fashioned an idiom that replicated both the clarity and the misperceptions of the vernacular: the direct poetry of the street that, sometimes, people use to conceal the truth from themselves. For Williams, what mattered was the common humanity that connects the uncommon, the outsider to the rest of us, the aberrant to the average. And to dramatize that, he devised a language that, at its best, was subtly poetic, rhythmic and emotional. These two major dramatists in effect measured the diverse potential of domestic realism: stretched out, when necessary, to incorporate borrowings from other forms and styles, notably symbolism and expressionism. They also mapped out the terrain that most subsequent American dramatists have occupied. Apart from a brief period in the 1960s and just after, when many playwrights struck out towards improvisation and more radical experiment, it is the dramatic land of Miller or Williams that most continue to inhabit. The domestic setting and some form of realistic speech – both of which, in Miller's and Williams's hands, became rich and variable instruments – have continued to dominate the American stage.

The first play by Arthur Miller (1915–) to reach Broadway, *The Man Who Had All the Luck* (1944), closed after only four performances. His second, *All My Sons* (1947), however, achieved success and introduced certain themes that would dominate his work: the pursuit of success and public approbation enshrined in the American dream, social and familial tension and the conflict between competing moralities, the economic and political system as a final cause of the problems and passionate misconceptions Miller's characters have to endure. The central character, Joe Keller, sold faulty airplane parts to the government during the war. Believing that he did what was necessary to support his family, he does not recognize his responsibility for the consequent death of several pilots: that is, until the discovery that his son killed himself in shame prompts him to see the higher moral obligation announced in the title of the play. Characteristically, Miller explores the past and its impact on the present, and the fundamental issues of moral and social responsibility, through a dramatization of family conflict. The story of the play is told entirely in domestic terms; and at its fictional centre is the question of whether Joe's surviving son, Chris, should marry the fiancée of his dead brother. Equally characteristically, Miller encourages us to pity Joe rather than damn him for his misrecognition. *All My Sons* may, finally, endorse the declaration made by Chris: that 'there's a universe outside and you're responsible to it'. But it shows that Joe's failure to recognize this is a fault of society rather than his own. And it lays the fundamental blame squarely on a system that would force a man to choose between competing imperatives of family and society, his sons and *all* his sons.

With *Death of a Salesman* (1949), unquestionably his finest play, Miller endowed similar issues and problems with a tragic dimension. It relates the story of a representative American, Willy Loman: an ordinary man, as his surname punningly indicates, but one whose choices and their consequences spell out the darker,

---

destructive side of the national dream. A salesman who, after thirty-five years on the road, has never achieved the rewards and recognition for which he had hoped, Willy is driven to despair by his failure in a system that seems to him to guarantee success. Measuring his worth by the volume of his sales – Miller never lets us know what Willy sells because, essentially, he is selling himself – Willy obsessively withdraws from the crises and disappointments of the present into memories of the past and into imaginary conversations with his brother Ben, his symbol of success. *Death of a Salesman* is, in a sense, a memory play, for which a working title was 'The Inside of his Head'. And everything here is seen double, as Willy sees it and as it is: a point sounded in the initial stage description of Willy's 'fragile-seeming home'. 'An air of the dream clings to the place,' we are told, 'a dream rising out of reality.' This is also a tale of domestic realism in which Miller uses elements of expressionism and symbolism to transmute the story into a tragedy. The dialogue is realistic vernacular: the idiom of a society that pursues images, illusion rather than fact, tawdry dreams rather than terrible reality. But the 'exploded house' in cross-section that appears in act one and supplies the setting for most of the play prepares us for a revelatory intimacy. We, the audience, are drawn into the family combustion, the crisis in the Loman household. We are drawn into the collapsing consciousness of Willy, in particular, into the past as an explanation of the present. And with the help of a rich tapestry of symbols (the symbols of success and successful father-figures that haunt Willy, for instance), we are invited to see this drama as the tragic crisis of a society as well as that of one unremarkable but representative man.

Good American that he is, Willy believes that success is his birthright. 'And that's the wonder, the wonder of this country,' he declares, 'that a man can end with diamonds here on the basis of being liked.' He can never give up this belief, or its corollary: that, in the land of opportunity that is America, failure can only be the fault of the individual. Despite his glimmering, growing sense of separation from the success ethic, he still judges himself in its terms. As Miller himself has put it, Willy is 'constantly haunted by the hollowness of all he had placed his faith in', but nevertheless, at the end, he stakes 'his very life on the ultimate assertion' of that faith: not least because, in terms of belief, he has nowhere else to go. His wife Linda watches helplessly as he tears himself apart. All she can do is care and ask others to care: 'attention,' she declares, 'attention must be finally paid to such a person.' His son Happy can only surrender to the same ethic. 'He had a good dream,' he says of his father at the end. 'It's the only dream you can have – to come out number-one man. He fought it out here, and this is where I'm gonna win it for him.' Willy's other son Biff, though, is different. Biff senses that he does not want what the world calls success. But, unfortunately, he cannot articulate, or properly know, what he does want. 'I don't know – what I'm supposed to want,' he confesses. All he can say to Willy, in a desperate declaration of personal love and social resistance, is, 'Pop! I'm a dime a dozen, and so are you!' 'Pop, I'm nothing,' he then adds, 'I'm just what I am, that's all.' Listening to Biff, Willy learns the value of love. Tragically, and typically, however, he then translates love into the only values he knows, the values of a salesman. What he gives Biff in return is the gift of himself, or rather his worth as an economic unit, a social commodity. Willy kills himself so that his family can have the insurance money and Biff, he hopes, can get a new start in life. 'He had the wrong dreams, All, all, wrong,' Biff observes of his father, as he stands beside his graveside. That was the tragedy of Willy Loman, and of that he was tormentingly, tremulously aware. And, Miller makes it clear, it was and is the tragedy of a society as well.

The challenge that Willy Loman never quite meets, to know and name himself, is also the challenge that confronts John Proctor, the central character in *The Crucible* (1953), and Eddie Carbone, the protagonist in *A View from the Bridge* (1955; revised 1956). As in *Death of a Salesman*, too, that challenge is a personal one rooted in a social landscape: people in Miller's plays, and especially the earlier ones, are compelled to confront themselves, and make the choices that define their lives, in terms that are determined by their history and their society. Eddie Carbone cannot meet the challenge. A Sicilian American longshoreman, Eddie is consumed with a love for his niece Catherine that approaches the incestuous. When Catherine falls in love with a cousin smuggled into the country, Eddie is driven to violate one of the taboos of his culture by reporting the illegal immigrant to the authorities. Equating the loss of honour with loss of name, he dies denying his guilt: 'I want my name!' he cries out, as he tries to recover his self-respect by seizing it, by violence. John Proctor does meet the challenge, however. Written at the height of the hysteria whipped up by the Un-American Activities Committee, *The Crucible* explores issues of personal conscience and social suppression through the dramatic analogy of the 1692 Salem witchcraft trials. With the help of this analogy, Miller, who was himself a victim of the Committee, touches on all the consequences of McCarthyism: the exploitation of legitimate cultural fears, conspiracy theories and social hysteria, the oppression of the innocent and the manipulation of power, the complicity of ordinary citizens and public officials in a pernicious, paranoid social process that appears to take on an irresistible life of its own. When John Proctor's wife is named as a witch by a young woman, Abigail, with whom he has had an adulterous liaison, he attempts to expose the accuser. This, however, leads to his own arrest. Tempted to save his skin by confessing, he decides that honour requires his death. He has been drawn into examining his life by the accusations levelled at him; and he recognizes that, while innocent of witchcraft, he has other responsibilities to answer for. His confession of adultery with Abigail initiates an intense spiritual revaluation of himself. This leads, in turn, to the belief that even his execution for witchcraft would be unearned, since he is guilty while those he would be dying with are truly innocent. John confesses because he believes himself too ridden with guilt to die with honour. He recants, however, out of a sense of responsibility to the innocents he is to die with, and to himself. The demand that his signed confession be displayed in public is one that he feels compelled, ultimately, to resist. It would steal innocence from the truly innocent: 'I blacken all of them when this is nailed to the church the very day they hang for silence!' John declares. And it would steal from him, however guilty, his own core of being, his fundamental sense of his worth; or, as he sees and puts it, his name. 'How may I live without my name,' John asks his accusers. 'I've given you my soul; leave me my name!'

After an absence of eight years from the New York stage, Miller returned in 1964 with *After the Fall* and *Incident at Vichy*. This was followed by *The Price*, in 1968, and *The Creation of the World and Other Business*, in 1972. The plays of this period are very different in terms of subject matter. *After the Fall* is a semi-autobiographical drama, based on Miller's marriage to Marilyn Monroe; *Incident at Vichy* deals with Nazi persecution of the Jews. In *The Price*, two brothers meet after the death of their father to arrange the sale of his furniture. In *The Creation of the World*, a serio-comic rewriting of the story of Adam and Eve, Adam must struggle to find a capacity for goodness and moral responsibility in himself to guide Eve towards forgiveness and Cain towards repentance. All of them, however, are marked by a shift from the social to the personal. Whatever the subject and setting, the focus is on individual experience and, in particular, the problem of individual guilt. So, in *After the Fall*, the central character Quentin prepares for his third marriage with the fear that his past history does not make him deserving of happiness. Talking to the audience about the past, then moving back to join in past events as he recollects them, Quentin is plagued with guilt over his failures and betrayals. He recalls, for instance, the neurotic demands made by his second wife Maggie, summed up in her insistent, 'Love me, and do what I tell you. And stop arguing.' He recognizes the demands as impossible, yet he feels guilty for not having met them. What he comes to realize, finally, is that the defects for which he blames himself are part of the human condition. As human beings, he, and we, must accept and forgive our imperfections, and then build for the future on the basis of that acceptance. We need 'to know, and even happily, that we meet unblessed', Quentin concludes; 'not in some garden of wax fruit and painted trees, that lie of Eden, but after, after the Fall'.

The personal resonance of plays like *After the Fall* has been sustained in some of Miller's later works. *Elegy for a Lady* (1982), for example, is an elegant and ambiguous exploration of love. A man enters a shop to buy a gift for his dying lover; the proprietress of the shop attempts to help him make a choice and seems gradually to take on the character, the persona of the dying woman. *Some Kind of Love Story* (1982), in a similarly intense, intimate way, investigates the strange relationship between a private detective and a prostitute he has been questioning about a murder over the years. *I Can't Remember Anything* (1987) again concentrates on a couple, this time an elderly one, to dramatize the pleasures and the pains of old age. A few other later dramas return, however, to the social emphasis of *Death of a Salesman* and *The Crucible*. *The Archbishop's Calling* (1977), for example, uses the setting of an unnamed East European country to consider the political and moral responsibilities of the artist. It is not clear to an American writer visiting the country if he is genuinely interested in the plight of the people he is visiting, or simply using them for his writing. It is not clear, either, if the two European writers he meets are spies or simply complicit in the suppression and constant surveillance that scar their country, where even the most innocent conversation loses its innocence because it might be overheard. Even more memorably, *The American Clock* (1986) returns to Miller's earlier dramatic explorations of the national democratic experiment. An epic history of the Depression of the 1930s, in both personal and public terms, the play focuses on the memories of two survivors. One, called Les Baum, dwells on the domestic: the decline of his middle-class Jewish family into poverty. The other, a financier named Arthur Robertson, concentrates on the social: his survival, thanks to his ability to anticipate the economic crash. Together, though, the recollections of the two men register an abiding faith in the ability of the American nation to repair and redefine itself. What the Depression did ultimately, Miller suggests, was strengthen and affirm democracy, to give Americans back their belief in themselves. 'She was so like the country,' Baum observes of his mother; 'money obsessed her but what she really longed for was some kind of height where she could stand and see out and around and breathe in the air of her own free life.' That catches perfectly the critical faith in America that characterizes all Miller's best work, as well as its intimate blend of the domestic and the political, family and history. So does Baum's next remark about the woman he loved and now sees as representative: 'With all her defeats she believed to the end that the world was meant to be better.'

For Tennessee Williams (1911–83), too, the world was meant to be better; however, he and many of his characters believed that it had little chance of ever being so. 'I write from my own tensions,' Williams once observed. 'For me, this is a form of therapy.' And those tensions drove him towards a series of intensely poetic examinations of the injured spirit: the private pains and passions of lonely individuals for whom the task of living in the world is almost unendurable. 'We're all of us sentenced to solitary confinement inside our own skins for life!' the main character, Val Xavier, in *Orpheus Descending* (1957) declares. 'What does anyone wait for? For something to happen, for anything to happen, to make things make more sense.' Waiting, and living in the meantime, so many of Williams's protagonists are concerned with nameless fears and insecurities – and with desperate desires, grasping at anything to numb them, to offer distraction from the pain. Williams called his fragile, deeply wounded characters 'the fugitive kind'. 'It appears to me, sometimes,' he explained, 'that there are only two kinds of people who live outside what e. e. cummings has defined as "this socalled world of ours" – the artists and the insane.' Williams added that, of course, 'there are those who are not practising artists and those who have not been committed to asylums' but who have, nevertheless, 'enough of one or both magical elements, lunacy and vision' to see into the dark heart of things, to sense the raw, cold, frightening nature of life. And he made those people, often leading ordinary, unheroic lives but far from ordinary otherwise, the core subject of his plays.

The Glass Menagerie (1945) was the first drama to announce Williams's voice and vision: his project of stretching ordinary domestic realism to explore extremes of sensibility and experience. The domestic setting of the play is transformed by being filtered through reminiscence. 'The play is memory,' Tom Wingfield, the narrator, announces at the beginning. 'Being a memory play, it is dimly lighted, it is sentimental, it is not realistic.' 'Yes, I have tricks in my pocket . . . But I am the very opposite of a stage magician,' Tom explains. 'He gives you illusion that has the appearance of truth. I give you truth in the pleasant disguise of illusion.' Williams deploys evocative language, elusive symbolism and sly, suggestive glimpses into processes of thought and emotion that are too ephemeral, too evanescent to be analysed or explained. And all of this is to describe this truth, which circulates around Tom's memories of his family, living in genteel poverty in St Louis during the Depression. Tom recalls his life with his mother Amanda, a faded Southern belle who clings persistently to glamorous illusions about her past, and with his sister Laura, a crippled, painfully shy young woman whose intensely private world is centred on a treasured collection of small glass animals. He recollects how he ached to leave home, but how his mother insisted he first supply a man to care for Laura in his absence. In a series of impressionistic scenes, intimate remembrances of things past, Tom conjures up for us how he brought a visitor to the house, 'an emissary from a world that we were somehow set apart from', and how the visit ended in disaster. And he remembers how he finally left home, never to return. Williams presents the Wingfield family as unable to function in reality, in this 'socalled world of ours'. But this seems more of a virtue than a weakness: the alternative space or place they inhabit seems as special and seductive as the world of glass animals that gives the play its title. Driven by guilt over his desertion of his mother and sister, too, Tom comes to realize this. 'Oh, Laura, Laura,' Tom cries to his lost sister, 'I tried to leave you behind me, but I am more faithful than I intended to be!' He is doomed to relive the past and to recognize that that is where, if anywhere, the emotional truth resides: a truth he has betrayed.

The intensely heightened realism, the poetic impressionism of feeling and method that characterize *The Glass Menagerie* mark all of Williams's finest work. They are there, above all, in his finest play, *A Streetcar Named Desire* (1947). Set in New Orleans, the plot is devastatingly simple. Blanche Dubois visits her sister Stella and finds her married to what she calls an 'animal', the crude, intensely physical Stanley Kowalski. Another faded Southern belle, Blanche has come 'to the last stop at the end of the line', as the director of the first Broadway production of the play, Elia Kazan, put it. This is her last chance. She struggles for control of Stella with Stanley. She also struggles for a new life, a new romance with Stanley's friend Mitch. She fails. After a violent and sexual confrontation with Stanley, she is defeated and broken. And the play ends with Blanche being taken off to the asylum and Stella and Stanley still together. Williams explained once that the idea for the play came from a time when he himself was living in New Orleans. Near where he lived ran 'two streetcars, one named DESIRE and the other named CEMETERY'. For him, the 'undiscourageable progress' of the two seemed to have 'some symbolic bearing', to express the opposing fundamentals of experience. And they are certainly the tensions that threaten to tear Blanche apart. Blanche Dubois is torn between death and its opposite desire, 'the long parade to the graveyard' as she calls it and the desperate longing to live and perhaps love. Torn and driven within, she is also driven into a wrenching, searing conflict with Stanley. Resisting death, reaching out to desire, she engages in mortal combat with her brother-in-law for some-where to be, somewhere where things might just make more sense. She 'tries to make a place for herself', as Kazan put it. But there is no place for her.

A Streetcar Named Desire has the elemental force of a struggle for survival. It begins when Blanche invades the space occupied by Stanley and Stella. It lasts for the duration of a primitive fight for that space between Blanche and Stanley. It ends with Blanche's defeat and departure. So it signals a fundamental need that humans share with all animals: the need to secure territory. Building on this founda-tion, however, Williams weaves a complex tapestry of oppositions, as he describes the conflicting, contesting personalities of Blanche and Stanley. In a series of eleven tight cinematic scenes, he uses every resource of theatrical language to tell us what, essentially, this man and woman are, and mean. Blanche is a Southern lady in a world that has no use for ladies. Her need is to find protection, to secure her image of herself in the gaze of the, mostly male, other. So her need for flattery ('How do I look?'), her pursuit of romance and illusion; so, also, the power and pathos of her famous closing line, addressed to the man who takes her to the asylum: 'Whoever you are – I have always depended on the kindness of strangers.' Endowed with an evocative idiom, a theatricality of gesture and behaviour, Blanche stands, as it were, for illusion, idealism, culture, purity, love, the romance of the past. As her name intimates, she is associated with whiteness, the virgin of the zodiac with soft colours and soft lights: 'I can't stand a naked light bulb,' she declares as she puts up an 'adorable little coloured paper lantern', 'any more than I can a rude remark or a vulgar action.' But, equally, she stands for 'lies', falsehood, fantasy and weakness: it is this, after all, that makes her vulnerable. 'I've been on to you from the start!' Stanley triumphantly declares just before the brutal climax of the play. 'Not once did you pull any wool over this boy's eyes!'

That is a typical remark. Stanley is as tough and terse in words as he is in action. He believes that, as he puts it, you have 'to hold front position in this rat-race' and, to do that, you have to have pluck and luck. His faith is in the facts, in prosaic reality rather than poetic idealism and illusion. His allegiance is to the rawly physical, the sexual rather than the spiritual. '*Animal Joy in his being is implicit in all his movements and attitudes,*' we are told in the stage directions. '*Since earliest manhood the center of his life has been pleasure with women . . . Branching out from this com-plete and satisfying center are all the auxiliary channels of his life.*' Associated with vivid colours, violent action, the goat of the zodiac and the strutting cockerel of folktale, he has next to no interest in the past. His commitment is to the present and the future, and what he can make out of them. 'We've had this date with each other from the beginning!' Stanley says to Blanche immediately before he rapes her. It is a remark typical of the play, in its mix of brutality and mystery, suggest-ing, as it does, that these two antagonists are strangely fascinated with each other and with their antagonism. The 'date' with each other, the conflict that is at the heart of *A Streetcar Named Desire*, operates on so many levels and carries with it so many intimations. It is a fairytale, of beauty and the beast. It is a social history, of a declining old world and an emergent new one, translated into sexual terms. It is a mythic contest between the material and the moral, the 'female' principle and the 'male'. It is also a perversely, painfully human tale of tension between two richly individualized characters. With its multiple levels of meaning and inflection, all of them founded on a raw base of feeling and longing, *A Streetcar Named Desire* is a play that is constantly available to the discovery of fresh nuances. It is also a play that leaves its audiences torn: between regret and recognition of necessity, the ineluctable nature of both reality and illusion, facts and lies, the material and ideal – above all, perhaps, between pity and fear as we contemplate the fate of Blanche Dubois.

Williams was only to approach the achievement of *A Streetcar Named Desire* in one or two of his later plays. *Cat on a Hot Tin Roof* (1955) is a powerful play with a dual narrative. Big Daddy Pollitt, a Mississippi landowner, has to decide who should inherit his estate. Practical considerations clearly favour his sensible, reliable son Gooper; emotion and empathy draw him towards his childless and tortured son Brick. Brick and his wife Maggie, the 'cat' of the title, have in turn to find some way of living together. Both narratives gravitate towards the discovery of emotional truth: the need to know and accept oneself. Big Daddy decides in favour of Brick, his natural heir and spiritual mirror – however warped that mirror may be. Brick and Maggie start to face the facts about themselves and their relationship. The facts may not be pleasant, far from it, but they offer the chance of real survival: 'I don't know why people have to pretend to be good,' Maggie declares, 'nobody's good . . . but I'm honest! . . . *I'm alive.* Maggie the cat is – *alive!*' By contrast, *The Night of the Iguana* (1961) has a minimal plot. Weaving together very different characters, Williams does, however, explore his chosen theme of waiting for meaning, watching out for emotional rescue with a characteristic mix of realism and poetic sensibility. This is not, unfortunately, the case with many of his other plays. Some, like *The Rose Tattoo* (1951) and *Period of Adjustment* (1960), are simply minor comedies. Others, such as *Suddenly Last Summer* (1958), stray into a sensationalism unanchored in emotional reality, the raw, intimate feeling that secures his best work. Still others, among them *Summer and Smoke* (1968), *Camino Real* (1953), *Orpheus Descending* and *Sweet Bird of Youth* (1959), suffer from an excess of symbolism, an overplus of heavily signposted meaning that swamps and obscures what Williams was always best at: the stories of lonely, frightened people wondering how on earth they can endure the pain of life.

Plagued by alcoholism, drugs and depressive illness in his later years, Williams never completely lost his touch. Even in the most disappointing work, there are moments of corrosive pathos that recall the writer at his best. So, in *The Milk Train Doesn't Stop Here Anymore* (1963), there is an extraordinary speech in which the speaker compares human beings to 'kittens or puppies'. No matter how 'secure in the house of their master' 'a pair of kittens or puppies' may seem during the day, the speaker observes, 'at night, when they sleep, they don't seem sure of their owner's care for them'. They 'draw close together, they curl up against each other'. 'We're all of us living in a house we're not used to,' the speaker concludes. 'We have to creep close to each other and give those gentle little nudges . . . before we can slip into – sleep and – rest for the next day's – playtime.' Moments like this, however, tend to exist in a vacuum. Williams himself seemed to sense the decline in his own powers, as he compulsively rewrote material in a desperate attempt to make it work. *The Milk Train Doesn't Stop Here Anymore*, for instance, was revised no fewer than three times. He also began to use his plays as confessionals. *In the Bar of a Tokyo Hotel* (1969) includes an artist suffering a mental and aesthetic breakdown, while, in *Clothes for a Summer Hotel* (1980), Williams used F. Scott and Zelda Fitzgerald as barely disguised projections of his own sense of falling off and failure. 'The losses accumulated in my heart, the disenchantments steadily increased,' Williams has his version of F. Scott Fitzgerald declare. 'Wouldn't accept it. Romantics won't, you know . . . I went back to the world of vision which was my only true home.' Williams was blessed, or cursed, with an acute sense of the abyss and a compassionate complicity with those who hurtle into it. In his finest work he could dramatize that sense in a way that made the ordinary seem extraordinary, the domestic mythic, and that infused the mundane particulars of life with a sensual mystery. The fact that he could not sustain the level of intensity that characterizes *A Streetcar Named Desire* is not, perhaps, remarkable. The fact that he could achieve it at all, there and in a few other plays, is. Indeed, it is little short of miraculous. And it makes him one of the two or three greatest American dramatists.

Between them, Williams and Miller, together with the later O'Neill, dominated the American stage for more than a decade after the Second World War. There were other new dramatists: among them, Lorraine Hansberry, Robert Anderson (1917–), whose *Tea and Sympathy* (1953) was an enormous success, and Paddy Chayefsky (1923–81), who established a reputation with such plays as *Middle of the Night* (1956) before departing for Hollywood to become a screenwriter. But the only playwright of the period who came even close to the triumvirate of Williams, Miller and O'Neill – and that was not very close at all – was William Inge (1913–73). Inge received help and encouragement from Williams; and, like his mentor, he wrote about scared, lonely people – who feel, as one of his characters puts it in *Bus Stop* (1955), 'left out in the cold'. But none of his plays has the exotic poetry, or the Gothicism, of Williams's work. Plays like *Come Back, Little Sheba* (1950), *Picnic* (1953), *Bus Stop* and *The Dark at the Top of the Stairs* (1957) depict, simply and with quiet sympathy, the lives of ordinary people leading ordinary lives. Even their dreams have only a muted romanticism to them. And, while they may enjoy moments of happiness, what most of Inge's characters have to learn is the peace, the quietude of resignation: a gentle, shrugging acceptance of their own mediocrity and the littleness of their lives. So, in *Come Back, Little Sheba*, the failed dreams and lost romance of a married couple are emblematized for them, and us, in the loss of their dog, little Sheba, who gives the play its title. At one point the husband, Doc, is driven to recall and record all their losses and disappointments, all the things the couple hoped for and never had. 'But we don't have any of those things,' he concludes. 'So what! We gotta keep on living, don't we? I can't stop just 'cause I made a few mistakes. I gotta keep goin'. . . . somehow.'

Inge enjoyed his last commercial success in the late 1950s. By that time, the dominance of Broadway was being challenged. Alternative theatre was appearing in New York City, first 'Off-Broadway' as it was called, and then, when 'Off-Broadway' came to acquire respectability and status, 'Off Off-Broadway'. New theatres and theatre companies were also developing in other parts of the country. With these new theatres, too, came new forms of organization and financing: theatres as non-profit corporations, support from private foundations, repertory companies and the sale of tickets for an entire season. By the 1980s, up to ten times as many new American plays were being produced outside Broadway as on; and the expanded theatrical arena inevitably encouraged a degree of experiment. Some new dramatists and companies, at least, challenged domestic realism. Especially in the 1960s, but even beyond that, a significant experimental theatre developed. Companies like the Performance Group and the Open Theatre in New York, the Firehouse Theatre in Minneapolis, the Odyssey Theatre in Los Angeles and the Living Theatre transplanted to Europe: all moved away from a drama that was author- and text-based. They turned to improvisation, using a text only as a departure point, to mime, dance and ritual. And they deployed techniques like 'transformation', in which actors would suddenly switch roles or even plays, or make some other radical alteration in the fictive reality they were creating. This was a theatre of change, process. And, quite apart from the very particularized forms of theatrical experiment that it produced, it was to have a significant impact on a much wider range of American drama. American playwrights, most of them, never surrendered their allegiance to domestic realism. But, even more than before, they were encouraged to expand and embellish it, to push it to new frontiers.

Among those dramatists who took advantage of the new opportunities for improvisation and experiment during this period were Jean-Claude van Italie (1936–), John Guare (1938–), Jack Gelber (1932–) and Arthur Kopit (1937–). Born in Belgium but raised in the United States from the age of four, van Italie became playwright in residence with the Open Theatre in the 1960s. His work with the group includes *America Hurrah* (1966) and *The Serpent* (1968). Both plays are determinately anti-realistic, using disconnected scenes, improvised responses, mime, ritual and stylized movement to explore national and Biblical themes. Similarly resistant to the constraints of realism are *The House of Blue Leaves* (1971) by Guare and *The Connection* (1952) by Gelber. In the Guare play, slapstick farce mixes with pathos and a series of bizarre events invokes a strange medley of characters that include a deaf starlet, an insane bomber, three nuns and the Pope. In *The Connection*, in turn, Gelber imitates the random, shapeless existence of the heroin addicts who form his subject in the free-form movement of his play. And the improvised, chaotic character of the addicts' lives meets its response in the presence on stage of jazz musicians, who break into music at apparently random moments in the action. Arthur Kopit achieved fame with *Oh Dad, Poor Dad, Mamma's Hung You in the Closet and I'm Feelin' So Sad* (1962). The absurd title is matched by the absurdist action of the play, in which the fabulously wealthy mamma of the title travels the world with the dead body of her husband, a talking fish, two giant

Venus fly-traps and a son whom she insists on calling by whatever name first comes to mind. There is, however, a serious point buried in Kopit's play, about the eccentric strategies people use to protect themselves from a fundamentally hostile, terrifying world. And the seriousness at the heart of the absurdism is even more noticeable in Kopit's other main success, *Indians* (1968). Here, Kopit uses the bizarrely symbolic figure of 'Buffalo' Bill Cody, and his travelling Wild West show, to explore American mythmaking, the way the nation has habitually suppressed knowledge of its past by transforming the actual into the apocryphal, moral guilt into mythical innocence.

Of the many dramatists who discovered the freedom first to experiment outside Broadway, the most notable are Edward Albee (1928–), Sam Shepard (1943–) and, to a lesser extent, Lanford Wilson (1937–) and David Mamet (1947–). The first play by Edward Albee to be produced, first in Berlin in 1959, then in New York in 1960, *The Zoo Story*, introduced many of his obsessive themes: alienation, the human need for and terror of contact, a nameless existential fear that seems to haunt all but especially modern life. *The Zoo Story* is basically an extended monologue by a young New Yorker so lost and alienated that he feels any contact, however painful or impermanent, would be a relief. 'A person has to have some way of dealing with SOMETHING,' he declares. 'If not with people . . . SOMETHING.' He lights on a very ordinary man in the park as his first attempt at contact. He cannot move the man enough, however, by simply telling him his story. So, desperate for some tangible proof of himself and his ability to impinge on another, he starts a knife fight, impales himself on the blade of his opponent, and dies giving thanks for the proof he believes he has now received. 'I came unto you,' the young New Yorker declares, 'and you have comforted me.' Two plays that followed this, *The Death of Bessie Smith* (1961) and *The American Dream* (1961), give a more specifically American edge to Albee's explorations of human anxiety and alienation. In *The Death of Bessie Smith*, the suggestion is clearly that it is precisely the rage and resentment that alienation provokes which find their issue, and the illusion of release, in racism. *The American Dream*, as its title implies, takes a broader canvas. Absurdist in many of its dramatic strategies, it combines this with a devastating analysis of national values. The typical American family in this play – an emasculated Daddy, abrasive Mommy and cynical Grandma – are empty, evacuated of feeling by the American dream of success. Their comical abuses of language reflect and express their abuse of life, their disconnection from real human emotion. And they find their natural heir in an equally anonymous Young Man who appears at the end of the play confessing that, since one traumatic moment in his past, 'I no longer have the capacity to feel anything'.

The success of *The American Dream* enabled Albee to move to Broadway. There, in 1962, his best and most well-received play was produced: *Who's Afraid of Virginia Woolf?* Set in a small New England college, it depicts the events of one night of passionate conflict and purgation. And, unlike Albee's earlier work, it gravitates towards domestic realism. To be more exact, this is domestic realism edged with a fiery poeticism. In this, as well as its portrait of characters who find everyday life emotionally exhausting, almost unendurable, it recalls the work of Tennessee Williams: a debt that Albee slyly acknowledges through brief allusions to *A Streetcar Named Desire*. George, a history professor, and his wife Martha bring a young colleague and his nervous wife back from a party. They involve the younger couple in a torrent of argument and abuse that appears to be a nightly ritual. After a second act that Albee has called 'Walpurgisnacht', when the pain and purgation are pushed to the limit, comes the 'Exorcism' of act three. The imaginary son that George and Martha have created, as some kind of sustenance and defence against the existential dread that haunts their lives, is declared dead by Martha. The couple acknowledge their illusions, and end the play facing an unknown future with a courage that comes from admitting their fear but not turning back, not trying to hide. To the question of who is afraid of Virginia Woolf – that is, afraid of all the despair and insecurity of modern life, and especially modern American life – the answer is that George and Martha are. But so is everybody. At least, George and Martha know they are, and know now even more fiercely than before. In that knowledge there is at least a measure of redemption.

What is curious about *Who's Afraid of Virginia Woolf?*, in the light of Albee's subsequent development, is the way the play ultimately forces us to see George and Martha's immersion in life as strangely heroic. For them, as for the young protagonist of *The Zoo Story*, if it resists, if it hurts, it is real. Life, it seems to them and the action seems to suggest, is painful, unbearably difficult for those committed to living rather than evading it. The passion of that perception, however, a passion that consequently fires up the story of George and Martha, is precisely what is lacking from most of Albee's later work. Many of the later plays explore familiar themes. *Tiny Alice* (1964), for example, explores the absurd but inescapable nature of faith, illusion. *A Delicate Balance* (1966) dramatizes human defence systems, how social and family rituals, even argument and aberrant behaviour, act as temporary stays against confusion, a way of shoring up the psyche against dread. *Box* (1968) and *Quotations from Chairman Mao* (1968) dwell on the banality of human relationships in America. *The Lady from Dubuque* (1980) presents dying, and the despair consequent on the knowledge of it, as a necessary adjunct of living. But none of these plays has the verve, the sometimes bitter vitality that characterises the early work. It is too abstracted, too intent on presenting an intellectual argument rather than a dramatic action. It lacks the urgent sense of need that drives, say, *The Zoo Story*, the absurdist rage of *The American Dream* or the verbal and emotional fervour of *Who's Afraid of Virginia Woolf?* Albee began by adventures into style encouraged Off-Broadway. Moving to Broadway, he moved into a form of realism, simultaneously domestic and poetic, that gave him his greatest success. Since then, he appears to have lost his way. Whatever dramatic language he chose in his earlier work, it was always the language of passion, a corrosive anxiety and anger. That language does not appear to be with him, or is perhaps not even what he wants, any more.

Sam Shepard saw his first play performed Off Off-Broadway in 1964: *Cowboys*. Between then and 1975 he wrote more than twenty-five more. They include *Icarus's*

Mother (1965), *La Tourista* (1966), *Operation Sidewinder* (1970), *Mad Dog Blues* (1971), *The Tooth of Crime* (1972), *Action* (1974) and *Geography of a Horse Dreamer* (1974). Most of them are notable for radical shifts of character, tone and even dramatic medium – shifting suddenly from, say, expressionism to realism to allegory – for jazz-like rhythms of action and speeches that resemble jazz riffs. Rarely linear, logical or consistent, they habitually use settings and symbolism in which cowboys collide with monsters, rock mythology is mixed with religion and folk-lore, and the America of small farms and wide open spaces, fast cars and jukeboxes is invaded by magic and the supernatural. Certain themes recur, and were to become characteristic of Shepard's work. *Action*, for example, begins with the remark, 'I'm looking forward to my life'; it ends with 'I had no idea what the world was. I had no idea how I got there or why or who did it. I had no references for this.' Midway, one character observes, 'You act yourself out'. And that spells it out: in a random, crazy world, without arbiters or guides, human beings tend and in fact have to experiment with identity. *Icarus's Mother* puts a further spin on this: that acting out, engaging in fictions, can be dangerous, seducing those who act in this way into a destructive escape from reality. The reality that Shepard intimates we must never try to escape from is not a narrowly materialistic, mundane one. The failure to acknowledge magic as a vital element in the world is another insist-ent theme, pulsating like a drumbeat through such plays as *La Tourista* and *Mad Dog Blues*. In *La Tourista*, in particular, that failure is seen as a characteristically American one. In American culture, the action suggests, alienation from the spiritual is endemic and indelibly linked to alienation from the past. What we see here is an American in Mexico forced to confront his own mortality, his own inhumanity: compared to the native traditions he encounters, he is, he finds, a kind of Frankenstein's monster, and a spiritual pauper. America, according to all these early plays, is heading in the wrong direction: away from the power of mystery to the power of the material. And nowhere is this clearer than in the best of them, *The Tooth of Crime*.

At the core of *The Tooth of Crime* is a mythic contest between Hoss, an ageing rock star, and Crow, a young newcomer with a new style. Typically of the work of this period, Shepard deploys a kaleidoscope of images, as his characters use a fast-talking, sharp-shooting range of styles in an attempt to impose alternative realities on each other. Hoss is a gypsy loner, a Mafia godfather, a boxing champion, the old pro; Crow is a teen gang leader, a lonely hit-man, the challenger, the new kid on the block. Above all, though, Hoss is a man with a history and roots, simultan-eously enriched and weakened by his accomplishments and his knowledge of his art. Crow, on the other hand, is a boy with no knowledge beyond his own limited experience, no sense of commitment to any community or communal inheritance, with the strength and freedom that his own alienation and amorality bring. Hoss is the past, Crow is the future; given that, the outcome of the contest between them is inevitable. All Hoss can do, finally, to reaffirm his identity, is kill himself with a stylishness, a grace under pressure, that Crow can only envy. To an extent, the antagonists here are hip versions of Blanche Dubois and Stanley Kowalski in

A Streetcar Named Desire. In this play, though, the victor is irredeemably crude, raw, empty; Crow has none of the latent vulnerability of Stanley (a vulnerability that, of course, helps drive him to brutality in the end). The future is seen as a decisive drift away from everything that, in the past, defined not only culture but also community and even humanity.

Not long after writing *The Tooth of Crime*, Shepard moved away from the disjunctive narrative rhythms and rapid tonal shifts of his earlier work. He remained committed to a theatre of extremes, emotional and actorly: the stage directions for his 1983 drama *Fool for Love*, for instance, insist that '*This play is to be performed relentlessly without a break*'. But his style gravitated closer to domestic realism, the dynamics of the familiar and obsessive intimacy. Bizarre events and brutal emotional violence still occurred, but there were no longer such radical shifts in language and form. This alteration of style was announced in *Curse of the Starving Class* (1977), the first play in a trilogy exploring the relationship of Americans to their land, family and history; the other two are *A Buried Child* (1979), probably his finest play to date, and *True West* (1980). In *Curse of the Starving Class*, Shepard uses the experiences of a family over two days to explore the national hunger. Everyone, it seems, is taught by American culture to feel incomplete without the endless chain of commodities the institutions of capitalism produce. Starvation is the natural condition of this family, and Americans generally, because they are stimulated to wants, to experience a need, that can never really be satisfied. Another family in *A Buried Child* supplies an even more powerful emblem for the corruption of the American spirit. The child that supplies the title of the play is the product of an incestuous union whom the family have killed and buried. Clearly, what Shepard is rehearsing here, personifying in this family, is what he sees as a general national compulsion to bury the past, to conceal guilt and deny responsibility: to rewrite history so as to retain the illusion of innocence. The process is not irreversible, the play intimates. In the final scene, the father of the buried child enters with its exhumed body in his arms. As he does so, the offstage voice of the mother of the family announces a miraculous abundance of vegetables springing up on a farm that, up until then, had been a wasteland. 'I've never seen such corn,' she declares. 'Tall as a man already . . . It's like a paradise out there.' The resurrection of the family, and by implication America, is possible, it seems. All it needs is courage to face and embrace the past, to recover the best and recognize the worst. With that, it will again be 'paradise out there'.

The power of *A Buried Child*, and of so many of Shepard's plays in his mature style, stems from his weaving together of the domestic and the mythic, volcanic emotions and vast landscapes. His people are the stuff of raw experience and legend, barely able to contain immeasurable emotions within measurable frames of flesh and bone. So, in *True West*, Shepard explores a uniquely American myth, perhaps the defining one of the continent, through the intensely claustrophobic tale of two brothers writing a script. The script is about a chase: one man pursuing another across the country in a drive for vengeance without a definite start or finish. Gradually, the two brothers become the two men in the script. The real and the fictional, the story of the play and the story in the play, coalesce; and this answers the question slyly posed in the play's title. The myth of America *is* its reality, Shepard suggests, the dream of the West *is* the true West. What dream and truth, myth and reality both involve, in turn, is the immensity of human feeling and setting: drives and desires that sweep through men and women like a whirlwind, mysteries that move, only partly hidden, through the vastnesses of the world that surrounds them. In *Fool for Love*, for instance, the two central characters are lovers, half-brother and sister, who cannot live apart or together. They are victims and agents of a passion that is like an elemental force; lurching from one extreme to another, tenderness is inseparable from violence for them, and love from hate. The motel on the margins of the desert where the passion is acted out translates their condition into material terms. It is, like each of them, each of their bodies, a small, frail enclosure in the middle of an empty immensity, which can barely contain the elements careering within it. To be human, it seems for Shepard both here and in all his work, is to be in the eye of the storm: a fragile structure in and through which powers both material and magical circulate, caught in a turbulence that has no measurable beginning or end.

Like Albee and Shepard, Lanford Wilson used the freedom of the theatre outside Broadway to find a style. With him, however, the experimentation tended to be less radical. In early plays like *Balm of Gilead* (1965), he experimented with theatrical versions of cinematic effects, such as freezing the action, deploying slow motion during death scenes, background music and choric voiceover. In some of this early work, like *The Hot l Baltimore* (1973) and *The Mound Builders* (1975), he also developed his dramatic skill with overlapping narratives, simultaneous conversations and fluid time flow to develop what were to become favourite themes. So, *The Hot l Baltimore* – set in a residential hotel the seediness of which is suggested by the title, a neon sign with the letter 'e' burned out – invites the audience to consider the necessity of illusion, the human need for community (even as rundown a community as the one in the hotel), and, perhaps above all, America's betrayal of its past. 'Baltimore used to be one of the most beautiful cities in America,' a character observes. 'Every city in America used to be one of the most beautiful cities in America,' comes the reply. And, in *The Mound Builders*, set at an archaeological dig near an ancient Indian site, the human need to build monuments – mounds, cities, plays – to create the illusion of permanence gives a quiet pathos and irony to the action. Later plays, like *5th of July* (1978) and *Angels Fall* (1982), build on Wilson's ability to explore the complex relations of a group, using a wry lyricism, drifting conversations and what may seem like a meandering plot. They also develop his perception that life is to be endured, occasionally enjoyed, but never conquered. 'The only good thing that comes from these silly emergencies,' concludes one character after the crisis has passed in *Angels Fall*, 'these rehearsals for the end of the world, is that it make us get our act together.'

David Mamet first achieved success with *The Duck Variations* (1972) and *Sexual Perversity in Chicago* (1974). They introduced his characteristic style. This is not so much the vernacular, or the idiom of an actual subculture, as an intensely poetic instrument. Repetition, intensification, a shared jargon and rhythm: all are used by the characters to create the feeling of a club, a closed world, with its own games, its own secret signs and codes. These two early plays also introduced Mamet's obsessive interest in how people use language, not just as a communicative tool but to give the truth of fiction, the illusion of substance and significance, to their lives. In the thirty-one short scenes of *Sexual Perversity in Chicago*, for instance, the separate idioms, the separate realities or fictions (the two terms seem interchangeable in Mamet's work), of a self-proclaimed swinger and a feminist collide. Both in their different ways afraid of sex, the two manage to break up the healthy sexual relationship of another couple. They do this not because what they separately say to the couple to persuade them is right, but because they manage to make it sound right. Sounding right is similarly important to the characters in *American Buffalo* (1975) and *Glengarry Glen Ross* (1984), two plays which also take us into the dark heart, the selling of America. In *American Buffalo*, some minor criminals planning a robbery use a language that combines the mannerly and the vulgar, the precious and the obscene. Bumbling and incompetent as they prove to be, their shared jargon, reminiscent of the stylized talk of the characters in the stories of Damon Runyan (1884–1946), nevertheless gives them bravura, the confidence to believe in themselves.

    Glengarry Glen Ross turns from robbers planning a robbery to salesmen planning a sale. Mamet makes the one seem in no way morally superior to the other. The salesmen are selling tracts of land in Florida; and the Scottish lilt of the title refers to the fantasy names given to what are worthless pieces of real estate, virtual swamp. The distinction of the play lies precisely in its revaluation of the desperate faith, the perverse resourcefulness of the salesmen. To earn a living, they have to combine the cynicism appropriate to their fraudulent trade with a belief in their skill, the power and value of their virtuoso sales techniques. Their language tells their story. It is the story of a group, a club of men for whom 'a great sale' is the fiction that gives false meaning to their lives. So, in its own way, the play is as devastating a critique of the American myth of success, selling yourself, as *Death of a Salesman*. Mamet has continued to explore characters who create a local habitation and a name for themselves out of fast talk, shared slang and smart conversation. *Speed-the-Plow* (1988) is set in Hollywood, with its flattery and fake intimacy, and it has many of its creator's familiar trademarks: language as a substitute for meaning, selling as a mask for substance, the special status of those deemed to be in the club, the game. Mamet has also sustained his interest in those moments when different word systems and worlds collide. His controversial play *Oleander* (1992) deals with the issue of sexual harassment in the story of a female student who denounces a university professor. Whether she has a legitimate grievance or is working with her 'group' to achieve a kind of ethical cleansing, or whether there is an intriguing mix of both at work here, is never made clear. The audience is left in suspension, to debate. And, in a way, this is how the typical Mamet play always leaves us. All his characters are not so much liars as accomplished fantasists, who use the wiles of words, sometimes knowingly and sometimes not, to suspend disbelief in the fantasies they inhabit. As such, they offer a comment not just on their own subcultures but on American culture generally. One thing it is not difficult to believe, in fact, is that Mamet is commenting not just on the fictions of a particular group but on the collective fictions, the myths of his country.

Other dramatists have used the theatre even more openly than Mamet to interrogate the myths of the country. Especially during the Vietnam War, there was a flowering of drama that offered a sometimes savage critique of American culture. Apart from several plays mentioned earlier, such as *America Hurrah* and *Indians*, these included *Where Has Tommy Flowers Gone?* by Terrence McNally (1939–), *That Championship Season* (1972) by Jason Miller (1939–) and *Kennedy's Children* (1973) by Robert Patrick (1940–). But the dramatist who caught most powerfully the destructive consequences of the Vietnam conflict, in particular, was David Rabe (1940–). Rabe spent two years in the army in Vietnam; and that experience feeds into his three most successful and effective plays, *The Basic Training of Pavlo Hummel* (1971), *Sticks and Bones* (1971) and *Streamers* (1976). Each play addresses the brutalizing effects of war, on the individual and on the national psyche, in a different way. *The Basic Training of Pavlo Hummel* describes the transformation of a sad, helpless young man into a soldier and then into a dead body. In this ironic *Bildungsroman*, the hero does not grow up; he simply hurtles, in eager innocence and ignorance, towards a random and pointless death. *Sticks and Bones* brings the war to the home front, contrasting a blinded Vietnam veteran, consumed with guilt and the horrors he has witnessed, with his family, who cannot begin to understand what has happened to him. By naming the various members of the family after a popular American television series, Ozzie, Harriet, David and Ricky, Rabe suggests its typicality. And it is typical too, Rabe intimates, in its stubborn, eventually violent refusal to accept the truth. In the end, rather than come to terms with their son and the obscenities he has experienced, they kill him. Set in an army camp in the United States, *Streamers* is more sympathetic and indirect in its approach. The characters are young soldiers awaiting their postings, among them two African Americans and a homosexual. The war in Vietnam is scarcely mentioned, but it does not have to be; it hangs over the characters as the imminent fate of some, or possibly every one, of them. And that fate is marked out in the title: 'streamers', we learn, is army slang for a parachute that does not open, billowing out uselessly above a man as he plunges to an inevitable death.

Like Mamet, Wilson, Shepard and Albee, Rabe has enjoyed intermittent success in and outside the commercial theatre. The success of Neil Simon (1927–), however, has been unstoppable and continuous. His first successful play, *Come Blow Your Horn*, appeared on Broadway in 1961. It was followed by a steady stream of hit comedies, at a rate of almost one a year: among them, *Barefoot in the Park* (1963), *The Odd Couple* (1965), *Plaza Suite* (1968) and *The Prisoner of Second Avenue* (1971). The structure of these comedies generally involves a collision of opposites: odd couples yoked humorously together who sometimes achieve reconciliation, and sometimes do not. This supplies the basis or pretext for a quick-fire succession of jokes, comic conflicts and misunderstandings. The sometimes formulaic nature of the humour may be one reason for Simon's success, but so is his familiarity with his usual dramatic setting, in middle-class, middle-aged, middle-of-the-road New York. In some of his later work Simon has moved into a more serious, if sentimental, mode, drawing on his own experiences. *Brighton Beach Memoirs* (1983) tells the story of a young man not unlike the youthful author, growing up in New York during the Depression. *Biloxi Blues* (1985) takes the young man into basic training in the army; *Broadway Bound* (1986), in turn, takes up his story just after the Second World War, when he has become an aspiring comic writer. Comic and inclined to gentle sentiment as they are, these plays show a new interest in developing character, and in relating that development to more general social and cultural change. In the portrait of the family of the young man, too, they reveal an understanding of the warmth and dynamics of domestic life, particularly lower-class Jewish life, that recalls the work of Clifford Odets. Like the work of Odets, as well, is the sympathy these plays show for the dignity of the poor. As one character in *Brighton Beach Memories* puts it, 'For people like us, sometimes the only thing we really own is our dignity'.

While Simon has continued to see his plays produced on Broadway, one result of the exponential growth in other theatrical arenas in America has been the increase in the production of plays by writers from previously marginalized groups. Notable here is the emergence of many women playwrights, including Marsha Norman (1947–), Wendy Wasserstein (1950–) and Beth Henley (1952–). Norman saw her first play, *Getting Out* (1977), produced in Louisville, Kentucky; other, later plays include *Circus Valentine* (1979) and *The Hold-Up* (1980). But it is *'night, Mother* (1982) that has brought her her greatest success so far. At the centre of the play is a woman in her forties, Jessie Cates, who tells her mother that she plans to commit suicide. Resisting every attempt her mother makes to dissuade her, she outlines her reasons for killing herself. 'I'm just not having a very good time,' she explains, 'and I don't have any reason to think it'll get anything but worse.' *'night, Mother* is not so much about the ethics of suicide as about the right of the individual to control her own destiny. After forty or so years, Jessie is taking control of her life. 'It's all I really have that belongs to me and I'm going to say what happens to it,' she says. Her mother can finally do no more than acknowledge her right to make her decision: 'Forgive me,' she declares, 'I thought you were mine.' In all this, *'night, Mother* is very much in the American grain. Very much in the Southern grain, by contrast, are the plays of Beth Henley, her most notable being *Crimes of the Heart* (1979) and *The Miss Firecracker Contest* (1981). The women who dominate her work offer persuasive variations on the Southern grotesque. Simultaneously feisty and fantastic, bold and bizarre, they tend to see life askew and respond to events in a quirky way that hardly distinguishes between the serious and the trivial. Their quirkiness turns out to be a survival technique, however. 'But, Babe, we've just got to learn how to get through these real bad days here,' one woman in *Crimes of the Heart* explains, 'I mean, it's getting to be a thing in our family.' And their oddness, their often freakish humour, is clearly how they learn to get through.

Survival is also an issue at the heart of the plays of Wendy Wasserstein. In *Uncommon Women and Others* (1977), *Isn't It Romantic?* (1983) and *The Heidi Chronicles* (1988), Wasserstein takes as her subject her own generation of women, shaped by the feminist aspirations of the 1970s. *Uncommon Women*, for example, explores the lives of a group of ambitious young women in an exclusive college. They receive ambiguous messages about their destiny from their teachers, their family and society. Told that 'today all fields are open to women', they are nevertheless also advised that they can achieve what they want 'without loss of gaiety, charm or femininity' – and offered courses in gracious domestic living. Confused by these messages, they pursue different destinies none of which seems entirely satisfactory or fulfilling. One woman retreats into dreams of an ideal mate, another into mindless domesticity; one becomes a professional, but still feels suppressed and thwarted – 'Just once it would be nice to wake up with nothing to prove,' she confesses. In a concluding section some six years after the main action, these 'uncommon women' are still trying to find ways of achieving and expressing their uncommonness, their difference from the norm prescribed for previous generations of women. Nothing has really been resolved. 'I'm afraid I haven't really been happy for some time,' the main character, Heidi Holland, in *The Heidi Chronicles* admits, 'It's just that I feel stranded. And I thought the whole point was that we wouldn't feel stranded.' That is a shared feeling among female characters in these plays: confusion, irresolution, the sense of an immeasurable gap between aspiration and achievement – what they want and what their society, and even their loved ones, tell them they can get. Despite that, these characters at some elemental level reveal an indestructible optimism: the belief that, as Heidi Holland puts it, 'maybe, just maybe, things will be a little better'. Woven through the dramatic texture of *The Heidi Chronicles*, and its predecessors, is a sustained if muted belief in the possible, a realization of a proper role for women, if not now, then in the next generation.

It was not until the late 1960s that another minority group was able openly to dramatize issues of identity. Up until then, a homosexual playwright like Tennessee Williams had to explore his homosexuality, if he wished to do so, by stealth and indirection. From one perspective, for example, Blanche Dubois can be seen as a mask, a convenient, concealed means of expressing what it feels like to be different from the moral majority. With plays like *The Boys in the Band* (1968) by Mart Crowley (1945–), however, the subject of male or female homosexuality came directly to be addressed. *The Boys in the Band*, although it suffers from a tendency to conform to the stereotype of the anguished, self-hating gay, was one of the first commercially successful plays to deal with its gay characters not only openly but with considerable sympathy. Other, later dramas that deal with the homosexual community and focus on homosexuals, and made their way into the mainstream theatre, include *As Is* (1985) by William M. Hoffman (1935–) and *The Normal Heart* (1985) by Larry Kramer (1935–). Above all, there is *The Torch Song Trilogy* (1981) by Harvey Fierstein (1954–). In three plays originally written and produced separately, Fierstein here uses a dramatic persona, Arnold Beckoff, to consider the evolution of homosexuals to social acceptance and, more important, acceptance of themselves. A deft blend of autobiography, comedy, domestic realism and social naturalism, the trilogy concludes with Beckoff mourning the loss of his lover and partner. By now, he has discovered that, in his own way, he is as 'normal' – if that is the right word – as everyone else: wanting a home, a loving partnership, the right to mourn his loved one openly. By now his mother recognizes this, too, acknowledging that his widowhood is the emotional and moral equivalent of her own, and that his sexual orientation and status have to be honoured.

Apart from some of the African American playwrights discussed earlier, the most notable dramatist from the racially marginalized minorities is, without doubt, David Henry Hwang (1957–). His first play, *F.O.B.* (1978), deals with the cultural conflict between those of Chinese origin born in America and those 'fresh off the boat', newly arrived immigrants. It was followed by *Family Devotion* (1981), which explores a similar theme, *The Dance and the Railroad* (1981), based on a strike in 1867 by Chinese workers on a railroad, *Sound and Beauty* (1983), consisting of two one-act plays, and *Rich Relations* (1986). Hwang consistently received support from the Public Theatre of New York, under the direction of Joseph Papp (1921–91). His early plays met with varying fortunes, but in 1988 Hwang achieved major success with *M. Butterfly*. The play was inspired by a 1986 newspaper account of a bizarre relationship. A French diplomat, on trial for espionage, was revealed to have had a twenty-six-year relationship with someone he believed to be a Chinese woman, whereas in fact 'she' was not only a spy but also a man. From this story, Hwang got his idea for what he called 'a deconstructivist *Madame Butterfly*' addressing a complex web of racial and sexual issues. The basic arc of the play, as Hwang has explained it in an Afterword, is simple. 'The Frenchman fantasises that he is Pinkerton and his lover Butterfly,' Hwang has said. 'By the end of the piece, he realises that it is he who has been Butterfly, in that the Frenchman has been duped in love; the Chinese spy, who exploited that love, is therefore the real Pinkerton.' What expands and enriches that arc, though, is Hwang's understanding of how issues of race and gender, cultural and imperial politics, intersect here; how the tragic blindness of the Frenchman involves multiple levels of misrecognition. Hwang has the Chinese lover Song allude to those levels in his courtroom testimony after the two are finally caught. 'As soon as a Western man comes in contact with the East – he's already confused,' Song points out. 'The West thinks of itself as masculine – big guns, big industry, big money – so the East is feminine – weak, delicate, poor.' For Hwang, as for Song, the tale of the French diplomat and his lover is not so extraordinary, given what the author calls 'the degree of misunderstanding between men and women and also between East and West'. 'Her mouth says no but her eyes say yes,' as Song sardonically puts it; 'The West believes the East, deep down, *wants* to be dominated.'

In *M. Butterfly*, Hwang offers a powerful metaphor for the way men misperceive women and the West misperceives the East. The events of the play coincide with the period of the Vietnam War, alluded to several times, which gives them a further resonance and contemporary relevance. The metaphor is powerful because it is dramatic. None of this would have worked, of course, if Hwang had not fashioned a passionate, compelling action that, besides being strong on insight, is a sad, strange kind of love story. René Gallimard, the Frenchman blinded to reality by his needs, his consuming desire *not* to see the truth, is a character who inspires sympathy as well as stupefaction – and simple wonder at what sightless fools mortals can be. Song, in turn, besides being given to what the judge at his trial caustically terms 'armchair political theory', is a man caught up in his own fantasies about women. The reason that he makes what Gallimard calls 'the Perfect Woman' is precisely that he knows what men intend by that phrase, what they and he want. 'There is a vision of the Orient that I have,' Gallimard eventually confesses, 'Of . . . women willing to sacrifice themselves for the love of a man.' Challenged with veritable fact, Gallimard will not surrender that vision. 'I've finally learned to tell fantasy from reality. And, knowing the difference, I choose fantasy,' he announces. 'I'm a man who loved a woman created by a man. Everything else – simply falls short.' For Gallimard, 'death with honour is better than life'. That, in his case, means killing himself with the declaration, 'My name is René Gallimard – also known as Madame Butterfly'. It is a strange kind of honour that compels him to become his own fantasy. It measures just how far men see themselves and their needs in women, how far the West projects its will to power and domination on to the East. But it, and the suicide it leads to, measures those things in terms that combine analysis with awe, pity for the predicament of Gallimard with fear over the deeper sources, the larger consequences, of his error. This is a genuine tragedy and, on one level, a genuinely American one.

New Journalists and dirty realists

Realism is a notoriously slippery term, but it is true to say that the realistic approach, allied to the domestic setting, has been the staple of the American theatre. In prose writing, fictional and non-fictional, it also became the weapon, in particular, of those who came to be known as the New Journalists. In fact, according to the man who has seen himself as the chief publicist and cheerleader for the New Journalism, Tom Wolfe (1931–), realism is now, or should be, the emotional and moral core of all serious writing. 'The introduction of realism into literature by people like Richardson, Fielding, and Smollett', Wolfe has insisted, 'was like the introduction of electricity into machine technology.' 'The genius of any writer – . . . in fiction or nonfiction –', Wolfe has argued, 'will be severely handicapped if he cannot master, or if he abandons, the techniques of realism.' Wolfe's specific argument here has been with those American writers who, as he sees it, have ignored their primary obligation, to catch the manners and comment on the morals of their times, and who have instead gone after the strange gods of fantasy and absurdism, myth, fable and magic. Too many writers, in his view, have abandoned 'the whole business of "the way we live now"' and sought to produce 'novels of ideas, Freudian novels, surrealistic novels . . . Kafkaesque novels . . . the catatonic novel or the novel of immobility'. Other, earlier writers, Wolfe has pointed

---

out, were proud to see themselves as the chroniclers of their society; but too many writers now give the appearance of having only 'fable, myth, and the sacred office to think about' – to be a chronicler, to give a brief abstract of their times, is evidently 'a menial role'. For Wolfe, the counterrevolutionary movement, a return to the imperatives of social realism, began in the early 1960s, with the appearance of articles and books that explored non-fictional subjects, events and characters symptomatic of their times, using some of the classic strategies of realist fiction. The main exponents of this new way of writing, registering the rich social fabric of contemporary America, were, he suggested, him, of course, Norman Mailer and Joan Didion, and Truman Capote (1924–84).

According to Wolfe, the good New Journalist should stick to the facts as far as he can, the ones he has gathered as a reporter. But in retelling those facts, he avails himself of certain novelistic devices: techniques that have helped give the realistic novel its unique power – what, Wolfe says, is 'variously known as its immediacy', its 'concrete quality', its 'emotional involvement', its 'gripping' or 'absorbing' quality. These techniques, as Wolfe describes them, are essentially four. First, what is required is an extensive use of dialogue: so the New Journalist needs to be a skilful interviewer and a careful recorder. Second, what is needed is a scrupulously detailed and exact recording of the everyday gestures, habits, manners of people, their styles of clothing, furniture and so on. Third, there needs to be a careful arrangement of the narrative, scene by scene. Finally, the New Journalist should deploy a consistent narrative point of view, so that the reader can see things just as the reporter saw them and be drawn into them just as he or she was. Curiously, this formula does not precisely inform Wolfe's own non-fiction. He has published many collections of essays commenting on contemporary American culture, from its popular heroes to its alternative lifestyles. The collections include *The Kandy-Kolored Tangerine-Flame Streamline Baby* (1965), *The Electric Kool-Aid Acid Test*, *Radical Chic and Mau-Mauing the Flak Catchers* (1970), *The Painted Word* (1975), about the pretensions of the art world, and *The Right Stuff* (1979), about the US astronauts, 'gods for a day'. But, as the titles of many of these collections suggest, what most of his essays are notable for is their wit, bravura and high-octane prose: a baroque pop style that offers a sardonic reflection of, and comment on, their subjects. Wolfe is, above all, a satirist or jet-set sociologist, intent on making sly fun of the shiny surfaces and strutting heroes of his culture. His prescription for the New Journalism does not really fit his own non-fiction; still less does it fit the immense Swiftian satire of his novels *The Bonfire of the Vanities* (1987) and *A Man in Full* (1998). Rather, it fits perfectly some of the work of Norman Mailer (*The Armies of the Night*, *The Executioner's Song*) and Joan Didion (*Slouching Towards Bethlehem*, *The White Album*), and the later writing of Truman Capote, above all *In Cold Blood* (1966).

Capote had already acquired a reputation before he published *In Cold Blood*, with books such as *Other Voices, Other Rooms* (1948), a Gothic tale about a homosexually inclined boy groping towards maturity, *The Grass Harp* (1951) and *Breakfast at Tiffany's* (1958), about a light-hearted, freewheeling, romantic playgirl living in New York City. *In Cold Blood* was something different, however. It was based on fact. In 1959, two ex-convicts, Perry Smith and Richard Hickock, broke into the isolated farmhouse of a respectable family called the Clutters, tied up the four family members who were there, then killed them. All they got, for loot, was between forty and fifty dollars. Having learned about the brutal incident, Capote worked on and off for five years, interviewing friends and family, surviving members and detectives investigating the murders. Then, once Smith and Hickock were caught, Capote got to know them as well, talking to them during the trial, after their conviction and right up until the time of their execution in 1965. Out of the mass of material he accumulated, Capote then produced what he called his 'Non-Fiction Novel'. His aim in writing it, he explained, was simple. He wanted to make the cold fact of the murder understandable. By implication, he wanted to make the violence characteristic of contemporary society understandable. And the best way he could do this, he felt, was by presenting that cold fact in the context of other facts: above all, by avoiding anything not derived from observation, interview and record. Capote tries to avoid commentary in the book; he also seeks to eschew analysis, social or psychological, simply presenting what he has seen or heard. He does, however, permit himself use of the four novelistic devices Wolfe prescribed for the New Journalism. In particular, the entire narrative is carefully structured scene by scene, section by section. The first section, for instance, leads slowly up to the killing, building tension by cutting between the Clutter family and Smith and Hickock driving towards them. The second concentrates on the search for the killers, the third describes them after their arrest and during their trial; and the fourth, final section brings them to death row and eventual execution.

Using this narrative arrangement, Capote avoids sensationalism. For example, the actual murders are only described in the third section, through the recollection and confessions of the murderers; there is no attempt made to step outside of this, in some kind of voyeuristic, melodramatic way. What he avoids, though, is less important than what he gains. *In Cold Blood* takes violence out of the backwoods and the city – their usual sites in American fiction – and into the heartland. In doing so, it vividly juxtaposes the contrasts and contradictions of American life. The dream and the nightmare, the everyday and the aberrant, American normalcy and its dark underbelly: these opposites are all powerfully registered thanks to Capote's method of presentation. More than that, they come together in direct conflict in the central event of the book. Capote cannot, of course, entirely absent himself in terms of sympathy from the narrative. He was clearly drawn to one of the murderers, the misfit Perry Smith, and it shows. He was also a stranger to the kind of middle American tastes and habits the Clutters embodied, and that occa-sionally shows too. But this is a book that works because, most of the time, it is coolly dispassionate. Capote captures, with a cold but uncynical eye, the bleak emptiness of life on the vast wheat plains of Kansas, that area of the Midwest where the Clutters lived and worked. With equal dispassion, he catches the quiet desperation of Smith and Hickock, as they wander across the country in search of a job or, more often, in search of someone to rob and perhaps kill. There is no explanation supplied for the killing. 'The crime was a psychological accident, virtually an impersonal act; the victims might as well have been killed by lightning,' we are told at one point. 'Except for one thing: they had experienced prolonged terror, they had suffered.' Things happen, people suffer; those who make them suffer must suffer in turn. That is the closest *In Cold Blood*, wedded to the cult of the fact, comes to a judgement. Otherwise, it is left to the reader to see the violence as random, gratuitous, meaningless – and, to that extent, peculiarly typical of America and, in particular, the contemporary American scene.

The prose style of *In Cold Blood* is one of scrupulous meanness. Capote was to use it again, with conspicuously less success, in later books like *Music for Chameleons* (1980), a collection of pieces, and his unfinished novel *Answered Prayers* (1986). It is also a style that is favoured by those writers known as dirty realists. They include Bobbie Ann Mason and Jayne Anne Phillips, at least in their early work, Larry Brown (1945–) and Harry Crews (1935–). What these writers honour and articulate are the lives of the working poor: people who have to sell their labour, or even their bodies, to live and who might, at any time, lose everything including the basic dignities that make human beings human. 'This is America, where money's more serious than death.' That remark, coined by Harry Crews, could act as an epigraph to the work of many of the dirty realists. For that matter, it could act as an epigraph to the work of the first and finest of them, Raymond Carver (1938–88). During his lifetime, Carver published several collections of short stories, among them *Will You Be Quiet, Please?* (1976), *What We Talk About When We Talk About Love* (1981), *Cathedral* (1984) and *Where I'm Calling From* (1988). Terse and toughly graceful, these stories sometimes recall the work of Hemingway in the way the writer uses omission, the spaces between the words to catch evanescent, elusive feelings. They also resemble the early short stories of Hemingway, in particular, in their quiet stoicism, their allegiance to the concrete, their cleaving to the stark surfaces and simple rituals of everyday life. What is remarkable about Carver's stories is the way they can combine weariness with wonder, an acknowledgement of the sheer grind and cruelty of life, especially for the poor, with the occasional moment of relief, revelation, the awareness of possibility. So, in a story called 'A Small, Good Thing', a small boy is killed in a road accident just before his birthday. The cake ordered for the birthday celebration is, naturally enough, not picked up by the parents. The baker, not knowing the reason, is outraged, and starts making a series of abusive phone calls. Confronted by the angry, heartbroken parents at his bakery, all he can say is, 'I'm just a baker', 'I'm sorry. Forgive me, if you can.' And a little more: he can offer them some freshly baked rolls. 'Eating is a small, good thing in a time like this,' he tells the mother and father of the dead boy. It is not much, next to nothing in a dark world, but it is *not* nothing. The three sit together in the clean, well-lighted place of the bakery, eating and talking. And the parents, the story concludes, 'did not think of leaving'.

Realism slips into stylistic minimalism in the work of Carver and the dirty realists. In *A Fan's Notes* (1968) by Frederick Exley (1929–92), a book reflecting the disturbances of a life of divorce, alcoholism and recurrent mental illness, it slithers into autobiography. In *Last Exit to Brooklyn* (1964) by Hubert Selby, Jr (1928–), a vivid, sometimes obscene account of the violence and corruption of contemporary urban life, it slides into Gothic documentary. It has often been the style of choice for writers specializing in a particular milieu, trying to capture the way not all but certain particular Americans live now. So, J. F. Powers (1917–99) has used it to record the Catholic parish world (*Morte D'Urban* [1962]), Alison Lurie, Randall Jarrell (*Pictures from an Institution* [1954]) and Howard Nemerov (*The Homecoming Game* [1957]) have all deployed it to describe life on the university campus. And James Gould Cozzens (1903–78) employed it to explore the worlds of the military (*Guard of Honour* [1948] and law (*By Love Possessed* [1957]). It also remains an invaluable form or style for examining political or cultural conflict. Peter Matthiessen (1927–), for instance, has used it in *At Play in the Fields of the Lord* (1965) to chart the invasion of more primitive, natural environments by the destructive forces of supposedly civilized cultures. And Paul Theroux (1941–) has found it useful in his portraits in fiction (*Saint Jack* [1973], *Mosquito Coast* [1982]) and non-fiction (*The Great Railway Bazaar* [1975], *Sailing Through China* [1984]) of the often abrasive encounters between old worlds and new. Outside of certain genre reading, though, such as the detective story, the thriller and the police procedural, the area where it has had most conspicuous impact in recent times is in the various accounts, in fictional or non-fictional terms, of the war in Vietnam.

Certain of the best of these accounts in fiction circulate around memories of the Vietnam War: *In Country* by Bobbie Ann Mason, *Machine Dreams* by Jayne Anne Phillips, *The Floatplane Notebooks* (1988) by Clyde Edgerton (1946–), *Ray* (1980) by Barry Hannah (1942–), whose protagonist, a Vietnam veteran, appears to live by the maxim, 'It is terribly, excruciatingly difficult to be at peace when all our history is war'. Others are devoted to the combat zone. The military experience of Tim O'Brien (1946–), for instance, has been the material of most of his novels, especially in the three most notable, thinly fictionalized ones. *If I Die in a Combat Zone, Box Me Up and Ship Me Home* (1973) is a series of linked sketches; *The Things They Carried* (1990) explores the futility of searching for the truth about what happens, or why, in war; *Going for Cacciato* (1978) stretches into magic realism as it follows a breakaway group of soldiers marching across Asia to Paris. O'Brien has also explored the legacy of the Vietnam past as it haunts the American present, in *Northern Lights* (1975) and *In the Lake of the Woods* (1994). So, in very different terms, have Robert Olen Butler (1945–) and Robert Stone (1937–). Butler, who served in the American army in Vietnam as a Vietnamese linguist, produced in *A Good Scent from a Strange Mountain* (1997) a collection of tales about Vietnamese Americans that capture the fluid world they navigate, caught between the memories of the Asia they have left and the mysteries of America they now encounter. In *Dog Soldiers* (1974), a story about drug dealing from Vietnam to California, Stone brought the Vietnam War to the home front. It is one of several fictions in which he has used the adventure story format to explore what he sees as the ineradicable American inclination towards violence. Others include *A Hall of Mirrors* (1967), *A Flag for Sunrise* (1982) and *Outerbridge Reach* (1992).

Among all the literary treatments of the Vietnam War, though, the one that stands out is a work of non-fiction, very much in the vein of the New Journalism, *Dispatches* (1977) by Michael Herr (1940–). There have been many other non-fictional accounts, of course, notably *A Rumor of War* (1977) by Philip Caputo (1941–) – which Caputo tersely described as 'simply a story about war, about the things men do in war and the things war does to them'. But no account matches *Dispatches* in its narrative power, its ability to capture the brutally material yet dreamlike, hallucinatory quality of combat, its strangely unreal reality. Almost at once, Herr plunges the reader into the middle of the action: 'Going out at night the medics gave you pills.' You the reader are snatched into the world of 'you' the narrator and 'you' the 'grunts', the ordinary infantrymen who are at the centre of the action. The erratic rhythms of war dictate the rhythm of the narrative. 'Sometimes everything stopped,' Herr records; then, suddenly, everything will slip into hysterical, high-velocity action. Herr deploys direct address, pacy language, the syncopations of jazz, rock and pop to register a battle landscape that is also a Sixties spectacle. Here, the phrase 'theatre of war' takes on a series of haunting multiple meanings since this is a real conflict shot through with alternative real-ities: media events, bad drug trips, John Wayne movies and rock concerts. Real and basic enough, however, are the 'shitty choices' with which the 'grunts' are con-fronted. They can have 'fear and motion' or 'fear and standstill', Herr observes. 'No preferred cut there, no way even to be clear about which was really worse, the wait or the delivery.' *Dispatches* is a great non-fiction novel about war because, caught in its panoramic field of vision, is the insanity of combat as it was experi-enced by men teetering on a precipice, standing on the edge of death every moment of every day. And, in its dark way, the book even has its own heroes: those men themselves, the 'grunts', who somehow made their way through things – with the help of black humour, bleak cynicism and the belief that, in a world without logic, the only logical thing to do was to go with the flow, stick to the job and try to stay alive.

Language and Genre

Watching nothing: Postmodernity in prose

When Wolfe was cataloguing the forms of the contemporary American novel that, he believed, had failed in the primary duty to the real, he picked out one group for particular condemnation. They were the postmodernists: those who, Wolfe scorn-fully suggested, wrote about 'The Prince of Alienation . . . sailing off to Lonesome Island on his Tarot boat with his back turned and his Timeless cape on, reeking of camphor balls'. For their part, some of those writers have returned the compli-ment. One of them, for example, clearly thinking of figures like Raymond Carver,

---

has referred to the school of 'Post Alcoholic Blue-Collar Minimalist Hyperrealism'. The opposition is not universal, of course, nor even inevitable. On the contrary, most contemporary American novelists exploit the possibilities of both realism and postmodernism, and others besides, as they attempt to navigate the two rivers of American history described by Mailer. Nevertheless, the opposition has been there at times: between the New Journalists and the Fabulators, the dirty realists and the fantasists or systems builders. And it is mapped out clearly in the gap that separates Wolfe, Carver and the Capote of *In Cold Blood* from the wholehearted postmodernists of contemporary American writing: notably Thomas Pynchon (1937–) and John Barth (1930–). Pynchon is perhaps the most acclaimed and personally the most elusive of the postmodernists. Relatively little is known about him, apart from the fact that he studied at Cornell, for some of the time under Vladimir Nabokov (who did not remember him), and that he worked for a while for the Boeing Aircraft Company in Seattle. He has chosen social invisibility, the last known photograph of him dating from the 1950s. Although this is almost certainly motivated by a desire to avoid the pitfalls of celebrity and the publicity machine, it has given the figure of Pynchon a certain alluring mystery. It also adds to the mystique his fiction projects, since that projection is of a world on the edge of apocalypse, threatened by a vast conspiracy directed by or maybe against an established power elite. This conspiracy, the intimation is, is decipherable through a series of arcane signs. The signs, however, require interpretation, decoding according to the rules of structural paranoia. And one of those rules is that structural paranoia is impossible to distinguish from clinical paranoia. So interpretation may be a symptom rather than a diagnosis. Pynchon's novels are extraordinarily intricate webs, self-reflexive halls of mirrors, precisely because they replicate the world as text – a system of signs that must but cannot be interpreted. Each of his books creates a lexical space, a self-referential verbal system, that imitates the post-humanist space, steadily running down and losing energy, that all of us now occupy.

Pynchon has been his own fiercest critic. In an introductory essay to his early stories, *Slow Learner* (1984), he has said that his fundamental problem when he began writing was an inclination 'to begin with a theme, symbol, or other unifying agent, and then try to force characters and events to conform to it'. His books are certainly packed with ideas and esoteric references; and, whether one agrees with this self-criticism or not, it is clear that Pynchon laid down his intellectual cards early. The title of his first important short story is 'Entropy' (1960). It contains specific references to Henry Adams; and it follows carefully the Adams formulation, 'Chaos was the law of nature; Order was the dream of man'. The use of entropy as a figure for civilization running down was to become structurally formative in his later fiction. So was his use of two kinds of characters, alternative central figures first sketched out here. The situation in 'Entropy' is simply and deliberately schematic. There is a downstairs and upstairs apartment. Downstairs, a character called Meatball Mulligan is holding a lease-breaking party, which moves gradually towards chaos and consequent torpor. Upstairs, another character, an intellectual called Callisto, is trying to warm a freezing bird back to life. In his room he maintains a small hothouse jungle, referred to as a 'Rousseau-like fantasy'. 'Hermetically sealed, it was a tiny enclave in the city's chaos,' the reader is told, 'alien to the vagaries of the weather, national politics, of any civil disorder.' The room is a fantasy, a dream of order, in which Callisto has 'perfected its ecological balance'. But the room leaves him in paralysis, the dream does not work; the bird dies, and Callisto's girlfriend, realizing that he is 'helpless in the past', smashes the window of their hermetically sealed retreat, breaking the shell surrounding his fantasy life. Meatball Mulligan, meanwhile, does what he can to stop his party 'deteriorating into total chaos' by tidying up, calming his guests, getting things mended.

'Entropy', in this way, mediates between binary opposites: which are the opposites of modern consciousness and culture. There is the pragmatist, active to the point of excess, doing what he can with the particular scene, working inside the chaos to mitigate it. And there is the theorist, passive to the point of paralysis, trying to shape and figure the cosmic process, standing outside as much as he can, constructing patterns for the chaos to explain it. Meatball is immersed, drowning in the riotous present; Callisto is imprisoned in the hermetically sealed glasshouse of the past. The text, which here and later is the dominant presence in Pynchon's writing, is the interface between these two figures, these two systems or levels of experience. As such, it sketches out human alternatives in a multiverse where mind and matter are steadily heading for extinction. Or, it may be, the alternatives of hyperactivity and containment, the open and the closed, between which the individual consciousness constantly vacillates. The two are not, in any event, mutually exclusive. To an extent, what Pynchon does in his work is to give a decidedly postmodernist spin to perennial American preoccupations. In the tradition of the American jeremiad, he presents a culture, if not bound for heaven, then bent towards hell, its own form of apocalypse or heat death. And in the grain of American writing structured around the figures of the wilderness and the clearing, he develops a sometimes bewildering series of systems, human and non-human, built around the fundamental, formative principles of spatial openness and closure, immersion and separation, the flexible and the fixed, the signified and the signifier – a world that is a totality of things, data, and a world that is a totality of fact, signs.

In his first novel, *V* (1963), Pynchon returned to two formative characters recalling Callisto and Meatball in the shape of Hubert Stencil and Benny Profane. The book confirms its author's sense of the modern world as an entropic wasteland, inhabited by men and women dedicated to the annihilation of all animatedness. It is bounded by dead landscapes, urban, mechanical, underground. A populous narrative, it is also packed with characters who are ciphers: seeing others and themselves not as people but as things, objects, they lapse into roles, masquerade and cliché. Blown along the mean streets, and even meaner sewers, of this story, Benny Profane is a schlemiel, the suffering absurd comedian of Jewish lore. A faded copy of a picaro, he drifts through life in such enterprises as hunting alligators underneath New York City; it is there, in fact, in the darkness and oblivion of the sewers, that he finds his greatest comfort and peace. Hubert Stencil, on the other hand, searches the world for V., the mysterious female spy and anarchist who is by turns Venus, Virgin, Void and seems to be everywhere and nowhere. Stencil appears to be on a significant quest. Described as 'a century's child' and born in 1901, he is pursuing the remnants of the Virgin in the world of the Dynamo. His father, a former British spy, has left behind enigmatic clues pointing to a vast conspiracy in modern history. So, whereas Profane lives in a world of sightlessness without signs or discernible patterns, Stencil enters a world of elusive signs and apparent patterns, all gravitating towards an absent presence, the lady V. His quest is for a fulcrum identity. In a sense, he is given an outline identity by his search, since he thinks of himself as 'quite purely He who looks for V. (and whatever impersonations that might involve)'. It is also for the identity of modern times. Using the oblique strategy of 'attack and avoid', Stencil moves through many of the major events of the twentieth century, seeking to recover the master plot, the meanings of modern history and this book. The only meaning found, however, is the erasure of meaning: the emptying of a significant human history and its sacrifice to mechanism and mass. The purposiveness of Stencil, it turns out, and the purposelessness of Profane are both forms of 'yo-yoing'; movement, often violent oscillation, bereft of all significance except the elemental one of postponing inanimatedness.

At the heart of *V*, in short, is a paradox characteristic of all Pynchon's work. Its enormous historical bulk and vast social fabric is so constructed that it may be deconstructed, so complexly created that it may be doubted then decreated. The deconstruction is there, centrally, in the controlling sign of V. herself, 'a remarkably scattered concept' as we are told. A human figure, passing through many stages and identities, she comes down to Stencil's final dream of her as a plasticated technological object. A shifting letter attached to a historical process of progressive deanimation, the human figure is translated into a figure of speech. The other two compositional principles of the novel, Stencil and Profane, may apparently be opposed, just as Callisto and Meatball are, as the creator of patterns and the man of contingency, the constructive and the deconstructive, he who seeks and he who floats. They are joined, however, not only in a failure of significance but a failure of identity. Stencil and Profane inhabit a textual world that simultaneously exhausts and drains meaning: there is a proliferation of data, in excess of possible systems and in denial of any need, any compulsion to explain. Not only that, they are created only to be decreated, just as that textual world is – and in the same terms as that elusive non-character, V. herself. Their names are parodies, their words and gestures gamesome or stereotypical, their physical bearing a series of masks. As such, they offer playful variations on a definition of life supplied during the novel: as 'a successive rejection of personalities'. In the simplest sense, *V* is not a book without a subject or a plot. Full of characters (of a sort) and events, it exploits a number of narrative genres to keep the action lively and the attention engaged: among them the mystery story, the tale of the quest and science fiction. But in another, more elemental sense, it is. Not only a text about indeterminacy, *V* is also an indeterminate text: its significance, its subject is the lack, the impossibility of one.

Almost the last reported words of V. are, 'How pleasant to watch Nothing'. In his subsequent fiction, Pynchon has continued this watching, and searching, the boundlessness of 'Nothing' in a variety of fictional guises. In his second novel, *The Crying of Lot 49* (1966), the main character, Oedipa Maas, learns that her onetime lover, Pierce Inverarity, has made her an executor of his estate. Now he is dead, she sets out to investigate Inverarity's property: an investigation that leads to the discovery of what she takes to be a conspiratorial underground communications system dating back to the sixteenth century. Following the clues, she finally believes she will solve the enigma through a mysterious bidder keen to buy Inverarity's stamp collection. But the novel ends with the enigma unsolved, the plot and its meaning unresolved, as Oedipa awaits the crying out at the auction of the relevant lot number 49. The subject, and its significance, still wait to be located. So do they in *Gravity's Rainbow* (1973), Pynchon's third novel. Set in the closing years of the Second World War, the story here, a complex web of plots and counterplots, involves a Nazi Lieutenant Weissman, disguised as a mysterious Captain Blicero, and an American sleuth, Lieutenant Tyrone Slothrop, while V-2 rockets rain down on London. Weissman, it appears, was once the lover of V.: in this elaborately intertextual world, Pynchon's texts echo his own as well as the texts of others. The gravitations of mood are characteristic: from black humour to lyricism to science fiction to fantasy. So is the feeling the reader experiences, while reading this book, that he or she is encountering not so much different levels of meaning or reality as different planes in fictive space, with each plane in its shadow box proving to be a false bottom, in an evidently infinite regression. So also, finally, is the suspicion of conspiracy: *Gravity's Rainbow* explores the possibility that, as one character puts it, 'war was never political at all, the politics was all theatre, all just to keep the people distracted'.

In this fictive maze, the V-2 rocket assumes an elusive significance. It answers 'to a number of shapes in the dreams of those who touch it – in combat, in tunnel, or on paper'; each rocket, the reader learns, 'will know its intended and hunt him . . . shining and pointed in the sky at his back . . . rushing in, rushing closer'. The intimations of a conspiratorial system, here 'dictated . . . by the needs of technology', is wedded, in a way characteristic of Pynchon, to a centrally, crucially indeterminate sign. Like V., the V-2 rocket is as compelling as it is mysterious, as beautiful as it is dangerous, constantly dissolving into nothingness, deadly. Compared to a rainbow arched downwards, as if by a force of gravity that is dragging humankind to its death, the rocket initiates the same need to find meaning as V. did. Similarly, it offers an excess of meaning, an excess that is an evacuation. Since *Gravity's Rainbow*, Pynchon has moved forwards to the landscape of the 1980s and, through ample reminiscence, the 1960s in *Vineland* (1990). Then, he has moved back to the early republic in *Mason and Dixon* (1997), to the days when men like the two famous surveyors mentioned in the title were trying to establish boundaries in the boundlessness of America, in order to appropriate it. America is memorably described in this novel as 'a very Rubbish-Tip for subjunctive Hopes, for all that *may yet be true*'. It is the realm, the landscape that inhabits all Pynchon's fiction: the realm of measurelessness and dream, the indicative and the subjunctive, the closed and appropriated and the open. And it is typical of the author that he should weave his speculations on legends, the rich 'Rubbish-Tip' of dreams ('Does Britannia when she sleeps, dream?' one character asks, 'Is America her dream?'), into a densely populated social fabric and a meditation on historical decline. The fictive energy of Pynchon seems inexhaustible, not least because it careers with tireless energy between contraries. But to an extent, what drives it is summed up in one simple question one central character asks the other in this novel: 'Good Christ, Dixon. What are we about?'

The narrator of John Barth's second novel, *The End of the Road* (1958), begins the story he is to tell with a sly parody of the opening sentence of *Moby-Dick*: '*In a sense, I am Jake Horner.*' That use of language to set up distances is characteristic. The distances are several: between reader and character (Horner is already asking us to look at him as only 'in a sense' what he names himself), between the narrator and character (who only 'in a sense' form a negotiable, nameable identity) – above all, between the world inside the text and the world outside. Barth has proved to be his own best critic and commentator precisely because his is a fiction that continually backs up on itself, subverting any temptation to link that fiction to reality by commenting on form. His texts and characters are constantly commenting on themselves, or inviting or insisting on such comment. His fourth novel, *Giles Goat-Boy* (1966), for instance, begins with fictive letters of introduction by several editors that suggest, among other things, that the author is 'unhealthy, embittered, desperately unpleasant, perhaps masturbative, perhaps alcoholic or insane, if not a suicide'. Or then, again, that he is a mysterious unknown, or even a computer. Besides creating multiple dubieties, making the book a series of masks, the letters both liberate the author from the authority of authorship and advise the reader as to how to read this fiction. Which is, as fiction: a series of signs that have no reference to objects outside themselves, and whose value lies in their intrinsic relationship, the play between them. 'This author', one editor complains, 'has maintained . . . that language *is* the matter of his books'; 'he turns his back on what *is the case*, rejects the familiar for the amazing, embraces artifice and extravagance; washing his hands of the search for Truth, he calls himself . . . "doorman of the Muses' Fancy-house"'.

'What *is the case*' is a sly allusion to a famous remark made by the philosopher Ludwig Wittgenstein: 'The world is all that is the case.' The world, Wittgenstein argues, is the sum of what we take to be true and believe that others take to be true. We construct our world from the inside out; and the crucial weapon in those configurations, those patternings of things, is the system of language we have at our disposal. We cannot, in fact, get outside of the prisonhouse of our language; all we can do, when we draw a picture of our world, is draw the bars. Inadvertently, one of the fictive editors reveals the project that is at the heart of all Barth's fiction, and all other work that is sometimes called postmodern and sometimes metafiction.

Everything is only 'in a sense' this or that it is named. The self is the sum of its rules, of its locutions; the world is the sum of our constructions of it; any apparent essence, any 'natural' being or feeling or presence, is really a social construct, a sign of culture trying to wear the mask of nature (and 'nature' is a cultural convention, too). And the text refers to nothing but itself. The ultimate postmodern protagonist is perhaps Echo in *Lost in the Funhouse* (1968), Barth's first collection of stories, who 'becomes no more than her voice'. That, together with the self-referential nature of his language and the self-reflexive character of his fiction, may make Barth's work sound abstract to the point of being ossified. It is not, on the whole, because the voice is vital: his novels and stories are as packed with voices, energetic, comically ebullient, often ironic, as Pynchon's are with masks and figures. Not only that, in his hands, the prisonhouse of language does become a funhouse, a place for play and passionate virtuosity.

As for voices: these range from the tones of the narrator of Barth's first novel, *The Floating Opera* (1956), recalling his experiences on the day in 1937 when he debates suicide, to the multiple voices of his fifth novel, *Letters* (1979). As its title implies, *Letters* is an unusual development of epistolary fiction. In it, seven more or less parallel narratives are revealed through correspondence written by seven characters from Barth's earlier fiction, including the author himself as just another imaginary figure. The intricate story that emerges is a characteristic enquiry into enclosure and liberation: the patterns into which all seven characters have previously been set, the degree of freedom they may possibly discover and possess. Typical of Barth's voices, that of Jake Horner, in turn, is notable for its sometimes playful, sometimes angry, irony, its humorous elusiveness. Horner is a man so aware of the plural possibilities of existence, the 'game' involved in living, that he often finds himself incapable of reacting, acting out a role. He can always find a reason for doing something, or its complete opposite. And the action of *The End of the Road* concerns a time when, on the advice of his doctor, he attempts to remedy this by becoming a college teacher, to 'teach the rules. Teach the truth about grammar', the vocabulary of life. The novel circles around a disastrous travesty of a love triangle, when Jake becomes briefly involved with the wife of a fellow teacher who does believe life can be contained within one version of it – who, as Jake marvels, is 'always sure of his ground'. Yet that triangular affair, and its dreadful outcome, is less in the foreground than Jake's sustained sense of the absence of identity, his or that of others, outside of roles, or the absence of action or meaning apart from performance. He and we the readers are constantly being reminded that this is a story, one possible version of the world among an infinite number. What gives the novel its power is the tricky movements of Jake's voice, always prone to tell us something then confide, 'in other senses, of course, I don't believe this at all'. And what gives it its passion is the vacillation, the constant movement Jake's awareness of his predicament instigates, between play and paralysis. The games enforced in *The End of the Road*, with their painful consequences, conclude, in fact, with Jake leaving the college and taking a taxi cab to the airport. Jake's last word is his ambiguous instruction to the driver, as he gets into the taxi: 'terminal'.

Jake seems to step out of life and motion as he steps into the cab and out of the narrative. Life equals language equals story. That is the formula animating Barth's work. To cease to narrate is to die: a point that Barth makes more or less explicit in his use of the figure of Scheherezade in the opening story in his collection *Chimera* (1972). Scheherezade was, of course, the figure in Arabian folktale who stayed alive simply by telling stories. Telling stories, in turn, spins into fantasy. Barth is fond of creating worlds within worlds, using parody and pastiche, verbal and generic play to produce multiple, layered simulacra: that is, copies, imitations of something for which the original never existed. It could and can never exist, because there was and is no reality prior to the imitation, to tales and telling. So, in *The Sot-Weed Factor* (1960), Barth takes up the author of the 1708 Maryland poem with the same title, Ebenezer Cooke, about whom virtually nothing is known. He then uses Cooke as the hero of a lusty picaresque tale that is a pastiche of history, conventional historical fiction, autobiography and much else besides. *The Sot-Weed Factor* also raises the issue of how history and identity are known, by slyly eliding them with all kinds of literary 'lies' from poetry to tall tales and braggadocio to mythology. *Giles Goat-Boy*, after its initial framing in the debate over authorship, continues this subversion through similarly comic devices. The whole modern world is conceived of as a university campus, controlled by a computer that is able to run itself and tyrannize people. The book is, in part, a satirical allegory of the Cold War, since it is divided into East and West. It is also a characteristically layered fiction, since it parodies several genres (myth, allegory, the quest and so on) and a variety of texts (including the Bible, *Don Quixote* and *Ulysses*). Above all, it translates the earth into an artifice. The world, the intimation is, is a fable, a structure created by language and, as such, comparable to the artificial structures created by the author of this novel (whoever he or it may be) and by all his characters (who practise their several disciplines, their different roles and subject vocabularies). Works written since *Giles Goat-Boy*, such as *Letters, Sabbatical: A Romance* (1982), *The Tidewater Tales* (1987) and *The Last Voyage of Sinbad the Sailor* (1991), continue Barth's passionate play with various forms, the numerous ways in which we tell ourselves stories to live them and live in them. For him, that play is at once imperative and inspiring, a form of necessity and a liberation, something co-extensive with breathing. Some of his characters, sometimes, may yearn, as one of them puts it, 'to give up language altogether'. But that, as Barth feels and indicates, is to 'relapse into numbness', to 'float voiceless in the wash of time like an amphora in the sea'. It may seem attractive occasionally, but to evacuate voice is to erase identity, place and presence. To abandon language, and its difficulties, is to surrender to death.

Two writers who have sketched out very different possibilities for postmodernism, and, in doing so, created distinctive fictive landscapes, are Donald Barthelme (1931–89) and John Hawkes (1925–98). The distances between them, despite their common allegiance to work of art as object, an opaque system of language, rather than transparent account of the world, are suggested by two remarks. 'Fragments are the only forms I trust,' observes the narrator in one of the stories in Barthelme's second collection, *Unspeakable Practices, Unnatural Acts* (1968). 'The need is to maintain the truth of the fractured picture,' Hawkes insisted in an early interview. Hawkes is interested in creating strange, phantasmagoric landscapes, dreamscapes in a way, that evoke, always in their own terms, what he has called 'the enormities of ugliness and potential failure within ourselves and in the world around us', 'our potential for violence and absurdity as well as for graceful action'. Barthelme is just as committed as Hawkes is to the displacement of the writer from the work. He is also committed to the displacement of the work from the world, so that the work becomes simply, as Barthelme puts it, 'something that is *there*, like a rock or a refrigerator'. But, whereas Hawkes's fiction has a quality of nightmare, entropic stillness, Barthelme's stories and novels are witty, formally elegant, slyly commenting on themselves as artefacts. Hawkes began his writing, he said, with 'something immediately and intensely visual – a room, a few figures'. Then, eschewing interest in plot, character, setting and theme, he aimed for what he called 'totality of vision or structure'. Using corresponding events, recurring images and actions, and a prose style that seems to freeze things in time and retard readerly attention, he created landscapes of evil and decay. As his characters traverse these landscapes almost somnambulistically, their and our feelings vacillate between fear, dread, and the bleakly, blackly humorous. Barthelme, however, begins *his* writing in the verbal rather than the visual. 'Oh I wish there were some words in the world that were not the words I always hear!' complains the title character in Barthelme's first novel, *Snow White* (1967). Barthelme obliges with a verbal collage, full of odd juxtapositions and unpredictable swerves: a linguistic equivalent of Pop Art, in a way, which picks up the shards and fragments, the detritus of modern life, and gives them a quality of surprise. 'We like books that have a lot of *dreck* in them,' admits the narrator of that same novel. And it is precisely the *dreck* of contemporary conversation, from the commonest clichés to intellectual chatter, that is picked up in his books and turned all to strangeness by omitting or fragmenting the habitual arrangements and separations by which we seek to retain a feeling of control over our environment. Waste is turned to magic in his work: but the sense of magic is also accompanied by unease. Barthelme's fiction constantly fluctuates between immersion in trash culture and the impulse to evade, an impulse that finds its emotional issue in irony, disappointment and a free-floating nostalgia. Everything doubles back on itself, nothing is not placed in implicit, ironic question marks in this fiction. Nevertheless, what Barthelme captures in his work along with what one of his characters has called 'the ongoing circus of the mind' is the sadness of the city: the suspicion that, after all, it may not be that easy to go with the junk flow – or to be what Barthelme has called himself, 'a student of surfaces'.

'Do you like the story so far?' asks the narrator of *Snow White* about halfway through. He then helpfully provides the reader with an opportunity to answer: 'Yes ( ) No ( )'. This is followed by a further fourteen questions for the reader to fill in his or her preferences. Quite apart from reminding us that this book is, after all, an artefact, an object, the product of play and planning, the questionnaire offers a slyly parodic comment on the currently fashionable ideas of the work of art as open and the reader as co-producer rather than a consumer of the text. But the last question sounds a slightly melancholic note. 'In your opinion, should human beings have more shoulders? ( ),' the narrator asks. 'Two sets of shoulders? ( ) Three? ( ).' Any world has its stringencies, its absences, restricting the room for magic and play. The absence of several shoulders is not the most pressing of these, perhaps. But how else would Barthelme intimate these limits and lacks but in a manner that subverts, pokes fun at his own intimation? Barthelme is resistant to message. One of his stories, 'The Balloon', in *Unspeakable Practices, Unnatural Acts*, even toys with the absurdity of meaning. An enormous balloon appears over the city. People argue over its significance. Some manage to 'write messages on the surface'. Mainly what people enjoy, though, is that it is 'not limited and defined'. It is delightfully random, amorphous, floating free above 'the grid of precise, rectangular pathways' beneath it. And 'this ability of the balloon to shift its shape, to change', the reader learns, 'was very pleasing, especially to people whose lives were rather rigidly patterned'. Clearly, the balloon is a paradigm of the art object, the kind of free-form product, plastic and ephemeral, that Barthelme is interested in making: resistant to understanding, interpretation or reflection. But, in its own odd, jokey way, as it floats free over the citizens, it generates a ruefulness, a wry regret that carries over into Barthelme's other fictions. 'I am in the wrong time,' Snow White reflects. 'How does the concept of "something better" arise?' the narrator of that same novel asks, 'what does it look like, this *something better*?' It is noticeable that the sportive fantasy and verbal trickery of Barthelme are often at their best when he is playing with loss and longing: '*Emily Dickinson, why have you left me and gone?*' goes a passage in *Snow White*, 'ah ah ah ah ah.' Readers can certainly walk around a Barthelme verbal object, seeing in it above all a model of how to free up language and feeling from stale associations. But what they are likely to catch, as they walk around, is a borderline melancholia. So, when Snow White writes a poem, the seven men who live with her have no doubt as to its theme. 'The theme is loss, we take it,' they ask caustically. Her reply is simple: '*I have not been able to imagine anything better.*'

Of John Hawkes's 1961 novel, *The Lime Twig*, his fellow novelist Flannery O'Connor has observed that 'You suffer it like a dream. It seems to be something that is happening to you, that you wait to escape from but can't.' That is true of all his fiction. His nominal subjects range far and wide, many of them, he has said, acquired from the newspapers or from other writers. So, for instance, *The Cannibal* (1949) explores the horrors of devastation in postwar Germany. *The Lime Twig* presents the psychopathic effects on a man of life during and after the blitz on London. *Travesty* (1967) is the monologue of a Frenchman that serves as a suicide note while he prepares to kill his daughter, his friend and himself. *Virginia* (1982) concerns a girl who has experienced two previous lives in France, both marked by strange sexual experience. And *Adventures in the Alaskan Skin Trade* (1985) is about a boy confronted with hunting and sexuality during a trip to Alaska. What characterizes all these and his other novels, however, is the vision of a dreamscape fractured by an appalling yet almost ritualized violence. Hawkes has said that he wanted, from the first, to create, 'a totally new and necessary fictional landscape'. 'My writing depends on absolute detachment,' he has explained, 'and the unfamiliar or invented landscape helps me to achieve and maintain that detachment . . . I want to try to create a world, not represent one.' What he is after is objectification, not representation. As Hawkes puts it, his aim is 'to objectify the terrifying similarity between the unconscious desires of the solitary man and the disruptive needs of the visible world', so as to achieve 'a formalising of our deepest urgencies'. His characters come and go across his frozen landscapes as if caught in a strange sort of repetition compulsion. They are not so much imitations of life as figures from an exhibition, waxwork curios from some subliminal house of horror. And the violence they inevitably encounter is as vivid and distant as violence seen through soundproof glass. In *The Cannibal*, the primary act of violent negation is signalled by the controlling metaphor of the book, which also gives it its title. Although the main setting is Germany after the war, it reaches back to 1914 and forwards to a future repetition of Nazi control, which will return the entire nation to an insane asylum. The dominant presence, and narrator, is Zizendorf, the leader of the Nazis. Set in contrast to him is a young girl, Selvaggia, who stands at a window, in innocent, impotent terror, watching the evil that men do. By the end, she is 'wild-eyed from watching the night and the birth of the Nation'. Zizendorf orders her to draw the blinds and sleep. The last sentence of the book gives us her response: 'She did as she was told.' The return to an evidently endless sleep, a nightmare of violent repression, seems inevitable, since there is no intimation, in this or any other book by Hawkes, that things can change or get better. Just as character and setting appear paralysed, so events are peculiarly without progressions. Hawkes so rearranges the fractured elements in his fictive picture that the temporal dimension drains away into a spatial patterning of detail. And he so contrives his prose, into complex sequences of baroque fragments, that the reader too is held back, left in suspense. We are doomed to watch the world Hawkes creates just as Selvaggia does, with helpless, horrified wonder. Or, to return to that remark of O'Connor, we have to suffer it, like a dream.

Two other writers associated with postmodernism, Thomas Berger (1924–) and John Gardner (1933–82), could hardly be more different from Barthelme and Hawkes, or from one another. Which goes to show, perhaps, that postmodernist is almost as capacious a term as realist. A prolific writer, Berger has produced a series of comic novels about his non-Jewish schlemiel hero Carlo Reinhart (*Crazy in Berlin* [1958], *Reinhart in Love* [1962], *Vital Parts* [1970], *Reinhart's Women* [1981]). He has written parodies of the detective novel (*Who is Teddy Villanova?* [1977]) and Arthurian romance (*Arthur Rex* [1978]), replayed *Oresteia* (*Ossie's Story* [1990]) and Robinson Crusoe (*Robinson Crews* [1994]) for modern times, and engaged in satirical fables about, for instance, a man with the power to become invisible (*Being Invisible* [1987]). Unquestionably his best novel, however, is *Little Big Man* (1964). The narrator of this novel, Jack Crabb, the Little Big Man, is by his own account 111 years old. He claims to be the sole survivor of Custer's last stand, to have knocked out Wyatt Earp, and to have been in a shootout with 'Wild

Bill' Hickock. Drawing on the traditions of frontier humour and the tall tale, Berger endows Crabb with a voice that is vernacular and vital, and a view of life that is shifty, amoral and unillusioned. 'Most of all troubles comes from having standards,' he declares. So, he careers between roles and between cultures with 'a brainy opportunism', as it is called by the prissy amateur historian, Ralph Fielding Snell, who frames the novel with a foreword and epilogue. Snell admits doubt as to whether Crabb is 'the most neglected hero in the history of this country or a liar of insane proportions'. From one point of view, however, that hardly matters. Either way, Snell and Berger intimate, Crabb is heroic: providing, either by deed or word, 'an image of human vitality holding its own in the world amid the surprises of unplanned coincidence'. Set in a classic American past though it is, *Little Big Man* is about the typical protean man of postmodern fiction, for whom there are no settled certainties, no sure codes, and roles are picked up or discarded like a set of clothes. There are no absolutes, no essences; that classic past and its myths are themselves demystified, mocked and parodied. The only constant here is the constant of self-fashioning: a self exploratory, in flux, that casually acts or voices itself into being – that makes itself up as it goes along.

As the title of one of his critical works, *On Moral Fiction* (1978), suggests, Gardner was nominally far from such moral relativism. 'Art leads, it doesn't follow,' he said in an interview in 1977. 'Art doesn't imitate life, art makes people do things,' he added; 'if we celebrate bad values in our arts, we're going to have a bad society; if we celebrate values which make you healthier, which make life better, we're going to have a better world.' Consistent with this, he produced in his 1976 novel *October Light* two interwoven stories concerned with the nihilism and alienation of contemporary life. One circles around popular culture: television, with its 'endless simpering advertising' and 'its monstrously obscene games of greed'. The other focuses on high culture: the literature of absurdism and entropy with its assumption that 'life . . . was a boring novel'. What the protagonist in both stories has to learn is a deeply traditional lesson: the difference between false art and real life. He has to return from the false worlds of mass culture and amoral literature to the true world of relationship; and, finally, he does. Gardner's finest novel, *Grendel* (1971), however, does not entirely conform to his own expressed views about art. The book tells the story of the Old English epic poem *Beowulf* from the point of view of the monster. Gardner himself was a medievalist scholar; and here he plays with medieval notions of psychology and numerological symbolism as he sets the materialism, nihilism and sheer brutishness of Grendel against heroic Christianity. What emerges from this extraordinary tale is the revelation that Grendel is indispensable to the civilizing forces of science and the arts. He is the brute existence on which humans depend for their definition of themselves. 'You stimulate them! You make them think and scheme. You drive them to poetry, science, religion, all that makes them what they are,' a sympathetic dragon tells Grendel. 'You *are* mankind, or man's condition: inseparable as the mountain-climber and the mountain.' A source of power for humanity, apparently, Grendel is also the source of power for the book. Like Satan in *Paradise Lost*, he may lose but the author seems secretly to be on his side. Edgy, unnatural, unreliable, Grendel is a typically postmodern narrator. Constantly dramatizing or changing himself, his strong, seductive voice leaves the reader without sure ground. 'I cry, and hug myself, and laugh,' he declares, 'letting out salt tears, he he! till I fall down and gasping and sobbing. (It's mostly fake.).' Gardner may have been suspicious of postmodernism and keen to give his work a moral dimension. Ironically, his finest character and narrator is irredeemably, necessarily amoral. And his best work is his best precisely because it has a postmodern edge.

The range of possibilities charted by writers as otherwise different as Gardner and Berger, Hawkes and Barthelme suggests that postmodernism is probably best seen not as a unified movement but as a cluster or constellation of motives, a generic field. It is a field that is itself marked by scepticism about specific generic types; in its disposition to parody, ironic inversion and metafictional insistence on its own modes of significance – and, in particular, language – it is the absolute reverse of the stable. On the contrary, the one constant in postmodernism may be instability and, beyond that, the capacity to challenge the stability of all that is signified, all that is supposedly real. This master paradox of postmodernism, that it is constant only in its inconstancy, was handily summarized by Ronald Sukenick (1932–) in *The Death of the Novel and Other Stories* (1969). There, he insisted that 'the contemporary' lived in 'the world of post-realism' and had 'to start from scratch'. 'Reality doesn't exist,' Sukenick argued. 'God was the omnipresent author, but he died: now no one knows the plot.' So, living in an age of epistemological redefinition, an urgently felt need to redraw the mental maps of the world, postmodernist writers thrive on the imperative of being aberrant, arbitrary – above all, different. And the loose, baggy monster of postmodernism can include such diverse radical experimentalists, aside from writers already mentioned and Sukenick himself (*Up* [1968], *98.6* [1975], *Blown Away* [1986]), as Nicholson Baker (1940–) (*The Mezzanine* [1988], *Vox* [1992], *The Everlasting Story of Wory* [1998]), William H. Gass (*Omensetter's Luck*), Steve Katz (1935–) (*The Exaggerations of Peter Prince* [1968], *Moving Parts* [1977]), Clarence Major (1936–) (*All-Night Visions* [1969], *No* [1973]), Stephen Schneck (1944–) (*The Nightclerk* [1965]), Gilbert Sorrentino (1929–) (*Imaginary Qualities of Actual Things* [1971], *Flawless Play Restored* [1975], *Aberration of Starlight* [1980]) and Rudolph Wurlitzer (1938–) (*Nog* [1969]). For that matter, it can incorporate Joseph McElroy (1930–), whose *Lookout Cartridge* (1974) conveys a sense of formal systems functioning in a void and one of whose novels, *Plus* (1977), is about a mind suspended in space. And Robert Coover, who in his finest novel, *The Public Burning* (1977), transfers actual events, including the Eisenhower years and the execution of the Rosenbergs for spying, to the figurative realm. The execution of the Rosenbergs is turned into a public burning in Times Square, New York. Times Square itself is presented not just as a public meeting place but as a source of a history, since it is here the records of the *New York Times* are created. Coover goes on to analyse how historical record is made, in a bold imaginative gesture which shows that fiction does not only aid fact in the rehearsal of the past; it can also, and does, draw it into

subjective reality. In doing so, he offers what is in effect a postmodernist meditation on history and on the urgencies, the origins, of story.

John Barth once suggested that the way postmodernism showed its distinctly
American face was through its 'cheerful nihilism', its comic and parodic texture.
That is, of course, too sweeping. But across from radical experimentalists like
McElroy and Coover, there are those many postmodern writers who have chosen
to pursue an absurd humour, a dark comedy that deconstructs and demystifies
all it surveys. Again, apart from those already mentioned, such writers include J. P.
Donleavy (1926–) (*The Ginger Man* [1955], *The Beastly Beatitudes of Balthazar
B* [1968]) and Terry Southern (1926–2000) (*Candy* (1958), *The Magic Christian*
[1959], *Blue Movie* [1970]), whose predilection for protean, amoral characters has
got them into trouble with the censorship laws. Notably, there is also John Kennedy
Toole (1937–69) who, in his posthumously published novel *A Confederacy of Dunces*
(1980), mocked everything to do with his region, the South, and his hometown of
New Orleans, making his hero, Ignatius Reilly, sound sometimes like a Southern
traditionalist on speed. And there is Stanley Elkin (1930–95), a novelist and storyteller who, during the course of a long career, produced satirical, surreal versions
of the success story (*A Bad Man* [1967], *The Franchiser* [1976]), a picaresque tale
about adventures in the media trade (*The Dick Gibson Show* [1971]) and comic
fantasies about death (*The Living End* [1979]) and reincarnation (*George Mills*
[1982]).

Postmodernism as black humour or brave fantasy tends to merge here with
contemporary confessional forms of male liberationists like John Irving (1942–)
(*The World According to Garp* [1978], *The Hotel New Hampshire* [1981], *A Prayer
for Owen Meany* [1989], *A Son of the Circus* [1994]) and female liberationists like
Erica Jong (*Fear of Flying, Fear of Fifty* [1994]) and Lisa Alther (1944–) (*Kinflicks*
[1976], *Original Sin* [1981]). At the other edge, postmodernism as radical, metafictional experiment is more inclined to reveal its international relations. Experiment is, of course, an American tradition; and the subversion of fictional forms, in
particular, goes back at least as far in American literature as Herman Melville. But
the specific terms in which postmodernists have interrogated word and thing,
language and its connection to reality, show the impact and sometimes the influence
of writers from outside America. Like other cultural movements, more so than
most, postmodernism is on one level an international phenomenon. And the sense
postmodernist writers have of living after realism is one shared with, say, European
poststructuralist critics, writers of *le nouveau roman* like Michel Butor and Raymond
Queneau, and Latin American magic realists. This international dimension is
foregrounded in the work of those postmodern novelists whose own story is one of
crossings between national boundaries, especially the European and American.
The fiction of Vladimir Nabokov, born in Russia, spending long years in Europe
before continuing his exile in America, is a case in point. So are the narrative
experiments of the French American Raymond Federman (1928–), whose *Take It
Or Leave It* (1976) announces itself as 'an exaggerated second hand tale to be read
aloud either standing or sitting', and the books of the Polish-born, Russian-reared

Jerzy Kosinski (1933–91) from *The Painted Bird* (1965) through *Being There* (1971) and *Blind Date* (1977) to his last novel, *The Hermit of 69th Street* (1988).

Another instance of international origins promoting international connections is the writing of Walter Abish (1931–). Abish was born in Austria and reared in China before taking United States citizenship. His first novel, *Alphabetical Africa* (1974), invites a comparison with *le nouveau roman* in its stern attention to verbal structure. Every word of the first chapter begins with the letter A, the second with A or B, the third with A, B or C, and so on. At Z, the process reverses, the final chapter beginning every word again with the letter A. Abish's second novel, *How German It Is* (1984), suggests other international relations. A postmodern political thriller, it concerns an American of German parentage who returns to a German town to investigate his father's wartime death and to seek an answer to his own question as to how German he is. The international, influential presences here are several. They include American writers like Pynchon and French ones like Butor, who have used popular genres to break and undercut them. More deeply, persuasively, though, they are other European writers such as Italo Calvino and Peter Handke. As in the work of Calvino and Handke, there is a bleak detachment, a flat materialism to *How German It Is*, the presentation of a world of signs without meanings under which dark meanings may hide. A writer like Abish, as he explores the crisis of relations between history and form and pursues the task of unlocking some hidden code that might interpret those relations, shows how postmodernism – like any other movement in American literature, at some point – has to be perceived within a frame of reference other than the American. It has to be, not only because postmodernist writers skip across national boundaries with such calculated and consummate skill – and not only because some of them, at least, cannot or will not shake off their own international origins. It is also, and more fundamentally, because – as it has been the peculiar fate of postmodernism to emphasize – no boundary of any kind is impermeable. No frame of reference, including the national one, is adequate, absolute or terminal.

The actuality of words: Postmodern poetry

Internationalism is also a marked feature of the postmodernist impulse in poetry, especially that form of postmodernism known as language poetry. The antecedents of the language poets, for instance, include not only American writers like the Gertrude Stein of *Tender Buttons*, Louis Zukovsky, Laura Riding and John Ashbery, but also the James Joyce of *Finnegans Wake* (1939) and the Russian futurist writer Velimir Khlebnikov, inventor of *zaum* or 'transrational language'. Reflecting the belief of one of the leading language poets, Charles Bernstein (1950–), that 'poetry, like philosophy, may be involved with the investigation of phenomena (events, objects, selves) and human knowledge of them', those antecedents and influences include a number of continental philosophers as well. Notable among these, from an earlier generation, are Ludwig Wittgenstein, Walter Benjamin and Theodor Adorno. Contemporary European poststructuralists have been just as important to the language poets, because they see their project as continuous with that of ideology critiques and literary theory. To quote Bernstein again, as they see it 'poetics is the extension of poetry by other means'. And, in constructing a poetic and a poetry, the language poets have turned to such figures as Jacques Lacan, Roland Barthes, Julia Kristeva, Luce Irigaray and Jacques Derrida. What that construction involves is suggested by one poet who became a point of origin for language poets and, to an extent, became one of them, Clark Coolidge (1939–). 'What I think is that you start with the materials,' Coolidge explained. 'You start with the matter, not with rules.' 'I was really trying to work with the words, look at the words, try to use all their qualities,' he added of his own work in a collection like *Polaroid* (1975). 'There's no question of meaning, in the sense of explaining and understanding the poem. Hopefully, it's a unique object, not just an object.'

Language poetry is as various in its manifestations as contemporary sculpture or photography, but Coolidge is alerting the reader here to one aim all language poets do have in common. Instead of employing language as a transparent window on experience, the language poet attends to the material nature of words. He or she insists on the materiality of the medium used and its distance from whatever we are inclined to think of as natural or immediate. An analogy might be made with the sculptor who draws attention to the stone with which he or she is working, its weight, texture and cleavage. A more specific comparison might be made with the famous, frequently reproduced paintings by Magritte of a pipe, accompanied by the words 'Ceci n'est pas une pipe' ('This is not a pipe'). In common with Magritte, or that sculptor, the language poet questions the status of the work being created, and forces us to question that question. Privileging technique, resisting any temptation to present the poem as a window on experience, the language poet builds up a mosaic structure by means of seemingly unrelated sentences and sentence fragments. This progression of non-sequiturs frustrates the reader's expectations for linear development at the same time as it discloses a more complete world of reference. The stress is laid on production rather than ease of consumption, on the use of artifice in such a way as to force open given forms and break habitual patterns of attention. Another poet who has served as a point of origin for the language poets, Jackson Maclow (1922–), has conceded that 'no language is really 'nonreferential'. 'If it's language, it consists of signs, and all signs point to what they signify.' However, he has argued, that hardly detracts from the core aim of language poetry: which, as Maclow puts it, is to centre the focus 'on linguistic details and the relation among them, rather than on what they might "point to"'. The language poet resists all inclination to totalize or account for diversity in literary productions – or in experience – by the imposition of unifying schemes or rigid constructs. By interrogating, subverting or even exaggerating the effects of formal logic and linguistic structures on our thinking, he or she demonstrates how those structures can have a determining influence on what we see, how we behave – and, not least, who we think we are.

Along with this emphasis on the materiality of the signifier, what language poets also have in common is the project of restoring the reader as a co-producer of the text. That follows inevitably from their resistance to closure. 'The text calls upon the reader to be actively involved in the process of constructing its meaning,' as Bernstein has put it. 'The text formally involves the process of response/interpretation and in doing so makes the reader aware of herself or himself as producer as well as consumer of meaning.' A poem is not about something, a paraphraseable narrative, symbolic nexus or theme. It is the actuality of words. And those words call the reader to attention and action. They also call the reader, as Bernstein expresses it, 'to a reconsideration and a remaking of the habits, automatisms, conventions, beliefs through which, and only through which, we see and interpret the world'. For some language poets, at least, the strenuous attention to opacity and openness has clear political implications. 'The question is always what is the meaning of this language practice,' Bernstein has insisted; 'what values does it propagate; to what degree does it encourage an understanding, a visibility, of its own values or to what degree does it repress that awareness?' 'Language control = thought control = reality control' for Bernstein, and for the more politically inclined language poets like Bob Perelman (1947–) and Bruce Andrews (1948–). So part of their task, as they see it, is to 'bring into visibility as chosen instruments of power what is taken as neutral or given': to expose those language practices that distribute meaning and authority, that underpin the system of assumptions, the series of naturalized collusions and constraints on which their society operates. What such writers are after, as Andrews has it, is 'a conception of writing *as* politics, not writing *about* politics': poetry that interrogates language habits to discover whether their social function is liberating or repressive. Perelman has put it more satirically: 'Question: How do you tell a language from a dialect? Answer: A language is a dialect that has an army and a navy.' Works that foreground the way that language works, the sense here is, reveal the weaponry that gives it social weight. More generally, they show language as a field of ideological contention, not a monolithic system: as a series of constructed practices, neither innocent nor inevitable, but a symptom and agent of power.

Even those language poets who do not share this political edge or intention tend to privilege the marginal over the mainstream. This is if only because the limits of structure and ideology come into view most noticeably at the point where structure and ideology break down: where, as in language poems, instead of disappearing into the unstated assumptions of an activity, they appear all too clearly as evidence. So, one of the finest language poets, Susan Howe (1937–) has explained that her poetic project is to piece together and 'lift from the dark side of history, voices that are anonymous, slighted – inarticulate'. They include the numerous, unnamed victims of economic depression and world war or women slighted by history. *The Europe of Trusts* (1990) addresses the anonymous victims. *The Liberties* (1980) is one among many of Howe's works to consider marginal female figures: in it, Esther Johnson, known to history as Jonathan Swift's Stella, takes centre stage. No longer Swift's creature, she speaks with words of her own, Swift himself appearing only as a ghost. Similarly, Lyn Hejinian (1941–) has constructed a discontinuous narrative of her own childhood in *My Life* (1987). 'Repetition, and the rewriting that repetition becomes, make a perpetual beginning,' Hejinian has written. True to that formula, and to her belief that 'language itself is never in a state of rest', Hejinian creates autobiography through a mosaic of discontinuous sentences and glimpses, in which the title of one section of the book-length sequence finds its way into the text of another. The result is fugitive and absorbing, producing a jumpiness of word and mood that Hejinian has described as 'so natural to my "real life" experience' as to 'seem inevitable – and "true"'. In her own way, with disjunction of surface and voice, Hejinian uses her own slighted, elusive life experience to pursue the central project of language poetry: which, as Bernstein once expressed it, is 'to cast doubt on each and every "natural" construction of reality'.

Historically, that project began around the early 1970s. In 1971, the first issue of *This* appeared, co-founded by Robert Grenier (1941–) and Barrett Watten (1948–). 'I HATE SPEECH,' Grenier declared in an essay in that issue. It was his particular aim, in saying this, and the aim of *This* generally, to reject a poetics based on the assumptions of speech: to raise the issue of reference and to suggest that any new direction would require poets to look at what a poem is actually made of – language itself. The resistance sounded here, to the simple, seemingly obvious idea that words should derive from speech and refer to things, was followed up on the West Coast, in San Francisco, by writers like Bob Perelman, Watten, Hejinian and Carla Harryman (1952–). From 1977 to 1981, for instance, Perelman founded and curated the San Francisco Talk Series, then edited *Writing/Talks* (1985), a collection of talks and writings from the series. The 'talks' consisted of a presentation by the poet, during which the audience responded with their own thoughts. Then, on the East Coast, in and around New York City, a number of writers converged: among them, Bernstein, Andrews and Ray Di Palma. From that convergence came *L=A=N=G=U=A=G=E*, the first American journal of poetics by and for poets. Its editors said that they were 'emphasizing a spectrum of writing that places attention primarily on language'. They were, they explained, intent on 'ways of making meaning' and taking nothing for granted, 'neither vocabulary, grammar, process, shape, syntax, program, or subject matter'. Their journal lasted from 1981 until 1984, dedicated throughout that period to its mission of 'repossessing the word'. It was followed, in 1984, by an extensive anthology of pieces from the different issues. Then, two years later, two further anthologies appeared, *'Language' Poetries*, edited by Douglas Messerli, and *In the American Tree: Language, Realism, Poetry*, edited by Ron Silliman (1946–). *In the American Tree* was particularly groundbreaking and influential. Silliman, himself an accomplished language poet, explained in his introductory essay that the issues debated in and by language poetry were 'not to be underestimated'. They included 'the nature of reality', 'the nature of the individual', 'the function of language in the constitution of either realm'. The debate, Silliman added, was 'situated within the larger question of what, in the last part of the twentieth century, it means to be human'. With that, language poetry boldly announced itself as a leading register of its times, and among the most important of contemporary American poetic forms.

What it means to be human covers a lot of territory, of course, even if the meanings are delimited to one or two decades. Beyond a commitment to writing as rescue, repossessing the word and restoring the reader, language poets shoot off in a number of directions. Robert Grenier, for example, shows an interest in visual as well as sonic design. He has published three books in special formats. *Sentences* (1978) consists of five hundred poems on small index cards. *CAMBRIDGE M'ASS* (1979) is two hundred and sixty-five poems on a large poster. *What I Believe Transpiration/Transpiring Minnesota* (1989) is composed of photocopied pages, most of which are hand-written poems 'drawn' from the other side of the paper, as if the poet were writing with his left hand. Barrett Watten, whose books include *Frame: 1971–1990* (1994), is a more formidable writer, a radical formalist who calls for 'resistance between writer and reader'. Quoting with approval De Kooning's remark, 'I keep painting until I've painted myself out of the picture', Watten pursues 'anarchy of production', verbal forms so disjunctive and detached that their author is conspicuous only by his absence. An understanding of the political implications of language poetry has led Bob Perelman to a satirical view of consumer society, and a search for the strange and unsettling. In books like *Braille* (1975), *Captive Audience* (1988) and *Virtual Reality* (1993), he has tried to answer his own call for a 'defamiliarisation' of poetry by removing it from the comforting orbit of the oral. 'Unlike the oral poet,' Perelman has said, 'who is reinforcing what the community already knows, the didactic *writer* will always have something new, and, possibly, unacceptable to get across.' And, to that extent, he clearly sees his own poetic project as didactic. Similarly political in intent, Bruce Andrews has declared his allegiance to a radical poetic practice, involving what he terms 'an infinitising, a wide-open exuberance, a perpetual motion machine, a transgression'. 'Are "make it new" and "make it even" compatible?' one poem, 'Species Means Guilt' (1992), asks. And his cunning machines made out of words seem always to be debating the possibility of an answer.

'Language is, first of all, a political question.' That annotation, made in one of the poems of Ron Silliman, would appear to align him with Andrews or Perelman. It does, in a way. But Silliman is much more of an experimentalist, an eccentric inventor of forms. His ongoing long poem, *The Alphabet* (1983–), as its title implies, will eventually grow to twenty-six volumes. His prose poem *Tjanting* (1981) is written according to the Fibunacci number sequence, the result being that the number of sentences in each paragraph equals the number of sentences in the previous two paragraphs. And his prose poems, in particular, feature what Silliman calls the 'new sentence': a form intended to frustrate the conventions, and the closure, of both the poetic line and ordinary prose, as a series of discrete units are accumulated into a kind of disjunctive verbal mosaic that recalls the writing of Gertrude Stein. Stein is also an influential presence in the poetry of Michael Davidson (1944–), whose work, gathered together in volumes like *Summer Letters* (1977) and *Post Hue* (1996), maps out what he has termed 'the space occupied by chiasmus': that is, the rift or rupture between the world and its articulations in language. Both Carla Harryman and Lyn Hejinian, on the other hand, gravitate towards forms that, as Harryman has put it, 'distribute narrative rather than deny it'. Hejinian does this not only in that abruptly self-reflexive version of autobiography she calls *My Life*, but also in, say, *Oxata: A Short Russian Novel* (1991), a series of 'sonnets' through which she creates a portrait of post-Soviet Russia. And Harryman does it in her often humorously erotic poetry, collected in such volumes as *The Middle* (1983) and *In the Mode of* (1991). A writer from a slightly earlier generation than most language poets, Hannah Weiner (1928–97) mixed techniques learned from language poetry with more random elements, automatic writing, in her attempt to capture her own psychic experiences (*Clairvoyant Journal* [1978]). A writer from a slightly younger one, Diane Ward (1956–) owes a debt to Virginia Woolf. In the poems collected in, say, *Relation* (1989) and *Imaginary Movie* (1992), she uses form to generate mood. In her own words, she puts 'things', 'two disparate objects or events' 'side by side', 'thereby creating a third feeling (state) of perception'. What all these poets, despite all their differences and diversions, have in common is revealed by two other writers associated with the language movement, Ray Di Palma (1943–) (whose works include *The Jukebox of Memnon* [1988]) and Bernadette Mayer (1945–) (a selection of whose poetry is to be found in *A Bernadette Mayer Reader* [1992]). 'When and where there / is no such thing /' writes Di Palma, 'the thought walked.' 'The best obfuscation', Mayer observes, 'bewilders old meanings while reflecting or imitating or creating a structure of beauty that we know.' There have been few more formidable expressions of a common impulse, a shared motivation, than these two: few more memorable expressions, that is, of that energetic, enigmatic relation between thing and thought and language that drives all workers in the field of language poetry to write.

Nobody shares that impulse more than those three writers who are, arguably, the leading exponents of language poetry: Charles Bernstein, Michael Palmer (1943–) and Susan Howe. Along with being the leading theorist of language poetry, Bernstein is an accomplished poet, his numerous collections of poetry including *Poetic Justice* (1979), *Islets/Irritations* (1983) and *Rough Trades* (1991). Sometimes, the two vocations – which are nevertheless linked for Bernstein – come together. *Artifice of Absorption* (1987), for example, is an essay in verse that makes a core distinction between *absorption* and *impermeability* in literature. The one, suggests Bernstein, connotes all that is 'rhapsodic, spellbinding, / mesmerising, hypnotic, total, riveting, / enthralling', the other everything that is to do with 'artifice, boredom, / exaggeration, attention scattering, distraction, digression, interruptive, transgressive'. Absorptive writing pursues the realistic, continuous and transparent; impermeable or anti-absorptive writing favours artifice, discontinuity, the opaque. It is the impermeable, clearly, that Bernstein prefers. 'In my poems, I / frequently use opaque & nonabsorbable / elements,' he declares, 'digressions & / interruptions, as part of a technological arsenal.' His aim, Bernstein writes, is for the reader 'to be actively involved in the process of constructing its meaning', and, as far as both reader and writer are concerned, 'to wake / us from the hypnosis of absorption'. In *Artifice of Absorption*, Bernstein cites his poem 'The Klupzy Girl' as an example of his poetic technique. With typically antic humour, he takes an all-American klutz of both French and British descent (since she bears a close resemblance to Keats's 'La Belle Dame Sans Merci') as his demonic muse here. He then uses a rich mix of styles, redundancies, clichés, awkward or irrelevant constructions to create what is called, towards the end of the poem, 'a manic / state of careless grace'. The artifice is foregrounded by various cinematic devices: cutting and shifting focus, unanticipated breaks, disturbing and distorted perspective. It is this disjunctive rate of change that dictates the poem's rhythm, as it lurches from statements so bald that they border on parody ('Poetry is like a swoon, with this difference: / it brings you to your senses'), through disconnected snatches of conversation, phrases that might be overheard in the street, comments that float unanchored. Art, Bernstein has insisted, must be extraordinary, aberrant, abnormal. 'It partakes of both good and ill, of the agreeable and the disagreeable,' as he puts it. 'Or rather, it is within its mass that these oppositions are able to sketch themselves out.' Bernstein pursues an oppositional writing: and, in 'The Klupzy Girl', he manages just that – with a style that distorts and a strange, disturbing lady as his muse and the poem's occasion.

Michael Palmer has said that he is 'a little bit outside' 'the way many of the so-called language poets work' because the way 'I inhabit language, or language inhabits me, is in a sense more traditional'. Certainly, his poetry betrays other debts, to the Black Mountain and New York poets in particular; and, in his critical writings, he has admitted the inevitability of narrative. But his work is fundamentally of the language movement because of his core commitment to what he calls 'radical discontinuities of surface and voice' – to a poetry that resists and interrogates. He is interested, he has said, in a poetry that 'will not stand as a kind of decor in one's life, not the kind of thing for hammock and lemonade, where at the end everything is in resolution'. He is also concerned with the political implications of style and form: his work questions the status quo on the rhetorical level, supplying a critique of 'the discourses of power by undermining assumptions about meaning and univocality'. He may be more interested in story than, say, Bernstein is. However, as Palmer himself has pointed out, story, as well as autobiography, always involves a measure of concealment. 'What is taken as a *sign* of openness – conventional narrative order –', he has said, 'may stand for concealment.' Conversely, 'what are understood generally as *signs* of withholding or evasion – ellipsis, periphrases, etc. – may from another point of view stand for disclosure'. So, in a work like *Notes for Echo Lake* (1981), he uses devices of concealment, like writing about himself in the third person, in order to disclose. But, even while disclosing, there is a gnomic, hermetic quality to his writing that issues from a radical scepticism: a fundamental uncertainty about, as he has it, 'whether I know whatever I know'. Palmer is a prolific poet. His many collections include *Plan of the City O* (1971), *First Figure* (1984) and *At Passage* (1995). Nearly all of his work is marked by a search for an evidence of order in the sound and structure of language and proof of life, love in the steadiness of companionship. As the third of his 'Six Hermetic Songs', dedicated to Robert Duncan, expresses it: 'Send me my dictionary / Write how you are.'

Structurally, the poetry of Susan Howe often registers her early training in the visual arts. Some of her work treats words like fragments in a collage. Others experiment with the significations that emerge from the irregular distribution of letters on the page. The lines, 'Do not come down the ladder / iforI / have eaten / ita / way', from 'White Foolscap: Book of Cordelia' (1983), distribute sense, a layer of potential meaning, on a specifically visual level. Howe grew up during the Second World War, however, and, as a young woman, came under the influence of Charles Olson. Both experiences ignited her interest in an often silenced, often slighted history. 'The deaths of millions of people in Europe and Asia', Howe has said, 'prevented me from ever being able to believe history is only a series of justifications, or that tragedy and savagery can be theorised away.' Her many books of poetry include *The Western Borders* (1976), *Defenestration of Prague* (1983), *Articulation of Sound Forms in Time* (1987) and *The Nonconformist's Memorial* (1993). And many of her poems, gathered here and elsewhere, show her extraordinary ability to transform historical documents, the archive and the chronicle, into an elusive, elliptical yet deeply personal drama: in which, say, the ancient Britain of Lear, the New England of the Indian wars or the New England of Thoreau enter the consciousness of a woman living and working at the end of the American century, and beyond. Unlike Olson, Howe has never constructed a central persona. Instead, her poems contain lines and phrases that just will not come together in a unifying speech, form or episode. Lines may pass with one or two others, then typically drift off by themselves or into new, temporary arrangements. A charged lyricism fuses with a critical examination of authorial voice as, using pun and word play, Howe calls meaning itself into question. Figures hover at the edge of memory and history, in her work, and on the borderlines of speech. They seize our attention momentarily, then they are gone. 'For we are language Lost / in language,' one poem, 'Speeches at the Barriers', declares, 'Wind sweeps over the wheat / mistmask on woods.' 'Sleet whips the page / flying leaves and fugitive,' that same poem continues later; 'Earth of ancient ballad / earth as thought of the sea / water's edge to say goodbye.' A feeling of dissolution marks out these lines, a perpetual erasing inherent in the endless ebb and flow of human language, consciousness and history. It is a characteristic of her poetry that makes Howe one of the most exceptional, extraordinary poets of her generation.

Signs and scenes of crime, science fiction and fantasy

Language poetry remains very much the literature of a small community, one that began by being alternative but that later – as, for instance, many language poets took up posts at universities – became mainstream and, within limits, influential. As postmodernists, though, language poets are inclined to resist the traditional division of culture into minority and mass, elite and popular. In their turn, writers of detective stories, thrillers, hardboiled and science fiction have shown or encouraged the same resistance over fifty or more years, producing work so powerful or pervasive in its influence that it has helped erase the line of demarcation between genre fiction and literature. As far as hardboiled and detective tales are concerned, the period from roughly the 1940s to the 1960s was notable for the development of paperback original series and mystery magazines. Publishers like Fawcett, Avon and Dell produced brand-new, easy-to-read novels in a convenient pocket-size format. They adapted the pulp formula of the 1930s and 1940s for postwar American society, with all its changes in lifestyle, its looser attitudes to sex and violence, and its newfound sophistication. They paid writers reasonably well, with initial payment in advance of royalties that were up to four times as much as hardcover publishers were paying. They relied on printing hundreds of thousands of copies of many titles to reach every possible outlet and buyer. And they were committed to rapid turnover: very few of these paperback originals ever got beyond an initial printing unless they were extraordinarily popular. In just the same way as the pulp magazines had engineered the decline of dime novels, so these paperbacks brought about the end of the pulps. All major pulp titles were finished by the middle of the 1950s. The new setting for shorter fiction was the digest-size detective story or thriller magazine. These magazines, too, were phenomenally successful until the late 1960s: one of the first, for example, *Manhunt*, sold half a million copies on its first issue.

Two very different writers who benefited from these new means of literary production and distribution were Mickey Spillane (1918–) and Jim Thompson (1906–76). Spillane leaped to success in 1947, when he created the private eye Mike Hammer for *I, the Jury*. Hammer is a veteran of the Second World War who sets out to avenge the murder of an old army buddy who once saved his life. Assisted by his loyal, sexy secretary, Velda, he vows to let nothing stand in his way. And, at the climax of the story, he shoots his naked fiancée in the abdomen when he finds out that she has killed his buddy and five others. An untrammelled id who is constantly exploding in messianic rage – against intellectuals and homosexuals, or anyone who oppresses the 'little guy' from the Mafia to the Communist Party – Hammer continued his pursuit of vigilante justice in a series of novels whose titles suggest their tone and tenor: *My Gun is Quick* (1950), *Vengeance Is Mine* (1950), *Kiss Me Deadly* (1952). The unrestrained violence, which approaches sadism at times, and overt sexuality register a loosening up of popular attitudes and tastes after the war. The right-wing politics, and the paranoia about 'reds' in particular, reflects the Cold War atmosphere in which the books were written. Altogether, there may be doubts about the value of the Hammer novels, with their fantasies of irresistible male potency (women are constantly ripping off their clothes in the presence of the great detective), but there can be no doubt about their impact and influence.

Jim Thompson is a much darker and more impressive writer than Spillane, although he also shows a taste for psychopathic violence. His noir fiction contains few detectives. What it has in abundance, however, is unreliable narrators and protagonists whose mental state constantly verges on and often topples over into psychosis. The condition they inhabit is measured by the scatological mathematics of Thompson's 1959 novel *South of Heaven*: 'shit and three are nine . . . screw and two is four and frig makes ten.' Typical is the narrator of *The Killer Inside Me*

(1952), Deputy Lou Ford. Ford pretends to be a simple-minded hick, when in fact he is a ruthless, sadistic killer, responsible for the murders he is supposed to be investigating. The world this smiling villain inhabits is a bleak one, where human nature festers, corrupts and disrupts. The narration is sly, fooling the reader much of the time as well as the other characters. And the narrative tone, darkening the brutal, gaudy landscapes the Deputy negotiates, is cold, comic and caustic, exposing what looks like an almost universal hypocrisy. Nick Corey, the narrator of *Pop. 1280* (1964), is a twin to Ford: another polite, even amusing law officer who happens to be murderously corrupt. Typically for Thompson, the story Corey tells bypasses the tenets of good taste, with monstrosities of action and narration that serve as a harsh abrasive, a corrective to all our assumptions about human dignity. 'You might think it wasn't real nice to kick a dying man,' Corey says to the reader, after he has done just that. 'Maybe it wasn't. But I'd been wanting to kick him for a long time; and it just never seemed safe until now.' In other novels, Thompson introduces us to con artists (*The Grifters* [1963]), lowlife criminals (*The Getaway* [1959]), and people cracking up in a figurative prison of tough talk, 'lowdown' behaviour and smalltown scheming (*After Dark, My Sweet* [1955]). The family offers no refuge here; it is riven with incestuous desires and violence. In *King Blood* (1954), for instance, the protagonist is aroused in the act of beating his mother. People are on their own in a world of 'sickness', trying to cope while maybe knowing that, as Lou Ford puts it, 'all of us started the game with a crooked cue'. The task of coping is inevitably a hopeless one. Nowhere is this more evident than in two of Thompson's most troubling fictions, *A Hell of a Woman* (1984) and *Savage Night* (1953). So, the narrator of *A Hell of a Woman* copes in the end by going insane. The 'I' of the story splits into two voices: 'I laughed and laughed when I read that story. I felt *safe. from what? not the thing I needed to be safe from.*' The narrator then throws himself out the window. And *Savage Night* has an equally chilling finale. The narrator this time is a diminutive hit man, Charlie 'Little' Bigger. Holed up in an isolated house with a woman sent to spy on him, he and his companion Ruthie slip into madness. Ruthie attacks and chops him to pieces with an axe. And Bigger leaves us in a condition, a plight, that somehow epitomizes all Thompson's major characters. 'The darkness and myself. Everything else was gone,' Bigger confides, as he drags what is left of him through the basement. 'Death was here,' he concludes. 'And he smelled good.'

There were several notable generic developments in crime and hardboiled fiction during the three decades or so following the Second World War. These included the emergence of police procedural fiction and a kind of crime novel in which motivation rather than detection was central. The police procedural form, in which the role of protagonist is given to an entire unit of police officers, was introduced by Lawrence Treat (1903–98). However, the writer who has achieved most marked success with it is Evan Hunter (1926–), working under the name of Ed McBain, who has produced more than forty novels set in the Eighty-seventh Precinct of a thinly disguised New York City. The detectiveless crime novel, in turn, became the particular forte of Patricia Highsmith (1921–95). Her first novel, *Strangers on a*

Train (1950), set the pattern and established her claustrophobic, irrational, perilous fictive world. Here, and in other novels like *This Sweet Sickness* (1960), strangers are emotionally tied to each other through acts of violence. People are twinned, find themselves with secret sharers of their lives, in relationships that vacillate between love and hatred. Highsmith seems especially interested in acts of doubling and disguise that expose the darker side of life, and the murkier depths of human personality. This is especially so in her most popular books, about the pleasant, totally amoral young American Tom Ripley. The first and probably the best of these, *The Talented Mr. Ripley* (1955), offers a sardonic variation on *The Ambassadors* by Henry James, as Ripley, despatched to rescue a wealthy young man from the cultural fleshpots of Europe, ends up by murdering him and assuming his identity. There are no puzzles in Highsmith's work, justice is rarely done in them, and the emphasis is generally on the perpetrator of the crime rather than the victim or detector. What there is, besides this shift of emphasis, is a disconcerting dissolution of the boundaries that serve to keep society safe and ourselves comfortable: between reality and fantasy, the permissible and the forbidden, good and evil.

Other women writers besides Highsmith began to explore the possibilities of crime and mystery at the same time as her: among them Leigh Brackett (1915–78) and Helen Nielsen (1918–2002). Other male writers, in turn, added a subtler shading and tone to the generic field of mystery writing. Rex Stout (1886–1975), for instance, introduced an eccentric armchair detective called Nero Wolfe in *Fer-de-Lance* (1934). Joined with his sidekick, a variation on the hardboiled private eye named Archie Goodwin, the two became the most successful team in American mystery fiction. Equally successful, and more interesting, were the protagonists in the novels of John D. Macdonald (1916–86) and Ross Macdonald (1915–83). John Macdonald produced a series of twenty-one novels with Travis McGee as their hero. An unofficial private eye, and an intelligent, honest con man who swindles the swindlers, McGee is a character of some subtlety and complexity. The abuses that money and power may engender fuel the plots of all the novels in which he appears; and John Macdonald uses the narrative spine of the mystery to examine serious social issues, notably pollution and the destruction of the environment (*Bright Orange for the Shroud* [1965], *The Turquoise Lament* [1973]). Of Ross Macdonald, Eudora Welty once wrote that he had produced 'the finest series of detective novels ever written by an American'. His main protagonist, Lew Archer, first appeared in *The Moving Target* (1949). At first, Archer was a relatively stereotypical version of the hardboiled hero. Even in this first book, however, he reflected his creator's conviction that nothing is clear-cut. 'Evil isn't so simple,' Archer explains here. 'Everybody has it in him, and whether it comes out in his actions depends on a number of things. Environment, opportunity, economic pressure, a piece of bad luck, a wrong friend.' Gradually, though, Archer evolved into a prototypical figure of the Vietnam years and after. 'Not the usual peeper', as one of the characters observes in *The Far Side of the Dollar* (1965), Archer becomes more reflective and coolly perceptive. More interested in listening than detecting, in understanding rather than meting out justice, in books like *The Drowning Pool*

(1950), *The Galton Case* (1959) and *The Underground Man* (1971), Archer discovers the roots of present traumas in past betrayals. He exposes the schemes and self-deception concealed below the comfortable surfaces and plastic moralities of the marketplace. And he shows how the older generation have disturbed and disoriented the younger. As a quiet moral centre rather than a focus of action, Archer reflects the view, expressed in *Sleeping Beauty* (1973), that 'every witness has his own way of creeping up on truth'. Interrogation becomes less a matter of intimidation, more a chance for the participant to unburden knowledge, to dig up a buried past and perhaps come to terms with it. That past, invariably, has a social dimension: since what, on a deeper level, these stories dig up involves the sins of the founding fathers being visited upon the sons and daughters – the dreams of a nation turned irrevocably sour.

From the 1970s, novels written in the general generic field of crime and mystery have largely been published first in hardback. The paperback original and mystery magazine died out. And those short stories in the field that were still published appeared mostly in non-specialist magazines or crime anthologies. What has been particularly remarkable about this period is the rapid growth in the use of the genre to address serious issues. The drugs epidemic, urban violence, racism, homelessness, AIDS, sexual abuse, the issue of abortion: these and many other problems endemic in contemporary society have been confronted in mystery novels over the last quarter of the twentieth century and into the twenty-first. At the same time, markedly more sophisticated approaches to narration and characterization shown by many American mystery novelists have further eroded the distinction between genre writing and literature. That growth of sophistication is perceptible in the work of three contemporary masters, Elmore Leonard (1925–), George V. Higgins (1939–99) and James Ellroy (1948–). Leonard began by writing Westerns, notable among which are *Hombre* (1961) and *Valdez is Coming* (1970). Then, after reading *The Friends of Eddie Coyle* (1972) by George V. Higgins, he turned to the mystery genre and new ways of telling stories. The work of Higgins portrays sleazy characters on both sides of the law, with a toughly realistic sympathy for their struggles. It depends, above all, on dialogue, a stylized vernacular that has the smell of authenticity, and draws the reader into a world of rough justice, hard money and fast deals. Leonard developed a similar sympathy for his morally dubious characters through an equally vigorous use of their speech. Voice is as important to him as it is to Higgins. And, in works from *Fifty-Two Pickup* (1974) through *La Brava* (1983) to *Glitz* (1985), *Get Shorty* (1990), *Pagan Babies* (2002) and beyond, he has used a variety of urban settings in which to place his humanized villains. There are no true villains in the work of Ellroy either. In his case, however, it is because there appears to be no moral code here to distinguish heroes from villains, or to hint at the possibility of redemption. What Ellroy describes, with darkly comic venom and in a prose as strung out as a telegraph wire, is a world of violence and betrayal and corruption – where the ugliness just keeps on getting uglier. This is particularly noticeable in his Los Angeles Quartet, consisting of *The Black Dahlia* (1987), *The Big Nowhere* (1988), *L.A. Confidential* (1990) and *White Jazz* (1992). Written in what sometimes seems like a frenetic shorthand, the quartet charts crime and corruption in the City of Angels from the end of the Second World War to the election of John Kennedy. It is not so much a series of mystery novels as an absurdist vision of urban hell.

Higgins sets *The Friends of Eddie Coyle* in Boston, and Leonard has used a variety of urban settings including Detroit, Atlantic City and Miami Beach. In one of his more recent novels, *American Tabloid* (1995), Ellroy appears to take all America, or its underbelly, for his canvas. This reflects a general gravitation of mystery writing beyond its traditional locations and into new areas: such as New Orleans in the books of James Lee Burke (1943–), among them *The Neon Rain* (1987) and *Black Cherry Blues* (1989), or Boston in those of Robert B. Parker (1932–). The novels of Parker, such as *Mortal Stakes* (1975) and *Paper Doll* (1993), also measure the further development of the private eye character into a person of considerable sophistication and internal conflict. But more interesting, perhaps, than this have been two other seminal developments. The hardboiled and mystery traditions have recently been reconstructed as a vehicle for feminism. They have also been subject to radical revision and rewriting along racial lines. The private eye originated as a descendant of the frontier hero, carrying with him a freight of assumptions about gender and race. White, male and unattached, he negotiated a world controlled and corrupted by men like him. Women were mostly distractions, when they were not dangerous femmes fatales. Men and women of other races were scarcely noticed by him at all. And although he constantly exposed social corruption, he almost never registered the racial segregation and institutional racism that were an integral part of it. That all changed, from about the 1970s on. In the process, the mystery genre further revealed itself as a field of possibilities, with a capacity both to register historical change and to reflect and address pressing social issues.

Among American women writers of mystery fiction, Sara Paretsky (1947–) is particularly notable. With her first novel, *Indemnity Only* (1982), Paretsky introduced a private investigator, Victoria Iphigenia Warshawski, known as 'Vic' or 'V.I.', who narrates her experiences just as the traditional, hardboiled hero does. As this and the other Warshawski books, such as *Deadlock* (1984), *Killing Orders* (1985), *Blood Shot* (1988) and *Total Recall* (2001) show, though, Paretsky entered the hardboiled tradition in order to revise it. Her protagonist may be as sharply observant and harshly reflective as the traditional private eye; the prose may crackle with the same urgency; the same cool eye is cast on the grainy textures of everyday life and vital revelations of character and motive. But this is a private eye, and private eye fiction, with a difference. For one thing, Warshawski wryly distances herself from earlier textbook heroes: 'I'm no Philip Marlowe,' she observes in *Tunnel Vision* (1994), 'forever pulling guns out of armpits or glove compartments.' For another, she is constantly concerned about her own toughness, worrying that her job diminishes human connection. And she seeks, and finds, that connection, not so much with men of her own age – her sexual relations, even her brief, past marriage, seem relatively peripheral to her – but with an older, male neighbour and, even more, with other women. Her closest relation is with another, older woman, Lotte Herschel. That, perhaps, is one measure of Warshawski's own sense of female solidarity. Very much a child of the Sixties, she is constantly reflecting on the raw deal women still have despite the women's liberation movement in which she participated. She is also constantly trying to help other women, in her capacity as private eye and through her involvement in various causes and groups, such as a women's shelter. The feminism Paretsky embodies and expresses through her central character is neither narrow nor shrill. Warshawski is an unsentimental, unself-pitying, acerbically intelligent character with an ironic sense of humour as well as a keen eye for injustice. And the wrongs to women Warshawski may uncover are always seen to be irrevocably tied to a wider web of corruption. The specific crimes she investigates, and solves, are usually committed to preserve or consolidate power and always relate to wider social problems. The power may involve men but it is never definitively male; the problems may involve women but they are never exclusively female.

What has been described as the first African American detective novel, *The Conjure-Man Dies* by Rudolph Fisher, appeared in 1932. Over twenty years later, Chester Himes (1909–84) published *For Love of Imabelle* (1957, reissued as *A Rage in Harlem* [1965]), the first in a series of urban thrillers, resembling the police procedural in form, whose main characters grew to be two African American police detectives, Coffin Ed Johnson and Grave Digger Jones. Himes had himself been in prison, for armed robbery. It was there that he became an apprentice writer. Once he was released, he began writing novels that reflected his preoccupation with the destructive power of racism (*If He Hollers Let Him Go* [1945]), his experiences in prison (*Cast the First Stone* [1952]) and his own problems as an intelligent, sensitive black man living in a world dominated by whites (*The Primitive* [1955]). 'The American black man is the most neurotic, complicated, schizophrenic, unanalysed, anthropologically advanced specimen of mankind in the history of the world,' Himes wrote in the first volume of his autobiography, *The Quality of Hurt* (1972). It was partly to escape the pain, the predicament outlined here, that he became an expatriate. Leaving for Europe in 1953, he made only occasional trips back to the United States, usually to New York City. After several lean years in Europe, Himes was given the opportunity to write for Éditions Gallimard's *Série noire*, a respected series of translated American crime fiction. And so it was in Europe that his own variations on the police procedural scored their first success: among them, *The Real Cool Killers* (1959), *Cotton Comes to Harlem* (1965) and *Blind Man With a Pistol* (1969). In each of these novels, Himes juxtaposes absurdly comic characters with sinister situations, setting everything against the grim background of a swarming, degraded ghetto. Many of them concern a goodhearted black male, just inching along, who finds himself involved in a desperate struggle for his life. A morally equivocal light-skinned woman may be at the heart of his trouble. In any event, the scene is packed with hard-nosed gamblers, religious freaks and drug-crazed killers. Armed with identical revolvers, dressed in black suits and driving a battered Plymouth sedan, Johnson and Jones do the best they can in this world. As they struggle to deal with the chaos and corruption that surround them, the two detectives inspire the same fear, respect and awe as the 'bad men' of African American folklore. For all that, however, their struggle seems increasingly hopeless. By the time of the last book in the series, *Blind Man With a Pistol*, chaos seems to have come to Harlem in earnest and Johnson and Jones seem unable to restore order. The final image of the novel, signalled by its title, sums it all up: people are helpless in the face of a scattershot destructiveness that is as wasteful as it is random.

Twenty years after Himes completed his series of novels with Coffin Ed Johnson and Grave Digger Jones at their centre, Walter Mosley (1952–) published *Devil in a Blue Dress* (1990). This was followed by several other novels, including *White Butterfly* (1992) and *A Little Yellow Dog* (1996), set in postwar Los Angeles and featuring a reluctant black investigator, Ezekiel 'Easy' Rawlins. The novels unfold in a developing history: *Devil in a Blue Dress* takes place in 1948, *A Little Yellow Dog* just before the assassination of President Kennedy in 1963. What is more, they show an acute sense of the racism endemic in American society, not least in its police force. A migrant from the South, financially secure yet still painfully aware of the precariousness of being black, Easy Rawlins is a Second World War veteran who recalls that 'the army was segregated just like the South'. 'The white boys hated me,' he remembers, 'but if they didn't respect me I was ready to fight.' Easy carves out a life for himself with a home, some rental properties and an unconventional family of two adopted children, all of it concealed from the gaze of white bureaucracy. He is socially invisible in a way, just like the protagonist of *Invisible Man*. And, as he manoeuvres his way in and around the absurdities of a world dominated by whites, he attends to the voice inside him to guide him. 'The voice . . . just tells me how it is if I want to survive: Survive like a man,' Rawlins confesses in *Devil in a Blue Dress*. 'When the voice speaks, I listen.' Not a detective as such but someone in the 'favour business' of the black community, he is drawn into each adventure by attending to that voice: in order, that is, to maintain some tenuous grasp on security for himself and his children. The danger Rawlins encounters comes from inside as well as around him. He is only too aware of his own capacity for violence: a capacity powerfully figured in Raymond 'Mouse' Alexander, a childhood friend and sidekick whom he both loves and fears. Alexander is gleefully amoral and murderous; and his casual, conscienceless approach to things adds depth and shade to the portrait of Rawlins – not only as a contrast but also as a reminder of dark currents running within the protagonist, just below the brooding, reflective surface. Mosley has said that he owes a debt to Albert Camus in his conception of Easy Rawlins. And it is clear that, like other African American writers before him, he has used existentialism to explore the trials of race. Whatever else he is, this amateur detective (anti-)hero is a man in process: using his quicksilver sensibility not just to get by but to make himself and make his own morality up, as he wanders around some of the meanest streets in the city.

Native American sleuths began appearing in fiction well before their African American counterparts. Popular interest in the West, and in what was seen as the exoticism of Native American cultures, led to the wide dissemination of books with titles like *Velvet Foot, the Indian Detective, or, The Taut Tiger* (1882) in the later part of the nineteenth century. Even 'Buffalo' Bill tried his hand with a mystery story that had a Native American detective, *Red Ruard, the Indian Detective, or, The Gold Buzzards of Colorado: a romance of the mines and dead trails* (1886). The 'Indian detective' in these and similar stories was adept at tracking, following footprints or investigating the scene of a crime. He had an intimate understanding of the terrain, and he could negotiate different cultures with aplomb. In other words, he was stereotypical: a heroic type, evolved out of a number of perceptions and received assumptions about Native American people, with varying degrees of accuracy. What is different about more recent developments in this area is that mystery writers now are far more alert to cultural difference. Writers such as Tony Hillerman (1925–), in novels like *The Blessing Way* (1970) and *Finding Moon* (1996), pursue their work on the intersection where Anglo and Native American cultures meet. They expand the methods of investigation to incorporate different value systems and processes of thought; they explore the uneasy meeting, the conflict and occasional congruence, between whites and Native Americans; and they open the genre to political processes, such as the rights of indigenous peoples or the impact of commercial exploitation of the land both on the harsh landscapes of the Southwest and on those cultures still closely tied to the earth. This opening up of the generic field of mystery, to the processes of history and in particular the problems of cultural conflict, is not just the work of those who take Native Americans or African Americans as their prime subject. Chicano culture enters the detective genre in the fiction of Rudolfo A. Anaya, concerned with Sonny Baca, an Albuquerque private eye who first appears in *Zia Summer* (1995). It does so, again, in *Partners in Crime* (1985) by Rolando Hinojosa. In turn, immigrant culture in general and Korean culture in particular is the scarcely hidden agenda in *Native Speaker* (1995) by Chang-Rae Lee (1965–), a book that uses the mystery formula to investigate what is called the 'ugly immigrant's truth' of social exploitation, cultural confusion and, sometimes, personal self-hatred. In novels like these, it becomes simply impossible to preserve a distinction between mystery fiction and serious literature. If there was ever a wall between genre writing and other forms, then that wall has now been torn down.

The challenging and breaking up of genres by some writers does not mean, of course, that others have not chosen to exploit genre formulas by staying within their limits. There is, it seems, an inexhaustible public appetite for formulaic fiction, as the career of Stephen King (1947–) testifies. King has achieved phenomenal success by simply and skilfully working within different genres, particularly horror, and utilizing their formulas, their rhythms of expectation, tension and release, to the full. Other writers have achieved as much success by developing new formulas. A variant on the police procedural, for instance, the legal procedural, was developed by Scott Turow (1949–) in *Presumed Innocent* (1987) and by John Grisham (1955–) in a series of best-sellers beginning with *A Time to Kill* (1989). And Thomas Harris (1940–), in *The Silence of the Lambs* (1988), probed the psychology of a serial killer in a form that might be called noir Gothic. Even here, however, the distinction between genre and literature tends to become blurred, to the point of disappearance. Another, equally unnerving journey into the mind of a serial killer, *American Psycho* (1991) by Bret Easton Ellis, is, quite clearly, a crossover. A surfeit of violence and horror, an obsession with commodity fetishism and a knowing use of narrator (it is never clear whether the killer, who tells the story, is recording fact or fantasizing): all turn this novel, not untypically for its times, into a work that seems to want to be sensationalistic and serious at one and the same moment. Books like *American Psycho* or *Generation X: Tales for an Accelerated Culture* (1991) by Douglas Coupland (1952–) seem, in fact, not so much to critique commodity culture as to be contained in it. In the new information age, the sign has been commodified, becoming the standard coinage, the fuel of the postmodern economy. So, the inference is, the author, in adding his signature to his series of signs – known as the story or poem – is simply signing on to the economy. He is acknowledging, however wryly or bleakly, his implication in a culture where, as the narrator of *Generation X* puts it, 'genuine capital H history' has ended, 'turned into a press release, a marketing strategy'. Writers like Coupland and Ellis are sometimes called 'the blank generation' (which itself sounds suspiciously like a marketing strategy). Their characters exist in a state of anomie, in a deadpan culture of empty television shows, 'Elvis moments', semi-disposable Swedish furniture, fast food and designer labels. And their fiction circulates in that culture as part of its currency, stamped with the blank, value-free mark of the times. To talk of any distinction between genre and other writing is peculiarly irrelevant here, since the world recorded *and the recording instrument* are themselves layerings of genres, series of imitations of life that have no evident existence outside the systems of exchange.

In *God Bless You, Mr. Rosewater* (1965) by Kurt Vonnegut, the protagonist drunkenly addresses a meeting of writers of science fiction. 'I love you sons of bitches,' he announces, 'You're all I read any more. You're the only ones who'll talk about the really *terrific* changes going on.' That echoes a sentiment expressed by many readers of science fiction. Given the enormous pace of technological change in the twentieth century, with its consequent transformation of every corner of our lives, its potential for further transformation and perhaps global annihilation, then, so the argument goes, science fiction is the only form of literature really addressing the truth. Separate and different from mainstream literature, it is so because it is *better*. As a distinct genre, it reveals 'what machines do to us, what wars do to us, what cities do to us', to quote Mr Rosewater again, 'what big, simple ideas do to us, what tremendous misunderstandings, mistakes, accidents, and catastrophes do to us'. It is also a distinctively American genre, since American writers have been at the forefront of developments in the genre since the time of H. G. Wells. A formative figure here was H. P. Lovecraft (1890–1937). Primarily remembered, perhaps, as a writer of Gothic fiction, Lovecraft also produced works that exploited dislocations of time and space and extraterrestrial encounters. He was an initiator in those forms of science fiction in which fantasy, rather than scientific knowledge, dominates. And many of his stories first appeared in the magazine

Weird Tales. As a promoter and disseminator of science fiction narratives, this magazine was soon complemented by the founding, in 1926, of *Amazing Stories* and then, in 1937, *Astounding Science Fiction*. *Amazing Stories* was particularly influential here. It was founded by Hugo Gernsback (1884–1967), an indefatigable publisher of periodicals committed to science and fantasy. Because of this, and to a lesser extent because of his 'Baron Munchausen' stories ('Munchausen on the Moon' [1915], 'Munchausen Departs for the Planet Mars' [1916]), Gernsback, an immigrant from Luxembourg, is sometimes called 'the father of science fiction'. In turn, another early writer, Edward Elmer Smith (1890–1965), usually known as 'Doc' Smith, is often referred to as 'the father of space opera'. Good and evil in his 'Lensman' novels, such as *Triplanetary* (1934; revised 1948), *First Lensman* (1954) and *Galactic Patrol* (1937–8; revised 1950) are parcelled out between the benevolent Arisians and the malign Eddorians. There is a wealth of space opera fantasy here. For example, certain members of the Galactic Patrol acquire telepathic powers by wearing a 'lens' or bracelet, which gives the 'lensman' series its title. At its core, however, this sprawling epic recalls earlier epics of American empire: this is a Western transported into space.

The work of a later science fiction writer like Robert Heinlein (1907–88) is more sophisticated than this, not least because his works negotiate a path between scientific literalism and fantasy. Heinlein is also capable of humour and social comment. *Double Star* (1956), for instance, is about a failed actor who claims to be a galactic politician. And he can use the genre to make intelligent guesses about the future – from which vantage point he can then cast a critical eye over the present. So, the novel for which he is best known, *Stranger in a Strange Land* (1961), concerns Mike Smith, a human who has been brought up on Mars. Initiated into an unearthly way of regarding reality, Smith has also acquired suprahuman powers. On returning to earth, he founds a new religion on more Martian habits, a good deal more pacifist and hedonist than most earthly creeds. At the end of the novel, though, he is torn to pieces by outraged humans, crucified for his beliefs and practices. Among those practices, and at the core of this new religion, is what is called 'grokking'. '"Grok" means "identity equal",' a Martian character explains. '"Grok" means to understand so thoroughly that the observer becomes a part of the observed – to merge, blend, intermarry, lose identity in a group experience.' In effect, *Stranger in a Strange Land* takes themes ingrained in the American experience and writing – the lonely hero, the clash with conventional society, exile, longing and the impulse to merge with older, deeper forms of community – and gives them a new twist. This is a new siting of a series of classic tropes. So is another novel, *Childhood's End* (1954), by an equally influential science fiction writer, Arthur C. Clarke (1917–). This is a story about the end of the world, not due to some humanly produced catastrophe but because the human race achieves a total breakthrough into pure mind. It is experienced by all the children under ten, who suddenly cease to be individuals and become a vast group endowed with extraordinary powers. Jan, the last man on earth and observer of its final hours, watches the children; 'their faces', he comments, 'were merging into a common mould' as they serve and merge into what is called here the Overmind. The whole trajectory of the narrative, with its driving impulse of life disentangling itself from the flesh to become pure intelligence, is in fact distinctly transcendentalist: Overmind, after all, seems to echo the Emersonian notion of the Over-Soul. This is another story that rewrites old American stories in new forms.

Apocalypse of a very different kind occurs in the *Dune* series of Frank Herbert (1920–86). *Dune* (1965), one of the most successful science fiction novels ever, is a complex story of intrigue, mysticism and ecological theory. Its messianic hero, Paul Atreides, known as 'Maud'dib'', is descended from a line of space migrants who have been guided by the simple precept, 'thou shalt not disfigure the soul'. Creating an alien, elaborate but credible environment, Herbert combines action with speculation. As the human species struggles for survival against terrible odds, the narrative invites the reader to consider questions of social control, free will and determinism and the relation between human nature, nature and technology. In the sequels to *Dune*, *Dune Messiah* (1969) and *Children of Dune* (1976), the perils of the messianic impulse are explored. 'We're locked into forms, of government, of belief and behaviour which draw us to keep repeating ourselves,' Herbert has said. 'That's one of the points I wanted to make in *Dune*.' He does so by showing the universe exploding in violence, in a 'jihad' or holy war, as the vision of Maud'dib' is debased by a theocratic bureaucracy and the messiah himself departs for the wilderness leaving his children to inherit the burden. With an ambition equal to that of Herbert, Isaac Asimov (1920–92) explored the nature of human history in his *Foundation* series: *Foundation* (1951), *Foundation and Empire* (1952), *Second Foundation* (1953), *Foundation's Edge* (1982) and *Foundation and Earth* (1986). Asimov was also prodigiously productive. He published his first science fiction tale in *Amazing Stories* in 1938; by the time of his death, he had published four hundred and seventy titles, in science fiction and a number of other forms and genres.

Ray Bradbury (1920–) published numerous short stories before establishing his reputation with *The Martian Chronicles* (1950). It describes the first attempts of earth people to conquer and colonize Mars, the thwarting of their efforts by the gentle, telepathic Martians, the eventual colonization and the eventual effect on the Martian settlers of a nuclear war on earth. As much a work of social criticism as anything, the novel explores some of the prevailing anxieties of the 1950s and beyond: the fear of war, the longing for a simpler life, the resistance to racism and censorship. *Fahrenheit 451* (1953) is also a cautionary tale that uses an imagined future to critique the present. The title refers to the temperature at which books are supposed to burn; and the book is set in a future world where the written word is banned. A group of rebels resist the ban by memorizing entire works of literature and philosophy. Here and in his other books (including numerous collections of stories like *The Golden Apples of the Sun* [1953]), Bradbury views technological change with a cautious sympathy. Not against such change in itself, he is nevertheless alert to potential dangers – above all, the possibility that the moral evolution of human beings will not keep pace with their mechanical development. The use of science fiction or fantasy as a critique and corrective is just as notable in the work of Ursula Le Guin (1929–). In fact, in her introduction to her novel *The Left Hand of Darkness* (1969), Le Guin has insisted that 'science fiction is not predictive; it is descriptive'. True to that formula, this novel describes and critically defines sexual prejudice. It is set on an imaginary planet populated by 'androgynes', people who can at different times be male, female and neuter. An ordinary human who falls in love with a member of this trisexual society is forced to examine the meaning of sexual roles. And the reader, in turn, is invited to imagine what it may mean to be simply human, living outside the social determinants of sexual identity. Other books are critical of contemporary American political and social values. *The Word for World Forest* (1972) is about Vietnam; *The Dispossessed* (1974) is a fantasy set on an anarchist moon colony and its capitalist mother planet; *The New Atlantis* (1975) presents a futuristic vision of a totalitarian United States. Her most ambitious and acclaimed work, though, the 'Earthsea' trilogy, is more preoccupied with fundamental values: addressing, in terms of scientific fantasy, the need to face the evil in oneself (*A Wizard of Earthsea* [1968]), the need for trust and truth (*The Tombs of Atuan* [1971]) and the need to accept the ineluctable fact of death (*The Farthest Shore* [1972]).

The scope of science fiction, its capacity to explore not only social and moral issues but matters of being and knowledge, is nowhere more evident than in the stories of Philip K. Dick (1928–82), Samuel R. Delany (1942–) and Octavia Butler (1947–). Preoccupied with problems of perception, Dick returned obsessively to the permeable boundaries separating the real from the illusory, fact from fiction. Which is a reason for his interest in hallucinatory drugs, and their impact on consciousness (*The Three Stigmata of Palmer Eldritch* [1964], *A Scanner Darkly* [1977]). As the title of his most famous novel, *Do Androids Dream of Electric Sheep?* (1968), indicates, it was also the reason for his imagining of cunning facsimiles of humanity that call into question all our ideas of what it means to be human. The work of Delany reflects his own belief that, as he has put it, 'the science fictional enterprise is richer than the enterprise of mundane fiction'. An African American, Delany began by writing relatively traditional science fiction. His first book, *The Jewels of Aptor* (1962), explores themes of quest, the capabilities of technology and the status of the artist, to all of which Delany would later return. *The Einstein Intersection* (1967) is an ambitious attempt to satirize forms of human life using a science fiction frame. *Nova* (1968) is a dense translation of the myths of Prometheus and the Holy Grail into futuristic terms. These novels reveal an increasing complexity. In *Nova*, for instance, cryptic narrative information alternates with passages of lyrical rhetoric and the characterization is consistently freakish and bizarre. In the early 1970s, however, Delany moved altogether away from conventional narrative logic. *Dhalgren*, published in 1975, marks the change. 'A book about many things', as Delany has described it, it presents a city that has suffered a disaster so catastrophic that the space-time continuum has been distorted. In a powerful image of society in chaos, buildings burn endlessly without being consumed; and the only possibility of redemption seems to shine in youth and art. Time, logic and narrative viewpoints are all cut loose from their traditional literary moorings, in this and the later *Atlantis: Model 1924* (1995). They function relativistically. An additional, disconcerting factor in *Dhalgren* is that Kid, the narrator, is dyslexic and epileptic. These later books take science fiction into the postmodern; as they do so, they carry the habit of the genre to speculate and subvert to a new and extraordinary extreme.

Both the earlier and later science fiction of Delany is also notable for extending the frontiers of the genre as far as the treatment of race and sex are concerned. His novels are striking for their black and mixed-blood characters and their uninhibited approach to sexuality. One novel, *Triton* (1976), presents the reader with more than forty different sexes. Those frontiers have been further stretched by Octavia Butler, who is also African American. Her Patternist series, for instance, which includes *Patternmaster* (1976), *Wild Seed* (1984) and *Clay's Ark* (1984), has as its central character a 4,000-year-old immortal, Doro, who is able to move at will from body to body. The movement is regardless of race and gender, although Doro prefers to inhabit the bodies of black males. A powerful Nubian patriarch, who sustains his power with the help of his psychic abilities and physical strength, Doro has fathered enough descendants to establish a dynasty known as 'the Pattern'. Complementing Doro, among many others, is one of his daughters, Mary, a gifted telepath, and the woman who adopts her, Emma, a strong but elegant woman. In many ways, the two of them are prototypical feminist science fiction characters; and it comes as little surprise to learn that Butler herself includes Ursula Le Guin among the foremost of her influences, as her literary foremother. Just how writers like Butler have stretched science fiction, generically, imaginatively and thematically, is suggested by her best-known book, *Kindred* (1988). This was originally meant to be a Patternist novel, but Butler found it too realistic to fit into the futurist frame of the series. Here, a young black woman call Dana is transported back in time, from the 1970s Los Angeles suburb where she lives with her white husband to a Maryland plantation before the Civil War. She then finds herself the property of a family whose eldest son Rufus has summoned her to save him. During the course of her journey back into the racial past, Dana loses an arm: a mark of how slavery inscribed itself on the bodies as well as the minds and memories of African Americans. Incorporating elements of social and historical realism and naturalist critique into its framework of fantasy, *Kindred* shows how porous and adaptable the genre of science fiction can be – and just how alert, perceptive and predictive science fiction writers can become, as they attend to what Eliot Rosewater called 'the really *terrific* changes going on'.

Creating New Americas

Dreaming history: European immigrant writing

Sometimes it has seemed more appropriate to designate the changes going on in and around America during the past half-century as terrible rather than terrific.

Those changes, in particular, have helped account for the waves of immigration that have turned the United States into even more of a 'universal nation' than it was in the first two centuries of its existence. Immigration from Europe, for instance, increased dramatically after the Second World War. Between 1945 and 1950, almost 350,000 displaced persons arrived in the United States. Despite restrictions imposed by a conservative political administration, many of these were Jewish people. Many, too, were from Eastern Europe, as growing anti-Communist sentiments during this period encouraged a welcome for refugees from this area. Welcome as refugees from Communism, often unwelcome if they were Jewish, these immigrants from old European cultures entered established communities in the United States, communities that perhaps retained their allegiance to the old ways and even the old language. Haunted by war and Holocaust, they brought their own special freight of memories, their own unbearable past with them, one that made it difficult, if not impossible, for them to embrace the millennial hopes associated with America. It sometimes made it difficult for them, too, to subscribe to the inherited beliefs of their culture. As a character in *Meshugah* (1994) by Isaac Bashevis Singer (1904–91) declares, 'I owe nothing to the Almighty as long as He keeps sending us Hitlers and Stalins. He is *their* God, not mine.' Singer himself came to the United States from Poland in 1935. He became a journalist, writing in Yiddish for the *Jewish Daily Forward*. It was there also that he published most of his fiction. Dealing with the mixed inheritance of Polish Jews, their traditional faith and folkways, their daily village life, their mysticism and sexuality, their lively personal relationships, he combined fantasy with humour. His first major work, *Satan in Gusay*, was published in Yiddish in 1935 and in English twenty years later. It describes the aftermath of a Polish pogrom in the seventeenth century, when the surviving Jews turned to a messianic sect with erotic and mystic beliefs. The first of his books to appear in English was *The Family Muskat* (1950), a naturalistic account of the decline of a Jewish family in Warsaw from the beginning of the twentieth century until the Second World War. It was followed by other books set in Poland, like *The Magician of Lublin* (1960), *The Manor* (1967) and *The Estate* (1969). Throughout his life, Singer also chronicled ghetto life in wry, pungent short stories, collected in such volumes as *Gimpel the Fool* (1957), *The Spinoza of Market Street* (1961) and *Passions* (1978).

Enemies: A Love Story (1972) was the first of his novels to be set in the United States. It comprises a kind of post-Holocaust trilogy with *The Penitent* (1983) and the posthumously published *Meshugah*. 'Although I did not have the privilege of going through the Hitler Holocaust,' Singer writes in a caustic author's note to *Enemies*, 'I have lived for years with refugees from this ordeal.' And, in each of these narratives, characters try to exorcise the millions of ghosts created by genocide. In *Enemies*, the protagonist, a refugee called Herman Broder, shuttles uneasily between three women, a mistress and two wives, one he married in America, the other he thought had died in Europe. At the same time, he careers between the ordeal of his European past and the challenge of his American present. Persistently reinventing himself, Herman encounters postwar culture as a mildly deranged survivor who is alienated from the grand narratives of history and trapped in wartime memories. 'Where are the Nazis?' his psychotic mistress asks him, when he takes her on a trip into the American pastoral of the Adirondack mountains. 'What kind of world is this without Nazis? A backward country, this America.' Like her, Herman suspects trauma and disruption everywhere; he cannot reconcile the Holocaust with his American experience and so form a new cultural identity. All he can manage, finally, after his mistress commits suicide, is to set up a strange but strangely touching *ménage à trois* with his two wives. It is not a reconciliation of the warring opposites of his life, perhaps, but it is a form of survival. In *The Penitent*, the protagonist survives in another way, by leaving 'the Golden Land' of America for Europe. In *Meshugah*, the narrator negotiates a sort of survival when he marries, in a muted, postlapsarian gesture of forgiveness, a woman who had collaborated with the Nazis. It is, we are told, 'the quietest wedding since the one between Adam and Eve'. Despite such gently or quirkily redemptive moments, though, all three books in the post-Holocaust trilogy are marked by a comic absurdism of tone and a carnivalesque nihilism of spirit. Meshugah, Singer reminds the reader, is a Yiddish word meaning 'crazy, senseless, insane'. That reflects the feeling, expressed by one character, that 'the whole world is an insane asylum'. Or, as another character puts it, 'the Hitler and Stalin catastrophes demonstrated that humanity's dreams of permanent peace and a united mankind were unreal'. The only genuine relief in this fiction comes from its antic narrative rhythms and mad, mordant humour. As Singer confessed, not long before he died, some of his characters may finally have 'made peace with the cruelty of life, and the violence of man's history . . . but I haven't'.

The characters in the stories of Tillie Olsen (1913–) are not so much haunted by the Holocaust as haunted by silence. What they are faced with are the numerous denials of voice and identity imposed by poverty, by suffering, the Depression and World War – by 'the unnatural thwarting of what struggles to come into being for them', as Olsen has put it, 'but cannot', particularly if they are women. Olsen experienced such silencing herself. The daughter of a couple who fled from Russia when the 1905 revolution failed, she began work, at the age of nineteen, on a novel concerned with the efforts of a family to survive on the farms and in the packing houses of the Midwest. Marriage, motherhood and the need to find a means to survive economically all intervened. It was only much later that she was able to return to the unfinished manuscripts. 'The book ceased to be solely the work of that long ago young writer', Olsen recalled, 'and, in arduous partnership, became this older one's as well.' 'But', she added, 'it is all the old manuscripts – no rewriting, no new writing.' And it was finally published in 1974, as *Yonnondio: From the Thirties*. Before that, in the 1950s, Olsen had already begun writing again, a series of stories, *Tell Me a Riddle*, that was published in 1962. Originally conceived as part of a novel about three generations of a Russian Jewish family, these stories retrieve not only the particular sufferings and triumphs of individual characters but the meaning of entire decades of the national experience, intensely lived but barely recorded. They were clearly inspired by what Olsen has called, in her critical work *Silences* (1978), her 'hatred for all that, societally rooted, unnecessarily lessens and denies' creative acts of consciousness and that 'slows, impairs, silences writers'. And what they tell is a kind of secret history.

The title story of *Tell Me a Riddle* is typical. With the density and force of a novel, as if the long silence of its author had pressed its subject into fiercely condensed form, the story concerns the life and death of an immigrant woman, Eva. The narrative present is the close of her life. That narrative, however, dips back in memory, voice and consciousness to recover forty-seven years of subordination in marriage, long, anxious years of poverty and child-rearing. As a child and young woman, Eva had been part of a movement for change. Full of optimism, she had known 'transport, meaning, community'. As a wife and mother, however, she had had to live 'for' and not 'with' others. Now old, her children grown and gone, she relishes the chance *'never again to be forced to move to the rhythms of others'*. Her husband, meanwhile, unnerved by the absence of social relations and appalled by his wife's delight in the solitude of an 'empty house', wants to sell up and retire to a 'haven' for pensioners. 'Tell Me a Riddle' is a touching, telling account of the loving war that is marriage. It is also a revelation of the real cost of the sexual division of labour. The husband, David, having lived 'with' people, has made his peace with modern America. He has abandoned the 'holiest dreams' he and his wife had shared in their radical youth; alone, on the other hand, Eva has stored up these dreams. Eva has seen her husband and her children make their compromises, bury themselves in making do. But with her, we are told, it is as if 'for seventy years she had hidden a tape recorder, infinitely microscopic within her, that it had coiled infinite mile on mile, trapping every song, every melody, every word read, heard, and spoken'. At last, as she lies dying from cancer, all the coiled tape is played back, the dammed speech is released. On her deathbed, the silence of Eva is broken. In a lyrically disjunctive prose, Olsen recreates her protagonist's recovery of all that has been repressed: Eva's fear of nuclear annihilation, her anger at the waste of human potential, her unextinguished belief in the possibility of progress and revolution. *'Death deepens the wonder'* are the final, dedicatory words in this story. The wonder is for an indomitable woman, an uncornered spirit. It is for human, particularly female, continuity, since Eva passes the secret of the 'riddle' of life – which is hope, and the speaking of hope – on to her granddaughter. It is also for a tale that, while figuring what are called 'the monstrous shapes of what had actually happened in the twentieth century', still has time to celebrate all that grudgingly, lovingly David perceives in his wife. As he gazes at the broken body of Eva, he sees there what he has lost but what, even in dying, she still possesses: *'that joyous certainty, that sense of mattering, of moving and being moved, of being one and indivisible with the great of the past, with all that freed, ennobled'*.

Memories of the Holocaust haunt immigrant survivors in several other notable fictions of this period. Arriving in America as the remnants of a murdered culture, rather than the fragments of a decaying one, the protagonists of these fictions, just like the central figures in Singer's trilogy, demonstrate a corrosive scepticism – particularly about the hopes and dreams enshrined in the supposedly new world they have entered. So, Arthur Sammler in *Mr. Sammler's Planet* by Saul Bellow sees New York City merely as a metaphor for global disintegration. The city, he observes, 'makes one think about Sodom and Gomorrah, about the end of the world'. And Sophia Sawistowska, the gentile survivor of a Polish concentration camp in *Sophie's Choice* by William Styron, seems wedded to death. Her past, the narrator Stingo observes, trails 'its horrible smoke – as if from the chimneys of Auschwitz – of anguish, confusion, self-deception and, above all, guilt'. She cannot believe in the American promise, or even live in America; in the end, she commits suicide, and she persuades Stingo, a thinly disguised avatar of the author, to surrender his attachment to the national pastoral, the fresh green breast of the new world. Cynthia Ozick (1928–), too, has explored characters unwilling to accept the notion of their new home, the United States, as Eden in her novel *The Cannibal Galaxy* (1983) and her two-part novella *The Shawl* (1980). Born in New York City, Ozick explores the dilemma of being Jewish in a Christian world. In her short stories, in particular, she expresses her oppositional difference by turning postmodernism against itself. Two of her most engaging tales, for instance, about a character called Ruth Puttermesser, included in *Levitation: Five Fictions* (1982), employ postmodernist techniques to undermine postmodernist values and reaffirm traditional Jewish values of conscientiousness and respect for the limits of the self. The first Puttermesser story, 'Puttermesser: Her Work History, Her Ancestry, Her Afterlife', ends with the challenge, 'Hey! Puttermesser's biographer! What will you do with her now?' And the second, 'Puttermesser and Xanthippe', responds to that challenge by showing the protagonist's utopian daydreams getting strangely out of hand, before she recognizes and accepts the fact that the imagination must have ethical limits.

It is in the longer fiction, however, that the limits to imagining America are seriously addressed, through the experience of Holocaust survivors. Tortured by what are called, in *The Shawl*, 'cannibal dreams', the human devastation they have witnessed, these survivors seem not only sceptical but also substanceless. Ghostlike, they appear hardly to inhabit their own bodies, or to belong, to be really there, in a culture that their own memories turn into something irredeemably mediocre, meaningless. The vision of America nurtured by Joseph Brill, the protagonist in *The Cannibal Galaxy*, is scarcely pastoral or paradisiacal. A French Jew who survived the war in hiding, he sees the United States, where he now works as a school principal, as a land of the mediocre. 'He saw himself in the middle of an ashen America, heading a school of middling reputation, beleaguered by middling parents and their middling offspring,' the reader is told. 'All of this was a surprise in his late middle age, but of only middling size. He was used to consorting with the Middle.' Obsessed with the breakdown of culture, Brill feels that he is trapped in a cannibal galaxy, a 'megalosaurian colony of primordial gases that devours smaller brother galaxies'. He also sees shadows of the past looming through the tenuous and banal surfaces of the present. The 'innocent' American architecture of the school campus, for example, with the buildings lined up symmetrically, takes on the ghostly contours of the boxcars that took his family away from Paris to death in Poland. Like Rosa Lublin, the protagonist of *The Shawl*, who treasures the shawl of her daughter, killed in a concentration camp, like a talisman, Brill is wrapped up and rapt in recollection. Rosa equates America with the trivial, the 'prevalent, frivolous'. So does Brill. She has no time for millennial dreams: 'Stella Columbus!' she declares contemptuously of her niece Stella; 'She thinks there's such a thing as the New World.' Neither does he. Lublin and Brill are fatally alike in their 'secret cynicism', their sense of only half living in a banal limbo. Both of them end up married, which might suggest a kind of making do and going on. But the suitor of Rosa is comic, and acceptance of him grudging. And, after taking a wife, Joseph Brill retires to a middle-class existence in Florida that sounds like a dire parody of the American dream. Neither has learned much more than to sojourn as a stranger in the promised land.

Two writers of European immigrant families who, like Tillie Olsen, have been more interested in giving speech to the silences, and hope or even release to the desperate, are Grace Paley and Marge Piercy (1936–). Paley, whose work was discussed earlier, is the daughter of Jewish immigrants from Russia; Piercy was born to a Welsh father and a Jewish mother of Russian descent. Both were encouraged, as Olsen was, to be politically active; and both have used their writing as a form of activism – a means of resistance to, and rescue from, the potentially overwhelming experiences of poverty and oppression, the fact of war and the threat of annihilation. So, from the perspective of immigrant experience, the artfully fragmented tales of Paley emerge as cultural kaleidoscopes, mosaics of different language and speech patterns: a verbal and narrative equivalent of the mixed medium, the overlapping cultures of old worlds and new, in which her characters have to navigate their way and make their choices. The persona of Faith Asbury, a recurrent figure in these stories, helps Paley articulate her own choices, she is also a source of intensification and expansion. Faith enables Paley to intensify her own vision and voice, which are engaged but quirky, serious but susceptible to flights of fantasy. And she allows her creator, too, to expand her concerns beyond the local and the immediate, as Faith meets and measures her bond with other women, often from other cultures, who share her interests and anxieties. A similar feeling of female solidarity is notable in the work of Piercy, particularly the poems collected in such volumes as *To Be of Us* (1973) and *My Mother's Body* (1985). In the autobiographical 'Putting the good things away', for instance, Piercy reveals how the feelings her mother repressed have toughened and tempered her. 'Her anger annealed me, /' Piercy declares. 'I was dipped into the cauldron of boiling rage and rose / a warrior and a witch.' But, the poet adds, she is 'still vulnerable / there where she held me' because 'our minds were woven together'. Other poems explore how ordinary women 'must learn again to speak / starting with I / starting with We' ('Unlearning to not speak'), or the potential for 'a woman peppery as curry' in even the most 'ordinary pudgy downcast girl' ('The woman in the ordinary'). Still others, such as 'The Chuppah' or 'The perpetual migration', expose the impulse Piercy has inherited from her immigrant family always to go forward towards 'the mountains of freedom'. 'If I turn back,' she says, 'it feels / wrong.' Like Paley, or for that matter Olsen, Piercy is a writer of conscience, who may admit to being haunted but who sees her work as an act of exorcism. For her, the ghosts of the past, from Europe or elsewhere, do not paralyse: on the contrary, they propel her on to the future.

It is difficult to think of a European émigré writer further from all this than Vladimir Nabokov (1899–1977). In fact, the verbal shift that seems required, from immigrant to émigré, suggests some of the difference. Nabokov was born into a wealthy, prominent family in St Petersburg, Russia, and as a youth travelled extensively. His father, a liberal aristocratic jurist, opposed the tyranny of the tsar then that of the bolsheviks. He took his family into exile, then was murdered in Berlin in 1922 by a reactionary White Russian who later became a Nazi official. Nabokov lived in Berlin and Paris between the two World Wars. There, he produced a critically acclaimed series of poems, short stories and novels in Russian. Then, in 1940, in flight from various forms of totalitarianism, he emigrated to the United States where he began teaching Russian literature. His first novel in English, *The Real Life of Sebastian Knight*, was published in 1941; it concerns a young Russian in Paris, the narrator, who discovers the true nature of his half-brother, an English novelist, while writing his biography. This was followed by *Bend Sinister* in 1947, about a politically uncommitted professor in a totalitarian state who tries to maintain personal integrity. Four years later, Nabokov published his first memoir, *Conclusive Evidence*, later retitled *Speak, Memory* and, under this title, revised and expanded in 1966. Four years after that, in turn, came the book that established his fortune, his reputation for some and his notoriety for others, *Lolita*, published first in France then, after censorship problems were resolved, in the United States in 1958. It tells of the passion of a middle-aged European émigré, who calls himself Humbert Humbert, for what he terms 'nymphets' in general and the twelve-year-old girl he calls Lolita in particular, and their wanderings across America. It was Nabokov's first novel set in his new home in the New World; and its success allowed him to devote himself full-time to his writing. Three more novels appeared after the first publication of *Lolita*: among them, *Pale Fire* (1962), a postmodernist tour de force purporting to be a poem about an exiled Balkan king in a New England college town and the involved critical commentary on the poem by an academic who admits to being the king himself. Along with the other two novels, *Pnin* (1957) and *Ada, or Ardor: A Family Chronicle* (1969), there were novellas, short stories, a play, critical studies and commentary, translations of his earlier, Russian novels, lectures and correspondence, and a monumental translation of Pushkin's *Eugene Onegin* (1964). All of the work reflects, in some way, Nabokov's aesthetic of subjective idealism. All of it plays variations on the observation made by the academic commentator in *Pale Fire*: '"reality" is neither the subject nor the object of true art,' that commentator observes, 'which creates its own special reality having nothing to do with the average "reality" perceived by the communal eye.'

Which suggests the fundamental difference between Nabokov and even a writer like Singer, let alone Olsen or Ozick. 'To be sure, there is an average reality, perceived by all of us,' Nabokov admits in *Strong Opinions* (1973), a collection of his answers to questions about himself, art and public issues. 'But that is not true reality: it is only the reality of general ideas, conventional forms of humdrummery, current editorials.' 'Average reality', Nabokov insists, 'begins to rot and stink as soon as the act of individual creation ceases to animate a subjectively perceived texture.' Any book he makes, any art anyone makes that is worth reading, is 'a subjective and specific affair', Nabokov suggests. It is the creative act that effectively maintains reality just as – and the analogy is his – electricity binds the earth together. As a writer, a creator, he has 'no purpose at all when composing the stuff except to compose it'. 'I work long, on a body of words,' as Nabokov puts it, 'until it grants me complete possession and pleasure.' According to this subjective idealist creed, there can be no totalizing, totalitarian reading of experience, no monolithic entity entitled 'life'. There is only the 'manifold shimmer' of separate, specific lives, *my* life, *your* life, *his* life or *her* life. As Nabokov has it, 'life does not exist without a possessive epithet'. Nor is there some kind of absolute truth or absolute morality attainable, a master narrative of history or ethics that the artists must discover and disclose. 'Reality is an infinite succession of stops, levels of perception, false bottoms, and hence unquenchable, unattainable,' Nabokov argues. 'You can never get near enough'; and so 'whatever the mind grasps it does so with the assistance of creative fancy, that drop of water on a glass slide which gives distinction and relief to the observed organism'. There is no place here for naturalism or didacticism. 'I am neither a reader nor a writer of didactic fiction,' Nabokov confesses. 'Why do I write books, after all? For the sake of pleasure, for the sake of the difficulty.' '*Lolita* has no moral in tow,' he adds. 'For me a work of fiction exists only insofar as it affords me what I bluntly call aesthetic bliss.' That bliss is the triumph of art, for Nabokov. Its tragedy is suggested by an anecdote Nabokov tells about the original inspiration for *Lolita*, which is a story about an ape who, after months of coaxing, produced the first ever drawing by an animal. 'This sketch showed the bars of the poor creature's cage.'

Lolita is certainly Nabokov's finest book. Before it was published, he wrote of it, to Edmund Wilson, 'its art is pure and its fun riotous'. The purity of its art has several dimensions. Structurally, Nabokov uses traditional romance patterns only to deconstruct them. Humbert Humbert reveals how he desired Lolita, possessed her, fled with her across America after the death of her mother, Charlotte Haze, lost her to a man named Quilty, then killed her new lover. It is the elemental romance structure used here to startling, inverted effect, with elements of quest, attainment, journey, loss, pursuit and revenge. The love plot is propelled forward in a straight line, in accordance with whose unrelating extension Charlotte loves Humbert, who loves Lolita, who loves Quilty, who seems to love no one at all. And, as in the courtly love story, the desire of the narrator becomes a metaphor for other kinds of daring, transgression and retribution. 'Oh, My Lolita, I have only words to play with!' Humbert declares early on in the novel. And that discloses another kind of artfulness. The narrator is telling his story as he awaits trial for murder. A 'Foreword' by one 'John Ray Jr. Ph.D.' informs us that Humbert died 'in legal captivity' after writing this 'Confession of a white Widowed Male' 'a few days before his trial was scheduled to start'. Humbert is a peculiarly knowing narrator. 'I shall not exist if you do not imagine me,' he tells the reader. Using a style both outrageously lyrical and outrageously jokey, he is constantly teasing, eluding his audience. Undercutting what might seem predictably valid responses, he plays on the whole literary history of dubious anti-heroes and duplicitous first-person protagonists from Diderot to Dostoevsky. 'I am writing this under observation,' Humbert admits. Within the narrative, this is literal, since he is in the psychiatric ward of the prison and his cell has an observation window. But Humbert is, additionally, acutely aware of being under our observation as well. That helps make his story slippery, his character protean, and his language radically, magically self-referential. Like all Nabokov's novels, but even more than most, *Lolita* is a verbal game, a maze: what one character in *Pale Fire* christens a 'lexical playfield'.

The lexical playfield belongs, of course, to the author eventually rather than the narrator. It is Nabokov who discovers pleasure and difficulty in the complex web of allusion and verbal play – 'the magic of games', as Humbert calls it – that constitutes the text. There is, in any event, a distinct difference between the games of the narrator and those of the author; or, if you will, 'Lolita' the confession and *Lolita* the novel. It is this. Humbert remains so trapped in his words, the 'signposts and tombstones' of his story, that he does not realize he is using Lolita. Nabokov does. A great deal of intercultural fun is derived from the contrast between the 'old-world politeness' of Humbert and what he perceives as the intriguing banality of America. This is an international novel, in one of its dimensions; and it offers a riotously comic contrast between different languages, different voices. The verbal hauteur of Humbert ('You talk like a book, *Dad*,' Lolita tells him) collides, in particular, with the unbuttoned slangy creativity that is a verbal element of the girl he pursues and possesses ('Yessir! The Joe-Rea marital enigma is making yaps flap'). And that collision has the dramatic advantage of allowing Lolita, as she is to herself, to escape through the chinks of the narrative. 'Lolita had been safely solipsised,' Humbert claims, after he has used her as an unsuspecting aid to masturbatory fantasy. But he does not really solipsize her, turn her, as he puts it, into 'my own creation, another, fanciful Lolita', even for the period that he writes or we read the text. Perversely, Nabokov once claimed that 'one day a reappraiser will come and declare that I was a rigid moralist kicking sin . . . and assigning sovereign power to tenderness, talent, and pride'. That reappraisal is clearly required here, for what we as readers witness is Humbert committing the cardinal sin in the subjective idealistic moral lexicon: he takes another human being as a means rather than an end. In the process, he commits child abuse and statutory rape. But that is subsumed, for Nabokov, under the determining, damning fact that he has acted like a moral totalitarian with Lolita. He has imprisoned her within his own reality, denying her her right to hers – and, as a corollary to that, her specific right to be an ordinary, vulgar, obnoxious yet charming but not charmed or enchanted or mesmerized child. Momentarily, Humbert senses this, when, in the last chapter of *Lolita*, he hears from his cell sounds coming from the valley below. 'What I heard was but the melody of children at play,' he confesses; 'and then I knew that the poignant thing was not Lolita's absence from my side, but the absence of her voice from that concord.' The note of longing, loss was one that Nabokov was particularly apt to sound. He once said that 'the type of artist who is always in exile' was one for whom he felt 'some affinity': which was, perhaps, natural for someone who spent nearly all his life as an émigré. What charges it with a tragic pathos here, however, is the pain of knowing, as Humbert does for a brief, enchanted moment, that there is nothing worse than this: to rob someone of their childhood – to steal from them the chance to say, right from the start, this is *my* reality, *my* life.

Remapping a nation: Chicano/a and Latino/a writing

Different, in turn, from those who came to the United States from the east or west are those who entered from the south: the Mexican Americans. Some trace their ancestry from the approximately 100,000 Mexicans who constituted the host culture of the Southwest and California when that area was taken from Mexico in the 1840s. Even more came over, or their ancestors did, in successive waves of migration. In the years after 1910, almost one-eighth of the population of Mexico, overwhelmingly rural in complexion, migrated to the United States. Those who arrived after 1940 were particularly numerous, thanks to the much heavier influx of immigrants during the fifty years of exceptional economic expansion in the Southwest that was initiated by the Second World War. By 1993, there were over fourteen million Mexican Americans, constituting more than 64 per cent of the Hispanic population. Many of them were the victims of hostile immigration policies: manipulated, it might be, to allow them across the border when cheap labour was required, only to be deported again when the demand was no longer there (the so-called 'revolving door' policy). Most were, and are, subject to a kind of colonial situation. Living in what has become known as occupied America, formerly Mexican land now owned and controlled by the United States, they form a richly hybrid culture, one founded on *mestizo* or mixed origins. Mexican Americans negotiate a border territory, *la frontera*, where competing languages and cultures encounter each other. Here, notions of migrants and natives, the local and the national, the periphery and the core, appear to coalesce, come together in a potent mix of transcultural forms. 'Every Mexican knows there are two Mexicos,' one Mexican American commentator, Américo Paredes, has observed, '– the real one and Mexico de Afuera (Mexico abroad) as Mexicans call it, composed of all the persons of Mexican origin in the United States.' And nowhere has this awareness of duality, two Mexicos, been more apparent than in the distinctive body of Chicano writing that began around 1960.

The term *chicano* probably derives from the sixteenth-century corruption in pronunciation of *mexicano* or *meschicano* which then, with the dropping of the *mes*, becomes *chicano* – or, for the female equivalent, *chicana*. Gaining momentum from the widespread civil rights activism of the 1960s, the Chicano movement found expression in both poetry and prose. In poetry, Chicano poets have been linked in particular with other performance poets, who are marked by their multiculturalism and their attachment to a past when the oral was primary: 'the past had a lot more / talking than writing,' one early performance poet, David Antin (1932–) declares in his talk poem 'what am i doing here' (1973), 'i'll make a bold hypothesis before / . . . there was writing there was / talking.' That has been the aboriginal belief, the impulse driving performance poets like John Giorno (1936–), who uses multiple voices and repetitions, sometimes by adding tape tracks to the spoken word in performance (his printed work may be sampled in *You Got to Burn to Shine: Selected Poetry and Prose* [1993]); Jayne Cortez (1936–), whose work, collected in *Coagulations* (1984), originates in African American traditions and who sing-shouts her poetry; and Kenward Elmslie (1929–) (*Moving Right Along* [1979]) and Ed Sanders (1939–2000) (*Hymn to the Rebel Cafe* [1993]), who make ample use of music and song. It also prompted the Puerto Rican poet Miguel Algarin (1941–) (whose 1980 collection *On Call* won a Before Columbus Foundation award) to found the Nuyorican Poets' Café in New York City. This became one centre for performance poetry; another was Beyond Baroque, on the other side of the continental United States in California, where performance poets like David Trinidad (1953–) (*Handover Heart* [1991]), Amy Gerstler (1956–) (*Bitter Anger* [1990]) and Dennis Cooper (1953–) (*He Cried* [1984]) appeared. Among the most notable performance poets have been two, in particular, who reveal very clearly the priorities, formal and ideological, of Chicano poetry: Gary Soto (1952–) and Jimmy Santiago Baca (1952–), who is, in fact, half-Chicano and half-Apache. The formal priorities are a clear, uncomplicated language, concrete imagery, a driving rhythm and a linking of personal experience to the social, autobiography to history. The ideological ones are plain enough from Soto's declaration, 'I believe in the culture of the poor', and what he has to say, in turn, about the work of Baca. Of the two long narrative poems that comprise *Mártin and Meditations on the South Valley* (1987), Soto has said, 'What makes this story succeed is its honesty, a brutal honesty, as well as Baca's original imagery and the passion of his writing'. 'A history is being written of a culture of poverty,' Soto added of his fellow Chicano, 'which, except for a few poets is absent from American poetry.' Those few, of course, include the author of these words, Soto himself, in works that commemorate and celebrate personal memories ('Braly Street' [1977]), his family ('The Cellar' [1978]) and the Mexican American community ('Kearney Park' [1985]).

What the poetry of Soto and Baca does not possess is suggested by someone else who maps out *la frontera*, the border territory inhabited by Mexican Americans: the Chicana poet Lorna Dee Cervantes (1954–). Certainly, Cervantes can rise to a powerful performance rhetoric just as Soto and Baca do. She is acutely aware, as other Chicano/a poets are, of division and dispossession. 'Everyday I am deluged with reminders / that this is not / my land,' she declares in 'Poem for the Young White Man Who Asked Me How I, An Intelligent, Well-Read Person, Could Believe in the War Between Races' (1981). '[A]nd this is my land,' Cervantes then adds; 'I do not believe in the war between races / but in this country / there is war.' What Cervantes adds to this, however, is a subtle use of speech and symbol, and an even subtler understanding of tensions sometimes within Mexican American culture. Specifically, these tensions have to do with machismo, the tradition of male dominance. Sometimes, as in a poem with the tell-tale title 'Macho' (1991), she exposes those tensions simply and directly. At other times, she links them with her notion of struggle as the sign and support of all life. What is the enemy is also the guide, Cervantes intimates. What is other to us can enslave or, through struggle, can liberate. In personal terms, that other for her is men; in ethnic terms it is machismo; in social terms, it is Anglo-America; in aesthetic terms, it is the English language. In the most elemental terms of all, it is nature. The alternative in either case is either to submit and surrender to the enemy and guide, or to enter into an encounter, an active engagement that can lead, in the long run, through mastery to harmony and unity. One of her finest poems, 'Beneath the Shadow of the Freeway' (1981), shows this process. On one level, it is a celebration of a multi-generation, all-women family: her grandmother, 'our innocent Queen', her mother, the 'Fearless Warrior', and their successors, surviving in the face of the 'shadow', oppressive social forces that are determinately male. On another, related to it, it is a celebration of her own life and art, as she builds a home in the world for herself: a harmonious identity with nature, with one 'gentle man', and with herself and her own needs. Linking the several forms of survival, homebuilding and harmony, are the images of birds that run through this complex piece. Drawing on the Native American element in her Mexican American past, Cervantes uses the traditional image of birds, mockingbirds singing all night, to describe the state of harmonious being in the world enjoyed, in turn, by the several generations of women in her family. Playing on *pluma*, which in Spanish means both feather and pen, she also links such harmony, earned through struggle, to her own vocation as writer, maker of words and the making of this poem. In that way, the poem itself becomes an interlingual, intercultural signpost to survival, personal and communal. 'I plant geraniums, / I tie up my hair into loose braids, /' as Cervantes puts it in the closing lines, 'and trust only what I have built / with my own hands.'

In fiction, the appearance of a distinctively Chicano literature was anticipated by the publication of *Pocho* by José Antonio Villareal (1924–) in 1959. Setting his story in the turbulent period from the Mexican Revolution of 1910–20, when Mexican migrants flowed across the border, to the beginning of the Second World War, Villareal concentrates on two characters: Juan Rubio and his son Richard. Juan, we are told, 'became a part of the great exodus that came of the Mexican Revolution': people who crossed the border by the thousands believing that 'a short walk through the open door would deposit them in Utopia'. Possessing no great love of either Spanish or 'gringo' civilization, he falls back on the values of honour, manliness and courage – machismo. Of the firm belief that 'people who are pushed around in the rest of the world' come to the United States '[b]ecause here they can maybe push someone else around', he eventually becomes a home-owner. As he does so, the narrative discloses, 'he was unaware that he was fashioning the last link of events that would bind him to America and the American way of life'. As a young man, his son Richard resists this 'strange metamorphosis' he witnesses in Juan and other members of his family. Yet, by the end of the book, Richard Rubio too is going through his own experience of acculturation. Joining the martial virtues of his father and his generation to a developing spirit of patriotism, he enlists in the armed forces of the United States. That message of assimilation meets its opposite in a novel published ten years after *Pocho*, *The Plum Pickers* (1969) by Raymond Barrio (1938–), which is set, as Villareal's book is, in the Santa Clara Valley of California, but sounds a note of radical resistance. *The Plum Pickers* is different from *Pocho* in formal terms. Highly experimental, it combines documentary realism with political allegory and satirical fantasy; sometimes, the prose breaks into a poetic riff or prophetic comment. It also differs in its conclusions. 'Moving, moving, always moving', the central characters of *The Plum Pickers*, the migrant couple Manuel and Lupe Guitterez, experience California as 'the newest of modern tortures'. They are also dimly, inexplicably aware that the new world they encounter is a bizarre system of oppression, a postmodern parody of Eden: 'quite a remarkable, sophisticated invention,' the narrator observes, 'as the US headed towards its glorious 21st century, combining big land combines with perpetual migrant slavism.' Lupe is torn between the old and the new, to neither of which she really belongs. 'Where did she come from? Why was she here?' She 'often talked about Mexico', we are told, 'but Mexico was nowhere to her. It was as foreign to her as Belgium.' Manuel, however, begins to feel 'a thrill of power' as he stands up to his oppressors. Another younger character called Ramiro Sanchez, in turn, embodies a still firmer hope. 'He would find a way, some way out,' Ramiro believes. And he begins to find that way through a will to action that does not stop short of violence – and that embraces both restoration of the past and revolution in the future. Ramiro anticipates 'the return of the natives', the recovery and reconstruction of an indigenous history based on authentic Mexican sources. He hopes, too, for a real share for his people of 'the most productive chunk of rich earth in the world'. Working towards all this, he seems to link up with myriad others involved in a struggle against oppression, 'from prehistory into glassbright civilization'. In an epic story of resistance, he is the rebel as culture hero.

Two books published shortly after *The Plum Pickers*, in the early 1970s, announced the arrival of Chicano fiction as a major presence in American literature. The first was . . . *y no se lo tragó la tierra / And the Earth Did Not Devour Him* (1971) by Tomás Rivera (1935–84). The son of Mexican citizens who migrated to Texas in the 1920s, Rivera worked as a migrant farm labourer in the 1950s; and this experience, together with his working-class background, formed the basis of his writing. 'In *Tierra* I wrote about the migrant worker in a ten-year period,' Rivera explained in an interview. 'I began to see that my role would be to document that period of time, but giving it some kind of spiritual strength or spiritual history.' As Rivera intimates here, *Tierra* has profound social concerns, but it is not a work of social realism. Instead, in covering the ten years from 1945 to 1955, it offers a complex narrative of subjective impressions. Concentrating on the lives and wanderings of Mexican workers, and with the Korean War serving as an immediate backdrop, *Tierra* eschews chronological presentation and linear plot development. What it has instead is a structure reminiscent of Ernest Hemingway's *In Our Time*. Two vignettes frame the book. Within that frame are twelve brief stories or *estempas* common to Spanish and Latin American fiction, interspersed with thirteen sketches. The links between these different elements are tonal and thematic, as Rivera reveals a dawning sense of communal solidarity among the Mexican migrants. A central character, an unnamed boy, appears in many but by no means all of the sections. On one level, *Tierra* narrates an allegorical year in the life of this anonymous young farmworker; and, on this level, what the reader witnesses is the growth of a consciousness. The host of migrant workers, caught in the flow of their feelings and thoughts, gradually register their ability to sustain their own imagined community. As they do so, and in a related movement, the central narrative persona constructs an identity for himself that enables him to mediate between his Mexican past and neo-colonial present. He also recognizes that this identity depends on identification with the people, the wretched of the earth who share his condition of wandering, perpetual arrivals and departures.

So, in its thematic inclination, *Tierra* is very different from *In Our Time*. The central character realizes himself with rather than without his people. Like the equally anonymous protagonist of Ralph Ellison's *Invisible Man*, it is his task to forge the uncreated conscience of his race. At the end of the book, he has even retreated as the invisible man does, although 'under the house' rather than under-ground, to ponder his individual and communal destiny – and to weave a usable past out of the web of family lore and Mexican American history that is his inher-itance. The fragmentary nature of *Tierra* may serve as a reflection of the frag-mented nature of the migrant life. But it also suggests the fragments out of which the consciousness in the book must and does construct a viable culture. Anglo-American society receives fierce analysis. But the indigenous culture of Mexican Americans is not immune from criticism. The title of the book, after all, refers to an occasion when the young protagonist curses God, and expects the earth to devour him in punishment; it does not, and so he begins to question the religion of his mother and of his community. *Tierra* is a novel that does not work in the easy, polarized terms of assimilation or resistance. Instead, it explores and enunciates the complex, richly layered character of Mexican American identity, as the nameless narrator, the anonymous bearer of his race, becomes a spiritual voyager, open to constant transformation as the old struggles with the new. A similar awareness of ethnic identity as a borderland, a meeting place between different cultures, marks the other novel that announced the arrival of Chicano fiction as a significant force, *Bless Me, Ultima* (1972) by Rudolfo A. Anaya (1937–). Rich in folklore, moving effortlessly between memory, reality and dream, the material, myth and magic, the book focuses on the experiences of Antonio Márez as he begins school towards the end of the Second World War. The novel is attentive to the specifics of the culture where it is set, a fairly remote area of New Mexico: a culture rooted in the rich traditions of pre-Columbian aboriginal America and the Spain of the golden age. It also draws on the early experiences of its author. It reaches out beyond that, however, to map the border territory that, spiritually, all Mexican Americans inhabit

– perhaps everyone, in a transcultural age. And, as Anaya himself has observed, Antonio is not so much a fragment of autobiography as a paradigmatic new world person, a cultural composite who 'incorporates the Español and the Indio, the old world and the new'.

As the last of four sons in the family, Antonio bears the burden of the increasingly desperate hopes of his parents. His mother is a Luna, a descendant of farmers and priests; his father a Márez, descended from sailors and vaqueros. Their family names sketch out their different allegiances. Both are alert to tradition. For the mother, though, tradition involves stillness. 'It is the blood of the Lunas to be quiet,' she tells Antonio, 'for only a quiet man can learn the secrets of the earth that are necessary for planting – They are quiet like the moon.' For the father, it involves independence, adventure. 'It is the blood of the Márez to be wild,' the mother explains, 'like the ocean from which they take their name, and the spaces of the llano that have become their home.' 'Oh, it was hard to grow up,' Antonio comments, as he recalls struggling with the conflicting ambitions of his parents for him: to be a farmer or a priest, or to be a vaquero. And, in growing up, he turns to the tutelage of Ultima who 'came to stay with us', Antonio remembers, 'the summer I was almost seven'. Ultima is 'a curandera, a woman who knew the herbs and remedies of the ancients, a miracle worker'. Through her, he learns of the cultures of the Indians of the region; he recovers an indigenous education in his cultural origins far more persuasive than the one offered in school. With her, he also learns what he calls 'the secret of my destiny'; and he experiences a sense of unity with his surroundings, as 'the granules of sand at my feet and the sun and sky above me seemed to dissolve into one strange, complete being'. 'My spirit shared in the spirit of all things,' Antonio confides. It is that experience, of sharing, that constitutes vital knowledge, the secret by which he can live. 'Does one have to choose?' the young man asks, when he is told he must decide 'between the god of the church, or the beauty that is here and now'. And quietly Ultima reveals that he does not. As she tells Antonio, when she appears to him in a dream, existence is interdependence, communality, 'the waters are one': moon and sea, earth and sun are all in a state of becoming, all part of the same fluid process. The task of the young protagonist, then, is not to choose between this or that, but to 'take the llano and the river valley, the moon and the sea', the God of the church and the gods of aboriginal folklore 'and make something new': to realize his deepest potential, for himself and for his people, out of the cycle, the confluence of elements that is his being. As the dying Ultima blesses Antonio at the end of the novel, she tells him, 'I shall be with you'; and she is still there with him, the reader infers, all the while he narrates this story. What Antonio has been blessed with, above all, is the power to liberate himself from the warring contraries of his inheritance by seeing and synthesizing them, then speaking of that synthesis here. The process of liberation, Anaya himself has suggested, is the crucial aspect of *Bless Me, Ultima*; it is a process that is at once personal and cultural – and a matter not only of action but also of narration.

At the end of *Tierra*, the anonymous narrator talks of the need to 'discover and rediscover and piece things together. This to that, that to that, all with all.' This is a need felt, with equal urgency, by the narrator of *Bless Me, Ultima*. For that matter, it is a need that drives the work of Rolando Hinojosa (1929–) and one that, in turn, he imposes on the reader. Hinojosa is the author of an ever-expanding work, sometimes described as a novel, known as the *Kansas City Death Trap Series*. The series began in 1972 with *Estampas del valle y otras obras*. This first volume appeared in English, not simply as a literal translation, in 1983 as *The Valley*. So far, the series has fourteen instalments constituting, as it were, one vast, unfinished jigsaw, the aim of which is to depict a place and its people. In *The Valley*, a prefatory remark warns the reader that the narrative structure may seem confusing; very much like the hair of one Mencho Saldaña, we are advised, 'the damn thing's dishevelled'. This, however, is dishevelment with a purpose. The use of narrative fragmentation in books like *The Valley* must be understood not in the Modernist sense of dissolution of meaning but in postmodernist terms, as a sign or symptom of cultural richness and as a source, too, of specifically social revelation. Taken together, the series constitutes an imaginative history of Belken County, Texas, a border territory that is also a battleground for Anglo and Mexican American cultures. Typically, as in *The Valley*, their history works through voice: the testimony of numerous people. It works through volume: we are introduced to a cast of well over two hundred named characters in this first book. And it works through vision: the subtitle of *The Valley*, after all, is 'a portfolio of etchings, engravings, sketches, and silhouettes by various artists in various styles', and Hinojosa begins the book with a county map. Here, and elsewhere in *Kansas City Death Trap*, what Hinojosa is clearly trying to do is take possession of their geography and history for Mexican Americans. A place, for him, is a space given substance, significance, by people (it is notable that, unlike Anaya, he is remarkably uninterested in describing the actual, physical contours of a landscape). A time, equally, is a temporal space endowed with meaning, given its story, by human action and narration. What Hinojosa is after is recovery, restitution of a land and its history, a restoration of what is rightly theirs, to his people. A simple illustration of this occurs in a section titled 'Sometimes It Just Happens That Way; That's All (A Study of Black and White Newspaper Photographs)'. Juxtaposing newspaper accounts of a murder with oral testimony, the narrative explores the difference between the official version and the oral tradition of the people. The one is superficial and wrong, the other digs up a buried history that helps explain the act of violence. The section resembles a detective novel with profound social overtones, as fragments of testimony slowly reveal the neglected truth; so, in a way, does *The Valley* and the series to which it belongs. This is historiography from the oral roots up, not from the standpoint of authorial omniscience, those in power. It reveals a history that might otherwise have been silenced, suppressed by those who have the authority, or simple force, required to get their stories heard: a history that, Hinojosa suggests, can and must be continually retold, renewed.

One of the distinctive features of Chicano fiction of a more recent generation is that it acknowledges the movement of many Mexican Americans into new urban environments. Another even more distinctive feature is that it is very often written by women and, as with the poetry of Lorna Dee Cervantes, adopts a critical view towards the cult of machismo and many of the tensions obtaining between the sexes in the Mexican American community. A notable illustration of both these features is the fiction of Sandra Cisneros (1954–): *The House on Mango Street* (1980), then later *Woman Hollering Creek and Other Stories* (1991). Born in Chicago, Cisneros spent her early years moving backwards and forwards between the United States and Mexico with her family. Moving to the border state of Texas, she then began to write what she later described as 'the stories that haven't been written . . . to fill a literary void'. The eventual result was the collection *The House on Mango Street*, which established her reputation. In this volume, Cisneros developed the form used by other Chicano/a writers, such as Rivera: a series of related stories and sketches, with a central character and narrator to provide them with a sense of continuity. The central character here is Esparanza Cordero, a young girl who moves into the house that gives the book its title. The trope of movement, migration, so rooted in Chicano fiction is still there. 'We didn't always live on Mango Street,' Esparanza explains. 'Before we lived on Loomis on the third floor, and before that we lived on Keeler. Before Keeler it was Pauline, and before that I can't remember. But what I remember is moving a lot.' However, this series of stories concentrates on Esparanza, her family and the rundown neighbourhood in Chicago where they live. 'Here there is too much sadness and not enough sky,' Esparanza observes. Giving her narrator an intimate idiom that moves between the colloquial and the lyrical, Cisneros explores the 'sadness' of these people's lives and their gazing at the 'sky', their yearning for something better. Telling her story ('I like to tell stories,' she confesses), Esparanza confides in few people apart from the reader (whom she calls 'my friend'). And her confidences begin to liberate her. 'You must keep writing,' someone tells her; 'it will keep you free.' By the end of the collection, she is beginning to realize that freedom.

The House on Mango Street, in fact, addresses several forms of enclosure and liberation: opposites figured throughout the story in terms of the polarities of house and sky, room and window (so many women in these stories spend their time gazing from their windows), streets and trees. This is a series of stories about growing up, coming of age: Esparanza breaks slowly out into the adult world of high heels and womanly hips, jobs and kisses, sex and death. It is also about the ghetto, the urban enclosure inhabited by Mexican Americans, where, as Esparanza puts it, 'we make the best of it', living in an exile that is cultural and also maybe linguistic – dreaming, perhaps, of 'the ones left behind . . . far away'. It is also, and more specifically, about the imprisonment of women, denied the possibility of realizing their dreams even, especially by their own men. 'I could've been somebody,' sighs Esparanza's mother, and she speaks for so many others. Finally, it is about the mind-forged manacles from which the narrator is freed through her writing: literally so, since by the end of the book she is ready to depart. 'One day I will go away,' Esparanza explains, to a house of her own: a true house that is, in part, the house of fiction, like the book she is telling and Cisneros is writing. 'They will not know I have gone away to come back,' she says of the friends and neighbours she will leave. 'For the ones I left behind. For the ones who cannot out.' Cisneros has continued to explore her ambivalent position as a woman and writer, and the rhythm of departure and return it seems to impose, in her second collection of stories. A similar rhythm is at work in *The Mixquiahuala Letters* (1986) by Ana Castillo (1953–), where the blueprint of the narrator for feminist liberation requires persistent returns to Mexico, 'home', she says, 'of my mother, grandmother, and great grandmother'. The feeling of solidarity with other Mexican American women that permeates *The House on Mango Street* is also a marked feature of other recent fiction by Chicana writers, as that remark from Castillo's novel illustrates. It is there, for instance, in *The Ultraviolet Sky* (1988) and *Naked Ladies* (1994) by Alma Luz Villanueva (1944–). And it is an even more marked feature of *Face of an Angel* (1995) by Denise Chávez (1948–), an account of the trials and tribulations of a waitress as she writes her Book of Service that incorporates the trinity of grand-mother, mother and daughter and the web of relationship between them.

As the work of Cisneros, her contemporaries and predecessors indicates, what is remarkable about Chicano/a writing is its sheer formal variety; it is not simply protest or political fiction. There are, of course, novels and stories that use naturalist techniques, the strategies of the documentary or the literature of commitment to make their point about life in occupied America. *Chicano* (1970), for instance, by Richard Vāsquez (1928–90), is a politically inclined chronicle of a family over several generations, from their passage through Mexico, torn by revolution, to the barrio of east Los Angeles. *The Revolt of the Cockroach People* (1973) by Oscar Zeta Acosta (1935–) is a harsh record of events in the heyday of Chicano nationalism. *Caras viejas y vina nuevo* (1975) by Alejandro Morales (1944–), reissued as *Barrio on the Edge* (1997), documents crises in the lives of two teenage boys in the urban barrio. And *Rain of Gold* (1991) by Victor Villaseñor (1940–) chronicles the lives of three generations of one family as they cross the Rio Grande to become 'border Mexicans with American citizenship'. Even here, however, in these fictions, there are cultural and linguistic tensions that the authors feel, and that then filter into their characters: a dual literary and verbal inheritance which pulls these stories away from simple naturalism. And other Chicano writing is even more notably experimental, on the edge. There is, perhaps, no better example of this than *The Road to Tamazunchale* (1975) by Ron Arias (1941–). In this novel, a dying man, Fausto Tejada, escapes the realities of a Los Angeles barrio for an imaginative land far away. He finds his own forms of resistance and rescue, as his creator does, in the fiercely relevant dreamscapes of magical realism.

The fiction of Helena Maria Viramontes (1954–) measures the capacity for experiment shown by Chicano/a writers, especially the more recent ones. It also reveals how permeable the barriers are between the Chicano/a and the wider Latino/a communities. In her short story collection *The Moths and Other Stories* (1985), Viramontes uses a fractured narrative technique to disrupt our reading of the text. The effect is one of strangeness, disorientation: so that we, the readers, experience a disturbance, a dismay analogous to that felt by her characters, the immig-rant workers entering a culture not their own – and one that values them only intermittently, as useful tools. It is a strangeness that the Chicana poet Pat Mora (1942–) also arouses in poems like 'Border Town: 1938' (1986) and 'Unnatural Speech' (1986). As readers, we are hurled here into forms of broken speech and narration that imitate precisely the immigrant experience of shifting, suspected, multiple identities. 'An American / to Mexicans / a Mexican to Americans /', as Mora observes of such people, in one of the poems, 'Legal Alien', from her first collection, *Chants* (1984): this is 'the discomfort / of being pre-judged / Bi-laterally', 'sliding back and forth / between the fringes of both worlds'. Viramontes adds to the discomfort announced and aroused by Mora, by subverting the traditional Mexican American notion of 'familia'. This she does in two ways: by opening up concepts of the family and the community to feminist perspectives, and by enlarging those concepts to embrace 'los otros Americanos' – other refugees and immigrants from other Hispanic cultures. Her characters are, many of them, women; many are also people fleeing oppression in Central America. They come to the United States in a state of fear: of men, of strangers (which is just about everybody), of the immigration authorities and of the police (who, they believe, are merely 'La Migra in disguise'). The only community they have is with those in the same state as themselves, others in flight in a world turned upside down. And Viramontes makes us share that state for a while, through the creation of a narrative that is the imaginative equivalent of trauma. Her books cut across the boundaries between Chicano and other Hispanic cultures, not only because they exploit the magical, experimental techniques of Latin American writers like Gabriel Garcia Marquez, but also because they incorporate people and memories from countries like El Salvador. They remind us, in effect, that there is a wider Hispanic community to which Mexican Americans belong: which is, more often than not, a community of the oppressed.

This is particularly true of those from Puerto Rico, who began coming to the mainland in large numbers after the Second World War. Puerto Rico has the unique status of an American commonwealth, so the more than half a million Puerto Ricans settled in the United States by 1955 were, and are, officially classified as migrants rather than immigrants. Nevertheless, concentrated mostly in New York City, they face the same sense of dispossession as Chicano immigrants, a similar experience of disorientation, division, that is simultaneously linguistic and cultural. One of the most outspoken writers, as far as the Puerto Rican experience is concerned, is the poet Pedro Pietri (1944–). One of the so-called Nuyorican poets who began to read at the Nuyorican Poets' Café in New York City, Pietri is typical of these poets as a group. He uses a harsh, demotic language, the street speech of African Americans and Puerto Ricans in the barrio, to reflect the problems and the pride of 'puertorriquenos'. In a key text for Nuyorican poetry, *Puerto Rican Obituary* (1973), Pietri even creates a mock epic about the Puerto Rican community. The image of communal death is deployed here to denounce the suffering, and the failure, of everyone in the barrio; men and women have died, the poet declares, and will continue to die, 'Always broke / Always owing / Never knowing / that they are a beautiful people'. Yet the poem concludes in a hopeful vein: with a vision of some place, some symbolic inner space, where 'puertor-riquenos' can achieve peace. That place is 'aquí', 'here', within each Puerto Rican man and woman. '*Aquí Se habla Español* all the time / Aquí you salute your flag first,' the poet insists. 'Aquí Qué Pasa Power is what's happening / Aquí to be called *negrito* / means to be called LOVE.' It is a vision of possible redemption that measures its distance from mainstream millennialism, the American dream, pre-cisely through its bilingualism, the poetic use of English and Spanish – and what has been called 'Spanglish', a mixture of the two.

Tato Laviera (1951–) is another Puerto Rican poet who mixes languages to register his mixed inheritance and uses a powerful orality to capture the rhythms of the street. Laviera has published several volumes, including *La Carreta Made a U-Turn* (1976) and *Mainstream Ethics* (1988), but he has always produced poems that are meant to be sung or spoken. He celebrates the Puerto Rican community, and his own Puertoricanness. However, he also insists on the presence of a new ethnic identity, the product of a convergence with other minority groups: with New York City as the exemplary space in which this cultural mixing, or 'mestizaje', occurs. 'We gave birth to a new generation,' Laviera announces in 'AmeRícan' (1985), and the title of this poem is the term he uses to describe this 'new genera-tion': a new America with the accents of many cultures. In his own way, Laviera is rewriting the line and vision of Whitman. His poems often have the oracular sweep of, say, 'Song of Myself', with Laviera stirring in new influences, such as the oral traditions of Puerto Rico and the Caribbean and Afro-Caribbean music. They equally often proclaim the arrival of a new dispensation in the New World, just as Whitman did. But this 'new america, humane america, admired america, loved america, harmonious america' that Laviera conjures, with insistent, driving rhythms, speaks in the tongues of many languages, far more than even Whitman ever imag-ined: among them, 'the soul gliding talk of gospel boogie music' and 'new words in spanglish tenements, fast tongue moving street corner "*que corta*" talk being invented at the insistence of a smile!' By comparison, Victor Hernández Cruz (1949–) is a more formal, introspective poet, whose work registers the influence of such different aesthetic movements as surrealism, concrete poetry and minimalism. He is attentive to the subtleties of word play, as the title of his 1982 collection *By Lingual Wholes* illustrates – alluding as it does to bilingualism and the warring concepts of totality and absence. And he is interested in literary experiment. *By Lingual Wholes*, for instance, is a collage, in which visual signs become part of the meaning and poetry and prose are intertwined with haikus, short stories, prose poems, one-word poems and an empty appendix. Nevertheless, Cruz is just as dedicated as Laviera and Pietri are to registering the truth of his culture. In 'Moun-tain Building', past and present converge, as the mountains where the Indians once lived metamorphose into high-rise buildings where Puerto Ricans now live side by side with other impoverished ethnic groups, among them later generations of Indians. 'It is', the poet observes, 'the same people in the windowed / Mountains.'

The poetry of Cruz represents, in a way, a transformation of literary English thanks to its contact with Spanish. Witty, often erudite and sometimes violent, it exists at the intersection between English and Spanish literary cultures. So, in another way, do the poetry and prose of Aurora Levins Morales (1954–) and Judith Ortiz Cofer (1952–). Morales was born in Puerto Rico, brought up in Chicago and rural New Hampshire and now lives in the San Francisco Bay area. Her ethnic origins are a similarly rich mix. 'I am a child of the Americas, /', she writes in 'Child of the Americas'(1986), 'a light-skinned mestiza of the Caribbean, / a child of many diaspora, born into this continent at a crossroads.' 'I am a U.S. Puerto Rican Jew, /' she adds in the same poem; 'my first language was spanglish.' And, in order to explain her life at the crossroads, she draws on several traditions, notably, Latin American writers like Pablo Neruda, American feminists such as Adrienne Rich, and the African American author who calls herself a womanist, Alice Walker. Morales identifies herself passionately not just with Latina women but with all American women of colour. She uses the signs and symbols of her Puerto Rican and Jewish inheritance to link the experiences of her own body to the body politic, not just on a national level but on an international level as well – she is, for example, deeply concerned with the Middle East conflict. Transnational and transcultural in her concerns, she is also transgenerational: her 1986 book *Getting Home Alive*, for instance, was co-authored with her mother Rosa, and she has described it as a 'cross-fertilisation' between her mother's voice and her own. Out of this rich brew, Morales seeks to produce a new identity for herself the strength of which derives precisely from its plural origins. 'I was born at the crossroads /', Morales declares, 'and I am whole.' And, like so many American writers before her, Morales sees this her life as representative; she is bragging for humanity rather than herself.

'It was Puerto Rico waking up inside her,' one of the prose pieces of Morales begins. That is a constant theme of the stories by Judith Ortiz Cofer gathered together in *An Island Like You* (1995). Born in Puerto Rico and brought up in Paterson, New Jersey, Cofer invests many of her characters with the duality of her own inheritance and experience. Typically, the American-born teenagers who form the continuous and recursive spine of the stories in this collection live between two competing cultures. And a moment of encounter with Puerto Rican heritage supplies the narrative substance and dramatic crisis. Her poems, in turn, show what Cofer herself has called the 'habit of movement' between the several levels or overlays of cultures. She has the habit of gathering words or expressions from Puerto Rican Spanish, then recasting them into English poems in which meaning is transported across linguistic borders. The result is a mapping of the experience of intercultural life. The characters in her poetry, like her grandmother ('Claims' [1987]), a jilted woman ('The Woman Who Was Left at the Altar' [1987]), and her father ('My Father in the Navy: A Childhood Memory' [1987]), are all exposed to alternative perspectives. And the reader, the privileged recipient of this defamiliarizing strategy, sees these characters released from the confines of habit and convention, the familiar words of a single language. Like many recent Latina writers, Cofer is preoccupied in particular with sexual politics: the disintegration of traditional family life, for example, under the pressure of migration and male absence.

'His homecomings', she says of her father, 'were the verses / we composed over the years making up / the siren's song that kept him coming back.' It is the position of women in particular in this fluid, plural world of the migrant that fascinates her, compels her imagination. This is not least for its ironies. 'Latin women pray / In incense sweet churches / They pray in Spanish to an Anglo God / with a Jewish heritage,' Cofer writes in one poem ('Latin Women Pray' [1983]), 'All fervently hoping / That if not omnipotent / At least he be bilingual.'

'In American literature, I, as a Puerto Rican child, did not exist,' the novelist and short story writer Nicholasa Mohr (1935–) has observed; 'and I as a Puerto Rican woman do not exist now.' That is a gap, an absence Mohr herself has attempted to fill. So has Esmerelda Santiago (1940–) in her memoir *When I Was Puerto Rican* (1993) and her novel *América's Dream* (1996). In novels like *Nilda* (1974) and *Felita* (1979), and in the twelve stories of *El Bronx Remembered* (1976), Mohr focuses on the experiences of children and adolescents, to show how, as she puts it in the Preface to *El Bronx Remembered*, Puerto Ricans are 'strangers in their own country . . . with a different language, culture, and racial mixture'. 'Like so many before them,' Mohr explains, 'they hoped for a better life, a new future . . . and a piece of that good life known as the "American Dream"'. In *Rituals of Survival: A Woman's Portfolio* (1985), Mohr then turns to the stories of older women. Six vignettes about Puerto Rican women, representing different circumstances and ages, reveal strategies of survival. Amy, for instance, the young widowed mother of four children in one episode, 'A Thanksgiving Celebration', resorts to the ingenious use of turkey eggs and the storytelling skills inherited from her grandmother to give the family a meaningful Thanksgiving Day. 'Yes,' Amy tells herself defiantly, 'today's for us, for me and the kids.' A similar defiance shines through the story of the immigrant woman América Gonzales, the central character in *América's Dream*. A hotel maid on the island of Vieques off the Puerto Rican coast, she is 'not ashamed' of her job. 'It's housework, women's work,' she tells herself, 'nothing to be ashamed of.' Nevertheless, she seems trapped in a system of power, her identity and her very body controlled not only by the work she is required to do but also by an abusive partner. By the close of the novel, however, América has made a new life for herself. Her partner killed by her when he abused her one time too often, she moves to a Puerto Rican section of the Bronx. She still bears the scars of the abusive relationship she has escaped. 'They're there to remind her that she fought for her life, and that, no matter how others may interpret it, she has a right to live her life as she chooses it,' the novel concludes. 'It is, after all, her life, and she's the one in the middle of it.' The other woman of so much American writing and discourse, América has laid claim to the right to be in charge and in the centre of her own story. *América's Dream*, as its title implies, is a novel that reconstructs the American dream, as an act of resistance to both the machismo of the old culture and the neo-colonial oppression of the new.

The largest source of new residents in New York City, for the past several decades, has not, however, been Puerto Rico but the Dominican Republic. Dominicans, in fact, accounted for one out of every five immigrants to the city in the 1990s. They have also been the subject of two remarkable novels by Julia Alvarez (1950–), a Dominican who emigrated to the United States in the 1960s: *How the Garcia Girls Lost Their Accents* (1991) and *Yo* (1997). The narrative of the earlier and finer of these novels centres on political turmoil and flight, with the Garcia family escaping to the United States after being implicated in a failed plot against the Dominican dictator Trujillo. Its tripartite structure, in turn, moves back in time: from 1989 to 1972, then 1970 to 1960, then 1960 to 1956. The Garcia family arrive in America in a condition of 'abrupt exile' and soon encounter an alien culture. 'At home there had always been a chauffeur opening a car door or a gardener tipping his hat'; here in the Bronx, by contrast, they live in a rented apartment and survive for a while on the generosity of others. Dr Garcia, the father, never shakes off all the residues of his former life as a prominent member of the Dominican community, such as his accent and his assumption of patriarchal authority. He is enough of a realist, though, to assimilate himself to the American work ethic and an agenda of social mobility. He is also sufficiently successful in his new clinical practice to move the family out to Long Island eventually. Very soon, he is proudly proclaiming his new identity as '*un dominican-york*', and takes out American citizenship. The real centre of the family is not Dr Garcia, however, but his wife Laura. Her abrupt exile may initially lead her to recall her old home 'through the lens of loss'. But she soon becomes the 'daughter of invention' in America. She rejects the chance to return to the island of her upbringing, declaring 'better an independent nobody than a high-class house slave'. And although she remains devoted to her husband, she loses much of her deference. 'This is America, Papi, America!' she tells Dr Garcia during a moment of confrontation. 'You are not in a savage country anymore!' To her four daughters, she is 'their Thomas Edison, their Benjamin Franklin Mom', the emotional matrix of their lives and their role model. Gathered together in an 'invisible sisterhood', the four Garcia girls learn independence from her. Acculturating rapidly, they also reject the notions of female subordination associated with the island nation from which they have fled. 'Island was the hair-and-nails crowd, chaperones and icky boys with their macho strutting,' the narrator tells us. 'By the end of a couple of years away from home, we had *more* than adjusted.' One of the daughters, Yolanda, who turns to writing as a vocation, does find adjustment difficult. The central consciousness of the novel, as her nickname 'Yoyo' implies, she finds herself yoyoing, oscillating between the old culture and the new in a way that the other Garcias do not. She even returns 'home' to the Dominican Republic for her birthday, after an absence of five years, and she reflects that she 'is not so sure she'll be going back'. But, as the narrative makes clear, her reluctance to become simply American is not a sign of her identification with her old home. Rather, it is a symptom of her subtle reaction to the alchemy of exile; she, at least, understands that she must recreate herself out of the two cultures to which she is heir.

Another potent source of Latino culture in the United States has been supplied by the successive waves of immigrants arriving from Cuba. As late as 1950, there were as few as 50,000 foreign-born Cubans in the whole country. In the wake of the revolution, however, close to a million Cubans left the island for America, the majority of them torn between an imagined Eden lost or left behind and their emergent status as secure Americans. In *The Mambo Kings Play Songs of Love* (1989), Oscar Hijuelos (1951–) centres his story on two Cuban brothers, Nestor and Cesar Castillo, who arrive in America a decade before the revolution in their homeland. It is 1949, and Latin American music is at the height of its popularity. 'Part of the wave of musicians who had been pouring out of Havana', they are lured by the chance, the hope of fame and fortune. They love 'the immensity of the United States', and they embrace the glamour of the metropolis. In New York City, they also find themselves cheerfully at home in a community of immigrants, 'apartments filled with travellers or cousins and friends from Cuba'. Their music, a mix of Cuban and American influences, enables them to make sense of their new world and navigate their way through their divided allegiances. However, the novel is no simple, straightforward success story. Even at the height of their fame, the songs of the Castillo brothers, full of the 'sadness and torment of love', reflect their lingering attachment to a lost, lamented world. Nestor writes letters to his mother: 'heartsick letters nostalgic for the security of the home he had – or thought he had – in Cuba'. And with the passing of the fashion for Latin music, the Castillo brothers find their fame fading away. Not a simple success story, neither is *The Mambo Kings* a naturalist tale of failure and decline. It is a magically realist account of the way celebration and sadness, consummation and loss, are all woven into the same tapestry. The story is structurally framed by the occasion when, at the apex of their fame, the Castillo brothers appear on the *I Love Lucy* television show. And it is emotionally framed by the Cuban American star of that show, Desi Arnaz, who invites them to appear after hearing, in their music, a poignant expression of 'his own past love, his love for . . . his family down in Cuba and old friends he had not seen in a long time'. In a paradigmatic moment, at the end of the novel, Desi grown old now reappears, living in seclusion in California. 'I chose this climate here', he explains, 'because it reminds me of Cuba.' Like the Castillo brothers, he remains torn emotionally between his old home and his new. Like them, too, he has shaped his life, and his art, out of the fusion between them.

'Cuba is a peculiar exile, I think, an island-colony,' says the narrator of *Dreaming in Cuban* (1992) by Christine Garcia (1958–). 'We can reach it by a thirty-minute charter flight from Miami, but never reach it at all.' The dreamlike rhythm of longing and attachment, exile and return, is as fundamental to this novel as it is to *The Mambo Kings*. It describes the condition out of which here too, like the Castillo brothers, the characters must construct an authentic reality: in this case, the four women of the del Pino family. The idea of Cuba is a shifting, ambiguous dream for all four: the different ways in which they try to come to terms with that dream determine their lives and describe quite different strands in the Cuban American experience. The oldest of the four, Celia del Pino, for instance, stays in Cuba, where she transfers an unrequited passion for a lost love to 'El Lider', Fidel Castro. Her daughter Lourdes, on the other hand, moves to Brooklyn where she embraces American opportunity, becoming a successful entrepreneur, head of her own

'Yankee Doodle Bakery' chain. The daughter of Lourdes, in turn, Pilar, the signature voice of the novel, experiences a dual exile, caught in the interstices between Cuban and American cultures. By the close of the story, she has returned to Cuba. 'I've started dreaming in Spanish,' Pilar confesses. 'I wake up feeling different, like something inside me is changing', 'there's a magic working its way through my veins'. Nevertheless, she realizes that 'sooner or later' she will return to New York. 'I know now', she says, 'its where I belong – not *instead* of here, but *more* than here.' Recent novels by Cuban Americans are packed with characters like Pilar, who labour just as she does under not just the opportunity but the necessity of reinventing themselves, dreaming their way into a new identity. There is, for instance, the protagonist of *The Doorman* (1987) by Reinaldo Arenas (1943–90), a surreal tale of exile in New York. Trapped in what he describes as 'an immense underwater city' full of people who look 'like fish seeking temporary refuge', he is constantly searching for some way to keep himself afloat. There is the family in *Raining Backwards* (1988) by Roberto Fernandez (1951–), who experience their life between cultures as a kind of montage, a clash of different aesthetic forms and styles. And there is, in turn, the central character in *The Pérez Family* (1990) by Christine Bell (1951–): Dorita, an enterprising 'Cuban madonna hip' who declares, 'the second I stepped into the United States, I am a new woman'. 'She was going to have a second chance to live the way she dreamed life should be,' Bell says of Dorita, 'and not the way it turned out.' That strikes a recurrent chord in the fiction by and about Cuban Americans, although it is not by any means a constant, invariable one. Dreaming mostly in metropolitan spaces, the characters in this fiction may have trouble weaving their way between memory and longing; 'there's only my imagination where our history should be,' the narrator of *Dreaming in Cuban* complains. But they never entirely surrender, or relinquish their dreams; on the contrary, they sometimes manage to give them momentary, magical life.

Improvising America: Asian American writing

As late as 1960, there were fewer than 900,000 people of Asian descent in the United States. Thirty years later, there were more than seven million. The largest group, in terms of national origins, were and are Chinese Americans, followed by Filipinos, Japanese, Asian Indians, Koreans, Vietnamese and, much lower down the numerical scale, Laotians, Cambodians and Hmong. With profoundly different histories, what these immigrants from a Greater Asia and the Pacific Rim have in common is something they share with some, but by no means all, immigrant peoples from other parts of the world. They came in quest of what earlier Chinese immigrants had christened the gold mountain, and what still earlier travellers had seen as the golden land in the golden West, the virgin territory or the city on a hill. As Bharati Mukherjee, who was born in Calcutta, puts it in her essay 'American Dreamer' (1997), they came from a traditional if often disrupted society, one governed by convention and consideration of class or caste, to a site of 'scary improvisations and heady explorations'. For an immigrant to 'desire America', as

Mukherjee puts it, is to move from a place where 'identity was fixed, derived from religion, caste, patrimony, and mother tongue' to somewhere where adjustment is required to a new repertoire of styles, to the rampant pace and frantic mobility of postmodern culture. For an immigrant to enter America, in turn, is to change not only himself or herself but also the character and complexion of the American nation. As Mukherjee has pointed out, along with other immigrant peoples Asian Americans are 'minute-by-minute transforming America'. 'The transformation is a two-way process,' Mukherjee adds. 'It affects both the individual and the national cultural identities'; it is part of the continuing process of imagining new communities, improvising America.

By the end of the Second World War, the Chinese American community was decimated, its ageing bachelor society waiting for an injection of new immigrants and a recovery of family life. *Eat a Bowl of Tea* (1961) by Louis Chu (1925–70) is one of several novels to capture the tone of this bachelor society; others include *Chinatown Family* (1948) by Lin Yutang (1895–1976) and *The Flower Drum Song* (1957) by Chin Yang Lee (1917–). Set among a group of older men in Chinatown in New York, *Eat a Bowl of Tea*, in particular, is a humorous, sympathetic account. However, it is sharply unsentimental in its depiction of the cramped, lonely lives of these men, their work in laundries and restaurants punctuated only by visits to prostitutes and mah-jong games. And it shows a younger generation of males apparently facing the same destiny. What has been remarkable, though, since the publication of the Chu novel is not only the exponential growth in the Chinese American population, but also the proliferation of Chinese American writing: poetry, autobiography and, above all, fiction. Reflecting the growth, too, not just as a growth in numbers but also as a growth in community, of women as well as men, the young as well as the old, many of the more notable new Chinese American writers have been female. Among poets, for example, the most distinguished has been Cathy Song (1955–). Song was born in Honolulu to a Chinese mother and Korean father. Her first book, *Picture Bride*, was published in 1983. Consisting of thirty-one poems divided into five sections, *Picture Bride* concentrates on autobiography to explore family and history – and, in particular, the equivocal nature of her own relation with the traditions of Asian culture. In 'The Youngest Daughter', for example, Song delicately sketches out her relation with her mother, 'the familiar silence' of their intimacy, her mother's unease about her and her own longing for flight. In 'The White Porch', through a carefully articulated development of imagery, Song pursues a similar conflict felt along her pulses between tradition and the new. The daughter is trapped in domestic duties, but lets her hair down 'like a measure of wealth' for her lover. From the daughter washing her hair, the poem moves seamlessly through the chores of the day and the intricacies of the mother–daughter relation, figured in the mother's grabbing of her daughter's hair ('So much hair, my mother / used to say'). And it ends with the daughter, in another fugitive gesture, this time taken from fairytale, smuggling her lover into her room through 'cloth, hair, and hands'. Other poems explore, with similar, mothlike precision, the routines of family life, a home where 'there was always something that needed fixing' ('The Tower of Pisa' [1987]), the 'magic island' of Hawaii where Song was born ('The Magic Island' [1988]), and a later generation – 'We love them more than life, /' as the poet puts it in 'The Binding' (1988), 'these children that are born to us.' Always, these poems hover gracefully between the old and the new, memory and adventure. As a result, the poetic persona that weaves her way through them, whose mellifluous voice shapes them, seems to belong with the 'beautiful iridescent' women whom the Japanese printmaker Utamuro depicted and whom Song celebrates in her poem 'Beauty and Sadness' (1983). Richly strange, and changing, these women resemble 'creatures from a floating world', Song confides; and so, in her own lines, does she.

As for prose, the three most renowned Chinese American writers of the past few decades have all also been female: Amy Tan (1952–), Gish Jen (1956–) and Maxine Hong Kingston (1940–). All three are preoccupied with what Jen, in *Typical American* (1991), jokingly refers to as being 'Chang-kees', or 'Chinese Yankees'. All turn their attention, at times, to the first generation born and brought up in the United States and their poignant, often problematical relationship with their immigrant parents. Their strategies for dramatizing and dealing with the bilingual, bicultural dilemmas of their protagonists are, however, very different. So, in *The Joy Luck Club* (1989), then later in *The Kitchen God's Wife* (1991), Amy Tan concentrates on the relation between mothers and daughters as a measure of changes and continuities that are, in equal measure, cultural and emotional. *The Joy Luck Club*, for instance, is a series of narratives telling the stories of eight women: the four original members of the Joy Luck Club of Gweilin and their four daughters, all born in the United States. The mothers initially met every week, despite deprivation and devastation, to devise their own moments of respite, gossip and anecdote, around the mah-jong table in China. In the United States, they continue to meet, to talk, praise and complain about their daughters until one of the mothers dies. The novel makes two complete rounds of the table. As it does so, it explores the generational contests that form its core. 'My mother believed you could be anything you wanted to be in America,' one of the daughters, Jing-Mei 'June' Woo, recalls. Despite such beliefs, the mother, Suyuan Woo, is outraged by the very American independence of her daughter. When Jing-Mei rebelliously refuses to practise the piano at her mother's command – 'I wasn't her slave,' she reflects, 'this wasn't China' – her mother scolds her in Chinese. 'Only two kinds of daughter,' Suyuan declares. 'Those who are obedient and those who follow their own mind! Only one kind of daughter can live in this house. Obedient daughter!' To begin with, Jing-Mei resists her mother's demand that she could and should mix 'American circumstances and Chinese character'. 'Inside', she feels and her mother suspects, ' – she is all American-made.' But, like the other daughters, she eventually learns that, as one of the other mothers, An-Mei Hsu, puts it, 'All of us are like stairs, one step after another, going up and down, but all going the same way'. There is continuity, connection: something that Jing-Mei, in particular, discovers when, following her mother's death, she travels to China. 'I am becoming Chinese,' she reflects; just as her mother had predicted, and hoped. There, in

China, she meets the twin daughters of her mother's first marriage. 'Now I also see', she says, 'what part of me is Chinese. It is so obvious. It is my family. It is in our blood.' By retrieving the past, the history of her mother, the daughter learns how to balance her Americanized identity against the competing claims of tradition. She is, she has come to understand, both Chinese and American, Jing-Mei and June.

Gish Jen has similarly centred her stories around family but in a much quirkier, seriocomic way. Her stories, many of them, and her novels, *Typical American* and *Mona in the Promised Land* (1996), are concerned with the Chang family, in particular the father, Ralph Chang, and the two daughters, Mona and Callie. 'It's an American story,' *Typical American* begins. It is also a story told with engaging, ironic wit. Ralph, born with the name Yifeng, comes to America in 1947. On the boat from China, he composes a list of aims for himself that recalls the self-help programme of Benjamin Franklin. Arriving in San Francisco, the 'splendour' and 'radiance' of the Golden Gate Bridge – all that he had dreamed of on his way from Shanghai – is wreathed in fog. That is the first sign of the paradoxical nature of the Golden Land he will encounter. As he then travels across the New World to New York City, 'the whole holy American spectacle', 'famous rivers, plains, canyons' 'lumbered by', but he does not notice them. He is too immersed in his studies. He does, however, notice and admire New York. This, after all, is 'the city of cities', Ralph tells himself: an intricate American machine, almost mythic in its mechanical grandeur and the opposite of his rural Chinese upbringing. Here, he embarks on his own eccentric quest to become a typical American: with a new name, given to him by a secretary at the university where he enrols, and a gradually acquired new language. The quest, Jen suggests in a recurrent image, is like a roller-coaster ride: full of surprises, slow rises, sudden falls, then gradual recoveries. Ralph careers from success as an academic to disaster as an entrepreneur, through marital crises, financial security then stringency, with a strangely touching optimism and absurdly quixotic faith. 'Anything could happen, this was America,' Ralph tells himself when he first arrives. 'He gave himself up to the country, and dreamt.' Just about anything and everything does then happen to him. As a result, he does appear to have learned his lesson, and begun to change, by the end of the novel. 'A man was as doomed here as he was in China. *Kan bu jian. Ting bu jian*,' Ralph finally tells himself. 'He was not what he made up his mind to be. A man was the sum of his limits: freedom only made him see how much so.' The Chinese phrases represent the 'old culture talking', advising him to temper the belief in success of the 'typical American' with the 'bleak understanding' fostered in the land he has left behind. '*Opposites begin in one another*,' Ralph's father once told him. Now, Ralph is starting to see how opposites begin in him, since Chinese past and American promise both form part of his character and fate.

Maxine Hong Kingston is certainly the most widely recognized contemporary Asian American writer. Her first book, *The Woman Warrior* (1975), is subtitled *Memoirs of a Girlhood Among Ghosts*. It is, however, not so much a memoir as an intentionally hybrid form, blending elements of several genres: myth, fiction, autobiography and biography as well as memoir. Negotiating both the sexism of traditional Chinese culture and the racism of white America, Kingston recounts the childhood experiences of a young girl. Interweaving adolescent confusion and uncertainty of perspective with ironic adult commentary, she describes someone caught between her Chinese inheritance and her American upbringing, between Canton and California. The narrative as a whole is separated into five sections or movements, each one pursuing the theme of the development of the young girl into the inspirational figure of the woman warrior. Each section, in turn, tells the story of a particular woman who has a formative influence on the protagonist, who is also the narrator. These maternal figures, who are both actual and mythical, ghostly and real presences in the life of the young girl, gradually, cumulatively promote a growth from silence to speech. For what the book slowly discloses is the power of story to shape character and behaviour: the opportunity, and even the necessity, to speak oneself into being and identity. To that extent, the woman warrior is the writer, the author of *The Woman Warrior*. Tellingly, the book opens with an injunction to silence. 'You must not tell anyone what I am about to tell you,' Kingston's mother warns her, before revealing the true story of Kingston's aunt's illegitimate pregnancy, shaming and eventual suicide. This is the 'no name woman' of the first movement. The story is told by the mother as a cautionary tale and as an injunction against the passing on of familial shame. The narrator, however, makes her own use of what she is told. As 'a story to grow up on', the history of her aunt is reimagined as an emancipatory narrative: the account of a woman who had her vengeance on Chinese patriarchal culture, and those who would shame and control her, by casting her body into the family drinking well. For Kingston, 'deliberately forgetting' her aunt has been the cruellest punishment meted out to her by her family. Now, by 'telling' about her, she is redressing the balance. She knows the perils attendant on this. Her aunt, she recognizes, is an unquiet ghost who 'does not always mean me well'. But she is willing to take that risk, in order to discover in the past what she needs for her own speech and survival.

Like the opening movement, the other four movements in *The Woman Warrior* show the ability of the protagonist and narrator to sift through the cultural fragments she inherits through her mother and reinvigorate, reinvent them for her own purposes. She acknowledges the dilemma of living in a divided world. 'Chinese-Americans, when you try to understand what things in you are Chinese,' she asks, 'how do you separate what is peculiar to childhood . . . from what is Chinese? What is Chinese tradition and what is the movies?' Nevertheless, she strenuously pursues a solution to that dilemma by separating out the different strands of her experience and aiming, somehow, for a new synthesis. So, in the second movement, 'White Tigers', Kingston revises the story of Fa Mu Lan, the woman warrior of ancient Chinese legend. The mother of the narrator, Brave Orchid, also tells this story. It is a measure of her ambivalence as a guide and mentor, in fact, that she can tell emancipatory tales as well as cautionary ones. Or, as the narrator says of her mother, 'she said I would grow up a wife and a slave, but she taught me the song of the warrior woman'. In the retelling of the story here, however, Kingston craftily reshapes the story, attributing some of the exploits and experiences normally associated with male legendary warriors to Fa Mu Lan. Her aim, she has said, was to take male power 'for women' and also to write myths that are 'new, American'. Like *The Woman Warrior* as a whole, 'White Tigers' is a reinvention of tradition that invests old stories with a new, liberating and feminist bias – and dramatizes the point that a diversity of cultural influences, Chinese, American and so on, may, and perhaps must, lead to the creation of hybrid narratives.

The solution *The Woman Warrior* offers to the problem of being both a 'Chinese "I"' and an 'American "I"', in effect, is not to collapse these dualities and differences but to accommodate them. The final story, 'A Song for a Barbarian Reed Pipe', offers further illustration of this. It is about an actual historical figure, Ts'ai Yen, who was captured and forced to live in 'barbarian' lands for many years. A mother, warrior and poet, to her 'the barbarians were primitives', we are told. But she heard a strange music among them, made on reed flutes; and she learned how to sing in a way that somehow 'matched the flutes'. Returned to her own people at last, Ts'ai Yen 'brought her songs back from savage lands'. One of these, the reader discovers, is called '"Eighteen Stanzas for a Barbarian Reed Pipe", a song that Chinese sing to their own instruments. It translated well.' Clearly, Ts'ai Yen supplies an analogue for the author and narrator's own status as a woman warrior of words: using the instruments or forms at her disposal to 'translate' her experiences, dramatize her own mixed heritage and diverse experience. Equally clearly, there is change here, since the old story is rewritten as it is retold, and there is also consistency – not least because *this* version of the story is retold by both mother and daughter. 'The beginning is hers,' Kingston discloses, 'the ending, mine.' The young girl remembered in *The Woman Warrior* is someone who seems habitually stifled and silenced: her inability, in particular, to speak with confidence in English is linked to a crisis in identity. What she learns is what the narrator demonstrates and discloses: how to find refuge and redemption in telling, writing books like this one. 'The reporting is the vengeance,' the narrator declares at one point. Words are the weapons of this woman warrior: her way of getting back at and getting into the world.

The book that followed *The Woman Warrior* in 1980, *China Men*, also depends on family history. As its title implies, however, it concentrates on men and on a difficult, uncommunicative relationship between father and daughter. A hybrid, like its predecessor, it also draws on history, law and imaginative revisioning of historical fact. Her aim, Kingston said, was to 'claim America' for Chinese Americans by showing how deeply in debt America is to the labour of Chinese men, her forebears among them, who cleared the land, built the railroads and created fertile farmland out of desert and swamp. *Tripmaster Monkey: His Fake Book*, published in 1989, is more of a novel, recounting the exploits of Wittman Ah Sing. Wittman, a 'Chinese beatnik' as he is called at one juncture in the story, is a protean figure, who gradually resolves his problems by embracing his immigrant past while singing the song of an American open road. And like its protagonist, the form of the book is fluid, evasive, with the borderlines between naturalism and myth, the material and the magical, constantly blurred. This may be the story of a beatnik playwright, a contemporary incarnation of Walt Whitman living in Berkeley, California, in the 1960s. It also alludes to and accommodates Chinese legend and fantasy, however. One constant source of reference, for example, is the Chinese classic, *Monkey* or *Journey to the West*, the story of a magical, mischievous monkey who accompanies a monk to India for the sacred books of Buddhism. 'Where's our name that shows that we aren't from anywhere but America!' Wittman demands towards the end of this book. 'Once and for all: I am not oriental,' he adds. 'An oriental is antipodal. I am a human being right here on land which I belong to and which belongs to me.' Resisting any monolithic notion of American identity – or, more simply, the use of '"American" interchangeably with "white"' – Wittman sees and names multiplicity as the core of personal and national selfhood. For him, as for his (almost) namesake, the author of 'Song of Myself', America is a 'teeming Nation of nations'. Both Wittman and Whitman, in turn, echo Kingston here: who, in *Tripmaster Monkey* as in all her other writing, creates a multidimensional fictive space to reflect and express the American mosaic. The secret that her work discloses, over and over again, is that the American voice does not speak simply in this way or in that. It is large; it contains multitudes; and it speaks in many tongues, many accents.

The differences between Tan, Jen and Kingston indicate that, even among Chinese American women writers, there is no set formal agenda. That is a point pressed home by two other seminal novels by Chinese American women, *The Frontiers of Love* (1956) by Diana Chang (1934–) and *Crossings* (1968) by Chuang Hua. Set in Shanghai in 1945, when it was occupied by the Japanese, *The Frontiers of Love* considers issues of personal and cultural identity in naturalistic terms. *Crossings* has similar preoccupations. As its title implies, Hua's novel charts movements that are both material and moral, as a Chinese American woman crosses over several kinds of border in order to find out who she is. Unlike Chang's book, however, it is determinately Modernist and experimental, the story itself crossing backwards and forwards between several different narrative forms. Difference, too, can sometimes develop into disagreement. Kingston, for instance, has come under considerable critical fire from other Chinese American writers. In the Introduction to an anthology of Asian American writing, *Aiiieeee!* (1974), several of those writers, among them Frank Chin and Shawn Wong, accuse Kingston of a failure to render Chinese myths and Chinese American experience accurately. Their charge is, briefly, that her rewriting of traditional stories and her use of hybrid forms constitute a kind of 'contamination', generic, cultural and even racial. What is needed, they argue, is a literature that resists racial stereotyping more actively and responds more fully to the present needs of the Chinese American community. This does not mean, however, that in their own work writers like Chin and Wong have been uncritical in their approach to that community. On the contrary, in both his short story collection *The Chinaman Pacific & Frisco R.R. Co.* (1998) and his novel *Donald Duk* (1991), Frank Chin (1940–) presents the Chinatowns of America as oppressive internal colonies and sites of grotesque cultural behaviour. Nor does it mean that they are resistant to the need for change, an active response to the challenge of America. In his first novel, *Homebase* (1979), for example, Shawn Wong (1949–) takes as his subject precisely that: the search for an American identity taken up by his protagonist, a Chinese American called Rainford Chan, as he travels psychically and physically across the continent. Chinese Americans 'are on the run through America', the reader learns in Wong's novel; they need a 'homebase', a point of cultural origin to supply a stable sense of identity in a shifting world. 'And today, . . . I do not want just a home that time allowed to have. America must give me legends with spirit,' Rainford Chan declares. 'I take myths to name this country's canyons, dry riverbeds, mountains, after my father, grandfather, great-grandfather. We are old enough to haunt this land.' The desire to 'haunt' the land by naming it, possessing it through story, is one that, despite their differences, Wong and Kingston, in fact all Chinese American writers, share. On this, the search for a foundation narrative pieced together out of the fragments of several histories, they can find common ground – not only with each other, it may be, but also with all those writing in and of America.

Unlike the Chinese, the Japanese had historically emigrated to America, before the Second World War, as families. They had no equivalent of the Chinese American 'bachelor society'. What Japanese Americans had with the outbreak of war, however, was far more dramatic and traumatic. The attack on Pearl Harbor in 1941 engendered a mood of national hysteria, one consequence of which was the creation of internment camps for people of Japanese ancestry. All mainland Japanese Americans living in the western halves of California, Oregon and Washington were relocated to what were, in effect, concentration camps by another name. It was a transformational moment, a radical displacement of humanity that became a dominant trope for Japanese American writers – as powerful for them as the trope of the Middle Passage was, and remains, for African American writers. Several Japanese American writers wrote highly critical retrospective narratives after the war, describing the experience of internment. These included two notable collections of short stories, *Yokohama, California* (1949) by Toshio Mori (1910–80) and *Seventeen Syllables and Other Stories* (1985) by Hisaye Yamamoto (1921–), and the autobiographical *Nisei Daughter* (1953) by Monica Sone (1919–). The stories of Mori offer a poignant contrast between the strong communal identity felt by Japanese Americans during the Depression and the disruptive, disintegrative effects of relocation. *Nisei Daughter*, in turn, pursues reconciliation: between Sone and her white readership, between Japanese and other Americans, and between what Sone herself describes as 'the Japanese and American parts of me'. The book follows a relatively conventional autobiographical pattern: beginning in childhood with many incidental details about family life, then moving into an adulthood that includes the experiences of internment and a visit to Japan. Sone is keen to present an accommodating image of Japanese Americans. She is insistent, too, on her own Americanness. 'I was a Yankee,' she declares proudly early on in the narrative; 'this America,' she insists much later on, 'where I was born, surrounded by people of different extractions, was still my home.' Yet Sone also admits that she experienced racial prejudice and oppression on a regular basis, which continually, painfully reminded her of her 'Asianness'. And, as these remembered experiences accumulate, the tone becomes notably more subdued, awkwardly self-conscious. She may claim, in her closing statement, that her Japanese and American selves 'were now blended into one', but this seems more a matter of wish than fulfilment. What the book expresses, really, is a desire for the several forms of reconciliation it pursues rather than their achievement.

The most remarkable book to come out of the Japanese American experience of the war, however, is *The No-No Boy* (1957) by John Okada (1923–71). It is also a milestone, one of the first Japanese American novels. The 'no-no boy' of the title is a twenty-five-year-old Japanese American, Ichiro Yamada. In 1943, all internees were given a 'loyalty questionnaire' containing two unsettling questions: whether or not the internee would be willing to serve in the American military and whether or not they would deny allegiance to Japan. Ichiro, we learn, has answered 'no-no' to these two questions; and when we meet him, at the beginning of the novel, he has just returned to Seattle, where his family lives, after two years in the internment camp and – following his refusal to be drafted – a further two years in a federal prison. He is no hero, but an alienated, disaffected stranger in his own land, doubly marginalized and conflicted because he rejects his Japanese as well as his American identity. Feeling 'like an intruder in a world to which he had no claim', he exists in a state of hopelessness (a word that Okada recapitulates throughout the novel). 'I wish with all my heart that I were Japanese or that I were American,' Ichiro reflects; 'I am neither.' His family, similarly conflicted, offers no refuge. On the basic level of communication, there is division and confusion, since his parents 'spoke virtually no English' while 'the children, like Ichiro, spoke almost no Japanese'. His father, a submissive, feminized reversal of traditional Japanese notions of patriarchy, seeks comfort and oblivion in drink, while his mother is so disoriented by the war and internment that she firmly believes Japan was victorious and that ships will soon be arriving to take them home. Ichiro rejects the mythmaking of his mother, together with 'her stories about gallant and fierce warriors' drawn from traditional Japanese lore. He cannot, and will not, embrace the foundation narratives – and, more specifically, the warrior values – of either America or Japan. So he becomes a wanderer, literally and figuratively. In an odyssey that begins and ends on the streets of Seattle, Ichiro appears to parody those legends of heroic mobility enshrined in both American and Japanese legends of pioneers and samurai. To use a trope that Okada weaves through the narrative, he is a traveller moving or driving without a map.

What compel *The No-No Boy* in new directions, gradually, are the relationships Ichiro has with his friend, Kenji, and his lover, Emi. Kenji is his foil and desired double. Kenji, a decorated and wounded war hero, is idolized, whereas Ichiro is despised; his family is brought together by the war, while the family of Ichiro is torn apart. 'They were two extremes,' the narrator observes, 'the Japanese who was more American than most Americans because he had crept to the brink of death for America, and the other who was neither Japanese nor American because he had failed to recognize the gift of his birthright when recognition meant everything.' Kenji offers Ichiro the chance of intimacy, the opportunity to break out of the descending spiral of his own hopelessness: not least when Ichiro is required to witness, and share in, Kenji's suffering and dying. A similar chance, to break out and perhaps believe in 'the great compassionate stream of life that is America', is offered by the woman to whom Kenji introduces him. Emi, whose father was repatriated to Japan and whose husband, a Japanese American soldier, has left her for a second tour of military duty and will never return, is freely compassionate and loving. Together with Kenji, she is vital to the protagonist's sometimes faint-hearted 'quest for completeness'. That quest is never accomplished, to the extent that the narrative circles back on itself: with Ichiro, at the end, still in motion. But, at least, there is the sense, as the book goes on, that this *is* a quest, not just a wandering but a seeking. Ichiro extends his sympathies to a former enemy injured in a bar-room brawl; his frozen emotional state starts to thaw; and his story closes, for us, on a carefully nuanced note of hope. 'He walked along, thinking, searching, thinking and probing,' the book concludes, 'and, in the darkness of the alley of the community that was a tiny bit of America, he chased that faint and elusive promise as it continued to take shape in mind and in heart.' *The No-No Boy* is a subtle story. It catches, for instance, the intricate network of tensions obtaining between several racial groups, not just Anglo and Japanese, and within the Japanese American community, between those born in Japan and those born in America. So the conclusion is not simply affirmative. What it is, is quietly reflective, delicately shaded: Ichiro leaves the story journeying towards redemption, the elusive promise of a recovery that is both personal and cultural. In that sense, he resembles the protagonist of *Invisible Man*, and so many other American novels that have at their core the dilemma of divided identity. He is an underground man, the conscience of a particular people and a nation, seeking a place where he can be truly and fully himself.

Janice Mirikitani (1942–) also experienced internment as a very young girl. It is an experience that supplies material for many of her poems. So do her memories of her mother and father, who were interned along with her. 'Your tears, mama, / have nourished us. / Your children /', Mirikitani confesses in 'Desert Flowers' (1978), 'like pollen / scatter in the wind.' 'He came over the ocean / carrying Mt. Fuji / on his back,' she recalls in 'For My Father' (1978), 'hacked through the brush of deserts / and made them grow / strawberries.' In 'Breaking Silence' (1987), she even uses excerpts from her mother's testimony to the Commission on Wartime Relocation and Internment. The quotations are inserted between stanzas, using Mirikitani's characteristically loose, idiomatic line, that celebrate her mother's courage – and her resistance to the traditional imperatives of female submission and silence. That resistance is shared by the daughter. In 'Recipe' (1987), Mirikitani mocks the absurd convention of Asian American women trying to conform to Western ideals of appearance. Elsewhere, in 'Bitches Don't Wait' (1978), for instance, she uses explicitly sexual material to defy the assumption that, as an Asian American female, she should be demure and modest. 'I don't think that Third

World writers can really afford to separate themselves from the ongoing struggle of their people,' Mirikitani has said. 'Nor can we ever not embrace our history.' That belief has led her to weave the lyrical and the political together, or sometimes be direct to the point of bluntness. It has also led her to celebrate rebellion as the only true tradition that one generation of Asian American women should pass down to the next. 'My daughter denies she is like me,' Mirikitani says in 'Breaking Tradition' (1987). 'She mirrors my ageing,' she adds. 'She is breaking tradition.' The daughter becomes like the mother in wanting to be unlike her. She reflects her, even honours her, by insisting on being herself, doing things her own way.

Another accomplished Japanese American poet, Garrett Hongo (1951–), offers a different nuance on the idea of tradition. Hongo has described his project as a poet as one 'motivated by a search for origins of various kinds – quests for ethnic and familial roots, cultural identity'. All of this, he has explained, is 'somehow connected' to his 'need for an active imaginative and spiritual life'. His 'obsession with origin', as he puts it, is 'more than a nostalgia'; 'it is rather a way to isolate, and to uphold moral and cultural value in a confusing time', 'to produce something of traditional learning, spiritual value, and personal experience out of the whirlwind' in which he lives. Hongo has a keen eye for what he has called the 'specificities' that 'bear culture'. In a manner that is sometimes reminiscent of the Imagists, he presses the telling detail into service, the random gesture or casual habit that carries a whole freight of cultural meaning. So, 'the essence / of garlic and black lotus root' can become a paradigm for the secrets of Japanese culture ('Who Among You Knows the Essence of Garlic?' [1982]). A woman walking down the street in Los Angeles, negotiating her way past Japanese and Chicano schoolboys and 'the Korean grocer's wife', becomes a sort of cultural catalyst: a guide through, and reflection of, the rich racial mosaic that is 'the Barrio' ('Yellow Light' [1982]). And the poet's own father, in 'Off from Swing Shift' (1982), betting on horse races with his constant dream that 'maybe tonight' would be 'his night / for winning, his night / for beating the odds', is made to epitomize, in an oddly heroic fashion, Japanese American suffering and stoicism. Hongo is adept, too, at secret histories. His anonymous characters voice their experiences of living 'on the frontier' ('The Unreal Dwelling: My Years in Volcano' [1985]). As they do so, they reveal an irrepressible spirit that has plainly cultural, communal origins. In 'Something Whispered in the *Shakukachi*' (1982), for instance, the speaker of the poem recalls his poverty in peacetime, internment in wartime, and subsequent survival. 'So, when it's bad now, / when I can't remember what I have lost,' he concludes, 'I go out back of the greenhouse / at the far end of my land,' where 'the rivers of weather' 'shape full-throated songs / out of wind, out of bamboo.' That reminds him, he intimates, of the bamboo flutes he used to fashion out of the bamboo on his farm, and play, when he was much younger. It is an apt image of someone making something out of nothing, or very little: 'my land was never thick with rice, /' the narrator reflects, 'only the bamboo.' It is also a compelling portrait of the artist as Japanese American, perhaps Hongo himself, making music out of his own territory and tradition.

Much of that music in prose, over the last two decades, has been produced by Japanese American women. There have been autobiographical narratives, developing the conventions of *Nisei Daughter*: among them, *Talking to High Monks in the Snow: An Asian American Odyssey* (1993) by Lydia Minatoya (1950–) and *The Dream of Water: A Memoir* (1995) by Kyoko Mori (1957–). There has also been a steady stream of fiction. In *Women of Silk* (1991), Gail Tsukiyama (1950–) writes about girl labourers; in *A Bridge Between Us* (1995), Julie Shigekuni concerns herself with the interwoven lives of four generations of Japanese American women. More remarkably still, Cynthia Kadohata (1956–) explores the experience of Japanese immigrants in the 1950s in *The Floating World* (1989). She then carries the action forward to 2052 in her second novel, *In the Heart of the Valley of Love* (1992), a complex dystopian narrative about a Japanese American woman's efforts to make sense of a world gone insane. *The Floating World*, in particular, may be the most important book written by a Japanese American since *The No-No Boy*. It embraces three generations of Japanese Americans, Issei, Nisei and Sansei (the Japanese terms for first-, second-, and third-generation immigrants), as it tells the story of one family and its search for America. The narrator is Olivia Osaka, or Livvie, who is twelve when the novel opens and twenty-one when it ends. What she recalls is that, as she tells us right at the beginning, her family 'travelled a lot'. Among those she recalls, in particular, is her grandmother, Hisae Fujitano or Obasan, a powerful woman who has had three husbands and several lovers and is the initiator of the family odyssey. Toughened by her passage from Japan to Hawaii then to the mainland, Obasan instils in her family the habit of movement and the myth of the floating world. The floating world, the grandmother tells the family, 'was the gas station attendants, restaurants, and jobs we depended on, the motel towns floating in the middle of fields and mountains'. In 'old Japan', she adds, it 'meant the districts full of brothels, teahouses, and public baths, but it also referred to change and the pleasures and loneliness change brings'. As an adult, Livvie remains faithful to this vision of immigrant rootlessness, which she sees as the essence of the American character and landscape. It is what maps America. 'I read once that there were three main rivers in the country, one on the West Coast, one on the East, and one in the Midwest,' she explains. 'The rivers, made up of migrant farmworkers, travelled down the country every year during the growing season.' Eventually her parents settle down, comfortably assimilated. Livvie, however, continues to live a life on the move that seems to connect her with both her Japanese past and her American future. She floats, just as her 'tormentor', her tyrannical grandmother, did, between cultures and identities, pursuing the elusive promise of America and performing, revising and remaking herself in her fluid environment from day to day.

Like the Japanese, many Korean immigrants travelled initially to Hawaii, escaping first from Japanese aggression at the beginning of the twentieth century and then, between 1930 and 1945, from Japanese occupation. Something of what Koreans had to contend with, during the years of occupation, is revealed in *Comfort Woman* (1997) by Nora Okja Keller (1965–). The novel is narrated from the perspective of

Akiko, a Korean refugee who has fled to the United States, and her daughter by an American missionary, Beccah. And it tells the story of a search for stability, and a secure identity, framed by the mother's secret past as a 'comfort woman', a prostitute in a 'recreation camp', forced to service the Japanese military. 'For years, we travelled from the east coast to the west coast, from north to south,' Beccah recalls, 'to every state in the Union.' Eventually, they stay in Hawaii. There it becomes Beccah's task to piece together the traumatic story of her mother, to 'claw' through memories to understand the atrocities she has suffered. As Akiko struggles to come to terms with her past, she tries to find a place for herself in America. That place is never really found, not least because she sees the United States only as a 'country of excess and extravaganza'. Her daughter, too, experiences dislocation and disorientation. 'When you see it for the first time, it glitters, beautiful, like a dream,' she says of America, 'but then, the longer you walk through it, the more you realize that dream is empty, false, sterile. You realize that you have no face and no place in this country.' Still, by the end of the narrative, she is beginning to break out of 'death thoughts' in a way that, understandably, her mother could never manage. With her mother dead, but the truth of her life and the love between them now acknowledged, Beccah seems to have achieved a kind of wholeness. Like the protagonists of so many stories of immigrant experience – *The No-No Boy* and *The Joy Luck Club*, for instance – Akiko ends with a beginning, by starting to understand and even cope with the diasporic currents of her life.

Notable writing by Korean Americans includes autobiography. In *The Dreams of Two Yi-min* (1989), for example, Margaret K. Pai (1900–) describes the life of her family in Hawaii, while Mary Paik Lee (1900–) tells the story of her own immigration in *Quiet Odyssey* (1990). Although these two books were only written towards the end of the twentieth century, both in fact deal with immigration experience towards the beginning. Like them, the novel *Clay Walls* (1987) by Kim Ronyoung (1926–87) looks back to an earlier part of the century, telling the story of Koreans arriving in California in the 1920s. Unlike them, however, it concentrates on the lives Korean immigrant women led once they arrived in America. A panoramic novel, *Clay Walls* pushes its story through to the 1940s. And, by emphasizing in particular the stories of a mother and daughter, it contrasts the experiences of first- and second-generation immigrants as they fight for job opportunities and encounter racism in their new home. *Dictee* (1982) by Theresa Hak Kyung Cha (1951–82) also documents both Korean life under Japanese control and Korean immigrant experience in America. Whereas Ronyoung is naturalistic in her approach, though, Cha is radically experimental and innovative. Weaving together a number of different narrative forms, including letters, journal entries, poetry and excerpts from histories, she also punctuates her text with photographs, maps and other visual material. The result is a cross between postmodern fiction, memoir and protest literature. A generic hybrid, *Dictee* dramatizes in its structure as well as in its story the complex, conflicted fate that is, very often, the lot of the immigrant.

For Filipino Americans that fate is, if anything, more conflicted than for most. Shaped by Spanish language, culture and religion since the sixteenth century, the inheritors as well of the English language and American popular culture, Filipinos are arguably more Western in their orientation than other Asian immigrant groups. They certainly enjoy a richly heterogeneous racial heritage. That is reflected in *what the hell for you left your heart in san francisco* (1987) by Bienvenido Santos (1911–96). Even the title of this remarkable novel, in its verbal play, gestures towards a mixed transnational heritage. And, as he describes his flight from the Philippines and his life of 'aimlessly wandering the United States', its immigrant protagonist insists on his complicated, composite identity. He is 'an oriental with broad hints of Malay-Indonesian, perhaps Chinese, strain, a kind of racial chopsuey', he explains. 'Better yet, for historical and ethnic accuracy, an oriental omelette flavoured with Spanish wine.' The contribution of American mass culture, in particular, to this rich ethnic mix is marked in two novels by Jessica Hagedorn (1949–), *Dogeaters* (1991) and *The Gangster of Love* (1996). In *Dogeaters* (a pejorative term for Filipinos), Hagedorn tells the stories of a range of Filipino characters, among them a pimp, a freedom fighter and a movie star. Told retrospectively by Rio Gonzaga, a young woman who as a teenager emigrates with her mother to the United States, these stories incorporate a variety of narrative forms, ranging from the discourses of history to vernacular forms such as gossip. What is remarkable, though, is the sense that the forms and imagery of the American media have penetrated Filipino culture so deeply that even memories of the Philippines are marked by it. The era of the Filipino dictator President Marcos, for instance, is recollected as if it were a series of Hollywood scripts, some romantic, some comic, some pornographic or the stuff of nightmare. Similarly, the protagonist of *The Gangster of Love*, Rocky Rivera, the member of a struggling rock band, admits that she is trapped in her 'media-saturated, wayward American skin'. Disappointed by her initial encounter with America, when she arrives to find the Golden Gate Bridge shrouded in fog – and, as it turns out, not really made of gold – Rocky becomes a countercultural 'gangster', crisscrossing the continent in a wild, geographic simulation of her own lack of a stable cultural base. The story she tells is equally, appropriately disjunctive, mixing narrative with poetry, dramatic skits and jokes. By the end, her careering backwards and forwards across America has brought her little beyond the dubious gift of being superficially Americanized. And, like many other immigrant protagonists, she makes the journey back to her old home in the belief, or perhaps just the hope, that there she may be able to resurrect and retrieve her origins.

It was not until several decades after the Second World War that, for quite different reasons, the United States experienced significant immigration from Vietnam and South Asia. The exodus from Vietnam that followed the disastrous military engagement there is the narrative occasion of *Monkey Bridge* (1997) by Lan Cao (1961–), which tells the story of a mother and a daughter, and a people, not accustomed to 'crossing boundaries' who suddenly have to do so. From farm life on the Mekong Delta to strategic hamlets to Saigon and then to Little Saigon in Virginia, the characters in this novel have to negotiate the perilous 'monkey bridge' from one 'shifting world' to another. They become wandering spirits, threatened with 'the complete absence of identity, of history', looking for an 'American future' but longing to 'hang onto their Vietnam lives' – and learning, some of them, to 'relocate one's roots and bend one's body in a new direction'. The arrival of South Asians in America in large numbers, in turn, has been the source and inspiration of a number of stories and novels published in the last two or three decades of the twentieth century. They include the poetry and fiction of Meena Alexander (1951–), two novels, *Arranged Marriage* (1995) and *The Mistress of Spices* (1997), by Chitra Banerjee Divakaruni (1957–), and the work in shorter and longer narrative forms by the most significant South Asian American writer, Bharati Mukherjee (1940–). 'I feel very American,' Mukherjee has declared. 'I knew the moment I landed as a student in 1961 . . . that this is where I belonged. It was an intense kind of love.' That, however, does not register the subtlety, or the variety, of her versions of the immigrant experience in her work. She may well believe that, as she has said, America gave her the chance to become 'a new person', 'to discard that part of my history that I want, and invent a whole new history for myself'. But her characters may not find such a chance easy or available. Or they may find themselves living in a more culturally mixed and confused world than the notion of beginning again, as a 'new person' suggests. 'The first time I heard of Karma', the narrator of Mukherjee's 1997 novel *Leave It to Me* explains, 'was from the Indian burger-muncher at McDonald's, the one who asked me out to an Indian movie.'

Wife, published in 1975, introduces one typical kind of Mukherjee protagonist: the immigrant woman who remains trapped inside her house, for fear of what lies outside, beyond the door. Dimple Dasgupta, the daughter of middle-class Indian parents, marries and emigrates to the United States. 'Dimple Dasgupta had set her heart on marrying a neuro-surgeon,' the novel begins with typical, ironic wit, 'but her father was looking for engineers in the matrimonial ads.' And it is with an engineer, eventually, that she makes her journey to the New World. Her expectations are high, and they are disappointed. Dimple encounters a world of, at best, indifference and, at worst, real prejudice. Her husband cannot get the work for which he is qualified. And she is frightened by what she sees as the perilous landscape of New York City. 'The air was never free of the sounds of sirens growing louder, or gradually fading,' Dimple notes. 'They were reminders of a dangerous world (even the hall was dangerous, she thought, let alone the playground and the streets).' So, she retreats into the safety and security of her apartment. Faced by the challenge of the new, she opts for memories of the old, isolation and a form of cultural stalemate. The novel that Mukherjee published fourteen years after *Wife*, *Jasmine*, tells a very different story and describes a quite different – but, in her own way, equally typical – kind of heroine. The eponymous Jasmine Vijh is born and raised in rural India, named 'Jyoti, Light' by her grandmother. She emigrates to the United States alone to escape her fate as a widow in a small village. There, she constantly reinvents and renames herself, as Jasmine, Jane or Jase, confessing, 'I changed because I wanted to'. 'We murder who we were so we can rebirth ourselves in the images of dreams,' Jasmine declares towards the beginning of her story. And pursuing what she calls a 'zigzag route' across America, she leads a life of 'adventure, risk, transformation'; 'the frontier is pushing indoors through uncaulked windows,' she declares triumphantly at the end of the novel, as she prepares to leave an old home for a new one.

Jasmine is not, however, a simple celebration of American innovation and the national imperative to 'shuttle between identities'. It is more barbed and rebarbative than that. 'I didn't know what to think of America,' Jasmine confesses to herself prior to her arrival in the United States. 'I'd read only *Shane* and seen only one movie.' What she encounters, when she first arrives with a group of 'outcasts' or illegal immigrants, is hardly the promised land. 'The first thing I saw were the two cones of a nuclear plant,' she remembered. 'I waded through Eden's waste,' she explains, as she describes stumbling from ship to shore, 'plastic bottles, floating oranges, boards, sodden boxes, white and green plastic sacks tied shut but picked open by birds and pulled apart by crabs.' This nautical wasteland is her entrance into what often appears to be an 'underworld of evil'. Washed up in America like so much flotsam and jetsam, Jasmine is confined and raped by a man called Half-Face, a paradigm of the disfigured landscape and perverted national myth. She has to kill Half-Face to escape: first to New York City, 'an archipelago of ghettoes seething with aliens', then to Iowa, which may seem rooted, reassuring, but has its own forms of poverty and violence, and is, besides, a place where people tend to regard her as 'different', an 'inscrutable' 'alien'. Throughout her trials, however, what sustains Jasmine is her spiritual buoyancy, her eager response to what she terms 'the fluidity of American character and American landscape'. 'In America, nothing lasts,' she reflects. That may be a cause for regret sometimes but, more often than not, it is a source of consolation, even cheer. It enables Jasmine to be 'many selves'; and it challenges her to become 'a fighter and adapter'. And even though Jasmine herself may claim at one moment, 'I became an American', the situation, as she elsewhere acknowledges, is richer, more layered than that. 'I am caught between the promise of America', she ends up confessing, 'and old-world dutifulness.' Not only that, she learns to find salvation eventually in a synthesis between old and new. Her newly acquired American belief in the reinvention of the self finds confirmation, it turns out, receives a further charge from her inherited Indian belief in reincarnation. She is able to connect up with the idea that she can be many women precisely because she is committed to the notion of spiritual metamorphosis. 'We do keep revisiting the world,' she tells a friend. 'I have also travelled in time and space. It is possible.' Shuttling between each of her identities as if it were 'a possible assignment from God', feeling wondrously, divinely inspired, she combines the cosmic rhythms of ancient belief with the New World rhythms of mobility and adventure. So Jasmine is not so much a divided or dual personality as a unified one, deriving her strength from the communion, the marriage between the cultures she is heir to. That strength enables her, as the novel closes, to strike out for a territory that inspires a connection with the oldest and newest of American stories. She is 'heading West'; and, as she does so, she tells us, she is 'greedy with wants and reckless from hope'.

Writing of those white settlers who were headed west over a hundred years before Jasmine, the poet Simon Ortiz (1941–) observes: 'It is a wonder / they ever made it to California. / But of course they did.' 'And they named it success. / Conquest. / Destiny /', he adds. 'Frontiers ended for them / and a dread settled upon them / and became remorseless / nameless / namelessness.' Ortiz is from the Acoma Pueblo tribe. The cycle of poems from which these lines are taken, *from Sand Creek* (1981), weaves together autobiography and history, as Ortiz rehearses his experiences as a veteran in a military hospital, the wars white Americans fought to wrest the land from its original inhabitants, and the wars the tribes still have to fight in a society that is oblivious to their presence, let alone their needs. 'I am a veteran of 30,000 years,' Ortiz declares in another work, 'The Significance of a Veteran's Day' (1992). Exploring personal and cultural dispossession, Ortiz finds the tools of survival in the ancient stories and songs, the oral traditions of the Acoma Pueblo people. 'I am talking about how much we have been able / to survive insignificance,' he explains. And the 'we' here includes other Native American tribes since, as he observes wryly in another, earlier collection of poems, *Going for Rain* (1974), 'You meet Indians everywhere'. All Native Americans, Ortiz insists in this collection – which was, of course, published at a moment of particularly fierce political activism – must work against the 'feeling of no self-esteem, insignificance, powerlessness'. They can do so by rediscovering their connection with the land and with the myths of their peoples. More specifically, he suggests, they can do so by striving for a holistic consciousness that is rooted in language: 'not necessarily only native languages but the consciousness of our true selves at the core of whatever language we use, including English'. *There is a revolution going on,* Ortiz announces in *from Sand Creek*; *'it is very spiritual and its manifestation is economic, political, and social. Look to the horizon and listen.'* It is, for him, a revolution that embraces both the traditions of the tribal past and the inspired talk of the present. Native Americans are 'caught now, in the midst of wars / against foreign disease, missionaries, / canned food, Dick and Jane textbooks, IBM cards, / Western philosophies and General Electric'. Their way of escaping this imprisonment, Ortiz suggests, is through a rediscovery of 'ancient and deep story' and 'song as language'. Only by such means can they make a place and presence for themselves and realize their dream of a true homeland. 'That dream / shall have a name / after all, /' Ortiz prophesies in *from Sand Creek*, in words that offer a triumphantly new variation on an old American theme. 'And it will not be vengeful / but wealthy with love / and compassion / and knowledge /', he concludes. 'And it will rise / in this heart / which is our America.'

A historical sense of dispossession, the search for a place and past rooted in the oral tradition, the presence and pleasure of a communal identity co-extensive with the land, the transformative power of language: these themes sounded in the poetry of Simon Ortiz are common in contemporary Native American writing. The writers speak them, however, and other themes, in a variety of voices. The poetic voice of Roberta Hill Wideman (1947–), for instance, a member of the Oneida tribe, is quieter, more indirect and economical. 'Indians know how to wait,' she writes in 'Lines for Marking Time' (1984); and her poems reveal the rewards of waiting, patient attention to a particular event or object – a house and museum ('In the Longhouse, Oneida Museum' [1984]), a familiar street ('Scraps Worthy of Wind' [1984]) – as a preliminary to emotional release and discovery. 'I think we (Indian people) . . . have an intuitive sense of our own exile,' Wideman has said. 'But it is never dealt with.' She adds, 'there's no comment on it'; 'we know this emotionally and spiritually and we understand it'. That understanding feeds into poems that capture the larger narratives of history in small nuances of event and feeling. So, in 'Underground Water' (1984), a child who 'awaking, takes the long way home' to his parents' bed becomes a paradigm, an emblem of exile and the comforts of community: compulsions and consolations that have a general resonance, of course, but also a particular pressing relevance for the Oneida and other Native American peoples that are the poet's main subject. As the title of her collection *Star Quilt* (1984), intimates, Wideman sees her project as a weaving together of the apparently trivial and mundane into a significant pattern, a knitting together of the scraps and fragments of memory into forms that invite revelation.

While sharing certain themes in common with Ortiz and Wideman, the poetic voice of Wendy Rose (1948–) is, in turn, different from either. Of mixed Hopi, Miwok, English, Scottish, Irish and German extraction, Rose also reaches out in her work to women of any race, although particularly to those of mixed-blood origin like herself. 'Remember I am a garnet woman,' one of her poems called 'If I Am Too Brown or Too White for You' (1985) begins. Through a series of linked images, of woman, water, stories and jewels, Rose then explores the fluid nature of her identity and the chance song gives her to celebrate what she calls here the 'small light / in the smoke, a tiny sun / in the blood, so deep / it is there and not there, / so pure / it is singing'. That light is a crystalline clarity of self that, for so many women like her, so often remains secret, unacknowledged. It is up to Rose, as she sees it, to lay bare the secret. Some poems turn from the lyrical to the historical, using a historical occasion to declare a humanity that has been consistently denied. In 'To the Hopi in Richmond (Santa Fe Village)' (1985), for example, it is what Rose calls 'my people my pain' that supplies the impulse, as she records how a colony of Hopi were dispossessed and denied, carried away in boxcars to help build a railroad. In 'Julia' (1985), the subject is the plight of one woman, a Mexican Indian of the nineteenth century known as 'The Ugliest Woman in the World'. A carnival performer, she was married eventually to her manager, who wanted to protect his investment; when she died, he had her body stuffed and mounted, so that she could continue to be put on display. The poem, spoken by Julia, is a plea for love: 'tell me, husband, how you love me,' she begs. It also reveals the power of song: in asking for acknowledgement of herself as a human being, Julia manifests just how complexly, poignantly human she is. Through the telling of her story, Julia confirms the truth of her self; and Rose, in fact, sees her own project in that of Julia. Storytelling, she tells us in 'Story Keeper' (1985), is something she learned from her family and her tribe. 'I feel the stories / settle under my bed,' she confesses. The stories 'go a winding way' back to 'the red clouds / our first / Hopi morning'. They offer a return to origins, and a means of rediscovering the personal by reconnecting it to the communal, a shared tradition and a shared humanity.

Joy Harjo (1951–), a poet born into the Creek Nation, also mixes Anglo and Native American influences in her work. Her poems deploy a free verse line that connects her with the tradition of Whitman; they are also marked, however, by a cadence that recalls the repetitions of the Indian ceremonial drum. There is song here, and chant, as Harjo describes Native American women living on a knife edge ('The Woman Hanging from the Thirteenth Floor Window' [1983]), the tragic past and grim present of most Native Americans ('New Orleans' [1983]), or rehearses her own memories and metamorphic sense of her own identity. 'Remember that you are all people and that all people / are you, /' she writes in 'Remember' (1983). 'Remember that you are this universe and that this / universe is you. / Remember that all is in motion, is growing, is you,' she concludes. 'Remember that language comes from this.' 'The dance that language is' is, in effect, the key for Harjo, the way to unlock what Native Americans have been, are and may become. Her work is packed with the dire particulars of Native American history: 'I have a memory, /' she says in 'New Orleans', 'It swims deep in blood.' But it is also brimming over with visions. So, in the appropriately titled 'Vision' (1983), Harjo transmutes a rainbow touching down 'somewhere in the Rio Grande' into 'horses / of colour / horses that were within us all of this time'. 'The thunder of their beating / hearts' and hooves becomes an emblem of the vitality lurking within her, her people and all life. Similarly, in 'Deer Dancer' (1990), a beautiful Indian woman who appears in a 'bar of misfits' suddenly, dances naked and then vanishes, seems to figure old dreams and new promises. Linked with elemental, elusive creatures of Native American myth, she is, we are told, 'the deer who entered our dream in white dawn, breathed mist / into pine trees, her fawn a blessing of meat, the ancestors who never left'. 'Give me back my language.' Harjo demands in 'We Must Call a Meeting' (1990). She is, she indicates, like her fellow Native American poets in her search for the right words that will enable her to tell the truth, the tale of her tribe. With those words found and carefully fashioned, the tale she tells is, she confesses, an almost incredible one, of a people still here despite everything, including war, disease and famine. 'Everybody laughed at the impossibility of it, / but also the truth,' Harjo admits in 'Anchorage' (1983). 'Because who would believe / the fantastic and terrible story of all of our survival / those who were never meant / to survive?'

'We are what we imagine,' N. Scott Momaday (1934–) from the Kiowa tribe once wrote. 'Our very existence consists in the imagination of ourselves . . . The greatest tragedy that can befall us is to go unimagined.' Momaday has also remarked that when he began writing the novel that established his reputation, *House Made of Dawn* (1968), he did not know any other works of Native American fiction existed. To that extent, he was faced with an 'unimagined' collective existence, the erasure of Native Americans from the national literature and life. And although this was more a matter of perception than fact – since works of Native American fiction were, after all, in existence before *House Made of Dawn* – it is nevertheless true that Momaday's remarkable first book helped to usher in a renaissance in Native American writing. Following its publication, and critical and commercial success, a whole series of works, especially in prose, has helped to establish the Native American presence, and helped Native American readers in particular to see, and imagine, who they were and what they might become. In non-fiction, notable works have included *Custer Died For Your Sins: An Indian Manifesto* (1969) by the Sioux writer Vine Deloria (1933–) and *The Sacred Hoop: Recovering the Feminine in American Indian Traditions* (1986) by the Native feminist and gay rights activist Paula Gunn Allen (1939–), from the Laguna Pueblo tribe. In fiction, among other key books there has been *Mean Spirit* (1990) by the Chickasaw novelist Linda Hogan (1947–), which describes how Osage Indians, after the discovery of oilfields on their reservations, endured a campaign of racial abuse from whites who would not stop at murder to make the oil theirs. There have been *Medicine River* (1989) and *Green Grass, Running Water* (1993) by the Cherokee writer Thomas King (1943–), the later book featuring the trickster figure Coyote and a host of other extraordinary characters gathering for the Sun Dance ceremony on a Blackfeet reservation. There has also been a series of milestone novels by Martin Cruz-Smith (1942–), from the Senecu del Sur and Yaqui tribes (among them, *Nightwing* [1977] and *Stallion Gate* [1986]), Janet Campbell Hale (1946–), from the Coeur d'Alene and Kootenai tribes (*Owl Song* [1974], *Jailing of Cecilia Capture* [1985]), and the Cheyenne Hyemeyohsts Storm (1935–) (*Seven Arrows* [1972], *His The Song of the Heyoehkah* [1981]) as well as shorter fiction from the Cherokee writer Diane Glancy (1941–), the Chippewa Basil H. Johnston (1929–) and Michael Dorris (1945–97) from the Modoc tribe. Significant or seminal though the work by all these writers is, however, the core texts in the Native American renaissance in fiction, following Momaday, have been written by five others: Leslie Marmon Silko (1948–), James Welch (1940–), Louise Erdrich (1954–), Gerald Vizenor (1934–) and Sherman Alexei (1966–). Key workers in prose fiction, each of these five has produced work worthy to stand with *House Made of Dawn*. As remarkable as they are remarkably different, all of them together with Momaday have been instrumental in producing a body of work that deserves to stand in the front row of contemporary writing, Native American or otherwise.

Momaday himself lived in several non-Indian communities as a child, as well as with several Southwestern tribes, especially the Jemez Pueblo. From his father's family he inherited Kiowa storytelling traditions and a love of the Rainy Mountain area of Oklahoma. His mother, whose paternal grandmother was a Cherokee, instilled in him both an affection for English literature and the example of how an act of imaginative will could help him forge an Indian identity. Gerald Vizenor, in 1981, was to make the celebrated remark, 'I believe we're all invented as Indians'. And Momaday, like so many other contemporary Native American writers, reflects that belief in his mixed, crossblood origins, his seizure of a plural, mobile identity, his experimenting with and mixing of different genres and his preference for hybrid forms. Typically, Momaday sees Americans of tribal descent, past or present, as anything but frozen in time, a species of immobile victimry. Survival, and the tragic wisdom it has engendered, remain for him dynamic not static, tokens of the Native living not dead. That, too, holds for the massive pluralities of tribal affiliation, many of which Momaday has shared. Educated at reservation, public and parochial schools, the universities of New Mexico, Virginia and Stanford, Momaday brought a catholic reading in Dickinson, Joyce and Faulkner among others, as well as the oral traditions of the Navajo, Pueblo and Kiowa, to his work. Diversity became a characteristic, as a result, not just of his writing as a whole but of individual texts. In *The Names: A Memoir* (1976), for example, he uses fictional techniques, as well as traditional autobiographical ones, to trace his passionate rediscovery and reinvention of himself. The poems in his collections *The Gourd Dancer* (1976) and *In the Presence of the Sun* (1992) range wide, from forms recollecting Native American orality through traditional to free verse. His 1989 novel *The Ancient Child* mixes ancient Kiowa bear stories, the contemporary tale of a male artist's midlife crisis and outlaw fantasies imagined by the young medicine woman who tries to cure the artist. More extraordinary still, his 1969 book *The Way to Rainy Mountain* welds together several genres. Here, Momaday collects stories from his Kiowa elders. To all but a few of these he attaches short historical and personal commentaries. He then arranges twenty-four of these triple-voiced movements into three sections titled 'The Setting Out', 'The Going On' and 'The Closing In'. Framed by two poems and three lyric essays that combine mythic, historical and personal perspectives, the three sections dramatize several kinds of journey, the two foregrounded being the historical migration of the Kiowa and the personal entry of the author into his Kiowa identity. As these journeys continue, *The Way to Rainy Mountain* sounds the themes that resonate through all Momaday's writing: the uses of memory, imagination and the oral in the formation of personal and communal presence, the land and language as extensions of being, the beauty and authority of the Native American sense of the sacred. And similarly resonant with these themes is the book that preceded *The Way to Rainy Mountain* by a year, that first established Momaday's reputation and influence – and that, by common consent, remains his finest work: *House Made of Dawn*.

Set circularly in Walatowa, a fictional version of Jemez Pueblo, Los Angeles and then, by eventual return, the pueblo again, *House Made of Dawn* tells the story of Abel, a Pueblo Indian. After fighting in the Second World War, Abel returns alienated from white America and from Pueblo culture. 'He had tried to pray, to sing, to enter into the old rhythm of the tongue,' the reader is told, 'but he was no longer attuned to it.' Abel is described, several times, as 'unlucky'. In an interview, however, Momaday has described his hero perhaps more accurately as tragic. The trauma suffered by Abel, Momaday explained, was shared by a 'tragic generation' of Indians who suffered 'a dislocation of the psyche'. 'Almost no Indian of my generation or of Abel's generation escaped that dislocation,' Momaday observed, 'that sense of having to deal immediately with, not only the traditional world but with the other world that was placed over the traditional world so abruptly and with great violence.' What Abel representatively has to do, and in the end manages to do, is to renegotiate his Indian identity through an empowering embrace of ritual and mythical precedent. And the prologue to the novel reveals how he will do it, as it anticipates the end by showing Abel running in a ceremonial race. As he runs, we are told, he appears to have become one with the 'still and strong' land around him. The prologue also begins with the traditional invocation, *Dypaloh*, of a Walatowa or Jemez Indian storyteller. It then announces: 'There was a house made of dawn. It was made of pollen and rain, and that land was very old and everlasting.' The motif that gives the book its title is taken from the songs of the Navajo Nightway ceremony, a long healing ritual. From the beginning Momaday alludes in this way to traditions of storytelling and healing within quite separate Indian cultures of the Southwest. *House Made of Dawn* consequently becomes a continuation of each tradition, as well as, in its alternately terse and densely referential prose, a continuation of the more Anglo-American lines of Hemingway and Faulkner.

In the prologue, Abel is running seven years after the time of the first section, 'The Longhair'. Set in the pueblo in 1945, this, the first of four sections into which the book is divided, introduces Abel as he stumbles drunkenly off a bus bringing him home from military service. Haunted though he is by war memories, it is clear that his sense of separation from the Pueblo community occurred before he entered the army. And his vulnerability to pressure is measured in two key moments or experiences: his involvement with a privileged white woman who is attracted to his 'primitive' masculinity, and his murder of an albino Indian whom he takes to be an incarnation of evil. The second section of the novel, 'The Priest of the Sun', is set in a miasmic Los Angeles. After a trial in '*their* language', the language of a white society that does not even begin to understand the terms and conditions of his life, Abel has been imprisoned and now relocated to the city. He has become one of any number of Native Americans who have not been so much relocated, in fact, as dislocated: adrift in an environment where they seem to lack the simplest words, the most basic tools required to cope. The third section, 'The Night Chanter', begins with a Navajo Indian called Benally, telling the tale of the departure of Abel from the city. Abel and Benally, it turns out, have become friends; and Benally has told Abel about the songs and chants associated with the Navajo healing ceremonies, the Beautyway and the Night Chant. 'I used to tell him about those old ways,' Benally recalls. He also sings about the house made of dawn: making a gift of the words that will help Abel find the right language to express himself, and a sense of an identity that is continuous, co-extensive with the land.

The final section of the book, 'The Dawn Runner', turns the wheel of the narrative full circle. Abel awakes at dawn, only a week after his return from Los Angeles, to find his grandfather dead. 'The old man had spoken six times in the dawn,' we are told, 'and the voice of his memory was whole and clear and growing like the dawn.' What 'the voice of his memory' has declared is a lesson in language and in living. The grandfather has taught his grandson about the land, its rhythms and rituals, he has acted as a guide, an initiator into the mysteries of sex and death. He has also, over the years and over the night, helped to give Abel the right words, pointed a way for him to articulate and celebrate his being. Abel now prepares the body of his grandfather in the ritual fashion. He then hurries off to run after the men who have set off in the ceremonial race. 'All of his being was concentrated in the sheer motion of running on,' the reader learns, 'and he was past caring about pain.' Abel runs to the point where 'he could see at last without having to think'. What he sees are 'the canyon and the mountains and the sky', 'the rain and river and the fields beyond', and 'the dark hills at dawn'. Entering body and soul into a holistic harmony with the land that, from time immemorial, has sustained his people, Abel begins to sing 'under his breath'. 'There was no sound, and he had no voice,' the book concludes, 'he had only the words of a song. And he went on running on the rise of the song. *House made of pollen, house made of dawn. Qtsedaba.*' Abel has at last found the right words: the words of the Night Chant that restore him to earth and to community. The Walatowa term *Qtsedaba*, indicating that the story is over, seals the healing process, an experience of restoration of being that is also a restoration in saying and seeing. It is a defining moment in contemporary Native American writing, not least because, in responding to the ancient rhythms and rituals, the novel itself has entered into a new language along with its protagonist. In wedding the forms of American fiction to the songs and storytelling of the Native American oral tradition, Momaday has fashioned a voice, the right voice for himself, just as his hero, Abel has done.

Like Momaday, Leslie Marmon Silko has a mixed ancestry. The family of her father was a mixture of Laguna and white; her mother came from a Plains tribe; and she also has some Mexican ancestors. As the title of her first book, *Laguna Woman* (1974), a collection of poems, indicates, however, it is the traditions and territory of the Laguna that have meant most to her. Many cultures have influenced the Laguna. Hopi, Zuni and Jemez people had married into the pueblo before it was established at its present site in New Mexico five hundred years ago. Later, Navajos, Spanish and other European settlers also intermarried with the Lagunas. Those who joined the pueblo brought with them their own rituals and myths, which were then incorporated into Laguna culture. 'Things which don't shift and grow are dead things,' says a medicine man in Silko's finest novel, *Ceremony* (1977). Silko registers this, the plural, changing nature of the ceremonies that underpin Laguna society. She also catches, as Momaday does, Native American culture as continuous with language and landscape. Silko describes what she calls, in *Ceremony*, 'a world made of stories'. 'You don't have anything / if you don't have the stories,' the poetic prologue to this novel announces. 'In the belly of this story / the rituals and the ceremony / are still growing.' Repetition and recurrence are the vital elements of ritual and narrative, a rhythm of continuity and change that links word to world, language to life, and the Laguna people as they tell their stories and perform their ceremonies to the earth that is their 'mother' and the sky that is their 'father'. 'It seems like I already heard these stories somewhere before,' declares a character called 'old Grandma', in *Ceremony*, 'only thing is the names sound different.' For Silko, fiction is a continuation of the oral tradition, in that it renews and retells old tales, marrying the fresh to the familiar, the signs of the past to the settings of the present so as to make 'the names sound different'. 'In the belly of this story /', the prologue to *Ceremony* announces, 'the rituals and the ceremony / are still growing.' Like 'a good ceremony', a good story, such as the one these lines preface, is curative because its element is growth; it both explores and enacts those compulsive, repetitive but constantly revitalized rhythms that are the determining characteristics of life.

Like *House Made of Dawn*, *Ceremony* has a veteran of the Second World War as its protagonist. Tayo, a man of mixed blood, returns to postwar New Mexico feeling dispossessed and disoriented. During the war, he and other Native American combatants had felt, 'they belonged to America'; now he and they have lost that 'new feeling'. The place to which he returns is a disconcerting mix of the old and the new. 'The fifth world had become entangled with European names: the names of the rivers, the hills, the names of the animals and plants,' the reader is told; '– all of creation suddenly had two names: an Indian name and a white name.' There is poverty and homelessness, white tourism and 'the dirty walls of the bars along Highway 66'. There is significant tension, too, between the new urban Indians cut off from their tribal cultures and the perpetuation of ceremonies by the medicine men. 'I'm sick,' Tayo admits. He goes to see a medicine man called Betonie, a man who, with all his allegiance to the ancient rituals, acknowledges the ineluctable nature of the new. 'Ceremonies have always been changing' since the arrival of the whites, Betonie tells Tayo, and 'only this growth keeps the ceremonies strong'. 'Bundles of newspapers', 'telephone books', 'Coke bottles' are all 'part of the pattern', Betonie says, 'all these things have stories in them'. 'Nothing is simple.' The ceremonies have to reflect this, accommodate change and complexity and not resort to a binary split of white against red, new against old. As a 'half-breed' Tayo is part of this hybrid culture. As a man in search of healing, he finds restoration in the hybrid rituals of Betonie, who teaches Tayo the difference between 'witchery', red or white, that treats the world as 'a dead thing', and ceremony through which Tayo came to learn 'the world was alive'. A sign or symbol of witchery is the atomic bomb. The first atomic explosion occurred, historically, little more than a hundred miles from the Laguna; and in *Ceremony*, Tayo, whose grandmother witnessed that explosion, sees the bomb as uniting humanity under the threat of annihilation. 'Human beings were one clan again,' he reflects, 'united by the fate the destroyers planned for all of them, for all living things.' The redemptive ceremony is the experience in the book, the one that Tayo undergoes, and the experience of the book, as it incorporates everything, old and new, into an inclusive vision of peace. Sitting among the rocks mined for uranium to make the atom bomb, Tayo sees in the stars a pattern of convergence with 'no boundaries, only transitions through all distances and time'. That pattern the protagonist sees is one that this narrative also performs, from its opening invocation to a close that repeats in a new key the old songs and chants: 'Sunrise, / accept this offering, / Sunrise.'

Several of the characters in the fiction of James Welch bear a haunting resemblance to Tayo in *Ceremony* and Abel in *House Made of Dawn*. 'I felt no hatred, no love, no guilt, no conscience,' the protagonist and narrator of Welch's first novel, *Winter in the Blood* (1974), admits, 'nothing but a distance that had grown through the years.' He is a drifter, marked by a sense of alienation and loss. So is the protagonist of Welch's second novel, *The Death of Jim Loney* (1979). Both men, after promising athletic careers in youth, now hardly live their lives. Estranged from their families, they see in their fathers haunting omens of what they might become, outsiders living on the fringes of white culture. Consumed by feelings of uselessness – 'What use', the protagonist of *Winter in the Blood* keeps asking himself, of everything – they are aimless, apathetic creatures, seeking relief in drink and casual sex. Welch, who is half Blackfeet and half Gros Ventre, has a far more laconic, terser narrative style than Momaday or Silko, however. Plot matters less than mood in these two novels. Mood and tone are set by a bleak, oblique humour and a tightly rhythmic, repetitive prose style that recalls the early fiction of Ernest Hemingway. That goes for Welch's fourth book, *Indian Lawyer* (1990), as well. As its title suggests, the hero here is more materially comfortable. With a shiny Saab and finely tailored suits, he has moved a long way from his impoverished childhood on a Blackfeet reservation. Like Welch's other sad young contemporary men, though, he moves between two worlds, one white and one Indian, feeling adrift, out of place in both. *Fool's Crow*, published in 1986, is different from Welch's other fiction. The year here is 1870, the location is a Blackfeet camp. And the story, replete with Native American custom and ceremony, retells an actual historical tale about the decline of tribal life. A young medicine man, the Fool's Crow of the title, sees the danger posed by the Napikwans, or white men. He knows that his people must either wage a brave but futile war, or simply surrender their land and way of life without a fight. Still, even *Fool's Crow* has the dark texture, the sombre tone and shadowy humour that are Welch's trademark. And, in its own way, it acts as a supplement. It forms part of a tetralogy that sets the pride of the Native American past against the pity of the present, and that suggests one small recompense, in a world of drift and loss, is a recovery of ancestry – to become aware, as the narrator of *Winter in the Blood* puts it, of 'the presence of ghosts'.

Just how he becomes aware of this is exemplary for Welch's fiction. He discovers that his grandfather is not the man he supposed but someone called Yellow Calf. This secret of his ancestry is never stated; it is simply understood, as Yellow Calf talks to him about the past of his family and his people. '*It was you, Yellow Calf, the hunter!*' the narrator says, to nobody but himself. 'And so we share this secret in the presence of ghosts,' he then recollects, 'in wind that called forth the muttering tepees, the blowing snow, the white air of the horse's nostrils.' Returning to the family land, he finds he has two tasks to perform. One is the burial of his grandmother, which is recollected in a tone of typical graveyard humour. 'The hole was too short', the reader is told, so someone had to jump up and down on the coffin until 'it went down a bit more, enough to look respectable'. Just prior to this seriocomic act of piety, the narrator has another, quite unexpected job to do, one that is dirty, dangerous and slightly ridiculous. He has to rescue a cow that has become stuck in the mud. The job is done with a will; and the performance of the job is described with a sly humour but serious attention to detail that lends it a modest heroism. One release from nothingness, it seems, is the one the heroes of Joseph Conrad and Ernest Hemingway found: in work, patient, practical attention to the task at hand. Rain falls just after the task is finished. 'Some people . . . will never know how pleasant it is to be distant in a clean rain, the driving rain of a summer storm,' the narrator concludes. 'It's not like you'd expect, nothing like you'd expect.' This is a small thing, perhaps, but a small, good thing. Along with the small ceremonies due to ancestors, the small consolations of the senses are like a good deed in a naughty world. They may not promise redemption but they provide a kind of temporary emotional rescue. That may not be enough, Welch intimates, but it is all that we can have.

Like James Welch, Louise Erdrich has devoted much of her career to writing a tetralogy. Of German and Chippewa descent, Erdrich grew up in the Turtle Mountain Band of Chippewa, in North Dakota. In 1984 she published the first of four books set on and around a fictional Chippewa reservation in her homestate. Titled *Love Medicine*, it consists of a series of free-standing narratives told by various members of two families, the Kashpaws and the Lamartines, living on the reservation between 1974 and 1984. Appearing in one another's stories, their fates intertwined, the narrators mix humour and despair as they tell stories of survival that focus in particular upon women. The second novel in the series, *The Beet Queen* (1986), begins in 1932 when two children, Karl and Mary Adare, leap from a boxcar. Orphaned, they have come to seek refuge with their Aunt Fritzie. The story then spans forty years, taking in what is for Erdrich a characteristically large gallery of characters. Erdrich is particularly adept not only at intercalating narratives, weaving the stories of several people together into one densely layered tapestry, but also at linking story to history. These are all extraordinary people; and Erdrich is not averse to stepping beyond the realms of naturalism, into folktale, myth, ritual and magic realism, in order to tell their tales. But she and her storytellers are always aware of their connection to the ordinary community. And she, in particular, always takes care to relate what happens with her exceptional characters to the larger narratives of what has happened, in the West, between American Indians and whites. To that extent, she is telling a tale that derives its power from its typicality, its roots in the history of a people. That is just as true of the fourth novel in the tetralogy, *The Bingo Palace* (1994). The title here refers to a bingo parlour owned by a member of the Lamartine family, Lyman. But another member of the Chippewa, Lipsha Morrissey, is the central character, a young man who has returned home from Fargo in search of a meaningful life. 'Money is alive', Lyman tells Lipsha, as he tries to persuade him to invest, to come in with him on 'a more enormous bingo hall'. Circulating around the tensions created by this proposal, the novel then explores the dualities and tensions in Native American culture: and, not least, the difference between the solidity of ritual, ceremony and community and the abstractions of power and money – between seeing the land as an extension of being and seeing it simply as 'real estate'.

The link Erdrich habitually forges between the extraordinary and the ordinary, personal story and Native American history, is particularly noticeable in the third and arguably the finest book in the tetralogy, *Tracks*, published in 1988. 'We started dying before the snow', the novel begins, as one narrator, Nanapush, takes his audience back to 1912. This was a crucial time. The challenge of white disease killing Native peoples, which Nanapush refers to here, becomes a paradigm of cultural invasion and crisis. The spread of epidemic disease, we learn, land loss, confinement on reservations, forced assimilation and intertribal conflicts, all had a traumatic effect on Indian communities. Covering the years from 1912 to 1924, *Tracks* then dramatizes the deep divisions between 'conservative' and 'progressive', or 'hostile' and 'friendly' members of these communities: that is, between those who were resistant to the pressure from federal government to assimilate into white society and culture and those who were more positively responsive. Rather than dramatizing those divisions in conventionally historical terms, however, Erdrich, typically for her, turns to the personal. History, for her, is not so much a singular objective narrative as a multidimensional, often magical, one created out of the conflict between various vibrant and often fallible voices. The voices are many, as Erdrich spreads her story out to an extended network of characters whose lives are all dramatically altered by the struggle to cope with the forces undermining traditional Chippewa culture. But two voices matter, in particular, since the story is structured around two alternating narrators. One is Nanapush, the storyteller whose story begins the book. His stance is clear from the fact that he refers to his people as the 'Anishinabe', meaning First or Original People, the tribal name for itself, rather than 'Chippewa', the name given by the United States government to the tribe in legal agreements. The other is a woman called Pauline Puyat, of mixed Chippewa and white ancestry, who tries to deny her Indian identity and leaves the Indian community to become a nun.

The life of Nanapush, as he recalls and narrates it, straddles the time from when the Chippewas still lived freely off the land to when they lived off government supplies on the reservation. 'I guided the last buffalo hunt. I saw the last bear shot. I trapped the last beaver with a pelt of more than two year's growth,' he recollects. 'I spoke aloud the words of the government treaty, and refused to sign the settlement papers that would take away our woods and lake. I axed the last birch that was older than I.' *Tracks* captures the conflicted state in which the Chippewas live, now that their culture and even their character have been invaded by the whites, and their lives of hunting and gathering, living with the earth, all but lost to anything but memory. But it also conjures up the animistic world that people like Nanapush still inhabit. In this novel, 'the spirits of the dead' accompany the living, people resort to magic and medicine to accomplish their aims, and a woman may drown three times and be three times saved – thanks, it seems, to the water spirit or manitou, Misshepeshu. The land may be subject to taxes, but it still seems alive; and, as Nanapush says, 'land is the only thing that lasts from life to life'. Nanapush may be a richly historical character, but he carries with him traces of Native American folktale and legend. His name links him, it turns out, with the Chippewa trickster Naanabozho, who appears in traditional oral narratives as a culture hero. 'Nanapush. That's what you'll be called,' his father tells him. 'Because it's got to do with trickery and living in the bush. The first Nanapush stole fire. You will steal hearts.' A joker, trickster and a storyteller, Nanapush is also a mediator, though. When young, he reveals, he served as a government interpreter. Older, accepting what he calls 'this new way of wielding influence, this method of leading others with a pen and piece of paper', he is elected tribal chairman. Mediating between white and Indian society, even while he maintains his traditional view of the world, Nanapush is no more simply one thing or another – man or trickster, tied to old ways or captivated by the new – than *Tracks* is simply a record of cultural resistance or surrender, survival or defeat. The strength of both the character and the novel lies, precisely, in their many dimensions, their density of texture. What is told here is a story of triumph not despite but through tragedy, the heroism of continuance against all the odds. As Nanapush recollects greeting his granddaughter Lulu, on her return from a boarding school off the reservation, the nature of that triumph is caught in a single, organic image that concludes the novel. 'We gave against your rush like creaking oaks,' he tells Lulu, 'held on, braced ourselves together in the fierce dry wind.'

'Postindian mixedblood': Gerald Vizenor uses that phrase several times in his self-chronicle, *Interior Landscapes: Autobiographical Myths and Metaphors* (1990). It could act as a mnemonic for a life and a career that includes more than thirty published books and a vast quantity of shorter pieces. Contrariety, a willingness to resist, even deconstruct, all cultural categories, has always been his trademark. And, in the pursuit of his transgressive project, he has drawn into his armoury both postmodern cultural theory and such Native American forms of resistance as the trickster or joker. Vizenor uses the term 'postindian' to express the notion that, since Native lives have been so encrusted in myth and stereotype, it is necessary to move on from, or leave behind, all fabricated versions of 'the Indian'. The 'survivance', as he calls it, of Native life, in all its variety, is imperative. But that, if it is to be realized, depends on what Vizenor, in a collection of essays titled *Crossbloods* (1992), has described as socioacupuncture, a cultural striptease which 'reverses the documents, deflates data, dissolves historical time, releases the pressure in captured images and exposes the pale inventors of the tribes'. Or, in other words, the most effective response to false images is not just more accuracy, better history, but a creative awareness – using humour, self-reflexivity, myth and dream – of how such images have to be deconstructed and used rather than ignored and dismissed. Vizenor uses the term 'crossblood', in turn, not just because he himself is of a radically mixed heritage, including Chippewa-Ojibwa origins among many others, but because he sees identity as dialogic, double-edged and mobile. Crucially, he uses this term, or 'tribal people', rather than the term 'Indian'. This is, not least, because he insists to be an Indian now is to be a mixedblood, both racially and culturally, even though the cultural traditions in which Indians have been represented have always associated pure blood with authenticity and 'half-breeds' or mixedbloods with degeneration. Waging war against what he regards as the 'terminal creeds' of American myth, Vizenor has tried to liberate 'Indianness' from its invented simulations and one-dimensional portrayals, whether originating in the white or Indian world. Both, as he sees it, serve to restrict Native people, producing only a 'narrative of tribal doom', fixed images of 'Vanishing Americans' caught at the moment of their vanishing. 'The trick', Vizenor explains in his novel *The Trickster of Liberty: Tribal Heirs to a Wild Baronage at Petronia* (1988), 'in seven words is to *elude historicism, racial representations, and remain historical.*' It is to create a new sense, and a new sensation, of tribal presence in the ruins of the old; using 'wonder, chance, coincidence' to produce a vision of individual and communal being that is always on the move, always cutting across and undercutting boundaries – and that flies forward through the 'shimmer of the imagination'.

Characteristically, Vizenor has said that he wants his work to 'break out of all restrictions', 'out of invented cultures and repression', to 'break out of the measures that people make'. So, although some of his work is more clearly fiction or non-fiction, he tends to move freely across genres. Fiction, autobiography, history, social or cultural commentary, folklore, myth and fantasy: all are always, in his writing, in unstable and exhilarating relation with each other. As a result, the reader is never permitted to forget the problematic nature of any representation of the American Indian, including self-representation. Boundaries are further blurred, to the point of invisibility, by Vizenor's habits of revision and repeating material, only slightly altered, from one book to another. Vizenor's first novel, for instance, *Darkness in Saint Louis Bearheart* (1978), was reissued as *Bearheart: The Heirship Chronicles* (1990). Since its initial publication, he has produced among other books that might be classed as novels (although not always are), *Griever: An American Monkey King in China* (1987), *The Heirs of Columbus* (1991), *Dead Voices: Natural Agonies in the New World* (1992) and *Hotline Healers: An Almost Browne Novel* (1997). Along with these there have been series of linked stories such as *Landfill Meditations* (1991), collections of essays (including *Manifest Manners: Postindian Warriors of Survivance* [1994]), as well as an autobiography, poems and journalism. All continue his project of mixing trickster language with the strategies of postmodernism so as to become a textual shapeshifter, deinventing and then reinventing the very notion of the 'Indian'. *Heirs of Columbus* is as typical of all these shapeshifting texts as any other: above all, in its author's refusal to conform to generic conventions or cultural expectations. Published a year before the quincentenary celebrations of the 'discovery' of America by Columbus, it is a cunning mix of science fiction, satire, fantasy, trickster tale and postmodern murder mystery. Not content with either simply celebrating or dismissing the concept of discovery, Vizenor expropriates the practice itself. This strange 'tribal story' makes its own 'discovery', that Columbus was a man of 'mixedblood', including Mayan. The controlling idea of Columbus as a 'crossblood', with its provocative rider that 'mongrels created the best humans', realizes several purposes. It reinforces the hybrid nature of the text; it comments on the doubtful nature of what the white world calls history; it puts in question the authority of any supposedly authoritative account. This revisionist version of American history, Vizenor intimates, is quite as plausible, as (un)reliable, as the standard one, which claims that Columbus 'discovered' a 'New World'. By reimagining the man who mistakenly called the tribes 'Indians', Vizenor not only rattles the bars of the national tradition and the history manuals. He also stakes a claim for his own teasing, transgressive styling of those tribes, one resistant to what is called here 'the notion of blood quantums, racial identification, and tribal enrolment'. The styling is, of course, to return to that phrase, as 'postindian mixedblood'.

The fiction of Sherman Alexei maps a territory in which the mysticism of Silko and the postmodern tricksterism of Vizenor are likely to coexist along with the contemporary reality of casinos and sweatlodges, rock music and ancient ritual, landfill and sacred sites. Alexei's first novel is titled *Reservation Blues* (1996) and reservation blues music, we are told, is a 'little bit of everything'. It is a 'tribal music' that cannibalizes elements from all kinds of distinctive idioms – delta blues, country and western, punk, heavy rock, American Indian traditions – to create 'new songs' responsive to the crisscross 'crossroads' culture Native Americans now inhabit. And it is the music of Alexei's stories. They are exhilaratingly ragged and freewheeling, with an immediacy, energy, rawness and sometimes downright clumsiness – clumsiness here seems almost a measure of authenticity – that contrasts with the measured tone of the work of Momaday – or, for that matter, the minimalist cadences of Welch. Alexei registers a 'cable-television reservation world' in which the 'reservation staples' include 'Diet Pepsi, Spam, Wonder bread, and a cornucopia of various carbohydrates, none of them complex'. It is a place where members of the tribe queue up at 'the Trading Post' to try out a new slot machine, and where poverty, alcoholism, domestic discord and community faction often lead to violence. And he registers this 'in-between' place, the 'rez' where identity always resembles a 'goofy . . . mixed drink', in multidimensional terms that are quite different from those of Erdrich. Nervous, edgy, with the syncopated rhythms of jazz, blues or rock – music, the guess is in *Reservation Blues*, 'just might be the most important thing there is' – his narratives concoct a strange brew of snappy one-liners and ghostly dreams, jokes and anger, laughter and pain. 'There's a little bit of magic in everything and then some loss to even things out': that line, borrowed from the rock singer Lou Reed, serves as an epitaph to one of Alexei's books. It offers another handy compass to the reader when entering all of them. This is a fiction on fast forward, careering wildly in tone and packed with characters close to caricature. But always, at the back, we can hear echoes of older, still enduring ways of understanding and being in the world that remain distinctive to Native American culture. Among the many other elements that coexist here, in this tense, dynamic fictive environment, are matter and memory, present and past.

Alexei, who comes from the Spokane and Coeur d'Alene tribes, produced a substantial body of work even before he reached the age of thirty. There have been three collections of poetry (*The Business of Fancydancing* [1992], *First Indian on the Moon* [1993], *Old Shirts and New Skins* [1993]), a volume of short stories (*The*

Lone Ranger and Tonto Fistfight in Heaven [1998]) and two novels (*Reservation Blues, Indian Killer* [1996]). Much of this work relates to the area in and around the Spokane reservation in the eastern part of Washington State. This is the setting, for instance, for most of *Reservation Blues*. It is a divided, dual territory that seems both disabling and empowering. 'The word *gone* echoed all over the reservation. The reservation was gone itself, just a shell of its former self, just a fragment of the whole,' we learn during the course of the novel. 'But the reservation still possessed power and rage, music and loss, joys and jealousy,' the narrator then adds. 'The reservation tugged at the lives of its Indians, stole from them in the middle of the night, watched impassively as the horses and salmon disappeared. But the reservation forgave too.' A crossroads near Wellpinit, 'the only town on the reservation', is appropriately the starting point for the story. The African American blues guitarist Robert Johnson miraculously arrives there. Having made a deal with the 'Gentleman', or the Devil, to become a great guitarist, he has, he says, been on the run since faking his death in 1938. 'Old and tired' now, and unable to play his guitar, he has 'walked from crossroads to crossroads'; he has travelled to the reservation in search of a cure for a sickness he 'can't get rid of'. His guitar is taken up by a young Spokane Indian on the reservation called Victor Joseph. With two other young Spokane Indians, Junior Polatkin and Thomas Builds-the-Fire, Victor then forms an 'all-Indian rock and blues band', calling themselves Coyote Springs. The blues they play are, we are told, 'ancient, aboriginal, indigenous'. Sticking to cover versions of songs by other musicians at first, they gradually turn to their own 'new songs'. Energetic, eclectic, chaotic, these songs are an apt expression for a generation of Indians who have grown up watching 'bad television', eating fast food or 'wish sandwiches' – 'two slices of bread with only wishes in between' – and who are constantly reminded that 'white people owned everything'. At first, the band enjoys some success. They are even invited to New York by an outfit called Cavalry Records to make some demonstration tapes. The trip and the recording tryout are, however, both disastrous. The band falls apart. Victor sinks into alcoholism and apathy; Junior kills himself; and Thomas, who gradually emerges as the central character, leaves the 'rez' for the city accompanied by Chess and Checkers Warm Water, two sisters from the Flathead reservation in Montana who had earlier joined the band. 'Songs were waiting for them in the city', Thomas believes. He has become a mobile adventurer, who nevertheless takes the memories, even some of the mysticism, of the 'rez' with him. Robert Johnson, meanwhile, chooses to stay where he is. 'I think this tribe's been waiting for me for a long time,' he says. 'I think these Indians might need me. Maybe need me and music. Besides, it's beautiful here.'

In dramatizing the fortunes of Coyote Springs, Alexei plays with several possibilities. The band and its music catch the tensions in contemporary Native American culture, convey ways of turning pain into poetry, loss into story and song, that are similar to Alexei's own, and concentrate the raw feeling and rough magic of the entire narrative. Also, in their rise and fall, the band connects up with history. After all, the record company that spurns Coyote Springs bears a name, Cavalry

---

816   American Literature since 1945

Records, that recalls earlier white interventions in Native American territory and culture. And, freewheeling between past and present, the narrative depicts the executives of the company, called Wright and Sheridan, as all too substantial ghosts. They are the nineteenth-century military leaders Colonel George Wright and General Philip Sheridan, living on into the late twentieth century. The link is clear, and clearly forged in its downbeat way, between the victimization of Native Americans in an earlier age and the exploitation, the cultural and commercial sidelining of Native Americans now. Wright, in particular, is described as the man who in 1858 ordered the killing of hundreds of Spokane horses. And the spirits of those horses appear sporadically throughout the novel, in a kind of collective narrative memorializing of pain, a mystic commemoration of a past that keeps repeating itself – that just will not, cannot, go away. After Coyote Springs fails to perform as required in the recording studio, Wright sees in the band 'the faces of millions of Indians, beaten, scarred, by smallpox and frostbite, split open by bayonets and bullets'. Gazing at his own hands, he sees 'the blood stains there'. That is his vision, the significant past that haunts him. The past that haunts the central Native American character Thomas and his travelling companions, at the end of *Reservation Blues*, is utterly, remarkably different. As Thomas, Chess and Checkers leave for the city in their van, they see shadows that become horses. 'The horses were following, leading Indians toward the city,' we are told, 'while other Indians were traditional dancing in the Longhouse after the feast, while drunk Indians stood outside the Trading Post, drinking and laughing.' In the van, the three travellers begin to sing. 'They sang together with the shadow horses: we are alive, we'll keep living. Songs were waiting for them up there in the dark.' It is with this visionary mix of myth, the material and magic, the past and the possible, that *Reservation Blues* ends: in an ending that is, of course, no ending at all. 'Thomas drove through the dark. He drove,' are the final words. 'Chess and Checkers reached out of their window and held tightly to the manes of those shadow horses running alongside the blue van.' In the end is the beginning, it seems. The first Americans have not vanished; they are journeying on, transforming mourning into music, commemorating the 'dead Indians' but also celebrating the living. Just like those generations that lived American lives for thousands of years before the arrival of Columbus, these are people turning their American world into their own American words. This is a new song perhaps, but it echoes an ancient one.

further reading

The following list of books is necessarily and highly selective, even though I have omitted works on individual authors. I have tried to choose a range of introductory and more advanced works that bear witness to the range and variety of American literatures and that might be useful to both those new to the subject and those pursuing more specialized studies. I have arranged most of the titles according to the chapters of this history. Inevitably, there are many books listed here that cut across one or more, or perhaps even all, of the chronological boundaries mapped out by the chapters. In such cases, I have simply placed books under the chapter heading, and in the period, where I myself have found them most useful as sources of information and guidance. Readers are advised, if they are interested in a particular subject or theme – and perhaps even if they are not – to browse through the list as a whole for advice about further reading.

Bibliographies and Reference Works

Andrews, William L., Foster, Frances Smith and Harris, Trudier (eds.), *The Concise Oxford Companion to African American Literature* (2001).

Bordman, Gerald (ed.), *The Oxford Companion to the American Theatre* (1984; 2nd ed., 1992).

Bradbury, Malcolm, Franco, Jean and Mottram, Eric (eds.), *The Penguin Companion to Literature: The United States and Latin America* (1971).

Cheung, King-kok (ed.), *An Interethnic Companion to Asian American Literature* (1996).

Cheung, King-kok and Yogi, Stan (eds.), *Asian American Literature: An Annotated Bibliography* (1988).

Davidson, Cathy and Wagner-Martin, Linda (eds.), *The Oxford Companion to Women's Writing in the United States* (1999).

Elliott, Emory Elliott (ed.), *The Columbia Literary History of the United States* (1988).

Gohdes, Clarence and Marovitz, Stanford (eds.), *Bibliographical Guide to the Study of the Literature of the U.S.A.* (1954; 5th revised ed., 1984).

Hart, James and Heininger, Philip W. (eds.), *The Oxford Companion to American Literature* (1941; 6th revised ed., 1995).

Herbert, Rosemary (ed.), *The Oxford Companion to Crime and Mystery Writing* (1999).

Kirkpatrick, D. L. (ed.), *Reference Guide to American Literature* (1987).

Leary, Lewis, *American Literature: A Study and Research Guide* (1954–71).

Lomeli, Francis A. and Shirley, Carl R. (eds.), *Chicano Writers: First, Second, and Third Series* (1989, 1992, 1999).

Martinez, Julio A. and Lomeli, Francisco A. (eds.), *Chicano Literature* (1985).

Perkins, George, Perkins, Barbara and Leininger, Philip, *HarperCollins Reader's Encyclopaedia of American Literature* (2002).

Salzman, Jack (ed.), *The Cambridge Handbook of American Literature* (1986).

Schweik, Robert C. and Riesner, Dieter (eds.), *Reference Sources in English and American Literature: An Annotated Bibliography* (1977).

Tuck, Donald Henry (ed.), *Encyclopedia of Science Fiction Through 1968* (1978).

Tuska, Jon and Piekawski, Vicki (eds.), *Encyclopedia of Frontier and Western Fiction* (1983).

Tuska, Jon and Piekawski, Vicki (eds.), *The Frontier Experience: A Reader's Guide to the Life and Literature of the American West* (1984).

Wiget, Andrew (ed.), *Dictionary of Native American Literature* (1994).

Witalec, Janet, Chapman, Jeffery and Giroux, Christopher (eds.), *Native North American Literature: Biographical and Critical Information on Native Writers and Orators from the United States and Canada from Histori* (1994).

Woodress, James and Robbins, J. Albert (eds.), *American Literary Scholarship: An Annual* (1965–).

Anthologies

Baym, Nina et al. (eds.), *The Norton Anthology of American Literature* (1998).

Eduardo, R. del Rio (ed.), *The Prentice Hall Anthology of Latino Literature* (2001).

Fowke, Edith and Glazer, Joe (eds.), *Songs of Work and Protest* (1973).

Gates, Henry Louis and McKay, Nellie (eds.), *The Norton Anthology of African American Literature* (1997).

Gilbert, Sandra M. (ed.), *The Norton Anthology of Literature by Women: The Traditions in English* (1996).

Horwitz, Richard P., *The American Studies Anthology* (2001).

Lauter, Paul et al. (eds.), *The Heath Anthology of American Literature* (1990; 3rd revised ed., 1998).

Lauter, Paul and Fitzgerald, Ann (eds.), *Literature, Class, and Culture: An Anthology* (2001).

Lim, Shirley (ed.), *Asian American Literature: An Anthology* (2000).

McQuade, Donald et al. (eds.), *The Harper American Literature* (1993).

McQuade, Donald and Atwan, Robert (eds.), *Popular Writing in America* (1993).

Parini, Jay (ed.), *The Columbia Anthology of American Poetry* (1995).

Purdy, John and Ruppert, James (eds.), *Nothing But the Truth: An Anthology of Native American Literature* (2000).

Rebolledo, Tey Diana et al. (eds.), *Infinite Divisions: An Anthology of Chicano Literature* (1993).

Rothenberg, Jerome and Quasha, George, *America A Prophecy* (1974).

Shell, Marc and Sollors, Werner (eds.), *The Multilingual Anthology of American Literature* (2000).

Wolf, Robert (ed.), *An American Mosaic: Prose and Poetry by Everyday Folk* (1999).

Zandy, Janet (ed.), *Calling Home: Working-class Women's Writings: An Anthology* (1990).

Chapter 1 The First Americans: American Literature Before and During the Colonial and Revolutionary Periods

Aldridge, A. Owen, *Early American Literature: A Comparatist Approach* (1982).

Amory, Hugh (ed.), *A History of the Book in America: The Colonial Book in the Atlantic World* (1999).

Andrews, William L. et al. (eds.), *Journeys in New Worlds: Early American Women's Narratives* (1991).

Arias, Santa (ed.), *Mapping Colonial Spanish Americas: Places and Commonplaces of Identity, Culture, and Experience* (2002).

Axtell, James, *After Columbus: Essays in the Ethnohistory of North America* (1989).

Bach, Rebecca Ann, *Colonial Transformations: The Cultural Production of the New Atlantic World, 1588–1640* (2000).

Bailyn, Bernard, *The Ideological Origins of the American Revolution* (1992).

Bercovitch, Sacvan (ed.), *The American Puritan Imagination: Essays in Revaluation* (1974).

Bercovitch, Sacvan, *The Puritan Origins of the American Self* (1975).

Bercovitch, Sacvan, *The American Jeremiad* (1978).

Bercovitch, Sacvan (ed.), *The Cambridge History of American Literature. Volume One: 1590–1820* (1994).

Bonomi, Patricia, *Under the Cope of Heaven: Religion, Society, and Politics in Colonial America* (1986).

Boorstin, Daniel, *The Americans: The Colonial Experience* (1958).

Brown, Richard D., *Knowledge is Power: The Diffusion of Information in Early America 1700–1865* (1989).

Bruce, Dickson D., *The Origins of African American Literature 1680–1865* (2001).

Brumm, Ursula, *American Thought and Religious Typology* (1970).

Burkhart, Louise M., *Before Guadalupe: The Virgin Mary in Early Colonial Nahuatl Literature* (2001).

Burnham, Michelle, *Captivity and Sentiment: Cultural Exchanges in American Literature, 1682–1861* (1997).

Burnstein, Andrew, *Sentimental Democracy* (1999).

Caldwell, Patricia, *The Puritan Conversion Narrative: The Beginnings of American Expression* (1983).

Carnup, John, *Out of the Wilderness: The Emergence of an American Identity in Colonial New England* (1990).

Carroll, Peter N., *Puritanism and the Wilderness: The Intellectual Significance of the New England Frontier 1629–1700* (1969).

Castiglia, Christopher, *Bound and Determined: Captivity, Culture-crossing, and White Womanhood from Mary Rowlandson to Patty Hearst* (1996).

Conforti, Joseph A., *Imagining New England: Explorations of Regional Identity from the Pilgrims to the Mid-Twentieth Century* (2001).

Copeland, David A., *Colonial American Newspapers: Character and Content* (1997).

Cressy, David, *Coming Over: Migration and Communication Between England and New England in the Seventeenth Century* (1987).

Daly, Robert, *God's Altar: The World and the Flesh in Puritan Poetry* (1978).

Dameron, J. Lesley, *No Fairer Land: Studies in Southern Literature Before 1900* (1986).

Davidson, Cathy, *Revolution and the Word: The Rise of the Novel in America* (1986).

Davis, Richard B., *Intellectual Life in the Colonial South* (3 vols; 1978).

Delbanco, Andrew, *The Puritan Ordeal* (1989).

Derounian-Stodola, Kathryn Zabelle (ed.), *Early American Literature: Essays Honoring Harrison T. Meserole* (1992).

Elliott, Emory (ed.), *American Colonial Writers, 1735–1781* (1978).

Elliott, Emory, *Revolutionary Writers: Literature and Authority in the New Republic, 1725–1810* (1982).

Elliott, Emory, *The Cambridge Introduction to Early American Literature* (2002).

Elliott, J. H., *The Old World and the New: 1492–1650* (1970).

Emerson, Everett H. (ed.), *Major Writers of Early American Literature* (1972).

Emerson, Everett H. (ed.), *American Literature 1764–1789* (1977).

Faery, Rebecca Blevins, *Cartographies of Desire: Captivity, Race, and Sex in the Shaping of an American Narrative* (1999).

Ferguson, Robert A., *The American Enlightenment* (1997).

Fliegelman, Jay, *Prodigals and Pilgrims: The American Revolution Against Patriarchal Authority, 1750–1800* (1982).

Foster, David Williams (ed.), *Writers of the Spanish Colonial Period: A Collection of Essays* (1997).

Franklin, Wayne, *Discoverers, Explorers, Settlers: The Diligent Writers of Early America* (1979).

Giles, Paul, *Transatlantic Insurrections: British Culture and the Formation of American Literature, 1730–1860* (2001).

Gilmore, Michael T. (ed.), *Early American Literature: A Collection of Critical Essays* (1981).

Gilroy, Paul, *The Black Atlantic: Modernity and Double Consciousness* (1994).

Gray, Richard, *Writing the South: Ideas of an American Region* (1986).

Greene, Jack P., *The Intellectual Construction of America: Exceptionalism and American Identity from 1492 to 1800* (1993).

Greene, Roland, *Unrequited Conquests: Love and Empire in the Colonial Americas* (2000).

Gunn, Giles (ed.), *Early American Writing* (1993).

Hammond, Jeffrey A., *The American Puritan Elegy: A Literary and Cultural Study* (2000).

Harris, Sharon M. (ed.), *American Women Writers to 1800* (1996).

Hartman, John D., *Providence Tales and the Birth of American Literature* (1999).

Herrera-Sobek, M., *Reconstructing a Chicano/a Literary Heritage: Hispanic Colonial Literature of the Southwest* (1993).

Hulme, Peter, *Colonial Encounters: Europe and the Native Caribbean, 1492–1797* (1986).

Jara, Rene and Spadaccini, Nicholas, *Re/Discovering Colonial Writing* (1989).

Jennings, Francis, *The Invasion of America: Indians, Colonialism and the Cant of Conquest* (1975).

Johnson, Julie Green, *Women in Colonial Spanish American Literature: Literary Images* (1983).

Johnson, Julie Green, *Satire in Colonial Spanish America: Turning the New World Upside Down* (1993).

Jones, Howard M., *O Strange New World: American Culture: The Formative Years* (1964).

Jones, Howard M., *The Literature of Virginia in the Seventeenth Century* (1968).

Jordan, Winthrop, *White Over Black: American Attitudes Toward the Negro, 1550–1812* (1968).

Josephy, Alvin M., Jr (ed.), *America in 1492: The World of the Indian Peoples Before the Arrival of Columbus* (1992).

Kammen, Michael, *A Season of Youth: The American Revolution and the Historical Imagination* (1978).

Kaufman, Michael W., *Institutional Individualism: Conversion, Exile, and Nostalgia in Puritan New England* (1998).

Kerber, Linda, *Women of the Republic: Intellect and Ideology in Revolutionary America* (1980).

Kibbey, Ann, *The Interpretation of Material Shapes in Puritanism: A Study of Rhetoric, Prejudice and Violence* (1986).

Kolodny, Annette, *The Land Before Her: Fantasy and Experience of the American Frontier 1630–1860* (1984).

Kopper, Philip, *The Smithsonian Book of North American Indians: Before the Coming of the Europeans* (1986).

Kroeber, Karl, *Traditional Literatures of the American Indian: Texts and Interpretations* (1981).

Landsman, Ned C., *From Colonials to Provincials: American Thought and Culture, 1680–1760* (1997).

Lawson-Peebles, R., *Landscape and Expression in Revolutionary America: The World Turned Upside Down* (1988).

Leverenz, David, *The Language of Puritan Feeling: An Exploration in Literature, Psychology, and Social History* (1980).

Lomeli, Francisco (ed.), *Handbook of Hispanic Cultures in the United States: Literature and Art* (1993).

Lowance, Mason I., *The Language of Canaan: Metaphor and Symbol in New England from the Puritans to the Transcendentalists* (1983).

McGiffert, Michael (ed.), *Puritanism and the American Experience* (1969).

Mackenthun, Gesa, *Metaphors of Dispossession: American Beginnings and the Translation of Empire, 1492–1637* (1997).

May, Henry F., *The Enlightenment in America* (1976).

Miller, Perry, *The New England Mind: The Seventeenth Century* (1939).

Miller, Perry, *The New England Mind: From Colony to Province* (1953).

Morgan, Edmund, *Visible Saints: The History of a Puritan Idea* (1963).

Morison, Samuel, *Intellectual Life in Early New England* (1956).

Mott, Frank Luther, *A History of American Magazines* (5 vols; 1938–68), *Volume One: 1741–1850.*

Mulford, Carla (ed.), *American Women Prose Writers to 1820* (1998).

Munk, Linda, *The Devil's Mousetrap: Redemption and Colonial American Literature* (1997).

Murdock, Kenneth B., *Literature and Theology in Colonial New England* (1949).

Norton, Mary B., *Liberty's Daughters: The Revolutionary Experience of American Women, 1750–1800* (1980).

Nye, Russell B., *The Cultural Life of the New Nation* (1960).

Nye, Russell B., *American Literary History, 1607–1830* (1970).

Pagden, Anthony, *European Encounters with the New World* (1993).

Percy, Josephine Ketcham, *Studies in Literary Types in Seventeenth-century America, 1607–1710* (1991).

Pratt, Mary Louise, *Imperial Eyes: Travel Writing and Transculturation* (1992).

Promis, Jose et al., *The Identity of Hispanoamerica: An Interpretation of Colonial Literature* (1991).

Regis, Pamela, *Describing Early America: Bartram, Jefferson, Crevecoeur, and the Rhetoric of Natural History* (1992).

Richards, Jeffrey H., *Theatre Enough: American Culture and the Metaphor of the World Stage, 1607–1789* (1991).

Richardson, Gary A., *American Drama from the Colonial Period through World War I: A Critical History* (1997).

Sayre, Gordon M., *Les Sauvages Americains: Representations of Native Americans in French and English Colonial Literature, 1730–1860* (2001).

Scanlan, Thomas, *Colonial Writing and the New World 1583–1671: Allegories of Desire* (1999).

Scheik, William J., *Design in Puritan American Literature* (1992).

Scheik, William J., *Authority and Female Authorship in Colonial America* (1998).

Schmidt, Klaus H. (ed.), *Early America Re-explained: New Readings in Colonial, Early National, and Antebellum Culture* (1997).

Schweitzer, Ivy, *The Work of Self-representation: Lyric Poetry in Colonial New England* (1991).

Seelye, John, *Beautiful Machine: Rivers and the Republican Plan 1755–1825* (1991).

Shields, David, *Oracles of Empire: Poetry, Politics, and Commerce in British America, 1690–1750* (1990).

Shields, David, *Civil Tongues and Polite Letters in British America* (1997).

Shields, John C., *The American Aeneas: Classical Origins of the American Self* (2001).

Shuffleton, Frank (ed.), *A Mixed Race: Ethnicity in Early America* (1993).

Shaw, Peter, *American Patriots and the Rituals of Revolution* (1981).

Shea, Daniel B., *Spiritual Autobiography in Early America* (1968).

Silverman, Kenneth A., *A Cultural History of the American Revolution 1763–1789* (1976).

Spengemann, William A., *A New World of Words: Redefining Early American Literature* (1994).

Spurr, David, *The Rhetoric of Empire: Colonial Discourse in Journalism, Travel Writing, and Imperial Administration* (1993).

Swann, Brian (ed.), *Smoothing the Ground: Essays on Native American Oral Literature* (1983).

Tilton, Robert S., *Pocahontas: The Evolution of an American Narrative* (1994).

Tichi, Cecelia, *New Earth: Environmental Reform in American Literature from the Puritans through Whitman* (1979).

Warner, Michael, *Letters of the Republic: Publication and the Public Sphere in Eighteenth-century America* (1990).

Watts, Emily Stipes, *The Poetry of American Women from 1632 to 1945* (1977).

Wright, Louis B., *The Cultural Life of the American Colonies, 1607–1763* (1957).

Yazawa, Melvin, *From Colonies to Commonwealth* (1985).

Ziff, Larzer, *Puritanism in America: New Culture in a New World* (1975).

Chapter 2 Inventing Americas: The Making of American Literature, 1800–1865

Aaron, Daniel, *The Unwritten War: American Writers and the Civil War* (1973).

Anderson, Quentin, *The Imperial Self: An Essay in American Literary and Cultural History* (1971).

Andrews, William L., *To Tell a Free Story: The First Century of Afro-American Autobiography 1760–1865* (1988).

Arms, George, *The Fields Were Green* (1953).

Barnes, Elizabeth, *States of Sympathy: Seduction and Democracy in the American Novel* (1997).

Bauer, Dale M. and Gould, Philip (eds.), *The Cambridge Companion to Nineteenth-century American Women's Writing* (2002).

Baym, Nina, *Women's Fiction: A Guide to Novels by and about Women, 1820–1870* (1978).

Baym, Nina, *Novels, Readers, and Reviewers in Antebellum America* (1984).

Baym, Nina, *Feminism and American Literary History* (1992).

Baym, Nina, *American Women Writers and the Work of History, 1790–1860* (1995).

Beetham, Margaret, *A Magazine of Her Own? Domesticity and Desire in the Woman's Magazine, 1800–1914* (1996).

Bell, Michael, *The Development of American Romance: The Sacrifice of Relation* (1980).

Bercovitch, Sacvan and Jehlen, Myra (eds.), *Ideology and Classic American Literature* (1983).

Bewley, Marius, *The Complex Fate: Hawthorne, Henry James, and Some Other American Writers* (1952).

Bewley, Marius, *The Eccentric Design: Form in the Classic American Novel* (1959).

Blair, Walter, *Native American Humor, 1800–1900* (1937).

Blair, Walter, *Tall Tale America* (1944).

Blair, Walter, *Horse Sense in American Humor from Benjamin Franklin to Ogden Nash* (1962).

Blair, Walter and Hill, Hamlin, *America's Humor, From Poor Richard to Doonesbury* (1978).

Boller, Paul F., Jr, *American Transcendentalism, 1830–1860: An Intellectual Inquiry* (1975).

Brodhead, Richard, *Hawthorne, Melville, and the Novel* (1976).

Brodhead, Richard, *Cultures of Letters: Scenes of Reading and Writing in Nineteenth-century America* (1997).

Brown, Gillian, *Domestic Individualism: Imagining Self in Nineteenth-century America* (1990).

Brown, Herbert R., *The Sentimental Novel in America, 1789–1860* (1942).

Buell, Lawrence, *New England Literary Culture: From Revolution Through Renaissance* (1986).

Buell, Lawrence, *The Environmental Imagination: Thoreau, Nature Writing and the Formation of American Culture* (1995).

Buell, Lawrence, *Writing for an Endangered World: Literature, Culture, and Environment in the U.S. and Beyond* (2001).

Bush, Clive, *The Dream of Reason: American Consciousness and Cultural Achievement from Independence to the Civil War* (1978).

Cady, E. H. (ed.), *Literature of the Early Republic* (1950).

Carby, Hazel, *Reconstructing Womanhood: The Emergence of the African American Woman Novelist* (1995).

Castranovo, Russ, *Fathering the Nation: American Genealogies of Slavery and Freedom* (1995).

Chapman, Mary and Hendler, Glenn, *Sentimental Men: Masculinity and the Politics of Affect in American Culture* (1999).

Chase, Richard, *The American Novel and its Tradition* (1957).

Cherniavsky, Eva, *That Pale Mother Rising: Sentimental Discourses and the Imitation of Motherhood in 19th Century America* (1995).

Cogan, Francis, *All-American Girl: The Ideal of Real Womanhood in Mid-Nineteenth-century America* (1989).

Connor, Kimberley Rae, *Conversions and Visions in the Writings of African-American Women* (1994).

Conrad, Susan P., *Perish the Thought: Intellectual Women in Romantic America, 1830–1860* (1976).

Cott, Nancy, *The Bonds of Womanhood: 'Woman's Sphere' in New England, 1780–1835* (1977).

Crain, Patricia, *The Story of A: The Alphabetization of America from the New England Primer to The Scarlet Letter* (2000).

Cullen, Jim, *The Civil War in Popular Culture: A Reusable Past* (1995).

Daerborn, Mary V., *Pocahontas's Daughters: Gender and Ethnicity in Early American Culture* (1986).

Davidson, Cathy (ed.), *Reading in America: Literature and Social History* (1989).

Dekker, George, *The American Historical Romance* (1987).

Elder, John (ed.), *American Nature Writers* (1996).

Ellis, Joseph J., *After the Revolution: Profiles of Early American Culture* (1979).

Ernest, John (ed.), *Resistance and Reformation in Nineteenth-century African-American Literature* (1995).

Erkkila, Betsy, *The Wicked Sisters: Women Poets, Literary History, and Discord* (1992).

Fabian, Ann, *The Unvarnished Truth: Personal Narratives in Nineteenth-century America* (2000).

Fahs, Alice, *The Imagined Civil War: Popular Literature of the North and South, 1861–1865* (2001).

Faust, Drew Gilpin, *A Sacred Circle: The Dilemma of the Intellectual in the Old South* (1977).

Feidelson, Charles S., Jr, *Symbolism and American Literature* (1953).

Fender, Stephen, *Plotting the Golden West: American Literature and the American West* (1982).

Fiedler, Leslie, *Love and Death in the American Novel* (1966).

Fisher, Philip, *Hard Facts: Setting and Form in the American Novel* (1985).

Fisher, Philip (ed.), *The New American Studies: Essays from Representations* (1991).

Foster, Francis Smith, *Written by Herself: Literary Production by African American Women, 1746–1892* (1993).

Foster, Francis Smith, *Witnessing Slavery: The Development of Ante-Bellum Slave Narratives* (1994).

Foster, Richard (ed.), *Six American Novelists of the Nineteenth Century: An Introduction* (1968).

Frederick, John T., *The Darkened Sky: Nineteenth-century American Novelists and Religion* (1989).

Fussell, Edwin, *Frontier: American Literature and the American West* (1965).

Gelpi, Albert, *The Tenth Muse: The Psyche of the American Poet* (1975).

Gilmore, Michael T., *The Middle Way: Puritanism and Ideology in American Romantic Fiction* (1977).

Gilmore, Michael T., *American Romanticism and the Marketplace* (1985).

Golden Taylor, J. et al. (eds.), *A Literary History of the American West* (1987).

Gould, Philip, *Covenant and Republic: Historical Romance and the Politics of Puritanism* (1996).

Grammer, John, *Pastoral and Politics in the Old South* (1996).

Gray, Janet, *She Wields a Pen: American Women Poets of the Nineteenth Century* (1997).

Griffin, Susan M., *'Who Set You Flowin?': The African American Migration Narrative* (1995).

Grossman, J. (ed.), *The Frontier in American Culture* (1994).

Gura, Philip, *The Wisdom of Words: Language, Theology, and Literature in the New England Renaissance* (1981).

Harris, Sharon M. (ed.), *Redefining the Political Novel: American Women Writers, 1797–1901* (1995).

Harris, Susan K., *Nineteenth-century American Women's Novels: Interpretive Strategies* (1990).

Hobbs, Catherine (ed.), *Nineteenth-century Women Learn to Write* (1995).

Hoffman, Daniel, *Form and Fable in American Fiction* (1961).

Holman, C. Hugh, *The Roots of Southern Writing* (1972).

Horwitz, Howard, *By the Law of Nature: Form and Value in Nineteenth-century America* (1991).

Hubbell, Jay B., *The South in American Literature, 1607–1900* (1954).

Irwin, John T., *American Hieroglyphics: The Symbol of the Egyptian Hieroglyphics in the American Renaissance* (1983).

Kaul, A. N., *The American Vision: Actual and Ideal Society in Nineteenth-century Fiction* (1963).

Kerber, Linda, *Federalists in Dissent: Imagery and Ideology in Jeffersonian America* (1970).

Kolodny, Annette, *The Lay of the Land: Metaphor as Experience and History in American Life and Literature* (1975).

Leary, Lewis, *Soundings: Some Early American Writers* (1975).

Lee, L. L. and Lewis, Merrill (eds.), *The Westering Experience in American Literature* (1977).

Lee, L. L. and Lewis, Merrill (eds.), *Women, Women Writers, and the West* (1980).

Lee, R. E., *From West to East: Studies in the Literature of the American West* (1966).

Levander, Caroline Field, *Voices of the Nation: Women and Public Speech in Nineteenth-century American Literature and Culture* (1998).

Levin, David, *History as Romantic Art: Bancroft, Prescott, Motley, Parkman* (1959).

Levin, Harry, *The Power of Blackness: Hawthorne, Poe, Melville* (1958).

Lewis, R. W. B., *The American Adam: Innocence, Tragedy, and Tradition in the Nineteenth Century* (1955).

Lively, Robert C., *Fiction Fights the Civil War* (1957).

Lynn, Kenneth, *The Comic Tradition in America* (1958).

Lyon, Thomas J. et al. (eds.), *A Literary History of the American West* (1974).

McKinsey, Elizabeth R., *Niagara Falls: Icon of the American Sublime* (1985).

McWilliams, John P., Jr, *Hawthorne, Melville, and the American Character* (1984).

McWilliams, John P., Jr, *The American Epic: Transforming the Genre, 1770–1860* (1990).

Matthiessen, F. O., *American Renaissance: Art and Expression in the Age of Emerson and Whitman* (1941).

Miller, David, *Dark Eden: The Swamp in Nineteenth-century American Culture* (1989).

Miller, Perry, *The Raven and the Whale: The War of Wits and Words in the Era of Poe and Melville* (1956).

Miller, Perry, *Nature's Nation* (1967).

Morrison, Toni, *Playing in the Dark: Whiteness and the Literary Imagination* (1992).

Mott, Frank Luther, *A History of American Magazines* (5 vols; 1938–68), *Volume Two: 1850–65*.

Papashvily, Helen White, *All the Happy Endings: A Study of the Domestic Novel in America, the Women Who Wrote It, the Women Who Read It, in the Nineteenth Century* (1956).

Pearce, Roy Harvey, *The Continuity of American Poetry* (1961).

Pease, Donald E., *Visionary Compacts: American Renaissance Writings in Cultural Contexts* (1987).

Pease, Donald E. (ed.), *National Identities and Post-Americanist Narratives* (1994).

Pease, Donald E. (ed.), *Revisionary Interventions into the Americanist Canon* (1994).

Peterson, Carla, *Doers of the Word: African-American Speakers and Writers in the North, 1830–1880* (1998).

Poirier, Richard, *A World Elsewhere: The Place of Style in American Literature* (1966).

Porte, Joel, *The Romance in America: Studies in Cooper, Poe, Hawthorne, Melville, and James* (1969).

Porte, Joel, *In Respect to Egotism: Studies in American Romantic Writing* (1991).

Pryse, Marjorie, *The Mark of Knowledge: Social Stigma in Classical American Fiction* (1979).

Radaway, Janice, *Reading the Romance: Women, Patriarchy, and Popular Literature* (1991).

Reynolds, David, *Beneath the American Renaissance: The Subversive Imagination in the Age of Emerson and Melville* (1988).

Reynolds, David, *Walt Whitman's America: A Cultural Biography* (1995).

Ridgely, J. V., *Nineteenth-century Southern Literature* (1980).

Romero, Lora, *Home Fronts: Domesticity and its Critics in the Antebellum United States* (1997).

Rose, Anne C., *Transcendentalism as a Social Movement* (1982).

Rose, Anne C., *Victorian America and the Civil War* (1992).

Rourke, Constance, *American Humor: A Study of the National Character* (1931).

Rowe, John Carlos, *At Emerson's Tomb: The Politics of Classic American Literature* (1997).

Ryan, Mary P., *The Empire of the Mother: American Writing About Domesticity, 1830–1860* (1982).

Samuels, Shirley (ed.), *The Culture of Sentiment: Race, Gender and Sentimentality in Nineteenth-century America* (1992).

Samuels, Shirley, *Romances of the Republic: Women, the Family, and Violence in the Literature of the Early American Nation* (1996).

Sanchez-Eppler, Karen, *Touching Liberty: Abolition, Feminism, and the Politics of the Body* (1993).

Seelye, John, *Prophetic Waters: The River in Early American Life and Literature* (1977).

Shell, Marc (ed.), *American Babel: Literatures of the United States from Abnaki to Zuni* (2002).

Sherman John R., *Invisible Poets: Afro-Americans in the Nineteenth Century* (1989).

Slotkin, Richard, *Regeneration Through Violence: The Mythology of the American Frontier, 1600–1860* (1973).

Smith, Henry Nash, *Virgin Land: The American West as Symbol and Myth* (1950).

Smith, Henry Nash, *Democracy and the Novel: Popular Resistance to Classic American Writers* (1978).

Smith, Stephanie A., *Conceived by Liberty: Maternal Figures and Nineteenth-century American Literature* (1995).

Sollors, Werner, *Neither Black Nor White Yet Both: Thematic Explorations of Interracial Literature* (1997).

Spiller, Robert (ed.), *The American Literary Revolution, 1787–1837* (1967).

Stern, Julia, *The Plight of Feeling: Sympathy and Dissent in the Early American Novel* (1997).

Stovall, Floyd, *The Development of American Literary Criticism* (1955).

Sundquist, Eric, *Home as Found: Authority and Genealogy in Nineteenth-century American Literature* (1979).

Sundquist, Eric, *To Wake the Nations: Race in the Making of American Literature* (1993).

Tanner, Tony, *The Reign of Wonder: Naivety and Reality in American Literature* (1965).

Taylor, Walter, *Cavalier and Yankee: The Old South and American National Character* (1961).

Tompkins, Jane, *Sensational Designs: The Cultural Work of American Fiction, 1790–1860* (1985).

Walker, Cheryl, *The Nightingale's Burden: Women Poets in American Culture Before 1900* (1982).

Walker, Cheryl, *Indian Nation: Native American Literature and Nineteenth-century Nationalism* (1997).

Ward, Geoff, *The Writing of America: Literature and Cultural Identity from the Puritans to the Present* (2002).

Weinstein, Cindy, *The Literature of Labor and the Labors of Literature: Allegory in Nineteenth-century American Fiction* (1995).

Weisbuch, Robert, *Atlantic Double-Cross: American Literature and British Influence in the Age of Emerson* (1986).

Wilson, Edmund, *Patriotic Gore: Studies in the Literature of the American Civil War* (1962).

Yellin, Jean Fagan, *The Intricate Knot: Black Figures in American Literature, 1776–1863* (1992).

Young, Elizabeth, *Disarming the Nation: Women's Writing and the Civil War* (1999).

Zaggari, Rosemarie, *The Politics of Size: Representation in the United States 1776–1850* (1988).

Ziff, Larzer, *Literary Democracy: The Declaration of Cultural Independence in America* (1981).

Ziff, Larzer, *Writing in the New Nation: Prose, Print, and Politics in the Early United States* (1991).

Chapter 3 Reconstructing the Past, Reimagining the Future: The Development of American Literature, 1865–1900

Ahnebrink, Lahrs, *The Beginnings of Naturalism in American Fiction* (1950).

Ammons, Elizabeth, *Conflicting Stories: American Women Writing at the Turn of the Twentieth Century* (1991).

Auchinloss, Louis, *Pioneers and Caretakers: A Study of Nine American Women Novelists* (1965).

Baker, Houston A., *Blues, Ideology, and Afro-American Literature: A Vernacular Theory* (1984).

Barrish, Philip, *American Literary Realism, Critical Theory, and Intellectual Prestige 1880–1995* (2001).

Bederman, Gail, *Manliness and Civilization: A Cultural History of Gender and Race in the United States, 1880–1917* (1995).

Bell, Bernard W., *The Afro-American Novel and its Tradition* (1987).

Bell, Michael Davitt, *The Problem of American Realism: Studies in the Cultural History of a Literary Idea* (1993).

Berthoff, Warner, *The Ferment of Realism: American Literature, 1884–1919* (1965).

Bone, Robert, *Down Home: Origins of the Afro-American Short Story* (1975).

Bordman, Gerald, *American Theatre: A Chronicle of Comedy and Drama, 1869–1914* (1994).

Borus, Daniel, *Writing Realism: Howells, James, and Norris in the Mass Market* (1989).

Braxton, Joanne M., *Black Women Writing Autobiography* (1989).

Bridgman, Richard, *The Colloquial Style in America* (1966).

Brooks, Van Wyck, *The Confident Years, 1885–1915* (1952).

Cady, Edwin H., *The Light of Common Day* (1971).

Campbell, Donna, *Resisting Regionalism: Gender and Naturalism in American Fiction, 1885–1915* (1997).

Carnes, Mark C. and Griffin, Clyde, *Meanings for Manhood: Constructions of Masculinity in Victorian America* (1990).

Cockrel, Dale, *Demons of Disorder: Early Blackface Minstrels and their World* (1997).

Condor, John, *Naturalism in American Fiction: The Classic Phase* (1984).

Conn, Peter, *The Divided Mind: Ideology and Imagination in America, 1898–1917* (1983).

Coultrap-McQuinn, Susan, *Doing Literary Business: American Women Writers in the Nineteenth Century* (1990).

Crumden, Robert M., *American Salons: Encounters with European Modernism, 1885–1917* (1993).

Derrick, Scott S., *Monumental Anxieties: Homoerotic Desire and Feminine Influence in 19th Century U.S. Literature* (1997).

Dictionary of Literary Biography: Afro-American Writers Before the Harlem Renaissance (1986).

Donovan, Josephine, *New England Local Color Literature: A Women's Tradition* (1983).

Dorson, Richard M., *American Negro Folktales* (1967).

Douglas, Ann, *The Feminization of American Culture* (1974).

Ducille, Ann, *The Coupling Convention: Sex, Text, and Tradition in Black Women's Fiction* (1993).

Duffey, Bernard, *The Chicago Renaissance in American Letters* (1954).

Dundes, Alan (ed.), *Mother Wit from the Laughing Barrel: Readings in the Interpretation of Afro-American Folklore* (1973).

Falk, Robert, *The Victorian Mode in American Fiction, 1865–1885* (1965).

Fanning, Charles (ed.), *The Irish Voice in America* (1987).

Fine, David M., *The City, the Immigrant and American Fiction, 1880–1920* (1977).

Folson, J. K., *The American Western Novel* (1966).

Foner, Philip (ed.), *Inside the Monster: Writings on the United States and American Imperialism* (1975).

Foster, Dennis, *Sublime Enjoyment: On the Perverse Motive in American Literature* (1997).

Franklin, H. B., *Future Perfect: American Science Fiction of the Nineteenth Century* (1966).

Geismar, Maxwell, *Rebels and Ancestors, 1890–1915* (1953).

Gelfant, Blanche, *The American City Novel* (1954).

Glazener, Nancy, *Reading for Realism: The History of a U.S. Literary Institution, 1850–1910* (1997).

Guttman, Allen, *The Jewish Writer in America: Assimilation and the Crisis of Identity* (1971).

Habegger, Alfred, *Gender, Fantasy, and Realism in American Literature* (1982).

Harap, Louis, *The Image of the Jew in American Literature: From Early Republic to Mass Immigration* (1974).

Harley, Sharon and Terborg-Penn, Rosalyn (eds.), *The Afro-American Woman: Struggles and Images* (1978).

Harris, Trudier, *Exorcising Blackness: Historical and Literary Lynching and Burning Rituals* (1984).

Hart, James, *The Popular Book: A History of America's Literary Taste* (1950).

Helttunen, Karen, *Confidence Men and Painted Women: A Study of Middle-class Culture in America, 1830–1870* (1982).

Herrera-Sobek, Maria, *The Mexican Corrido: A Feminist Analysis* (1990).

Houchens, Sue E. (ed.), *Spiritual Narratives* (1988).

Howard, June, *Form and Function in American Literary Naturalism* (1985).

Jones, Anne Goodwyn, *Tomorrow is Another Day: The Woman Writer in the South, 1859–1936* (1981).

Jones, Howard Mumford, *The Age of Energy: Varieties of American Experience, 1865–1915* (1971).

Kaplan, Amy, *The Social Construction of American Realism* (1988).

Kasson, John F., *Civilizing the Machine: Technology and Republican Values in America 1776–1900* (1977).

Kazin, Alfred, *On Native Grounds: An Interpretation of Modern American Prose Literature* (1942).

Kelley, Mary, *Private Women, Public Stage: Literary Domesticity in Nineteenth-century America* (1984).

Kim, Elaine H., *Asian American Literature: An Introduction to the Writings and their Social Contexts* (1982).

Kolb, Harold, *The Illusion of Life: American Realism as a Literary Form* (1969).

Lears, T. Jackson, *No Place of Grace: Antimodernism and the Transformation of American Culture, 1880–1920* (1981).

Liberty, Margot (ed.), *American Indian Intellectuals* (1978).

Ling, Amy, *Between Worlds: Women Writers of Chinese Ancestry* (1990).

Loewenberg, Bert James and Bogin, Ruth (eds.), *Black Women in Nineteenth-century American Life: Their Words, Their Thoughts, Their Feelings* (1976).

Lott, Eric W., *Love and Theft: Blackface Minstrelsy and the American Working Class* (1993).

Love, Glen A., *New Americans: The Westerner and the Modern Experience in the American Novel* (1982).

Machor, James L., *Readers in History: Nineteenth-century American Literature and the Contexts of Response* (1993).

McKay, Janet Holmgrin, *Narration and Discourse in American Realistic Fiction* (1982).

MacKethan, Lucinda, *The Dream of Arcady: Place and Time in Southern Literature* (1980).

Martin, Jay, *Harvests of Change: American Literature, 1865–1914* (1967).

Martin, Ronald E., *American Literature and the Universe of Force* (1981).

Marx, Leo, *The Machine in the Garden: Technology and the Pastoral Ideal in America* (1964).

Michaels, Walter Benn, *The Gold Standard and the Logic of Naturalism: American Literature at the Turn of the Century* (1987).

Miller, Ruth, *Backgrounds to Black American Literature* (1971).

Mitchell, Lee Clark, *Determined Fictions: American Literary Naturalism* (1989).

Mott, Frank Luther, *A History of American Magazines* (5 vols; 1938–68), *Volume Three: 1865–85* and *Volume Four: 1885–1905*.

Mumford, Lewis, *The Brown Decades: A Study of the Arts in America, 1865–1895* (2nd ed., 1955).

Nettels, Elsa, *Language and Gender in American Fiction: Howells, James, Wharton, and Cather* (1997).

Nye, Russell B., *The Unembarrassed Muse: The Popular Arts in America* (1970).

Ostriker, Alicia, *Stealing the Language: The Emergence of Women's Poetry in America* (1986).

Oostrum, Duco van, *Male Authors, Female Subjects: The Woman Within/Beyond the Borders of Henry Adams, Henry James and Others* (1995).

Padilla, Genaro, *My History, Not Yours: The Formation of Mexican-American Autobiography* (1994).

Perkins, David, *A History of Modern Poetry: From the 1890s to the High Modernist Mode* (1976).

Peyser, Thomas, *Utopia and Cosmopolis: Globalization in the Era of American Literary Realism* (1998).

Pizer, Donald (ed.), *American Thought and Writing: The 1890s* (1976).

Pizer, Donald, *Realism and Naturalism in Nineteenth-century American Literature* (1984).

Pizer, Donald, *The Theory and Practice of American Literary Naturalism: Selected Essays and Reviews* (1993).

Pizer, Donald (ed.), *The Cambridge Companion to American Realism and Naturalism: From Howells to London* (1995).

Porter, Carolyn, *Seeing and Believing: The Plight of the Participant Observer in Emerson, James, Adams, and Faulkner* (1981).

Rebolledo, Tey Diana, *Women Singing in the Snow: A Cultural Analysis of Chicana Literature* (1995).

Roemer, Kenneth M., *The Obsolete Necessity: America in Utopian Writings, 1888–1900* (1976).

Rowe, John Carlos, *Through the Custom-House: Nineteenth-century American Fiction and Modern Theory* (1982).

Saldivar, Ramon, *Chicano Narrative: The Dialectics of Difference* (1990).

Schneider, Robert W., *Five Novelists of the Progressive Era* (1965).

Sedgwick, Ellery, *The Atlantic Monthly, 1857–1909: Yankee Humanism at High Tide and Ebb* (1994).

Segal, Howard P., *Technological Utopianism in American Culture* (1985).

Shockley, Ann Allen, *Afro-American Women Writers, 1746–1933* (1988).

Shockley, Ann Allen (ed.), *Afro-American Women Writers, 1746–1933: An Anthology and Critical Guide* (1989).

Skaggs, H. M., *The Folk of Southern Fiction* (1972).

Snyder, Katherine V., *Bachelors, Manhood and the Novel, 1850–1925* (1999).

Spindler, Michael, *American Literature and Social Change* (1984).

Sterling, Dorothy, *We Are Your Sisters: Black Women in the Nineteenth Century* (1984).

Sundquist, Eric (ed.), *American Realism: New Essays* (1982).

Tate, Claudia, *Domestic Allegories of Political Desire: The Black Heroine's Text at the Turn of the Century* (1992).

Taylor, Gordon O., *The Passages of Thought: Psychological Representation in the American Novel, 1870–1900* (1962).

Taylor, W. F., *The Economic Novel in America* (1942).

Thomas, Brook, *American Literary Realism and the Failed Promise of Contract* (1997).

Tracy, Karen, *Plots and Proposals: American Women's Fiction, 1850–90* (2000).

Wagoner, Jean, *Black Poets of the United States: From Paul Laurence Dunbar to Langston Hughes* (1978).

Walcutt, Charles C., *American Naturalism: A Divided Stream* (1956).

Walker, Robert H., *The Poet and the Gilded Age: Social Themes in Late Nineteenth-century American Verse* (1963).

Warren, Kenneth W., *Black and White Strangers: Race and American Literary Realism* (1993).

Weintraub, Stanley, *London Yankees: Portraits of American Writers and Artists in England, 1894–1914* (1979).

Weiss, R., *The American Myth of Success* (1969).

Weissman, Judith, *Half Savage and Hardy and Free: Women and Rural Radicalism in the Nineteenth-century Novel* (1987).

Westbrook, P. D., *Free Will and Determinism in American Literature* (1979).

Ziff, Larzer, *The American 1890s: Life and Times of a Lost Generation* (1966).

Chapter 4 Making it New: The Emergence of Modern American Literature, 1900–1945

Aaron, Daniel, *Writers on the Left: Episodes in American Literary Communism* (1961).

Abrahamson, Edward A., *The Immigrant Experience in Literature* (1982).

Abramson, Doris E., *New Playwrights in the American Theatre, 1925–1959* (1969).

Auerbach, Nina, *Communities of Women: An Idea in Fiction* (1978).

Aldridge, John, *After the Lost Generation: A Critical Study of the Writers of the Two Wars* (1951).

Altieri, Charles, *Painterly Abstraction in Modernist American Poetry* (1989).

Anderson, Elliott, *The Little Magazine in America* (1981).

Aquila, Richard, *Wanted Dead or Alive: The American West in Popular Culture* (1996).

Armitage, S. and Jameson, E. (eds.), *The Women's West* (1987).

Armstrong, Tim, *Modernism, Technology, and the Body: A Cultural Study* (1998).

Baker, Houston A., Jr, *The Journey Back: Issues in Black Literature and Criticism* (1980).

Baker, Houston A., Jr, *Modernism and the Harlem Renaissance* (1991).

Baker, Houston A., Jr, *Workings of the Spirit: The Poetics of Afro-American Women's Writing* (1991).

Beach, Joseph Warren, *American Fiction 1920–1940* (1960).

Berkowitz, Gerald M., *American Drama of the Twentieth Century* (1992).

Bigsby, C. W. E., *A Critical Introduction to Twentieth-century American Drama* (3 vols; 1985).

Bloom, Harold, *The Anxiety of Influence: A Theory of Poetry* (1973).

Bloom, Harold, *Figures of Capable Imagination* (1976).

Blotner, Joseph, *The American Political Novel 1900–1960* (1960).

Boelhower, William, *Through a Glass Darkly: Ethnic Semiosis in American Literature* (1987).

Bogardus, Ralph and Hobson, Fred (eds.), *Literature at the Barricades: The American Writer in the 1930s* (1982).

Bone, Robert A., *The Negro Novel in America* (1965).

Bradbury, John M., *The Fugitives: A Critical Account* (1958).

Bradbury, John M., *Renaissance in the South: A Critical History of the Literature 1920–1960* (1963).

Bradbury, Malcolm, *The Expatriate Tradition in American Literature* (1982).

Bradbury, Malcolm, *The Modern American Novel* (1983).

Bradbury, Malcolm and Palmer, David (eds.), *The American Novel and the 1920s* (1971).

Bryant, J. A., Jr, *Twentieth-century Southern Literature* (1997).

Butterfield, R. W. (ed.), *Modern American Poetry* (1986).

Cambon, Glauco, *The Inclusive Flame: Studies in American Poetry* (1963).

Cantwell, Robert, *When We Were Good: The Folk Revival* (1996).

Castro, Michael, *Interpreting the Indian: Twentieth-century Poets and the Native American* (1983).

Chapman, Abraham, *Jewish-American Literature* (1974).

Christian, Barbara, *Black Women Novelists: The Development of a Tradition, 1892–1976* (1984).

Clurman, Harold, *The Story of the Group Theatre and the Thirties* (1945).

Coffman, Stanley, *Imagism: A Chapter for the History of Modern Poetry* (1951).

Conkin, Paul K., *The Southern Agrarians* (1988).

Cook, Sylvia Jenkins, *From Tobacco Road to Route 66: The Southern Poor White in Fiction* (1976).

Cooley, John, *Savages and Naturals: Black Portraits by White Writers in Modern American Literature* (1982).

Cooperman, Stanley J., *World War I and the American Novel* (1967).

Cowan, Louise, *The Fugitive Group: A Literary History* (1959).

Cowley, Malcolm, *Exile's Return: A Literary Odyssey of the 1920's* (1934).

Cowley, Malcolm, *Think Back on Us: A Contemporary Chronicle of the 1930's* (1967).

Cowley, Malcolm, *A Second Flowering: Works and Days of the Lost Generation* (1973).

Crumden, Robert M., *Body and Soul: The Making of American Modernism* (2000).

Cutler, Edward C., *Recovering the New: Transatlantic Roots of Modernism* (2002).

Dardis, Tom, *Some Time in the Sun* (1976).

Dardis, Tom, *The Thirsty Muse: Alcohol and the American Writer* (1989).

Dembo, Louise, *Conceptions of Reality in Modern American Poetry* (1966).

De Jongh, James, *Vicious Modernism: Black Harlem and the Literary Imagination* (1990).

Dixon, Melvin, *Ride Out the Wilderness: Geography and Identity in Afro-American Literature* (1987).

Donoghue, Denis, *Connoisseurs of Chaos: Ideas of Order in Modern American Poetry* (1966).

Downer, Alan S., *Fifty Years of American Drama 1900–1950* (1951).

Downer, Alan S. (ed.), *American Drama and its Critics: A Collection of Critical Essays* (1965).

Dukore, Bernard F., *American Dramatists 1918–1945* (1984).

Du Plessis, Rachel Blau, *Writing Beyond the Ending: Narrative Strategies of Twentieth-century Women Writers* (1985).

Du Plessis, Rachel Blau, *Genders, Races, and Religious Cultures in Modern American Poetry, 1908–1934* (2001).

Earnest, Ernest, *Expatriates and Patriots: American Artists, Scholars, and Writers in Europe* (1968).

Eisinger, Chester, *Fiction of the Forties* (1963).

Emmett, S., *Loaded Fictions: Social Critiques in the Twentieth-century Western* (1996).

Etulain, Richard W., *The American Literary West* (1980).

Fabre, Michel, *From Harlem to Paris: Black American Writers in France* (1991).

Ferraro, Thomas J., *Ethnic Passages: Literary Immigrants in Twentieth-century America* (1993).

Fetterley, Judith, *The Resisting Reader: A Feminist Approach to American Fiction* (1978).

Fine, Richard, *West of Eden: Writers in Hollywood, 1928–1940* (1993).

Fisher, Philip, *Still the New World: American Literature in a Culture of Creative Destruction* (1999).

Folsom, James K., *The American Western Novel* (1966).

Fredman, Stephen, *Poet's Prose: The Crisis in American Verse* (1983).

Frohock, W. M., *The Novel of Violence in America* (1957).

Gambrell, Alice, *Women Intellectuals, Modernism, and Difference: Transatlantic Culture, 1919–1945* (1997).

Gates, Henry Louis, Jr, *Black Literature and Literary Theory* (1984).

Gates, Henry Louis, Jr, *The Signifying Monkey: A Theory of African-American Literary Criticism* (1988).

Gayle, Addison, *The Way of the New World: The Black Novel in America* (1975).

Geismar, Maxwell, *Writers in Crisis: The American Novel 1925–1940* (1942).

Geismar, Maxwell, *The Last of the Provincials: The American Novel 1915–1925* (1947).

Geismar, Maxwell, *American Moderns: Rebellion to Conformity* (1958).

Gelfant, Blanche (ed.), *The Columbia Companion to the Twentieth-century American Short Story* (2000).

Gelpi, Albert, *A Coherent Splendour: The American Poetic Renaissance 1910–1950* (1988).

Gilbert, James, *Writers and Partisans: A History of Literary Radicalism in America* (1968).

Godden, Richard, *Fictions of Capital: The American Novel from James to Mailer* (1990).

Gould, Jean, *Modern American Playwrights* (1966).

Gould, Jean, *Modern American Women Poets* (1985).

Gray, Richard, *The Literature of Memory: Modern Writers of the American South* (1977).

Gray, Richard (ed.), *American Fiction: New Readings* (1980).

Gray, Richard, *American Poetry of the Twentieth Century* (1990).

Gressley, G. M., *Old West/New West* (1997).

Gwin, Minrose, *Black and White Women of the Old South: The Peculiar Sisterhood in American Literature* (1985).

Hamilton, Ian, *Writers in Hollywood, 1915–1951* (1990).

Harap, Louis, *In the Mainstream: The Jewish Presence in Twentieth-century American Literature* (1978).

Haslam, Gerald W. (ed.), *Western Writing* (1974).

Hilfer, Tony, *The Revolt from the Village* (1969).

Himelstein, Morgan Y., *Drama Was a Weapon: The Left-wing Theatre in New York, 1929–1941* (1963).

Hobson, Fred, *Tell About the South: The Southern Rage to Explain* (1983).

Hoffman, Frederick, *The Twenties: American Writing in the Postwar Decade* (1949).

Hoffman, Frederick, *The Modern Novel in America* (1951).

Hoffman, Frederick, *The Art of Southern Fiction* (1967).

Hoffman, Michael J. and Murphy, Patrick D. (eds.), *Critical Essays in American Modernism* (1992).

Homberger, Eric, *American Writers and Radical Politics, 1900–1939* (1985).

Howard, Maureen, *Seven American Women Writers of the Twentieth Century* (1977).

Huang, Yunte, *Transpacific Development: Ethnography, Translation, and Intertextual Travel in Twentieth-century American Literature* (2002).

Huggins, Nathan, *Harlem Renaissance* (1971).

Hughes, Glenn, *Imagism and the Imagists: A Study in Modern Poetry* (1960).

Jade, Cathy L., *Modernismo, Modernity, and the Development of Spanish American Literature* (1998).

Jordan, June (ed.), *Soulscript: Afro-American Poetry* (1970).

Juhasz, Suzanne, *Naked and Fiery Forms: Modern American Poetry by Women: A New Tradition* (1976).

Kazin, Alfred, *Contemporaries: Essays on Modern Life and Literature* (1962).

Kazin, Alfred, *Bright Book of Life: American Novelists and Storytellers from Hemingway to Mailer* (1973).

Kellner, Bruce, *The Harlem Renaissance: An Historical Dictionary for the Era* (1984).

Kennedy, J. Gerald, *Imagining Paris: Exile, Writing, and American Identity* (1993).

Kenner, Hugh, *A Homemade World: American Modernist Writers* (1975).

Kern, Robert, *Orientalism, Modernism, and the American Poem* (1996).

King, Richard H., *A Southern Renaissance: The Cultural Awakening of the American South, 1930–1955* (1980).

Kirkpatrick, Marcus, *After Alienation: American Novels at Mid-Century* (1962).

Klein, Marcus, *Foreigners: The Making of American Literature, 1900–1940* (1981).

Kramer, Victor A., *The Harlem Renaissance Re-examined* (1987).

Krupat, Arnold, *The Voice in the Margin: Native American Literature and the Canon* (1989).

Lee, Brian, *American Fiction 1865–1940* (1987).

Lee, R. E., *From West to East: Studies in the Literature of the American West* (1966).

Lensink, Judy Nolte (ed.), *Old Southwest/New Southwest: Essays on a Region and its Literature* (1987).

Levin, Jonathan, *The Poetics of Transition: Emerson, Pragmatism, and American Literary Modernism* (1999).

Lewis, Allan, *American Plays and Playwrights of the Contemporary Theatre* (1970).

Lewis, David L., *When Harlem Was In Vogue* (1981).

Londre, Felicia Hardison and Watermeier, Daniel J., *The History of North American Theater* (1998).

Madden, David (ed.), *Proletarian Writers of the Thirties* (1968).

Madden, David (ed.), *Tough Guy Writers of the Thirties* (1968).

Magny, C. E., *The Age of the American Novel: The Film Aesthetic of Fiction Between the Two Wars* (1972).

Manning, Carol S. (ed.), *The Female Tradition in Southern Literature* (1993).

Mariani, Paul, *A Usable Past: Essays on Modern and Contemporary American Poetry* (1984).

Mazzaro, Jerome (ed.), *Modern American Poetry: Essays in Criticism* (1970).

Mellard, James M., *The Exploded Form: The Modernist Novel in America* (1980).

Meserve, Walter J., *An Outline History of American Drama* (1965).

Messent, Peter, *New Readings of the American Novel: Narrative Theory and its Application* (1990).

Meyer, Roy W., *The Middle Western Farm Novel in the Twentieth Century* (1965).

Michaels, Walter Benn, *Our America: Nativism, Modernism, and Pluralism* (1995).

Middlebrook, Diane Wood and Yalom, Marilyn (eds.), *Coming to Light: American Women Poets in the Twentieth Century* (1985).

Millgate, Michael, *American Social Fiction: James to Cozzens* (1964).

Milton, John R., *The Novel of the American West* (1980).

Mizener, Arthur, *Twelve Great American Novels* (1967).

Mootry, Maria Katella, *Studies in Black Pastoral: Five Afro-American Writers* (1974).

Morrison, Mark S., *The Public Face of Modernism: Little Magazines, Audiences, and Reception, 1905–1920* (2000).

Mott, Frank Luther, *A History of American Magazines* (5 vols, 1938–68), *Volume Five: 1905–1930*.

Murphy, Brenda, *American Realism and American Drama, 1880–1940* (1987).

Myers, Jack and Wojahn, David (eds.), *A Profile of Twentieth-century American Poetry* (1991).

Nevius, Blake, *The American Novel: Sinclair Lewis to the Present* (1970).

Nicholls, Peter, *Modernisms: A Literary Guide* (1995).

North, Michael, *The Dialect of Modernism: Race, Language, and Twentieth-century Literature* (1974).

O'Connor, William Van, *Seven Modern American Novelists: An Introduction* (1964).

Payne, L., *Black Writers and the Southern Literary Renaissance* (1981).

Pells, Richard, *Radical Visions and American Dreams* (1973).

Perkins, David, *A History of Modern Poetry: Modernism and After* (1987).

Perloff, Marjorie, *The Poetics of Indeterminacy: From Rimbaud to Cage* (1981).

Perloff, Marjorie, *The Dance of the Intellect: Studies in the Poetry of the Pound Tradition* (1986).

Perry, Margaret, *Silence to the Drums: A Survey of the Literature of the Harlem Renaissance* (1976).

Pizer, Donald, *Twentieth-century American Literary Naturalism: An Interpretation* (1982).

Pizer, Donald, *American Expatriate Writing and the Paris Movement* (1992).

Quartermain, Peter, *Disjunctive Poetics: From Gertrude Stein and Louis Zukofsky to Susan Howe* (1992).

Rabinowitz, Paula, *Black and White Noir: America's Pulp Modernism* (2001).

Rabkin, Gerald, *Drama and Commitment: Politics in the American Theatre of the Thirties* (1964).

Redmond, Eugene, *Drumvoices: The Mission of Afro-American Poetry, A Critical History* (1976).

Reynolds, Guy, *Twentieth-century American Women's Fiction* (1999).

Rideout, Walter B., *The Radical Novel in the United States, 1900–1954* (1956).

Robinson, F. G., *Having it Both Ways: Self-subversion in Western Popular Classics* (1993).

Rocard, Marcienne, *The Children of the Sun: Mexican Americans in the Literature of the United States* (1989).

Rosenblatt, Roger, *Black Fiction* (1974).

Rubin, Louis D., Jr, *The Faraway Country: Writers of the Modern South* (1963).

Rubin, Louis D., Jr, *The Wary Fugitives: Four Poets and the South* (1978).

Rubin, Louis D., Jr, *A Gallery of Southerners* (1982).

Rubin, Louis D., Jr et al. (eds.), *The History of Southern Literature* (1985).

Rubin, Louis D., Jr and Jacobs, Robert D. (eds.), *Southern Renascence: The Literature of the Modern South* (1953).

Rubin, Louis D., Jr and Jacobs, Robert D. (eds.), *South: Modern Southern Literature in its Cultural Setting* (1961).

Ruland, Richard, *The Rediscovery of American Literature: Premises of Critical Taste, 1900–1940* (1967).

Sanders, Leslie Catherine, *The Development of Black Theatre in America* (1988).

Scanlan, Tom, *Family, Drama, and American Dreams* (1978).

Schlueter, June (ed.), *Modern American Theatre: The Female Canon* (1990).

Seed, David (ed.), *Anticipations: Essays on Early Science Fiction and its Precursors* (1995).

Shiach, Don, *American Drama 1900–1990* (2000).

Simpson, Lewis P., *The Dispossessed Garden: Pastoral and History in Southern Literature* (1975).

Simpson, Lewis P., *The Fable of the Southern Writer* (1994).

Singal, Daniel J., *The War Within: From Victorian to Modernist Thought in the South* (1982).

Singh, Amrijit, *The Novels of the Harlem Renaissance* (1976).

Slotkin, Richard, *The Fatal Environment: The Myth of the Frontier in the Twentieth Century* (1985).

Slotkin, Richard, *Gunfighter Nation: The Myth of the Frontier in Twentieth-century America* (1992).

Stanford, Donald, *Revolution and Convention in Modern Poetry* (1983).

Stauffer, Donald, *A Short History of American Poetry* (1974).

Stepto, Robert, *From Behind the Veil: A Study of Afro-American Narrative* (1979).

Stewart, John L., *The Burden of Time: The Fugitives and Agrarians* (1965).

Stott, William, *Documentary Expression and Thirties America* (1973).

Tallack, Douglas, *Twentieth-century America* (1991).

Taylor, Gordon O., *Chapters of Experience: Studies in Twentieth-century American Autobiography* (1983).

Teague, D., *The Southwest in American Literature and Art* (1997).

Tichi, Cecelia, *Shifting Gears: Technology, Literature, Culture in Modernist America* (1987).

Tompkins, Jane, *West of Everything: The Inner Life of Westerns* (1992).

Truettner, W. (ed.), *The West as America: Reinterpreting Images of the Frontier* (1991).

Tuma, Keith, *Fishing by Obstinate Isles: Modern and Postmodern British and American Poetry and American Readers* (1998).

Tuttleton, J., *The Novel of Manners in America* (1972).

Unger, Leonard (ed.), *Seven Modern American Poets: An Introduction* (1967).

Vendler, Helen, *Part of Nature, Part of Us: Modern American Poets* (1980).

Waldau, Roy S., *Vintage Years of the Theatre Guild* (1972).

Watts, Emily S., *The Poetry of American Women from 1612 to 1945* (1977).

West, R. B., *The Short Story in America 1900–1950* (1952).

Williams, Jay, *Stage Left* (1974).

Willis, Susan B., *Specifying: Black Women Writing the American Experience* (1987).

Wilmeth, Don B. and Bigsbee, C. W. E. (eds.), *The Cambridge History of American Theatre: Three-Volume Set* (2000).

Wilmeth, Don B. and Miller, Tice L. (eds.), *The Cambridge Guide to American Theatre* (1996).

Wilson, Edmund, *American Earthquake: A Documentary of the Twenties and Thirties* (1958).

Young, James O., *Black Writers of the Thirties* (1973).

Young, R., *White Mythologies: Writing History and the West* (1995).

Chapter 5 Negotiating the American Century: American Literature since 1945

Alexander, M., *Flights from Realism: Themes and Strategies in Postmodernist British and American Fiction* (1990).

Allen, Paula Gunn, *The Sacred Hoop: Recovering the Feminine in American Indian Tradition* (1986).

Allmendinger, Blake, *Ten Most Wanted: The New Western Literature* (1998).

Alter, Robert, *Partial Magic: The Novel as a Self-conscious Genre* (1975).

Altieri, Charles, *Enlarging the Temple: New directions in American Poetry during the 1960s* (1979).

Altieri, Charles, *Self and Sensibility in Contemporary American Poetry* (1984).

Anderson, Eric Gary, *American Indian Literature and the Southwest* (1999).

Anzaldúa, Gloria, *Borderlands/La Frontera: The New Mestiza* (1987).

Anzaldúa, Gloria (ed.), *Making Face/Making Soul: Hacienda Caras: Creative and Critical Perspectives by Feminists of Color* (1990).

Apt Russell, Sharman, *Kill the Cowboy: A Battle of Mythology in the New West* (1993).

Aronson, Arnold, *American Avant-Garde Theatre* (2000).

Barthold, Bonnie J., *Black Time: Fiction of Africa, the Caribbean, and the United States* (1981).

Baumbach, Jonathan, *The Landscape of Nightmare: Studies in the Contemporary American Novel* (1965).

Bawer, Bruce, *The Middle Generation: The Lives and Poetry of Delmore Schwartz, Randall Jarrell, John Berryman, and Robert Lowell* (1986).

Beidler, Philip, *Re-writing America: Vietnam Authors in their Generation* (1991).

Bercovitch, Sacvan (ed.), *The Cambridge History of American Literature: Volume Eight: Poetry and Criticism, 1940–1995* (1996).

Bercovitch, Sacvan (ed.), *The Cambridge History of American Literature: Volume Seven: Prose Writing, 1940–1995* (1998).

Berger, Alan L., *Crisis and Covenant: The Holocaust in American Jewish Fiction* (1985).

Berke, Roberta, *Bounds out of Bounds: A Compass for Recent American and British Poetry* (1981).

Berkowitz, Gerald M., *New Broadways: Theatre Across America 1950–1980* (1982).

Berman, N. D., *Playful Fictions and Fictional Players: Game, Sport and Survival in Contemporary American Fiction* (1981).

Berthoff, Warner, *A Literature Without Qualities: American Writing since 1945* (1979).

Bigsby, C. W. E., *Confrontation and Commitment: A Study of Contemporary American Drama 1959–1966* (1968).

Bigsby, C. W. E., *The Second Black Renaissance: Essays in Black Literature* (1980).

Bigsby, C. W. E., *Contemporary American Playwrights* (1999).

Bigsby, C. W. E., *Modern American Drama, 1945–2000* (2000).

Bilik, Dorothy, *Immigrant Survivors: Post-Holocaust Consciousness in Recent Jewish American Fiction* (1981).

Blasing, Mutlu K., *American Poetry: The Rhetoric of its Forms* (1987).

Boyers, Robert (ed.), *Contemporary Poetry in America: Essays and Interviews* (1974).

Braxton, Joanne M. and McLaughlin, Nicola (eds.), *Wild Women in the Whirlwind: Afro-American Culture and the Continuing Literary Renaissance* (1991).

Breslin, James E. B., *From Modern to Contemporary: American Poetry 1945–1965* (1980).

Breslin, Paul, *The Psycho-political Muse: American Poetry since the Fifties* (1987).

Bryant, J., *The Open Decision: The Contemporary American Novel and its Intellectual Background* (1970).

Calderon, Hector and Saldivar, Jose David (eds.), *Criticism in the Borderlands: Studies in Chicano Literature, Culture, and Ideology* (1991).

Campbell, Neil, *The Cultures of the American New West* (2000).

Cambon, Glauco, *Recent American Poetry* (1962).

Carroll, Paul, *The Poem in its Skin* (1968).

Chametzky, J., *Our Decentralized Literature: Cultural Mediations in Selected Jewish and Southern Writers* (1986).

Charters, Samuel, *Some Poems/Poets: Studies in American Underground Poetry since 1945* (1968).

Chattarji, Subarno, *Memories of a Lost War: American Poetic Responses to the Vietnam War* (2001).

Cheung, Kink-kok, *Articulate Silences: Hoaye Yamamoto, Maxine Hong Kingston, Joy Kogawa* (1993).

Chinoy, Helen Krich and Jenkins, Linda Walsh (eds.), *Women in American Theatre* (1981).

Christian, Karen, *Show and Tell: Identity as Performance in U.S. Latino/Latina Fiction* (1997).

Clark, Tom, *The Poetry Beat: Reviewing the Eighties* (1990).

Clayton, J., *The Pleasures of Babel: Contemporary American Literature and Theory* (1993).

Cohn, Ruby, *New American Dramatists 1960–1980* (1982; 2nd ed., 1991).

Comer, Krista, *Landscapes of the New West: Gender and Geography in Contemporary Women's Writing* (1999).

Coser, Stelemaris, *Bridging the Americas: The Literature of Paule Marshall, Toni Morrison, and Gayl Jones* (1995).

Conte, Joseph, *Unending Design: The Forms of Postmodern Poetry* (1991).

Cook, B., *The Beat Generation* (1971).

Corpi, Lucha, *Mascaras* (1997).

Currie, M., *Metafiction* (1995).

Damon, Maria, *The Dark End of the Street: Margins in American Vanguard Poetry* (1993).

Davidson, Michael, *The San Francisco Renaissance: Poets and Community at Mid-Century* (1989).

Dewey, J., *The Apocalyptic Temper in the American Novel of the Nuclear Age* (1989).

Diehl, Joanne Feit, *Women Poets and the American Sublime* (1990).

Dixon, Melvin, *Ride Out the Wilderness: Geography and Identity in African-American Literature* (1987).

Dodd, Wayne, *Toward the End of the Century: Essays into Poetry* (1992).

Duberman, Martin, *Black Mountain: An Exploration in Community* (1974).

Dunaway, D. K. (ed.), *Writing the Southwest* (1995).

Dickstein, Morris, *Gates of Eden: American Culture in the Sixties* (1977).

Evans, Mari (ed.), *Black Women Writers: Arguments and Interviews* (1985).

Eysturoy, Annie O., *Daughters of Self-creation: The Contemporary Chicana Novel* (1996).

Fabre, Genevieve and O'Meally, Robert (eds.), *History and Memory in African-American Culture* (1994).

Federman, Raymond (ed.), *Surfiction: Fiction Now and Tomorrow* (1975).

Finkelstein, Norman, *The Utopian Moment in Contemporary American Poetry* (1993).

Fitzgerald, F., *Cities on a Hill: A Journey through Contemporary American Cultures* (1986).

Francaviglia, R. and Narrett, D. (eds.), *Essays on the Changing Images of the Southwest* (1994).

Friedman, M. J. and Siegel, B. (eds.), *Traditions, Voices, and Dreams: The American Novel since the 1960s* (1995).

Fusco, Coco, *English is Broken Here: Notes on Cultural Fusion in the Americas* (1995).

Galloway, David, *The Absurd Hero in American Fiction* (1970).

Gates, Henry Louis, Jr (ed.), *Reading Black, Reading Feminist: A Critical Anthology* (1990).

Gibson, Donald, *Five Black Writers: Essays on Wright, Ellison, Baldwin, Hughes, and Leroi Jones* (1970).

Gilbert, Roger, *Walks in the World: Representation and Experience in Modern American Poetry* (1991).

Giles, Paul, *Virtual Americas: Transnational Fictions and the Transatlantic Imaginary* (2002).

Gilman, Owen, Jr, *Vietnam and the Southern Imagination* (1992).

Gilman, R., *The Confusion of Realism* (1969).

Gish, Robert Franklin, *Beyond Bounds: Cross-cultural Essays on Anglo-American, Indian, and Chicano Literature* (1996).

Gossett, Louise Y., *Violence in Recent Southern Fiction* (1965).

Gotera, Vince, *Radical Visions: Poetry by Vietnam Veterans* (1994).

Gottfried, Martin, *A Theatre Divided: The Postwar American Stage* (1967).

Graff, Gerald, *Literature Against Itself: Literary Ideas in Modern Society* (1979).

Gray, Richard, *Southern Aberrations: Writers of the American South and the Problems of Regionalism* (2000).

Grice, Helena, Hepworth, Candida, Lauret, Maria and Padget, Martin, *Beginning Ethnic American Literatures* (2001).

Guinn, Matthew, *After Southern Modernism: Fiction of the Contemporary South* (2000).

Hansen, E. T., *Mother Without Child: Contemporary Fiction and the Crisis of Motherhood* (1997).

Harap, L., *The Jewish Presence in Twentieth-century American Literature* (1978).

Harper, Howard M., *Desperate Faith: A Study of Bellow, Salinger, Mailer, Baldwin, and Updike* (1978).

Harris, C. B., *Contemporary American Novelists of the Absurd* (1971).

Hassan, Ihab, *Radical Innocence: Studies in the Contemporary American Novel* (1961).

Hassan, Ihab, *The Dismemberment of Orpheus: Towards a Postmodern Literature* (1971).

Hassan, Ihab, *Paracriticism: Seven Speculations on the Times* (1975).

Hauck, Richard B., *A Cheerful Nihilism: 'Confidence' and 'The Absurd' in American Humorous Fiction* (1971).

Haut, Woody, *Pulp Culture: Hardboiled Fiction and the Cold War* (1992).

Haut, Woody, *Neon Noir: Contemporary American Crime Fiction* (1999).

Hendin, Josephine, *Vulnerable People: A View of American Fiction since 1945* (1978).

Herrera-Sobek, Maria and Viramontes, Helena Maria (eds.), *Chicana Creativity and Criticism: New Frontiers in American Literature* (1996).

Hicks, J., *In the Singer's Temple: Prose Fictions of Barthelme, Gaines, Brautigan, Percy, Kesey, and Kosinski* (1981).

Hilfer, Tony, *American Fiction since 1940* (1992).

Hobson, Fred, *The Southern Writer in the Postmodern World* (1991).

Holden, Jonathan, *Style and Authenticity in Postmodern Poetry* (1986).

Homberger, Eric, *The Art of the Real: Poetry in England and America since 1939* (1977).

Howard, Richard, *Alone with America: Studies in the Art of Poetry in the United States since 1950* (1970).

Hughes, Catharine, *American Playwrights 1945–1975* (1976).

Hutchens, L., *A Poetics of Postmodernism* (1988).

Jackson, Richard, *The Dismantling of Time in Contemporary Poetry* (1988).

Jarvis, Brian, *Postmodern Cartographies: The Geographical Imagination in Contemporary American Culture* (1998).

Jeffords, S., *The Remasculinization of America: Gender and the Vietnam War* (1989).

Jimenez, Francisco (ed.), *The Identification and Analysis of Chicano Literature* (1979).

Johnson, C., *Being and Race: Black Writing since 1970* (1988).

Johnson, M. K., *The New Westerners: The West in Contemporary American Culture* (1996).

Jones, Gayl, *Liberating Voices: Oral Tradition in African American Literature* (1991).

Karl, Frederick R., *American Fictions 1940–1980: A Comprehensive History and Critical Evaluation* (1983).

Keller, Lynn, *Re-making it New: Contemporary American Poetry and the Modernist Tradition* (1986).

King, Richard H. and Taylor, Helen (eds.), *Dixie Debates: Perspectives on Southern Cultures* (1996).

Kirby, Michael (ed.), *The New Theatre* (1974).

Klein, Marcus (ed.), *The American Novel since World War II* (1969).

Klinkowitz, Jerome, *Literary Disruptions: The Making of a Post-contemporary American Fiction* (1975).

Klinkowitz, Jerome, *The Life of Fiction* (1977).

Klinkowitz, Jerome, *The Practice of Fiction in America* (1980).

Knight, Brenda, *Women Writers of the Beat Generation* (1996).

Kowalewski, M. (ed.), *Reading the West* (1997).

Kuhl, J., *Alternate Worlds: A Study of Postmodern Antirealistic American Fiction* (1989).

Lattin, Vernon E., *Contemporary Chicano Fiction: A Critical Survey* (1986).

Lee, A. Robert (ed.), *Black Fiction: New Studies in the Afro-American Novel since 1945* (1980).

Lee, A. Robert (ed.), *The Beat Generation Writers* (1996).

Lee, A. Robert, *Designs of Blackness: Mappings in the Literature and Culture of Afro-America* (1998).

Lee, Rachel C., *The Americas of Asian American Literature: Gendered Fictions of Nation and Transnation* (1999).

Lensing, George and Moran, Ronald, *Four Poets and the Emotive Imagination: Robert Bly, James Wright, Louis Simpson, and William Stafford* (1976).

Li, David Leiwei, *Imagining the Nation: Asian American Literature and Cultural Consent* (1998).

Libby, Anthony, *Mythologies of Nothing: Mystical Death in American Poetry, 1940–1970* (1984).

Lieberman, Laurence, *Unassigned Frequencies: American Poetry in Review, 1964–1977* (1977).

Lim, Shirley Geok-lin and Ling, Amy (eds.), *Reading the Literatures of Asian America* (1992).

Lincoln, Kenneth, *Ind'n Humor: Bicultural Play in Native America* (1993).

Ling, Jinqui, *Narrating Nationalisms: Ideology and Form in Asian American Literature* (1998).

McCaffery, L., *The Metafictional Muse* (1982).

McCarthy, Mary, *The Writing on the Wall and Other Literary Essays* (1970).

McClatchy, J. D., *White Paper: On Contemporary American Poetry* (1989).

McConnell, F., *Four Postwar America Novelists: Bellow, Mailer, Barth, and Pynchon* (1977).

McCorkle, James, *The Still Performance: Writing, Self, and Interconnection in Five Postmodern American Poets* (1989).

McKenna, Theresa, *Migrant Song: Politics and Process in Contemporary Chicano Literature* (1997).

Madsen, Deborah L., *Understanding Chicana Literature* (2001).

Malin, Irving, *New American Gothic* (1962).

Malin, Irving (ed.), *Contemporary American-Jewish Literature* (1983).

Malkoff, Karl, *Escape from the Self: A Study in Contemporary American Poetry and Poetics* (1972).

Malkoff, Karl, *Crowell's Handbook of Contemporary American Poetry: A Critical Handbook of American Poetry since 1940* (1973).

Maltby, Paul, *Dissident Postmodernists: Barthelme, Coover, Pynchon* (1991).

Marcus, Greil, *Invisible Republic: Bob Dylan's Basement Tapes* (1997).

Marranca, Bonnie and Dasgupta, Gautam (eds.), *American Playwrights: A Critical Survey* (1981).

May, John R., *Towards a New Earth: Apocalypse in the American Novel* (1972).

Mazzaro, Jerome, *Postmodern American Poetry* (1980).

Meltzer, David (ed.), *The San Francisco Poets* (1971).

Mersman, James F., *Out of the Vietnam Vortex: A Study of Poets and Poetry against the War* (1974).

Millard, Kenneth, *Contemporary American Fiction: An Introduction to American Fiction since 1970* (2000).

Mills, Ralph J., *Contemporary American Poetry* (1965).

Mills, Ralph J., *Creation's Very Self: On the Personal in Recent American Poetry* (1969).

Mills, Ralph J., *Cry of the Human: Essays on Contemporary American Poetry* (1974).

Molesworth, Charles, *The Fierce Embrace; A Study of Contemporary American Poetry* (1979).

Montefiore, Jan, *Feminism and Poetry: Language, Experience, Identity in Women's Writing* (1987).

Moore, Harry T. (ed.), *Contemporary American Novelists* (1964).

Muller, Gilbert H., *New Strangers in Paradise: The Immigrant Experience in Contemporary American Fiction* (1999).

Nelson, Cary, *Our Last First Poets: Vision and History in Contemporary American Poetry* (1981).

Newman, C., *The Post-modern Aura: The Art of Fiction in the Age of Inflation* (1985).

Norwood, V. and Monk, J. (eds.), *The Desert is No Lady: Southwestern Landscapes in Women's Writing and Art* (1987).

O'Donnell, P., *Passionate Doubts: Designs of Interpretation in Contemporary American Fiction* (1986).

Olderman, Raymond, *Beyond the Waste Land: A Study of the American Novel in the 1960s* (1972).

Ortega, Eliana and Sternbach, Nancy Saporta (eds.), *Breaking Boundaries: Latina Writing and Critical Readings* (1989).

Owens, L., *Other Destinies: Understanding the American Indian Novel* (1992).

Parkinson, Tom (ed.), *A Casebook on the Beats* (1961).

Paul, Sherman, *Hewing to Experience: Essays and Reviews on Recent American Poetry and Poetics, Nature and Culture* (1989).

Peden, W., *The American Short Story: Continuity and Change 1940–1975* (1975).

Pepper, Andrew, *The Contemporary American Crime Novel: Race, Ethnicity, Gender, Class* (2000).

Perloff, Marjorie, *Radical Artifice: Writing Poetry in the Age of the Media* (1991).

Phillips, Robert, *The Confessional Poets* (1973).

Pinsky, Robert, *The Situation of Poetry: Contemporary Poetry and its Traditions* (1977).

Poirier, Richard, *The Performing Self: Compositions in the Language of Contemporary Life* (1971).

Prenshaw, Peggy (ed.), *Women Writers of the Contemporary South* (1984).

Pryse, Marjorie and Spillers, Hortense J. (eds.), *Conjuring: Black Women, Fiction, and Literary Tradition* (1985).

Putz, Manfred, *The Story of Identity: American Fiction of the Sixties* (1979).

Quantic, D. Dufra, *The Nature of Place: A Study of Great Plains Fiction* (1997).

Quintana, Alvina E., *Home Girls: Chicana Literary Voices* (1996).

Rainwater, C. and Scheik, W. (eds.), *Contemporary American Women Writers: Narrative Strategies* (1985).

Reinfeld, Linda, *Language Poetry: Writing as Rescue* (1992).

Roller, J. M., *The Politics of the Feminist Novel* (1986).

Rosenthal, M. L., *The New Poets: American and British Poetry since World War II* (1967).

Safer, E., *The Contemporary American Comic Epic: The Novels of Barth, Pynchon, Gaddis, and Kesey* (1988).

Sage, Lorna, *Women in the House of Fiction* (1992).

Saltzman, A., *Designs of Darkness in Contemporary American Fiction* (1990).

Sarris, Greg, *Keeping Slug Woman Alive: A Holistic Approach to American Indian Texts* (1993).

Schaub, T. H., *American Fiction and the Cold War* (1991).

Scholes, Robert, *Fabulation and Metafiction* (1979).

Schulz, M., *Radical Sophistication* (1969).

Schulz, M., *Black Humour Fiction of the Sixties: A Pluralistic Definition of Man and his World* (1973).

Schweik, Susan, *A Gulf So Deeply Cut: American Women Poets and the Second World War* (1991).

Seed, David, *American Science Fiction and the Cold War: Literature and Film* (1999).

Shank, Theodore, *American Alternative Theatre* (1982).

Shaw, Robert B. (ed.), *American Poetry since 1960: Some Critical Perspectives* (1974).

Shippey, Tom, *Fictional Space: Essays on Contemporary Science Fiction* (1991).

Showalter, Elaine (ed.), *The New Feminist Criticism* (1985).

Simmons, P. E., *Deep Surfaces, Mass Culture and History in Postmodern American Fiction* (1997).

Smith, Dave, *Local Assays: On Contemporary American Poetry* (1985).

Spiegelman, Willard, *The Didactic Muse: Scenes of Instruction in Contemporary American Poetry* (1989).

Stepanchev, Stephen, *American Poetry since 1945: A Critical Survey* (1965).

Stevick, P., *Alternative Pleasures: Postrealist Fiction and the Tradition* (1981).

Summers, Joseph and Ybarra-Frausto, Tomas, *Modern Chicano Writers* (1979).

Tanner, Tony, *Scenes of Nature, Signs of Man* (1987).

Tate, Linda, *A Southern Weave of Women: Fiction of the Contemporary South* (1994).

Tatum, Charles, *Chicano Literature* (1982).

Temple, J. Nolte (ed.), *Open Spaces, City Places: Contemporary Writers on the Changing Southwest* (1994).

Thurley, Geoffrey, *The American Moment: American Poetry in the Mid-Century* (1977).

Tytell, John, *Naked Angels: The Lives and Literature of the Beat Generation* (1986).

Vendler, Helen, *The Music of What Happens: Poems, Poetics, Critics* (1988).

Vendler, Helen, *Soul Says: Recent Poetry* (1995).

Vizenor, Gerald (ed.), *Narrative Chance: Postmodern Discourses on Native American Indian Literatures* (1989).

von Hallberg, R., *American Poetry and Culture 1945–80* (1984).

Waldmeir, Joseph J., *Recent American Fiction: Some Critical Views* (1963).

Walsh, R., *Novel Arguments: Reading Innovative American Fiction* (1997).

Waugh, Patricia, *Metafiction* (1984).

Waugh, Patricia, *Feminine Fiction: Revisiting the Postmodern* (1989).

Weales, Gerald, *American Drama since World War II* (1962).

Weales, Gerald, *The Jumping Off Place: American Drama in the 1960s* (1969).

Weaver, J., *That the People Might Live: Native American Literatures and Native American Community* (1997).

Webster, Grant, *The Republic of Letters: A History of Postwar American Literary Opinion* (1979).

Wilentz, Gay, *Binding Cultures: Black Women Writers in Africa and the Diaspora* (1992).

Williams, Mance, *Black Theatre in the 1960s and 1970s* (1985).

Wong, Sau-ling Cynthia, *Reading Asian American Literature: From Necessity to Extravagance* (1993).

Yorke, Liz, *Impertinent Voices: Subversive Strategies in Contemporary Women's Poetry* (1991).

Young, Elizabeth and Caveney, Graham, *Shopping in Space: Essays on America's Blank Generation Fiction* (1992).

Zamora, L., *Contemporary American Women Writers: Gender, Class, Ethnicity* (1998).

Zaverzadeh, Mas'ud, *The Mythopoeic Reality: The Postwar American Nonfiction Novel* (1975).

Zeigler, Joseph Wesley, *Regional Theatre* (1973).

Index

African Americans: writings
  18th century, 83–8
  19th century, 160–4, 176,
    181–94, 260, 278–81
  19th-century women's,
    309–12, 323–4
  bibliographies, 511
  effect of white culture, 164
  first detective novel, 512,
    755
  first novel, 184
  first novel with first-person
    narrator, 354
  first published novel by
    woman, 193–4
  first short story, 183
  first travel writing, 186
  journals, 104
  publication, problems of,
    86–7, 88
  regionalist, 260
  slave narratives, 84–5, 86,
    144–51, 181, 185–6
  slave writings, 62
  spirituals, 220–2
  studies, 525
African Americans: writings
  of the 20th century
  Black Arts movement,
    664–8
  crime novels and thrillers,
    755–6
  early, 342–3, 344, 348–55
  Harlem Renaissance and
    beyond, 342–3, 509–37
  postwar drama, 686–91
  postwar poetry, 598,
    599–600
  postwar prose, 674–86,
    691–701
  protest writing, 663–74
  science fiction, 761–2
  slave narratives, modern
    versions, 682, 685, 693,
    699
After the Fall (Miller), 706
'Aftermath' (Longfellow),
  229
Agassiz, Louis, 165

The Age of Innocence
  (Wharton), 356–8
The Age of Reason (Paine),
  75–6
Agee, James, 347
Agnes of Sorrento (Stowe),
  200
Agrarians, 466, 471, 490
Ah, Wilderness (O'Neill), 460
Ahab, Captain (*Moby-Dick*),
  111, 132, 209–10,
  211–12, 213
Ai, 598–9
Aiiieeee!, 792
Aiken, Conrad, 396–7, 403
*The Air-Conditioned
  Nightmare* (Miller), 658
'Ajanta' (Rukeyser), 425
Albee, Edward, 713–14
Alcott, Bronson, 131, 135,
  312
Alcott, Louisa M., 312–14
Alcuin (Brown), 96
Aldington, Richard, 388–9
Alexander, Meena, 800
Alexei, Sherman, 805,
  815–17
Algarin, Miguel, 772
Alger, Horatio, 248–9
Algren, Nelson, 605
The Alhambra (Irving), 107
alienation
  1950s society, 556
alienation: literary treatments
  Albee, 713–14
  Anderson, 372–3
  beat poets, 641
  Bowles, 605
  Didion, 628
  Gardner, 739
  Kincaid, 701
  Momaday, 806–8
  Okada, 794–5
  Salinger, 659–61
  Shepard, 715–17
  Sontag, 627–8
  Tuckerman, 232
  Updike, 614–15
  Welch, 810

All (Zukofsky), 393–4
All God's Chillun (O'Neill),
  459–60
'All My Pretty Ones' (Sexton),
  572
All My Sons (Miller), 703
All the King's Men (Warren),
  474–5
All the Pretty Horses
  (McCarthy), 618–19
Allan, John, 119
allegory
  in Barth, 735
  in Cabell, 368–9
  in Hawthorne, 201, 205
  in Melville, 208–9
  reasons for prevalence,
    34
  in Shepard, 715
Allen, James Lane, 267, 268
Allen, Paula Gunn, 805
Allison, Dorothy, 626, 627
allusion
  in Eliot, 229, 397, 403–4
  in Longfellow, 229
  in Melville, 209–10, 212
  in Pound, 400
almanacs
  Crockett Almanacs, 124,
    125
  and Franklin, 71
The Alphabet (Silliman), 746
Alphabetical Africa (Abish),
  742
Alsea people, 13
Alsop, George, 41
alternative culture, *see* culture,
  alternative
Alther, Lisa, 741
Alvarez, Julia, 784
Amazing Stories, 759
The Ambassadors (James),
  295–6, 752
The Amber Gods (Spofford),
  314
ambiguity, Welty on, 620–1
America
  19th century, 100–1,
    246–7

animals
  Moore on, 419
  in Native American stories,
    5–6, 8, 10, 14–15
  see also nature
'Animals are Passing from
    our Lives' (Levine),
    576–7
Anna Christie (O'Neill),
    459
Annie John (Kincaid), 701
'Annunciation' (Le Sueur),
    493
Another Country (Baldwin),
    678
Anthology of Magazine Verse,
    527
Anthony, Susan B., 432
Anti-Slavery Catechism
    (Child), 175–6
Antin, David, 772
Antin, Mary, 329
'Antique Harvesters'
    (Ransom), 468–9
antiquity
  Pound's use of, 397–9
  see also classical writers;
    myths and legends
Anzaldúa, Gloria, 159
Apache people, 7, 13
Apess, William, 154
apocalypse
  in early 20th-century works,
    347
  Merrill on, 653
  in Native American stories,
    7
  Pynchon on, 729
  and science fiction,
    759–60, 761–2
Appeal for the Indians (Child),
    176
An Appeal in Favor of That
    Class of Americans
    Called Africans (Child),
    175–6
An Appeal to the Christian
    Women of the South
    (Weld), 176–7

The Archbishop's Calling
    (Miller), 706–7
Archer, Isabel (The Portrait
    of a Lady), 291–4
Archer, Lew (Macdonald
    character), 752–3
Archer, Newland (The Age of
    Innocence), 356–8
Arenas, Reinaldo, 786
Argosy, 539
Arias, Ron, 779
Ariel (Plath), 594–6
Armies of the Night (Mailer),
    604
Armstrong, Louis, 531
Armstrong, Samuel, 349
Army Life in a Black Regiment
    (Higginson), 166
Arnaz, Desi: literary
    treatments, 785
Arnow, Harriette S., 490
The Arrivistes (Simpson),
    565
'Arrow' (Dove), 672–3
art, and New York poets,
    645, 647, 648, 650–1
Art Decoration Applied to
    Furniture (Spofford),
    314
'The Art of Fiction' (James),
    289, 290
Arthur Mervyn (Brown), 96,
    98
Artifice of Absorption
    (Bernstein), 747–8
As I Lay Dying (Faulkner),
    449, 450
Asa Vickers (Lewis), 371
Ash Wednesday (Eliot), 402,
    405
Ashbery, John, 645, 646–7,
    649, 650–2, 742
Ashbridge, Elizabeth, 65
Asian Americans: writings
    early and mid-20th
    century, 332–5, 502–5,
    559
    late 20th century, 600,
    722–3, 757, 786–801

Asimov, Isaac, 760
'Asphodel, That Greeny
    Flower' (Williams),
    408–9, 581
The Assistant (Malamud),
    609–10
Astoria (Irving), 107
Astounding Science Fiction,
    759
'At Melville's Tomb' (Crane),
    428
'At the Bomb Testing Site'
    (Stafford), 580
'At the Fishhouses' (Bishop),
    585
'The Atlantic Cable' (Ridge),
    153
Atlantic Monthly, 231, 239,
    262, 282, 289
Auchincloss, Louis, 604–5
Auden, W. H., 566, 591
audience, see readers, authors'
    relationship with
Audubon (Warren), 472,
    473
Augie March, The Adventures
    of (Bellow), 610–11
'Aunt Jennifer's Tigers'
    (Rich), 572
Aupaumut, Hendrick, 81–2
Austen, Jane, influence, 293
Auster, Paul, 617
Austin, Mary, 326–7
authority, resistance to
  in Native American
    stories, 13–14
  in 1950s, 556
  postwar novels, 654–63
  Twain on, 254
  Whitman on, 234
  see also beat movement;
    protest; social
    convention and
    conditioning
autobiographies
  Adams, 318–21, 336
  Apess, 154–5
  Asian American writers,
    793–4, 797, 798

Craft, William, 185, 187
Crafts, Hannah, 187–92
Crane, Hart, 347, 373, 424, 426–9, 470
Crane, Helga (*Quicksand*), 516–17
Crane, Stephen, 299–300, 303–5
Crashaw, William, 27
Crawford, Cheryl, 456
The Crayon Miscellany (Irving), 107
creation
　in Miller, 706
　in Native American stories, 4, 5, 6, 7–10
The Creation of the World (Miller), 706
creative process
　Ashbery on, 651–2
　Barth on, 735
　Barthelme on, 736
　Cather on, 362
　Ciardi on, 575
　Crane on, 426, 427
　cummings on, 422–3
　Dugan on, 575
　Duncan on, 635–6
　Ellison on, 674–5
　Faulkner on, 447–8
　Ferlinghetti on, 637
　Gardner on, 739
　Ginsberg on, 642, 643
　H. D. on, 391
　Hawkes on, 736
　Hawthorne on, 204
　Hemingway on, 444–5
　Ignatow on, 575
　James on, 289, 290, 296
　language poets on, 742–9
　Merrill on, 653
　Moore on, 418
　Nabokov on, 768–9
　O'Hara on, 645–6
　Olson on, 629–30
　Pound on, 388–90, 397, 398
　Pynchon on, 729
　Rexroth on, 482–3

(Riding) Jackson on, 426
Rukeyser on, 425
Schwartz on, 575
Spicer on, 638–9
Stafford on, 575
Stein on, 429–30, 432
Stevens on, 412–13
Wharton on, 356
Wilbur on, 566–7
Williams on, 390, 408
Wolfe on, 723–4
Wright on, 537
Zukofsky on, 393
Creek people, 260
Creeley, Robert, 633–4, 635, 646
Creoles: literary treatments, 274–7
Crèvecoeur, Hector St Jean de, 73–4
Crews, Harry, 618, 726
The Cricket (Tuckerman), 232
crime novels, 122, 540–2, 751–7
　first African American, 512, 755
　postmodern, 618, 738, 814–15
　see also thrillers
Crimes of the Heart (Henley), 720
The Crisis, 351, 510, 518, 525
Crisis papers (Paine), 75
criticism: New Criticism, 466–7, 471
Criticism and Fiction (Howells), 282, 286
'Critics' (Fern), 179
Crockett, Davy, 124–5
Croft, Sergeant (*The Naked and the Dead*), 602, 603
The Cross and the Arrow (Maltz), 489
Crossbloods (Vizenor), 813–14
The Crossing (McCarthy), 618–19

'Crossing Brooklyn Ferry' (Whitman), 235
Crossings (Hua), 559, 792
Crouse, Russel, 455
Crow (*The Tooth of Crime*), 715–16
Crow Indians, 7
Crowley, Mart, 721
The Crucible (Miller), 705–6
Crumbling Idols (Garland), 297
Cruz, Victor Hernández, 781–2
Cruz-Smith, Martin, 805
The Crying of Lot 49 (Pynchon), 732
Cuba and Cuban Americans, 2
　writings, 784–6
Cullen, Countee, 510, 512, 520, 527
culture
　MacLeish on, 484–5
　Pound on, 400–1
culture, alternative, 560–1
　African American drama, 688–90
　African American protest writing, 663–74
　language poetry, 742–9
　newspapers, 680
　postwar novels, 654–63
　theatre, 712–17
culture, mass: literary treatments
　Alexei, 815, 816–17
　DeLillo, 616–17
　Dorn, 635
　Gardner, 739
　Hagedorn, 799
　Olson, 631–2
A Cumberland Vendetta (Fox), 269
Cummings, General (*The Naked and the Dead*), 602, 603
cummings, e. e., 393, 411, 422–4
Cummins, Maria, 104

guilt: literary treatments
Hawthorne, 201–2, 203
Ignatow, 576
Logan, 571
Miller, 703–7
Schwartz, 574–5
Styron, 606
'Gulls' (Nemerov), 582
Gurdjieff, Georgei I., 520
Guy Domville (James), 294
Gyles, John, 51
Gysin, Brion, 657

H. D. (Hilda Doolittle),
388–9, 390–2, 416, 636
Hagedorn, Jessica, 799
Hahn, Kimiko, 599, 600
Haines, John, 597
The Hairy Ape (O'Neill),
458, 459, 460
Hakluyt, Richard, the elder,
26
Hakluyt, Richard, the
younger, 24, 26–7
Haida people, 14
Hale, Janet Campbell, 805
Hale, Sara Josepha, 104
Haley, Alex, 679
Hall, Donald, 574
Hall, Prince, 83–4
Hallek, Fitz-Greene, 105
Hamilton, Alexander, 96
The Hamlet (Faulkner), 449
Hammer, Mike (Spillane
character), 750
Hammerstein, Oscar, 702
Hammett, Dashiel, 491,
541–2
Hammon, Briton, 185
Hammon, Jupiter, 83, 86
Hammond, James Henry,
168, 170
Hammond, John, 28–9
Hamor, Ralph, 27–8
Handke, Peter, 742
Handsome Lake, 32
Handy, W. C., 520, 530, 531
Hannah, Barry, 618, 727
Hansberry, Lorraine, 686–7

Hanson, Elizabeth Meader,
51
'The Happiest Man on Earth'
(Maltz), 489
Harding, Warren, 343
Harjo, Joy, 804
Harlem (Thurman), 511
Harlem Gallery (Tolson), 528
Harlem Renaissance, 342–3,
509–27
Harlem Shadows (McKay),
513
Harmonium (Stevens), 393,
411, 413
Harper, Frances E. W.,
182–4
Harper, Michael, 671–2
Harper's Ferry raid, 166
Harper's Monthly Magazine,
282
Harris, George Washington,
128–9
Harris, Joel Chandler, 267–8
Harris, Thomas, 757–8
Harrison, William Henry,
102
Harryman, Carla, 745, 746–7
Hart, Lorenz, 702
Hart, Moss, 455, 702
Harte, Francis Bret, 251, 258
Hartigan, Grace, 647
'The Hasty Pudding' (Barlow),
90
Hathorne, John, 201–2
Hathorne, William, 201
Haun, Mildred, 490
Hawkes, John, 735, 736,
737–8
Hawthorne, Nathaniel,
200–7
and cooperative
communities, 135
on Eliot, 53
and Emerson, 131
and human behaviour, 34
and literary magazines, 104
precursors, 99
and Stoddard, 217
on Tuckerman, 232

Hayden, Robert, 528–9
Hayes, Alfred, 481
Haynes, Lemuel, 83
A Hazard of New Fortunes
(Howells), 286
Heading West (Betts), 628
'Heart's Needle' (Snodgrass),
571
Hecht, Anthony, 567, 582
Hecht, Ben, 372, 455
Hedged In (Phelps), 315
The Heidi Chronicles
(Wasserstein), 721
Heinlein, Robert, 759
Heirs of Columbus (Vizenor),
814–15
Hejinian, Lyn, 744–5, 746–7
A Hell of a Woman
(Thompson), 751
Heller, Joseph, 602
Hellman, Lillian, 348, 490–1,
541–2
Hemingway, Ernest, 347,
348, 442–7
and Anderson, 371, 373
and Crane, 303
and Gold, 488
influence, 619
and Stein, 432
on Twain, 255–6
Hemphill, Essex, 674
Henderson, David, 665
Henley, Beth, 720
Henri, Robert, 365
Hentz, Caroline Lee, 171–3
Hepburn, Katharine, 546
Herbert, Frank, 760
'Heritage' (Cullen), 527
Herland (Gilman), 316
heroes and heroism: literary
treatments
baseball players as heroes,
609
Berger, 739
Cooper, 108–9, 111
democratic epic, 91, 236–7
detectives as heroes, 540,
542, 754
Ellison, 675

Ray (*Home to Harlem*), 513
readers, authors' relationship
    with
  Barth, 733
  Barthelme, 736–7
  language poets, 743–4
  McClure, 639
  Morrison, 693–4
  Nabokov, 770
  O'Hara, 647
  postwar poets, 567
  Whitman, 235–7
  Wieners, 633
Reagan, Ronald, 554, 561
*The Real Life of Sebastian
    Knight* (Nabokov), 768
realism
  19th-century drama,
    453–4
  19th-century novels, 250,
    282–6
  dirty realism, 601, 726–8
  domestic realism, in
    postwar drama, 702–12,
    713–14, 716–17
  Hansberry on, 686
  and New Journalists,
    723–5
reality
  Nabokov on, 768–9
  Stevens on, 411–12
The Rebels (Child), 175
'Recipe' (Mirikitani), 795
Recollections of a Forest Life
    (Copway), 155
The Red Badge of Courage
    (Crane), 304–5
Red Rock (Page), 267
Redburn (Melville), 208, 209
*The Redeemed Captive
    Returning to Zion*
    (Williams), 51
redemption: literary
    treatments
  Crane, 427
  Delany, 761
  Fugitives, 464, 472–5
  Grey, 539
  Merrill, 653

O'Connor, 621–3
  Welch, 811
The Redskins (Cooper), 112
Redwood (Sedgwick), 115–16
Reed, Ishmael, 562, 680–2
Reed, John, 487
Reed, Lou, 815
regionalism
  African American and
    Native American,
    259–61
  definition, 257
  Fugitives and traditionalists,
    463–77
  New England, 261–5
  South, 265–81
  Twain, 250–7
  West and Midwest, 258–9
religion
  in 18th-century works,
    65–8
  in 19th-century works,
    195, 196, 224
  African American services,
    174
  and Baldwin, 676–7
  in colonial poetry, 42–4,
    48–9
  Douglass on, 146–7
  in early 20th-century
    literature, 299
  Edwards on emotion's
    place in, 67
  Emerson on, 130, 133, 135
  evangelical writings, 18th
    century, 82–3
  evangelism, 55, 65–7, 102
  and Foote, 309–10
  and King, 680
  and Lowell, 588
  Melville on faith, 211–12,
    213, 214
  Native American, 40,
    324–5
  and O'Connor, 621–3
  and O'Neill, 458–9, 462
  and Puritan writings,
    33–6, 42, 50–4
  Stevens on, 413–14

and Tate, 470–1
  see also Buddhism;
    Catholicism;
    Christianity; Islam;
    spirituality
'Remember' (Harjo), 804
Remember to Remember
    (Miller), 658
renewal: literary treatments
  Douglass, 147
  Native American stories,
    16–17
  naturalists, 302
  Thoreau, 142
repetition
  and Everson, 638
  and Faulkner, 447–53
  Hejinian on, 744–5
  and Le Sueur, 494
  and Olson, 631
  and Stein, 431
  and Welch, 810
  and Whitman, 233–4
The Repository (Murray),
    81
repression: literary
    treatments
  Gilman, 316–18
  Glasgow, 359–60
  Thurber, 545
  Wharton, 357–8
Requiem for a Nun (Faulkner),
    447
'Requiem for the Spanish
    Dead' (Rexroth), 483
Reservation Blues (Alexei),
    815, 816–17
reservations: literary
    treatments, 815–16
Resolutions (Edwards), 66
'A Respectable Woman'
    (Chopin), 271
'The Return of the Private'
    (Garland), 297
revenge: literary treatments,
    203, 205–6
*Review of the Debate in the
    Virginia Legislature*
    (Dew), 170

violence
African American protest
writing, 663–74, 679–80
Capote, 724–6
'hardboiled' novels, 541–4
O'Connor, 621–3
postmodern novels, 737–8
postwar novels, 727,
750–1
see also protest; war
The Violent Bear It Away
(O'Connor), 622–3
Viramontes, Helena Maria,
779–80
Virgil, influence
on Cather, 363
on Lewis, 63
on Longfellow, 228
on Mather, 54
on Villagrá, 23
Virgin, Adams on, 318,
319–20
Virgin of Guadalupe, 64–5,
159
Virginia
18th century, 56–60
exploration and
colonization, 25–30
slavery, 101
Virginia (Hawkes), 737
Virginia Company, 29–30
The Virginian (Wister),
538–9
'Vision' (Hinojosa), 804
The Vision of Columbus
(Barlow), 63, 90
The Vision of Sir Launfal
(Lowell), 231
Vizenor, Gerald, 805, 813–15
A Voice from the South
(Cooper), 323–4
Vonnegut, Kurt, 602, 758
Vorticism, 389
'Voyages' (Crane), 428

Wadsworth, Rev. Charles, 239
Wagner, Richard, 688
Wah'kon-tah (Matthews),
508

Waiting for Lefty (Odets),
457
Waiting for the Verdict
(Davis), 220
Waiting to Exhale (McMillan),
699
'Wakefield' (Hawthorne),
202
'Waking Early Sunday
Morning' (Lowell), 580
Wakoski, Diane, 599
Walden (Thoreau), 138–42
Walker, Alice, 516, 695–8,
782
Walker, David, 160–2
Walker, Margaret, 521,
531–2, 532–3
Wall Street Crash, 345
Wallace, David Foster, 619
Wallace, Lew, 249
The Walls Do Not Fall
(H. D.), 391–2
Walter, Eugene, 453
The Wapshot Chronicle
(Cheever), 605
war: literary treatments
19th-century prose, 286–7
Chesnut, 173–5
Crane, 304–5
Dos Passos, 440
Ginsberg, 560, 579, 642,
644
Harper, 184
Hemingway, 444, 445
Japanese American writers,
793–5
Komunyakaa, 673
Le Guin, 761
Lowell, 560, 580, 588
Mailer, 602–3
Mason, 626
Miller, 706
Mitchell, 546–9
Moody, 299
postwar novels, 601–2,
727–8
postwar poetry, 564–6
Pynchon, 732
Rabe, 719

regionalists, 265–6
Styron, 606
Tate, 469–70
Vietnam War protest
poetry, 579–80
Whitman, 233–4
Ward, Diane, 747
Warner, Charles Dudley, 251
Warner, Susan, 104
Warren, Mercy Otis, 62
Warren, Robert Penn, 464,
471–5
Warshawski, Victoria
Iphigenia (Paretsky
character), 754–5
Washington, Booker T.,
348–51
Washington, Madison, 185
Wasserstein, Wendy, 720,
721
The Waste Land (Eliot),
404–5
allusiveness, 229, 397,
404
and Fugitives, 470
and Pound, 397
publication, 393
and the sea, 402
Williams on, 407
Watch on the Rhine
(Hellman), 491
Waters, Frank, 606
Waters, Muddy, 668
The Waterworks (Doctorow),
608
Watten, Barrett, 745, 746
The Way to Rainy Mountain
(Momaday), 806
The Way to Wealth (Franklin),
71
'We Real Cool' (Brooks),
529–30
wealth, individual
19th century, 248–9
20th century, 345–6,
557–8
'Weaving' (Larcom), 226
The Web and the Rock
(Wolfe), 496–7

Williams, John, 51–2
Williams, John A., 684
Williams, Jonathan, 632
Williams, Oscar, 565
Williams, Paulette, *see*
    Shange, Ntozake
Williams, Raymond, x
Williams, Roger, 37, 39–41
Williams, Sherley Anne, 516,
    699
Williams, Tennessee, 688,
    702–3, 707–11, 714
Williams, William Carlos,
    347, 392, 406–11
  on the bomb, 581
  on creative process, 390,
    408
  on Ginsberg, 642
  influence, 576, 589, 646
  Moore on, 416
  and Objectivism, 393
  and Pound, 388
  on Rexroth, 483, 484
Willis, Nathaniel Parker, 179
Willis, Sarah Payson, *see*
    Fern, Fanny
Wilson, August, 688, 690–1
Wilson, Edmund, 475, 491,
    769
Wilson, Harriet E., 193–4,
    354
Wilson, Lanford, 713, 717
Wilson, Woodrow, 339
Windy McPherson's Son
    (Anderson), 372
Winesburg, Ohio (Anderson),
    371, 372–3
Winona (Hopkins), 310
Winter in the Blood (Welch),
    810
'Winter Remembered'
    (Ransom), 467, 468
Winters, Yvor, 421, 477
Winterset (Anderson), 456
Winthrop, John, 32, 35–7
Wise Blood (O'Connor),
    622–3
'Wiser than a God' (Chopin),
    271

Wister, Owen, 538–9
witchcraft
  Franklin on, 72
  see also Salem witch trials
The Witches of Eastwick
    (Updike), 615
With Shuddering Fall (Oates),
    624
Wittgenstein, Ludwig, 733,
    742
A Wizard of Earthsea (Le
    Guin), 761
Wolfe, Hugh ('Life in the
    Iron Mills'), 220
Wolfe, Thomas, 495–7, 504
Wolfe, Tom, 663, 723–4, 728
*Woman in the Nineteenth
    Century* (Fuller), 136–8
'Woman Poem' (Giovanni),
    670–1
The Woman Warrior
    (Kingston), 789–91
The Woman Within
    (Glasgow), 358, 360
women
  and abolitionism, 178
  Adams on feminine force,
    318, 319–20
  Byrd on, 59
  colonial expectations of,
    44–5
  Fuller on, 136–8
  Hawthorne on, 206
  housekeeping manuals,
    175, 179
  Hwang on male
    perceptions, 722–3
  and slavery, 146, 148–51,
    173–4, 177–8, 186–7
  see also feminism
women: conditions
  18th century, 61
  19th century, 103, 179–80,
    249–50, 261–5
  20th century, 340–1
  Austin on, 326–7
  frontier life, 215–16
  Hopkins on, 310–12
  plantation life, 173–4

women: literary treatments
  19th century, 92–3, 117
  African American, 519, 688
  Hispanic folklore, 159
  marginalized subjects, 744
  Mexican American, 482
  Modernist prose, 450–2
  Native American stories, 7
  postwar drama, 708–10
  see also women: writings
women: rights
  and Adams, 318
  African American women,
    323–4
  Asian immigrants, 503–4
  and Alcott, 313–14
  James on, 294
  Le Sueur on, 493–4
  Revolutionary period,
    79–81, 96
  and Smith, 490
  voting, 340
women: writings
  first autobiography by
    Native American,
    325–6
  first novel by African
    American, 193–4
  first novel by African
    American to sell
    1 million-plus, 532
  first novel by Native
    American, 509
  mutual support networks,
    355
  writing style and attitude
    to, 104
women: writings, 17th and
    18th centuries, 44–6,
    61–2, 93–5
women: writings, 19th century
  novels, 214–16, 217–20,
    309, 310–14, 315–16
  short stories, 314–15,
    316–18
women: writings, 20th
    century
  African American drama,
    686–8

Also available from Blackwell Publishing

A History of American Literature
Richard Gray

A Companion to the Regional Literatures of America
Edited by Charles L. Crow

A Companion to the Literature and Culture of the American South
Edited by Richard Gray and Owen Robinson

The Literatures of Colonial America: An Anthology
Edited by Susan Castillo

American Gothic: An Anthology 1787–1916
Edited by Charles L. Crow

Native American Women's Writing:
An Anthology *c.* 1800–1924
Edited by Karen Kilcup

Nineteenth-Century American Women Writers: An Anthology
Edited by Karen Kilcup

Nineteenth-Century American Women Writers: A Critical Reader
Edited by Karen Kilcup

Twentieth-Century American Poetry
Christopher MacGowan

For further details about these titles, visit the Blackwell Publishing
website at: www.blackwellpublishing.com

To receive regular e-mail updates on new publications in your field,
register for Blackwell E-mail Alerts at:
www.blackwellpublishing.com/ealerts